k_{SIMPLE}	Nominal risk-free rate of interest; also referred to
k_{ps}	Cost of preferred stock
k_{RF}	Rate of return on a risk-free security
k_s	(1) Cost of retained earnings
	(2) Required return on a stock
M	Maturity value of a bond
M/B	Market-to-book ratio
MCC	Marginal cost of capital
MIRR	Modified internal rate of return
N	Calculator key denoting number of periods
n	Life of a project
NPV	Net present value
NWC	Net working capital
P_o	Price of stock today
P	Sales price per unit of product sold
P/E	Price/earnings ratio
PMT	Periodic level payment of an annuity
PV	Present value
PVA_n	Present value of an annuity for n years
PVIF	Present value interest factor for a lump sum
PVIFA	Present value interest factor for an annuity
Q	Quantity produced or sold
r	Correlation coefficient
ROA	Return on assets
ROE	Return on equity
RP	Risk premium
RP_M	Market risk premium
S	Sales in dollars
SML	Security Market Line
Σ	Summation sign (capital sigma)
σ	Standard deviation (lowercase sigma)
σ^2	Variance
t	Time period
T	Marginal income tax rate
TIE	Times interest earned
v	Variable cost as a percent of selling price
V	Variable cost per unit
V_d	Bond value
V_{ps}	Preferred stock value
VC	Total variable costs
WACC	Weighted average cost of capital
YTC	Yield to call
YTM	Yield to maturity

Principles of Finance

Scott Besley
University of South Florida

Eugene F. Brigham
University of Florida

THE DRYDEN PRESS
Harcourt Brace College Publishers

Fort Worth   Philadelphia   San Diego   New York   Orlando   Austin   San Antonio
Toronto   Montreal   London   Sydney   Tokyo

Executive Editor: Mike Reynolds
Developmental Editor: Terri House
Project Editor: Becky Dodson
Art Director: Bill Brammer
Production Manager: Eddie Dawson
Product Manager: Charles Watson
Project Management: Elm Street Publishing Services, Inc.
Compositor: The Clarinda Company
Cover Image: Bob Asbille

ISBN: 0-03-025253-9
Library of Congress Catalog Card Number: 98-73874

Address for Domestic Orders
The Dryden Press, 6277 Sea Harbor Drive, Orlando, FL 32887-6777
800-782-4479

Address for International Orders
International Customer Service
The Dryden Press, 6277 Sea Harbor Drive, Orlando, FL 32887-6777
407-345-3800
(fax) 407-345-4060
(e-mail) hbintl@harcourtbrace.com

Address for Editorial Correspondence
The Dryden Press, 301 Commerce Street, Suite 3700, Fort Worth, TX 76102

Web Site Address
http://www.hbcollege.com

THE DRYDEN PRESS, DRYDEN, and the DP LOGO are registered trademarks of Harcourt Brace & Company.

Printed in the United States of America

9 0 1 2 3 4 5 6 7 8 048 9 8 7 6 5 4 3 2 1

The Dryden Press
Harcourt Brace College Publishers

Amling and Droms
Investment Fundamentals

Berry and Young
Managing Investments: A Case Approach

Besley and Brigham
Principles of Finance

Boone, Kurtz, and Hearth
Planning Your Financial Future

Brigham
Brigham's Interactive Guide to Finance
CD-ROM

Brigham, Gapenski, and Daves
Intermediate Financial Management
Sixth Edition

Brigham, Gapenski, and Ehrhardt
Financial Management: Theory and Practice
Ninth Edition

Brigham, Gapenski, and Klein
1999 Cases in Financial Management: Dryden Request

Brigham and Houston
Fundamentals of Financial Management
Eighth Edition

Brigham and Houston
Fundamentals of Financial Management: Concise Second Edition

Chance
An Introduction to Derivatives
Fourth Edition

Clark, Gerlach, and Olson
Restructuring Corporate America

Cooley
Advances in Business Financial Management: A Collection of Readings
Second Edition

Dickerson, Campsey, and Brigham
Introduction to Financial Management
Fourth Edition

Eaker, Fabozzi, and Grant
International Corporate Finance

Gardner, Mills, and Cooperman
Managing Financial Institutions: An Asset/Liability Approach
Fourth Edition

Gitman and Joehnk
Personal Financial Planning
Eighth Edition

Greenbaum and Thakor
Contemporary Financial Intermediation

Harrington and Eades
Case Studies in Financial Decision Making
Third Edition

Hayes and Meerschwam
Financial Institutions: Contemporary Cases in the Financial Services Industry

Hearth and Zaima
Contemporary Investments: Security and Portfolio Analysis
Second Edition

Johnson
Issues and Readings in Managerial Finance
Fourth Edition

Kidwell, Peterson, and Blackwell
Financial Institutions, Markets, and Money
Sixth Edition

Koch and MacDonald
Bank Management
Fourth Edition

Leahigh
Pocket Guide to Finance

Maness and Zietlow
Short-Term Financial Management

Martin, Cox, and MacMinn
The Theory of Finance: Evidence and Applications

Mayes and Shank
Financial Analysis with Lotus 1-2-3 for Windows

Mayes and Shank
Financial Analysis with Microsoft Excel

Mayo
Financial Institutions, Investments, and Management: An Introduction
Sixth Edition

Mayo
Investments: An Introduction
Fifth Edition

Osteryoung, Newman, and Davies
Small Firm Finance: An Entrepreneurial Analysis

Reilly and Brown
Investment Analysis and Portfolio Management
Fifth Edition

Reilly and Norton
Investments
Fifth Edition

Sears and Trennepohl
Investment Management

Seitz and Ellison
Capital Budgeting and Long-Term Financing Decisions
Third Edition

Siegel and Siegel
Futures Markets

Smith and Spudeck
Interest Rates: Principles and Applications

Stickney and Brown
Financial Reporting and Statement Analysis: A Strategic Perspective
Fourth Edition

Weston, Besley, and Brigham
Essentials of Managerial Finance
Eleventh Edition

Preface

Principles of Finance is intended for use in an introductory finance course. The book represents a survey of key concepts by covering the three general areas of study in finance: (1) financial markets and institutions, (2) investments, and (3) managerial finance. The book begins with a discussion of the principles of financial systems—markets, institutions, and assets—and business organizations. The next set of chapters covers valuation concepts, which include the time value of money, valuing financial and real assets, and fundamentals of risk and return. Then, corporate decision making, or managerial finance, is presented. The discussions here center on how financial managers can help maximize their firms' values by improving decisions in such areas as capital budgeting, choice of capital structure, and working capital management. Finally, in the last two chapters, investment fundamentals are explained. This organization has three important advantages:

1. Explaining early in the book how financial markets operate and how security prices are determined helps students understand how managerial finance can affect the value of the firm. Also, early coverage of such key concepts as risk analysis, time value, and valuation techniques permits their use and reinforcement throughout the remainder of the book.
2. Structuring the book around markets and valuation enhances continuity because this organization helps students see how the various topics relate to one another.
3. Most students—even those who do not plan to major in finance—are generally interested in *investment* concepts, such as stock and bond valuation and selection, how financial markets work, how risk and rates of return affect financial decision making, and the like. Because people's ability to learn a subject is a function of their interest and motivation, and because *Principles* begins by showing the relationships among security markets, valuing financial assets, and managerial finance, this organization is good from a pedagogic standpoint.

Although this book is intended to be a survey of general finance, we could not include discussions of every area associated with the field of finance. Thus, we included those topics considered most relevant to presenting a basic understanding of the diversity of finance as an area of study. Because most students who read this book will probably not become finance majors, this book will be their only exposure to finance, including investment concepts that seemingly are intriguing to all of us. For that reason, we have structured the book so that (1) its content is sufficient to provide students with a good basic understanding of finance and (2) it can be used as a reference, or guide, for answering fundamental questions about finance.

Relationship with Our Other Books

Clearly it is impossible to provide everything one needs to know about finance in one text, especially an undergraduate text. This recognition has led us to limit the scope of this book and also to write other texts to deal with the materials that cannot be included in *Principles*. We have authored a text that emphasizes more detailed material about managerial finance (*Essentials of Managerial Finance*, twelfth edition). Also, Gene Brigham, Lou Gapenski, and Phillip Daves have co-authored an intermediate undergraduate text (*Intermediate Financial Management*, sixth edition), and Gene Brigham, Lou Gapenski, and Mike Ehrhardt have coauthored a comprehensive book aimed primarily at MBAs (*Financial Management: Theory and Practice*, ninth edition).

The relationship between *Principles* and the more advanced books deserves special comment. First, we recognize that the advanced books are often used by students who have also used *Principles* in the introductory undergraduate course. So we wanted to avoid excessive overlap but wanted to be sure to expose students to alternative points of view on controversial subjects. We should note, though, that our students in advanced courses invariably tell us that they find it helpful to have the more difficult materials repeated—they need the review. Students also say they like the fact that the style and notation used in our upper-level books are consistent with those in the introductory text, as this makes learning easier. Regarding alternative points of view, we have made every effort to take a moderate, middle-of-the-road approach, and where serious controversy exists, we have tried to present the alternative points of view. Reviewers were asked to consider this point, and their comments have helped us eliminate potential biases.

Intended Market and Use

As noted earlier, *Principles* is intended for use as an introductory text. The key chapters can be covered in a one-term course, and, supplemented with cases and some outside readings, the book can also be used in a two-term course. If it is used in a one-term course, the instructor might cover only selected chapters, leaving the others for students either to examine on their own or to use as reference in conjunction with work in later courses. Also, we have made every effort to write the chapters in a flexible, modular format, which helps instructors cover the material in a different sequence should they choose to do so.

Important Features of the Book

We must present the material contained in the book in a structured manner to ensure continuity and cogency in the coverage of the topics. To enhance the pedagogy, we have included some important features, which are discussed on the following page.

Time Line and Solutions Approach to TVM Analysis

In our discussions of time value of money topics (Chapter 6), we begin each major section with a verbal discussion of a time value issue, then we present a time line to show graphically the cash flows that are involved, after which we give the equation that must be solved to obtain the required answer. Finally, we present three methods which can be used to solve the equation: (1) a numerical solution, (2) a solution based on the time value tables, and (3) a financial calculator solution. The time line helps students visualize the problem at hand and see how to set it up for solution, the equation helps them understand the mathematics, and the three-pronged solution approach helps them see that time value problems can be solved in alternative ways. Each student will focus on the particular solution technique he or she will actually use, which generally calls for using a financial calculator. One advantage of our approach is that with it a financial calculator is not considered a "black box"; rather, it is viewed as an efficient way to solve a particular time value problem. The same general approach is used in subsequent chapters, especially in the chapters dealing with stock and bond valuation and capital budgeting.

Globalization

The movement toward the globalization of financial markets and businesses is continuing more rapidly than ever. Foreign corporations and financial institutions, such as banks, are aggressively moving into areas that have traditionally been dominated by U.S. firms. While this situation subjects all U.S. companies, including banks and brokerage firms, to increasing competition, it also gives U.S. companies access to additional markets and sources of funds. Clearly, then, individuals involved in business in the United States, whether it is related to a multinational firm or a purely domestic company, must have some knowledge about foreign firms' operations and international capital markets and securities and their impacts on business conditions in the United States. Thus, because the business arena truly is global, we have incorporated aspects of international finance throughout the text in an effort to make students recognize that success in today's world requires a multinational perspective. We are not attempting to make multinational finance experts out of introductory finance students, but even introductory students should understand that successful financial decisions must be made within a global context.

Ethical Dilemmas

In the 1990s, ethics became an important buzzword in business education. We felt that it was crucial to introduce students to ethical issues in finance throughout the book. Therefore, in some of the chapters we have included a feature called "Ethical Dilemma," in which we present an ethical situation based on a true story and ask students to decide what they would do if they were faced with such a situation. These Ethical Dilemmas expose students to the relationship between ethics and business, promote critical thinking and decision-making skills, and provide interesting vehicles for class discussion. The real-world situation upon which the Ethical Dilemma is based is contained in the *Instructor's Manual,* with information about the situation and key discussion points for the class.

A Managerial Perspective

Each chapter begins with "A Managerial Perspective," which describes actual events that relate to the material contained in the chapter. These boxes set up interesting and engaging situations that provoke thought about subjects covered in the chapter. The situations come into perspective as the chapters progress and some of the queries are described in greater detail.

Margin Definitions

Throughout the book, we include definitions of important terms and concepts in the margins. This allows students to easily refer to the definitions as they read the book.

End-of-Chapter Problems

We have included a substantial number and variety of questions and problems at the end of each chapter. Exam-type problems are included to give students practice with problems similar to some of the more difficult ones in the *Test Bank.* In addition, integrative problems appear in each chapter after the regular end-of-chapter problems. The integrative problems cover, in a comprehensive manner, the major concepts discussed in the chapters. We use these problems as the basis for our lectures, but other instructors assign them as comprehensive study problems. Finally, in an effort to encourage students to utilize spreadsheets, we have included Computer-Related Problems that must be solved using the predefined models that are contained on the *Problem Disk.* Note, though, that it is not necessary for students using the text to be proficient (or even literate) in computer usage. However, students who do continue their studies in finance and who later use spreadsheets (either to analyze cases or in real-world applications) will benefit from solving these problems.

Supplementary Materials

A number of items are available free of charge to adopting instructors:

1. **Instructor's Manual.** This comprehensive manual contains answers to all text questions and problems, a set of lecture notes, discussion guidelines for the Ethical Dilemmas, detailed solutions to integrative problems, and suggested course outlines. If a computerized version of the *Instructor's Manual* would help in class preparation, instructors can contact The Dryden Press for a copy.
2. **Lecture Presentation Software.** To facilitate classroom presentations, a computer graphics slide show written in Microsoft *PowerPoint* is available. The slides feature all the essential topics presented in each chapter.
3. **Test Bank.** The *Test Bank* contains a substantial number of class-tested questions and problems in an objective format. There is a generous offering of

true/false questions, multiple-choice conceptual questions, multiple-choice problems (that can easily be modified to short-answer problems by removing the answer choices), and financial calculator problems. Complete solutions are given for all numerical problems, and explanations for many conceptual questions are also provided. The *Test Bank* is available in computerized format, featuring Dryden's computerized test bank program EXAMaster+. EXAMaster+ has many features that allow the instructor to modify test questions, select items by key words, scramble tests for multiple sections, and test completely on the computer. EXAMaster+ is available in Windows. For instructors more comfortable with Microsoft Word, we also offer the *Test Bank* in that format.

4. **Problem Diskette.** A diskette containing spreadsheet models for the computer-related end-of-chapter problems is also available.

A number of additional items are available for purchase by students:

1. **Study Guide.** This supplement outlines the key sections of each chapter, provides students with self-test questions, and also provides a set of problems and solutions similar to those in the text and in the *Test Bank*. Because many instructors use multiple-choice exams, we include exam-type questions and problems in the *Study Guide.*

2. **Cases.** *Cases in Financial Management: Dryden Request,* by Eugene F. Brigham and Lin Klein, is well suited for use with *Principles.* The cases provide real-world applications of the methodologies and concepts developed in this book. In addition, all of the cases are available in a customized format, so your students pay only for cases you decide to use.

3. **Readings Books.** One readings book, *Issues and Readings in Managerial Finance,* fourth edition, edited by Ramon E. Johnson, provides an excellent mix of theoretical and practical articles that can be used to supplement the text. Another supplemental reader is *Advances in Business Financial Management: A Collection of Readings,* second edition, edited by Philip L. Cooley, which provides a broader selection of articles from which to choose.

4. **Spreadsheet Analysis Books.** *Financial Analysis with Microsoft Excel* and *Financial Analysis with Lotus for Windows,* by Timothy Mayes and Todd Shank, fully integrate the teaching of spreadsheet analysis with the basic finance concepts. These books make good companions to *Principles* in courses in which computer work is highly emphasized.

5. **Blueprints.** This supplement consists of the *Lecture Presentation Software* slides in a printed format in order to facilitate notetaking in the classroom.

The Dryden Press will provide complimentary supplements or supplement packages to those adopters qualified under our adoption policy. Please contact your sales representative to learn how you can qualify. If you receive supplements you do not need, please return them to your sales representative or send them to the following address:

Attn: Returns Department
Troy Warehouse
465 South Lincoln Drive
Troy, MO 63379

Acknowledgments

We would like to thank the following reviewers for their valuable comments and suggestions:

Nasser Arshadi, *University of Missouri*
Robert E. Chatfield, *University of Nevada, Las Vegas*
K. C. Chen, *California State University, Fresno*
John H. Crockett, Jr., *George Mason University*
Mary M. Cutler, *Central Connecticut State University*
Dean Drenk, *Montana State University*
Shawn M. Forbes, *Georgia Southern University*
Beverly Hadaway, *University of Texas, Austin*
William C. Handorf, *George Washington University*
Stephen Peters, *University of Connecticut*
Marianne Plunkert, *University of Colorado, Denver*
Gary Sanger, *Louisiana State University*
Harold B. Tamule, *Providence College*
David E. Upton, *Virginia Commonwealth University*
Howard R. Whitney, *Franklin University*

Errors in the Text

At this point, most authors make a statement like this: "We appreciate all the help we received from the people listed above, but any remaining errors are, of course, our own responsibility." And generally there are more than enough remaining errors. Having experienced difficulty with errors ourselves, both as students and as instructors, we resolved to avoid this problem in *Principles*. As a result of our error-detection procedures, we are convinced that it is relatively free of mistakes.

Partly due to our confidence that there are few errors in this book, but primarily because we want to correct any errors that might exist in this printing in future printings of the book, we have decided to offer a reward of $10 per error to the first person who reports it to us. For purposes of this reward, errors are defined as spelling errors, computational errors, errors in finance content and facts, and other errors that inhibit comprehension. Typesetting errors, such as spacing, or differences in opinion concerning grammatical or punctuation convention do not qualify for the reward. Finally, any qualifying error that has follow-through effect is counted as two errors only. Errors should be reported to Scott Besley at the address given below.

Conclusion

Finance is, in a real sense, the cornerstone of the enterprise system—good financial management is vitally important to the economic health of business firms, and hence to the nation and the world. Because of its importance, finance should be widely and thoroughly understood, but this is easier said than done. The field is relatively complex, and it is undergoing constant change in response to shifts in economic conditions. All of this makes finance stimulating and exciting but also challenging and sometimes perplexing. We sincerely hope that *Principles* will meet its own challenge by contributing to a better understanding of our financial system.

Scott Besley
University of South Florida
College of Business Administration, BSN 3403
Tampa, FL 33620-5500

Eugene F. Brigham
University of Florida
College of Business
Gainesville, Florida 32611-7160

December 1998

Brief Contents

Appendixes

Contents

PART   IV   Investor Decision Making   631

Appendixes

PART I

General Finance Concepts

An Overview of Finance

Have you ever heard of John Studzinski, Eric Schwartz, Ana Particia Botín, Andrei Kozlov, or Martin Warner? According to *BusinessWeek*, these are some of the up-and-coming stars of finance. Significant political and technological changes throughout the world have reshaped the financial arena, resulting in a milieu that requires well-trained, innovative participants. Finance frenzy is spreading throughout the world, and many international businesses are recognizing the benefits of the American approach to financial decision making. Some of the reasons for this "finance revolution" include major events that have occurred during the past couple of decades — communism is nearly extinct, and socialism is waning, thus the global economy is more monolithic than ever before. "Capitalism Rules" is the new motto of Russia and many Eastern European countries, who have created financial markets and adopted financial strategies with characteristics familiar to financial managers in the United States. Even traditionally capitalistic European countries have taken measures to improve the efficiency of their financial markets and to create companies with operations that are more open than ever before. For example, John Studzinski, a 41-year-old investment banker with Morgan Stanley, Dean Witter, Discover & Co., and one of the rising stars mentioned by *BusinessWeek*, currently helps firms in Europe with "American-style" mergers, refinancing plans, and so forth.

According to *BusinessWeek*, global finance is becoming much more "Americanized," and much of the current financial breakthroughs result from innovative ideas developed in the United States. At 34, Eric Schwartz of Goldman, Sachs & Co. used such innovation to raise $1.15 billion for Loews Corporation via convertible securities — the transaction took place overnight, from 4 P.M. to 9 A.M., when most American financial markets were closed. Ana Patricia Botín, who is in charge of the investment banking operations at Spain's second largest bank, Banco Santander, is largely responsible for the bank's presence in Latin America and its success in brokering stocks of firms in Latin American countries to institutional investors in the United States. Before joining Santander, Botín was with J.P. Morgan & Co., and some members of her investment banking group previously worked at firms such

Continued

as Morgan Stanley, Merrill Lynch, and Salomon Brothers. Andrei Kozlov, who is a 32-year-old top executive of the Central Bank of Russia, introduced the Russian Treasury bill, which he patterned after the U.S. Treasury bill. Martin Warner received his degree from Yale. At 34, he is currently the Mexican Finance Under Secretary, and he was instrumental in the resurgence of the economic welfare of Mexico. Edward D. Horwitz, from Citicorp, and Dudley M. Nigg, from Wells Fargo Bank have been instrumental in the development of electronic banking in recent years. We could go on — there are many more.

BusinessWeek chose the up-and-coming stars of finance by polling experts in various areas of finance from around the world. The "stars" are those individuals who are expected to be at the forefront of financial development as we enter the new millennium. According to *BusinessWeek*, the new stars of finance have a common bond — they all believe a global marketplace should be free of artificial barriers or restrictions. Thus, the trend in international business is *laissez-faire* finance — "Capitalism Rules."

Finance is centuries old, but it truly is an evolving discipline, with no limits in sight. As you read this chapter, as well as the rest of the book, keep in mind that finance is a dynamic, ever-changing field. If you are looking for a career in which you are not likely to become bored, finance just might be the answer.

SOURCE: "The New Stars of Finance," *BusinessWeek,* October 27, 1997, 122-125.

"Why should I study finance?" As a student, you might be asking yourself this question right now. To answer this question, we need to ask: What role does "finance" play in your life and in the successful operation of a firm? As we will see throughout this text, we are exposed to finance and related areas on a daily basis.

We will show you that proper management of the financial function of a firm will help any business provide better products to its customers at lower prices, pay higher salaries to its employees, and still provide greater returns to investors who put up the funds needed to form and operate the business. Because the economy — both national and worldwide — consists of customers, employees, and investors, sound financial management contributes to the well-being of both individuals and the general population.

The purpose of this chapter is to provide an overview of finance. After you finish the chapter, you should have a reasonably good idea of how finance knowledge is used in the business world. You should also have a better understanding of some of the forces that will affect finance in the future.

Career Opportunities in Finance

The study of finance consists of three interrelated areas: (1) *financial markets,* which deals with many of the topics covered in macroeconomics; (2) *investments,* which focuses on the decisions of individuals and financial and other institutions as they choose securities for their investment portfolios; and (3) *manage-*

rial finance, or "business finance," which involves the actual management of the firm. Each of these areas is related to the other, so an individual who works in any one of the areas should have a good understanding of the other areas as well. The career opportunities within each field are many and varied. The purpose of this section is to give you a general idea of the areas in which finance graduates can expect to work.

Financial Markets

Many finance majors go to work for financial institutions, including banks, insurance companies, savings and loans, and credit unions, which are an integral part of the financial marketplace. For success in the financial services industry, one needs a knowledge of the factors that cause interest rates to rise and fall, the regulations to which financial institutions are subject, and the various types of financial instruments (mortgages, auto loans, certificates of deposit, and so on). One also needs a general knowledge of all aspects of business administration, because the management of a financial institution involves accounting, marketing, personnel, and computer systems, as well as managerial finance. For example, as a corporate bank officer, you will be responsible for (1) calling on companies that are existing customers to ensure they are satisfied with the services offered by the bank; (2) calling on companies that are prospective customers to inform them of the services and benefits the bank can provide them; (3) identifying opportunities and innovations for the bank to improve existing services; (4) staying current with respect to technology in the financial services industry, especially information technology; and (5) performing administrative tasks, including hiring personnel, approving loan applications, determining rates used by the bank, and so forth. The responsibilities of a corporate banker truly represent an amalgamation of job descriptions.

Investments

Finance graduates who go into investments generally work for stock brokerage firms, banks, investment companies, or insurance companies. The three main functions in the investments area are (1) sales, (2) the analysis of individual securities, and (3) determining the optimal mix of securities for a given investor. As a finance graduate, you might get a job performing any one or some combination of these tasks. Even if you do not go into a career that has a direct link to finance, a basic understanding of the subject is necessary to be able to evaluate the performance of your personal investments, such as retirement funds in which you have a choice about where your contributions are invested. Investments is an area that fascinates most individuals because we constantly hear about investors who started with very little and turned their investments into fortunes. But, as you read this book, you will find that there is great risk in investments, which means investors can lose substantial amounts just as easily as they can gain. A basic knowledge of finance will help you understand how to (1) review companies and industries to determine prospects for future growth and gain the ability to maintain the safety of your investment, (2) determine how much risk you are willing to take with your investment position, and (3) evaluate how well your investments are performing so you can better ensure your funds are invested "appropriately."

Managerial Finance

Managerial finance is the broadest of the three areas, and the one with the greatest number of job opportunities. Managerial finance is important in all types of businesses, whether they are public or private, deal with financial services, or are manufacturers. The types of jobs one encounters in managerial finance range from decisions regarding plant expansions to choosing what types of securities to issue to finance expansion. Financial managers also have the responsibility for deciding the credit terms under which customers can buy, how much inventory the firm should carry, how much cash to keep on hand, whether to acquire other firms (merger analysis), and how much of the firm's earnings to plow back into the business versus pay out as dividends.

Regardless of which area you go into, you will need a knowledge of all three areas. For example, a banker lending to businesses cannot do his or her job well without a good understanding of managerial finance because he or she must be able to judge how well a business is operated. The same thing holds for one of Merrill Lynch's security analysts, and even stockbrokers must have an understanding of general financial principles if they are to give intelligent advice to their customers. At the same time, corporate financial managers need to know what their bankers are thinking about and how investors are likely to judge their corporations' performances and thus determine their stock prices. So, if you decide to make finance your career, you will need to know something about all three areas.

Self-Test Questions

What are the three main areas of finance?

If you have definite plans to go into one area, why is it necessary that you know something about the other areas?

Finance in the Twentieth Century[1]

In this book, we examine aspects of each of the three areas in finance — financial markets, investments, and corporate, or managerial, finance. Therefore, in this section, we provide you with a brief overview of each area in terms of its evolution in the twentieth century and its role in the current business world. Later in the book, you will find that much of our discussions emphasize managerial finance. The primary reason for such treatment is because (1) managerial finance encompasses both of the other areas, and (2) in general, the techniques we examine in managerial finance can also be applied to financing and investment decisions faced by individuals.

---

[1]For an excellent discussion of the evolution of finance in the twentieth century, see J. Fred Weston, "A (Relatively) Brief History of Finance Ideas." *Financial Practice and Education,* Spring/Summer 1994, 7-26.

Financial Markets

Because the financial markets in the United States are well developed, we have been able to achieve a higher standard of living than otherwise would be possible. Without financial institutions, such as banks, credit unions, and savings and loan associations, it would be much more difficult for us to finance such purchases as houses and automobiles. But, during the twentieth century, financial markets and financial institutions have experienced substantial changes.

In the early 1900s, the "banking" community consisted of thousands of independent banking organizations, which were mostly small, hometown banks. The larger banks offered a variety of services, including what we traditionally associate with banks, as well as other financial functions, such as investment services and insurance. By 1920, many of the large commercial banks included investment departments and affiliated organizations that helped companies issue stocks and bonds. A decade later, banks or their affiliates originated nearly 50 percent of new issues of stocks and bonds. During this period, banks truly were full-service financial organizations.

But, a series of financial catastrophes — including a devastating financial crisis in 1907, the failure of nearly 6,000 banks during the 1920s, and the Great Depression of 1929-1933 — resulted in legislation that severely restricted where and how banks could operate and formed the foundation for our current banking structure. During this period, branch banking as we know it today did not exist because it was either prohibited by law or condemned by the banking industry. In addition, banking reforms enacted in the 1930s significantly narrowed the financial activities banks could undertake. The general sentiment was that unscrupulous banking organizations contributed to earlier financial panics, including the Great Depression; thus reform was needed to require banks to concentrate on the principal activities associated with the banking industry — taking deposits and making loans. Such focus could be achieved only through cogent regulation and supervision.

The restrictions imposed on banking operations placed banks at a competitive disadvantage in the financial markets, both domestically and abroad. In the 1970s and 1980s, the financial markets experienced rapid increases in interest rates, as well as significant technological advances in communications and information systems, which resulted in the emergence of nonbank organizations that threatened the presence of banks and other financial institutions. As a result, a great deal of deregulation has occurred in the banking industry since the 1970s. Recent legislation and legislative proposals, for example, have called for barriers to national branch banking to be torn down and have permitted banking organizations to venture into such financial areas as investments and insurance, which have been prohibited since the 1930s. The deregulation has been supported as a means to improve competition; proponents argue that severely restrictive regulation threatens the existence of financial institutions.

In the past, as banking regulations became more restrictive, so did regulation of the financial markets as a whole. It will be interesting to see the sentiment of future legislation — generally when the economy, thus the financial markets, are performing well, there is a tendency to deregulate, while the opposite is true during, or immediately following, calamitous economic events.

Investments

We have experienced a variety of types of stock markets since the beginning of the twentieth century. In addition, participation in investments and the types of instruments offered have changed considerably. In the early 1900s, the investments arena was dominated by a small group of very wealthy investors and opulent corporations. Few small, individual investors ventured into corporate stocks and bonds because managers rarely disclosed financial information to the public — disclosure of such information was not mandated at the time. Because information was controlled by insiders and those who could afford to pay for it, the small investor was considerably disadvantaged and often exploited by the more informed investor. Thus, most individuals invested in instruments considered relatively safe, such as savings accounts at banks or government securities.

Industrialization and government financing of World War I resulted in increased financial prosperity and provided substantial wealth for those who had invested in the financial markets. The performance of the markets attracted greater interest from individual investors. By the 1920s, the number of investment firms had grown substantially, and corporate stocks and bonds were no longer viewed as investments for the elite only. Unfortunately, as the popularity of the securities markets increased, so did the fraudulent and manipulative practices of investment organizations, including those affiliated with commercial banks. It is interesting to note that mutual funds were introduced to the American financial markets during this period. Nearly all of these funds focused on common stock, and many were very speculative in nature and helped fuel the "fire" associated with the 1929 stock market crash.

From 1929 to 1932, the stock market declined by more than 80 percent — from nearly $90 billion to less than $16 billion. Many felt that the market crash was precipitated by unethical trading practices and abuses of investment organizations and individuals. Consequently, during the 1930s, there was significant pressure to regulate the behavior of the participants in the financial markets, and much of the legislation that forms the foundation of the regulatory tenor that exists today was enacted at the time. The principal impetus of the regulation was to ban fraudulent behavior and abusive practices of investors and investment organizations and to require greater disclosure of financial information by issuers of securities. The requirements to disclose greater amounts of financial information created opportunities in the investments arena: The accounting profession exploded, investment organizations introduced security analysis, and investments became a popular field of study at many universities.

Prosperity after World War II and a growing interest in investments by the average individual helped popularize mutual funds in the 1950s and 1960s. But, the 1970s was a period of rising interest rates and high inflation, which created a great deal of uncertainty in the economy and very volatile securities markets. Thus, investors withdrew from mutual funds, which was primarily a single-product industry at the time — stocks. It was during this period, though, that mutual fund companies began introducing new products, such as money market funds and municipal bond funds, in an attempt to recapture some of the lost demand. And, since the 1970s, mutual fund organizations have continued to expand the types of funds offered, mostly to satisfy investors' demands. Currently, there exist mutual funds for just about any type of investment you can imagine, and the popularity of any one type of fund shifts with changes in the financial markets — inevitably, when the stock market is performing well, stock funds are in greater demand, and when the economy is stagnant or decreasing, short-term, money market funds are more popular.

Since World War II, both institutional investors, which include pension funds, mutual funds, insurance companies, and the like, and individual investors have increased their presence in the securities markets. For instance, prior to 1950, institutional investors held less than 20 percent of corporate stock; but, by 1990, the proportion had increased to greater than 40 percent. At the same time, after the 1929 market crash, less than 5 percent of the population owned stock; currently greater than one-fourth of the population invests directly in common stock. With the recent successes of the stock markets and advanced information technologies that are available, the number of individual stockholders surely will increase in the future.

As the attitudes of both investors and regulators have changed, so have the types of investments and the methods used to evaluate investment opportunities. At the beginning of the twentieth century, in most cases, the only investments available to individuals were corporate stocks and bonds. And, because useful, timely financial information was rarely disclosed publicly, for the common investor, evaluation of securities generally consisted of observing the behavior of, and reacting to, those with access to financial information. But, as information disclosure became standardized and the common investor obtained greater investment knowledge, greater varieties of investment instruments and investing techniques were introduced, including interest-rate swaps, Treasury strips, program trading, junk bonds, and indexing. In addition, investment analysis evolved into a more sophisticated process. The analytical tools we use today find their roots in theory developed in the 1930s. During that period, it was suggested there exists a relationship among earnings, dividends, and stock prices such that value should be determined by computing the present value of the future cash flows associated with the stock. And, as you will see in this book, we still use this approach today.

Managerial Finance

When managerial finance emerged as a separate field of study in the early 1900s, the emphasis was on the legal aspects of mergers, the formation of new firms, and the various types of securities firms could issue to raise funds. This was a time when industrialization was sweeping the country; "big" was considered power, so many takeovers and mergers were used to create large corporations. To illustrate the sentiment of the times, consider the fact that almost 4,300 companies were merged into 300 corporations during the period from 1890 to 1905. The most famous merger was the combination of eight large steel companies to form U.S. Steel Corporation. The deal was worth $1.4 billion, which was equivalent to 7 percent of the country's gross national product at the time. In today's economy, a comparable merger would be valued at more than $500 billion.

Another wave of mergers occurred during the 1920s, fueled primarily by consolidations within the utilities industry. During the Depression era of the 1930s, however, an unprecedented number of business failures caused the emphasis in managerial finance to shift to bankruptcy and reorganization, to corporate liquidity, and to regulation of security markets. During this period, new rules were enacted that required firms to maintain and publicly disclose certain financial information.

Even with the frenzy of mergers in the early 1900s and the 1920s, and the large numbers of bankruptcies that followed the Depression in the 1930s, finance was mostly a descriptive discipline that emphasized organizational relationships of firms and legal matters. For the most part, finance theory consisted of anecdotes and "rules of thumb." If you read books about financial decision-making practices that were published during this period, you find little, if any, analytical procedures applied to complex decisions such as appropriate levels of liquidity; many decisions were based on subjective, or "seat-of-the-pants," logic. Analytical models based on time value of money principles were sometimes used to help make decisions about long-term, high-priced capital investments; but, even then, subjective techniques, such as payback, were considered the best method to make such decisions.

During the 1940s and early 1950s, finance continued to be taught as a descriptive, institutional subject, viewed more from the standpoint of an outsider rather than from that of management. Financial managers emphasized liquidity — cash budgeting and management of short-term assets and liabilities were stressed. At the same time, the scope of financial management began to widen some, primarily because the responsibilities associated with proper liquidity management included knowledge of accounts receivable activities, manufacturing operations, and short-term financing alternatives.

In the late 1950s and the 1960s, increased competition in established industries reduced the profit opportunities available to corporations. Financial managers shifted their focus toward techniques used to evaluate investment opportunities. Emphasis was given to finding investments that would improve the firm's ability to generate profits in the future. At about the same time, the computer was introduced as a tool for general business use. Thus, the focus of managerial finance began to shift more toward the insider's point of view and the importance of financial decision making to the firm. A movement toward theoretical analysis began during the 1960s, and the emphasis of managerial finance shifted to managerial decisions regarding the choice of assets and liabilities necessary to maximize the value of the firm. This era is considered the birth of modern finance, from which many of the decision-making techniques we use today evolved.

The 1970s was a period of increased international competition, fast-paced innovation and technological changes, and, perhaps most important, persistent inflation and economic uncertainty fueled by deficits in government spending and international trade. Changes in the business arena saw the beginning of a financial revolution of sorts in the late 1970s. Firms discovered innovative ways to manage financial risk and finance the firm. Stockholders became more concerned with how firms were managed and how managers' actions affected the value of the firm.

The focus on valuation continued through the 1980s, but the analysis was expanded to include (1) inflation and its effects on business decisions; (2) deregulation of financial institutions and the resulting trend toward large, broadly diversified financial services companies; (3) the dramatic increase in both the use of computers for analysis and the electronic transfer of information; (4) the increased importance of global markets and business operations; and (5) innovations in the financial products offered to investors. For example, it was the 1980s that saw an increase in the popularity of leveraged buyouts, or LBOs, which are transactions to purchase a company with huge amounts of debt to form a new privately owned, highly leveraged company.

In today's fast-paced, technologically driven world, the area of managerial finance continues to evolve. Mergers and acquisitions are still an important part of the financial world. But, to this point, the most important trends during the 1990s have been (1) the continued globalization of business, (2) a further increase in the use of electronic technology, and (3) the regulatory attitude of the government.

THE GLOBALIZATION OF BUSINESS   Four factors have made the trend toward globalization mandatory for many businesses:

1. Improvements in transportation and communications have lowered shipping costs and made international trade more feasible.
2. The political clout of consumers who desire low-cost, high-quality products has helped lower trade barriers designed to protect inefficient, high-cost domestic manufacturers.
3. As technology has become more advanced, the cost of developing new products has increased, and, as development costs rise, so must unit sales if the firm is to be competitive.
4. In a world populated with multinational firms able to shift production to wherever costs are lowest, a firm whose manufacturing operations are restricted to one country cannot compete unless costs in its home country happen to be low, a condition that does not necessarily exist for many U.S. corporations.

As a result of these four factors, survival requires that most manufacturers produce and sell globally.

Service companies, including banks, advertising agencies, and accounting firms, are also being forced to "go global" because such firms can better serve their multinational clients if they have worldwide operations. There will, of course, always be some purely domestic companies, but you should keep in mind that the most dynamic growth, and the best opportunities, are often with companies that operate worldwide. Recent events in eastern Asia prove the interrelationship of the world's marketplaces — economic catastrophes in Japan and Southeast Asia have caused American investors to become skittish and the financial markets in the United States to become more uncertain than previously. Many investors are sitting on the sidelines waiting to see if the economic problems in Asia will affect large American companies that have multinational operations.

INFORMATION TECHNOLOGY   Most large companies currently have networks of personal computers linked to one another, to the firm's own mainframe computers, and to their customers' and suppliers' computers. Some companies, like General Motors, require their suppliers to be linked electronically so that orders and payments can be made via the computer. As we enter the next millennium, we will see continued advances in the use of electronic technology in managerial finance, and this technology will revolutionize the way financial decisions are made, just as it has in the past. One result of this "electronic revolution" that we have seen during the last couple of decades is the increased use of quantitative analysis via computer models for financial decision making. Therefore, it is clear that the next generation of financial managers will need stronger computer and quantitative skills than were required in the past.

REGULATORY ATTITUDE OF THE GOVERNMENT   In the past 20 years, the government has taken fairly friendly positions with respect to legislative enactments and regulatory enforcements affecting businesses. Much of the legislation has focused on deregulation of highly regulated industries. Industries that have been deregulated include financial services, transportation, communications, and utilities. In addition, for the most part, the government has not discouraged mergers and acquisitions — since 1985 record numbers of mergers at historically high values have taken place. During this period, economic conditions generally were very favorable, as evidenced by record levels posted by the stock markets. In the future, if economic conditions sour, causing decreases in the securities markets, you can bet legislators will favor re-regulation if they believe deregulation contributed to the economic woes of the country. Historically, after the country has experienced economic tragedy, cries for new, tougher regulations have been abundant, and, for the most part, Congress has obliged.

Self-Test Questions

How have financial markets and institutions changed from the early 1900s to the 1990s?

How have investments changed from the early 1900s to the 1990s?

How has managerial finance changed from the early 1900s to the 1990s?

How might a person become better prepared for a career in managerial finance?

Importance of Managerial Finance

The historical trends discussed in the previous section have greatly increased the importance of finance, especially managerial finance. Because much of this book is concerned with the decision-making framework faced by corporate financial managers, in this section, we provide you with an indication of the role of managerial finance in business decisions.

In earlier times the marketing manager would project sales, the engineering and production staffs would determine the assets necessary to meet those demands, and the financial manager's job was simply to raise the money needed to purchase the required plant, equipment, and inventories. That situation no longer exists; decisions now are made in a much more coordinated manner, and the financial manager generally has direct responsibility for the control process.

Eastern Airlines and Delta Airlines can be used to illustrate both the importance of managerial finance and the effects of financial decisions. In the 1960s, Eastern's stock sold for more than $60 per share while Delta's sold for just $10. By the mid 1990s, Delta had become one of the world's strongest airlines, and its stock was selling for nearly $50 per share; and, in 1998, its price approached $120 per share. Eastern, on the other hand, had gone bankrupt and was no longer in existence. Although many factors combined to produce these divergent results, financial decisions exerted a major influence. Because Eastern had traditionally used a great deal of debt while Delta had not, Eastern's costs increased significantly, and its profits were lowered, when interest rates rose during the late 1970s and the early 1980s. Rising rates had only a minor effect on Delta. Further, when fuel price increases made it imperative for the airlines to buy new, fuel-efficient planes,

Delta was able to do so, but Eastern was not. Finally, when the airlines were deregulated, Delta was strong enough to expand into developing markets and to cut prices as necessary to attract business, but Eastern was not.

The Delta-Eastern story, and others like it, are now well known, so all companies today are greatly concerned with financial planning, and this has increased the importance of corporate financial staffs. Indeed, the value of managerial finance is reflected in the fact that more chief executive officers (CEOs) in the top 1,000 U.S. companies started their careers in finance than in any other functional area.

It also is becoming increasingly important for people in marketing, accounting, production, personnel, and other areas to understand finance in order to do a good job in their own fields. People in marketing, for instance, must understand how marketing decisions affect and are affected by funds availability, by inventory levels, by excess plant capacity, and so on. Similarly, accountants must understand how accounting data are used in corporate planning and are viewed by investors. Also, financial managers must have an understanding of marketing, accounting, and so forth, to make more informed decisions about replacement or expansion of plant and equipment and about how to best finance their firms.

Thus, *there are financial implications in virtually all business decisions, and nonfinancial executives simply must know enough finance to work these implications into their own specialized analyses.*[2] Because of this, every student of business, regardless of major, should be concerned with finance.

Self-Test Questions

Explain why financial planning is important to today's chief executives.

Why do marketing people need to know something about managerial finance?

The Financial Manager's Responsibilities

The financial manager's task is to make decisions concerning the acquisition and use of funds for the greatest benefit of the firm. Here are some specific activities that are involved:

1. **Forecasting and planning.** The financial manager must interact with other executives as they look ahead and lay the plans that will shape the firm's future position.
2. **Major investment and financing decisions.** A successful firm generally has rapid growth in sales, which requires investments in plant, equipment, and inventory. The financial manager must help determine the optimal sales growth rate, and he or she must help decide on the specific assets to acquire and the best way to finance those assets. For example, should the firm raise funds by borrowing (debt) or by selling stock (equity)? If the firm uses debt (borrows), should it be long term or short term?

---

[2]It is an interesting fact that the course "Managerial Finance for Nonfinancial Executives" has the highest enrollment in most executive development programs.

3. **Coordination and control.** The financial manager must interact with other executives to ensure that the firm is operated as efficiently as possible. All business decisions have financial implications, and all managers — financial and otherwise — need to take this into account. For example, marketing decisions affect sales growth, which, in turn, influences investment requirements. Thus, marketing decision makers must consider how their actions affect (and are affected by) such factors as the availability of funds, inventory policies, and plant capacity utilization.

4. **Dealing with the financial markets.** The financial manager must deal with the money and capital markets. As we will see in Chapter 2, each firm affects and is affected by the general financial markets where funds are raised, where the firm's securities are traded, and where its investors are either rewarded or penalized.

In summary, financial managers make decisions regarding which assets their firms should acquire, how those assets should be financed, and how the firm should manage its existing resources. If these responsibilities are performed optimally, financial managers will help to maximize the values of their firms, and this will also maximize the long-term welfare of those who buy from or work for the company, as well as the community where the firm is located.

Self-Test Question

What are four specific activities with which financial managers are involved?

Organization of the Book

This book is intended to provide you with an overview of finance. As the discussions in the previous sections indicate, the general area of finance includes numerous subjects that are related to either financial markets, investments, or managerial finance. There are many too many topics to cover in one book, so we have chosen to include those areas we believe will provide you with a good survey of finance topics. When you finish this book, you should be better informed about how financial managers and investors approach their decision-making tasks, and this knowledge should help you to make more informed decisions concerning your personal finances.

To accomplish our goal, in Part I of this book we present background material that is primarily descriptive in nature. In this chapter, we introduced you to the subject of finance. Chapter 2 describes the characteristics of financial markets and how they operate, the investment banking process, and how interest rates are determined. Chapter 3 describes financial institutions and the U.S. banking system, while Chapter 4 defines the characteristics of the various instruments (assets) traded in the financial markets. Finally, Chapter 5 includes a description of business organizations, a discussion about the goals of the firm, and an indication of the tax structure of our country.

Part II includes topics related to the theory of valuation. First, in Chapter 6, we discuss the concept of time value of money and its effects on asset values and rates of return. Then, Chapter 7 explains how asset values are determined in the marketplace. And, in Chapter 8 we see how risk is measured and how it affects asset prices and rates of return.

Part III deals specifically with managerial finance. First, Chapter 9 describes capital budgeting techniques and how to make decisions about major capital expenditures. Decisions in this area generally are not reversible and hence affect the firm's operations for many years, so their effect on the firm's value is significant. In Chapters 10 and 11, we examine the costs of the funds used to finance the firm and determine whether the method of financing affects the value of the firm. Chapters 9, 10, and 11 use the valuation concepts developed in Chapters 6, 7, and 8 to analyze such key issues as what projects to purchase, and the optimal debt/equity mix. In Chapter 12, we examine short-term, day-to-day operating decisions. Chapter 13 describes the key financial statements, shows how analysts appraise a firm's performance, and explains how the various aspects of managerial finance relate to one another. Then, in Chapter 14, we focus on projecting future financial statements under different strategic plans and operating conditions.

Part IV deals with issues associated with investments. We describe some general characteristics of investing as well as techniques used by investors to make investment decisions.

Each chapter begins with a "Managerial Perspective" that provides a real-world example of the subject to be discussed. Some chapters conclude with "Ethical Dilemma" boxes that set up predicaments for you to evaluate and decide a course of action. In addition, throughout the book, we discuss small business issues and incorporate descriptions of international business where appropriate.

It is worth noting that some instructors may choose to cover the chapters in a different sequence from their order in the book. The chapters are written in a modular, self-contained manner, so such a reordering will present no major difficulties.

Summary

This chapter has provided an overview of finance. The key concepts covered in the chapter are listed below.

- The study of finance consists of three interrelated areas: (1) **financial markets,** (2) **investments,** and (3) **managerial finance.**
- Finance has undergone significant changes over time, but four issues have received the most emphasis in recent decades: (1) **inflation** and its effects on interest rates, (2) **deregulation** of highly regulated industries, (3) a dramatic increase in **technology,** such as the use of telecommunications for transmitting information and the use of computers for analyzing the effects of alternative financial decisions, and (4) the increased importance of **global financial markets and business operations.**
- **Financial managers** are responsible for obtaining and using funds in a way that will **maximize the value of their firms.**
- **Small businesses** are quite important in the aggregate, so we shall discuss small business issues throughout the text.

Questions

1-1 How has the study of finance changed since the beginning of the twentieth century?

1-2 Why is it important for business students to study finance, even if it is not their major?

1-3 Can you think of how knowledge of how financial decisions are made by corporate financial managers can help you make personal financial decisions?

1-4 What are the major responsibilities of financial managers, and why is each important for proper management of a company?

1-5 Under what circumstances do you think the government will impose greater regulations on financial markets and businesses? When does the government tend to favor deregulation and take a more *laissez-faire* attitude toward business?

CHAPTER 2

Financial Markets, the Investment Banking Process, and Interest Rates*

A MANAGERIAL PERSPECTIVE

In December 1991, after 17 months of recession, the Federal Reserve took drastic actions to lower interest rates in the financial markets in an attempt to halt the recession. Rates were lowered to levels not seen in nearly three decades. Previous Fed actions had been small, cautious reductions which had been announced with minimum fanfare to keep the financial markets convinced of the Fed's commitment to fight inflation.

The actions came in response to growing criticism from the White House, Congress, and private economists, who accused the Fed of worrying too much about bond market psychology and too little about the rapidly deteriorating confidence of both consumers and business executives in other financial markets. In addition, new forecasts by the Fed's economists (who had earlier been confident that the economy was recovering) showed an economy "dead in the water." Their revised forecasts predicted no growth, or even negative growth, for both the fourth quarter of 1991 and the first quarter of 1992.

The financial system responded immediately to the Fed's actions. Morgan Guaranty Trust Co. cut its prime lending rate from 7.5 percent to 6.5 percent, and other large banks followed Morgan's actions. Long-term rates in the bond market decreased to levels not seen in years.

In an attempt to "prop up the economy" and push it toward recovery, the Fed continued its support for lower interest rates for the next couple of years. In fact, at the end of 1993, the yield on 30-year Treasury bonds had dipped to a record low of 5.8 percent, and the yield on Treasury bills was

Continued

*Throughout much of this chapter, as well as the next couple of chapters, we primarily refer to corporations as the users, or issuers, of such financial assets as debt and equity. In reality, governments, government agencies, and individuals also issue debt. For example, an individual "issues" a mortgage when he or she finances the purchase of a house. But, because corporations issue a variety of debt and can also issue equity, we will identify them as the issuers more often than governments or individuals in the examples.

around 3 percent. These low rates helped encourage borrowing and capital investment, which, in turn, helped the economy move closer to recovery. The policy makers at the Fed were happy — right? Not exactly. The Fed was worried that the record low interest rates would result in a recovery with too much growth too quickly, which would create "runaway" inflation.

To slow the pace of the economy, the Fed increased interest rates six times during 1994. This action caused short-term interest rates to increase by more than 2 percent during the year. But, just as the Fed had hoped, economic growth slowed to about 2.5 percent, and inflation leveled off at about 3 percent.

From 1995 until 1998 interest rates have remained fairly stable. But during the latter half of 1998, the Fed felt the need to lower rates several times to ensure economic growth did not stall. Such changes affect both businesses and individuals. Whether a business or an individual, when we borrow we would like the rates to be low. On the other hand, when rates are low, those who depend on the income from their investments suffer. Thus, interest rate changes affect all of us.

As you read this chapter, think about (1) all the factors the Fed must consider before attempting to change interest rates, and (2) the effects of interest rate changes on inflation, on the financial markets, and on the economy as a whole.

Financial markets are extremely important to the economic well-being of our country. Thus, it is important that both investors and financial managers understand the environment and markets within which securities are traded and businesses operate. Therefore, in this chapter, we examine the markets where firms raise funds, securities are traded, and the prices for stocks and bonds are established. In the process, we will explore the principal factors that determine money costs in the economy.

What Are Financial Markets?

Businesses, individuals, and government units often need to raise capital (funds). For example, suppose Carolina Power & Light (CP&L) forecasts an increase in the demand for electricity in North Carolina, and the company decides to build a new power plant. Because CP&L almost certainly will not have the billions of dollars necessary to pay for the plant, the company will have to raise these funds in the financial markets. Or suppose Mr. Chang, the proprietor of a San Francisco hardware store, decides to expand into appliances. Where will he get the money to buy the initial inventory of TV sets, washers, and freezers? Similarly, if you want to buy a home that costs $100,000, but you only have $20,000 in savings, how can you raise the additional $80,000?

On the other hand, some individuals and firms have incomes that are greater than their current expenditures, so they have funds available to invest, or save. For example, Alexandra Trottier has an annual income of $36,000, but her expenses are only $30,000, while Microsoft recently announced its desire to invest a few billion dollars for expanding into related businesses and for research and development.

People and organizations that need money are brought together with those having surplus funds in the *financial markets.* Note that "markets" is plural — there are a great many different financial markets, each one consisting of many institutions and individuals, in a developed economy such as ours. Unlike *physical asset markets,* which are those for such products as wheat, autos, real estate, computers, and machinery, *financial asset markets* deal with stocks, bonds, mortgages, and other *claims on real assets* with respect to the distribution of future cash flows.

In a general sense, the term *financial market* refers to a conceptual "mechanism" rather than a physical location or a specific type of organization or structure. We usually describe the **financial markets** as being a system comprised of individuals and institutions, instruments, and procedures that bring together borrowers and savers, no matter the location. In this chapter, we describe the concepts and procedures of financial markets; in the next chapter, we describe some of the institutions that participate in borrowing and savings activities that take place in the financial markets; and, in Chapter 4, we describe some of the instruments utilized to facilitate the borrowing and savings processes.

FINANCIAL MARKETS
A system comprised of individuals and institutions, instruments, and procedures that bring together borrowers and savers.

Self-Test Questions

What is a financial market?

Why is it important to have a basic understanding of financial markets?

Importance of Financial Markets

The primary role of financial markets is to help bring together *borrowers* and savers (*lenders*) by facilitating the flow of funds from individuals and businesses with surplus funds to individuals, businesses, and governments that have needs for funds in excess of their incomes.[1] In developed economies, financial markets help efficiently allocate excess funds of savers to individuals and organizations in need of funds for investment or consumption. The more efficient the process of funds flow, the more productive the economy, both in terms of manufacturing and financing.

Flow of Funds

By providing *mechanisms* by which borrowers and lenders get together to transfer funds, the financial markets allow us to consume amounts different than our current incomes. Thus, financial markets provide us with the ability to transfer

---

[1]Throughout the chapter, we often refer to the parties involved in financial market transactions as *borrowers* or *lenders,* which implies that only loans are traded in the financial markets. But, as you will see, stocks, options, and many other financial assets also are traded in the financial markets. But, throughout our general discussions, we will use the term "borrowers" to refer to such parties as individuals and government units that raise needed funds using various types of loans, as well as corporations that use both loans and stock issues to raise needed funds. Further, we will use the term "lenders" to refer to those parties that provide funds, whether the medium is a loan or a stock.

income through time. When we borrow, for example, we sacrifice future income to increase current income; when we save, or invest, we sacrifice current income in exchange for greater expected income in the future. For example, as young adults we borrow funds to go to college or to buy such high-priced items as a house or a car; thus we tend to save little or nothing. But, as older adults, when we become established in our careers and reach, or are near, our peak income years, we generally save (invest) greater percentages of our incomes. Finally, when we retire, we rely on funds accumulated from prior years' savings to provide our retirement income. Consequently, as adults, we go through three general phases that would not be possible without financial markets — as young adults we desire to consume more than our incomes, so we must borrow; as older working adults we earn more than our consumption needs, so we save; and, as retired adults, the funds accumulated in earlier years are used to at least partially replace income lost due to retirement. Without financial markets, consumption would be restricted to income earned each year plus any amounts put aside (perhaps in a coffee can) in previous years; thus, our standard of living would be much lower than is now possible.

Funds are transferred from those with surpluses (savers) to those with needs (borrowers) by the three different processes diagrammed in Figure 2-1:

1. A *direct transfer* of money and securities, as shown in the top section occurs when a business sells its stocks or bonds directly to savers (investors), without going through any type of intermediary, or financial institution. The business delivers its securities to savers, who, in turn, give the firm the money it needs.

2. As shown in the middle section, a transfer can also go through an *investment banking house* such as Goldman Sachs, which serves as a middleman and

FIGURE 2-1

Diagram of the Capital Formation Process

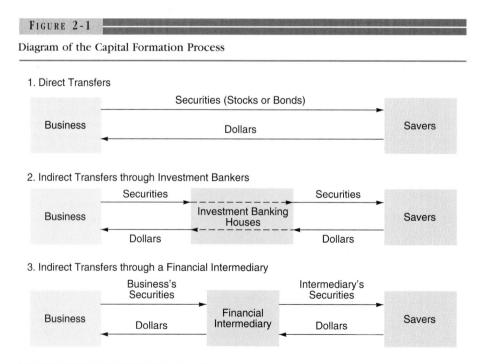

1. Direct Transfers

2. Indirect Transfers through Investment Bankers

3. Indirect Transfers through a Financial Intermediary

facilitates the issuance of securities. The company sells its stocks or bonds to the investment bank, which, in turn, sells these same securities to savers. The business's securities and the savers' money merely "pass through" the investment banking house. For example, the next time IBM raises funds by issuing stock, it probably will utilize the services of an investment banker, such as Goldman Sachs or Merrill Lynch, to sell the issue in the financial markets. We describe the investment banking process later in the chapter.

3. Transfers can also be made through a *financial intermediary* such as a bank or a mutual fund. Here the intermediary obtains funds from savers, and then it uses the money to lend out or to purchase another business's securities. For example, when you deposit money in a savings account at your local bank, the bank takes those funds along with other depositors' funds and creates such loans as mortgages, business loans, and automobile loans. The existence of intermediaries greatly increases the efficiency of the financial markets. More information concerning the roles and descriptions of financial intermediaries is provided in the next chapter.

For simplicity, in Figure 2-1, we assumed the entity that needs capital is a business, and specifically a corporation, but it is easy to visualize the demander of funds as a home purchaser or a government unit. Direct transfers of funds from savers to borrowers are possible and do occur on occasion, but generally corporations and government entities use investment bankers to help them raise needed capital in the financial markets, and savers often use such intermediaries as banks and mutual funds to help them lend their funds or to borrow needed funds.

Market Efficiency

If the financial markets did not provide efficient funds transfers, the economy simply could not function as it now does: Carolina Power & Light would have difficulty raising needed capital, so Raleigh's citizens would pay more for electricity; you would not be able to buy the house you want; and, Alexandra Trottier would have no place to invest her savings. Obviously, the level of employment and productivity, hence our standard of living, would be much lower. Therefore, it is absolutely essential that our financial markets function efficiently — not only quickly, but also at a low cost. The types of market efficiency include economic efficiency and informational efficiency.

ECONOMIC EFFICIENCY
Funds are allocated to their optimal use at the lowest costs in the financial markets.

ECONOMIC EFFICIENCY   The financial markets are said to have **economic efficiency** if funds are allocated to their optimal use at the lowest costs. In other words, in economically efficient markets, businesses and individuals invest funds in assets that yield the highest returns, and the costs of searching for such opportunities are lower than in less efficient markets. Often individuals hire brokers, who charge commissions, to help search for, and then buy or sell investments in the financial markets. If the commissions and other costs associated with transactions, called **transaction costs,** are very high, investments will not be as attractive as when transaction costs are low.

TRANSACTION COSTS
Costs associated with buying and selling investments, including commissions, search costs, taxes, and so on.

INFORMATION EFFICIENCY   The prices of investments bought and sold in the financial markets are based on available information. If the prices of investments reflect existing information and adjust very quickly when new information becomes

INFORMATIONAL EFFICIENCY
The prices of investments reflect existing information and adjust quickly when new information enters the markets.

available, then the financial markets have achieved **informational efficiency.** When the financial markets have a large number of participants in search of the most profitable investments, informational efficiency generally exists. For instance, in the United States, there are millions of individual investors, as well as more than 100,000 highly trained professionals, who participate in the financial markets, so you would expect investment prices to adjust almost instantaneously to new information because a large number of the market participants will evaluate the new information as soon as possible in an effort to find more profitable investments. Informational efficiency generally is divided into the following three categories:

1. *Weak-form* efficiency states that all information contained in past price movements is fully reflected in current market prices. Therefore, information about recent, or past, trends in investment prices is of no use in selecting investments — the fact that an investment has risen for the past three days, for example, gives us no useful clues as to what it will do today or tomorrow.

2. *Semistrong-form* efficiency states that current market prices reflect all *publicly available* information. If this is true, it does no good to pore over such published data as a corporation's financial statements because market prices will have adjusted to any good or bad news contained in such reports as soon as they were made public. However, insiders (say, the presidents of companies), even under semistrong-form efficiency, can still make abnormal returns on their own companies' investments (stocks).[2]

3. *Strong-form* efficiency states that current market prices reflect all pertinent information, whether publicly available or privately held. If this form of efficiency holds, even insiders would find it impossible to earn abnormal returns in the financial markets.[3]

The informational efficiency of the financial markets has received a great deal of attention during the past three decades. The results of most of the studies suggest that the financial markets are highly efficient in the weak form and reasonably efficient in the semistrong form, but strong-form efficiency does not hold.

Financial markets that are informationally efficient also tend to be economically efficient because investors can expect prices to reflect appropriate information and thus make intelligent choices about which investments are expected to provide the highest returns.

 Self-Test Questions

What are the three ways funds are transferred from savers, or lenders, to borrowers?

Why do you think that most transfers of money and securities are indirect rather than direct?

---

[2]An abnormal return is one that exceeds the return justified by the riskiness of the investment.

[3]Several cases of illegal insider trading have made the news headlines in the past. In a famous case, Ivan Boesky admitted to making $50 million by purchasing the stock of firms he knew were about to merge. He went to jail, and he had to pay a large fine, but he helped disprove strong-form efficiency.

What does it mean to have economically efficient financial markets? What does it mean to have informationally efficient markets?

What are the three forms (degrees) of informational efficiency?

Types of Financial Markets

There exist a number of different types of financial markets with a variety of investments and participants. We generally differentiate among financial markets according to the types of investments, maturities of investments, types of borrowers and lenders, locations of the markets, and types of transactions. There are too many different types of financial markets to discuss here. Instead, we describe the more common classifications and provide some indication of the function of each type of market.

Money Markets versus Capital Markets

Some borrowers need funds for short periods, while others need funds for extended periods. For example, a company that finances its inventories generally uses loans with maturities ranging from 30 to 90 *days,* while an individual who purchases a house uses loans with maturities from 15 to 30 *years.* Similarly, some investors prefer to invest for short periods, while others invest for longer periods. For example, a college student who has funds she does not need for another six months, perhaps to pay tuition, might invest the extra funds in a six-month certificate of deposit (CD). On the other hand, a couple who is investing for the college education of their eight-year-old child might choose to invest in longer-term investments, say, ten-year corporate bonds.

MONEY MARKETS
The segments of the financial markets in which the instruments that are traded have maturities equal to one year or less.

The markets for short-term financial instruments are termed the *money markets,* while the markets for long-term financial instruments are termed the *capital markets.* More specifically, the **money markets** include instruments with maturities equal to one year or less when originally issued, and the **capital markets** include instruments with original maturities greater than one year. By definition, then, money markets include only debt instruments, because equity instruments (i.e., stocks) have no specific maturity, while capital markets include both equity instruments and such long-term debt instruments as mortgages, corporate bonds, and government bonds.[4]

CAPITAL MARKETS
The segments of the financial markets in which the instruments that are traded have maturities greater than one year.

The primary function of the money markets is to provide liquidity to businesses, governments, and individuals to meet short-term needs for cash, because, in most cases, the timings of cash inflows and cash outflows do not coincide exactly. But, the existence of money market instruments with different maturities permits us to better match our cash inflows with cash outflows. For example, the college student who has funds that are not needed for tuition payments until six months from now can invest the funds and earn a positive return rather than allowing the funds to sit in a checking account that earns little or no interest. If she invests in a six-month CD, the college student will effectively match the timing of her cash inflow (maturity of the CD) with her cash need (payment of

---

[4]The characteristics of various financial instruments, called financial assets, are discussed in Chapter 4.

tuition). On the other hand, consider a corporation that needs to pay for the purchase of inventory, but cash from the sale of the inventory will not be received for another 30 days. The company has the opportunity to raise the needed funds through a 30-day loan, and thus it can match the timing of the cash outflow (payment for inventory) with the timing of the cash inflow (collection for inventory sale). Individuals, companies, and governments use the money markets similarly — to better align short-term cash flows. Thus, when cash surpluses exist for short periods, short-term investments are desirable; when cash deficits exist for short periods, short-term loans (debt instruments) are desirable.

The primary function of the capital markets is to provide us with the opportunity to transfer cash surpluses or deficits to future years. For example, without the availability of mortgages, most individuals could not afford to buy houses when they are young and just starting their careers because they have little or no savings and their incomes are not sufficient to pay for such houses. But, mortgages and other long-term loans permit us to borrow funds we do not have today based on our abilities to generate sufficient funds from future years' incomes to repay the debts. Thus, we can spend more than our incomes today because we expect to provide greater incomes in the future. Similarly, corporations issue stocks and bonds to get funds to support such current investment needs as expansion, and investors who provide the funds receive promises that cash flows generated by the corporations will be distributed some time in the future. In essence, then, individuals, corporations, and governments use the capital markets to spend more than the funds generated in the current period at the expense of the ability to spend funds generated in future periods or to invest current income to enable greater consumption in the future.

Debt Markets versus Equity Markets

Simply stated, the debt markets are the markets where loans are traded, while the equity markets are the markets where stocks of corporations are traded. A debt instrument is a contract that specifies the amounts, as well as the times, a borrower must repay a lender. On the other hand, equity represents "ownership" in a corporation and entitles the stockholder to share in cash distributions generated from income (dividends) and from liquidation of the firm. The debt markets provide individuals, companies, and governments with opportunities to consume future income in the current period through such loans as mortgages, corporate bonds, and Treasury bonds. Each of these loans requires repayment, with interest, from income (cash flows) generated during the loan period. On the other hand, the equity markets permit corporations to raise funds by selling ownership interests, thus transferring some risks associated with the businesses to individuals and other companies. Purchasers of equity receive the right to distributions of cash flows made by the firm from income generated in the future. But, unlike debt, equity is not a specific contract that guarantees cash distributions will be made or the investment will be repaid. Because debt typically has a maturity, it can be considered temporary funding, while equity is more permanent because it has no specific maturity.

Equity markets, which also are called stock markets, are familiar to most of us. In fact, more than 50 million Americans invest in stocks, either directly or through mutual funds. In addition, there are more than 10,000 institutions, such as pension funds and insurance companies, that invest in the equity markets. It is apparent,

TABLE 2-1

TABLE 2-1

Debt Markets in the United States, 1997

Type of Debt	Amount (billions of dollars)	Percent of Total
Treasury	$ 3,450	29.7%
Corporate	2,135	18.4
Mortgage-backed (agency)	1,780	15.3
Money market	1,530	13.2
Municipal	1,325	11.4
Federal agencies	950	8.2
Asset-backed	450	3.9
Total debt	$11,620	

SOURCE: Federal Reserve System

then, that stock markets are very important in the United States. For that reason, we discuss further the characteristics of stock markets in the next section.

Debt markets generally are described according to the characteristics of the debt that is traded. There are many different types of debt, hence many different types of debt markets. For example, short-term debt instruments, such as those issued by the U.S. Treasury, are traded in the *money markets,* while such long-term debt instruments as corporate bonds and mortgages are traded in the *capital markets.* In addition, the debt markets are clearly divided by type of participant, whether issuer (borrower) or investor (lender). The portion of the debt markets where government bonds are traded differs from the corporate bonds market, and the market for consumer debt differs further. Thus, the segmentation of the debt markets is based on the maturity of the instrument, the issuer, and the investor.

The largest segment of the debt markets is represented by the bond markets, where government, corporate, and foreign bonds are traded. Table 2-1 shows the values of the various debt markets in the United States in 1997. At that time, the value of the bond markets in the United States was more than $11.5 trillion. As you can see, Treasury issues and corporate bonds accounted for almost 50 percent of the entire debt market. Corporate debt is held principally by corporations and institutions, such as mutual funds and insurance companies.

Primary Markets versus Secondary Markets

PRIMARY MARKETS
Markets in which corporations raise funds by issuing new securities.

SECONDARY MARKETS
Markets in which securities and other financial assets are traded among investors after they have been issued by corporations and public agencies such as municipalities.

The primary markets are the markets where "new" securities are traded, while the secondary markets are the markets where "used" securities are traded. **Primary markets** are the markets in which corporations raise new capital. If IBM were to sell a new issue of common stock to raise capital, this would be a primary market transaction. The corporation selling the newly created stock receives the proceeds from the sale in a primary market transaction. **Secondary markets** are markets in which existing, previously issued securities are traded among investors. Thus, if Jessica Rogers decided to buy 1,000 shares of existing IBM stock, the purchase would occur in the secondary market. The New York Stock Exchange is a secondary market, because it deals in outstanding, or previously issued, stocks and bonds as opposed to newly issued stocks and bonds. Secondary markets also exist for mortgages, various other types of loans, and other financial assets. The corporation whose securities are being traded in the secondary market is not involved in the transaction and, thus, does not receive any funds from such a sale.

Derivatives Markets

Options, futures, and swaps are some of the securities traded in the derivatives markets. These securities are called derivatives because their values are determined, or "derived," directly from other assets. For example, if an individual owns a call option written on AT&T stock, he or she has the ability to purchase shares of AT&T at a price specified in the option contract. Because the purchase price of AT&T is fixed in the contract, the value of the call option changes as the actual *market value* of AT&T changes.

Although derivatives often are used to speculate about the movements of prices in the financial markets and the markets for such commodities as wheat and soy beans, they typically are used to help manage risk. Individuals, corporations, and governments use derivatives to *hedge* risk by offsetting exposures to uncertain price changes in the future. Chapter 4 includes a description of some characteristics of different derivatives as well as other financial assets.

Self-Test Questions

How are the financial markets differentiated?

What are the differences between (1) the money markets and the capital markets, (2) the primary markets and the secondary markets, and (3) the debt markets and the equity markets?

How are the debt markets differentiated?

What types of assets are traded in the derivatives markets?

Stock Markets

In recent years, individuals have expressed greater interest in stocks than ever before. A major reason for this increased interest is the fact that the stock markets have generated record-breaking results in recent years. For example, from 1995 to 1997 the annual returns in the stock markets averaged more than 20 percent, which is unprecedented. During the period we wrote this book in 1998, the markets experienced several swings — from record highs to very substantial decreases. Much of the record upward movement in the markets has resulted from enthusiastic buying by individual investors, which has resulted from a greater interest in stocks expressed by individuals in recent years. Although the markets might have slowed or even turned around by the time you read this text, the popularity and intrigue of the stock markets will always be evident. Therefore, in this section, we describe the characteristics of the stock markets.

Types of Stock Market Transactions

We can classify stock market transactions into three distinct types:

1. **Trading in the outstanding, previously issued shares of established, publicly owned companies: the secondary market.** If the owner of 100 shares of Microsoft sells his or her stock, the trade is said to have occurred in the *secondary market*. The company receives no new money when sales occur in this market.

2. **Additional shares sold by established, publicly owned companies: the primary market.** If Microsoft decides to sell (or issue) additional shares to raise funds for expansion, this transaction is said to occur in the *primary market*.

3. **New public offerings by privately held firms — the initial public offering (IPO) market: the primary market.** When Coors Brewing Company, which was owned by the Coors family at the time, decided to sell some stock to raise capital needed for a major expansion program, it took its stock public. Whenever stock in a privately held corporation is offered to the public for the first time, the company is said to be **going public.** The market for stock that has recently gone public is called the **initial public offering (IPO) market.**

GOING PUBLIC
The act of selling stock to the public at large for the first time by a corporation or its principal stockholders.

INITIAL PUBLIC OFFERING (IPO) MARKET
The market consisting of stocks of companies that have just gone public.

Nearly all stock transactions occur in the secondary markets, either on the organized exchanges or in the over-the-counter market. But, primary market transactions are very important to corporations that need to raise funds for capital projects. In this section we describe the general characteristics of stock markets, which function principally as secondary markets; then in the next section we describe how stocks and bonds are issued in the primary markets.

There are two basic types of stock markets in the United States: (1) *organized exchanges,* which include the New York Stock Exchange (NYSE), the American Stock Exchange (AMEX), and several regional exchanges, and (2) the less formal *over-the-counter market* (OTC). In most cases, the stocks of smaller publicly owned firms are not listed on an exchange; they trade in the over-the-counter (OTC) market, and the companies and their stocks are said to be *unlisted.* However, larger publicly owned companies generally apply for listing on an organized exchange, and they and their stocks are said to be *listed.* As a general rule, companies are first traded in the over-the-counter market. Then, as they grow, companies list on a regional organized exchange, such as the Philadelphia Stock Exchange or the Pacific Exchange. As the company matures and becomes even larger, its stock moves to the American Stock Exchange and the New York Stock Exchange. Because the organized exchanges have actual physical market locations and are easier to describe and understand, we consider them first.

The Stock Exchanges

ORGANIZED SECURITY EXCHANGES
Formal organizations with physical locations that facilitate trading in designated (listed) securities. The two major U.S. stock exchanges are the New York Stock Exchange (NYSE) and the American Stock Exchange (AMEX).

The **organized security exchanges** are tangible physical entities. The organized exchanges in the United States include national exchanges, such as the New York Stock Exchange (NYSE) and American Stock Exchange (AMEX), and regional exchanges, such as the Philadelphia Stock Exchange (PHLX) and the Chicago Stock Exchange (CHX). The NYSE, which is more than 200 years old, is the largest organized stock exchange in the world in terms of the total value of stocks traded. The PHLX, which was established in 1790, is the oldest organized exchange in the United States.

Each of the larger stock exchanges occupies its own building, has specifically designated members, and has an elected governing body — its board of governors. Members are said to have *seats* on the exchange, although everybody stands up. These seats, which are bought and sold, give the holder the right to trade on the exchange. The number of seats, or memberships, available on each exchange varies. For example, the number of seats on the NYSE has remained at 1,366 since 1868, the AMEX has 864 seats, and the CHX has 445 seats. The cost of exchange membership also varies considerably; it generally is greater for national exchanges than for regional exchanges. In 1998, a seat on the NYSE was selling for more than $1.5 million, a seat on the AMEX was selling for more than $400,000, and a seat on the CHX averaged about $30,000.[5]

Most of the larger stock brokerage firms own seats on the exchanges and designate one or more of their officers as members. The exchanges are open on all normal working days, with the members meeting in a large room equipped with telephones and other electronic equipment that enable each member to communicate with his or her firm's offices throughout the country.

Not all exchange seats have the same membership responsibility. And, to be listed, companies must have certain minimum qualifications. The types of exchange membership and the listing requirements are discussed next.

EXCHANGE MEMBERS   Exchange members are charged with different trading responsibilities, depending on the type of seat that is owned. For example, the seats on the NYSE can be classified into one of four categories: commission brokers, independent (floor) brokers, competitive (registered) traders, and specialists. The responsibilities of each NYSE member are given here:

1. *Commission brokers* are individuals employed by brokerage firms that are members of the exchange. These brokers act as agents for individual investors, such as Alexandra Trottier, who want to buy or sell stocks. As the title implies, commission brokers are paid commissions for their services. Commission brokers are allowed to trade only for other investors; they are not allowed to trade for their own accounts.

2. *Independent brokers,* sometimes called *floor brokers,* are independent, freelance brokers who work for themselves rather than for a brokerage firm. Independent brokers "farm out" their services to brokerage firms that need additional help because trading activity is too high for their commission brokers to handle. Like commission brokers, independent brokers are not allowed to trade for their own accounts.

3. *Competitive traders,* also known as *registered floor traders,* represent a small group of individuals who trade only for their own accounts. Such traders try to find disparities in stock prices by continuously searching for mispriced (overvalued and undervalued) stocks. Competitive traders are not allowed to trade for other investors; they can only trade for themselves.

4. *Specialists* are considered the most important participants in NYSE transactions because their role is to bring buyers and sellers together. Each specialist is assigned a group of stocks to oversee. Specialists make certain the auction process is completed in a fair and efficient manner. To accomplish his or her job, a specialist might have to buy stock when not enough sellers exist or to

---

[5]NYSE stocks were not continuously traded until 1871. Prior to that time, stocks were traded sequentially according to their position on a stock roll, or roster, sheet. Members were assigned chairs, or "seats," to sit in while the roll call of stocks proceeded. The number of "seats" changed as the number of members changed, until the number was fixed at 1366 in 1868. The highest price paid for a seat on the NYSE was $20 million on March 9, 1998.

sell stock when not enough buyers exist; he or she must be ready to *make a market* when buyers or sellers are needed. To accomplish this, a specialist is required to maintain inventories in the stocks he or she is assigned. The specialist sets a *bid price* (the price the specialist will pay for the stock) and an *asked price* (the price at which shares will be sold out of inventory) in an effort to keep the inventory in balance. If many buy orders start coming in because of favorable developments or if sell orders come in because of unfavorable events, the specialist will raise or lower prices to keep supply and demand in balance. Bid prices are somewhat lower than asked prices, with the difference, or *spread,* representing the specialist's profit margin.[6] On the NYSE, supply/demand imbalances require specialists to participate in buying or selling shares only about 10 percent of the time.

LISTING REQUIREMENTS For a stock to be traded on an exchange, it must be *listed.* Each exchange has established **listing requirements,** which indicate the quantitative and qualitative characteristics a firm must possess to be listed. Examples of the listing requirements for some exchanges in the United States are provided in Table 2-2. As you can see, even for the NYSE, firms do not have to be extremely large to qualify for listing. The primary purpose for the listing requirements is to ensure that investors have some interest in the company so its stock will be actively traded on the exchange.

Approximately 3,000 companies in the United States and worldwide have shares listed for trade on the NYSE, more than 900 are listed on the AMEX, more than 4,000 are listed on the Chicago Stock Exchange, and the Philadelphia Exchange and Pacific Exchange each has more than 2,500 listed companies. The NASDAQ, which stands for the National Association of Security Dealers Automated

LISTING REQUIREMENTS
Characteristics a firm must possess to be listed on an exchange.

TABLE 2-2

Listing Requirements for Exchanges and NASDAQ

	NYSE	AMEX and Regional Exchanges[a]	NASDAQ
Round lot (100 shares) shareholders	2,000	800	300
Number of public shares (million)	1.1	0.5	0.5
Market value of public shares (millions of dollars)	$40	$3	$1
Net tangible assets (millions of dollars)	$4	$4	$2
Pre-tax income (millions of dollars)	$2.50	$0.75	$0.50

[a]These numbers are indicative of the listing requirements for larger regional stock exchanges, including the Chicago Stock Exchange, the Pacific Exchange, and the Philadelphia Stock Exchange. The listing requirements for smaller regional exchanges generally are not as restrictive.

---

[6]Special facilities are available to help institutional investors such as mutual funds or pension funds sell large blocks of stock without depressing their prices. In essence, brokerage houses that cater to institutional clients will purchase blocks (defined as 10,000 or more shares) and then resell the stock to other institutions or individuals. Also, when a firm has a major announcement that is likely to cause its stock price to change sharply, it will ask the exchanges to halt trading in its stock until the announcement has been made and digested by investors. Thus, when Texaco announced that it planned to acquire Getty Oil, trading was halted for one day in both Texaco and Getty stocks.

Quotation, has the greatest number of listed companies, with more than 5,500. The NASDAQ evolved from the over-the-counter market (OTC), which is described in the next section.

Listed firms pay relatively small annual fees to the exchange to receive such benefits as the marketability offered by continuous trading activity and the publicity and prestige associated with being an exchange-listed firm. Many people believe that listing has a beneficial effect on the sales of the firm's products, and it probably is advantageous in terms of lowering the return demanded by investors to buy its common stock. Investors respond favorably to increased information, increased liquidity, and confidence that the quoted price is not being manipulated. It is not required that a qualified firm be listed on an exchange — listing is the choice of the firm.

The Over-the-Counter Market (OTC)

OVER-THE-COUNTER MARKET
A large collection of brokers and dealers, connected electronically by telephones and computers, that provides for trading in securities not listed on the organized exchanges.

If a security is not traded on an organized exchange, it is said to be traded *over the counter.* In contrast to the organized security exchanges, the **over-the-counter market** is an intangible organization that consists of a network of brokers and dealers around the country. An explanation of the term "over-the-counter" will help clarify exactly what this market is. The exchanges operate as auction markets — buy and sell orders come in more or less simultaneously, and exchange members match these orders. If a stock is traded less frequently, perhaps because it is the stock of a new or a small firm, few buy and sell orders come in, and matching them within a reasonable length of time would be difficult. To avoid this problem, some brokerage firms maintain an inventory of such stocks — they buy when individual investors want to sell and sell when investors want to buy. At one time the inventory of securities was kept in a safe, and the stocks, when bought and sold, literally were passed *over the counter.*

Traditionally, the over-the-counter market has been defined to include all facilities that are needed to conduct security transactions not conducted on the organized exchanges. These facilities consist of (1) the relatively few *dealers* who hold inventories of over-the-counter securities and who are said to "make a market" in these securities, (2) the thousands of *brokers* who act as *agents* in bringing these dealers together with investors, and (3) the computers, terminals, and electronic networks that provide a communications link between dealers and brokers. Unlike most organized exchanges, the OTC does not operate as an auction market. The dealers who make a market in a particular stock continuously quote a price at which they are willing to buy the stock (the bid price) and a price at which they will sell shares (the asked price). Each dealer's prices, which are adjusted as supply and demand conditions change, can be read off computer screens all across the country. The spread between bid and asked prices represents the dealer's markup, or profit.

Many of the brokers and dealers who make up the over-the-counter market are members of a self-regulating body known as the *National Association of Security Dealers* (NASD), which licenses brokers and oversees trading practices. The computerized trading network used by NASD is known as the NASD Automated Quotation System (NASDAQ), and *The Wall Street Journal* and other newspapers contain information on NASDAQ transactions. Today, the NASDAQ is considered a sophisticated market of its own, separate from the OTC. Unlike the OTC, the NASDAQ has market makers who continuously monitor trading activities in various stocks to ensure stocks are available to traders who want to buy, and vice versa. The role of the NASDAQ market maker is similar to that of the specialist on the NYSE. Also, there are minimum financial requirements for companies to be listed, or included, on the NASDAQ (see Table 2-2), while the OTC has no such requirements.[7]

In terms of *numbers of issues,* most stocks are traded over the counter. Even though the OTC market and NASDAQ include some very large companies, such as Microsoft and Intel, most of the stocks traded over the counter are from small companies that do not meet the requirements to be listed on an organized exchange. On the other hand, because the stocks of larger companies generally are listed on the exchanges, about two-thirds of the *dollar volume of stock trading* takes place on the exchanges. In fact, the NYSE generates about 60 percent of the daily dollar trading with its listing of nearly 3,000 stocks.

 Self-Test Questions

What are the two basic types of stock markets, and how do they differ?

Are the greatest number of stocks traded over the counter or on the organized exchanges?

Why do stock exchanges have listing requirements?

What are the four types of membership (seats) available on the NYSE?

How do stocks traded on the NASDAQ differ from other stocks traded over the counter?

The Investment Banking Process

INVESTMENT BANKER
An organization that underwrites and distributes new issues of securities; helps businesses and other entities obtain needed financing.

When a business (or government unit) needs to raise funds in the financial markets, it generally enlists the services of an **investment banker** (see panel 2 in Figure 2-1). Merrill Lynch, Morgan Stanley Dean Witter, and Goldman Sachs are examples of companies that offer investment banking services. Such organizations (1) help corporations design securities with the features that are most attractive to investors given existing market conditions, (2) buy these securities from the corporations, and (3) then resell them to investors (savers). Although the securities are sold twice, this process really is one primary market transaction, with the investment banker acting as a middleman (agent) as funds are transferred from savers to businesses.

---

[7]At the time we write this text in 1998, The National Association of Securities Dealers (NASD) and the American Stock Exchange (AMEX) have reached an agreement to merge the AMEX into the NASD. According to the agreement, the AMEX would still function as a separate market from the NASD; it would continue to have its own members and listed companies that would be traded much the way they are today. The NASD would add substantial automation so that some trades could be executed off the exchange floor. In addition, both the AMEX and the NASD recently announced that an agreement has been reached to add the Philadelphia Stock Exchange (PHLX) to its new joint organization, currently referred to as the NASD/AMEX "family of companies." The primary reason for the mergers of these markets is to increase their ability to compete with the NYSE and with international markets. In the past few years, trading on the AMEX and the PHLX has decreased relative to the NYSE and other major international stock markets. It is felt that the combinations will help add diversity to, and increase the presence of, these markets. The final structure of these mergers is unclear at this time.

We should note that investment banking has nothing to do with the traditional banking process as we know it — investment banking deals with the issuance of new securities, not deposits and loans. The major investment banking houses often are divisions of large financial service corporations engaged in a wide range of activities. For example, Merrill Lynch has a brokerage department that operates thousands of offices worldwide, as well as an investment banking department that helps companies issue securities, take over other companies, and the like. Merrill Lynch's brokers sell previously issued stocks as well as stocks that are issued through their investment banking departments. Thus, financial service organizations such as Merrill Lynch sell securities in both the secondary markets and the primary markets.

In this section we describe how securities are issued in the financial markets, and we explain the role of investment bankers in this process.

Raising Capital: Stage I Decisions

The corporation itself makes some preliminary decisions on its own, including the following:[8]

1. **Dollars to be raised.** How much new capital do we need?
2. **Type of securities used.** Should stock, bonds, or a combination be used? Further, if stock is to be issued, should it be offered to existing stockholders or sold to the general public?
3. **Competitive bid versus negotiated deal.** Should the company simply offer a block of its securities for sale to the investment banker that bids highest, or should it sit down and negotiate a deal? These two procedures are called *competitive bids* and *negotiated deals*. Only a handful of the largest firms on the NYSE, whose securities are already well known to the investment banking community, are in a position to use the competitive bid process. The investment banks would have to do a large amount of investigative work in order to bid on an issue unless they were already quite familiar with the firm, and the costs involved would be too high to make it worthwhile unless the investment bank was sure of getting the deal. Therefore, the vast majority of offerings of stocks or bonds are made on a negotiated basis.[9]
4. **Selection of an investment banker.** Assuming the issue is to be negotiated, which investment banker should the firm use? Older firms that have "been to market" before will already have established a relationship with an investment banker, although it is easy enough to change bankers if the firm is dissatisfied. However, a firm that is just going public will have to choose an investment bank, and different investment banking houses are better suited for different companies. The older, larger "establishment houses" such as Morgan Stanley Dean Witter deal mainly with large companies such as AT&T, IBM, and Exxon. Other bankers specialize in more speculative issues such as initial public offerings. Table 2-3 lists in ranked order the top ten investment bankers in the United States, as measured by the dollar amount of securities underwritten

---

[8]For the most part, the procedures described in this section also apply to government entities. However, governments only issue debt; they do not issue stock.

[9]It should be noted that most government entities are required by law to solicit competitive bids for bond issues.

TABLE 2-3

Largest Underwriters of Debt and Equity in the United States in 1997 (billions of dollars)

Rank	Investment Banker	Amount Issued	Market Share	Number of Issues
1	Merrill Lynch	$ 208.1	16.1%	1,815
2	Salomon Smith Barney	167.0	12.9	1,203
3	Morgan Stanley Dean Witter	139.5	10.8	1,489
4	Goldman Sachs	137.3	10.6	1,094
5	Lehman Brothers	121.0	9.4	910
6	J.P. Morgan	104.0	8.0	840
7	Credit Suisse First Boston	67.7	5.2	541
8	Bear Sterns	57.5	4.4	—
9	Donaldson, Lufkin & Jenrette	46.0	3.6	329
10	Chase Manhattan	33.1	2.6	—
	Others	211.8	16.4	4,240
	Total	$1,293.0	100.0%	12,461

Source: *The Wall Street Journal,* January 2, 1998.

during 1997. Notice that the top four companies handled more than 50 percent of the total amount of debt and equity issued.

Raising Capital: Stage II Decisions

Stage II decisions, which are made jointly by the firm and its selected investment banker, include the following:

1. **Reevaluating the initial decisions.** The firm and its investment banker will reevaluate the initial decisions about the size of the issue and the type of securities to use. For example, the firm initially might have decided to raise $50 million by selling common stock, but the investment banker might convince management that it would be better, in view of existing market conditions, to limit the stock issue to $25 million and to raise the other $25 million as debt.

UNDERWRITTEN ARRANGEMENT
Agreement for the sale of securities in which the investment bank guarantees the sale by purchasing the securities from the issuer, thus agreeing to bear any risks involved in the transaction.

BEST EFFORTS ARRANGEMENT
Agreement for the sale of securities in which the investment bank handling the transaction gives no guarantee that the securities will be sold.

2. **Best efforts or underwritten issues.** The firm and its investment banker must decide whether the investment banker will work on a best efforts basis or underwrite the issue. In an **underwritten arrangement,** the investment banker generally assures the company that the entire issue will be sold, so the investment banker bears significant risks in such an offering. With this type of arrangement, the investment banking firm typically buys the securities from the issuing firm and then sells the securities in the primary markets, hoping to make a profit. In a **best efforts arrangement,** the investment banker does not guarantee that the securities will be sold or that the company will get the cash it needs. With this type of arrangement, the investment banker does not buy the securities from the issuing firm; rather the securities are handled on a contingency basis, and the investment banker is paid a commission based on the amount of the issue that is sold. The investment banker essentially promises to exert its *best efforts* when selling the securities. With a best efforts arrangement, the issuing firm takes the chance the entire issue will not be sold and that all the needed funds will not be raised. For example, the very day IBM

signed an underwritten agreement to sell $1 billion of bonds in 1979, interest rates rose sharply, and bond prices fell. IBM's investment bankers lost somewhere between $10 million and $20 million. Had the offering been on a best efforts basis, IBM would have been the loser.

3. **Issuance (flotation) costs.** The investment banker's fee must be negotiated, and the firm also must estimate the other expenses it will incur in connection with the issue — lawyers' fees, accountants' costs, printing and engraving, and so forth. Usually, the investment banker will buy the issue from the company at a discount below the price at which the securities are to be offered to the public, and this **underwriter's spread** covers the investment banker's costs and provides a profit.

Table 2-4 gives an indication of the **flotation costs** associated with public issues of bonds and common stock. As the table shows, costs as a percentage of the proceeds are higher for stocks than for bonds, and costs are also higher for small issues than for large issues. The relationship between size of issue and flotation costs is primarily due to the existence of fixed costs: Certain costs must be incurred regardless of the size of the issue, so the percentage flotation cost is quite high for small issues.

4. **Setting the offering price.** If the company already is publicly owned, the **offering price** will be based on the existing market price of the stock or the yield on the bonds. For common stock, the most typical arrangement calls for the investment banker to buy the securities at a prescribed number of points below the closing price on the last day of registration, which is the day the issue is released for sale by the Securities and Exchange Commission (SEC). Investment bankers have an easier job if an issue is priced relatively low, but the issuer of the securities naturally wants as high a price as possible. Therefore, an inherent conflict of interest on price exists between the investment banker and the issuer. However, if the issuer is financially sophisticated and

UNDERWRITER'S SPREAD The difference between the price at which the investment banking firm buys an issue from a company and the price at which the securities are sold in the primary market — it represents the investment banker's gross profit on the issue.

FLOTATION COSTS The costs associated with issuing new stocks or bonds.

OFFERING PRICE The price at which securities are sold to the public.

TABLE 2-4

Flotation (Issuance) Costs for Issuing Debt and Equity[a]

Issue Size (millions of dollars)	Bonds			Common Stock		
	Underwriting Commission	Other Costs	Total Costs	Underwriting Commission	Other Costs	Total Costs
Under 1.0	10.0%	4.0%	14.0%	13.0%	9.0%	22.0%
1.0–1.9	8.0	3.0	11.0	11.0	5.9	16.9
2.0–4.9	4.0	2.2	6.2	8.6	3.8	12.4
5.0–9.9	2.4	0.8	3.2	6.3	1.9	8.2
10.0–19.9	1.2	0.7	1.9	5.1	0.9	6.0
20.0–49.9	1.0	0.4	1.4	4.1	0.5	4.6
50.0 and above	0.9	0.2	1.1	3.3	0.2	3.5

[a]The numbers presented in this table are intended to provide an indication of the costs associated with issuing debt and equity. Such costs rise somewhat when interest rates are cyclically high, because when money is in relatively tight supply, the investment bankers will have a more difficult time placing issues. So, actual flotation costs vary somewhat over time.

SOURCE: Securities and Exchange Commission, *Cost of Flotation of Registered Issues,* December 1974; Robert Hansen, "Evaluating the Costs of a new Equity Issue," *Midland Corporate Finance Journal,* Spring 1986; and informal surveys of common stock and bond issues conducted by the authors.

makes comparisons with similar security issues, the investment banker will be forced to price close to the market.

If the company is going public for the first time (an IPO), it will have no established price (or demand curve), so the investment bankers will have to estimate the equilibrium price at which the stock will sell after issue. The Small Business box at the end of this chapter illustrates in some detail the process involved. If the offering price is set below the true equilibrium price, the stock will rise sharply after issue, and the company and its original stockholders will have given away too many shares to raise the required capital. If the offering price is set above the true equilibrium price, either the issue will fail or, if the bankers succeed in selling the stock, their investment clients will be unhappy when the stock subsequently falls to its equilibrium level. Therefore, it is important that the equilibrium price be approximated as closely as possible.

Selling Procedures

REGISTRATION STATEMENT
A statement of facts filed with the SEC about a company that plans to issue securities.

PROSPECTUS
A document describing a new security issue and the issuing company.

Once the company and its investment bankers have decided how much money to raise, the types of securities to issue, and the basis for pricing the issue, they will prepare and file a registration statement and prospectus with the SEC. The **registration statement** provides financial, legal, and technical information about the company, while the **prospectus** summarizes the information in the registration statement and is provided to prospective investors for use in selling the securities. Lawyers and accountants at the Securities and Exchange Commission (SEC) analyze both the registration statement and the prospectus; if the information is inadequate or misleading, the SEC will delay or stop the public offering. It generally takes from 20 days to six months for the issue to be approved by the SEC. The final price of the stock (or the interest rate on a bond issue) is set at the close of business the day the issue clears the SEC, and the securities are then offered to the public the following day.

Investment bankers must pay the issuing firm within four days of the time the offering officially begins, so, typically, the investment bankers sell the stock within a day or two after the offering begins. On occasion, however, investment bankers miscalculate, set the offering price too high, and are unable to move the issue. Similarly, the market might decline during the offering period, which again would force the investment bankers to reduce the price of the stock. In either instance, on an underwritten offering, the firm would still receive the price that was agreed upon, and the investment bankers would have to absorb any losses that were incurred.

UNDERWRITING SYNDICATE
A group of investment banking firms formed to spread the risk associated with the purchase and distribution of a new issue of securities.

Because they are exposed to large potential losses, investment bankers typically do not handle the purchase and distribution of an issue singlehandedly unless it is very small. If the amount of money involved is large and the risk of price fluctuations substantial, an investment banker forms an **underwriting syndicate,** where the issue is distributed to a number of investment firms in an effort to minimize the amount of risk each one carries. The investment banking house that sets up the deal is called the *lead,* or *managing, underwriter.*

In addition to the underwriting syndicate, on larger offerings still more investment bankers are included in a *selling group,* which handles the distribution of securities to individual investors. The selling group includes all members of the underwriting syndicate plus additional dealers who take relatively small participations (or shares of the total issue) from the syndicate members. Members of the selling group act as selling agents and receive commissions for their efforts — they do not purchase the securities, so they do not bear the same risk the underwriting syndicate does. Thus, the underwriters act as wholesalers and bear the risk associated with the issue, whereas members of the selling group act as retailers. The number of investment banking houses in a selling group depends partly on the size of the issue; for example, the one set up when Communications Satellite Corporation (Comsat) went public consisted of 385 members.

SHELF REGISTRATIONS   The selling procedures described previously, including the 20-day minimum waiting period between registration with the SEC and sale of the issue, apply to most security sales. However, large, well-known public companies that issue securities frequently file a master registration statement with the SEC and then update it with a short-form statement just prior to each individual offering. In such a case, a company could decide at 10 A.M. to sell registered securities and have the sale completed before noon. This procedure is known as **shelf registration** because, in effect, the company puts its new securities "on the shelf" and then sells them to investors when it thinks the market is right.

MAINTENANCE OF THE SECONDARY MARKET   In the case of a large, established firm such as General Motors, the investment banking firm's job is finished once it has disposed of the stock and turned the net proceeds over to the company. However, in the case of a company going public for the first time, the investment banker is under an obligation to maintain a market for the shares after the issue has been completed. Such stocks typically are traded in the over-the-counter market, and the lead underwriter generally agrees to "make a market" in the stock and to keep it reasonably liquid. The company wants a good market to exist for its stock, as do its stockholders. Therefore, if the investment banking house wants to do business with the company in the future, to keep its own brokerage customers happy, and to have future referral business, it will hold an inventory of the shares and help maintain an active secondary market in the stock.

SHELF REGISTRATION
Securities are registered with the SEC for sale at a later date; the securities are held "on the shelf" until the sale.

Self-Test Questions

How does an investment bank differ from a commercial bank?

What is the sequence of events when a firm decides to issue new securities?

What is an underwriting syndicate, and why is it important in the investment banking process?

What type of firm would use a shelf registration? Explain.

Regulation of Securities Markets

SECURITIES AND EXCHANGE COMMISSION (SEC)
The U.S. government agency that regulates the issuance and trading of stocks and bonds.

Sales of new securities, such as stocks and bonds, as well as operations in the secondary markets, are regulated by the **Securities and Exchange Commission (SEC)** and, to a lesser extent, by each of the 50 states. For the most part, the SEC regulations are intended to (1) ensure investors receive fair financial disclosure from publicly traded companies and (2) discourage fraudulent and misleading behavior by firms' investors, owners, and employees to manipulate stock prices. The primary elements of SEC regulations are as follows:

1. The SEC has jurisdiction over most interstate offerings of new securities to the general investing public in amounts of $1.5 million or more. As we mentioned earlier, firms that wish to issue new stock must file both a registration statement and a prospectus with the SEC. The primary purpose of such filings is to require disclosure of specific information, financial and nonfinancial, concerning the issuing firm and the intended use of the funds to be raised from the issue. When the SEC approves the registration statement and the prospectus, it only validates that the required information has been furnished. The SEC does not provide judgment concerning the quality of the issue — that task is left to potential investors.

2. The SEC also regulates all national securities exchanges, and companies whose securities are listed on an exchange must file annual reports similar to the registration statement with both the SEC and the exchange.

INSIDERS
Officers, directors, major stockholders, or others who might have inside information on a company's operations.

3. The SEC has control over stock trades by corporate **insiders.** Officers, directors, and major stockholders must file monthly reports of changes in their holdings of the corporation's stock. Any short-term profits from such transactions must be handed over to the corporation.

4. The SEC has the power to prohibit manipulation of securities' prices by such devices as pools (aggregations of funds used to affect prices artificially) or wash sales (sales between members of the same group to record artificial trading volume and transaction prices). The essence of such prohibition is that deliberate manipulation of securities' prices is illegal.

Self-Test Question

What is the primary purpose for regulating securities trading?

International Financial Markets

Financial markets have become much more global during the last few decades. As the economies of countries in southeast Asia and the former Soviet Union have developed and experienced enormous growth in their financial markets, greater numbers of investors have provided funds to these regions. To illustrate, consider the fact that U.S. stocks accounted for nearly two-thirds of the value of worldwide stock markets in 1970. But, as Table 2-5 shows, U.S. stock markets now represent less than 50 percent of the total value worldwide.[10] The areas of greatest growth are in the emerging markets of the Pacific Rim countries, including Malaysia, Thailand, and Indonesia, which currently are experiencing great economic difficulty due to unstable financial markets. Much of the troubles evident in this region can be traced to insufficient regulation and monitoring of financial markets, which allowed a few influential individuals or groups to wield significant power and control in determining economic events. Still, many experts predict the growth potential that exists in southeast Asian countries will attract investors from around the world for many years to come.

---

[10]The value given for U.S. stock exchanges is based on the combined values of the New York Stock Exchange, the American Stock Exchange, and NASDAQ.

TABLE 2-5

Foreign Stock Market Values (billions of dollars)[a]

	Year-End 1988		Year-End 1997		10-Year Growth	Number of Domestic Companies Listed — 1997
	Market Value	Percent of Total	Market Value	Percent of Total		
I. Developed Stock Markets						
United States[b]	$2,793.8	28.72%	$11,308.8	48.04%	305%	8,851
Japan[c]	3,906.7	40.16	2,216.7	9.42	−43	2,387
United Kingdom	771.2	7.93	1,996.2	8.48	159	2,046
Germany	251.8	2.59	825.2	3.51	228	700
Australia	138.3	1.42	696.7	2.96	404	1,219
France	244.8	2.52	674.4	2.86	175	683
Switzerland	140.5	1.44	575.3	2.44	309	216
Canada	241.9	2.49	567.6	2.41	135	1,362
Netherlands	113.6	1.17	468.7	1.99	313	201
Hong Kong	74.4	0.76	413.3	1.76	456	658
Italy	135.4	1.39	344.7	1.46	155	235
Other developed markets	415.7	4.27	1,244.3	5.20	195	2,098
All developed markets	$9,228.1	94.86%	$21,311.9	90.53%	131%	20,656
II. Emerging Stock Markets						
Taiwan, China	120.0	1.23%	287.8	1.22%	140%	404
Brazil	32.1	0.33	255.5	1.09	696	536
South Africa	126.1	1.30	232.1	0.99	84	642
China	—	—	206.4	0.88	—	764
Mexico	13.8	0.14	156.6	0.67	1,035	198
India	23.6	0.24	128.5	0.55	444	5,843
Malaysia	23.3	0.24	93.6	0.40	302	708
Korea	94.2	0.97	41.9	0.18	−56	776
Philippines	4.3	0.04	31.4	0.13	630	221
Indonesia	0.3	0.00	29.1	0.12	9,600	282
Thailand	8.8	0.09	23.5	0.10	167	431
Other emerging markets	53.9	0.55	743.1	3.16	1,279	9,132
All emerging markets	500.4	5.14%	2,229.5	9.47%	346	19,937
All stock markets	9,728.5	100.00%	23,541.4	100.00%	142%	40,593

NOTES:

[a]All market values are stated in U.S. dollars. Thus, some of the changes in market values from 1988 to 1997 resulted from changes in the value of the dollar relative to foreign currencies (exchange rate changes). Also, all the numbers are rounded, so the totals might reflect rounding errors.

[b]Based on the combined values of the New York Stock Exchange, the American Stock Exchange, and NASDAQ.

[c]Based on the combined values of all Japanese stock exchanges.

SOURCE: *Emerging Stock Markets Factbook 1998.*

Even with the expansion of stock markets internationally, exchanges in the United States still conduct the greatest numbers of trades, both with respect to volume and value. In 1996, stock trades in the United States exceeded $10 trillion, which was eight times greater than the value of stocks traded in Japan ($1.25 trillion) and about ten times greater than the value of stocks traded in Germany

($1.03 trillion). In fact, trading activity in the United States accounted for more than 50 percent of worldwide trading activity in 1997.

The international market for bonds has experienced growth similar to the international stock markets. Table 2-6 shows the values of some of the foreign bond markets in 1994. The value of the U.S. bond market is substantial, but the bond markets in such countries as Japan, Germany, and Italy have experienced substantial growth in the past few years.

On January 1, 1999, the European Monetary Union (EMU) is slated to begin. The EMU will include from 8 to 11 countries and will create a common bond that will be traded in a unified financial market called the Euro market. According to Salomon Brothers, the bonds from the countries expected to comprise the EMU had a combined value greater than $6 trillion in 1996, which was approximately 63 percent of the world market for U.S. dollar bonds. It is estimated that seven of the ten countries listed in Table 2-6 will be members of the EMU. Thus, you can imagine that the importance of international markets will increase greatly during the next few decades. The financial markets truly are global in nature — events that influence the markets in Asia and Europe also influence the markets in the United States, and vice versa.

While the globalization of financial markets continues and international markets offer investors greater frontiers of opportunities, investing overseas can be difficult due to restrictions or barriers erected by foreign countries. In many cases, individual investors find it difficult or unattractive to invest directly in foreign stocks because many countries prohibit or severely limit the ability of foreigners to invest in their financial markets, or they make it extremely difficult to access reliable information concerning the companies that are traded in the stock markets. Therefore, most individuals interested in investing internationally do so *indirectly* by purchasing financial instruments that represent foreign stocks, bonds, and other investments but that are offered by institutions in the United

TABLE 2-6

Foreign Bond Market Values, 1994 (billions of U.S. dollars)

Country	Total Bonds	Government Bonds	Corporate Bonds	Other Bonds[a]
United States	$8,592	$5,489	$2,247	$856
Japan	4,533	2,977	1,221	335
Germany	2,598	1,236	927	435
Italy	981	799	136	46
France	792	513	144	135
United Kingdom	523	331	29	163
Canada	467	335	51	81
Belgium	335	193	115	27
Netherlands	327	253	24	50
Denmark	232	72		160
Other countries[b]	1,725	996	515	214

NOTES:

[a]For most of the countries, the "other" category includes foreign bonds, but some countries, including Denmark, included the values of corporate bonds in combination with foreign bonds.

[b]Includes 26 other countries for which data were given.

SOURCE: "Size and Structure of the World Bond Market: 1995," Merrill Lynch & Company, 1995.

States. Investors can participate internationally by purchasing (1) American Depository Receipts (ADRs), (2) mutual funds that hold international stocks, or (3) foreign securities certificates issued in dollar denominations. We describe each of these instruments in Chapter 4, which includes descriptions of the more common financial assets, or securities, traded in the financial markets.

 ### Self-Test Questions

Why should investors in the United States be concerned with financial markets in other countries?

What effect do you think the European Monetary Union (EMU) will have on the international financial markets?

The Cost of Money

PRODUCTION OPPORTUNITIES
The returns available within an economy from investment in productive (cash-generating) assets.

TIME PREFERENCES FOR CONSUMPTION
The preferences of consumers for current consumption as opposed to saving for future consumption.

RISK
In a financial market context, the chance that a financial asset will not earn the return promised.

INFLATION
The tendency of prices to increase over time.

In a free economy such as ours, funds are allocated in the financial markets through a pricing system. *Interest rates represent the prices paid to borrow funds, whereas in the case of equity capital, investors expect to receive dividends and capital gains.* Factors that affect the supply of and demand for investment capital, and hence the cost of money, are discussed in this section.

The four most fundamental factors affecting the cost of money are (1) **production opportunities,** (2) **time preferences for consumption,** (3) **risk,** and (4) **inflation.** To see how these factors operate, visualize an isolated island community where the people survive on fish. They have a stock of fishing gear that permits them to live reasonably well, but they would like to have more fish. Now suppose Mr. Crusoe has a bright idea for a new type of fishnet that would enable him to double his daily catch. However, it would take him a year to perfect his design, to build his net, and to learn how to use it efficiently; and Mr. Crusoe probably would starve before he could put his new net into operation. Therefore, he might suggest to Ms. Robinson, Mr. Friday, and several others that if they would give him one fish each day for a year, he would return two fish a day during all of the next year. If someone accepted the offer, then the fish which Ms. Robinson or one of the others gave to Mr. Crusoe would constitute *savings,* these savings would be *invested* in the fishnet, and the extra fish the net produced would constitute a *return on the investment.*

Obviously, the more productive Mr. Crusoe thought the new fishnet would be, the higher his expected return on the investment would be, and the more he could afford to offer potential investors for their savings. In this example, we assume that Mr. Crusoe thinks he will be able to pay, and thus he has offered, a 100 percent rate of return — he has offered to give back two fish for every one he received. He might have tried to attract savings for less, say, only 1.5 fish next year for every one he receives this year.

How attractive Mr. Crusoe's offer appears to a potential saver would depend in large part on the saver's *time preference for consumption.* For example, Ms. Robinson might be thinking of retirement, and she might be willing to trade fish today for fish in the future on a one-for-one basis. On the other hand, Mr. Friday might be unwilling to "lend" a fish today for anything less than three fish next year, because he has a wife and several young children to feed with his current fish. Mr. Friday would be said to have a high time preference for consumption and

Ms. Robinson a low time preference. Note also that if the entire population is living right at the subsistence level, time preferences for current consumption would necessarily be high, aggregate savings would be low, interest rates would be high, and capital formation would be difficult.

The risk inherent in the fishnet project, and thus in Mr. Crusoe's ability to repay the loan, also affects the return investors require: The higher the perceived risk, the higher the required rate of return. Also, in a more complex society there are many businesses like Mr. Crusoe's, many goods other than fish, and many savers like Ms. Robinson and Mr. Friday. Further, people use money as a medium of exchange rather than barter with fish. When money is used, rather than fish, its value in the future, which is affected by inflation, comes into play: The higher the expected rate of *inflation,* the larger the required return.

Thus, we see that the interest rate paid to savers depends in a basic way (1) on the rate of return producers expect to earn on invested capital, (2) on savers' time preferences for current versus future consumption, (3) on the riskiness of the loan, and (4) on the expected future rate of inflation. The returns borrowers expect to earn by investing the funds they borrow set an upper limit on how much they can pay for savings, while consumers' time preferences for consumption establish how much consumption they are willing to defer, hence how much they will save at different levels of interest offered by borrowers. Higher risk and higher inflation also lead to higher interest rates.

Self-Test Questions

What is the price paid to borrow money called?

What is the "price" of equity capital?

What four fundamental factors affect the cost of money?

Interest Rate Levels

Funds are allocated among borrowers by interest rates: Firms with the most profitable investment opportunities are willing and able to pay the most for capital, so they tend to attract it away from less efficient firms or from those whose products are not in demand. Of course, our economy is not completely free in the sense of being influenced only by market forces. Thus, the federal government has agencies that help designated individuals or groups obtain credit on favorable terms. Among those eligible for this kind of assistance are small businesses, certain minorities, and firms willing to build plants in areas with high unemployment. Still, most capital in the U.S. economy is allocated through the price system.

Figure 2-2 shows how supply and demand interact to determine interest rates in two capital markets. Markets A and B represent two of the many capital markets in existence. The going interest rate, which can be designated as either k or i, but for purposes of the discussion here is designated as k, initially is 10 percent for the low-risk securities in Market A. Borrowers whose credit is strong enough to qualify for this market can obtain funds at a cost of 10 percent, and investors who want to put their money to work without much risk can obtain a 10 percent return. Riskier borrowers must obtain higher cost funds in Market B. Investors who are more willing to take risks invest in Market B expecting to earn a 12

FIGURE 2-2

Interest Rates as a Function of Supply and Demand for Funds

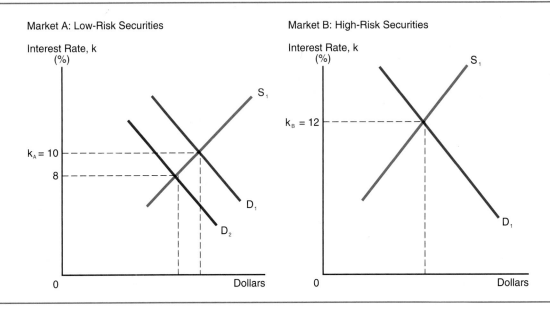

percent return, but also realizing that they might actually receive much less (or much more).

If the demand for funds declines, as it typically does during business recessions, the demand curves will shift to the left, as shown in Curve D_2 in Market A. The market-clearing, or equilibrium, interest rate in this example declines to 8 percent. Similarly, you should be able to visualize what would happen if the supply of funds tightens: The supply curve, S_1, would shift to the left, and this would raise interest rates and lower the level of borrowing in the economy.

Financial markets are interdependent. For example, if Markets A and B were in equilibrium before the demand shift to D_2 in Market A, this means that investors were willing to accept the higher risk in Market B in exchange for a risk premium of 12% − 10% = 2%. After the shift to D_2, the risk premium would initially increase to 12% − 8% = 4%. In all likelihood, this much larger premium would induce some of the lenders in Market A to shift to Market B; this, in turn, would cause the supply curve in Market A to shift to the left (or up) and that in Market B to shift to the right. The transfer of capital between markets would raise the interest rate in Market A and lower it in Market B, thus bringing the risk premium back closer to the original level, 2 percent. For example, when rates on Treasury securities increase, the rates on corporate bonds and mortgages generally follow.

As we discussed in previous sections, there are many financial markets in the United States and throughout the world. There are markets for short-term debt, long-term debt, home loans, farm loans, business loans, government loans, and so forth. For each type of funds, there is a price, and these prices change over time as shifts occur in supply and demand conditions. Figure 2-3 shows how long- and short-term interest rates to business borrowers have varied since the 1960s. Notice that short-term interest rates are especially prone to rise during booms and then fall during recessions. (The shaded areas of the chart indicate recessions.) When the economy is expanding, firms need capital, and this demand for capital

FIGURE 2-3

Long- and Short-Term Interest Rates, 1965–1998

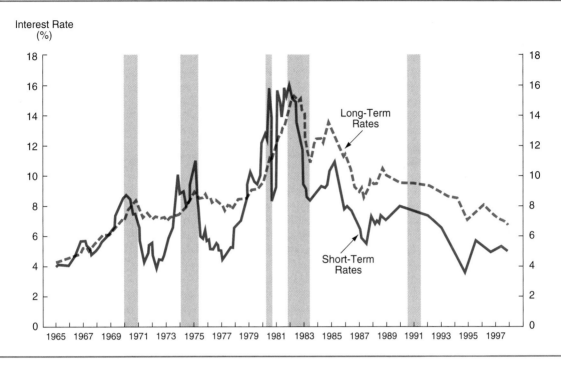

NOTES:

a. The shaded areas designate business recessions.

b. Short-term rates are measured by three-month loans (commercial paper) to very large, strong corporations, and long-term rates are measured by AAA corporate bonds.

SOURCE: *Federal Reserve Bulletin.*

pushes rates up. Also, inflationary pressures are strongest during business booms, and that also exerts upward pressure on rates. Conditions are reversed during recessions such as the one in 1991 and 1992. Slack business reduces the demand for credit, the rate of inflation falls, and the result is a drop in interest rates.

These tendencies do not hold exactly — the period after 1984 is a case in point. The price of oil fell dramatically in 1985 and 1986, reducing inflationary pressures on other prices and easing fears of serious long-term inflation. Earlier, these fears had pushed interest rates to record levels. The economy from 1984 to 1987 was fairly strong, but the declining fears about inflation more than offset the normal tendency of interest rates to rise during good economic times, and the net result was lower interest rates.[11]

The relationship between inflation and long-term interest rates is highlighted in Figure 2-4, which plots rates of inflation along with long-term interest rates. Prior to 1965, when the average rate of inflation was about 1 percent, interest

---

[11]Short-term rates are responsive to current economic conditions, whereas long-term rates primarily reflect long-run expectations for inflation. As a result, short-term rates are sometimes above and sometimes below long-term rates. The relationship between long-term and short-term rates is called the *term structure of interest rates*. This topic is discussed later in the chapter.

FIGURE 2-4

Relationship between Annual Inflation Rates and Long-Term Interest Rates 1965–1998

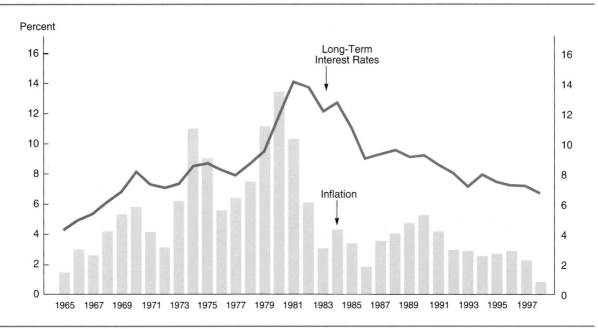

NOTES:

a. Interest rates are those on AAA long-term corporate bonds.

b. Inflation is measured as the annual rate of change in the Consumer Price Index (CPI).

SOURCE: *Federal Reserve Bulletin.*

rates on the least risky bonds generally ranged from 4 to 5 percent. As the war in Vietnam accelerated in the late 1960s, the rate of inflation increased, and interest rates began to rise. The rate of inflation dropped after 1970 and so did long-term interest rates. However, the 1973 Arab oil embargo was followed by a quadrupling of oil prices in 1974, which caused a spurt in inflation, which, in turn, drove interest rates to new record highs in 1974 and 1975. Inflationary pressures eased in late 1975 and 1976 but then rose again after 1976. In 1980, inflation rates hit the highest level on record, and fears of continued double-digit inflation pushed interest rates up to historic highs. From 1981 through 1986, the inflation rate dropped sharply, and in 1986 inflation was only 1.1 percent, the lowest level in 25 years. In 1993, interest rates dropped to historical lows — the Treasury bill yield actually dropped below 3 percent. Currently (1998), inflation is negligible, Treasury bill rates are about 4.5 percent, and interest rates charged to strong corporations are about 6.5 percent.

 Self-Test Questions

How are interest rates used to allocate capital among firms?

What happens to market-clearing, or equilibrium, interest rates in a capital market when the demand for funds declines? What happens when inflation increases or decreases?

Why does the price of capital change during booms and recessions?

How does risk affect interest rates?

How does a change in rates in one financial market affect the rates in other financial markets?

The Determinants of Market Interest Rates

In general, the quoted (or nominal) interest rate on a debt security, k, is composed of a *real* risk-free rate of interest, k*, plus several premiums that reflect inflation, the riskiness of the security, and the security's marketability (or liquidity). This relationship can be expressed as follows:

> **2-1**   Quoted interest rate = k = k* + IP + DRP + LP + MRP

In Equation 2-1, the variables are defined as follows:

k = the quoted, or *nominal,* rate of interest on a given security.[12] There are many different securities, hence many different quoted interest rates.

k* = the *real risk-free rate of interest;* k* is pronounced "k-star."

k_{RF} = the quoted, or *nominal risk-free rate* of interest.

IP = inflation premium.

DRP = default risk premium.

LP = liquidity, or marketability, premium.

MRP = maturity risk premium.

We discuss the components whose sum makes up the quoted, or nominal, rate on a given security in the following sections.

The Real Risk-Free Rate of Interest, k*

REAL RISK-FREE RATE OF INTEREST, k*
The rate of interest that would exist on default-free U.S. Treasury securities if no inflation were expected.

The **real risk-free rate of interest, k*,** is defined as the interest rate that would exist on a security with a *guaranteed* payoff (termed a riskless, or risk-free security) if inflation was expected to be zero during the investment period. It can be thought of as the rate of interest that would exist on short-term U.S. Treasury securities in an inflation-free world. The real risk-free rate changes over time depending on economic conditions, especially (1) on the rate of return corporations and other borrowers are willing to pay to borrow funds and (2) on people's time preferences for current versus future consumption. It is difficult to measure the real risk-free rate precisely, but most experts think that in the United States k* has fluctuated in the range of 1 to 4 percent in recent years.

---

[12]The term *nominal* as it is used here means the stated rate as opposed to the real rate, which is adjusted to remove the effects of inflation. If you bought a ten-year Treasury bond in May 1998, the quoted, or nominal, rate would be about 5.5 percent, but if inflation was expected to average 2 percent over the next ten years, the real rate would be about 5.5% − 2% = 3.5%.

The Nominal, or Quoted, Risk-Free Rate of Interest, k_{RF}

The **nominal,** or **quoted, risk-free rate, k_{RF},** is the *real risk-free rate plus a premium for expected inflation:* $k_{RF} = k^* + IP$. If we combine $k^* + IP$ and let this sum equal k_{RF}, then Equation 2-1 becomes:

2-2	
	$$k = k_{RF} + DRP + LP + MRP$$

NOMINAL (QUOTED) RISK-FREE RATE, k_{RF}
The rate of interest on a security that is free of all risk; k_{RF} is proxied by the T-bill rate or the T-bond rate; k_{RF} includes an inflation premium.

To be strictly correct, the risk-free rate should mean the interest rate on a security that has absolutely no risk at all — one that has no risk of default, no maturity risk, no liquidity risk, and no risk of loss if inflation increases. No such security exists in the real world; hence there is no observable truly risk-free rate. However, there is one security that is free of most risks — a U.S. Treasury bill (T-bill), which is a short-term security issued by the U.S. government. Treasury bonds (T-bonds), which are longer-term government securities, are free of default and liquidity risks, but T-bonds are exposed to some risk because of changes in the general level of interest rates.

If the term "risk-free rate" is used without either the term "real" or the term "nominal," people generally mean the quoted (nominal) rate, and we will follow that convention in this book. Therefore, when we use the term risk-free rate, k_{RF}, we mean the nominal risk-free rate, which includes an inflation premium equal to the average expected inflation rate over the life of the security. In general, we use the T-bill rate to approximate the short-term risk-free rate and the T-bond rate to approximate the long-term risk-free rate. So, whenever you see the term "risk-free rate," assume that we are referring either to the quoted U.S. T-bill rate or to the quoted T-bond rate.

Inflation Premium (IP)

Inflation has a major impact on interest rates because it erodes the purchasing power of the dollar and lowers the real rate of return on investments. To illustrate, suppose you saved $1,000 and invested it in a certificate of deposit that matures in one year and will pay 5 percent interest. At the end of the year you will receive $1,050 — your original $1,000 plus $50 of interest. Now suppose the inflation rate during the year is 10 percent, and it affects all items equally. If beer had cost $1 per bottle at the beginning of the year, it would cost $1.10 at the end of the year. Therefore, your $1,000 would have bought $1,000/$1 = 1,000 bottles at the beginning of the year but only $1,050/$1.10 = 955 bottles at year's end. Thus, *in real terms,* you would be worse off — you would receive $50 of interest, but it would not be sufficient to offset inflation. In this case, you would be better off buying 1,000 bottles of beer (or some other storable asset such as land, timber, apartment buildings, wheat, or gold) than investing in the certificate of deposit.

INFLATION PREMIUM (IP)
A premium for expected inflation that investors add to the real risk-free rate of return.

Investors are well aware of all this, so when they lend money, they build in an **inflation premium (IP)** equal to the *average inflation rate expected over the life of the security.* Therefore, if the real risk-free rate of interest, k^*, is 3 percent, and if inflation is expected to be 4 percent (and hence IP = 4%) during the next year, then the quoted rate of interest on one-year T-bills would be 7 percent.

Default Risk Premium (DRP)

The risk that a borrower will *default* on a loan, which means not to pay the interest or the principal, also affects the market interest rate on a security: The greater the default risk, the higher the interest rate lenders charge (demand). Treasury securities have no default risk; thus, they generally carry the lowest interest rates on taxable securities in the United States. For corporate bonds, the better the bond's overall credit rating (AAA is the best), the lower its default risk, and, consequently, the lower its interest rate.[13] Here are some representative interest rates on long-term bonds in March 1998:

	Rate	DRP
U.S. Treasury	6.0%	—
AAA	6.7	0.7%
AA	6.9	0.9
A	7.1	1.1

DEFAULT RISK PREMIUM (DRP)
The difference between the interest rate on a U.S. Treasury bond and a corporate bond of equal maturity and marketability.

The difference between the quoted interest rate on a T-bond and that on a corporate bond with similar maturity, liquidity, and other features is the **default risk premium (DRP)**. Therefore, if the bonds listed above were *otherwise similar,* the default risk premium would be DRP = $k - k_{RF}$, which are the values given above. Default risk premiums vary somewhat over time, but the March 1998 figures are representative of levels in recent years.

Liquidity Premium (LP)

LIQUIDITY PREMIUM (LP)
A premium added to the rate on a security if the security cannot be converted to cash on short notice and at close to the original cost.

Liquidity generally is defined as the ability to convert an asset to cash on short notice and "reasonably" capture the amount initially invested. The more easily an asset can be converted to cash at a price that substantially recovers the initial amount invested, the more liquid it is considered. Consequently, short-term financial assets generally are more liquid than long-term financial assets. Because liquidity is important, investors evaluate liquidity and include **liquidity premiums (LP)** when market rates of securities are established. Although it is very difficult to accurately measure liquidity premiums, a differential of at least two and probably four or five percentage points exists between the least liquid and the most liquid financial assets of similar default risk and maturity.

Maturity Risk Premium (MRP)

INTEREST RATE RISK
The risk of capital losses to which investors are exposed because of changing interest rates.

The prices of bonds decline whenever interest rates rise, and because interest rates can and do occasionally rise, *all* bonds, even Treasury bonds, have an element of risk called **interest rate risk.** As a general rule, the bonds of any organization, from the U.S. government to General Motors, have more interest rate risk

---

[13]Bond ratings, and bonds' riskiness in general, will be discussed in more detail in Chapter 4. For now, merely note that bonds rated AAA are judged to have less default risk than bonds rated AA, AA bonds are less risky than A bonds, and so on.

MATURITY RISK PREMIUM (MRP)
A premium that reflects interest rate risk; bonds with longer maturities have greater interest rate risk.

the longer the maturity of the bond.[14] Therefore, a **maturity risk premium (MRP),** which is higher the longer the years to maturity, must be included in the required interest rate. The effect of maturity risk premiums is to raise interest rates on long-term bonds relative to those on short-term bonds. This premium, like the others, is extremely difficult to measure, but (1) it seems to vary over time, rising when interest rates are more volatile and uncertain, then falling when interest rates are more stable, and (2) in recent years, the maturity risk premium on 30-year T-bonds appears to have generally been in the range of one or two percentage points.[15]

We should mention that although long-term bonds are heavily exposed to maturity risk, short-term investments are heavily exposed to **reinvestment rate risk.** When short-term investments mature and the proceeds are reinvested, or "rolled over," a decline in interest rates would necessitate reinvestment at a lower rate, and hence would lead to a decline in interest income. Thus, although "investing short" preserves one's principal, the interest income provided by short-term investments varies from year to year, depending on reinvestment rates.[16]

REINVESTMENT RATE RISK
The risk that a decline in interest rates will lead to lower income when bonds mature and funds are reinvested.

Self-Test Questions

Write out an equation for the nominal interest rate on any debt security.

Distinguish between the real risk-free rate of interest, k^*, and the nominal, or quoted, risk-free rate of interest, k_{RF}.

How is inflation considered when interest rates are determined by investors in the financial markets? Explain.

Does the interest rate on a T-bond include a default risk premium? Explain.

Briefly explain the following statement: "Although long-term bonds are heavily exposed to maturity risk, short-term bills are heavily exposed to reinvestment rate risk."

The Term Structure of Interest Rates

A study of Figure 2-3 reveals that at certain times, such as in 1998, short-term interest rates are lower than long-term rates, whereas at other times, such as in

---

[14]For example, if someone had bought a 30-year Treasury bond for $1,000 in 1972, when the long-term interest rate was 7 percent, and held it until 1981, when long-term T-bond rates were about 14.5 percent, the value of the bond would have declined to about $514. That would represent a loss of almost half the money, and it demonstrates that long-term bonds, even U.S. Treasury bonds, are not riskless. However, had the investor purchased short-term T-bills in 1972 and subsequently reinvested the principal each time the bills matured, he or she would still have had $1,000.

[15]The MRP has averaged 1.3 percentage points over the last 65 years. See *Stocks, Bonds, Bills, and Inflation: 1998 Yearbook* (Chicago: Ibbotson Associates, 1998).

[16]Long-term bonds also have some reinvestment rate risk. To actually earn the quoted rate on a long-term bond, the interest payments must be reinvested at the quoted rate. However, if interest rates fall, the interest payments must be reinvested at a lower rate; thus, the realized return would be less than the quoted rate. Note, though, that the reinvestment rate risk is lower on a long-term bond than on a short-term bond because only the interest payments (rather than interest plus principal) on the long-term bond are exposed to reinvestment rate risk. Only zero coupon bonds, discussed in Chapter 4, are completely free of reinvestment rate risk.

TERM STRUCTURE
OF INTEREST RATES
The relationship between
yields and maturities of
securities.

YIELD CURVE
A graph showing the
relationship between yields
and maturities of securities.

1980 and 1981, short-term rates were higher than long-term rates. The relationship between long- and short-term rates, which is known as the **term structure of interest rates,** is important to corporate treasurers, who must decide whether to borrow by issuing long- or short-term debt, and to investors, who must decide whether to buy long- or short-term bonds. Thus, it is important to understand (1) how long- and short-term rates are related to each other and (2) what causes shifts in their relative positions.

To begin, we can find in a source such as *The Wall Street Journal* or the *Federal Reserve Bulletin* the interest rates on Treasury bonds of various maturities on a specific date. For example, the tabular section of Figure 2-5 presents interest rates for different maturities on two different dates. The set of data for a given date, when plotted on a graph such as that in Figure 2-5, is called the **yield curve**

FIGURE 2-5

U.S. Treasury Bond Interest Rates on Different Dates

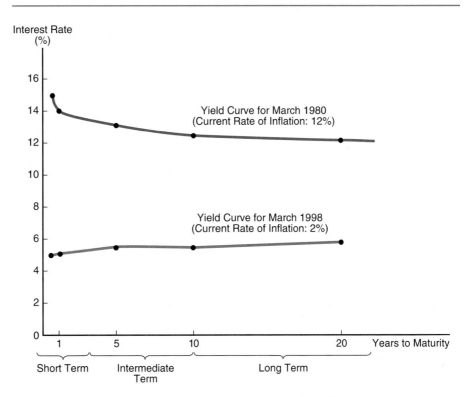

	Interest Rate	
Term to Maturity	March 1980	March 1998
6 months	15.0%	5.0%
1 year	14.0	5.1
5 years	13.5	5.6
10 years	12.8	5.7
20 years	12.5	6.0

for that date. The yield curve changes both in position and in slope over time. In March 1980, all rates were relatively high, and short-term rates were higher than long-term rates, so the yield curve on that date was *downward sloping*. However, in March 1998, all rates had fallen, and short-term rates were lower than long-term rates, so the yield curve at that time was *upward sloping*. Had we drawn the yield curve during January 1982, it would have been essentially horizontal, because long-term and short-term bonds on that date had about the same rate of interest (see Figure 2-3).

"NORMAL" YIELD CURVE
An upward-sloping yield curve.

Historically, in most years, long-term rates have been above short-term rates, so usually the yield curve has been upward sloping. For this reason, people often call an upward-sloping yield curve a **"normal" yield curve** and a yield curve that slopes downward an **inverted, or "abnormal," yield curve.** Thus, in Figure 2-5, the yield curve for March 1980 was inverted, but the one for March 1998 was normal. In the next section, we discuss three explanations for the shape of the yield curve and why an upward sloping yield curve is considered normal.

INVERTED ("ABNORMAL")
YIELD CURVE
A downward-sloping yield curve.

Term Structure Theories (Explanations)

Several theories have been proposed to explain the shape of the yield curve. The three major ones are (1) the expectations theory, (2) the liquidity preference theory, and (3) the market segmentation theory.

EXPECTATIONS THEORY
The theory that the shape of the yield curve depends on investors' expectations about future inflation rates.

EXPECTATIONS THEORY   The **expectations theory** states that the yield curve depends on *expectations* concerning future inflation rates. Specifically, k_t, the nominal interest rate on a U.S. Treasury bond that matures in t years, is found as follows under the expectations theory:

$$k_t = k^* + IP_t$$

Here k^* is the real risk-free interest rate, and IP_t is an inflation premium that is equal to the *average expected rate of inflation* over the t years until the bond matures. Under the expectations theory, the maturity risk premium (MRP) is assumed to be zero, and, for Treasury securities, the default risk premium (DRP) and liquidity premium (LP) also are zero.

To illustrate, suppose that in late December 1998 the real risk-free rate of interest was $k^* = 3\%$ and expected inflation rates for the next three years were as follows[17]:

Year	Expected Annual (1-year) Inflation Rate	Expected Average Inflation Rate from 1998 to Indicated Year (IP_t)
1999	2%	2%/1 = 2%
2000	4%	(2% + 4%)/2 = 3%
2001	9%	(2% + 4% + 9%)/3 = 5%

---

[17]Technically, we should be using geometric averages rather than arithmetic averages, but the differences are not material in this example. For a discussion of this point, see Chapter 15.

Given these expectations, the following interest rate pattern should exist:

Bond Type	Real Risk-free Rate (k^*)		Inflation Premium: Average Expected Inflation Rate (IP_t)		Nominal Treasury Bond Rate for Each Maturity (k_{T-bond})
1-year bond	3%	+	2%	=	5%
2-year bond	3%	+	3%	=	6%
3-year bond	3%	+	5%	=	8%

If the yields on these hypothetical bonds were plotted, the yield curve would be upward sloping, similar to the March 1998 yield curve in Figure 2-5. Had the pattern of expected inflation rates been reversed, with inflation expected to fall from 9 percent to 2 percent during the three-year period, the pattern of interest rates would produce an inverted yield curve like the March 1980 yield curve in Figure 2-5.

LIQUIDITY PREFERENCE THEORY
The theory that, all else equal, lenders prefer to make short-term loans rather than long-term loans; hence, they will lend short-term funds at lower rates than long-term funds.

LIQUIDITY PREFERENCE THEORY The **liquidity preference theory** states that long-term bonds normally yield more than short-term bonds for two reasons: (1) Investors generally prefer to hold short-term securities, because such securities are more liquid in the sense that they can be converted to cash with little danger of loss of principal. Investors will, therefore, generally accept lower yields on short-term securities, and this leads to relatively low short-term rates. (2) Borrowers, on the other hand, generally prefer long-term debt, because short-term debt exposes them to the risk of having to repay the debt under adverse conditions. Accordingly, borrowers want to "lock into" long-term funds, which means they are willing to pay higher rates, other things held constant, for long-term funds than for short-term funds — this also leads to relatively low short-term rates. Thus, both lender and borrower preferences operate to cause short-term rates to be lower than long-term rates. Taken together, these two sets of preferences — and hence the liquidity preference theory — imply that under normal conditions, a positive maturity risk premium (MRP) exists, and the MRP increases with years to maturity, causing the yield curve to be upward sloping.

MARKET SEGMENTATION THEORY
The theory that each borrower and lender has a preferred maturity and that the slope of the yield curve depends on the supply of and demand for funds in the long-term market relative to the short-term market.

MARKET SEGMENTATION THEORY Briefly, the **market segmentation theory** states that each lender and each borrower has a preferred maturity. For example, a person borrowing to buy a long-term asset such as a house, or an electric utility borrowing to build a power plant, would want a long-term loan. However, a retailer borrowing in September to build its inventories for Christmas would prefer a short-term loan. Similar differences exist among savers — for example, a person saving up to take a vacation next summer would want to save in the short-term market, but someone saving for retirement 20 years hence would probably buy long-term securities.

The thrust of the market segmentation theory is that the slope of the yield curve depends on supply/demand conditions in the long- and short-term markets. Thus, according to this theory, the yield curve could at any given time be either flat, upward sloping, or downward sloping. An upward-sloping yield curve would occur when there was a large supply of short-term funds relative to demand, but a shortage of long-term funds. Similarly, a downward-sloping curve would indicate relatively strong demand for funds in the short-term market compared with that in the long-term market. A flat curve would indicate a balance between the two markets.

Various tests of the theories explaining the shape of the yield curve have been conducted, and these tests indicate that all three theories have some validity. Thus, the shape of the yield curve at any given time is affected (1) by expectations about future inflation, (2) by liquidity preferences, and (3) by supply/demand conditions in long- and short-term markets. One factor might dominate at one time, another at another time, but all three affect the term structure of interest rates.

Self-Test Questions

What is a yield curve, and what information would you need to draw this curve?

Discuss each of the following theories:

(1) market segmentation theory.

(2) liquidity preference theory.

(3) expectations theory.

Distinguish between the shapes of a "normal" yield curve and an "abnormal" yield curve, and explain when each might exist.

Other Factors That Influence Interest Rate Levels

Factors other than those discussed above also influence both the general level of interest rates and the shape of the yield curve. The four most important factors are (1) Federal Reserve policy, (2) the level of the federal budget deficit, (3) the foreign trade balance, and (4) the level of business activity.

Federal Reserve Policy

As you probably learned in your economics courses, (1) the money supply has a major effect on both the level of economic activity and the rate of inflation, and (2) in the United States, the Federal Reserve Board controls the money supply. If the Fed wants to control growth in the economy, it slows growth in the money supply. The initial effect of such an action is to cause interest rates to increase and inflation to stabilize. The reverse holds if the Fed loosens the money supply.

In the next chapter, we describe the operations of the Fed in greater detail. For our current discussion, it is important to know that the reason the Fed intervenes in the financial markets is to help stabilize economic conditions. And, during periods when the Fed is actively intervening in the markets, the yield curve will be distorted. Short-term rates will be temporarily "too low" if the Fed is easing credit and "too high" if it is tightening credit. Long-term rates are not affected as much as short-term rates by Fed intervention.

Federal Deficits

If the federal government spends more than it takes in from tax revenues, it runs a deficit, and that deficit must be covered either by borrowing or by printing money. If the government borrows, this added demand for funds pushes up interest rates. If it prints money, this increases expectations for future inflation, which also drives up interest rates. Thus, the larger the federal deficit, other things held constant, the higher the level of interest rates. Whether long- or short-term rates are more affected depends on how the deficit is financed, so we cannot state, in general, how deficits will affect the slope of the yield curve.

Foreign Trade Balance

Businesses and individuals in the United States buy from and sell to people and firms in other countries. If we buy more than we sell (that is, if we import more than we export), we are said to be running a *foreign trade deficit*. When trade deficits occur, they must be financed, and the main source of financing is debt.[18] Therefore, the larger our trade deficit, the more we must borrow, and as we increase our borrowing, this drives up interest rates. Also, foreigners are willing to hold U.S. debt only if the interest rate on this debt is competitive with interest rates in other countries. Therefore, if the Federal Reserve attempts to lower interest rates in the United States, causing our rates to fall below rates abroad, then foreigners will sell U.S. bonds, which will depress bond prices and cause U.S. interest rates to increase. Thus, the existence of a deficit trade balance hinders the Fed's ability to combat a recession by lowering interest rates.

The United States has been running annual trade deficits since the mid-1970s, and the cumulative effect of these deficits is that the United States is by far the largest debtor nation of all time. As a result, our interest rates are very much influenced by interest rate trends in other countries around the world (higher rates abroad lead to higher U.S. rates). Because of all this, U.S. corporate treasurers — and anyone else who is affected by interest rates — must keep up with developments in the world economy.

Business Activity

Figure 2-3, presented earlier, can be examined to see how business conditions influence interest rates. Here are the key points revealed by that graph:

1. Because inflation increased from the 1960s to 1981, the general tendency during this period was toward higher interest rates. However, since the 1981 peak, the trend has generally been downward.
2. Until 1966, short-term rates were almost always below long-term rates. Thus, in those years the yield curve was almost always "normal" in the sense that it was upward sloping.
3. The shaded areas in the graph represent recessions, during which both the demand for money and the rate of inflation tend to fall, and, at the same time, the Federal Reserve tends to increase the money supply in an effort to stimulate the economy. As a result, there is a tendency for interest rates to decline during recessions. Currently, in 1998, the economy is strong, so any actions taken by the Fed to change interest rates are efforts to control the economy so that growth does not result in high inflation.

---

[18]The deficit could also be financed by selling assets, including gold, corporate stocks, entire companies, and real estate. The United States has financed its massive trade deficits by all of these means in recent years, but the primary method has been by borrowing.

4. During recessions, short-term rates decline more sharply than long-term rates. This occurs because (a) the Fed operates mainly in the short-term sector, so its intervention has the strongest effect here, and (b) long-term rates reflect the average expected inflation rate over the next 20 to 30 years, and this expectation generally does not change much, even when the current rate of inflation is low because of a recession.

Self-Test Questions

Other than inflationary expectations, liquidity preferences, and normal supply/demand fluctuations, name four additional factors that influence interest rates. Explain their effects.

How does the Fed stimulate the economy? How does the Fed affect interest rates?

Interest Rate Levels and Stock Prices

Interest rates have two effects on corporate profits. First, because interest is a cost, the higher the rate of interest, the lower a firm's profits, other things held constant. Second, interest rates affect the level of economic activity, and economic activity affects corporate profits. Interest rates obviously affect stock prices because of their effects on profits, but, perhaps even more important, they have an effect due to competition in the marketplace between stocks and bonds. If interest rates rise sharply, investors can get higher returns in the bond market, which induces them to sell stocks and to transfer funds from the stock market to the bond market. A massive sale of stocks in response to rising interest rates obviously would depress stock prices. Of course, the reverse occurs if interest rates decline. Indeed, the bull market of December 1991, when the Dow Jones Industrial Index rose 10 percent in less than a month, was caused almost entirely by the sharp drop in long-term interest rates. On the other hand, the poor performance exhibited by the market in 1994 — common stocks declined on average by more than 3 percent — resulted from sharp increases in interest rates. Since that period, as interest rates declined, the stock market has been the "hot" investment. In the past few years, rates in the debt markets have remained at relatively low levels, while rates in the stock markets have been high.

Self-Test Question

In what two ways do changes in interest rates affect stock prices?

SMALL BUSINESS

Why Go Public for Less Than You're Worth?

For many entrepreneurs, making an initial public offering (IPO) of their company's equity is a dream come true. After their years of sacrifice and hard work, the company finally is a success. The value of that sacrifice is realized by going public. Many observers are amazed that the successful entrepreneur appears

Continued

willing to sell equity in his or her firm for too little money — on average, IPOs are *underpriced.*

Stocks are underpriced if they begin trading in the public markets at a price that is higher than the offering price. An example would be a stock that was sold in an IPO for $12.00 that begins trading immediately after the IPO for $15.00 per share.

This underpricing is a puzzle. The company going public, and any current shareholders of the privately owned firm who are selling as part of the public offering, receive, on average, the IPO price minus a commission or "discount" of roughly 8 percent. Even if the shareholders do not sell any of their own shares in the IPO, but instead sell only the company's shares, they still are hurt by underpricing because their ownership in the firm is diluted more than it would have been had the shares been fully priced.

The large returns of IPOs in the public market are not caused by the companies' performance after the IPOs. They do not mean that the firms showed high earnings growth after the IPOs — the higher returns generally occur on the *first trading day.* This simply means that the IPO securities were sold at a price below their value.

Why would issuers in IPOs (i.e., selling companies) willingly sell their stocks for less than their true value? There are a number of theories to explain underpricing, but there is no widespread consensus on the reasons for underpricing. Some possible explanations are described next.

One explanation for underpricing is that the issuing companies' owners are not as knowledgeable as their underwriters; if owners have the same knowledge as underwriters, issues would be fully priced. This theory might explain some occurrences of underpricing, such as isolated instances in which an unethical underwriter (who presumably would not last long in the business) knowingly misinforms the issuer. However, some underwriters themselves have gone public, acting as their own underwriters, and they also have had substantial first-day returns — underpricing.

A popular theory among academicians is that underpricing occurs to keep *uninformed* investors in the market. According to this theory, there are some

well-informed investors who regularly watch the IPO market to identify those that are mispriced. These *informed* investors, therefore, buy only the underpriced issues. However, such informed investors do not have enough capital to buy all of the shares of any offering. On the other hand, uninformed investors tend to buy every IPO, believing significant returns will be realized. Thus, uninformed investors tend to buy a lot of stock in the overpriced or correctly priced offerings, but will obtain only a small portion of the offerings in which the informed investors are active. And, unless the set of all offerings is underpriced on average, then uninformed investors would consistently lose money, they would leave the market, and the market would break down. Thus, this theory argues, the IPO market must experience general underpricing to function. Early empirical evidence is consistent with this theory.

The most popular theory with underwriters and venture capitalists is what might be called the "good taste in the mouth" theory. According to this theory, if the company underprices its issue in an IPO, investors will be more receptive to future "seasoned" issues from the same firm. Note, too, that most IPOs involve only 10 to 20 percent of the stock, so the original owners still have 80 to 90 percent of the shares.

All of these theories have a similar implication: An IPO with less uncertainty concerning its value will tend to be more fully priced. This suggests that firms can prepare themselves for public offerings at higher prices by using more prestigious underwriters to issue IPOs, using reputable, visible accountants for their audits, and acquiring venture capital investment from more reputable capitalists.

The phenomenon of underpricing IPO shares remains a puzzle to finance academicians. We think we have some of the answers, but the questions are not yet settled. Meanwhile, an issuer should be aware that most IPOs are underpriced by a meaningful amount and that this underpricing is almost certainly related to the risk and uncertainty of the business. This is important information to consider when deciding when the firm should make its initial public offering.

Summary

In this chapter we described the nature of financial markets. The key concepts covered in the chapter are listed below.

- The **financial markets** make up a system comprised of individuals and organizations, instruments, and procedures that bring together borrowers and savers.
- Transfers of capital between "borrowers" and savers take place (1) by **direct transfers** of money and securities; (2) by transfers through **investment banking houses,** which act as middlemen; and (3) by transfers through **financial intermediaries,** which create new securities.
- Many would attest the financial markets have achieved **informational efficiency** either in the *weak form, semi-strong form,* or *strong form.*
- There are many different types of *financial markets.* Each market serves a different region or deals with a different type of security. **Money markets** are the markets in which short-term financial assets are traded, while **capital markets** are the markets for long-term financial assets. Bonds and other types of loans are traded in the **debt markets,** and corporate stock is traded in the **equity markets.** When a company or government issues new securities to raise funds, they "visit" the **primary markets.** When investors trade previously issued securities among themselves, they are said to be trading in the **secondary markets.**
- The **stock market** is an especially important market because this is where stock prices (which are used to "grade" managers' performances) are established.
- There are two basic types of stock markets — the **organized exchanges** and the **over-the-counter market.**
- Membership on the New York Stock Exchange (NYSE) is classified in one of the following categories: **commission broker, independent broker, competitive traders,** or **specialist.**
- The **listing requirements** of the various stock exchanges differ, depending on whether the exchange is national or regional.
- To raise funds in the capital markets, firms and governments generally engage **investment bankers,** which assist in the issuing of securities by helping the firm determine the size of the issue and the type of securities to be issued, by establishing the selling price, by selling the issue, and, in some cases, by maintaining an after-market for the stock.
- Financial markets are regulated by the **Securities and Exchange Commission (SEC),** which encourages disclosure of financial information by corporations and discourages fraudulent behavior by investors, companies, employees, and so on.
- **International financial markets** have experienced significant growth, and the domination of the U.S. markets has decreased in recent years. Generally, we invest in foreign companies *indirectly* through financial instruments sold in the United States.
- Capital is allocated through the price system — a price must be paid to "rent" money. Lenders charge interest on funds they lend, while equity investors receive dividends and capital gains in return for letting firms use their money.
- Four fundamental factors affect the cost of money: (1) **production opportunities,** (2) **time preferences for consumption,** (3) **risk,** and (4) **inflation.**
- The **risk-free rate of interest, k_{RF},** is defined as the real risk-free rate, k^*, plus an inflation premium (IP): $k_{RF} = k^* + IP$.
- The **nominal (or quoted) interest rate** on a debt security, k, is composed of the real risk-free rate, k^*, plus premiums that reflect inflation (IP), default risk (DRP), liquidity (LP), and maturity risk (MRP):

$$k = k^* + IP + DRP + LP + MRP.$$

- If the **real risk-free rate of interest and the various premiums were constant over time,** interest rates in the economy would be stable. However, both the real rate and the risk premiums — especially the premium for expected inflation — **do change over time, causing market interest rates to change.** Also, Federal Reserve intervention to increase or decrease the money supply, as well as international currency flows, lead to fluctuations in interest rates.
- The relationship between the yields on securities and the securities' maturities is known as the **term structure of interest rates,** and the **yield curve** is a graph of this relationship.
- The yield curve is normally **upward sloping,** but the curve can **slope downward** if the demand for short-term funds is relatively strong or if the rate of inflation is expected to decline.
- **Interest rate levels have a profound effect on stock prices.** Higher interest rates (1) slow down the economy, (2) increase interest expenses and thus lower corporate profits, and (3) cause investors to sell stocks and transfer funds to the bond market. Each of these factors tends to depress stock prices.
- A small firm's stock sold in an **initial public offering (IPO)** often increases in price immediately after issue, with the largest price increases being associated with issues where uncertainties are greatest.

Questions

2-1 What would happen to the standard of living in the United States if people lost faith in our financial markets? Why?

2-2 How does a cost-efficient capital market help to reduce the prices of goods and services?

2-3 The SEC attempts to protect investors who are purchasing newly issued securities by requiring issuers to provide relevant financial information to prospective investors. However, the SEC does not provide an opinion about the real value of the securities; hence, an investor might pay too much for some stock and consequently lose heavily. Do you think the SEC should, as a part of every new stock or bond offering, render an opinion to investors on the proper value of the securities being offered? Explain.

2-4 How do you think each of the following items would affect a company's ability to attract new capital and the flotation (issuing) costs involved in doing so?
  a. A decision to list a company's stock; the stock now trades in the over-the-counter market.
  b. A decision of a privately held company to go public.
  c. The increasing importance of institutions in the stock and bond markets.
  d. The trend toward financial conglomerates as opposed to stand-alone investment banking houses.
  e. The introduction of shelf registrations.

2-5 Before entering a formal agreement, investment bankers carefully investigate the companies whose securities they underwrite; this is especially true of the issues of firms going public for the first time. Because the bankers do not themselves plan to hold the securities but intend to sell them to others as soon as possible, why are they so concerned about making careful investigations?

2-6 Why would management be interested in getting a wide distribution of its shares?

2-7   Microsoft and Intel qualify to be listed on the New York Stock Exchange, but both have chosen to be traded on the NASDAQ portion of the over-the-counter market. Can you think of reasons the companies would choose to be traded OTC? (Hint: Both companies deal with products that relate to electronic/computer media.)

2-8   Both organized exchanges and the OTC are markets for trading stocks. Why do you think companies want to be listed on organized exchanges rather than stay OTC?

2-9   What types of companies enter the markets for initial public offerings (IPOs)? Why do companies choose to go public? Why not stay private?

2-10   Suppose interest rates on residential mortgages of equal risk were 8 percent in California and 10 percent in New York. Could this differential persist? What forces might tend to equalize rates? Would differentials in borrowing costs for businesses of equal risk located in California and New York be more or less likely to exist than differentials in residential mortgage rates? Would differentials in the cost of money for New York and California firms be more likely to exist if the firms being compared were very large or if they were very small? What are the implications of all this for the pressure now being put on Congress to permit banks to engage in nationwide branching?

2-11   Which fluctuate more, long-term or short-term interest rates? Why?

2-12   Suppose a new process was developed that could be used to make oil out of seawater. The equipment required is quite expensive but it would, in time, lead to very low prices for gasoline, electricity, and other types of energy. What effect would this have on interest rates?

2-13   Suppose a new and much more liberal Congress and administration were elected, and their first order of business was to take away the independence of the Federal Reserve System and to force the Fed to greatly expand the money supply. What effect would this have
   a. On the level and slope of the yield curve immediately after the announcement?
   b. On the level and slope of the yield curve that would exist two or three years in the future?

2-14   Suppose interest rates on Treasury bonds rose from 7 to 14 percent as a result of higher interest rates in Europe. What effect would this have on the price of an average company's common stock?

Self-Test Problems   *Solutions Appear in Appendix B*

Key terms   **ST-1**   Define each of the following terms:
   a. Informational efficiency; economic efficiency
   b. Money market; capital market
   c. Debt market; equity market
   d. Primary market; secondary market
   e. Over-the-counter (OTC) market; organized security exchange
   f. Commission broker; independent broker; competitive trader; specialist
   g. Investment banker
   h. Going public; new issue market; initial public offering (IPO)
   i. Prospectus; registration statement
   j. Shelf registration
   k. Best efforts arrangement; underwritten arrangement
   l. Underwriters' spread; flotation costs; offering price

m. Underwriting syndicate; lead, or managing, underwriter; selling group

n. Securities and Exchange Commission (SEC); insiders

o. Production opportunities; time preferences for consumption

p. Real risk-free rate of interest, k*; nominal risk-free rate of interest, k_{RF}

q. Inflation premium (IP)

r. Default risk premium (DRP)

s. Liquidity; liquidity premium (LP)

t. Interest rate risk; maturity risk premium (MRP)

u. Term structure of interest rates; yield curve

v. "Normal" yield curve

w. Market segmentation theory; liquidity preference theory; expectations theory

Inflation rates   **ST-2**   Assume that it is now January 1, 2000. The rate of inflation is expected to be 6 percent throughout 2000. However, increased government deficits and renewed vigor in the economy are then expected to push inflation rates higher. Investors expect the inflation rate to be 7 percent in 2001, 8 percent in 2002, and 9 percent in 2003. The real risk-free rate, k*, currently is 3 percent. Assume that no maturity risk premiums are required on bonds with 5 years or less to maturity. The current interest rate on 5-year T-bonds is 11 percent.

a. What is the average expected inflation rate over the next 4 years?

b. What should be the prevailing interest rate on 4-year T-bonds?

c. What is the implied expected inflation rate in 2004, or Year 5, given that bonds which mature in that year yield 11 percent?

Problems

Profit (loss) on   **2-1**   Security Brokers Inc. specializes in underwriting new issues by small firms. On a
a new stock issue   recent offering of Barenbaum Inc., the terms were as follows:

Price to public	$7.50 per share
Number of shares	3 million
Proceeds to Barenbaum	$21,000,000

The out-of-pocket expenses incurred by Security Brokers in the design and distribution of the issue were $450,000. What profit or loss would Security Brokers incur if the issue were sold to the public at an average price of

a. $7.50 per share?

b. $9.00 per share?

c. $6.00 per share?

Yield curves   **2-2**   Suppose you and most other investors expect the rate of inflation to be 7 percent next year, to fall to 5 percent during the following year, and then to remain at a rate of 3 percent thereafter. Assume that the real risk-free rate, k*, is 2 percent and that maturity risk premiums on Treasury securities rise from zero on very short-term bonds (those that mature in a few days) by 0.2 percentage point for each year to maturity, up to a limit of 1.0 percentage point on 5-year or longer-term T-bonds.

a. Calculate the interest rate on 1-, 2-, 3-, 4-, 5-, 10-, and 20-year Treasury securities, and plot the yield curve.

b. Now suppose Exxon, an AAA-rated company, had bonds with the same maturities as the Treasury bonds. As an approximation, plot an Exxon yield curve on the same graph with the Treasury bond yield curve. (Hint: Think about the default risk premium on Exxon's long-term versus its short-term bonds.)

c. Now plot the approximate yield curve of Long Island Lighting Company, a risky nuclear utility.

Yield curve **2-3** The following yields on U.S. Treasury securities were taken from *The Wall Street Journal* of May 27, 1998:

Term	Rate
6 months	5.4%
1 year	5.6
2 years	5.6
3 years	5.7
4 years	5.7
5 years	5.7
10 years	5.8
20 years	6.0
30 years	6.0

Plot a yield curve based on these data. Discuss how each term structure theory can explain the shape of the yield curve you plot.

Inflation and interest rates **2-4** It is January 1, 2000. Inflation currently is about 2 percent; throughout 1999, the Fed took action to maintain inflation at this level. However, the economy is starting to grow too quickly, and reports indicate that inflation is expected to increase during the next 5 years. Assume that *at the beginning* of 2000, the rate of inflation *expected* for 2000 is 4 percent; for 2001, it is *expected* to be 5 percent; for 2002, it is *expected* to be 7 percent; and, for 2003 and every year thereafter, it is *expected* to settle at 4 percent.

a. What was the average expected inflation rate over the 5-year period 2000–2004? (Use the arithmetic average.)

b. What average nominal interest rate would, over the 5-year period, be expected to produce a 2 percent real risk-free rate of return on 5-year Treasury securities?

c. Assuming a real risk-free rate of 2 percent and a maturity risk premium that starts at 0.1 percent and increases by 0.1 percent *each year,* estimate the interest rate in January 2000 on bonds that mature in 1, 2, 5, 10, and 20 years, and draw a yield curve based on these data.

d. Describe the general economic conditions that could be expected to produce an upward-sloping yield curve.

e. If the consensus among investors in early 2000 had been that the expected rate of inflation for every future year was 5 percent (that is, $I_t = I_t + 1 = 5\%$ for t = 1 to ∞), what do you think the yield curve would have looked like? Consider all the factors that are likely to affect the curve. Does your answer here make you question the yield curve you drew in part c?

Exam-Type Problems

The problems included in this section are set up in such a way that they could be used as multiple-choice exam problems.

Underwriting and flotation expenses **2-5** The Taussig Company, whose stock price now is $30, needs to raise $15 million in common stock. Underwriters have informed Taussig's management that it must price the new issue to the public at $27.53 per share to ensure the shares will be sold. The underwriters' compensation will be 7 percent of the issue price, so Taussig will net $25.60 per share. Taussig will also incur expenses in the amount of $360,000. How many shares must Taussig sell to net $15 million after underwriting and flotation expenses?

Expected rate of interest **2-6** Suppose the annual yield on a 2-year Treasury bond is 11.5 percent, while that on a 1-year bond is 10 percent; k* is 3 percent, and the maturity risk premium is zero.

a. Using the expectations theory, forecast the interest rate on a 1-year bond during the second year. (Hint: Under the expectations theory, the yield on a 2-year bond is equal to the average yield on 1-year bonds in Years 1 and 2.)

b. What is the expected inflation rate in Year 1? Year 2?

Expected rate of interest   **2-7**   Assume that the real risk-free rate is 4 percent and that the maturity risk premium is zero. If the nominal rate of interest on 1-year bonds is 11 percent and that on comparable-risk 2-year bonds is 13 percent, what is the 1-year interest rate that is expected for Year 2? What inflation rate is expected during Year 2? Comment on why the average interest rate during the 2-year period differs from the 1-year interest rate expected for Year 2.

Interest rates   **2-8**   The rate of inflation for the coming year is expected to be 3 percent, and the rate of inflation in Year 2 and thereafter is expected to be constant at some level above 3 percent. Assume that the real risk-free rate is $k^* = 2$ percent for all maturities and the expectations theory fully explains the yield curve, so there are no maturity premiums. If 3-year Treasury bonds yield 2 percentage points more than 1-year bonds, what rate of inflation is expected after Year 1?

Integrative Problem

Financial markets   **2-9**   Assume that you recently graduated with a degree in finance and have just reported to work as an investment advisor at the firm of Balik and Kiefer Inc. Your first assignment is to explain the nature of the U.S. financial markets and institutions to Michelle Delatorre, a professional tennis player who has just come to the United States from Chile. Delatorre is a highly ranked tennis player who expects to invest substantial amounts of money through Balik and Kiefer. She is also very bright, and, therefore, she would like to understand in general terms what will happen to her money. Your boss has developed the following questions, which you must ask and answer to explain the U.S. financial system to Delatorre.

a. What is a financial market? How are financial markets differentiated from markets for physical assets?

b. Differentiate between money markets and capital markets.

c. Differentiate between a primary market and a secondary market. If Microsoft decided to issue additional common stock, and Delatorre purchased 100 shares of this stock from Merrill Lynch, the underwriter, would this transaction be a primary market transaction or a secondary market transaction? Would it make a difference if Delatorre purchased previously outstanding Apple stock in the over-the-counter market?

d. Describe the three primary ways in which capital is transferred between savers and borrowers.

e. Securities can be traded on organized exchanges or in the over-the-counter market. Define each of these markets, and describe how stocks are traded in each of them.

f. What do we call the price that a borrower must pay for debt capital? What is the price of equity capital? What are the four most fundamental factors that affect the cost of money, or the general level of interest rates, in the economy?

g. What is the real risk-free rate of interest (k^*) and the nominal risk-free rate (k_{RF})? How are these two rates measured?

h. Define the terms inflation premium (IP), default risk premium (DRP), liquidity premium (LP), and maturity risk premium (MRP). Which of these premiums is included when determining the interest rate on (1) short-term U.S. Treasury securities, (2) long-term U.S. Treasury securities, (3) short-term corporate securities, and (4) long-term corporate securities? Explain how the premiums would vary over time and among the different securities listed above.

i. What is the term structure of interest rates? What is a yield curve? At any given time, how would the yield curve facing a given company such as AT&T or Chrysler compare with the yield curve for U.S. Treasury securities? Draw a graph to illustrate your answer.

j. Several theories have been advanced to explain the shape of the yield curve. The three major ones are (1) the market segmentation theory, (2) the liquidity preference theory, and (3) the expectations theory. Briefly describe each of these theories. Do economists regard one as being "true"?

k. Suppose most investors expect the rate of inflation to be 5 percent next year, 6 percent the following year, and 8 percent thereafter. The real risk-free rate is 3 percent. The maturity risk premium is zero for bonds that mature in 1 year or less, 0.1 percent for 2-year bonds, and the MRP increases by 0.1 percent per year thereafter for 20 years, after which it is stable. What is the interest rate on 1-, 10-, and 20-year Treasury bonds? Draw a yield curve with these data. Is your yield curve consistent with the three term structure theories?

CHAPTER 3

Financial Intermediaries
and the Banking System

Are banks becoming less important to Americans? Perhaps. During the past couple of decades, the visage of banking has changed significantly, primarily the result of deregulation in the financial services industry. Banks no longer have a monopoly on checking accounts like they did prior to the mid 1970s. Now, checking services, as well as other services traditionally offered by banks, also are available at such nonbank organizations as mutual funds and brokerage firms. Consider the fact that about 36 percent of the financial assets held by individuals was in banks in 1975, while the amount held in banks today is less than 17 percent.

Why has there been a relative decline in individuals' financial assets held in banks? The simple answer is that "nonbanks" have been able to offer more of the same products as banks, and they have been very good at creating other products with the same qualities as those offered by banks. For example, to many of us, there is no real difference between money market mutual funds and savings accounts at banks — both offer a safe medium to invest, and funds are easily accessible. In an effort to regain customers' funds, banks have recently begun to fight back by expanding into areas previously considered "taboo." For instance, in 1998, Citicorp, one of the largest banking organizations in the United States, and Travelers Group, which operates large insurance and investment organizations, agreed to a merger that would create the largest financial services organization in the world with combined assets greater than $700 billion. The company created by the Travelers-Citicorp merger can offer an array of products and services demanded by a wide range of individuals and other businesses.

Other large mergers that have taken place in the financial services industry in the past couple of years have been among banks. In 1997, NationsBank acquired Barnett Banks and then merged with BankAmerica in 1998 to create the largest bank in the United States. Banc One and First Chicago also merged in 1998. Mergers of financial services organizations are not expected to slow any time soon, which illustrates the current attitude of

Continued

many financial intermediaries — big is better. It is expected that banking, as well as the financial services industry in general, will undergo major changes during the next decade or two, because the future success of financial institutions lies in the ability to offer a variety of financial products and services. Financial intermediaries that exist today will look significantly different tomorrow.

As you read this chapter, think about why particular types of financial intermediaries evolved, as well as about how such intermediaries will be transformed in the future. How different will a bank and an insurance company be in the year 2020?

In Chapter 2 we noted that most people do not provide funds directly to such users, or borrowers, as companies, governments, and individuals; rather, they transfer funds through firms known as financial intermediaries. In this chapter, we describe in more detail the functions and types of financial intermediaries as well as the banking system and the role of the Federal Reserve as the central bank of the United States. Finally, we will give an indication of how the U.S. banking system differs from banking systems in other countries.

Roles of Financial Intermediaries

FINANCIAL INTERMEDIARIES
Specialized financial firms that facilitate the *indirect* transfer of funds from savers to borrowers by offering savings instruments, such as pension plans and mutual funds, and borrowing instruments, such as credit cards and mortgages.

Financial intermediaries include such financial services organizations as commercial banks, savings and loan associations, pension funds, and insurance companies. In simple terms, **financial intermediaries** facilitate the transfer of funds from those who have funds (savers) to those who need funds (borrowers). However, financial intermediaries do more than simply transfer money and securities between borrowers and savers — they literally *manufacture* a variety of financial products, including mortgages, automobile loans, NOW accounts, money market mutual funds, and pension funds. Such products allow savers to *indirectly* provide funds to borrowers, using whichever savings method (product) is most preferred. At the same time, borrowers can raise funds by using debt instruments created by intermediaries that have characteristics suitable for their needs, including maturity, denomination, and payment structure.

FINANCIAL INTERMEDIATION
The process by which financial intermediaries transform funds provided by savers into funds used by borrowers.

In reality, when intermediaries take funds from savers, they issue *securities* with such names as savings accounts, money market funds, and pension plans, which represent claims, or liabilities, against the intermediaries. The funds received by intermediaries are, in turn, lent to businesses, individuals, and governments via debt instruments created by intermediaries, such as automobile loans, mortgages, and commercial loans. The process by which financial intermediaries transform funds provided by savers into funds used by borrowers is called **financial intermediation.** Figure 3-1 illustrates the financial intermediation process. The arrows at the top of the boxes (pointing to the right) show the flow of funds from savers to borrowers through intermediaries, and the arrows at the bottom of the boxes (pointing to the left) indicate the changes in the balance sheets of savers, borrowers, and intermediaries that result from the intermediation process. Basically, savers *exchange* funds for such claims, or liabilities, from intermediaries as deposits at banks, retirement plans, or money market funds. The

FIGURE 3-1

The Financial Intermediation Process

intermediaries then *exchange* funds provided by savers for claims, or liabilities, of borrowers that are packaged as debt or other instruments created by the intermediaries, including mortgages, commercial loans, and many other types of loans.

Financial intermediaries have created a variety of products to facilitate the savings and borrowing processes both for individuals and businesses. To illustrate, consider again Alexandra Trottier, who currently has an income equal to $36,000 but only spends (consumes) $30,000 annually. Because there exists a variety of savings instruments, Alexandra can choose the instrument that best fits her needs. If she decides to put her funds in a savings instrument offered by Valrico State Bank, the bank will pay her interest on the funds deposited. To pay interest to Alexandra, the bank must create loans for which it receives interest payments from such borrowers as individuals and businesses. The funds the bank uses to create such loans come from Alexandra's deposits, as well as those of other individuals and businesses. Thus, by depositing money in Valrico State Bank, Alexandra and other depositors *indirectly* lend funds through the bank to individuals and businesses. Without financial intermediaries such as Valrico State Bank, savers would have to provide funds *directly* to borrowers, which would be a difficult task for savers who do not possess such expertise — such loans as mortgages and automobile financing would be much more costly; thus the financial markets would be much less efficient. Therefore, the presence of intermediaries improves economic well-being. In fact, financial intermediaries were created to fulfill specific needs of both savers and borrowers, and thus reduce inefficiencies that would exist if users of funds could get loans only by borrowing directly from savers.

Improving economic well-being is only one of the benefits associated with intermediaries. Some additional benefits include the following:

1. **Reduced costs.** Without intermediaries, the net cost of borrowing would be greater, and the net return earned by savers would be less, because individuals with funds to lend would have to seek out appropriate borrowers themselves, and vice versa. Intermediaries are more cost efficient than individuals because they create combinations of financial products that better match funds provided by savers with the needs of borrowers, and they are able to spread costs associated with such activities over large numbers of transactions. For example, financial intermediaries have greater expertise than individuals when it comes to gathering, verifying, and evaluating information concerning borrowers, because such functions are performed continuously by intermediaries but not by individuals; thus, it is less costly for intermediaries than individuals to evaluate the attractiveness of each borrower. Similarly, other costs associated with transforming savings into loans are less because intermediaries have expertise and achieve economies of scale that individuals do not. Consider what would happen if you had savings you wanted to invest, but you had to personally search for potential borrowers. The costs associated with the time and effort needed to ensure your funds are invested safely might be so extraordinary compared with the potential return that you might decide to keep your savings under your mattress.

2. **Risk/diversification.** The loan portfolios of intermediaries generally are well diversified because they provide funds to a large number and variety of borrowers by offering many different types of loans. Therefore, just like investors who purchase varied financial securities, intermediaries spread their risk by "not putting all their financial eggs in one basket."

3. **Funds divisibility/pooling.** Intermediaries can pool funds provided by individuals to offer loans or other financial products with different denominations to borrowers. Thus, an intermediary can offer a large loan to a single borrower by combining the funds provided by many small savers. In essence, then, intermediaries permit the "small guys" to be a part of large loans and the "big guys" to get large amounts of funds without the need to find individuals with sufficient wealth.

4. **Financial flexibility.** Because intermediaries offer a variety of financial products, both savers and borrowers have greater choices, or financial flexibility, than can be achieved with direct placements. For instance, banks offer savers such products as regular passbook savings accounts, certificates of deposit, and money market accounts, and they offer borrowers such products as commercial loans, mortgages, and lines of credit. Still different financial products are offered by other types of intermediaries. In general, the financial products created by intermediaries are quite varied with respect to denominations, maturities, and other characteristics; hence intermediaries attract many different types of savers and borrowers.

5. **Related services.** A system of specialized intermediaries offers more than just a network of "mechanisms" to transfer funds from savers to borrowers. Many intermediaries provide financial services in areas in which they achieve comparative advantages, such as expertise or economies of scale, over individuals. For example, banks provide individuals with a convenient method to make payments through checking accounts, and life insurance companies offer financial protection for individuals' beneficiaries.

Think about the complications that would exist if we could not pay our bills using checks or we could not borrow funds to purchase cars or houses. In general, financial intermediaries increase the standard of living in the economy. The financial products offered by intermediaries help both individuals and businesses invest in opportunities that otherwise might be unreachable. For example, without the mortgages offered by savings and loan associations, individuals would find it much more difficult to purchase houses — other sources of funds would exist, but great amounts of time, effort, and cost would have to be expended to search for an individual, or group of individuals, willing to lend the correct amount at an appropriate rate. Similarly, financial intermediaries offer loans to businesses that increase growth, hence improve manufacturing abilities and increase employment. Thus, intermediaries are good for the economy.

Self-Test Questions

What is the principal role of financial intermediaries?

In what ways do financial intermediaries benefit society?

Types of Financial Intermediaries

In the United States, a large set of specialized, highly efficient financial intermediaries has evolved. Competition and government policy have created a rapidly changing arena, however, such that different types of institutions currently create financial products and perform services that previously were reserved for others. This trend, which is destined to continue into the future, has caused institutional distinctions to become blurred. Still, there remains a degree of institutional identity among various financial intermediaries, and such differences are discussed in this section.

Each type of intermediary originated because there existed a particular need in the financial markets that was not satisfied at the time. And, for that reason, historically, it generally has been easy to distinguish among various types of intermediaries with respect to the characteristics of assets and liabilities. Even though various organizations are more alike today than at any time in modern history, there still exist differences in the specific assets/liabilities structures among the intermediaries. For that reason, as we describe each type of intermediary, we also include an indication of the combination of assets and liabilities. At this point, we should mention that the combinations of assets and liabilities of financial institutions differ from the combinations of assets and liabilities of individuals and businesses. The assets of financial institutions primarily consist of loans and other instruments that are comparable to the accounts receivable held by businesses. On the other side of the balance sheet, the liabilities of financial institutions primarily result from savers providing funds in the form of deposits or shares, which are similar to the accounts payable or notes payable used by businesses to raise funds. But, as you will discover, while there exist many similarities, the *types* of loans, deposits, and other products offered by intermediaries differ among the various intermediaries.

Commercial Banks

COMMERCIAL BANK
"Department stores of finance" that offer a variety of deposits, loans, and other products and services to a variety of customers.

Commercial banks, commonly referred to simply as banks, are the traditional "department stores of finance" because they offer a wide variety of products and services to a variety of customers. Historically, banks were the institutions that handled checking accounts and provided mechanisms for clearing checks. Also, banks traditionally provided the medium through which the supply of money was expanded or contracted. Today, however, several other institutions also provide checking and check-clearing services and significantly influence the money supply. Conversely, banking companies provide an ever-widening range of services, including trust operations, stock brokerage services, and insurance.

Originally, banks were established to serve the needs of commerce, or business, hence the name commercial banks. Today, commercial banks represent the largest depository intermediaries, and their operations impact nearly everyone either directly or indirectly. Most individuals have at least one checking account or savings account at a commercial bank, and many have borrowed from banks to finance automobile purchases and also use bank-issued credit cards. Even those who do not specifically use such services are affected by commercial lending activities, which support business operations. For example, banks provide funds that allow firms to grow, which, in turn, increases wage and employment levels.

Table 3-1 shows the combination of assets and liabilities for the approximately 9,000 federally insured commercial banks in the United States in 1997. As the balance sheet shows, almost 60 percent of commercial banks' assets is in the form of loans, with about 70 percent of the loans consisting of business loans or real estate financing, much of which is commercial land, and less than 20 percent classified as consumer, or individual, loans. The loans created by banks are funded by liabilities, which consist primarily of deposits; according to Table 3-1, deposits from businesses and individuals represent nearly 70 percent of banks' liabilities.

TABLE 3-1

FDIC-Insured Commercial Banks: Assets and Liabilities, June 30, 1998 (billions of dollars)

	Amount	Percent of Total Assets
Assets		
Cash	$ 331.5	6.4%
Investments		
Treasury and government agencies	667.3	12.9
Other investments	227.2	4.4
Total investments	$ 894.5	17.3%
Loans		
Business	850.4	16.4
Real estate	1,284.6	24.8
Consumer	547.9	10.6
To depository institutions	100.5	1.9
Other loans	251.9	4.9
Total loans	$3,035.3	58.6%
Other assets	921.5	17.8
Total assets	$5,182.8	100.1%[a]
Liabilities and Equity		
Deposits		
Noninterest-bearing	$ 687.0	13.3
Interest-bearing	2,819.6	54.4
Total deposits	$3,506.6	67.7%
Borrowed funds	1,083.2	20.9
Other liabilities	147.0	2.8
Equity capital	446.0	8.6
Total liabilities and equity	$5,182.8	100.0%

[a]Number does not add to 100.0% due to rounding.

SOURCE: Federal Deposit Insurance Company, *Statistics on Banking,* Second Quarter, 1998; http://www.fdic.gov/data.bank

Credit Unions

CREDIT UNION
A depository institution owned by depositors who have a common association, such as an occupation or a religion.

A **credit union** is a depository institution that is owned by its depositors, who are members of a common organization or association, such as an occupation, a religious group, or a community. Credit unions operate as nonprofit businesses and are managed by member depositors elected by other members.

The first credit unions can be traced to financial pools, or cooperatives, established in England nearly 200 years ago. The purpose of these financial groups originally was to create savings pools that could be used to provide credit to neighboring farmers who suffered temporary losses of income due to crop failures or other catastrophes. The common bonds possessed by the members generated a "help thy neighbor" attitude within the savings pools. As credit unions developed, they became known as financial institutions that served the "common worker," because many were originally established to serve members of particular occupations, such as the military or railroad workers.

Today, credit unions differ significantly from their earliest forms — they are much larger, hence less personal. But, the spirit of credit unions remains unchanged — to serve depositor members. Members' savings are still loaned to other members, but the loans are primarily for automobile purchases, home improvements, and the like. Because of the common bond members possess, loans from credit unions often are the cheapest source of funds available to individual borrowers.

Table 3-2 gives an indication of the mix of assets and liabilities of credit unions for the 11,125 federally insured credit unions. As you can see, 64 percent of the assets are loans. Most of the loans are made to individuals and take the form of balances outstanding on credit cards (individual loans), home equity loans (real estate), or automobile financing — about two-thirds of the loans are classified as either individual or automobile. The funds used to make these loans primarily come from members' deposits, which generally are checkable deposits called *share drafts*, regular savings accounts called *share accounts*, or such other types of savings as certificates of deposit and IRA accounts.

Thrift Institutions

THRIFTS
Institutions that cater to savers, especially individuals who have relatively small amounts of money to deposit or need long-term loans to purchase houses.

Thrifts are financial institutions that cater to savers, especially individuals who have relatively small savings or need long-term loans to purchase houses. Thrifts originally were established because the services offered by commercial banks were designed for businesses rather than individuals, whose needs differed greatly. The two basic types of thrifts are savings and loan associations (S&Ls) and mutual savings banks.

Historically, S&Ls have been viewed as the place to go to get real estate mortgages. In fact, when S&Ls originally were established, depositors pooled their savings to create loans that were used to help other depositors build houses in a particular geographic area, and each savings association was liquidated once the building goals were achieved and all the loans were repaid. Today, S&Ls take the funds of many small savers and then lend this money to home buyers and other types of borrowers. Without institutions such as S&Ls, savers would not be able to invest in mortgages unless they were willing to lend directly to borrowers, such as home buyers, which would require funds to be "tied up" for long time periods. Savings accounts provide savers with greater flexibility, because funds do not have to be committed for long periods, and, in many cases, savings can be easily

TABLE 3-2

Federally Insured Credit Unions: Assets and Liabilities, June 30, 1998
(billions of dollars)

	Amount	**Percent of Total Assets**
Assets		
Cash	$ 7.9	2.1%
Investments		
Treasury and government		
agencies	52.9	14.3
Mutual funds	3.1	0.8
Deposits at institutions	56.2	15.1
Other investments	4.6	1.2
Total investment	$116.8	31.4%
Loans		
Individual	$ 56.5	15.2
Automobile	94.4	25.4
Real estate	86.0	23.2
Other	0.9	0.2
Total loans	$237.8	64.0%
Other assets	9.1	2.5
Total assets	$371.6	100.0%
Liabilities and Equity		
Deposits		
Share draft (checkable)	$ 38.4	10.3%
Regular share accounts	129.8	34.9
Other savings	155.9	42.0
Nonmember deposits	0.8	0.2
Total deposits	$324.9	87.4%
Borrowings	6.1	1.7
Equity/reserves	40.6	10.9
Total liabilities and equity	$371.6	100.0%

SOURCE: National Credit Union Association;
htttp://www.ncua.gov/ref/data

liquidated (withdrawn) with little or no restriction. Thus, perhaps the most significant economic function of the S&Ls is to "create liquidity" that otherwise would be lacking.

Mutual savings banks, which operate mainly in the northeastern states, are similar to S&Ls, except they are owned and managed by their depositors. Thus, mutual savings banks operate like credit unions.

About 70 percent of thrifts are savings associations, which have more than 90 percent of thrift deposits. Table 3-3 shows the mix of assets and liabilities of the 1,728 thrift institutions insured by the Federal Deposit Insurance Corporation (FDIC). More than two-thirds of the assets are in the form of loans, and 90 percent of the loans are mortgages. Thus, thrifts still are viewed primarily as mortgage lending institutions. About two-thirds of the liabilities consist of deposits, and nearly 95 percent of the deposits are termed "nontransaction" deposits, which represent some form of savings account or other savings instrument.

| TABLE 3-3 | | |

Savings Institutions Insured by the FDIC: Assets and Liabilities, June 30, 1998
(billions of dollars)

	Amount	**Percent of Total Assets**
Assets		
Cash	$ 26.8	2.6%
Investments		
Treasury and government agencies	211.3	20.2
Other investments	40.7	3.9
Total investment	$ 252.0	24.1%
Loans		
1-4 family mortgages	$ 508.0	48.6
Multifamily mortgages	56.7	5.4
Other mortgages	46.7	4.5
Construction and land loans	20.8	2.0
Commercial loans	17.8	1.7
Consumer loans	48.9	4.7
Other loans	3.1	0.3
Total loans	$ 702.0	67.2%
Other assets	64.0	6.1
Total assets	$1,044.8	100.0%
Liabilities and Equity		
Deposits		
Demand deposits	$ 41.2	3.9%
Nontransaction deposits	661.4	63.3
Total deposits	$ 702.6	67.2%
Borrowings	15.2	1.5
Other liabilities	233.6	22.4
Equity	93.4	8.9
Total liabilities and equity	$1,044.8	100.0%

SOURCE: Federal Deposit Insurance Corporation;
http://www.fdic.gov/databank

Mutual Funds

Mutual funds are *investment companies* that accept money from savers and then use these funds to buy various types of financial assets, including stocks, long-term bonds, short-term debt instruments, and so forth. These organizations pool funds and thus reduce risks through diversification. They also achieve economies of scale, which lower the costs of analyzing securities, managing portfolios, and buying and selling securities.

There are literally hundreds of different types of mutual funds with a variety of goals and purposes that meet the objectives of different types of savers. For instance, investors who prefer current income can invest in mutual funds referred to as *income funds*. Such funds invest primarily in instruments that generate fairly constant annual incomes, including bonds with constant annual interest payments and stocks with constant dividend payments. In contrast, investors who are willing to accept higher risks in hopes of higher returns can invest in mutual funds referred to as *growth funds*. Such funds are comprised of investments that generate little or no income each year but exhibit high growth potential, which could result in significant increases in the values of the investments (i.e., capital gains) in the future.

MONEY MARKET MUTUAL FUND
A mutual fund that invests in short-term, low-risk securities and allows investors to write checks against their accounts.

One of the newest savings mediums available in the financial markets is the *money market fund.* A **money market mutual fund** includes short-term, low-risk securities and generally allows investors to write checks against their accounts. From their beginning in the mid-1970s, money market funds have experienced unparalleled growth. In 1975, the total value of money market funds was under $10 million, while in 1997 the total value was greater than $1 trillion. Other mutual funds have shown similar, albeit somewhat slower, growth patterns. With more than $4.4 trillion in assets in 1997, mutual fund investment companies represented the second largest financial institution in the United States — second only to commercial banks. Today there are more than 7,000 individual mutual funds offered by various investment companies, and according to the Investment Company Institute (ICI), which monitors the performances of mutual funds, more than 60 million Americans own shares in mutual funds. The primary reason individuals invest in mutual funds is for retirement.

The combination of assets and liabilities of investment companies is evident — assets principally include stocks, bonds, and other financial instruments the companies purchase, while the major liability is represented by investors' (savers') shares, which provide the funds used to purchase the financial assets. The actual composition of the portfolio of investments held by mutual funds changes as economic and financial market conditions change. Table 3-4 shows the breakdown of the value of mutual funds in 1998 into stock funds, bond funds, and money market funds. As you can see, stock funds represent more than 50 percent of the value, while bonds and money market funds make up between 23 percent and 26 percent. In contrast, in 1970, before money market funds existed, nearly 95 percent of mutual funds were stock funds, and the remaining 5 percent were bond funds. In 1980, when the economy was in the middle of a recession, the mixture was about 33 percent stock funds, 10 percent bond funds, and 57 percent money market funds. And, in 1990, the mixture was 23 percent stock funds, about 30 percent bond funds, and nearly 47 percent money market funds. In general, when the economy is doing well and stock markets are moving upward, mutual funds tend to invest greater amounts in stocks; when the economy is stagnant and movements in stock markets are very uncertain or exhibit a downward

---

TABLE 3-4

Mutual Funds Net Assets, September 1998 (billions of dollars)

Type of Fund	Amount	Percent of Total
Stock	$2,482.8	50.7%
Bond/Income	1,143.0	23.4
Money market — taxable	1,086.1	22.2
Money market — tax-free	180.8	3.7
Total assets	$4,892.7	100.0%

SOURCE: Investment Company Institute,
http://www.ici.org

trend, funds then tend to invest greater amounts in short-term, liquid assets (money market instruments).

Whole Life Insurance Companies[1]

WHOLE LIFE INSURANCE COMPANIES Receive premiums from individuals — a portion of the funds is invested and a portion is used to cover the insured.

Whole life insurance companies differ from other financial institutions because they provide two services to individuals: insurance and savings. In recent years, many life insurance companies have also offered a variety of tax-deferred savings plans designed to provide benefits to the participants when they retire.

Broadly speaking, the purpose of life insurance is to provide a beneficiary, such as a spouse or family member(s), with protection against financial distress or insecurity that might result from the premature death of a "breadwinner," or other wage earner. And, in a general sense, life insurance can be labeled either term insurance or whole life insurance. *Term life insurance* is a relatively short-term contract that provides protection for a temporary period, perhaps for one year or for five years at a time, and it must be renewed each period to continue such protection. On the other hand, *whole life insurance* is a long-term contract that provides lifetime protection. The cost of term insurance, called the *premium,* generally increases with each renewal, because the risk of premature death increases as the insured ages. In contrast, the premiums associated with *whole* life insurance policies are fixed payments computed as an average of the premiums required over the expected life of the person insured. This means the premiums in the early years exceed what is needed to cover the insured, and the premiums in the later years are less than what is needed. The excess amounts in the early years are invested to make up for the deficits in later years. The invested amounts provide savings features that create cash values for the whole life insurance policies. Term life insurance policies do not provide savings features, because the premiums are fixed only for a short time period, which generally is five years or less; thus, the premiums are based on the existing risks only and are changed at renewal if risks change. Thus, life insurance companies offer both insurance coverage and a savings feature with their whole life policies, but not with their term life policies.[2]

Life insurance companies use statistical tables, called actuarial tables, to estimate the amounts of cash that will be needed each year to satisfy insurance claims. The actuarial tables, which are based on various risk factors, such as age and lifestyle, as well as previous experiences with claims in the life insurance industry, provide companies with fairly accurate forecasts of the amounts and the timings of future claims. Thus, companies that offer whole life insurance can project their cash needs with good precision. And, because such policies are

---

[1]The concept of insurance is to reduce the consequences of risk by transferring some of the economic consequences to others, namely, insurance companies, who are better able to absorb such risks. Insurance companies achieve risk reduction by pooling, or diversifying, the risks of individuals, companies, and governments.

[2]Premiums charged by other insurance companies, such as health insurance, property and casualty insurance, and the like, are based only on the risks faced and are changed over time as the risks change. In other words, the premiums are based on the cost of the peril (risk) that is insured at the time the premium is paid. There is no savings function, because individuals pay only for the insurance services offered by such companies. These insurance companies do not perform the same intermediary function as life insurance companies.

TABLE 3-5		
Life Insurance Companies: Assets Composition, December 31, 1996 (billions of dollars)		
	Amount	**Percent of Total Assets**
Assets		
Cash	$ 4.6	0.2%
Investments		
Government securities	396.7	17.1
Corporate bonds	951.7	41.0
Corporate stock	477.5	20.6
Mortgages	207.8	8.9
Real estate	49.5	2.1
Total investments	$2,083.2	89.7%
Policy loans	100.5	4.3
Other assets	135.3	5.8
Total assets	$2,323.6	100.0%
Liabilities and Equity		
Reserves	$1,965.0	84.6%
Other liabilities	192.8	8.3
Surplus and net worth	165.8	7.1
Total liabilities and equity	$2,323.6	100.0%

SOURCE: *Life Insurance Fact Book,* 1997.

long-term contracts, the companies invest significant portions of their funds in such long-term assets as corporate bonds, stocks, and government bonds. Table 3-5 gives an indication of the structure of assets and liabilities for all life insurance companies. As you can see, these companies invest primarily in long-term instruments, and the principal source of funds is represented by the reserves associated with the whole life insurance policies and pension plans sold by the companies. The liability labeled "Reserves" represents obligations of the companies associated with future commitments derived from currently outstanding policies.

Because life insurance companies are able to invest in corporate bonds and stocks, they provide an important source of long-term funds for companies. Table 3-5 shows that investment in corporate bonds and stocks accounts for nearly 60 percent of total assets, and about 65 percent of total investments. To some degree, then, life insurance companies compete with commercial banks to provide funds to corporations. However, for the most part, life insurance companies operate in different financial markets than banks. While banks primarily help corporations meet their needs for short-term funds, the accuracy of the actuarial tables used in the life insurance industry allows insurance companies to support long-term funding needs.

Pension Funds

PENSIONS
Employee retirement plans funded by corporations or government agencies.

Pensions are retirement plans funded by corporations or government agencies for their workers and administered primarily by the trust departments of commercial banks or by life insurance companies. Probably the most famous pension plan is Social Security, which is a government-sponsored plan funded by tax revenues. Most state and municipal governments and large corporations offer pen-

TABLE 3-6

Major Pension and Retirement Programs: Assets and Reserves, December 31, 1996 (billions of dollars)

Type of Program	Amount	Percent of Total Assets
Private Plans		
With life insurance companies	$ 916.0	15.5%
Other private plans	2,794.2	47.3
Total	$3,710.2	62.8%
Public (Government) Plans		
Railroad retirement	$ 14.9	0.3%
Federal civilian employees	416.7	7.1
State and local employees	1,195.6	20.2
Total	$1,627.2	27.6%
Social Security	567.0	9.6
Sum total	$5,904.4	100.0%

SOURCE: *Life Insurance Fact Book,* 1997.

sion plans to their employees. Many of these plans have been established to accept both employer and employee contributions, which often are shielded from taxes until the assets are withdrawn from the plan.

The earliest pensions in the United States were created by railroad companies more than a century ago. As the country became more industrialized, pension plans expanded greatly. As pensions grew, so did some of the problems associated with managing such plans. Many pensions did not survive the financial turmoil that occurred in the 1920s and 1930s because they were "pay-as-you-go" plans with benefits paid out of the contributions made by the existing employees. "Pay-as-you-go" plans are termed *unfunded pensions.* Social Security, which was established in 1935 to supplement the retirement income provided by private pensions, is the largest unfunded pension.

Since World War II, private pensions have grown significantly compared with government pensions, and today they account for more than 60 percent of the total assets held in retirement plans. And, as Table 3-6 shows, the assets in Social Security represent less than 10 percent of the total value of pensions in the United States today.

Like life insurance companies, pension funds are long-term contracts for fairly predictable payments. Therefore, pension plan assets are similar to those of life insurance companies presented in Table 3-5; funds are invested primarily in long-term assets such as bonds, stocks, mortgages, and real estate.

Self-Test Questions

List the major types of financial intermediaries, and briefly describe each one's function.

What is the primary asset of savings institutions? Why?

Why do you think the assets in Social Security represent less than 10 percent of the value of the assets in all pension plans?

Safety (Risk) of Financial Institutions

As we have seen in the previous sections, the services provided by financial intermediaries help the economy function more efficiently and increase the general standard of living of the population. Each financial institution was originally established to meet certain needs, or inefficiencies, that existed in the financial markets. Because intermediaries play such a critical role in the welfare of the economy, the financial services industry has been heavily regulated in an effort to ensure stability and safety in the nation's financial markets. Proponents of regulation argue that the parties involved in the financial intermediation process — savers, borrowers, and intermediaries — do not possess equal levels of expertise or have access to the same information, so legislation is needed to provide a more "even playing field" and to help maintain public confidence in the financial system. Most of the financial panics we have experienced in the past can be traced to actions of intermediaries, such as engaging in unscrupulous behavior or taking on too much risk, which contributed to a public loss of faith in the country's financial system.

The primary reason financial institutions are regulated is because it is generally accepted that the public needs protection from financial environments that can cause economic disasters precipitated by a "domino effect" triggered by the failures of financial intermediaries. When the public loses faith in the financial system, individuals tend to pull funds out of intermediaries, thus sources of credit shrink considerably and the economy suffers. Therefore, much of the regulation that currently exists restricts the activities of financial institutions, presumably to maintain public confidence by helping to assure some degree of safety in the financial system. In addition, the regulations require intermediaries to periodically report certain information. Regulatory attitudes have shaped the structure of the banking system that exists in the United States. In the next section, we describe the U.S. banking system and outline how previous regulatory actions affected the infrastructure of the financial system. Therefore, in this section we describe a major aspect of regulation that affects the overall risk associated with various intermediaries: the safety of funds provided by savers.

Individuals and businesses are willing to provide funds to borrowers through intermediaries because they have confidence their savings are safe. If the public lost faith in the safety of intermediaries, very few, if any, funds would be available through such institutions. Thus, to help maintain confidence, the funds provided to most financial institutions are insured by agencies established through federal or state legislation. The primary purpose of such insurance is to assure savers their funds will be safe even if the financial intermediary fails. In this section, we provide some indication of the principal insuring agencies of the financial intermediaries described in the previous section.

Banks, Thrifts, and Credit Unions

Probably the most familiar insuring agency is the Federal Deposit Insurance Corporation (FDIC), which insures the deposits at most banks and thrift institutions. Even though the FDIC has changed considerably since it was established in 1933, the primary objective of the federal insurance fund has not changed — to maintain safety and depositor confidence by shifting the risk of losing deposited funds from the saver/depositor to the FDIC. There also is federal deposit insurance available for credit unions through the National Credit Union Share Insurance Funds (NCUSIF). Both the FDIC and the NCUSIF insure deposits for amounts up to $100,000. Banks, thrifts, and credit unions that are chartered by the federal government must use a federal insurance fund. Institutions chartered by state governments can use federal insurance if they are qualified; otherwise, they must use the insurance fund provided by the state that charters them.

The Federal Reserve (Fed), which is discussed in the next section, traditionally has been considered the regulatory agency of commercial banking. But, the Fed actually has the power to impose such regulations as reserve requirements on other financial institutions that accept deposits from savers or make conventional loans to borrowers. While Fed regulations affect thrifts and credit unions, federally chartered thrifts are also regulated/supervised by the Office of Thrift Supervision (OTS), and federally chartered credit unions are regulated/supervised by the National Credit Union Administration (NCUA).

Insurance Companies

Insurance companies are primarily regulated by the states in which they operate. For the most part, the purpose of regulations in the insurance industry is to help assure the financial stability of insurance companies. Insurance companies require prepayment for policies that extend into future periods, so financial stability is important to ensure policyholders receive all the future coverage purchased. The National Association of Insurance Commissioners (NAIC) is a group of state insurance commissioners that meets on a regular basis to discuss concerns in the insurance industry and to try to coordinate legislative efforts in each state to attain more uniform regulations nationwide.

Pensions

The major legislation affecting pension plans is the Employee Retirement Income Security Act (ERISA), which became law in 1974. Although the law does not require firms to have pension plans, it does specify the conditions necessary for a retirement program to receive favorable tax benefits, such as tax-deferred contributions. ERISA and its subsequent improvements have been instrumental in reforming the management of pension plans, thus ensuring greater safety of workers' retirement funds. ERISA includes provisions that mandate certain information be disclosed by pension funds and provide insurance of benefits in case an employer defaults or terminates a plan. The federal insurance organization established by ERISA is the Pension Benefit Guarantee Corporation (PBGC), which insures benefits up to about $2,000 per month, with the maximum amount adjusted for inflation in future periods. Each year, every pension plan must file a statement with the U.S. Department of Labor reporting information about the operation and financial position of the fund.

Mutual Funds

The regulation of mutual funds is the responsibility of the Securities and Exchange Commission (SEC), except in a few instances where state regulations apply. Specifically, regulations that apply to mutual funds are included in the

Investment Company Act of 1940 and its subsequent changes. The regulations provide that certain information is disclosed to investors, that the funds be diversified, and that managers and employees of funds avoid conflicts of interest associated with the investments held by the funds. In addition, the practices used to sell funds and to compensate for such sales (i.e., commissions) should not be considered unethical or appear to take advantage of investors. Because mutual funds represent investment pools that include such risky assets as stocks, bonds, and options, there is no federal insurance agency to assure the safety of savers' funds. Instead, each fund is required to inform investors/savers concerning the investment goal (e.g., income or growth) and an indication of the risk associated with pursuing that goal. It is the responsibility of the individual to determine the amount of risk he or she is willing to accept. There are many different types of mutual funds with many different levels of risk, so investors can choose from funds with amounts of risk that range from very low to very high.

Self-Test Questions

Why is it necessary to regulate financial institutions?

Why have federal insurance agencies been established for financial intermediaries?

Why is there no specific insurance available for mutual funds?

Banking Systems

In this section, we describe the structure of our banking system and illustrate the role it plays in our business environment and our personal lives. It is important to have a basic knowledge of how the banking system works to understand how the nation's monetary policy is managed and the role of financial intermediaries in this process.

Evolution of Banking Systems

There is evidence that such banking activities as lending took place in civilizations as early as ancient Babylon. But, the beginning of banking as we know it today probably did not start until the Middle Ages. During these times, widespread unrest and wars resulted in a great deal of anarchy. Wealthy individuals felt compelled to protect their fortunes by storing their valuables with merchants — usually metalsmiths, such as goldsmiths and silversmiths — who maintained facilities that were considered safe havens for property. When the valuables were *deposited,* the merchants would *issue* a receipt that verified the deposit and ownership of the property. And, when individuals wanted to purchase goods and services, they would redeem their *depository receipts* for the needed gold or silver. But, in time, individuals found the depository receipts of the better known and more trusted metalsmiths could be used for trade; metal deposits did not actually have to be withdrawn, which was easier and safer than physically redeeming the depository receipts. It was not long before metalsmiths discovered that they always had positive inventories of gold and silver because only a portion of the receipts was redeemed at any point in time. Further, the "safekeepers" realized a profit could be made by lending some of their idle inventories to other merchants and individuals who found themselves temporarily short of funds needed for trade. As this process became more prevalent, the metalsmiths began to issue standardized depository receipts that could be more easily used for purchasing goods and services. Often, the depository receipts were also deposited with the issuing metalsmiths, which provided them with additional sources of loans. Thus, metalsmiths found themselves with more depository receipts outstanding than the amount of gold and silver that was held for safekeeping. But, as they discovered, it was not necessary to hold gold and silver equal to the amount of total deposits as long as all depositors did not demand payment all at once. Consequently, the *safekeepers* needed to maintain metal *reserves* equal to only a fraction of the total deposits. The use of depository receipts as exchange mediums became more widespread as knowledge and confidence improved. And banks, which dealt primarily with deposits and loans, emerged as such transactions became more sophisticated and specialization became more profitable.[3]

The rather simplistic banking operations created by the metalsmiths of the Middle Ages have evolved into the more sophisticated banking systems we observe in the world today. An important concept discovered by the metalsmiths was that "money" could be created by lending some of the deposits of others, but only if there were assurances that less than 100 percent of deposits was required to meet depositors' withdrawals at any point in time. Thus, the metalsmiths originated the *fractional reserve system,* which forms the basis of our current banking system. In the next section, we describe how a fractional reserve banking system allows banks to "create" money.

Fractional Reserve System

FRACTIONAL RESERVE SYSTEM
When the amount of reserves maintained by a financial institution to satisfy requests for withdrawals is less than 100 percent of total deposits.

In a **fractional reserve system**, the amount of reserves maintained to satisfy requests for withdrawal of deposits is less than 100 percent of the total deposits. As the metalsmiths discovered, a fractional reserve system actually increases, or creates, money in the economy. To see how money is created, consider a banking system that has one bank, which initially has total deposits equal to $100. If the bank is required to maintain reserves equal to 100 percent of deposits, then the bank would have to keep all $100 in reserves to "back up" deposits; it could not lend any of the funds deposited, so the $100 deposits would represent exactly $100 in money. Now suppose the bank is required to maintain reserves equal to only a fraction of the total deposits, say, 10 percent. Thus, of the original $100 deposits, $90 would represent **excess reserves** because the bank is required to maintain reserves equal to only $10 to "back up" the $100 deposit. The bank can lend the excess reserves to an individual or a company. Consider what would happen if an individual borrows the entire $90 initial excess reserves and redeposits the funds in the bank. Now the bank would have new deposits equal to $90, and because only 10 percent of each deposit has to be maintained in reserves, the

EXCESS RESERVES
Reserves at a bank, or other institution affected by reserve requirements, in excess of the amount required; equal to the total reserves minus required reserves.

[3]History seems to indicate that the term "bank" originated from the word "bancos," which is Italian for "benches." Often merchants conducted their transactions from benches at a central meeting location. Merchants who did not honor their deals had their benches broken so they could not enter new transactions; the term "bankrupt" evolved from this practice.

new deposit would create excess reserves equal to $81 = $90 × (1 − 0.10) that could be loaned to other borrowers. You can imagine what happens as this process continues until excess reserves are totally eliminated — the $90 excess reserves from the original $100 deposit magnifies to produce much greater deposits, or funds in the form of money. The amount of additional money produced by the original deposit is dependent on the *fraction* that must be held in reserves — if the reserve requirement is 100 percent, then there is no magnification; if there is no reserve requirement, the magnification is unlimited. In general, the maximum change in the money supply created by a fractional reserve system is computed as:

3-1	
	$$\frac{\text{Maximum change in}}{\text{the money supply}} = \frac{\text{Excess reserves}}{\text{Reserve requirement}}$$

Thus, if all the excess reserves are loaned to individuals and subsequently redeposited in the bank, the initial $100 deposit would create $900 = ($100 − $10)/(0.10) new money through additional deposits. At the same time, the amount of loans, or credit, created in the banking system also would be $900 because the additional money was created through the loans produced by the bank. Table 3-7 indicates the changes in deposits and loans associated with our fractional reserve banking system illustration. Note that when the bank has loaned the maximum amount based on the 10 percent reserve requirement, there are no excess reserves, the total deposits in the banking system equal $1,000, and the total required reserves are $100, the amount of the initial deposit.

This simple example shows how a fractional reserve system can be used to expand money through deposits in a system with a single bank. The same change would occur in a banking system consisting of many banks or intermediaries, as long as the excess reserves are used to create loans that are redeposited in the intermediaries. If deposits are withdrawn from the bank, the process reverses, so money would contract according to Equation 3-1.

TABLE 3-7

Fractional Reserve System

	New Deposits	Total Deposits	Total Reserve Requirement	Total Loans
Initial depositor	$100.00	$ 100.00	$ 10.00	$ 0.00
Second depositor	90.00	190.00	19.00	90.00
Third depositor	81.00	271.00	27.10	171.00
Fourth depositor	72.90	343.90	34.39	243.90
	.	.	.	.
	.	.	.	.
	.	.	.	.
Final depositor	0.01	1,000.00	100.00	900.00

The U.S. Banking System (Structure)

The U.S. banking system is a fractional reserve system consisting of various depository institutions, such as banks and thrifts, chartered either by the federal government or by the state in which they are located. Institutions whose names contain the words "national" or "federal" have federal charters; likewise, institutions whose names contain the word "state" have state charters. Because the U.S. banking system includes both national and state charters, it is referred to as a **dual banking system.**[4] The roots of the current banking structure can be traced to financial developments that occurred early in the history of the nation.

DUAL BANKING SYSTEM
A banking system in which bank chartering exists both at the national and the state level.

In the early years of its existence, the U.S. economy was agriculturally oriented, with the populace located in somewhat fragmented farming communities. Thus, banking structures and financial markets were also quite segmented, or territorial, in nature. During this period, large communities created self-sufficient banking systems, which often issued their own bank notes that were used as currency, or money, for transactions with local businesses and residents. Only the currencies of the most reliable banks were accepted in other banking communities. Over time, the federal government made a couple of attempts to form a unified banking system by creating central, or national, banks. But, until the Federal Reserve was established in 1913, such attempts were not very successful.

Although banking changed dramatically as the country became more industrialized, the influence of early banking systems is very evident in contemporary banking. Today there exist more than 9,000 individual, or unit, banking organizations, which is fewer than the 12,500 banks that existed at the beginning of the twentieth century and the 31,000 banks that existed in 1920. Many more banks were needed when transportation and communications were not sufficient to support an integrated and efficient banking system.

Fewer banks might exist today if federal and state regulations enacted from 1900 to 1930 had not restricted the ability of banks to open multiple offices, or branches, especially across state lines. At the time, such legislation was favored by the banking industry, because it was believed more banks promoted competition, thus efficiency, in the banking system. But, in reality, many bankers feared that unrestricted branching would result in a concentration of financial power in the hands of a few very large banks, and such a banking structure would favor industry and commerce at the expense of agriculture and individuals, resulting in the ruin of the nation's financial system.

INTRASTATE BRANCHING
Establishing branch banks within the same state.

INTERSTATE BRANCHING
Establishing branch banks in more than one state; i.e., across state lines.

Even though legislation passed since 1930 has relaxed some of the branching restrictions, the banking system in the United States is still dominated by a large number of individual banks that generally are allowed to branch within the states they are located (**intrastate branching**) but are limited when it comes to branching across state lines (**interstate branching**). However, during the past couple of decades, interest in unrestricted branch banking has increased greatly. In fact, Congress recently passed, and will continue to examine, legislation that promotes elimination of the barriers that currently restrict interstate banking.[5]

---

[4]Banking regulations are enacted both at the federal level and at the state level. When a conflict arises between federal and state laws, generally the one that is more restrictive applies.

[5]The Reigle-Neal Interstate Banking and Branching Efficiency Act of 1994 allowed large bank holding companies to purchase banks in any state beginning in 1995. This legislation also allowed large banks to merge with banks in other states, subject to the state banking laws, starting in June 1997.

BANK HOLDING COMPANY
A corporation that owns controlling interest in one bank or more.

Even with the barriers to interstate banking, some banking organizations attained quasi-branch banking via bank holding companies, which were developed in the 1950s. A **bank holding company** is a corporation that owns controlling interest in one bank or more. Bank holding companies often were allowed to own multiple banks in the same state, and, in some cases, unusual circumstances led to ownership of banks in other states. Thus, where a particular bank could not branch across state lines, a bank holding company could effectively achieve branching by operating separate banks in different states.

Another restriction faced by banks is the type of business activity they are permitted to undertake. Since the Banking Act of 1933, also known as the Glass-Steagall Act, banks have been prohibited from engaging in activities that are not related to banking services. For instance, banks could neither have significant ownership in corporations nor help corporations issue stocks and bonds. This law effectively prohibited banks from combining commerce and banking activities. But, recent legislation has removed some of these restrictions. Banks can now establish nonbank subsidiaries that engage in bank-related activities. In addition, well-run bank holding companies face fewer barriers to integrating banking operations with nonbank activities.

Size of Banks

Table 3-8 shows the ten largest commercial banking organizations in the United States at the end of 1998. There has been a great deal of recent interest in mergers and acquisitions of large banks. For example, in 1997, Nations-Bank, which was the 5th largest banking company at the time, acquired Barnett Banks, the 25th largest banking company, and then in 1998 it merged with BankAmerica to form the nation's largest banking company. Banking experts expect such mergers and acquisitions to continue, so the rankings of the banks in Table 3-8 most likely will change during the next few years.

TABLE 3-8

Ten Largest Banking Companies in the United States, 1998

Rank	Name	State	Total Assets (billions of dollars)
1	BankAmerica Corp.	California	$549.0
2	Citigroup Inc.	New York	357.3
3	Chase Manhattan Corp.	New York	348.5
4	Bank One Corp.	Ohio	253.4
5	First Union	North Carolina	224.5
6	J.P. Morgan & Company	New York	198.2
7	Bankers Trust Corp.	New York	123.1
8	Fleet Financial Group Inc.	Rhode Island	110.3
9	Washington Mutual	California	105.9
10	Wells Fargo & Company	California	96.6

NOTE: A great deal of merger activity is currently taking place in the banking industry. This list includes mergers that occurred through June 1998.

SOURCE: Federal Deposit Insurance Corporation.

Central Banking—The Federal Reserve System

FEDERAL RESERVE SYSTEM
The central banking system charged with managing the monetary policy of the country.

The **Federal Reserve System**, which was established in 1913, is the central banking system charged with managing the monetary policy of the United States. The Fed was established by the Federal Reserve Act to reform the U.S. banking system following the Wall Street Panic of 1907, which resulted in financial ruin for much of the country. Even before this financial crisis, the banking system was plagued by periods of financial panic and was prone to significant bank failures during economic downturns. Thus, when it was originally created, the primary purpose of the Fed was to supervise banking activities such that bank operations were more stable and economic conditions would not cause widespread ruin in the banking industry. While it still views banking stability as an important goal, the responsibilities of the Fed have expanded as time has passed.

STRUCTURE OF THE FED   To ensure control of the banking system was not consolidated in the hands of a few, the central bank of the U.S. was created with a *decentralized* network of regional, or district, banks. The Fed is comprised of 12 independent district banks located in major cities throughout the country. The district banks, which have branches in larger cities within their Federal Reserve districts, provide such services as loans and deposits to banks and other financial institutions, but not to individuals. Thus, the Fed often is referred to as a *banker's bank*. The Fed is also used by the government for its banking needs. The U.S. Treasury has a checking account at the Fed, which is used to collect the taxes we pay and to pay government employees and other expenses.

BOARD OF GOVERNORS
The central governing body of the Federal Reserve System.

The Fed banks are supervised by a central governing body called the **Board of Governors**. The members of the Board of Governors are appointed by the President and approved by the Senate. The Board consists of seven members, each appointed to a 14-year term. Even though the terms are staggered to expire every two years, often members of the Board do not serve full terms, allowing the President to appoint a majority of the Board.

In addition to the district banks and the Board of Governors, the other important components of the Federal Reserve include the commercial banks and other financial institutions that are members of the Fed, advisory committees, which provide various kinds of recommendations to the Board of Governors and the district banks, and the Federal Open Market Committee, which oversees the principal instrument used by the Fed to manage monetary policy.

RESPONSIBILITIES OF THE FED   The responsibilities of the Federal Reserve System include the following:

MONETARY POLICY
The policy by which the Fed influences economic conditions, especially interest rates, by managing the nation's money supply.

1. According to the Federal Reserve Act, the Fed should direct the **monetary policy** of the United States "to promote effectively the goals of maximum employment, stable prices, and moderate long-term interest rates." The primary means by which the Fed attempts to achieve these goals is by changing the nation's money supply through the reserves held at banks and other financial institutions. For instance, if the desire is to increase the nation's money supply, the Fed will take actions to provide excess reserves to the banking system, which will be channeled into the economy through loans made to individuals and businesses. And, because our banking system is characterized by a fractional reserve system, a $1 addition to reserves will create more than $1 in new loans, or money, in the economy, and vice versa. The Fed affects reserves in the banking system through its lending policy, with changes in reserve requirements, and by buying and selling U.S. government securities.

The most important tool used by the Fed to manage the supply of money is **open market operations**, which involves buying or selling U.S. Treasury securities to change bank reserves. Figure 3-2 diagrams the process involved. When the Fed wants to increase the money supply, government securities are purchased from **primary dealers** who have established trading relationships with the Federal Reserve. The Fed pays for the securities by sending funds to the banks where the primary dealers have accounts so that the deposit balances of the dealers can be increased, which results in an increase in the overall reserves of the banking system. Banks have additional funds to lend, so the money supply increases. The Fed carries out "normal" open market operations on a continuous basis to maintain economic activity within defined limits, and it shifts its open market strategies toward heavier than normal buying or selling when a more substantial adjustment is needed.

The potential by which the money supply can change when the reserves are changed depends on the existing reserve requirement. Currently, a reserve requirement exists only for checking (transactions) deposits — the requirement is 10 percent.[6] Thus, for every $1 of government securities purchased through open market operations, the money supply can potentially increase by about $9 = $1(1 − 0.10)/0.10 (see Equation 3-1). If the Fed wanted to

OPEN MARKET OPERATIONS
The Federal Reserve buys or sells Treasury securities to expand or contract the nation's money supply.

PRIMARY DEALER
Used by the Fed to modify the money supply, such a dealer has established a relationship with the Federal Reserve to buy and sell government securities.

FIGURE 3-2

Diagram of Federal Reserve Open Market Operations

I. Increase the money supply—Fed buys government securities

Make payment—increase bank reserves

| Federal Reserve | → | Bank of Primary Dealer |

Receive securities from bank/dealer

II. Decrease the money supply—Fed sells government securities

Receive payment—decrease bank reserves

| Federal Reserve | ← | Bank of Primary Dealer |

Deliver securities to bank/dealer

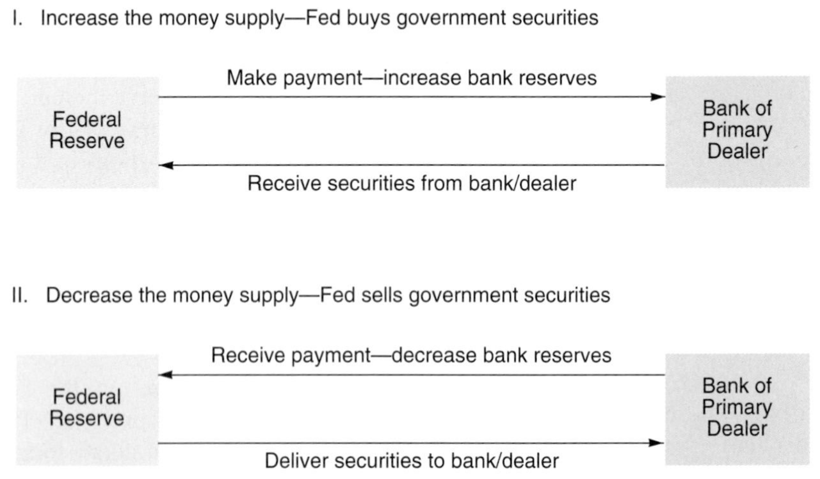

[6]Actually, the first $4.0 million of deposits are not subject to reserve requirements, transaction deposits up to $51.9 million are subject to a 3 percent reserve requirement, and all transaction deposits above $51.9 million are subject to a 10 percent reserve requirement. Because most banks have deposits substantially greater than $51.9 million, the average reserve requirement is close to 10 percent.

decrease the money supply, the process would be reversed — government securities would be sold to primary dealers, thus their bank accounts would be decreased.

The Fed can also affect the supply of money by changing the reserve requirement. Consider what would happen if the Fed increased the reserve requirement from 10 percent to 20 percent. After the change, 80 percent rather than 90 percent of deposits could be loaned to individuals and businesses. How would this change affect the money supply? To find the answer, let's return to the example we used earlier to describe a fractional reserve system, where the reserve requirement was 10 percent. Because only fractional reserves needed to be held by the bank, we discovered that the initial deposit of $100 could be multiplied via the lending process to expand the money supply by an additional $900, such that the total funds in our simple one-bank system were $1,000. If the reserve required is 20 percent rather than 10 percent, the total funds would decrease to $500. The $100 now would be able to expand the money supply by $400 = ($100 − $20)/0.2. As this example illustrates, when the Fed changes the reserve requirement, there is an immediate impact on the ability of banks to lend funds because excess reserves are affected. Unlike open market operations, this method is not used to manage the supply of money on a day-to-day basis; reserve requirements are changed infrequently.

DISCOUNT RATE
The rate the Fed charges for loans it makes to banks to meet temporary shortages in required reserves.

Another tool the Fed uses to direct monetary policy is the **discount rate**, which is the interest rate banks and other financial institutions have to pay when they borrow from one of the Fed district banks to meet temporary shortages in required reserves. Changes in the discount rate affect the amounts banks are willing to borrow and thus ultimately affect the money supply. For example, if the Fed lowers the discount rate, banks would tend to depend more on loans from the Fed to meet temporary reserve shortfalls, so more loans could be made to individuals and businesses than if the discount rate was higher. In reality, the discount rate is related to the market rates on other types of debt, such as Treasury securities and interest rates on short-term loans at commercial banks. Thus, a discount rate change generally is the result, rather than the cause, of movements in other rates, and this instrument is neither as effective nor as prominent as open market operations for managing monetary policy.

2. The Federal Reserve also is charged with *regulating and supervising* depository financial institutions operating in the United States. The Fed monitors such institutions through audits and "bank examinations" to ensure that the U.S. banking system remains sound. In addition, the Fed authorizes bank mergers and any nonbanking activities bank holding companies undertake.

3. One very important service offered by the Fed is the *check clearing operations* provided by its payment system, which clears millions of paper checks and electronic payments each day. The Fed's payment system helps ensure that the funds represented by checks or other payment mechanisms are transferred as efficiently as possible among various financial institutions.

The importance of the Fed and its influence on the financial markets cannot be overstated. Decisions made by the Fed generally cause significant movements in the financial markets. For example, when the decision is to increase interest rates, the markets decline, often substantially.

U.S. Banking in the Future

The banking system of the United States has changed significantly during the last couple of decades, and additional changes are certain to continue in the future. The banking industry has always been very heavily regulated, primarily to ensure the safety of the financial institutions and thus protect depositors. However, many of these regulations have tended to impede the free flow of funds around the country and thus have been detrimental to the efficiency of our financial markets. Recent legislative changes have removed some of the competitive obstacles created by previous regulations, and more changes are forthcoming.

During the past several decades, deregulation of depository intermediaries has erased many of the differences among such institutions. For the most part, deregulation that has been enacted since 1980 has encouraged increased competition among various types of financial intermediaries by eliminating some restrictions limiting both the products offered by such intermediaries as commercial banks and savings institutions and the locations where intermediaries can do business. The principal results of the move toward deregulation in the financial services industry are that intermediaries have become much more similar in their operations and the numbers of intermediaries have decreased because mergers and acquisitions have been facilitated. The impact of deregulation is illustrated by the data given in Table 3-9. As you can see, the number of commercial banks in the United States has decreased from approximately 31,000 in 1920 to less than 10,000 in 1997. At the same time, the number of bank branches has increased from fewer than 2,000 to more than 60,000 over the same period.

The trend in the United States today is toward huge financial service corporations, which own banks, S&Ls, investment banking houses, insurance companies, pension plan operations, and mutual funds, and which have branches across the country and even around the world. Interestingly, at one time, Sears, Roebuck, which is one of the largest retailing organizations in the United States, also owned a large insurance company (Allstate Insurance), a leading brokerage and investment banking firm (named Dean Witter at the time), the largest real estate brokerage firm (Coldwell Banker), a mortgage company (Sears Mortgage), a huge

---

TABLE 3-9

Number of Banks and Branches in the United States

Year	Banks	Branches	Year	Banks	Branches
1997	9,144	60,320	1950	13,446	4,832
1995	9,942	56,512	1940	13,442	3,489
1990	12,347	50,406	1930	22,500	4,000
1985	14,417	43,293	1920[a]	31,000	1,200
1980	14,434	38,738	1910[a]	25,000	<1,000
1970	13,511	21,839	1900[a]	12,500	<1,000
1960	13,126	10,556			

[a]These figures were estimated from graphs.

SOURCES: *FDIC Historical Statistics on Banking;*
http://www.fdic/databank/sob/hist96
Federal Reserve Chart Book on Financial and Business Statistics, Historical Supplement.

credit card business, and a host of other related businesses. By the end of 1994, though, Sears had sold or spun off most of these financial services businesses in an effort to pare down its own operations. Other financial service corporations, most of which started in one area and have now diversified to cover wide financial spectra, include Transamerica, Merrill Lynch, American Express, Citicorp, Fidelity, Prudential, and Travelers. And, in the future, we should see many finance-related companies that have traditionally been focused in a single area such as insurance or real estate branching into related businesses. In recent times, Congress has shown a willingness to permit financial services organizations greater latitude in the products they offer, and it appears such sentiment will continue.[7]

Self-Test Questions

Explain how money is created in a fractional reserve banking system.

Why do so many banks exist in the United States today?

What are the primary roles of the Federal Reserve System?

What effect do you think regulatory changes and competitive pressures will have on financial institutions in the future?

International Banking

There are two notable factors that distinguish the banking system in the United States from banking structures in other countries. Both factors can be traced to the regulatory climate that has existed historically in the United States. Generally speaking, financial institutions in the United States are much more heavily regulated and face significantly greater limitations with regard to branching activity and nonbanking business relationships than their foreign counterparts. Such regulations have imposed an organizational structure and competitive environment that have curbed the ability of individual banking organizations to grow in size.

First, it was noted earlier that the United States banking system traditionally has been characterized by a large number of independent banks of various sizes rather than a few very large banks that might exist with unrestricted branch banking. For that reason, the country has approximately 23,000 individual banks, credit unions, and thrift institutions. In contrast, the banking companies of nearly every other country in the world have been allowed to branch with few, if any, limitations; thus, their banking systems include far fewer individual, or unit, institutions than exist in the United States. Japan, for example, has fewer than 175 such institutions, Australia has about 20 local banks, and Canada has only 59 chartered banks, seven of which operate nationally and internationally. Even India, which has a population nearly four times larger than the United States, has fewer

---

[7]In May 1998, the House of Representatives passed the Financial Services Act of 1998, which would eliminate many of the barriers that restrict banks and other financial services organizations from engaging in related business activities. For example, the law would allow banks, securities firms, and insurance companies to offer common services — banks could offer insurance and investment banking services, while securities firms could offer insurance and conduct some banking activities. As we write this text, though, neither the Senate nor the President has approved the Act, so its fate is unknown.

than 300 individual banks (about 3 percent of the number in the United States). But, in India as well as other countries, each bank generally has many branches. For instance, the State Bank of India alone has more than 8,700 offices (branches).

The second major difference between U.S. banks and their foreign counterparts is that most foreign banks are allowed to engage in nonbanking business activities while U.S. banks are not. Such developed countries as the United Kingdom, France, Germany, and Switzerland, to name a few, permit banking firms and commercial firms to interact without restriction; banking firms can own commercial firms, and vice versa. Other countries, including Canada, Japan, and Spain, allow the mixing of banking firms and commercial firms with some restrictions. In aggregate, banks in countries that permit banking and commerce to be combined account for nearly 75 percent of banking assets throughout the world. Thus, regulations that restrict the nonbanking activities of U.S. banks have positioned these institutions such that they are at a competitive disadvantage internationally. But, as Congress has demonstrated recently, the legislative trend is to remove existing "competitive restraints" so U.S. institutions can better compete in the global financial arena.

Because foreign banks are less regulated and have fewer restrictions concerning the types of business activities they can pursue than their U.S. counterparts, such banks often engage in numerous aspects of multilayer financial deals. For example, a foreign bank might use its investment banking division to help a business raise funds through a new stock issue, even though the bank owns shares of stock and is the primary lender of the company. Being able to operate as a company's lender, owner, investment banker, and insurer permits foreign banking organizations to offer financial products not available to U.S. banking organizations. In addition, because such financial products can be packaged together by a single bank, it is possible to reduce the aggregate costs associated with financial services.

With less restrictive regulations and other limitations on banking activities than in the United States, foreign banking organizations have tended to develop huge, one-stop financial service arrangements. The ten largest banks in the world are shown in Table 3-10. Note that only one of the banks on the list is located in the United States, but five of the top ten banks are Japanese. In all, fewer than 15 U.S. banks are ranked in the list of the world's largest 100 banks.

It should not be surprising that foreign banks dominate international banking activities. Certainly, fewer restrictions have helped foreign banks attain such dominance, but, in addition, foreign banks have been involved in international banking much longer than U.S. banks. The worldwide presence of foreign banks can be documented as far back as the twelfth century when banks from Italy dominated international trade, which is long before the United States became a country. In fact, American banks were not permitted to have operations outside the United States until 1913, when the Federal Reserve Act was passed. And, until about 40 years ago, not many U.S. banks operated internationally.

While the Federal Reserve Act originally allowed banks with certain qualifications to engage in banking outside the United States, it was the Edge Act, which was approved in 1919, that allowed U.S. banks to operate subsidiary organizations in other countries to offer banking and financial services beyond those considered traditional "American" banking activities, including investment in stocks of foreign companies. And, in 1981, the Fed established another tool to help U.S. banks compete for international funds by allowing banks to create International

TABLE 3-10

World's Ten Largest Banks, 1998 (billions of dollars)

Rank	Bank Name	Country	Assets
1	Bank of Tokyo-Mitsubishi	Japan	$631.0
2	Deutsche Bank	Germany	582.0
3	BankAmerica Corporation	United States	524.6
4	Sumitomo Bank	Japan	495.6
5	Industrial & Commerce Bank	China	489.0
6	Credit Suisse Group	Switzerland	473.8
7	HSBC Holdings	United Kingdom	473.6
8	Dai-Ichi Kangyo Bank	Japan	443.8
9	Sanwa Bank	Japan	438.5
10	Fuji Bank	Japan	424.4

NOTE: Ranks are based on December 31, 1997, data, except for Japanese banks, which are based on March 31, 1998, data.

SOURCE: "The World's 100 Largest Banks," *Institutional Investor,* August 1998, on LEXIS-NEXIS Academic Universe.

Banking Facilities (IBFs), which take foreign deposits that are not subject to the same restrictions as domestic deposits, such as reserve requirements and deposit insurance (FDIC). An IBF is not a separate banking organization; it is a method of accounting for international deposits separately from domestic deposits. In reality, an IBF is a set of financial statements associated with international deposits that is separated from the other financial statements of the bank and subject to different restrictions. Whether a bank establishes an Edge Act organization or an IBF, its international banking activities are still subject to limitations imposed by the Fed. And, although American banks generally face fewer restrictions in their overseas operations than their domestic operations, for the most part, the overseas organizations are not allowed to engage in all the business activities available to the "native" banks they are competing against.

The presence of foreign banks in the United States has grown significantly in the past couple of decades. To ensure foreign banking organizations do not have an unfair competitive edge, Congress established regulations that specifically apply to foreign banks operating in the United States. The International Banking Act (IBA), passed in 1978, essentially obligates foreign banking organizations to follow the same rules that are applicable to American banks. And, the Foreign Bank Supervision Enhancement Act (FBSEA), passed in 1991, requires foreign banks to get the Fed's approval before establishing offices in the United States.

Even with the restrictions on American banking operations overseas, the presence of U.S. banks in international banking has increased rapidly in recent years. At the same time, the limitations overseas banking operations face in the United States have not discouraged the presence of foreign banks, especially in California, where large Japanese banks have established significant market shares. As the world becomes more globally oriented, so will the banking industry — American banks will become more important internationally, while foreign banks will increase their presence in the United States.

Self-Test Questions

How do U.S. financial institutions differ from their counterparts in other countries?

What are the two factors that distinguish the banking system in the United States from banking structures in other countries?

What changes are needed for U.S. financial institutions to become more competitive with financial institutions in other countries? Do you think such changes will occur in the near future?

Summary

In this chapter we described the roles and characteristics of financial institutions and the banking system present in the United States, and we indicated how institutions in the United States differ from their counterparts in other countries. The key concepts covered in the chapter are listed below.

- **Financial intermediaries** facilitate the transfer of funds from those who save to those who borrow by issuing their own securities and purchasing securities of others.
- Some of the benefits provided by financial intermediaries include **economic efficiency**, **reduced costs** associated with borrowing and lending, **diversification and pooling of risks**, **financial flexibility** through various financial products, and the ability to offer **related financial services**.
- Intermediaries include **commercial banks**, which are major lenders to businesses, **credit unions**, which are major lenders to consumers, **thrift institutions**, which lend mostly to house buyers, and organizations that offer a savings function as well as other services, such as **mutual funds**, **life insurance companies**, and **pension funds**.
- Today's banking system is based on a **fractional reserve system**, which was developed by metalsmiths during the Middle Ages.
- A **fractional reserve banking system** permits intermediaries to create money through loans because not all deposits have to be maintained in reserves. The **maximum amount** the money supply can be changed by a change in deposits in a fractional reserve system equals (Excess reserves)/(Reserve requirement).
- The U.S. has a **dual banking system**, which means financial intermediaries are chartered both by the federal government and state governments.
- The **Federal Reserve System** is the central bank of the United States, and it is responsible for managing the money supply and ensuring the banking system remains financially stable.
- **Banking legislation** historically has **restricted** the ability of U.S. banks (1) to branch from one state to another and (2) to enter into nonbanking business activities. Recent legislation has removed some of these restrictions, and legislative actions to remove even more restrictions are expected in the future.
- As a result of previous regulatory restrictions, the **number of banks** in the United States is much greater than the number in most other countries. In addition, the **average size** of U.S. banks is much smaller than the average size of banks in other countries.

Questions

3-1 What are financial intermediaries, and what economic functions do they perform?

3-2 In what ways do financial intermediaries improve the standard of living in an economy?

3-3 What would happen to the standard of living in the United States if people lost faith in the safety of our financial institutions? Why?

3-4 It is a fact that the federal government (1) encouraged the development of the savings and loan industry, (2) virtually forced the industry to make long-term, fixed-interest-rate mortgages, and (3) forced the savings and loans to obtain most of their capital as deposits that were withdrawable on demand.
   a. Would the savings and loans be better off in a world with a "normal" or an inverted yield curve? (Hint: Yield curves were discussed in Chapter 2.)
   b. Would the savings and loan industry be better off if the individual institutions sold their mortgages to federal agencies and then collected servicing fees or if the institutions held the mortgages that they originated?

3-5 Name some of the different types of financial intermediaries described in the chapter, and indicate the primary reason(s) each was created.

3-6 How has deregulation of the financial services industry changed the makeup of financial intermediaries? How do you think intermediaries' characteristics will change in the future?

3-7 How do bank organizations in the United States differ from banking organizations in other countries? Why?

3-8 How is money created in a banking system that has fractional reserve requirements (i.e., a fractional reserve system)?

3-9 Describe the open market operations of the Federal Reserve. What type of trades would the Fed undertake if it wanted to increase interest rates?

Self-Test Problems   *Solutions Appear in Appendix B*

Key terms **ST-1** Define each of the following terms:
   a. Financial intermediary; financial intermediation
   b. Commercial bank; thrift institution; credit union
   c. Mutual fund; money market fund
   d. Pension fund
   e. Fractional reserve system; excess reserves
   f. Dual banking system
   g. Branch banking; bank holding company
   h. Federal Reserve System; Board of Governors
   i. Monetary policy; open market operations

Fractional reserves **ST-2** Assume the reserve requirement in the United States currently is 10 percent on all deposits at financial institutions. Also, assume excess reserves do not exist in these institutions — as soon as reserves become excess, they are loaned out.
   a. If the Fed wants to increase the money supply by $110 billion, should it buy or sell Treasury securities? In what amount?
   b. If the Fed wants to decrease the money supply by $50 billion, should it buy or sell Treasury securities? In what amount?

Problems

Reserve requirements **3-1** Deposits in all financial institutions equal $2 trillion. The total reserves held by these institutions are $110 billion, $20 billion of which is in excess of reserve requirements.

a. What is the percentage reserve requirement?

b. What would the percentage reserve requirement have to be to maintain the existing amount of reserves ($110 billion) but eliminate excess reserves?

c. What would happen to deposits at all financial institutions if the existing excess reserves were eliminated? Assume elimination of excess reserves affects deposits only, and use the reserve requirement computed in part a.

Excess reserves **3-2** It has been determined that, in aggregate, financial institutions with depository accounts currently hold excess reserves equal to $3 billion — there is $3 billion more than is necessary to meet the reserve requirements associated with existing deposits. The reserve requirement applicable to *all* deposits is 15 percent. Assume changes in reserves held by financial institutions affect deposits only (i.e., amounts lent out are always redeposited in the financial institutions).

a. All else equal, what would be the effect on deposits if financial institutions immediately eliminated all excess reserves?

b. All else equal, what would be the effect on deposits if financial institutions adjusted reserves so that excess reserves were decreased to $1.2 billion?

c. Describe the impact you think either of the above actions would have on interest rates in the financial markets.

Bank deposits and reserves **3-3** According to statistics provided by the Federal Reserve, total reserves of commercial banks currently equal $45.4 billion. Required reserves are $45.1 billion, so excess reserves are about $300 million. The reserve requirement is 10 percent on transaction deposits, which include accounts that offer unlimited checking privileges, and 0 percent on nontransaction deposits. Nontransaction deposits currently total $2.5 trillion. Assume changes in reserves held by banks affect transaction deposits only.

a. According to the information given, determine the total amount of transaction deposits in commercial banks.

b. What are total deposits, transaction and nontransaction, at commercial banks?

c. What would happen to deposits if the Fed mandated the commercial banks to eliminate excess reserves?

d. How much would total required reserves be if total deposits remained at the level computed in part b, but the Fed imposed a 2 percent reserve requirement on nontransaction deposits and maintained the same 10 percent requirement on transaction deposits?

e. Would the existing reserves be sufficient to meet reserve requirements if the Fed imposed a 10 percent requirement for both transaction deposits and existing nontransaction deposits?

Reserve requirements **3-4** In recent years, the Fed has shown a willingness to decrease existing reserve requirements. Assume the total transaction deposits at banks and other financial institutions are $900 billion, and a reserve requirement of 10 percent applies only to these deposits. Also assume financial institutions never have excess reserves, and all monies they lend are deposited in transaction accounts (i.e., none of the funds is held as cash or deposited in non-transaction accounts).

a. By what *dollar* amount will transactions deposits increase if the Fed reduces the reserve requirement to 8 percent?

b. By what percentage will transaction deposits increase if the Fed changes the reserve requirement to 8 percent?

c. How will transaction deposits change if the Fed increases the reserve requirement to 12 percent?

Exam-Type Problems

The problems included in this section are set up in such a way that they could be used as multiple-choice exam problems.

Impact of deposit increase   **3-5**   Through its open market operations, the Federal Reserve recently increased deposits at financial institutions by $90 billion. If the reserve requirements for all deposits is 8 percent, what is the maximum impact the Fed's actions can have on total deposits?

Impact of reserve requirements   **3-6**   Compute the maximum change in total deposits that would result if deposits at financial institutions were immediately *increased* by $120 billion, and the reserve requirements applicable to all deposits are
  a. 5 percent.
  b. 10 percent.
  c. 50 percent.
  d. 100 percent.

Impact of reserve requirements   **3-7**   Compute the maximum change in total deposits that would result if deposits at financial institutions were immediately *decreased* by $120 billion, and the reserve requirements applicable to all deposits are
  a. 5 percent.
  b. 10 percent.
  c. 50 percent.
  d. 100 percent.

Change in reserves   **3-8**   The Federal Reserve has decided interest rates need to be increased to maintain relatively low inflation in the economy. To accomplish this, it has been determined that the money supply needs to be decreased by $188 billion. The Fed wants to affect the decrease in the money supply through reserves at financial institutions. Assume the current reserve requirement is 6 percent, and it applies to all deposits. By how much must reserves be decreased for the Fed to accomplish its goal?

Reserve requirement   **3-9**   Assume the reserve requirement for transaction deposits is 15 percent, and it is 4 percent for nontransaction deposits. Compute the reserve requirement for a bank that has $340 million deposited in transaction accounts and $120 million deposited in nontransaction accounts.

Integrative Problem

Financial intermediaries   **3-10**   Michelle Delatorre, the professional tennis player we introduced in the Integrative Problem in Chapter 2, has some questions about banks and other financial institutions that she wants answered so she can better understand the U.S. banking system and make more informed decisions concerning the investment of her money. Your boss at Balik and Kiefer Inc. has asked you to provide Ms. Delatorre answers to the following questions:
  a. What is a financial intermediary? What is the financial intermediation process?
  b. What are the roles of financial intermediaries? How have intermediaries helped improve our standard of living as well as the efficiency of the financial markets?
  c. What are the different types of financial intermediaries? Give some characteristics that differentiate the various types of intermediaries.
  d. Describe the banking system in the United States. What role does the Federal Reserve play in the U.S. banking system?
  e. How does the U.S. banking system differ from banking systems in other countries?
  f. How has the U.S. banking system changed in recent years? What are the arguments for and against such changes? What changes are expected in the future?
  g. How can Michelle Delatorre utilize the services provided by financial intermediaries?

CHAPTER 4

Financial Assets (Instruments)

Suppose you just received a modest amount of money because you won the lottery, a sweepstakes, or some other contest. Also, suppose you don't need this windfall gain for current expenses, so you have decided to invest the funds for future use. What investment(s) would (should) you choose? Would you invest in stocks or bonds? If you decide to invest in stocks, would you invest in preferred stock or common stock? Maybe you like common stock because it has the potential for substantial gains, and the stock market seems "hot" — it has received a great deal of publicity lately. But, which kind of common stock should you purchase — growth stock or income stock? If bonds are your choice, what types of bonds would you prefer, long-term or short-term, secured or unsecured? What about mutual funds? Are they appropriate for you? Or, would you just put the money in the bank in a certificate of deposit?

Now suppose you are the financial manager of a large corporation, and you are charged with making decisions about how to finance current operations as well as capital projects needed for future expansion. Should you recommend the firm issue commercial paper, mortgage bonds, common stock, or some other type of financial instrument? If bonds are issued, should they have a conversion feature, should they have a call provision, or should both features be included in the indenture?

Procedures and techniques to answer the questions just posed are described in later chapters. But, before we can make such decisions, we need to have some understanding of the types of financial assets available both to investors who use them as savings instruments and to corporations and governments that use them as instruments to raise funds. It should be apparent from these questions that there exist many different types of financial instruments with numerous characteristics. At times, the choices facing investors and borrowers seem boundless. But, as you will see, not all financial assets serve the same purpose — different circumstances call for different instruments.

As you read this chapter, try to answer the questions we posed here. As each financial asset is described, put yourself in the place of an investor, and

Continued

consider the circumstances in which you would invest in that instrument. Then "switch hats" — put yourself in the place of a borrower — and think about when it would be appropriate to use that same instrument to raise funds. You should find this an interesting exercise. And, by the time you finish this chapter, you should be able to give cursory answers to the questions we posed.

In the last two chapters, we described financial markets and the financial intermediaries that operate in those markets. Throughout the discussions, we referred to such financial securities as stocks, bonds, money market funds, and certificates of deposit, among others. These securities represent the actual instruments by which savers provide funds to borrowers, and they come in many different forms. Therefore, in this chapter, we describe various financial assets that exist in the financial markets, some of which are created by financial intermediaries and others by businesses and governments.

Before describing financial assets, we should differentiate between a *real asset* and a *financial asset,* the two general categories of asset classification in the business world. Although any asset generally is regarded as something that provides value to its owner, there is a significant difference between how value is provided by a real asset and a financial asset. A **real asset,** sometimes called a physical asset, is typically a tangible, or physically observable item, such as a computer, a building, or an inventory item. On the other hand, a **financial asset** is intangible; it represents an expectation, or promise, that future cash flows will be paid to the owner of such an asset.

Different groups of investors prefer different types of financial instruments, and investors' tastes change over time. Thus, corporations and governments offer a variety of securities, and they package their new security offerings at each point in time to appeal to the greatest possible number of potential investors. For the most part, though, a financial asset can be classified as either debt, equity, or a derivative. Table 4-1 lists the most important financial instruments traded in the various financial markets. The instruments are arranged from those with the shortest maturities (money market securities) to those with the longest maturities (capital market securities).

To give some perspective of the role of financial instruments in business, we begin the chapter with a discussion of some accounting issues relating to securities used (issued) by firms. Then, in the remainder of the chapter, we describe each security included in Table 4-1, along with a short discussion of derivatives. We should note that individuals can invest in each of the financial instruments described in this chapter either through direct investment or through intermediaries.

TANGIBLE ASSET
A physically observable, or touchable, item.

FINANCIAL ASSET
An asset that represents a promise to distribute cash flows some time in the future.

Financial Instruments and the Firm's Balance Sheet

Remember from your accounting course(s) that a company invests in such real assets as inventories and fixed assets to generate positive returns called income. Also, remember that a corporation issues financial instruments called debt and equity to raise funds to acquire its assets. In other words, a firm issues *financial*

TABLE 4-1

Major Financial Instruments

Instrument	Market	Market Participants	Riskiness	Maturity	Rates on 6/8/98
Treasury bills	Money	Sold to institutional investors by the Treasury to finance the government	Default-free	91 days to 1 year	5.2%
Repurchase agreements	Money	Used by banks to adjust reserves — sell investments with a repurchase promise	Low degree of risk	Very short/ overnight	5.5
Federal funds	Money	Interbank loans used to adjust reserves	Low degree of risk	Very short/ overnight	5.5
Bankers' acceptances	Money	Firm's promise to pay; guaranteed by a bank	Low degree of risk if bank is strong	Up to 180 days	5.5
Commercial paper	Money	Issued by large, financially secure firms to large investors	Low default risk	Up to 270 days	5.5
Negotiable CDs	Money	Issued by large, financially sound banks to large investors	Riskier than Treasury bills	Up to 1 year	5.6
Eurodollars	Money	Dollar-denominated deposits in banks outside the U.S.	Risk depends on soundness of issuing bank (foreign)	Up to 1 year	5.7
Money market funds	Money	Invested in T-bills, CDs, and other short-term instruments; held by individuals and businesses	Low degree of risk	No specific maturity (instant liquidity); funds reinvested	5.2
Treasury notes/bonds	Capital	Issued by the U.S. government to finance expenditures	No default risk, but prices change with changes in market interest rates	1 to 30 years	5.8
Municipal bonds	Capital	Issued by state and local governments to individuals and institutional investors	Riskier than Treasury bonds; exempt from federal taxes	Up to 30 years	5.0
Term loans	Capital	Negotiated with financial institutions	Risk depends on borrower; riskier than government bonds	2 to 30 years	6.4

(Continued)

TABLE 4-1

(Continued)

Instrument	Market	Market Participants	Riskiness	Maturity	Rates on 6/8/98
Mortgages	Capital	Loans from financial intermediaries to individuals and businesses	Risk depends on the borrower; much riskier than government bonds	Up to 30 years	7.0
Corporate bonds	Capital	Issued by corporations to individuals, institutional investors, and corporations	Risk depends on company; riskier than government bonds, but not as risky as stock	Up to 40 years	6.6
Preferred stock	Capital	Issued by corporations to individuals, institutional investors, and corporations	Riskier than corporate bonds, but not as risky as common stock	None	6-8
Common stock	Capital	Issued by corporations to individuals, and institutional investors	Risky	None	12-20

instruments so that the *assets* necessary to produce and sell inventories can be purchased. In addition, firms use derivatives to hedge, or insure, against a variety of risks. An understanding of the legal and accounting terminology and explanations of financial instruments issued by firms is vital to both investors and financial managers if they are to avoid misinterpretations and possibly costly mistakes.

First, consider Table 4-2, which shows a simplified balance sheet for Sydex Corporation. At the end of 1999, the book value of Sydex's assets was $740 million, and these assets were financed by (1) debt in the form of current liabilities (short-term) and bonds (long-term), which totaled $410 million, and (2) equity, which totaled $330 million. During the year, Sydex's investment in total assets increased by $60 million, from $680 million at the beginning of 1999 to $740 million at the end of the year. The company raised the funds needed to purchase the additional assets by using $10 million more of short-term debt (current liabilities increased from $220 million to $230 million), by issuing bonds worth $30 million (long-term debt increased from $150 million to $180 million), and by retaining $20 million of the income earned during the year (retained earnings increased from $150 million to $170 million).

At the end of 1999, Sydex had total liabilities equal to $410 million, which represents funds borrowed from such creditors as banks, materials suppliers, and investors in bonds. Thus, Sydex owes its creditors $410 million, but, only $230 million is "current," which means it has to be paid during the year 2000 — the rest is due in future years.

COMMON EQUITY
The sum of the firm's common stock, paid-in capital, and retained earnings, which equals the common stockholders' total investment in the firm stated at book value.

According to the **common equity** section of the balance sheet, Sydex's owners — its stockholders — have authorized management to issue a total of 75 million shares of stock, and management actually has issued, or sold, 40 million

TABLE 4-2

Sydex Corporation: Balance Sheet, December 31 (millions of dollars)

	1999	1998
Assets		
Cash and receivables	$280	$290
Inventory	180	150
Current assets	460	440
Net plant and equipment	280	240
Total assets	$740	$680
Liabilities and Equity		
Current liabilities	$230	$220
Long-term debt (bonds)	180	150
Total liabilities	410	370
Common stock (75 million shares authorized,		
40 million shares outstanding, $1 par)	40	40
Additional paid-in capital	120	120
Retained earnings	170	150
Total common stockholders' equity	330	310
Total liabilities and equity	$740	$680

PAR VALUE
The nominal or face value of a stock or bond.

RETAINED EARNINGS
The balance sheet account that indicates the total amount of earnings the firm has not paid out as dividends throughout its history; these earnings have been reinvested in the firm.

ADDITIONAL PAID-IN CAPITAL
The difference between the value of newly issued stock and its par value.

shares thus far. Each share has a **par value** of $1; this is the minimum amount for which new shares of common stock can be issued.[1]

Sydex's income statement (not included for brevity) shows that net income generated in 1999 was $50 million. A portion of the earnings was paid as dividends to stockholders, while the remainder was added to retained earnings. Total dividend payments were $30 million, so $20 million was added to accumulated **retained earnings** to produce the $170 million balance shown at year-end 1999. This means Sydex has retained, or plowed back into the company, a total of $170 million since it began business. This is money that belongs to the stockholders; it represents funds that could have been paid as dividends in previous years. Instead, the stockholders "allowed" management to reinvest the $170 million in the business so growth could be achieved.

Now consider the $120 million **additional paid-in capital.** This account shows the difference between the stock's par value and what stockholders paid when they bought newly issued shares of common stock. For example, in 1990, when Sydex was formed, 15 million shares were issued at par value; thus, the first balance sheet showed a zero for paid-in capital and $15 million for the common stock account. However, in 1993, to raise funds for expansion projects, Sydex issued 25 million additional shares at a market price of $5.80 per share — total value of the issue was $145 million. At that time, the common stock account was increased by $25 million ($1 par value for the 25 million shares issued), and the

---

[1]A stock's value is an arbitrary figure that originally indicated the minimum amount of money stockholders had put up. Today, firms generally are not required to establish a par value for their stock. Thus, Sydex Corporation could have elected to use "no-par" stock, in which case the common stock and additional paid-in capital accounts would have been consolidated under one account called *common stock,* which would show a 1999 balance of $160 million.

remainder of the $145 million issue value, $120 million, was added to additional paid-in capital. Sydex has not issued any more stock since 1993, so the only change in the common equity section since that time has been in retained earnings.

As Table 4-2 shows, Sydex used both debt and equity to raise funds to support its 1999 operations. The debt and equity instruments issued by the company, which were purchased by individuals, other corporations, and financial institutions, represent some of the financial assets that are traded in the financial markets. In the remainder of this chapter, we describe the characteristics of debt and equity, as well as other types of financial instruments.

Self-Test Questions

How are financial instruments recognized on the balance sheets of firms?

What differences would there be in the stockholders' equity accounts of a firm that has par value stock and one that has no-par stock?

How does the amount of earnings retained by a firm affect its common equity accounts?

Debt

DEBT
A loan to an individual, company, or government.

Simply stated, **debt** is a loan to a firm, government, or individual. There are many types of debt instruments: commercial paper, term loans, bonds, secured and unsecured notes, and marketable and nonmarketable debt, among others.

Debt Features

Often, when we refer to debt we identify it using three major features: principal repayment value, interest payments, and the time to maturity. For instance, a $1,000, ten-year, 8 percent bond is debt with a $1,000 principal due in ten years that pays interest equal to 8 percent of the principal amount, or $80, per year. In this section, we describe what these terms mean and some of the general features associated with debt.

PRINCIPAL VALUE, FACE VALUE, MATURITY VALUE, AND PAR VALUE   The principal value of debt represents the amount owed to the lender, which must be repaid some time during the life of the debt. For much of the debt issued by corporations, the principal amount is repaid at maturity, so, often, we also refer to the principal value as the *maturity value*. In addition, the principal value generally is written on the "face" of the debt instrument, so it also is called the *face value*. Further, when the market value of debt is the same as its face value, it is said to be selling at *par,* thus the principal amount also is referred to as the *par value.* Thus, for most debt, the terms *par value, face value, maturity value,* and *principal value* generally are used interchangeably to indicate the amount repaid by the borrower.

INTEREST PAYMENTS   In many cases, owners of debt instruments receive periodic payments of interest, which are computed as a percent of the principal amount. Some debt does not pay interest; to generate a positive return for investors, such financial assets must sell for less than their par, or maturity values when issued.

DISCOUNTED SECURITIES
Securities that sell for less
than par value when issued.

Securities that sell for less than their par values when they are issued are called **discounted securities** because they sell for less than their par values. Most discounted debt securities have maturities of one year or less.

MATURITY DATE   The maturity date represents the date the principal amount of a debt is due. As long as interest has been paid when due, once the principal amount is repaid, the debt obligation has been satisfied. Some debt instruments, called *installment loans,* require the principal amount to be repaid in several payments during the life of the loan. In such cases, the maturity date is the date the last installment payment of principal is made. The time to maturity varies — some debt has maturity as short as a few hours, while other debt has no specific maturity.

We often refer to debt instruments as either short-term debt or long-term debt. In the next section, we briefly describe familiar short-term debt instruments and long-term debt instruments.

PRIORITY TO ASSETS AND EARNINGS   In the corporation, debtholders have priority over stockholders with regard to distribution of earnings and liquidation of assets. In other words, debtholders must be paid before stockholders can be paid — interest on debt is paid before dividends are paid, and the principals of outstanding debt must be paid before stockholders can receive any proceeds from liquidation of the company.

CONTROL OF THE FIRM (VOTING RIGHT)   In the corporation, debtholders do not have voting rights, thus they cannot attain control. Yet, debtholders can affect the management and the operations of a firm by including restrictions on the use of the funds as part of the loan agreement.

Short-Term Debt

Short-term debt generally refers to debt with a maturity of one year or less. Some of the more common short-term debt instruments are discussed in this section.

TREASURY BILLS (T-BILLS)
Discounted debt
instruments issued by the
U.S. government.

TREASURY BILLS   **Treasury bills (T-bills)** are discounted securities issued by the U.S. government. When the Treasury issues T-bills, prices are determined by an auction process — interested investors and investing organizations submit competitive bids for the T-bills offered.[2] T-bills are issued with face values ranging from $10,000 to $1 million, and with maturities of 13, 26, or 52 weeks at the time of issue.

REPURCHASE AGREEMENT
An arrangement in which
one firm sells some of its
financial assets to another
firm with a promise to
repurchase the securities at
a later date.

REPURCHASE AGREEMENT (REPO)   A **repurchase agreement** is an arrangement in which one firm sells some of its financial assets to another firm with a promise to repurchase the securities at a higher price at a later date. The price at which the securities will be repurchased is agreed to at the time the "repo" is arranged. A firm agrees to sell securities because it needs funds, while another firm agrees to

---

[2]The Treasury also sells T-bills on a noncompetitive basis to investors or investment organizations offering to buy a certain dollar amount. In such cases, the purchase price is based on the average of the competitive bids received by the Treasury.

purchase the securities because it has excess funds. Thus with this arrangement, the repo seller effectively borrows funds from the repo buyer. Often the parties involved in repurchase agreements are banks, and the securities that are sold and repurchased are such government securities as T-bills. While some repos last for days or even weeks, the maturity for most repurchase agreements is overnight.

FEDERAL FUNDS
Overnight loans from one bank to another.

FEDERAL FUNDS   Often referred to simply as "fed funds," **federal funds** represent overnight loans from one bank to another. Banks generally use the fed funds market to adjust their reserves — banks that need additional funds to meet the reserve requirements of the Federal Reserve borrow from banks with excess reserves. The interest rate associated with such debt is known as the *federal funds rate.*

BANKER'S ACCEPTANCE
An instrument issued by a bank that obligates the bank to pay a specified amount at some future date.

BANKER'S ACCEPTANCE   A **banker's acceptance** might be best described as a post-dated check. But, in reality, a banker's acceptance is a time draft issued by a bank that obligates the bank to pay the owner of the banker's acceptance at some future date.[3] Generally used in international trade, a banker's acceptance arrangement is established between a bank and a firm so the firm can ensure its international trading partner that payment for goods and services essentially is guaranteed at some future date, which is sufficient time to verify the completion of the transaction. Banker's acceptances are generally sold by the original owner in the secondary market to raise immediate cash. Banker's acceptances are sold at discounts because they do not pay interest.

COMMERCIAL PAPER
A discounted instrument that is a type of promissory note, or legal IOU, issued by large, financially sound firms.

COMMERCIAL PAPER   **Commercial paper** is a type of promissory note, or legal IOU, issued by large, financially sound firms. Like T-bills, commercial paper does not pay interest, so it must be sold at a discount. The maturity on commercial paper varies from one to nine months, with an average of about five months.[4] Generally, commercial paper is issued in denominations of $100,000 or more, so few individuals can afford to *directly* invest in the commercial paper market; instead, commercial paper is sold primarily to other businesses, to insurance companies, to pension funds, to money market mutual funds, and to banks.

CERTIFICATE OF DEPOSIT
An interest-earning time deposit at a bank or other financial intermediary.

NEGOTIABLE CD
Certificate of deposit that can be traded to other investors prior to maturity; redemption is made by the investor who owns the CD at maturity.

CERTIFICATE OF DEPOSIT (CD)   A **certificate of deposit** represents a time deposit at a bank or other financial intermediary. Traditional CDs generally earn periodic interest and must be kept at the institution for a specified time period. To liquidate a traditional CD prior to maturity, the owner must return it to the issuing institution, where an interest penalty will be incurred. **Negotiable CDs,** however, can be traded to other investors prior to maturity because they can be redeemed by whomever owns them at maturity. Often called jumbo CDs, these financial assets typically have denominations in increments of $1 million to $5 million, and they have maturities that range from a few months to a few years.

EURODOLLARS
Deposits in banks outside the United States that are denominated in U.S. dollars.

EURODOLLAR DEPOSIT   A **Eurodollar deposit** is a deposit in a bank outside the United States that is not converted into the currency of the foreign country;

---

[3]A time draft simply is a checklike (checkable) instrument that has a future payment, or maturity date.

[4]The maximum maturity without SEC registration is 270 days. Also, commercial paper can be sold only to "sophisticated" investors; otherwise, SEC registration would be required even for maturities of less than 270 days.

instead it is denominated in U.S. dollars. Such deposits are not exposed to *exchange rate risk,* which is the risk associated with converting dollars into foreign currencies. Eurodollar deposits earn rates offered by foreign banks and are not subject to the same regulations imposed on deposits in U.S. banks. Thus, there are times when the rate that can be earned on Eurodollars is considerably greater than the rate that can be earned in the United States.

MONEY MARKET MUTUAL FUNDS
Pools of funds managed by investment companies that are primarily invested in short-term financial assets.

MONEY MARKET MUTUAL FUNDS **Money market mutual funds** are investment funds pooled and managed by investment companies for the purpose of investing in short-term financial assets, including those described above. These funds offer individual investors the ability to *indirectly* invest in such short-term securities as T-bills, commercial paper, Eurodollars, and so forth, which they otherwise would not be able to purchase because such investments either are sold in denominations that are too high or are not sold to individuals.[5]

Long-Term Debt

Long-term debt refers to debt instruments with maturities greater than one year. Owners of such debt generally receive periodic payments of interest. Some more common types of long-term debt are discussed in this section.

TERM LOAN
A loan, generally obtained from a bank or insurance company, in which the borrower agrees to make a series of payments consisting of interest and principal on specific dates.

TERM LOANS A **term loan** is a contract under which a borrower agrees to make a series of interest and principal payments on specific dates to the lender. Term loans usually are negotiated directly between the borrowing firm and a financial institution, such as a bank, an insurance company, or a pension fund. Although term loans' maturities vary from 2 to 30 years, most are for periods in the 3- to 15-year range.[6]

Term loans have three major advantages over public debt offerings such as corporate bonds — *speed, flexibility,* and *low issuance costs.* Because they are negotiated directly between the lender and the borrower, formal documentation is minimized. The key provisions of a term loan can be worked out much more quickly than those for a public issue, and it is not necessary for the loan to go through the Securities and Exchange Commission registration process. A further advantage of term loans has to do with future flexibility. If a bond issue is held by many different bondholders, it is virtually impossible to obtain permission to alter the terms of the agreement, even though new economic conditions might make such changes desirable. With a term loan, however, the borrower generally can sit down with the lender and work out mutually agreeable modifications to the contract.

The interest rate on a term loan can be either fixed for the life of the loan or variable. If a fixed rate is used, generally it will be set close to the rate on bonds of equivalent maturity and risk. If the rate is variable, it usually will be set at a certain number of percentage points above an index representing either the prime rate, the commercial paper rate, the T-bill rate, or some other designated rate.

---

[5]Mutual funds are discussed in greater detail in Chapter 3.

[6]Most term loans are amortized, which means they are paid off in equal installments over the life of the loan. Amortization protects the lender against the possibility that the borrower will not make adequate provisions for the loan's retirement during the life of the loan. See Chapter 6 for a review of amortization. Also, if the interest and principal payments required under a term loan agreement are not met on schedule, the borrowing firm is said to have defaulted, and it can then be forced into bankruptcy.

BOND
A long-term debt instrument.

COUPON RATE
Interest paid on a bond or other debt instrument stated as a percentage of its face, or maturity, value.

GOVERNMENT BONDS
Debt issued by federal, state, or local governments.

MUNICIPAL BONDS
Bonds issued by state and local governments.

REVENUE BONDS
Municipal bonds that generate revenues that can be used to make interest payments and to repay the principal.

GENERAL OBLIGATION BONDS
Municipal bonds backed by the local government's ability to impose taxes.

CORPORATE BONDS
Long-term debt instruments issued by corporations.

Then, when the index rate goes up or down, periodic adjustments are made to the rate charged on the outstanding balance of the term loan. With the increased volatility of interest rates, banks and other lenders have become increasingly reluctant to make long-term, fixed-rate loans, so variable-rate term loans have become more common in recent years.

BONDS A **bond** is a long-term contract under which a borrower agrees to make payments of interest and principal on specific dates to the holder of the bond. The interest payments are determined by the *coupon rate* and the principal, or face value, of the bond. The **coupon rate** represents the total interest paid each year stated as a percentage of the bond's face value.[7] Interest generally is paid semiannually, although bonds that pay interest annually, quarterly, and monthly also exist. For example, a typical 10 percent coupon bond with a face value equal to $1,000 would pay $50 interest every six months, or a total of $100 each year.

Now, we describe some of the more common bonds issued by both governments and corporations.

1. **Government bonds** are issued by the U.S. government, state governments, and local, or municipal governments. U.S. government bonds are issued by the Treasury, and are called either *Treasury notes* or *Treasury bonds.* Both types of debt pay interest semiannually. The primary difference between Treasury notes and Treasury bonds is the maturity when the debt is issued: The original maturity on notes is from greater than one year to ten years, while the original maturity on bonds is greater than ten years.

    Municipal bonds, or *munis,* are similar to Treasury bonds, except they are issued by state and local governments. The two principal types of munis are revenue bonds and general obligation bonds. **Revenue bonds** are used to raise funds for projects that generate *revenues* that are used to make interest payments and repay the debt. **General obligation bonds** are backed by the government's ability to impose taxes. Generally, the income an investor earns from munis is exempt from federal taxes.

2. As the name implies, **corporate bonds** are issued by businesses called corporations.[8] Although corporate bonds traditionally have been issued with maturities of between 20 and 30 years, in recent years shorter maturities, such as 7 to 10 years, have been used to an increasing extent. Bonds are similar to term loans, but a bond issue is generally advertised, offered to the public, and actually sold to many different investors. Indeed, thousands of individual and institutional investors might purchase bonds when a firm sells a bond issue,

---

[7]The term "coupon" comes from the fact that some time ago, most bonds literally had a number of small (½- by 2-inch), dated coupons attached to them, and on the interest payment date, the owner would clip off the coupon for that date and either cash it at his or her bank or mail it to the company's paying agent, who then mailed back a check for the interest. Today most bonds are registered — no physical coupons are involved, and interest checks are mailed automatically to the registered owners of the bonds. Even so, people continue to use the terms "coupon" and "coupon interest rate" when discussing registered bonds.

[8]The forms of business organizations — proprietorships, partnerships, and corporations — are described in the next chapter. At this point, we need only point out that corporate bonds are issued by businesses formed as corporations; proprietorships and partnerships cannot use corporate bonds to raise funds.

whereas there generally is only one lender in the case of a term loan.[9] With bonds, the interest rate generally is fixed, although in recent years there has been an increase in the use of various types of floating rate bonds. There also are a number of different types of corporate bonds, the more important of which are discussed in the remainder of this section.

MORTGAGE BOND
A bond backed by fixed assets. First mortgage bonds are senior in priority to claims of second mortgage bonds.

3. With a **mortgage bond,** the corporation pledges certain assets as security, or collateral, for the bond. To illustrate, in 1998 Ottley Corporation needed $10 million to build a major regional distribution center. Bonds in the amount of $4 million, secured by a mortgage on the property, were issued. (The remaining $6 million was financed with stock, or equity capital.) If Ottley defaults on the bonds, the bondholders can foreclose on the property and sell it to satisfy their claims. At the same time, if Ottley chooses to, it can issue *second mortgage bonds* secured by the same $10 million facility. In the event of liquidation, the holders of these second mortgage bonds would have a claim against the property, but only after the first mortgage bondholders had been paid off in full. Thus, second mortgages are sometimes called *junior mortgages,* because they are junior in priority to the claims of *senior mortgages,* or *first mortgage bonds.*

DEBENTURE
A long-term bond that is not secured by a mortgage on specific property.

4. A **debenture** is an unsecured bond, and, as such, it provides no lien, or claim, against specific property as security for the obligation. Therefore, debenture holders are general creditors whose claims are protected by property not otherwise pledged as collateral. In practice, the use of debentures depends both on the nature of the firm's assets and on its general credit strength. An extremely strong company, such as IBM, will tend to use debentures; it simply does not need to put up property as security for its debt. Debentures also are issued by companies in industries in which it would not be practical to provide security through a mortgage on fixed assets. Examples of such industries are the large mail-order houses and commercial banks, which characteristically hold most of their assets in the form of inventories or loans, neither of which is satisfactory security for a mortgage bond.

SUBORDINATED DEBENTURE
A bond that has a claim on assets only after the senior debt has been paid off in the event of liquidation.

5. A **subordinated debenture** is an unsecured bond that ranks below, or is "inferior to," other debt with respect to claims on cash distributions made by the firm. In the event of bankruptcy, for instance, subordinated debt has claims on assets only after senior debt has been paid off. Subordinated debentures might be subordinated either to designated notes payable (usually bank loans) or to all other debt.

INCOME BOND
A bond that pays interest to the holder only if the interest is earned by the firm.

PUTABLE BOND
A bond that can be redeemed at the bondholder's option.

INDEXED (PURCHASING POWER) BOND
A bond that has interest payments based on an inflation index to protect the holder from inflation.

6. Several other types of corporate bonds are used sufficiently often to merit mention. **Income bonds** pay interest only when the firm has sufficient income to cover the interest payments. Thus, missing interest payments on these securities cannot bankrupt a company, but from an investor's standpoint they are riskier than "regular" bonds. **Putable bonds** are bonds that can be turned in and exchanged for cash at the bondholder's option. Generally, the option to turn in the bond can be exercised only if the firm takes some specified action, such as being acquired by a weaker company or increasing its outstanding debt by a large amount. With an **indexed,** or **purchasing power,**

---

[9]However, for very large term loans, 20 or more financial institutions might form a syndicate to grant the credit. Also, it should be noted that a bond issue can be sold to one lender (or to just a few); in this case, the issue is said to be "privately placed." Companies that place bonds privately do so for the same reasons that they use term loans — speed, flexibility, and low issuance costs.

FLOATING RATE BOND
A bond whose interest rate fluctuates with shifts in the general level of interest rates.

ZERO COUPON BOND
A bond that pays no annual interest but is sold at a discount below par, thus providing compensation to investors in the form of capital appreciation.

JUNK BOND
A high-risk, high-yield bond used to finance mergers, leveraged buyouts, and troubled companies.

bond, which is popular in countries plagued by high rates of inflation, the interest payment is based on an inflation index such as the consumer price index; the interest paid rises automatically when the inflation rate rises, thus protecting the bondholders against inflation. **Floating rate bonds** are similar to indexed bonds except the coupon rates on these bonds "float" with market interest rates; when interest rates increase, the coupon rates will increase, and vice versa. In many cases, limits are imposed on how high or low (referred to as "caps" and "collars") the rates on such debt can change, both each period and over the life of the bond.

7. During the 1980s, a couple of interesting debt instruments were introduced that illustrated how flexible and innovative issuers have been in recent years. *Original issue discount bonds (OIDs),* commonly referred to as **zero coupon bonds** were created. These securities were offered at substantial discounts below their par values because they paid little or no coupon interest. OIDs have lost interest with many individual investors, primarily because the interest income that must be reported each year for tax purposes includes any cash interest actually received, which is $0 for zero coupons, plus the annual pro rated capital appreciation that would be received if the bond was held to maturity. Thus, capital appreciation is taxed prior to when it actually is received. For this reason, most OID bonds currently are held by institutional investors, such as pension funds and mutual funds, rather than individual investors.[10] Another innovation from the 1980s is the **junk bond,** which is a high-risk, high-yield bond often issued to finance a management buyout, a merger, or a troubled company. In junk bond deals, firms generally have a significant amount of debt, so bondholders must bear as much risk as stockholders normally would. The yields on these bonds reflect this fact — junk bonds issued by the Public Service of New Hampshire to finance construction of its troubled Seabrook nuclear plant had a coupon rate of 25 percent. The emergence of junk bonds as an important type of debt is another example of how the investment banking industry adjusts to and facilitates new developments in capital markets.[11]

---

[10]It is interesting to note that shortly after corporations began to issue zeros, investment bankers figured out a way to create zeros from U.S. Treasury bonds, which are issued only in coupon form. In 1982 Salomon Brothers bought $1 billion of 12 percent, 30-year Treasuries. Each bond had 60 coupons worth $60 each, which represented the interest payments due every six months. Salomon then in effect clipped the coupons and placed them in 60 piles; the last pile also contained the now "stripped" bond itself, which represented a promise of $1,000 in the year 2012. These 60 piles of U.S. Treasury promises were then placed with the trust department of a bank and used as collateral for "zero coupon U.S. Treasury Trust Certificates," which are, in essence, zero coupon Treasury bonds. A pension fund that expected to need money in 2000 could have bought 18-year certificates backed by the interest the Treasury will pay in 2000. Treasury zeros are, of course, safer than corporate zeros, so they are very popular with pension fund managers.

[11]The development of junk bond financing has done as much as any single factor to reshape the U.S. financial scene. The existence of these securities led directly to the loss of independence of Gulf Oil and hundreds of other companies, and it led to major shakeups in such companies as CBS, Union Carbide, and USX (formerly U.S. Steel). The phenomenal growth of the junk bond market was impressive, but controversial. Significant risk, combined with unscrupulous dealings, created significant losses for investors. For example, in 1990 Michael Milken, who was considered the "junk bond king," was sent to jail for his role in misleading investors in the junk bond market. Additionally, the realization that high leverage can spell trouble — as when Campeau, with $3 billion in junk financing, filed for bankruptcy in early 1990 — has slowed the growth in the junk bond market from its glory days. Recent trends, however, indicate a slight resurgence.

Self-Test Questions

Differentiate between the characteristics of short-term debt and the characteristics of long-term debt.

What are the three major advantages that term loans have over public offerings?

Differentiate between term loans and bonds.

Differentiate between mortgage bonds and debentures.

Define income bonds, putable bonds, and indexed bonds.

What problem was solved by the introduction of long-term floating rate debt, and how is the rate on such bonds actually set?

Why would you expect junk bonds to have higher yields than traditional bonds with similar coupons?

Bond Contract Features[12]

A firm's managers are concerned with both the effective cost of debt and any restrictions in debt contracts that might limit the firm's future actions. In this section, we discuss features that generally are included in bond contracts; thus they can affect either the cost of the firm's debt or the firm's future flexibility.

Bond Indenture

Bondholders have a legitimate fear that once they lend money to a company and are "locked in" for up to 30 years, the company will take some action that is designed to benefit stockholders but that harms bondholders. For example, RJR Nabisco, when it was highly rated, sold 30-year bonds with a low coupon rate, and investors bought those bonds in spite of the low yield because of their low risk. Then, after the bonds had been sold, the company announced plans to issue a great deal more debt, increasing the expected rate of return to stockholders but also increasing the riskiness of the bonds. RJR's bonds fell 20 percent the week the announcement was made. A number of other companies have done the same thing, and their bondholders also lost heavily as the market yield on the bonds rose and drove the prices of the bonds down.

Bondholders attempt to reduce the potential for financial problems by use of legal restrictions designed to ensure, insofar as possible, that the company does nothing to cause the quality of its bonds to deteriorate after they have been issued. The **indenture** is the legal document that spells out any legal restrictions associated with the bond, as well as the rights of the bondholders (lenders) and the corporation (bond issuer). A **trustee,** usually a bank, is assigned to represent the bondholders and to make sure that the terms of the indenture are carried out. The indenture might be several hundred pages in length, and it will include **restrictive covenants** that cover such points as the conditions under which the

INDENTURE
A formal agreement (contract) between the issuer of a bond and the bondholders.

TRUSTEE
An official who ensures that the bondholders' interests are protected and that the terms of the indenture are carried out.

RESTRICTIVE COVENANT
A provision in a debt contract that constrains the actions of the borrower.

---

[12]In this section, as well as the rest of the chapter, we refer primarily to corporate debt when discussing features and characteristics of bonds and other debt. The reason for this emphasis is because much of the remainder of the book is devoted to financial management within a corporation or investment decisions made by individuals that affect corporations. Many of the corporate bond features we discuss here also apply to government bonds.

issuer can pay off the bonds prior to maturity, the level at which various financial measures, such as the maximum amount of debt a firm can have, must be maintained if the company is to sell additional bonds, and restrictions against the payment of dividends when earnings do not meet certain specifications.

The trustee is responsible both for making sure the covenants are not violated and for taking appropriate action if they are. What constitutes "appropriate action" varies with the circumstances. It might be that to insist on immediate compliance would result in bankruptcy, which, in turn, might lead to large losses on the bonds. In such a case, the trustee might decide that the bondholders would be better served by giving the company a chance to work out its problems rather than by forcing it into bankruptcy.

The Securities and Exchange Commission approves indentures for publicly traded bonds and makes sure that all indenture provisions are met before allowing a company to sell new securities to the public. The indentures of many larger corporations were written back in the 1930s or 1940s, and many issues of new bonds, all covered by the same indenture, have been sold down through the years. The interest rates on the bonds, and perhaps also the maturities, will change from issue to issue, but bondholders' protection as spelled out in the indenture will be the same for all bonds of a given type.[13]

Call Provision

CALL PROVISION
A provision in a bond contract that gives the issuer the right to redeem the bonds under specified terms prior to the normal maturity date.

Most corporate bonds contain a **call provision,** which gives the issuing corporation the right to call the bonds for redemption prior to maturity. The call provision generally states that the company must pay the bondholders an amount greater than the par value for the bonds when they are called. The additional amount, which is termed a *call premium,* typically is set equal to one year's interest if the bonds are called during the first year a call is permitted, and the premium declines at a constant rate each year thereafter. Bonds usually are not callable until several years (generally five to ten) after they are issued; bonds with these *deferred calls* are said to have *call protection.* Call provisions allow firms to refinance debt much like we individuals refinance our mortgages — when interest rates decline, firms can recall some existing debt and replace it with lower cost debt.

Sinking Fund

SINKING FUND
A required annual payment designed to amortize a bond or preferred stock issue.

A **sinking fund** is a provision that facilitates the orderly retirement of a bond issue. Typically, the sinking fund provision requires the firm to retire a portion of the bond issue each year. On rare occasions the firm might be required to deposit money with a trustee, which invests the funds and then uses the accumulated sum to retire the bonds when they mature. A failure to meet the sinking fund requirement causes the bond issue to be thrown into default, which might force the company into bankruptcy. Obviously, a sinking fund can constitute a dangerous cash drain on the firm.

---

[13]A firm will have different indentures for each major type of bonds it issues, including its first mortgage bonds, its debentures, and so forth.

In most cases, the firm is given the right to handle the sinking fund in either of two ways:

1. The company can call in for redemption (at par value) a certain percentage of the bonds each year; for example, it might be able to call 2 percent of the total original amount of the issue at a price of $1,000 per bond. The bonds are numbered serially, and those called for redemption are determined by a lottery administered by the trustee.
2. The company might buy the required amount of bonds on the open market.

The firm will choose the least-cost method. If interest rates have risen, causing bond prices to fall, it will buy bonds in the open market at a discount; if interest rates have fallen, it will call the bonds. Note that a call for sinking fund purposes is quite different from a refinancing call as discussed above. A sinking fund call requires no call premium, but only a small percentage of the issue normally is callable in any one year.

Convertible Feature

CONVERSION FEATURE Permits investors in bonds or preferred stock to exchange their investments for shares of common stock at a fixed price.

A **conversion feature** permits the bondholder (investor) to exchange *(convert)* the bond for shares of common stock at a fixed price. Investors have greater flexibility with *convertible bonds* compared with straight bonds, because they can choose whether to hold the company's bond or convert into its stock. We discuss convertible securities further later in the chapter.

Self-Test Questions

How do trustees and indentures reduce potential problems for bondholders?

What are the two ways a sinking fund can be handled? Which method will be chosen by the firm if interest rates have risen? If interest rates have fallen?

What is the difference between a call for sinking fund purposes and a refinancing call?

Are securities that provide for a sinking fund regarded as being riskier than those without this type of provision? Explain.

Why is a call provision so advantageous to a bond issuer? When will the issuer initiate a refunding call? Why?

Bond Ratings

Since the early 1900s, bonds have been assigned quality ratings that reflect their probability of going into default. The two major rating agencies are Moody's Investors Service (Moody's) and Standard & Poor's Corporation (S&P). These agencies' rating designations are shown in Table 4-3.[14] The triple-A and double-A bonds

---

[14] In the discussion to follow, reference to the S&P code is intended to imply the Moody's code as well. Thus, triple-B bonds mean both BBB and Baa bonds; double-B bonds mean both BB and Ba bonds; and so on.

TABLE 4-3

Moody's and S&P Bond Ratings

| | High Quality | | Investment Grade | | Junk Bonds | | | |
					Substandard		Speculative	
Moody's	Aaa	Aa	A	Baa	Ba	B	Caa	C
S&P	AAA	AA	A	BBB	BB	B	CCC	D

NOTE: Both Moody's and S&P use "modifiers" for bonds rated below triple A. S&P uses a plus and minus system; thus, A+ designates the strongest A-rated bonds and A− the weakest. Moody's uses a 1, 2, or 3 designation, with 1 denoting the strongest and 3 the weakest; thus, within the double-A category, Aa1 is the best, Aa2 is average, and Aa3 is the weakest.

INVESTMENT GRADE BONDS
Bonds rated A or triple-B; many banks and other institutional investors are permitted by law to hold only investment grade or better bonds.

are extremely safe. Single-A and triple-B bonds are strong enough to be called **investment grade bonds,** and they are the lowest-rated bonds that many banks and other institutional investors are permitted by law to hold. Double-B and lower bonds are speculative, or *junk bonds;* they have a significant probability of going into default, and many financial institutions are prohibited from buying them.

Bond Rating Criteria

Bond ratings are based on both qualitative and quantitative factors. Some of the factors considered by the bond rating agencies include the financial strength of the company as measured by various ratios, collateral provisions, seniority of the debt, restrictive covenants, provisions such as a sinking fund or a deferred call, litigation possibilities, regulation, and so forth. Representatives of the rating agencies have consistently stated that no precise formula is used to set a firm's rating; all the factors listed, plus others, are taken into account, but not in a mathematically precise manner. Statistical studies have borne out this contention: researchers who have tried to predict bond ratings on the basis of quantitative data have had only limited success, indicating that the agencies use subjective judgment when establishing a firm's rating.[15]

Importance of Bond Ratings

Bond ratings are important both to issuers and to investors. First, because a bond's rating is an indicator of its default risk, the rating has a direct, measurable influence on the bond's interest rate and the firm's cost of using such debt. Second, most bonds are purchased by institutional investors rather than individuals, and many institutions are restricted to investment grade or higher rated securities. Thus, if a firm's bonds fall below BBB, it will have a difficult time selling new bonds because many potential purchasers will not be allowed to buy them.

As a result of their higher risk and more restricted market, lower grade bonds offer higher returns than high-grade bonds. Figure 4-1 illustrates this point. In each of the years shown on the graph, U.S. government bonds have had the lowest yields, corporate AAA have been next, and corporate BBB bonds have had the highest yields. The figure also shows that the gaps between yields on the three

---

[15]See Ahmed Belkaoui, *Industrial Bonds and the Rating Process* (London: Quorum Books, 1983).

FIGURE 4-1

Yields on Selected Long-Term Bonds, 1965–1998

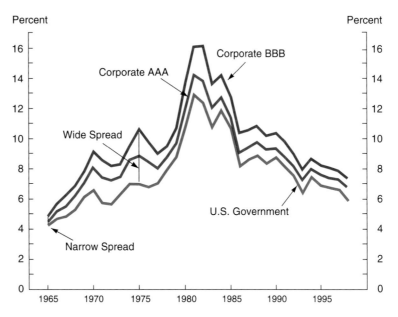

SOURCE: *Federal Reserve Bulletin,* various issues.

types of bonds vary over time, indicating that the cost differentials, or risk premiums, fluctuate from year to year. This point is highlighted in Figure 4-2, which gives the yields on the three types of bonds and the risk premiums for AAA bonds and BBB bonds in January 1965 and January 1998.[16] Note first that the risk-free rate, or vertical axis intercept, rose more than 1.6 percentage points from 1965 to 1998, primarily reflecting the increase in realized and anticipated inflation. Second, the slope of the line also has increased since 1965, indicating an increase in investors' risk aversion. Thus, the penalty for having a low credit rating varies over time. Occasionally, as in 1965, the penalty is relatively small, but at other times, as in 1998, it becomes larger. These slope differences reflect investors' risk aversion. When there is fear of an increase in inflation, there is a "flight to quality;" Treasuries are in great demand, and the premium on low-quality over high-quality bonds increases. Such periods included 1970–1976 and 1981–1982, which were

---

[16]The term "risk premium" ought to reflect only the difference in expected (and required) returns between two securities that results from differences in their risk. However, the differences between yields to maturity on different types of bonds consist of (1) a true risk premium; (2) a liquidity premium, which reflects the fact that U.S. Treasury bonds are more readily marketable than most corporate bonds; (3) a call premium, because most Treasury bonds are not callable whereas corporate bonds are; and (4) an expected loss differential, which reflects the probability of loss on the corporate bonds. As an example of the last point, suppose the yield to maturity on a BBB bond was 10 percent versus 7 percent on government bonds, but there was a 5 percent probability of total default loss on the corporate bond. In this case, the expected return on the BBB bond would be 0.95(10%) + 0.05(0%) = 9.5%, and the risk premium would be 2.5 percent, not the full 3 percentage point difference in "promised" yields to maturity. Because of all these points, the risk premiums given in Figure 4-2 overstate somewhat the true (but unmeasurable) risk premiums.

FIGURE 4-2

Relationship between Bond Ratings and Bond Yields, 1965 and 1998

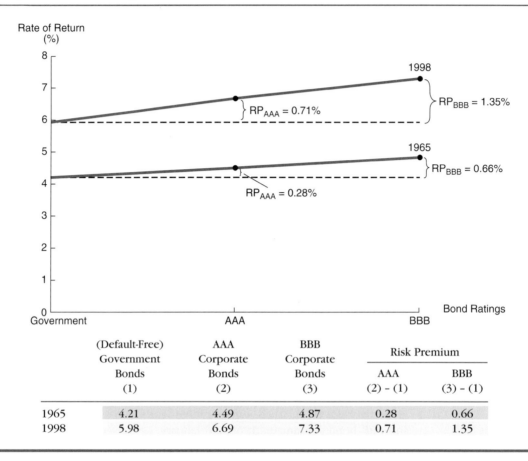

	(Default-Free) Government Bonds (1)	AAA Corporate Bonds (2)	BBB Corporate Bonds (3)	Risk Premium	
				AAA (2) – (1)	BBB (3) – (1)
1965	4.21	4.49	4.87	0.28	0.66
1998	5.98	6.69	7.33	0.71	1.35

periods characterized by high inflation relative to earlier times and low investors' confidence (high risk aversion). For example, in 1982, rates for government bonds were greater than 12 percent, rates for AAA corporate bonds were nearly 14 percent, and rates for BBB corporate bonds were greater than 16 percent. So, the premium on AAA bonds in 1982 was twice the 1998 premium, and on BBB bonds it was about three times current levels.

Changes in Ratings

Changes in a firm's bond rating affect both its ability to borrow long-term capital and the cost of those funds. Rating agencies review outstanding bonds on a periodic basis, occasionally upgrading or downgrading a bond as a result of its issuer's changed circumstances. For example, in January 1998, *Standard & Poor's CreditWeek* reported that Service Merchandise's debt ratings were lowered from BB– to B+, reflecting a weakened market position that was exhibited by a trend of "weak" sales and continued decreases in profits. During the previous five years, the company's operating income decreased 40 percent, and most analysts were not optimistic that proposed changes would help Service Merchandise regain lost market share. In the same month, S&P upgraded Fitzgeralds Gaming Corporation from CCC+ to B–, because the casino owner and operator had improved its operating performance and made favorable changes to its capital structure.

Self-Test Questions

Name the two major rating agencies and some factors that affect bond ratings.

Why are bond ratings important both to firms and to investors?

Stock (Equity)

Each corporation issues at least one type of stock, or equity, called *common stock.* Some corporations issue more than one type of common stock, and some issue *preferred stock* in addition to common stock. As the names imply, most equity is in the form of common stock, and preferred shareholders have preference over common shareholders when a firm distributes funds to stockholders — dividends, as well as liquidation proceeds resulting from bankruptcy, are paid to preferred stockholders before common stockholders. But, preferred stockholders generally are paid the same dividend every year, regardless of the company's earnings or growth during the year, while the dividends paid to common stockholders can vary each year and often are dependent on current and previous earnings levels and the future growth plans of the firm.

The amount of stock sold by a corporation is reflected in the "Owner's Equity" section of its balance sheet. Returning to Table 4-2, you can see that the owner's equity, or net worth, for Sydex Corporation was $330 million in 1999. And, according to Sydex's balance sheet, the company has issued only common stock.

In this section, we describe the basic characteristics of both preferred and common stock.

Preferred Stock

PREFERRED STOCK
Equity that has preference over common stock in the distribution of dividends and assets; dividend payments are fixed.

Preferred stock often is referred to as a *hybrid* security, because it is similar to bonds in some respects and to common stock in others. The hybrid nature of preferred stock becomes apparent when we try to classify it in relation to bonds and common stock. Like bonds, preferred stock has a par, or face, value. Preferred dividends are also similar to interest payments in that they are fixed in amount and must be paid before common stock dividends can be paid. However, if the preferred dividend is not earned, the directors can omit (or "pass") it without throwing the company into bankruptcy. So, although preferred stock has a fixed payment like bonds, a failure to make this payment will not lead to bankruptcy.

Accountants classify preferred stock as equity and report it in the equity portion of the balance sheet under "preferred stock" or "preferred equity." However, financial analysts sometimes treat preferred stock as debt and sometimes treat it as equity, depending on the type of analysis being made. If the analysis is being made by a common stockholder, the key consideration is the fact that the preferred dividend is a fixed charge that reduces the amount that can be distributed to common shareholders; from the common stockholder's point of view, preferred stock is similar to debt. Suppose, however, that the analysis is being made by a bondholder studying the firm's vulnerability to failure in the event of a decline in sales and income. If the firm's income declines, the debtholders have a prior claim to the available income ahead of preferred stockholders, and if the firm fails, debtholders have a prior claim to assets when the firm is liquidated. Thus, to a bondholder, preferred stock is similar to common equity.

From management's perspective, preferred stock lies between debt and common equity. Because failure to pay dividends on preferred stock will not force the firm into bankruptcy, preferred stock is safer to use than debt. At the same time, if the firm is highly successful, the common stockholders will not have to share that success with the preferred stockholders because preferred dividends are fixed. Remember, however, that the preferred stockholders do have a higher priority claim than the common stockholders. We see, then, that preferred stock has some of the characteristics of debt and some of the characteristics of common stock, and it is used in situations where neither debt nor common stock is entirely appropriate. For instance, a corporation might find that preferred stock is an ideal instrument to use to raise needed funds if it already has a considerable amount of debt; its creditors would be reluctant to lend more funds, and, at the same time, its common stockholders would not want their ownership shares diluted.

Preferred stock has a number of features, the most important of which are described next.

Priority to Assets and Earnings   Preferred stockholders have priority over common stockholders with regard to earnings and assets. Thus, dividends must be paid on preferred stock before they can be paid on the common stock, and, in the event of bankruptcy, the claims of the preferred shareholders must be satisfied before the common stockholders receive anything. To reinforce these features, most preferred stocks have coverage requirements similar to those on bonds. These restrictions limit the amount of preferred stock a company can use, and they also require a minimum level of retained earnings before common dividends can be paid.

Par Value   Preferred stock always has a par value (or its equivalent under some other name), and this value is important. First, the par value establishes the amount due the preferred stockholders in the event of liquidation. Second, the preferred dividend frequently is stated as a percentage of the par value. For example, an issue of Duke Power's preferred stock has a par value of $100 and a stated dividend of 7.8 percent of par. The same results would, of course, be produced if this issue of Duke's preferred stock simply called for an annual dividend of $7.80.

Cumulative Dividends
A protective feature on preferred stock that requires preferred dividends previously unpaid to be paid before any common dividends can be paid.

Cumulative Dividends   Most preferred stock provides for **cumulative dividends**; that is, any preferred dividends not paid in previous periods must be paid before common dividends can be paid. The cumulative feature is a protective device, because if the preferred stock dividends were not cumulative, a firm could avoid paying preferred and common stock dividends for, say, ten years, plowing back all of its earnings, and then pay a huge common stock dividend but pay only the stipulated annual dividend to the preferred stockholders. Obviously, such an action would effectively void the preferred position the preferred stockholders are supposed to have. The cumulative feature helps prevent such abuses.[17]

---

[17]Note, however, that compounding is absent in most cumulative plans — in other words, the unpaid preferred dividends themselves earn no return. Also, many preferred issues have a limited cumulative feature; for example, unpaid preferred dividends might accumulate for only three years.

CONVERTIBILITY   Approximately 40 percent of the preferred stock that has been issued in recent years is convertible into common stock. For example, each share of the Series B preferred stock JCPenney issued in 1988 can be converted into 20 shares of common stock at the option of the preferred shareholders.

OTHER PROVISIONS   Some other provisions occasionally found in preferred stocks include the following:

1. **Voting rights (control of the firm).** Although preferred stock is not voting stock, preferred stockholders generally are given the right to vote for directors if the company has not paid the preferred dividend for a specified period, such as ten quarters. This feature motivates management to make every effort to pay preferred dividends.

2. **Participating.** A rare type of preferred stock is one that participates with the common stock in sharing the firm's earnings. Participating preferred stocks generally work as follows: (a) The stated preferred dividend is paid — for example, $5 a share; (b) the common stock is then entitled to a dividend in an amount up to the preferred dividend; and (c) if the common dividend is raised, say, to $5.50, the preferred dividend must likewise be raised to $5.50.

3. **Sinking fund.** In the past (before the mid-1970s), few preferred issues had sinking funds. Today, however, most newly issued preferred stocks have sinking funds that call for the purchase and retirement of a given percentage of the preferred stock each year.

4. **Call provision.** A call provision gives the issuing corporation the right to call in the preferred stock for redemption. As in the case of bonds, call provisions generally state that the company must pay an amount greater than the par value of the preferred stock, the additional sum being termed a **call premium.** For example, Bangor Hydro-Electric Company has various issues of preferred stock outstanding, two of which are callable. The call prices on the two issues are $100 and $110. Before it was called in December 1997, Bangor had another callable preferred issue that included a sinking fund provision.

5. **Maturity.** Before the mid-1970s, most preferred stock was perpetual — it had no maturity and never needed to be paid off. However, today most new preferred stock has an effective maturity date with call provisions.

CALL PREMIUM
The amount in excess of par value that a company must pay when it calls a security.

Common Stock

We usually refer to common stockholders as the "owners" of the firm, because investors in **common stock** have certain rights and privileges generally associated with property ownership. The most common characteristics and rights associated with common stock are described here.

COMMON STOCK
Equity that represents ownership in a corporation; common stockholders vote for members of the board of directors and other important matters; last claim on the distribution of earnings and assets.

PRIORITY TO ASSETS AND EARNINGS   Common stockholders can be paid dividends only after the interest on debt and the preferred dividends are paid. Further, in the event of liquidation resulting from bankruptcy, common stockholders are last to receive any funds. Thus, as investors, the common stockholders are "last in line" to receive any cash distributions from the corporation.

DIVIDENDS   The firm has no obligation, contractual or implied, to pay common stock dividends. Some firms pay relatively constant dividends from year to year, while other firms do not pay dividends at all. The return investors receive when

INCOME STOCKS
Stocks of firms that
traditionally pay large,
relatively constant
dividends each year.

GROWTH STOCKS
Stocks that generally pay
little or no dividends in
order to retain earnings to
help fund growth
opportunities.

PROXY
A document giving one
person the authority to act
for another, typically the
power to vote shares of
common stock.

PROXY FIGHT
An attempt by a person or
group of people to gain
control of a firm by getting
its stockholders to grant
that person or group the
authority to vote their
shares in order to elect a
new management team.

TAKEOVER
An action whereby a
person or group succeeds
in ousting a firm's
management and taking
control of the company.

they own a company's common stock is based on both the change in the stock's market value (capital gain) and the dividend paid by the company. Some investors prefer current income to future capital gains, so they invest in firms that pay large dividends; thus, their returns are based primarily on the dividends earned from owning such stocks. These types of stocks traditionally are called **income stocks** — utility companies usually are considered income stocks. On the other hand, there are investors who prefer capital gains to current income, so they invest in firms that pay little or no dividends; thus their returns are based primarily on the capital gains earned from owning such stocks. Generally these types of firms retain most, if not all, of their earnings each year to help fund growth opportunities, so their stocks are referred to as **growth stocks.** Microsoft Corporation is a good example of a growth stock — the company has never paid a dividend, and its growth rate during the past few years has been phenomenal.

CONTROL OF THE FIRM (VOTING RIGHTS)   The common stockholders have the right to elect the firm's directors, who, in turn, elect the officers who manage the business. Stockholders also vote on shareholders' proposals, mergers, and changes in the firm's charter. In a small firm, the major stockholder typically assumes the positions of president and chairperson of the board of directors. In a large, publicly owned firm, the managers typically have some stock, but their personal holdings are insufficient to provide voting control. Thus, the managements of most publicly owned firms can be removed by the stockholders if they decide a management team is not effective.

Various state and federal laws stipulate how stockholder control is to be exercised. First, corporations must hold an election of directors periodically, usually once a year, with the vote taken at the annual meeting. Each share of stock normally has one vote; thus, the owner of 1,000 shares has 1,000 votes. Stockholders can appear at the annual meeting and vote in person, but typically they transfer their right to vote to a second party by means of an instrument known as a **proxy.** Management always solicits stockholders' proxies and usually gets them. However, if earnings are poor and stockholders are dissatisfied, an outside group might solicit the proxies in an effort to overthrow management and take control of the business. This is known as a **proxy fight.**

The question of corporate control has become a central issue in finance in recent years. The frequency of proxy fights has increased, as have attempts by one corporation to take over another by purchasing a majority of the outstanding stock. This action is called a **takeover.** Some well-known examples of takeover battles include Kohlberg Kravis Roberts & Company's acquisition of RJR Nabisco, Chevron's acquisition of Gulf Oil, AT&T's takeover of NCR, and NationsBank's takeover of Barnett Banks and BankAmerica.

Managers who do not have majority control (more than 50 percent of their firms' stock) are very much concerned about proxy fights and takeovers, and many attempt to get stockholder approval for changes in their corporate charters that would make takeovers more difficult. For example, a number of companies have gotten their stockholders to agree (1) to elect only one-third of the directors each year (rather than electing all directors each year), (2) to require 75 percent of the stockholders (rather than 50 percent) to approve a merger, and (3) to vote in a "poison pill" provision that would allow the stockholders of a firm that is taken over by another firm to buy shares in the second firm at a reduced price. The third provision makes the acquisition unattractive and, thus, wards off hostile takeover attempts. Managements seeking such changes generally cite a fear that the firm will be picked up at a bargain price, but it often appears that managers' concerns about their own positions might be an even more important consideration.

PREEMPTIVE RIGHT
A provision in the corporate charter or bylaws that gives common stockholders the right to purchase on a pro rata basis new issues of common stock.

PREEMPTIVE RIGHT   Common stockholders often have the right, called the **preemptive right,** to purchase any additional shares of common stock sold by the firm. The preemptive right requires a firm to offer existing stockholders shares of a new stock issue in proportion to their ownership holdings before such shares can be offered to other investors. In some states the preemptive right is automatically included in every corporate charter; in others it is necessary to insert it specifically into the charter.

The purpose of the preemptive right is twofold. First, it protects the power of control of current stockholders. If it were not for this safeguard, the management of a corporation under criticism from stockholders could prevent stockholders from removing it from office by issuing a large number of additional shares and purchasing these shares itself. Management could thereby secure control of the corporation and frustrate the will of the current stockholders.

The second, and more important, reason for the preemptive right is that it protects stockholders against a dilution of value. For example, suppose 1,000 shares of common stock, each with a price of $100, were outstanding, making the total market value of the firm $100,000. If an additional 1,000 shares were sold at $50 a share, or for $50,000, this would raise the total market value of the firm to $150,000. When the total market value is divided by the new total shares outstanding, a value of $75 a share is obtained. The old stockholders thus lose $25 per share, and the new stockholders have an instant profit of $25 per share.[18] Thus, selling common stock at a price below the market value would dilute its price and would transfer wealth from the present stockholders to those who were allowed to purchase the new shares. The preemptive right prevents such occurrences.

CLASSIFIED STOCK
Common stock that is given a special designation, such as Class A, Class B, and so forth, to meet special needs of the company.

TYPES OF COMMON STOCK   Although most firms have only one type of common stock, in some instances **classified stock** is used to meet the special needs of the company. Generally, when special classifications of stock are used, one type is designated Class A, another Class B, and so on. Small, new companies seeking to obtain funds from outside sources frequently use different types of common stock. For example, when Genetic Concepts went public, its Class A stock was sold to the public and paid a dividend, but this stock did not have voting rights until five years after its issue. Its Class B stock, which was retained by the organizers of the company, had full voting rights for five years, but the legal terms stated that dividends could not be paid on the Class B stock until the company had established its earning power by building up retained earnings to a designated level. The use of classified stock thus enabled the public to take a position in a conservatively financed growth company without sacrificing income, while the founders retained absolute

---

[18]In reality, the values given in this example would be correct *only* if the funds raised by the firm with the new issue are put into cash, thus not invested in projects with positive returns. But, even if the funds are invested, there probably still would be some decrease in the price per share because there will exist more shares of common stock in the stock markets.

FOUNDERS' SHARES
Stock owned by the firm's
founders that has sole
voting rights but generally
has restricted dividends for
a specified number of years.

CLOSELY HELD CORPORATION
A corporation that is owned
by a few individuals who
are typically associated with
the firm's management.

PUBLICLY OWNED CORPORATION
A corporation that is owned
by a relatively large number
of individuals who are not
actively involved in its
management.

control during the crucial early stages of the firm's development. At the same time, outside investors were protected against excessive withdrawals of funds by the original owners. As is often the case in such situations, the Class B stock was called **founders' shares.** Note that "Class A," "Class B," and so on, have no standard meanings. Most firms have no classified shares, but a firm that does could designate its Class B shares as founders' shares and its Class A shares as those sold to the public, while another could reverse these designations. Still other firms could use stock classifications for entirely different purposes.[19]

Some companies are so small that their common stocks are not actively traded; they are owned by only a few people, usually the companies' managers. Such firms are said to be *privately owned,* or **closely held, corporations,** and their stock is called *closely held stock.* In contrast, the stocks of most larger companies are owned by a large number of investors, most of whom are not active in management. Such companies are said to be **publicly owned corporations,** and their stock is called *publicly held stock.*

Self-Test Questions

Explain the following statement: "Preferred stock is a hybrid."

Identify and briefly explain some of the key features of preferred stock and common stock.

Identify some actions that companies have taken to make takeovers more difficult.

What are the two primary reasons for the existence of the preemptive right?

What are some reasons a company might use classified stock?

What is a closely held stock?

Derivatives

DERIVATIVES
Financial assets whose
values depend on the value
of some underlying asset,
such as a stock or a bond.

The term **derivatives** refers to a group of financial assets whose values are dependent on, or *derived* from, the value of some other asset(s), such as a stock or a bond. Because their values depend on the values of other assets, derivative securities can be rather complex investments. Thus, a detailed discussion of derivative securities is beyond the scope of this textbook. To provide an indication of the nature of derivatives, we briefly describe options, futures, convertibles, and swaps.

---

[19]When General Motors acquired Hughes Aircraft for $5 billion, it paid in part with a new Class H common, GMH, which had limited voting rights and whose dividends were tied to Hughes's performance as a GM subsidiary. The reasons for the new stock were reported to be (1) that GM wanted to limit voting privileges on the new classified stock because of management's concern about a possible takeover and (2) that Hughes employees wanted to be rewarded more directly on Hughes's own performance than would have been possible through regular GM stock. GM's deal posed a problem for the NYSE, which had a rule against listing any company's common stock if the company had any nonvoting common stock outstanding. GM made it clear that it was willing to delist if the NYSE did not change its rules. The NYSE concluded that such arrangements as GM had made were logical and were likely to be made by other companies in the future, so it changed its rules to accommodate GM.

Options

An **option** is a contract that gives its holder the right to buy or sell an asset at some predetermined price within a specified period of time. "Pure options" are instruments that are created by outsiders (generally investment banking firms) rather than by the firm itself; they are bought and sold primarily by investors (or speculators).

The most basic types of options include a *call* and a *put.* A **call option** gives the holder the right to purchase, or *call in,* shares of a stock for purchase at a predetermined price any time during the option period. In contrast, a **put option** gives the holder the right to sell, or *put out,* shares of a stock at a specified price during the option period. The transaction price established in the option contract (i.e., purchase price for a call, selling price for a put) is called the **striking,** or **exercise, price.**

Because options are created by parties outside the firm, such as investment bankers or investors, the companies are not directly involved in the options markets. Therefore, corporations do not raise money in the options markets, and option holders neither receive dividends nor vote for corporate directors (unless they exercise their options to purchase the stock, which few actually do).[20]

Convertibles

Convertible securities are bonds or preferred stocks that can be exchanged for, or converted into, common stock at the option of the holder. Conversion does not bring in additional capital for the issuing firm — debt or preferred stock simply is replaced by common stock. Of course, this reduction of debt or preferred stock will strengthen the firm's balance sheet and make it easier to raise additional capital, but this is a separate action. Often a convertible is issued as a temporary substitute for common stock when the market price of a firm's stock is depressed but is expected to improve in the future. If the company wants to ensure that a convertible will be converted into common stock once stock prices rise, the original convertible will include a call provision. The firm will then call the bond (or preferred stock) when the market price of the common stock has risen to a point where bondholders would prefer to convert rather than return the bonds to the firm.

One of the most important provisions of a convertible security is the *conversion ratio,* defined as the number of shares of stock the convertible holder receives upon conversion. Related to the conversion ratio is the conversion price, which is the effective price paid for the common stock obtained by converting a convertible security. For example, a $1,000 convertible bond with a conversion ratio of 20 can be converted into 20 shares of common stock, so the conversion price is $50 = $1,000/20. If the market value of the stock rises above $50 per share, it would be beneficial for the bondholder to convert (ignoring any costs associated with conversion).

---

[20]Corporations sometimes issue options called *warrants.* The holder of a warrant has the right to buy a stated number of shares of the company's stock at a specified price. Generally, warrants are distributed along with debt, and they are used to induce investors to buy a firm's long-term debt at a lower interest rate than otherwise would be required. Often warrants cannot be exercised for several years after their issue, so their lives are longer than "pure options." When a warrant is exercised, unlike a "pure option," the issuing company does receive funds from the investor.

Futures

FUTURES CONTRACT
An arrangement for delivery of an item at some date in the future, where the delivery details are determined when the contract is created.

A **futures contract** represents an arrangement for delivery of an item at some date in the future, where the details of the delivery, including the amount to be delivered and the price that will be paid at delivery, are specified when the futures contract is created. Multinational corporations often enter into futures contracts for foreign currencies used in their transactions. For example, consider a U.S. firm that has to pay for products purchased from a British manufacturer. The terms of the transactions require the firm to pay £500,000 30 days from today. If the firm exchanges U.S. dollars into British pounds today, it would need $750,000, because each dollar can be exchanged for about 0.67 British pound (each $1.00 buys £0.67, or $1.50 buys £1.00). But, when the firm makes payment in 30 days, the exchange rate could be different, and it could cost the firm more than $750,000. So, to avoid the risk of the exchange rate changing in an unfavorable direction, the firm can enter into a futures contract today to purchase £500,000 in 30 days at a price specified today, say, $1.52 per British pound. In 30 days, the firm could take delivery of £500,000 and pay $760,000 = $1.52 × 500,000, no matter what exchange rate exists at that time. The futures contract provides the company with *insurance* against unfavorable changes in exchange rates — the company has hedged its risk.

Swaps

SWAP
An agreement to exchange, or swap, cash flows or assets at some time in the future.

A **swap** is an agreement to exchange, or swap, cash flows or assets at some time in the future. For example, firms might agree to exchange interest payments on outstanding debt. One firm might have fixed-rate debt outstanding but it would rather have floating-rate debt, while the other firm might have floating-rate debt outstanding but it would rather have fixed-rate debt. Perhaps market conditions make it too costly for each firm to refinance or convert into the desired debt. So the firms could agree to swap interest payments such that the firm with the fixed-rate debt pays the variable interest on the floating-rate debt, and vice versa. As long as the principal amounts of the two debts are the same, the swap agreement allows the two firms to create the desired interest payments. Such an arrangement is referred to as a "plain vanilla" swap, because it is a very simple strategy. More complex arrangements include combination swaps in which multiple items are exchanged. An example would be a combination interest-rate, exchange-rate swap. Combination swaps can be very complex.

Self-Test Questions

Differentiate between a call option and a put option.

Do the corporations on whose stocks options are written raise money in the options market? Explain.

Does the exchange of convertible securities for common stock bring in additional funds to the firm? Explain.

Why are convertibles with call provisions considered "delayed" equity offerings?

What are futures contracts, and how are they used to reduce risk?

What is a swap agreement?

Rationale for Using Different Types of Securities

Why are there so many different types of securities? At least a partial answer to this question might be seen in Figure 4-3, which depicts the trade-off between the risk and expected after-tax return for the various securities issued by Taxton Products.[21] First, U.S. Treasury bills, which represent the risk-free rate, are shown for reference. The lowest risk, long-term securities offered by Taxton are its floating rate notes; these securities are free of risk associated with changes in interest rates (interest rate risk), but they are exposed to some risk of default, or nonpayment by the company. The first mortgage bonds are somewhat riskier than the notes (because the bonds are exposed to interest rate risk), and they sell at a somewhat higher after-tax return. The second mortgage bonds are even riskier, so they have a still higher return. Subordinated debentures, income bonds, and preferred stocks are all increasingly risky, and their returns increase accordingly. Taxton's common stock is the riskiest security it issues; thus, it has the highest return.

Why does Taxton issue so many different classes of securities? Why not offer just one type of bond, plus common stock? The answer lies in the fact that different investors have different risk/return trade-off preferences, so to appeal to the

---

[21]The returns in Figure 4-3 are on an after-tax basis to the recipient. If yields were on a before-tax basis, those on preferred stocks would lie below those on bonds because of the tax treatment of preferreds. In essence, 70 percent of preferred dividends are tax exempt to corporations owning preferred shares, so a preferred stock with a 10 percent pre-tax yield will have a higher after-tax return to a corporation in the 34 percent tax bracket than will a bond with a 12 percent yield.

FIGURE 4-3

Risk and Returns on Different Classes of Financial Instruments

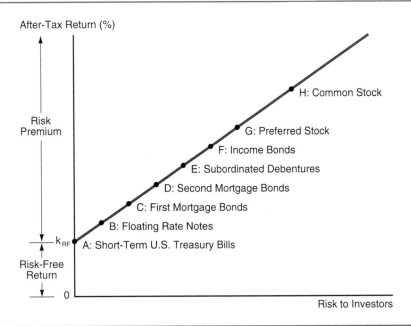

broadest possible market, Taxton must offer securities that attract as many different types of investors as possible. Also, different securities are more popular at different points in time, and firms tend to issue whatever is popular at the time they need money. Used wisely, a policy of selling differentiated securities to take advantage of market conditions can lower a firm's overall cost of funds below what it would be if the firm used only one class of debt or equity.

Self-Test Questions

List the different types of securities in order of highest to lowest risk.

Why do corporations issue so many different classes of securities?

Which Financial Instrument Is Best?

In this chapter, we have described numerous financial instruments used by firms to raise funds and used by investors as tools for saving funds. At this point, you might be wondering which financial instrument is best. Simply stated, what is best for one individual or firm is not necessarily best for another individual or firm, and, to complicate matters, what is best for one individual or firm when certain market conditions or circumstances exist might not be best when other market conditions or circumstances exist. For example, the decisions you make concerning your investments most certainly will change as you approach retirement age — when you first start investing, you probably will take greater chances, and thus invest in riskier financial assets, than when you are near retirement age. Similarly, your confidence in the financial markets most certainly will change with market conditions, and thus affect the types of financial instruments purchased. Generally, as your confidence in the markets increases, so do the chances you are willing to take, and vice versa. With this in mind, let's consider when firms might prefer to use debt and equity to raise funds, as well as when investors might have a preference for one of these investments compared to another.

Issuer's Viewpoint

Traditional bonds, as well as many other forms of debt, require fixed interest payments no matter the level of operating earnings for a firm. Thus, a principal advantage to debt issues is that a firm can limit its financial costs, which is beneficial when the firm prospers because earnings above the interest payments can be distributed to stockholders or reinvested in the firm to fund growth opportunities. Bondholders do not share in the firm's prosperity; only stockholders do. Unfortunately, debt can be a drawback during times of economic and financial adversity because the interest obligation must be paid even if the firm's operating earnings are very low. Another advantage of using debt financing is that it does not represent ownership, so debtholders do not have voting rights, and thus there is no dilution of ownership when additional debt is issued. However, bond indentures and other debt contracts generally contain clauses that restrict certain actions the firm can make, such as the amount of common stock dividends that can be paid each year. And, if the firm violates any of the contractual provisions, debtholders might force it to liquidate.

Remember that preferred stock has many of the same characteristics as debt, including a fixed payment and no voting rights. Thus, a firm might consider issuing preferred stock if prosperous times are expected so that existing common stockholders do not have to share the prosperity. Unlike debt, preferred stock does not "legally" obligate the firm to make payments to stockholders, and it has no maturity date. However, preferred stock does have a major disadvantage from the issuer's standpoint: It has a higher after-tax cost than debt. The major reason for this higher cost is taxes: Preferred dividends are not deductible as a tax expense, whereas interest expense is deductible.[22] This makes the cost of preferred stock much greater than that of bonds.

Common stock offers several advantages to the corporation.

1. Like preferred stock, common stock does not legally obligate the firm to make payments to stockholders — only if the company generates earnings and has no pressing internal needs for them will it pay dividends.
2. Common stock carries no fixed maturity date — it never has to be "repaid" as would a debt issue.
3. The sale of common stock generally increases the creditworthiness of the firm because common stock cushions creditors against losses.
4. If a company's prospects look bright, then common stock often can be sold on better terms than debt.

Stock appeals to certain groups of investors because it typically carries a higher expected total return (dividends plus capital gains) than does preferred stock or debt, and it provides the investor with a means to hedge against unanticipated inflation because common dividends tend to rise during inflationary periods.[23]

Disadvantages associated with issuing common stock include the following:

1. The sale of common stock gives some voting rights, and perhaps even control, to new stockholders. For this reason, additional equity financing often is avoided by managers who are concerned about maintaining control.
2. Common stock gives new owners the right to share in the income of the firm; if profits soar, then new stockholders will share in this bonanza, whereas if debt had been used, new investors would have received only a fixed return, no matter how profitable the company had been.[24]

---

[22]One would think that a given firm's preferred stock would carry a higher coupon rate than its bonds because of the preferred's greater risk from the holder's viewpoint. However, 70 percent of preferred dividends received by corporate owners are exempt from income taxes, and this has made preferred stock very attractive to corporate investors. Therefore, most preferred stock is owned by corporations, and in recent years high-grade preferreds, on average, have sold on a lower-yield basis, before taxes, than high-grade bonds. On an after-tax basis, though, the yield on preferred stock generally is greater than the yield on high-grade corporate bonds.

[23]For common stock in general, the rate of increase in dividends has slightly exceeded the rate of inflation since 1970.

[24]This point has given rise to an important theory: "If a firm sells a large issue of bonds, this is a signal that management expects the company to earn high profits on investments financed by the new capital and that it does not wish to share these profits with new stockholders. On the other hand, if the firm issues stock, this is a signal that its prospects are not so bright."

3. As we saw in Chapter 2, the costs of underwriting and distributing common stock usually are higher than those for debt or preferred stock.
4. Like preferred stock, under current tax laws, common stock dividends are not deductible as an expense for tax purposes.

Convertibles can be used to take advantage of some of the benefits associated with both debt and equity. Debt with a conversion feature offers investors greater flexibility by providing them the opportunity to ultimately be either a debtholder or a stockholder, thus such a feature generally allows the firm to sell debt with lower coupon interest rates and with fewer restrictive covenants. Even though convertibles do not bring in additional funds to the firm at the time of conversion, they are useful features that help the firm achieve "delayed equity financing" when conversion takes place. Convertibles are generally subordinated to mortgage bonds, bank loans, and other senior debt, so financing with convertibles leaves the company's access to "regular" debt unimpaired. Also, convertibles provide a way of selling common stock at prices higher than those prevailing when the issue was made. Many companies actually want to sell common stock and not debt, but they believe that the price of their stock is temporarily depressed and "too many" shares would have to be sold to raise a given amount of money. Such firms might use convertibles if they expect the prices of common stocks to rise sufficiently in the future to make conversion attractive; when the conversions take place, the firms have obtained "delayed equity financing" that eliminates the original debt. However, if stock prices do not increase sufficiently, hence conversions do not occur, the companies could be saddled with debt in the face of low earnings, which could prove disastrous.

Convertibles are useful, but they do have important disadvantages. The use of a convertible feature might, in effect, give the issuer the opportunity to sell common stock at a price higher than it could sell stock otherwise. However, if the common stock price increases greatly, the company probably would have been better off if it had used straight debt, in spite of its higher interest rate, and then later sold common stock to refund the debt. Also, convertibles typically have a low coupon interest rate, an advantage that will be lost when conversion occurs.

Investor's Viewpoint

In designing securities, the financial manager must consider the investor's point of view. Both debt and preferred stock provide investors with a steadier, more assured income than common stock, and debtholders and preferred stockholders have preference over common stockholders in the event of liquidation. Probably the primary advantage of debt from an investor's standpoint is that the firm is legally obligated to make the interest payments, and, if payments are missed, debtholders have legal recourse that might include forcing the firm into bankruptcy in an attempt to recover what is owed.

Many firms find preferred stock a very attractive investment, because 70 percent of the preferred dividends received by corporations are not taxable. For this reason, most preferred stock is owned by corporations. But, preferred stock is somewhat unattractive to investors because their returns are limited due to fixed dividend payments, even though preferred stockholders bear some of the ownership risks. And, for individual investors as opposed to corporations, *after-tax* bond yields generally are higher than those on preferred stock, even though the preferred is riskier.

From a social viewpoint, common stock is a desirable form of financing because it makes businesses less vulnerable to the consequences of declines in sales and earnings. Common stock financing involves no fixed charge payments, which might force a faltering firm into bankruptcy. From the standpoint of the economy as a whole, if too many firms used too much debt, business fluctuations would be amplified, and minor recessions could turn into major ones.

Derivatives are used by investors either to manage risk associated with their portfolios or to speculate as to the direction prices will change in the future. Options and futures essentially are created by investors; they are not used by firms to raise funds. Both these derivatives involve two parties — one on each side of the transaction. In aggregate, such derivatives do not create wealth in the financial markets because, when an investor on one side of the transaction gains from a price movement, the investor on the other side loses an equivalent amount. From an investor's viewpoint, derivatives can be quite complex. You can learn more details about derivatives as well as other complex investments by taking a course that covers "investments."

Self-Test Questions

What are the advantages and disadvantages of debt and preferred stock from an issuer's viewpoint?

What are the advantages and disadvantages of debt and preferred stock from an investor's viewpoint?

How are warrants and convertibles used to help firms raise funds?

What are some advantages and disadvantages of including warrants and convertibles as features in debt indentures?

What are the major advantages and disadvantages of common stock financing?

From a social viewpoint, why is common stock a desirable form of financing?

Financial Instruments in International Markets

For the most part, the financial securities of companies and institutions in other countries are similar to those in the United States. There are some differences, however, which we discuss in this section. Also, there exist financial securities that have been created to permit investors easier access to international investments, such as *American Depository Receipts.*

American Depository Receipts

AMERICAN DEPOSITORY RECEIPTS (ADRs)
Certificates representing ownership in stocks of foreign companies that are held in trust by a bank located in the country the stock is traded.

Foreign companies can be traded internationally through *depository receipts,* which represent shares of the underlying stocks of foreign companies. In the United States, most foreign stock is traded through **American Depository Receipts (ADRs).** ADRs are not foreign stocks; rather they are "certificates" created by such organizations as banks. The certificates represent ownership in stocks of foreign companies that are held in trust by a bank located in the country in which the stock is traded. ADRs provide Americans the ability to invest in foreign companies with less complexity and difficulty than might otherwise be possible. Each ADR certificate represents a certain number of shares of stock of a foreign company, and it entitles the owner to receive any dividends paid by the company in U.S. dollars. In addition, ADRs are traded in the stock markets in the United States, which often are more liquid than foreign markets. All financial information, including value, is denominated in dollars and stated in English; thus there are no problems with exchange rates and language translations.

In many cases, investors can purchase foreign securities directly. But, such investments might be complicated by legal issues, the ability to take funds such as dividends out of the country, and interpretation into domestic terms. Thus, ADRs provide investors the ability to participate in the international financial markets without having to bear risks greater than those associated with the corporations in which the investments are made. The market values of ADRs move in tandem with the market values of the underlying stocks that are held in trust.

Debt Instruments

Like the U.S. debt markets, the international debt markets offer a variety of instruments with many different features. In this section, we discuss a few of the more familiar types of debt that are traded internationally.

Any debt sold outside the country of the borrower is called an international debt. However, there are two important types of international debt: foreign debt and Eurodebt. **Foreign debt** is debt sold by a foreign borrower but denominated in the currency of the country in which the issue is sold. For instance, Bell Canada might need U.S. dollars to finance the operations of its subsidiaries in the United States. If it decides to raise the needed capital in the domestic U.S. bond market, the bond will be underwritten by a syndicate of U.S. investment bankers, denominated in U.S. dollars, and sold to U.S. investors in accordance with SEC and applicable state regulations. Except for the foreign origin of the borrower (Canada), this bond will be indistinguishable from those issued by equivalent U.S. corporations. Because Bell Canada is a foreign corporation, however, the bond will be called a *foreign bond.* Foreign bonds generally are labeled according to the country in which they are issued. For example, if foreign bonds are issued in the United States they are called *Yankee bonds,* if they are issued in Japan they are called *Samurai bonds,* and if they are issued in England they are called *Bulldog bonds.*

The term **Eurodebt** is used to designate any debt sold in a country other than the one in whose currency the debt is denominated. Examples include *Eurobonds,* such as a British firm's issue of pound bonds sold in France or a Ford Motor Company issue denominated in dollars and sold in Germany. The institutional arrangements by which Eurobonds are marketed are different than those for most other bond issues, with the most important distinction being a far lower level of required disclosure than normally is found for bonds issued in domestic markets, particularly in the United States. Governments tend to be less strict when regulating securities denominated in foreign currencies than they are on home-currency securities because the bonds' purchasers generally are more "sophisticated." The lower disclosure requirements result in lower total transaction costs for Eurobonds.

Eurobonds appeal to investors for several reasons. Generally, they are issued in *bearer* form rather than as registered bonds, so the names and nationalities of investors are not recorded. Individuals who desire anonymity, whether for privacy reasons or for tax avoidance, find Eurobonds to their liking. Similarly, most governments do not withhold taxes on interest payments associated with Eurobonds.

More than half of all Eurobonds are denominated in dollars; bonds in Japanese yen, German marks, and Dutch guilders account for most of the rest. Although

FOREIGN DEBT
A debt instrument sold by a foreign borrower but denominated in the currency of the country in which it is sold.

EURODEBT
Debt sold in a country other than the one in whose currency the debt is denominated.

centered in Europe, Eurobonds truly are international. Their underwriting syndicates include investment bankers from all parts of the world, and the bonds are sold to investors not only in Europe but also in such faraway places as Bahrain and Singapore. Until recently, Eurobonds were issued solely by multinational firms, by international financial institutions, or by national governments. Today, however, the Eurobond market also is being tapped by purely domestic U.S. firms such as electric utilities, which find that by borrowing overseas they can lower their debt costs.

Some other types of Eurodebt include the following:

1. *Eurocredits.* Eurocredits are bank loans that are denominated in the currency of a country other than where the lending bank is located. Many of these loans are very large, so the lending bank often forms a loan syndicate to help raise the needed funds and to spread out some of the risk associated with the loan.

LIBOR
The London InterBank Offer Rate, which represents the interest rate offered by the best London banks on deposits of other large, very creditworthy banks.

Interest rates on Eurocredits, as well as other short-term Eurodebt, typically are tied to a standard rate known by the acronym **LIBOR,** which stands for *London InterBank Offer Rate.* LIBOR is the rate of interest offered by the largest and strongest London banks on deposits of other large banks of the highest credit standing. In June 1998, LIBOR rates were 0.5 percentage point above domestic U.S. bank rates on time deposits of the same maturity — 5.25 percent for three-month CDs versus 5.75 percent for three-month LIBOR CDs.

2. *Euro-commercial paper (Euro-CP).* Euro-CP is similar to commercial paper issued in the United States. It is a short-term debt instrument issued by corporations, and it has typical maturities of one, three, and six months. The principal difference between Euro-CP and U.S. commercial paper is that there is not as much concern about the credit quality of Euro-CP issuers.

3. *Euronotes.* Euronotes, which represent medium-term debt, typically have maturities from one to ten years. The general features of Euronotes are much like those of longer-term debt instruments like bonds. The principal amount is repaid at maturity and interest is often paid semiannually. Most foreign companies use Euronotes like they would a line of credit, continuously issuing notes to finance medium-term needs.

Equity Instruments

The equities of foreign companies are like those of U.S. corporations. The primary difference between stocks of foreign companies and American companies is that U.S. regulations provide greater protection of stockholders' rights than those of most other countries. In the international markets, equity generally is referred to as Euro stock or Yankee stock:

- *Euro stock* refers to stock that is traded in countries other than the "home" country of the company, not including the United States. Thus, if the stock of a Japanese company is sold in Germany, it would be considered a Euro stock.
- *Yankee stock* is stock issued by foreign companies that is traded in the United States. If a Japanese company sold its stock in the United States, it would be called Yankee stock in the international markets.

As the financial markets become more "global" and more sophisticated, the financial instruments offered both domestically and internationally will change. Already, foreign companies and governments have discovered that financial markets in the United States provide excellent sources of funds because there exist a great variety of financial outlets. As technology improves and regulations that bar or discourage foreign investing are repealed, the financial markets of other developed countries will become more prominent, and new, innovative financial products will emerge.

Self-Test Questions

Differentiate between foreign debt and Eurodebt.

Why do Eurobonds appeal to investors?

What are Eurocredits, Euro-commercial paper, and Euronotes?

What is a Yankee stock?

What changes do you think will occur in the international markets during the next couple of decades?

Summary

This chapter is more descriptive than analytical, but a knowledge of the financial instruments described in the chapter is essential to an understanding of finance. The key concepts covered in the chapter are listed below.

- **Stockholders' equity** consists of the firm's common stock, paid-in capital (funds received in excess of the par value), and retained earnings (earnings not paid out as dividends).
- **Short-term debt** includes such instruments as Treasury bills, commercial paper, banker's acceptances, etc., which have maturities less than or equal to one year. **Long-term debt** instruments have maturities greater than one year.
- **Term loans** and **bonds** are long-term debt contracts under which a borrower agrees to make a series of interest and principal payments on specific dates to the lender. A term loan generally is sold to one lender (or a few), while a bond typically is offered to the public and sold to many different investors.
- There are many different types of bonds. They include **mortgage bonds, debentures, convertibles, bonds with warrants, income bonds, putable bonds,** and **purchasing power (indexed) bonds.** The return required on each type of bond is determined by the bond's riskiness.
- Some innovations in long-term financing include **zero coupon bonds,** which pay no annual interest but which are issued at a discount; **floating rate debt,** whose interest payments fluctuate with changes in the general level of interest rates; and **junk bonds,** which are high-risk, high-yield instruments issued by firms that use a great deal of financial leverage.
- A bond's **indenture** is a legal document that spells out the rights of the bondholders and of the issuing corporation. A **trustee** is assigned to make sure that the terms of the indenture are carried out.
- A **call provision** gives the issuing corporation the right to redeem the bonds prior to maturity under specified terms, usually at a price greater than the maturity value (the difference is a **call premium**). A firm typically will call a bond and refund it if interest rates fall substantially.
- A **sinking fund** is a provision that requires the bond issuer to retire a portion of the bond issue each year. The purpose of the sinking fund is to provide for the orderly retirement of the issue.

- Bonds are assigned **ratings** that reflect the probability of their going into default. The higher a bond's rating, the less risky it is considered, so the lower its interest rate.
- **Preferred stock** is a hybrid security having some characteristics of debt and some of equity. Equity holders view preferred stock as being similar to debt because it has a claim on the firm's earnings ahead of the claim of the common stockholders. Bondholders, however, view preferred as equity because debtholders have a prior claim on the firm's income and assets.
- **Common stockholders** are "last in line" to receive cash distributions made by the firm; they get paid only after both debtholders and preferred stockholders are paid.
- A **proxy** is a document that gives one person the power to act for another person, typically the power to vote shares of common stock. A proxy fight occurs when an outside group solicits stockholders' proxies in order to vote a new management team into office.
- Stockholders often have the right to purchase any additional shares sold by the firm. This right, called the **preemptive right,** protects the control of the present stockholders and prevents dilution of the value of their stock.
- Firms sometimes issue more than one type of common stock. **Classified stock** is used to meet special needs of the firm.
- A **derivative security** is a financial instrument whose value is dependent on, or derived from, the value of an underlying asset, such as a stock or a bond.
- An **option** is a contract that gives its holder the right to buy (or sell) an asset at some predetermined price within a specified period of time.
- A **convertible security** is a bond or preferred stock that can be exchanged for common stock. When conversion occurs, debt or preferred stock is replaced with common stock, but no money changes hands.
- **Futures** are contracts for delivery of commodities, currencies, and other products at some future date. Futures can be used to reduce risk associated with business or investment.
- The firm can **fix its financial costs** by issuing debt. But, if the fixed financial costs are not paid, the firm can be forced into **bankruptcy.** Also, interest is tax deductible.
- The primary **advantages of preferred stock to the issuer** are (1) that preferred dividends are limited and (2) that failure to pay them will not bankrupt the firm. The primary disadvantage to the issuer is that the cost of preferred is higher than that of debt because preferred dividend payments are not tax deductible.
- To the **investor,** preferred stock offers the advantage of **more dependable income** than common stock, and, to a corporate investor, **70 percent of such dividends are not taxable.** The principal disadvantages to the investor are that the **returns are limited** and the investor has **no legally enforceable right to a dividend.**
- The major **advantages of common stock financing** are as follows: (1) There is no obligation to make fixed payments, (2) common stock never matures, (3) the use of common stock increases the creditworthiness of the firm, and (4) stock often can be sold on better terms than debt.
- The major **disadvantages of common stock financing** are as follows: (1) It extends voting privileges to new stockholders, (2) new stockholders share in the firm's profits, (3) the costs of stock financing are high, and (4) dividends paid on common stock are not tax deductible.

- The **conversion** of bonds or preferred stock by their holders **does not provide additional funds** to the company, but it does result in a lower amount of debt.
- Financial instruments available in the international markets are similar to those issued in the United States. But, most Americans invest in foreign companies through **American Depository Receipts (ADRs),** which are certificates that represent foreign stocks held in trust, generally by a bank, in the country where the company is located.
- The **Eurodebt** market includes any debt sold in a country other than the one in whose currency the debt is denominated. Examples of Eurodebt are **Eurobonds, Eurocredits, Euro-commercial paper,** and **Euronotes.**
- Stock traded internationally generally is referred to as either **Euro stock** or **Yankee stock.** Euro stock is stock traded in countries other than the country where the company is located, except the United States, where such foreign stock is called Yankee stock.

Questions

4-1 What effect would each of the following items have on the interest rate a firm must pay on a new issue of long-term debt? Indicate whether each factor would tend to raise, lower, or have an indeterminate effect on the interest rate, and then explain why.

  a. The firm uses bonds rather than a term loan.

  b. The firm uses debentures rather than first mortgage bonds.

  c. The firm makes its bonds convertible into common stock.

  d. If the firm makes its debentures subordinate to its bank debt, what will the effect be

   (1) On the cost of the debentures?

   (2) On the cost of the bank debt?

   (3) On the average cost of total debt?

  e. The firm sells income bonds rather than debentures.

  f. The firm must raise $100 million, all of which will be used to construct a new plant, and it is debating the sale of first mortgage bonds or debentures. If it decides to issue $50 million of each type, as opposed to $75 million of first mortgage bonds and $25 million of debentures, how will this affect

   (1) The cost of debentures?

   (2) The cost of mortgage bonds?

   (3) The overall cost of the $100 million?

  g. The firm puts a call provision on its new issue of bonds.

  h. The firm includes a sinking fund on its new issue of bonds.

  i. The firm's bonds are downgraded from A to BBB.

4-2 Rank the following securities from lowest (1) to highest (8) in terms of their riskiness for an investor. All securities (except the Treasury bond) are for a given firm. If you think two or more securities are equally risky, indicate so.

  a. Income bond   _____

  b. Subordinated debentures — noncallable   _____

  c. First mortgage bond — no sinking fund   _____

  d. Common stock   _____

  e. U.S. Treasury bond   _____

  f. First mortgage bond — with sinking fund   _____ *g.* Subordinated debentures — callable   _____

h. Term loan   _____

4-3 A sinking fund can be set up in one of two ways:
(1) The corporation makes annual payments to the trustee, who invests the proceeds in securities (frequently government bonds) and uses the accumulated total to retire the bond issue at maturity.
(2) The trustee uses the annual payments to retire a portion of the issue each year, either calling a given percentage of the issue by a lottery and paying a specified price per bond or buying bonds on the open market, whichever is cheaper.
Discuss the advantages and disadvantages of each procedure from the viewpoint of both the firm and its bondholders.

4-4 Examine Table 4-2. Suppose Sydex sold 2 million shares of common stock, with the company netting $25 per share. Construct a statement of the equity accounts to reflect this sale.

4-5 It frequently is stated that the primary purpose of the preemptive right is to allow individuals to maintain their proportionate share of the ownership and control of a corporation.
a. How important do you suppose this consideration is for the average stockholder of a firm whose shares are traded on the New York Stock Exchange?
b. Is the preemptive right likely to be of more importance to stockholders of publicly owned or closely held firms? Explain.

4-6 Should preferred stock be classified as debt or equity? Does it matter if the classification is being made (a) by the firm's management, (b) by creditors, or (c) by equity investors?

4-7 Evaluate the following statement: "Issuing convertible securities represents a means by which a firm can sell common stock at a price above the existing market price."

4-8 Suppose a company simultaneously issues $50 million of convertible bonds with a coupon rate of 9 percent and $50 million of pure bonds with a coupon rate of 12 percent. Both bonds have the same maturity. Does the fact that the convertible issue has the lower coupon rate suggest that it is less risky than the pure bond? Would you regard its cost of the funds as being lower on the convertible than on the pure bond? Explain. (Hint: Although it might appear at first glance that the convertible's cost is lower, this is not necessarily the case because the interest rate on the convertible understates its cost. Think about this.)

Self-Test Problems   *Solutions Appear in Appendix B*

Key terms   **ST-1** Define each of the following terms:
a. Term loan; bond
b. Mortgage bond
c. Debenture; subordinated debenture
d. Convertible bond; income bond; putable bond; indexed, or purchasing power, bond
e. Indenture; restrictive covenant
f. Trustee
g. Call provision; sinking fund
h. Zero coupon bond; original issue discount bond (OID)
i. Floating rate bond
j. Junk bond
k. Investment grade bonds

l. Common equity; paid-in capital; retained earnings

m. Par value

n. Proxy; proxy fight; takeover

o. Preemptive right

p. Classified stock; founders' shares

q. Closely held corporation; publicly owned corporation

r. Cumulative dividends

s. Option; call option; put option

t. Convertible security; convertible preferred stock

u. Swaps

v. Eurodebt, Yankee stock

Sinking fund   **ST-2**   The Vancouver Development Company has just sold a $100 million, 10-year, 12 percent bond issue. A sinking fund will retire the issue over its life. Sinking fund payments are of equal amounts and will be made *annually*, and the proceeds will be used to retire bonds as the payments are made. Bonds can be called at par for sinking fund purposes, or the funds paid into the sinking fund can be used to buy bonds in the open market.

a. How large must each annual sinking fund payment be?

b. What will happen, under the conditions of the problem thus far, to the company's debt service requirements (interest and sinking fund payments) per year for this issue over time?

c. Now suppose Vancouver Development set up its sinking fund so that equal annual amounts, payable at the end of each year, are paid into a sinking fund trust held by a bank, with the proceeds being used to buy government bonds that pay 9 percent interest. The payments that will be made to the sinking fund each year equal $6,582,009. What are the annual cash requirements for covering bond service costs under this trusteeship arrangement? (Note: Interest must be paid on Vancouver's outstanding bonds but not on bonds that have been retired.)

d. What would have to happen to bond prices to cause the company to buy bonds on the open market rather than call them under the original sinking fund plan?

Perpetual bond analysis   **ST-3**   In 1936 the Canadian government raised $55 million by issuing bonds at a 3 percent annual rate of interest. Unlike most bonds issued today, which have a specific maturity date, these bonds can remain outstanding forever.

At the time of issue, the Canadian government stated in the bond indenture that cash redemption was possible at face value ($100) on or after September 1966; in other words, the bonds were callable at par after September 1966. Believing that the bonds would in fact be called, many investors purchased these bonds in 1965 with expectations of receiving $100 in 1966 for each perpetual bond they had. In 1965 the bonds sold for $55, but a rush of buyers drove the price to just below the $100 par value by 1966. Prices fell dramatically, however, when the Canadian government announced that these bonds would not be paid off.

The bonds' market price declined to $42 in December 1966. Because of their severe losses, hundreds of Canadian bondholders formed the Perpetual Bond Association to lobby for face value redemption of the bonds, claiming that the government had reneged on an implied promise to redeem the bonds. Government officials in Ottawa insisted that claims for face value payment were nonsense, for the bonds were and always had been clearly identified as perpetual bonds with no maturity. One Ottawa official stated, "Our job is to protect the taxpayer. Why should we pay $55 million for less than $25 million worth of bonds?"

Here are some questions relating to the Canadian issue that will test your understanding of bonds in general:

a. Do you think it would it make sense for a business firm to issue bonds like the Canadian government bonds described here?

b. Suppose the U.S. government today sold $100 million each of these types of bonds: 5-year bonds, 50-year bonds, and Canadian-type perpetual bonds. Rank the bonds from the one with the lowest to the one with the highest expected interest rate. Explain your answer.

c. Do you think the Canadian government would have taken the same action with regard to retiring the bonds if the interest rate had fallen rather than risen after they were issued?

d. Do you think the Canadian government was fair or unfair in its actions? Give the pros and cons, and justify your reason for thinking that one outweighs the other. Would it matter if the bonds had been sold to "sophisticated" as opposed to "naive" purchasers?

Problems

Zero coupon bond **4-1** Filkins Farm Equipment needs to raise $4.5 million for expansion, and its investment bankers have indicated that 5-year zero coupon bonds could be sold at a price of $567.44 for each $1,000 bond.

a. How many $1,000 par value zero coupon bonds would Filkins have to sell to raise the needed $4.5 million? Ignore flotation (issuing) costs.

b. What will be the burden of this bond issue on the future cash flows generated by Filkins? What will be the annual debt service costs?

Balance sheet effects of raising funds **4-2** Two textile companies, Meyer Manufacturing and Haugen Mills, began operations with identical balance sheets. A year later, both required additional manufacturing capacity, which could be attained by purchasing a new machine for $200,000. To raise the needed funds, Meyer issued a 5-year, $200,000 bond with a coupon rate equal to 8 percent. Haugen, on the other hand, decided to sell common stock to raise the $200,000. The stock was sold for $50 per share, and the issue increased the number of outstanding, or existing, shares by 20 percent from the pre-issue level. The balance sheet for each company, before the asset increases, is as follows:

		Debt	$200,000
		Equity	200,000
Total assets	$400,000	Total liabilities and equity	$400,000

a. Show the balance sheet of each firm after the asset is purchased.

b. How many shares of stock did Haugen have outstanding before the equity issue? How many are outstanding after the issue?

c. With the additional manufacturing capacity provided by the machine, the operating earnings (before taxes and interest payments) of each company will increase by $100,000. How much of this amount could be paid to the shareholders of each company? Assume the tax rate for both companies is 40 percent.

d. How much of the $100,000 operating earnings could be paid as dividends to *each* share of stock for each company (i.e., the additional earnings per share)? Assume both companies had the same number of outstanding shares of stock prior to the purchase of the new machine.

Convertible bond **4-3** The Swift Company was planning to finance an expansion in the summer of 2000. The principal executives of the company agreed that an industrial company such as theirs should finance growth by means of common stock rather than by debt. However, they believed that the price of the company's common stock did not reflect its true worth, so they decided to sell a convertible bond. Each convertible bond has a face value equal to $1,000, and can be converted into five shares of common stock.

a. What would be the minimum price of the stock that would make it beneficial for bondholders to convert? Ignore the effects of taxes or other costs.

b. What would be the benefits of including a call provision with these convertible bonds?

Financing alternatives   **4-4**   The Cox Computer Company has grown rapidly during the past 5 years. Recently its commercial bank urged the company to consider increasing its permanent financing. Its bank loan has risen to $150,000, carrying a 10 percent interest rate, and Cox has been 30 to 60 days late in paying its suppliers.

Discussions with an investment banker have resulted in the decision to raise $250,000 at this time. Investment bankers have assured Cox that the following alternatives are feasible (flotation costs will be ignored):

- *Alternative 1:* Sell common stock at $10 per share.
- *Alternative 2:* Sell convertible bonds at a 10 percent coupon, convertible into 80 shares of common stock for each $1,000 bond (i.e., the conversion price is $12.50 per share).
- *Alternative 3:* Sell debentures with a 12 percent coupon; each bond will sell at its face value of $1,000, and will have a maturity of 10 years.

Charles Cox, the president, owns 80 percent of Cox's common stock and wishes to maintain control of the company; 50,000 shares are outstanding. The following are summaries of Cox's latest financial statements:

Balance Sheet

		Short-term debt (bank loans, etc.)	$175,000
		Bonds	25,000
		Common stock, $1 par	50,000
		Retained earnings	25,000
Total assets	$275,000	Total liabilities and equity	$275,000

Income Statement

Sales	$550,000
All costs except interest	495,000
EBIT	$ 55,000
Interest	15,000
EBT	$ 40,000
Taxes at 40%	16,000
Net income	$ 24,000
Shares outstanding	50,000
Earnings per share	$0.48
Market price of stock	$8.64

a. Show the new balance sheet under each alternative. For Alternative 2, show the balance sheet after conversion of the bond into stock. Assume that $150,000 of the funds raised will be used to pay off the bank loan and the rest to increase total assets.

b. Show Charles Cox's control position under each alternative, assuming that he does not purchase additional shares.

c. What is the effect on earnings per share of each alternative if it is assumed that earnings before interest and taxes will be 20 percent of total assets? [Hint: Earnings per share = (Net income)/(Shares outstanding).]

d. Which of the three alternatives would you recommend to Charles Cox, and why?

Exam-Type Problems

The problems included in this section are set up in such a way that they could be used as multiple-choice exam problems.

Gain (loss) from options   **4-5**   Suppose you purchased a call option that permits you to purchase 100 shares of the stock of Silicon Graphics for $15 per share any time in the next 3 months. Silicon Graphics has a current market price of $12 per share.

    a. Should you exercise the option and purchase the stock if its price increases to $18? What would be your gain (loss) if you exercised the option and then immediately sold the stock? Ignore taxes and commissions.

    b. Should you exercise the option and purchase the stock if its price increases to $13? What would be your gain (loss) if you exercised the option and then immediately sold the stock? Ignore taxes and commissions.

    c. Would your answer to part b change if the option was a put rather than a call? Remember, a put gives you the right to sell stock at a pre-determined price. Assume the exercise price is $15.

Futures contract   **4-6**   Fibertech Corporation just received an invoice from a German manufacturer. The invoice states that Fibertech must pay the German company 7,500,000 deutschemarks (the German currency) in 90 days. If Fibertech pays the bill today, it needs $4,215,000, because each deutschemark currently costs $0.562 (i.e., each $1 can purchase 1.779 deutschemarks). But, Fibertech is considering waiting to pay until the bill is due, because, to pay today, it would have to borrow the needed funds at a very high interest rate. In 90 days, the firm expects to have collected funds from outstanding sales that will be more than sufficient to pay the German manufacturer.

    a. Give some reasons Fibertech might want to pay the bill today rather than wait for 90 days. Give some reasons for not paying the bill until it is due.

    b. Suppose Fibertech can obtain a futures contract for delivery of 7,500,000 deutschemarks in 90 days, but it will cost $0.567 for each deutschemark at delivery. In U.S. dollars, how much will Fibertech have to pay to settle its bill in 90 days with this contract?

    c. Assume Fibertech chooses not to take the futures contract described in part b. In U.S. dollars, how much will the company have to pay if the exchange rate in 90 days is $0.60 per deutschemark? What if it is $0.54 per deutschemark?

    d. What primary benefit would Fibertech derive from entering into the futures contract?

Integrative Problem

Debt/equity financing   **4-7**   Gonzales Food Stores, a family-owned grocery store chain headquartered in El Paso, has hired you to make recommendations concerning financing needs for the two situations given below.

Situation I: Initial Expansion
Gonzales is a closely-held corporation considering a major expansion. The proposed expansion would require Gonzales to raise $10 million in additional capital. Because Gonzales currently has 50 percent debt, and because the family members already have all their funds tied up in the business, the owners cannot supply any additional equity, so the company will have to sell stock to the public. However, the family wants to ensure that they retain control of the company. This would be Gonzales's first stock sale, and the owners are not sure just what would be involved. Therefore, they have asked you to research the process and to help them decide exactly how to raise the needed capital. In doing so, you should answer the following questions.

    a. What are the advantages to Gonzales of financing with stock rather than bonds? What are the disadvantages of using stock?

b. Is the stock of Gonzales Food Stores currently publicly held or privately owned? Would this situation change if the stock sale were made?

c. What is classified stock? Would there be any advantage to Gonzales of designating the stock currently outstanding as "founders' shares"? What type of common stock should Gonzales sell to the public to allow the family to retain control of the business?

d. If some of the Gonzales family members wanted to sell some of their own shares in order to diversify at the same time the company was selling new shares to raise expansion capital, would this be feasible?

Situation II: Subsequent Expansions

A few years after the initial expansion, Gonzales wants to build a plant and finance an operation that would manufacture and distribute its homemade salsa and related products to supermarkets throughout the United States and Mexico. Mr. Gonzales, CEO and family head, already has begun planning this venture, even though construction is not expected to begin until the current expansion is complete and the company is financially stable, which might take several years. Even so, Mr. Gonzales has some ideas he would like you to examine.

The project's estimated cost is $30 million, which will be used to build a manufacturing facility and to set up the necessary distribution system. Gonzales tentatively plans to raise the $30 million by selling 10-year bonds, and its investment bankers have indicated that either regular or zero coupon bonds can be used. Regular coupon bonds would sell at par and would have annual payment coupons of 12 percent and would be callable after 3 years, on the anniversary date of the issue.

As part of your analysis, you have been asked to answer the following questions.

a. What is the difference between a bond and a term loan? What are the advantages of a term loan over a bond?

b. Suppose Gonzales issues bonds and uses the manufacturing facility (land and buildings) as collateral to secure the issue. What type of bond would this be? Suppose that instead of using secured bonds Gonzales decides to sell debentures. How would this affect the interest rate that Gonzales would have to pay on the $30 million of debt?

c. What is a bond indenture? What are some typical provisions the bondholders would require Gonzales to include in its indenture?

d. Gonzales's bonds will be callable after 3 years. If the bonds were not callable, would the required interest rate be higher or lower than 12 percent? What would be the effect on the rate if the bonds were callable immediately? What are the advantages to Gonzales of making the bonds callable?

e. (1) Suppose Gonzales's indenture included a sinking fund provision that required the company to retire one-tenth of the bonds each year. Would this provision raise or lower the interest rate required on the bonds?

 (2) How would the sinking fund operate?

 (3) Why might Gonzales's investors require it to use a sinking fund?

 (4) For this particular issue, would it make sense to include a sinking fund?

f. At the time of the bond issue Gonzales expects to be an A-rated firm. Suppose Gonzales's bond rating was (1) lowered to triple-B or (2) raised to double-A. Who would make these changes, and what would the changes mean? What would be the effect of these changes on the interest rate required on Gonzales's new long-term debt and on the market value of Gonzales's outstanding debt?

g. What are some of the factors a firm such as Gonzales should consider when deciding whether to issue long-term debt, short-term debt, or equity? Why might long-term debt be Gonzales's best choice for this project?

CHAPTER 5

Business Organizations and the Tax Environment

For two decades, William Bennett headed Circus Circus Enterprises, which he and co-founder William Pennington built into a major gaming organization through their vision that gambling could be mass-marketed with the allure of cheap travel junkets and low-stakes games. But, on July 8, 1994, relenting to pressure from stockholders, Bennett resigned from his powerful position as chairman of the board of directors. One of the primary reasons the stockholders forced Bennett out was because they saw the price of Circus Circus stock drop by almost 60 percent during the previous six months, and much of the blame for this devaluation was attributed to the fact that Bennett ruled the firm much like a dictator with his own agenda. The bottom line was that stockholders believed the value of their investment suffered under Bennett's administration — in their minds, the stockholders' best interests were not being served. Maurice Saatchi, chairman and co-founder of Saatchi & Saatchi PLC, which is a worldwide advertising agency with accounts such as Procter & Gamble and Hewlett-Packard, can empathize with Bennett because he was forced to resign in December 1994, also because stockholders did not believe he had their best interests in mind. For the same reason, in the same year, the stockholders of Circus Circus and John Labatt Ltd., which is a Toronto-based beer brewer, turned down proposals from top management that would make the firms less attractive as takeover candidates, because the proposals were viewed as being beneficial to management rather than the stockholders.

In each of these instances, stockholders sent clear messages to management — it is the stockholders who are the owners of the firms, and, as such, top management should strive to achieve the stockholders' primary goal of value maximization. And, recently, stockholders also have made it clear that no one is immune from the "corporate ax" if it is felt shareholders' interests are not being pursued. For instance, in June 1998, "Chainsaw Al" Dunlap was fired as CEO of Sunbeam, a small appliance manufacturer. Dunlap got his

Continued

moniker because he became famous as a "turnaround artist" who would breathe life into a floundering business by paring down its operations through sales of inefficient divisions and layoffs of large numbers of employees — he would bring his "chainsaw" to the corporate table to save the business. Unfortunately, Dunlap could not work miracles at Sunbeam. Just before he was fired, the price of Sunbeam's stock had dropped to $14 per share, which represented nearly a 73 percent loss in value from its 1997 high of $51. One of Sunbeam's biggest shareholders saw his nearly $1 billion investment decrease to less than $300 million. The stockholders, as well as the others, believed Dunlap was not acting in the best interests of the owners; otherwise, the stock value would not have decreased so significantly.

When conflicts occur between managements' goals (e.g., job security, substantial compensation, etc.) and the owners' goal (increased value), management should "do what is right for the company and its owners." To reduce the chances of conflicts in goals and ensure the goals of stockholders are pursued, many firms now require their senior managers to own stock in the companies they run. Firms such as Eastman Kodak, Xerox, Union Carbide, and Hershey Foods, to name a few, have policies that force those who are in top management positions to also be owners of the firms. It is believed that if managers also are owners, they will be more "in tune" with the other stockholders' interests and less inclined to pursue activities harmful to the stock's value. There is evidence that supports this contention — firms with executives that own substantial amounts of stock do very well.

As you read this chapter, think about some of the issues raised here: As a stockholder in a company, what goal (or set of goals) would you like to see pursued? To what extent should top managers let their own personal goals influence the decisions they make concerning how the firm is run? Would you, as an outside stockholder, feel more comfortable that your interests were being represented better if the firm's top managers also owned large amounts of the firm's stock? What factors should management consider when trying to "boost" the value of the firm's stock?

In the last few chapters, we described financial markets and the instruments traded in those markets. As we saw, many of the financial instruments are issued by businesses to raise funds to support current operations and future growth. It is reasonable to assume that investors will provide funds to firms only if they believe the funds will be used "appropriately." But, how do investors know when their funds are used "appropriately," or when a firm is doing well? To answer this question, we need to understand the goals of the firm and the way financial managers can contribute to achieving these goals. Therefore, the purpose of this chapter is to give you an overview of business organizations, including appropriate goals that should be pursued by financial managers and how finance fits in a firm's organizational structure. In addition, because taxes affect every financial decision, whether related to individuals or businesses, we discuss some key features of the U.S. tax laws.

Alternative Forms of Business Organization

There are three main forms of business organization: (1) sole proprietorships, (2) partnerships, and (3) corporations. In terms of numbers, about 75 percent of businesses are operated as proprietorships, nearly 7 percent are partnerships, and the remaining 18 percent are corporations. Based on dollar value of sales, however, almost 90 percent of all business is conducted by corporations, while the remaining 10 percent is generated by both partnerships and proprietorships.[1] Because most business is conducted by corporations, we will concentrate on them in this book. However, it is important to understand the differences among the three forms of business.

Sole Proprietorship

SOLE PROPRIETORSHIP
An unincorporated business owned by one individual.

A **sole proprietorship** is an unincorporated business owned by one individual, in which the sole owner has unlimited personal liability for any debts incurred by the business. Starting a proprietorship is fairly easy — just begin business operations. For instance, if you mowed yards when you were younger to earn money, you technically operated as a sole proprietorship. In most cases, though, even the smallest business must be licensed by the municipality (city, county, or state) in which it operates.

The proprietorship has three important advantages: (1) It is easily and inexpensively formed, (2) it is subject to few government regulations, and (3) the business is taxed like an individual, not a corporation.

The proprietorship also has three important limitations: (1) The proprietor has unlimited personal liability for business debts, which can result in losses that exceed the money he or she has invested in the company; (2) it is difficult for a proprietorship to obtain large sums of capital, because the firm's financial strength often is based on the financial strength of the sole owner; (3) transferring ownership is somewhat difficult — disposing of the business is similar to selling a house in that the proprietor has to seek out and negotiate with a potential buyer; and (4) the life of a business organized as a proprietorship is limited to the life of the individual who created it. For these reasons, individual proprietorships are confined primarily to small business operations. In fact, only about 1 percent of all proprietorships have assets that are valued at $1 million or greater, and nearly 90 percent have assets valued at $100,000 or less. However, businesses frequently are started as proprietorships and then are converted to corporations when their growth causes the disadvantages of being a proprietorship to outweigh the advantages.

Partnership

PARTNERSHIP
An unincorporated business owned by two or more persons.

A **partnership** is like a proprietorship, except there are two or more owners. Partnerships can operate under different degrees of formality, ranging from

---

[1]The statistics provided in this section are based on business tax filings reported by the Internal Revenue Service (IRS). Additional statistics can be found on the IRS website at http://www.irs.ustreas.gov/tax_stats.

informal, oral understandings to formal agreements filed with the secretary of the state in which the partnership does business. Most legal experts recommend that the partnership agreement be put in writing.

The advantages of a partnership are the same as for a proprietorship: (1) formation is easy and relatively inexpensive, (2) it is subject to few government regulations, and (3) the business is taxed like an individual, not a corporation.

The disadvantages also are similar to those associated with proprietorships: (1) unlimited liability, (2) limited life of the organization, (3) difficulty of transferring ownership, and (4) difficulty of raising large amounts of capital.

Regarding liability, the partners can potentially lose all of their personal assets, even those assets not invested in the business, because under partnership law each partner is liable for the debts of the business. Therefore, if any partner is unable to meet his or her *pro rata* claim in the event the partnership goes bankrupt, the remaining partners must make good on the unsatisfied claims, drawing on their personal assets if necessary. Thus, the business-related activities of any of the firm's partners can bring ruin to the other partners, even though those partners were not a direct party to such activities. For example, the partners of the national accounting firm Laventhol and Horwath, a huge partnership that went bankrupt at the end of 1992 as a result of suits filed by investors who relied on faulty audit statements, learned all about the perils of doing business as a partnership — they discovered that a Texas partner who audits a savings and loan that goes under can bring ruin to a millionaire New York partner who never went near the S&L.[2]

The first three disadvantages — unlimited liability, impermanence of the organization, and difficulty of transferring ownership — lead to the fourth, the difficulty partnerships have in attracting substantial amounts of funds. This is no particular problem for a slow-growing business, but if a business's products really catch on, and if it needs to raise large amounts of funds in order to capitalize on its opportunities, the difficulty in attracting funds becomes a real drawback. Thus, growth companies such as Hewlett-Packard and Microsoft generally begin life as a proprietorship or partnership, but at some point they find it necessary to convert to a corporation.

Corporation

CORPORATION
A legal entity created by a state, separate and distinct from its owners and managers, having unlimited life, easy transferability of ownership, and limited liability.

A **corporation** is a legal entity created by a state, which is separate and distinct from its owners and managers. This separateness gives the corporation three major advantages:

1. **Easy transferability of ownership interest.** Ownership interests can be divided into shares of stock, which, in turn, can be transferred far more easily than can proprietorship or partnership interests.

---

[2]However, it is possible to limit the liabilities of some of the partners by establishing a *limited partnership,* wherein one (or more) partner is designated the *general partner* and the others *limited partners.* Limited partnerships are quite common in the area of real estate investment, but they do not work well with most types of businesses, including accounting firms, because one partner rarely is willing to assume all of the risks of the business. Not long ago, large accounting firms reorganized themselves as *limited liability partnerships,* which are partnerships in which only the assets of the partnership and the "engagement" partner (partner in charge of the situation) are at risk.

2. **Unlimited life.** Because ownership is represented by shares of stock that do not mature, a corporation can continue after its original owners and managers no longer are part of the firm.

3. **Limited liability.** To illustrate the concept of limited liability, suppose you invested $10,000 to become a partner in a business that subsequently went bankrupt, owing creditors $1 million. Because the owners are liable for the debts of a partnership, you could be assessed for a share of the company's debt, and you could be held liable for the entire $1 million if your partners could not pay their shares — this is what we mean by unlimited liability. On the other hand, if you invested $10,000 in the stock of a corporation that then went bankrupt, your potential loss on the investment would be limited to your $10,000 investment.[3]

These three factors — unlimited life, easy transferability of ownership interest, and limited liability — make it much easier for corporations than for proprietorships or partnerships to raise money in the capital markets.

The corporate form of business offers significant advantages over proprietorships and partnerships, but it does have two primary disadvantages: (1) Corporate earnings are subject to double taxation — the earnings of the corporation are taxed, and then any earnings paid out as dividends are taxed again as income to the stockholders. (2) Setting up a corporation, and filing required state and federal reports, is more complex and time-consuming than for a proprietorship or a partnership.

CORPORATE CHARTER
A document filed with the secretary of the state in which the firm is incorporated that provides information about the company, including its name, address, directors, and amount of capital stock.

Although a proprietorship or a partnership can commence operations without much paperwork, setting up a corporation requires that the incorporators hire a lawyer to prepare a charter and a set of bylaws. The **corporate charter** includes the following information: (1) name of the proposed corporation, (2) types of activities it will pursue, (3) amount of capital stock, (4) number of directors, and (5) names and addresses of directors. The charter is filed with the secretary of the state in which the firm will be incorporated, and, when it is approved, the corporation is officially in existence.[4] Then, after the corporation is in operation, quarterly and annual financial and tax reports must be filed with state and federal authorities.

BYLAWS
A set of rules drawn up by the founders of the corporation that indicate how the company is to be governed; includes procedures for electing directors, whether common stock has a preemptive right, and how to change the bylaws when necessary.

The **bylaws** represent a set of rules drawn up by the founders of the corporation to aid in governing the internal management of the company. Included are such points as (1) how directors are to be elected (all elected each year, or perhaps one-third each year for three-year terms); (2) whether the existing stockholders will have the first right to buy any new shares the firm issues (the preemptive right); and (3) procedures for changing the bylaws themselves, should conditions require it.

The value of any business other than a very small one probably will be maximized if it is organized as a corporation for these reasons:[5]

---

[3]In the case of small corporations, the limited liability feature is often a fiction, because bankers and credit managers frequently require personal guarantees from the stockholders of small, weak businesses.

[4]A majority of major U.S. corporations are chartered in Delaware, which has, over the years, provided a favorable legal environment for corporations. It is not necessary for a firm to be headquartered, or even to conduct operations, in its state of incorporation.

[5]Each of these reasons (topics) will be discussed in more detail later in the text.

1. Limited liability reduces the risks borne by investors, and, other things held constant, *lower risk means higher value.*
2. Corporations can attract funds more easily than can unincorporated businesses, and these funds can be invested in *growth opportunities* that help increase the firm's value.
3. Corporate ownership can be transferred more easily than ownership of either a proprietorship or a partnership. Therefore, all else equal, investors would be willing to pay more for a corporation than a proprietorship or partnership — this means that the corporate form of organization can enhance the value of a business.
4. Corporations are taxed differently than proprietorships and partnerships, and some of the differences are beneficial for corporations.

As we will see later in the chapter, most firms are managed with value maximization in mind, which, in turn, has caused most large businesses to be organized as corporations.

 Self-Test Questions

What are the key differences among sole proprietorships, partnerships, and corporations?

Explain why the value of any business other than a very small one probably will be maximized if it is organized as a corporation.

Finance in the Organizational Structure of the Firm

Organizational structures vary from firm to firm, but Figure 5-1 presents a fairly typical picture of the role of finance within a corporation. The chief financial officer — who has the title of vice-president: finance — reports to the president. The financial vice-president's key subordinates are the treasurer and the controller. In most firms the treasurer has direct responsibility for managing the firm's cash and marketable securities, for planning how funds are raised, for selling stocks and bonds to raise funds, and for overseeing the corporate pension fund. The treasurer also supervises the credit manager, the inventory manager, and the director of capital budgeting (who analyzes decisions related to investments in fixed assets). The controller is responsible for the activities of the accounting and tax departments.

 Self-Test Question

Identify the two subordinates who report to the firm's chief financial officer, and indicate the primary responsibilities of each.

The Goals of the Corporation

Business decisions are not made in a vacuum — decision makers have some objective in mind. *Throughout this book we operate on the assumption that manage-*

FIGURE 5-1

Place of Finance in a Typical Business Organization

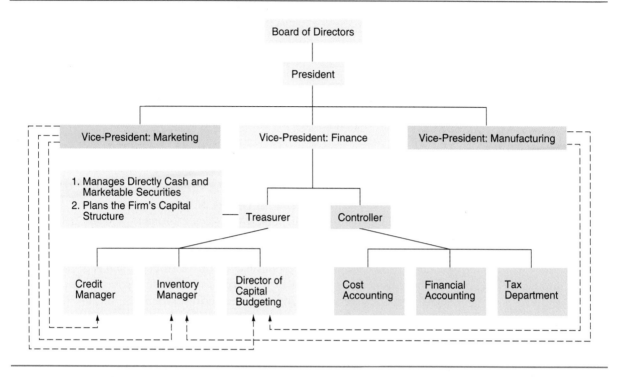

**STOCKHOLDER WEALTH
MAXIMIZATION**
The appropriate goal for
management decisions;
considers the risk and
timing associated with
expected earnings per
share in order to maximize
the price of the firm's
common stock.

ment's primary goal is **stockholder wealth maximization**, which, as we will
see, translates into *maximizing the value of the firm, which is measured by the
price of the firm's common stock.* Firms do, of course, have other objectives — in
particular, managers, who make the actual decisions, are interested in their own
personal satisfaction, in their employees' welfare, and in the good of the community and of society at large. Still, for the reasons set forth in the following sections,
stock price maximization is the principal goal of most corporations.

Managerial Incentives to Maximize Shareholder Wealth

It is the stockholders who own the firm and elect the management team. Management, in turn, is supposed to operate in the best interests of the stockholders.
As a stockholder of a company, you probably would want the managers to make
decisions that would maximize the value of the stock you own, including dividends. We know, however, that because the stock of most large firms is widely
held, ownership is dispersed and managers of large corporations have a great deal
of latitude in making business decisions. This being the case, might not managers
pursue goals other than stock price maximization? For example, some have
argued that the managers of a large, well-established corporation could work just
hard enough to keep stockholder returns at a "reasonable" level and then devote
the remainder of their efforts and resources to public service activities, to
employee benefits, to higher executive salaries, or to golf.

It is almost impossible to determine whether a particular management team
is trying to maximize shareholder wealth or is merely attempting to keep

stockholders satisfied while pursuing other goals. For example, how can we tell whether employee or community benefit programs are in the long-run best interests of the stockholders? Similarly, are relatively high executive salaries really necessary to attract and retain excellent managers, or just another example of managers taking advantage of stockholders?

It is impossible to give definitive answers to these questions. However, we do know that the managers of a firm operating in a competitive market will be forced to undertake actions that are reasonably consistent with shareholder wealth maximization. If they depart from this goal, they run the risk of being removed from their jobs. We will have more to say about the conflict between managers and shareholders later in the chapter.

Social Responsibility

SOCIAL RESPONSIBILITY
The concept that businesses should be actively concerned with the welfare of society at large.

NORMAL PROFITS/RATES OF RETURN
Those profits and rates of return that are close to the average for all firms and are just sufficient to attract capital.

Another issue that deserves consideration is **social responsibility**: Should businesses operate strictly in their stockholders' best interests, or are firms also responsible for the welfare of their employees, customers, and the communities in which they operate? Certainly firms have an ethical responsibility to provide a safe working environment, to avoid polluting the air or water, and to produce safe products. However, socially responsible actions have costs, and it is questionable whether businesses would incur these costs voluntarily. If some firms do act in a socially responsible manner while others do not, then the socially responsible firms will be at a disadvantage in attracting funds. To illustrate, suppose the firms in a given industry have **profits** and **rates of return on investment** that are close to **normal**, that is, close to the average for all firms and just sufficient to attract capital. If one company attempts to exercise social responsibility, it will have to raise prices to cover the added costs. If the other businesses in its industry do not follow suit, their costs and prices will be lower. The socially responsible firm will not be able to compete, and it will be forced to abandon its efforts. Thus, any voluntary socially responsible acts that raise costs will be difficult, if not impossible, in industries that are subject to keen competition.

What about oligopolistic firms, or firms that face little competition, with profits above normal levels — cannot such firms devote resources to social projects? Undoubtedly they can, and many large, successful firms do engage in community projects, employee benefit programs, and the like to a greater degree than would appear to be called for by pure profit or wealth maximization goals.[6] Still, publicly owned firms are constrained in such actions by capital market factors. To illustrate, suppose a saver who has funds to invest is considering two alternative firms. One firm devotes a substantial part of its resources to social actions, while the other concentrates on profits and stock prices. Most investors are likely to shun the socially oriented firm in favor of higher returns from other firms. Thus, the socially oriented firm would be at a disadvantage in the capital market. After all, why should the stockholders of one corporation subsidize society to a greater extent than those of other businesses? For this reason, even highly profitable firms (unless they are closely held rather than publicly owned) generally are constrained against taking unilateral cost-increasing social actions.

---

[6]Even firms like these often find it necessary to justify such projects at stockholder meetings by stating that these programs will contribute to long-run profit maximization.

Does all this mean that firms should not exercise social responsibility? Not at all, but it does mean that most significant cost-increasing actions will have to be put on a *mandatory* rather than a voluntary basis, at least initially, to ensure that the burden falls uniformly on all businesses.

Stock Price Maximization and Social Welfare

If a firm attempts to maximize its stock price, is this good or bad for society? In general, it is good. Aside from such illegal actions as attempting to form monopolies, violating safety codes, and failing to meet pollution control requirements, *the same actions that maximize stock prices also benefit society.* First, note that stock price maximization requires efficient, low-cost plants that produce high-quality goods and services at the lowest possible cost. Second, stock price maximization requires the development of products that consumers want and need, so the profit motive leads to new technology, to new products, and to new jobs. Finally, stock price maximization necessitates efficient and courteous service, adequate stocks of merchandise, and well-located business establishments — these factors all are necessary to maintain a customer base that is necessary for producing sales, and thus profits. Therefore, actions that help a firm increase the price of its stock also are beneficial to society at large. This is why profit-motivated, free-enterprise economies have been so much more successful than socialistic and communistic economic systems. Because managerial finance plays a crucial role in the operation of successful firms, and because successful firms are absolutely necessary for a healthy, productive economy, it is easy to see why finance is important from a social standpoint.[7]

Self-Test Questions

What is management's primary goal?

What would happen if one firm attempted to exercise costly social responsibility, while its competitors did not exercise social responsibility?

How does the goal of stock price maximization benefit society at large?

Managerial Actions to Maximize Shareholder Wealth

PROFIT MAXIMIZATION
The maximization of the firm's net income.

To maximize the price of a firm's stock, what types of actions should its management take? First, consider the question of stock prices versus profits: Will **profit maximization** also result in stock price maximization? In answering this

---

[7]People sometimes argue that firms, in their efforts to raise profits and stock prices, increase product prices and gouge the public. In a reasonably competitive economy, which we have, prices are constrained by competition and consumer resistance. If a firm raises its prices beyond reasonable levels, it will simply lose its market share. Even giant firms such as General Motors lose business to the Japanese and Germans, as well as to Ford and Chrysler, if they set prices above levels necessary to cover production costs plus a "normal" profit. Of course, firms want to earn more, and they constantly try to cut costs, to develop new products, and so on, and thereby to earn above-normal profits. Note, though, that if they are indeed successful and do earn above-normal profits, those very profits will attract competition, which will eventually drive prices down, so again the main long-term beneficiary is the consumer.

EARNINGS PER SHARE (EPS)
Net income divided by the number of shares of common stock outstanding.

question, we must consider the matter of total corporate profits versus **earnings per share (EPS)**.

For example, suppose Xerox had 300 million shares outstanding and earned $1,200 million, or $4 per share (EPS). If you owned 100 shares of the stock, your share of the total profits would be $400. Now suppose Xerox sold another 300 million shares and invested the funds received in assets that produced $300 million of income. Total income would rise to $1,500 million, but earnings per share would decline from $4 to $2.50 = $1,500/600. Now your share of the firm's earnings would be only $250, down from $400. You (and other current stockholders) would have suffered an earnings dilution, even though total corporate profits had risen. Therefore, other things held constant, *if management is interested in the well-being of its current stockholders, it should concentrate on earnings per share rather than on total corporate profits.*

Will maximization of expected earnings per share always maximize stockholder welfare, or should other factors be considered? Think about the *timing of the earnings.* Suppose Xerox had one project that would cause earnings per share to rise by $0.20 per year for five years, or $1 in total, while another project would have no effect on earnings for four years but would increase earnings by $1.25 in the fifth year. Which project is better — in other words, is $0.20 per year for five years better or worse than $1.25 in Year 5? The answer depends on which project adds the most to the value of the stock, which, in turn, depends on the time value of money to investors. Thus, timing is an important reason to concentrate on wealth as measured by the price of the stock rather than on earnings alone.

Another issue relates to *risk.* Suppose one project is expected to increase earnings per share by $1, while another is expected to raise earnings by $1.20 per share. The first project is not very risky — if it is undertaken, earnings will almost certainly rise by about $1 per share. However, the other project is quite risky, so, although our best guess is that earnings will rise by $1.20 per share, we must recognize the possibility that there might be no increase whatsoever, or even a loss. Depending on how averse stockholders are to risk, the first project might be preferable to the second.

The riskiness inherent in projected earnings per share (EPS) also depends on *how the firm is financed.* As we shall see, many firms go bankrupt every year, and the greater the use of debt, the greater the threat of bankruptcy. *Consequently, while the use of debt financing might increase projected EPS, debt also increases the riskiness of projected future earnings.*

Another issue is the matter of paying dividends to stockholders versus retaining earnings and reinvesting them in the firm, thereby causing the earnings stream to grow over time. Stockholders like cash dividends, but they also like the growth in EPS that results from plowing earnings back into the business. The financial manager must decide exactly how much of the current earnings to pay out as dividends rather than to retain and reinvest — this is called the **dividend policy decision**. The optimal dividend policy is the one that maximizes the firm's stock price.

DIVIDEND POLICY DECISION
The decision as to how much of current earnings to pay out as dividends rather than to retain for reinvestment in the firm.

We see, then, that the firm's stock price is dependent on the following factors:

1. Projected earnings per share.
2. Timing of the earnings stream.
3. Riskiness of the projected earnings.

4. Use of debt.
5. Dividend policy.

Every significant corporate decision should be analyzed in terms of its effect on these factors and hence on the price of the firm's stock. For example, suppose Occidental Petroleum's coal division is considering opening a new mine. If this is done, can it be expected to increase EPS? Is there a chance that costs will exceed estimates, that prices and output will fall below projections, and that EPS will be reduced because the new mine was opened? How long will it take for the new mine to show a profit? How should the capital required to open the mine be raised? If debt is used, by how much will this increase Occidental's riskiness? Should Occidental reduce its current dividends and use the cash thus saved to finance the project, or should it maintain its dividends and finance the mine with outside funds? Managerial finance is designed to help answer questions like these, plus many more. In the chapters that follow, we present the methods used to provide managers and investors with information necessary to make "educated" decisions relating to such questions.

Self-Test Questions

Will profit maximization always result in stock price maximization?

Identify five factors that affect the firm's stock price, and explain the effects of each of them.

Agency Relationships

An *agency relationship* exists when one or more people which have *principal ownership rights* hire another person, or *agent,* to perform a service and then delegate decision-making authority to that agent — the agent acts on behalf of the principal. Important agency relationships exist (1) between stockholders and managers and (2) between stockholders and creditors (debtholders).

Stockholders versus Managers

AGENCY PROBLEM
A potential conflict of interest between (1) the principals (outside shareholders) and the agent (manager) or (2) stockholders and creditors (debtholders).

A potential **agency problem** arises whenever the manager of a firm owns less than 100 percent of the firm's common stock. If a firm is a proprietorship managed by the owner, the owner-manager will presumably operate the business in a fashion that will improve his or her own welfare, with welfare measured in the form of increased personal wealth, more leisure, or perquisites.[8] However, if the owner-manager incorporates and sells some of the firm's stock to outsiders, a potential conflict of interests arises immediately. For example, the owner-manager might now decide not to work as hard to maximize shareholder wealth because less of this wealth will go to him or her, or to take a higher salary or enjoy more perquisites because part of those costs will be borne by the outside stockholders.

---

[8]Perquisites are executive fringe benefits such as luxurious offices, use of corporate planes and yachts, personal assistants, and general use of business assets for personal purposes.

This potential conflict between two parties, the principals (outside shareholders) and the agent (manager), is an agency problem.

In general, if a conflict of interest exists, what can be done to ensure that management treats the outside stockholders fairly? Several mechanisms are used to motivate managers to act in the shareholders' best interests. These include (1) the threat of firing, (2) the threat of takeover, and (3) managerial compensation.

1. **The threat of firing.** It wasn't long ago that the management teams of large firms felt secure in their positions, because the chances of being ousted by stockholders were so remote that managers rarely felt their jobs were in jeopardy. This situation existed because ownership of most firms was so widely distributed, and management's control over the proxy (voting) mechanism was so strong, that it was almost impossible for dissident stockholders to gain enough votes to overthrow the managers. However, today much of the stock of an average large corporation is owned by a relatively few large institutions rather than by thousands of individual investors, and the institutional money managers have the clout to influence a firm's operations. Major corporations whose managements have been ousted include United Airlines, Disney, and IBM.

HOSTILE TAKEOVER
The acquisition of a company over the opposition of its management.

2. **The threat of takeover. Hostile takeovers** (where management does not want the firm to be taken over) are most likely to occur when a firm's stock is undervalued relative to its potential. In a hostile takeover, the managers of the acquired firm generally are fired, and any who are able to stay on lose the power they had prior to the acquisition. Thus, managers have a strong incentive to take actions that maximize stock prices. In the words of one company president, "If you want to keep control, don't let your company's stock sell at a bargain price."

Actions to increase the firm's stock price and to keep it from being a bargain obviously are good from the standpoint of the stockholders, but other tactics that managers can use to ward off a hostile takeover might not be. Two examples of questionable tactics are *poison pills* and *greenmail.* A **poison pill** is an action a firm can take that practically kills it when certain events or actions are taken, and thus makes it unattractive to potential suitors. Examples include Disney's plan to sell large blocks of its stock at low prices to "friendly" parties, Scott Industries' decision to make all of its debt immediately payable if its management changed, and Carleton Corporation's decision to give huge retirement bonuses, which represented a large part of the company's wealth, to its managers if the firm was taken over (such payments are called *golden parachutes).* **Greenmail,** which is like blackmail, occurs when (a) a potential acquirer (firm or individual) buys a block of stock in a company, (b) the target company's management becomes frightened that the acquirer will make a takeover offer and gain control of the company and oust them, and (c) to head off a possible takeover, management offers to pay greenmail, buying the stock owned by the potential raider at a price above the existing market price without offering the same deal to other stockholders. A good example of greenmail was Disney's buy-back of 11.1 percent of its stock from Saul Steinberg's Reliance Group in 1984, which gave Steinberg a quick $60 million profit (he held the stock only a few months). The day the buy-back was announced, the price of Disney's stock dropped approximately 10 percent. A group of stockholders sued, and Steinberg and the Disney directors were forced to pay $45 million to Disney stockholders.

POISON PILL
An action taken by management to make a firm unattractive to potential buyers and thus to avoid a hostile takeover.

GREENMAIL
A situation in which a firm, trying to avoid a takeover, buys back stock at a price above the existing market price from the person(s) trying to gain control of the firm.

3. **Structuring managerial incentives.** Increasingly, firms are tying managers' compensation to the company's performance, and this motivates managers to operate in a manner consistent with stock price maximization.

EXECUTIVE STOCK OPTION
A type of incentive plan that allows managers to purchase stock at some future time at a given price.

In the 1950s and 1960s, most performance-based incentive plans involved **executive stock options**, which allowed managers to purchase stock at some future time at a given price. Because the value of the options was tied directly to the price of the stock, it was assumed that granting options would provide an incentive for managers to take actions that would maximize the stock's price. This type of managerial incentive lost favor in the 1970s, however, because the general stock market declined, and stock prices did not necessarily reflect companies' earnings growth. Incentive plans should be based on those factors over which managers have control, and because they cannot control the general stock market, stock option plans were not good incentive devices. Therefore, while 61 of the 100 largest U.S. firms used stock options as their sole incentive compensation in 1970, not even one of the largest 100 companies relied *exclusively* on such plans in 1998.

PERFORMANCE SHARES
A type of incentive plan in which managers are awarded shares of stock on the basis of the firm's performance over given intervals with respect to earnings per share or other measures.

An important incentive plan now is **performance shares**, which are shares of stock given to executives on the basis of performance as measured by earnings per share, return on assets, return on equity, and so on. For example, Honeywell uses growth in earnings per share as its primary performance measure. If the company achieves a targeted average growth in earnings per share, the managers will earn 100 percent of their shares. If the corporate performance is above the target, Honeywell's managers can earn even more shares. But, if growth is below the target, they get less than 100 percent of the shares.

All incentive compensation plans — executive stock options, performance shares, profit-based bonuses, and so forth — are designed to accomplish two things. First, these plans provide inducements to executives to act on those factors under their control in a manner that will contribute to stock price maximization. Second, the existence of such performance plans helps companies attract and retain top-level executives. Well-designed plans can accomplish both goals.

Stockholders versus Creditors

A second agency problem involves conflicts between stockholders and creditors (debtholders). Creditors lend funds to the firm at rates that are based on (1) the riskiness of the firm's existing assets, (2) expectations concerning the riskiness of future asset additions, (3) the firm's existing capital structure (i.e., the amount of debt financing it uses), and (4) expectations concerning future capital structure changes. These are the factors that determine the riskiness of the firm's debt, so creditors base the interest rate they charge on expectations regarding these factors.

Now suppose the stockholders, acting through management, cause the firm to take on new ventures that have much greater risk than was anticipated by the creditors. This increased risk will cause the value of the outstanding debt to fall. If the risky ventures turn out to be successful, all of the benefits will go to the stockholders because the creditors only get a fixed return. However, if things go sour, the bondholders will have to share the losses. What this amounts to, from the stockholders' point of view, is a game of "heads I win, tails you lose," which obviously is not a good game for the bondholders.

Similarly, if the firm increases its use of debt in an effort to boost the return to stockholders, the value of the old debt will decrease, so we have another "heads I win, tails you lose" situation. To illustrate, consider what happened to RJR Nabisco's bondholders when, in 1988, RJR's chief executive officer announced his plan to take the company private with funds the company would borrow (termed a *leveraged buyout*). Stockholders saw their shares jump in value from $56 to over $90 in just a few days, but RJR's bondholders suffered losses of approximately 20 percent. Investors immediately realized that taking RJR Nabisco private would cause the amount of its debt to rise dramatically, and thus its riskiness would soar. This, in turn, led to a huge decline in the price of RJR's outstanding bonds. Ultimately, RJR's management was not successful in its buyout attempt. But, Nabisco was purchased by another company for more than $100 per share — what a gain for the stockholders!

Can and should stockholders, through their managers/agents, try to expropriate wealth from the firm's creditors? In general, the answer is no. First, because such attempts have been made in the past, creditors today protect themselves reasonably well against stockholder actions through restrictions in credit agreements (covenants). Second, if potential creditors perceive that a firm will try to take advantage of them in unethical ways, they will either refuse to deal with the firm or require a much higher than normal rate of interest to compensate for the risks of such "sneaky" actions. Thus, firms that try to deal unfairly with creditors either lose access to the debt markets or are saddled with higher interest rates, both of which decrease the long-run value of the stock.

STAKEHOLDERS
Individuals or entities that have an interest in the well-being of a firm — stockholders, creditors, employees, customers, suppliers, and so on.

In view of these constraints, it follows that the goal of maximizing shareholder wealth requires fair play with creditors: Stockholder wealth depends on continued access to capital markets, and access depends on fair play and abiding by both the letter and the spirit of credit agreements. Managers, as agents of both the creditors and the stockholders, must act in a manner that is fairly balanced between the interests of these two classes of security holders. Similarly, because of other constraints and sanctions, management actions that would expropriate wealth from any of the firm's **stakeholders** (employees, customers, suppliers, and the like) will ultimately be to the detriment of shareholders. Therefore, maximizing shareholder wealth requires the fair treatment of all stakeholders.

Self-Test Questions

What is an agency relationship, and what two major agency relationships affect managerial finance?

Give some examples of potential agency problems between stockholders and managers.

List several factors that motivate managers to act in the shareholders' interests.

Give an example of how an agency problem might arise between stockholders and creditors.

The External Environment

Although managerial actions affect the value of a firm's stock, external factors also influence stock prices. Included among these factors are legal constraints, the gen-

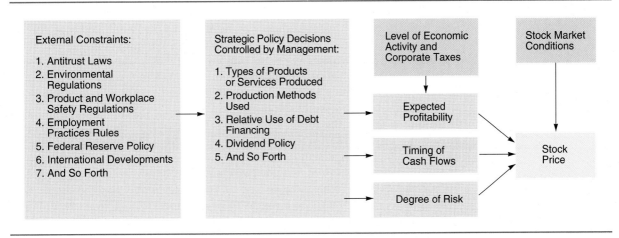

Summary of Major Factors Affecting Stock Prices

eral level of economic activity, the tax laws, and conditions in the stock market. Figure 5-2 diagrams these general relationships. Working within the set of external constraints shown in the box at the extreme left, management makes a set of long-run strategic policy decisions that chart a future course for the firm. These policy decisions, along with the general level of economic activity and the level of corporate income taxes, influence the firm's expected profitability, the timing of its cash flows, their eventual transfer to stockholders in the form of dividends, and the degree of risk inherent in projected earnings and dividends. Profitability, timing, and risk all affect the price of the firm's stock, but so does another factor, conditions in the stock market as a whole, because all stock prices tend to move up and down together to some extent.

Self-Test Question

Identify some factors beyond a firm's control that influence its stock price.

Business Ethics

BUSINESS ETHICS
A company's attitude and conduct toward its stakeholders (employees, customers, stockholders, and so forth); ethical behavior requires fair and honest treatment toward all parties.

The word *ethics* is defined in Webster's dictionary as "standards of conduct or moral behavior." **Business ethics** can be thought of as a company's attitude and conduct toward its employees, customers, community, and stockholders. High standards of ethical behavior demand that a firm treat each party that it deals with in a fair and honest manner. A firm's commitment to business ethics can be measured by the tendency of the firm and its employees to adhere to laws and regulations relating to such factors as product safety and quality, fair employment practices, fair marketing and selling practices, the use of confidential information for personal gain, community involvement, bribery, and illegal payments to foreign governments to obtain business.

There are many instances of firms engaging in unethical behavior. For example, since 1985, the employees of several prominent Wall Street investment banking houses have been sentenced to prison for illegally using insider information on proposed mergers for their own personal gain, and E. F. Hutton, a large brokerage firm, lost its independence through a forced merger after it was convicted of cheating its banks out of millions of dollars in a check kiting scheme. Drexel Burnham Lambert, one of the largest investment banking firms, went bankrupt, and its "junk bond king," Michael Milken, who had earned $550 million in just one year, was sentenced to ten years in prison plus charged a huge fine for securities-law violations. And, even more recently, Salomon Brothers Inc. was implicated in a Treasury-auction bidding scandal that resulted in the removal of key officers and a significant reorganization of the firm.

In spite of all this, the results of a recent study indicate that the executives of most major firms in the United States believe that their firms should, and do, try to maintain high ethical standards in all of their business dealings. Further, most executives believe that there is a positive correlation between ethics and long-run profitability because ethical behavior (1) avoids fines and legal expenses, (2) builds public trust, (3) attracts business from customers who appreciate and support the firm's policies, (4) attracts and keeps employees of the highest caliber, and (5) supports the economic viability of the communities in which it operates.

Most firms today have in place strong codes of ethical behavior, and they conduct training programs designed to ensure that all employees understand the correct behavior in different business situations. However, it is imperative that top management — the chairman, president, and vice-presidents — be openly committed to ethical behavior, and that they communicate this commitment through their own personal actions as well as through company policies, directives, and punishment/reward systems.

Self-Test Questions

How would you define "business ethics"?

Do you think "being ethical" is good for profits in the long run? In the short run?

Forms of Businesses in Other Countries

Large corporations in the United States can best be described as "open" companies because they are publicly traded organizations that, for the most part, are independent of each other as well as the government. And, as we described in previous sections, such companies offer limited liability to owners who usually do not participate in the day-to-day operations, and who can easily transfer ownership by trading stock in the capital markets. While most developed countries with free economies have similar types of business organizations as U.S. corporations, there exist some differences relating to ownership structure and management of operations. Although a comprehensive discussion is beyond the scope of this book, in this section, we provide some examples of differences between U.S. companies and non-U.S. companies.

Firms in most developed economies, such as corporations in the United States, offer equities with limited liability to stockholders that can be traded in domestic financial markets. Such firms are not always called corporations, though. For instance, a comparable firm in England is called a "public limited company," or

PLC, while in Germany it is known as an *Aktiengesellschaft,* or AG, and in Mexico, Spain, and Latin America it is called a *Sociedad Anónima,* or SA. Some of these firms are publicly traded, while others are privately held.

Like corporations in the United States, most of the large companies in England and Canada are "open," and the stock is widely dispersed among a number of different investors. Of note, though, is that about two-thirds of the traded stocks of English companies are owned by institutional investors rather than individuals. On the other hand, in much of continental Europe, stock ownership is more concentrated; major investor groups include families, banks, and corporations. In Germany and France, for instance, corporations represent the primary group of shareholders, followed by families. Although banks do not hold a large number of shares of stock, they can greatly influence companies because many shareholders assign banks their proxy votes. Also, often the family unit has concentrated ownership and thus is a major influence in many of the large companies in developed countries such as these. The ownership structures of these firms and many other non-U.S. companies, including very large organizations, are often concentrated in the hands of a relatively few investors or investment groups. Such firms are considered "closed" because shares of stock are not publicly traded, there are relatively few individuals or groups that own the stock, and major stockholders often are involved in the daily operations of the firms.

The primary reason non-U.S. firms are likely to be more "closed," thus have more concentrated ownership, than U.S. firms results from the "universal" banking relationships that exist outside the United States. Remember from our discussion in Chapter 3 that financial institutions in other countries generally are less regulated than in the United States, which means foreign banks, for instance, can provide businesses with a greater variety of services, including short-term loans, long-term financing, investment banking services, and even stock ownership. And, these services are available at many locations, or branches, throughout the country. Thus, non-U.S. firms tend to have a close relationship with individual banking organizations, which also might have ownership positions in the firms. What this means is that banks in countries such as Germany can meet the financing needs of family-owned businesses, even if they are very large, so such companies do not have to "go public," and thus relinquish some control, to finance additional growth. Consider the fact that in both France and Germany about 75 percent of the gross domestic product (GDP) comes from firms not publicly traded, or "closed" firms. The opposite is true in the United States, because large firms do not have "one-stop" financing outlets; thus, growth generally has to be financed by bringing in outside owners, which results in more widely dispersed ownership.

INDUSTRIAL GROUPS
Organizations comprised of companies in different industries with common ownership interests, which include firms necessary to manufacture and sell products — a network of manufacturers, suppliers, marketing organizations, distributors, retailers, and creditors.

In some parts of the world, firms are part of **industrial groups**, which are organizations comprised of companies in different industries with common ownership interests and, in some instances, shared management. Firms in the industrial group are "tied" by a major lender, typically a bank, which often also has a significant ownership interest along with other firms in the group. The objective of an industrial group is to include firms that provide materials and services required to manufacture and sell products; that is, to create an organization that ties together all the functions of production and sales from start to finish. Thus, an industrial group includes firms involved in manufacturing, financing, marketing, and distribution of products, which includes suppliers of raw materials, production organizations, retail stores, and creditors. A portion of the stocks of firms that are members of an industrial group might be traded publicly, but the "lead" company, which is typically a major creditor, controls the management of the entire group. Industrial groups are most prominent in Asian countries. In Japan, an industrial group is called a *keiretsu,* and it is called a *chaebol* in Korea. Well-known *keiretsu* groups include Mitsubishi, Toshiba, and Toyota, while the best known *chaebol* probably is Hyundai. The success of industrial groups in Japan and Korea has resulted in similar organizations in developing countries located in Latin America and Africa, as well as other parts of Asia.

The differences in ownership concentration of non-U.S. firms might cause the behavior of managers, thus the goals they pursue, to differ. For instance, it is often argued that the greater concentration of ownership of non-U.S. firms permits managers to focus more on long-term objectives, especially wealth maximization, than short-term earnings, because firms have easier access to credit in times of financial difficulty — creditors who also are owners generally have greater interest in supporting short-term survival. On the other hand, it also has been argued that the ownership structures of non-U.S. firms create an environment in which it is difficult to change managers, especially if they are significant stockholders. Such "entrenchment" could be very detrimental to firms if management is extremely inefficient. Consider, for example, firms in Japan that generally are very reluctant to fire employees, because losing your job is a disgrace in the Japanese culture. Whether the ownership structure of non-U.S. firms is an advantage or a disadvantage is debatable. But, we do know that the greater concentration of ownership in non-U.S. firms permits greater control by individuals or groups than the more dispersed ownership structures of U.S. firms.

Self-Test Questions

What is the primary difference between U.S. corporations and non-U.S. firms?

What is an industrial group?

What are some of the names given to firms in other countries?

Multinational Corporations

MULTINATIONAL CORPORATION
A firm that operates in two or more countries.

Large firms, both U.S. and non-U.S., generally do not operate in a single country; rather they do business throughout the world. In fact, the largest firms in the world truly are "multinational" rather than "domestic" operations. As you can see from the names in Table 5-1, the world's largest companies are those with operations in many countries. Managers of such "multinational" companies face a wide range of issues that are not present when a company operates in a single country. In this section, we highlight the key differences between multinational and domestic corporations, and we discuss the impact of these differences on managerial finance for U.S. businesses.

The term **multinational corporation** is used to describe a firm that operates in two or more countries. During the period since World War II, a new and fundamentally different form of international commercial activity has developed, and it has increased greatly worldwide economic and political interdependence. Rather than merely buying resources from foreign concerns, multinational firms now make direct investments in fully integrated operations, with worldwide entities controlling all phases of the production process — from extraction of raw materials, through the manufacturing process, to distribution to consumers

TABLE 5-1

The World's Largest Public Companies, 1997

Rank	Company Name	Country	Market Value (millions of dollars)
1	General Electric	United States	$214,454
2	Royal Dutch/Shell	Netherlands/ United Kingdom	177,537
3	Coca-Cola	United States	167,334
4	Nippon Telegraph	Japan	152,784
5	Exxon	United States	152,706
6	Microsoft	United States	151,438
7	Merck	United States	124,936
8	Intel	United States	116,144
9	Toyota Motors	Japan	111,924
10	Philip Morris	United States	107,778

SOURCE: *Wall Street Journal Interactive Edition,* http://www.wsj.com

throughout the world. Today, multinational corporate networks control a large and growing share of the world's technological, marketing, and productive resources.

There are five principal reasons companies, both U.S. and foreign, go "international":

1. **To seek new markets.** After a company has saturated its home market, growth opportunities are often better in foreign markets. Thus, such home-grown firms as Coca-Cola and McDonald's have aggressively expanded into overseas markets, and foreign firms such as Sony and Toshiba are major competitors in the U.S. consumer electronics market.

2. **To seek raw materials.** It is not surprising that many U.S. oil companies, such as Exxon, have major subsidiaries around the world to ensure access to the basic resources needed to sustain the company's primary business line.

3. **To seek new technology.** No single nation holds a commanding advantage in all technologies, so companies scour the globe for leading scientific and design ideas. For example, Xerox has introduced more than 80 different office copiers in the United States that were engineered and built by its Japanese joint venture, Fuji Xerox.

4. **To seek production efficiency.** Companies in high-production-cost countries are shifting production to low-cost countries. For example, GM has production and assembly plants in Mexico and Brazil, and even Japanese manufacturers have shifted some of their production to lower cost countries in the Pacific Rim. The ability to shift production from country to country has important implications for labor costs in all countries. For example, when Xerox threatened to move its copier rebuilding work to Mexico, its union in Rochester, New York, agreed to work rule and productivity improvements that kept the operation in the United States.

5. **To avoid political and regulatory hurdles.** The primary reason for Japanese auto companies to move production to the United States was to get around U.S. import quotas. Now, Honda, Nissan, and Toyota all assemble automobiles or trucks in the United States. Similarly, one of the factors that prompted U.S. pharmaceutical maker SmithKline and Britain's Beecham to merge was that they wanted to avoid licensing and regulatory delays in their largest markets, Western Europe and the United States. Now, SmithKline Beecham can identify itself as an inside player in both Europe and the United States.

During the 1980s and the 1990s, investments in the United States by foreign corporations have increased significantly. This "reverse" investment is of increasing concern to U.S. government officials because of its implication for eroding the traditional doctrine of independence and self-reliance that always has been a hallmark of U.S. policy. Just as U.S. corporations with extensive overseas operations are said to use their economic power to exert substantial economic and political influence over host governments around the world, it is feared that foreign corporations might gain similar sway over U.S. policy. However, these developments suggest an increasing degree of mutual influence and interdependence among business enterprises and nations, to which the United States is not immune.

During the past couple of decades, some dramatic international changes have taken place, including the breakup, both politically and economically, of the former Soviet Union, the collapse of communism in many Eastern European countries, the reunification of Germany, the political revolution in South Africa, and economic disasters in Japan and southeast Asia. Future events will include the continued phasing in of the European Economic Community with one Eurocurrency and the determination of how to help the cash-starved Eastern Bloc nations. Also, there has been a war with Iraq and continuing turbulence in the Middle East. These events, and others that surely will occur, have an impact on the world economy.

Self-Test Questions

What is a multinational corporation?

Why do companies go "international"?

Multinational versus Domestic Managerial Finance

In theory, the concepts and procedures we discuss in the remaining chapters of the text are valid for both domestic and multinational operations. However, several problems uniquely associated with the international environment increase the complexity of the manager's task in a multinational corporation, and they often force the manager to alter the way alternative courses of action are evaluated and compared. Six major factors distinguish managerial finance as practiced by firms operating entirely within a single country from management by firms that operate in several different countries:

1. **Different currency denominations.** Cash flows in various parts of a multinational corporate system are generally denominated in different currencies. Hence, an analysis of exchange rates, and the effects of fluctuating currency values, must be included in all financial analyses.
2. **Economic and legal ramifications.** Each country in which the firm operates will have its own unique political and economic institutions, and institutional differences among countries can cause significant problems when a firm tries to coordinate and control the worldwide operations of its sub-

sidiaries. For example, differences in tax laws among countries can cause a particular transaction to have strikingly dissimilar after-tax consequences, depending on where the transaction occurred. Similarly, differences in legal systems of host nations complicate many matters, from the simple recording of a business transaction to the role played by the judiciary in resolving conflicts. Such differences can restrict multinational corporations' flexibility to deploy resources as they wish, and they can even make procedures illegal in one part of the company that are required in another part. These differences also make it difficult for executives trained in one country to operate effectively in another.

3. **Language differences.** The ability to communicate is critical in all business transactions, and here persons who are American born and raised are often at a disadvantage because they are generally fluent only in English, while European and Japanese businesspeople are usually fluent in several languages, including English. Thus, it is easier for internationals to invade U.S. markets than it is for Americans to penetrate international markets.

4. **Cultural differences.** Even within geographic regions long considered fairly homogeneous, different countries have unique cultural heritages that shape values and influence the role of business in the society. Multinational corporations find that such matters as defining the appropriate goals of the firm, attitudes toward risk taking, dealings with employees, the ability to curtail unprofitable operations, and so on, can vary dramatically from one country to the next.

5. **Role of governments.** Most traditional models in finance assume the existence of a competitive marketplace in which the terms of trade are determined by the participants. The government, through its power to establish basic ground rules, is involved in this process, but its participation is minimal. Thus, the market provides both the primary barometer of success and the indicator of the actions that must be taken to remain competitive. This view of the process is reasonably correct for the United States and a few other major developed nations, but it does not accurately describe the situation in most of the world. Frequently, the terms under which companies compete, the actions that must be taken or avoided, and the terms of trade on various transactions are determined not in the marketplace, but by direct negotiation between the host government and the multinational corporation. This is essentially a political process, and it must be treated as such.

6. **Political risk.** The distinguishing characteristic of a nation that differentiates it from a multinational corporation is that the nation exercises sovereignty over the people and property in its territory. Hence, a nation is free to place constraints on the transfer of corporate resources and even to expropriate (take for public use) the assets of a firm without compensation. This is political risk, and it tends to be largely a given rather than a variable that can be changed by negotiation. Political risk varies from country to country, and it must be addressed explicitly in any financial analysis. Another aspect of political risk is terrorism against U.S. firms or executives abroad. For example, in years past, U.S. executives have been captured and held for ransom in several South American and Middle Eastern countries.

These six factors complicate managerial finance within multinational firms, and they increase the risks faced by the firms involved. However, prospects for high profits often make it worthwhile for firms to accept these risks, and to learn how to minimize or at least live with them.

Self-Test Question

Identify and briefly explain six major factors that complicate managerial finance within multinational firms.

The Federal Income Tax System

The value of any financial asset, including stocks, bonds, and mortgages, as well as the values of most real assets, such as manufacturing plants or even entire firms, depends on the stream of cash flows produced by the asset. For the most part, cash flows from an asset consist of usable income plus depreciation, and usable income means income after taxes. Therefore, in this section, we describe the federal tax system to show how cash flows produced both by individuals and businesses are influenced by taxes and to provide a fundamental background of the tax system in the United States.

Congress and the administration continuously debate the merits of different changes in the tax laws. Some people want to raise taxes to reduce our huge deficits and to help rebuild our inner cities. But, others think reducing taxes will help stimulate the economy and reduce deficits by producing greater revenues for the government. No matter the reason, it is clear the tax laws will change in coming years — they always do. Indeed, a major change has occurred, on average, every three to four years since 1913, when our federal income tax system began. Further, certain parts of our tax system are tied to the rate of inflation, so changes occur automatically each year, depending on the rate of inflation during the previous year. Therefore, although this section gives you a background on the basic nature of our tax system, you should consult current rate schedules and other data published by the Internal Revenue Service (and available in U.S. post offices, as well as on the Internet at http://www.irs.ustreas.gov) to determine your personal or business taxes.

Taxes are so complicated that university law schools offer master's degrees in taxation to practicing lawyers, many of whom also have CPA (Certified Public Accountant) certifications. In a field complicated enough to warrant such detailed study, we can cover only the highlights. This really is enough, though, because business managers and investors should, and do, rely on tax specialists rather than trusting their own limited knowledge. Still, it is important to know the basic elements of the tax system to understand the impact taxes have on cash flows.

Individual Income Taxes

PROGRESSIVE TAX
A tax that requires a higher percentage payment on higher incomes. The personal income tax in the U.S. is progressive.

Individuals pay taxes on wages and salaries, on investment income (dividends, interest, and profits from the sale of securities), and on the profits of *proprietorships and partnerships*. Our tax rates are **progressive** — that is, the higher one's income, the larger the percentage paid in taxes. The individual tax rates for 1998 are provided in Table 5A-1 in the appendix to this chapter. In this section, we discuss some of the general topics applicable to those who are affected by the individual tax code section:

TAXABLE INCOME
Gross income minus exemptions and allowable deductions as set forth in the Tax Code.

1. **Taxable income** is defined as gross income less a set of exemptions and deductions that are spelled out in the instructions to the tax forms individuals must file. When filing a tax return in 1999 for the tax year 1998, every taxpayer will receive an exemption of $2,700 for each dependent, including the taxpayer, which reduces taxable income. However, this exemption is indexed to rise with inflation, and the exemption is phased out for high-income taxpayers. Also, certain expenses, such as mortgage interest paid, state and local income taxes paid, and charitable contributions, can be deducted and thus be used to reduce taxable income; but again, high-income taxpayers lose some of this benefit.

MARGINAL TAX RATE
The tax applicable to the last unit of income.

2. The **marginal tax rate** is defined as the tax on the last unit of income. The marginal tax rate is represented by the tax bracket you are in. For example, if you are single and your taxable income is $50,000, then your marginal tax rate is 28 percent. As Table 5A-1 shows, marginal rates begin at 15 percent, rise to 28, then to 31 percent, and so on.

AVERAGE TAX RATE
Taxes paid divided by taxable income.

3. One can calculate **average tax rates** from the data in Table 5A-1. The average tax rate equals the percent of taxable income that is paid in taxes. For example, if Jill Smith, a single individual, had taxable income of $35,000, her tax bill would be $3,802.50 + ($35,000 − $25,350)(0.28) = $3,802.50 + $2,702.00 = $6,504.50. Her average tax rate would be $6,504.50/$35,000 = 18.6% versus a marginal rate of 28 percent. If Jill received a raise of $1,000, bringing her income to $36,000, she would have to pay $280 of it as taxes, so her after-tax raise would be $720. In addition, her Social Security and Medicare taxes would increase.

TAXES ON DIVIDEND AND INTEREST INCOME   Dividend and interest income received by individuals from investments is added to other income and thus is taxed at the rates shown in Table 5A-1. Because corporations pay dividends out of earnings that already have been taxed, there is *double taxation* of corporate income.

Under U.S. tax laws, interest on most state and local government bonds (municipals) is not subject to federal income taxes. Thus, investors get to keep all the interest received from most municipal bonds but only a fraction of the interest received from bonds issued by corporations or by the U.S. government. This means that a lower-yielding municipal bond can provide the same after-tax return as a higher-yielding corporate bond. For example, a taxpayer in the 31 percent marginal tax bracket who could buy a municipal bond that yielded 10 percent would have to receive a before-tax yield of 14.5 percent on a corporate or U.S. Treasury bond to have the same after-tax income:

$$\frac{\text{Equivalent pretax yield}}{\text{on a taxable investment}} = \frac{\text{Yield on tax-free investment}}{1 - \text{Marginal tax rate}}$$

$$= \frac{10\%}{1 - 0.31} = 14.5\%$$

If we know the yield on the taxable bond (investment), we can use the following equation to find the equivalent yield on a municipal bond or other tax-free investment:

$$\frac{\text{Yield on}}{\text{tax-free investment}} = \left(\frac{\text{Pretax yield on}}{\text{taxable investment}}\right) \times (1 - \text{Marginal tax rate})$$

$$= 14.5\% \times (1 - 0.31) = 14.5\%(0.69) = 10.0\%$$

The exemption from federal taxes stems from the separation of federal and state powers, and its primary effect is to help state and local governments borrow at lower rates than otherwise would be available to them.

INTEREST PAID BY INDIVIDUALS For the most part, the interest paid by individuals on loans is *not* tax deductible. The principal exception to this is the interest paid on mortgage financing used to purchase a house for personal residence, which is tax deductible. The effect of tax-deductible interest payments is to lower the actual cost of the mortgage to the tax payer. For example, if Staci Jones has an 8 percent mortgage on her house and she has an average tax rate equal to 30 percent, the after-tax cost of her mortgage is

$$\text{After-tax rate} = 8\%(1 - 0.30) = 5.6\%$$

CAPITAL GAINS VERSUS ORDINARY INCOME Assets such as stocks, bonds, and real estate are defined as *capital assets*. If you buy a capital asset and later sell it for more than your purchase price, the profit is called a **capital gain**; if you suffer a loss, it is called a **capital loss**. An asset sold within one year of the time it was purchased produces a *short-term gain or loss,* whereas one held for more than one year produces a *long-term gain or loss.* Thus, if you buy 100 shares of Disney stock for $100 per share and sell it for $110 per share, you will have a capital gain of $100 \times \$10$, or $1,000. However, if you sell the stock for $90 per share, you will have a $1,000 capital loss. If you hold the stock for more than one year, the gain or loss is long-term; otherwise, it is short-term. If you sell the stock for exactly $100 per share, you will have neither a gain nor a loss; you simply get back the $10,000 you originally invested, and no tax is due.

> **CAPITAL GAIN OR LOSS**
> The profit (loss) from the sale of a capital asset for more (less) than its purchase price.

While short-term capital gains are taxed at the same rate as other income, long-term capital gains traditionally have received favorable treatment. From 1921 through 1986, long-term capital gains were taxed at substantially lower rates than ordinary income. For example, in 1986 long-term capital gains were taxed at only 40 percent of the tax rate on ordinary income. The tax law changes that took effect in 1987 eliminated this differential, and from 1987 through 1990 all capital gains income (both long- and short-term) was taxed as if it were ordinary income. However, in 1990 the maximum tax rate on long-term capital gains was capped at 28 percent, and in 1998 the rate was changed so that the maximum rate was 20 percent for assets held greater than 12 months and 18 percent for assets held for more than five years.

There has been a great deal of controversy over the proper tax rate for capital gains. It has been argued that lower tax rates on capital gains (1) stimulate the flow of venture capital to new, startup businesses, which generally provide capital gains as opposed to dividend income, and (2) cause companies to retain and reinvest a high percentage of their earnings in order to provide their stockholders with lightly taxed capital gains as opposed to highly taxed dividend income. Thus, it has been argued that elimination of the favorable rates on capital gains has retarded investment and economic growth. The proponents of preferential capital gains tax rates lost the argument in 1986, but in 1990 and 1996 they did succeed in getting the rate capped at rates lower than the top marginal rate of about 40 percent. You should not be surprised if the capital gains differential is changed again sometime in the future.

BUSINESS VERSUS PERSONAL EXPENSES *Individuals* pay taxes on the income generated by proprietorships and partnerships they own — the income *"passes through"* to the owners of these types of businesses. Therefore, we need to differentiate business expenses, which are tax deductible, from personal expenses, which are not tax deductible. Generally speaking, an allowable business expense is a cost incurred to generate business revenues. On the other hand, if the expense is incurred for personal benefit (use), it is considered a personal expense. For instance, Loretta Kay owns a house in which she lived until last month, at which time she moved and rented the house to a group of college students. Three months ago, the plumbing burst in the kitchen, and Loretta had to call the plumber for repairs. The repairs cost $1,000. Is this a tax-deductible expense? No, because the house was Loretta's personal residence at the time. Last night, Loretta had to call the plumber again to fix pipes that had burst in the house she now has rented to the students — the repairs cost $1,200. Is this a tax-deductible expense? Yes, the expense was incurred for business purposes because the house is now rental property, which is considered a business operation.

Corporate Income Taxes

The corporate tax structure is shown in Table 5A-2 in Appendix 5A. The structure is similar to the individual rates. However, there are some areas in which the corporate tax code and the individual tax code differ significantly. We discuss some of the differences in this section.

INTEREST AND DIVIDEND INCOME RECEIVED BY A CORPORATION Interest income received by a corporation is taxed as ordinary income at regular corporate tax rates. However, 70 percent of the dividends received by one corporation from another corporation is excluded from taxable income, while the remaining 30 percent is taxed at the ordinary tax rate.[9] Thus, a corporation earning more than $12 million and paying a 35 percent marginal tax rate would pay only $(0.30)(0.35) = 0.105 = 10.5\%$ of its dividend income as taxes, so its effective tax rate on intercorporate

---

[9]The size of the dividend exclusion actually depends on the degree of ownership. Corporations that own less than 20 percent of the stock of the dividend-paying company can exclude 70 percent of the dividends received; firms that own more than 20 percent but less than 80 percent can exclude 80 percent of the dividends; and firms that own more than 80 percent can exclude the entire dividend payment. Because most companies own less than 20 percent of other companies, we will assume a 70 percent dividend exclusion.

dividends would be 10.5 percent. If this firm received $10,000 in dividends from another corporation, its after-tax dividend income would be $8,950:

$$\text{After-tax income} = \text{Before-tax income} - \text{Taxes}$$

$$= \$10,000 - \$10,000[(0.30)(0.35)]$$

$$= \$10,000(1 - 0.105) = \$10,000(0.895) = \$8,950$$

If the corporation that receives dividends pays its own after-tax income out to its stockholders as dividends, the income is ultimately subjected to triple taxation: (1) The original corporation is taxed first, (2) then the second corporation is taxed on the dividends it receives, and (3) the individuals who receive the final dividends are taxed again. This is the reason for the 70 percent exclusion on intercorporate dividends.

Interest and Dividends Paid by a Corporation   A firm's operations can be financed with either debt or equity capital. If the firm uses debt, it must pay interest on this debt (to banks and to bondholders), whereas if it uses equity, it will pay dividends to the equity investors (stockholders). The interest paid by a corporation is deducted from its operating income to obtain its taxable income, but the dividends paid are not deductible. Therefore, a firm needs $1 of pre-tax income to pay $1 of interest, but if it is in the 35 percent tax bracket, it needs $1.54 of pre-tax income to pay $1 of dividends:

$$\frac{\text{Pre-tax income needed}}{\text{to pay \$1 of dividends}} = \frac{\$1}{1 - \text{Tax rate}} = \frac{\$1}{1 - 0.35} = \$1.54$$

Of course, it generally is not possible to finance exclusively with debt capital, and the risk of doing so would offset the benefits of the higher expected income. Still, *the fact that interest is a deductible expense has a profound effect on the way businesses are financed — our tax system favors debt financing over equity financing.* This point is discussed in more detail in Chapters 10 and 11.

Corporate Capital Gains   Before 1987, corporate long-term capital gains were taxed at lower rates than ordinary income, as was true for individuals. Under current law, however, corporations' capital gains are taxed at the same rates as their operating income.

Corporate Loss Carryback and Carryover   Beginning in 1997, ordinary operating losses can be carried back (**carryback**) to each of the preceding two years (decreased from three years) and carried over (**carryover**) to the next 20 years (increased from 15 years) to offset taxable income in those years. For example, an operating loss reported in 1998 could be carried back and used to reduce taxable income in 1996 and 1997, and carried forward, if necessary, and used in 1999, 2000, and so on, to the year 2018 to offset future taxable income. The loss is applied first to the earliest year, then to the next earliest year, and so on, until losses have been used up or the 20-year carryover limit has been reached.

> **Tax Loss Carryback and Carryover**
> Losses that can be carried backward or forward in time to offset taxable income in a given year.

To illustrate, partial income statements for Apex Corporation are given in Table 5-2. In 1996 and 1997, Apex produced positive taxable income amounts, and it paid the appropriate taxes each of these years, which totaled $154 million. However, in 1998, Apex experienced a taxable loss equal to $700 million. The

TABLE 5-2

Apex Corporation: Partial Income Statements for 1996–1998 (millions of dollars)

	1996	1997	1998
Original Statement			
Taxable income	$260	$180	$(700)
Taxes (35%)	91	63	(245)
Net income	$169	$117	$(455)
			Total Effect of Carryback
Adjusted Statement			
Original taxable income	$260	$180	
Carryback credit	(260)	(180)	$440
Adjusted taxable income	0	0	
Taxes (35%)	0	0	
Adjusted net income	$ 0	$ 0	
Taxes originally paid	91	63	$154

Tax refund = $154

Loss available to carry forward in 1999–2018 = $700 − $440 = $260

carryback feature allows Apex to write off this taxable loss against positive taxable income beginning in 1996. Note, the loss is large enough that the *adjusted* taxable incomes for 1996 and 1997 equal zero. This permits Apex to recover the amount of taxes paid in those years. Thus, Apex would amend the tax forms filed in 1996 and 1997, and it would receive a tax refund equal to $154 million. After adjusting the previous two years' tax forms, Apex still would have $260 million of unrecovered loss from 1998 to carry forward through the year 2018, if necessary. The purpose of permitting firms to treat losses like this is to avoid penalizing corporations whose incomes fluctuate substantially from year to year.

ACCUMULATED EARNINGS TAX   Corporations could refrain from paying dividends to permit their stockholders to avoid personal income taxes on dividends. To prevent this, the Tax Code contains an **improper accumulation** provision that states that earnings accumulated by a corporation are subject to penalty rates *if the purpose of the accumulation is to enable stockholders to avoid personal income taxes.* A cumulative total of $250,000 (the balance sheet item "retained earnings") is by law exempted from the accumulated earnings tax for most corporations. This is a benefit primarily to small corporations.

The improper accumulation penalty applies only if the retained earnings in excess of $250,000 are shown to be *unnecessary to meet the reasonable needs of the business.* A great many companies do indeed have legitimate reasons for retaining more than $250,000 of earnings. For example, earnings might be retained and used to pay off debt, to finance growth, or to provide the corporation with a cushion against possible cash drains caused by losses. How much a firm should properly accumulate for uncertain contingencies is a matter of judgment.

IMPROPER ACCUMULATION Retention of earnings by a business for the purpose of enabling stockholders to avoid personal income taxes.

CONSOLIDATED CORPORATE TAX RETURNS   If a corporation owns 80 percent or more of another corporation's stock, it can aggregate income and file one consolidated tax return; thus, the losses of one company can be used to offset the profits of another. (Similarly, one division's losses can be used to offset another division's profits.) No business ever wants to incur losses (you can go broke losing $1 to save 34¢ in taxes), but tax offsets do make it more feasible for large, multidivisional corporations to undertake risky new ventures or ventures that will suffer losses during a developmental period and earn profits thereafter.

Taxation of Small Businesses: S Corporations

S CORPORATION
A small corporation that, under the Internal Revenue Code, elects to be taxed as a proprietorship or a partnership yet retains limited liability and other benefits of the corporate form of organization.

The Internal Revenue Code provides that small businesses (fewer than 75 stockholders) that meet certain restrictions as spelled out in the code can be set up as corporations and thus receive the benefits of the corporate form of organization — especially limited liability — yet still be taxed as proprietorships or partnerships rather than as corporations. These corporations are called **S corporations**. For a corporation that elects S corporation status for tax purposes, all of the income of the business is reported as personal income by the owners, and it is taxed at the rates that apply to individuals. This would be preferred by owners of small corporations in which all or most of the income earned each year is distributed as dividends because the income would be taxed only once at the individual level.

Self-Test Questions

Explain what is meant by the statement: "Our tax rates are progressive."

Are tax rates progressive for all income ranges?

Explain the difference between marginal tax rates and average tax rates.

What are capital gains and losses, and how are they differentiated from ordinary income?

How does the federal income tax system tax corporate dividends received by a corporation and those received by an individual? Why is this distinction made?

Briefly explain how tax loss carry-back and carry-forward procedures work.

Corporate Tax Rates in Other Countries

Earlier in the chapter, we described some of the major differences between the organizational structures of U.S. and non-U.S firms. We discovered that much of the difference can be attributed to the regulatory environment that prevails in other countries — for the most part, non-U.S. firms are not exposed to as many regulations as U.S. firms. In addition, businesses in other countries do not face complicated tax laws such as those we have in the United States. Although a discussion of the structure of taxes in foreign countries is beyond the scope of this chapter, we can give you some indication of the tax rates multinational organizations face. Table 5-3 gives the tax rates applied to corporate earnings in various countries.

It is clear from the table that the corporate tax rates differ significantly among the various countries listed. Chile's tax rate is only 15 percent, while Germany has a rate that is nearly 57 percent on income not distributed to shareholders. On

---

TABLE 5-3

1998 Corporate Tax Rates for Selected Countries

	Tax Rate[a]
I. Developed Markets	
Australia	36.0%
Canada	44.6
France	41.7
Germany	56.7/43.6[b]
Italy	41.3
Japan	51.6
Netherlands	35.0
Switzerland	27.8
United Kingdom	31.0
United States	40.0
II. Emerging Markets	
Brazil	25.0
Chile	15.0
China, PR	33.0
India	35.0
Indonesia	30.0
Korea	30.8
Malaysia	28.0
Mexico	34.0
Philippines	34.0
Thailand	30.0

[a]The tax rates represent the maximum percent applied to income.

[b]The first number represents the average tax rate on earnings retained by the firm, and the second number represents the rate on earnings distributed to shareholders.

SOURCE: *KPMG Corporate Tax Rate Survey,* July 1998.

average, the tax rates of countries with developed markets are 5 to 10 percent higher than the rates of countries with emerging markets.

According to a survey by KPMG Peat Marwick, corporate tax rates are lowest in Latin America. Chile has the lowest tax rate of all the countries surveyed — 15 percent. Twelve other Latin American countries have rates that do not exceed 30 percent, and the rates in half of those countries are 25 percent or less. The low corporate tax rates in Latin American countries have helped attract some of the operations of multinational firms, which have bolstered the economic conditions, in this region of the world.

 Self-Test Question

Why might one country have a lower corporate tax rate than other countries?

Depreciation

Depreciation is the means by which the price of a long-term asset is written off, or expensed, over time. Depreciation plays an important role in income tax calculations. Congress specifies, in the Tax Code, the life over which assets can be depreciated for tax purposes and the methods of depreciation that can be used. Because these factors have a major influence on the amount of depreciation a firm can take in a given year, and thus on the firm's taxable income, depreciation has an important effect on taxes paid and cash flows from operations. Because depreciation relates to the valuation of long-term, or capital, assets, we will discuss how it is calculated, and how it affects income and cash flows, when we discuss the subject of capital budgeting in Chapter 9.

ETHICAL DILEMMA

Chances Are What They Don't Know Won't Hurt Them!

Futuristic Electronic Technologies (FET) recently released a new advanced electronic microsystem to be used by financial institutions, large corporations, and governments to process and store financial data, including taxes, automatic payroll payments, and so on. Even though the technology used in the creation of the product was developed by FET, it is expected FET's competitors will soon possess similar technology. In order to beat the competition to the market, FET introduced its new microsystem a little earlier than originally planned. In fact, laboratory testing had not been fully completed before the product reached the market. The tests are complete now, and the final results suggest the microsystem might be flawed with respect to how some data are retrieved and processed. The tests are not conclusive, though, and even if additional testing proves a flaw does exist, according to FET, it is of minuscule importance because the problem seems to occur for only 1 out of 100 million retrieval and processing attempts. The financial ramifications associated with the flaw are unknown at this time.

Assume you are one of FET's senior executives whose annual salary is based on the performance of the firm's common stock. You realize that if FET recalls the affected microsystem the stock price will suffer, thus your salary for the year will be less than you expected. To complicate matters, you just purchased a very expensive house based on your salary expectations for the next few years — those expectations will not come true unless the new microsystem is a success for FET. As one of the senior executives, you will help determine what course of action FET will follow with respect to the microsystem. What should you do? Should you encourage FET to recall the microsystem until further testing is completed? Or, is there another course of action you can suggest?

SMALL BUSINESS

Goals and Resources in the Small Firm

Although small business is a vital contributor to the financial health of our economy, the businesses themselves are often fragile and susceptible to failure because of poor management, particularly financial management.

Significant differences exist between small and big businesses regarding the way they are owned, the way they are managed, and the financial and managerial resources at their disposal. These differences make it necessary to modify managerial finance principles for application in the small business area. Two especially important differences are resource shortages and goal conflicts.

RESOURCE SHORTAGES

It is not unusual for the founders of a small business to have full responsibility for all phases of the firm's operations. In fact in many cases, these individuals are reluctant to relinquish any responsibilities, even when the firm grows significantly. Thus, management in small firms often is spread very thin, with one or two key individuals taking on far more responsibility than they can handle properly. If you talk to small business operators, you often will hear, "This is my business, and I need to keep active in every aspect of the operation in order to monitor its pulse — no one can do this for me."

Continued

SMALL BUSINESS

Continued

Unfortunately, it is this attitude that keeps most small businesses small.

Not only is management often spread thin in small firms, but such firms have great difficulty acquiring the new funds needed for expansion. Until a firm achieves a fairly substantial size, say, $15 million or so in sales, it cannot sell stock or bonds to the general public. Further, if the company does have a public stock offering at the first opportunity, its costs will be quite high in comparison with larger firms' costs of issuing stock. For example, it took Richard Smyth four tries and substantial expense to find a company that was willing to underwrite a $5.5 million initial public offering for Vista 2000 Inc., a small firm that develops and markets home safety devices in Roswell, Georgia. In general, small firms have very limited access to public capital markets. Access to nonpublic markets also is limited. For example, banks sometimes are reluctant to lend substantial amounts to small firms that lack a financial history, and relatives' resources only extend so far.

Small firms thus have constraints both on their managerial talent and on their ability to obtain adequate capital. It is no wonder small firms often fail, given their poor (or overworked) management and lack of capital.

GOAL CONFLICTS

Small businesses also differ from large firms with regard to corporate goals. Earlier in the chapter we pointed out that share price maximization is taken to be the goal of all firms. For a small firm, often the owner's livelihood is the business, because a substantial portion of the owner's wealth is bet on the success of the business. Generally, the small business owner is not diversified at all — every bit of wealth is invested in the business.

Given this level of commitment and lack of a fall-back position, small business owners take a very different posture toward risk-taking than would a typical investor in a public company. Most public investors hold a well-diversified portfolio of assets, and their employment incomes generally come from jobs in altogether separate industries. On the other hand, both the salary and investment income of a small business owner are generally dependent on the success of one company. This makes the risk exposure of the small business owner quite high.

The owner-managers of small firms are keenly interested in the value of their firms, even if this value cannot be observed in the market. But the motives of small business owners are complex. Some owners are motivated primarily by such considerations as the desire to be their "own boss," even if this means not letting the firm grow at the fastest rate possible or be as profitable as it could be. In other words, there is value to being in control, and that value is not easily measurable. As a result, we often observe small businesses taking actions, such as refusing to bring in new stockholders even when they badly need new capital, that do not make sense when judged on the basis of value maximization but that do make sense when seen in the light of the personal objectives of the owners.

To the extent that the goals of the small firm differ from value maximization, some of the prescriptions in this text might not be entirely applicable. However, most of the tools we develop will be useful for small businesses, even though the tools might have to be modified somewhat. In any event, brief "Small Business" boxes in various chapters will serve as our vehicle for discussing issues of special importance to small firms.

Summary

In this chapter, we described the forms of business organizations evident in the United States, as well as the primary objective such organizations should pursue. We also indicated some of the differences between U.S. firms and non-U.S. firms and provided reasons a firm might choose to be a multinational organization. The end of the chapter contains a description of the taxes in the United States, and how taxes affect individuals and businesses. The key concepts covered in the chapter are listed below.

- The three main forms of business organization are the **proprietorship**, the **partnership**, and the **corporation**.

- Although each form of organization offers some advantages and disadvantages, **most business is conducted by corporations because this organizational form maximizes most firms' values.**
- The **primary goal** of management should be to **maximize stockholders' wealth**, and this means **maximizing the price of the firm's stock.** Further, actions that maximize stock prices also increase social welfare.
- An **agency problem** is a potential conflict of interests that can arise between (1) the owners of the firm and its management or (2) the stockholders and the creditors (debtholders).
- There are a number of ways to **motivate managers to act in the best interests of stockholders**, including (1) the **threat of firing**, (2) the **threat of takeovers**, and (3) properly structured **managerial incentives.**
- The **price of the firm's stock** depends on the firm's **projected earnings per share**, the **timing of its earnings**, the **riskiness of the projected earnings**, its **use of debt**, and its **dividend policy.**
- **Non-U.S. firms** generally have more concentrated ownership than U.S. firms. In some cases, firms in other countries are part of an **industrial group**, which is a network of firms with common ownership ties, that provides the different functions required to manufacture and sell a product from "start to finish." Examples of industrial groups include the *keiretsu* in Japan and the *chaebol* in Korea.
- **International operations** have become increasingly important to individual firms and to the national economy. A **multinational corporation** is a firm that operates in two or more nations.
- Companies go "international" for five primary reasons: (1) to **seek new markets**, (2) to **seek raw materials**, (3) to **seek new technology**, (4) to **seek production efficiency**, and (5) to **avoid trade barriers.**
- Six major factors distinguish managerial finance as practiced by domestic firms from that of multinational corporations: (1) **different currency denominations**, (2) **economic and legal ramifications**, (3) **languages**, (4) **cultural differences**, (5) **role of governments**, and (6) **political risk.**
- The value of any asset depends on the stream of **after-tax cash flows** it produces. Tax rates and other aspects of our tax system are changed by Congress every few years.
- In the United States, income tax rates are *progressive* — the higher one's income, the larger the percentage paid in taxes, up to a point.
- Assets such as stocks, bonds, and real estate are defined as **capital assets**. If a capital asset is sold for more than the purchase price, the profit is called a **capital gain**. If the capital asset is sold for a loss, it is called a **capital loss**. A capital gain earned by individuals might be taxed at a rate less than ordinary income, depending on how long the asset is held.
- **Interest income** received by a corporation is taxed as ordinary income; however, **70 percent of the dividends received by one corporation from another is excluded from taxable income.**
- Because **interest paid by a corporation is a deductible expense** while dividends are not, our tax system favors debt financing over equity financing.
- Ordinary corporate operating losses can be **carried back** to each of the preceding 2 years and **carried forward** for the next 20 years to offset taxable income in those years.

- **S corporations** are small businesses that have the limited-liability benefits of the corporate form of organization yet obtain the benefits of being taxed as a partnership or a proprietorship.

Questions

5-1 What are the three principal forms of business organization? What are the advantages and disadvantages of each?

5-2 Would the "normal" rate of return on investment be the same in all industries? Would "normal" rates of return change over time? Explain.

5-3 Would the role of the financial manager be likely to increase or decrease in importance relative to other executives if the rate of inflation increased? Explain.

5-4 Should stockholder wealth maximization be thought of as a long-term or a short-term goal? For example, if one action would probably increase the firm's stock price from a current level of $20 to $25 in six months and then to $30 in five years, but another action would probably keep the stock at $20 for several years but then increase it to $40 in five years, which action would be better? Can you think of some specific corporate actions that might have these general tendencies?

5-5 Drawing on your background in accounting, can you think of any accounting procedure differences that might make it difficult to compare the relative performance of different firms?

5-6 Would the management of a firm in an oligopolistic or in a competitive industry be more likely to engage in what might be called "socially conscious" practices? Explain your reasoning.

5-7 What is the difference between stock price maximization and profit maximization? Under what conditions might profit maximization not lead to stock price maximization?

5-8 If you were the president of a large, publicly owned corporation, would you make decisions to maximize stockholders' welfare or your own personal interests? What are some actions stockholders could take to ensure that management's interests and those of stockholders coincided? What are some other factors that might influence management's actions?

5-9 The president of United Semiconductor Corporation made this statement in the company's annual report: "United's primary goal is to increase the value of the common stockholders' equity over time." Later on in the report, the following announcements were made:

   a. The company contributed $1.5 million to the symphony orchestra in San Francisco, its headquarters city.

   b. The company is spending $500 million to open a new plant in Mexico. No revenues will be produced by the plant for 4 years, so earnings will be depressed during this period versus what they would have been had the decision not been made to open the new plant.

   c. The company is increasing its relative use of debt. Whereas assets were formerly financed with 35 percent debt and 65 percent equity, henceforth the financing mix will be 50-50.

   d. The company uses a great deal of electricity in its manufacturing operations, and it generates most of this power itself. Plans are to utilize nuclear fuel rather than coal to produce electricity in the future.

     e. The company has been paying out half of its earnings as dividends and retaining the other half. Henceforth, it will pay out only 30 percent as dividends.

        Discuss how each of these actions would be reacted to by United's stockholders, customers, and labor force, and then how each action might affect United's stock price.

5-10 Why do U.S. corporations build manufacturing plants abroad when they could build them at home?

5-11 Compared with the ownership structure of U.S. firms, which are "open" companies, what are some advantages of the ownership structure of non-U.S. firms, many of which are "closed" companies? Can you think of any disadvantages?

5-12 Suppose you owned 100 shares of General Motors stock, and the company earned $6 per share during the last reporting period. Suppose further that GM could either pay all its earnings out as dividends (in which case you would receive $600) or retain the earnings in the business, buy more assets, and cause the price of the stock to go up by $6 per share (in which case the value of your stock would rise by $600).

     a. How would the tax laws influence what you, as a typical stockholder, would want the company to do?

     b. Would your choice be influenced by how much other income you had? Why might the desires of a 35-year-old doctor differ with respect to corporate dividend policy from those of a pension fund manager or a retiree living on a small income?

     c. How might the corporation's decision with regard to the dividends it pays influence the price of its stock?

5-13 What does *double taxation of corporate income* mean?

5-14 If you were starting a business, what tax considerations might cause you to prefer to set it up as a proprietorship or a partnership rather than as a corporation? Would you consider the average or the marginal tax rate more relevant?

5-15 Explain how the federal income tax structure affects the choice of financing (use of debt versus equity) of U.S. business firms.

Self-Test Problems   *Solutions Appear in Appendix B*

Key terms   **ST-1** Define each of the following terms:

     a. Proprietorship; partnership; corporation
     b. Stockholder wealth maximization
     c. Hostile takeover
     d. Social responsibility; business ethics
     e. Normal profits; normal rate of return
     f. Agency problem; agency costs
     g. Poison pill; greenmail
     h. Performance shares; executive stock option
     i. Profit maximization
     j. Earnings per share
     k. Dividend policy decision
     l. Multinational corporation
     m. Political risk
     n. Industrial group; *chaebol*; *keiretsu*
     o. Progressive tax
     p. Marginal and average tax rates
     q. Capital gain or loss

r. Tax loss carry-back and carry-forward

s. S corporation

Form of business and taxes **ST-2** John Thompson is planning to start a new business, JT Enterprises, and he must decide whether to incorporate or to do business as a sole proprietorship. Under either form, Thompson will initially own 100 percent of the firm, and tax considerations are important to him. He plans to finance the firm's expected growth by drawing a salary just sufficient for his family living expenses, which he estimates will be about $40,000, and by retaining all other income in the business. Assume that as a married man with one child, Thompson has income tax exemptions of 3 × $2,700 = $8,100, and he estimates that his itemized deductions for each of the 3 years will be $9,000. He expects JT Enterprises to grow and to earn income of $60,000 in 2000, $90,000 in 2001, and $110,000 in 2002. Which form of business organization will allow Thompson to pay the lowest taxes (and retain the most income) during the period from 2000 to 2002? Assume that the tax rates given in Appendix 5A are applicable for all future years. (Social Security taxes would also have to be paid, but ignore them.)

Problems

Note: By the time this book is published, Congress may have changed rates and/or other provisions of current tax law — as noted in the chapter, such changes occur fairly often. Work all problems on the assumption that the information in the chapter is still current.

Loss carryback, carryover **5-1** The Angell Company has made $150,000 before taxes during each of the last 15 years, and it expects to make $150,000 a year before taxes in the future. However, in 1998 the firm incurred a loss of $650,000. The firm claimed a tax credit at the time it filed its 1998 income tax return, and it will receive a check from the U.S. Treasury. Show how it calculated this credit, and then indicate the firm's tax liability for each of the following 5 years. Assume a 30 percent tax rate on all income to ease the calculations.

Tax loss carryback, carryover **5-2** The projected taxable income of the Glasgo Corporation, formed in 1999, is indicated in the table below. (Losses are shown in parentheses.) What is the corporate tax liability for each year? Use tax rates as shown in the appendix.

Year	Taxable Income
1999	($ 95,000)
2000	70,000
2001	55,000
2002	80,000
2003	(150,000)

Form of organization **5-3** Kate Brown has operated her small repair shop as a sole proprietorship for several years, but projected changes in her business's income have led her to consider incorporating.

Brown is married and has two children. Her family's only income, an annual salary of $45,000, is from operating the business. (The business actually earns more than $45,000, but Kate reinvests the additional earnings in the business.) She itemizes deductions, and she is able to deduct $8,000. These deductions, combined with her four personal exemptions for 4 × $2,700 = $10,800, give her a taxable income of $45,000 − $8,000 − $10,800. (Assume the personal exemption remains at $2,700.)

Of course, her actual taxable income, if she does not incorporate, would be higher by the amount of reinvested income. Brown estimates that her business earnings before salary and taxes for the period 2000 to 2002 will be:

Year	Earnings before Salary and Taxes
2000	$65,000
2001	85,000
2002	95,000

a. What would her total taxes (corporate plus personal) be in each year under
   (1) A non-S corporate form of organization? (2000 tax = $6,930.)
   (2) A proprietorship? (2000 tax = $7,430.50.)
b. Should Brown incorporate? Discuss.

Personal taxes   **5-4**   Margaret Considine has this situation for the year 2000: salary of $60,000; dividend income of $10,000; interest on IBM bonds of $5,000; interest on state of Florida municipal bonds of $10,000; proceeds of $22,000 from the sale of IBM stock purchased in 1985 at a cost of $9,000; and proceeds of $22,000 from the November 2000 sale of IBM stock purchased in October 2000 at a cost of $21,000. Margaret gets one exemption ($2,650), and she has allowable itemized deductions of $5,000; these amounts will be deducted from her gross income to determine her taxable income.
a. What is Margaret's federal tax liability for 2000?
b. What are her marginal and average tax rates?
c. If she had some money to invest and was offered a choice of either state of Florida bonds with a yield of 9 percent or more IBM bonds with a yield of 11 percent, which should she choose, and why?
d. At what marginal tax rate would Margaret be indifferent in her choice between the Florida and IBM bonds?

Personal taxes   **5-5**   Lexy Ballinger and her 4-year-old son currently live in an apartment owned by Lexy's parents. Her parents charge her very little for rent — $200 per month for a luxurious two-bedroom townhouse. Lexy works at a local hospital as a physician's assistant, where she earns $42,540 per year.
a. What is Lexy's tax liability?
b. How would Lexy's tax liability change if she had a $15,000 automobile loan with monthly payments equal to $484 and the interest paid this year was $1,300?

Tax liability   **5-6**   Donald Jefferson and his wife Maryanne live in a modest house located in a Los Angeles suburb. Donald has a job at Pittsford CastIron that pays him $50,000 annually. In addition, he and Maryanne receive $2,500 interest from bonds they purchased 10 years ago. To supplement his annual income, Donald bought rental property a few years ago. Every month he collects $3,500 rent from all the property he owns. Maryanne manages the rental property, and she is paid $15,000 annually for her work. During 1999, Donald had to have the plumbing fixed in the houses he rents and the house in which he and his wife live. The plumbing bill for the rented houses was $1,250, and it was $550 for the Jeffersons' personal residence. In 1999, Donald paid $18,000 for mortgage interest and property taxes — $12,650 was for the rental houses, and the remaining $5,350 was for the house occupied by him and his wife. Donald and Maryanne have three children who have graduated from medical college and now are working as physicians in other states.
a. What is the Jeffersons' tax liability for 1999?
b. What would the tax liability be if the Jeffersons did not have the rental property? (Assume Maryanne would not get another job if the Jeffersons did not own the rental property.)

c. Why is the plumbing expense a tax deduction for the rental property but not for the house in which the Jeffersons live?

Exam-Type Problems

The problems in this section are set up in such a way that they could be used as multiple-choice exam problems.

Corporate tax liability   **5-7** The Ramjah Corporation had $200,000 of taxable income from operations in 1999.
  a. What is the company's federal income tax bill for the year?
  b. Assume the firm receives an additional $40,000 of interest income from some Treasury bonds it owns. What is the tax on this interest income?
  c. Now assume that Ramjah does not receive the interest income but does receive an additional $40,000 as dividends on some stock of other companies that it owns. What is the tax on this dividend income?

Corporate tax liability   **5-8** The Zocco Corporation had a 1999 taxable income of $365,000 from operations after all operating costs, but before (1) interest charges of $50,000, (2) dividends received of $15,000, (3) dividends paid of $25,000, and (4) income taxes.
  a. What is the firm's income tax liability, and its after-tax income?
  b. What are the company's marginal and average tax rates on taxable income?

Capital gains tax liability   **5-9** A couple of days ago, Deanna purchased 100 shares of Microsoft common stock for $95 per share. Deanna is single, and her taxable income (after all deductions and exemptions) is $75,000. Compute the capital gains tax liability for the following situations:
  a. Deanna holds the stock for 5 months and then sells it for $100 per share.
  b. Deanna sells the stock for $110 per share 13 months after it was purchased.
  c. Deanna doesn't sell the stock until 5 years from today, and the selling price is $230.

Capital gains tax liability   **5-10** Compute the capital gains tax liability for each of the following:
  a. An individual sold a municipal bond for $1,150, 2 years after it was purchased for $950.
  b. An individual sold 100 shares of a stock for $12 per share, 2 years after it was purchased at a price equal to $10 per share.
  c. A corporation bought 100 shares of stock of another company for $55 per share, and then sold it for $57 per share 2 years later.

Integrative Problems

Taxes   **5-11** Working with Michelle Delatorre, the tennis pro we introduced in the Integrative Problem in Chapter 2, has required you to put in a lot of overtime, so you have had very little time to spend on your private finances. It is now April 1, and you have only 2 weeks left to file your income tax return. You have managed to get all the information together that you will need to complete your return.
  a. Balik and Kiefer Inc. paid you a salary of $45,000, and you received $3,000 in dividends from common stock that you own. You are single, so your personal exemption is $2,700, and your itemized deductions are $4,650.
    (1) On the basis of the information above and the 1998 individual tax rate schedule, what is your tax liability?
    (2) What are your marginal and average tax rates?
  b. You also compute the taxes for the corporation your parents own. It has $100,000 of taxable income from operations plus $5,000 of interest income and

$10,000 of dividend income. And, during the year, the company paid its stockholders dividends equal to $8,000. What is the company's tax liability?

c. Assume that after paying your personal income tax, as calculated in part a, you have $5,000 to invest. You have narrowed your investment choices down to California bonds with a yield of 7 percent or IBM bonds with a yield of 10 percent. Which one should you choose, and why? At what marginal tax rate would you be indifferent to the choice between California and IBM bonds?

Multinational finance   **5-12** Until now, your parents have confined their company's operations sales to the United States, but they are considering an expansion into Europe. They have asked you to develop a tutorial package that explains the basics of multinational finance to be presented at the next board of director's meeting. In particular, your parents would like you to address the following questions:

a. What is a multinational corporation? Why do firms expand into other countries?

b. What are the six major factors that distinguish multinational managerial finance from managerial finance as practiced by a purely domestic firm?

c. What are the major differences between the structures of U.S. firms and firms from other countries? Why is knowledge of such differences important to U.S. multinational firms?

Computer-Related Problem

Work the problem in this section only if you are using the computer problem diskette.

Effect of form   **5-13** The problem requires you to rework Problem 5-3, using the data given below. Use
of organization on taxes   File C5 on the computer problem diskette.

a. Suppose Brown decides to pay out (1) 50 percent or (2) 100 percent of the after-salary corporate income in each year as dividends. Would such dividend policy changes affect her decision about whether to incorporate?

b. Suppose business improves, and actual earnings before salary and taxes in each year are twice the original estimate. Assume that if Brown chooses to incorporate she will continue to receive a salary of $45,000 and to reinvest additional earnings in the business. (No dividends would be paid.) What would be the effect of this increase in business income on Brown's decision to incorporate or not incorporate?

| **APPENDIX 5A** | Tax Rate Schedules |

Table 5A-1 gives the 1998 tax rates for individuals, and Table 5A-2 gives the 1998 tax rates for corporations. Even though these rates probably have changed, they should be used for all of the problems in this chapter that require the computation of tax liabilities.

Individual Tax Rates for 1998

UNMARRIED TAXPAYERS, NOT HEADS OF HOUSEHOLDS

Taxable Income Bracket			Base Tax Amount		Plus This Percent	of the Amount Over	Average Tax Rate at the Top of the Bracket
$ 0	–	$ 25,350	$ 0.00	+	15.0%	$ 0	15.0%
25,351	–	61,400	3,802.50	+	28.0	25,350	22.6
64,401	–	128,100	12,896.50	+	31.0	61,400	27.0
128,101	–	278,450	34,573.50	+	36.0	128,100	31.9
		Above 278,450	88,699.50	+	39.6	278,450	40.0

MARRIED TAXPAYERS FILING JOINT RETURNS

Taxable Income Bracket			Base Tax Amount		Plus This Percent	of the Amount Over	Average Tax Rate at the Top of the Bracket
$ 0	–	$ 42,350	$ 0.00	+	15.0%	$ 0	15.0%
42,351	–	102,300	6,352.50	+	28.0	42,350	22.6
102,301	–	155,950	23,138.50	+	31.0	102,350	25.5
155,951	–	278,450	39,770.00	+	36.0	155,950	30.1
		Above 278,450	83,870.00	+	39.6	278,450	40.0

NOTES:

[a]The personal exemption for 1998 was $2,700 per person or dependent. The total amount of this exemption can be deducted from income to compute taxable income. For example, for a family of four, the total personal exemption would be $10,800 = 4 × $2,700.

[b]If the taxpayer does not want to itemize deductions such as interest payments made on mortgages, charitable contributions, and so on, the standard deduction can be taken. In 1998, the standard deduction for an unmarried taxpayer, not the head of a household, was $4,250, and it was $7,100 for married taxpayers filing joint returns.

[c]The tax rate applied to capital gains equals the marginal tax rate of the taxpayer up to a maximum of 20 percent for assets held greater than 12 months.

Corporate Tax Rates for 1998

Taxable Income Bracket			Base Tax Amount		Plus This Percent	of the Amount Over	Average Tax Rate at the Top of the Bracket
$ 0	–	$ 50,000	$ 0	+	15%	$ 0	15.0%
50,001	–	75,000	7,500	+	25	50,000	18.3
75,001	–	100,000	13,750	+	34	75,000	22.3
100,001	–	335,000	22,250	+	39	100,000	34.0
335,001	–	10,000,000	113,900	+	34	335,000	34.0
10,000,001	–	15,000,000	3,400,000	+	35	10,000,000	34.3
$15,000,001	–	18,333,333	5,150,000	+	38	15,000,000	35.0
		Above 18,333,333	6,416,667	+	35	18,333,333	35.0

NOTES:

[a]The tax rates given above are adjusted for appropriate tax surcharges.

[b]Personal service corporations pay a 35 percent flat tax.

[c]Capital gains are taxed at the same rate as ordinary income.

PART II

Fundamentals of Valuation

CHAPTER 6

The Time Value of Money

Even as a student, you should be thinking about retirement. Don't laugh — most experts would agree you should have some financial plan for achieving your retirement goals when you start your professional career, or very soon afterward, or you will find those goals will be difficult, if not impossible, to attain. Chances are that unless you create a savings plan for retirement as soon as you start your career, either you will have to work longer than you planned to attain the retirement lifestyle you desire or you will have to live below the standard of living you planned for your retirement years. According to the experts, saving for retirement cannot begin too soon. Unfortunately, most Americans are professional procrastinators when it comes to saving and investing for retirement. The savings rate in the United States is the lowest of any developed country — currently it is only about 4 percent, down from 9 percent at its peak in 1974. One reason many people give for their lack of savings is that they expect to receive Social Security when they retire. But, don't bet on it! The ratio of workers paying into Social Security to retirees receiving benefits, which was 16.5 in 1950, was down to 3.3 in 1998, and it is expected to be less than 2.0 by the year 2030. What does all this mean? Unless Congress takes some action and the funds going into Social Security are increased substantially relative to the benefits expected to be paid out in the future, it is estimated the government retirement system will go bankrupt sometime between 2018 and 2030. There are a number of reasons the future of Social Security is in doubt:

1. The life expectancy of Americans has increased by more than 15 years, from 61 to over 76, since the inception of Social Security in 1935, and it is expected to increase further in the future.
2. The number of elderly as a percentage of the American population has increased significantly. Consider the fact that the proportion of Americans 65 or older was only 4 percent in 1900, it was about 12.5 percent in 1998, and it is expected to be 25 percent by the year 2040.
3. More than 77 million "baby boomers" born between 1946 and 1964 are beginning to retire, which will add a tremendous burden to the system.

Continued

At some point in the future, there might be more retirees receiving Social Security benefits than workers making contributions to the plan, because birth rates since the mid-1960s have fallen sharply — from 1946 to 1964, the average family had three children, but, from 1970 to 1990 the average number of children dropped to two.

What does the retirement plight of the baby boomers (and their children) have to do with the time value of money? Actually, a great deal. According to a study published by the National Commission on Retirement Policy, Social Security is currently the primary source of retirement income for 66 percent of beneficiaries, and it represents the only income for 16 percent. And, an earlier study conducted by *Money* magazine and Oppenheimer Management Corporation indicated that Americans do little more than talk about retirement plans until late in their professional careers; in many cases it is too late for their retirement goals to be achievable. To retire comfortably, 10 to 20 percent of your income should be set aside each year. For example, it is estimated that a 35-year-old who is earning $55,000 would need at least $1 million to retire at the current standard of living in 30 years. To achieve this goal, the individual would have to save about $10,600 each year at a 7 percent return, which represents nearly a 20 percent annual savings. The annual savings would have been about one-half this amount (just over $5,000) if the individual had begun saving for retirement at age 25.

The techniques and procedures covered in this chapter are exactly the ones used by experts to forecast the boomers' retirement needs, their probable wealth at retirement, and the resulting shortfall. If you study this chapter carefully, perhaps you can avoid the trap into which many people seem to be falling — spending today rather than saving for tomorrow.

SOURCES: Penelope Wang, "How to Retire with Twice as Much Money," *Money,* October 1994; "Can America Afford to Retire: The Retirement Security Challenge Facing You and the Nation," National Commission on Retirement Policy, Center for Strategic International Studies, 1998.

Financial decision making, whether from the perspective of firms or investors, is primarily concerned with determining how value will be affected by the expected outcomes (payoffs) associated with alternative choices. For example, if you have $5,500 to invest today, you must decide what to do with the money. If you have the opportunity to purchase an investment that will return $7,020 after five years or an investment that will return $8,126 after eight years, which should you choose? To answer this question, you must determine which investment alternative has greater value to you.

All else equal, a dollar received soon is worth more than a dollar expected in the distant future, because the sooner a dollar is received the quicker it can be invested to earn a positive return. So, does that mean the five-year investment is more valuable than the eight-year investment? Not necessarily, because the eight-year investment promises a higher dollar payoff than the five-year investment. To determine which investment is more valuable, the dollar payoffs for the investments need to be compared at the same point in time. Thus, for these two investments, we could determine the current values of both investments by restating, or revaluing, the payoffs expected in the future ($7,020 in five years and $8,126 in eight years) in terms of current (today's) dollars. The concept used to revalue payoffs such as those associated with these investments is termed the *time value of money*. It is essential that both financial managers and investors have a clear understanding of the time value of money and its impact on the value of an asset. These concepts are discussed in this chapter, where we show how the timing of cash flows affects asset values and rates of return.

The principles of time value analysis that are developed in this chapter have many applications, ranging from setting up schedules for paying off loans to decisions about whether to acquire new equipment. *In fact, of all the techniques used in finance, none is more important than the concept of the time value of money.* Because this concept is used throughout the remainder of the book, it is vital that you understand time value before you move on to other topics.

Cash Flow Time Lines

CASH FLOW TIME LINE
An important tool used in time value of money analysis; a graphical representation used to show the timing of cash flows.

One of the most important tools in time value of money analysis is the **cash flow time line**, which is used to help us visualize when the cash flows associated with a particular situation occur. Constructing a cash flow time line will help you solve problems related to the time value of money, because illustrating what happens in a particular situation generally makes it easier to set up the problem for solution. To illustrate the time line concept, consider the following diagram:

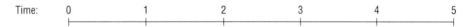

Time 0 is today; Time 1 is one period from today, or the end of Period 1; Time 2 is two periods from today, or the end of Period 2; and so on. Thus, the values on top of the tick marks represent end-of-period values. Often the periods are years, but other time intervals such as semiannual periods, quarters, months, or even days also are used. If each period on the time line represents a year, the interval from the tick mark corresponding to 0 to the tick mark corresponding to 1 would be Year 1, the interval from the tick mark corresponding to 1 to the tick mark corresponding to 2 would be Year 2, and so on. Note that each tick mark corresponds to the end of one period as well as the beginning of the next period. In other words, the tick mark at Time 1 represents the *end* of Year 1; it also represents the *beginning* of Year 2 because Year 1 has just passed.[1]

Cash flows are placed directly below the tick marks, and interest rates are shown directly above the cash flow time line. Unknown cash flows, which you are trying to find in the analysis, are indicated by question marks. For example, consider the following time line:

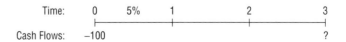

---

[1]For our discussions, the difference between the end of one period and the beginning of the next period is the same as one day ending and the next day beginning — it occurs in less than one second.

OUTFLOW
A payment, or disbursement, of cash for expenses, investments, and so on.

Here the interest rate for each of the three periods is 5 percent; a single amount (or lump sum) cash **outflow** is made at Time 0; and the Time 3 value is an unknown **inflow**. Because the initial $100 is an outflow (an investment), it has a minus sign. Because the Period 3 amount is an inflow, it does not have a minus sign. Note that no cash flows occur at Time 1 and Time 2. Note also that we do not show dollar signs on time lines; this reduces clutter.

INFLOW
A receipt of cash from an investment, an employer, or other source.

The cash flow time line is an essential tool for better understanding time value of money concepts — even experts use cash flow time lines to analyze complex problems. We use time lines throughout the book, and you should get into the habit of using them when you work problems.

Self-Test Question

Draw a three-year time line to illustrate the following situation: (1) An outflow of $5,000 occurs at Time 0. (2) Inflows of $2,000 occur at the end of Years 1, 2, and 3. (3) The interest rate during the three years is 12 percent.

Future Value

A dollar in hand today is worth more than a dollar to be received in the future because, if you had it now, you could invest it, earn interest, and end up with more than a dollar in the future. The process of going from today's values, which are termed present values (PVs), to future values (FVs) is called **compounding**. To illustrate, suppose you deposited $100 in a bank account that paid 5 percent interest each year. How much would you have at the end of one year? To begin, we define the following terms:

COMPOUNDING
The process of determining the value of a cash flow or series of cash flows some time in the future when compound interest is applied.

PV = present value, or beginning amount, in your account. Here PV = $100.

i = interest rate the bank pays on the account per year. The interest earned is based on the balance in the account at the beginning of each year, and we assume that it is paid at the end of the year. Here i = 5%, or, expressed as a decimal, i = 0.05. Throughout this chapter, we designate the interest rate as i because that symbol is used on most financial calculators. Note, though, that in later chapters we use the symbol k to denote interest rates because k is used more often in the financial literature.

INT = dollars of interest you earn during the year = (Beginning account balance) × i. Here INT = $100(0.05) = $5.

FV_n = future value, or value of the account at the end of n periods (years in this case) after the interest earned has been added to the account.

n = number of periods interest is earned. Here n = 1.

In our example, n = 1, so FV_n can be calculated as follows:

$$FV_n = FV_1 = PV + INT$$
$$= PV + PV(i)$$
$$= PV(1 + i)$$

$$= \$100(1 + 0.05) = \$100(1.05) = \$105$$

FUTURE VALUE (FV)
The amount to which a cash flow or series of cash flows will grow over a given period of time when compounded at a given interest rate.

Thus, the **future value (FV)** at the end of one year, FV_1, equals the present value multiplied by 1.0 plus the interest rate. So you will have $105 in one year if you invest $100 today and 5 percent interest is paid at the end of the year.

What would you end up with if you left your $100 in the account for five years? Here is a cash flow time line set up to show the amount at the end of each year:

Time:	0	5%	1	2	3	4	5
Initial deposit:	−100		$FV_1 = ?$	$FV_2 = ?$	$FV_3 = ?$	$FV_4 = ?$	$FV_5 = ?$
Interest earned this year:			5.00	5.25	5.51	5.79	6.08
Interest from previous years:			0.00	5.00	10.25	15.76	21.55
Total amount at the end of each year:			105.00	110.25	115.76	121.55	**127.63**

Note the following points: (1) You start by depositing $100 in the account — this is shown as an outflow at time period 0. (2) You earn $100(0.05) = $5 of interest during the first year, so the amount at the end of Year 1 is $100 + $5 = $105. (3) You start the second year with $105, so, in the second year, you earn 5 percent interest both on the $100 you invested originally and on the $5 paid to you as interest in the first year; $5.25 interest is earned in the second year, so at the end of the second year you have $110.25. Your interest during Year 2, $5.25, is higher than the first year's interest of $5, because you earned $5(0.05) = $0.25 interest on the first year's interest. (4) This process continues, and because the beginning balance is higher in each succeeding year, the annual amount of interest earned increases. (5) The total interest earned, $27.63, is reflected in the final balance at the end of the fifth year, $127.63. As you can see, the total interest earned is greater than $5 per year, which is 5 percent of the original $100 investment, because each year the interest paid was left in the account to earn additional interest the next year. The total *additional* interest earned would be $2.63 — this

COMPOUNDED INTEREST
Interest earned on interest.

results because interest is earned on interest already paid, which means **compounded interest** is received.

Note that the value at the end of Year 2, $110.25, is equal to

$$FV_2 = FV_1(1 + i)$$
$$= PV[(1 + i)](1 + i)$$
$$= PV(1 + i)^2$$
$$= \$100(1.05)^2 = \$110.25$$

Continuing, the balance at the end of Year 3 is

$$FV_3 = FV_2 (1 + i)$$
$$= [PV_2(1 + i)^2](1 + i)$$
$$= PV(1 + i)^3$$
$$= \$100(1.05)^3 = \$115.76$$

and

$$FV_5 = \$100(1.05)^5 = \$127.63$$

In general, the future value of an initial sum at the end of n years can be found by applying Equation 6-1:

6-1

$$FV_n = PV(1 + i)^n$$

Equation 6-1 and most other time value of money problems can be solved in three ways: numerically with a regular calculator, with interest tables, or with a financial calculator.

Numerical Solution

According to Equation 6-1, to compute the future value, FV, of an amount invested today, PV, we need to determine by what multiple the amount invested will increase in the future. As you can see, the multiple by which any amount will increase is based on the total dollar interest earned, which depends on both the interest rate and the length of time interest is earned. This multiple, termed the **Future Value Interest Factor for i and n (FVIF$_{i,n}$)** is defined as $(1 + i)^n$.

FUTURE VALUE INTEREST FACTOR FOR i AND n (FVIF$_{i,n}$) The future value of $1 left on deposit for n periods at a rate of i percent per period; the multiple by which an initial investment grows because of the interest earned.

The value for FVIF$_{i,n}$ can be computed using a regular calculator either by (1) multiplying $(1 + i)$ by itself $n - 1$ times, or (2) using the exponential function to raise $(1 + i)$ to the nth power. For our example, you can enter $1 + i = 1.05$ into your calculator, and then multiply 1.05 by itself four times; or, if you have an exponential function key on your calculator, which generally is labeled y^x, you can enter 1.05 into your calculator, press the y^x function key, enter 5, and then press the = (equal) key. In either case, your answer would be 1.276282, which you would multiply by $100 to get the final answer, $127.6282, which would be rounded to $127.63.

In certain time value of money problems, it is difficult to arrive at a solution using a regular calculator. We will tell you this when we have such a problem, and in these cases we will not show a numerical solution. Also, at times we show the numerical solution just below the time line, as a part of the diagram, rather than in a separate section.

Interest Tables (Tabular Solution)

As we showed in the previous section, computing the values for FVIF$_{i,n}$ is not a very difficult task if you have a calculator handy. Table 6-1 gives the future value interest factors for i values from 4 percent to 6 percent and n values from one to six periods, while Table A-3 in Appendix A at the back of the book contains FVIF$_{i,n}$ values for a wide range of i and n values.

Because $(1 + i)^n = $ FVIF$_{i,n}$, Equation 6-1 can be rewritten as follows:

6-1a

$$FV_n = PV(1 + i)^n = PV(FVIF_{i,n})$$

TABLE 6-1

Future Value Interest Factors: $FVIF_{i,n} = (1 + i)^n$

Period (n)	4%	5%	6%
1	1.0400	1.0500	1.0600
2	1.0816	1.1025	1.1236
3	1.1249	1.1576	1.1910
4	1.1699	1.2155	1.2625
5	1.2167	**1.2763**	1.3382
6	1.2653	1.3401	1.4185

To illustrate, the FVIF for our five-year, 5 percent interest problem can be found in Table 6-1 by looking down the first column to Period 5, and then looking across that row to the 5% column, where we see that $FVIF_{5\%,5} = 1.2763$. Then, the value of $100 after five years is found as follows:

$$FV_n = PV(FVIF_{i,n})$$

$$= \$100(FVIF_{5\%,5})$$

$$= \$100(1.2763)$$

$$= \$127.63$$

Financial Calculator Solution

Equation 6-1 and a number of other equations have been programmed directly into *financial calculators,* and such calculators can be used to find future values. Note that calculators have five keys that correspond to the five most commonly used time value of money variables:

Here

N = the number of periods; some calculators use n rather than N.

I = interest rate per period; some calculators use i, INT, or I/Y rather than I.

PV = present value.

PMT = annuity payment. This key is used only if the cash flows involve a series of equal, or constant, payments (an annuity). If there are no periodic payments in the particular problem, then PMT = 0. We will use this key later in the chapter.

FV = future value.

On some financial calculators, these keys actually are buttons on the face of the calculator, while on others they are shown on a screen after going into the time value of money (TVM) menu.

In this chapter, we will deal with equations that involve only four of the variables at any one time — three of the variables will be known, and the calculator will then solve for the fourth (unknown) variable. In the next chapter, when we deal with bonds, we will use all five variables in the bond valuation equation.[2]

To find the future value of $100 after five years at 5 percent interest using a financial calculator, note again that we are dealing with Equation 6-1:

$$FV_n = PV(1 + i)^n \qquad \qquad \textbf{(6-1)}$$

The equation has four variables, FV_n, PV, i, and n. If we know any three, we can solve for the fourth. In our example, we can enter PV = −100, I = 5, PMT = 0, and N = 5. Then, when we press the FV key, we will get the answer, FV = 127.6282 (rounded to four decimal places). Note that on some calculators you are required to press a "Compute" (sometimes labeled CPT or COMP) key before pressing the FV key to get the answer.

Most financial calculators require that all cash flows be designated as either inflows or outflows, because the computations are based on the fact that we generally pay (cash outflows) to receive benefits (cash inflows). For these calculators, you must enter cash outflows as negative numbers. In our illustration, you deposit, or put in, the initial amount (which is an outflow to you) and you take out, or receive, the ending amount (which is an inflow to you). If your calculator requires that you input outflows as negative numbers, the PV would be entered as −100. If you forget the negative sign and enter 100, then the calculator assumes you received $100 in the current period and that you must pay it back with interest in the future, so the FV appears as −127.63, a cash outflow. Sometimes the convention of changing signs can be confusing, but, if you think about what you are doing, you should not have a problem with whether the calculator gives you a positive or a negative answer.

We also should note that financial calculators permit you to specify the number of decimal places that are displayed. For most calculators, at least 12 significant digits are used in the actual calculations. But, for the purposes of reporting the results of the computations, generally we use two places for answers when working with dollars or percentages and four places when working with decimals. *The nature of the problem dictates how many decimal places should be displayed* — to be safe, you might want to set your calculator so the floating decimal format is used, and round the final results yourself.

Technology has progressed to the point where it is far more efficient to solve most time value of money problems with a financial calculator. *However, you must understand the concepts behind the calculations and know how to set up cash flow time lines in order to work complex problems.* This is true for stock and bond valuation, capital budgeting, and many other important types of problems such as retirement planning, mortgage payments, and other situations that affect you personally.

---

[2]The equation programmed into the calculators actually has five variables, one for each key. In this chapter, the value of one of the variables is always zero. It is a good idea to get into the habit of inputting a zero for the unused variable (whose value automatically is set equal to zero when you clear the calculator's memory); if you forget to clear your calculator, this procedure will help you avoid trouble.

Problem Format

To help you understand the various types of time value problems, we generally will use a standard format in the book. First, we state the problem in words. Next, we diagram the problem using a cash flow time line. Then, beneath the time line, we show the equation that must be solved. Finally, we present three alternative procedures for solving the equation to obtain the answer: (1) use a regular calculator to obtain a numerical solution, (2) use the tables, or (3) use a financial calculator.

To illustrate the format, we use the five-year, 5 percent example:

CASH FLOW TIME LINE:

EQUATION:

$$FV_n = PV(1 + i)^n = \$100(1.05)^5$$

1. NUMERICAL SOLUTION:

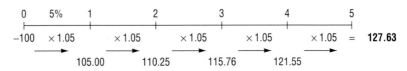

Using a regular calculator, raise 1.05 to the 5th power and multiply by \$100 to get $FV_5 = \$100(1.05)^5 = \$100(1.2763) = \$127.63$.

2. TABULAR SOLUTION:

Look up $FVIF_{5\%,5}$ in Table 6-1 or Table A-3 at the end of the book and then multiply by \$100:

$$FV_5 = \$100(FVIF_{5\%,5}) = \$100(1.2763) = \$127.63$$

3. FINANCIAL CALCULATOR SOLUTION:

Inputs:	5	5	−100	0	?
	N	I	PV	PMT	FV
Outputs:					= 127.63

Note that the calculator diagram tells you to input N = 5, I = 5, PV = −100, and PMT = 0, and then to press the FV key to get the answer, 127.63. Also, note that in this particular problem, the PMT key does not really come into play, as no constant series of payments is involved.[3] Finally, you should recognize that small

---

[3] We input PMT = 0, but if you cleared the calculator before you started, that already would have been done for you.

rounding differences often occur among the various solution methods because tables use fewer significant digits (4) than do calculators (12 to 14), and also because rounding sometimes is done at intermediate steps in long problems rather than only in the final solution.

Graphic View of the Compounding Process: Growth

Figure 6-1 shows how $1 (or any other sum) grows over time at various interest rates. The data used to plot the curves could be obtained from Table A-3, or it could be generated with a calculator. The higher the rate of interest, the faster the rate of growth. *The interest rate is, in fact, a growth rate:* If a sum is deposited and earns 5 percent interest, then the funds on deposit will grow at a rate of 5 percent per period. Note also that time value concepts can be applied to anything that is growing — sales, population, earnings per share, or whatever.

Self-Test Questions

Explain what is meant by the following statement: "A dollar in hand today is worth more than a dollar to be received next year."

What is compounding? What is "interest on interest"?

Explain the following equation: $FV_1 = PV + INT$.

FIGURE 6-1

Relationships among Future Value, Growth or Interest Rates, and Time

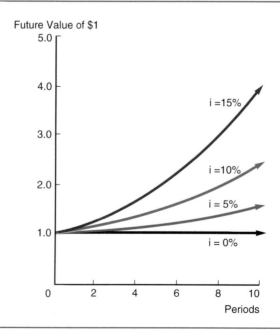

Set up a time line that shows the following situation: (1) Your initial deposit is $100. (2) The account pays 5 percent interest annually. (3) You want to know how much money you will have at the end of three years.

What equation could you use to solve the preceding problem?

What are the five TVM (time value of money) input keys on a financial calculator?

Present Value

OPPORTUNITY COST RATE
The rate of return on the best available alternative investment of equal risk.

PRESENT VALUE (PV)
The value today of a future cash flow or series of cash flows.

Suppose you have some extra cash, and you have a chance to buy a low-risk security that will pay $127.63 at the end of five years. Your local bank currently is offering 5 percent interest on five-year certificates of deposit, and you regard the security as being very safe. The 5 percent rate is defined as being your **opportunity cost rate**, or the rate of return you could earn on alternative investments of *similar risk*. How much should you be willing to pay for the security?

From the future value example presented in the previous section, we saw that an initial amount of $100 invested at 5 percent per year would be worth $127.63 at the end of five years. As we will see in a moment, you should be indifferent to the choice between $100 today and $127.63 at the end of 5 years, and the $100 is defined as the **present value**, or **PV**, of $127.63 due in five years when the opportunity cost rate is 5 percent. If the price of the security is anything less than $100, you should definitely buy it because it would cost you exactly $100 to produce the $127.63 in five years if you earned a 5 percent return. Therefore, if you could find another investment with the same risk that would produce the same future amount ($127.63) but it cost less than $100, say, $95.00, then you could earn a return higher than 5 percent by purchasing that investment. Similarly, if the price of the security is greater than $100, you should not buy it because it would cost you only $100 to produce the same future amount at the given rate of return. If the price is exactly $100, then you could either buy it or turn it down, because $100 is the security's fair value if it has a 5 percent expected return.

In general, *the present value of a cash flow due n years in the future is the amount that, if it were on hand today, would grow to equal the future amount.* Because $100 would grow to $127.63 in five years at a 5 percent interest rate, $100 is the present value of $127.63 due five years in the future when the opportunity cost rate is 5 percent.

DISCOUNTING
The process of finding the present value of a cash flow or a series of cash flows; the reverse of compounding.

Finding present values is called **discounting**, and it simply is the reverse of compounding — if you know the PV, you can compound to find the FV, while if you know the FV, you can discount to find the PV. When discounting, you would follow these steps:

CASH FLOW TIME LINE:

```
0    5%    1         2         3         4         5
|----------|---------|---------|---------|---------|
PV = ?                                           127.63
```

EQUATION:
To develop the present value, or discounting, equation, we begin with Equation 6-1:

$$FV_n = PV(1 + i)^n = PV(FVIF_{i,n})$$ **(6-1)**

and then solve for PV to yield:

6-2

$$PV = \frac{FV_n}{(1+i)^n} = FV_n \left[\frac{1}{(1+i)^n} \right] = FV_n \, (PVIF_{i,n})$$

The last form of Equation 6-2 recognizes that the interest factor $PVIF_{i,n}$ is equal to

6-2a

$$PVIF_{i,n} = \frac{1}{(1+i)^n}$$

The term given in Equation 6-2a is called the **Present Value Interest Factor for i and n ($PVIF_{i,n}$)**.

PRESENT VALUE INTEREST FACTOR FOR i AND n ($PVIF_{i,n}$)
The present value of $1 due n periods in the future discounted at i percent per period.

1. NUMERICAL SOLUTION:

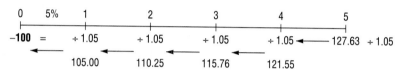

Using a regular calculator, raise 1.05 to the 5th power and divide $127.63 by the result, or divide $127.63 by 1.05 five times:

$$PV = \frac{\$127.63}{(1.05)^5}$$

$$= \frac{\$127.63}{1.2763} = \$127.63(0.7835)$$

$$= \$100$$

2. TABULAR SOLUTION:

Table A-1 in Appendix A contains present value interest factors for selected values of i and n, $PVIF_{i,n}$. The value of $PVIF_{i,n}$ for i = 5% and n = 5 periods is 0.7835, so the present value of $127.63 to be received after five years when the opportunity cost rate is 5 percent equals:

$$PV = \$127.63(PVIF_{5\%,5}) = \$127.63(0.7835) = \$100$$

3. FINANCIAL CALCULATOR SOLUTION:

Inputs:	5	5	?	0	127.63
	N	**I**	**PV**	**PMT**	**FV**
Output:			= −100		

Enter N = 5, I = 5, PMT = 0, and FV = 127.63, and then press PV to get PV = −100.

FIGURE 6-2

Relationships among Present Value, Interest Rates, and Time

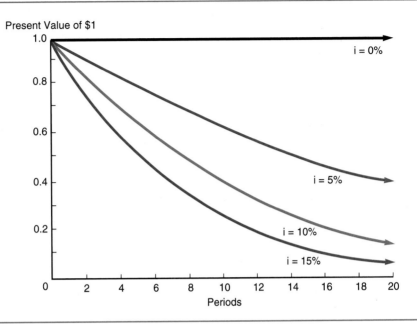

Graphic View of the Discounting Process

Figure 6-2 shows how the present value of $1 (or any other sum) to be received in the future diminishes as the years to receipt increase. Again, the data used to plot the curves could be obtained either with a calculator or from Table A-1, and the graph shows (1) that the present value of a sum to be received at some future date decreases and approaches zero as the payment date is extended further into the future, and (2) that the rate of decrease is greater the higher the interest (discount) rate. At relatively high interest rates, funds due in the future are worth very little today, and even at a relatively low discount rate, the present value of a sum due in the very distant future is quite small. For example, at a 20 percent discount rate, $5 million due in 100 years is worth only about 6¢ today. (However, 6¢ would grow to $5 million in 100 years at 20 percent.)

Self-Test Questions

What is meant by the term "opportunity cost rate"?

What is discounting? How is it related to compounding?

How does the present value of an amount to be received in the future change as the time is extended and as the interest rate increases?

Solving for Time and Interest Rates

At this point, you should realize that the compounding and discounting processes are reciprocals, or inverses, of one another and that we have been dealing with one equation in two different forms:

FV FORM:

6-1

$$FV_n = PV(1 + i)^n = PV(FVIF_{i,n})$$

PV FORM:

6-2

$$PV = \frac{FV_n}{(1 + i)^n} = FV_n \left[\frac{1}{(1 + i)^n}\right] = FV_n (PVIF_{i,n})$$

There are four variables in these equations — PV, FV, i, and n — and if you know the values of any three, you (or your financial calculator) can find the value of the fourth. To this point, we have known the interest rate (i) and the number of years (n) plus either the PV or the FV. In many situations, though, you will need to solve for either i or n, as we discuss below.

Solving for i

Suppose you can buy a security at a price of $78.35 that will pay you $100 after five years. Here we know PV, FV, and n, but we do not know i, the interest rate you will earn on your investment. Problems such as this are solved as follows:

CASH FLOW TIME LINE:

EQUATION:

$$FV_n = PV(1 + i)^n \qquad \text{(6-1)}$$

$100 = $78.35(1 + i)^5$. Solve for i.

1. NUMERICAL SOLUTION:

One method of finding the value of i is to go through a trial-and-error process in which you insert different values of i into Equation 6-1 until you find a value that "works" in the sense that the right side of the equation equals $100. The solution value is i = 0.05, or 5 percent. This trial-and-error procedure is extremely tedious and inefficient for most time value problems, so it is rarely used in the "real world." Alternatively, in this case, you could solve this problem by using relatively simple algebra to find i directly:

$$FV_n = PV(1 + i)^n = PV(FVIF_{i,n})$$

$$\$100 = \$78.35(1 + i)^5$$

$$(1 + i)^5 = \frac{\$100}{\$78.35} = 1.2763 = FVIF_{i,5}$$

$$(1 + i) = (1.2763)^{\frac{1}{5}} = 1.05$$

$$i = 1.05 - 1 = 0.05$$

2. TABULAR SOLUTION:

As the computations given above show, $FVIF_{i,5} = 1.2763$. Using Table A-3, look across the Period 5 row until you find $FVIF = 1.2763$. This value is in the 5% column, so the interest rate at which $78.35 grows to $100 over five years is 5 percent.[4] This procedure can be used only if the interest rate is in the table; therefore, it will not work for fractional interest rates or where n is not a whole number. Approximation procedures can be used, but they can be laborious and inexact.

3. FINANCIAL CALCULATOR SOLUTION:

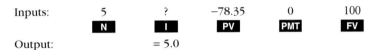

Inputs:	5	?	−78.35	0	100
	N	**I**	**PV**	**PMT**	**FV**
Output:		= 5.0			

Enter N = 5, PV = −78.35, PMT = 0, and FV = 100, and then press I to get I = 5. This procedure can be used for any interest rate or any value of n, including fractional values.

Solving for n

Suppose you know that the security will provide a return of 10 percent per year, that it will cost $68.30, and that you will receive $100 at maturity, but you do not know when the security matures. Thus, you know PV, FV, and i, but you do not know n, the number of periods. Here is the situation:

CASH FLOW TIME LINE:

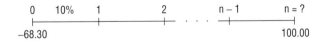

EQUATION:

$$FV_n = PV(1 + i)^n \qquad \text{(6-1)}$$

$$\$100 = \$68.30(1.10)^n. \qquad \text{Solve for n.}$$

1. NUMERICAL SOLUTION:

Again, you could go through a trial-and-error process wherein you substitute different values for n into the equation. You would find (eventually) that n = 4

---

[4]The solution could also be set up in present value format:

$$PV = FV_n(PVIF_{i,n})$$

$$\$78.35 = \$100(PVIF_{i,5})$$

$$PVIF_{i,5} = \$78.35/\$100 = 0.7835$$

This value corresponds to i = 5 percent in Table A-1.

"works," so 4 is the number of years it takes for $68.30 to grow to $100 if the interest rate is 10 percent.[5]

2. TABULAR SOLUTION:

$$FV_n = PV(1 + i)^n = PV(FVIF_{i,n})$$

$$\$100 = \$68.30(FVIF_{10\%,n})$$

$$FVIF_{10\%,n} = \frac{\$100}{\$68.30} = 1.4641$$

Now look down the 10% column in Table A-3 until you find FVIF = 1.4641. This value is in Row 4, which indicates that it takes four years for $68.30 to grow to $100 at a 10 percent interest rate.[6]

3. FINANCIAL CALCULATOR SOLUTION:

Inputs:	?	10	−68.30	0	100
	N	I	PV	PMT	FV
Output:	= 4.0				

Enter I = 10, PV = −68.30, PMT = 0, and FV = 100, and then press N to get N = 4.

Self-Test Questions

Assuming that you are given PV, FV, and the interest rate, i, write out an equation that can be used to determine the time period, n.

Assuming that you are given PV, FV, and the time period, n, write out an equation that can be used to determine the interest rate, i.

Explain how a financial calculator can be used to solve for i and for n.

---

[5]The value of n also can be found as follows:

$$\$100 = \$68.30(1.10)^n$$

$$(1.10)^n = \frac{\$100}{\$68.30} = 1.4641$$

$$\ln[(1.10)^n] = n[\ln(1.10)] = \ln(1.4641)$$

$$n = \frac{\ln(1.4641)}{\ln(1.10)} = \frac{0.3812}{0.0953} = 4.00$$

You can use your calculator to find ln, which is the natural logarithm. For most calculators, you insert the number, say, 1.4641, and then press the LN key (or its equivalent) — the result is 0.3812.

[6]The problem could also be solved as follows:

$$PV = FV_n(PVIF_{i,n})$$

$$\$68.30 = \$100(PVIF_{10\%,n})$$

$$PVIF_{10\%,n} = \$68.30/\$100 = 0.6830$$

This value corresponds to n = 4 years in Table A-1.

Future Value of an Annuity

ANNUITY
A series of payments of an equal amount at fixed intervals for a specified number of periods.

An **annuity** is a series of equal payments made at fixed intervals for a specified number of periods. For example, $100 at the end of each of the next three years is a three-year annuity. The payments are given the symbol PMT, and they can occur at either the beginning or the end of each period. If the payments occur at the *end* of each period, as they typically do in business transactions, the annuity is called an **ordinary**, or **deferred**, annuity. If payments are made at the *beginning* of each period, the annuity is an **annuity due.** Because ordinary annuities are more common in finance, when the term "annuity" is used in this book, you should assume that the payments occur at the end of each period unless otherwise noted.

ORDINARY (DEFERRED) ANNUITY
An annuity whose payments occur at the end of each period.

Ordinary Annuities

ANNUITY DUE
An annuity whose payments occur at the beginning of each period.

If you deposit $100 at the end of each year for three years in a savings account that pays 5 percent interest per year, how much will you have at the end of three years? To answer this question, we must find the future value of an ordinary annuity, FVA_n. Each payment is compounded out to the end of Period n, and the sum of the compounded payments is the future value of the annuity.

FVA_n
The future value of an annuity over n periods.

CASH FLOW TIME LINE:

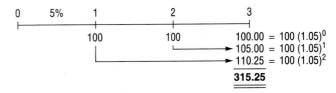

Here we show the regular cash flow time line as the top portion of the diagram, but we also show how each cash flow is processed to produce the value FVA_n in the lower portion of the diagram.

EQUATION:

The cash flow time line shows that we can compute the future value of the annuity simply by determining the future values of the individual payments and summing the results. Thus, the equation for the future value of an ordinary annuity can be written[7]:

---

[7]The second form of the equation is simply a shorthand expression in which sigma Σ, means "sum up," or add the values of n factors. If $t = 0$, then $(1 + i)^0$; if $t = 1$, then $(1 + i)^1$; if $t = 2$, then $(1 + i)^2$; and so on until $t = n - 1$, the last possible outcome. The symbol $\sum_{t=1}^{n-1}$ simply says, "Go through the following process: First, let $t = 0$ and find the first interest factor, $FVIF_{i,0}$; then let $t = 1$ and find the second interest factor, $FVIF_{i,1}$; then continue until each individual interest factor, FVIF, up to $t = n - 1$ has been found, and then add these individual FVIFs to find the total FVIF for an annuity." Finally, according to Equation 6-3, the sum of the FVIFs is multiplied by PMT to compute FVA_n.

6-3

$$FVA_n = PMT(1 + i)^0 + PMT(1 + i)^1 + PMT(1 + i)^2 + \cdots + PMT(1 + i)^{n-1}$$
$$= PMT\sum_{t=1}^{n} (1 + i)^{n-t} = PMT \sum_{t=0}^{n-1} (1 + i)^t$$

Note that the first line of Equation 6-3 presents the annuity payments in reverse order of payment, and the superscript in each term indicates the number of periods of interest each payment receives. In other words, because the first annuity payment was made at the end of Period 1, interest would be earned in Period 2 through Period n only; thus, compounding would be for $n - 1$ periods rather than n periods, compounding for the second annuity payment would be for Period 3 through Period n, or $n - 2$ periods, and so on. The last annuity payment is made at the same time the computation is made, so there is no time for interest to be earned; thus, the superscript 0 represents the fact that no interest is earned. Simplifying the first line produces the last line of Equation 6-3.

1. NUMERICAL SOLUTION:

The lower section of the time line shows the numerical solution. The future value, FV, of each cash flow is found, and those FVs are summed to find the FV of the annuity. This is a tedious process for long annuities.

We can simplify the numerical solution somewhat by simplifying Equation 6-3[8]:

6-3a

$$FVA_n = PMT \left[\sum_{t=1}^{n} (1 + i)^{n-t}\right] = PMT \left[\frac{(1 + i)^n - 1}{i}\right]$$

Using Equation 6-3a, the future value of $100 deposited at the end of each year for three years in a savings account that earns 5 percent interest per year is

FUTURE VALUE INTEREST FACTOR FOR AN ANNUITY ($FVIFA_{i,n}$) The future value interest factor for an annuity of n periods compounded at i percent.

$$FVA_3 = \$100 \left[\frac{(1.05)^3 - 1}{0.05}\right]$$
$$= \$100(3.1525)$$
$$= \$315.25$$

2. TABULAR SOLUTION:

The summation term in Equation 6-3 is called the **Future Value Interest Factor for an Annuity of n payments at i interest ($FVIFA_{i,n}$)**:

---

[8]The simplification shown in Equation 6-3a is found by applying the algebra of geometric progressions. This equation is useful in situations in which the required values of i and n are not in the tables or when a financial calculator is not available.

6-3b

$$FVIFA_{i,n} = \sum_{t=1}^{n} (1 + i)^{n-t} = \frac{(1 + i)^n - 1}{i}$$

FVIFAs have been calculated for various combinations of i and n; Table A-4 in Appendix A contains a set of FVIFA factors. To find the answer to the three-year, $100 annuity problem, first refer to Table A-4 and look down the 5% column to the third period; the FVIFA is 3.1525. Thus, the future value of the $100 annuity is $315.25:

$$FVA_n = PMT(FVIFA_{i,n})$$

$$FVA_3 = \$100(FVIFA_{5\%,3})$$

$$= \$100(3.1525)$$

$$= \$315.25$$

3. FINANCIAL CALCULATOR SOLUTION:

Inputs:	3	5	0	−100	?
	N	**I**	**PV**	**PMT**	**FV**
Output:					= 315.25

Note that in annuity problems, the PMT key is used in conjunction with the N and I keys, plus either the PV or the FV key, depending on whether you are trying to find the PV or the FV of the annuity. In our example, you want the FV, so press the FV key to get the answer, $315.25. Because there is no initial payment, we input PV = 0.

Annuities Due

Had the three $100 payments in the previous example been made at the *beginning* of each year, the annuity would have been an *annuity due.* In the cash flow time line, each payment would be shifted to the left one year; therefore, each payment would be *compounded for one extra year (period),* which means each payment would earn interest for an additional year.

CASH FLOW TIME LINE:

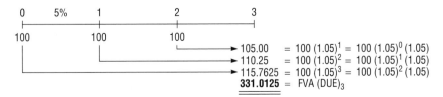

Again, the regular time line is shown at the top of the diagram, and the future value of each annuity payment at the end of Year 3 is shown in the Year 3 column, with the actual computations shown to the right.

1. NUMERICAL SOLUTION:

We can find the FV of each cash flow and then sum the results to find the FV of the annuity due, $FVA(DUE)_n$. This procedure is shown in the lower section of the cash flow time line. Note from the diagram that the difference between an ordinary annuity and an annuity due is that *each of the payments of the annuity due earns interest for one additional year.* So the numerical solution for an annuity due also can be found by adjusting Equations 6-3 and 6-3a to account for the fact that *each* annuity payment is able to earn an additional year's interest when compared to an ordinary annuity. The solution for $FVA(DUE)_n$ is

6-3c

$$FVA(DUE)_n = PMT\left[\sum_{t=1}^{n}(1+i)^t\right] = PMT\left[\left\{\sum_{t=1}^{n}(1+i)^{n-t}\right\} \times (1+i)\right]$$

$$= PMT\left[\left\{\frac{(1+i)^n - 1}{i}\right\} \times (1+i)\right]$$

The future value of the three $100 deposits made at the beginning of each year into a savings account that earns 5 percent annually is

$FVIFA(DUE)_{i,n}$
The future value interest factor for an annuity due —
$FVIFA(DUE)_{i,n} = FVIFA_{i,n} \times (1+i)$.

$$FVA(DUE)_3 = \$100\left[\left\{\frac{(1.05)^3 - 1}{0.05}\right\} \times (1.05)\right]$$

$$= \$100[(3.1525) \times 1.05]$$

$$= \$331.0125$$

2. TABULAR SOLUTION:

As we have shown, for an annuity due, each payment is compounded for one additional period, so the future value interest factor for an annuity due, **$FVIFA(DUE)_{i,n}$**, is equal to the $FVIFA_{i,n}$ for an ordinary annuity compounded for one additional period. In other words,

$$FVIFA(DUE)_{i,n} = \left[\left\{\frac{(1+i)^n - 1}{i}\right\} \times (1+i)\right]$$

$$= [(FVIFA_{i,n})(1+i)]$$

Here is the tabular solution for $FVA(DUE)_n$:

$$FVA(DUE)_n = PMT[FVIFA(DUE)_{i,n}] = PMT[(FVIFA_{i,n})(1+i)]$$

$$FVA(DUE)_n = \$100[(3.1525)(1.05)] = \$331.0125$$

The payments occur earlier, so more interest is earned. Therefore, the future value of the annuity due is larger — $331.01 versus $315.25 for the ordinary annuity.

3. FINANCIAL CALCULATOR SOLUTION:

Most financial calculators have a switch, or key, marked DUE or BEG that allows you to switch from end-of-period payments (ordinary annuity) to beginning-of-period payments (annuity due). When the beginning mode is activated, the display normally will show the word BEGIN, or the letters BGN. Thus, to deal with annuities due, switch your calculator to BEGIN and proceed as before:

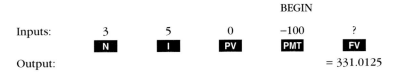

				BEGIN	
Inputs:	3	5	0	−100	?
	N	**I**	**PV**	**PMT**	**FV**
Output:					= 331.0125

Enter N = 3, I = 5, PV = 0, PMT = −100, and then press FV to get the answer, $331.01. Because most problems specify end-of-period cash flows, you should always switch your calculator back to END mode after you work an annuity due problem.

Self-Test Questions

What is the difference between an ordinary annuity and an annuity due?

How do you modify the $FVIFA_{i,n}$ for determining the value of an ordinary annuity in order to determine the value of an annuity due?

Which annuity has the greater future value: an ordinary annuity or an annuity due? Why?

Explain how financial calculators can be used to solve future value of annuity problems.

Present Value of an Annuity

Suppose you were offered the following alternatives: (1) a three-year annuity with payments of $100 at the end of each year or (2) a lump sum payment today. You have no need for the money during the next three years, so if you accept the annuity, you would simply deposit the payments in a savings account that pays 5 percent interest per year. Similarly, the lump sum payment would be deposited into the same account. How large must the lump sum payment today be to make it equivalent to the annuity? Here is the setup:

CASH FLOW TIME LINE:

$$\frac{100}{(1.05)^1} = 95.238$$

$$\frac{100}{(1.05)^2} = 90.703$$

$$\frac{100}{(1.05)^3} = 86.384$$

272.325

0	5%	1	2	3
		100	100	100

The regular time line is shown at the top of the diagram, and the numerical solution values are on the left. The PV of the three annuity payments, PVA_3, is $272.325.

EQUATION:

As you can see from the cash flow time line, the present value of an annuity can be determined by computing the PV of the individual payments and summing the results. The general equation used to find the PV of an ordinary annuity consisting of n payments, designated PVA_n, is shown below:

6-4

$$PVA_n = PMT\left[\frac{1}{(1+i)^1}\right] + PMT\left[\frac{1}{(1+i)^2}\right] + \cdots + PMT\left[\frac{1}{(1+i)^n}\right]$$

$$= PMT\left[\sum_{t=1}^{n}\frac{1}{(1+i)^t}\right]$$

1. NUMERICAL SOLUTION:

One method of determining the present value of the annuity is to compute the present value of each cash flow and then sum the results. This procedure is shown in the lower section of the cash flow time line diagram, where we see that the PV of the annuity is $272.325. This approach can be tedious if there are a large number of annuity payments.

The numerical solution is easier if we simplify Equation 6-4[9]:

6-4a

$$PVA_n = PMT\left[\sum_{t=1}^{n}\frac{1}{(1+i)^t}\right] = PMT\left[\frac{1 - \dfrac{1}{(1+i)^n}}{i}\right]$$

Using Equation 6-4a, the PV of the three-year annuity with end-of-year payments of $100 is

$$PVA_3 = \$100\left[\frac{1 - \dfrac{1}{(1.05)^3}}{0.05}\right]$$

$$= \$100(2.72325)$$

$$= \$272.325$$

---

[9]Like Equation 6-3a, the simplification shown in Equation 6-4a is found by applying the algebra of geometric progressions. This equation is useful in situations in which the required values of i and n are not in the tables or when a financial calculator is not available.

2. TABULAR SOLUTION:

The summation term in Equation 6-4 is called the **Present Value Interest Factor for an Annuity of n payments at i interest (PVIFA$_{i,n}$):**

6-4b

$$PVIFA_{i,n} = \sum_{t=1}^{n} \frac{1}{(1+i)^t} = \frac{1 - \dfrac{1}{(1+i)^n}}{i}$$

PRESENT VALUE INTEREST FACTOR FOR AN ANNUITY (PVIFA$_{i,n}$)
The present value interest factor for an annuity of n periods discounted at i percent.

The values for PVIFA at different values of i and n are shown in Table A-2 at the back of the book.

To find the answer to the three-year, $100 annuity problem, simply refer to Table A-2 and look down the 5% column to the third period. The PVIFA is 2.7232, so the present value of the $100 annuity is $272.32:

$$PVA_n = PMT(PVIFA_{i,n})$$

$$PVA_3 = \$100(PVIFA_{5\%,3}) = \$100(2.7232) = \$272.32$$

3. FINANCIAL CALCULATOR SOLUTION:

Inputs:	3	5	?	−100	0
	N	**I**	**PV**	**PMT**	**FV**
Output:			= 272.325		

Enter N = 3, I = 5, PMT = −100, and FV = 0, and then press the PV key to find the PV, $272.32.

One especially important application of the annuity concept relates to loans with constant payments, such as mortgages and auto loans. With such loans, called amortized loans, the *amount borrowed is the present value of an ordinary annuity,* and the payments constitute the annuity stream. We will examine constant payment loans in more depth in a later section of this chapter.

Annuities Due

Had the three $100 payments in our earlier example been made at the *beginning* of each year, the annuity would have been an *annuity due.* On the cash flow time line, each payment would be shifted to the left one year, so each payment would be *discounted for one less year.* Here is the cash flow time line setup:

CASH FLOW TIME LINE:

$$\frac{100}{(1.05)^1} \times (1.05) = \frac{100}{(1.05)^0} = 100.000$$

$$\frac{100}{(1.05)^2} \times (1.05) = \frac{100}{(1.05)^1} = 95.238$$

$$\frac{100}{(1.05)^3} \times (1.05) = \frac{100}{(1.05)^2} = 90.703$$

$$PVA(DUE)_3 = \mathbf{285.941}$$

Time line: 0 — 5% — 1 — 2 — 3, with cash flows 100, 100, 100 at periods 0, 1, 2.

1. NUMERICAL SOLUTION:

Again, we can find the PV of each cash flow and then sum these PVs to find the PV of the annuity due, $PVA(DUE)_n$. This procedure is illustrated in the lower section of the time line diagram. Because the cash flows occur sooner, the PV of the annuity due exceeds that of the ordinary annuity — $285.94 versus $272.32.

The cash flow time line shows that the difference between the PV of an annuity due and the PV of an ordinary annuity is that *each of the payments of the annuity due is discounted one less year.* So, the numerical solution for an annuity due also can be found by adjusting Equations 6-4 and 6-4a to account for the fact each annuity payment will have the *opportunity* to earn an additional year's (period's) interest when compared with an ordinary annuity:

6-4c

$$PVA(DUE)_n = PMT\left[\sum_{t=0}^{n-1}\frac{1}{(1+i)^t}\right] = PMT\left[\left\{\sum_{t=1}^{n}\frac{1}{(1+i)^t}\right\} \times (1+i)\right]$$

$$= PMT\left[\left\{\frac{1 - \dfrac{1}{(1+i)^n}}{i}\right\} \times (1+i)\right]$$

Therefore, if the three $100 payments were made at the beginning of the year, the PV of the annuity would be:

$$PV(DUE)_3 = \$100\left[\left\{\frac{1 - \dfrac{1}{(1.05)^3}}{0.05}\right\} \times (1.05)\right]$$

$$= \$100[(2.72325)(1.05)]$$

$$= \$100(2.85941)$$

$$= \$285.941$$

2. TABULAR SOLUTION:

We can use the PVIFAs given in Table A-2, which are computed for ordinary annuities, if we adjust these values to account for the fact that the payments associated with an annuity due occur one period earlier than the payments associated with

PVIFA(DUE)$_{i,n}$
The present value interest
factor for an annuity due —
PVIFA(DUE)$_{i,n}$ =
PVIFA$_{i,n}$ × (1 + i).

an ordinary annuity. As the cash flow time line and the numerical solution indicate, the adjustment is rather simple — just multiply the PVIFA for an ordinary annuity by (1 + i). So, the present value interest factor for an annuity due, **PVIFA(DUE)$_{i,n}$**, is

$$
PVIFA(DUE)_{i,n} = \left[\left\{ \frac{1 - \dfrac{1}{(1 + i)^n}}{i} \right\} \times (1 + i) \right]
$$

$$
= [(PVIFA_{i,n})(1 + i)]
$$

The tabular solution for PVA(DUE)$_n$ is

$$
PVA(DUE)_n = PMT[PVIFA(DUE)_{i,n}] = PMT[(PVIFA_{i,n})(1 + i)]
$$

$$
PVA(DUE)_3 = \$100[(2.7232)(1.05)]
$$

$$
= \$100(2.85941) = \$285.941
$$

3. Financial Calculator Solution:

BEGIN

Inputs:	3	5	?	−100	0
	N	**I**	**PV**	**PMT**	**FV**

Output: = 285.941

Switch to the beginning-of-period mode, and then enter N = 3, I = 5, PMT = −100, and FV = 0, and then press PV to get the answer, $285.94. *Again, because most problems deal with end-of-period cash flows, don't forget to switch your calculator back to the END mode.*

Self-Test Questions

Which annuity has the greater present value: an ordinary annuity or an annuity due? Why?

Explain how financial calculators can be used to find present values of annuities.

Solving for Interest Rates with Annuities

Suppose you pay $846.80 for an investment that promises to pay you $250 per year for the next four years. If the payments are made at the end of each year, what interest rate (rate of return) will you earn on this investment? We can solve this problem as follows:

CASH FLOW TIME LINE:

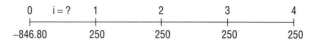

EQUATION:

$$PVA_n = PMT(PVIFA_{i,n})$$ **(6-4)**

$$\$846.80 = \$250(PVIFA_{i = ?, 4})$$

1. NUMERICAL SOLUTION:

To solve this problem numerically, you would have to use a trial-and-error process in which you plug different values for i into either Equation 6-4 or Equation 6-4a until you find the value for i where the present value of the six-year $250 annuity is equal to $846.80. The solution is i = 0.07, or 7%.

2. TABULAR SOLUTION:

If we solve the equation given above for the PVIFA, we find

$$PVIFA_{i=?, 4} = \frac{\$846.80}{\$250} = 3.3872$$

Using Table A-1, look across the Period 4 row until you find PVIFA = 3.3872. This value is in the 7% column, so the interest rate at which a four-year $250 annuity has a present value equal to $846.80 is 7 percent. This method cannot be used if the interest rate is not in the table; instead, you would have to use your financial calculator to solve the problem.

3. FINANCIAL CALCULATOR SOLUTION:

Inputs: 4   ?   -846.80   250   0
           N   I   PV   PMT   FV
Output: = 7.0

Enter N = 4, PV = -846.80, PMT = 250, and FV = 0, and then press I to get the answer, 7.0%.

In the problem we just solved, the information that was given included the amount of the annuity payment, the *present value* of the annuity, and the number of years the annuity payment is received. If the *future value* of the annuity was given instead of the present value, to find i, we would follow the same procedures outlined above, but Equation 6-3 would be used because it applies to future values. For example, let's assume a financial institution has an investment that requires you to make annual payments equal to $250 starting at the end of this year, and in four years the financial institution will pay you $1,110. In this case, we know the amount of the annuity — $250 — the length of the annuity — six years — and the future value of the annuity — $1,110. What is the interest rate that you would earn on this investment? The procedure to solve this problem is the same as outlined earlier, except you use the FVA_n equation (Equation 6-3) instead of the PVA_n equation for the numerical and tabular solution, and the FV key ($1,110) instead of the PV key for the financial calculator solution. Try it — you should get i = 7%.

Self-Test Question

Describe how you would solve for interest rates with annuities using the numerical solution.

Perpetuities

PERPETUITY
A stream of equal payments expected to continue forever.

Most annuities call for payments to be made over some finite period of time — for example, $100 per year for three years. However, some annuities go on indefinitely, or perpetually, and these annuities are called **perpetuities**. The present value of a perpetuity, PVP, is found by applying Equation 6-5.[10]

6-5

$$PVP = \frac{Payment}{Interest\ rate} = \frac{PMT}{i}$$

CONSOL
A perpetual bond issued by the British government to consolidate past debts; in general, any perpetual bond.

Perpetuities can be illustrated by some British securities issued after the Napoleonic Wars. In 1815, the British government sold a huge bond issue and used the proceeds to pay off many smaller issues that had been floated in prior years to pay for the wars. Because the purpose of the bonds was to consolidate past debts, the bonds were called **consols**. Suppose each consol promised to pay $100 per year in perpetuity. (Actually, interest was stated in pounds.) What would each bond be worth if the opportunity cost rate, or discount rate, was 5 percent? The answer is $2,000:

$$PVP = \frac{\$100}{0.05} = \$2,000$$

Suppose the interest rate rose to 10 percent; what would happen to the consol's value? The value would drop to $1,000:

$$PVP = \frac{\$100}{0.10} = \$1,000$$

We see that the value of a perpetuity changes dramatically when interest rates change. Perpetuities are discussed further in Chapter 7, where procedures for finding the value of various types of securities are discussed.

---

[10]The derivation of Equation 6-5 is given in the Extension section of Chapter 28 of Eugene F. Brigham, Louis C. Gapenski, and Phillip R. Daves, *Intermediate Financial Management*, 6th ed. (Fort Worth, TX: Dryden Press, 1999).

Self-Test Questions

What happens to the value of a perpetuity when interest rates increase?

What happens when interest rates decrease? Why do these changes occur?

Uneven Cash Flow Streams

UNEVEN CASH FLOW STREAM
A series of cash flows in which the amount varies from one period to the next.

The definition of an annuity includes the words *constant amount* — in other words, annuities involve payments that are equal in every period. Although many financial decisions do involve constant payments, some important decisions involve uneven, or nonconstant, cash flows. For example, common stocks typically pay an increasing stream of dividends over time, and fixed asset investments such as new equipment normally do not generate constant cash flows. Consequently, it is necessary to extend our time value discussion to include **uneven cash flow streams**.

PAYMENT (PMT)
This term designates constant cash flows.

Throughout the book, we will follow convention and reserve the term **payment (PMT)** for annuity situations where the cash flows are constant, and we will use the term **cash flow (CF)** to denote cash flows in general, which includes uneven cash flows. Financial calculators are set up to follow this convention, so if you are using one and dealing with uneven cash flows, you will need to use the cash flow register.

CASH FLOW (CF)
This term designates cash flows in general, including uneven cash flows.

Present Value of an Uneven Cash Flow Stream

The PV of an uneven cash flow stream is found as the sum of the PVs of the individual cash flows of the stream. For example, suppose we must find the PV of the following cash flow stream, discounted at 6 percent:

```
0    6%    1        2        3        4        5
|         |        |        |        |        |
PV = ?    100      300      200      200      1,000
```

The PV is found by applying this general present value equation:

$$\text{6-6} \quad PV = CF_1 \left[\frac{1}{(1+i)^1} \right] + CF_2 \left[\frac{1}{(1+i)^2} \right] + \cdots + CF_n \left[\frac{1}{(1+i)^n} \right]$$

$$= \sum_{t=1}^{n} CF_t \left[\frac{1}{(1+i)^t} \right] = \sum_{t=1}^{n} CF_t \, (PVIF_{i,t})$$

We can find the PV of each individual cash flow using the numerical, tabular, or financial calculator methods, and then sum these values to find the present value of the stream. Here is what the process would look like:

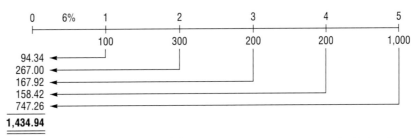

All we did was to apply Equation 6-6, show the individual PVs in the left column of the diagram, and then sum these individual PVs to find the PV of the entire stream.

The present value of any cash flow stream can always be found by summing the present values of the individual cash flows as shown above. However, when cash flows are constant, we can simplify our computations by applying the annuity solutions discussed earlier.

Problems involving uneven cash flows can be solved in one step with most financial calculators. First, you input the individual cash flows, in chronological order, into the cash flow register. Cash flows usually are designated CF_0, CF_1, CF_2, CF_3, and so on. Next, you enter the interest rate. At this point, you have substituted in all the known values of Equation 6-6, so you only need to press the NPV key to find the present value of the cash flow stream. The calculator has been programmed to find the PV of each cash flow, including CF_0, and then to sum these values to find the PV of the entire stream. To input the cash flows for this problem, enter 0 (because $CF_0 = 0$), 100, 300, 200, 200, and 1000 in that order into the cash flow register, enter I = 6, and then press NPV to obtain the answer, \$1,434.94.

Two points should be noted. First, when dealing with the cash flow register, the calculator uses the term NPV rather than PV. The N stands for *net,* so NPV is the abbreviation for Net Present Value, which simply is the net present value of a series of positive and negative cash flows, including CF_0. Our example has no negative cash flows, but if it did, we simply would input them with negative signs. Also, because we wanted to compute the PV, $CF_0 = 0$.

The second point to note is that annuities can be entered into the cash flow register more efficiently by using the N_j key. (On some calculators, you are prompted to enter the number of times the cash flow occurs, and on still other calculators the procedures for inputting data, as we discuss next, might be different. You should consult your calculator manual to determine the appropriate steps for your specific calculator.) In this illustration, you would enter $CF_0 = 0$, $CF_1 = 100$, $CF_2 = 300$, $CF_3 = 200$, $N_j = 2$ (which tells the calculator that the 200 occurs two times), and $CF_5 = 1000$. Then enter I = 6, and press the NPV key; 1,434.94 will appear in the display. Also, note that amounts entered into the cash flow register remain in the register until they are cleared. Thus, if you had previously worked a problem with eight cash flows and then moved to a problem with only four cash flows, the calculator would assume that the last four cash flows from the first problem belonged to the second problem. Therefore, *you must be sure to clear the cash flow register before starting a new problem.*

Future Value of an Uneven Cash Flow Stream

TERMINAL VALUE
The future value of a cash flow stream.

The future value of an uneven cash flow stream (sometimes called the **terminal value**) is found by compounding each payment to the end of the stream and then summing the future values:

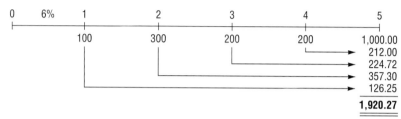

6-7

$$FV_n = CF_1 (1 + i)^{n-1} + CF_2(1 + i)^{n-2} + \cdots + CF_n (1 + i)^0$$

$$= \sum_{t=1}^{n} CF_t (1 + i)^{n-t} = \sum_{t=1}^{n} CF_t (FVIF_{i,n-t})$$

The future value of our illustrative uneven cash flow stream is \$1,920.27:

```
 0     6%     1         2         3         4         5
 ├─────────────┼─────────┼─────────┼─────────┼─────────┤
              100       300       200       200   1,000.00
                                              └──────► 212.00
                                    └────────────────► 224.72
                          └──────────────────────────► 357.30
               └─────────────────────────────────────► 126.25
                                                      1,920.27
```

Some financial calculators have a net future value (NFV) key that, after the cash flows and interest rate have been entered into the calculator, can be used to obtain the future value of an uneven cash flow stream. In any event, it is easy enough to compound the individual cash flows to the terminal year and then to sum them to find the FV of the stream. Also, we generally are more interested in the present value of an asset's cash flow stream than in the future value because the present value represents today's value, which we can compare with the price of the asset.

ANNUAL COMPOUNDING
The arithmetic process of determining the final value of a cash flow or series of cash flows when interest is added once a year.

SEMIANNUAL COMPOUNDING
The arithmetic process of determining the final value of a cash flow or series of cash flows when interest is added twice a year.

Solving for i with Uneven Cash Flow Streams

It is relatively easy to solve for i *numerically* or *with the tables* when the cash flows are lump sums or annuities. However, it is extremely difficult to solve for i if the cash flows are uneven, as you will have to go through tedious trial-and-error calculations. With a financial calculator, though, it is easy to find the value of i. Simply input the CF values into the cash flow register and then press the IRR key. IRR stands for *internal rate of return*, which is the return on an investment. We will defer further discussion of this calculation for now, but we will take it up later in our discussion of capital budgeting methods in Chapter 9.

Self-Test Questions

Give two examples of financial decisions that would typically involve uneven flows of cash.

What is meant by the term *terminal value?*

Semiannual and Other Compounding Periods

In our examples thus far, we have assumed that interest is compounded once a year, or annually. This is called **annual compounding**. Suppose, however, that you put \$100 into a bank that states it pays a 10 percent annual interest rate, but that interest is added each six months. This is called **semiannual compounding**.

How much would you accumulate at the end of one year, two years, or some other period under semiannual compounding?

To illustrate semiannual compounding, assume that $100 is placed into an account at an interest rate of 10 percent and left there for three years. First, consider again what happens under annual compounding:

1. TIME LINE, EQUATION, AND NUMERICAL SOLUTION:

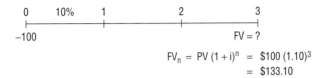

$$FV_n = PV(1+i)^n = \$100(1.10)^3$$
$$= \$133.10$$

2. TABULAR SOLUTION:

$$FV_3 = \$100(FVIF_{10\%,3}) = \$100(1.3310) = \$133.10$$

3. FINANCIAL CALCULATOR SOLUTION:

Inputs:	3	10	−100	0	?
	N	**I**	**PV**	**PMT**	**FV**
Output:					= 133.10

Now consider what happens under semiannual compounding. Here we have n = 2 × 3 = 6 semiannual periods, and you will earn i = 10% ÷ 2 = 5% every six months. Note that on all types of contracts, interest is always quoted as an annual rate, and if compounding occurs more frequently than once a year, that fact is stated, along with the rate. In our example, the quoted rate is *10 percent, compounded semiannually.* Here is how we find the FV after three years at 10 percent with semiannual compounding:

1. EQUATION AND NUMERICAL SOLUTION:

$$FV_n = PV(1+i)^n = \$100(1.05)^6$$
$$= \$100(1.3401) = \$134.01$$

Here i = Rate per period = (Annual rate) ÷ (Compounding periods per year) = 10% ÷ 2 = 5%, and n = Total number of periods = (Years) × (Compounding periods per year) = 3 × 2 = 6.

2. TABULAR SOLUTION:

$$FV_6 = \$100(FVIF_{5\%,6}) = \$100(1.3401) = \$134.01.$$

Look up FVIF for 5 percent and 6 periods in Table A-3 and complete the arithmetic.

3. FINANCIAL CALCULATOR SOLUTION:

Inputs:	6	5	−100	0	?
	N	**I**	**PV**	**PMT**	**FV**
Output:					= 134.01

Enter N = (Years) × (Periods per year) = 3 × 2 = 6, I = (Annual rate) ÷ (Periods per year) = 10/2 = 5, PV = −100, and PMT = 0, and then press FV to find the answer, $134.01 versus $133.10 under annual compounding. The FV is larger under semi-annual compounding because interest on interest is being earned more frequently.

Throughout the world economy, different compounding periods are used for different types of investments. For example, bank accounts generally compute interest on a daily basis; most bonds pay interest semiannually; and stocks generally pay dividends quarterly.[11] If we are to properly compare securities with different compounding periods, we need to put them on a common basis. This requires us to distinguish between the **simple**, or **quoted**, **interest rate** and the **effective annual rate (EAR)**.

The simple, or quoted, interest rate in our example is 10 percent. *The effective annual rate (EAR) is defined as the rate that would produce the same ending (future) value if annual compounding had been used.* In our example, the effective annual rate is the rate that would produce an FV of $134.01 at the end of Year 3.

We can determine the effective annual rate, given the simple rate and the number of compounding periods per year, by solving this equation:

6-8

$$\text{Effective annual rate} = \text{EAR} = \left(1 + \frac{i_{\text{SIMPLE}}}{m}\right)^m - 1.0$$

Here i_{SIMPLE} is the simple, or quoted, interest rate, and m is the number of compounding periods per year. For example, to find the effective annual rate if the simple rate is 10 percent and semiannual compounding is used, we have[12]

$$\frac{\text{Effective}}{\text{annual rate}} = \text{EAR} = \left(1 + \frac{0.10}{2}\right)^2 - 1.0 = (1.05)^2 - 1.0$$

$$= 1.1025 - 1.0 = 0.1025 = 10.25\%$$

Semiannual compounding (or any nonannual compounding) can be handled in two ways: (1) State everything on a periodic basis rather than on an annual basis. For example, use n = 6 periods rather than n = 3 years, and use i = 5% per period

---

SIMPLE (QUOTED) INTEREST RATE The contracted, or quoted, interest rate that is used to compute the interest paid per period.

EFFECTIVE ANNUAL RATE (EAR) The annual rate of interest actually being earned, as opposed to the quoted rate, considering the compounding of interest.

---

[11]Some banks and savings and loans even pay interest compounded continuously. For a discussion of continuous compounding, see Chapter 2, in Eugene F. Brigham and Louis C. Gapenski, *Financial Management,* 9th ed. (Fort Worth, TX: Dryden Press, 1999).

[12]Many financial calculators are programmed to find the EAR or, given the EAR, to find the simple interest rate. This is called "interest rate conversion," and you simply enter the simple interest rate and the number of compounding periods per year, and then press the EFF% key to find the EAR.

rather than i = 10% per year. (2) Alternatively, find the effective annual rate by applying Equation 6-8, and then use this rate as an annual rate over the given number of years. In our example, use i = 10.25% and n = 3 years. Here are the time lines for the two alternative procedures:

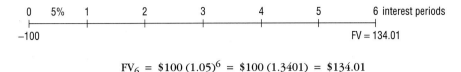

$$FV_6 = \$100\,(1.05)^6 = \$100\,(1.3401) = \$134.01$$

$$FV_3 = \$100\,(1.1025)^3 = \$100\,(1.3401) = \$134.01$$

We see that both procedures produce the same result, $134.01. Of course, once you start dealing with noninteger interest rates such as 10.25 percent, the use of a calculator or the numerical solution is essential.

The points made about semiannual compounding can be generalized as follows. When compounding occurs more frequently than once a year, we can use a modified version of Equation 6-1 to find the future value of any lump sum:

$$\text{Annual compounding: } FV_n = PV(1 + i)^n \qquad \textbf{(6-1)}$$

6-9

$$\text{More frequent compounding: } FV_n = PV\left(1 + \frac{i_{\text{SIMPLE}}}{m}\right)^{m \times n}$$

Here i_{SIMPLE} is the simple, or quoted, rate, m is the number of times compounding occurs per year, and n is the number of years. For example, when banks pay daily interest, the value of m is set at 365, and Equation 6-9 is applied.[13]

ANNUAL PERCENTAGE RATE (APR)
The periodic rate multiplied by the number of periods per year.

To illustrate further the effects of compounding more frequently than once a year, consider the interest rate charged on credit cards. Many banks charge 1.5 percent per month, and, in their advertising, they state that the **Annual Percentage Rate (APR)** is 18.0 percent. However, the true rate is the effective annual rate of 19.6 percent[14]:

---

[13]To illustrate, the future value of $1 invested at 10 percent for one year under daily compounding (using a 365-day year) is $1.1052:

$$FV_n = \$1\left(1 + \frac{0.10}{365}\right)^{365} = \$1(1.105156) = \$1.1052$$

[14]The *annual percentage rate (APR)* is the rate often used in bank loan advertisements because it meets the minimum requirements contained in "truth in lending" laws. Typically, the APR is defined as (Periodic rate) × (Number of periods in one year). For example, the APR on a credit card with interest charges of 1.5 percent per month is 1.5%(12) = 18.0%. The APR understates the effective annual rate because compounding is not taken into consideration. So, banks tend to use the APR when advertising what they charge on loans, but they use the effective annual rate when advertising rates on savings accounts and certificates of deposit because they want to make their deposit rates look high.

$$\text{Effective annual rate} = \text{EAR} = \left(1 + \frac{0.18}{12}\right)^{12} - 1$$

$$= (1.015)^{12} - 1$$

$$= 0.196 = 19.6\%$$

Semiannual and other compounding periods can also be used for discounting, and for both lump sums and annuities. First, consider the case where we want to find the PV of an ordinary annuity of $100 per year for three years when the interest rate is 8 percent, compounded annually:

CASH FLOW TIME LINE:

```
0      8%      1           2           3
├──────────────┼───────────┼───────────┤
PV = ?       −100        −100        −100
```

1. NUMERICAL SOLUTION:

Find the PV of each cash flow and sum them. Alternatively, compute the PV directly as follows:

$$\text{PVA}_3 = \$100 \left[\frac{1 - \dfrac{1}{(1.08)^3}}{0.08}\right] = \$100(2.5771) = \$257.71$$

2. TABULAR SOLUTION:

$$\text{PVA}_3 = \text{PMT}(\text{PVIFA}_{8\%,3})$$

$$= \$100(2.5771) = \$257.71$$

3. FINANCIAL CALCULATOR SOLUTION:

Inputs:	3	8	?	−100	0
	N	**I**	**PV**	**PMT**	**FV**
Output:			= 257.71		

Now let's change the situation so that the annuity calls for payments of $50 each six months rather than $100 per year, and the rate is 8 percent, compounded semiannually. Here is the time line:

CASH FLOW TIME LINE:

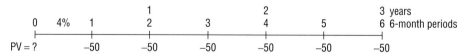

```
                  1           2           3 years
0     4%    1     2     3     4     5     6 6-month periods
├──────────┼─────┼─────┼─────┼─────┼─────┤
PV = ?    −50   −50   −50   −50   −50   −50
```

1. NUMERICAL SOLUTION:

Find the PV of each cash flow by discounting at 4 percent. Treat each tick mark on the time line as a period, so there would be 6 periods. The PV of the annuity is \$262.11 versus \$257.71 under annual compounding. Solving directly, the computation is:

$$PVA_6 = \$50 \left[\frac{1 - \frac{1}{(1.04)^6}}{0.04} \right] = \$50(5.2421) = \$262.11$$

2. TABULAR SOLUTION:

$$PVA_6 = PMT(PVIFA_{4\%,6})$$

$$= \$50(5.2421) = \$262.11$$

3. FINANCIAL CALCULATOR SOLUTION:

Inputs:	6	4	?	−50	0
	N	**I**	**PV**	**PMT**	**FV**

Output: = 262.11

The semiannual payments come in sooner, so they can be invested sooner, which means the \$50 semiannual annuity is more valuable than the \$100 annual annuity.

Self-Test Questions

What changes must you make in your calculations to determine the future value of an amount that is being compounded at 8 percent semiannually versus one being compounded annually at 8 percent?

Why is semiannual compounding better than annual compounding from a saver's standpoint?

What are meant by the terms *annual percentage rate, effective annual rate,* and *simple interest rate?*

Amortized Loans

AMORTIZED LOAN
A loan that is repaid in equal payments over its life.

One of the most important applications of compound interest involves loans that are paid off in installments over time. Included are automobile loans, home mortgages, student loans, and most business debt other than very short-term loans and long-term bonds. If a loan is to be repaid in equal periodic amounts (monthly, quarterly, or annually), it is said to be an **amortized loan**.[15]

To illustrate, suppose a firm borrows \$15,000, and the loan is to be repaid in three equal payments at the end of each of the next three years. The lender is to receive 8 percent interest on the loan balance that is outstanding at the beginning of each year. The first task is to determine the amount the firm must repay each year, or the annual payment. To find this amount, recognize that the \$15,000

---

[15]The word *amortized* comes from the Latin *mors,* meaning "death," so an amortized loan is one that is "killed off" over time.

represents the present value of an annuity of PMT dollars per year for three years, discounted at 8 percent:

CASH FLOW TIME LINE AND EQUATION:

0	8%	1	2	3
15,000		PMT	PMT	PMT

$$PVA_3 = \frac{PMT}{(1+i)^1} + \frac{PMT}{(1+i)^2} + \frac{PMT}{(1+i)^3} = \sum_{t=1}^{3} \frac{PMT}{(1+i)^t}$$

$$\$15,000 = \sum_{t=1}^{3} \frac{PMT}{(1.08)^t}$$

Here we know everything except PMT, so we can solve the equation for PMT.

1. NUMERICAL SOLUTION:

You could follow the trial-and-error procedure, inserting values for PMT in the equation until you find a value that "works" and causes the right side of the equation to equal $15,000. This would be a tedious process, but you would eventually find PMT = $5,820.50. Or, you could solve for PMT as follows:

$$\$15,000 = \sum_{t=1}^{3} \frac{PMT}{(1.08)^t} = PMT\left[\sum_{t=1}^{3} \frac{1}{(1.08)^t}\right] = PMT\left[\frac{1 - \frac{1}{(1.08)^3}}{0.08}\right]$$

$$\$15,000 = PMT(2.5771)$$

$$PMT = \frac{\$15,000}{2.5771} = \$5,820.50$$

2. TABULAR SOLUTION:

Substitute in known values and look up PVIFA for 8%, 3 periods in Table A-2:

$$PVA_n = PMT(PVIFA_{i,n})$$

$$\$15,000 = PMT(2.5771)$$

$$PMT = \frac{\$15,000}{2.5771} = \$5,820.50$$

3. FINANCIAL CALCULATOR SOLUTION:

Inputs:	3	8	15000	?	0
	N	**I**	**PV**	**PMT**	**FV**
Output:				= −5820.50	

Enter N = 3, I = 8, PV = 15000 (the firm receives the cash), and FV = 0, and then press the PMT key to find PMT = −5820.50.

TABLE 6-2

Loan Amortization Schedule, 8 Percent Interest Rate

Year	Beginning Amount (1)	Payment (2)	Interest[a] (3)	Repayment of Principal[b] (2) – (3) = (4)	Remaining Balance (1) – (4) = (5)
1	$15,000.00	$5,820.50	$1,200.00	$4,620.50	$10,379.50
2	10,379.50	5,820.50	830.36	4,990.14	5,389.36
3	5,389.36	5,820.50	431.15	5,389.35	0.01[c]

NOTES:

[a]Interest is calculated by multiplying the loan balance at the beginning of the year by the interest rate. Therefore, interest in Year 1 is $15,000(0.08) = $1,200.00; in Year 2, it is $10,379.50(0.08) = $830.36; and in Year 3, it is $5,389.36(0.08) = $431.15 (rounded).

[b]Repayment of principal is equal to the payment of $5,820.50 minus the interest charge for each year.

[c]The $0.01 remaining balance at the end of Year 3 results from rounding differences.

Therefore, the firm must pay the lender $5,820.50 at the end of each of the next three years, and the percentage cost to the borrower, which is also the rate of return to the lender, will be 8 percent.

Each payment consists partly of interest and partly of repayment of principal. This breakdown is given in the **amortization schedule** shown in Table 6-2. The interest component is largest in the first year, and it declines as the outstanding balance of the loan decreases. For tax purposes, a *business* borrower reports the interest component shown in Column 3 as a deductible cost each year, while the lender reports this same amount as taxable income.

AMORTIZATION SCHEDULE
A schedule showing precisely how a loan will be repaid. It gives the required payment on each payment date and a breakdown of the payment, showing how much is interest and how much is repayment of principal.

Most financial calculators are programmed to calculate amortization tables; you simply enter the input data, and then press one key to get each entry in Table 6-2. If you have a financial calculator, it is worthwhile to read the appropriate section of the manual and learn how to use its amortization feature.

Self-Test Questions

To construct an amortization schedule, how do you determine the amount of the periodic payments?

How do you determine the amount of each payment that goes to interest and to principal?

Comparison of Different Types of Interest Rates

Up to this point, we have discussed three different types of interest rates. It is useful to compare the three types and to know when each should be used, as we discuss below.

1. **Simple, or quoted, rate, i_{SIMPLE}.** This is the rate that is quoted by borrowers and lenders, and it is used to determine the rate earned per compounding period (periodic rate). Practitioners in the stock, bond, mortgage, loan, banking, and other markets generally express financial contracts in terms of simple rates. So, if you talk with a banker, broker, mortgage lender, auto finance company, or student loan officer about rates, the simple rate is the one he or she normally quotes you. However, to be meaningful, the simple rate quotation also must include the number of compounding periods per year. For example, a bank might offer 8.5 percent, compounded quarterly, on CDs, or a mutual fund might offer 8 percent, compounded monthly, on its money market account.

Simple rates can be compared with one another, *but only if the instruments being compared use the same number of compounding periods per year.* Thus, to compare an 8.5 percent, annual payment CD with an 8 percent, daily payment money market fund, we would need to put both instruments on an effective annual rate (EAR) basis as discussed later in this section.

Note also that the simple rate never is shown on a time line, and it is never used as an input in a financial calculator unless compounding occurs only once a year (in which case i_{SIMPLE} = periodic rate = EAR). If more frequent compounding occurs, you must use either the periodic rate or the effective annual rate as discussed below.[16]

2. **Periodic rate.** This is the rate charged by a lender or paid by a borrower *each interest period.* It can be a rate per year, per six-month period, per quarter, per month, per day, or per any other time interval (usually one year or less). For example, a bank might charge 1 percent per month on its credit card loans, or a finance company might charge 3 percent per quarter on consumer loans. We find the periodic rate as follows:

$$\text{6-10} \qquad \text{Periodic rate} = \frac{i_{SIMPLE}}{m}$$

which implies that

$$\text{6-11} \qquad i_{SIMPLE} = (\text{Periodic rate}) \times (m) = APR$$

Here i_{SIMPLE} is the simple annual rate and m is the number of compounding periods per year. APR, which is the annual percentage rate, represents the periodic rate stated on an annual basis without considering interest compounding; it is i_{SIMPLE}. *The APR never is used in actual calculations; it is simply reported to borrowers.*

If there is one payment per year, or if interest is added only once a year, then m = 1, and the periodic rate is equal to the simple rate. *But, in all cases where*

---

[16]Some calculators have a switch that permits you to specify the number of payments per year. We find it less confusing to set this switch to 1 and then leave it there. We prefer to work with *periods* when more than one payment occurs each year because this maintains a consistency between number of periods and the periodic interest rate.

interest is added or payments are made more frequently than annually, the periodic rate is less than the simple rate.

The periodic rate is used for calculations in problems where these two conditions hold: (a) payments occur on a regular basis more frequently than once a year, and (b) a payment is made on each compounding (or discounting) date. Thus, if you are dealing with an auto loan that requires monthly payments, with a semiannual payment bond, or with an education loan that calls for quarterly payments, then your time line and in your calculations you would use the Periodic rate = $i_{SIMPLE} \div m$, and the appropriate number of periods would be $n \times m$.

3. **Effective annual rate, EAR.** This is the rate with which, under annual compounding (m = 1), we would obtain the same result as if we had used a given periodic rate with m compounding periods per year. The EAR is found as follows:

6-8

$$EAR = \left(1 + \frac{i_{SIMPLE}}{m}\right)^m - 1.0$$

$$= (1 - \text{Periodic rate})^m - 1$$

In the EAR equation, $i_{SIMPLE} \div m$ is the periodic rate, and m is the number of periods per year. For example, suppose you could borrow using either a credit card that charges 1 percent per month or a bank loan with a 12 percent quoted simple interest rate that is compounded quarterly. Which should you choose? To answer this question, the cost rate of each alternative must be expressed as an EAR:

Credit card loan: EAR = $(1 + 0.01)^{12} - 1.0 = (1.01)^{12} - 1.0$

$$= 1.126825 - 1.0 = 0.126825 = 12.6825\%$$

Bank loan: EAR = $(1 + 0.03)^4 - 1.0 = (1.03)^4 - 1.0$

$$= 1.125509 - 1.0 = 0.125509 = 12.5509\%$$

Thus, the credit card loan costs a little more than the bank loan. This result should have been intuitive to you — both loans have the same 12 percent simple rate, yet you would have to make monthly payments on the credit card versus quarterly payments under the bank loan.

Self-Test Questions

Define the simple (or quoted) rate, the periodic rate, and the effective annual rate.

How are the simple rate, the periodic rate, and the effective annual rate related? Can you think of a situation where all three of these rates will be the same?

Summary

Financial decisions often involve situations in which someone pays (receives) money at one point in time and receives (pays) money at some later time. Dollars

FIGURE 6-3

Illustration for Chapter Summary

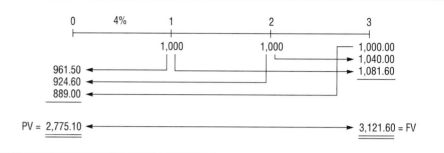

that are paid or received at two different points in time are different, and this difference is recognized and accounted for by time value of money (TVM) analysis. We summarize below the types of TVM analyses and the key concepts covered in this chapter, using the data shown in Figure 6-3 to illustrate the various points. Refer to the figure constantly, and try to find in it an example of the points covered as you go through this summary.

- **Compounding** is the process of determining the **future value (FV)** of a cash flow or a series of cash flows. The compounded amount, or future value, is equal to the beginning amount plus the interest earned.
- Future value (single payment): $FV_n = PV(1 + i)^n = PV(FVIF_{i,n})$
  Example: $924.56 compounded for two years at 4 percent:

$$FV_2 = \$924.56(1.04)^2 = \$1,000$$

- **Discounting** is the process of finding the **present value (PV)** of a future cash flow or a series of cash flows; discounting is the reciprocal (inverse) of compounding.
- Present value (single payment): $PV = \dfrac{FV_n}{(1 + i)^n} = FV_n\left[\dfrac{1}{(1 + i)^n}\right] = PVIF_{i,n}$
  Example: $1,000 discounted back for two years at 4 percent:

$$PV = \frac{\$1,000}{(1.04)^2} = \$1,000\left[\frac{1}{(1.04)^2}\right] = \$1,000(0.9246) = \$924.60$$

- An **annuity** is defined as a series of equal periodic payments (PMT) for a specified number of periods.
- Future value of an annuity:

$$FVA_n = PMT(1 + i)^0 + PMT(1 + i)^1 + \cdots + PMT(1 + i)^{n-1}$$

$$= PMT\sum_{t=1}^{n}(1 + i)^{n-t} = PMT\left[\frac{(1 + i)^n - 1}{i}\right] = PMT(FVIFA_{i,n})$$

Example: FVA of three payments of $1,000 when i = 4%:

$$FVA_3 = \$1,000(3.1216) = \$3,121.60$$

- Present value of an annuity:

$$PVA_n = \frac{PMT}{(1 + i)^1} + \frac{PMT}{(1 + i)^2} + \cdots + \frac{PMT}{(1 + i)^n}$$

$$= PMT\left[\sum_{t=1}^{n}\frac{1}{(1 + i)^t}\right] = PMT\left[\frac{1 - \dfrac{1}{(1 + i)^n}}{i}\right] = PMT(PVIFA_{i,n})$$

Example: PVA of three payments of $1,000 when i = 4%:

$$PVA_3 = \$1,000(2.7751) = \$2,775.10$$

- An annuity whose payments occur at the end of each period is called an **ordinary annuity**. The formulas just presented are for ordinary annuities.
- If each payment occurs at the beginning of the period rather than at the end, then we have an **annuity due**. In Figure 6-3, the payments would be shown at Years 0, 1, and 2 rather than at Years 1, 2, and 3. The PV of each payment would be larger, because each payment would be discounted back one year less; hence, the PV of the annuity also would be larger.

    Similarly, the FV of the annuity due also would be larger because each payment would be compounded for an extra year. The following formulas can be used to convert the PV and FV of an ordinary annuity to an annuity due:

$$PVA(DUE)_n = PMT[(PVIFA_{i,n}) \times (1 + i)] = PMT[PVIFA(DUE)_{i,n}]$$

Example: PVA of three beginning-of-year payments of $1,000 when i = 4%:

$$PVA(DUE)_3 = \$1,000[(2.7751)(1.04)] = \$2,886.10$$

$$FVA(DUE)_n = PMT[(FVIFA_{i,n}) \times (1 + i)] = PMT[FVIFA(DUE)_{i,n}]$$

Example: FVA of three beginning-of-year payments of $1,000 when i = 4%:

$$FVA(DUE)_3 = \$1,000[(3.1216)(1.04)] = \$3,246.46$$

- If the cash flow time line in Figure 6-3 was extended out forever so that the $1,000 payments went on forever, we would have a **perpetuity** whose value could be found as follows:

$$\text{Value of a perpetuity} = PVP = \frac{PMT}{i} = \frac{\$1,000}{0.04} = \$25,000$$

- If the cash flows in Figure 6-3 were unequal, we could not use the annuity formulas. To find the PV or FV of an **uneven cash flow stream (series)**, find the PV or FV of each individual cash flow and then sum them.
- **Financial calculators** have built-in programs that perform all the operations discussed in this chapter. It would be useful for you to buy such a calculator

and to learn how to use it. Even if you do, though, it is essential that you understand the logical processes involved.

- Thus far in the summary we have assumed that interest is earned, at the end of each year, or annually. However, many contracts call for more frequent payments; for example, mortgage and auto loans call for monthly payments, and most bonds pay interest semiannually. Similarly, most banks compute interest daily. When compounding occurs more frequently than once a year, this fact must be recognized. We can use the Figure 6-3 example to illustrate the procedures. First, the following formula is used to find an **effective annual rate (EAR)**:

$$\text{Effective annual rate} = \text{EAR} = \left(1 + \frac{i_{\text{SIMPLE}}}{m}\right)^m - 1.0$$

- For semiannual compounding, the effective annual rate is 4.04 percent:

$$\left(1 + \frac{0.04}{2}\right)^2 - 1.0 = (1.02)^2 - 1.0 = 1.0404 - 1.0 = 0.0404 = 4.04\%$$

This rate could then be used (with a calculator but not with the tables) to find the PV or FV of each payment in Figure 6-3.

If the $1,000 per-year payments were actually payable as $500 each six months, you would simply redraw Figure 6-3 to show six payments of $500 each, but you would also need to use a periodic interest rate of 4% ÷ 2 = 2% for determining the PV or FV of the payments.

- The general equation for finding the future value of a single payment for any number of compounding periods per year is:

$$\text{FV}_n = \text{PV}\left(1 + \frac{i_{\text{SIMPLE}}}{m}\right)^{n \times m}$$

where

i_{SIMPLE} = quoted interest rate.
  m = number of compounding periods per year.
  n = number of years.

- An **amortized loan** is one that is paid off in equal payments over a specified period. An **amortization schedule** shows how much of each payment constitutes interest, how much is used to reduce the principal, and the remaining balance of the loan at each point in time.

The concepts covered in this chapter are used throughout the remainder of the book. For example, in Chapter 7 we apply present value concepts to determine the values of stocks and bonds, and we see that the market prices of securities are established by determining the present values of the cash flows they are expected to provide. In later chapters, the same basic concepts are applied to corporate decisions involving both expenditures on capital assets and determining the types of capital that should be used to pay for such assets.

Questions

6-1 What is an opportunity cost rate? How is this rate used in time value analysis, and where is it shown on a time line? Is the opportunity rate a single number that is used in all situations?

6-2 An annuity is defined as a series of payments of a fixed amount for a specific number of periods. Thus, $100 a year for 10 years is an annuity, but $100 in Year 1, $200 in Year 2, and $400 in Years 3 through 10 does *not* constitute an annuity. However, the second series *contains* an annuity. Is this statement true or false?

6-3 If a firm's earnings per share grew from $1 to $2 over a 10-year period, the total growth would be 100 percent, but the annual growth rate would be *less than* 10 percent. True or false? Explain. Under what conditions would the annual growth rate *actually* be 10 percent per year?

6-4 Would you rather have a savings account that pays 5 percent interest compounded semiannually or one that pays 5 percent interest compounded daily? Explain.

6-5 To find the present value of an uneven series of cash flows, you must find the PVs of the individual cash flows and then sum them. Annuity procedures can never be of use, even if some of the cash flows constitute an annuity (e.g., $100 each for Years 3, 4, 5, and 6), because the entire series is not an annuity. Is this statement true or false? Explain.

6-6 The present value of a perpetuity is equal to the payment on the annuity, PMT, divided by the interest rate, i: $PVP = PMT/i$. What is the sum, or future value, of a perpetuity of PMT dollars per year? (Hint: The answer is infinity, but explain why.)

Self-Test Problems   *Solutions Appear in Appendix B*

Key terms   **ST-1** Define each of the following terms:
    a. PV; i; INT; FV_n; n; PVA_n; FVA_n; PMT; m; i_{SIMPLE}
    b. $FVIF_{i,n}$; $PVIF_{i,n}$; $FVIFA_{i,n}$; $PVIFA_{i,n}$; $FVIFA(DUE)_{i,n}$; $PVIFA(DUE)_{i,n}$
    c. Opportunity cost rate
    d. Annuity; lump-sum payment; cash flow; uneven cash flow stream
    e. Ordinary (deferred) annuity; annuity due
    f. Perpetuity; consol
    g. Outflow; inflow; cash flow time line
    h. Compounding; discounting
    i. Annual, semiannual, quarterly, monthly, and daily compounding
    j. Effective annual rate (EAR); simple (quoted) interest rate; annual percentage rate (APR); periodic rate
    k. Amortization schedule; principal component versus interest component of a payment; amortized loan
    l. Terminal value

Rates of return   **ST-2** Remember in the introduction to this chapter that we asked whether you would prefer to invest $5,500 today and receive either $7,020 in 5 years or $8,126 in 8 years? You should now be able to determine which investment alternative is better.
    a. Based only on the return you would earn from each investment, which is better?
    b. Can you think of any factors other than the expected return that might be important to consider when choosing between the two investment alternatives?

Future value **ST-3** Assume that it is now January 1, 2000. On January 1, 2001, you will deposit $1,000 into a savings account that pays 8 percent.

    a. If the bank compounds interest annually, how much will you have in your account on January 1, 2004?

    b. What would your January 1, 2004, balance be if the bank used quarterly compounding rather than annual compounding?

    c. Suppose you deposited the $1,000 in 4 payments of $250 each on January 1 of 2001, 2002, 2003, and 2004. How much would you have in your account on January 1, 2004, based on 8 percent annual compounding?

    d. Suppose you deposited 4 equal payments in your account on January 1 of 2001, 2002, 2003, and 2004. Assuming an 8 percent interest rate, how large would each of your payments have to be for you to obtain the same ending balance as you calculated in part a?

Time value of money **ST-4** Assume that it is now January 1, 2000, and you will need $1,000 on January 1, 2004. Your bank compounds interest at an 8 percent annual rate.

    a. How much must you deposit on January 1, 2001, to have a balance of $1,000 on January 1, 2004?

    b. If you want to make equal payments on each January 1 from 2001 through 2004 to accumulate the $1,000, how large must each of the 4 payments be?

    c. If your father were to offer either to make the payments calculated in part b ($221.92) or to give you a lump sum of $750 on January 1, 2001, which would you choose?

    d. If you have only $750 on January 1, 2001, what interest rate, compounded annually, would you have to earn to have the necessary $1,000 on January 1, 2004?

    e. Suppose you can deposit only $186.29 each January 1 from 2001 through 2004, but you still need $1,000 on January 1, 2004. What interest rate, with annual compounding, must you seek out to achieve your goal?

    f. To help you reach your $1,000 goal, your father offers to give you $400 on January 1, 2001. You will get a part-time job and make 6 additional payments of equal amounts each 6 months thereafter. If all of this money is deposited in a bank which pays 8 percent, compounded semiannually, how large must each of the 6 payments be?

    g. What is the effective annual rate being paid by the bank in part f?

    h. Reinvestment rate risk was defined in Chapter 2 as being the risk that maturing securities (and coupon payments on bonds) will have to be reinvested at a lower rate of interest than they were previously earning. Is there a reinvestment rate risk involved in the preceding analysis? If so, how might this risk be eliminated?

Effective annual rates **ST-5** Bank A pays 8 percent interest, compounded quarterly, on its money market account. The managers of Bank B want its money market account to equal Bank A's effective annual rate, but interest is to be compounded on a monthly basis. What simple, or quoted, rate must Bank B set?

Problems

Present and future values for different periods **6-1** Find the following values, *using the numerical solution approach,* and then work the problems using a financial calculator or the tables to check your answers. Disregard rounding errors. (Hint: If you are using a financial calculator, you can enter the known values and then press the appropriate key to find the unknown variable. Then, without clearing the TVM register, you can "override" the variable that changes by simply entering a new value for it and then pressing the key for the unknown variable to obtain the second answer. This procedure can be used in parts b and d, and in many other situations, to see how changes in input variables affect the output variable.)

a. An initial $500 compounded for 1 year at 6 percent.
b. An initial $500 compounded for 2 years at 6 percent.
c. The present value of $500 due in 1 year at a discount rate of 6 percent.
d. The present value of $500 due in 2 years at a discount rate of 6 percent.

Present and future values
for different interest rates

6-2 Use the tables or a financial calculator to find the following values. See the hint for Problem 6-1.
a. An initial $500 compounded for 10 years at 6 percent.
b. An initial $500 compounded for 10 years at 12 percent.
c. The present value of $500 due in 10 years at a 6 percent discount rate.
d. The present value of $1,552.90 due in 10 years at (1) a 12 percent discount rate, and (2) a 6 percent rate. Give a verbal definition of the term *present value,* and illustrate it using a cash flow time line with data from this problem. As a part of your answer, explain why present values depend on interest rates.

Time for a lump sum to double

6-3 To the closest year, how long will it take $200 to double if it is deposited and earns the following rates? [Notes: See the hint for Problem 6-1. You can also look up FVIF = 400/200 = 2 in the tables for parts a, b, and c, but you must figure out part d.]
a. 7 percent.
b. 10 percent.
c. 18 percent.
d. 100 percent.

Future value of an annuity

6-4 Find the *future values* of the following annuities. The first payment in these annuities is made at the *end* of Year 1; that is, they are *ordinary annuities.* (Note: See the hint to Problem 6-1. Also, note that you can leave values in the TVM register, switch to "BEG," press FV, and find the FV of the *annuity due*.)
a. $400 per year for 10 years at 10 percent.
b. $200 per year for 5 years at 5 percent.
c. $400 per year for 5 years at 0 percent.
d. Now rework parts a, b, and c, assuming that payments are made at the beginning of each year; that is, they are *annuities due.*

Present value of an annuity

6-5 Find the present values of the following ordinary annuities (see note to Problem 6-4):
a. $400 per year for 10 years at 10 percent.
b. $200 per year for 5 years at 5 percent.
c. $400 per year for 5 years at 0 percent.
d. Now rework parts a, b, and c assuming that payments are made at the beginning of each year; that is, they are *annuities due.*

Uneven cash flow stream

6-6 Find the present values of the following cash flow streams under the following conditions:

Year	Cash Stream A	Cash Stream B
1	$100	$300
2	400	400
3	400	400
4	400	400
5	300	100

a. The appropriate interest rate is 8 percent. (Hint: It is fairly easy to work this problem dealing with the individual cash flows. However, if you have a financial calculator, read the section of the manual that describes how to enter cash flows such as the ones in this problem. This will take a little time, but the investment will pay huge dividends throughout the course. Note, if you do work with the cash flow register, that you must enter $CF_0 = 0$.)

b. What is the value of each cash flow stream at a 0 percent interest rate?

Effective rate of interest   **6-7**   Find the interest rates, or rates of return, on each of the following:

  a. You *borrow* $700 and promise to pay back $749 at the end of 1 year.

  b. You *lend* $700 and receive a promise to be paid $749 at the end of 1 year.

  c. You *borrow* $85,000 and promise to pay back $201,229 at the end of 10 years.

  d. You *borrow* $9,000 and promise to make payments of $2,684.80 per year for 5 years.

Future value of various
compounding periods   **6-8**   Find the amount to which $500 will grow under each of the following conditions:

  a. 12 percent compounded annually for 5 years.

  b. 12 percent compounded semiannually for 5 years.

  c. 12 percent compounded quarterly for 5 years.

  d. 12 percent compounded monthly for 5 years.

Present value of various
compounding periods   **6-9**   Find the present value of $500 due in the future under each of the following conditions:

  a. 12 percent simple rate, compounded annually, discounted back 5 years.

  b. 12 percent simple rate, semiannual compounding, discounted back 5 years.

  c. 12 percent simple rate, quarterly compounding, discounted back 5 years.

  d. 12 percent simple rate, monthly compounding, discounted back 1 year.

FV of an annuity for various
compounding periods   **6-10**   Find the future values of the following ordinary annuities:

  a. FV of $400 each 6 months for 5 years at a simple rate of 12 percent, compounded semiannually.

  b. FV of $200 each 3 months for 5 years at a simple rate of 12 percent, compounded quarterly.

  c. The annuities described in parts a and b have the same amount of money paid into them during the 5-year period and both earn interest at the same simple rate, yet the annuity in part b earns $101.76 more than the one in part a over the 5 years. Why does this occur?

Effective versus
nominal interest rates   **6-11**   The First City Bank pays 7 percent interest, compounded annually, on time deposits. The Second City Bank pays 6.5 percent interest, compounded quarterly.

  a. Based on effective interest rates, in which bank would you prefer to deposit your money?

  b. Could your choice of banks be influenced by the fact that you might want to withdraw your funds during the year as opposed to at the end of the year? In answering this question, assume that funds must be left on deposit during the entire compounding period in order for you to receive any interest.

Amortization schedule   **6-12**   Lorkay Seidens Inc. just borrowed $25,000. The loan is to be repaid in equal installments at the end of each of the next 5 years, and the interest rate is 10 percent.

  a. Set up an amortization schedule for the loan.

  b. How large must each annual payment be if the loan is for $50,000? Assume that the interest rate remains at 10 percent and that the loan is paid off over 5 years.

  c. How large must each payment be if the loan is for $50,000, the interest rate is 10 percent, and the loan is paid off in equal installments at the end of each of the next 10 years? This loan is for the same amount as the loan in part b, but the payments are spread out over twice as many periods. Why are these payments not half as large as the payments on the loan in part b?

Effective rates of return   **6-13**   Assume that AT&T's pension fund managers are considering two alternative securities as investments: (1) Security Z (for zero intermediate year cash flows), which costs $422.41 today, pays nothing during its 10-year life, and then pays $1,000 after

10 years or (2) Security B, which has a cost today of $500 and pays $74.50 at the end of each of the next 10 years.

a. What is the rate of return on each security?

b. Assume that the interest rate AT&T's pension fund managers can earn on the fund's money falls to 6 percent immediately after the securities are purchased and is expected to remain at that level for the next 10 years. What would the price of each security change to, what would the fund's profit be on each security, and what would be the percentage profit (profit divided by cost) for each security?

c. Assuming that the cash flows for each security had to be reinvested at the new 6 percent market interest rate, (1) what would be the value attributable to each security at the end of 10 years and (2) what "actual, after-the-fact" rate of return would the fund have earned on each security? (Hint: The "actual" rate of return is found as the interest rate which causes the PV of the compounded Year 10 amount to equal the original cost of the security.)

d. Now assume all the facts as given in parts b and c except assume that the interest rate rose to 12 percent rather than fell to 6 percent. What would happen to the profit figures as developed in part b and to the "actual" rates of return as determined in part c? Explain your results.

Required annuity payments   **6-14** A father is planning a savings program to put his daughter through college. His daughter is now 13 years old. She plans to enroll at the university in 5 years, and it should take her 4 years to complete her education. Currently, the cost per year (for everything — food, clothing, tuition, books, transportation, and so forth) is $12,500, but a 5 percent inflation rate in these costs is forecasted. The daughter recently received $7,500 from her grandfather's estate; this money, which is invested in a bank account paying 8 percent interest compounded annually, will be used to help meet the costs of the daughter's education. The rest of the costs will be met by money the father will deposit in the savings account. He will make 6 equal deposits to the account in each year from now until his daughter starts college. These deposits will begin today and will also earn 8 percent interest.

a. What will be the present value of the cost of four years of education at the time the daughter becomes 18? [Hint: Calculate the future value of the cost (at 5%) for each year of her education, then discount three of these costs back (at 8%) to the year in which she turns 18, then sum the four costs.]

b. What will be the value of the $7,500 that the daughter received from her grandfather's estate when she starts college at age 18? (Hint: Compound for 5 years at 8%.)

c. If the father is planning to make the first of 6 deposits today, how large must each deposit be for him to be able to put his daughter through college?

Future value of a retirement fund   **6-15** As soon as she graduated from college, Kay began planning for her retirement. Her plans were to deposit $500 semiannually into an IRA (a retirement fund), beginning six months after graduation and continuing until the day she retired, which she expected to be 30 years later. Today is the day Kay retires (happy retirement!). She just made the last $500 deposit into her retirement fund, and now she wants to know how much she has accumulated for her retirement. The fund earned 10 percent compounded semiannually since it was established.

a. Compute the balance of the retirement fund assuming all of the payments were made on time.

b. Although Kay was able to make all of the $500 deposits she planned, 10 years ago she had to withdraw $10,000 from the fund to pay some medical bills incurred by her mother. Compute the balance in the retirement fund based on this information.

Exam-Type Problems

The problems in this section are set up in such a way that they could be used as multiple-choice exam problems.

Present value comparisons

6-16 Which amount is worth more at 14 percent: $1,000 in hand today or $2,000 due in 6 years?

Growth rates

6-17 Martell Corporation's 1999 sales were $12 million. Sales were $6 million 5 years earlier (in 1994).
   a. To the nearest percentage point, at what rate have sales been growing?
   b. Suppose someone calculated the sales growth for Martell Corporation in part a as follows: "Sales doubled in 5 years. This represents a growth of 100 percent in 5 years, so, dividing 100 percent by 5, we find the growth rate to be 20 percent per year." Explain what is wrong with this calculation.

Effective rate of return

6-18 Krystal Magee invested $150,000 18 months ago. Currently, the investment is worth $168,925. Krystal knows the investment has paid interest every 3 months (i.e., quarterly), but she doesn't know what the yield on her investment is. Help Krystal. Compute both the annual percentage rate (APR) and the effective annual rate of interest.

Effective rate of interest

6-19 Your broker offers to sell you a note for $13,250 that will pay $2,345.05 per year for 10 years. If you buy the note, what rate of interest (to the closest percent) will you be earning?

Effective rate of interest

6-20 A mortgage company offers to lend you $85,000; the loan calls for payments of $8,273.59 per year for 30 years. What interest rate is the mortgage company charging you?

Required lump-sum payment

6-21 To complete your last year in business school and then go through law school, you will need $15,000 per year for 4 years, starting next year (that is, you will need to withdraw the first $15,000 one year from today). Your rich uncle offers to put you through school, and he will deposit in a bank paying 7 percent interest a sum of money that is sufficient to provide the four payments of $15,000 each. His deposit will be made today.
   a. How large must the deposit be?
   b. How much will be in the account immediately after you make the first withdrawal? After the last withdrawal?

Repaying a loan

6-22 Sue wants to buy a car that costs $18,000. She has arranged to borrow the total purchase price of the car from her credit union at a simple interest rate equal to 12 percent. The loan requires quarterly payments for a period of 3 years. If the first payment is due in 3 months (1 quarter) after purchasing the car, what will be the amount of Sue's quarterly payments on the loan?

Repaying a loan

6-23 While Steve Bouchard was a student at the University of Florida, he borrowed $12,000 in student loans at an annual interest rate of 9 percent. If Steve repays $1,500 per year, how long, to the nearest year, will it take him to repay the loan?

Reaching a financial goal

6-24 You need to accumulate $10,000. To do so, you plan to make deposits of $1,750 per year, with the first payment being made a year from today, in a bank account that pays 6 percent annual interest. Your last deposit will be more than $1,750 if more is needed to round out to $10,000. How many years will it take you to reach your $10,000 goal, and how large will the last deposit be?

Present value of a perpetuity

6-25 What is the present value of a perpetuity of $100 per year if the appropriate discount rate is 7 percent? If interest rates in general were to double and the appropriate discount rate rose to 14 percent, what would happen to the present value of the perpetuity?

Loan amortization **6-26** Assume that your aunt sold her house on December 31 and that she took a mortgage in the amount of $10,000 as part of the payment. The mortgage has a quoted (or simple) interest rate of 10 percent, but it calls for payments every 6 months, beginning on June 30, and the mortgage is to be amortized over 10 years. Now, 1 year later, your aunt must file a Form 1099 with the IRS and with the person who bought the house, informing them of the interest that was included in the two payments made during the year. (This interest will be income to your aunt and a deduction to the buyer of the house.) To the closest dollar, what is the total amount of interest that was paid during the first year?

Automobile loan comparison **6-27** Sarah is on her way to the local Chevrolet dealership to buy a Cavalier. The list, or "sticker," price of the car is $13,000. Sarah has $3,000 in her checking account that she can use as a down payment toward the purchase of a new car. Sarah has carefully evaluated her finances, and she has determined she can afford payments that total $2,400 per year on a loan to purchase the car. Sarah can borrow the money to purchase the car either through the dealer's "special financing package," which is advertised as 4.0 percent financing, or from a local bank, which has automobile loans at 12 percent interest. Each loan would be outstanding for a period of 5 years, and the payments would be made quarterly (every 3 months). Sarah knows the dealer's "special financing package" requires that she will have to pay the "sticker" price for the car. But, if she uses the bank financing, she thinks she can negotiate with the dealer for a better price. Assume Sarah wants to pay $600 per payment, regardless of which loan she chooses, and the remainder of the purchase price will be a down payment that can be satisfied with any of the $3,000 in Sarah's checking account. Ignoring charges for taxes, tag, and title transfer, how much of a reduction in the sticker price must Sarah negotiate in order to make the bank financing more attractive than the dealer's special financing package?

Annuity withdrawals — ordinary annuity versus annuity due **6-28** Jason worked various jobs during his teenage years to save money for college. Now it is his 20th birthday, and he is about to begin his college studies at the University of South Florida (USF). A few months ago, Jason received a scholarship that will cover all of his college tuition for a period not to exceed 5 years. The money he has saved will be used for living expenses while he is in college; in fact, Jason expects to use all of his savings while attending USF. The jobs he worked as a teenager allowed him to save a total of $10,000, which currently is invested at 12 percent in a financial asset that pays interest monthly. Because Jason will be a full-time student, he expects to graduate 4 years from today, on his 24th birthday.
   a. How much can Jason withdraw every month while he is in college if the first withdrawal occurs today?
   b. How much can Jason withdraw every month while he is in college if he waits until the end of this month to make the first withdrawal?

Simple rate of return **6-29** Sue Sharpe, manager of Oaks Mall Jewelry, wants to sell on credit, giving customers 3 months in which to pay. However, Sue will have to borrow from her bank to carry the accounts payable. The bank will charge a simple 15 percent, but with monthly compounding. Sue wants to quote a simple rate to her customers (all of whom are expected to pay on time) that will exactly cover her financing costs. What simple annual rate should she quote to her credit customers?

Required annuity payments **6-30** Janet just graduated from a women's college in Mississippi with a degree in business administration, and she is about to start a new job with a large financial services firm based in Cleveland, Ohio. From reading various business publications while she was in college, Janet has concluded it probably is a good idea to begin planning for her retirement now. Even though she is only 25 years old and just beginning her career, Janet is concerned that Social Security will not be able to meet her needs when she retires. Fortunately for Janet, the company that has hired her has created a good retirement/investment plan that permits her to make contributions every year. So, Janet is now evaluating the amount she needs to contribute to satisfy her financial requirements at retirement. She has decided that she would like to take a trip as soon as her retirement begins (a reward to herself for many years of excellent work). The estimated cost of the trip, including all expenses such as meals and souvenirs, will be $120,000, and it will last for 1 year (no other funds will be needed during the first year of retirement). After she returns from her trip, Janet plans to settle down to enjoy her retirement. She estimates she will need $70,000 each year to be able to live comfortably and enjoy her "twilight years." The retirement/investment plan available to employees where Janet is going to work pays 7 percent interest compounded annually, and it is expected this rate will continue as long as the company offers the opportunity to contribute to the fund. When she retires, Janet will have to move her retirement "nest egg" to another investment so she can withdraw money when she needs it. Her plans are to move the money to a fund that allows withdrawals at the beginning of each year; the fund is expected to pay 5 percent interest compounded annually. Janet expects to retire in 40 years, and, after looking at the actuarial tables, she has decided she will live another 20 years after she returns from her retirement trip around the world. If Janet's expectations are correct, how much must she contribute to the retirement fund to satisfy her retirement plans if she plans to make her first contribution to the fund 1 year from today and if the last contribution will be made on the day she retires?

Integrative Problem

Time value of money analysis

6-31 Assume that you are nearing graduation and that you have applied for a job with a local bank. As part of the bank's evaluation process, you have been asked to take an examination that covers several financial analysis techniques. The first section of the test addresses time value of money analysis. See how you would do by answering the following questions.

a. Draw cash flow time lines for (1) a $100 lump sum cash flow at the end of Year 2, (2) an ordinary annuity of $100 per year for 3 years, and (3) an uneven cash flow stream of -$50, $100, $75, and $50 at the end of Years 0 through 3.

b. (1) What is the future value of an initial $100 after 3 years if it is invested in an account paying 10 percent annual interest?

   (2) What is the present value of $100 to be received in 3 years if the appropriate interest rate is 10 percent?

c. We sometimes need to find how long it will take a sum of money (or anything else) to grow to some specified amount. For example, if a company's sales are growing at a rate of 20 percent per year, approximately how long will it take sales to triple?

d. What is the difference between an ordinary annuity and an annuity due? What type of annuity is shown here? How would you change it to the other type of annuity?

e. (1) What is the future value of a 3-year ordinary annuity of $100 if the appropriate interest rate is 10 percent?

   (2) What is the present value of the annuity?

   (3) What would the future and present values be if the annuity were an annuity due?

f. What is the present value of the following uneven cash flow stream? The appropriate interest rate is 10 percent, compounded annually.

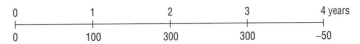

```
0          1          2          3        4 years
├──────────┼──────────┼──────────┼──────────┤
0         100        300        300        −50
```

g. What annual interest rate will cause $100 to grow to $125.97 in 3 years?

h. (1) Will the future value be larger or smaller if we compound an initial amount more often than annually, for example, every 6 months, or semiannually, holding the stated interest rate constant? Why?

    (2) Define (a) the stated, or quoted, or simple, rate, (b) the periodic rate, and (c) the effective annual rate (EAR).

    (3) What is the effective annual rate for a simple rate of 10 percent, compounded semiannually? Compounded quarterly? Compounded daily?

    (4) What is the future value of $100 after 3 years under 10 percent semiannual compounding? Quarterly compounding?

i. Will the effective annual rate ever be equal to the simple (quoted) rate?

j. (1) Construct an amortization schedule for a $1,000, 10 percent annual rate loan with 3 equal installments.

    (2) What is the annual interest expense for the borrower, and the annual interest income for the lender, during Year 2?

Computer-Related Problem

Work the problem in this section only if you are using the computer problem diskette.

Amortization schedule   **6-32** Use the computerized model in File C6 to solve this problem.

a. Set up an amortization schedule for a $30,000 loan to be repaid in equal installments at the end of each of the next 20 years at an interest rate of 10 percent. What is the annual payment?

b. Set up an amortization schedule for a $60,000 loan to be repaid in 20 equal annual installments at an interest rate of 10 percent. What is the annual payment?

c. Set up an amortization schedule for a $60,000 loan to be repaid in 20 equal annual installments at an interest rate of 20 percent. What is the annual payment?

CHAPTER 7

Valuation Concepts

On January 3, 1994, Treasury notes were selling at prices that promised investors an average return of about 5.5 percent if they were held until the year 2001. Therefore, a seven-year Treasury note with a face, or par, value equal to $10,000 that paid $275 in interest every six months had a market value equal to $10,000 on January 3, 1994. By January 3, 1995, the value of the same Treasury note was approximately $8,910. So, if you had purchased the note one year earlier, at least on paper, you would have incurred a capital loss equal to $1,090 during 1994. How could the market value of the Treasury note lose so much value in one year? The primary reason the value of this investment, as well as other debt instruments, decreased so significantly was because the Federal Reserve purposely increased interest rates six times during 1994. So at the beginning of 1995, the average return on a Treasury note with a 2001 maturity was 7.81 percent. In a single year, the return demanded by investors in Treasury notes increased about 2.3 percent, and this caused the values of these financial instruments to decrease greatly. Investors who bought the seven-year Treasury notes on January 3, 1994 experienced a loss in value equal to $1,090, but they received interest payments of $550 ($275 each six months); those investors who sold their Treasury notes on January 3, 1995 lost 5.4 percent ($540) on their original $10,000 investment. On the other hand, if investors held their Treasury notes until June 1998, they would have earned an average annual return equal to about 5.5 percent, because the average market return on such investments had fallen back to 5.62 percent; the lower rates caused the price to increase to $9,962, which was close to the original purchase price.

Could investors have fared better in the stock market or in other types of investments? Probably. In 1994, according to the S&P 500 Index, the values of stocks increased by about 2 percent on average; and, after considering dividends paid by the companies, the average return earned by investors was nearly 5 percent. Although this return was well below the return considered "normal" for the equity markets, an individual who invested in stocks at the beginning of 1994 and held them until June 1998 would have nearly doubled his or her investment — the return on stocks averaged about 25

Continued

percent from 1995 through 1997. As we write this text in 1998, the stock market has begun to fluctuate some — the Dow Jones Industrial Average pushed above the 9300 level for the first time in history in July 1998, but since that time it has mostly fluctuated between 8800 and 9100. In addition, interest rates have been relatively constant in 1998, so investors have greater confidence the values of their investments will not decrease significantly if the stock markets experience downward "adjustments" during the next year.

As you read this chapter, think about why the value of the Treasury notes decreased so significantly from January 1994 to January 1995 when interest rates increased 2.3 percent. What happens to the value of financial assets when the returns demanded by investors change? Are bonds and stocks affected the same? Answering these questions will help you to get a basic understanding of how stocks and bonds are valued in the financial markets. Such an understanding will help you make investments decisions, including those that are critical when establishing a retirement plan.

In the last chapter we examined time value of money (TVM) analysis. These TVM concepts are used by managers and investors to establish the worth of any asset whose value is derived from future cash flows, including such assets as real estate, factories, machinery, oil wells, coal mines, farmland, stocks, and bonds. Now, in this chapter, we use TVM techniques to explain how the values of assets are determined. The material covered in the chapter is important to investors who want to establish the values of their investments. But, knowledge of valuation is also important to financial managers because all important corporate decisions should be analyzed in terms of how they will affect the value of the firm. Remember that in Chapter 5 we noted the goal of managerial finance is to maximize the value of the firm. Thus, it is critical that we understand the valuation process so we can determine what affects the value of the firm.

Basic Valuation

After learning about the time value of money, you should realize that the *value* of anything, whether it is a financial asset like a stock or a bond or it is a real asset like a building or a piece of machinery, *is based on the present value of the cash flows the asset is expected to produce in the future.* On a cash flow time line, value can be depicted as follows:

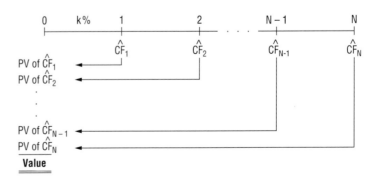

Therefore, the value of any asset can be expressed in general form as:

$$7\text{-}1 \quad \frac{\text{Asset}}{\text{value}} = V = \frac{\hat{CF}_1}{(1 + k)^1} + \frac{\hat{CF}_2}{(1 + k)^2} + \cdots + \frac{\hat{CF}_N}{(1 + k)^N} = \sum_{t=1}^{N} \frac{\hat{CF}_t}{(1 + k)^t}$$

Here, and on the cash flow time line,

$\hat{CF}_t$ = the cash flow *expected* to be generated by the asset in period t.

k = the return investors consider appropriate for holding such an asset. This return usually is termed the *required return,* and it is based on both economic conditions and the riskiness of the asset. We discuss risk/return concepts in the next chapter.

According to Equation 7-1, the value of an asset is affected by the cash flows it is expected to generate, $\hat{CF}$, and the return required by investors, k. As you can see, the higher the expected cash flows, the greater the asset's value; also, the lower the required return, the greater the asset's value. In the remainder of this chapter, we discuss how this general valuation concept can be applied to determine the value of various types of assets. First, we examine the valuation process for financial assets, and then we apply the process to value real assets.

Self-Test Questions

Describe the general methodology used to value any asset.

All else equal, how would an increase in an asset's expected future cash flows affect its value? What would be the impact of an increase in the required rate of return?

Valuation of Financial Assets — Bonds

BOND
A long-term debt instrument.

As we saw in Chapter 4, corporations raise capital in two forms — debt and equity. Our first task is to examine the valuation process for bonds, the principal type of long-term debt.

Remember, a **bond** is a long-term promissory note issued by a business or governmental unit. The conditions of the bond are contractually specified, such that the principal amount (or par value), the coupon interest rate, the maturity date, and any other features are known by investors. For example, suppose on January 2, 1999, Genesco Manufacturing borrowed $25 million by selling 25,000 individual bonds for $1,000 each. Genesco received the $25 million, and it promised to pay the bondholders annual interest equal to $150 per bond per year and to repay the $25 million at the end of 15 years. The lenders, who wanted to earn a 15 percent return on their investment, were willing to give Genesco $25 million, so the value of the bond issue was $25 million on January 2, 1999. But, how did investors decide that the issue was worth $25 million? Would the value have been different if investors demanded a different rate of return, say, 10 percent?

As we shall see, a bond's market price is determined primarily by the cash flows it generates, or the interest it pays, which depends on the coupon interest rate — the higher the coupon rate, other things held constant, the higher the market price of the bond. At the time a bond is issued, the coupon is generally set at a level that will cause the market price of the bond to equal its par value. If a lower coupon were set, investors simply would not be willing to pay $1,000 for the bond, while if a higher coupon were set, investors would clamor for the bond and bid its price up over $1,000. Investment bankers can judge quite precisely the coupon rate that will cause a bond to sell at its $1,000 par value.

A bond that has just been issued is known as a *new issue*. (*The Wall Street Journal* classifies a bond as a new issue for about one month after it has first been issued.) Once the bond has been on the market for a while, it is classified as an *outstanding bond,* also called a *seasoned issue.* Newly issued bonds generally sell very close to par, but the prices of outstanding bonds vary widely from par. Coupon interest payments are constant, so when economic conditions change, a bond with a $150 coupon that sold at par when it was issued will sell for more or less than $1,000 thereafter.

The Basic Bond Valuation Model[1]

Equation 7-1 shows that the value of a financial asset is based on the cash flows expected to be generated by the asset in the future. In the case of a bond, the cash flows consist of interest payments during the life of the bond plus a return of the principal amount borrowed, generally the par value, when the bond matures. In a time line format, here is the situation:

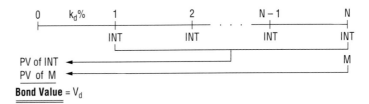

Here

k_d = the average rate of return investors require to invest in the bond. So, for the Genesco Manufacturing bond issue k_d = 15%. We used the term "i" or "I" to designate the interest rate in Chapter 6 because those terms are used on financial calculators, but "k," with the subscript "d" to designate the rate on a debt security, is normally used in finance.[2]

N = the number of years before the bond matures. For the Genesco bonds, N = 15. Note that N declines each year after the bond has been issued, so a bond that had a maturity of 15 years when it was issued (original maturity = 15) will have N = 14 after one year, N = 13 after two years, and so on.

---

[1]In finance, the term *model* refers to an equation or set of equations designed to show how one or more variables affect some other variable. Thus, a bond valuation model shows the mathematical relationship between a bond's price and the set of variables that determine the price.

[2]The appropriate interest rate on debt securities was discussed in Chapter 2. The bond's riskiness, liquidity, and years to maturity, as well as supply and demand conditions in the capital markets, all influence the interest rate on bonds.

Note also that at this point we assume that the bond pays interest once a year, or annually, so N is measured in years. Later on, we will deal with semi-annual payment bonds, which pay interest each six months.[3]

INT = dollars of interest paid each year = Coupon rate × Par value. In our example, each bond issued by Genesco requires an interest payment equal to $150. Thus, the coupon rate for these bonds must be 15 percent, because $150 = 0.15($1,000). In calculator terminology, INT = PMT = 150.

M = the par, or face, value of the bond = $1,000. This amount must be paid off at maturity.

We can now redraw the time line to show the numerical values for all variables except the bond's value:

0	15%	1	2		14	15
Value		150	150	. . .	150	150
						1,000
						1,150

Now the following general equation can be solved to find the value of any bond:

7-2

$$\text{Bond value} = V_d = \frac{INT}{(1+k_d)^1} + \frac{INT}{(1+k_d)^2} + \cdots + \frac{INT}{(1+k_d)^N} + \frac{M}{(1+k_d)^N}$$

$$= \sum_{t=1}^{N} \frac{INT}{(1+k_d)^t} + \frac{M}{(1+k_d)}$$

Note that the interest payments represent an annuity, and repayment of the par value at maturity represents a single, or lump sum, payment. Thus, Equation 7-2 can be rewritten for use with the tables:

7-2a

$$V_d = INT(PVIFA_{k_d,N}) + M(PVIF_{k_d,N})$$

Inserting values for Genesco's, we have

$$V_d = \sum_{t=1}^{15} \frac{\$150}{(1.15)^t} + \frac{\$1,000}{(1.15)^{15}}$$

$$= \$150(PVIFA_{15\%,15}) + \$1,000(PVIF_{15\%,15})$$

---

[3]We should note that some bonds that have been issued either pay no interest during their lives (*zero coupon bonds*) or else pay very low coupon rates. Such bonds are sold at a discount below par, and hence they are called *original issue discount bonds*. The "interest" earned on a zero coupon bond comes at the end when the company pays off at par ($1,000) a bond that was purchased for, say, $321.97. The discount of $1,000 - $321.97 = $678.03 substitutes for interest.

The value of the bond can be computed by using the three procedures discussed in Chapter 6: (1) numerically, (2) using the tables, and (3) with a financial calculator.

1. NUMERICAL SOLUTION:

Simply discount each cash flow back to the present and sum these PVs to find the value of the bond; see Figure 7-1 for an example. This procedure is not very efficient, especially if the bond has many years to maturity. So, alternatively, we can use the equations presented in Chapter 6 to find the solution:

$$V_d = \$150 \left[\frac{1 - \dfrac{1}{(1.15)^{15}}}{0.15} \right] + \$1,000 \left[\frac{1}{(1.15)^{15}} \right]$$

$$= \$150(5.8474) + \$1,000(0.12289)$$

$$= \$877.11 + \$122.89 = \$1000$$

2. TABULAR SOLUTION:

Simply look up the appropriate PVIF and PVIFA values in Tables A-1 and A-2 at the end of the book, insert them into the equation, and complete the arithmetic:

$$V_d = \$150(5.8474) + \$1,000(0.1229)$$

$$= \$877.11 + \$122.90 = \$1000.01 \approx \$1,000$$

FIGURE 7-1

Cash Flow Time Line for Genesco Manufacturing Bonds, 15% Interest Rate

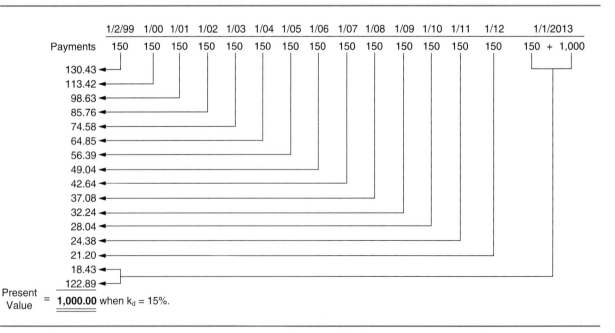

There is a one-cent rounding difference, which results from the fact that the tables only go to four decimal places.

3. FINANCIAL CALCULATOR SOLUTION:

In Chapter 6 we worked problems where only four of the five time value of money (TVM) keys were used, but all five keys are used with bond problems. Here is the setup:

Inputs:	15	15	?	150	1000
	N	**I**	**PV**	**PMT**	**FV**
Output:			$= -1{,}000$		

Simply input $N = 15$, $I = k = 15$, PMT = INT = 150, M = FV = 1000, and then press the PV key to find the value of the bond, $1,000. Because the PV is an outflow to the investor, it is shown with a negative sign.

Changes in Bond Values over Time

If k_d remained constant at 15 percent, what would the value of the bond be one year after it was issued? We can find this value using Equation 7-2a and the tables, but now the term to maturity is only 14 years, so $N = 14$. We see that V_d remains constant at $1,000:

$$V_d = \$150(\text{PVIFA}_{15\%,14}) + \$1{,}000(\text{PVIF}_{15\%,14})$$

$$= \quad \$150(5.7245) \quad + \quad \$1{,}000(0.1413) \quad = \$999.98 \approx \$1{,}000$$

With a financial calculator, just override $N = 15$ with $N = 14$, press the PV key, and you will get the same answer. The value of the bond will remain at $1,000 as long as the appropriate interest rate, k_d, remains constant at 15 percent, and k_d equals the coupon interest rate. In other words, *if the market rate associated with a bond, k_d, equals the coupon rate of interest, the bond will sell at its par value.*[4]

Now suppose interest rates in the economy fell after the Genesco Manufacturing bonds were issued, and, as a result, k_d fell *below the coupon rate,* decreasing from 15 to 10 percent. *Both the coupon interest payments and the maturity value remain constant,* but now the PVIF and PVIFA values used in Equation 7-2 would have to be based on a k_d equal to 10 percent. The value of the bond at the end of the first year (so, $N = 14$) would be $1,368.31:

$$V_d = \$150(\text{PVIFA}_{10\%,14}) + \$1{,}000(\text{PVIF}_{10\%,14})$$

$$= \$150(7.3667) + \$1{,}000(0.2633)$$

$$= \$1{,}105.01 + \$263.30 = \$1{,}368.31$$

---

[4]The bond prices quoted by brokers are calculated as described. However, if you bought a bond between interest payment dates, you would have to pay the basic price plus accrued interest. Thus, if you purchased a Genesco bond six months after it was issued, your broker would send you an invoice stating that you must pay $1,000 as the basic price of the bond plus $75 interest, representing one-half the annual interest of $150. The seller of the bond would receive $1,075. If you bought the bond the day before its interest payment date, you would pay $1,000 + (364/365)($150) = $1,149.59. Of course, you would receive an interest payment of $150 at the end of the next day.

Throughout the chapter we assume that the bond is being evaluated immediately after an interest payment date. The more expensive financial calculators have a built-in calendar that permits the calculation of exact values between interest payment dates.

Thus, if k_d fell *below* the coupon rate, the bond would sell above par, or at a *premium*. With a financial calculator, just change $k_d = I$ from 15 to 10, and then press the PV key to get the answer, $1,368.33. (The calculator solution and the tabular solution differ due to rounding.)

The arithmetic of the bond value increase should be clear, but what is the logic behind it? The fact that k_d has fallen to 10 percent means that if you had $1,000 to invest, you could buy new bonds like Genesco Manufacturing's (every day some 10 to 12 companies sell new bonds), except that these new bonds would pay $100 of interest each year rather than $150. Naturally, you would prefer $150 to $100, so you would be willing to pay more than $1,000 for Genesco Manufacturing's bonds to obtain its higher coupons. All investors would recognize these facts, and, as a result, the Genesco Manufacturing bonds would be bid up in price to $1,368.31, at which point they would provide the same rate of return to a potential investor as the new bonds — 10 percent.

Assuming that interest rates remain constant at 10 percent for the next 14 years, what would happen to the value of a Genesco Manufacturing bond? It would fall gradually from $1,368.31 on January 2, 2000, to $1,000 at maturity, when Genesco Manufacturing will redeem each bond for $1,000. This point can be illustrated by calculating the value of the bond on January 2, 2001, when it has 13 years remaining to maturity. With a financial calculator, merely input the values for N, I, PMT, and FV, now using N = 13, and press the PV key to find the value of the bond, $1,355.17. Using the tables, we have

$$V_d = \$150(PVIFA_{10\%,13}) + \$1,000(PVIF_{10\%,13})$$

$$= \$150(7.1034) + \$1,000(0.2897) = \$1,355.21 \text{ (rounding)}$$

Thus, the value of the bond will have fallen from $1,368.31 to $1,355.21, or by $13.10. If you were to calculate the value of the bond at other future dates, the price would continue to fall as the maturity date is approached. At maturity, the value of the bond would have to equal $1,000 (as long as the firm does not go bankrupt).

Note that if you purchased the bond at a price of $1,368.31 and then sold it one year later with k_d still at 10 percent, you would have a capital loss of $13.10, or a total return of $150.00 − $13.10 = $136.90. Your percentage rate of return would consist of an *interest yield* (also called a *current yield*) plus a *capital gains yield*. The computations for the current yield and the capital gains yield are defined as follows:

$$\frac{\text{Current}}{\text{yield}} = \frac{\text{INT}}{V_d}$$

$$\frac{\text{Capital}}{\text{gains yield}} = \frac{\left(\begin{array}{c}\text{Beginning}\\\text{bond value}\end{array}\right) - \left(\begin{array}{c}\text{Ending}\\\text{bond value}\end{array}\right)}{\left(\begin{array}{c}\text{Beginning}\\\text{bond value}\end{array}\right)} = \frac{V_{d,\,End} - V_{d,\,Begin}}{V_{d,\,Begin}}$$

The yields for Genesco's bond after one year are as follows:

Current yield $= \$150.00/\$1{,}368.31 = 0.1096 = 10.96\%$
Capital gains yield $= -\$13.10/\$1{,}368.31 = -0.0096 = -0.96\%$
Total rate of return (yield) $= \$136.90/\$1{,}368.31 = 0.1001 \approx \underline{\underline{10.00\%}}$

Had interest rates risen from 15 to 20 percent during the first year after issue rather than fallen, the value of the bond would have declined to $769.49:

$$V_d = \$150(\text{PVIFA}_{20\%,\, 14}) + \$1{,}000(\text{PVIF}_{20\%,\, 14})$$

$$= \$150(4.6106) + \$1{,}000(0.0779)$$

$$= \$691.59 + \$77.90 = \$769.49$$

In this case, the bond would sell at a *discount* of $230.51 below its par value:

$$\text{Discount} = \text{Price} - \text{Par value} = \$769.49 - \$1{,}000.00$$

$$= -\$230.51$$

CURRENT YIELD
The annual interest payment on a bond divided by its current market value.

The total expected future yield on the bond would again consist of a **current yield** and a capital gains yield, but now the capital gains yield would be positive. The total yield would be 20 percent. To see this, calculate the price of the bond with 13 years left to maturity, assuming that interest rates remain at 20 percent. With a calculator, enter $N = 13$, $I = 20$, $\text{PMT} = 150$, and $\text{FV} = 1000$, and then press PV to obtain the bond's value, $773.37. Using the tables, proceed as follows:

$$V_d = \$150(\text{PVIFA}_{20\%,\, 13}) + \$1{,}000(\text{PVIF}_{20\%,\, 13})$$

$$= \$150(4.5327) + \$1{,}000(0.0935)$$

$$= \$679.91 + \$93.50 = \$773.41 \text{ (rounding)}$$

Note that the capital gain for the year is the difference between the value of the bond when $N = 14$ years and when $N = 13$ years, which equals $773.41 - $769.49 = $3.92. The current yield, capital gains yield, and total yield are calculated as follows:

Current yield $= \$150.00/\$769.49 = 0.1949 = 19.49\%$
Capital gains yield $= \$3.92/\$769.49 = 0.0051 = 0.51\%$
Total rate of return (yield) $= \$153.92/\$769.49 = 0.2000 = \underline{\underline{20.00\%}}$

Figure 7-2 graphs the value of the bond over time, assuming that interest rates in the economy (1) remain constant at 15 percent, (2) fall to 10 percent and then remain constant at that level, or (3) rise to 20 percent and remain constant at that level. Of course, if interest rates do not remain constant, then the price of the bond will fluctuate. However, *regardless of what future interest rates do, the bond's price will approach $1,000 as it nears the maturity date* (barring bankruptcy, in which case the bond's value might drop to zero). Figure 7-2 illustrates the following key points:

1. Whenever the going rate of interest, k_d, is equal to the coupon rate, a bond will sell at its par value. Normally, the coupon rate is set equal to the going interest rate when a bond is issued, so it sells at par initially.

FIGURE 7-2

Time Path of the Value of a 15% Coupon, $1,000 Par Value Bond
When Interest Rates Are 10%, 15%, and 20%

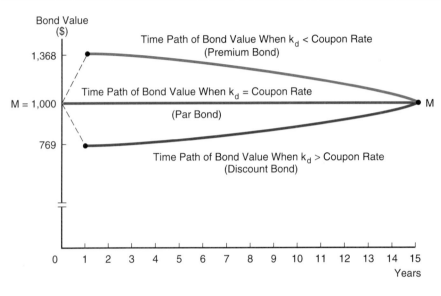

Year	$k_d = 10\%$	$k_d = 15\%$	$k_d = 20\%$
0	—	$1,000.00	—
1	$1,368.31	1,000.00	$ 769.49
.	.	.	.
.	.	.	.
.	.	.	.
15	1,000.00	1,000.00	1,000.00

NOTE: The curves for 10% and 20% have a slight bow.

2. Interest rates do change over time, but the coupon rate remains fixed after the bond has been issued. Whenever the going rate of interest is *greater than* the coupon rate, a bond's price will fall *below* its par value. Such a bond sells at a discount from its face value, so it is called a **discount bond**.

3. Whenever the going rate of interest is *less than* the coupon rate, a bond's price will rise *above* its par value. Such a bond sells at a premium compared to this face value, so it is called a **premium bond**.

4. Thus, an *increase* in interest rates will cause the price of an outstanding bond to *fall*, whereas a *decrease* in rates will cause it to *rise*.

5. The market value of a bond always will approach its par value as its maturity date approaches, provided the firm does not go bankrupt (see Figure 7-2).

These points are very important, because they show that bondholders can suffer capital losses or make capital gains, depending on whether interest rates rise or fall after the bond is purchased. And, as we saw in Chapter 2, interest rates do indeed change over time.

DISCOUNT BOND
A bond that sells below its par value, which occurs whenever the going rate of interest rises above the coupon rate.

PREMIUM BOND
A bond that sells above its par value, which occurs whenever the going rate of interest falls below the coupon rate.

Finding the Interest Rate on a Bond: Yield to Maturity

YIELD TO MATURITY (YTM)
The average rate of return earned on a bond if it is held to maturity.

Suppose you were offered a 14-year, 15 percent coupon, $1,000 par value bond at a price of $1,368.31. What rate of interest would you earn on your investment if you bought the bond and held it to maturity? This rate is called the bond's **yield to maturity (YTM)**, and it is the interest rate discussed by bond traders when they talk about rates of return. To find the yield to maturity, you could solve Equation 7-2 or 7-2a for k_d:

$$V_d = \$1,368.31 = \frac{\$150}{(1 + k_d)^1} + \cdots + \frac{\$150}{(1 + k_d)^{14}} + \frac{\$1,000}{(1 + k_d)^{14}}$$

$$= \$150(\text{PVIFA}_{k_d,14}) + \$1,000(\text{PVIF}_{k_d,14})$$

If you have a financial calculator, you would simply enter N = 14, PMT = 150, FV = 1000, and PV = −1368.31, and then press the I key. The calculator will blink (or perhaps go blank) for a few seconds, and then the answer, 10 percent, will appear.

If you do not have a financial calculator, you can substitute values for PVIFA and PVIF until you find a pair that "works" so that the present value of the interest payments combined with the present value of the repayment of the face value at maturity equals the current price of the bond. But, what would be a good interest rate to use as a starting point? First, you know that the bond is selling at a premium over its par value ($1,368.31 versus $1,000), so the bond's yield to maturity must be below its 15 percent coupon rate. Therefore, you might start by trying rates below 15 percent. It could take you a while to "zero in" on the appropriate rate. It probably would be better to get an estimate of the rate by computing the *approximate* yield to maturity, which can be found with the following equation[5]:

7-3

$$\begin{aligned} \frac{\text{Approximate}}{\text{yield to maturity}} &= \frac{\text{Annual} + \text{Accrued}}{\text{interest} + \text{capital gains}}{\text{Average value of bond}} \\[2mm] &= \frac{\text{INT} + \left(\dfrac{M - V_d}{N}\right)}{\left[\dfrac{2(V_d) + M}{3}\right]} \end{aligned}$$

Equation 7-3 is based on computations of approximate yields in the past and it does not consider the time value of money, so it should be used only to approximate a bond's yield to maturity. For the bond we are examining, the approximate yield to maturity is

---

[5]The form of Equation 7-3, which gives a "good" approximation for a bond's yield to maturity, is based on the work of Gabriel A. Hawawini and Ashok Vora, "Yield Approximations: A Historical Perspective," *Journal of Finance,* March 1982, 145-156.

$$\text{Yield to maturity} = k_d \approx \cfrac{\left(\$150 + \cfrac{\$1,000 - \$1,368.31}{14} \right)}{\left[\cfrac{2(\$1,368.31) + \$1,000}{3} \right]}$$

$$= \frac{\$150 + (-\$26.31)}{\$1,245.54} = 0.0993 \approx 10\%$$

Inserting interest factors for 10 percent, you obtain

$$V_d = \$150(7.3667) + \$1,000(0.2633)$$

$$= \$1,105.01 + \$263.30 = \$1,368.31$$

This calculated value is equal to the market price of the bond, so 10 percent is the bond's actual yield to maturity: $k_d = \text{YTM} = 10.0\%$.[6]

The yield to maturity is identical to the total annual rate of return discussed in the preceding section. The YTM for a bond that sells at par consists entirely of an interest yield, but if the bond sells at a price other than its par value, the YTM consists of the interest yield plus a positive or negative capital gains yield. Note also that a bond's yield to maturity changes whenever interest rates in the economy change, and this is almost daily. One who purchases a bond and holds it until it matures will receive the YTM that existed on the purchase date, but the bond's calculated YTM will change frequently between the purchase date and the maturity date.[7]

---

[6]Many years ago, bond traders all had specialized tables called *bond tables* that gave yields on bonds of different maturities selling at different premiums and discounts. Because calculators are so much more efficient (and accurate), bond tables are rarely used any more.

[7]Bonds that contain call provisions (callable bonds) often are called by the firm prior to maturity. In cases where a bond issue is called, investors do not have the opportunity to earn the yield to maturity (YTM), because the bond issue is retired before the maturity date arrives. Thus, for callable bonds, we often compute the *yield to call (YTC),* rather than the yield to maturity. The computation for the yield to call is the same as the yield to maturity, except the *call price* of the bond is substituted for the maturity (par) value, and the number of years until the bond can be called is substituted for the years to maturity. So, to calculate the yield to call (YTC), we modify Equation 7-2, and solve the following equation for k_d:

$$\text{Price of bond} = \sum_{t=1}^{N_C} \frac{\text{INT}}{(1 + kd)^t} + \frac{\text{Call price}}{(1 + k_d)^{N_C}}$$

Here N_C is the number of years until the company can call the bond; Call price is the price the company must pay in order to call the bond (it is often set equal to the par value plus one year's interest); and k_d is the yield to call (YTC). To solve for the YTC, proceed just as with the solution for the yield to maturity of a bond. For example, suppose Genesco's 15 percent coupon bonds, which have a current price of $1,368.31, are callable in nine years at $1,150. The setup for computing the YTC is as follows:

$$\$1,368.31 = \frac{\$150}{(1 + k_d)^1} + \frac{\$150}{(1 + k_d)^2} + \cdots + \frac{\$150}{(1 + k_d)^9} + \frac{\$1,150}{(1 + k_d)^9}$$

Using your calculator, you would find the solution for the yield to call is 9.78 percent.

Bond Values with Semiannual Compounding

Although some bonds pay interest annually, most actually pay interest semiannually. To evaluate semiannual payment bonds, we must modify the valuation equations the same as we did in Chapter 6 to take into consideration that interest compounding can occur more than once a year. So, Equations 7-2 and 7-2a become

7-2b

$$V_d = \sum_{t=1}^{2N} \frac{\dfrac{INT}{2}}{\left(1 + \dfrac{k_d}{2}\right)^t} + \frac{M}{\left(1 + \dfrac{k_d}{2}\right)^{2N}}$$

$$= \frac{INT}{2}\left(PVIFA_{\frac{k_d}{2}, 2N}\right) + M\left(PVIF_{\frac{k_d}{2}, 2N}\right)$$

To illustrate, assume now that Genesco's 14-year bonds pay $75 interest each six months rather than $150 at the end of each year. Thus, each interest payment is only half as large, but there are twice as many of them. When the going (simple) rate of interest is 10 percent with semiannual compounding, the value of this 15-year bond is found as follows[8]:

$$V_d = \$75(PVIFA_{5\%, 28}) + \$1,000(PVIF_{5\%, 28})$$

$$= \$75(14.8981) + \$1,000(0.2551)$$

$$= \$1,117.36 + \$255.10 = \$1,372.46$$

With a financial calculator, enter N = 30, k = I = 5, PMT = 75, FV = 1000, and then press the PV key to obtain the bond's value, $1,372.45 (rounding). The value with semiannual interest payments is slightly larger than $1,380.32, the value when interest is paid annually. This higher value occurs because interest payments are received, and therefore can be reinvested, somewhat faster under semiannual compounding.

Students sometimes want to discount the *maturity (par) value* at 10 percent over 14 years rather than at 5 percent over 28 six-month periods. This is incorrect. Logically, all cash flows in a given contract must be discounted at the same periodic rate, the 5 percent semiannual rate in this instance, because this is the opportunity rate for the investor. For consistency, bond traders must use the same discount rate for all cash flows, including the cash flow at maturity; and they do.

---

[8]We are also assuming a change in the effective annual interest rate, from 10 percent to EAR = $(1.05)^2 - 1 = 1.1025 - 1.0 = 0.1025 = 10.25\%$. Most bonds pay interest semiannually, and the rates quoted are simple rates compounded semiannually. Therefore, effective annual rates for most bonds are somewhat higher than the quoted rates, which, in effect, represent the annual percentage rates, APRs, for the bonds.

Interest Rate Risk on a Bond

As we saw in Chapter 2, interest rates go up and down over time. Further, changes in interest rates affect the bondholders in two ways:

INTEREST RATE PRICE RISK
The risk of changes in bond prices to which investors are exposed due to changing interest rates.

INTEREST RATE REINVESTMENT RATE RISK
The risk that income from a bond portfolio will vary because cash flows have to be reinvested at current market rates.

1. An increase in interest rates leads to a decline in the values of outstanding bonds. Because interest rates can rise, bondholders face the risk of losses in the values of their portfolios. This risk is called **interest rate price risk**.

2. Many bondholders (including such institutional bondholders as pension funds and life insurance companies) buy bonds to build funds for some future use. These bondholders reinvest the cash flows (interest payments plus repayment of principal when the bonds mature or are called). If interest rates decline, the bondholders will earn a lower rate of return on reinvested cash flows, and this will reduce the future value of their portfolios relative to the values they would have had if interest rates had not fallen. This is called **interest rate reinvestment rate risk**.

We see, then, that any given change in interest rates has two separate effects on bondholders: It changes the current values of their portfolios (price risk), and it also changes the rates of return at which the cash flows from their portfolios can be reinvested (reinvestment rate risk). Note that these two risks tend to offset one another. For example, an increase in interest rates will lower the *current* value of a bond portfolio, but because the future cash flows produced by the portfolio will then be reinvested at a higher rate of return, the *future* value of the portfolio will be increased. In this section we look at just how these two effects operate to affect bondholders' positions.[9]

Suppose you bought some 15 percent Genesco Manufacturing bonds at a price of $1,000, and interest rates subsequently rose to 20 percent. As we saw before, the price of the bonds would fall to $769.49, so you would have a loss of $230.51 per bond.[10] Interest rates can and do rise, and rising rates cause a loss of value for bondholders, but you now can reinvest the $150 interest received each year at 20 percent. Thus, people or firms who invest in bonds are exposed to risk from changing interest rates.

Exposure to interest rate price risk is higher on bonds with long maturities than on those maturing in the near future. This point can be demonstrated by showing how the value of a 1-year bond with a 15 percent coupon fluctuates with changes in k_d and then comparing these changes with those on a 14-year bond as calculated previously. The values for a 1-year bond and a 14-year bond at several different market interest rates, k_d, are shown in Figure 7-3. The values

---

[9]Actually, we will stop far short of a full examination of the effects of interest rate changes on bondholders' positions because such an examination would go well beyond the scope of the text. We can note, though, that a concept called "duration" has been developed to help fixed-income investors deal with changing interest rates, and, with a properly structured portfolio (one that has the proper duration), most of the risks of changing interest rates can be eliminated because price risk and reinvestment rate risk can be made to exactly offset one another.

[10]You would have an *accounting* (and tax) loss only if you sold the bond; if you held it to maturity, you would not have such a loss. However, even if you did not sell, you would still have suffered a *real economic loss in an opportunity cost sense* because you would have lost the opportunity to invest at 20 percent and would be stuck with a 15 percent bond in a 20 percent market. Thus, in an economic sense, "paper losses" are just as bad as realized accounting losses.

FIGURE 7-3

Value of Long- and Short-Term 15% Annual Coupon Rate Bonds
at Different Market Interest Rates

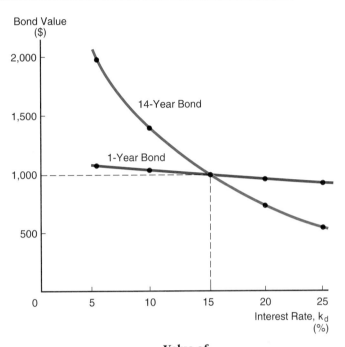

Current Market Interest Rate, k_d	Value of	
	1-Year Bond	**14-Year Bond**
5%	$1,095.24	$1,989.86
10	1,045.45	1,368.33
15	1,000.00	1,000.00
20	958.33	769.47
25	920.00	617.59

NOTE: Bond values were calculated using a financial calculator.

for the bonds were computed assuming the coupon interest payments for the bonds occur annually. Note how much more sensitive the price of the long-term bond is to changes in interest rates. At a 15 percent interest rate, both the long- and the short-term bonds are valued at $1,000. When rates rise to 20 percent, the long-term bond falls to $769.47, but the short-term bond falls only to $958.33.

For bonds with similar coupons, this differential sensitivity to changes in interest rates always holds true — the longer the maturity of the bond, the greater its price changes in response to a given change in interest rates. Thus, even if the risk of default on two bonds is exactly the same, the one with the longer maturity typically is exposed to more price risk from a change in interest rates.[11]

The logical explanation for this difference in interest rate price risk is simple. Suppose you bought a 14-year bond that yielded 15 percent, or $150 a year. Now suppose interest rates on comparable-risk bonds rose to 20 percent. You would be stuck with only $150 of interest for the next 14 years. On the other hand, had you bought a 1-year bond, you would have had a low return for only 1 year. At the end of the year, you would get your $1,000 back, and you could then reinvest it and receive 20 percent, or $200 per year, for the next 13 years. Thus, interest rate price risk reflects the length of time one is committed to a given investment.

Although a 1-year bond has less interest rate *price* risk than a 14-year bond, the 1-year bond exposes the buyer to more interest rate *reinvestment* rate risk. Suppose you bought a 1-year bond that yielded 15 percent, and then interest rates on comparable-risk bonds fell to 10 percent. After 1 year, when you got your $1,000 back, you would have to invest it at only 10 percent, so you would lose $150 − $100 = $50 in annual interest. Had you bought the 14-year bond, you would have continued to receive $150 in annual interest payments even if rates fell. If you reinvested those coupon payments, you would have to accept a lower rate of return, but you would still be much better off than if you had been holding the 1-year bond.

Bond Prices in Recent Years

We know from Chapter 2 that interest rates fluctuate, and we have just seen that the prices of outstanding bonds rise and fall inversely with changes in interest rates. Figure 7-4 shows what has happened to the price of a typical bond, Florida Power Corporation's $7\frac{1}{4}$ percent, 30-year bond that matures in 2002. The bond prices given on the graph are the prices for the last trading day of each year; for example, on December 30, 1997, the bond sold for $1,015. Some of the yields associated with the bond are also reported on the graph to give you an indication of the changes in interest rates that caused the bond price changes from 1977 to 1998.

When Florida Power first issued this bond in 1972, it was worth $1,000, but in 1981, when corporate bond rates hovered around 16 percent, it sold for only $479, a significant discount from its par value. As interest rates decreased from the extraordinarily high levels of the early 1980s, the price of Florida Power's bond rose, and in 1993 was selling at a premium for $1,023. By the end of 1997 (beginning of 1998), the bond was still selling for a premium, at $1,015, and by the end of May 1998 the bond price had dropped slightly to $1,014. As the graph shows, if the interest rates stay at the 1998 level of 6.88 percent for the remaining four years of the bond's life, the price of the bond will gradually decrease to its maturity value of $1,000 just before it matures in 2002.

---

[11]If a 10-year bond were plotted in Figure 7-3, its curve would lie between those of the 14-year bond and the 1-year bond. The curve of a one-month bond would be almost horizontal, indicating that its price would change very little in response to an interest rate change, but a perpetuity would have a very steep slope.

FIGURE 7-4

Florida Power Corporation 7¼%, 30-Year Bond:
Market Value (Yield to Maturity) from 1977–1998

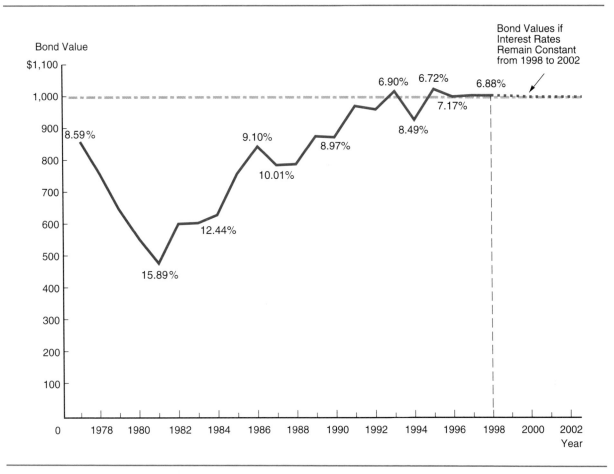

Self-Test Questions

In what two primary forms do corporations raise capital?

What is meant by the terms "new issue" and "seasoned issue"?

Explain, verbally, the following equation:

$$V_d = \sum_{t=1}^{N} \frac{INT}{(1 + k_d)^t} + \frac{M}{(1 + k_d)^N}$$

Explain what happens to the price of a bond if (1) interest rates rise above the bond's coupon rate or (2) interest rates fall below the bond's coupon rate.

Write out a formula that can be used to calculate the discount or premium on a bond, and explain it.

Differentiate between interest rate price risk and reinvestment rate risk.

Differentiate between a bond's yield to maturity and its current yield.

How is the bond valuation formula shown above changed to deal with bonds that have semiannual coupons rather than annual coupons?

Valuation of Financial Assets — Equity (Stock)

Remember from our discussion in Chapter 4 that corporations can issue two forms of equity — preferred stock and common stock. We indicated that preferred stock is generally considered a hybrid security because it is similar to bonds in some respects and to common stock in other respects. Preferred dividends are similar to interest payments on bonds in that they are fixed in amount and generally must be paid before common stock dividends can be paid. However, like common dividends, preferred dividends can be omitted without bankrupting the firm, and preferred issues generally have no specific maturity date. But, preferred stock does not represent an ownership interest — it is the common stockholders, not the preferred stockholders, who elect members of the board of directors. Further, it is the common stockholders who benefit when extraordinary growth occurs because cash distributions (dividends) to preferred stockholders do not vary with the success of the firm. Thus, preferred stockholders do not receive additional (lower) dividends when the firm's earnings are above (below) normal — the growth in earnings (whether positive or negative) "belongs to" common stockholders.

In this section, we examine the process to value stock, both preferred and common. We begin by introducing a general stock valuation model. Then, we apply the model to three scenarios: (1) when there is no growth in dividends so the amount paid each year remains constant (such as preferred dividends), (2) when dividends increase at a constant rate each year, and (3) when dividends grow at different rates.

Definitions of Terms Used in the Stock Valuation Models

Stocks provide an expected future cash flow stream, and a stock's value is found in the same manner as the values of other assets — namely, as the present value of the expected future cash flow stream. The expected cash flows consist of two elements: (1) the dividends expected to be paid each year and (2) the price investors expect to receive when they sell the stock. The expected final stock price includes the return of the original investment plus a capital gain or loss.

Before we present the general stock valuation model, let's define some terms and notations we will use throughout this section:

$\hat{D}_t$ = dividend the stockholder expects to receive at the end of Year t (pronounced "D hat t"). D_0 is the most recent dividend, which already has been paid; $\hat{D}_1$ is the next dividend expected to be paid, and it will be paid at the end of this year; $\hat{D}_2$ is the dividend expected at the end of two years; and so forth. $\hat{D}_1$ represents the first cash flow a new purchaser of the stock will receive. Note that D_0, the dividend that has just been paid, is known with certainty (thus, there is no "hat" over the D).

MARKET PRICE, P_0
The price at which a stock sells in the market.

INTRINSIC VALUE, $\hat{P}_0$
The value of an asset that, in the mind of a particular investor, is justified by the facts; $\hat{P}_0$ may be different from the asset's current market price, its book value, or both.

GROWTH RATE, g
The expected rate of change in dividends per share.

REQUIRED RATE OF RETURN, k_s
The minimum rate of return on a common stock that stockholders consider acceptable.

DIVIDEND YIELD
The expected dividend divided by the current price of a share of stock.

CAPITAL GAINS YIELD
The change in price (capital gain) during a given year divided by the price at the beginning of the year.

EXPECTED RATE OF RETURN, $\hat{k}_s$
The rate of return on a common stock that an individual stockholder expects to receive; equal to the expected dividend yield plus the expected capital gains yield.

However, all future dividends are *expected* values, so the estimate of $\hat{D}_t$ may differ among investors for some stocks.[12]

P_0 = actual **market price** of the stock today.

$\hat{P}_t$ = expected price of the stock at the end of each Year t. $\hat{P}_0$ is the **intrinsic**, or *theoretical*, **value** of the stock today as seen by the particular investor doing the analysis; $\hat{P}_1$ is the price *expected* at the end of one year; and so on. Note that $\hat{P}_0$ is the intrinsic value of the stock today based on a particular investor's estimate of the stock's expected dividend stream and the riskiness of that stream. Hence, whereas P_0 is fixed and is identical for all investors because it represents the price at which the stock currently can be purchased in the stock market, P_0 could differ among investors depending on what they feel the firm is actually worth. $\hat{P}_0$, the individual investor's estimate of the intrinsic value today, could be above or below P_0, the current stock price, but an investor would buy the stock only if his or her estimate of $\hat{P}_0$ were equal to or greater than P_0.

Because there are many investors in the market, there can be many values for $\hat{P}_0$. However, we can think of a group of "average," or "marginal," investors whose actions actually determine the market price. For these marginal investors, P_0 must equal $\hat{P}_0$; otherwise, a disequilibrium would exist, and buying and selling in the market would change P_0 until $P_0 = \hat{P}_0$ for a marginal (average) investor.

g = expected **growth rate** in dividends as predicted by a marginal, or average, investor. (If we assume that dividends are expected to grow at a constant rate, g also is equal to the expected rate of growth in the stock's price.) Different investors may use different g's to evaluate a firm's stock, but the market price, P_0, is set on the basis of the g estimated by marginal investors.

k_s = minimum acceptable, or **required**, **rate of return** on the stock, considering both its riskiness and the returns available on other investments. Again, this term generally relates to average investors. The determinants of k_s are discussed in detail in the next chapter.

$\dfrac{\hat{D}_1}{P_0}$ = expected **dividend yield** on the stock during the coming year. If the stock is expected to pay a dividend of \$1 during the next 12 months, and if its current price is \$10, then the expected dividend yield is \$1 ÷ \$10 = 0.10 = 10%.

$\dfrac{\hat{P}_1 - P_0}{P_0}$ = expected **capital gains yield** on the stock during the coming year. If the stock sells for \$10 today, and if it is expected to rise to \$10.50 at the end of one year, then the expected capital gain is $\hat{P}_1 - P_0$ = \$10.50 − \$10.00 = \$0.50, and the expected capital gains yield is \$0.50 ÷ \$10 = 0.05 = 5%.

$\hat{k}_s$ = **expected rate of return** that an investor who buys the stock actually expects to receive. $\hat{k}_s$ could be above or below k_s, but one would buy

---

[12]Stocks generally pay dividends quarterly, so theoretically we should evaluate them on a quarterly basis. However, in stock valuation, most analysts work on an annual basis because the data are generally not precise enough to warrant refinement to a quarterly model. For additional information on the quarterly model, see Charles M. Linke and J. Kenton Zumwalt, "Estimation Biases in Discounted Cash Flow Analysis of Equity Capital Cost in Rate Regulation," *Financial Management*, Autumn 1984, 15-21.

the stock only if $\hat{k}_s$ was equal to or greater than k_s. $\hat{k}_s$ = expected dividend yield plus expected capital gains yield; in other words,

$$\hat{k}_s = \frac{\hat{D}_1}{P_0} + \frac{\hat{P}_1 - P_0}{P_0}$$

ACTUAL (REALIZED) RATE OF
RETURN, $\bar{k}_s$
The rate of return on a
common stock actually
received by stockholders. $\bar{k}_s$
may be greater than or less
than $\hat{k}_s$ and/or k_s.

In our example, the expected total return = $\hat{k}_s$ = 10% + 5% = 15%.

$\bar{k}_s$ = **actual**, or **realized**, *after the fact* **rate of return** (pronounced "k bar s"). You may expect to obtain a return of $\hat{k}_s$ = 15% if you buy IBM stock today, but if the market goes down, you may end up next year with an actual realized return that is much lower, perhaps even negative (e.g., $\bar{k}_s$ = 8%).

Expected Dividends as the Basis for Stock Values

Remember that according to Equation 7-1 the value of any asset is the present value of the cash flows expected to be generated by the asset in the future. In our discussion of bonds, we found that the value of a bond is the present value of the interest payments over the life of the bond plus the present value of the bond's maturity (or par) value. Stock prices are likewise determined as the present value of a stream of cash flows, and the basic stock valuation equation is similar to the bond valuation equation (Equation 7-2). What are the cash flows that corporations provide to their stockholders? First, think of yourself as an investor who buys a stock with the intention of holding it (in your family) forever. In this case, all that you (and your heirs) will receive is a stream of dividends, and the value of the stock today is calculated as the present value of an infinite stream of dividends, which is depicted on a cash flow time line as:

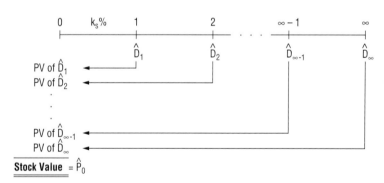

Thus, to compute the value of the stock, we must solve the following equation:

7-4

Value of stock = $V_s = \hat{P}_0$ = PV of expected future dividends

$$= \frac{\hat{D}_1}{(1 + k_s)^1} + \frac{\hat{D}_2}{(1 + k_s)^2} + \cdots + \frac{\hat{D}_\infty}{(1 + k_s)^\infty}$$

$$= \sum_{t=1}^{\infty} \frac{\hat{D}_t}{(1 + k_s)^t}$$

What about the more typical case, where you expect to hold the stock for a specific (finite) period and then sell it — what will be the value of $\hat{P}_0$ in this case? Unless the company is likely to be liquidated and thus to disappear, *the value of the stock still is determined by Equation 7-4.* To see this, recognize that for any individual investor, the expected cash flows consist of expected dividends plus the expected sale price of the stock. However, the sale price the current investor receives will depend on the dividends the future investor expects. Therefore, for all present and future investors in total, expected cash flows must be based on all of the expected future dividends. To put it another way, the cash flows a firm provides to its stockholders will consist only of a stream of dividends; therefore, the value of a share of its stock must be established as the present value of that expected dividend stream that will be paid throughout the life of the company.

The general validity of Equation 7-4 can also be confirmed by asking the following question: Suppose I buy a stock and expect to hold it for one year. I will receive dividends during the year plus the value $\hat{P}_1$ when I sell the stock at the end of the year. But what will determine the value of $\hat{P}_1$? The answer is that it will be determined as the present value of the dividends during Year 2 plus the stock price at the end of that year, which, in turn, will be determined as the present value of another set of future dividends and an even more distant stock price. This process can be continued forever, and the ultimate result is Equation 7-4.[13]

Equation 7-4 is a generalized stock valuation model in the sense that the time pattern of $\hat{D}_t$ can be anything: $\hat{D}_t$ can be rising, falling, or constant, or it can even be fluctuating randomly, and Equation 7-4 will still hold. Often, however, the projected stream of dividends follows a systematic pattern, in which case we can develop a simplified (i.e., easier to apply) version of the stock valuation model expressed in Equation 7-4. In the following sections we consider the cases of zero growth, constant growth, and nonconstant growth.

Stock Values with Zero Growth

ZERO GROWTH STOCK
A common stock whose future dividends are not expected to grow at all; that is, $g = 0$, and $D_1 = D_2 = \cdots = \hat{D}_\infty = \hat{D}_0$.

Suppose dividends are not expected to grow at all; instead they are expected to stay the same every year. Here we have a **zero growth stock**, for which the dividends expected in future years are equal to some constant amount — the current dividend. That is, $\hat{D}_1 = \hat{D}_2 = \cdots = \hat{D}_\infty = D_0$. Therefore, we can drop the subscripts and the "hats" on D and rewrite Equation 7-4 as follows:

7-4a
$$\hat{P}_0 = \frac{D}{(1 + k_s)^1} + \frac{D}{(1 + k_s)^2} + \cdots + \frac{D}{(1 + k_s)^\infty}$$

---

[13]We should note that investors periodically lose sight of the long-run nature of stocks as investments and forget that in order to sell a stock at a profit, one must find a buyer who will pay the higher price. If you analyzed a stock's value in accordance with Equation 7-4, concluded that the stock's market price exceeded a reasonable value, and then bought the stock anyway, then you would be following the "bigger fool" theory of investment—you think that you may be a fool to buy the stock at its excessive price, but you also think that when you get ready to sell it, you can find someone who is an even bigger fool. The bigger fool theory was widely followed in the summer of 1987, just before the stock market lost more than one-third of its value in the October 1987 crash.

As we noted in Chapter 6 in connection with the British consol bond, a security that is expected to pay a constant amount each year forever is called a perpetuity. *Therefore, a zero growth stock is a perpetuity.*

Remember that the value of any perpetuity is simply the payment divided by the discount rate, so the value of a zero growth stock reduces to this formula:

7-5

$$\text{Value of zero growth stock} = \hat{P}_0 = \frac{D}{k_s}$$

Therefore, if we have a stock that is expected to always pay a dividend equal to $1.20, and the required rate of return associated with such an investment is 12 percent, the stock's value should be[14]

$$\hat{P}_0 = \frac{\$1.20}{0.12} = \$10.00$$

Generally, we can find the price of a stock and the most recent dividend paid to the stockholders by looking in a financial newspaper such as *The Wall Street Journal*. Therefore, if we have a stock with constant dividends, we can solve for the expected rate of return by rearranging Equation 7-5 to produce

7-5a

$$\hat{k}_s = \frac{D}{P_0}$$

Because we are dealing with an *expected rate of return,* we put a "hat" on the k value. Thus, if we bought a stock at a price of $10 and expected to receive a constant dividend of $1.20, our expected rate of return would be

$$\hat{k}_s = \frac{\$1.20}{\$10.00} = 0.12 = 12.0\%$$

By now, you have probably recognized that Equation 7-5 can be used to value preferred stock. Recall that preferred stocks entitle their owners to regular, or fixed, dividend payments. And, if the payments last forever, the issue is a *perpetuity* whose value is defined by Equation 7-5. Equation 7-5 can be used to value any asset, including common stock, with expected future cash flows that exhibit the properties of a perpetuity — constant cash flows forever.

---

[14]If you think that having a stock pay dividends forever is unrealistic, then think of it as lasting only for 50 years. Here you would have an annuity of $1.20 per year for 50 years. The PV of a 50-year annuity of $1.20 with an opportunity rate of interest equal to 12 percent would be $1.20(8.3045) = $9.97, which would differ by only a few pennies from that of the perpetuity. Thus, the dividends from Years 51 to infinity contribute little to the value of the stock.

Normal, or Constant, Growth

In general, investors expect the earnings and dividends of most companies to increase each year. Even though expected growth rates vary from company to company, it is not uncommon for investors to expect dividend growth to continue in the foreseeable future at about the same rate as that of the nominal gross national product (real GNP plus inflation). On this basis, we might expect the dividend of an average, or "normal," company to grow at a rate of 3 to 6 percent a year. Thus, if a **normal**, or **constant, growth** company's last dividend, which has already been paid, was D_0, its dividend in any future Year t can be forecasted as $\hat{D}_t = D_0(1 + g)^t$, where g is the constant expected rate of growth. For example, if Genesco Manufacturing just paid a dividend of $1.20 (i.e., $D_0 = \$1.20$), and if investors expect a 5 percent growth rate, then the estimated dividend one year hence would be $\hat{D}_1 = \$1.20(1.05) = \$1.26$; $\hat{D}_2$ would be $1.323; and the estimated dividend five years hence would be

$$\hat{D}_5 = D_0(1 + g)^5 = \$1.20(1.05)^5 = \$1.532$$

Using this method for estimating future dividends, we can determine the current stock value, $\hat{P}_0$, using Equation 7-4 as set forth previously — in other words, we can find the expected future cash flow stream (the dividends), then calculate the present value of each dividend payment, and finally sum these present values to find the value of the stock. Thus, the intrinsic value of the stock is equal to the present value of its expected future dividends.

If g is constant, Equation 7-4 can be rewritten as follows[15]:

7-6

$$\hat{P}_0 = \frac{D_0(1 + g)^1}{(1 + k_s)^1} + \frac{D_0(1 + g)^2}{(1 + k_s)^2} + \cdots + \frac{D_0(1 + g)^\infty}{(1 + k_s)^\infty}$$

$$= \frac{D_0(1 + g)}{k_s - g} = \frac{\hat{D}_1}{k_s - g}$$

Inserting values into the last version of Equation 7-6, we find the value of our illustrative stock is $18.00:

$$\hat{P}_0 = \frac{\$1.20(1.05)}{0.12 - 0.05} = \frac{\$1.26}{0.07} = \$18.00$$

The **constant growth model** as set forth in the last term of Equation 7-6 is often called the Gordon Model, after Myron J. Gordon, who did much to develop and popularize it.

NORMAL (CONSTANT) GROWTH
Growth that is expected to continue into the foreseeable future at about the same rate as that of the economy as a whole; g = a constant.

CONSTANT GROWTH MODEL
Also called the Gordon Model, it is used to find the value of a stock that is expected to experience constant growth.

---

[15]The last term in Equation 7-6 is derived in the Extensions section of Chapter 28 of Eugene F. Brigham, Louis C. Gapenski, and Phillip R. Daves, *Intermediate Financial Management,* 6th ed. (Fort Worth, TX: The Dryden Press, 1999). In essence, the full-blown version of Equation 7-6 is the sum of a geometric progression, and the last term is the solution value of the progression.

Note that Equation 7-6 is sufficiently general to encompass the zero growth case described earlier. If growth is zero, this is simply a special case of constant growth, and Equation 7-6 is equal to Equation 7-5. Note also that a necessary condition for the derivation of the simplified form of Equation 7-6 is that k_s be greater than g. If the equation is used in situations where k_s is not greater than g, the results will be meaningless.

The concept underlying the valuation process for a constant growth stock is graphed in Figure 7-5. Dividends are growing at the rate g = 5%, but because $k_s >$ g, the present value of each future dividend is declining. For example, the dividend in Year 1 is $\hat{D}_1 = D_0(1 + g)^1 = \$1.20(1.05) = \$1.26$. However, the present value of this dividend, discounted at 12 percent, is $PV(\hat{D}_1) = \$1.26/(1.12)^1 = \$1.125$. The dividend expected in Year 2 grows to $\$1.26(1.05) = \$1.323$, but the present value of this dividend falls to $\$1.055$. Continuing, $\hat{D}_3 = \$1.389$ and $PV(\hat{D}_3) = \$0.989$, and so on. Thus, the expected dividends are growing, but the present value of each successive dividend is declining, because the dividend growth rate (5 percent) is less than the rate used for discounting the dividends to the present (12 percent).

If we summed the present values of each future dividend, this summation would be the value of the stock, $\hat{P}_0$. When g is a constant, this summation is equal to $\hat{D}_1/(k_s - g)$, as shown in Equation 7-6. Therefore, if we extended the lower step function curve in Figure 7-5 on out to infinity and added up the present values of

FIGURE 7-5

Present Values of Dividends of a Constant Growth Stock: $D_0 = 1.20$, g = 5%, $k_s = 12\%$

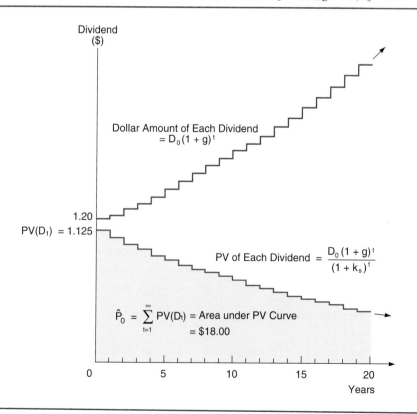

each future dividend, the summation would be identical to the value given by Equation 7-6, $18.

Growth in dividends occurs primarily as a result of growth in *earnings per share (EPS)*. Earnings growth, in turn, results from a number of factors, including (1) inflation, (2) the amount of earnings the company retains and reinvests, and (3) the rate of return the company earns on its equity (ROE). Regarding inflation, if output (in units) is stable and if both sales prices and input costs rise at the inflation rate, then EPS also will grow at the inflation rate. EPS also will grow as a result of the reinvestment, or plowback, of earnings. If the firm's earnings are not all paid out as dividends (i.e., if some fraction of earnings is retained), the dollars of investment behind each share will rise over time, which should lead to growth in future earnings and dividends.

Expected Rate of Return on a Constant Growth Stock

We can solve Equation 7-6 for k_s, again using the hat to denote that we are dealing with an expected rate of return[16]:

7-7		

$$\text{Expected rate of return} = \frac{\text{Expected dividend yield}}{} + \text{Expected growth rate, or capital gains yield}$$

$$\hat{k}_s = \frac{\hat{D}_1}{P_0} + g$$

Thus, if you buy a stock for a price $P_0 = \$18$, and if you expect the stock to pay a dividend $\hat{D}_1 = \$1.26$ one year from now and to grow at a constant rate $g = 5\%$ in the future, then your expected rate of return will be 12 percent:

$$\hat{k}_s = \frac{\$1.26}{\$18} + 0.05 = 0.07 + 0.05 = 0.12 = 12.0\%$$

In this form, we see that $\hat{k}_s$ is the *expected total return* and that it consists of an *expected dividend yield*, $\hat{D}_1/P_0 = 7\%$, plus an *expected growth rate or capital gains yield*, $g = 5\%$.

Suppose this analysis had been conducted on January 1, 2000, so $P_0 = \$18$ is the January 1, 2000, stock price and $\hat{D}_1 = \$1.26$ is the dividend expected at the end of 2000 (December 31). What is the expected stock price at the end of 2000 (or the beginning of 2001)? We would again apply Equation 7-6, but this time we would use the expected 2001 dividend, $\hat{D}_2 = \hat{D}_1(1 + g) = \$1.26(1.05) = \$1.323$:

$$\hat{P}_{1/1/01} = \frac{\hat{D}_{2001}}{k_s - g} = \frac{\$1.323}{0.12 - 0.05} = \$18.90$$

---

[16]The k_s value of Equation 7-7 is a *required* rate of return, but when we transform to obtain Equation 7-8, we are finding an *expected* rate of return. Obviously, the transformation requires that $k_s = \hat{k}_s$. This equality holds if the stock market is in equilibrium, a condition that will be discussed later in the chapter.

Now note that $18.90 is 5 percent greater than P_0, the $18 price on January 1, 2000:

$$P_{1/1/01} = \$18(1.05) = \$18.90$$

Thus, we would expect to make a capital gain of $18.90 − $18.00 = $0.90 during the year, which is a capital gains yield of 5 percent:

$$\text{Capital gains yield} = \frac{\text{Capital gain}}{\text{Beginning price}} = \frac{\overset{\text{Ending}}{\text{price}} - \overset{\text{Beginning}}{\text{price}}}{\text{Beginning price}}$$

$$= \frac{\$18.90 - \$18.00}{\$18.00} = \frac{\$0.90}{\$18.00} = 0.05 = 5.0\%$$

We could extend the analysis on out, and in each future year the expected capital gains yield would equal $g = 5\%$, the expected dividend growth rate.

Continuing, the dividend yield in 2001 could be estimated as follows:

$$\text{Dividend yield}_{2001} = \frac{\hat{D}_{2001}}{P_{1/1/01}} = \frac{\$1.323}{\$18.90} = 0.07 = 7.0\%$$

The dividend yield for 2002 could also be calculated, and again it would be 7 percent. Thus, for a constant growth stock, the following conditions must hold:

1. The dividend is expected to grow forever at a constant rate, g.
2. The stock price is expected to grow at this same rate.
3. The expected dividend yield is a constant.
4. The expected capital gains yield is also a constant, and it is equal to g.
5. The expected total rate of return, $\hat{k}_s$, is equal to the expected dividend yield plus the expected growth rate: $\hat{k}_s$ = dividend yield + g.

The term *expected* should be clarified — it means expected in a probabilistic sense, as the statistically expected outcome. Thus, if we say the growth rate is expected to remain constant at 5 percent, we mean that the best prediction for the growth rate in any future year is 5 percent, not that we literally expect the growth rate to be exactly equal to 5 percent in each future year. In this sense, the constant growth assumption is a reasonable one for many large, mature companies.

Nonconstant Growth

Firms typically go through *life cycles*. During the early part of their lives, their growth is much faster than that of the economy as a whole, then they match the economy's growth, and finally their growth is slower than that of the economy.[17]

---

[17]The concept of life cycles could be broadened to *product cycle*, which would include both small, startup companies and large companies such as IBM that periodically introduce new products to give sales and earnings a boost. We should also mention *business cycles*, which alternately depress and boost sales and profits. The growth rate just after a major new product has been introduced, or just after a firm emerges from the depths of a recession, is likely to be much higher than the "expected long-run average growth rate," which is the proper value to use for evaluating the project.

Illustrative Dividend Growth Rates

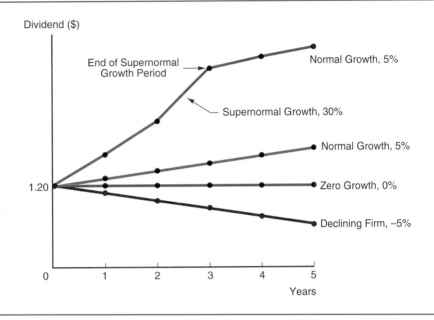

NONCONSTANT GROWTH
The part of the life cycle of a firm in which its growth is either much faster or much slower than that of the economy as a whole.

Automobile manufacturers in the 1920s and computer software firms such as Microsoft in the 1990s are examples of firms in the early part of the cycle. Other firms, such as those in tobacco industry or coal industry, are in the waning stages of their life cycles, so their growth is not keeping pace with the general economic growth (in some cases growth is negative). Firms whose growths are not about the same as the economy's growth are called **nonconstant growth** firms. Figure 7-6 illustrates nonconstant growth and also compares it with normal growth and zero growth.[18]

In the figure, the dividends of the supernormal growth firm (growth much greater than the economy) are expected to grow at a 30 percent rate for three years, after which the growth rate is expected to fall to 5 percent, the assumed average for the economy. The value of this firm, like any other, is the present value of its expected future dividends as determined by Equation 7-4. In the case in which $\hat{D}_t$ is growing at a constant rate, we simplified Equation 7-4 to $\hat{P}_0 = \hat{D}_1/(k_s - g)$. In the supernormal case, however, the expected growth rate is not a constant — it declines at the end of the period of supernormal growth. To find the value of

---

[18]A negative growth rate indicates a declining company. A mining company whose profits are falling because of a declining ore body is an example. Someone buying such a company would expect its earnings, and consequently its dividends and stock price, to decline each year, and this would lead to capital losses rather than capital gains. Obviously, a declining company's stock price will be relatively low, and its dividend yield must be high enough to offset the expected capital loss and still produce a competitive total return. Students sometimes argue that they would not be willing to buy a stock whose price was expected to decline. However, if the annual dividends are large enough to *more than* *offset* the falling stock price, the stock could still provide a good return.

such a stock, or of any nonconstant growth stock when the growth rate will eventually stabilize, we proceed in three steps:

1. Compute the value of the dividends that experience nonconstant growth, and then find the PV of these dividends.
2. *Find the price of the stock* at the end of the nonconstant growth period, *at which point it has become a constant growth stock,* and discount this price back to the present.
3. Add these two components to find the intrinsic value of the stock, $\hat{P}_0$.

Figure 7-7 can be used to illustrate the process for valuing nonconstant growth stocks, assuming the following five facts exist:

k_s = stockholders' required rate of return = 12%. This rate is used to discount the cash flows.

N = years of supernormal growth = 3.

g_s = rate of growth in both earnings and dividends during the supernormal growth period = 30%. (Note: The growth rate during the supernormal growth period could vary from year to year. Also, there could be several different supernormal growth periods — for example, 30% for three years, then 20% for three years, and then a constant rate.) This rate is shown directly on the time line.

g_n = rate of normal, constant growth after the supernormal period = 5%. This rate also is shown on the cash flow time line, after Year 3.

D_0 = last dividend the company paid = $1.20.

The valuation process as diagrammed in Figure 7-7 is explained in the steps set forth below the time line. The value of the supernormal growth stock is calculated to be $33.03.

Changes in Stock Prices

Stock prices are not constant — they sometimes change significantly, as well as very quickly. For example, on October 19, 1987, the Dow Jones Industrial Average (DJIA) dropped 508 points, and the average stock lost about 23 percent of its value in just one day. Some stocks lost more than half of their value that day. To see how changes can occur, let's assume we have a stock of a company that just paid a $2.50 dividend ($D_0$ = $2.50). The company's growth has been constant for many years, so it is expected that the company will continue to grow at the same rate, 6 percent, in the future (g = 6%). Currently, investors require a return equal to 15 percent for such investments, so the value of the company's stock should be

$$\hat{P}_0 = \frac{\$2.50(1.06)}{0.15 - 0.06} = \frac{\$2.65}{0.09} = \$29.44$$

Consider what would happen to the stock price if the value of any of the variables used to compute the current price changed. For instance, how would the price be affected if investors demanded a higher rate of return, say, 18 percent? If we change the value for k_s to 18 percent in the equation, we find that the value of the stock would be

$$P_0 = \frac{\$2.50\ (1.06)}{0.18 - 0.06} = \frac{\$2.65}{0.12} = \$22.08$$

The new price is lower because investors demand a higher return for receiving the same future cash flows. But, how would the price change if the future cash flows are different than expected, but the required return is 15 percent? Consider the effect if the company's growth rate is 4 percent rather than 6 percent:

FIGURE 7-7

Process for Finding the Value of a Nonconstant Growth Stock

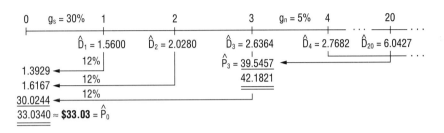

STEP 1. Calculate the dividends for each year during the nonconstant growth period — $\hat{D}_t = D_0\ (1 + g_s)^t$:

$$\hat{D}_1 = \$1.20\ (1.30)^1 = \$1.5600$$

$$\hat{D}_2 = \$1.20\ (1.30)^2 = \$2.0280$$

$$\hat{D}_3 = \$1.20\ (1.30)^3 = \$2.6364$$

Show these values on the cash flow time line as cash flows for Years 1 through 3.

STEP 2. The price of the stock is the PV of dividends from Year 1 to infinity. So, in theory, we could continue projecting each future dividend beyond Year 3, when normal growth of 5 percent occurs. In other words, use $g_n = 5\%$ to compute $\hat{D}_4, \hat{D}_5$, and so on with $\hat{D}_3$ as the base dividend for normal growth:

$$\hat{D}_4 = \$2.6364\ (1.05)^1 = \$2.7682$$

$$\hat{D}_5 = \$2.6364\ (1.05)^2 = \$2.9066$$

$$\vdots$$

$$\hat{D}_{20} = \$2.6364\ (1.05)^{17} = \$6.0427$$

We can continue this process, and then find the PV of this stream of dividends. However, we know that after $\hat{D}_3$ has been paid in Year 3, the stock becomes a constant growth stock, so we can apply the constant growth formula at that point and find $\hat{P}_3$, which is the PV of the dividends from Year 4 through infinity as evaluated in Year 3. After the Year 3 dividend has been paid, all of the future dividends will grow at a constant rate equal to 5 percent, so

$$\hat{P}_3 = \frac{\hat{D}_4}{k_s - g_n} = \frac{\$2.7682}{0.12 - 0.05} = \$39.5457$$

We show this $39.5457 on the cash flow time line as a second cash flow at Year 3. The $39.5457 is a Year 3 cash flow in the sense that the owner of the stock could sell it for $39.5457 at the end of Year 3, and also in the sense that $39.5457 is the present value equivalent of the dividend cash flows from Year 4 to infinity. Therefore, the *total cash flow* we recognize in Year 3 is the sum of $\hat{D}_3 + P_3 = \$2.6364 + \$39.5457 = \$42.1821$.

STEP 3. Now that the cash flows have been placed on the cash flow time line, we need to discount each cash flow at the required rate of return, $k_s = 12\%$. To find the present value, you either (a) compute the PVs directly, (b) use the PV tables, or (c) use the cash flow registers on your calculator. You can compute the PVs directly by dividing each cash flow by $(1.12)^t$. If you use the cash flow registers on your calculator, input $CF_0 = 0$, $CF_1 = 1.5600$, $CF_2 = 2.0280$, $CF_3 = 42.1821, I = 12$. The result is shown to the left below the cash flow time line.

$$P_0 = \frac{\$2.50\ (1.04)}{0.15 - 0.04} = \frac{\$2.60}{0.11} = \$23.64$$

Again, the new price is lower. But, in this case, the price is lower because investors demand the same return, but the cash flows the stock is expected to provide are less than expected previously.

From this simple example, you should have concluded that changes in stock prices occur because (1) investors change the rates of return required to invest in stocks or (2) expectations about the cash flows associated with stocks change. And, from the example, we can generalize the impact we would expect such changes to have on stock prices: *Stock prices move opposite changes in rates of return, but they move the same as changes in future cash flows expected from the stock in the future.* Therefore, if investors demand higher (lower) returns to invest in stocks, prices (values) should fall (increase); if investors expect their investments to generate lower (higher) future cash flows, prices should also fall (increase). What do you think would happen to the price of Microsoft's stock if Bill Gates announced the company's future growth opportunities looked to be better than previously expected? Because most investors would interpret such an announcement as "good news" concerning future cash flows, specifically that future cash flows should be higher than previously anticipated, you should expect the price of Microsoft to increase.

Self-Test Questions

In what way is preferred stock similar to bonds, and in what respect is it similar to common stock?

Explain the following statement: "Whereas a bond contains a promise to pay interest, common stock provides an expectation but no promise of dividends."

What are the two elements of a stock's expected returns?

Write out and explain the valuation model for a zero growth stock.

Write out and explain the valuation model for a constant growth stock.

How do you calculate the capital gains yield and the dividend yield of a stock?

Explain how you would find the value of a stock with nonconstant growth.

All else equal, how should prices change if investors demand lower rates of return to purchase stock?

Valuation of Real (Tangible) Assets

In the previous sections, we found that the values of financial assets, bonds and stocks, are based on the present value of the future cash flows expected from the assets. Valuing real assets is no different. We need to compute the present value of the expected cash flows associated with the asset. For example, suppose Genesco Manufacturing is considering purchasing a machine so that it can manufacture a new line of products. After five years, the machine will be worthless because it will be used up. But, during the five years Genesco uses the machine, the firm will be able to increase its net cash flows by the following amounts:

Year	Expected Cash Flow, $\widehat{CF}$
1	$120,000
2	100,000
3	150,000
4	80,000
5	50,000

If Genesco wants to earn a 14 percent return on investments like this machine, what is the value of the machine to the company? To find the answer, we need to solve for the present value of the uneven cash flow stream produced by the machine. Thus, the value of this machine can be depicted as follows:

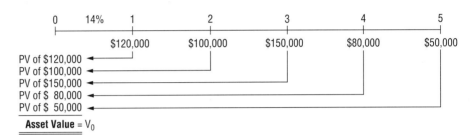

To compute the value of the machine, we simply apply Equation 7-1:

$$V_0 = \frac{\$120,000}{(1.14)^1} + \frac{\$100,000}{(1.14)^2} + \frac{\$150,000}{(1.14)^3} + \frac{\$80,000}{(1.14)^4} + \frac{\$50,000}{(1.14)^5}$$

The value of the machine can be computed by using the three procedures discussed in Chapter 6: (1) numerically, (2) using the tables, and (3) with a financial calculator.

1. NUMERICAL SOLUTION:

Because the stream of cash flows is uneven (i.e., it is not an annuity), we must discount each cash flow back to the present and sum these PVs to find the machine's value:

$$V_0 = \$120,000 \times \left[\frac{1}{(1.14)^1}\right] + \$100,000 \times \left[\frac{1}{(1.14)^2}\right] + \$150,000 \times \left[\frac{1}{(1.14)^3}\right]$$

$$+ \$80,000 \times \left[\frac{1}{(1.14)^4}\right] + \$50,000 \times \left[\frac{1}{(1.14)^5}\right]$$

$$= \$105,263.16 + \$76,946.75 + \$101,245.73 + \$47,366.42 + \$25,968.43$$

$$= \$356,790.49$$

2. TABULAR SOLUTION:

Simply look up the appropriate PVIF values in Table A-1 at the end of the book, insert them into the equation, and complete the arithmetic:

$$V_d = \$120{,}000(PVIF_{14\%,1}) + \$100{,}000(PVIF_{14\%,2}) + \$150{,}000(PVIF_{14\%,3})$$

$$+ \$80{,}000(PVIF_{14\%,4}) + \$50{,}000(PVIF_{14\%,5})$$

$$= \$120{,}000(0.8772) + \$100{,}000(0.7695) + \$150{,}000(0.6750)$$

$$+ \$80{,}000(0.5921) + \$50{,}000(0.5194)$$

$$= \$356{,}802$$

There is a rounding difference, which results from the fact that the tables only go to four decimal places.

3. FINANCIAL CALCULATOR SOLUTION:

To find the answer using your financial calculator, you must input the individual cash flows, in chronological order, into the cash flow register. On most financial calculators, cash flows are designated CF_0, CF_1, CF_2, and so on. Because the machine will not produce a cash flow until the end of the first year, $CF_0 = 0$. According to the cash flow time line, the cash flows entered into the calculator are $CF_1 = \$120{,}000$, $CF_2 = \$100{,}000$, $CF_3 = \$150{,}000$, $CF_4 = \$80{,}000$, and $CF_5 = \$50{,}000$. After entering these values, enter the required rate of return, $k = 14\%$ (remember the appropriate key is usually labeled INT or I). At this point, you have entered all the known information, so you only need to press the NPV key to find the present value of the cash flows. You should find the answer is $356,790.49.

The valuation of real assets is a critical concern for financial managers because they need to know whether the plant (e.g., buildings) and equipment (e.g., machines) and other long-term assets they purchase will help achieve the goal of wealth maximization. To determine how investing in a particular asset will affect the value of the firm, the financial manager must be able to determine whether the asset is worth its purchase price and if the asset will increase the firm's wealth. Although the general valuation procedures we outlined in this section can be used to value real assets, other factors often need to be considered before a final purchasing decision can be made. The process of evaluating projects and deciding which projects should be purchased is called *capital budgeting*. The capital budgeting decision-making process is crucial to the firm's success, and it is especially important if the firm is to achieve the goal of wealth maximization. Therefore, we devote an entire chapter to the topic of capital budgeting. In Chapter 9, we explain in great detail the procedures firms use to make capital budgeting decisions — procedures that you can apply to make decisions when purchasing personal assets.

SMALL BUSINESS

Valuation of Small Firms

In this chapter we presented several equations for valuing a firm's common stock. These equations had one common element: They all assumed that the firm is currently paying a dividend. However, many small firms, even highly profitable ones whose stock is traded in the market, have never paid a dividend. How does one value the stock of such firms? If a firm is expected to begin

Continued

Continued

paying dividends in the future, we can modify the equations presented in the chapter and use them to determine the value of the stock.

A new business often expects to have very low sales during its first few years of operation as it develops its product. Then, if the product catches on, sales will grow rapidly for several years. For example, Compaq Computer Company had only three employees when it was incorporated in 1982. Its first year was devoted to product development, and 1982 sales were zero. In 1983, however, Compaq began marketing its personal computer, and its sales hit $111 million, a record first-year volume for any new firm, and by 1986 Compaq was included in *Fortune's* 500 largest U.S. industrial firms. Obviously, Compaq has been more successful than most new businesses, but it is common for small firms to have growth rates of 100 percent, 500 percent, or even 1,000 percent during their first few years of operation.

Sales growth brings with it the need for additional assets — Compaq could not have increased its sales as it did without also increasing its assets, and asset growth requires an increase in liability and/or equity accounts. Small firms can generally obtain some bank credit, but they must maintain a reasonable balance between debt and equity. Thus, additional bank borrowings require increases in equity, and getting the equity capital needed to support growth can be difficult for small firms. They have limited access to the capital markets, and, even when they can sell common stock, the owners of small firms are reluctant to do so for fear of losing voting

control. Therefore, the best source of equity for most small businesses is retained earnings, and for this reason most small firms pay no dividends during their rapid growth years. Eventually, though, successful small firms do pay dividends, and those dividends generally grow rapidly at first but slow down to a sustainable constant rate once the firm reaches maturity.

Finding the value of the stock of a small firm is the same as was described earlier in the chapter in the section about nonconstant growth companies, except, for most small firms, there might be numerous years in which no dividend payments are expected. If a small firm currently pays no dividend but is expected to pay dividends in the future, the value of its stock can be found as follows:

1. Estimate when dividends will be paid, the amount of the first dividend, the growth rate during the supernormal growth period, the length of the supernormal period, the long-run (constant) growth rate, and the rate of return required by investors.
2. Use the constant growth model to determine the price of the stock after the firm reaches a stable growth situation.
3. Set out on a time line the cash flows (dividends during the supernormal growth period and the stock price once the constant growth state is reached) and then find the present value of these cash flows. *That present value represents the value of the stock today.*

Summary

Corporate decisions should be analyzed in terms of how alternative courses of action are likely to affect the value of a firm. However, it is necessary to know how value is determined before attempting to measure how a given decision will affect a specific firm's value. Accordingly, this chapter showed how assets are valued as well as how investors go about estimating the rates of return they expect to earn. The key concepts covered in the chapter are listed below.

- The **value** of any asset can be found by computing the **present value of the cash flows** the asset is expected to generate during its life.
- A **bond** is a long-term promissory note issued by a business or governmental unit. The firm receives the selling price of the bond in exchange for promising to make interest payments and to repay the principal on a specified future date.

- The **value of a bond** is found as the present value of an **annuity** (the interest payments) plus the present value of a lump sum (the **principal**). The bond is evaluated at the appropriate periodic interest rate over the number of periods for which interest payments are made.
- The equation used to find the value of a bond is as follows:

$$V_d = \sum_{t=1}^{N \times m} \frac{INT}{\left(1 + \frac{k_d}{m}\right)^t} + \frac{M}{\left(1 + \frac{k_d}{m}\right)^{N \times m}}$$

$$= INT\left(PVIFA_{\frac{k_d}{m}, N \times m}\right) + M\left(PVIF_{\frac{k_d}{m}, N \times m}\right)$$

where m equals the number of times interest is paid during the year.
- The return earned on a bond held to maturity is defined as the bond's **yield to maturity (YTM)**.
- The longer the term to maturity of a bond, the more its price will change in response to a given change in interest rates; this is called **interest rate price risk.** Bonds with short maturities, however, expose the investor to high **interest rate reinvestment rate risk,** which is the risk that income will differ from what is expected because cash flows received from bonds will have to be reinvested at different interest rates.
- The **value of a share of stock** is calculated as the **present value of the stream of dividends** it is expected to provide in the future.
- Most **preferred stocks are perpetuities**, and the value of a share of perpetual preferred, or any zero growth stock, stock is found as the dividend divided by the required rate of return: $P_0 = D/k_s$.
- The equation used to find the **value of a constant**, or **normal, growth** stock is $\hat{P}_0 = \hat{D}_1/(k_s - g)$.
- The **expected total rate of return** from a stock consists of an **expected dividend yield** plus an **expected capital gains yield**. For a constant growth firm, both the expected dividend yield and the expected capital gains yield are constant.
- The equation for $\hat{k}_s$, **the expected rate of return on a constant growth stock**, can be expressed as follows: $\hat{k}_s = \hat{D}_1/P_0 + g$.
- A **zero growth stock** is one whose future dividends are not expected to grow at all, while a **nonconstant growth stock** is one whose earnings and dividends are expected to grow at a rate different from the economy as a whole over some specified time period.
- To find the **present value of a nonconstant growth stock,** (1) find the dividends expected during the nonconstant growth period, (2) find the price of the stock at the end of the nonconstant growth period, (3) discount the dividends and the projected price back to the present, and (4) sum these PVs to find the current value of the stock, $\hat{P}_0$.
- Like a financial asset, the value of a **real asset** is computed as the present value of the cash flows the asset is expected to provide in the future.
- Determining the value of the stock of a **small firm** is the same as for larger companies with nonconstant growth, except small firms often do not pay dividends until later in their lives, which might be many years from the current period.

Questions

7-1   Describe how you should determine the value of an asset, whether it is a real asset or a financial asset.

7-2   Two investors are evaluating IBM's stock for possible purchase. They agree on the expected value of $\hat{D}_1$ and also on the expected future dividend growth rate. Further, they agree on the riskiness of the stock. However, one investor normally holds stocks for 2 years, while the other normally holds stocks for 10 years. On the basis of the type of analysis done in this chapter, they should both be willing to pay the same price for IBM's stock. True or false? Explain.

7-3   A bond that pays interest forever and has no maturity date is a perpetual bond. In what respect is a perpetual bond similar to a no-growth common stock and to a share of preferred stock?

7-4   "The rate of return you would get if you bought a bond and held it to its maturity date is called the bond's yield to maturity. If interest rates in the economy rise after a bond has been issued, what will happen to the bond's price and to its YTM? Does the length of time to maturity affect the extent to which a given change in interest rates will affect the bond's price?

7-5   If you buy a callable bond and interest rates decline, will the value of your bond rise by as much as it would have risen if the bond had not been callable? Explain.

7-6   If you bought a share of common stock, you would typically expect to receive dividends plus capital gains. Would you expect the distribution between dividend yield and capital gains to be influenced by the firm's decision to pay more dividends rather than to retain and reinvest more of its earnings?

7-7   How do you think the price of AT&T's stock will change if investors decide they want to earn a higher return for purchasing the stock? Assume all else remains constant. Do you think the price of AT&T's stock would change if the CEO announced that the company was going to have to pay a 10-year, $10,000,000 fine for unfair trade practices? Explain your rationale.

7-8   How do you think valuing a real asset, such as a building, differs from valuing a financial asset, such as a stock or bond?

Self-Test Problems   *Solutions Appear in Appendix B*

Key terms   **ST-1**   Define each of the following terms:
  a. Bond
  b. Premium bond; discount bond
  c. Current yield (on a bond); yield to maturity (YTM)
  d. Interest rate price risk; interest rate reinvestment rate risk
  e. Intrinsic value, $\hat{P}_0$; market price, P_0
  f. Required rate of return, k_s; expected rate of return, $\hat{k}_s$; actual, or realized, rate of return, $\bar{k}_s$
  g. Capital gains yield; dividend yield; expected total return
  h. Zero growth stock
  i. Normal, or constant, growth; nonconstant growth

Stock growth rates
and valuation   **ST-2**   You are considering buying the stocks of two companies that operate in the same industry; they have very similar characteristics except for their dividend payout policies. Both companies are expected to earn $6 per share this year. However, Company

D (for "dividend") is expected to pay out all of its earnings as dividends, while Company G (for "growth") is expected to pay out only one-third of its earnings, or $2 per share. D's stock price is $40. G and D are equally risky. Which of the following is most likely to be true?

a. Company G will have a faster growth rate than Company D. Therefore, G's stock price should be greater than $40.

b. Although G's growth rate should exceed D's, D's current dividend exceeds that of G, and this should cause D's price to exceed G's.

c. An investor in Stock D will get his or her money back faster because D pays out more of its earnings as dividends. Thus, in a sense, D is like a short-term bond, and G is like a long-term bond. Therefore, if economic shifts cause k_d and k_s to increase and if the expected streams of dividends from D and G remain constant, Stocks D and G will both decline, but D's price should decline more.

d. D's expected and required rate of return is $\hat{k}_s = k_s = 15\%$. G's expected return will be higher because of its higher expected growth rate.

e. On the basis of the available information, the best estimate of G's growth rate is 10 percent.

Bond valuation **ST-3** The Pennington Corporation issued a new series of bonds on January 1, 1976. The bonds were sold at par ($1,000), have a 12 percent coupon, and mature in 30 years, on December 31, 2005. Coupon payments are made semiannually (on June 30 and December 31).

a. What was the YTM of Pennington's bonds on January 1, 1976?

b. What was the price of the bond on January 1, 1981, 5 years later, assuming that the level of interest rates had fallen to 10 percent?

c. Find the current yield and capital gains yield on the bond on January 1, 1981, given the price as determined in part b.

d. On July 1, 1999, Pennington's bonds sold for $916.42. What was the YTM at that date?

e. What were the current yield and capital gains yield on July 1, 1999?

Constant growth stock valuation **ST-4** Ewald Company's current stock price is $36, and its last dividend was $2.40. In view of Ewald's strong financial position and its consequent low risk, its required rate of return is only 12 percent. If dividends are expected to grow at a constant rate, g, in the future, and if k_s is expected to remain at 12 percent, what is Ewald's expected stock price 5 years from now?

Nonconstant growth stock valuation **ST-5** Snyder Computer Chips Inc. is experiencing a period of rapid growth. Earnings and dividends are expected to grow at a rate of 15 percent during the next 2 years, at 13 percent in the third year, and at a constant rate of 6 percent thereafter. Snyder's *last* dividend was $1.15, and the required rate of return on the stock is 12 percent.

a. Calculate the value of the stock today.

b. Calculate $\hat{P}_1$ and $\hat{P}_2$.

c. Calculate the dividend yield and capital gains yield for Years 1, 2, and 3.

Problems

Bond valuation **7-1** Suppose Ford Motor Company sold an issue of bonds with a 10-year maturity, a $1,000 par value, a 10 percent coupon rate, and semiannual interest payments.

a. Two years after the bonds were issued, the going rate of interest on bonds such as these fell to 6 percent. At what price would the bonds sell?

b. Suppose that, 2 years after the initial offering, the going interest rate had risen to 12 percent. At what price would the bonds sell?

c. Suppose that the conditions in part a existed — that is, interest rates fell to 6 percent 2 years after the issue date. Suppose further that the interest rate remained at 6 percent for the next 8 years. Describe what would happen to the price of the Ford Motor Company bonds over time.

Perpetual bond valuation   **7-2**   The bonds of the Lange Corporation are perpetuities with a 10 percent coupon. Bonds of this type currently yield 8 percent, and their par value is $1,000.

a. What is the price of the Lange bonds?

b. Suppose interest rate levels rise to the point where such bonds now yield 12 percent. What would be the price of the Lange bonds?

c. At what price would the Lange bonds sell if the yield on these bonds were 10 percent?

d. How would your answers to parts a, b, and c change if the bonds were not perpetuities but had a maturity of 20 years?

Constant growth stock valuation   **7-3**   Your broker offers to sell you some shares of Wingler & Co. common stock that paid a dividend of $2 *yesterday.* You expect the dividend to grow at the rate of 5 percent per year for the next 3 years, and if you buy the stock you plan to hold it for 3 years and then sell it.

a. Find the expected dividend for each of the next 3 years; that is, calculate $\hat{D}_1, \hat{D}_2$, and $\hat{D}_3$. Note that $D_0 = \$2$.

b. Given that the appropriate discount rate is 12 percent and that the first of these dividend payments will occur 1 year from now, find the present value of the dividend stream; that is, calculate the PV of $\hat{D}_1, \hat{D}_2$, and $\hat{D}_3$, and then sum these PVs.

c. You expect the price of the stock 3 years from now to be $34.73; that is, you expect $\hat{P}_3$ to equal $34.73. Discounted at a 12 percent rate, what is the present value of this expected future stock price? In other words, calculate the PV of $34.73.

d. If you plan to buy the stock, hold it for 3 years, and then sell it for $34.73, what is the most you should pay for it?

e. Use Equation 7-6 to calculate the present value of this stock. Assume that g = 5%, and it is constant.

f. Is the value of this stock dependent upon how long you plan to hold it? In other words, if your planned holding period were 2 years or 5 years rather than 3 years, would this affect the value of the stock today, $\hat{P}_0$?

Return on common stock   **7-4**   You buy a share of Damanpour Corporation stock for $21.40. You expect it to pay dividends of $1.07, $1.1449, and $1.2250 in Years 1, 2, and 3, respectively, and you expect to sell it at a price of $26.22 at the end of 3 years.

a. Calculate the growth rate in dividends.

b. Calculate the expected dividend yield.

c. Assuming that the calculated growth rate is expected to continue, you can add the dividend yield to the expected growth rate to get the expected total rate of return. What is this stock's expected total rate of return?

Constant growth stock valuation   **7-5**   Investors require a 15 percent rate of return on Goulet Company's stock ($k_s = 15\%$).

a. What will be Goulet's stock value if the previous dividend was $D_0 = \$2$ and if investors expect dividends to grow at a constant compound annual rate of (1) −5 percent, (2) 0 percent, (3) 5 percent, and (4) 10 percent?

b. Using data from part a, what is the constant growth model value for Goulet's stock if the required rate of return is 15 percent and the expected growth rate is (1) 15 percent or (2) 20 percent? Are these reasonable results? Explain.

c. Is it reasonable to expect that a constant growth stock would have g > k_s?

Nonconstant growth   **7-6**   Bayboro Sails is expected to pay dividends of $2.50, $3.00, and $4.00 in the next 3
stock valuation   years — $\hat{D}_1, \hat{D}_2$, and $\hat{D}_3$, respectively. After 3 years, the dividend is expected to grow at a constant rate equal to 4 percent per year indefinitely. Stockholders require a return of 14% to invest in the common stock of Bayboro Sails.

a. Compute the present value of the dividends Bayboro is expected to pay over the next 3 years.

b. For what price should investors expect to be able to sell the common stock of Bayboro at the end of 3 years? (Hint: The dividend will grow at a constant 4 percent in Year 4, Year 5, and every year thereafter, so Equation 7-6 can be used to find $\hat{P}_3$ — the appropriate dividend to use in the numerator is $\hat{D}_4$.)

c. Compute the value of Bayboro's common stock today, $\hat{P}_0$.

Bond valuation   **7-7**   In January 1994, the yield on AAA rated corporate bonds averaged about 5 percent; by the end of the year the yield on these same bonds was about 8 percent because the Federal Reserve increased interest rates six times during the year. Assume IBM issued a 10-year, 5 percent coupon bond on January 1, 1994. On the same date, GM issued a 20-year, 5 percent coupon bond. Both bonds pay interest *annually.* Also assume that the market rate on similar risk bonds was 5 percent at the time the bonds were issued.

a. Compute the market value of each bond at the time of issue.

b. Compute the market value of each bond 1 year after issue if the market yield for similar risk bonds was 8 percent on January 1, 1995.

c. Compute the 1994 capital gains yield for each bond.

d. Compute the current yield for each bond in 1994.

e. Compute the total return each bond would have generated for investors in 1994.

f. If you invested in bonds at the beginning of 1994, would you have been better off to have held long-term or short-term bonds? Explain.

g. Assume interest rates stabilize at the January 1995 rate of 8.0 percent, and they stay at this level indefinitely. What would be the price of each bond on January 1, 2000, after 6 years have passed? Describe what should happen to the prices of these bonds as they approach their maturities.

Nonconstant growth   **7-8**   It is now January 1, 2000. Swink Electric Inc. has just developed a solar panel capa-
stock valuation   ble of generating 200 percent more electricity than any solar panel currently on the market. As a result, Swink is expected to experience a 15 percent annual growth rate for the next 5 years. By the end of 5 years, other firms will have developed comparable technology, and Swink's growth rate will slow to 5 percent per year indefinitely. Stockholders require a return of 12 percent on Swink's stock. The most recent annual dividend (D_0), which was paid yesterday, was $1.75 per share.

a. Calculate Swink's expected dividends for 2000, 2001, 2002, 2003, and 2004.

b. Calculate the value of the stock today, $\hat{P}_0$. Proceed by finding the present value of the dividends expected at the end of 2000, 2001, 2002, 2003, and 2004 plus the present value of the stock price that should exist at the end of 2004. The year-end 2004 stock price can be found by using the constant growth equation (Equation 7-6). Note that to find the December 31, 2004, price, you use the dividend expected in 2005, which is 5 percent greater than the 2004 dividend.

c. Calculate the expected dividend yield, $\hat{D}_1/P_0$, the capital gains yield expected in 2000, and the expected total return (dividend yield plus capital gains yield) for 2000. (Assume that $\hat{P}_0 = P_0$, and recognize that the capital gains yield is equal to the total return minus the dividend yield.) Also calculate these same three yields for 2004.

d. How might an investor's tax situation affect his or her decision to purchase stocks of companies in the early stages of their lives, when they are growing rapidly, versus stocks of older, more mature firms? When does Swink's stock become "mature" in this example?

e. Suppose your boss tells you she believes that Swink's annual growth rate will be only 12 percent during the next 5 years and that the firm's normal growth rate will be only 4 percent. Without doing any calculations, what general effect would these growth-rate changes have on the price of Swink's stock?

f. Suppose your boss also tells you that she regards Swink as being quite risky and that she believes the required rate of return should be 14 percent, not 12 percent. Again without doing any calculations, how would the higher required rate of return affect the price of the stock, its capital gains yield, and its dividend yield?

Supernormal growth stock valuation

7-9 Tanner Technologies Corporation (TTC) has been growing at a rate of 20 percent per year in recent years. This same growth rate is expected to last for another 2 years.

a. If $D_0 = \$1.60$, $k = 10\%$, and $g_n = 6\%$, what is TTC's stock worth today? What are its expected dividend yield and capital gains yield at this time?

b. Now assume that TTC's period of supernormal growth is expected to last another 5 years rather than 2 years. How would this affect its price, dividend yield, and capital gains yield? Answer in words only.

c. What will be TTC's dividend yield and capital gains yield once its period of supernormal growth ends? (Hint: These values will be the same regardless of whether you examine the case of 2 or 5 years of supernormal growth; the calculations are very easy.)

d. Of what interest to investors is the changing relationship between dividend yield and capital gains yield over time?

Constant growth stock valuation

7-10 The stock of Gerlunice Company has a rate of return equal to 15.5 percent.

a. If the dividend expected during the coming year, $\hat{D}_1$, is \$2.25, and if $g = 5\%$ and is constant, at what price should Gerlunice's stock sell?

b. Now suppose the Federal Reserve Board increases the money supply, causing the risk-free rate to drop, and thus the return expected for investing in Gerlunice will fall to 13.5 percent. What would this do to the price of the stock?

c. In addition to the change in part b, suppose investors' risk aversion declines; this fact, combined with the decline in k_{RF}, causes k_s for Gerlunice's stock to fall to 12 percent. At what price would Gerlunice's stock sell?

d. Now suppose Gerlunice has a change in management. The new group institutes policies that increase the expected constant growth rate to 6 percent. Also, the new management stabilizes sales and profits, which causes the return demanded by investors to decline to 11.6 percent. After all these changes, what is Gerlunice's new equilibrium price? (Note: $\hat{D}_1$ goes to \$2.27.)

Exam-Type Problems

The problems included in this section are set up in such a way that they could be used as multiple-choice exam problems.

Bond valuation

7-11 The Desreumaux Company has two bond issues outstanding. Both bonds pay \$100 annual interest plus \$1,000 at maturity. Bond L has a maturity of 15 years and Bond S a maturity of 1 year.

a. What will be the value of each of these bonds when the going rate of interest is (1) 5 percent, (2) 8 percent, and (3) 12 percent? Assume that there is only one more interest payment to be made on Bond S.

b. Why does the longer-term (15-year) bond fluctuate more when interest rates change than does the shorter-term bond (1-year)?

Yield to maturity

7-12 1t is now January 1, 2000, and you are considering the purchase of an outstanding Puckett Corporation bond that was issued on January 1, 1998. The Puckett bond has a 9.5 percent annual coupon and a 30-year original maturity (it matures on December 31, 2028). Interest rates have declined since the bond was issued, and the bond now is selling at 116.575 percent of par, or \$1,165.75. You want to determine the yield to maturity for this bond.

a. Use Equation 7-3 to approximate the yield to maturity for the Puckett bond in 2000.

b. What is the actual yield to maturity in 2000 for the Puckett bond?

Yield to maturity **7-13** The Severn Company's bonds have 4 years remaining to maturity. Interest is paid annually; the bonds have a $1,000 par value; and the coupon interest rate is 9 percent.

a. Compute the *approximate* yield to maturity for the bonds if the current market price is either (1) $829 or (2) $1,104.

b. Would you pay $829 for one of these bonds if you thought that the appropriate rate of interest was 12 percent — that is, if $k_d = 12\%$? Explain your answer.

Rate of return for a perpetual bond **7-14** What will be the rate of return on a perpetual bond with a $1,000 par value, an 8 percent coupon rate, and a current market price of (a) $600, (b) $800, (c) $1,000, and (d) $1,500? Assume interest is paid annually.

Declining growth stock valuation **7-15** McCue Mining Company's ore reserves are being depleted, so its sales are falling. Also, its pit is getting deeper each year, so its costs are rising. As a result, the company's earnings and dividends are declining at the constant rate of 5 percent per year. If $D_0 = \$5$ and $k_s = 15\%$, what is the value of McCue Mining's stock?

Supernormal growth stock valuation **7-16** Assume that the average firm in your company's industry is expected to grow at a constant rate of 6 percent, and its dividend yield is 7 percent. Your company is about as risky as the average firm in the industry, but it has just successfully completed some R&D work that leads you to expect that its earnings and dividends will grow at a rate of 50 percent $[\hat{D}_1 = D_0(1 + g) = D_0(1.50)]$ this year and 25 percent the following year, after which growth should match the 6 percent industry average rate. The last dividend paid (D_0) was $1. What is the value per share of your firm's stock?

Effective annual rate **7-17** Assume that as investment manager of Florida Electric Company's pension plan (which is exempt from income taxes), you must choose between IBM bonds and AT&T preferred stock. The bonds have a $1,000 par value, they mature in 20 years, they pay $40 each 6 months, and they sell at a price of $897.40 per bond. The preferred stock is a perpetuity; it pays a dividend of $2 each quarter, and it sells for $95 per share. What is the effective annual rate of return (EAR) on the *higher* yielding security?

Simple interest rate **7-18** Tapley Corporation's 14 percent coupon rate, semiannual payment, $1,000 par value bonds mature in 30 years. The bonds sell at a price of $1,353.54, and the yield curve is flat. Assuming that interest rates in the economy are expected to remain at their current level, what is the best estimate of Tapley's simple interest rate on *new* bonds?

Nonconstant growth stock valuation **7-19** Microtech Corporation is expanding rapidly, and it currently needs to retain all of its earnings, hence it does not pay any dividends. However, investors expect Microtech to begin paying dividends, with the first dividend of $1.00 coming 3 years from today. The dividend should grow rapidly — at a rate of 50 percent per year — during Years 4 and 5. After Year 5, the company should grow at a constant rate of 8 percent per year. If the required return on the stock is 15 percent, what is the value of the stock today?

Valuation of real assets **7-20** Currently, there is so much demand for Anderson Electric's products that the company cannot manufacture enough inventory to satisfy demand. Consequently, Anderson is considering purchasing a new machine that will increase inventory production. Anderson estimates that the new machine will generate the following net cash flows during its lifetime:

Year	Net Cash Flow, $\widehat{CF}$
1	$18,000
2	12,000
3	15,000
4	10,000
5	10,000
6	10,000

a. If Anderson normally requires a return equal to 12 percent for such projects, what is the *maximum* amount it should pay for the machine?

b. How would your answer to part a change if the appropriate rate of return is 15 percent?

Integrative Problem

Section I: Bond Valuation

Valuation **7-21** Robert Campbell and Carol Morris are senior vice presidents of the Mutual of Chicago Insurance Company. They are co-directors of the company's pension fund management division, with Campbell having responsibility for fixed-income securities (primarily bonds) and Morris being responsible for equity investments. A major new client, the California League of Cities, has requested that Mutual of Chicago present an investment seminar to the mayors of the represented cities, and Campbell and Morris, who will make the actual presentation, have asked you to help them by answering the following questions:

a. What are the key features of a bond?

b. How is the value of any asset whose value is based on expected future cash flows determined?

c. How is the value of a bond determined? What is the value of a 1-year, $1,000 par value bond with a 10 percent annual coupon if its required rate of return is 10 percent? What is the value of a similar 10-year bond?

d. (1) What would be the value of the bond described in part c if, just after it had been issued, the expected inflation rate rose by 3 percentage points, causing investors to require a 13 percent return? Would we now have a discount or a premium bond? (Hint: $PVIF_{13\%,1} = 0.8850$; $PVIF_{13\%,10} = 0.2946$; $PVIFA_{13\%,10} = 5.4262$.)

  (2) What would happen to the bond's value if inflation fell, and k_d declined to 7 percent? Would we now have a premium or a discount bond?

  (3) What would happen to the value of the 10-year bond over time if the required rate of return remained at 13 percent or remained at 7 percent?

e. (1) What is the yield to maturity on a 10-year, 9 percent annual coupon, $1,000 par value bond that sells for $887.00? That sells for $1,134.20? What does the fact that a bond sells at a discount or at a premium tell you about the relationship between k_d and the bond's coupon rate?

  (2) What is the current yield, the capital gains yield, and the total return in each case?

f. What is interest rate price risk? Which bond in part c has more interest rate price risk, the 1-year bond or the 10-year bond?

g. What is interest rate reinvestment rate risk? Which bond in part c has more interest rate reinvestment rate risk, assuming a 10-year investment horizon?

h. Redo parts c and d, assuming the bonds have semiannual rather than annual coupons. (Hint: $PVIF_{6.5\%,2} = 0.8817$; $PVIFA_{6.5\%,2} = 1.8206$; $PVIF_{6.5\%,20} = 0.2838$;

$\text{PVIFA}_{6.5\%,20} = 11.0185$; $\text{PVIF}_{3.5\%,2} = 0.9335$; $\text{PVIFA}_{3.5\%,2} = 1.8997$; $\text{PVIF}_{3.5\%,20} = 0.5026$; $\text{PVIFA}_{3.5\%,20} = 14.2124$.)

    i. Suppose you could buy, for $1,000, either a 10 percent, 10-year, annual payment bond or a 10 percent, 10-year, semiannual payment bond. They are equally risky. Which would you prefer? If $1,000 is the proper price for the semiannual bond, what is the proper price for the annual payment bond?

    j. What is the value of a perpetual bond with an annual coupon of $100 if its required rate of return is 10 percent? 13 percent? 7 percent? Assess the following statement: "Because perpetual bonds match an infinite investment horizon, they have little interest rate price risk."

Section II: Stock Valuation

To illustrate the common stock valuation process, Campbell and Morris have asked you to analyze the Bon Temps Company, an employment agency that supplies word processor operators and computer programmers to businesses with temporarily heavy workloads. You are to answer the following questions.

    a. (1) Write out a formula that can be used to value any stock, regardless of its dividend pattern.

        (2) What is a constant growth stock? How are constant growth stocks valued?

        (3) What happens if the growth is constant, and $g > k_s$? Will many stocks have $g > k_s$?

    b. Assume that Bon Temps is a constant growth company whose last dividend (D_0, which was paid yesterday) was $2.00 and whose dividend is expected to grow indefinitely at a 6 percent rate. The appropriate rate of return for Bon Temps' stock is 16 percent.

        (1) What is the firm's expected dividend stream over the next 3 years?

        (2) What is the firm's current stock price?

        (3) What is the stock's expected value 1 year from now?

        (4) What are the expected dividend yield, the capital gains yield, and the total return during the first year?

    c. Now assume that the stock is currently selling at $21.20. What is the expected rate of return on the stock?

    d. What would the stock price be if its dividends were expected to have zero growth?

    e. Now assume that Bon Temps is expected to experience supernormal growth of 30 percent for the next 3 years, then to return to its long-run constant growth rate of 6 percent. What is the stock's value under these conditions? What is its expected dividend yield and capital gains yield in Year 1? In Year 4?

    f. Suppose Bon Temps is expected to experience zero growth during the first 3 years and then to resume its steady-state growth of 6 percent in the fourth year. What is the stock's value now? What is its expected dividend yield and its capital gains yield in Year 1? In Year 4?

    g. Finally, assume that Bon Temps's earnings and dividends are expected to decline by a constant 6 percent per year, that is, $g = -6\%$. Why would anyone be willing to buy such a stock, and at what price should it sell? What would be the dividend yield and capital gains yield in each year?

Section III: Real Asset Valuation

Mutual of Chicago currently is examining the possibility of purchasing a piece of equipment that will scan data into its main computer. The new scanner will eliminate the need to hire part-time help to make sure information about clients is recorded accurately and in a timely manner. After evaluating all future costs and benefits, management has determined the new scanner will generate the following cash flows during its 10-year life:

Year/Period	Expected Cash Flow, $\hat{CF}$
1-3	$30,000
4-6	15,000
7	−20,000
8-10	10,000

Campbell and Morris would like you to evaluate the value of the scanner.

a. If Mutual of Chicago believes the appropriate return for investments like the scanner is 15 percent, what is the value of the scanner to the company?

b. Would you recommend the machine be purchased if its current cost is $100,000? Explain your reasoning.

c. Would the scanner be more attractive if the appropriate return was 10 percent, rather than 15 percent? Explain your answer.

Computer-Related Problem

Work the problem in this section only if you are using the computer problem diskette.

Nonconstant growth
stock valuation

7-22 Use the model in File C7 to solve this problem.

a. Refer back to Problem 7-8. Rework part e using the computerized model to determine what Swink's expected dividends and stock price would be under the conditions given.

b. Suppose your boss tells you that she regards Swink as being quite risky and that she believes the required rate of return should be higher than the 12 percent originally specified. Rework the problem under the conditions given in part e, except change the required rate of return to (1) 13 percent, (2) 15 percent, and (3) 20 percent to determine the effects of the higher required rates of return on Swink's stock price.

CHAPTER 8

Risk and Rates of Return

A MANAGERIAL PERSPECTIVE

The performance of the major stock markets from 1995 through 1997 can best be described as remarkable — a period investors would love to repeat again and again. During this three-year period, stocks traded on the New York Stock Exchange (NYSE), on the American Stock Exchange (AMEX), and the NASDAQ increased by an average of more than 20 percent each year. In 1997, companies such as Microsoft and AT&T increased by about 50 percent. Other companies such as Best Buy, which is a discount outlet, and Jackson Hewitt, which is a national tax preparation company, increased by more than 250 percent. Consider the return you would have earned in 1997 if you purchased Jackson Hewitt at the beginning of the year for $4.75, and at the end of the year it was selling for $68 — that's a one-year return of nearly 1,332 percent. Even as these stocks experienced unbelievable gains, other stocks suffered debilitating losses. Financial difficulties at L.A. Gear caused the stock to decline from $1.92 at the beginning of the year to 9¢ by the end of the year — a return equal to a *loss* of 95 percent. At the same time, the price of Apple Computer's stock declined by more than 37 percent. As these examples show, investors who "put all their eggs in one basket" faced considerable risk in the stock markets — they would have won big if the "basket" they chose was Jackson Hewitt's stock, but they would have lost almost everything if the "basket" they chose was L.A. Gear. Investors who diversified by spreading their investments among many stocks, perhaps through mutual funds, would have earned a return somewhere between the extraordinary increases posted by Jackson Hewitt and Microsoft and the extraordinary decreases posted by L.A. Gear and Apple Computer — very large "baskets" of such diversified investments would have earned returns fairly close to the average of the stock markets.

Investing is risky! Although the stock markets performed well from 1995 through 1997, they also go through periods of decreasing prices, or average returns that are negative. For instance, in 1990 and 1994, the average stock listed on the New York Stock Exchange decreased in value. And, more recently, during a six-week period in the summer of 1998, the market tumbled nearly 20 percent, and more than half of the drop occurred within one

Continued

week. In mid-July 1998, the Dow Jones Industrial Average (DJIA) reached 9338, a record high; by the end of August the DJIA was at 7539, which was less than the 7908 level at which it began the year. What a roller-coaster ride! What risk!

Who knows what the stock market will be doing when you read this book — it could be an up market, which is referred to as a "bull," or it could be a down market, which is referred to as a "bear." But, we know that as times change, investment strategies and portfolio mixes need to be changed to meet new conditions. Thus, it is important for you to understand the basic concepts of risk and return and how diversification affects investment decisions. You will discover that investors can create portfolios of securities to reduce risk without reducing the average return on their investments. After reading this chapter, you should have a better understanding of how risk affects investment returns and how to evaluate risk when selecting investments such as those described here.

In this chapter we take an in-depth look at how investment risk should be measured and how it affects assets' values and rates of return. Recall that in Chapter 2, when we examined the determinants of interest rates, we defined the real risk-free rate, k*, to be the rate of interest on a risk-free security in the absence of inflation. The actual interest rate on a particular debt security was shown to be equal to the real risk-free rate plus several premiums that reflect both inflation and the riskiness of the security in question. In this chapter we define more precisely what the term *risk* means as it relates to investments, we examine procedures used to measure risk, and we discuss the relationship between risk and return. It is important for both investors and financial managers to understand these concepts and use them when considering investment decisions, whether the decisions concern financial assets or real assets.

We demonstrate in this chapter that each investment — each stock, bond, or physical asset—has two different types of risk: (1) diversifiable risk and (2) nondiversifiable risk. The sum of these two components is the investment's total risk. Diversifiable risk is not important to rational, informed investors, because they will eliminate its effects by diversifying it away. The really significant risk is nondiversifiable risk — this risk is bad in the sense that it cannot be eliminated, and if you invest in anything other than riskless assets, such as short-term Treasury bills, you will be exposed to it. In the balance of the chapter we explain these risk concepts and show you how risk enters into the investment decision process.

Defining and Measuring Risk

Risk is defined in *Webster's* as "a hazard; a peril; exposure to loss or injury." Thus, risk refers to the chance that some unfavorable event will occur. If you engage in skydiving, you are taking a chance with your life — skydiving is risky. If you bet on the horses, you are risking your money. If you invest in speculative stocks (or, really, *any* stock), you are taking a risk in the hope of making an appreciable return.

Most people view risk in the manner we just described — a chance of loss. In reality, risk occurs when we cannot be certain about the outcome of a particular activity or event, so we are not sure what will occur in the future. Consequently, risk results from the fact that an action such as investing can produce more than one outcome in the future. To illustrate the riskiness of financial assets, suppose you have a large amount of money to invest for one year. You could buy a Treasury security that has an expected return equal to 6 percent. The rate of return expected from this investment can be determined quite precisely because the chance of the government defaulting on Treasury securities is negligible; the outcome essentially is guaranteed, which means this is a risk-free investment. On the other hand, you could buy the common stock of a newly formed company that has developed technology that can be used to extract petroleum from the mountains in South America without defacing the landscape and without harming the ecology. The technology has yet to be proven economically feasible, so it is not known what returns the common stockholders will receive in the future. Experts who have analyzed the common stock of the company have determined that the *expected,* or average long-run, return for such an investment is 30 percent; each year, the investment could yield a positive return as high as 900 percent, but there also is the possibility the company will not survive, in which case, the entire investment will be lost and the return will be −100 percent. The return investors receive each year cannot be determined precisely because more than one outcome is possible — this is a risky investment. Because there is a significant danger of actually earning considerably less than the expected return, investors probably would consider the stock to be quite risky. But, there also is a very good chance the actual return will be greater than expected, which, of course, is an outcome we gladly accept. So, when we think of investment risk, along with the chance of actually receiving less than expected, we should consider the chance of actually receiving more than expected. If we consider investment risk from this perspective, then we can define **risk** as the chance of receiving an actual return other than expected, which simply means there is *variability in the returns* or outcomes from the investment. Therefore, investment risk can be measured by the variability of the investment's returns.

RISK
The chance that an outcome other than expected will occur.

Investment risk, then, is related to the possibility of actually earning a return other than expected — the greater the variability of the possible outcomes, the riskier the investment. However, we can define risk more precisely, and it is useful to do so.

Probability Distributions

An event's *probability* is defined as the chance that the event will occur. For example, a weather forecaster might state, "There is a 40 percent chance of rain today and a 60 percent chance that it will not rain." If all possible events, or outcomes, are listed, and if a probability is assigned to each event, the listing is called a **probability distribution**. For our weather forecast, we could set up the following probability distribution:

PROBABILITY DISTRIBUTION
A listing of all possible outcomes, or events, with a probability (chance of occurrence) assigned to each outcome.

Outcome (1)	Probability (2)	
Rain	0.40 =	40%
No rain	0.60 =	60
	1.00	100%

The possible outcomes are listed in Column 1, while the probabilities of these outcomes, expressed both as decimals and as percentages, are given in Column 2. Notice that the probabilities must sum to 1.0, or 100 percent.

Probabilities can also be assigned to the possible outcomes (or returns) from an investment. If you buy a bond, you expect to receive interest on the bond, and those interest payments will provide you with a rate of return on your investment. The possible outcomes from this investment are (1) that the issuer will make the interest payments or (2) that the issuer will fail to make the interest payments. The higher the probability of default on the interest payments, the riskier the bond; and the higher the risk, the higher the rate of return you would require to invest in the bond. If instead of buying a bond you invest in a stock, you will again expect to earn a return on your money. As we saw in the last chapter, a stock's return will come from dividends plus capital gains. Again, the riskier the stock — which means the greater the variability of the possible payoffs — the higher the stock's expected return must be to induce you to invest in it.

With this in mind, consider the possible rates of return (dividend yield plus capital gain or loss) that you might earn next year on a $10,000 investment in the stock of either Martin Products Inc. or U.S. Electric. Martin Products manufactures and distributes computer terminals and equipment for the rapidly growing data transmission industry. Because its sales are cyclical, its profits rise and fall with the business cycle. Further, its market is extremely competitive, and some new company could develop better products that could literally bankrupt Martin. U.S. Electric, on the other hand, supplies electricity, which is an essential service, and because it has city franchises that protect it from competition, its sales and profits are relatively stable and predictable.

The rate-of-return probability distributions for the two companies are shown in Table 8-1. Here we see that there is a 20 percent chance of a boom, in which case both companies will have high earnings, pay high dividends, and enjoy capital gains; there is a 50 percent probability of a normal economy and moderate returns; and there is a 30 percent probability of a recession, which will mean low earnings and dividends as well as capital losses. Note, however, that Martin Products' rate of return could vary far more widely than that of U.S. Electric. There is a fairly high probability that the value of Martin's stock will vary substantially, resulting in a loss of 60 percent or a gain of 110 per-

---

TABLE 8-1

Probability Distributions for Martin Products and U.S. Electric

State of the Economy	Probability of This State Occurring	Rate of Return on Stock if This State Occurs	
		Martin Products	**U.S. Electric**
Boom	0.2	110%	20%
Normal	0.5	22	16
Recession	0.3	−60	10
	1.0		

cent, while there is no chance of a loss for U.S. Electric and its maximum gain is 20 percent.[1]

Self-Test Questions

What does "investment risk" mean?

Set up illustrative probability distributions for (1) a bond investment and (2) a stock investment.

Expected Rate of Return

EXPECTED RATE OF RETURN, k̂
The rate of return expected to be realized from an investment; the mean value of the probability distribution of possible results.

Table 8-1 provides the probability distributions showing the possible outcomes for investing in Martin Products and U.S. Electric. We can see that the most likely outcome is for the economy to be normal, in which case Martin will return 22 percent and U.S. Electric will return 16 percent. But other outcomes also are possible, so we need to somehow summarize the information contained in the probability distributions into a single measure that considers all these possible outcomes: That measure is the expected value, or expected rate of return, for the investments.

Simply stated, the **expected value (return)** is the *weighted average* of the outcomes, where the weights we use are the probabilities. Table 8-2 shows how the expected rates of return for Martin Products and U.S. Electric are computed: We multiply each possible outcome by the probability it will occur and then sum the results. We designate the expected rate of return, k̂, which is termed "k-hat."[2]

TABLE 8-2

Calculation of Expected Rates of Return: Martin Products and U.S. Electric

State of the Economy (1)	Probability of This State Occurring (Pr_i) (2)	Martin Products		U.S. Electric	
		Return if This State Occurs (k_i) (3)	Product: (2) × (3) = (4)	Return if This State Occurs (k_i) (5)	Product: (2) × (5) = (6)
Boom	0.2	110%	22%	20%	4%
Normal	0.5	22	11	16	8
Recession	0.3	−60	−18	10	3
	1.0		$\hat{k}_M =$ 15%		$\hat{k}_{US} =$ 15%

[1]It is, of course, completely unrealistic to think that any stock has no chance of a loss. Only in hypothetical examples could this occur. To illustrate, the price of Columbia Gas's stock dropped from $34.50 to $20.00 in just three hours on June 19, 1991. All investors were reminded that any stock is exposed to some risk of loss, and those investors who bought Columbia Gas learned this lesson the hard way.

[2]In Chapter 7, we used k_d to signify the return on a debt instrument and k_s to signify the return on a stock. In this section, however, we discuss only returns on stocks; thus, the subscript s is unnecessary, and we use the term $\hat{k}$ rather than $\hat{k}_s$.

The expected rate of return can be calculated using the following equation:

8-1

$$\text{Expected rate of return} = \hat{k} = Pr_1k_1 + Pr_2k_2 + \cdots + Pr_nk_n$$
$$= \sum_{i=1}^{n} Pr_ik_i$$

Here k_i is the ith possible outcome, Pr_i is the probability the ith outcome will occur, and n is the number of possible outcomes. Thus, $\hat{k}$ is a weighted average of the possible outcomes (the k_i values), with each outcome's weight being its probability of occurrence. Using the data for Martin Products, we obtain its expected rate of return as follows:

$$\hat{k} = Pr_1(k_1) + Pr_2(k_2) + Pr_3(k_3)$$
$$= 0.2(110\%) + 0.5\,(22\%) + 0.3\,(-60\%)$$
$$= 15\%$$

Note that the expected rate of return does not equal any of the possible payoffs for Martin Products given in Table 8-2. Stated simply, the expected rate of return represents the average payoff investors will receive from Martin Products if the probability distribution given in Table 8-2 does not change over a long period of time. If the probability distribution for Martin Products is correct, then 20 percent of the time the future economic condition will be termed a boom, so investors will earn a 110 percent rate of return; 50 percent of the time the economy should be normal, and the investment payoff will be 22 percent; and, 30 percent of the time the economy should be recessionary, and the payoff will be a loss equal to 60 percent. On average, then, Martin Products' investors will earn 15 percent.

We can graph the rates of return to obtain a picture of the variability of possible outcomes; this is shown in the Figure 8-1 bar charts. The height of each bar signifies the probability that a given outcome will occur. The range of probable returns for Martin Products is from +110 to −60 percent, with an expected return of 15 percent. The expected return for U.S. Electric also is 15 percent, but its range is much narrower.

Continuous versus Discrete Probability Distributions

DISCRETE PROBABILITY DISTRIBUTION
The number of possible outcomes is limited, or finite.

Thus far we have assumed that only three states of the economy can exist: recession, normal, and boom. So, the distributions given in Table 8-1 are called **discrete probability distributions** because there are a finite, or limited, number of outcomes. Actually, of course, the state of the economy could range from a deep depression to a fantastic boom, and there are an unlimited number of possibilities in between. Suppose we had the time and patience to assign a probability to each possible state of the economy (with the sum of the probabilities still equaling 1.0) and to assign a rate of return to each stock for each state of

FIGURE 8-1

Probability Distributions of Martin Products' and U.S. Electric's Rates of Return

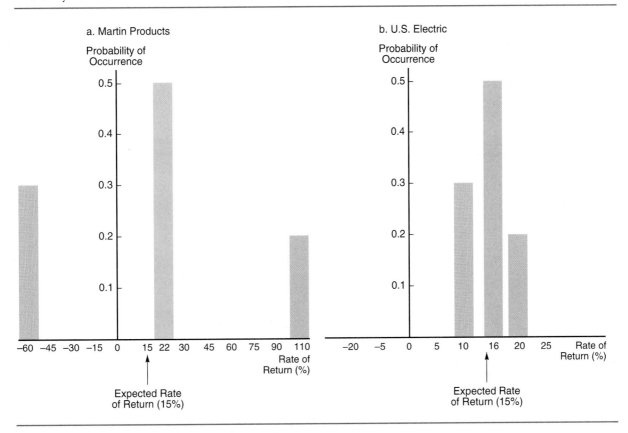

the economy. We would have a table similar to Table 8-1, except that it would have many more entries in each column. This table could be used to calculate expected rates of return as shown previously, and the probabilities and outcomes could be approximated by continuous curves such as those presented in Figure 8-2. Here we have changed the assumptions so that there is essentially a zero probability that Martin Products' return will be less than −60 percent or more than 110 percent, or that U.S. Electric's return will be less than 10 percent or more than 20 percent, but virtually any return within these limits is possible. These are **continuous probability distributions** because, in each case, the number of outcomes possible is unlimited — U.S. Electric's return could be 10.01 percent, 10.001 percent, and so on.

CONTINUOUS PROBABILITY DISTRIBUTION
The number of possible outcomes is unlimited, or infinite.

The *tighter the probability distribution*, the *less variability* there is, and the more likely it is that the actual outcome will be close to the expected value; consequently, the less likely it is that the actual return will be much different from the expected return. Thus, the *tighter the probability distribution, the lower the risk assigned to a stock*. Because U.S. Electric has a relatively tight probability distribution, its *actual* return is likely to be closer to its 15 percent expected return than is that of Martin Products.

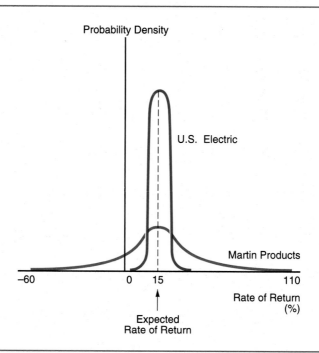

FIGURE 8-2

Continuous Probability Distributions of Martin Products' and
U.S. Electric's Rates of Return

NOTE: The assumptions regarding the probabilities of various outcomes have been changed from those in Figure 8-1. There the probability of obtaining exactly 16 percent return for U.S. Electric was 50 percent; here it is *much smaller,* because there are many possible outcomes instead of just three. With continuous distributions, it is more appropriate to ask what the probability is of obtaining at least some specified rate of return than to ask what the probability is of obtaining exactly that rate. This topic is covered in detail in statistics courses.

Measuring Risk: The Standard Deviation

Because we defined risk as the variability of returns, we can measure risk by examining the tightness of the probability distribution associated with the possible outcomes. In general, the width of a probability distribution indicates the amount of scatter, or variability, of the possible outcomes. Therefore, *the tighter the probability distribution of expected returns, the less its variability — thus the smaller the risk associated with the investment.* According to this definition, U.S. Electric is much less risky than Martin Products, because the actual payoffs that are possible are closer to the expected return for U.S. Electric than for Martin Products.

To be most useful, any measure of risk should have a definite value — we need a measure of the tightness of the probability distribution. The measure we use most often is the **standard deviation**, the symbol for which is σ, pronounced "sigma." The smaller the standard deviation, the tighter the probability distribution, and, accordingly, the lower the riskiness of the investment. To calculate the standard deviation, we proceed as shown in Table 8-3, taking the following steps:

STANDARD DEVIATION, σ
A measure of the tightness, or variability, of a set of outcomes.

TABLE 8-3

Calculating Martin Products' Standard Deviation

Payoff k_i (1)		Expected Return $\hat{k}$ (2)		$k_i - \hat{k}$ (3)	$(k_i - \hat{k})^2$ (4)	Probability (5)	$(k_j - \hat{k})^2 Pr_j$ (4) × (5) = (6)
110%	−	15%	=	95	9,025	0.2	(9,025)(0.2) = 1,805.0
22	−	15	=	7	49	0.5	(49)(0.5) = 24.5
(60)	−	15	=	−75	5,625	0.3	(5,625)(0.3) = 1,687.5

Variance = σ^2 = 3,517.0

Standard deviation = σ_m = $\sqrt{\sigma_m^2}$ = $\sqrt{3,517}$ =   59.3%

1. We calculate the expected rate of return:

8-1

$$\text{Expected rate of return} = \hat{k} = \sum_{i=1}^{n} Pr_i k_i$$

For Martin, we previously found $\hat{k}$ = 15%.

2. In Column 3 of Table 8-3, we subtract the expected rate of return ($\hat{k}$) from each possible outcome (k_i) to obtain a set of deviations from $\hat{k}$:

$$\text{Deviation}_i = k_i - \hat{k}$$

VARIANCE, σ^2
The standard deviation squared.

3. In Columns 4 and 6 of the table, we square each deviation, then multiply the result by the probability of occurrence for its related outcome, and then sum these products to obtain the **variance** of the probability distribution:

8-2

$$\text{Variance} = \sigma^2 = \sum_{i=1}^{n} (k_i - \hat{k})^2 Pr_i$$

4. Finally, we take the square root of the variance to obtain the standard deviation:

8-3

$$\text{Standard deviation} = \sigma = \sqrt{\sigma^2} = \sqrt{\sum_{i=1}^{n} (k_i - \hat{k})^2 Pr_i}$$

Thus, the standard deviation is a weighted average deviation from the expected value, and it gives an idea of how far above or below the expected value the

COEFFICIENT OF VARIATION (CV)
Standardized measure of the risk per unit of return; calculated as the standard deviation divided by the expected return.

actual value is likely to be. Martin's standard deviation is seen in Table 8-3 to be $\sigma = 59.3\%$, and, using these same procedures, we find U.S. Electric's standard deviation to be 3.6 percent. The larger standard deviation of Martin Products indicates a greater variation of returns, thus a greater chance that the expected return will not be realized; therefore, Martin Products would be considered a riskier investment than U.S. Electric, according to this measure of risk.[3]

Another useful measure to evaluate risky investments is the **coefficient of variation (CV)**, which is the standard deviation divided by the expected return:

8-4
$$\text{Coefficient of variation} = CV = \frac{\text{Risk}}{\text{Return}} = \frac{\sigma}{\hat{k}}$$

The coefficient of variation shows the risk per unit of return, and it provides a more meaningful basis for comparison when the expected returns on two alternatives are not the same. Because U.S. Electric and Martin Products have *the same expected return, it is not necessary to compute the coefficient of variation* to compare the two investments. In this case, most people would prefer to invest in U.S. Electric, because it offers the same expected return with lower risk. The firm with the larger standard deviation, Martin, must have the larger

---

[3]In the example we described the procedure for finding the mean and standard deviation when the data are in the form of a known probability distribution. If only sample returns data over some *past period* are available, the standard deviation of returns can be estimated using this formula:

$$\text{Estimated } \sigma = S = \sqrt{\frac{\sum_{t=1}^{n} (\bar{k}_t - \bar{k}_{Avg})^2}{n - 1}} \qquad \textbf{8-3a}$$

Here $\bar{k}_t$ ("k bar t") denotes the past realized rate of return in Period t, and $\bar{k}_{Avg}$ is the average annual return earned during the last n years. Here is an example:

Year	$\bar{k}_t$
1996	15%
1997	−5
1998	20

$$\bar{k}_{Avg} = \frac{15 + (-5) + 20}{3} = 10\%$$

$$\text{Estimated } \sigma = S = \sqrt{\frac{(15 - 10)^2 + (-5 - 10)^2 + (20 - 10)^2}{3 - 1}}$$

$$= \sqrt{\frac{350}{2}} + 13.2\%$$

The historical σ often is used as an estimate of the future σ. Much less often, and generally incorrectly, $\bar{k}_{Avg}$ for some past period is used as an estimate of $\hat{k}$, the *expected* future return. Because past variability is likely to be repeated, σ might be a good estimate of future risk, but it is much less reasonable to expect that the past *level* of return (which could have been as high as +100 percent or as low as −50 percent) is the best expectation of what investors think will happen in the future.

coefficient of variation because the means for the two stocks are equal, but the numerator in Equation 8-4 will be greater for Martin. In fact, the coefficient of variation for Martin is 59.3%/15% = 3.95 and that for U.S. Electric is 3.6%/15% = 0.24. Thus, Martin is more than 16 times riskier than U.S. Electric on the basis of this criterion.

The coefficient of variation is more useful when we consider investments that have different expected rates of return *and* different levels of risk. For example, Biobotics Corporation is a biological research and development firm that, according to stock analysts, offers investors an expected rate of return equal to 35 percent with a standard deviation of 7.5 percent. Biobotics offers a higher expected return than U.S. Electric, but it is also riskier. So, with respect to both risk and return, which is a better investment? If we calculate the coefficient of variation for Biobotics, we find it equals 7.5%/35% = 0.21, which is slightly less than U.S. Electric's coefficient of variation of 0.24. Consequently, Biobotics actually has less risk per unit of return than U.S. Electric, even though its standard deviation is higher. In this case, the additional return offered by the Biobotics investment is more than sufficient to compensate for the additional risk.

The probability distributions for U.S. Electric and Biobotics are graphed in Figure 8-3. U.S. Electric has the smaller standard deviation, hence the more peaked probability distribution. But, it is clear from the graph that the chances of a really high return are higher for Biobotics than for U.S. Electric, because Biobotics' expected return is so high. *Because the coefficient of variation captures the effects of both risk and return, it is a better measure for evaluating risk in situations where investments differ with respect to both their amounts of total risk and their expected returns.*

FIGURE 8-3

Comparison of Probability Distributions and Rates of Return for U.S. Electric and Biobotics Corporation

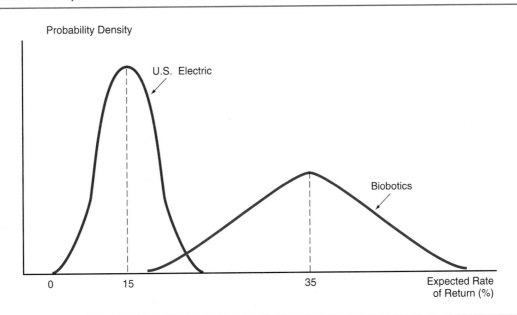

Risk Aversion and Required Returns

Suppose you have worked hard and saved $1 million, which you now plan to invest. You can buy a 10 percent U.S. Treasury note, and at the end of one year you will have a sure $1.1 million, which is your original investment plus $100,000 in interest. Alternatively, you can buy stock in R&D Enterprises. If R&D's research programs are successful, your stock will increase in value to $2.2 million; however, if the research is a failure, the value of your stock will go to zero, and you will be penniless. You regard R&D's chances of success or failure as being 50-50, so the expected value of the stock investment is 0.5($0) + 0.5($2,200,000) = $1,100,000. Subtracting the $1 million cost of the stock leaves an expected profit of $100,000, or an expected (but risky) 10 percent rate of return:

$$\frac{\text{Expected rate}}{\text{of return}} = \frac{\text{Expected ending value} - \text{Beginning value}}{\text{Beginning value}}$$

$$= \frac{\$1,100,000 - \$1,000,000}{\$1,000,000}$$

$$= \frac{\$100,000}{\$1,000,000} = 0.10 = 10\%$$

Thus, you have a choice between a sure $100,000 profit (representing a 10 percent rate of return) on the Treasury note and a risky expected $100,000 profit (also representing a 10 percent expected rate of return) on the R&D Enterprises stock. Which one would you choose? *If you choose the less risky investment, you are risk averse. Most investors are indeed risk averse, and certainly the average investor is risk averse, at least with regard to his or her "serious money." Because this is a well-documented fact, we shall assume* **risk aversion** *throughout the remainder of the book.*

RISK AVERSION
Risk-averse investors require higher rates of return to invest in higher-risk securities.

What are the implications of risk aversion for security prices and rates of return? The answer is that, other things held constant, the higher a security's risk, the higher the return investors demand, thus the less they are willing to pay for the investment. To see how risk aversion affects security prices, we can analyze the situation with U.S. Electric and Martin Products stocks. Suppose each stock sold for $100 per share and each had an expected rate of return of 15 percent. Investors are averse to risk, so there would be a general preference for U.S. Electric because there is less variability in its payoffs (less uncertainty). People with money to invest would bid for U.S. Electric rather than Martin stock, and Martin's stockholders would start selling their stock and using the money to buy U.S. Electric stock. Buying pressure would drive up the price of U.S. Electric's stock, and selling pressure would simultaneously cause Martin's price to decline.

RISK PREMIUM, RP
The portion of the expected return that can be attributed to the additional risk of an investment; the difference between the expected rate of return on a given risky asset and that on a less risky asset.

These price changes, in turn, would cause changes in the expected rates of return on the two securities. Suppose, for example, that the price of U.S. Electric stock was bid up from $100 to $150, whereas the price of Martin's stock declined from $100 to $75. This would cause U.S. Electric's expected return to fall to 10 percent, while Martin's expected return would rise to 20 percent. The difference in returns, 20% − 10% = 10%, is a **risk premium, RP,** which represents the compensation investors require for assuming the *additional* risk of Martin stock.

This example demonstrates a very important principle: In a market dominated by risk-averse investors, *riskier securities* ***must*** *have higher expected returns,* as estimated by the average investor, than less risky securities because, if this situation does not hold, investors will buy and sell investments, and prices will continue to change until the higher risk investments have higher expected returns than the lower risk investments. We consider the question of how much higher the returns on risky securities must be later in the chapter, after we see how diversification affects the way risk should be measured.

 Self-Test Questions

Which of the two stocks graphed in Figure 8-2 is less risky? Why?

How is the standard deviation associated with an investment calculated?

Why is the standard deviation used as a measure of risk?

Which is a better measure of risk: (1) standard deviation or (2) coefficient of variation? Explain.

What is meant by the following statement: "Most investors are risk averse"?

How does risk aversion affect relative rates of return?

Portfolio Risk and the Capital Asset Pricing Model

CAPITAL ASSET PRICING MODEL (CAPM)
A model based on the proposition that any stock's required rate of return is equal to the risk-free rate of return plus a risk premium, where risk reflects diversification.

In the preceding section we considered the riskiness of investments held in isolation. We used the standard deviation to measure the risk of an investment because it provides an indication of the total variability of the investment's possible payoffs. Now we analyze the riskiness of investments held in portfolios.[4] As we shall see, holding an investment, whether a stock, bond, or other asset, as part of a portfolio is generally less risky than holding the same investment all by itself. This fact has been incorporated into a procedure called the **Capital Asset Pricing Model**, or **CAPM**, used to analyze the relationship between risk and rates of return. The CAPM is an extremely important analytical tool in both managerial finance and investment analysis. In fact, the 1990 Nobel Prize was awarded to the developers of the CAPM, Professors Harry Markowitz and William F. Sharpe, in part because of their work in this area.

In the following sections we discuss the elements of the CAPM.[5] We emphasize application of the CAPM to evaluate the riskiness of stocks. But, we should note that, at least theoretically, the CAPM can be applied to any asset, including such financial assets as stocks and bonds, and such real assets as real estate and manufacturing equipment.

Portfolio Risk and Return

Most financial assets are not held in isolation; rather, they are held as parts of portfolios. Banks, pension funds, insurance companies, mutual funds, and other financial institutions are required by law to hold diversified portfolios. Even individual

---

[4]A *portfolio* is a collection of investment securities or assets. If you owned some General Motors stock, some Exxon stock, and some IBM stock, you would be holding a three-stock portfolio. For the reasons set forth in this section, the majority of all stocks are held as parts of portfolios.

[5]The CAPM is a relatively complex subject, and we present only its basic elements in this text. For a more detailed discussion, see any standard investments textbook.

investors — at least those whose security holdings constitute a significant part of their total wealth — generally hold stock portfolios, not the stock of only one firm. This being the case, from an investor's standpoint the fact that a particular stock goes up or down is not very important; what is important is the return on his or her portfolio and the portfolio's risk. Logically, then, the risk and return characteristics of an investment should *not* be evaluated in isolation; rather, the risk and return of an individual security should be analyzed in terms of how that security affects the risk and return of the portfolio in which it is held.

To illustrate, Payco American is a collection agency company that operates several offices nationwide. The company is not well known, its stock is not very liquid, its earnings have fluctuated quite a bit in the past, and it doesn't even pay a dividend. All this suggests that Payco is risky and that its required rate of return, k, should be relatively high. However, Payco's k has always been quite low in relation to those of most other companies. This indicates that investors regard Payco as being a low-risk company in spite of its uncertain profits and its nonexistent dividend stream. The reason for this somewhat counterintuitive fact has to do with diversification and its effect on risk. Payco's stock price rises during recessions, whereas other stocks tend to decline when the economy slumps. Therefore, holding Payco in a portfolio of "normal" stocks tends to stabilize returns on the entire portfolio.

EXPECTED RETURN ON A PORTFOLIO, $\hat{k}_p$
The weighted average expected return on the stocks held in the portfolio.

PORTFOLIO RETURNS   The **expected return on a portfolio, $\hat{k}_p$**, is simply the weighted average of the expected returns on the individual stocks in the portfolio, with the weights being the fraction of the total portfolio invested in each stock:

$$8\text{-}5 \qquad \hat{k}_p = w_1\hat{k}_1 + w_2\hat{k}_2 + \cdots + w_N\hat{k}_N$$
$$= \sum_{j=1}^{N} w_j\hat{k}_j$$

Here the $\hat{k}_j$'s are the expected returns on the individual stocks, the w_j's are the weights, and there are N stocks in the portfolio. Note (1) that w_j is the proportion of the portfolio's dollar value invested in Stock $_j$ (i.e., the value of the investment in Stock j divided by the total value of the portfolio) and (2) that the w_j's must sum to 1.0 (100 percent) to account for every dollar invested.

In January 1999, a security analyst estimated that the following returns could be expected on four large companies:

	Expected Return, $\hat{k}$
AT&T	8%
General Electric	13
Microsoft	30
Citigroup	18

If we formed a $100,000 portfolio, investing $25,000 in each stock, the expected portfolio return would be 17.25%:

$$\hat{k}_p = \quad w_1\hat{k}_1 \quad + \quad w_2\hat{k}_2 \quad + \quad w_3\hat{k}_3 \quad + \quad w_4\hat{k}_4$$

$$= \quad 0.25(8\%) \quad + 0.25(13\%) + 0.25(30\%) + 0.25(18\%)$$

$$= 17.25\%$$

REALIZED RATE OF RETURN, $\bar{k}$
The return that is actually earned. The actual return ($\bar{k}$) is usually different from the expected return ($\hat{k}$).

Of course, after the fact and a year later, the actual **realized rates of return, $\bar{k}$**, on the individual stocks — the $\bar{k}_j$, or "k-bar," values — will almost certainly be different from their expected values, so $\bar{k}_P$ will be somewhat different from $\hat{k}_P = 17.25\%$. For example, General Electric stock might double in price and provide a return of +100%, whereas Citigroup stock might have a terrible year, fall sharply, and have a return of −75%. Note, though, that those two events would be somewhat offsetting, so the portfolio's return might still be close to its expected return, even though the individual stocks' actual returns were far from their expected returns.

PORTFOLIO RISK   As we just saw, the expected return of a portfolio is simply a weighted average of the expected returns of the individual stocks in the portfolio. However, unlike returns, the riskiness of a portfolio, σ_P, generally is *not* a weighted average of the standard deviations of the individual securities in the portfolio; the portfolio's risk usually is *smaller* than the weighted average of the stocks' σs. In fact, at least theoretically, it is possible to combine two stocks that, by themselves, are quite risky as measured by their standard deviations and to form a portfolio that is completely riskless, or risk-free, with $\sigma_P = 0$.

To illustrate the effect of combining securities, consider the situation in Figure 8-4. The bottom section gives data on rates of return for Stocks W and M individually and also for a portfolio invested 50 percent in each stock. The three top graphs show the actual historical returns for each investment from 1995 to 1999, and the lower graphs show the probability distributions of returns, assuming that the future is expected to be like the past. The two stocks would be quite risky if they were held in isolation, but when they are combined to form Portfolio WM, they are not risky at all. (Note: These stocks are called W and M because their returns graphs in Figure 8-4 resemble a W and an M.)

CORRELATION COEFFICIENT, r
A measure of the degree of relationship between two variables.

The reason Stocks W and M can be combined to form a riskless portfolio is that their returns move opposite to each other — when W's returns fall, those of M rise, and vice versa. The relationship between two variables is called *correlation,* and the **correlation coefficient, r,** measures the degree of the relationship between the variables.[6] In statistical terms, we say that the returns on Stocks W and M are perfectly negatively correlated, with r = −1.0.

The opposite of perfect negative correlation, with r = −1.0, is perfect positive correlation, with r = +1.0. Returns on two perfectly positively correlated stocks would move up and down together, and a portfolio consisting of two such stocks

[6]The correlation coefficient, r, can range from +1.0, denoting that the two variables move in the same direction with exactly the same degree of synchronization every time movement occurs, to −1.0, denoting that the variables always move with the same degree of synchronization, but in opposite directions. A correlation coefficient of zero suggests that the two variables are not related to each other — that is, changes in one variable are *independent* of changes in the other.

FIGURE 8-4

Rate of Return Distributions for Two Perfectly Negatively Correlated Stocks (r = −1.0) and for Portfolio WM

a. Rates of Return

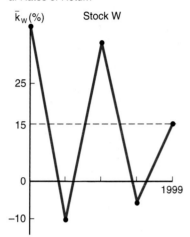 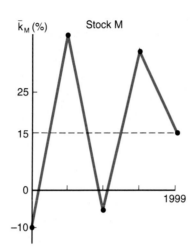 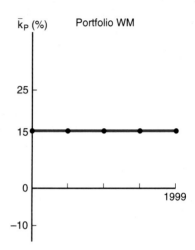

b. Probability Distributions of Returns

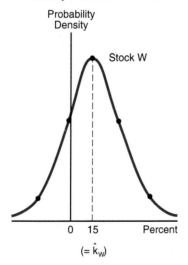 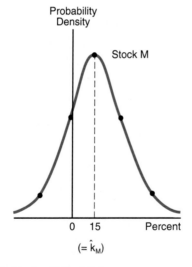 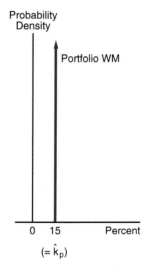

Year	Stock W ($\bar{k}_W$)	Stock M ($\bar{k}_M$)	Portfolio WM ($\bar{k}_p$)
1995	40%	(10%)	15%
1996	(10)	40	15
1997	35	(5)	15
1998	(5)	35	15
1999	15	15	15
Average return	15%	15%	15%
Standard deviation	22.6	22.6%	0.0%

FIGURE 8-5

Rate of Return Distributions for Two Perfectly Positively Correlated Stocks (r = +1.0) and for Portfolio MM'

a. Rates of Return

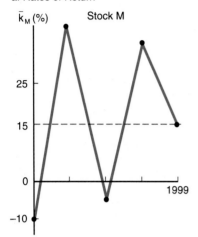
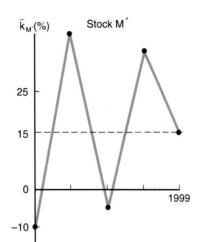
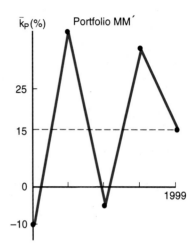

b. Probability Distributions of Returns

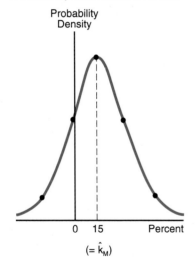
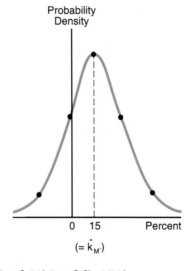
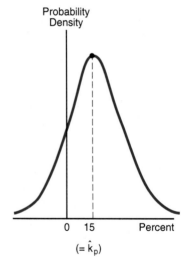

Year	Stock M ($\bar{k}_M$)	Stock M' ($\bar{k}_{M'}$)	Portfolio MM' ($\bar{k}_p$)
1995	(10%)	(10%)	(10%)
1996	40	40	40
1997	(5)	(5)	(5)
1998	35	35	35
1999	15	15	15
Average return	15%	15%	15%
Standard deviation	22.6%	22.6%	22.6%

would be exactly as risky as the individual stocks. This point is illustrated in Figure 8-5, where we see that the portfolio's standard deviation is equal to that of the individual stocks. Thus, diversification does nothing to reduce risk if the portfolio consists of perfectly positively correlated stocks.

Figures 8-4 and 8-5 demonstrate that when stocks are perfectly negatively correlated (r = −1.0), all risk can be diversified away, but when stocks are perfectly positively correlated (r = +1.0), diversification is ineffective. In reality, most stocks are positively correlated, but not perfectly so. On average, the correlation coefficient for the returns on two randomly selected stocks would be about +0.5, and for most pairs of stocks, r would lie in the range of +0.4 to +0.6. *Under such conditions, combining stocks into portfolios reduces risk but does not eliminate it completely.* Figure 8-6 illustrates this point with two stocks whose correlation coefficient is r = +0.67. The portfolio's average return is 15.0 percent, which is exactly the same as the average return for each of the two stocks, but its standard deviation is 20.6 percent, which is less than the standard deviation of either stock. Thus, the portfolio's risk is *not* an average of the risks of its individual stocks — diversification has reduced, but not eliminated, risk.

From these two-stock portfolio examples, we have seen that in one extreme case (r = −1.0), risk can be completely eliminated, while in the other extreme case (r = +1.0), diversification does no good. In between these extremes, combining two stocks into a portfolio reduces, but does not eliminate, the riskiness inherent in the individual stocks.

What would happen if we included more than two stocks in the portfolio? *As a rule, the riskiness of a portfolio is reduced as the number of stocks in the portfolio increases.* If we added enough stocks, could we completely eliminate risk? In general, the answer is no, but the extent to which adding stocks to a portfolio reduces its risk depends on the *degree of correlation* among the stocks: *The smaller the positive correlation coefficient, the lower the risk in a large portfolio.* If we could find a set of stocks whose correlations were negative, all risk could be eliminated. *In the typical case, where the correlations among the individual stocks are positive but less than +1.0, some, but not all, risk can be eliminated.*

To test your understanding, would you expect to find higher correlations between the returns on two companies in the same or in different industries? For example, would the correlation of returns on Ford's and General Motors' stocks be higher, or would the correlation coefficient be higher between either Ford or GM and Procter & Gamble (P&G), and how would those correlations affect the risk of portfolios containing them?

Answer: Ford's and GM's returns have a correlation coefficient of about 0.9 with one another because both are affected by auto sales, but only about 0.4 with those of P&G.

Implications: A two-stock portfolio consisting of Ford and GM would be riskier than a two-stock portfolio consisting of Ford or GM, plus P&G. Thus, to minimize risk, portfolios should be diversified across industries.

Firm-Specific Risk versus Market Risk

As noted earlier, it is very difficult, if not impossible, to find stocks whose expected returns are not positively correlated — most stocks tend to do well

FIGURE 8-6

Rate of Return Distributions for Two Partially Correlated Stocks (r = +0.67) and for Portfolio WY

a. Rates of Return

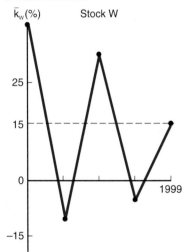
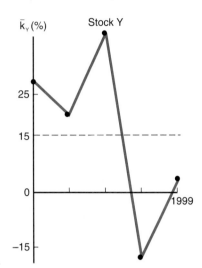
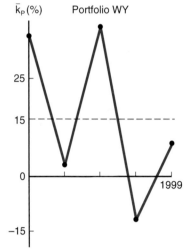

b. Probability Distribution of Returns

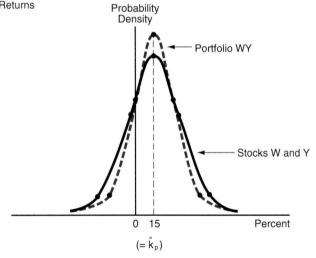

Year	Stock W ($\bar{k}_W$)	Stock Y ($\bar{k}_Y$)	Portfolio WY ($\bar{k}_p$)
1995	40%	28%	34%
1996	(10)	20	5
1997	35	41	38
1998	(5)	(17)	(11)
1999	15	3	9
Average return	15%	15%	15%
Standard deviation	22.6%	22.6%	20.6%

when the economy is strong and do poorly when it is weak.[7] Thus, even very large portfolios end up with a substantial amount of risk, but the risk is generally less than if all of the money was invested in only one stock.

To see more precisely how portfolio size affects portfolio risk, consider Figure 8-7, which shows how portfolio risk is affected by forming larger and larger portfolios of randomly selected stocks listed on the NYSE. Standard deviations are plotted for an average one-stock portfolio, for a two-stock portfolio, and so on, up to a portfolio consisting of all 1,500-plus common stocks that were listed on the NYSE at the time the data were graphed. The graph illustrates that, in general, the riskiness of a portfolio consisting of average NYSE stocks tends to decline and to approach some minimum limit as the size of the portfolio increases. According to the data, σ_1, the standard deviation of a one-stock portfolio (or an average stock), is approximately 28 percent. A portfolio consisting of all of the stocks in the market, which is called the *market portfolio,* would have a standard deviation, σ_M, of about 15.1 percent, which is shown as the horizontal dashed line in Figure 8-7.

Figure 8-7 shows that almost half of the riskiness inherent in an average individual stock can be eliminated if the stock is held in a reasonably well-diversified portfolio, which is one containing 40 or more stocks. Some risk always remains, however, so it is virtually impossible to diversify away the effects of broad stock market movements that affect almost all stocks.

The part of a stock's risk that can be eliminated is called *diversifiable,* or *firm-specific,* or *unsystematic, risk;* the part that cannot be eliminated is called *non-diversifiable,* or *market,* or *systematic, risk.* The name is not especially important, but the fact that a large part of the riskiness of any individual stock can be eliminated through portfolio diversification is vitally important.

Firm-specific risk is caused by such things as lawsuits, strikes, successful and unsuccessful marketing programs, the winning and losing of major contracts, and other events that are unique to a particular firm. Because the actual outcomes of these events are essentially random, their effects on a portfolio can be eliminated by diversification — bad events in one firm will be offset by good events in another. **Market risk**, on the other hand, stems from factors that systematically affect most firms, such as war, inflation, recessions, and high interest rates. Because most stocks tend to be affected similarly (negatively) by these *market* conditions, systematic risk cannot be eliminated by portfolio diversification.

We know that investors demand a premium for bearing risk; that is, the higher the riskiness of a security, the higher the expected return required to induce investors to buy (or to hold) it. However, if investors are primarily concerned with *portfolio risk* rather than the risk of the individual securities in the portfolio, how should the riskiness of an individual stock be measured? The answer, as provided by the Capital Asset Pricing Model (CAPM), is this: *The relevant riskiness of an individual stock is its contribution to the riskiness of a well-diversified portfolio.* In other words, the riskiness of General Electric's stock to a doctor who has a portfolio of 40 stocks or to a trust officer managing a 150-stock portfolio, is the contribution that the GE stock makes to the portfolio's riskiness. The stock might be quite risky if held by itself, but if most of its risk can be eliminated by diversification, then its **relevant risk,** which is its *contribution to the portfolio's risk,* might be small.

FIRM-SPECIFIC RISK
That part of a security's risk associated with random outcomes generated by events, or behaviors, specific to the firm; it can be eliminated by proper diversification.

MARKET RISK
That part of a security's risk that cannot be eliminated by diversification because it is associated with economic, or market, factors that systematically affect most firms.

RELEVANT RISK
The risk of a security that cannot be diversified away, or its market risk. This reflects a security's contribution to the risk of a portfolio.

---

[7]It is not too hard to find a few stocks that happened to rise because of a particular set of circumstances in the past while most other stocks were declining; it is much harder to find stocks that could logically be *expected* to go up in the future when other stocks are falling. Payco American, the collection agency discussed earlier, is one of those rare exceptions.

FIGURE 8-7

Effects of Portfolio Size on Portfolio Risk for Average Stocks

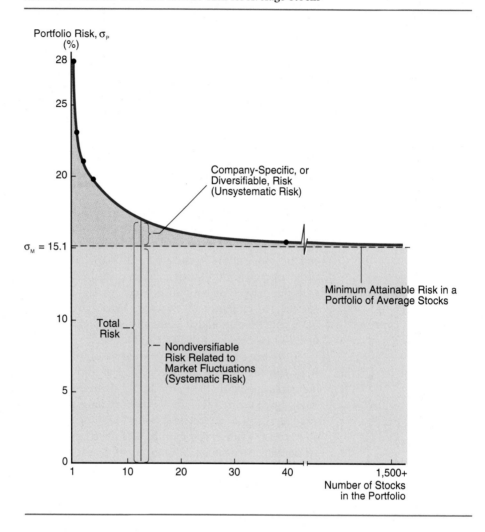

A simple example will help make this point clear. Suppose you are offered the chance to flip a coin once; if a head comes up, you win $20,000, but if it comes up tails, you lose $16,000. This is a good bet — the expected return is 0.5($20,000) + 0.5(–$16,000) = $2,000. However, it is a highly risky proposition because you have a 50 percent chance of losing $16,000. Thus, you might well refuse to make the bet. Alternatively, suppose you were offered the chance to flip a coin 100 times, and you would win $200 for each head but lose $160 for each tail. It is possible that you would flip all heads and win $20,000, and it is also possible that you would flip all tails and lose $16,000, but the chances are very high that you would actually flip about 50 heads and about 50 tails, winning a net of about $2,000. Although each individual flip is a risky bet, collectively you have a low-risk proposition, because most of the risk has been diversified away. This is the idea behind holding portfolios of stocks rather than just one stock, except that with stocks all of the risk cannot be eliminated by diversification — those risks related to broad, systematic changes in the stock market will remain.

Are all stocks equally risky in the sense that adding them to a well-diversified portfolio would have the same effect on the portfolio's riskiness? The answer is no. Different stocks will affect the portfolio differently, so different securities have different degrees of relevant risk. How can the relevant risk of an individual stock be measured? As we have seen, all risk except that related to broad market movements can, and presumably will, be diversified away. After all, why accept risk that can easily be eliminated? *The risk that remains after diversifying is market risk, or risk that is inherent in the market, and it can be measured by evaluating the degree to which a given stock tends to move up and down with the market.* In the next section, we develop a measure of a stock's market risk, and then, in a later section, we introduce an equation for determining the required rate of return on a stock, given its market risk.

The Concept of Beta

BETA COEFFICIENT, β
A measure of the extent to which the returns on a given stock move with the stock market.

Remember the relevant risk associated with an individual stock is based on its systematic risk, which depends on how sensitive the firm's operations are to economic events such as interest rate changes and inflationary pressures. Because the general movements in the financial markets reflect movements in the economy, the market risk of a stock can be measured by observing its tendency to move with the market, or with an average stock that has the same characteristics as the market. The measure of a stock's sensitivity to market fluctuations is called its **beta coefficient**, and it generally is designated with the Greek symbol beta, β. Beta is a key element of the CAPM.

An *average-risk stock* is defined as one that tends to move up and down in step with the general market as measured by some index, such as the Dow Jones Industrial Index, the S&P 500 Index, or the New York Stock Exchange Composite Index. Such a stock will, *by definition,* have a beta, β, of 1.0, which indicates that, in general, if the market moves up by 10 percent, the stock also will move up by 10 percent, while if the market falls by 10 percent, the stock likewise will fall by 10 percent. A portfolio of such β = 1.0 stocks will move up and down with the broad market averages, and it will be just as risky as the averages. If β = 0.5, the stock is only half as volatile as the market — it will rise and fall only half as much — and a portfolio of such stocks will be half as risky as a portfolio of β = 1.0 stocks. On the other hand, if β = 2.0, the stock is twice as volatile as an average stock, so a portfolio of such stocks will be twice as risky as an average portfolio. The value of such a portfolio could double — or halve—in a short time, and if you held such a portfolio, you could quickly become a millionaire — or a pauper.

Figure 8-8 graphs the relative volatility of three stocks. The data below the graph assume that in 1997 the "market," defined as a portfolio consisting of all stocks, had a total return (dividend yield plus capital gains yield) of $k_M = 14\%$, and Stocks H, A, and L (for High, Average, and Low risk) also had returns of 14 percent. In 1998 the market went up sharply, and the return on the market portfolio was $k_M = 28\%$. Returns on the three stocks also went up: H soared to 42 percent; A went up to 28 percent, the same as the market; and L only went up to 21 percent. Now suppose that the market dropped in 1999, and the market return was $k_M = -14\%$. The three stocks' returns also fell — H plunging to −42 percent, A falling to −14 percent, and L going down only to $k_L = 0\%$. Thus, the three stocks all moved in the same direction as the market, but H was by far the most volatile; A was just as volatile as the market; and L was less volatile than the market.

FIGURE 8-8

Relative Volatility of Stocks H, A, and L

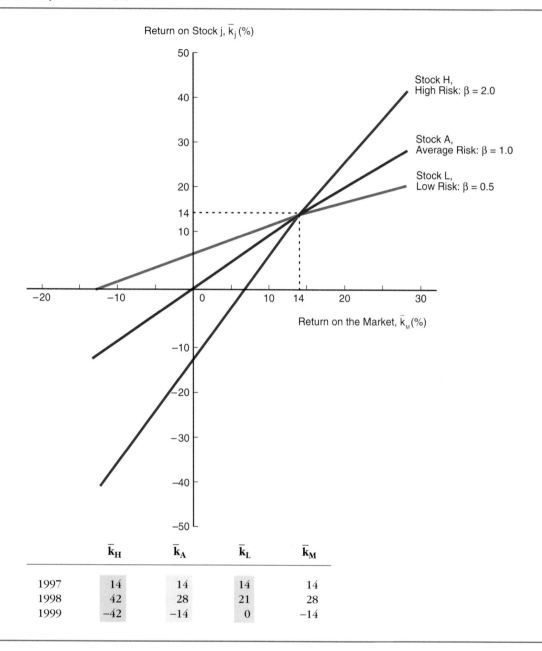

	$\bar{k}_H$	$\bar{k}_A$	$\bar{k}_L$	$\bar{k}_M$
1997	14	14	14	14
1998	42	28	21	28
1999	−42	−14	0	−14

Beta measures a stock's volatility relative to an average stock (or the market), which has $\beta = 1.0$, and a stock's beta can be calculated by plotting a line like those in Figure 8-8. The slopes of the lines show how each stock moves in response to a movement in the general market — indeed, *the slope coefficient of such a "regression line" is defined as a beta coefficient.* (Procedures for actually calculating betas are described in Appendix 8A.) Betas for literally thousands of companies are calculated and published by Merrill Lynch, *Value Line,* and numerous other organizations. The beta coefficients of some well-known companies are shown in Table 8-4. Most stocks have betas in the range of 0.50 to 1.50, and the average for all stocks is 1.0 by definition.[8]

If a higher-than-average-beta stock (one whose beta is greater than 1.0) is added to an average-beta ($\beta = 1.0$) portfolio, then the beta, and consequently the riskiness, of the portfolio will increase. Conversely, if a lower-than-average-beta stock (one whose beta is less than 1.0) is added to an average-risk portfolio, the portfolio's beta and risk will decline. *Thus, because a stock's beta measures its contribution to the riskiness of a portfolio, theoretically beta is the correct measure of the stock's riskiness.*

The preceding analysis of risk in a portfolio setting is part of the Capital Asset Pricing Model (CAPM), and we can summarize our discussion to this point as follows:

1. A stock's risk consists of two components — *market risk* and *firm-specific risk.*
2. Firm-specific risk can be eliminated through diversification, and most investors do indeed diversify, either by holding large portfolios or by purchasing shares in a mutual fund. We are left, then, with *market risk,* which is caused by general movements in the stock market and which reflects the fact that most stocks are systematically affected by certain overall economic events like war, recessions, and inflation. Market risk is the only relevant risk to a rational, diversified investor, because he or she should already have eliminated firm-specific risk.

TABLE 8-4

Illustrative List of Beta Coefficients

Stock	Beta
America Online	1.55
Citigroup	1.40
General Electric	1.25
Microsoft	1.10
Pepsico Inc.	1.00
Avon Products	1.00
Anheuser Busch	0.85
Winn-Dixie Stores	0.80
Energen Corp.[a]	0.75
Pacific Gas & Electric	0.60

[a]Energen is a gas distribution company. It has a monopoly in much of Alabama, and its rates are adjusted every three months or so to keep its profits relatively constant.

SOURCE: *Value Line,* June 26, 1998.

---

[8]In theory, betas can be negative — if a stock's returns tend to rise when those of other stocks decline, and vice versa, then the regression line in a graph such as Figure 8-8 will have a downward slope, and the beta will be negative. Note though, that *Value Line* follows 1,700 stocks, and none has a negative beta. Payco American, the collection agency company, might have a negative beta, but it is too small to be followed by *Value Line* and most other services that calculate and report betas.

3. Investors must be compensated for bearing risk — *the greater the riskiness of a stock, the higher its required return.* However, compensation is required only for risk that cannot be eliminated by diversification. If risk premiums existed on stocks with high diversifiable risk, well-diversified investors would start buying these securities and bidding up their prices, and their final (equilibrium) expected returns would reflect only nondiversifiable market risk.

An example might help clarify this point. Suppose half of Stock A's risk is market risk (it occurs because Stock A moves up and down with the market), and the other half of A's risk is diversifiable. You hold only Stock A, so you are exposed to all of its risk. As compensation for bearing so much risk, you *want* a risk premium of 8 percent above the 6 percent T-bond rate. Thus, the return you demand from this investment is 14% = 6% + 8%. But suppose other investors, including your professor, are well diversified; they also hold Stock A, but they have eliminated its diversifiable risk and thus are exposed to only half as much risk as you. Therefore, their risk premium will be only half as large as yours, and they will *require* a return of only 10% = 6% + (8%/2) to invest in the stock.

If the stock actually yielded more than 10 percent in the market, others, including your professor, would buy it. If it yielded the 14 percent you demand, you would be willing to buy the stock, but the well-diversified investors would compete with you to acquire it, thus bid its price up and its yield down, and this would keep you from getting the stock at the return you need to compensate you for taking on its *total risk.* In the end, you would have to accept a 10 percent return or else keep your money in the bank. Thus, risk premiums in a market populated with *rational* investors will reflect only market risk.

4. The market risk of a stock is measured by its *beta coefficient,* which is an index of the stock's relative volatility. Some benchmark values for beta are as follows:

$\beta = 0.5$: Stock is only half as volatile, or risky, as the average stock.
$\beta = 1.0$: Stock is of average risk.
$\beta = 2.0$: Stock is twice as risky as the average stock.

5. *Because a stock's beta coefficient determines how the stock affects the riskiness of a diversified portfolio, beta is the most relevant measure of a stock's risk.*

Portfolio Beta Coefficients

A portfolio consisting of low-beta securities will itself have a low beta, because the beta of any set of securities is a weighted average of the individual securities' betas:

8-6

$$\beta_p = w_1\beta_1 + w_2\beta_2 + \cdots + w_n\beta_n$$

$$= \sum_{j=1}^{N} w_j\beta_j$$

Here β_P is the beta of the portfolio, and it reflects how volatile the portfolio is in relation to the market; w_j is the fraction of the portfolio invested in the jth stock; and β_j is the beta coefficient of the jth stock. For example, if an investor holds a $105,000 portfolio consisting of $35,000 invested in each of three stocks, and each of the stocks has a beta of 0.7, then the portfolio's beta will be $\beta_{P1} = 0.7$:

$$\beta_{P1} = 0.33(0.7) + 0.33(0.7) + 0.33(0.7) = 0.7$$

Such a portfolio will be less risky than the market; it should experience relatively narrow price swings and have relatively small rate-of-return fluctuations. In terms of Figure 8-8, the slope of its regression line would be 0.7, which is less than that for a portfolio of average stocks.

Now suppose one of the existing stocks is sold and replaced by a stock with $\beta_j = 2.5$. This action will increase the riskiness of the portfolio from $\beta_{P1} = 0.7$ to $\beta_{P2} = 1.3$:

$$\beta_{P2} = 0.33(0.7) + 0.33(0.7) + 0.33(2.5) = 1.3$$

Had a stock with $\beta_j = 0.1$ been added, the portfolio beta would have declined from 0.7 to 0.5. Adding a low-beta stock, therefore, would reduce the riskiness of the portfolio.

Self-Test Questions

Explain the following statement: "A stock held as part of a portfolio is generally less risky than the same stock held in isolation."

What is meant by perfect positive correlation, perfect negative correlation, and zero correlation?

In general, can the riskiness of a portfolio be reduced to zero by increasing the number of stocks in the portfolio? Explain.

What is meant by diversifiable risk and nondiversifiable risk?

What is an average-risk stock?

Why is beta the theoretically correct measure of a stock's riskiness?

If you plotted the returns on a particular stock versus those on the Dow Jones Industrial Average index over the past five years, what would the slope of the line you obtained indicate about the stock's risk?

The Relationship between Risk and Rates of Return

In the preceding section we saw that under the CAPM theory, beta is the appropriate measure of a stock's relevant risk. Now we must specify the relationship between risk and return: For a given level of beta, what rate of return will investors require on a stock in order to compensate them for assuming the risk? To begin, let us define the following terms:

$\hat{k}_j$ = *expected* rate of return on the jth stock.

k_j = *required* rate of return on the jth stock. Note that if $\hat{k}_j$ is less than k_j, you would not purchase this stock, or you would sell it if you owned it. If $\hat{k}_j$ is greater than k_j, you would want to buy the stock, and you would be indifferent if $\hat{k}_j = k_j$.

k_{RF} = risk-free rate of return. In this context, k_{RF} is generally measured by the return on long-term U.S. Treasury securities.

β_j = beta coefficient of the jth stock. The beta of an average stock is $\beta_A = 1.0$.

k_M = required rate of return on a portfolio consisting of all stocks, which is the market portfolio. k_M also is the required rate of return on an average, or $\beta_A = 1.0$, stock.

$RP_M = (k_M - k_{RF})$ = market risk premium. This is the additional return above the risk-free rate required to compensate an average investor for assuming an average amount of risk ($\beta_A = 1.0$).

$RP_j = (k_M - k_{RF})\beta_j$ = risk premium on the jth stock. The stock's risk premium is less than, equal to, or greater than the premium on an average stock, depending on whether its beta is less than, equal to, or greater than 1.0. If $\beta_j = \beta_A = 1.0$, then $RP_j = RP_M$.

MARKET RISK PREMIUM, RP_M
The additional return over the risk-free rate needed to compensate investors for assuming an average amount of risk.

The **market risk premium, RP_M**, depends on the degree of aversion that investors on average have to risk.[9] Let us assume that at the current time, Treasury bonds yield $k_{RF} = 6\%$ and an average share of stock has a required return of $k_A = k_M = 14\%$. Therefore, the market risk premium is 8 percent:

$$RP_M = k_M - k_{RF} = 14\% - 6\% = 8\%.$$

It follows that if one stock were twice as risky as another, its risk premium would be twice as high, and, conversely, if its risk were only half as much, its risk premium would be half as large. Further, we can measure a stock's relative riskiness by its beta coefficient. Therefore, if we know the market risk premium, RP_M, and the stock's risk as measured by its beta coefficient, β_j, we can find its risk premium as the product $RP_M \times \beta_j$. For example, if $\beta_j = 0.5$ and $RP_M = 8\%$, then RP_j is 4 percent:

8-7

$$\text{Risk premium for Stock } j = RP_j = RP_M \times \beta_j$$

$$= 8\% \times 0.5$$

$$= 4.0\%$$

---

[9]This concept, as well as other aspects of CAPM, is discussed in more detail in Chapter 26 of Eugene F. Brigham, Louis C. Gapenski, and Phillip R. Daves, *Intermediate Financial Management*, 6th ed. (Fort Worth, TX: The Dryden Press, 1999). It should be noted that the risk premium of an average stock, $k_M - k_{RF}$, cannot be measured with great precision because it is impossible to obtain precise values for the expected future return on the market, k_M. However, empirical studies suggest that where long-term U.S. Treasury bonds are used to measure k_{RF} and where k_M is an estimate of the expected return on the S&P 400 Industrial Stocks, the market risk premium varies somewhat from year to year, and it has generally ranged from 4 to 8 percent during the last 20 years.

Chapter 26 of *Intermediate Financial Management* also discusses the assumptions embodied in the CAPM framework. Some of the assumptions of the CAPM theory are unrealistic, and, because of this, the theory does not hold exactly.

As the discussion in Chapter 2 implies, the required return for any investment can be expressed in general terms as:

Required return = Risk-free return + Premium for risk

$$k_j \quad = \quad k_{RF} \quad + \quad RP_j$$

According to the discussion presented above, then, the required return for Stock j can be written as

8-8

$$k_j = k_{RF} + (RP_M)\beta_j$$
$$= k_{RF} + (k_M - k_{RF})\beta_j$$

$$= 6\% + (14\% - 6\%)(0.5)$$

$$= 6\% + 8\% \ (0.5)$$

$$= 10\%$$

SECURITY MARKET LINE (SML)
The line that shows the relationship between risk as measured by beta and the required rate of return for individual securities.
SML = Equation 8-8.

Equation 8-8 is the equation for CAPM equilibrium pricing, and it generally is called the **Security Market Line (SML)**.

If some other stock were riskier than Stock j and had β_{j2} = 2.0, then its required rate of return would be 22 percent:

$$k_{j2} = 6\% + (8\%) \ 2.0 = 22\%$$

An average stock, with β = 1.0, would have a required return of 14 percent, the same as the market return:

$$k_A = 6\% + (8\%)1.0 = 14\% = k_M$$

As noted above, Equation 8-8 is called the Security Market Line (SML) equation, and it is often expressed in graph form, as in Figure 8-9, which shows the SML when k_{RF} = 6% and k_M = 14%. Note the following points:

1. *Required rates of return* are shown on the vertical axis, while risk as measured by beta is shown on the horizontal axis. This graph is quite different from the one shown in Figure 8-8, where the returns on individual stocks were plotted on the vertical axis and returns on the market index were shown on the horizontal axis. The slopes of the three lines in Figure 8-8 represented the three stocks' betas, and these three betas are now plotted as points on the horizontal axis in Figure 8-9.
2. Riskless securities have β_j = 0; therefore, k_{RF} appears as the vertical axis intercept in Figure 8-9.
3. The slope of the SML reflects the degree of risk aversion in the economy; the greater the average investor's aversion to risk, (a) the steeper the slope of the line, (b) the greater the risk premium for any stock, and (c) the higher the

FIGURE 8-9

The Security Market Line (SML)

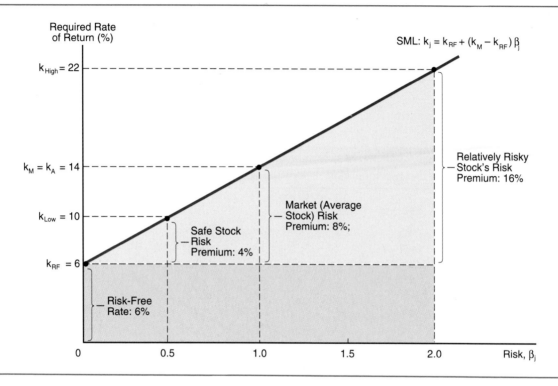

required rate of return on stocks.[10] These points are discussed further in a later section.

4. The values we worked out for stocks with $\beta_j = 0.5$, $\beta_j = 1.0$, and $\beta_j = 2.0$ agree with the values shown on the graph for k_{Low}, $k_A = k_M$, and k_{High}.

Both the Security Market Line and a company's position on it change over time due to changes in interest rates, investors' risk aversion, and individual companies' betas. Such changes are discussed in the following sections.

The Impact of Inflation

As we learned in Chapter 2, interest amounts to "rent" on borrowed money, or the price of money; thus, k_{RF} is the price of money to a riskless borrower. We also learned that the risk-free rate as measured by the rate on U.S. Treasury securities is called the *nominal,* or *quoted,* rate, and it consists of two elements: (1) a *real*

---

[10]Students sometimes confuse beta with the slope of the SML. This is a mistake. The slope of any line is equal to the "rise" divided by the "run," or $(Y_1 - Y_0)/(X_1 - X_0)$. Consider Figure 8-9. If we let $Y = k$ and $X = \beta$, and we go from the origin to $\beta = 1.0$, we see that the slope is $(k_M - k_{RF})/(\beta_M - \beta_{RF}) = (14 - 6)/(1 - 0) = 8$. Thus, the slope of the SML is equal to $(k_M - k_{RF})$, the market risk premium. In Figure 8-9, $k_j = 6\% + (8\%)\beta_j$, so a doubling of beta (e.g., from 1.0 to 2.0) would produce an 8 percentage point increase in k_j.

inflation-free rate of return, k*, and (2) an *inflation premium, IP,* equal to the anticipated rate of inflation.[11] Thus, $k_{RF} = k^* + IP$.

If the expected rate of inflation rose by 2 percent, this would cause k_{RF} to increase 2 percent. Such a change is shown in Figure 8-10. Note that under the CAPM, the increase in k_{RF} also causes an *equal* increase in the rate of return on all risky assets because the inflation premium is built into the required rate of return of both riskless and risky assets.[12] For example, the risk-free return increases from 6 to 8 percent, and the rate of return on an average stock, $k_A = k_M$,

---

FIGURE 8-10

Shift in the SML Caused by an Increase in Inflation

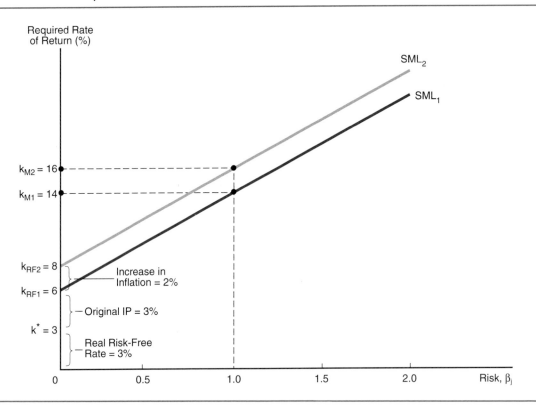

---

increases from 14 to 16 percent — all securities' returns increase by two percentage points.

Changes in Risk Aversion

The slope of the Security Market Line reflects the extent to which investors are averse to risk — the steeper the slope of the line, the greater the average investor's risk aversion. If investors were *indifferent* to risk, and if k_{RF} were 6 percent, then risky assets would also provide an expected return of 6 percent: If there were no risk aversion, there would be no risk premium, so the SML would be horizontal. *As risk aversion increases, so does the risk premium* and, thus, the slope of the SML.

Figure 8-11 illustrates an increase in risk aversion. The market risk premium rises from 8 to 10 percent, and k_M rises from $k_{M1} = 14\%$ to $k_{M2} = 16\%$. The returns on other *risky* assets also rise, with the effect of this shift in risk aversion being more pronounced on riskier securities. For example, the required return on a stock with $\beta_j = 0.5$ increases by only one percentage point, from 10 to 11 percent, whereas that on a stock with $\beta_j = 1.5$ increases by three percentage points, from 18 to 21 percent.

FIGURE 8-11

Shift in the SML Caused by Increased Risk Aversion

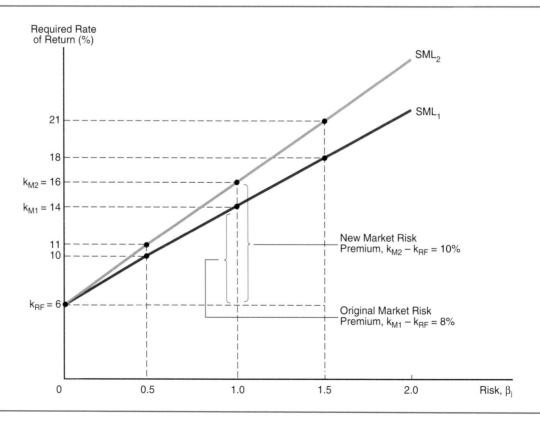

Changes in a Stock's Beta Coefficient

As we shall see later in the book, a firm can affect its beta risk through changes in the composition of its assets as well as through its use of debt financing. A company's beta can also change as a result of external factors, such as increased competition in its industry or the expiration of basic patents. When such changes occur, the required rate of return also changes, and, as we saw in Chapter 7, this will affect the price of the firm's stock. For example, consider United Textiles, with a beta equal to 1.0. Now suppose some action occurred that caused United's beta to increase from 1.0 to 1.5. If the conditions depicted in Figure 8-9 held, United's required rate of return would increase from

$$k_1 = k_{RF} + (k_M - k_{RF})\beta_j$$

$$= 6\% + (14\% - 6\%)1.0$$

$$= 14\%$$

to

$$k_2 = 6\% + (14\% - 6\%)1.5$$

$$= 18\%$$

Any change that affects the required rate of return on a security, such as a change in its beta coefficient or in expected inflation, will have an impact on the price of the security.

Self-Test Questions

Differentiate between the expected rate of return ($\hat{k}$) and the required rate of return (k) on a stock. Which would have to be larger to get you to buy the stock?

What are the differences between the relative volatility graph (Figure 8-8), where "betas are made," and the SML graph (Figure 8-9), where "betas are used"? Consider both how the graphs are constructed and the purpose for which they were developed.

What happens to the SML graph (1) when inflation increases or (2) when it decreases?

What happens to the SML graph (1) when risk aversion increases or (2) when it decreases? What would the SML look like if investors were indifferent to risk — that is, had zero risk aversion?

How can a firm influence its market, or beta, risk?

Stock Market Equilibrium

According to our discussion in the previous sections, we know we can find the *required return* for an investment, say, Stock A, k_A, by using the CAPM. Suppose the risk-free return is 6 percent, the market risk premium is 8 percent, and Stock

A has a beta of 1.5 ($\beta_A = 1.5$). Thus, the marginal, or average, investor will require a return of 18 percent on Stock A:

$$k_A = 6\% + 8\%(1.5) = 18\%$$

This 18 percent return is shown as a point on the SML in Figure 8-12.

The average investor will want to buy Stock A if the expected rate of return is more than 18 percent, will want to sell it if the expected rate of return is less than 18 percent, and will be indifferent, hence will hold but not buy or sell, if the expected rate of return is exactly 18 percent. Now suppose the investor's portfolio contains Stock A, and he or she analyzes the stock's prospects and concludes that its earnings, dividends, and price can be expected to grow at a constant rate of 5 percent per year forever. The last dividend was $D_0 = \$3$, so the next expected dividend is

$$\hat{D}_1 = \$3.00(1.05) = \$3.15$$

Our "average" (marginal) investor observes that the present price of the stock, P_0, is $26.25. Should he or she purchase more of Stock A, sell the present holdings, or maintain the present position?

FIGURE 8-12

Expected and Required Returns on Stock A

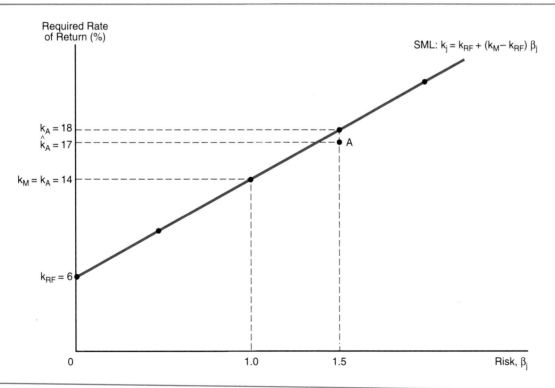

Remember from Chapter 7, we can calculate Stock A's *expected rate of return* as follows:

$$k_A = \frac{\hat{D}_1}{P_0} + g = \frac{\$3.15}{\$26.25} + 0.05 = 0.12 + 0.005 = 0.17 = 17\%$$

This value is plotted on Figure 8-12 as Point A, which is below the SML. Because the expected rate of return, $\hat{k}_A$, is less than the required return, k_A, this marginal investor would want to sell the stock, as would other holders. However, few people would want to buy at the $26.25 price, so the present owners would be unable to find buyers unless they cut the price of the stock. Thus, the price would decline, and this decline would continue until the stock's price reached $24.23, at which point the market for this security would be in **equilibrium**, because the expected rate of return, 18 percent, would be equal to the required rate of return:

EQUILIBRIUM
The condition under which the expected return on a security is just equal to its required return, $\hat{k} = k$, and the price is stable.

$$\hat{k}_A = \frac{\$3.15}{\$24.23} + 0.05 = 0.13 + 0.05 = 0.18 = 18\% = k_A$$

Had the stock initially sold for less than $24.23, say, at $22, events would have been reversed. Investors would have wanted to buy the stock because its expected rate of return would have exceeded its required rate of return, and buy orders would have driven the stock's price up to $24.23.

To summarize, in equilibrium these two conditions must hold:

1. The expected rate of return as seen by the marginal investor must equal the required rate of return: $\hat{k}_j = k_j$.
2. The actual market price of the stock must equal its intrinsic value as estimated by the marginal investor: $P_0 = \hat{P}_0$.

Of course, some individual investors may believe that $\hat{k}_j > k_j$ and $P_0 < \hat{P}_0$, and hence they would invest most of their funds in the stock, while other investors may have an opposite view and would sell their shares. However, it is the marginal investor who establishes the actual market price, and for this investor, $\hat{k}_j = k_j$ and $P_0 = \hat{P}_0$. If these conditions do not hold, trading will occur until they do hold.

Changes in Equilibrium Stock Prices

We know stock market prices are not constant — they undergo violent changes at times, such as on October 19, 1987, when the Dow Jones Industrial Average dropped 508 points. To see how such changes can occur, let us assume that Stock A is in equilibrium, selling at a price of $24.23 per share. If all expectations were met exactly, during the next year the price would gradually rise to $25.44, or by 5 percent. However, many different events could occur to cause a change in the equilibrium price of the stock. To illustrate, consider again the set of inputs used to develop Stock A's price of $24.23, along with a new set of assumed input variables:

	Variable Value	
	Original	New
Risk-free rate, k_{RF}	6%	5%
Market risk premium, $k_M - k_{RF}$	8%	7%
Stock X's beta coefficient, β_X	1.5	1.0
Stock X's expected growth rate, g_X	5%	6%
Current dividend, D_0	$3.00	$3.00
Price of Stock X	$24.23	?

Now give yourself a test: How would the change in each variable, by itself, affect the stock's return, and thus its price? What is your guess as to the new stock price?

Every change, taken alone, would lead to an increase in the price. The first three variables influence k_A, which declines from 18 to 12 percent:

$$\text{Original } k_A = 6\% + 8\%(1.5) = 18\%$$

$$\text{New } k_A = 5\% + 7\%(1.0) = 12\%$$

Using these values, together with the new g value, and applying the stock valuation model for constant growth that we discussed in Chapter 7, we find $\hat{P}_0$ rises from $24.23 to $53.00[13]:

$$\text{Original } \hat{P}_0 = \frac{\$3.00(1.05)}{0.18 - 0.05} = \frac{\$3.15}{0.13} = \$24.23$$

$$\text{New } \hat{P}_0 = \frac{\$3.00(1.06)}{0.12 - 0.06} = \frac{\$3.18}{0.06} = \$53.00$$

At the new price, the expected and required rates of return will be equal[14]:

$$\hat{k}_A = \frac{\$3.18}{\$53.00} + 0.06 = 0.06 + 0.06 = 0.12 = 12\% = k_A$$

Evidence suggests that stocks, especially those of large NYSE companies, adjust rapidly to disequilibrium situations. Consequently, equilibrium ordinarily exists for any given stock, and, in general, required and expected returns are equal. Stock prices certainly change, sometimes violently and rapidly, but this simply reflects changing conditions and expectations. There are, of course, times when a stock

---

[13]A price change of this magnitude is by no means rare. The prices of *many* stocks double or halve during a year. For example, during 1997 Yahoo, which produces Internet technology, increased in value by 511 percent; on the other hand, the price of Levitz Furniture fell 86 percent.

[14]It should be obvious by now that *actual realized* rates of return are not necessarily equal to expected and required returns. Thus, an investor might have *expected* to receive a return of 25 percent if he or she had bought Yahoo or L.A. Gear stock in 1997, but, after the fact, the realized return on Yahoo was far above 15 percent, whereas that on L.A. Gear was far below.

continues to react for several months to a favorable or unfavorable development, but this does not signify a long adjustment period; rather, it simply illustrates that as more new pieces of information about the situation become available, the market adjusts to them.

Actual Stock Prices and Returns

Our discussion thus far has focused on expected stock prices and expected rates of return. Anyone who has ever invested in the stock market knows that there can be, and there generally are, large differences between expected and realized prices and returns.

Figure 8-13 shows how the price of an average share of stock has varied in recent years, and Figure 8-14 shows how total realized returns have varied. The market trend has been strongly up, but it has gone up in some years and down in others, and the stocks of individual companies have likewise gone up and down. We know from theory that expected returns as estimated by a marginal investor are always positive, but in some years, as Figure 8-14 shows, negative returns have been realized. Of course, even in bad years some individual companies do well, so the "name of the game" in security analysis is to pick the winners. Financial managers attempt to take actions that will put their companies into the winners' col-

FIGURE 8-13

S&P 500 Index, 1970–1998

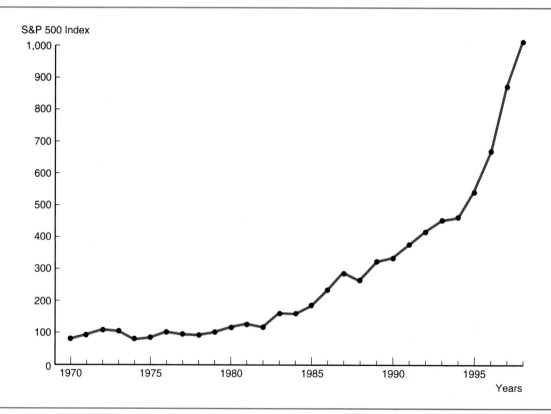

NOTE: 1998 figure is for the month of September.

SOURCE: *Federal Reserve Bulletin.*

FIGURE 8-14

S&P 500 Index, Total Returns: Dividend Yield + Capital Gain or Loss, 1970–1998

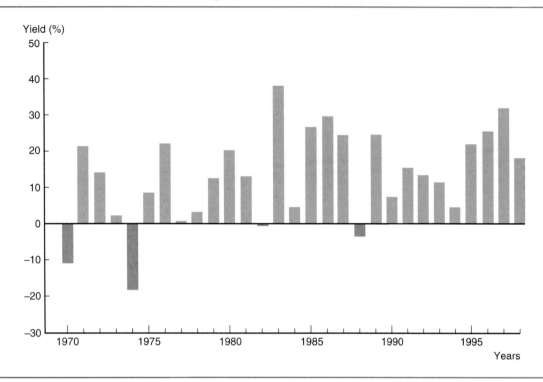

umn, but they don't always succeed. In subsequent chapters, we examine the actions that managers can take to increase the odds of their firms doing relatively well in the marketplace.

Self-Test Questions

When a stock is in equilibrium, what two conditions must hold?

If a stock is not in equilibrium, explain how financial markets adjust to bring it into equilibrium.

Physical Assets versus Securities

In this chapter, much of the discussion relates to the riskiness of financial assets, especially stocks. But, it seems financial managers should be more concerned with the riskiness of such business, or real, assets as plant and equipment. So, why not examine the riskiness of real assets? The reason is that, *for a financial manager whose goal is stock price maximization, the overriding consideration is the riskiness of the firm's stock, and the relevant risk of any physical asset must be measured in terms of its effect on the stock's risk.* For example, suppose Goodyear Tire Company is considering a major investment in a new product, recapped tires. Sales of recaps and hence earnings on the new operation are highly uncertain, so it would appear that the new venture is quite risky. However, suppose returns on the recap business are negatively correlated with Goodyear's regular operations — when times are good and people have plenty of money, they buy new tires, but when times are bad, they tend to buy more recaps. Therefore, returns would be high on regular operations and low on the recap division during good times, but the opposite situation would occur during recessions. The result might be a pattern like that shown in Figure 8-4 earlier in the chapter for Stocks W and M. Thus, what appears to be a risky investment when viewed on a stand-alone basis might not be very risky when viewed within the context of the company as a whole.

This analysis can be extended to the corporation's owners, the stockholders. Because the stock of Goodyear is owned by diversified stockholders, the real issue each time the company makes a major asset investment is this: How does this investment affect the risk of our stockholders? Again, the stand-alone risk of an individual project may look quite high, but viewed in the context of the project's effect on stockholders' risk, it may not be very large. We address this subject again in the next chapter, where we examine the effects of capital budgeting projects on companies' beta coefficients and thus on their risk to stockholders.

Self-Test Questions

Explain the following statement: "The stand-alone risk of an individual project may look quite high, but viewed in the context of a project's effect on stockholders' risk, the project's risk might not be very large."

How would the correlation between returns on the project and other assets' returns affect the preceding statement?

A Word of Caution

A word of caution about betas and the Capital Asset Pricing Model is in order. Although these concepts are logical, the entire theory is based on *ex ante,* or expected, conditions, yet we have available only *ex post,* or past, data. Thus, the betas we calculate show how volatile a stock has been in the *past,* but conditions may change, and the stock's *future volatility,* which is the item of real concern to investors, might be quite different from its past volatility. Although the CAPM represents a significant step forward in security pricing theory, it does have some potentially serious deficiencies when applied in practice, so estimates of k_j found through use of the SML may be subject to considerable error — many investors and analysts use the CAPM and the concept of β to provide "ballpark" figures for further analysis.

ETHICAL DILEMMA

RIP — Retire in Peace

Retirement Investment Products (RIP) offers a full complement of retirement planning services and a diverse line of retirement investments that have varying degrees of risk. With the investment products available at RIP, investors could form retirement funds with any level of risk preferred, from risk-free to extremely risky. RIP's reputation in the investment community is impeccable, because the service agents who advise clients are required to fully inform their clients of the risk possibilities that exist for any investment position, whether it is recommended by an agent or requested by a client.

Since 1950, RIP has built its investment portfolio of retirement funds to $60 billion, which makes it one of the largest providers of retirement funds in the United States.

You work for RIP as an investment analyst. One of your responsibilities is to help form recommendations for the retirement fund managers to evaluate when making investment decisions. Recently, Howard, a close friend from your college days who now works for SunCoast Investments, a large brokerage firm, called to tell you about a new investment that is expected to earn very high returns during the next few years. The investment is called a "Piggy-back Asset Investment Device," or PAID for short. Howard told you that he really does not know what this acronym means or how the investment is constructed, but all the reports he has read indicate PAIDs should be a hot investment in the future, therefore the returns should be very handsome for those who get in now. The one piece of information he did provide you was that a PAID is a rather complex investment that consists of a combination of securities whose values are based on numerous debt instruments issued by government agencies, including the Federal National Mortgage Association, the Federal Home Loan Bank, and so on. Howard made it clear that he would like you to consider recommending to RIP that PAIDs be purchased through SunCoast Investments. The commissions from such a deal would bail him and his family out of a financial crisis that resulted because they had bad luck with their investments in the 1999 financial markets. Howard has indicated that somehow he would reward you if RIP invests in PAIDs through SunCoast, because, in his words: "You would literally be saving my life." You told Howard you would think about it, and call him back.

Further investigation into PAIDs has yielded little additional information beyond what previously was provided by Howard. The new investment is intriguing because its expected return is extremely high compared with similar investments. So, earlier this morning, you called Howard to quiz him a little more about the return expectations and to try to get an idea concerning the riskiness of PAIDs. But Howard was unable to adequately explain the risk associated with the investment, though he reminded you that the debt of U.S. government agencies is involved. As he says, "How much risk is there with government agencies?"

The PAIDs are very enticing because RIP can attract more clients if it can increase the return offered on its investments. If you recommend the new investment and the higher returns pan out, you will earn a very sizable commission. In addition, you will be helping Howard out of his financial situation, because his commissions will be substantial if the PAIDs are purchased through SunCoast Investments. Should you recommend the PAIDs as an investment?

Summary

The primary goals of this chapter were (1) to show how risk is measured in financial analysis and (2) to explain how risk affects rates of return. The key concepts covered in the chapter are listed below.

- **Risk** can be defined as the chance that some event other than expected will occur.
- Most rational investors hold **portfolios of stocks**, and they are more concerned with the risks of their portfolios than with the risks of individual stocks.
- The **expected return** on an investment is the mean value of its probability distribution of possible returns.
- The **higher the probability** that the actual return will be *significantly different* from the expected return, the **greater the risk** associated with owning an asset.
- The average investor is **risk averse**, which means that he or she must be compensated for holding risky securities; therefore, riskier securities must have higher expected returns than less risky securities.

- A stock's risk consists of (1) **company-specific risk**, which can be eliminated by diversification, plus (2) **market, or beta, risk**, which cannot be eliminated by diversification.
- The **relevant risk** of an individual security is its contribution to the riskiness of a well-diversified portfolio, which is the security's **market risk**. Because market risk cannot be eliminated by diversification, investors must be compensated for it.
- A stock's **beta coefficient,** β, is a measure of the stock's market risk. Beta measures the extent to which the stock's returns move with the market.
- A **high-beta stock** is more volatile than an average stock, while a **low-beta stock** is less volatile than an average stock. An **average stock** has $\beta = 1.0$.
- The **beta of a portfolio** is a **weighted average** of the betas of the individual securities in the portfolio.
- The **Security Market Line (SML)** equation shows the relationship between a security's risk and its required rate of return. The return required for any security j is equal to the **risk-free rate** plus the **market risk premium** times the **security's beta**: $k_j = k_{RF} + (k_M - k_{RF})\beta_j$.
- Even though the expected rate of return on a stock is generally equal to its required return, a number of things can happen to cause the required rate of return to change: (1) the **risk-free rate can change** because of changes in anticipated inflation, (2) a **stock's beta can change**, or (3) **investors' aversion to risk can change**.
- Also, we saw that differences can and do exist between expected and actual returns in the stock and bond markets. **But, in general, expected and actual (or realized) returns are equal; otherwise, investors will take corrective actions.**

In the next few chapters, we examine the ways in which a firm's management can influence a stock's riskiness and hence its price.

Questions

8-1 The probability distribution of a less risky expected return is more peaked than that of a riskier return. What shape would the probability distribution have for (a) completely certain returns and (b) completely uncertain returns?

8-2 Security A has an expected return of 7 percent, a standard deviation of expected returns of 35 percent, a correlation coefficient with the market of −0.3, and a beta coefficient of −0.5. Security B has an expected return of 12 percent, a standard deviation of returns of 10 percent, a correlation with the market of 0.7, and a beta coefficient of 1.0. Which security is riskier? Why?

8-3 Suppose you owned a portfolio consisting of $250,000 worth of long-term U.S. government bonds.
   a. Would your portfolio be riskless?
   b. Now suppose you hold a portfolio consisting of $250,000 worth of 30-day Treasury bills. Every 30 days your bills mature and you reinvest the principal ($250,000) in a new batch of bills. Assume that you live on the investment income from your portfolio and that you want to maintain a constant standard of living. Is your portfolio *truly* riskless?
   c. Can you think of any asset that would be completely riskless? Could someone develop such an asset? Explain.

8-4 A life insurance policy is a financial asset. The premiums paid represent the investment's cost.

    a. How would you calculate the expected return on a life insurance policy?

    b. Suppose the owner of a life insurance policy has no other financial assets — the person's only other asset is "human capital," or lifetime earnings capacity. What is the correlation coefficient between returns on the insurance policy and returns on the policyholder's human capital?

    c. Life insurance companies have to pay administrative costs and sales representatives' commissions; hence, the expected rate of return on insurance premiums is generally low, or even negative. Use the portfolio concept to explain why people buy life insurance in spite of negative expected returns.

8-5 If investors' aversion to risk increased, would the risk premium on a high-beta stock increase more or less than that on a low-beta stock? Explain.

Self-Test Problems   *Solutions Appear in Appendix B*

Key terms **ST-1** Define the following terms, using graphs or equations to illustrate your answers wherever feasible:

    a. Risk; probability distribution

    b. Expected rate of return, $\hat{k}$, required rate of return, k

    c. Continuous probability distribution

    d. Standard deviation, σ; variance, σ^2; coefficient of variation, CV

    e. Risk aversion; realized rate of return, $\bar{k}$

    f. Risk premium for Stock j, RP_j; market risk premium, RP_M

    g. Capital Asset Pricing Model (CAPM)

    h. Expected return on a portfolio, $\hat{k}_p$

    i. Correlation coefficient, r

    j. Market risk; company-specific risk; relevant risk

    k. Beta coefficient, β; average stock's beta, β_A

    l. Security Market Line (SML); SML equation

    m. Slope of SML as a measure of risk aversion

Realized rates of return **ST-2** Stocks A and B have the following historical returns:

Year	Stock A's Returns, k_A	Stock B's Returns, k_B
1995	−10.00%	−3.00%
1996	18.50	21.29
1997	38.67	44.25
1998	14.33	3.67
1999	33.00	28.30

    a. Calculate the average rate of return for each stock during the period 1995 through 1999. Assume that someone held a portfolio consisting of 50 percent of Stock A and 50 percent of Stock B. What would have been the realized rate of return on the portfolio in each year from 1995 through 1999? What would have been the average return on the portfolio during this period?

    b. Now calculate the standard deviation of returns for each stock and for the portfolio. Use Equation 8-3a in Footnote 3.

    c. Looking at the annual returns data on the two stocks, would you guess that the correlation coefficient between returns on the two stocks is closer to 0.9 or to −0.9?

d. If you added more stocks at random to the portfolio, which of the following is the most accurate statement of what would happen to σ_p?
   (1) σ_p would remain constant.
   (2) σ_p would decline to somewhere in the vicinity of 15 percent.
   (3) σ_p would decline to zero if enough stocks were included.

Problems

Expected returns   **8-1**   Suppose you won the Florida lottery and were offered (1) $0.5 million or (2) a gamble in which you would get $1 million if a head were flipped but zero if a tail came up.
   a. What is the expected value of the gamble?
   b. Would you take the sure $0.5 million or the gamble?
   c. If you choose the sure $0.5 million, are you a risk averter or a risk seeker?
   d. Suppose you actually take the sure $0.5 million. You can invest it in either a U.S. Treasury bond that will return $537,500 at the end of a year or a common stock that has a 50-50 chance of being either worthless or worth $1,150,000 at the end of the year.
      (1) What is the expected *dollar profit* on the stock investment? (The expected profit on the T-bond investment is $37,500.)
      (2) What is the expected *rate of return* on the stock investment? (The expected rate of return on the T-bond investment is 7.5 percent.)
      (3) Would you invest in the bond or the stock?
      (4) Exactly how large would the expected profit (or the expected rate of return) have to be on the stock investment to make you invest in the stock, given the 7.5 percent return on the bond?
      (5) How might your decision be affected if, rather than buying one stock for $0.5 million, you could construct a portfolio consisting of 100 stocks with $5,000 invested in each? Each of these stocks has the same return characteristics as the one stock — that is, a 50-50 chance of being worth either zero or $11,500 at year-end. Would the correlation between returns on these stocks matter?

Security Market Line   **8-2**   The McAlhany Investment Fund has total capital of $500 million invested in five stocks:

Stock	Investment	Stock's Beta Coefficient
A	$160 million	0.5
B	120 million	2.0
C	80 million	4.0
D	80 million	1.0
E	60 million	3.0

The current risk-free rate is 8 percent, whereas market returns have the following estimated probability distribution for the next period:

Probability	Market Return
0.1	10%
0.2	12
0.4	13
0.2	16
0.1	17

a. Compute the expected return for the market.

b. Compute the beta coefficient for the investment fund. (Remember, this is a portfolio.)

c. What is the estimated equation for the Security Market Line (SML)?

d. Compute the fund's required rate of return for the next period.

e. Suppose John McAlhany, the president, receives a proposal for a new stock. The investment needed to take a position in the stock is $50 million, it will have an expected return of 18 percent, and its estimated beta coefficient is 2.0. Should the new stock be purchased? At what expected rate of return should McAlhany be indifferent to purchasing the stock?

Realized rates of return   8-3   Stocks A and B have the following historical returns:

Year	Stock A's Returns, k_A	Stock B's Returns, k_B
1995	−18.00%	−14.50%
1996	33.00	21.80
1997	15.00	30.50
1998	−0.50	−7.60
1999	27.00	26.30

a. Calculate the average rate of return for each stock during the period 1995 through 1999.

b. Assume that someone held a portfolio consisting of 50 percent of Stock A and 50 percent of Stock B. What would have been the realized rate of return on the portfolio in each year from 1995 through 1999? What would have been the average return on the portfolio during this period?

c. Calculate the standard deviation of returns for each stock and for the portfolio. (Use Equation 8-3a in Footnote 3.)

d. Calculate the coefficient of variation for each stock and for the portfolio.

e. If you are a risk-averse investor, would you prefer to hold Stock A, Stock B, or the portfolio? Why?

Exam-Type Problems

The problems included in this section are set up in such a way that they could be used as multiple-choice exam problems.

Expected returns   8-4   The market and Stock S have the following probability distributions:

Probability	k_M	k_S
0.3	15%	20%
0.4	9	5
0.3	18	12

a. Calculate the expected rates of return for the market and Stock S.

b. Calculate the standard deviations for the market and Stock S.

c. Calculate the coefficients of variation for the market and Stock S.

Expected returns   8-5   Stocks X and Y have the following probability distributions of expected future returns:

Probability	X	Y
0.1	−10%	−35%
0.2	2	0
0.4	12	20
0.2	20	25
0.1	38	45

a. Calculate the expected rate of return, $\hat{k}$, for Stock Y. ($\hat{k}_X = 12\%$.)

b. Calculate the standard deviation of expected returns for Stock X. ($\sigma_Y = 20.35\%$) Now calculate the coefficient of variation for Stock Y. Is it possible that most investors might regard Stock Y as being less risky than Stock X? Explain.

8-6 Suppose $k_{RF} = 8\%$, $k_M = 11\%$, and $k_B = 14\%$.

a. Calculate Stock B's beta.

b. If Stock B's beta were 1.5, what would be B's new required rate of return?

8-7 Suppose $k_{RF} = 9\%$, $k_M = 14\%$, and $\beta_X = 1.3$.

a. What is k_X, the required rate of return on Stock X?

b. Now suppose k_{RF} (1) increases to 10 percent or (2) decreases to 8 percent. The slope of the SML remains constant. How would this affect k_M and k_X?

c. Now assume k_{RF} remains at 9 percent, but k_M (1) increases to 16 percent or (2) falls to 13 percent. The slope of the SML does not remain constant. How would these changes affect k_X?

Portfolio beta   **8-8** Suppose you hold a diversified portfolio consisting of a $7,500 investment in each of 20 different common stocks. The portfolio beta is equal to 1.12. Now, suppose you have decided to sell one of the stocks in your portfolio with a beta equal to 1.0 for $7,500 and to use these proceeds to buy another stock for your portfolio. Assume the new stock's beta is equal to 1.75. Calculate your portfolio's new beta.

Portfolio required return   **8-9** Suppose you are the money manager of a $4 million investment fund. The fund consists of 4 stocks with the following investments and betas:

Stock	Investment	Beta
A	$ 400,000	1.50
B	600,000	−0.50
C	1,000,000	1.25
D	2,000,000	0.75

If the market required rate of return is 14 percent and the risk-free rate is 6 percent, what is the fund's required rate of return?

Required rate of return   **8-10** Stock R has a beta of 1.5, Stock S has a beta of 0.75, the expected rate of return on an average stock is 15 percent, and the risk-free rate of return is 9 percent. By how much does the required return on the riskier stock exceed the required return on the less risky stock?

Integrative Problem

Risk and return   **8-11** Assume that you recently graduated with a major in finance, and you just landed a job in the trust department of a large regional bank. Your first assignment is to invest $100,000 from an estate for which the bank is trustee. Because the estate is expected to be distributed to the heirs in about one year, you have been instructed to plan for a one-year holding period. Further, your boss has restricted you to the following investment alternatives, shown with their probabilities and associated outcomes. (Disregard for now the items at the bottom of the data; you will fill in the blanks later.)

State of the Economy	Probability	Returns on Alternative Investments					
		Estimated Rate of Return					
		T-Bills	High Tech	Collec-tions	U.S. Rubber	Market Portfolio	2-Stock Portfolio
Recession	0.1	8.0%	−22.0%	28.0%	10.0%	−13.0%	
Below Average	0.2	8.0	(2.0)	14.7	−10.0	1.0	
Average	0.4	8.0	20.0	0.0	7.0	15.0	
Above Average	0.2	8.0	35.0	−10.0	45.0	29.0	
Boom	0.1	8.0	50.0	−20.0	30.0	43.0	—
$\hat{k}$							
σ							
CV							

The bank's economic forecasting staff has developed probability estimates for the state of the economy, and the trust department has a sophisticated computer program that was used to estimate the rate of return on each alternative under each state of the economy. High Tech Inc. is an electronics firm; Collections Inc. collects past due debts; and U.S. Rubber manufactures tires and various other rubber and plastics products. The bank also maintains an "index fund" that owns a market-weighted fraction of all publicly traded stocks; you can invest in that fund and thus obtain average stock market results. Given the situation as described, answer the following questions:

a. (1) Why is the T-bill's return independent of the state of the economy? Do T-bills promise a completely risk-free return?

(2) Why are High Tech's returns expected to move with the economy whereas Collections' are expected to move counter to the economy?

b. Calculate the expected rate of return on each alternative, and fill in the row for $\hat{k}$ in the table above.

c. You should recognize that basing a decision solely on expected returns is only appropriate for risk-neutral individuals. Since the beneficiaries of the trust, like virtually everyone, are risk averse, the riskiness of each alternative is an important aspect of the decision. One possible measure of risk is the standard deviation of returns.

(1) Calculate this value for each alternative, and fill in the row for σ in the table above.

(2) What type of risk is measured by the standard deviation?

(3) Draw a graph which shows *roughly* the shape of the probability distributions for High Tech, U.S. Rubber, and T-bills.

d. Suppose you suddenly remembered that the coefficient of variation (CV) is generally regarded as being a better measure of total risk than the standard deviation when the alternatives being considered have widely differing expected returns. Calculate the CVs for the different securities, and fill in the row for CV in the table above. Does the CV produce the same risk rankings as the standard deviation?

e. Suppose you created a two-stock portfolio by investing $50,000 in High Tech and $50,000 in Collections.

(1) Calculate the expected return ($\hat{k}_p$), the standard deviation (σ_p), and the coefficient of variation (CV_p) for this portfolio and fill in the appropriate rows in the table above.

(2) How does the riskiness of this two-stock portfolio compare to the riskiness of the individual stocks if they were held in isolation?

f. Suppose an investor starts with a portfolio consisting of one randomly selected stock. What would happen (1) to the riskiness and (2) to the expected return of the portfolio if more and more randomly selected stocks were added to the portfolio? What is the implication for investors? Draw two graphs to illustrate your answer.

g. (1) Should portfolio effects impact the way investors think about the riskiness of individual stocks?

(2) If you chose to hold a one-stock portfolio and consequently were exposed to more risk than diversified investors, could you expect to be compensated for all of your risk; that is, could you earn a risk premium on that part of your risk that you could have eliminated by diversifying?

h. The expected rates of return and the beta coefficients of the alternatives as supplied by the bank's computer program are as follows:

Security	Return ($\hat{k}$)	Risk (Beta)
High Tech	17.4%	1.29
Market	15.0	1.00
U.S. Rubber	13.8	0.68
T-bills	8.0	0.00
Collections	1.7	−0.86

(1) What is a beta coefficient, and how are betas used in risk analysis?

(2) Do the expected returns appear to be related to each alternative's market risk?

(3) Is it possible to choose among the alternatives on the basis of the information developed thus far?

(4) Use the data given at the start of the problem to construct a graph which shows how the T-bill's, High Tech's, and Collections' beta coefficients are calculated. Then discuss what betas measure and how they are used in risk analysis.

i. (1) Write out the Security Market Line (SML) equation, use it to calculate the required rate of return on each alternative, and then graph the relationship between the expected and required rates of return.

(2) How do the expected rates of return compare with the required rates of return?

(3) Does the fact that Collections has a negative beta make any sense? What is the implication of the negative beta?

(4) What would be the market risk and the required return of a 50-50 portfolio of High Tech and Collections? Of High Tech and U.S. Rubber?

j. (1) Suppose investors raised their inflation expectations by 3 percentage points over current estimates as reflected in the 8 percent T-bill rate. What effect would higher inflation have on the SML and on the returns required on high- and low-risk securities?

(2) Suppose instead that investors' risk aversion increased enough to cause the market risk premium to increase by 3 percentage points. (Inflation remains constant.) What effect would this have on the SML and on returns of high- and low-risk securities?

Computer-Related Problem

Work the problem in this section only if you are using the computer problem diskette.

Realized rates of return   **8-12** Using the model in File C8, rework Problem 8-3, assuming that a third stock, Stock C, is available for inclusion in the portfolio. Stock C has the following historical returns:

Year	Stock C's Return, k_C
1995	32.00%
1996	−11.75
1997	10.75
1998	32.25
1999	−6.75

    a. Calculate (or read from the computer screen) the average return, standard deviation, and coefficient of variation for Stock C.

    b. Assume that the portfolio now consists of 33.33 percent of Stock A, 33.33 percent of Stock B, and 33.33 percent of Stock C. How does this affect the portfolio return, standard deviation, and coefficient of variation versus when 50 percent was invested in A and in B?

    c. Make some other changes in the portfolio, making sure that the percentages sum to 100 percent. For example, enter 25 percent for Stock A, 25 percent for Stock B, and 50 percent for Stock C. (Note that the program will not allow you to enter a zero for the percentage in Stock C.) Notice that $\hat{k}_p$ remains constant and that σ_p changes. Why do these results occur?

    d. In Problem 8-3, the standard deviation of the portfolio decreased only slightly, because Stocks A and B were highly positively correlated with one another. In this problem, the addition of Stock C causes the standard deviation of the portfolio to decline dramatically, even though $\sigma_C = \sigma_A = \sigma_B$. What does this indicate about the correlation between Stock C and Stocks A and B?

    e. Would you prefer to hold the portfolio described in Problem 8-3 consisting only of Stocks A and B or a portfolio that also included Stock C? If others react similarly, how might this affect the stocks' prices and rates of return?

APPENDIX 8A

Calculating Beta Coefficients

The CAPM is an *ex ante* model, which means that all of the variables represent before-the-fact, *expected* values. In particular, the beta coefficient used in the SML equation should reflect the expected volatility of a given stock's return versus the return on the market during some *future* period. However, people generally calculate betas using data from some *past* period and then assume that the stock's relative volatility will be the same in the future as it was in the past.

To illustrate how betas are calculated, consider Figure 8A-1. The data at the bottom of the figure show the historical realized returns for Stock J and for the market over the last five years. The data points have been plotted on the scatter diagram, and a regression line has been drawn. If all the data points had fallen on a straight line, as they did in Figure 8-8 in the chapter, it would be easy to draw an accurate line. If they do not, as in Figure 8A-1, then you must fit the line either "by eye" as an approximation or with a calculator or a computer.

Recall what the term *regression line,* or *regression equation,* means: The equation $Y = \alpha + \beta X + \varepsilon$ is the standard form of a simple linear regression. It states that the dependent variable, Y, is equal to a constant, α (the Y intercept), plus β times X, where β is the slope coefficient and X is the independent variable, plus an error term, ε. Thus, the rate of return on the stock during a given time period (Y) depends on what happens to the general stock market, which is measured by $X = \bar{k}_M$.

Once the data have been plotted and the regression line has been drawn on graph paper, we can estimate its intercept and slope, the α and β values in $Y = \alpha + \beta X$. The intercept, α, simply is the point where the line cuts the vertical axis. The slope coefficient, β, can be estimated by the "rise over run" method. This involves calculating the amount by which $\bar{k}_J$ increases for a given increase in $\bar{k}_M$. For example, we observe in Figure 8A-1 that $\bar{k}_J$ increases from -8.9 to $+7.1$ percent (the rise) when $\bar{k}_M$ increases from 0 to 10 percent (the run). Thus β, the beta coefficient, can be measured as follows:

$$\text{Beta} = \beta = \frac{\text{Rise}}{\text{Run}} = \frac{\Delta Y}{\Delta X} = \frac{7.1 - (-8.9)}{10.0 - 0.0} = \frac{16.0}{10.0} = 1.6$$

Note that rise over run is a ratio, and it would be the same if measured using any two arbitrarily selected points on the line.

FIGURE 8A-1

Calculating Beta Coefficients

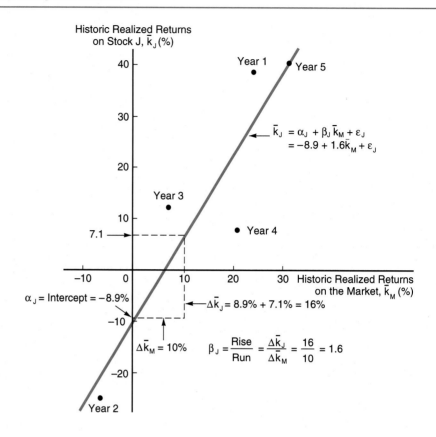

Year	Market ($\bar{k}_M$)	Stock J ($\bar{k}_J$)
1	23.8%	38.6%
2	−7.2	−24.7
3	6.6	12.3
4	20.5	8.2
5	30.6	40.1
Average $\bar{k}$	14.9%	14.9%
$\sigma_{\bar{k}}$	15.1%	26.5%

The regression line equation enables us to predict a rate of return for Stock J, given a value of $\bar{k}_M$. For example, if $\bar{k}_M$ = 15%, we would predict $\bar{k}_J$ = −8.9% + 1.6(15%) = 15.1%. However, the actual return probably would differ from the predicted return. This deviation is the error term, ε_J, for the year, and it varies randomly from year to year depending on company-specific factors. Note, though, that the higher the stock's correlation with the market, the closer the points lie to the regression line, and the smaller the errors.

If you have taken a statistics course that covered regression analysis, you are aware that five observations are not sufficient to attain valid results. In actual practice, monthly (or daily) rather than annual returns are generally used for $\bar{k}_J$ and $\bar{k}_M$, and five years of data are often employed; thus, there would be $5 \times 12 = 60$ data points on the scatter diagram. Also, in practice one would use the *least squares method* for finding the regression coefficients α and β; this procedure minimizes the squared values of the error terms. It is discussed in statistics courses.

The least squares value of beta can be obtained quite easily with a financial calculator or a spreadsheet such as *Excel* or *Lotus 1-2-3*.

PART III

Corporate Decision Making

CHAPTER 9

Capital Budgeting

When RJR Nabisco canceled its smokeless cigarette project, *The Wall Street Journal* called it "one of the most stunning new product disasters in recent history." RJR had spent more than $300 million on the product and had test marketed it for five months. The company had even built a new plant and was all set to produce smokeless cigarettes in huge quantities.

The new cigarette had two fatal flaws — it had to be lit with a special lighter and even then it was hard to light, and many, if not most, smokers didn't like the taste. These problems were well known early on, yet RJR still pumped money into the project.

What led RJR's top managers to downplay the flaws and to spend $300 million on a bad product? According to industry observers, many people inside the company were aware of the seriousness of the situation, but they were afraid to voice their concerns because they were afraid they would offend the top managers. The top managers, meantime, were so infatuated with their "new toy" that they assumed consumers would embrace the smokeless cigarette in spite of its obvious flaws. Interestingly, most of the top managers smoked, but none smoked the new smokeless cigarette!

RJR was not a well-run company, even though it was entrenched in highly profitable markets and was generating billions of dollars of cash each year. The smokeless cigarette project didn't kill the company, but it did contribute to the downfall of the management team that backed the project. Had RJR's top managers followed the procedures set forth in this chapter, perhaps they would still be in control of the company.

CAPITAL BUDGETING
The process of planning expenditures on assets whose cash flows are expected to extend beyond one year.

In the previous two chapters we saw how to value assets and determine required rates of return. Now we apply these concepts to investment decisions involving the fixed assets of a firm, or *capital budgeting*. Here the term *capital* refers to fixed assets used in production, while a *budget* is a plan that details projected inflows and outflows during some future period. Thus, the capital budget is an outline of planned expenditures on fixed assets, and **capital budgeting** is the process of analyzing projects and deciding which are acceptable investments and which actually should be purchased.

Our treatment of capital budgeting is divided into two general areas. First, we give an overview and description of the basic techniques used in capital budgeting analysis. Then, we consider how the cash flows associated with capital budgeting projects are estimated and how risk is considered in capital budgeting decisions.

Importance of Capital Budgeting

A number of factors combine to make capital budgeting decisions perhaps the most important ones financial managers must make. First, the impact of capital budgeting is long term, thus the firm loses some decision-making flexibility when capital projects are purchased. For example, when a firm invests in an asset with a ten-year economic (useful) life, its operations are affected for ten years — the firm is "locked in" by the capital budgeting decision. Further, because asset expansion is fundamentally related to expected future sales, a decision to buy a fixed asset that is expected to last ten years involves an implicit ten-year sales forecast. An error in the forecast of asset requirements can have serious consequences — investing too much will result in unnecessarily heavy expenses; investing too little might create inefficient production and inadequate capacity that result in lost sales.

Timing is also important in capital budgeting — capital assets must be ready to come "on line" when they are needed; otherwise, opportunities might be lost. A firm that forecasts its needs for capital assets in advance will have an opportunity to purchase and install the assets before they are needed. Consider what happened to Decopot when it began to experience intermittent spurts of additional demand for the decorative tiles it produces. At the time, Decopot did not have the capacity to manufacture products to meet the additional demand, so customers were turned away. By the time senior management decided to add capacity so that production could be increased, it was too late. Decopot's competitors already had expanded their operations, which allowed them to satisfy the additional demand; thus many of Decopot's customers became the competitors' customers. Unfortunately, like Decopot, many firms do not order capital goods until they approach full capacity or are forced to replace worn-out equipment, which often is too late.

Finally, capital budgeting is also important because the acquisition of fixed assets typically involves substantial expenditures, and before a firm can spend a large amount of money, it must have the funds available — large amounts of money are not available automatically. Therefore, a firm contemplating a major capital expenditure program must arrange its financing well in advance to be sure the funds required are available.

Self-Test Questions

Why are capital budgeting decisions so important to the success of a firm?

Why is the sales forecast a key element in a capital budgeting decision?

Generating Ideas for Capital Projects

The ideas for capital budgeting projects are generally created by the firm. For example, a sales representative might report that customers are asking for a particular product that the company does not currently produce. The sales manager then discusses the idea with the marketing research group to determine the size of the market for the proposed product. If it appears likely that a significant market does exist, and the product can be produced and sold at a sufficient profit, the project will be undertaken.

A firm's growth, and even its ability to remain competitive and to survive, depends on a constant flow of ideas for new products, ways to make existing products better, and ways to produce output more efficiently. Accordingly, a well-managed firm will go to great lengths to develop good capital budgeting proposals. Some firms even provide incentives to employees to encourage suggestions that lead to beneficial investment proposals.

Because some capital investment ideas will be good and others will not, procedures must be established for evaluating the worth of such projects to the firm. Our topic in the remainder of this chapter is the evaluation of the acceptability of capital projects.

Self-Test Question

How does a firm generate ideas for capital projects?

Project Classifications

REPLACEMENT DECISIONS
Decisions to determine whether to purchase capital assets to take the place of existing assets to maintain existing operations.

EXPANSION DECISIONS
Decisions to determine whether to purchase capital projects and add them to existing assets to increase existing operations.

INDEPENDENT PROJECTS
Projects whose cash flows are not affected by the acceptance or nonacceptance of other projects.

Capital budgeting decisions generally are termed either *replacement decisions* or *expansion decisions*. **Replacement decisions** involve determining whether capital projects should be purchased to take the place of (replace) existing assets that might be worn out, damaged, or obsolete. Usually the replacement projects are necessary to maintain or improve profitable operations using the *existing* production levels. On the other hand, if a firm is considering whether to *increase* operations by adding capital projects to existing assets that will help produce either more of its existing products or entirely new products, **expansion decisions** are made.

Some of the capital budgeting decisions involve *independent projects,* while others will involve *mutually exclusive projects*. **Independent projects** are projects whose cash flows are not affected by one another, so the acceptance of one project does not affect the acceptance of the other project(s) — *all independent projects can be purchased if they all are acceptable.* For example, if Ziff-Davis Publishing Company, which publishes magazines for personal computer users, decided to purchase the ABC television network, it still could publish a new PC magazine. On the other hand, if a capital budgeting decision involves **mutually exclusive projects,** then when one project is taken on, the other(s) must be rejected — *only one mutually exclusive project can be purchased, even if they all are acceptable.* For example, Alldome Sports Ltd. has a parcel of land on which it wants to build either a children's amusement park or a domed baseball stadium.

MUTUALLY EXCLUSIVE PROJECTS
A set of projects where the acceptance of one project means the others cannot be accepted.

The land is not large enough for both alternatives, so if Alldome chooses to build the amusement park, it could not build the stadium, and vice versa.

In general, relatively simple calculations, and only a few supporting documents, are required for replacement decisions, especially maintenance-type investments in profitable plants. More detailed analysis is required for cost-reduction replacements, for expansion of existing product lines, and especially for investments in new products or areas. Also, more expensive projects, whether replacement or expansion, usually require both more detailed analysis and approval at a higher level within the firm. For instance, a plant manager might be authorized to approve maintenance expenditures up to $10,000 using relatively unsophisticated analysis, but upper management might be responsible for capital budgeting decisions involving investments greater than $1 million.

Self-Test Question

Identify and briefly explain how capital project classification categories are used.

Steps in the Valuation Process

Capital budgeting decisions involve valuation of assets, or projects. Therefore, capital budgeting involves the same steps used in general asset valuation, which were described in Chapters 7 and 8:

1. Determine the cost, or purchase price, of the asset.
2. Estimate the cash flows expected from the asset.
3. Evaluate the riskiness of the projected cash flows to determine the appropriate rate of return to use for computing the present value of the estimated cash flows.
4. Compute the present value of the expected cash flows.
5. Compare the present value of the expected cash inflows with the initial investment, or cost, required to acquire the asset.

If a firm invests in a project with a present value greater than its cost, the value of the firm will increase. Thus, there is a very direct link between capital budgeting and stock values: The more effective the firm's capital budgeting procedures, the higher the price of its stock.

Self-Test Questions

List the steps in the capital budgeting process, and compare them with the steps in security valuation.

Explain how capital budgeting is related to the wealth-maximization goal that should be pursued by the financial manager of a firm.

Capital Budgeting Evaluation Techniques

The basic methods used by businesses to evaluate capital budgeting projects are (1) payback, (2) net present value (NPV), and (3) internal rate of return (IRR). We

FIGURE 9-1

Net Cash Flows for Projects S and L

Year	Expected After-Tax Net Cash Flows, $\widehat{CF}_t$	
(t)	Project S	Project L
0^a	$ (3,000)	$ (3,000)
1	1,500	400
2	1,200	900
3	800	1,300
4	300	1,500

PROJECT S:

0	1	2	3	4
-3,000	1,500	1,200	800	300

PROJECT L:

0	1	2	3	4
-3,000	400	900	1,300	1,500

[a] $\widehat{CF}_0$ represents the initial investment, or net cost of the project.

explain how each evaluation criterion is calculated, and then we determine how well each performs in terms of identifying those projects that will maximize the firm's stock price.

We use the tabular and time line cash flow data shown in Figure 9-1 for Projects S and L to illustrate each capital budgeting method, and throughout this section we assume that the projects are equally risky. Note that the cash flows, $\widehat{CF}_t$, are expected values. Later in the chapter we show how these cash flows are estimated. But, at this point, we assume the net cash flows are given — they have been adjusted to reflect taxes, depreciation, salvage values, and any other changes in cash flows associated with the capital projects — so we can focus on our main area of concern, the capital budgeting evaluation techniques. Also, we assume that all cash flows occur at the end of the designated year. Incidentally, the S stands for *short* and the L for *long:* Project S is a short-term project in the sense that its cash inflows tend to come in sooner than those for Project L.

Payback Period

PAYBACK PERIOD
The length of time before the original cost of an investment is recovered from the expected cash flows.

The **payback period,** defined as the expected number of years required to recover the original investment, is the simplest and, as far as we know, the oldest *formal* method used to evaluate capital budgeting projects. To compute a project's payback period, simply add up the expected cash flows for each year until the cumulative value is equal to the amount initially invested. The total amount of time, including the fraction of a year if appropriate, that it takes to recapture the original amount invested is the payback period. The payback calculation process for both Project S and Project L is diagrammed in Figure 9-2.

Figure 9-2

Payback Period for Project S and Project L

Project S:	0	1	2 PB$_S$	3	4
Net cash flow	-3,000	1,500	1,200	800	300
Cumulative net cash flow	-3,000	-1,500	-300	500	800

Project L:	0	1	2	3 PB$_L$	4
Net cash flow	-3,000	400	900	1,300	1,500
Cumulative net cash flow	-3,000	-2,600	-1,700	-400	1,100

The *exact* payback period can be found using the following formula:

9-1

$$\text{Payback} = \left(\begin{array}{c} \text{Number of years before} \\ \text{full recovery of} \\ \text{original investment} \end{array} \right) + \left(\dfrac{\begin{array}{c} \text{Unrecovered cost at start} \\ \text{of full-recovery year} \end{array}}{\begin{array}{c} \text{Total cash flow during} \\ \text{full-recovery year} \end{array}} \right)$$

The diagram in Figure 9-2 shows that the payback period for Project S is between two and three years, so, using Equation 9-1, the exact payback period is

$$\text{Payback}_S = 2 + \frac{300}{800} = 2.4 \text{ years}$$

Applying the same procedure to Project L, we find Payback$_L$ = 3.3 years.

Using payback to make capital budgeting decisions is based on the concept that it is better to recover the cost of (investment in) a project sooner rather than later. Therefore, Project S is considered better than Project L because it has a lower payback. *As a general rule, a project is considered acceptable if its payback is less than the maximum cost recovery time established by the firm.* For example, if the firm requires projects to have a payback of three years or less, Project S would be acceptable but Project L would not.

The payback method is very simple, which explains why it traditionally has been one of the most popular capital budgeting techniques. But payback ignores the time value of money, so relying solely on this method could lead to incorrect decisions — at least if our goal is to maximize value. If a project has a payback of three years, we know how quickly the initial investment will be covered by the expected cash flows, but this information does not provide any indication of whether the return on the project is sufficient to cover the cost of the funds invested. In addition, when payback is used, the cash flows beyond the payback period are ignored. For example, even if Project L had a fifth year of cash flows equal to $50,000, its payback would remain 3.3 years, which is less desirable than the payback of 2.4 years for Project S. But, with the additional $50,000 cash flow, Project L probably would be preferred.

Net Present Value (NPV)

To correct for the fact that payback and other *nondiscounting* techniques ignore the time value of money, methods were developed to include consideration of the time value of money. One such method is the **net present value (NPV) method,** which relies on **discounted cash flow (DCF) techniques.**

NPV is computed using the following equation:

9-2

$$NPV = \widehat{CF}_0 + \frac{\widehat{CF}_1}{(1 + k)^1} + \frac{\widehat{CF}_2}{(1 + k)^2} + \cdots + \frac{\widehat{CF}_n}{(1 + k)^n}$$

$$= \sum_{t=0}^{n} \frac{\widehat{CF}_t}{(1 + k)^t}$$

NET PRESENT VALUE (NPV) METHOD
A method of evaluating capital investment proposals by finding the present value of future net cash flows, discounted at the rate of return required by the firm.

DISCOUNTED CASH FLOW (DCF) TECHNIQUES
Methods of evaluating investment proposals that employ time value of money concepts; two of these are the net present value and internal rate of return methods.

Here $\widehat{CF}_t$ is the expected net cash flow at Period t, and k is the rate of return required by the firm to invest in this project.[1] Cash outflows (expenditures on the project, such as the cost of buying equipment or building factories) are treated as negative cash flows. For our Projects S and L, only $\widehat{CF}_0$ is negative, but for many large projects such as the Alaska Pipeline or an electric generating plant, outflows occur for several years before operations begin and cash flows turn positive.

If you look at Equation 9-2, the rationale for the NPV method is straightforward. An NPV of zero signifies that the project's cash flows are just sufficient to repay the invested capital and to provide the required rate of return on that capital, k. If a project has a positive NPV, then it generates a return that is greater than is needed to pay for the funds provided by investors, and this excess return accrues solely to the firm's stockholders. Therefore, if a firm takes on a project with a positive NPV, the position of the stockholders is improved because the firm's value is greater. In general, then, we can say that *a project is considered acceptable if its NPV is positive; it is not acceptable if its NPV is negative.* If projects with positive NPVs are purchased, the value of the firm will increase; purchasing negative NPV projects will lower the value of the firm. Further, higher NPV projects are better than lower NPV projects. So, if two projects are mutually exclusive, and *both have positive NPVs,* the one with the higher NPV should be chosen.

At a 10 percent required rate of return, Project S's NPV is $161.33:

CASH FLOW TIME LINE FOR PROJECT S:

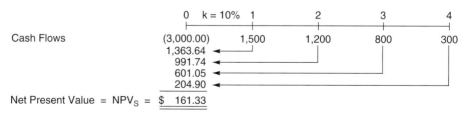

	0	k = 10%	1	2	3	4
Cash Flows	(3,000.00)		1,500	1,200	800	300
	1,363.64					
	991.74					
	601.05					
	204.90					
Net Present Value = NPV$_S$ =	$ 161.33					

---

[1]The rate of return required by the firm is generally termed the firm's cost of capital, because it is the average rate the firm must pay for the funds used to purchase capital projects. The concept of cost of capital is discussed in the next chapter.

By a similar process, we find $NPV_L = \$108.67$. On this basis, both projects should be accepted if they are independent, but S should be the one chosen if they are mutually exclusive.

Note when $NPV > 0$, the project's discounted cash flows (DCF) are greater than its initial investment, $DCF > \widehat{CF}_0$, which indicates the initial investment is recovered on a present value basis prior to the end of the project's life. In fact, if we use the payback concept developed in the previous section, we can compute how long it would take to recapture the initial outlay of $3,000 using the discounted cash flows given in the cash flow time line — the sum of the present values of the cash flows for Project S for the first three years is $2,956.43, so all of the $3,000 cost is not recovered until 3.2 years = 3 years + [($3,000 − $2,956.43) ÷ $204.90] years. Therefore, on a present value basis, it takes 3.2 years for Project S to recover, or pay back, its original cost. This is called the **discounted payback** of Project S — it is the length of time it takes for a project's *discounted* cash flows to repay the cost of the investment. The discounted payback for Project L is 3.9 years, so Project S is more acceptable. Unlike the traditional payback computation discussed in the previous section, the discounted payback computation *does* consider the time value of money. Using the discounted payback method, a project should be accepted when the value of its discounted payback is less than its expected life because, in such instances, $DCF > \widehat{CF}_0$; thus, $NPV > 0$.

It is not hard to calculate the NPV as was done with the time line by using Equation 9-2 and a regular calculator, along with the interest rate tables. However, the most efficient way to find the NPV is with a financial calculator. Different calculators are set up somewhat differently, but they all have a section of memory called the "cash flow register," which is used for uneven cash flows such as those in Projects S and L (as opposed to equal annuity cash flows). A solution process for Equation 9-2 is literally programmed into financial calculators, and all you have to do is enter the cash flows (being sure to observe the signs) in the order they occur, along with the value of $k = I$. At that point you have (in your calculator) this equation for Project S:

$$NPV_S = \frac{-3,000}{(1.10)^0} + \frac{1,500}{(1.10)^1} + \frac{1,200}{(1.10)^2} + \frac{800}{(1.10)^3} + \frac{300}{(1.10)^4}$$

As you can see, the equation has one unknown — NPV. Now all you need to do is to ask the calculator to solve the equation for you, which you do by pressing the NPV key (and, on some calculators, the "compute" key). The answer, 161.33, will appear on the screen.[2]

Internal Rate of Return (IRR)

INTERNAL RATE OF RETURN (IRR)
The discount rate that forces the PV of a project's expected cash flows to equal its cost. IRR is similar to the YTM on a bond.

In Chapter 7, we presented procedures for finding the yield to maturity, or average rate of return, on a bond — if you invest in the bond and hold it to maturity, you can expect to earn the YTM on the money you invested. Exactly the same concepts are employed in capital budgeting when the internal rate of return method is used. The **internal rate of return (IRR)** is the rate of return the firm expects to earn if the project is purchased; thus it is defined as the discount rate that equates the present

DISCOUNTED PAYBACK
The length of time it takes for a project's discounted cash flows to repay the cost of the investment.

---

[2]Refer to the manual that came with your calculator to determine how the CF function is used. The steps for the Texas Instruments BAII PLUS are shown in Appendix 9A.

value of a project's expected cash flows to the investment outlay, or initial cost. As long as the project's IRR is greater than the rate of return *required* by the firm for such an investment, the project is acceptable.

We can use the following equation to solve for a project's IRR:

9-3

$$\widehat{CF}_0 + \frac{\widehat{CF}_1}{(1 + IRR)^1} + \frac{\widehat{CF}_2}{(1 + IRR)^2} + \cdots + \frac{\widehat{CF}_n}{(1 + IRR)^n} = 0$$

$$\sum_{t=0}^{n} \frac{\widehat{CF}_t}{(1 + IRR)^t} = 0$$

For Project S, the cash flow time line for the IRR computation is as follows:

CASH FLOW TIME LINE FOR PROJECT S:

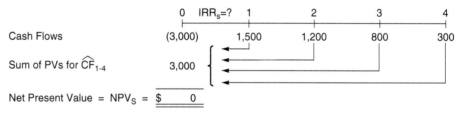

Using Equation 9-3, here is the setup for computing IRR_S:

$$-3,000 + \frac{1,500}{(1 + IRR)^1} + \frac{1,200}{(1 + IRR)^2} + \frac{800}{(1 + IRR)^3} + \frac{300}{(1 + IRR)^4} = 0$$

Although it is easy to find the NPV without a financial calculator, this is *not* true of the IRR. If the cash flows are constant from year to year, then we have an annuity, and we can use annuity factors discussed in Chapter 6 to find the IRR. However, if the cash flows are not constant, as is generally the case in capital budgeting, then it is difficult to find the IRR without a financial calculator. Without a financial calculator, you basically have to solve Equation 9-3 by trial and error — try different discount rates until you the find one that forces the equation to equal zero. The discount rate that causes the equation to equal zero is defined as the IRR. For a realistic project with a fairly long life, the trial and error approach is a tedious, time-consuming task.

Fortunately, it is easy to find IRRs with a financial calculator. You follow almost identical procedures to those used to find the NPV. First, you enter the cash flows as shown on the cash flow time line into the calculator's cash flow register. In effect, you have entered the cash flows into Equation 9-3. Note that we now have one unknown, IRR, or the discount rate that forces the equation to equal zero. The calculator has been programmed to solve for the IRR, and you activate this program by pressing the key labeled "IRR." Here are the IRRs for Projects S and L found using a financial calculator[3]:

---

[3]See Appendix 9A for the steps that should be followed to find the IRR using a Texas Instruments BAII PLUS.

$$IRR_S = 13.1\%$$
$$IRR_L = 11.4\%$$

REQUIRED RATE OF RETURN, OR HURDLE RATE
The discount rate (cost of funds) that the IRR must exceed for a project to be considered acceptable.

Projects that have IRRs greater than their **required rates of return,** *or* **hurdle rates** *are acceptable investments.* If the hurdle rate required by the firm is 10 percent, then both Projects S and L are acceptable. If they are mutually exclusive, Project S is more acceptable than Project L because $IRR_S > IRR_L$.

Why is a project acceptable if its IRR is greater than its required rate of return? Because the IRR on a project is its expected rate of return, if the IRR exceeds the cost of the funds used to finance the project, a surplus remains after paying for the funds — this surplus accrues to the firm's stockholders. Therefore, *taking on a project whose IRR exceeds its required rate of return, or cost of funds, increases shareholders' wealth.* Consider what would happen if you borrowed funds at a 15 percent interest rate to invest in the stock market. The 15 percent interest rate is your *cost of funds,* which is what you must *require* your investments to earn to break even — you lose money if you earn less than 15 percent, and you gain if you earn more than 15 percent. It is this "breakeven" characteristic that makes the IRR useful in evaluating capital projects.

Self-Test Questions

What three methods for evaluating capital budgeting proposals were discussed in this section?

Describe each method, and give the rationale for its use.

Comparison of the NPV and IRR Methods

We found the NPV for Project S is $161.33. This means that if the project is purchased, the value of the firm will increase by $161.33. The IRR for Project S is 13.1 percent. This means that if the firm purchases Project S, it will earn a 13.1 percent rate of return on its investment. We generally measure wealth in dollars, so the NPV method should be used to accomplish the goal of maximizing shareholders' wealth. In reality, using the IRR method could lead to investment decisions that increase, but do not maximize, wealth. We choose to discuss the IRR method and compare it with the NPV method because many corporate executives are familiar with the meaning of IRR, it is entrenched in the corporate world, and it does have some virtues. Therefore, it is important to understand the IRR method and be prepared to explain why, at times, a project with a lower IRR might be preferable to one with a higher IRR.

NET PRESENT VALUE (NPV) PROFILE
A curve showing the relationship between a project's NPV and various discount rates (required rates of return).

NPV Profiles

A graph that shows a project's NPV at various discount rates (required rates of return) is termed the project's **net present value (NPV) profile;** profiles for Projects L and S are shown in Figure 9-3. To construct the profiles, we calculate the projects' NPVs at various discount rates, say, 0, 5, 10, and 15 percent, and plot

FIGURE 9-3

NPV Profiles for Project S and Project L

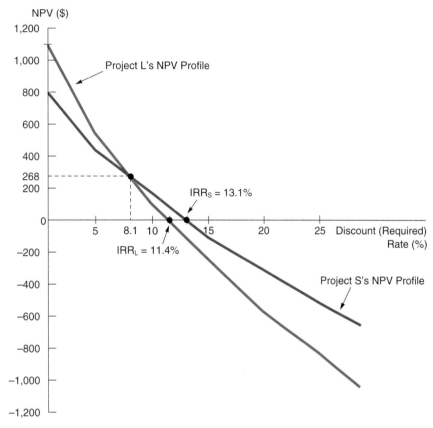

Discount Rate	NPV$_S$	NPV$_L$
0%	$800.00	$1,100.00
5	454.89	554.32
10	161.33	108.67
15	(90.74)	(259.24)
20	(309.03)	(565.97)

these values. The points plotted on our graph for each project are shown at the bottom of Figure 9-3.[4]

Because the IRR is defined as the discount rate at which a project's NPV equals zero, the point where its *NPV profile crosses the X axis indicates a project's internal rate of return.*

[4]Note that the NPV profiles are curved — they are *not* straight lines. Also, the NPVs approach the t = 0 cash flow (the cost of the project) as the discount rate increases without limit. The reason is that, at an infinitely high discount rate, the PV of the inflows would be zero, so NPV at (k = ∞) is $\widehat{CF}_0$, which, in our example, is −$3,000.

NPVs and the Required Rate of Return

Figure 9-3 shows that the NPV profiles of both Projects L and S decline as the discount rate increases. But note that Project L has the higher NPV at low discount rates, while NPV_S exceeds NPV_L if the discount rate is greater than 8.1 percent, which we term the **crossover rate** because, at a discount rate equal to 8.1 percent, $NPV_S = NPV_L = \$268$. If k < 8.1 percent, $NPV_S < NPV_L$, and if k > 8.1 percent, $NPV_S > NPV_L$.[5]

Figure 9-3 indicates that Project L's NPV is "more sensitive" to changes in the discount rate than is NPV_S; that is, Project L's net present value profile has the steeper slope, indicating that a given change in k has a larger effect on NPV_L than on NPV_S. Project L is more sensitive to changes in k because the cash flows from Project S are received faster than those from Project L — in a payback sense, S is a short-term project, while L is a long-term project. As a general rule, the impact of an increase in the discount rate is much greater on distant than on near-term cash flows.[6] Consequently, if a project has most of its cash flows coming in the early years, its NPV will not be lowered very much if the required rate of return increases, but a project whose cash flows come later will be severely penalized by high capital costs.

Independent Projects

Note that the internal rate of return formula, Equation 9-3, is simply the NPV formula, Equation 9-2, solved for the particular discount rate that forces the NPV to equal zero. Thus, the same basic equation is used for both methods. Mathematically, the NPV and IRR methods will always lead to the same accept/reject decisions for independent projects: *If a project's NPV is positive, its IRR will exceed k, while if NPV is negative, k will exceed the IRR.* To see why this is so, look back at Figure 9-3, focus on Project L's profile, and note (1) that the IRR criterion for acceptance is that the required rate of return is less than (or to the left of) the IRR = 11.4% and (2) that whenever the required rate of return is less than IRR = 11.4%, its NPV is positive.

---

[5]The crossover rate is easy to calculate. Simply go back to Figure 9-1, where we first show the two projects' cash flows. Now calculate the difference in the cash flows for Projects S and L in each year. The differences are $\widehat{CF}_S - \widehat{CF}_L = \$0, +\$1,100, +\$300, -\$500$, and $-\$1,200$, respectively. Enter these values into the cash flow register of a financial calculator, press the IRR key, and the crossover rate, 8.1 appears. Be sure to enter $\widehat{CF}_0 = 0$.

[6]To illustrate, consider the present value of $100 to be received in one year versus $100 to be received in ten years. The present values of each $100 discounted at 10 percent and at 15 percent are as follows:

Future Value	Year Received	PV at 10%	PV at 15%	Percent Difference
$100	1	$90.91	$86.96	−4.3%
$100	10	38.55	24.72	−35.9

As you can see, the farther into the future the cash flows are, the greater their sensitivity to discount rate changes.

Mutually Exclusive Projects

Now assume that Projects S and L are mutually exclusive rather than independent — only one project can be accepted. Note in Figure 9-3 that as long as the required rate of return is *greater than* the crossover rate of 8.1 percent, $NPV_S > NPV_L$ and $IRR_S > IRR_L$; so the two capital budgeting techniques lead to the selection of the same project. However, if the required rate of return is less than 8.1 percent, then $NPV_S < NPV_L$ and $IRR_S > IRR_L$, so a conflict exists, because NPV says choose Project L over Project S, while IRR says the opposite. Which answer is correct? Logic suggests that the NPV method is better because it selects the project that adds the most to shareholder wealth.

There are two basic conditions that can cause NPV profiles to cross and thus lead to conflicts between NPV and IRR: (1) when *project size (or scale) differences* exist, meaning that the cost of one project is larger than that of the other, or (2) when *timing differences* exist, meaning that the timing of cash flows from the two projects differs such that most of the cash flows from one project come in the early years and most of the cash flows from the other project come in the later years, as occurs with Projects S and L.[7]

The critical issue in resolving conflicts between mutually exclusive projects is this: How useful is it to generate cash flows earlier rather than later? The value of early cash flows depends on the rate at which we can reinvest these cash flows. *The NPV method implicitly assumes that the rate at which cash flows can be reinvested is the required rate of return, whereas the IRR method implies that the firm has the opportunity to reinvest at the project's IRR.* These assumptions are inherent in the mathematics of the discounting process. But, which is the better assumption — that cash flows can be reinvested at the required rate of return or that they can be reinvested at the project's IRR?

To reinvest at the IRR associated with a capital project, the firm would have to be able to reinvest a project's cash flows in another project with an identical IRR — such projects generally do not exist, or it is not feasible to reinvest in such projects. On the other hand, at the very least, a firm could repurchase the bonds and stock it has issued to raise capital budgeting funds and thus repay some of its investors, which would be the same as investing at its required rate of return. Thus, we conclude that the *more realistic* **reinvestment rate assumption** *is the required rate of return, which is implicit in the NPV method.* This, in turn, leads us to prefer the NPV method.

We should reiterate that, *when projects are independent, the NPV and IRR methods both make exactly the same accept/reject decision.* However, *when evaluating mutually exclusive projects,* especially those that differ in scale and/or timing, *the NPV method should be used.*

REINVESTMENT RATE ASSUMPTION
The assumption that cash flows from a project can be reinvested (1) at the cost of capital, if using the NPV method, or (2) at the internal rate of return, if using the IRR method.

Multiple IRRs

There is one other situation in which the IRR approach might not be usable — when projects have unconventional cash flow patterns. A project has a *conventional*

---

[7]Of course, it is possible for mutually exclusive projects to differ with respect to both scale and timing. Also, if mutually exclusive projects have different lives (as opposed to different cash flow patterns over a common life), this introduces further complications, and for meaningful comparisons, some mutually exclusive projects must be evaluated over a common life.

cash flow pattern if it has cash outflows (costs) in one or more periods at the beginning of its life followed by a series of cash inflows. If, however, a project has a large cash outflow either sometime during or at the end of its life, then it has an *unconventional* cash flow pattern. Projects with unconventional cash flow patterns present unique difficulties when the IRR method is used, including the possibility of **multiple IRRs.**[8]

MULTIPLE IRRS
The situation in which a project has two or more IRRs.

There exists an IRR solution for each time the *direction* of the cash flows is interrupted (i.e., inflow to outflow, and vice versa). For example, a conventional cash flow pattern only has one net cash outflow at the beginning of the project's life that is followed by a series of cash inflows, so the direction of the cash flows changes (is interrupted) once from negative (outflow) to positive (inflow), and there is only one IRR solution. A project with a ten-year life that has cash inflows every year except $\widehat{CF}_0 < 0$ and $\widehat{CF}_5 < 0$ will have two IRR solutions because the cash flow pattern has two direction changes, or interruptions — one after the initial cost is paid and another five years later. Figure 9-4 illustrates the multiple IRR problem with a strip mining project that costs $1.6 million. The mine will produce a cash inflow of $10 million at the end of Year 1, but $10 million must be spent at the end of Year 2 to restore the land to its original condition. Two IRRs

---

FIGURE 9-4

NPV Profile for Project M

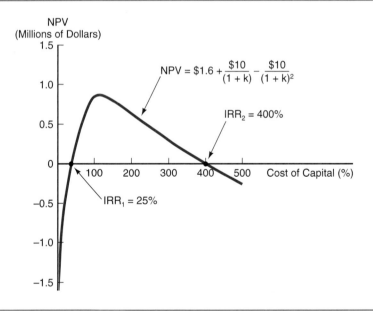

---

[8]Multiple IRRs result from the manner in which Equation 9-3 must be solved to arrive at a project's IRR. The mathematical rationale and the solution to multiple IRRs are not discussed here. Instead, we want you to be aware that multiple IRRs can exist, because this possibility complicates capital budgeting evaluation using the IRR method. In addition, some financial calculators cannot compute the IRR for projects that have unconventional cash flows because there is not a single solution. In such cases, you would have to use NPV profiles, which essentially is a trial-and-error process.

exist for this project — 25 percent and 400 percent. The NPV profile for the mine shows that the project would have a positive NPV, and thus be acceptable, if the firm's required rate of return is between 25 percent and 400 percent.

Self-Test Questions

Describe how NPV profiles are constructed.

What is the crossover rate, and how does it affect the choice between mutually exclusive projects?

Why do the NPV and IRR methods always lead to the same accept/reject decision for independent projects?

What are the two basic conditions that can lead to conflicts between the NPV and IRR methods?

If a conflict exists, should the capital budgeting decision be made on the basis of the NPV or the IRR ranking? Why?

What is the "multiple IRR problem," and what condition is necessary for its occurrence?

Conclusions on the Capital Budgeting Decision Methods

In the previous section, we compared the IRR and NPV methods to highlight their relative strengths and weaknesses, and in the process we probably created the impression that "sophisticated" firms should use only one method in the decision process — NPV. However, virtually all capital budgeting decisions are analyzed by computer, so it is easy to calculate and list all the decision measures described in the preceding sections: payback, discounted payback, NPV, and IRR. In making the accept/reject decision, most large, sophisticated firms calculate and consider multiple measures because each provides decision makers with a somewhat different piece of relevant information.

Payback and discounted payback provide an indication of both the risk and the *liquidity* of a project. A long payback means (1) that the investment dollars will be locked up for many years, hence the project is relatively illiquid, and (2) that the project's cash flows must be forecast far out into the future, which is difficult (as we shall see in the next section), hence the project probably is quite risky.

NPV is important because it gives a direct measure of the dollar benefit (on a present value basis) to the firm's shareholders, so we regard *NPV as the best single measure of profitability*. IRR also measures profitability, but here it is expressed as a percentage rate of return, which many decision makers, especially nonfinancial managers, seem to prefer. Further, IRR contains information concerning a project's "safety margin," which is not inherent in NPV. To illustrate, consider the following two projects: Project T costs $10,000 and is expected to return $16,500 at the end of one year, while Project B costs $100,000 and has an expected payoff of $115,500 after one year. At a 10 percent required rate of return, $NPV_T = NPV_B = \$5,000$. So, by the NPV rule we should be indifferent between the two. However, Project T provides a much larger margin for error, because its actual cash inflow could be nearly 40 percent below the expected amount of $16,500 and the firm would still recover its $10,000 investment. On the other hand, if Project B's inflow was only 14 percent less than expected, the firm would not recover its investment. Further, if no inflows were generated at all, the firm would lose only $10,000 with Project T but $100,000 if it took on Project B.

By comparing the projects' IRRs, we can see that the cash flows of Project T provide a greater "safety margin" than the cash flows of Project B. Project T's IRR is a whopping 65.0 percent, while Project B's IRR is only 15.5 percent. As a result, the realized return could fall substantially for Project T, and it would still make money. Remember, though, that the IRR method has a reinvestment assumption that probably is unrealistic, and it is possible for projects to have multiple IRRs.[9]

In summary, the different methods provide different types of information to decision makers. Because it is easy to calculate them, all should be considered in the decision process. For any specific decision, more weight might be given to one method than another, but it would be foolish to ignore the information provided by any of the methods.

Self-Test Questions

Describe the advantages and disadvantages of the capital budgeting methods discussed in this chapter.

Should capital budgeting decisions be made solely on the basis of a project's NPV?

Cash Flow Estimation

In the first part of the chapter, we described the general techniques used to evaluate capital budgeting projects. In the remainder of the chapter, we examine

---

[9]Both of these problems can be corrected using a modified IRR calculation, which we choose not to discuss here because it is beyond the scope of this chapter. For a discussion of the modified IRR, see Chapter 6 of Eugene F. Brigham, Louis C. Gapenski, and Phillip R. Daves, *Intermediate Financial Management,* 6th ed. (Fort Worth, Tex.: The Dryden Press, 1999). The modified IRR is defined as follows:

$$PV \text{ costs} = PV \text{ terminal value}$$

$$\sum_{t=0}^{n} \frac{COF_t}{(1+k)^t} = \frac{\sum_{t=0}^{n} CIF_t (1+k)^{n-t}}{(1 + MIRR)^n}$$

$$PV \text{ costs} = \frac{TV}{(1 + MIRR)^n}$$

Here COF refers to cash outflows (negative numbers), and CIF refers to cash inflows (all positive numbers). The left term is simply the PV of the investment outlays discounted at the project's required rate of return, and the numerator of the right term is the future value of the inflows, or terminal value, assuming that the cash inflows are reinvested at the project's required rate of return. The discount rate that forces the PV of the TV to equal the PV of the costs is defined as the MIRR.

The modified IRR has a significant advantage over the regular IRR. MIRR assumes that cash flows are reinvested at the required rate of return, while the regular IRR assumes that cash flows are reinvested at the project's own IRR. Because reinvestment at the required rate of return (cost of funds) is generally more correct, the modified IRR is a better indicator of a project's true profitability. MIRR also solves the multiple IRR problem.

some additional issues, including cash flow estimation and incorporating risk into the capital budgeting decision. We begin by discussing cash flow estimation, which is the most important, as well as the most difficult, step in the analysis of a capital project. The process of cash flow estimation is problematic because it is difficult to make accurate forecasts of the costs and revenues associated with large, complex projects or projects that are expected to affect sales and operating costs for long periods of time. Consider, for example, the Alaska Pipeline — original cost estimates were in the neighborhood of $700 million, but the final cost was closer to $7 billion. But, such estimates are required for evaluation of capital budgeting projects, and the individuals responsible for developing reliable estimates of relevant cash flows must use methods they believe are most appropriate. In this section, we give you a sense of some of the inputs involved in the estimation of the cash flows associated with a capital project.

Relevant Cash Flows

Many variables are involved in cash flow estimation, and many individuals and departments participate in the process. For example, the forecasts of unit sales and prices are normally made by the marketing group; the capital outlays associated with a new product are determined by the engineering and product development staffs; and operating costs are estimated by cost accountants, production experts, and so forth. When all the information about a project is collected, financial managers provide estimates of its **cash flows** — the investment outlays and the net cash flows expected after the project is purchased.

CASH FLOWS
The actual cash, as opposed to accounting profits, that a firm receives or pays during some specified period.

Although estimating the cash flows can be rather difficult, two cardinal rules can help financial analysts avoid mistakes: (1) Capital budgeting decisions must be based on *cash flows after taxes,* not accounting income, and (2) only *incremental cash flows are relevant* to the accept/reject decision.

CASH FLOW VERSUS ACCOUNTING INCOME   In capital budgeting analysis, *after-tax cash flows, not accounting profits,* are used — it is cash that pays the bills and can be invested in capital projects, not profits. Cash flows and accounting profits can be very different. To illustrate, consider Table 9-1, which shows how accounting profits and cash flows are related to one another. We assume that Argile Textiles is planning to start a new division at the end of 2000; that sales and all costs, except depreciation, represent actual cash flows and are projected to be constant over time; and that the division will use accelerated depreciation, which will cause its reported depreciation charges to decline over time.[10]

Section I of the table shows the situation in the first year of operations, 2001. Accounting profits are $7 million, but the division's net cash flow — money that is available to Argile — is $22 million. The $7 million profit is the *return on the funds* originally invested, while the $15 million of depreciation is a *return of part*

---

[10]Depreciation procedures are discussed in detail in accounting courses, but we do provide a summary and review in Appendix 9B at the end of this chapter. The tables provided in Appendix 9B are used to calculate depreciation charges used in the chapter examples. In some instances, we simplify the depreciation assumptions in order to reduce the arithmetic. Because Congress changes depreciation procedures fairly frequently, it is always necessary to consult the latest tax regulations before developing actual capital budgeting cash flows.

TABLE 9-1

Accounting Profits versus Net Cash Flow (thousands of dollars)

	Accounting Profits	Cash Flows
I. 2001 Situation		
Sales	$50,000	$50,000
Costs except depreciation	(25,000)	(25,000)
Depreciation	(15,000)	—
Net operating income or cash flow	$10,000	$25,000
Taxes based on operating income (30%)	(3,000)	(3,000)
Net income or net cash flow	$ 7,000	$22,000

Net cash flow = Net income plus depreciation = $7,000 + $15,000 = $22,000

II. 2006 Situation		
Sales	$50,000	$ 50,000
Costs except depreciation	(25,000)	(25,000)
Depreciation	(5,000)	—
Net operating income or cash flow	$20,000	$25,000
Taxes based on operating income (30%)	(6,000)	(6,000)
Net income or net cash flow	$14,000	$19,000

Net cash flow = Net income plus depreciation = $14,000 + $5,000 = $19,000

---

of the funds originally invested, so the $22 million cash flow consists of both a return *on* and a return *of* part of the invested capital.

Section II of the table shows the situation projected for 2006. Here reported profits have doubled because of the decline in depreciation, but net cash flow is down sharply because taxes have doubled. The amount of money received by the firm is represented by the cash flow figure, not the net income figure. And, although accounting profits are important for some purposes, it is cash flows that are relevant for the purposes of setting a value on a project using DCF techniques — cash flows can be reinvested to create value; profits cannot.[11]

INCREMENTAL CASH FLOWS   In evaluating a capital project, we are concerned only with those cash flows that occur as a direct result of accepting the project. To determine if a specific cash flow is considered relevant, we need to find out whether it is affected by the purchase of the project. Cash flows that will change

---

[11]In Table 9-1, we defined net cash flows as net income plus depreciation. Actually, net cash flow should be adjusted to reflect all noncash charges, not just depreciation. However, for most projects, depreciation is by far the largest noncash charge. Also, note that Table 9-1 ignores interest charges, which would be present if the firm used debt. Most firms do use debt and hence finance part of their capital budgets with debt. Therefore, the question has been raised as to whether interest charges should be reflected in capital budgeting cash flow analysis. The consensus is that interest charges should *not* be dealt with explicitly in capital budgeting — rather, the effects of debt financing are reflected in the required rate of return that is used to discount the cash flows. If interest were subtracted, and cash flows were then discounted, we would be double counting the cost of debt.

INCREMENTAL CASH FLOW
The change in a firm's net cash flow attributable to an investment project.

because the project is purchased are **incremental cash flows** that need to be included in the capital budgeting evaluation; cash flows that are not affected by the purchase of the project are not relevant to the capital budgeting decision. Unfortunately, identifying the relevant cash flows for a project is not always as simple as it seems. Some special problems in determining incremental cash flows include the following:

SUNK COST
A cash outlay that already has been incurred and that cannot be recovered regardless of whether the project is accepted or rejected.

1. **Sunk costs.** A **sunk cost** is an outlay that already has been committed or that already has occurred and hence is not affected by the accept/reject decision under consideration, so it should *not* be included in the cash flow analysis. To illustrate, in 1998 Argile Textiles hired a consulting firm to examine the feasibility of building a distribution center in New England. The study, which cost $100,000, was expensed for tax purposes in 1998. This expenditure is *not* a cost that should be included in the capital budgeting evaluation of the prospective distribution center because Argile cannot recover this money, regardless of whether the new distribution center is built.

OPPORTUNITY COST
The return on the best alternative use of an asset; the highest return that will not be earned if funds are invested in a particular project.

2. **Opportunity costs.** Another potential problem relates to **opportunity costs,** defined here as the cash flows that could be generated from assets the firm already owns, provided they are not used for the project in question. For example, Argile already owns a piece of land in New England that is suitable for a distribution center; the land could be sold for $150,000. When evaluating the prospective center, the cost of the land is considered an opportunity cost associated with the project, because use of the site for the distribution center would require forgoing a cash inflow equal to $150,000. Note that the proper land cost in this example is the $150,000 market-determined value, no matter what Argile originally paid for the property.

3. **Externalities: effects on other parts of the firm.** A third potential problem involves the effects of a project on other parts of the firm; economists call these effects **externalities.** For example, Argile has some existing customers in New England who would use the new distribution center because its location would be more convenient than the North Carolina distribution center they currently use. The sales, and hence profits, generated by these customers would not be new to Argile; rather, they would represent a transfer from one distribution center to another. Thus, the net cash flows produced by these customers should not be included in the capital budgeting decision. Although they often are difficult to quantify, externalities such as these should be considered.

EXTERNALITIES
The effect accepting a project will have on the cash flows in other parts (areas) of the firm.

4. **Shipping and installation costs.** When a firm acquires fixed assets, it often must incur substantial costs for shipping and installing the equipment. These charges are important because, for depreciable assets, *the total amount that can be depreciated, termed the depreciable basis, includes the purchase price and any additional expenditures required to make the asset operational, including shipping and installation.* Although *depreciation is a noncash expense* (cash is not needed to pay the depreciation expense each year), it affects the taxable income of a firm; thus, it affects the amount of taxes paid by the firm, which is a cash flow.

5. **Inflation.** Inflation is a fact of life, and it should be recognized in capital budgeting decisions. If expected inflation is not built into the determination of expected cash flows, then the calculated net present value and internal rate of return will be incorrect — both will be artificially low. It is easy to avoid

inflation bias — simply build inflationary expectations into the cash flows used in the capital budgeting analysis. The required rate of return does not have to be adjusted by the firm for inflation expectations because investors include such expectations when establishing the rate at which they are willing to permit the firm to use their funds: Investors decide at what rates a firm can raise funds in the capital markets.

Identifying Incremental (Relevant) Cash Flows

Generally, when we identify the incremental cash flows associated with a capital project, we separate them according to when they occur during the life of the project. In most cases, we can classify a project's incremental cash flows as (1) cash flows that occur *only at the start* of the project's life — time period 0, (2) cash flows that *continue throughout* the project's life — time periods 1 through n, and (3) cash flows that occur *only at the end,* or the termination, of the project — time period n. We discuss these three incremental cash flow classifications and identify some of the relevant cash flows in this section.

INITIAL INVESTMENT OUTLAY
Includes the incremental cash flows associated with a project that will occur only at the start of a project's life, $\widehat{CF}_0$.

INITIAL INVESTMENT OUTLAY   The **initial investment outlay** refers to the incremental cash flows that occur only at the start of a project's life, $\widehat{CF}_0$. The initial investment includes such cash flows as the purchase price of the new project and shipping and installation costs. If the capital budgeting decision is a replacement decision, the initial investment also must take into account the cash flows associated with the disposal of the old, or replaced, asset, which include any cash received or paid to scrap the old asset and any tax effects associated with the disposal. Also, in many cases, the addition or replacement of a capital asset has an impact on the firm's short-term assets and liabilities, which are called the working capital accounts. For example, additional inventories might be required to support a new operation, and increased inventory purchases also lead to additional accounts payable. The difference between the required increase in current assets and the increase in current liabilities is the change in net working capital. If this change is positive, as it generally is for expansion projects, then additional financing, over and above the cost of the project, is needed to fund the increase.[12] Thus, *the change in net working capital that results from the acceptance of a project is an incremental cash flow that must be considered in the capital budgeting analysis.* And, because the change in net working capital requirements occurs at the start of the project's life, this cash flow impact is an incremental cash flow that is included as a part of the initial investment outlay.

INCREMENTAL OPERATING CASH FLOWS
The changes in day-to-day cash flows that result from the purchase of a capital project and continue until the firm disposes of the asset.

INCREMENTAL OPERATING CASH FLOW   Incremental operating cash flows occur throughout the life of the project. Thus, we define **incremental operating cash flows** as the changes in day-to-day cash flows that result from the purchase of a

---

[12]We should note that there are instances in which the change in net working capital associated with a capital project actually results in a decrease in the firm's current funding requirements, which frees up cash flows for investment. Usually this occurs if the project being considered is much more efficient than the existing asset(s).

capital project. The impact of incremental operating cash flows continues until the firm disposes of the asset.

In most cases, the incremental operating cash flows for each year can be computed directly by using the following equation:

9-4

$$\text{Incremental operating cash flow}_t = \Delta\text{Revenue} - \Delta\text{Cash Expenses} - \Delta\text{Taxes}$$

$$= \Delta NI_t + \Delta Depr_t$$

$$= \Delta EBT_t \times (1 - T) + \Delta Depr_t$$

$$= (\Delta S_t - \Delta OC_t - \Delta Depr_t) \times (1 - T) + \Delta Depr_t$$

$$= (\Delta S_t - \Delta OC_t) \times (1 - T) + T(\Delta Depr_t)$$

The symbols in Equation 9-4 are defined as follows:

Δ = the Greek symbol delta, which represents the change in something.

$\Delta NI_t = NI_{t,accept} - NI_{t,reject}$ = the change in net income in period t that results from accepting the capital project. The subscript *accept* is used to indicate the firm's operations that would exist if the project is accepted, and the subscript *reject* indicates the level of operations that would exist if the project is rejected, that is, the existing situation *without* the project.

$\Delta Depr_t = Depr_{t,accept} - Depr_{t,reject}$ = the change in depreciation expense in period t that results from accepting the project.

$\Delta EBT_t = EBT_{t,accept} - EBT_{t,reject}$ = the change in earnings before taxes in period t that results from accepting the project.

$\Delta S_t = S_{t,accept} - S_{t,reject}$ = the change in sales revenues in period t that results from accepting the project.

$\Delta OC_t = OC_{t,accept} - OC_{t,reject}$ = the change in operating costs, excluding depreciation, in period t that results from accepting the project.

T = marginal tax rate.

We emphasized that depreciation is a *noncash* expense. But, the change in depreciation expense needs to be included when computing incremental operating cash flows because, when depreciation changes, taxable income changes, and so does the amount of income taxes paid — the amount of taxes paid is a cash flow.

TERMINAL CASH FLOW
The net cash flow that occurs at the end of the life of a project, including the cash flows associated with (1) the final disposal of the project and (2) returning the firm's operations to where they were before the project was accepted.

TERMINAL CASH FLOW   The **terminal cash flow** occurs at the end of the life of the project, and it is associated with (1) the final disposal of the project and (2) returning the firm's operations to where they were before the project was accepted. Consequently, the terminal cash flow includes the salvage value, which could be either positive (selling the asset) or negative (paying for removal), and the tax impact of the disposition of the project. In addition, we generally assume the firm returns to the operating level that existed prior to the acceptance of the project;

thus, any working capital accounts changes that occurred at the beginning of the project's life will be reversed at the end of its life. For example, as an expansion project's life approaches termination, we assume inventories will be sold off and not replaced; thus the firm will receive an end-of-project cash inflow equal to the net working capital requirement (cash outflow) that occurred when the project was begun.

Self-Test Questions

Briefly explain the difference between accounting income and net cash flow. Which should be used in capital budgeting? Why?

Explain what these terms mean, and assess their relevance in capital budgeting: incremental cash flow, sunk cost, opportunity cost, externality, shipping plus installation costs, and depreciable basis.

How should inflation expectations be included in analysis of capital projects?

Identify the three classifications for the incremental cash flows associated with a project, and give examples of the cash flows that would be in each category.

Why are the changes in net working capital recognized as incremental cash flows both at the beginning and the end of a project's life?

Cash Flow Estimation and the Evaluation Process

In the previous section, we discussed important aspects of cash flow analysis. Now we illustrate the estimation and evaluation of cash flows for expansion projects and for replacement projects.

Expansion Projects

Earlier we defined an *expansion project* as one that calls for the firm to invest in new assets to *increase* sales. Here we illustrate expansion project analysis with a project that is being considered by Household Energy Products (HEP), a Dallas-based technology company. HEP wants to decide whether it should proceed with full-scale production of a computerized home appliance control device its R&D department has developed. The computer device will increase a home's energy efficiency by simultaneously controlling all household appliances, large and small.

The marketing vice president believes that annual sales would be 15,000 units if the selling price is $2,000 each, so annual sales are estimated at $30 million. The engineering department determined the firm would need no additional manufacturing or storage space; it would just need the new machinery required to manufacture the devices. The necessary equipment would be purchased and installed late in 2000 and would cost $9.5 million, not including the $500,000 that would have to be paid for shipping and installation. Although the equipment's estimated economic, or useful, life is four years, it would fall into the MACRS five-year class for the purposes of depreciation (see Appendix 9B). At the end of its useful life, the equipment would have a market value of $2 million and a book value of $1.7 million.

The project would require an initial increase in net working capital equal to $4 million, primarily because the raw materials needed to produce the devices will require more inventory than HEP currently holds. The investment necessary to increase net working capital will be made at the time the equipment is installed. The production department estimated that variable manufacturing costs will total 60 percent of sales, and fixed overhead costs, excluding depreciation, will be $5 million a year. Depreciation expenses will vary from year to year in accordance with the MACRS rates.

HEP's marginal tax rate is 40 percent; its cost of funds, or required rate of return, is 15 percent; and, for capital budgeting purposes, the company's policy is to assume that operating cash flows occur at the end of each year. Because manufacture of the new product would begin on January 1, 2001, the first incremental operating cash flows would occur on December 31, 2001.

ANALYSIS OF THE CASH FLOWS   The first step in the analysis is to summarize the initial investment outlays required for the project; this is done in the 2000 column of Table 9-2. For HEP's appliance control device project, the cash outlays consist of the purchase price of the needed equipment, the cost of shipping and installation, and the required investment in net working capital (NWC). Notice that these cash flows do not carry over in the years 2001 to 2004 — they occur only at the start of the project. Thus, the initial investment outlay is $14 million.

Having estimated the investment requirements, we must now estimate the cash flows that will occur once production begins; these are set forth in the 2001 through 2004 columns of Table 9-2. The operating cash flow estimates are based on information provided by HEP's various departments. The depreciation amounts were obtained by multiplying the depreciable basis (purchase price plus shipping and installation) by the MACRS recovery allowance rates as set forth in the footnote to Table 9-2. As you can see from the values given in the table, the incremental operating cash flow differs each year only because the depreciation expense, and thus the impact depreciation has on taxes, differs each year.

The final cash flow component we need to compute is the terminal cash flow. For this computation, remember the $4 million investment in net working capital will be recovered in 2004. Also, we need an estimate of the net cash flows from the disposal of the equipment in 2004. Table 9-3 shows the calculation of the net salvage value for the equipment. It is expected that the equipment will be sold for more than its book value, which means the company will have to pay taxes on the gain because, in essence, the equipment was depreciated too quickly, allowing HEP to reduce its tax liability by too much from 2001 through 2004. The net cash flow from salvage is simply the sum of the salvage value and the tax impact resulting from the sale of the equipment, $1.88 million in this case. Thus, the terminal cash flow is $5.88 million = $4 million + $1.88 million.

Note that the total net cash flow for 2004 in Table 9-2 is the sum of the incremental cash flow for the year and the terminal cash flow. Thus, in the final year of a project's economic life, the firm incurs two types of cash flows — the final year's

---

TABLE 9-2

HEP Expansion Project Net Cash Flows, 2000–2004 (thousands of dollars)

	2000	2001	2002	2003	2004
I. Initial Investment Outlay					
Cost of new asset	$(9,500)				
Shipping and installation	(500)				
Increase in net working capital	(4,000)				
Initial investment	$(14,000)				
II. Incremental Operating Cash Flow[a]					
Sales revenues		$ 30,000	$ 30,000	$ 30,000	$ 30,000
Variable costs (60% of sales)		(18,000)	(18,000)	(18,000)	(18,000)
Fixed costs		(5,000)	(5,000)	(5,000)	(5,000)
Depreciation on new equipment[b]		(2,000)	(3,200)	(1,900)	(1,200)
Earnings before taxes (EBT)		$ 5,000	$ 3,800	$ 5,100	$ 5,800
Taxes (40%)		(2,000)	(1,520)	(2,040)	(2,320)
Net income		$ 3,000	$ 2,280	$ 3,060	$ 3,480
Add back depreciation		2,000	3,200	1,900	1,200
Incremental operating cash flows		$ 5,000	$ 5,480	$ 4,960	$ 4,680
III. Terminal Cash Flow					
Return of net working capital					4,000
Net salvage value (see Table 9-3)					1,800
Terminal cash flow					$ 5,880
IV. Annual Net Cash Flow					
Total net cash flow each year	$(14,000)	$5,000	$5,480	$4,960	$ 10,560
Net present value (15%)	$ 3,790				

---

[a]Using Equation 9-4, the incremental operating cash flows can be computed as follows:

Year	Incremental Operating Cash Flow Computation
2001	$5,000 = ($30,000 − $18,000 − $5,000) (1 − 0.40) + $2,000)0.40)
2002	5,480 = (30,000 − 18,000 − 5,000) (1 − 0.40) + 3,200(0.40)
2003	4,960 = (30,000 − 18,000 − 5,000) (1 − 0.40) + 1,900(0.40)
2004	4,600 = (30,000 − 18,000 − 5,000) (1 − 0.40) + 1,200(0.40)

[b]Depreciation for new equipment was calculated using MACRS (see Appendix 9B):

Year	2001	2002	2003	2004
Percent depreciated	20%	32%	19%	12%

These percentages were multiplied by the depreciable basis of $10,000 to get the depreciation expense each year.

incremental operating cash flow and the terminal cash flow associated with the disposal of the project. For the appliance control device project HEP is considering, the total expected net cash flow in 2004 is $10.56 million.

MAKING THE DECISION   A summary of the data and the computation of the project's NPV are provided with the cash flow time line below. The amounts are in thousands of dollars, just like in Table 9-2.

TABLE 9-3

HEP Expansion Project Net Salvage Value, 2004 (thousands of dollars)

I. Book Value of HEP's Project in 2004	
Cost of new asset in 2000	$ 9,500
Shipping and installation	500
Depreciable basis of asset	$10,000
Depreciation from 2001–2004 = (0.20 + 0.32 + 0.19 + 0.12) × $10,000	(8,300)
Book value in 2004	$ 1,700
II. Tax Impact of the Sale of HEP's Project in 2004	
Selling price of asset in 2004	$2,000
Book value of asset in 2004	(1,700)
Gain (loss) on sale of asset	$ 300
Taxes (40%)	$ 120
III. Net Salvage Value, CF, in 2004	
Cash flow from sale of project	$2,000
Tax impact of sale	(120)
Net salvage value cash flow	$1,880

CASH FLOW TIME LINE FOR HEP'S APPLIANCE CONTROL DEVICE PROJECT:

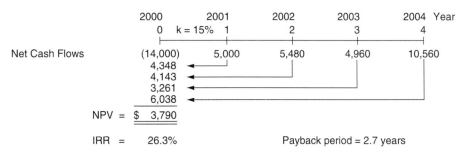

The project appears to be acceptable using the NPV and IRR methods, and it also would be acceptable if HEP required a payback period of three years. Note, however, that the analysis thus far has been based on the assumption that the project has the same degree of risk as the company's average project. If the project was judged to be riskier than an average project, it would be necessary to increase the required rate of return used to compute the NPV. Later in this chapter, we extend the evaluation of this project to include a risk analysis.

Replacement Analysis

All companies make decisions about replacing existing assets. The analysis relating to replacements is the same as for expansion projects, except, to some extent, identifying the incremental cash flows associated with a replacement project is more complicated than for an expansion project, because the *cash flows both from the new asset and from the old asset must be considered.* We illustrate replacement analysis with another HEP example.

A lathe for trimming molded plastics was purchased ten years ago at a cost of $7,500. The machine had an expected life of 15 years at the time it was purchased, and management originally estimated, and still believes, that the salvage value will be zero (five years from now). The machine is being depreciated on a straight line basis; therefore, its annual depreciation charge is $7,500/15 = $500, and its book value currently is $7,500 − 10($500) = $2,500.

HEP is considering the purchase of a new special-purpose machine to replace the lathe. The new machine, which can be purchased for $12,000 (including freight and installation), will reduce labor and raw materials usage sufficiently to cut operating costs from $7,500 to $4,000, so before-tax profits will increase by $3,500 per year. It is estimated that the new machine will have a useful life of five years, after which it will be sold for $2,000. By an IRS ruling, the new machine falls into the three-year MACRS class. The current market value of the old machine is $1,000, which is below its $2,500 book value. Net working capital requirements will increase by $1,000 if the lathe is replaced by the new machine; this increase will occur at the time of replacement. And, because the risk associated with the new machine is considered average for HEP, the project's required rate of return is 15 percent. Should the replacement be made?

Table 9-4 shows the worksheet format HEP uses to analyze replacement projects. To determine the relevant cash flows for a replacement decision, we need to consider the fact that *the cash flows associated with the new asset will take the place of the cash flows associated with the old asset.* Therefore, we must compute the increase or decrease in cash flows that results from the replacement of the old asset with the new asset. Table 9-4 shows the results of our computations.

ANALYSIS OF THE CASH FLOWS   First, the initial investment outlay of $11,400 includes the cash flows associated with the cost of the new asset and the change in net working capital, which is also included in the initial investment computation for the expansion decision shown in Table 9-2. But, with a replacement decision, because the asset being replaced is removed from operations, the cash flows associated with the disposal of the old asset must be considered when computing the initial investment outlay. In our example, the old asset has a book value equal to $2,500, but it can be sold for only $1,000. So HEP will incur a capital loss equal to − $1,500 = $1,000 − $2,500 if the lathe is replaced with the new machine. This loss will result in a tax savings equal to (Loss) × (T) = ($1,500)(0.4) = $600 to account for the fact that HEP did not adequately depreciate the old asset to reflect its market value. Consequently, the disposal of the old asset will generate a positive cash flow equal to $1,600 — the $1,000 selling price plus the $600 tax savings, which effectively reduces the amount of cash required to purchase the new machine and thus the initial investment outlay.[13]

Next, we need to compute the incremental operating cash flow each year. Section II of Table 9-4 shows these computations. The procedure is the same as before: Determine how operating cash flows will change if the new machine is purchased to replace the lathe. Remember, the lathe is expected to increase oper-

---

[13]If you think about it, the computation of the initial investment outlay for replacement decisions is similar to determining the amount you would need to purchase a new automobile to replace your old one — if the purchase price of the new car is $15,000 and the dealer is willing to give you $5,000 for your car as a trade-in, then the amount you need is only $10,000; but, if you need to pay someone to take your old car out of the garage because that is where you are going to keep the new car at night, then the total amount you need to purchase the new car actually is greater than $15,000.

TABLE 9-4

HEP Replacement Project Net Cash Flows, 2000–2005

	2000	2001	2002	2003	2004	2005
I. Initial Investment Outlay						
Cost of new asset	$(12,000)					
Change in net working capital	(1,000)					
Net cash flow from sale of old asset[a]	1,600					
Initial investment	$(11,400)					
II. Incremental Operating Cash Flows						
Δ Operating costs		$ 3,500	$ 3,500	$ 3,500	$ 3,500	$ 3,500
Δ Depreciation[b]		(3,460)	(4,900)	(1,300)	(340)	500
Δ Earnings before taxes (EBT)		40	(1,400)	2,200	3,160	4,000
Δ Taxes (40%)		(16)	560	(880)	(1,264)	(1,600)
Δ Net income		24	(840)	1,320	1,896	2,400
Add back Δ depreciation		3,460	4,900	1,300	340	(500)
Incremental operating cash flows		$ 3,484	$ 4,060	$ 2,620	$ 2,236	$ 1,900
III. Terminal Cash Flow						
Return of net working capital						$ 1,000
Net salvage value of new asset[c]						1,200
Terminal cash flow						$ 2,200
IV. Annual Net Cash Flows						
Total net cash flow each year	$(11,400)	$ 3,484	$ 4,060	$ 2,620	$ 2,236	$ 4,100
Net present value (15%)	$ (261)					

NOTES:

[a]The net cash flow from the sale of the old (replaced) asset is computed as follows:

Selling price (market value)	$ 1,000
Subtract book value	(2,500)
Gain (loss) on sale of asset	(1,500)
Tax impact of sale of asset	600
Net cash flow from the sale of asset = $1,000 + $600 = $1,600	

[b]The change in depreciation expense is computed by comparing the depreciation of the new asset with the depreciation that would have existed if the old asset was *not* replaced. The old asset has been depreciated on a straight-line basis, with five years of $500 depreciation remaining. The new asset will be depreciated using the rates for the three-year MACRS class (see Appendix 9B). So the change in annual depreciation would be as follows:

Year	New Asset Depreciation		Old Asset Depreciation		Change in Depreciation
2001	$12,000 × 0.33 = $ 3,960	–	$500	=	$3,460
2002	12,000 × 0.45 = 5,400	–	500	=	4,900
2003	12,000 × 0.15 = 1,800	–	500	=	1,300
2004	12,000 × 0.07 = 840	–	500	=	340
2005	= 0	–	500	=	(500)
	Accumulated depreciation = $12,000				

[c]The book value of the new asset in 2005 will be zero, because the entire $12,000 has been written off. So the net salvage value of the new asset in 2005 is computed as follows:

Selling price (market value)	$2,000
Subtract book value	(0)
Gain (loss) on sale of asset	2,000
Tax impact of sale of asset	(800)
Net salvage value of the new asset = $2,000 – $800 = $1,200	

ating profits by $3,500; thus less cash will have to be spent to operate the new machine. Had the replacement also resulted in a change in sales or the annual savings been expected to change over time, these facts would have to be built into the analysis.

The change in depreciation expense must be computed to determine the impact such a change will have on the taxes paid by the firm. If the new machine is purchased, the $500 depreciation expense of the lathe (old asset) will no longer be relevant for tax purposes; instead, the depreciation expense for the new machine will be used. For example, according to the percentages given in Appendix 9B for an asset in the three-year MACRS class, the depreciation expense for the new machine will be $3,960 in 2001. Therefore, the existing $500 depreciation from the *old* lathe will be replaced by the *new* machine's depreciation expense of $3,960, and depreciation will increase by $3,460 = $3,960 − $500. The computations for the remaining years are completed similarly. Note, in 2005 the change in depreciation is negative because the new machine will be fully depreciated at the end of 2004, so there is nothing left to write off in 2005 — the $500 depreciation from the old machine is replaced with the new machine's depreciation of $0, which is a change of −$500.

The terminal cash flow includes $1,000 for the return of the original net working capital investment and the net salvage value of the new machine, which is $1,200. It is expected that the new machine can be sold in 2005 for $2,000, but $800 in taxes will have to be paid on the sale because the new machine will be fully depreciated by the time of the sale.[14] Thus, the terminal cash flow equals $2,200 = $1,000 + $1,200.

Making the Decision

A summary of the data and the computation of the project's NPV are provided with the following cash flow time line:

CASH FLOW TIME LINE FOR HEP'S REPLACEMENT PROJECT:

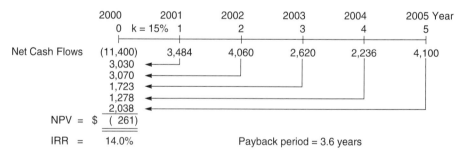

According to the NPV and IRR methods, HEP should *not* replace the lathe with the new machine.

---

[14]In this analysis, the salvage value of the old machine is zero. However, if the old machine was expected to have a positive salvage value at the end of five years, replacing the old machine now would eliminate this cash flow. Thus, the after-tax salvage value of the old machine would represent an opportunity cost to the firm, and it would be included as a Year 5 cash outflow in the terminal cash flow section of the worksheet.

Before we leave our discussion of replacement decisions, we should note that a replacement decision involves comparing two mutually exclusive projects: retaining the old asset versus buying a new one. To simplify matters, in our replacement example we assumed that the new machine had a life equal to the remaining life of the old machine. If, however, we were choosing between two mutually exclusive alternatives with significantly different lives, an adjustment would be necessary to make the results of the capital budgeting analysis for the two projects comparable. To attain comparability, we can either (1) use a common life for the evaluation of the two projects or (2) compute the annual annuity that could be produced from the dollar amount of the NPV of each project. Both these procedures are described in Appendix 9C. We mention the unequal life problem here to make you aware that the evaluation of mutually exclusive projects with significantly different lives requires a slightly different analysis to ensure a correct decision.

Self-Test Question

Explain and differentiate between the capital budgeting analyses required for expansion projects and for replacement projects.

Incorporating Risk in Capital Budgeting Analysis

STAND-ALONE RISK
The risk an asset would have if it were a firm's only asset; measured by the variability of the asset's expected returns.

CORPORATE (WITHIN-FIRM) RISK
Risk not considering the effects of stockholders' diversification; measured by a project's effect on the firm's earnings variability.

BETA (MARKET) RISK
That part of a project's risk that cannot be eliminated by diversification; measured by the project's beta coefficient.

To this point, we assumed the capital budgeting projects being evaluated have the same risk as the projects the firm currently possesses, because such projects can be evaluated using the firm's average required rate of return. However, there are three types of project risk that need to be examined to determine if the required rate of return used to evaluate a project should be different than the average required rate of the firm. The three risks are (1) the project's own **stand-alone risk,** or the risk it exhibits when evaluated alone rather than as part of a combination, or portfolio, of assets; (2) **corporate,** or **within-firm, risk,** which is the effect a project has on the total (overall) riskiness of the company; and (3) **beta,** or **market, risk,** which is project risk assessed from the standpoint of a stockholder who holds a well-diversified portfolio.

Evaluating the risk associated with a capital budgeting project is similar to evaluating the risk of a financial asset such as a stock. Therefore, much of our discussion in this section relies on the concepts introduced in Chapter 8. As we discovered in Chapter 8, an asset might have high stand-alone risk, often measured by σ, yet taking it on might not have much effect on the overall risk of a combination of assets because of portfolio, or diversification, effects.

To examine the three risks associated with capital budgeting projects, we will again refer to Household Energy Products' appliance control computer project. When we first introduced the HEP project, we suggested that the cash flows given in Table 9-2 were easily estimated. But, in reality, the individual cash flows associated with the project might be subject to great uncertainty.

Stand-Alone Risk

When we compute a project's NPV, we use cash flows that are forecasted by management. Unless management has perfect knowledge, the estimation of the cash flows included in capital budgeting analysis — for example, unit sales — employs expected values taken from probability distributions that define the outcomes management considers viable. We know that probability distributions could be relatively "tight," reflecting small standard deviations and low risk, or they could be "flat," denoting a great deal of uncertainty, or high risk. Thus, the nature of the individual cash flow distributions determines a project's stand-alone risk.

Techniques for assessing a project's stand-alone risk include (1) sensitivity analysis, (2) scenario analysis, and (3) Monte Carlo simulation.

SENSITIVITY ANALYSIS   **Sensitivity analysis** is a technique that shows exactly how much the NPV will change in response to a given change in an input variable, other things held constant. In a sensitivity analysis, each variable is changed by specific percentage points above and below the value originally estimated, holding other things constant; then a new NPV is calculated for each new value; and, finally, the set of NPVs is plotted against the variable that was changed. Figure 9-5 shows sensitivity graphs for three of the key input variables required to evaluate HEP's appliance control project. The table below the graphs gives the NPVs that were used to construct the graphs. The slopes of the lines in the graphs show how sensitive NPV is to changes in each of the inputs: *the steeper the slope, the more sensitive the NPV is to a change in the variable.* In the figure we see that the project's NPV is very sensitive to changes in variable costs, less sensitive to changes in unit sales, and not very sensitive to changes in the required rate of

> **SENSITIVITY ANALYSIS**
> A risk analysis technique in which key variables are changed and the resulting changes in the NPV and the IRR are observed.

FIGURE 9-5

Sensitivity Analysis (thousands of dollars)

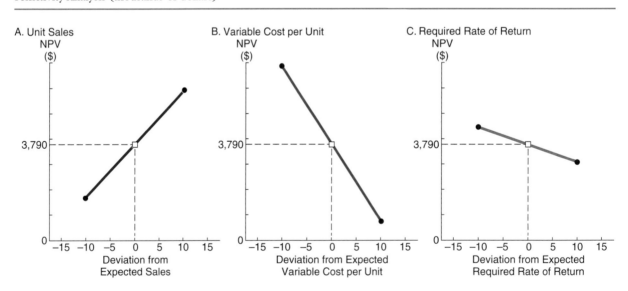

Deviation from Base Level (%)	Net Present Value		
	Units Sold	**Variable Cost/Unit**	**Required Rate of Return**
−10	$1,735	$6,874	$4,415
0 (base case)	3,790	3,790	3,790
+10	5,846	707	3,199

SCENARIO ANALYSIS
A risk analysis technique in which "bad" and "good" sets of financial circumstances are compared with a most likely, or base-case, situation.

WORST-CASE SCENARIO
An analysis in which all of the input variables are set at their worst reasonably forecasted values.

BEST-CASE SCENARIO
An analysis in which all of the input variables are set at their best reasonably forecasted values.

BASE CASE
An analysis in which all of the input variables are set at their most likely values.

MONTE CARLO SIMULATION
A risk analysis technique in which probable future events are simulated on a computer, generating estimated rates of return and risk indexes.

return.[15] So, when estimating these variables' values, HEP's management should take extra care to ensure the accuracy of the forecast for variable costs per unit.

SCENARIO ANALYSIS   **Scenario analysis** is a risk analysis technique that considers not only the sensitivity of NPV to changes in key variables but also the likely range of variable values. In a scenario analysis, the financial analyst asks operating managers to pick a "bad" set of circumstances (low unit sales, low sales price, high costs, and so on) and a "good" set. The NPVs under the bad and good conditions are then calculated and compared to the expected, or base-case, NPV. For example, HEP's managers are fairly confident of their estimates of all the project's cash flow variables except price and unit sales, but they believe the likely range for sales is from 10,000 units to 20,000 units, and the sales price will fall within the range of $1,500 to $2,500. Thus, 10,000 units at a price of $1,500 defines the lower bound, or the **worst-case scenario,** whereas 20,000 units at a price of $2,500 defines the upper bound, or the **best-case scenario.** Remember that the **base-case** values are 15,000 units selling for $2,000 each. Table 9-5 shows the NPVs for each scenario associated with the HEP project.[16]

We can use the results of the scenario analysis to determine the expected NPV, the standard deviation of NPV, and the coefficient of variation (CV). Table 9-5 shows the results of these computations, assuming there is a 20 percent probability of the worst-case scenario occurring, a 60 percent probability of the base case, and a 20 percent probability of the best case. The expected NPV is $4.475 million, and the coefficient of variation is 1.7.[17] The project's coefficient of variation can be compared with HEP's "average" CV to get an idea of the relative riskiness of the appliance control computer project. If HEP's "average" CV is about 1.0, on the basis of this stand-alone risk measure, the appliance control project would be considered riskier than the firm's "average" project.

MONTE CARLO SIMULATION   Scenario analysis provides useful information about a project's stand-alone risk. However, it is limited in that it only considers a few discrete outcomes (NPVs) for the project, even though there really are many more possibilities. **Monte Carlo simulation,** so named because this type of analysis grew out of work on the mathematics of casino gambling, ties together sensitivities and input variable probability distributions.

---

[15]We should note that spreadsheet computer models, such as *Lotus 1-2-3* and *Excel,* are ideally suited for performing sensitivity analysis. We used a *Lotus 1-2-3* model to conduct the analyses represented in Figure 9-5; it generated the NPVs and then drew the graphs. Also, we could have plotted all of the sensitivity lines on one graph; this would have facilitated direct comparisons of the sensitivities among different input variables.

[16]We could have included worst- and best-case values for fixed and variable costs, income tax rates, salvage values, and so on. For illustrative purposes, we limited the changes to only two variables. Also, note that we are treating sales price and quantity as independent variables; that is, a low sales price could occur when unit sales were low, and a high sales price could be coupled with high unit sales, or vice versa. As we discuss in the next section, it is relatively easy to vary these assumptions if the facts of the situation suggest a different set of conditions.

[17]Note that the expected NPV is *not* the same as the base case NPV, $3,790 (in thousands). This is because the two uncertain variables, sales volume and sales price, are multiplied together to obtain dollar sales, and this process causes the NPV distribution to be skewed to the right. A big number times another big number produces a very big number, which, in turn, causes the average, or expected value, to be increased.

TABLE 9-5

Scenario Analysis (dollars, except sales price, in thousands)

Scenario	Sales Volume (Units)	Sales Price	NPV	Probability of Outcome (Pr_i)	NPV × Pr_i
Best case	20,000	$2,500	$17,494	0.20	$3,499
Most likely case	15,000	2,000	3,790	0.60	2,274
Worst case	10,000	1,500	(6,487)	0.20	(1,297)
				1.00 Expected NPV =	$ 4,475
				σ_{NPV} =	$ 7,630
				CV_{NPV} =	1.7

$$\text{Expected NPV} = \sum_{i=1}^{n} Pr_i \, (NPV_i) = 0.20(\$17,494) + 0.60(\$3,790) + 0.20(-\$6,487) = \$4,475$$

$$\sigma_{NPV} = \sqrt{\sum_{i=1}^{n} Pr_i \, (NPV_i - \text{Expected NPV})^2}$$

$$= \sqrt{0.20(\$17,494 - \$4,475)^2 + 0.60(\$3,790 - \$4,475)^2 + 0.20\,(-\$6,487 - \$4,475)^2} = \$7,630$$

$$CV_{NPV} = \frac{\sigma_{NPV}}{\text{Expected NPV}} = \frac{\$7,630}{\$4,475} = 1.7$$

Simulation is more complicated than scenario analysis because the probability distribution of each uncertain cash flow variable has to be specified. Once this has been done, a value from the probability distribution for each variable is randomly chosen to compute the project's cash flows, and then the selected values are used to determine the project's NPV. Using a computer, this process is repeated again and again, say, 500 times, resulting in 500 NPVs, which make up a probability distribution for the NPVs. Thus, the output produced by simulation is a probability distribution that can be used to determine the most likely range of outcomes to be expected from a project. This provides the decision maker with a better idea of the various outcomes that are possible than is available from a point estimate of the NPV.

Unfortunately, Monte Carlo simulation is not easy to apply, because it is often difficult to specify the correlations among the uncertain cash flow variables. The problem is not insurmountable, but it is important not to underestimate the difficulty of obtaining valid estimates of probability distributions and correlations among the variables.

Corporate (Within-Firm) Risk

To measure corporate, or within-firm, risk, we need to determine how the capital budgeting project is related to the firm's existing assets. Remember from our discussion in Chapter 8 that two assets can be combined to reduce risk if their payoffs move in opposite directions — when the payoff from one asset falls, the payoff from the other asset rises. In reality, it is not easy to find assets with payoffs that move opposite each other. But, as we discovered in Chapter 8, as long as assets are *not* perfectly positively related (r = +1.0), some diversification, or risk reduction, can still be achieved. Many firms use this principle to reduce the risk associated with their operations — adding new projects that are not highly related to existing assets can help reduce corporate risk.

Corporate risk is important because the firm's stability is important to its managers, workers, customers, suppliers, and creditors, as well as to the community in which it operates and to undiversified stockholders. Firms that are in serious danger of bankruptcy, or even of suffering low profits and reduced output, have difficulty attracting and retaining good managers and workers, both suppliers and customers are reluctant to depend on weak firms, and such firms have difficulty borrowing money at reasonable interest rates. These factors tend to reduce risky firms' profitability and hence the prices of their stocks, and, thus, they also make corporate risk significant.

Beta (or Market) Risk

In Chapter 8 we developed the concept of beta, β, as a risk measure for individual stocks. From our discussion, we concluded that systematic risk is the relevant risk of a stock because unsystematic, or firm-specific, risk can be reduced significantly or eliminated through diversification. This same concept can be applied to capital budgeting projects because the firm can be thought of as a composite of all the projects it has undertaken. Thus, the relevant risk of a project can be viewed as the impact it has on the firm's systematic risk. This line of reasoning leads to the conclusion that if the beta coefficient for a project, β_{proj}, can be determined, then the **project required rate of return, k_{proj},** can be found using the following form of the CAPM equation:

$$k_{proj} = k_{RF} + (k_M - k_{RF})\beta_{proj}$$

PROJECT REQUIRED RATE OF RETURN, k_{proj}
The risk-adjusted required rate of return for an individual project.

To apply the CAPM to HEP's appliance control project, let's assume the company is financed only with equity, so the average required rate of return it needs to earn on capital budgeting projects is based solely on the average return demanded by stockholders (i.e., there is no debt that might require a different return). HEP's existing beta = β_{HEP} = 1.2, k_{RF} = 6%, and k_M = 13.5%. Thus, HEP's cost of equity is 15% = k_S = 6% + (13.5% − 6%)1.2, which suggests that investors should be willing to give HEP money to invest in average-risk projects if the company expects to earn 15 percent or more on this money.[18]

Suppose, however, the appliance control project (ACP) has a beta greater than HEP's average beta of 1.2, say, β_{ACP} = 1.7. Because the firm itself can be regarded as a "portfolio of assets," just like the beta of any portfolio, HEP's beta is a weighted average of the betas of its individual assets. If the project is accepted, 80 percent of HEP's total funds will be invested in its basic operations and 20 percent in operations associated with the appliance control project. Thus, accepting the project will increase HEP's beta to 1.3 = 0.8(1.2) + 0.2(1.7). This beta increase will cause its stock price to decline unless HEP earns at least a 15.75 percent

---

[18]To simplify things somewhat, we assume at this point that the firm uses only equity capital. If debt is used, the cost of capital used must be a weighted average of the costs of debt and equity. This point is discussed at length in Chapter 10.

return, because $k_{HEP\text{-}new}$ = 6% + (7.5%)1.3 = 15.75%. This higher *average* rate can be earned only if the new project generates a return substantially higher than the existing assets are providing. Of course, the opposite would be true if the project's β was lower than 1.2 (HEP's average).

With a β of 1.7, the new appliance control project should be evaluated at an 18.75 percent required rate of return:

$$k_{ACP} = 6\% + (7.5\%)1.7 = 18.75\%$$

Remember that the IRR for the appliance control device is 26.3 percent; so the project is acceptable, even if the appropriate required return is 18.75 percent.

The major problem with evaluating beta risk is that it is very difficult to measure betas for capital budgeting projects. One way a firm can try to measure the beta risk of a project is to find single-product companies in the same line of business as the project being evaluated and then use the betas of those companies to determine the required rate of return for the project being evaluated. This technique is termed the **pure play method,** and the single-product companies that are used for comparisons are called *pure play firms.* Generally, this method can only be used for major projects such as whole divisions, and even then it is frequently difficult to implement because pure play proxy firms are scarce. Can you think of any? Would you consider Apple Computers to be a pure play proxy firm for personal computers?

PURE PLAY METHOD
An approach used for estimating the beta of a project in which a firm identifies companies whose only business is the product in question, determines the beta for each firm, and then averages the betas to find an approximation of its own project's beta.

Self-Test Questions

What are the three types of project risk?

How would you measure a project's (1) stand-alone risk, (2) corporate risk, and (3) beta risk?

Differentiate between sensitivity and scenario analyses. Why might scenario analysis be preferable to sensitivity analysis?

What is Monte Carlo simulation?

What is meant by the term "average-risk project"? How could you find the required rate of return for projects with average risk, low risk, and high risk?

Complete the following sentence: "An increase in a company's beta coefficient would cause its stock price to decline unless . . ."

How Project Risk Is Considered in Capital Budgeting Decisions

RISK-ADJUSTED DISCOUNT RATE
The discount rate (required rate of return) that applies to a particular risky stream of income; it is equal to the risk-free rate of interest plus a risk premium appropriate to the level of risk attached to a particular project's income stream.

Thus far, we have seen that purchasing a capital project can affect a firm's beta risk, its corporate risk, or both. We also have seen that it is difficult to quantify either type of risk because it is difficult to develop a specific *measure* of project risk. But, it can be argued that it is possible to evaluate whether one project is riskier than another in a general sense.

In reality, most firms incorporate project risk in capital budgeting decisions using the **risk-adjusted discount rate** approach. With this approach, the required rate of return used to find a project's NPV is adjusted if its risk is substantially different from the firm's average risk. Therefore, average-risk projects would require an "average" rate of return; above-average-risk projects would

---

TABLE 9-6

Capital Budgeting Decisions Using Risk-Adjusted Discount Rates*

Project	Project Risk	Required Return	Estimated Life	Initial Investment Outlay, $\widehat{CF_0}$	Incremental Operating Cash Flows, $\widehat{CF_1}$–$\widehat{CF_5}$	NPV	IRR
A	Low	12%	5	$(10,000)	$2,850	$273.61	13.1%
B	Average	15	5	(11,000)	3,210	(239.58)	14.1
C	Average	15	5	(9,000)	2,750	218.43	16.0
D	High	20	5	(12,000)	3,825	(560.91)	17.9

*Note: The following classifications and rates of return apply to this table:

Project Risk Classification	Required Rate of Return
Low	12%
Average	15
High	20

require a higher-than-average rate; and below-average-risk projects would require a lower-than-average rate. Unfortunately, because risk cannot be measured precisely, there is no accurate way of specifying exactly how much higher or lower these required rates should be; thus, *risk adjustments are necessarily judgmental and somewhat arbitrary.*

Although the process is not exact, many companies use a two-step procedure to develop risk-adjusted discount rates for use in capital budgeting. First, the overall required rate of return is established for the firm's existing assets. This process is completed on a division-by-division basis for very large firms, perhaps using the CAPM. Second, all projects are generally classified into three categories — high risk, average risk, and low risk. Then, the firm or division uses the average required rate of return to evaluate average-risk projects, reduces the average rate by one or two percentage points when evaluating low-risk projects, and raises the average rate by several percentage points for high-risk projects. For example, HEP estimated its average required rate of return to be 15 percent, and it decided a 20 percent discount rate should be used for high-risk projects and a 12 percent rate for low-risk projects.

Table 9-6 contains an example of the application of risk-adjusted discount rates for the evaluation of four projects. Each of the four projects has a five-year life, and each is expected to generate a constant cash flow stream during its life. The analysis shows that only Projects A and C are acceptable when risk is considered. But, when the average required rate of return is used to evaluate all the projects, Projects C and D would be considered acceptable because their IRRs are greater than 15 percent. Thus, *if project risk is not considered in capital budgeting analysis, incorrect decisions are possible.*

This risk-adjusted discount rate approach is far from precise, but it recognizes that different projects have different risks, and projects with different risks should be evaluated using different required rates of return.

Self-Test Questions

How are risk-adjusted discount rates used to incorporate project risk into the capital budgeting decision process?

Briefly explain the two-step process many companies use to develop risk-adjusted discount rates for use in capital budgeting.

Capital Rationing

CAPITAL RATIONING
A situation in which a constraint is placed on the total size of the firm's capital investment.

Capital budgeting decisions are typically made on the basis of the techniques presented in this chapter: Independent projects are accepted if their NPVs are positive, and choices among mutually exclusive projects are made by selecting the one with the highest NPV. In this analysis, it is assumed that if in a particular year the firm has an especially large number of good projects, management simply will go into the financial markets and raise whatever funds are required to finance all of the acceptable projects. However, some firms do set limits on the amount of funds they are willing to raise, and, if this is done, the capital budget must also be limited. This situation is known as **capital rationing.**

Elaborate and mathematically sophisticated models have been developed to help firms maximize their values when they are subject to capital rationing. However, a firm that subjects itself to capital rationing is deliberately forgoing *profitable* projects, and hence it is not truly maximizing its value. This point is well known, so few sophisticated firms ration capital today. Therefore, we shall not discuss it further, but you should know what the term *capital rationing* means.

Self-Test Questions

What is meant by the term *capital rationing*?

Why do few sophisticated firms ration capital today?

The Post-Audit

POST-AUDIT
A comparison of the actual and expected results for a given capital project.

Because capital budgeting decisions involve large investments for long periods, it is important that the firm conducts a post-audit for each project that is accepted. The **post-audit** involves (1) comparing actual results with those predicted by the project's sponsors and (2) explaining why any differences occurred. Post-audits can help the firm improve both the forecasts and the efficiency of operations associated with a project by making those involved in the capital budgeting decision-making process accountable for their actions.

Self-Test Question

Why is it important to conduct a post-audit?

Multinational Capital Budgeting

Although the basic principles of capital budgeting analysis are the same for both domestic and foreign operations, some key differences need to be mentioned. First, cash flow estimation is generally much more complex for overseas investments. Most multinational firms set up a separate subsidiary in each foreign country in which they operate, and the relevant cash flows for these subsidiaries are the dividends and royalties returned to the parent company. Moving funds from a foreign subsidiary to the parent company is called **repatriation of earnings.** Second, these cash flows must be converted into the currency of the parent company, and thus are subject to future exchange rate changes. For example, General Motors' German subsidiary might make a profit of 150 million deutsche marks in 2000, but the value of these profits to GM will depend on the dollar/mark exchange rate. Third, dividends and royalties are normally taxed by both foreign and home-country governments. Furthermore, a foreign government might restrict the amount of cash that can be repatriated to the parent company, perhaps to force multinational firms to reinvest earnings in the host country or to prevent large currency outflows, which might affect the exchange rate. Whatever the host country's motivation, the result is that the parent corporation cannot use cash flows blocked in the foreign country to pay current dividends to its shareholders, nor does it have the flexibility to reinvest cash flows elsewhere in the world. Therefore, from the perspective of the parent organization, *the cash flows relevant for the analysis of a foreign investment are the cash flows that the subsidiary can legally send back to the parent.*

In addition to the complexities of the cash flow analysis, the rate of return required for a foreign project might be different than for an equivalent domestic project because foreign projects might be more or less risky. A higher risk could arise from two primary sources — exchange rate risk and political risk — while a lower risk might result from international diversification.

Exchange rate risk reflects the inherent uncertainty about the home-currency value of cash flows sent back to the parent. In other words, foreign projects have an added risk element that relates to what the basic cash flows will be worth in the parent company's home currency. The foreign currency cash flows to be turned over to the parent must be converted into U.S. dollars by translating them at *expected* future exchange rates — actual exchange rates might differ substantially from expectations.

Political risk refers to any action (or the chance of such action) by a host government that reduces the value of a company's investment. It includes at one extreme the expropriation (seizure) without compensation of the subsidiary's assets, but it also includes less drastic actions that reduce the value of the parent firm's investment in the foreign subsidiary such as higher taxes, tighter repatriation or currency controls, and restrictions on prices charged. The risk of expropriation of U.S. assets abroad is small in traditionally friendly and stable countries such as Great Britain or Switzerland. However, in Latin America and Africa, for example, the risk might be substantial. Past expropriations include those of ITT and Anaconda Copper in Chile, Gulf Oil in Bolivia, Occidental Petroleum in Libya, and the assets of many companies in Iraq, Iran, and Cuba.

Generally, political risk premiums are not added to the required rate of return to adjust for this risk. If a company's management has a serious concern that a given country might expropriate foreign assets, it simply will not make significant investments in that country. Expropriation is viewed as a catastrophic or ruinous event, and managers have been shown to be extraordinarily risk averse when faced with ruinous loss possibilities. However, companies can take steps to reduce the potential loss from expropriation in three major ways: (1) by financing the subsidiary with local capital, (2) by structuring operations so that the subsidiary has value only as a part of the integrated corporate system, and (3) by

REPATRIATION OF EARNINGS
The process of sending cash flows from a foreign subsidiary back to the parent company.

EXCHANGE RATE RISK
The uncertainty associated with the price at which the currency from one country can be converted into the currency of another country.

POLITICAL RISK
The risk of expropriation of a foreign subsidiary's assets by the host country, or of unanticipated restrictions on cash flows to the parent company.

obtaining insurance against economic losses from expropriation from a source such as the Overseas Private Investment Corporation (OPIC). In the latter case, insurance premiums would have to be added to the project's cost.

Self-Test Questions

List some key differences in capital budgeting as applied to foreign versus domestic operations.

What are the relevant cash flows for an international investment?

Why might the required rate of return for a foreign project differ from that of an equivalent domestic project? Could it be lower?

ETHICAL DILEMMA

This Is a Good Investment—Be Sure the Numbers Show That It Is!

Oliver Greene is the assistant to the financial manager at Cybercomp Inc., a company that develops software to drive network communications for personal computers. Oliver joined Cybercomp three years ago, following his graduation from college. His primary responsibility has been to evaluate capital budgeting projects and make investment recommendations to the board of directors. Oliver enjoys his job very much—he often finds himself challenged with interesting tasks, and he is paid extremely well for what he does.

Last week, Oliver started evaluating the capital projects that have been proposed for investment this year. One of the proposals is to purchase NetWare Products, a company that manufactures circuit boards, called network cards, that are required to achieve communication connectivity between personal computers. Cybercomp packages network cards with the software it sells, but it currently purchases them from another manufacturer. The proposal, which was submitted by Nadine Wilson, Cybercomp's CEO, suggests the company can reduce costs and increase profit margins by producing the network cards in-house.

Oliver barely had time to scan the proposal when he was summoned to Wilson's office. The meeting was short and to the point. Wilson instructed Oliver to "make the numbers for NetWare Products look good, because we *want* to buy that company." She also gave Oliver an evaluation of NetWare completed two years ago by an independent appraiser that suggests NetWare might not be worth the amount Cybercomp is willing to pay. Wilson instructed Oliver to find a way to rebut the findings of the report.

Oliver was troubled by the meeting he had with Wilson. His "gut feeling" was that something was wrong. But, he hadn't yet had time to carefully examine the proposal—his evaluation was very cursory, and he was far from making a final decision concerning the acceptability of the capital budgeting project proposed by Wilson. Oliver felt like he needed much more information before forming a final recommendation.

Oliver spent the entire day examining the appraisal report provided by Wilson and trying to gather additional information about the proposed investment. The report contains some background information concerning NetWare's operations, but crucial financial data are missing. Further investigation into NetWare Products has produced little information. Oliver discovered that the company's stock is closely held by a small group of investors who own numerous businesses and who generously contribute to the local university, which happens to be Wilson's alma mater. In addition, Oliver's secretary has informed him that the gossip around the "water cooler" at Cybercomp is that Wilson and the owners of NetWare are old college buddies, and she might even have a stake in NetWare.

This morning, Wilson called Oliver and repeated her feelings concerning the purchase of NetWare. This time she said: "We really want to purchase NetWare. Some people might not believe so, but this is a very good deal. It's your job to make the numbers work—that's why we pay you the big bucks!" As a result of the conversation, Oliver has the impression his job might be jeopardized if he doesn't make the "right" decision. This added pressure has made Oliver very tense. What should he do? What would you do if you were Oliver? Would your answer change if you knew Wilson had recently sold much of her Cybercomp stock?

SMALL BUSINESS

Capital Budgeting in the Small Firm

The allocation of capital in small firms is as important as it is in large ones. In fact, given their lack of access to the capital markets, it is often more important in the small firm because the funds necessary to correct mistakes might not be available. Also, large firms with capital budgets of $100 million or more allocate capital to numerous projects, so a mistake on one project can be offset by successes with others — large firms benefit from project diversification.

In spite of the importance of capital expenditures to small business, studies of the way capital budgeting decisions are made generally suggest that many small firms use "back-of-the-envelope" analysis, or perhaps no analysis at all. For example, when L. R. Runyon studied 214 firms with net worths of from $500,000 to $1,000,000, he found that almost 70 percent relied upon either payback or some other questionable criteria, only 14 percent used a discounted cash flow analysis, and about 9 percent indicated that they used no formal analysis at all.[a] Studies of larger firms, on the other hand, generally find that most analyze capital budgeting decisions using discounted cash flow techniques.

We are left with a puzzle. Capital budgeting is clearly important to small firms, yet these firms tend not to use the tools that have been developed to improve capital budgeting decisions. Why does this situation exist? One argument is that managers of small firms are simply not well trained; they are unsophisticated. This argument suggests that the managers would make greater use of sophisticated techniques if they understood them better. Another argument relates to the fact that management talent is a scarce resource in small firms, and the demands on their time might be such that they simply cannot afford the time to analyze projects using sophisticated methods, even if they did understand them. A third argument relates to the cost of analyzing capital projects. Some of the analysis costs are fixed, and it might not be economical to incur them if the project itself is relatively small. This argument suggests that small firms with small projects might actually be making the sensible decision when they rely upon management's "gut feeling."

In his study, Runyon also found that small firms tend to be cash oriented. They are concerned with basic survival, so they tend to look at expenditures from the standpoint of near-term effects on cash. This cash and survival orientation leads to a focus on a relatively short time horizon, and this, in turn, might lead to an emphasis on the payback method. The limitations of payback are well known, but in spite of those limitations, the technique is popular in small business because it gives the firm a "feel" for when the cash committed to an investment will be recovered and thus be available to repay loans or for new opportunities. Therefore, small firms that are cash oriented and have limited managerial resources might find the payback method an appealing compromise between the need for extensive analysis on the one hand and the high costs of analysis on the other.

Remember from our discussion in the chapter that the single most appealing argument for the use of net present value in capital budgeting decisions is that NPV gives an explicit measure of the effect of the investment on the value of the firm: If NPV is positive, the investment will increase the value of the firm and make its owners wealthier. In small firms, however, the stock often is not traded in public markets, so its value cannot be observed. Also, for reasons of control many small business owners and managers might not want to broaden ownership by going public. It is difficult to argue for value-based techniques when the value of the firm and its required rate of return are unobservable. Furthermore, in a closely held firm the objectives of the individual owner-manager might extend beyond the firm's monetary value.

In general, we know that small firms make less extensive use of DCF techniques than larger firms. This might be a rational decision resulting from a conscious or subconscious conclusion that the costs of sophisticated analyses outweigh their benefits; it might reflect nonmonetary goals of small businesses' owner-managers; or it might reflect difficulties in estimating the values needed for DCF analysis but not payback. However, nonuse of DCF methods might also reflect a

Continued

Continued

weakness in many small business organizations. We simply do not know. We do know that small businesses must do all they can to compete effectively with big business, and, to the extent that a small business fails to use DCF methods because its manager is

unsophisticated or uninformed, it might be putting itself at a serious competitive disadvantage.

[a]L. R. Runyon, "Capital Expenditure Decision Making in Small Firms," *Journal of Business Research*, September 1983, 389–397.

Summary

In this chapter, we discussed the capital budgeting process, including the techniques used for decision making and the estimation, evaluation, and risk analysis of cash flows. The key concepts covered in the chapter are listed below.

- **Capital budgeting** is the process of analyzing potential fixed-asset investments.
- The **payback period** is defined as the expected number of years required to recover a project's cost. The regular payback method does not consider the time value of money. The **discounted payback method** is similar to the regular payback method except that it discounts cash flows at the project's required rate of return. Like the regular payback, it ignores cash flows beyond the discounted payback period.
- The **net present value (NPV) method** discounts all cash flows at the project's required rate of return and then sums those cash flows. The project is acceptable if this sum, called the NPV, is positive.
- The **internal rate of return (IRR)** is defined as the discount rate that forces a project's NPV to equal zero. The project is acceptable if the IRR is greater than the project's required rate of return.
- The NPV and IRR methods make the same accept/reject decisions for **independent projects,** but if projects are **mutually exclusive,** ranking conflicts can arise. If conflicts arise, the NPV method generally should be used because NPV is the single best measure of a project's profitability.
- The NPV method assumes that cash flows can be reinvested at the firm's required rate of return, while the IRR method assumes reinvestment at the project's IRR. Because **reinvestment at the required rate of return is generally a better (closer to the truth) assumption,** the NPV is superior to the IRR.
- Sophisticated managers consider more than one of the project evaluation measures because the **different measures provide different types of information.**
- The most important, but also the most difficult, step in analyzing a capital budgeting project is estimating the **incremental after-tax cash flows** the project will produce.
- In determining incremental cash flows, **opportunity costs** (the cash flow forgone by using an asset) must be included, but **sunk costs** (cash outlays that have been made and that cannot be recouped) should not be included. Any **externalities** (effects of a project on other parts of the firm) should also be

reflected in the analysis. In addition, **inflation** effects must be considered in project analysis.

- Capital projects often require an additional investment in **net working capital (NWC).** An increase in NWC must be included in the Year 0 initial cash outlay and then shown as a cash inflow in the project's final year.
- **Replacement analysis** is slightly different from that for **expansion projects** because the cash flows from the old asset must be considered in replacement decisions.
- A project's **stand-alone risk** is the risk the project would have if it were the firm's only asset and if the firm's stockholders held only that one stock.
- **Within-firm,** or **corporate, risk** reflects the effects of a project on the firm's risk when combined with the existing assets.
- **Beta risk** reflects the effects of a project on the risks borne by stockholders, assuming stockholders hold diversified portfolios. In theory, beta risk should be the most relevant type of risk.
- **Sensitivity analysis** is a technique that shows how much an output variable such as NPV will change in response to a given change in an input variable such as sales, other things held constant.
- **Scenario analysis** is a risk analysis technique in which the best- and worst-case NPVs are compared with the project's expected NPV.
- **Monte Carlo simulation** is a risk analysis technique used to simulate probable future events and thus to estimate the NPV probability distribution and riskiness of a project.
- The **risk-adjusted discount rate** is the rate used to evaluate a particular project. The discount rate is increased for projects that are riskier than the firm's average project but is decreased for less risky projects.
- **Capital rationing** occurs when management places a constraint on the size of the firm's capital budget during a particular period.
- A **post-audit** review of capital budgeting decisions helps the firm determine if expectations are being met.
- Investments in **international capital projects** expose the investing firm to **exchange rate risk** and **political risk.** The relevant cash flows in international capital budgeting are the dollar cash flows that can be turned over to the parent company.
- Small firms tend to use the payback method rather than a "sophisticated" method. This might be a rational decision because (1) the **cost** of a DCF analysis **might outweigh the benefits** for the project being considered, (2) the firm's **required rate of return cannot be estimated accurately,** or (3) the small business owner might be considering **nonmonetary goals.**

Questions

9-1 Explain why the NPV of a relatively long-term project, defined as one for which a high percentage of its cash flows are expected in the distant future, is more sensitive to changes in the required rate of return than is the NPV of a short-term project.

9-2 Explain why, if two mutually exclusive projects are being compared, the short-term project might have the higher ranking under the NPV criterion if the required rate of return is high, but the long-term project might be deemed better if the required rate of return is low. Would changes in the required rate of return ever cause a change in the IRR ranking of two such projects?

9-3 In what sense is a reinvestment rate assumption embodied in the NPV and IRR methods? What is the assumed reinvestment rate of each method?

9-4 "If a firm has no mutually exclusive projects, only independent ones, and it also has both a constant required rate of return and projects with conventional cash flow patterns, then the NPV and IRR methods will always lead to identical capital budgeting decisions." Discuss this statement. What does it imply about using the IRR method in lieu of the NPV method? If each of the assumptions made in the question were changed (one by one), how would these changes affect your answer?

9-5 Are there conditions under which a firm might be better off if it were to choose a machine with a rapid payback rather than one with a larger NPV?

9-6 Cash flows rather than accounting profits are listed in Table 9-2. What is the basis for this emphasis on cash flows as opposed to net income?

9-7 Look at Table 9-4 and answer these questions:
   a. Why is the net salvage value shown in Section III reduced for taxes?
   b. How is the change in depreciation computed?
   c. What would happen if the new machine permitted a reduction in net working capital?
   d. Why are the cost savings shown as a positive amount?

9-8 Explain why sunk costs should not be included in a capital budgeting analysis but opportunity costs and externalities should be included.

9-9 Explain how net working capital is recovered at the end of a project's life and why it is included in a capital budgeting analysis.

9-10 Why is it true, in general, that a failure to adjust expected cash flows for expected inflation biases the calculated NPV downward?

9-11 Define (a) simulation analysis, (b) scenario analysis, and (c) sensitivity analysis. If AT&T were considering two investments, one calling for the expenditure of $200 million to develop a satellite communications system and the other involving the expenditure of $12,000 for a new truck, on which one would the company be more likely to use simulation analysis?

9-12 Distinguish between beta (or market) risk, within-firm (or corporate) risk, and stand-alone risk for a project being considered for inclusion in the capital budget. Which type of risk do you believe should be given the greatest weight in capital budgeting decisions? Explain.

9-13 Suppose Reading Engine Company, which has a high beta as well as a great deal of corporate risk, merged with Simplicity Patterns Inc. Simplicity's sales rise during recessions, when people are more likely to make their own clothes, and, consequently, its beta is negative but its corporate risk is relatively high. What would the merger do to the required rates of return in the consolidated company's locomotive engine division and in its patterns division?

9-14 Suppose a firm estimates its required rate of return for the coming year to be 10 percent. What are reasonable required rates of return for evaluating average-risk projects, high-risk projects, and low-risk projects?

Self-Test Problems   *Solutions Appear in Appendix B*

Key terms   **ST-1** Define each of the following terms:
   a. Capital budget; capital budgeting
   b. Regular payback period; discounted payback period
   c. Independent projects; mutually exclusive projects

d. Net present value (NPV) method; internal rate of return (IRR) method
e. NPV profile; crossover rate
f. Unconventional cash flow patterns; multiple IRRs
g. Reinvestment rate assumption
h. Cash flow; accounting income; relevant cash flow
i. Incremental cash flow; sunk cost; opportunity cost; externalities; inflation bias
j. Initial investment outlay; incremental operating cash flow; terminal cash flow
k. Change in net working capital
l. Expansion analysis; replacement analysis
m. Stand-alone risk; within-firm risk; market risk
n. Sensitivity analysis; scenario analysis; Monte Carlo simulation
o. Project beta versus corporate beta
p. Risk-adjusted discount rate; project required rate of return
q. Capital rationing

Project analysis **ST-2** You are a financial analyst for Damon Electronics Company. The director of capital budgeting has asked you to analyze two proposed capital investments, Projects X and Y. Each project has a cost of $10,000, and the required rate of return for each project is 12 percent. The projects' expected net cash flows are as follows:

	Expected Net Cash Flows	
Year	**Project X**	**Project Y**
0	$(10,000)	$(10,000)
1	6,500	3,500
2	3,000	3,500
3	3,000	3,500
4	1,000	3,500

a. Calculate each project's payback period, net present value (NPV), and internal rate of return (IRR).
b. Which project (or projects) should be accepted if they are independent?
c. Which project should be accepted if they are mutually exclusive?
d. How might a change in the required rate of return produce a conflict between the NPV and IRR rankings of these two projects? Would this conflict exist if k were 5%? (Hint: Plot the NPV profiles.)
e. Why does the conflict exist?

New project analysis **ST-3** You have been asked by the president of Ellis Construction Company, headquartered in Toledo, to evaluate the proposed acquisition of a new earthmover. The mover's basic price is $50,000, and it will cost another $10,000 to modify it for special use by Ellis Construction. Assume that the mover falls into the MACRS 3-year class. (See Table 9B-2 for MACRS recovery allowance percentages.) It will be sold after 3 years for $20,000, and it will require an increase in net working capital (spare parts inventory) of $2,000. The earthmover purchase will have no effect on revenues, but it is expected to save Ellis $20,000 per year in before-tax operating costs, mainly labor. Ellis's marginal tax rate is 40 percent.
a. What is the company's net initial investment outlay if it acquires the earthmover? (What are the Year 0 cash flows?)
b. What are the incremental operating cash flows in Years 1, 2, and 3?
c. What is the terminal cash flow in Year 3?
d. If the project's required rate of return is 10 percent, should the earthmover be purchased?

Replacement analysis **ST-4** The Dauten Toy Corporation currently uses an injection molding machine that was purchased 2 years ago. This machine is being depreciated on a straight line basis toward a $500 salvage value, and it has 6 years of remaining life. Its current book

value is $2,600, and it can be sold for $3,000 at this time. Thus, the annual depreciation expense is ($2,600 − $500)/6 = $350 per year.

Dauten is offered a replacement machine that has a cost of $8,000, an estimated
useful life of 6 years, and an estimated salvage value of $800. This machine falls into
the MACRS 5-year class. (See Table 9B-2 for MACRS recovery allowance percentages.)
The replacement machine would permit an output expansion, so sales would rise by
$1,000 per year; even so, the new machine's much greater efficiency would still
cause operating expenses to decline by $1,500 per year. The new machine would
require that inventories be increased by $2,000, but accounts payable would simul-
taneously increase by $500.

Dauten's marginal tax rate is 40 percent, and its required rate of return is 15 percent. Should it replace the old machine?

Corporate risk analysis   **ST-5** The staff of Heymann Manufacturing has estimated the following net cash flows and
probabilities for a new manufacturing process:

	Net Cash Flows		
Year	**$Pr = 0.2$**	**$Pr = 0.6$**	**$Pr = 0.2$**
0	$(100,000)	$(100,000)	$(100,000)
1	20,000	30,000	40,000
2	20,000	30,000	40,000
3	20,000	30,000	40,000
4	20,000	30,000	40,000
5	20,000	30,000	40,000
5*	0	20,000	30,000

Line 0 gives the cost of the process, Lines 1 through 5 give operating cash flows,
and Line 5* contains the estimated salvage values. Heymann's required rate of
return for an average-risk project is 10 percent.

  a. Assume that the project has average risk. Find the project's expected NPV. (Hint:
     Use expected values for the net cash flow in each year.)
  b. Find the best-case and worst-case NPVs. What is the probability of occurrence of
     the worst case if the cash flows are perfectly dependent (perfectly positively cor-
     related) over time? If they are independent over time?
  c. Assume that all the cash flows are perfectly positively correlated; that is, there are
     only three possible cash flow streams over time: (1) the worst case, (2) the most
     likely, or base, case, and (3) the best case, with probabilities of 0.2, 0.6, and 0.2,
     respectively. These cases are represented by each of the columns in the table.
     Find the expected NPV, its standard deviation, and its coefficient of variation.
  d. The coefficient of variation of Heymann's average project is in the range 0.8 to
     1.0. If the coefficient of variation of a project being evaluated is greater than 1.0,
     2 percentage points are added to the firm's required rate of return. Similarly, if the
     coefficient of variation is less than 0.8, 1 percentage point is deducted from the
     required rate of return. What is the project's required rate of return? Should Hey-
     mann accept or reject the project?

Problems

Payback, NPV, and   **9-1** Project K has a cost of $52,125, and its expected net cash inflows are $12,000 per
IRR calculations   year for 8 years.
  a. What is the project's payback period (to the closest year)?
  b. The required rate of return for the project is 12 percent. What is the project's
     NPV?
  c. What is the project's IRR? (Hint: Recognize that the project is an annuity.)

d. What is the project's discounted payback period, assuming a 12 percent required rate of return?

NPV and IRR analysis **9-2** Derek's Donuts is considering two mutually exclusive investments. The projects' expected net cash flows are as follows:

	Expected Net Cash Flows	
Year	Project A	Project B
0	$(300)	$(405)
1	(387)	134
2	(193)	134
3	(100)	134
4	500	134
5	500	134
6	850	134
7	100	0

a. Construct NPV profiles for Projects A and B.

b. What is each project's IRR?

c. If you were told that each project's required rate of return was 12 percent, which project should be selected? If the required rate of return was 15 percent, what would the proper choice be?

d. Looking at the NPV profiles constructed in part a, what is the *approximate* crossover rate, and what is its significance?

Timing differences **9-3** The Southwestern Oil Exploration Company is considering two mutually exclusive plans for extracting oil on property for which it has mineral rights. Both plans call for the expenditure of $12,000,000 to drill development wells. Under Plan A, all the oil will be extracted in 1 year, producing a cash flow at t = 1 of $14,400,000. Under Plan B, cash flows will be $2,100,000 per year for 20 years.

a. Construct NPV profiles for Plans A and B, identify each project's IRR, and indicate the approximate crossover rate of return.

b. Suppose a company has a required rate of return of 12 percent, and it can get unlimited capital at that cost. Is it logical to assume that it would take on all available independent projects (of average risk) with returns greater than 12 percent? Further, if all available projects with returns greater than 12 percent have been taken on, would this mean that cash flows from past investments would have an opportunity cost of only 12 percent, because all the firm could do with these cash flows would be to replace money that has a cost of 12 percent? Finally, does this imply that the required rate of return is the correct rate to assume for the reinvestment of a project's cash flows?

Scale differences **9-4** The Huckin Publishing Company is considering two mutually exclusive expansion plans. Plan A calls for the expenditure of $40 million on a large-scale, integrated plant that will provide an expected cash flow stream of $6.4 million per year for 20 years. Plan B calls for the expenditure of $12 million to build a somewhat less efficient, more labor-intensive plant that has an expected cash flow stream of $2.72 million per year for 20 years. Huckin's required rate of return is 10 percent.

a. Calculate each project's NPV and IRR.

b. Graph the NPV profiles for Plans A and B. From the NPV profiles constructed, approximate the crossover rate.

c. Give a logical explanation, based on reinvestment rates and opportunity costs, as to why the NPV method is better than the IRR method when the firm's required rate of return is constant at some value such as 10 percent.

New project analysis **9-5** You have been asked by the president of your company to evaluate the proposed acquisition of a spectrometer for the firm's R&D department. The equipment's base price is $140,000, and it would cost another $30,000 to modify it for special use by your firm. The spectrometer, which falls into the MACRS 3-year class, would be sold after 3 years for $60,000. (See Table 9B-2 for MACRS recovery allowance percentages.) Use of the equipment would require an increase in net working capital (spare parts inventory) of $8,000. The spectrometer would have no effect on revenues, but it is expected to save the firm $50,000 per year in before-tax operating costs, mainly labor. The firm's marginal tax rate is 40 percent.

a. What is the initial investment outlay in Year 0 associated with this project?

b. What are the incremental operating cash flows in Years 1, 2, and 3?

c. What is the terminal cash flow in Year 3?

d. If the project's required rate of return is 12 percent, should the spectrometer be purchased?

New project analysis   **9-6**   The Ewert Company is evaluating the proposed acquisition of a new milling machine. The machine's base price is $108,000, and it would cost another $12,500 to modify it for special use by the firm. The machine falls into the MACRS 3-year class, and it would be sold after 3 years for $65,000. (See Table 9B-2 for MACRS recovery allowance percentages.) The machine would require an increase in net working capital (inventory) of $5,500. The milling machine would have no effect on revenues, but it is expected to save the firm $44,000 per year in before-tax operating costs, mainly labor. Ewert's tax rate is 34 percent.

a. What is the initial investment outlay in Year 0 of the machine for capital budgeting purposes?

b. What are the incremental operating cash flows in Years 1, 2, and 3?

c. What is the terminal cash flow in Year 3?

d. If the project's required rate of return is 12 percent, should the machine be purchased?

Replacement analysis   **9-7**   Atlantic Control Company purchased a machine 4 years ago at a cost of $70,000. At that time, the machine's expected economic life was 6 years and the expected salvage value at the end of its life was $10,000. It is being depreciated using the straight line method so that its book value at the end of 6 years is $10,000.

A new machine can be purchased for $80,000, including shipping and installation costs. The new machine has an estimated economic life of 4 years. MACRS depreciation will be used, and the machine will be depreciated over its 3-year class life rather than its 4-year economic life. (See Table 9B-2 for MACRS recovery allowance percentages.) During its 4-year life, the new machine will reduce cash operating expenses by $20,000 per year. Sales are not expected to change. But, the new machine will require net working capital to be increased by $4,000. At the end of its useful life, the machine is estimated to have a market value of $2,500.

The old machine can be sold today for $20,000. If it is not replaced, the company believes the old machine can be used for another 4 years; in 4 years the old machine will be worthless, so its market value will be $0. The firm's tax rate is 40 percent. The appropriate required rate of return is 10 percent.

a. If the new machine is purchased, what is the amount of the initial investment outlay at Year 0?

b. What incremental operating cash flows will occur at the end of Years 1 through 4 as a result of replacing the old machine?

c. What is the terminal cash flow at the end of Year 4 if the new machine is purchased?

d. What is the NPV of this project? Should Atlantic replace the old machine?

Replacement analysis   **9-8**   The Boyd Bottling Company is contemplating the replacement of one of its bottling machines with a newer and more efficient one. The old machine has a book value of $600,000 and a remaining useful life of 5 years. The firm does not expect to realize any return from scrapping the old machine in 5 years, but it can sell it now to another firm in the industry for $265,000. The old machine is being depreciated toward a zero salvage value, or by $120,000 per year, using the straight line method.

The new machine has a purchase price of $1,175,000, an estimated useful life and MACRS class life of 5 years, and an estimated market value of $145,000 at the end of 5 years. (See Table 9B-2 for MACRS recovery allowance percentages.) It is expected to economize on electric power usage, labor, and repair costs, which will save Boyd $230,000 each year. In addition, it is expected that the new machine will reduce the number of defective bottles, which will save an additional $25,000 annually. The company's tax rate is 40 percent and it has a 12 percent required rate of return.

a. What is the initial investment outlay required for the new machine?

b. Calculate the annual depreciation allowances for both machines, and compute the change in the annual depreciation expense if the replacement is made.

c. What are the incremental operating cash flows in Years 1 through 5?

d. What is the terminal cash flow in Year 5?

e. Should the firm purchase the new machine? Support your answer.

Risky cash flows   **9-9**   The Singleton Company must decide between two mutually exclusive investment projects. Each project costs $6,750 and has an expected life of 3 years. Annual net cash flows from each project begin 1 year after the initial investment is made and have the following probability distributions:

Project A		Project B	
Probability	**Net Cash Flow**	**Probability**	**Net Cash Flow**
0.2	$6,000	0.2	$ 0
0.6	6,750	0.6	6,750
0.2	7,500	0.2	18,000

Singleton decided to evaluate the riskier project at a 12 percent rate and the less risky project at a 10 percent rate.

a. What is the expected value of the annual net cash flows from each project? What is the coefficient of variation (CV_{NPV})? (Hint: Use Equation 8-3 from Chapter 8 to calculate the standard deviation of Project A. $\sigma_B = \$5,798$ and $CV_B = 0.76$.)

b. What is the risk-adjusted NPV of each project?

c. If it were known that Project B was negatively correlated with other cash flows of the firm whereas Project A was positively correlated, how would this knowledge affect the decision? If Project B's cash flows were negatively correlated with gross national product (GNP), would that influence your assessment of its risk?

CAPM approach to   **9-10**   Goodtread Rubber Company has two divisions: the tire division, which manufactures risk adjustments   tires for new autos, and the recap division, which manufactures recapping materials that are sold to independent tire recapping shops throughout the United States. Because auto manufacturing fluctuates with the general economy, the tire division's earnings contribution to Goodtread's stock price is highly correlated with returns on most other stocks. If the tire division were operated as a separate company, its beta coefficient would be about 1.50. The sales and profits of the recap division, on the other hand, tend to be countercyclical because recap sales boom when people cannot afford to buy new tires. The recap division's beta is estimated to be 0.5. Approximately 75 percent of Goodtread's corporate assets are invested in the tire division, and 25 percent are invested in the recap division.

Currently, the rate of interest on Treasury securities is 9 percent, and the expected rate of return on an average share of stock is 13 percent. Goodtread uses only common equity capital, so it has no debt outstanding.

a. What is the required rate of return on Goodtread's stock?

b. What discount rate should be used to evaluate capital budgeting projects? Explain your answer fully, and, in the process, illustrate your answer with a project that costs $160,000, has a 10-year life, and provides expected after-tax net cash flows of $30,000 per year.

Exam-Type Problems

The problems included in this section are set up in such a way that they could be used as multiple-choice exam problems.

NPVs, IRRs, and payback for independent projects

9-11 Olsen Engineering is considering including two pieces of equipment, a truck and an overhead pulley system, in this year's capital budget. The projects are independent. The cash outlay for the truck is $17,100 and that for the pulley system is $22,430. Each piece of equipment has an estimated life of 5 years. The annual after-tax cash flow expected to be provided by the truck is $5,100; for the pulley, it is $7,500. The firm's required rate of return is 14 percent. Calculate the IRR, the NPV, and the payback period for each project, and indicate which project(s) should be accepted.

NPVs and IRRs for mutually exclusive projects

9-12 Horrigan Industries must choose between a gas-powered and an electric-powered forklift truck for moving materials in its factory. Since both forklifts perform the same function, the firm will choose only one. (They are mutually exclusive investments.) The electric-powered truck will cost more, but it will be less expensive to operate; it will cost $22,000, whereas the gas-powered truck will cost $17,500. The required rate of return that applies to both investments is 12 percent. The life for both types of truck is estimated to be 6 years, during which time the net cash flows for the electric-powered truck will be $6,290 per year, and those for the gas-powered truck will be $5,000 per year. Annual net cash flows include depreciation expenses. Calculate the NPV and IRR for each type of truck, and decide which to recommend.

Capital budgeting decisions

9-13 Project S costs $15,000 and is expected to produce benefits (cash flows) of $4,500 per year for 5 years. Project L costs $37,500 and is expected to produce cash flows of $11,100 per year for 5 years. Calculate the NPV, IRR, and payback period for each project, assuming a required rate of return of 14 percent. If the projects are independent, which project(s) should be selected? If they are mutually exclusive projects, which project actually should be selected?

Present value of costs

9-14 The Cordell Coffee Company is evaluating the within-plant distribution system for its new roasting, grinding, and packing plant. The two alternatives are (1) a conveyor system with a high initial cost but low annual operating costs and (2) several forklift trucks, which cost less but have considerably higher operating costs. The decision to construct the plant has already been made, and the choice here will have no effect on the overall revenues of the project. The required rate of return for the plant is 9 percent, and the projects' expected net costs are listed as follows:

	Expected Net Cash Flows	
Year	Conveyor	Forklift
0	($300,000)	($120,000)
1	(66,000)	(96,000)
2	(66,000)	(96,000)
3	(66,000)	(96,000)
4	(66,000)	(96,000)
5	(66,000)	(96,000)

a. What is the present value of costs of each alternative? Which method should be chosen?

b. What is the IRR of each alternative?

NPV and IRR   **9-15** The after-tax cash flows for two mutually exclusive projects have been estimated, and the following information has been provided:

Year	Machine D	Machine Q
0	($2,500)	($2,500)
1	2,000	0
2	900	1,800
3	100	1,000
4	100	900

The company's required rate of return is 14 percent, and it can get an unlimited amount of capital at that cost. What is the IRR of the *better* project? (Hint: Note that the better project might not be the one with the higher IRR.)

NPV and IRR   **9-16** Diamond Hill Jewelers is considering the following independent projects:

Year	Project Y	Project Z
0	($25,000)	($25,000)
1	10,000	0
2	9,000	0
3	7,000	0
4	6,000	36,000

Which project(s) should be accepted if the required rate of return for the projects is 10 percent? Compute the NPVs and the IRRs for both projects.

Replacement analysis   **9-17** The Gehr Company is considering the purchase of a new machine tool to replace an obsolete one. The machine being used for the operation has both a tax book value and a market value of zero; it is in good working order, however, and will last physically for at least another 10 years. The proposed replacement machine will perform the operation so much more efficiently that Gehr engineers estimate it will produce after-tax cash flows (labor savings and depreciation) of $9,000 per year. The new machine will cost $40,000 delivered and installed, and its economic life is estimated to be 10 years, at which time its salvage value will be zero. The firm's required rate of return is 10 percent, and its tax rate is 40 percent. Should Gehr buy the new machine?

Replacement analysis   **9-18** Galveston Shipyards is considering the replacement of an 8-year-old riveting machine with a new one that will increase earnings before depreciation from $27,000 to $54,000 per year. The new machine will cost $82,500, and it will have an estimated life of 8 years and no salvage value. The new machine will be depreciated over its 5-year MACRS recovery period. (See Table 9B-2 for MACRS recovery allowance percentages.) The firm's marginal tax rate is 40 percent, and the firm's required rate of return is 12 percent. The old machine has been fully depreciated and has no salvage value. Should the old riveting machine be replaced by the new one?

Risk adjustment   **9-19** The risk-free rate of return is 9 percent, and the market risk premium is 5 percent. The beta of the project under analysis is 1.4, with expected net cash flows estimated to be $1,500 per year for 5 years. The required investment outlay on the project is $4,500.
a. What is the required risk-adjusted return on the project?
b. Should the project be accepted?

Beta risk   **9-20** Capital Computer Corporation, a producer of office equipment, currently has assets of $15 million and a beta of 1.4. The risk-free rate is 8 percent and the market risk premium is 5 percent. Capital would like to expand into the risky home computer market. If the expansion is undertaken, Capital would create a new division with $3.75 million in assets. The new division would have a beta of 1.8.

a. What is Capital's current required rate of return?

b. If the expansion is undertaken, what would be the firm's new beta? What is the new overall required rate of return, and what rate of return must the home computer division produce to leave the new overall required rate of return unchanged?

Integrative Problems

Capital budgeting and cash flow estimation

9-21 Argile Textiles is evaluating a new product, a silk/wool blended fabric. Assume that you were recently hired as assistant to the director of capital budgeting, and you must evaluate the new project.

The fabric would be produced in an unused building adjacent to Argile's Southern Pines, North Carolina, plant; Argile owns the building, which is fully depreciated. The required equipment would cost $200,000, plus an additional $40,000 for shipping and installation. In addition, inventories would rise by $25,000, while accounts payable would go up by $5,000. All of these costs would be incurred at t = 0. By a special ruling, the machinery could be depreciated under the MACRS system as 3-year property.

The project is expected to operate for 4 years, at which time it will be terminated. The cash inflows are assumed to begin 1 year after the project is undertaken, or at t = 1, and to continue out to t = 4. At the end of the project's life (t = 4), the equipment is expected to have a salvage value of $25,000.

Unit sales are expected to total 100,000 5-yard rolls per year, and the expected sales price is $2.00 per roll. Cash operating costs for the project (total operating costs less depreciation) are expected to total 60 percent of dollar sales. Argile's marginal tax rate is 40 percent, and its required rate of return is 10 percent. Tentatively, the silk/wool blend fabric project is assumed to be of equal risk to Argile's other assets.

You have been asked to evaluate the project and to make a recommendation as to whether it should be accepted or rejected. To guide you in your analysis, your boss gave you the following set of questions:

a. What is capital budgeting? Are there any similarities between a firm's capital budgeting decisions and an individual's investment decisions?

b. What is the difference between independent and mutually exclusive projects? Between projects with conventional cash flows and projects with unconventional cash flows? Between replacement analysis and expansion analysis?

c. Draw a cash flow time line that shows when the net cash inflows and outflows will occur, and explain how the time line can be used to help structure the analysis.

d. Argile has a standard form that is used in the capital budgeting process (see Table IP9-1). Part of the table has been completed, but you must replace the blanks with the missing numbers. Complete the table in the following steps:

(1) Complete the unit sales, sales price, total revenues, and operating costs excluding depreciation lines.

(2) Complete the depreciation line.

(3) Now complete the table down to net income and then down to net operating cash flows.

(4) Now fill in the blanks under Year 0 and Year 4 for the initial investment outlay and the terminal cash flows, and complete the cash flow time line (net cash flow). Discuss working capital. What would have happened if the machinery were sold for less than its book value?

e. (1) Argile uses debt in its capital structure, so some of the money used to finance the project will be debt. Given this fact, should the projected cash flows be revised to show projected interest charges? Explain.

TABLE IP9-1

Argile's Silk/Wool Blend Project (thousands of dollars)

		End of Year			
	0	1	2	3	4
Unit sales (thousands)			100		
Price/unit		$ 2.00	$ 2.00		
Total revenues				$200.0	
Costs excluding depreciation			($120.0)		
Depreciation				36.0	(16.8)
Total operating costs		($199.2)	($228.0)		
Earnings before taxes (EBT)				$ 44.0	
Taxes		(0.3)			(25.3)
Net income				$ 26.4	
Depreciation		79.2		36.0	
Incremental operating CF		$ 79.7			$54.7
Equipment cost					
Installation					
Increase in inventory					
Increase in accounts payable					
Salvage value					
Tax on salvage value					
Return of net working capital					
Cash flow time line (Net CF)	$(260.0)				$89.7
Cumulative CF for payback	(260.0)	(180.3)			63.0
NPV =					
IRR =					
Payback =					

(2) Suppose you learned that Argile had spent $50,000 to renovate the building last year, expensing these costs. Should this cost be reflected in the analysis? Explain.

(3) Now suppose you learned that Argile could lease its building to another party and earn $25,000 per year. Should that fact be reflected in the analysis? If so, how?

(4) Now assume that the silk/wool blend fabric project would take away profitable sales from Argile's cotton/wool blend fabric business. Should that fact be reflected in your analysis? If so, how?

Disregard all the assumptions made in part e, and assume there was no alternative use for the building over the next 4 years.

    f. (1) What is the regular payback period and the discounted payback period for the project?

    (2) What is the rationale for the payback? According to the payback criterion, should the project be accepted if the firm's maximum acceptable payback is 2 years?

    (3) What is the difference between the regular payback and the discounted payback?

    (4) What are the main disadvantages of the regular payback? Is the payback method of any real usefulness in capital budgeting decisions?

    g. (1) Define the term net present value (NPV). What is the project's NPV?

    (2) What is the rationale behind the NPV method? According to NPV, should the project be accepted?

    (3) Would the NPV change if the required rate of return changed?

b. (1) Define the term internal rate of return (IRR). What is the project's IRR?

    (2) How is the IRR on a project related to the YTM on a bond?

    (3) What is the logic behind the IRR method? According to IRR, should the project be accepted?

    (4) Would the project's IRRs change if the required rate of return changed?

i. Draw the NPV profile for the project. What information does the NPV profile provide?

j. If this project had been a replacement rather than an expansion project, how would the analysis have changed? Think about the changes that would have to occur in the cash flow table, but no calculations are required.

k. Assume that inflation is expected to average 5 percent over the next 4 years; that this expectation is reflected in the required rate of return; and that inflation will increase variable costs and revenues by the same percentage, 5 percent. Does it appear that inflation has been dealt with properly in the analysis? If not, what should be done, and how would the required adjustment affect the decision?

Risk analysis   **9-22** Problem 9-21 contained the details of a new-project capital budgeting evaluation being conducted by Argile Textiles. Although inflation was considered in the initial analysis (part k), the riskiness of the project was not. The expected cash flows considering inflation as they were estimated in Problem 9-21 (in thousands of dollars) are given in Table IP9-2. Argile's required rate of return is 10 percent. You have been asked to answer the following questions:

TABLE IP9-2

Argile's Silk/Wool Blend Project Adjusted for Inflation (thousands of dollars)

			Year		
	0	**1**	**2**	**3**	**4**
Investment in:					
Fixed assets	($240.0)				
Net working capital	(20.0)				
Unit sales (thousands)		100	100	100	100
Sales price (dollars)		$2.100	$2.205	$2.315	$2.431
Total revenues		$210.0	$220.5	$231.5	$243.1
Cash operating costs (60%)		(126.0)	(132.3)	(138.9)	(145.9)
Depreciation		(79.2)	(108.0)	(36.0)	(16.8)
Earnings before taxes (EBT)		$ 4.8	($ 19.8)	$ 56.6	$ 80.4
Taxes 40%		(1.9)	7.9	(22.6)	(32.2)
Net income		$ 2.9	($ 11.9)	$ 34.0	$ 48.2
Plus depreciation		79.2	108.0	36.0	16.8
Net operating cash flow		$ 82.1	$ 96.1	$ 70.0	$ 65.0
Salvage value					25.0
Tax on SV (40%)					(10.0)
Recovery of NWC					20.0
Net cash flow	($260.0)	$ 82.1	$ 96.1	$ 70.0	$100.0
Cumulative cash flow for payback	(260.0)	(177.9)	(81.8)	(11.8)	88.2

NPV at 10% cost of capital   = $15.0

IRR   = 12.6%

a. (1) What are the three levels, or types, of project risk that are normally considered?

    (2) Which type is the most relevant?

    (3) Which type is the easiest to measure?

    (4) Are the three types of risk generally highly correlated?

b. (1) What is sensitivity analysis?

    (2) Discuss how one would perform a sensitivity analysis on the unit sales, salvage value, and required rate of return for the project. Assume that each of these variables deviates from its base-case, or expected, value by plus-and-minus 10, 20, and 30 percent. Explain how you would calculate the NPV, IRR, and the payback for each case.

    (3) What is the primary weakness of sensitivity analysis? What are its primary advantages?

c. Assume that you are confident about the estimates of all the variables that affect the project's cash flows except unit sales. If product acceptance is poor, sales would be only 75,000 units a year, while a strong consumer response would produce sales of 125,000 units. In either case, cash costs would still amount to 60 percent of revenues. You believe that there is a 25 percent chance of poor acceptance, a 25 percent chance of excellent acceptance, and a 50 percent chance of average acceptance (the base case).

    (1) What is the worst-case NPV? The best-case NPV?

    (2) Use the worst-, most likely (or base-), and best-case NPVs and probabilities of occurrence to find the project's expected NPV, standard deviation (σ_{NPV}), and coefficient of variation (CV_{NPV}).

d. (1) Assume that Argile's average project has a coefficient of variation (CV_{NPV}) in the range of 1.25 to 1.75. Would the silk/wool blend fabric project be classified as high risk, average risk, or low risk? What type of risk is being measured here?

    (2) Based on common sense, how highly correlated do you think the project would be to the firm's other assets? (Give a correlation coefficient, or range of coefficients, based on your judgment.)

    (3) How would this correlation coefficient and the previously calculated σ combine to affect the project's contribution to corporate, or within-firm, risk? Explain.

e. (1) Based on your judgment, what do you think the project's correlation coefficient would be with respect to the general economy and thus with returns on "the market"?

    (2) How would correlation with the economy affect the project's market risk?

f. (1) Argile typically adds or subtracts 3 percentage points to the overall required rate of return to adjust for risk. Should the project be accepted?

    (2) What subjective risk factors should be considered before the final decision is made?

g. Define scenario analysis and simulation analysis, and discuss their principal advantages and disadvantages. (Note that you have already done scenario analysis in part c.)

h. (1) Assume that the risk-free rate is 10 percent, the market risk premium is 6 percent, and the new project's beta is 1.2. What is the project's required rate of return on equity based on the CAPM?

    (2) How does the project's market risk compare with the firm's overall market risk?

    (3) How does the project's stand-alone risk compare with that of the firm's average project?

    (4) Briefly describe how you could estimate the project's beta. How feasible do you think that procedure actually would be in this case?

(5) What are the advantages and disadvantages of focusing on a project's market risk?

Computer-Related Problems

Work the problems in this section only if you are using the computer problem diskette.

NPV and IRR analysis   **9-23** Use the model in File C9 to solve this problem. West Coast Chemical Company (WCCC) is considering two mutually exclusive investments. The projects' expected net cash flows are as follows:

Expected Net Cash Flows

Year	Project A	Project B
0	($45,000)	($50,000)
1	(20,000)	15,000
2	11,000	15,000
3	20,000	15,000
4	30,000	15,000
5	45,000	15,000

a. Construct NPV profiles for Projects A and B.
b. Calculate each project's IRR.
c. If the required rate of return for each project is 13 percent, which project should West Coast select? If the required rate of return were 9 percent, what would be the proper choice? If the required rate of return were 15 percent, what would be the proper choice?
d. At what rate do the NPV profiles of the two projects cross?
e. Project A has a large cash flow in Year 5 associated with ending the project. WCCC's management is confident of Project A's cash flows in Years 0 to 4 but is uncertain about what its Year 5 cash flow will be. (There is no uncertainty about Project B's cash flows.) Under a worst-case scenario, Project A's Year 5 cash flow will be $40,000, whereas under a best-case scenario, the cash flow will be $50,000. Redo parts a, b, and d for each scenario, assuming a 13 percent required rate of return. If the required rate of return for each project is 13 percent, which project should be selected under each scenario?

Expansion project   **9-24** Use the model in File C9 to solve this problem. Golden State Bakers Inc. (GSB) has an opportunity to invest in a new dough machine. GSB needs more productive capacity, so the new machine will not replace an existing machine. The new machine costs $260,000 and will require modifications costing $15,000. It has an expected useful life of 10 years, will be depreciated using the MACRS method over its 5-year class life, and has an expected salvage value of $12,500 at the end of Year 10. (See Table 9B-2 for MACRS recovery allowance percentages.) The machine will require a $22,500 investment in net working capital. It is expected to generate additional sales revenues of $125,000 per year, but its use will also increase annual cash operating expenses by $55,000 (excluding depreciation). GSB's required rate of return is 10 percent, and its marginal tax rate is 40 percent. The machine's book value at the end of Year 10 will be zero, so GSB will have to pay taxes on the $12,500 salvage value.
a. What is the NPV of this expansion project? Should GSB purchase the new machine?
b. Should GSB purchase the new machine if it is expected to be used for only 5 years and then sold for $31,250? (Note that the model is set up to handle a 5-year life; you need only enter the new life and salvage value.)

c. Would the machine be profitable if revenues increased by only $105,000 per year? Assume a 10-year project life and a salvage value of $12,500.

d. Suppose that revenues rose by $125,000 but that expenses rose by $65,000. Would the machine be acceptable under these conditions? Assume a 10-year project life and a salvage value of $12,500.

APPENDIX 9A

Computing NPV and IRR Using a Financial Calculator

To compute the NPV and the IRR of a project using your financial calculator, you need to determine how the CF function is used. You should refer to the manual that came with your calculator. The steps for computing the NPV and the IRR for Project S using the Texas Instruments BAII PLUS are shown below:

1. Enter the cash flow function by pressing **CF**. Press one of the arrow keys, either **↑** or **↓**, to see if the registers are clear. If there are numbers in any of the registers, you can clear them by pressing the 2nd key, **2nd**, and then pressing **CE/C**, which has "CLR Work" written above (this is a secondary function).

2. Enter CF_0 as follows: 3,000 **+/−** **ENTER**.

3. Enter CF_1 as follows: **↓** 1,500 **ENTER**. Press **↓** again, and you will see F01 = 1 displayed on the screen — the calculator is telling you that it has assumed the 1,500 cash flow will occur (its frequency) only once. For capital budgeting problems where the same cash flow occurs more than once in consecutive periods, you can enter the frequency of the CFs, and then press **ENTER** to change the F01 value (the frequency for consecutive CFs received later in a project's life can be similarly changed).

4. Enter the remaining CFs in the same manner:

CF_2: **↓** 1,200 **ENTER**, **↓**
CF_3: **↓** 800 **ENTER**, **↓**
CF_4: **↓** 300 **ENTER**, **↓**

5. Once all the CFs have been entered, press **NPV**. I = 0 will appear on the display. Enter 10 and press **ENTER** **↓** **CPT** to get the answer: NPV =161.3277782.

6. To compute the IRR after all the CFs have been entered, press **IRR** **CPT** to get IRR = 13.11397895.

APPENDIX 9B

Depreciation

Suppose a firm buys a milling machine for $100,000 and uses it for five years, after which it is scrapped. The cost of the goods produced by the machine each year must include a charge for using the machine and reducing its value, and this charge is called *depreciation*. In this appendix we review some of the depreciation concepts covered in your accounting course(s).

Companies often calculate depreciation one way when figuring taxes and another way when reporting income to investors: many use the *straight line* method for stockholder reporting (or "book" purposes), but they use the fastest rate permitted by law for tax purposes. According to the straight line method, you normally would take the cost of the asset, subtract its estimated salvage value, and divide the net amount by the asset's useful economic life. For an asset with a five-year life that costs $100,000 and has a $12,500 salvage value, the annual straight line depreciation charge is ($100,000 − $12,500)/5 = $17,500. Note, however, as we discuss later in this appendix, that salvage value is not considered for tax depreciation purposes.

For tax purposes, Congress changes the permissible tax depreciation methods from time to time. Prior to 1954, the straight line method was required for tax purposes, but in 1954 accelerated methods (double-declining balance and sum-of-years'-digits) were permitted. Then, in 1981, the old accelerated methods were replaced by a simpler procedure known as the Accelerated Cost Recovery System (ACRS). The ACRS system was changed again in 1986 as a part of the Tax Reform Act, and it is now known as the Modified Accelerated Cost Recovery System (MACRS).

Tax Depreciation Life

For tax purposes, the *entire* cost of an asset is expensed over its depreciable life. Historically, an asset's depreciable life was determined by its estimated useful economic life; it was intended that an asset would be fully depreciated at approximately the same time that it reached the end of its useful economic life. However, MACRS totally abandoned that practice and set simple guidelines that created several classes of assets, each with a more-or-less arbitrarily prescribed life called a *recovery period* or *class life*. The MACRS class life bears only a rough relationship to the expected useful economic life.

A major effect of the MACRS system has been to shorten the depreciable lives of assets, thus giving businesses larger tax deductions and thereby increasing their cash flows available for reinvestment. Table 9B-1 describes the types of property that fit into the different class life groups, and Table 9B-2 sets forth the MACRS recovery allowances (depreciation rates) for selected classes of investment property.

Consider Table 9B-1 first. The first column gives the MACRS class life, while the second column describes the types of assets that fall into each category. Property classified with lives equal to or greater than 27.5 years (real estate) must be depreciated by the straight line method, but assets classified in the other categories can be depreciated either by the accelerated method using the rates shown in Table 9B-2 or by an alternate straight line method.

As we saw earlier in the chapter, higher depreciation expenses result in lower taxes, hence higher cash flows. Therefore, because a firm has the choice of using the alternate straight line rates or the accelerated rates shown in Table 9B-2, most elect to use the accelerated rates. The yearly recovery allowance, or depreciation expense, is determined by multiplying each asset's *depreciable basis* by the applicable recovery percentage shown in Table 9B-2. Calculations are discussed in the following sections.

HALF-YEAR CONVENTION   Under MACRS, the assumption is generally made that property is placed in service in the middle of the first year. Thus, for three-year class life property, the

---

Major Classes and Asset Lives for MACRS

Class	Type of Property
3-year	Certain special manufacturing tools
5-year	Automobiles, light-duty trucks, computers, and certain special manufacturing equipment
7-year	Most industrial equipment, office furniture, and fixtures
10-year	Certain longer-lived equipment and many water vessels
15-year	Certain land improvement, such as shrubbery, fences, and roads; service station buildings
20-year	Farm buildings
27.5-year	Residential rental real property such as apartment buildings
39-year	All nonresidential real property, including commercial and industrial buildings

TABLE 9B-2

Recovery Allowance Percentages for Personal Property

Ownership Year	Class of Investment			
	3-Year	5-Year	7-Year	10-Year
1	33%	20%	14%	10%
2	45	32	25	18
3	15	19	17	14
4	7	12	13	12
5		11	9	9
6		6	9	7
7			9	7
8			4	7
9				7
10				6
11				3
	100%	100%	100%	100%

NOTE: These recovery allowance percentages were taken from the Internal Revenue Service web site, http://www.irs.ustreas.gov. The percentages are based on the 200 percent declining balance method prescribed by MACRS, with a switch to straight line depreciation at some point in the asset's life. For example, consider the five-year recovery allowance percentages. The straight line percentage would be 20 percent per year, so the 200 percent declining balance multiplier is 2.0(20%) = 40% = 0.4. However, because the half-year convention applies, the MACRS percentage for Year 1 is 20 percent. For Year 2, there is 80 percent of the depreciable basis remaining to be depreciated, so the recovery allowance percentage is 0.40(80%) = 32%, and so on. Although the tax tables carry the allowance percentages to two decimal places, we have rounded to the nearest whole number for ease of illustration.

recovery period begins in the middle of the year the asset is placed in service and ends three years later. The effect of the *half-year convention* is to extend the recovery period out one more year, so three-year class life property is depreciated over four calendar years, five-year property is depreciated over six calendar years, and so on. This convention is incorporated into Table 9B-2's recovery allowance percentages.[1]

DEPRECIABLE BASIS The *depreciable basis* is a critical element of MACRS because each year's allowance (depreciation expense) depends jointly on the asset's depreciable basis and its MACRS class life. The depreciable basis under MACRS is equal to the purchase price of the asset plus any shipping and installation costs. The basis is not adjusted for salvage value.

DEPRECIATION ILLUSTRATION Assume that Argile Textiles buys a $150,000 machine that falls into the MACRS five-year class life and places it into service on March 15, 2000. Argile must pay an additional $30,000 for delivery and installation. Salvage value is not considered, so the machine's depreciable basis is $180,000. (Delivery and installation charges are included in the depreciable basis rather than expensed in the year incurred.) Each year's recovery

[1]The half-year convention also applies if the straight line alternative is used, with half of one year's depreciation taken in the first year, a full year's depreciation taken in each of the remaining years of the asset's class life, and the remaining half-year's depreciation taken in the year following the end of the class life. You should recognize that virtually all companies have computerized depreciation systems. Each asset's depreciation pattern is programmed into the system at the time of its acquisition, and the computer aggregates the depreciation allowances for all assets when the accountants close the books and prepare the financial statements and tax returns.

allowance (tax depreciation expense) is determined by multiplying the depreciable basis by the applicable recovery allowance percentage. Thus, the depreciation expense for 2000 is 0.20($180,000) = $36,000, and for 2001 it is 0.32($180,000) = $57,600. Similarly, the depreciation expense is $34,200 for 2002, $21,600 for 2003, $19,800 for 2004, and $10,800 for 2005. The total depreciation expense over the six-year recovery period is $180,000, which is equal to the depreciable basis of the machine.

As noted earlier, most firms use straight line depreciation for stockholder reporting purposes but MACRS for tax purposes. For these firms, for capital budgeting, MACRS should be used, because in capital budgeting, we are concerned with cash flows, not reported income.

Problem

Depreciation effects

9B-1   Christina Manning, great granddaughter of the founder of Manning Tile Products and current president of the company, believes in simple, conservative accounting. In keeping with her philosophy, she has decreed that the company shall use alternative straight line depreciation, based on the MACRS class lives, for all newly acquired assets. Your boss, the financial vice-president and the only nonfamily officer, has asked you to develop an exhibit that shows how much this policy costs the company in terms of market value. Manning is interested in increasing the value of the firm's stock because she fears a family stockholder revolt, which might remove her from office. For your exhibit, assume that the company spends $100 million each year on new capital projects; that the projects have, on average, a 10-year class life; that the company has a 9 percent required return; and that its tax rate is 34 percent. (Hint: Show how much the NPV of projects in an average year would increase if Manning used the standard MACRS recovery allowances.)

APPENDIX 9C

Comparing Projects with Unequal Lives

Two procedures used to compare capital projects with unequal lives are (1) the replacement chain (common life) method, and (2) the equivalent annual annuity method.

Suppose the company we followed throughout the chapter, HEP, is planning to modernize its production facilities, and as a part of the process, it is considering either a conveyor system (Project C) or some forklift trucks (Project F) for moving materials from the parts department to the main assembly line. Both the expected net cash flows and the NPVs for these two mutually exclusive alternatives are shown in Figure 9C-1. We see that Project C, when discounted at a 15 percent required rate of return, has the higher NPV and thus appears to be the better project, in spite of the fact that F has the higher IRR.

REPLACEMENT CHAIN (COMMON LIFE) APPROACH
A method of comparing projects of unequal lives that assumes each project can be replicated as many times as necessary to reach a common life span; the NPVs over this life span are then compared, and the project with the higher common life NPV is chosen.

Replacement Chain (Common Life) Approach

Although the analysis in Figure 9C-1 suggests that Project C should be selected, this analysis is incomplete, and the decision to choose Project C is actually incorrect. If we choose Project F, we will have the opportunity to make a similar investment in three years, and if cost and revenue conditions continue at the Figure 9C-1 levels, this second investment also will be profitable. However, if we choose Project C, we will not have this second investment opportunity. Therefore, to make a proper comparison of Projects C and F, we could apply the **replacement chain (common life) approach;** that is, we could find the NPV of Project F over a six-year period and then compare this extended NPV with the NPV of Project C over the same six years.

FIGURE 9C-1

Expected Net Cash Flows for Project C and Project F

PROJECT C:

	0 k = 15% 1	2	3	4	5	6
Net CF	(40,000) 13,000	8,000	14,000	12,000	11,000	15,000

$$NPV_C \text{ at } 15\% = \$5,374$$

$$IRR_C = 19.7\%$$

PROJECT F:

	0 k = 15% 1	2	3
Net CF	(20,000) 7,000	13,000	12,000

$$NPV_F \text{ at } 15\% = \$3,807$$

$$IRR_F = 25.2\%$$

The NPV for Project C as calculated in Figure 9C-1 already is over the six-year common life. For Project F, however, we must expand the analysis to include the replacement of F in Year 3, resulting in the following six-year time line[2]:

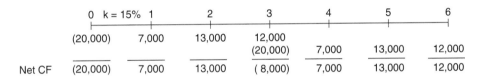

	0 k = 15% 1	2	3	4	5	6
	(20,000) 7,000	13,000	12,000			
			(20,000)	7,000	13,000	12,000
Net CF	(20,000) 7,000	13,000	(8,000)	7,000	13,000	12,000

$$\text{Extended life } NPV_C \text{ at } 15\% = \$6,310$$

Here we make the assumption that Project F's cost and annual cash inflows will not change if the project is repeated in three years and that HEP's required rate of return will remain at 15 percent. Project F's extended NPV is $6,310. This is the value that should be compared with Project C's NPV, $5,374. Because Project F's "true" NPV is greater than that of Project C, Project F should be selected.

Equivalent Annual Annuity Approach

Although the preceding example illustrates why an extended analysis is necessary if we are comparing mutually exclusive projects with different lives, the arithmetic is generally more

---

[2]We also could set up Project F's extended time line as follows:

1. The Stage 1 NPV is $3,807.
2. The Stage 2 NPV is also $3,807, but this value will not accrue until Year 3, so its value today, discounted at 15 percent, is $2,503.
3. The extended life NPV is thus $3,807 + $2,503 = $6,310.

complex in practice. For example, one project might have a six-year life versus a ten-year life for the other. This would require a replacement chain analysis over 30 years, the lowest common denominator of the two lives. In such a situation, it often is simpler to use a second procedure, the **equivalent annual annuity (EAA) method,** which involves three steps:

EQUIVALENT ANNUAL ANNUITY (EAA) METHOD
A method that calculates the annual payments a project would provide if it were an annuity. When comparing projects of unequal lives, the one with the higher equivalent annual annuity should be chosen.

1. Find each project's NPV over its initial life. In Figure 9C-1, we found $NPV_C = \$5,374$ and $NPV_F = \$3,807$.

2. Find the constant annuity cash flow that has the same present value as each project's NPV. For Project F, here is the cash flow time line:

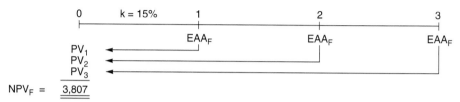

To find the value of EAA_F with a financial calculator, enter -3807 as the PV, k = I = 15, and N = 3, and solve for PMT. The answer is $1,667. This cash flow stream, when discounted back three years at 15 percent, has a present value equal to Project F's original NPV, $3,807. The payment figure we found, $1,667, is called the project's equivalent annual annuity (EAA). The EAA for Project C was similarly found to be $1,420. Thus, Project C has an NPV that is equivalent to an annuity of $1,420 per year, while Project F's NPV is equivalent to an annuity of $1,667.

3. Assuming that continuous replacements can and will be made each time a project's life ends, these EAAs will continue on out to infinity; that is, they will constitute perpetuities. Recognizing that the value of a perpetuity is V = PMT/k, we can find the net present values of the infinite EAAs of Projects C and F as follows:

$$\text{Infinite horizon } NPV_C = \$1,420/0.15 = \$ 9,467$$

$$\text{Infinite horizon } NPV_F = \$1,667/0.15 = \$11,113$$

In effect, the EAA method assumes that each project will, if taken on, be replaced each time it wears out and will provide cash flows equivalent to the calculated annuity value. The PV of this infinite annuity is then the infinite horizon NPV for the project. Because the infinite horizon NPV of F exceeds that of C, Project F should be accepted. Therefore, the EAA method leads to the same decision rule as the replacement chain method — accept Project F.

The EAA method often is easier to apply than the replacement chain method, but the replacement chain method is easier to explain to decision makers. Still, the two methods always lead to the same decision if consistent assumptions are used. Keep in mind that we do not need to make adjustments for unequal lives for independent projects, because we should always accept any project that is independent if its NPV is positive.

Problems

Unequal lives   **9C-1** Keenan Clothes Inc. is considering the replacement of its old, fully depreciated knitting machine. Two new models are available: Machine 190-3, which has a cost of $190,000, a 3-year expected life, and after-tax cash flows (labor savings and depreciation) of $87,000 per year, and Machine 360-6, which has a cost of $360,000, a 6-year life, and after-tax cash flows of $98,300 per year. Knitting machine prices are not expected to rise because inflation will be offset by cheaper components (microprocessors) used in the machines. Assume that the required rate of return appropriate for evaluating the machines is 9 percent.

a. Should the firm replace its old knitting machine, and, if so, which new machine should it use?

b. Suppose the firm's basic patents will expire in 9 years, and the company expects to go out of business at that time. Assume further that the firm depreciates its assets using the straight line method, that its marginal tax rate is 40 percent, and that the used machines can be sold at their book values. Under these circumstances, should the company replace the old machine? Explain.

Unequal lives   **9C-2** Zappe Airlines is considering two alternative planes. Plane A has an expected life of 5 years, will cost $100 million, and will produce net cash flows of $30 million, per year. Plane B has a life of 10 years, will cost $132 million and will produce net cash flows of $25 million per year. Zappe plans to serve the route for 10 years. Inflation in operating costs, airplane costs, and fares is expected to be zero, and the company's required rate of return is 12 percent. By how much would the value of the company increase if it accepted the better project (plane)?

CHAPTER 10

The Cost of Capital

A few years ago, Boomtown Inc., a small Nevada gaming company, announced its intention to purchase National Gaming, a New Jersey casino developer. According to Boomtown's management, the purpose of the acquisition was to improve liquidity and strengthen the company's financial position. But the stockholders balked at the deal, primarily because they believed the transaction would boost Boomtown's cost of capital to more than 20 percent. With such a high cost of capital, Boomtown would have difficulty finding growth opportunities (acceptable capital budgeting projects) in the future, and, quite possibly, the burden of the high financing costs could eventually force the firm into bankruptcy. Thus, Boomtown's stockholders wanted the deal blocked or restructured to reduce the impact on the company's cost of capital. The stockholders realized that a high cost of capital would be detrimental to their wealth position. And, just as home buyers prefer to avoid high mortgage rates, companies try to avoid using funds with high costs.

On the other side of the coin, Federated Department Stores was successful in its attempt to acquire R. H. Macy & Company in 1994. Federated, which had emerged from bankruptcy in 1992, was able to purchase Macy, which had been in bankruptcy since 1992, primarily because Citibank and Chemical Bank arranged a $2.8 billion loan package with a moderate interest rate. The arrangement did not increase Federated's debt position much; thus its cost of debt was not affected significantly — in fact, Federated was able to *save* about $40 million in interest with the bank arrangement compared with similar borrowing alternatives. The fact that the new capital needed for the acquisition was not expected to change Federated's existing cost of capital position was critical to the success of the deal.

Firms raise capital in the financial markets, where interest rates and other yields change continuously. We know that as interest rates change, so do the costs associated with the various types of capital. For instance, in 1994, interest rates increased dramatically while stock prices dropped, which meant that companies had to pay higher costs for using investors' funds.

Continued

Since then, the trend has reversed — in 1998, interest rates were very low, and the stock market reached record highs.

As you read this chapter, keep in mind that firms need funds provided by investors to take advantage of acceptable capital budgeting projects. The financial marketplace, which consists of investors like you, determines the "price" firms will have to pay for the funds they use. It is essential for us to be able to determine the "price," or the cost, of the capital used by a firm so that we know if the funds are being invested appropriately.

COST OF CAPITAL
The firm's average cost of funds, which is the average return required by the firm's investors; what must be paid to attract funds.

It is vitally important that a firm knows how much it pays for the funds used to purchase assets. The average return required by the firm's investors determines how much must be paid to attract funds — it is the firm's average cost of funds, which more commonly is termed the **cost of capital.** The firm's cost of capital is very important because it represents the minimum rate of return that must be earned from investments, such as capital budgeting projects, to ensure the value of the firm does not decrease — the cost of capital is the firm's *required rate of return*. For example, if investors provide funds to a firm for an average cost of 15 percent, wealth will decrease if the funds are used to generate returns less than 15 percent, wealth will not change if exactly 15 percent is earned, and wealth will increase if returns greater than 15 percent can be generated.

In this chapter, we discuss the concept of cost of capital, how the average cost of capital is determined, and how the cost of capital is used in financial decision making. Most of the models and formulas used in this chapter are the same ones we developed in Chapter 7, where we described how assets are valued. How much it costs a firm for its funds is based on the return demanded by investors — if the return offered by the firm is not high enough, then investors will not provide sufficient funds. In other words, the rate of return an investor earns on a corporate security is effectively a cost to the firm of using those funds, so the same models are used by investors and by corporate treasurers to determine required rates of return.

Our first topic in this chapter is the logic of the weighted average cost of capital. Next, we consider the costs of the major types of capital, after which we see how the costs of the individual components of the capital structure are brought together to form a weighted average cost of capital.

The Logic of the Weighted Average Cost of Capital

It is possible to finance a firm entirely with equity funds by issuing only stock. In that case, the cost of capital used to analyze capital budgeting decisions should be the company's required return on equity. However, most firms raise a substantial portion of their funds as long-term debt, and some also use preferred stock. For these firms, their cost of capital must reflect the average cost of the various sources of long-term funds used, not just the firms' costs of equity.

Assume that Daflex Inc. has a 10 percent cost of debt and a 14 percent cost of equity. Further, assume that Daflex has made the decision to finance next year's projects by selling debt only. The argument is sometimes made that the cost of capital for these new projects is 10 percent because only debt will be used to finance them. However, this position is incorrect. If Daflex finances a particular set of projects with debt, the firm will be using up some of its potential for obtaining new debt in the future. As expansion occurs in subsequent years, Daflex will at some point find it necessary to raise additional equity to prevent the debt/assets ratio from becoming too large.

To illustrate, suppose Daflex borrows heavily at 10 percent during 2000, using up its debt capacity in the process, to finance projects yielding 11 percent. In 2001 it has new projects available that yield 13 percent, well above the return on 2000 projects, but it cannot accept them because they would have to be financed with 14 percent equity money. To avoid this problem, Daflex should be viewed as an ongoing concern, and *the cost of capital used in capital budgeting should be calculated as a weighted average, or combination, of the various types of funds generally used, regardless of the specific financing used to fund a particular project.*

 ## Self-Test Question

Why should the cost of capital used in capital budgeting be calculated as a weighted average of the various types of funds the firm generally uses, regardless of the specific financing used to fund a particular project?

Basic Definitions

CAPITAL COMPONENT
One of the types of capital used by firms to raise money.

The items on the right side of a firm's balance sheet — various types of debt, preferred stock, and common equity — are its **capital components.** Any increase in total assets must be financed by an increase in one or more of these capital components.

Capital is a necessary factor of production, and, like any other factor, it has a cost. The cost of each component is called the *component cost* of that particular type of capital; for example, if Daflex can borrow money at 10 percent, its component cost of debt is 10 percent. Throughout this chapter we concentrate on debt, preferred stock, retained earnings, and new issues of common stock, which are the four major capital structure components. We use the following symbols to designate specific component costs of capital:

k_d = interest rate on the firm's debt = before-tax component cost of debt. For Daflex, k_d = 10%.

$k_{dT} = k_d(1 - T)$ = after-tax component cost of debt, where T is the firm's marginal tax rate. k_{dT} is the debt cost used to calculate the weighted average cost of capital. For Daflex, T = 40%, so $k_{dT} = k_d(1 - T) = 10\%(1 - 0.4) = 10\%(0.6) = 6.0\%$.

k_{ps} = component cost of preferred stock. Daflex has no preferred stock at this time, but, as new funds are raised, the company plans to issue preferred stock. The cost of preferred stock, k_{ps}, will be 11 percent.

k_s = component cost of retained earnings (or internal equity). It is identical to the k_s developed in Chapters 7 and 8 and defined there as the required rate of return on common stock. As we will see shortly, for Daflex, $k_s \approx 14\%$.

k_e = component cost of external equity obtained by issuing new common stock as opposed to retaining earnings. As we shall see, it is necessary to distinguish between common equity needs that can be satisfied by retained earnings and the common equity needs that are satisfied by selling new stock. This is why we distinguish between internal and external equity, k_s and k_e. Further, k_e is always greater than k_s. For Daflex, $k_e \approx 15\%$.

WACC = the weighted average cost of capital. In the future, when Daflex needs *new* capital to finance asset expansion, it will raise part of the new funds as debt, part as preferred stock, and part as common equity (with common equity coming either from retained earnings or from the issuance of new common stock).[1] We calculate WACC for Daflex Inc. shortly.

CAPITAL STRUCTURE
The combination or mix of different types of capital used by a firm.

These definitions and concepts are explained in detail in the remainder of the chapter, where we develop a marginal cost of capital (MCC) schedule that can be used in capital budgeting. Later, in Chapter 11, we extend the analysis to determine the mix of types of capital, which is termed the **capital structure,** that will minimize the firm's cost of capital and thereby maximize its value.

Self-Test Question

Identify the firm's four major capital structure components, and give their respective component cost symbols.

Cost of Debt, k_{dT}

The **after-tax cost of debt, k_{dT},** is the interest rate on debt, k_d, less the tax savings that result because interest is deductible. This is the same as k_d multiplied by $(1 - T)$, where T is the firm's marginal tax rate:

10-1

$$\frac{\text{After-tax}}{\text{component cost of debt}} = k_{dT} = \frac{\text{Bondholders' required}}{\text{rate of return}} - \frac{\text{Tax}}{\text{savings}}$$

$$= k_d - k_d \times T = k_d(1 - T)$$

AFTER-TAX COST OF DEBT, k_{dT}
The relevant cost of new debt, taking into account the tax deductibility of interest; used to calculate the WACC.

In effect, the government pays part of the cost of debt because interest is deductible. Therefore, if Daflex can borrow at an interest rate of 10 percent, and if it has a marginal tax rate of 40 percent, then its after-tax cost of debt is 6 percent:

---

[1]Firms try to keep their debt, preferred stock, and common equity in optimal proportions; we will learn how they establish these proportions in Chapter 11. However, firms do not try to maintain any proportional relationship between the common stock and retained earnings accounts as shown on the balance sheet — for capital structure purposes, common equity is common equity, whether it comes from selling new common stock or from retaining earnings.

$$k_{dT} = k_d(1 - T) = 10\%(1.0 - 0.4) = 10\%(0.6) = 6.0\%$$

We use the after-tax cost of debt because the value of the firm's stock, which we want to maximize, depends on *after-tax* cash flows. Because interest is a deductible expense, it produces tax savings that reduce the net cost of debt, making the after-tax cost of debt less than the before-tax cost. We are concerned with after-tax cash flows, so after-tax rates of return are appropriate.[2]

Note that the cost of debt is the interest rate on *new* debt, not that on already outstanding debt; in other words, we are interested in the *marginal* cost of debt. Our primary concern with the cost of capital is to use it for capital budgeting decisions — for example, a decision about whether to obtain the capital needed to acquire a new machine tool. The rate at which the firm has borrowed in the past is a sunk cost, and it is irrelevant for cost of capital purposes.

In Chapter 7, we solved the following equation to find k_d, the rate of return, or yield to maturity, for a bond:

$$V_d = \sum_{t=1}^{N} \frac{INT}{(1 + k_d)^t} + \frac{M}{(1 + k_d)^N}$$

where V_d is the current market price of the bond, INT is the dollar coupon interest paid per period, M is the face value repaid at maturity, and N is the number of interest payments remaining until maturity.

Assume that Daflex is going to issue a new 9 percent coupon bond in a few days. The bond has face value of $1,000 and a 20-year life, and interest is paid annually. If the market price of similar risk bonds is $915, what is Daflex's k_d? The solution is set up as follows:

$$\$915 = \frac{\$90}{(1 + k_d)^1} + \frac{\$90}{(1 + k_d)^2} + \cdots + \frac{\$1,090}{(1 + k_d)^{20}}$$

Whether you use the trial-and-error method, the time value of money functions on your calculator, or the approximation equation given in Chapter 7, you should find k_d is 10 percent, which is the before-tax cost of debt for this bond.[3] For

---

[2]The tax rate is zero for a firm with losses. Therefore, for a company that does not pay taxes, the cost of debt is not reduced; that is, in Equation 10-1 the tax rate equals zero, so the after-tax cost of debt is equal to the interest rate.

[3]It should also be noted that we have ignored flotation costs (the costs incurred for new issuances) on debt because nearly all the debt issued by small and medium-sized firms is privately placed and hence has no flotation cost. However, if bonds are publicly placed and do involve flotation costs, the solution value of k_d in this formula is used as the before-tax cost of debt:

$$V_d (1 - F) = \sum_{t=1}^{N} \frac{INT}{(1 + k_d)^t} + \frac{M}{(1 + k_d)^N}$$

Here F is the percentage (in decimal form) amount of the bond flotation, or issuing, cost, and the other variables are as defined in the body of the text; thus k_d is the cost of debt adjusted to reflect flotation costs. If we assume that the bond in the example calls for annual payments, that it has a 20-year maturity, and that F = 2%, then the flotation-adjusted, before-tax cost of debt is 10.23 percent versus 10 percent before the flotation adjustment.

example, using the equation to approximate the yield to maturity (Equation 7-3), we find

$$\text{Yield to maturity} \approx \frac{\$90 + \left[\dfrac{\$1,000 - \$915}{20}\right]}{\left[\dfrac{2(\$915) + \$1,000}{3}\right]} = \frac{\$94.25}{\$943.33} = 0.100 = 10.0\%$$

Daflex's marginal tax rate is 40 percent, so the after-tax cost of debt, k_{dT}, is 6% = 10%(1 − 0.40).

Self-Test Questions

Why is the after-tax cost of debt rather than the before-tax cost used to calculate the weighted average cost of capital?

Is the relevant cost of debt the interest rate on already outstanding debt or that on new debt? Why?

Cost of Preferred Stock, k_{ps}

In Chapter 7, we found that the dividend associated with preferred stock, which we designate D_{ps} here, is constant and that preferred stock has no stated maturity. Thus, D_{ps} represents a perpetuity, and the component **cost of preferred stock, k_{ps},** is the preferred dividend, D_{ps}, divided by the net issuing price, NP, or the price the firm receives after deducting the costs of issuing the stock:

10-2
$$\text{Component cost of preferred stock} = k_{ps} = \frac{D_{ps}}{NP} = \frac{D_{ps}}{P_0 - \text{Flotation costs}}$$

COST OF PREFERRED STOCK, k_{ps}
The rate of return investors require on the firm's preferred stock. k_{ps} is calculated as the preferred dividend, D_{ps}, divided by the net issuing price, NP.

For example, Daflex expects to issue preferred stock that pays a $10.25 dividend per share and sells for $96 per share in the market. It will cost 3 percent, or $2.88 per share, to issue the new preferred stock, so Daflex will net $93.12 per share. Therefore, Daflex's cost of preferred stock is 11 percent:

$$k_{ps} = \frac{\$10.25}{\$96.00 - \$2.88} = \frac{\$10.25}{\$93.12} = 0.110 = 11.0\%$$

No tax adjustments are made when calculating k_{ps} because preferred dividends, unlike interest expense on debt, are not tax deductible, so there are no tax savings associated with the use of preferred stock.

Self-Test Questions

Does the component cost of preferred stock include or exclude flotation costs? Explain.

Is a tax adjustment made to the cost of preferred stock? Why or why not?

Cost of Retained Earnings, k_s

The costs of debt and preferred stock are based on the returns investors require on these securities. Similarly, the **cost of retained earnings, k_s,** is the rate of return stockholders require on equity capital the firm obtains by retaining earnings that otherwise could be distributed to common stockholders as dividends.[4]

The reason we must assign a cost of capital to retained earnings involves the *opportunity cost principle.* The firm's after-tax earnings literally belong to its stockholders. Bondholders are compensated by interest payments and preferred stockholders by preferred dividends, but the earnings remaining after interest and preferred dividends belong to the common stockholders, and these earnings serve to compensate stockholders for the use of their capital. Management might either pay out the earnings in the form of dividends or retain earnings and reinvest them in the business. If management decides to retain earnings, there is an opportunity cost involved — stockholders could have received the earnings as dividends and invested this money in other stocks, in bonds, in real estate, or in anything else. Thus, the firm should earn a return on earnings it retains that is at least as great as the stockholders themselves could earn on alternative investments of comparable risk.

What rate of return can stockholders expect to earn on equivalent-risk investments? First, recall from Chapter 8 that stocks are normally in equilibrium, with the expected and required rates of return being equal: $\hat{k}_s = k_s$. Therefore, we can assume that Daflex's stockholders expect to earn a return of k_s on their money. *If the firm cannot invest retained earnings and earn at least k_s, it should pay these funds to its stockholders and let them invest directly in other assets that do provide this return.*[5]

Whereas debt and preferred stocks are contractual obligations that have easily determined costs, it is not as easy to measure k_s. However, we can employ the principles developed in Chapters 7 and 8 to produce reasonably good cost of equity estimates. To begin, we know that if a stock is in equilibrium (which is the typical situation), then its required rate of return, k_s, is also equal to its expected rate of return, $\hat{k}_s$. Further, its required return is equal to a risk-free rate, k_{RF}, plus a risk premium, RP, whereas the expected return on a constant growth stock is equal to the stock's dividend yield, $\hat{D}_1/P_0$, plus its expected growth rate, g:

10-3

$$\text{Required rate of return} = \text{Expected rate of return}$$

$$k_s = k_{RF} + RP = \frac{\hat{D}_1}{P_0} + g = \hat{k}_s$$

---

[4]The term *retained earnings* can be interpreted to mean either the balance sheet item "retained earnings," consisting of all the earnings retained in the business throughout its history, or the income statement item "additions to retained earnings." The income statement item is used in this chapter; for our purpose, *retained earnings* refers to that part of current earnings not paid out in dividends and hence available for reinvestment in the business this year.

[5]Dividends and capital gains are taxed differently, with long-term gains being taxed at a lower rate than dividends for many stockholders. That makes it beneficial for companies to retain earnings rather than to pay them out as dividends, and that, in turn, results in a relatively low cost of capital for retained earnings. This point is discussed in Chapter 11.

Because the two must be equal, we can estimate k_s either as $k_s = k_{RF} + RP$ or as $\hat{k}_s = \hat{D}_1/P_0 + g$. Actually, three methods are commonly used for finding the cost of retained earnings: (1) the CAPM approach, (2) the bond-yield-plus-risk-premium approach, and (3) the discounted cash flow (DCF) approach. These three approaches are discussed in the following sections.

The CAPM Approach

We developed the Capital Asset Pricing Model (CAPM) in Chapter 8:

| 10-4 | $$k_s = k_{RF} + (k_M - k_{RF})\beta_s$$ |

Equation 10-4 shows that the CAPM estimate of k_s begins with the risk-free rate, k_{RF}, to which is added a risk premium that is based on the stock's relation to the market as measured by its β_s and the magnitude of the market risk premium, which is the difference between the market return, k_M, and the risk-free rate, k_{RF}.

To illustrate the CAPM approach, assume that $k_{RF} = 6\%$, $k_M = 14\%$, and $\beta_s = 0.95$ for Daflex's common stock. Using the CAPM approach, Daflex's cost of retained earnings, k_s, is calculated as follows:

$$k_s = 6\% + (14\% - 6\%)\,(0.95) = 6\% + 7.6\% = 13.6\%$$

It should be noted that although the CAPM approach appears to yield an accurate, precise estimate of k_s, there are actually several problems with it. First, as we saw in Chapter 8, if a firm's stockholders are not well diversified, they might be concerned with total risk rather than with market risk only (measured by β); in this case the firm's true investment risk will not be measured by its beta, and the CAPM procedure will understate the correct value of k_s. Further, even if the CAPM method is valid, it is difficult to obtain correct estimates of the inputs required to make it operational: (1) There is controversy about whether to use long- or short-term Treasury yields for k_{RF}, and (2) both β_s and k_M should be estimated values, which often are difficult to obtain.

Bond-Yield-plus-Risk-Premium Approach

Although it is a subjective procedure, analysts often estimate a firm's cost of common equity by adding a risk premium of 3 to 5 percentage points to the interest rate on the firm's own long-term debt. It is logical to think that firms with risky, low-rated, and consequently high-interest-rate debt will also have risky, high-cost equity. Using this logic to estimate the cost of common stock is relatively easy because all we have to do is add a risk premium to a readily observable debt cost. For example, Daflex's cost of equity might be estimated as follows:

$$k_s = \text{Bond yield} + \text{Risk premium} = 10\% + 4\% = 14\%$$

Because the 4 percent risk premium is a judgmental estimate, the estimated value of k_s also is judgmental. Empirical work suggests that the risk premium over a firm's own bond yield generally has ranged from 3 to 5 percentage points, so this method is not likely to produce a precise cost of equity — about all it can do is get us "into the right ballpark."

Discounted Cash Flow (DCF) Approach

In Chapter 7 we learned that both the price and the expected rate of return on a share of common stock depend, ultimately, on the dividends expected on the stock. The value of a share of stock can then be written as

10-5

$$P_0 = \frac{\hat{D}_1}{(1 + k_s)^1} + = \frac{\hat{D}_2}{(1 + k_s)^2} + \cdots + \frac{\hat{D}_\infty}{(1 + k_s)^\infty}$$

$$= \sum_{t=1}^{\infty} \frac{\hat{D}_t}{(1 + k_s)^t}$$

Here P_0 is the current price of the stock, $\hat{D}_t$ is the dividend expected to be paid at the end of Year t, and k_s is the required rate of return. If dividends are expected to grow at a constant rate, then, as we saw in Chapter 7, Equation 10-5 reduces to

10-5a

$$P_0 = \frac{\hat{D}_1}{k_s - g}$$

We can solve Equation 10-5a for k_s to estimate the required rate of return on common equity, which for the marginal investor is also equal to the expected rate of return:

10-6

$$k_s = \hat{k}_s = \frac{\hat{D}_1}{P_0} + g$$

Thus, investors expect to receive a dividend yield, $\hat{D}_1/P_0$, plus a capital gain, g, for a total expected return of $\hat{k}_s$, and in equilibrium this expected return is also equal to the required return, k_s. From this point on, we assume that equilibrium exists, and we use the terms k_s and $\hat{k}_s$ interchangeably.

It is relatively easy to determine the dividend yield, but it is difficult to establish the proper growth rate. If past growth rates in earnings and dividends have been relatively stable, and if investors appear to be projecting a continuation of past trends, then g can be based on the firm's historical growth rate. However, if the company's past growth has been abnormally high or low, either because of its own unique situation or because of general economic fluctuations, then historical growth probably should not be used. Security analysts regularly make earnings and dividend growth forecasts, looking at such factors as projected sales, profit margins, and competitive factors. For example, *Value Line,* which is available in most libraries, provides growth rate forecasts for about 1,700 companies, and Merrill Lynch, Salomon Smith Barney, and other organizations make similar forecasts. Therefore, someone making a cost of capital estimate can obtain several analysts' forecasts, average them, and use the average as a proxy for the growth expectations, g.[6]

To illustrate the DCF approach, suppose Daflex's stock sells for $50; it is expected that the next dividend (in 2000) will be $4.70; and its expected long-term growth rate is 5 percent. Daflex's expected and required rate of return, and hence its cost of retained earnings, is 14.4 percent:

$$\hat{k}_s = k_s = \frac{\$4.70}{\$50.00} + 0.05 = 0.094 + 0.05 = 0.144 = 14.4\%$$

This 14.4 percent is the minimum rate of return that management must expect to earn to justify retaining earnings and plowing them back into the business rather than paying them out to stockholders as dividends.

We have used three methods to estimate the cost of retained earnings, which actually is a single number. To summarize, we found the cost of common equity to be (1) 13.6 percent using the CAPM method, (2) 14.0 percent with the bond-yield-plus-risk-premium approach, and (3) 14.4 percent using the constant growth model of the DCF approach. It is not unusual to get different estimates, because each of the approaches is based on different assumptions — the CAPM assumes investors are well diversified, the bond-yield-plus-risk-premium approach assumes the cost of equity is closely related to the firm's cost of debt, and the constant growth model assumes the firm's dividends and earnings will grow at a constant rate far into the future. So, which estimate should be used? Probably all of them. Many analysts use multiple approaches to estimate a single value and then average the results. For Daflex, then, the average of the estimates is 14.0% = (13.6% + 14.0% + 14.4%)/3.

People experienced in estimating equity capital costs recognize that both careful analysis and sound judgment are required. It would be nice to pretend that judgment is unnecessary and to specify an easy, precise way of determining the exact cost of equity capital. Unfortunately, this is not possible — finance is in large part a matter of judgment, and we simply must face that fact.

Self-Test Questions

Why must a cost be assigned to retained earnings?

What are the three approaches for estimating the cost of retained earnings?

Identify some problems with the CAPM approach.

What is the reasoning behind the bond-yield-plus-risk-premium approach?

---

[6]Analysts' growth rate forecasts are usually for five years into the future, and the rates provided represent the average growth rate over that five-year horizon. Studies have shown that analysts' forecasts represent the best source of growth rate data for DCF cost of capital estimates. See Robert Harris, "Using Analysts' Growth Rate Forecasts to Estimate Shareholder Required Rates of Return," *Financial Management,* Spring 1986, 58–67.

Which of the components of the constant growth DCF formula is most difficult to estimate? Why?

Cost of Newly Issued Common Stock, or External Equity, k_e

COST OF NEW COMMON EQUITY, k_e
The cost of external equity; based on the cost of retained earnings, but increased for flotation costs.

The **cost of new common equity, k_e,** or external equity capital, is higher than the cost of retained earnings, k_s, because there is a cost to issuing new stock. Because the firm incurs costs when selling new securities, called **flotation costs,** the full market value of the stock cannot be used by the company for investing in capital projects — only the amount left after paying flotation costs is available. Thus, the cost of issuing new common stock (external equity), k_e, is greater than the cost of retained earnings (internal equity), k_s, because there are no flotation costs associated with retained earnings.

FLOTATION COSTS
The expenses incurred when selling new issues of securities.

In general, the cost of issuing new equity, k_e, can be found by modifying the DCF formula used to compute the cost of retained earnings, k_s, to obtain the following equation:

10-7

$$k_e = \frac{\hat{D}_1}{NP} + g = \frac{\hat{D}_1}{P_0\,(1 - F)} + g$$

Here F is the percentage flotation cost incurred in selling the new stock issue, so $P_0(1 - F)$ is the net price per share received by the company.

If Daflex can issue new common stock at a flotation cost of 6 percent, k_e is computed as follows:

$$k_e = \frac{\$4.70}{\$50(1 - 0.06)} + 0.05 = \frac{\$4.70}{\$47} + 0.05 = 0.150 = 15.0\%$$

Using the DCF approach to estimate the cost of retained earnings, we found that investors require a return of $k_s = 14\%$ on the stock. However, because of flotation costs, the company must earn more than 14 percent on funds obtained by selling stock if it is to provide a 14 percent return. Specifically, if the firm earns 15 percent on funds obtained from new stock, then earnings per share will not fall below previously expected earnings, the firm's expected dividend can be maintained, and, as a result, the price per share will not decline. If the firm earns less than 15 percent, then earnings, dividends, and growth will fall below expectations, causing the price of the stock to decline. If it earns more than 15 percent, the price of the stock will rise.

The reason for the flotation adjustment can be made clear by a simple example. Suppose Coastal Realty Company has $100,000 of assets and no debt, it earns a 20 percent return (or $20,000) on its assets, and it pays all earnings out as dividends; thus, its growth rate is zero. The company has 1,000 shares of stock outstanding, so EPS = DPS = $20 = $20,000/1,000, and $P_0 = \$100 = \$100,000/1,000$. Coastal's cost of equity is thus $k_s = \$20/\$100 + 0 = 20\%$. Now suppose Coastal can get a return of 20 percent on new assets. Should it sell new stock to acquire new assets? If it sells 1,000 new shares of stock to the public for $100 per share, but it incurs a 10 percent flotation cost on the issue, it will net $100 − 0.10($100) = $90 per share, or $90,000 in total. It will then invest this $90,000 and earn 20 percent, or $18,000. Its new total earnings will be $38,000, which will consist of $20,000 generated from the old assets plus $18,000 from the new assets. But, the $38,000 will have to be distributed equally to the 2,000 shares of stock that now will be outstanding. Therefore, Coastal's EPS and DPS will decline from $20 to $19 = $38,000/2,000. Because its EPS and DPS will fall, the price of the stock will also fall from $P_0 = 100 to $P_1 = $19/0.20 = 95. This result occurs because investors have put up $100 per share, but the company has received and invested only $90 per share. Thus, we see that the $90 must earn more than 20 percent to provide investors with a 20 percent return on the $100 they put up.

We can use Equation 10-7 to compute the return Coastal must earn on the $90,000 of new assets — that is, the amount raised with the new issue:

$$k_e = \frac{\$20}{\$100(1 - 0.10)} + 0 = 0.2222 = 22.22\%$$

If Coastal invests the funds from the new common stock issue at 22.22 percent, here is what would happen:

New total earnings = $20,000 + $90,000(0.2222) = $40,000

New EPS and DPS = $40,000/2,000 = $20

New price = $20/0.20 = $100 = Original price

Thus, if the return on the new assets is equal to k_e as calculated by Equation 10-7, then EPS, DPS, and the stock price will all remain constant. If the return on the new assets exceeds k_e, then EPS, DPS, and P_0 will rise. This confirms the fact that because of flotation costs, the cost of external equity exceeds the cost of equity raised internally from retained earnings.

Self-Test Questions

Why is the cost of external equity capital higher than the cost of retained earnings?

How can the DCF model be changed to account for flotation costs?

Weighted Average Cost of Capital, WACC

As we will see in the next chapter, each firm has an optimal capital structure, or mix of debt, preferred stock, and common equity, that causes its stock price to be maximized. Therefore, a rational, value-maximizing firm will establish a **target (optimal) capital structure** and then raise new capital in a manner that will keep the actual capital structure on target over time. In this chapter we assume that the firm has identified its optimal capital structure, it uses this optimum as

TARGET (OPTIMAL) CAPITAL STRUCTURE
The percentages of debt, preferred stock, and common equity that will maximize the price of the firm's stock.

WEIGHTED AVERAGE COST OF CAPITAL (WACC)
A weighted average of the component costs of debt, preferred stock, and common equity.

the target, and it raises funds so it remains constantly on target. How the target is established is examined in Chapter 11.[7]

The target proportions of debt, preferred stock, and common equity, along with the component costs of capital, are used to calculate the firm's **weighted average cost of capital (WACC).** To illustrate, suppose Daflex Inc. has determined that in the future it will raise new capital according to the following proportions: 40 percent debt, 10 percent preferred stock, and 50 percent common equity (retained earnings plus common stock). In the preceding sections, we found that its before-tax cost of debt, k_d, is 10 percent, so its after-tax cost of debt, k_{dT}, is 6.0%; its cost of preferred stock, k_{ps}, is 11 percent; and its cost of common equity from retained earnings, k_s, is 14 percent if all of its equity financing comes from retained earnings. Now we can calculate Daflex's weighted average cost of capital (WACC) as follows:

$$10\text{-}8 \quad WACC = \left[\left(\begin{array}{c}\text{Proportion}\\\text{of}\\\text{debt}\end{array}\right) \times \left(\begin{array}{c}\text{After-tax}\\\text{cost of}\\\text{debt}\end{array}\right)\right] + \left[\left(\begin{array}{c}\text{Proportion}\\\text{of preferred}\\\text{stock}\end{array}\right) \times \left(\begin{array}{c}\text{Cost of}\\\text{preferred}\\\text{stock}\end{array}\right)\right] + \left[\left(\begin{array}{c}\text{Proportion}\\\text{of common}\\\text{equity}\end{array}\right) \times \left(\begin{array}{c}\text{Cost of}\\\text{common}\\\text{equity}\end{array}\right)\right]$$

$$= \quad w_d \quad \times \quad k_{dT} \quad + \quad w_{ps} \quad \times \quad k_{ps} \quad + \quad w_s \quad \times \quad k_s$$

$$= 0.40(6\%) + 0.10(11\%) + 0.50(14\%) = 10.5\%$$

Here w_d, w_{ps}, and w_s are the weights used for debt, preferred stock, and common equity, respectively.

Every dollar of new capital that Daflex obtains consists of 40¢ of debt with an after-tax cost of 6 percent, 10¢ of preferred stock with a cost of 11 percent, and 50¢ of common equity (all from additions to retained earnings) with a cost of 14 percent. The average cost of each whole dollar, WACC, is 10.5 percent as long as these conditions continue. If the component costs of capital change when new funds are raised in the future, then WACC changes. We discuss changes in the component costs of capital in the next section.

Self-Test Question

How does one calculate the weighted average cost of capital? Write out the equation.

---

[7]Note that only long-term debt is included in the capital structure. Daflex uses its cost of capital in the capital budgeting process, which involves long-term assets, and it finances those assets with long-term capital. Thus, current liabilities do not enter the calculation. We discuss this point in more detail in Chapter 11. Also, see Eugene F. Brigham, Louis C. Gapenski, and Phillip R. Daves, *Intermediate Financial Management,* 6th ed. (Fort Worth, Tex.: The Dryden Press, 1999), Chapter 5.

The Marginal Cost of Capital, MCC

The marginal cost of any item is the cost of another unit of that item; for example, the marginal cost of labor is the cost of adding one additional worker. The marginal cost of labor might be $25 per person if 10 workers are added but $35 per person if the firm tries to hire 100 new workers because it will be harder to find that many people willing and able to do the work. The same concept applies to capital. As the firm tries to attract more new dollars, at some point, the cost of each dollar will increase. Thus, the **marginal cost of capital (MCC)** is defined as the cost of the last dollar of new capital that the firm raises, and the marginal cost rises as more and more capital is raised during a given period.

MARGINAL COST OF CAPITAL (MCC)
The cost of obtaining another dollar of new capital; the weighted average cost of the last dollar of new capital raised.

In the preceding section, we computed Daflex's WACC to be 10.5 percent. As long as Daflex keeps its capital structure on target, and as long as its debt has an after-tax cost of 6 percent, its preferred stock a cost of 11 percent, and its common equity a cost of 14 percent, then its weighted average cost of capital will be 10.5 percent. Each dollar the firm raises will consist of some long-term debt, some preferred stock, and some common equity, and the cost of the whole dollar will be 10.5 percent — its marginal cost of capital (MCC) will be 10.5 percent.

The MCC Schedule

MARGINAL COST OF CAPITAL SCHEDULE
A graph that relates the firm's weighted average cost of each dollar of capital to the total amount of new capital raised.

A graph that shows how the WACC changes as more and more new capital is raised by the firm is called the **marginal cost of capital schedule.** Figure 10-1 shows Daflex's MCC schedule if the cost of debt, cost of preferred stock, and cost of common equity never change. Here the dots represent dollars raised, and because each dollar of new capital will have an average cost equal to 10.5 percent, the marginal cost of capital for Daflex is constant at 10.5 percent under the assumptions we have used to this point.

Do you think Daflex could actually raise an unlimited amount of new capital at the 10.5 percent cost? Probably not, because, as a practical matter, as a company raises larger and larger amounts of funds during a given time period, the costs of those funds begin to rise, and as this occurs, the weighted average cost of each new dollar also rises. Thus, companies cannot raise unlimited amounts of capital at a constant cost — at some point, the cost of each new dollar will increase, no matter what its source (debt, preferred stock, or common equity).

If we assume Daflex has $800 million in long-term debt and equity, how much can Daflex raise before the cost of its funds increases? As a first step to determining the point at which the MCC begins to rise, recognize that although the company's balance sheet shows total long-term capital of $800 million at the end of 1999, all of this capital was raised in the past, and it has been invested in assets that are now being used in operations. If Daflex wants to raise any new (marginal) capital so that the total amount consists of 40 percent debt, 10 percent preferred stock, and 50 percent common equity, then to raise $1,000,000 in new capital, the company should issue $400,000 of new debt, $100,000 of new preferred stock, and $500,000 of new common equity. The new common equity could come from two sources: (1) retained earnings, defined as that part of this year's profits that management decides to retain in the business rather than pay out as dividends (but not earnings retained in the past, because these amounts already have been invested in existing assets), or (2) proceeds from the sale of new common stock.

FIGURE 10-1

Marginal Cost of Capital (MCC) Schedule for Daflex Inc.

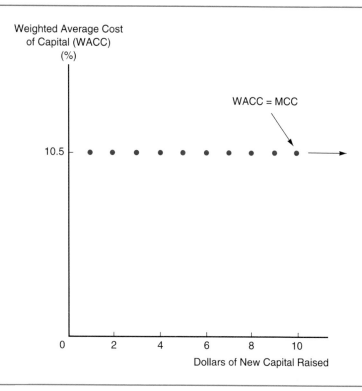

We know that Daflex's WACC will be 10.5 percent as long as the after-tax cost of debt is 6 percent, the cost of preferred stock is 11 percent, and the funds needed from common equity can be satisfied by retained earnings with a cost of 14 percent (k_s = 14%). But, what happens if Daflex expands so rapidly that the retained earnings for the year are not sufficient to meet the common equity needs, forcing the firm to sell new common stock? Earlier, we determined that the cost of issuing new common stock, k_e, will be 15 percent, because the flotation costs associated with the new issue will be 6 percent. Because the cost of common equity increases when common stock has to be issued, the WACC also increases.

How much new capital can Daflex raise before it exhausts its retained earnings and is forced to sell new common stock? In other words, where will an increase in the MCC schedule occur?

Let's assume analysts have forecast that Daflex's 2000 net income will be $80 million, that $30 million would be paid out as dividends, so $50 million would be added to retained earnings (the payout ratio would be 37.5 percent). Thus, Daflex can invest in capital projects to the point where the common equity needs equal $50 million before new common stock has to be issued. Remember, though, that when Daflex needs new funds, the target capital structure indicates only 50 percent of the total should be common equity; the remainder of the funds should come from issues of bonds (40 percent) and preferred stock (10 percent).

Because common equity makes up 50 percent of the total capital raised, we know the following:

$$\text{Common equity} = 0.50(\text{Total new capital raised})$$

We can use this relationship to determine how much total new capital — debt, preferred stock, and retained earnings — can be raised before the $50 million of retained earnings is exhausted and Daflex is forced to sell new common stock. Just set the common equity needs equal to the retained earnings amount, and solve for the total new capital amount:

$$\frac{\text{Common}}{\text{equity}} = \frac{\text{Retained}}{\text{earnings}} = \$50 \text{ million} = 0.50\left(\frac{\text{Total new}}{\text{capital raised}}\right)$$

$$\frac{\text{Total new}}{\text{capital raised}} = \frac{\$50 \text{ million}}{0.50} = \$100 \text{ million}$$

Thus, Daflex can raise a total of $100 million before it has to sell new common stock to finance its capital projects.

If Daflex needs *exactly* $100 million in new capital, the breakdown of the amount that would come from each source of capital and the computation for the weighted average cost of capital (WACC) would be as follows:

Capital Source	Weight	Amount in Millions	After-Tax Component Cost	WACC
Debt	0.40	$ 40	6%	2.4%
Preferred stock	0.10	10	11	1.1
Common equity	0.50	50	14	7.0
	1.00	$100		WACC$_1$ = 10.5%

Therefore, if Daflex needs $100 million or less in new capital in 2000, retained earnings will be just enough to satisfy the common equity requirement, so the firm will not need to sell new common stock and its weighted average cost of capital (WACC) will be 10.5 percent. But, what will happen if Daflex needs more than $100 million in new capital in 2000? If Daflex needs $110 million, for example, retained earnings will not be sufficient to cover the $55 million common equity requirements (50 percent of the total funds), so new common stock will have to be sold. The cost of issuing new common stock, k_e, is greater than the cost of retained earnings, k_s, hence the WACC will be greater. If Daflex raises $110 million in new capital, the breakdown of the amount that would come from each source of capital, and the computation for the weighted average cost of capital (WACC) would be as follows:

Capital Source	Weight	Amount in Millions	After-Tax Component Cost	WACC
Debt	0.40	$ 44	6%	2.4%
Preferred stock	0.10	11	11	1.1
Common equity	0.50	55	15	7.5
	1.00	$110		WACC$_2$ = 11.0%

BREAK POINT (BP)
The dollar value of new capital that can be raised before an increase in the firm's weighted average cost of capital occurs.

The WACC will be greater because Daflex will have to sell new common stock, which has a higher component cost than retained earnings. Consequently, if Daflex's capital budgeting needs are greater than $100 million, new common stock will need to be sold, and its WACC will increase. The $100 million in total new capital is defined as the *retained earnings break point,* because above this amount of total capital, a break, or jump, in Daflex's MCC schedule occurs. In general, a **break point (BP)** is defined as the dollar value of new total capital that can be raised before an increase in the firm's weighted average cost of capital occurs.

Figure 10-2 graphs Daflex's MCC schedule with the retained earnings break point. Each dollar has a weighted average cost of 10.5 percent until the company raises a total of $100 million. This $100 million will consist of $40 million of new debt with an after-tax cost of 6 percent, $10 million of preferred stock with a cost of 11 percent, and $50 million of retained earnings with a cost of 14 percent. However, if Daflex raises $1 over $100 million, each new dollar will contain 50¢ of equity *obtained by selling new common equity at a cost of 15 percent;* therefore, WACC jumps from 10.5 percent to 11.0 percent, as calculated earlier and shown in Table 10-1.

Note that we really don't think the MCC jumps by precisely 0.5 percent when we raise $1 over $100 million. Thus, Figure 10-2 should be regarded as an approximation rather than as a precise representation of reality. We return to this point later in the chapter.

FIGURE 10-2

Marginal Cost of Capital Schedule for Daflex Inc. Using Both Retained Earnings and New Common Stock

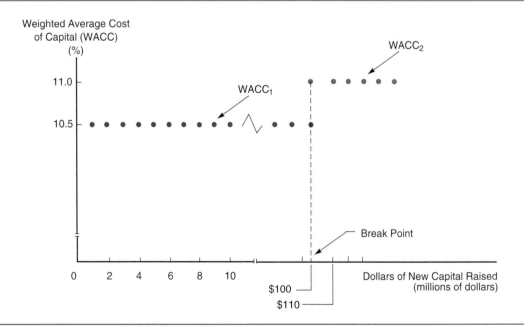

TABLE 10-1	

WACC and Break Points for Daflex's MCC Schedule

I. Break Points

1. $\qquad$ $BP_{\text{Retained earnings}} = \$50,000,000/0.50 = \$100,000,000$
2. $\qquad$ $BP_{\text{Debt}} = \$60,000,000/0.40 = \$150,000,000$

II. Weighted Average Cost of Capital (WACC)

  1. *New Capital Needs: $0–$100,000,000*

	Breakdown of Funds at $100,000,000	Weight	×	After-Tax Component Cost	=	WACC
Debt (k_d = 10%)	$40,000,000	0.40		6.0%		2.4%
Preferred stock	10,000,000	0.10		11.0		1.1
Common equity (Retained earnings)	50,000,000	0.50		14.0		7.0
	$100,000,000	1.00			$WACC_1$ =	10.5%

  2. *New Capital Needs: $100,000,001–$150,000,000*

	Breakdown of Funds at $150,000,000	Weight	×	After-Tax Component Cost	=	WACC
Debt (k_d = 10%)	$ 60,000,000	0.40		6.0%		2.4%
Preferred stock	15,000,000	0.10		11.0		1.1
Common equity (New stock issue)	75,000,000	0.50		15.0		7.5
	$150,000,000	1.00			$WACC_2$ =	11.0%

  3. *New Capital Needs: Above $150,000,000*

	Breakdown of Funds at $160,000,000	Weight	×	After-Tax Component Cost	=	WACC
Debt (k_d = 12%)	$ 64,000,000	0.40		7.2%		2.9%
Preferred stock	16,000,000	0.10		11.0		1.1
Common equity (New stock issue)	80,000,000	0.50		15.0		7.5
	$160,000,000	1.00			$WACC_3$ =	11.5%

Other Breaks in the MCC Schedule

There is a jump, or break, in Daflex's MCC schedule at $100 million of new capital because new common stock needs to be sold. Could there be other breaks in the schedule? Yes, there could. For example, suppose Daflex could obtain only $60 million of debt at a 10 percent interest rate, with any additional debt costing 12 percent. This would result in a second break point in the MCC schedule, at the point where the $60 million of 10 percent debt is exhausted. At what amount of total financing would the 10 percent debt be used up? We know that this total financing will amount to $60 million of debt plus some amount of preferred stock and common equity. If we let BP_{Debt} represent the total financing at this second break point, then we know that 40 percent of BP_{Debt} will be debt, so

$$0.40(BP_{\text{Debt}}) = \$60 \text{ million}$$

Solving for BP_{Debt}, we have

$$BP_{\text{Debt}} = \frac{\text{Maximum amount of 10\% debt}}{\text{Proportion of debt}} = \frac{\$60 \text{ million}}{0.40} = \$150 \text{ million}$$

Thus, there will be another break in the MCC schedule after Daflex has raised a total of $150 million, and this second break results from an increase in the cost of debt. The higher after-tax cost of debt (7.2 percent versus 6.0 percent) will result in a higher WACC. For example, if Daflex needs $160 million for capital budgeting projects, the WACC would be 11.5 percent:

Capital Source	Weight	Amount in Millions	After-Tax Component Cost	WACC
Debt	0.40	$64	7.2%	2.9%
Preferred stock	0.10	16	11.0	1.1
Common equity	0.50	80	15.0	7.5
	1.00	$160		WACC$_3$ $\approx$ 11.5%

In other words, the next dollar beyond $150 million will consist of 40¢ of 12 percent debt (7.2 percent after taxes), 10¢ of 11 percent preferred stock, and 50¢ of new common stock at a cost of 15 percent (retained earnings were used up much earlier), and this marginal dollar will have a cost of WACC$_3$ $\approx$ 11.5%.

The effect of this second WACC increase is shown in Figure 10-3. Now there are two break points, one caused by using up all the retained earnings and the other by using up all the 10 percent debt. With the two breaks, there are three different WACCs: WACC$_1$ = 10.5% for the first $100 million of new capital, WACC$_2$ = 11.0% in the interval between $100 million and $150 million, and WACC$_3$ = 11.5% for all new capital beyond $150 million.[8]

There could, of course, still be more break points; they would occur if the cost of debt continued to increase with more debt, if the cost of preferred stock increased at some level(s), or if the cost of common equity rose as more new common stock is sold.[9] In general, a break point will occur whenever the cost of

---

[8]When we use the term *weighted average cost of capital,* we are referring to the WACC, which is the cost of $1 raised partly as debt, partly as preferred stock, and partly as common equity. We could also calculate the average cost of all the capital the firm raised during a given year. For example, if Daflex raised $160 million, the first $100 million would have a cost of 10.5 percent, the next $50 million a cost of 11.0 percent, and the last $10 million a cost of 11.5 percent. The entire $160 million would have an average cost of

$$\left(\frac{\$100}{\$160}\right) \times (10.5\%) + \left(\frac{\$50}{\$160}\right) \times (11.0\%) + \left(\frac{\$10}{\$160}\right) \times (11.5\%) = 0.1072 = 10.72\%$$

In general, this particular cost of capital should not be used for financial decisions — it usually has no relevance in finance. The only exception to this rule occurs when the firm is considering a very large asset that must be accepted in total or else rejected, and the capital required for it includes capital with different WACCs. For example, if Daflex were considering one $160 million project, that project should be evaluated with a 10.72 percent cost.

[9]The first break point is not necessarily the point at which retained earnings are used up; it is possible for low-cost debt to be exhausted *before* retained earnings have been used up. For example, if Daflex had available only $30 million of 10 percent debt, BP$_{Debt}$ would occur at $75 million:

$$BP_{Debt} = \frac{\$30 \text{ million}}{0.40} = \$75 \text{ million}$$

Thus, the break point for debt would occur before the break point for retained earnings, which occurs at $100 million.

Marginal Cost of Capital Schedule for Daflex Inc. Using Retained Earnings, New Common Stock, and Higher-Cost Debt

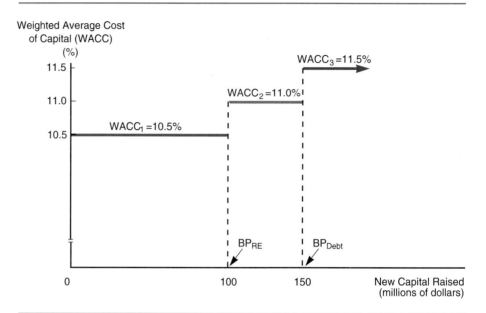

one of the capital components increases, and the break point can be determined by the following equation:

10-9

$$\text{Break point} = \frac{\text{Total amount of lower cost capital of a given type}}{\text{Proportion of this type of capital in the capital structure}}$$

We see, then, that numerous break points can occur. At the limit, we can even think of an MCC schedule with so many break points that it rises almost continuously beyond some given level of new financing. Such an MCC schedule is shown in Figure 10-4.

The easiest sequence for calculating MCC schedules is as follows:

1. Use Equation 10-9 to determine each point at which a break occurs. A break will occur any time the cost of one of the capital components rises. (It is possible, however, that two capital components could both increase at the same point.) After determining the exact break points, make a list of them.
2. Determine the cost of capital for each component in the intervals between the *different* breaks.
3. Calculate the weighted averages of these component costs to obtain the WACCs in each interval, as we did in Table 10-1. The WACC is constant within each interval, but it rises at each break point.

FIGURE 10-4

Smooth, or Continuous, Marginal Cost of Capital Schedule

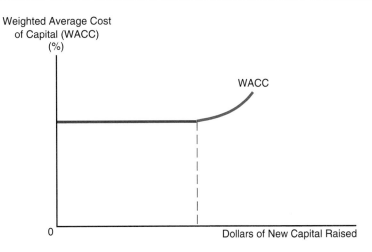

Note that if there are n separate breaks, there will be n + 1 different WACCs. For example, in Figure 10-3 we see two breaks and three different WACCs. Also, we should note again that a different MCC schedule would result if a different capital structure was used.

Self-Test Questions

What are break points, and why do they occur in MCC schedules?

Write out and explain the equation for determining break points.

How is an MCC schedule constructed?

If there are n breaks in the MCC schedule, how many different WACCs are there? Why?

Combining the MCC and Investment Opportunity Schedules

Now that we have calculated the MCC schedule, we can use it to develop a discount rate for use in the capital budgeting process; that is, *we can use the MCC schedule to find the cost of capital for determining projects' net present values (NPVs)* as discussed in Chapter 9.

To understand how the MCC schedule is used in capital budgeting, assume that Daflex Inc. has three financial executives: a financial vice-president (VP), a treasurer, and a director of capital budgeting (DCB). The financial VP asks the treasurer to develop the firm's MCC schedule, and the treasurer produces the schedule shown earlier in Figure 10-3. At the same time, the financial VP asks the DCB to draw up a list of all projects that are potentially acceptable. The list

FIGURE 10-5

Combining the MCC and IOS Schedules to Determine the Optimal Capital Budget

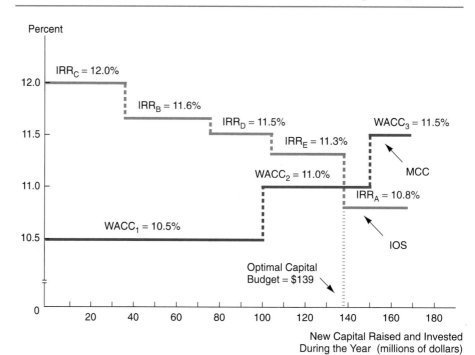

Project	Initial Cost (dollars in millions)	Annual Net Cash Flows (dollars in millions)	Life (years)	IRR
A	$26	$ 7	5	10.8%
B	40	11	5	11.6
C	37	9	6	12.0
D	25	6	6	11.5
E	37	12	4	11.3

INVESTMENT OPPORTUNITY SCHEDULE (IOS)
A graph of the firm's investment opportunities ranked in order of the projects' internal rates of return.

shows each project's cost, projected annual net cash inflows, life, and IRR. These data are presented at the bottom of Figure 10-5. For example, Project A has a cost of $26 million, it is expected to produce inflows of $7 million per year for five years, and, therefore, it has an IRR of 10.8 percent. Similarly, Project C has a cost of $37 million, it is expected to produce inflows of $9 million per year for six years, and thus it has an IRR of 12.0 percent. (NPVs cannot be shown yet because we do not yet know the marginal cost of capital.) For simplicity, we assume that all projects are independent as opposed to mutually exclusive, that they are equally risky, and that their risks are all equal to those of the firm's average existing assets.

The DCB then plots the IRR data shown at the bottom of Figure 10-5 as the **investment opportunity schedule (IOS)** shown in the graph. The IOS schedule shows, in rank order, how much money Daflex could invest at different rates of return (IRRs). Figure 10-5 also shows Daflex's MCC schedule as it was developed by the treasurer and plotted in Figure 10-3. Now consider Project C: Its IRR is 12.0 percent, and it can be financed with capital that costs only 10.5 percent; consequently, it should be accepted. Recall from Chapter 9 that if a project's IRR exceeds its cost of capital, its NPV also will be positive; therefore, Project C also must be acceptable by the NPV criterion. Projects B, D, and E can be analyzed similarly; they are all acceptable because IRR > MCC = WACC and hence NPV > 0. Project A, on the other hand, should be rejected because its IRR < MCC and therefore its NPV < 0.

People sometimes ask this question: "If we took Project A first, it would be acceptable because its 10.8 percent return would exceed the 10.5 percent cost of money used to finance it. Why couldn't we do this?" The answer is that we are seeking, in effect, to maximize the excess of returns over costs, or the area that is above the WACC but below the IOS. We accomplish this by graphing (and accepting) the most profitable projects first.

Another question that sometimes arises is this: "What would happen if the MCC cut through one of the projects? For example, suppose the second break point in the MCC schedule had occurred at $120 million rather than at $150 million, causing the MCC schedule to cut through Project E. Should we then accept Project E?" If Project E could be accepted in part, we would take on only part of it. Otherwise, the answer would be determined by (1) finding the average cost of the funds needed to finance Project E (some of the money would cost 11 percent and some 11.5 percent) and (2) comparing the average cost of this money with the 11.3 percent return on the project. We should accept Project E if its return exceeds the average cost of the $40 million needed to finance it.

The preceding analysis, as summarized in Figure 10-5, reveals a very important point: *The cost of capital used in the capital budgeting process as discussed in Chapter 9 actually is determined at the intersection of the IOS and MCC schedules. If the cost of capital at the intersection ($WACC_2 = 11\%$ in Figure 10-5) is used, then the firm will make correct accept/reject decisions, and its level of financing and investment will be optimal. If it uses any other rate, its capital budget will not be optimal.*

The intersection WACC as determined in Figure 10-5 should be used to find the NPVs of new projects that are about as risky as the firm's existing assets, but this cost of capital should be adjusted up or down to find NPVs for projects with higher or lower risk than the average project. This point was discussed in Chapter 9, in connection with the Home Energy Products appliance control computer example.

Self-Test Questions

Differentiate between the MCC and IOS schedules.

How is the corporate cost of capital, which is used to evaluate average-risk projects, found?

As a general rule, should a firm's cost of capital as determined in this chapter be used to evaluate all of its capital budgeting projects? Explain.

SMALL BUSINESS

The Cost of Equity Capital for Small Firms

The three equity cost estimating techniques discussed in this chapter (DCF, bond-yield-plus-risk-premium, and CAPM) have serious limitations when applied to small firms. First, many small, rapidly growing firms do not now and will not in the foreseeable future pay dividends. For firms such as this, the constant growth model is simply not applicable. In fact, it is difficult to imagine any dividend model that would be of practical benefit for such firms because of the difficulty of estimating dividends and growth rates. Second, the bond-yield-plus-risk-premium technique cannot be used for firms that do not have bond issues outstanding, and many small firms do not issue bonds. And, third, the CAPM is often not usable because the stocks of many small firms are not traded publicly, so we cannot calculate those firms' betas. For the privately owned firm, we might use the "pure play" CAPM technique, which involves finding a firm in the same line of business with publicly held stock, estimating that firm's beta, and then using this second firm's beta as a replacement for that of the small business in question. But, these "large" firms' betas would have to be subjectively modified to reflect their larger sizes and more established positions, as well as to take account of the differences in the nature of their products and their capital structures as compared with the smaller firms.

FLOTATION COSTS FOR SMALL ISSUES

We know that when external equity capital is raised, flotation costs increase the cost of equity capital beyond what it would be for internal funds. These external flotation costs are especially significant for smaller firms, and they can substantially affect capital budgeting decisions involving external equity funds. According to the latest Securities and Exchange Commission data, the average flotation costs of small common stock offerings are generally four to five times greater than those of large firms (greater than $50 million). Thus, small firms are at a substantial disadvantage because of the effects of flotation costs.

THE SMALL-FIRM EFFECT

A number of researchers have observed that portfolios of small-firm stocks have earned consistently higher average returns than those of large-firm stocks; this is called the "small-firm effect." On the surface, it would seem to be advantageous to the small firm to provide average returns in the stock market that are higher than those of large firms. In reality, this is bad news for the small firm — what the small-firm effect means is that the capital market demands higher returns on stocks of small firms than on otherwise similar stocks of large firms. Therefore, the basic cost of equity capital is higher for small firms. This compounds the high flotation cost problem noted earlier.

It might be argued that stocks of small firms are riskier than those of large ones and that this accounts for the differences in returns. However, the larger returns for small firms remain larger even after adjusting for the effects of their higher risks. Higher returns reflect higher costs of capital, so we must conclude that small firms do have higher capital costs than otherwise similar large firms. The manager of a small firm should take this factor into account when estimating the firm's cost of equity capital. In general, the cost of equity capital appears to be about 4 percentage points higher for small firms than for large, New York Stock Exchange firms with similar risk characteristics.

Summary

This chapter showed (1) how the weighted average cost of capital (WACC) is computed for a firm and (2) how the MCC schedule is developed for use in the capital budgeting process. The key concepts covered in the chapter are listed below.

- The cost of capital to be used in capital budgeting decisions is the **weighted average** of the various types of capital the firm uses, typically debt, preferred stock, and common equity.
- The **component cost of debt** is the after-tax cost of new debt. It is found by multiplying the cost of new debt by $(1 - T)$, where T is the firm's marginal tax rate: $k_{dT} = k_d(1 - T)$.

- The **component cost of preferred stock** is calculated as the preferred dividend divided by the net issuing price, where the net issuing price is the price the firm receives after deducting flotation costs: $k_{ps} = D_{ps}/[P(1 - F)] = D_{ps}/NP$.
- The **cost of common equity** is the cost of retained earnings as long as the firm has retained earnings, but the cost of equity becomes the cost of new common stock once the firm has exhausted its retained earnings.
- The **cost of retained earnings** is the rate of return required by stockholders on the firm's common stock, and it can be estimated using one of three methods: (1) the **CAPM approach**, (2) the **bond-yield-plus-risk-premium approach,** and (3) the **dividend-yield-plus-growth-rate, or DCF, approach.**
- To use the **CAPM approach,** one (1) estimates the firm's beta, (2) multiplies this beta by the market risk premium to determine the firm's risk premium, and (3) adds the firm's risk premium to the risk-free rate to obtain the firm's cost of retained earnings: $k_s = k_{RF} + (k_M - k_{RF})\beta_s$.
- The **bond-yield-plus-risk-premium approach** calls for adding a risk premium of from 3 to 5 percentage points to the firm's interest rate on long-term debt: $k_s = $ Bond yield + RP.
- To use the **dividend-yield-plus-growth-rate approach,** which is also called the **DCF approach,** one adds the firm's expected growth rate to its expected dividend yield: $k_s = \hat{D}_1/P_0 + g$.
- The **cost of new common equity** is higher than the cost of retained earnings because the firm incurs **flotation expenses** to sell stock. To find the cost of new common equity, the stock price is first reduced by the flotation expense, then the dividend yield is calculated on the basis of the price the firm actually will receive, and finally the expected growth rate is added to this **adjusted dividend yield**: $k_e = \hat{D}_1/[P_0(1 - F)] + g$.
- Each firm has an **optimal capital structure,** defined as that mix of debt, preferred stock, and common equity that *minimizes* its **weighted average cost of capital (WACC)**:

$$WACC = w_d k_{dT} + w_p k_{ps} + w_s(k_s \text{ or } k_e)$$

- The **marginal cost of capital (MCC)** is defined as the cost of the last dollar of new capital that the firm raises. The MCC increases as the firm raises more and more capital during a given period. A graph of the MCC plotted against dollars raised is the **MCC schedule.**
- A **break point** will occur in the MCC schedule each time the cost of one of the capital components increases.
- The **investment opportunity schedule (IOS)** is a graph of the firm's investment opportunities, ranked in order of their internal rates of return (IRR).
- The MCC schedule is combined with the IOS schedule, and the intersection defines the **corporate cost of capital,** which is used to evaluate average-risk capital budgeting projects.
- The three equity cost estimation techniques discussed in this chapter have **serious limitations when applied to small firms,** thus increasing the need for the small-business manager to use judgment.
- The average flotation cost for small firms is much greater than for large firms. As a result, a small firm would have to earn considerably more on the same project than a large firm. Also, the capital market demands higher returns on stocks of small firms than on otherwise similar stocks of large firms — this is called the **small-firm effect.**

The concepts developed in this chapter are extended in Chapter 11, where we consider the effect of the capital structure on the cost of capital.

Questions

10-1 In what sense does the marginal cost of capital schedule represent a series of average costs?

10-2 The financial manager of a large national firm was overheard making the following statement: "We try to use as much retained earnings as possible for capital budgeting purposes because there is no *explicit* cost to these funds, and this allows us to invest in relatively low yielding projects that would not be feasible if we had to issue new common stock. We actually use retained earnings to invest in projects with yields below the coupon rate on our bonds." Comment on the validity of this statement.

10-3 How would each of the following affect a firm's cost of debt, k_{dT}; its cost of equity, k_s; and its weighted average cost of capital, WACC? Indicate by a plus (+), a minus (−), or a zero (0) if the factor would raise, lower, or have an indeterminate effect on the item in question. Assume other things are held constant. Be prepared to justify your answer, but recognize that several of the parts probably have no single correct answer; these questions are designed to stimulate thought and discussion.

	Effect on		
	k_{dT}	k_s	WACC
a. The corporate tax rate is lowered.	___	___	___
b. The Federal Reserve tightens credit.	___	___	___
c. The firm uses more debt; that is, it increases its debt/assets ratio.	___	___	___
d. The dividend payout ratio (percentage of earnings paid as dividends) is increased.	___	___	___
e. The firm doubles the amount of capital it raises during the year.	___	___	___
f. The firm expands into a risky new area.	___	___	___
g. The firm merges with another firm whose earnings are countercyclical both to those of the first firm and to the stock market.	___	___	___
b. The stock market falls drastically, and the firm's stock falls along with the rest.	___	___	___
i. Investors become more risk averse.	___	___	___
j. The firm is an electric utility with a large investment in nuclear plants. Several states propose a ban on nuclear power generation.	___	___	___

10-4 Suppose a firm estimates its MCC and IOS schedules for the coming year and finds that they intersect at the point 10%, $10 million. What cost of capital should be used to evaluate average projects, high-risk projects, and low-risk projects?

Self-Test Problems   *Solutions Appear in Appendix B*

Key terms **ST-1** Define each of the following terms:

   a. After-tax cost of debt, k_{dT}; capital component cost

   b. Cost of preferred stock, k_{ps}

c. Cost of retained earnings, k_s
d. Cost of new common equity, k_e
e. Flotation cost, F
f. Target capital structure; capital structure components
g. Weighted average cost of capital, WACC
h. Marginal cost of capital, MCC
i. Marginal cost of capital schedule; break point, BP
j. Investment opportunity schedule, IOS

Optimal capital budget   **ST-2** Lancaster Engineering Inc. (LEI) has the following capital structure, which it considers to be optimal:

Debt	25%
Preferred stock	15
Common equity	60
	100%

LEI's expected net income this year is $34,285.72; its established dividend payout ratio is 30 percent; its marginal tax rate is 40 percent; and investors expect earnings and dividends to grow at a constant rate of 9 percent in the future. LEI paid a dividend of $3.60 per share last year, and its stock currently sells at a price of $60 per share. LEI can obtain new capital in the following ways:

Common: New common stock has a flotation cost of 10 percent for up to $12,000 of new stock and 20 percent for all common over $12,000.
Preferred: New preferred stock with a dividend of $11 can be sold to the public at a price of $100 per share. However, flotation costs of $5 per share will be incurred for up to $7,500 of preferred, and flotation costs will rise to $10 per share, or 10 percent, on all preferred over $7,500.
Debt: Up to $5,000 of debt can be sold at an interest rate of 12 percent; debt in the range of $5,001 to $10,000 must carry an interest rate of 14 percent; all debt over $10,000 will have an interest rate of 16 percent.

LEI has the following independent investment opportunities:

Project	Cost at t = 0	Annual Net Cash Flow	Project Life (years)	IRR
A	$10,000	$2,191.20	7	12.0%
B	10,000	3,154.42	5	17.4
C	10,000	2,170.18	8	14.2
D	20,000	3,789.48	10	13.7
E	20,000	5,427.84	6	?

a. Find the break points in the MCC schedule.
b. Determine the cost of each capital structure component.
c. Calculate the weighted average cost of capital in the interval between each break in the MCC schedule.
d. Calculate the IRR for Project E.
e. Construct a graph showing the MCC and IOS schedules.
f. Which project(s) should LEI accept?

Problems

Cost of retained earnings   **10-1** The earnings, dividends, and stock price of Talukdar Technologies Inc. are expected to grow at 7 percent per year in the future. Talukdar's common stock sells for $23 per share, its last dividend was $2.00, and the company will pay a dividend of $2.14 at the end of the current year.

a. Using the discounted cash flow approach, what is its cost of retained earnings?

b. If the firm's beta is 1.6, the risk-free rate is 9 percent, and the average return on the market is 13 percent, what will be the firm's cost of equity using the CAPM approach?

c. If the firm's bonds earn a return of 12 percent, what will k_s be using the bond-yield-plus-risk-premium approach? (Hint: Use the midpoint of the risk premium range discussed in the text.)

d. Based on the results of parts a, b, and c, what would you estimate Talukdar's cost of retained earnings to be?

Cost of retained earnings   **10-2**   The Shrieves Company's EPS was $6.50 in 1999 and $4.42 in 1994. The company pays out 40 percent of its earnings as dividends, and the stock sells for $36.

a. Calculate the past growth rate in earnings. (Hint: This is a 5-year growth period.)

b. Calculate the next expected dividend per share, $\hat{D}_1$. [$D_0 = 0.4(\$6.50) = \$2.60$.] Assume that the past growth rate will continue.

c. What is the cost of retained earnings, k_s, for the Shrieves Company?

Break point calculations   **10-3**   The Simmons Company expects earnings of $30 million next year. Its dividend payout ratio is 40 percent, and its debt/assets ratio is 60 percent. Simmons uses no preferred stock.

a. What amount of retained earnings does Simmons expect next year?

b. At what amount of financing will there be a break point in the MCC schedule?

c. If Simmons can borrow $12 million at an interest rate of 11 percent, another $12 million at a rate of 12 percent, and any additional debt at a rate of 13 percent, at what points will rising debt costs cause breaks in the MCC schedule?

Calculations of g and EPS   **10-4**   Rowell Products' stock is currently selling for $60 a share. The firm is expected to earn $5.40 per share this year and to pay a year-end dividend of $3.60.

a. If investors require a 9 percent return, what rate of growth must be expected for Rowell?

b. If Rowell reinvests retained earnings in projects whose average return is equal to the stock's expected rate of return, what will be next year's EPS? [Hint: $g = b \times ROE$, where b = fraction of earnings retained.]

Weighted average cost of capital   **10-5**   On January 1, 2000, the total assets of the Dexter Company are $270 million. The firm's present capital structure, which follows, is considered to be optimal. Assume that there is no short-term debt.

Long-term debt	$135,000,000
Common equity	135,000,000
Total liabilities and equity	$270,000,000

New bonds will have a 10 percent coupon rate and will be sold at par. Common stock, currently selling at $60 a share, can be sold to net the company $54 a share. Stockholders' required rate of return is estimated to be 12 percent, consisting of a dividend yield of 4 percent and an expected growth rate of 8 percent. (The next expected dividend is $2.40, so $2.40/$60 = 4%.) Retained earnings are estimated to be $13.5 million. The marginal tax rate is 40 percent. Assuming that all asset expansion (gross expenditures for fixed assets plus related working capital) is included in the capital budget, the dollar amount of the capital budget, ignoring depreciation, is $135 million.

a. To maintain the present capital structure, how much of the capital budget must Dexter finance by equity?

b. How much of the new equity funds needed will be generated internally? Externally?

c. Calculate the cost of each of the equity components.

d. At what level of capital expenditure will there be a break in Dexter's MCC schedule?

e. Calculate the WACC (1) below and (2) above the break in the MCC schedule.

f. Plot the MCC schedule. Also, draw in an IOS schedule that is consistent with both the MCC schedule and the projected capital budget. (Any IOS schedule that is consistent will do.)

Weighted average cost of capital 10-6 The following tabulation gives earnings per share figures for the Brueggeman Company during the preceding 10 years. The firm's common stock, 7.8 million shares outstanding, is now (January 1, 2000) selling for $65 per share, and the expected dividend at the end of the current year (2000) is 55 percent of the 1999 EPS. Because investors expect past trends to continue, g may be based on the earnings growth rate. (Note that 9 years of growth are reflected in the data.)

Year	EPS	Year	EPS
1990	$3.90	1995	$5.73
1991	4.21	1996	6.19
1992	4.55	1997	6.68
1993	4.91	1998	7.22
1994	5.31	1999	7.80

The current interest rate on new debt is 9 percent. The firm's marginal tax rate is 40 percent. Its capital structure, considered to be optimal, is as follows:

Debt	$104,000,000
Common equity	156,000,000
Total liabilities and equity	$260,000,000

a. Calculate Brueggeman's after-tax cost of new debt and of common equity, assuming that new equity comes only from retained earnings. Calculate the cost of equity as $k_s = \hat{D}_1/P_0 + g$.

b. Find Brueggeman's weighted average cost of capital, again assuming that no new common stock is sold and that all debt costs 9 percent.

c. How much can be spent on capital investments before external equity must be sold? (Assume that retained earnings available for 2000 are 45 percent of 1999 earnings. Obtain 1999 earnings by multiplying 1999 EPS by the shares outstanding.)

d. What is Brueggeman's weighted average cost of capital (cost of funds raised in excess of the amount calculated in part c) if new common stock can be sold to the public at $65 a share to net the firm $58.50 a share? The cost of debt is constant.

Optimal capital budget 10-7 Ezzell Enterprises has the following capital structure, which it considers to be optimal under present and forecasted conditions:

Debt (long-term only)	45%
Common equity	55
Total liabilities and equity	100%

For the coming year, management expects after-tax earnings of $2.5 million. Ezzell's past dividend policy of paying out 60 percent of earnings will continue. Present commitments from its banker will allow Ezzell to borrow according to the following schedule:

Loan Amount	Interest Rate
$0 to $500,000	9% on this increment of debt
$500,001 to $900,000	11% on this increment of debt
$900,001 and above	13% on this increment of debt

The company's marginal tax rate is 40 percent, the current market price of its stock is $22 per share, its *last* dividend was $2.20 per share, and the expected growth rate is 5 percent. External equity (new common) can be sold at a flotation cost of 10 percent.

Ezzell has the following investment opportunities for the next year:

Project	Cost	Annual Cash Flows	Project Life (years)	IRR
1	$675,000	$155,401	8	?
2	900,000	268,484	5	15.0%
3	375,000	161,524	3	?
4	562,500	185,194	4	12.0
5	750,000	127,351	10	11.0

Management asks you to help determine which projects (if any) should be undertaken. You proceed with this analysis by answering the following questions (or performing the tasks) as posed in a logical sequence:

a. How many breaks are there in the MCC schedule? At what dollar amounts do the breaks occur, and what causes them?

b. What is the weighted average cost of capital in each of the intervals between the breaks?

c. What are the IRR values for Projects 1 and 3?

d. Graph the IOS and MCC schedules.

e. Which projects should Ezzell's management accept?

f. What assumptions about project risk are implicit in this problem? If you learned that Projects 1, 2, and 3 were of above-average risk, yet Ezzell chose the projects you indicated in part e, how would this affect the situation?

g. The problem stated that Ezzell pays out 60 percent of its earnings as dividends. How would the analysis change if the payout ratio was changed to zero, to 100 percent, or somewhere in between? (No calculations are necessary.)

Exam-Type Problems

The problems included in this section are set up in such a way that they could be used as multiple-choice exam problems.

After-tax cost of debt   **10-8**   Calculate the after-tax cost of debt under each of the following conditions:
a Interest rate, 13 percent; tax rate, 0 percent.
b. Interest rate, 13 percent; tax rate, 20 percent.
c. Interest rate, 13 percent; tax rate, 34 percent.

After-tax cost of debt   **10-9**   The McDaniel Company's financing plans for next year include the sale of long-term bonds with a 10 percent coupon. The company believes it can sell the bonds at a price that will provide a yield to maturity of 12 percent. If the marginal tax rate is 34 percent, what is McDaniel's after-tax cost of debt?

Cost of preferred stock   **10-10**   Maness Industries plans to issue some $100 par preferred stock with an 11 percent dividend. The stock is selling on the market for $97.00, and Maness must pay flotation costs of 5 percent of the market price. What is the cost of the preferred stock for Maness?

Cost of new common stock   **10-11**   The Choi Company's next expected dividend, $\hat{D}_1$, is $3.18; its growth rate is 6 percent; and the stock now sells for $36. New stock can be sold to net the firm $32.40 per share.

a. What is Choi's percentage flotation cost, F?

b. What is Choi's cost of new common stock, k_e?

Weighted average cost of capital   **10-12**   The Gupta Company's cost of equity is 16 percent. Its before-tax cost of debt is 13 percent, and its marginal tax rate is 40 percent. The stock sells at book value. Using the following balance sheet, calculate Gupta's after-tax weighted average cost of capital:

Assets		**Liabilities and Equity**	
Cash	$ 120	Long-term debt	$1,152
Accounts receivable	240	Equity	1,728
Inventories	360		
Net plant and equipment	2,160		
Total assets	$2,880	Total liabilities and equity	$2,880

Optimal capital budgets   **10-13**   The Mason Corporation's present capital structure, which is also its target capital structure, calls for 50 percent debt and 50 percent common equity. The firm has only one potential project, an expansion program with a 10.2 percent IRR and a cost of $20 million but which is completely divisible; that is, Mason can invest any amount up to $20 million. The firm expects to retain $3 million of earnings next year. It can raise up to $5 million in new debt at a before-tax cost of 8 percent, and all debt after the first $5 million will have a cost of 10 percent. The cost of retained earnings is 12 percent, and the firm can sell any amount of new common stock desired at a constant cost of new equity of 15 percent. The firm's marginal tax rate is 40 percent. What is the firm's optimal capital budget?

Optimal capital budget   **10-14**   The management of Ferri Phosphate Industries (FPI) is planning next year's capital budget. FPI projects its net income at $7,500, and its payout ratio is 40 percent. The company's earnings and dividends are growing at a constant rate of 5 percent; the last dividend, D_0, was $0.90; and the current stock price is $8.59. FPI's new debt will cost 14 percent. If FPI issues new common stock, flotation costs will be 20 percent. FPI is at its optimal capital structure, which is 40 percent debt and 60 percent equity, and the firm's marginal tax rate is 40 percent. FPI has the following independent, indivisible, and equally risky investment opportunities:

Project	Cost	IRR
A	$15,000	17%
B	20,000	14
C	15,000	16
D	12,000	15

What is FPI's optimal capital budget?

Risk-adjusted optimal capital budget   **10-15**   Refer to Problem 10-14. Management now decides to incorporate project risk differentials into the analysis. The new policy is to add 2 percentage points to the cost of capital of those projects significantly riskier than average and to subtract 2 percentage points from the cost of capital of those that are substantially less risky than average. Management judges Project A to be of high risk, Projects C and D to be of average risk, and Project B to be of low risk. None of the projects is divisible. What is the optimal capital budget after adjustment for project risk?

Weighted average cost of capital   **10-16**   Florida Electric Company (FEC) uses only debt and equity. It can borrow unlimited amounts at an interest rate of 10 percent as long as it finances at its target capital structure, which calls for 45 percent debt and 55 percent common equity. Its last dividend was $2; its expected constant growth rate is 4 percent; its stock sells at a price of $25; and new stock would net the company $20 per share after flotation costs. FEC's marginal tax rate is 40 percent, and it expects to have $100 million of retained earnings this year. Two projects are available: Project A has a cost of $200 million and an IRR of 13 percent, while Project B has a cost of $125 million and an IRR of 10 percent. All of the company's potential projects are equally risky.

a. What is FEC's cost of equity from newly issued stock?

b. What is FEC's marginal cost of capital; that is, what WACC cost rate should it use to evaluate capital budgeting projects (these two projects plus any others that might arise during the year, provided the cost of capital schedule remains as it is currently)?

After-tax cost of debt   **10-17**   A company's 6 percent coupon rate, semiannual payment, $1,000 par value bond that matures in 30 years sells at a price of $515.16. The company's marginal tax rate is 40 percent. What is the firm's component cost of debt for purposes of calculating the WACC? (Hint: Base your answer on the simple rate, not the effective annual rate, EAR.)

Marginal cost of equity   **10-18**   Chicago Paint Corporation has a target capital structure of 40 percent debt and 60 percent common equity. The company expects to have $600 of after-tax income during the coming year, and it plans to retain 40 percent of its earnings. The current stock price is $P_0 = \$30$, the last dividend was $D_0 = \$2.00$, and the dividend is expected to grow at a constant rate of 7 percent. New stock can be sold at a flotation cost of F = 25 percent. What will Chicago Paint's marginal cost of *equity* capital (not the WACC) be if it raises a total of $500 of new capital?

Integrative Problem

Cost of capital   **10-19**   Assume that you were recently hired as assistant to Jerry Lehman, financial VP of Coleman Technologies. Your first task is to estimate Coleman's cost of capital. Lehman has provided you with the following data, which he believes may be relevant to your task:

(1) The firm's marginal tax rate is 40 percent.

(2) The current price of Coleman's 12 percent coupon, semiannual payment, noncallable bonds with 15 years remaining to maturity is $1,153.72. Coleman does not use short-term interest-bearing debt on a permanent basis. New bonds would be privately placed with no flotation cost.

(3) The current price of the firm's 10 percent, $100 par value, quarterly dividend, perpetual preferred stock is $113.10. Coleman would incur flotation costs of $2.00 per share on a new issue.

(4) Coleman's common stock is currently selling at $50 per share. Its last dividend (D_0) was $4.19, and dividends are expected to grow at a constant rate of 5 percent in the foreseeable future. Coleman's beta is 1.2; the yield on T-bonds is 7 percent; and the market risk premium is estimated to be 6 percent. For the bond-yield-plus-risk-premium approach, the firm uses a 4 percentage point risk premium.

(5) Up to $300,000 of new common stock can be sold at a flotation cost of 15 percent. Above $300,000, the flotation cost would rise to 25 percent.

(6) Coleman's target capital structure is 30 percent long-term debt, 10 percent preferred stock, and 60 percent common equity.

(7) The firm is forecasting retained earnings of $300,000 for the coming year.

To structure the task somewhat, Lehman has asked you to answer the following questions:

a. (1) What sources of capital should be included when you estimate Coleman's weighted average cost of capital (WACC)?

    (2) Should the component costs be figured on a before-tax or an after-tax basis?

    (3) Should the costs be historical (embedded) costs or new (marginal) costs?

b. What is the market interest rate on Coleman's debt and its component cost of debt?

c. (1) What is the firm's cost of preferred stock?

    (2) Coleman's preferred stock is riskier to investors than its debt, yet the yield to investors is lower than the yield to maturity on the debt. Does this suggest that you have made a mistake? (Hint: Think about taxes.)

d. (1) Why is there a cost associated with retained earnings?

    (2) What is Coleman's estimated cost of retained earnings using the CAPM approach?

    (3) Why is the T-bond rate a better estimate of the risk-free rate for cost of capital purposes than the T-bill rate?

e. What is the estimated cost of retained earnings using the discounted cash flow (DCF) approach?

f. What is the bond-yield-plus-risk-premium estimate for Coleman's cost of retained earnings?

g. What is your final estimate for k_s?

b. What is Coleman's cost for up to $300,000 of newly issued common stock, k_{e1}? What happens to the cost of equity if Coleman sells more than $300,000 of new common stock?

i. Explain in words why new common stock has a higher percentage cost than retained earnings.

j. (1) What is Coleman's overall, or weighted average, cost of capital (WACC) when retained earnings are used as the equity component?

    (2) What is the WACC after retained earnings have been exhausted and Coleman uses up to $300,000 of new common stock with a 15 percent flotation cost?

    (3) What is the WACC if more than $300,000 of new common equity is sold?

k. (1) At what amount of new investment would Coleman be forced to issue new common stock? To put it another way, what is the largest capital budget the company could support without issuing new common stock? Assume that the 30/10/60 target capital structure will be maintained.

    (2) At what amount of new investment would Coleman be forced to issue new common stock with a 25 percent flotation cost?

    (3) What is a marginal cost of capital (MCC) schedule? Construct a graph that shows Coleman's MCC schedule.

l. Coleman's Director of Capital Budgeting has identified the following potential projects:

Project	Cost	Life (years)	Cash Flow	IRR
A	$700,000	5	$218,795	17.0%
B	500,000	5	152,705	16.0
B′	500,000	20	79,881	15.0
C	800,000	5	219,185	11.5

Projects B and B′ are mutually exclusive, whereas the remainder are independent. All of the projects are equally risky.

    (1) Plot the IOS schedule on the same graph that contains your MCC schedule. What is the firm's marginal cost of capital for capital budgeting purposes?

    (2) What are the dollar size and the included projects in Coleman's optimal capital budget? Explain your answer fully.

(3) Would Coleman's MCC schedule remain constant at 12.8 percent beyond $2 million regardless of the amount of capital required?

(4) If WACC$_3$ had been 18.5 percent rather than 12.8 percent, but the second WACC break point had still occurred at $1,000,000, how would that have affected the analysis?

m. Suppose you learned that Coleman could raise only $200,000 of new debt at a 10 percent interest rate and that new debt beyond $200,000 would have a yield to investors of 12 percent. Trace back through your work and explain how this new fact would change the situation.

Computer-Related Problem

Work the problem in this section only if you are using the computer problem diskette.

Marginal cost of capital   **10-20**   Use the model in File C10 to solve this problem.

a. Refer back to Problem 10-7. Now assume that the debt ratio is increased to 65 percent, causing all interest rates to rise by 1 percentage point, to 10 percent, 12 percent, and 14 percent, and causing g to increase from 5 to 6 percent. What happens to the MCC schedule and the capital budget?

b. Assume the facts as in part a, but suppose Ezzell's marginal tax rate falls (1) to 20 percent or (2) to 0 percent. How would this affect the MCC schedule and the capital budget?

c. Ezzell's management would now like to know what the optimal capital budget would be if earnings were as high as $3.25 million or as low as $1 million. Assume a 40 percent marginal tax rate.

d. Would it be reasonable to use the model to analyze the effects of a change in the payout ratio without changing other variables?

CHAPTER 11

Capital Structure
and Dividend Policy Decisions

Unisys Corporation, a manufacturer of computers and related products for commercial and defense companies, had paid a regular dividend to common stockholders for almost 100 years. But, in September 1990, the board of directors decided to suspend the payment of future common stock dividends. According to James Unruh, president and CEO at the time, the dividend suspension was in the "best interests" of shareholders — the board felt Unisys needed to strengthen its financial condition to improve *shareholder wealth*.

Suspending the common stock dividend saved Unisys more than $162 million a year and allowed the company to use the funds internally to reduce debt. By eliminating the cash drain associated with the common stock dividend payment, Unisys was able to reduce its amount of debt substantially in four years — the debt/assets ratio fell from nearly 75 percent in 1990 to just over 60 percent in 1993. At the same time, Unisys increased its net income from a loss of a little more than $500 million in 1990 to a gain of $400 million in 1993. The dividend-cutting strategy helped Unisys improve its financial position by lowering its debt/assets ratio. Unfortunately, in 1995 the company increased its debt considerably, and its debt/assets ratio again was above 75 percent.

Unisys has not abandoned its goal to reduce debt. In September 1997, the company appointed Lawrence A. Weinbach chairman, president, and CEO. One of his first actions was to announce that Unisys would decrease debt by $1 billion by the year 2000. True to his word, Weinbach decreased debt by more than $800 million in the first four months of his tenure. It was estimated that the debt reduction saved more than $58 million annually in interest and debt-related expenses. Although more improvement is needed, the capital structure changes Unisys made have improved both its financial strength and its profit position. Even so, there is no clear indication when Unisys will resume dividend payments to its common stockholders. Many experts believe Unisys is risky, but a good investment for the future.

Continued

How has the stock of Unisys been affected by the dividend policy change made by the board in 1990 and by the capital structure changes made since that time? When Unisys announced the dividend suspension, the price of its common stock dropped more than 25 percent in one day and by about one-third of its value within one week — trading at just under $5 per share, the value of Unisys common stock was 76 percent lower than its high during the previous 12-month period, and 90 percent lower than its high value during the previous five years. Obviously the dividend suspension was not greeted favorably by the stockholders. By 1994, Unisys stock was selling for $11 per share and in 1998, the price was nearly $26. Thus, even though dividends were not being paid, the stock's value has grown by about 20 percent per year since the dividend suspension. It seems the stockholders realized the dividend suspension in 1990 was beneficial for long-run stability and wealth maximization.

As you can see from the Unisys example, a firm's capital structure and dividend policy can affect its cash position and value. As you read this chapter, keep in mind the reasons Unisys suspended its common stock dividend and wanted to decrease the proportion of debt in its capital structure. Consider the impact a particular capital structure or dividend policy can have on the cash position of a firm and how a change in either can affect the value of a firm.

In Chapter 10, when we calculated the weighted average cost of capital for use in capital budgeting, we took the capital structure weights, or the mix of securities the firm uses to finance its assets, as a given. However, if the weights are changed, the calculated cost of capital, and thus the set of acceptable projects, will also change. Further, changing the capital structure will affect the riskiness inherent in the firm's common stock, and this will affect the return demanded by stockholders, k_s, and the stock's price, P_0. Therefore, choosing a particular capital structure is an important decision. In addition, decisions concerning the amount of earnings that are paid to stockholders as dividends affects the amount of external equity a firm needs, and thus affects capital structure decisions. In this chapter, we discuss concepts relating to capital structure and dividend policy decisions.

The Target Capital Structure

CAPITAL STRUCTURE
The combination of debt and equity used to finance a firm.

Firms can choose whatever mix of debt and equity they desire to finance their assets, subject to the willingness of investors to provide such funds. And, as we shall see, there exist many different mixes of debt and equity, or **capital structures** — in some firms, such as Chrysler Corporation, debt accounts for more than 70 percent of the financing, while other firms, such as Microsoft, have little or no debt. In the next few sections, we discuss factors that affect a firm's capital structure, and we conclude a firm should attempt to determine what its optimal, or best, mix of financing should be. But, you will find that determining the exact *optimal capital structure* is not a science, so after analyzing a number of factors, a firm establishes

TARGET CAPITAL STRUCTURE
The mix of debt, preferred stock, and common equity with which the firm plans to finance its investments.

a **target capital structure** it believes is optimal, which is then used as a guide for raising funds in the future. This target might change over time as conditions vary, but at any given moment the firm's management has a specific capital structure in mind, and individual financing decisions should be consistent with this target. If the actual proportion of debt is below the target level, new funds will probably be raised by issuing debt, whereas if the proportion of debt is above the target, stock will probably be sold to bring the firm back in line with the target debt/assets ratio.

Capital structure policy involves a trade-off between risk and return. Using more debt raises the riskiness of the firm's earnings stream, but a higher proportion of debt generally leads to a higher expected rate of return; and, from the concepts we discussed in Chapter 8, we know that the higher risk associated with greater debt tends to lower the stock's price. At the same time, however, the higher expected rate of return makes the stock more attractive to investors, which, in turn, ultimately increases the stock's price. Therefore, *the optimal capital structure is the one that strikes a balance between risk and return to achieve our ultimate goal of maximizing the price of the stock.*

Four primary factors influence capital structure decisions:

1. The first is the firm's *business risk,* or the riskiness that would be inherent in the firm's operations if it used no debt. The greater the firm's business risk, the lower the amount of debt that is optimal.

2. The second key factor is the firm's *tax position.* A major reason for using debt is that interest is tax deductible, which lowers the effective cost of debt. However, if much of a firm's income is already sheltered from taxes by accelerated depreciation or tax loss carryforwards, its tax rate will be low, and debt will not be as advantageous as it would be to a firm with a higher effective tax rate.

3. The third important consideration is *financial flexibility,* or the ability to raise capital on reasonable terms under adverse conditions. Corporate treasurers know that a steady supply of capital is necessary for stable operations, which, in turn, are vital for long-run success. They also know that when money is tight in the economy, or when a firm is experiencing operating difficulties, a strong balance sheet is needed to obtain funds from suppliers of capital. Thus, it might be advantageous to issue equity to strengthen the firm's capital base and financial stability.

4. The fourth debt-determining factor has to do with *managerial attitude (conservatism or aggressiveness)* with regard to borrowing. Some managers are more aggressive than others, hence some firms are more inclined to use debt in an effort to boost profits. This factor does not affect the optimal, or value-maximizing, capital structure, but it does influence the target capital structure a firm actually establishes.

These four points largely determine the target capital structure, but, as we shall see, operating conditions can cause the actual capital structure to vary from the target at any given time. For example, as discussed in the Managerial Perspective at the beginning of the chapter, the debt/assets ratio of Unisys clearly has been much higher than its target, and the company has taken some significant corrective actions in recent years to improve its financial position.

Self-Test Questions

What are the four factors that affect a firm's target capital structure?

In what sense does capital structure policy involve a trade-off between risk and return?

Business and Financial Risk

When we examined risk in Chapter 8, we distinguished between *market risk,* which is measured by the firm's beta coefficient, and *total risk,* which includes both beta risk and a type of risk that can be eliminated by diversification (firm-specific risk). Then, in Chapter 9, we considered how capital budgeting decisions affect the riskiness of the firm. There again we distinguished between *beta risk* (the effect of a project on the firm's beta) and *corporate risk* (the effect of the project on the firm's total risk).

Now we introduce two new dimensions of risk:

BUSINESS RISK
The risk associated with projections of a firm's future returns on assets (ROA) or returns on equity (ROE) if the firm uses no debt.

1. **Business risk** is defined as the uncertainty inherent in projections of future returns, either on assets (ROA) or on equity (ROE), if the firm uses no debt, or debtlike financing (i.e., preferred stock); it is the risk associated with the firm's operations.
2. **Financial risk** is defined as the additional risk, over and above basic business risk, placed on common stockholders that results from using financing; alternatives with fixed periodic payments, such as debt and preferred stock; it is the risk associated with using debt or preferred stock.

FINANCIAL RISK
The portion of stockholders' risk, over and above basic business risk, resulting from the manner in which the firm is financed.

Conceptually, the firm has a certain amount of risk inherent in its production and sales operations; this is its business risk. When it uses debt, it partitions this risk and concentrates most of it on one class of investors — the common stockholders; this is its financial risk.[1] Both business risk and financial risk affect the capital structure choices a firm makes.

Business Risk

Business risk is the single most important determinant of capital structure. To illustrate the effects of business risk, consider Bigbee Electronics Company, a firm that currently uses 100 percent equity. Figure 11-1 shows the trend in ROE (defined as net income divided by common equity) from 1989 through 1999, and it gives both security analysts and Bigbee's management an idea of the degree to which ROE has varied in the past and might vary in the future. Comparing the actual results to the trend line, you can see that Bigbee's ROE has fluctuated significantly since 1989. These fluctuations in ROE were caused by many factors — booms and recessions in the national economy, successful new products introduced both by Bigbee and by its competitors, labor strikes, and so on. Similar events will doubtless occur in the

---

[1]Using preferred stock also adds to financial risk. To simplify matters somewhat, in this chapter we consider only debt and common equity.

FIGURE 11-1

Bigbee Electronics Company: Trend in ROE, 1989–1999
and Subjective Probability Distribution of ROE, 1999

a. Trend in Return on Equity (ROE)

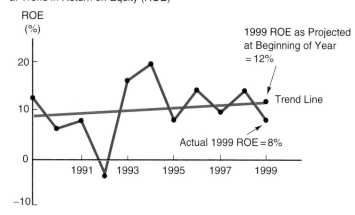

b. Subjective Probability Distribution of ROE

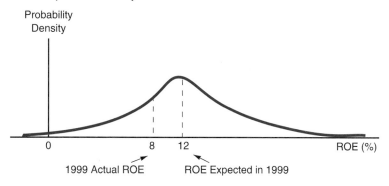

future, and when they do, Bigbee's ROE will rise or fall. Further, there is always the possibility that a long-term disaster might strike, permanently depressing the company's earning power. For example, a competitor could introduce a new product that would permanently lower Bigbee's earnings.[2] This element of uncertainty about Bigbee's future ROE is the company's *basic business risk*.

Business risk varies from one industry to another and also among firms in a given industry. Further, business risk can change over time. For example, the

---

[2]Two examples of "safe" industries that turned out to be risky are the railroads just before automobiles, airplanes, and trucks took away most of their business and the telegraph business just before telephones came on the scene.

electric utilities were regarded for years as having little business risk, but a combination of events in the 1970s and 1980s altered their situation, producing sharp declines in ROE for some companies and greatly increasing the industry's business risk. Today, food processors and grocery retailers are frequently cited as examples of industries with low business risk, whereas cyclical manufacturing industries, such as steel and construction, are regarded as having especially high business risk. Smaller companies, especially single-product firms, also have a relatively high degree of business risk.[3]

Business risk depends on a number of factors, the more important of which include the following:

1. **Sales variability (volume and price).** The more stable the unit sales (volume) and prices of a firm's products, other things held constant, the lower its business risk.
2. **Input price variability.** A firm whose input prices (labor, product costs, and so forth) are highly uncertain is exposed to a high degree of business risk.
3. **Ability to adjust output prices for changes in input prices.** Some firms have little difficulty in raising the prices of their products when input costs rise, and the greater the ability to adjust selling prices, the lower the degree of business risk. This factor is especially important during periods of high inflation.
4. **The extent to which costs are fixed: operating leverage.** If a high percentage of a firm's operating costs are fixed and hence do not decline when demand falls off, this increases the company's business risk. This factor is called *operating leverage,* and it is discussed at length in Chapter 14 when we describe financial planning and control. To illustrate the effects of operating leverage, consider the two companies shown in Table 11-1. Deesen Inc. and Westlex Corporation have identical operating sales/cost structures, and both are financed with stock only. Both companies sell their products for $50 per unit, the variable operating costs are $30 per unit, so the *gross margin* for each unit sold is $20. But, as you can see, Deesen's fixed operating costs are twice those of Westlex — $80,000 versus $40,000. Table 11-1 illustrates two important concepts. First, a firm with lower fixed operating costs, or operating leverage, which is Westlex in this case, does not have to sell as many units to reach the same level of operating income as a firm with higher operating leverage: EBIT = $120,000 at 8,000 units of sales for Westlex, but Deesen has to sell 10,000 to produce the same EBIT. Second, note that when actual sales are different than forecasted, the impact on earnings is greater for the firm with higher operating leverage: EBIT increases (decreases) by $20,000 when Deesen's sales are 10 percent above (below) the forecasted level, while Westlex's EBIT increases (decreases) only $16,000. This leads us to conclude that *a firm with greater operating leverage has greater business risk than a firm*

---

[3]We have avoided any discussion of market versus company-specific risk in this section. We note now (1) that any action that increases business risk will generally increase a firm's beta coefficient, but (2) that a part of business risk as we define it will generally be company specific and hence subject to elimination through diversification by the firm's stockholders.

TABLE 11-1

Operating Leverage Example: Deesen Inc. and Westlex Corporation

	Deesen Inc.			Westlex Corporation		
	10% below Forecast	Forecasted Amounts	10% above Forecast	10% below Forecast	Forecasted Amounts	10% above Forecast
Sales in units	9,000	10,000	11,000	7,200	8,000	8,800
Sales in dollars	$450,000	$500,000	$550,000	$360,000	$400,000	$440,000
Variable operating costs	(270,000)	(300,000)	(330,000)	(216,000)	(240,000)	(264,000)
Gross profit	180,000	200,000	220,000	144,000	160,000	176,000
Fixed operating costs	(80,000)	(80,000)	(80,000)	(40,000)	(40,000)	(40,000)
Earnings before taxes (EBT = EBIT)	100,000	120,000	140,000	104,000	120,000	136,000
Taxes (40%)	(40,000)	(48,000)	(56,000)	(41,600)	(48,000)	(54,400)
Net income	$ 60,000	$ 72,000	$ 84,000	$ 62,400	$ 72,000	$ 81,600

Notes:
(1) Both Deesen and Westlex finance only with equity; thus there is no interest expense, and EBIT = EBT.
(2) The sales price per unit equals $50, and the per unit variable cost is $30.

> *with lower operating leverage because its earnings will exhibit greater variability when sales vary.*

Each of these factors is determined partly by the firm's industry characteristics, but each is also controllable to some extent by management. For example, most firms can, through their marketing policies, take actions to stabilize both unit sales and sales prices. However, this stabilization might require either large expenditures on advertising or price concessions to induce customers to commit to purchasing fixed quantities at fixed prices in the future. Similarly, firms such as Bigbee Electronics can reduce the volatility of future input costs by negotiating long-term labor and materials supply contracts, but they might have to agree to pay prices somewhat above the current market price to obtain these contracts.

Financial Risk

FINANCIAL LEVERAGE
The extent to which fixed-income securities (debt and preferred stock) are used in a firm's capital structure.

Financial risk results from using **financial leverage**, which exists when a firm uses fixed-income securities, such as debt and preferred stock, to raise capital. When financial leverage is created, a firm intensifies the business risk borne by the common stockholders. To illustrate, suppose ten people decide to form a corporation to produce operating systems for personal computers. There is a certain amount of business risk in the operation. If the firm is capitalized only with common equity, and if each person buys 10 percent of the stock, then each investor will bear an equal share of the business risk. However, suppose the firm is capitalized with 50 percent debt and 50 percent equity, with five of the investors putting up their capital as debt and the other five putting up their money as equity. In this case, the cash flows received by the debtholders are based on a contractual agreement, so the investors who put up the equity will have to bear essentially all of the business risk, and their position will be twice as risky as it would have been had the firm been financed only with equity.

Thus, *the use of debt intensifies the firm's business risk borne by the common stockholders.*

In the next section, we explain how financial leverage affects a firm's expected earnings per share, the riskiness of those earnings, and, consequently, the price of the firm's stock. As you will see, the value of a firm that has no debt first rises as it substitutes debt for equity, then hits a peak, and finally declines as the use of debt becomes excessive. The objective of our analysis is to determine the capital structure at which *value is maximized;* this point is then used as the *target capital structure.*[4]

Self-Test Questions

What is the difference between business risk and financial risk?

Identify and briefly explain some of the more important factors that affect business risk.

Why does business risk vary from one industry to another?

What creates financial risk?

Determining the Optimal Capital Structure

We can illustrate the effects of financial leverage using the data shown in Table 11-2 for an illustrative company which we will call OptiCap. As shown in the top section of the table, the company has no debt. Should it continue the policy of using no debt, or should it start using financial leverage? If it does decide to substitute debt for equity, how far should it go? As in all such decisions, the correct answer is that it should *choose the combination of debt and equity, or a capital structure, that will maximize the price of the firm's stock.*

EBIT/EPS Analysis of the Effects of Financial Leverage

Changes in the use of debt will cause changes in earnings per share (defined as net income divided by the number of common shares outstanding) and, consequently, in the stock price. To understand the relationship between financial leverage and earnings per share (EPS), first consider Table 11-3, which shows how OptiCap's cost of debt would vary if it used different percentages of debt in its

---

[4]In this chapter we examine capital structures on a book value (or balance sheet) basis. An alternative approach is to calculate the market values of debt, preferred stock, and common equity and then to reconstruct the balance sheet on a market value basis. Although the market value approach is more consistent with financial theory, bond rating agencies and most financial executives focus their attention on book values. Moreover, the conversion from book to market values is a complicated process, and because market value capital structures change with stock market fluctuations, they are thought by many to be too unstable to serve as operationally useful targets. Finally, exactly the same insights are gained from the book value and market value analyses. For all these reasons, a market value analysis of capital structure is better suited for advanced finance courses.

TABLE 11-2

Data on OptiCap

I. Balance Sheet on 12/31/99

Current assets	$100,000	Debt	$ 0
Net fixed assets	100,000	Common equity (10,000 shares)	200,000
Total assets	$200,000	Total liabilities and equity	$200,000

II. Income Statement for 1999

Sales		$200,000
Fixed operating costs	($40,000)	
Variable operating costs (60%)	(120,000)	(160,000)
Earnings before interest and taxes (EBIT)		$ 40,000
Interest		0
Taxable income		$ 40,000
Taxes (40%)		(16,000)
Net income		$ 24,000

III. Other Data
1. Earnings per share = EPS = $24,000/10,000 shares = $2.40.
2. Dividends per share = DPS = $24,000/10,000 shares = $2.40. (Thus, OptiCap pays out all its earnings as dividends.)
3. Book value per share = $200,000/10,000 shares = $20.
4. Market price per share = P_0 = $20. (Thus, the stock sells at its book value, so Market price)/(Book price) = M/B = 1.0.)
5. Price/earnings ratio = P/E = $20/$2.40 = 8.33 times.

---

capital structure. Naturally, the higher the percentage of debt, the riskier the debt, hence the higher the interest rate lenders will charge.

Now consider Table 11-4, which shows how expected EPS varies with changes in financial leverage. Section I of the table begins with a probability distribution of sales; we assume for simplicity that sales can take on only three values, $100,000, $200,000, or $300,000. In the remainder of Section I, we calculate earnings before interest and taxes (EBIT) at each of the three sales levels. Note that

---

TABLE 11-3

Interest Rates for OptiCap with Different Debt/Assets Ratios

Amount Borrowed[a]	Debt/Assets Ratio	Interest Rate, k_d, on All Debt
$ 20,000	10%	8.0%
40,000	20	8.3
60,000	30	9.0
80,000	40	10.0
100,000	50	12.0
120,000	60	15.0

[a]We assume that the firm must borrow in increments of $20,000. We also assume that OptiCap is unable to borrow more than $120,000, or 60 percent of assets, because of restrictions in its corporate charter.

TABLE 11-4

OptiCap: EPS with Different Amounts of Financial Leverage
(thousands of dollars, except per-share figures)

I. Calculation of EBIT

Probability of indicated sales	0.2	0.6	0.2
Sales	$100.0	$200.0	$300.0
Fixed costs	(40.0)	(40.0)	(40.0)
Variable costs (60% of sales)	(60.0)	(120.0)	(180.0)
Total costs (except interest)	($100.0)	($160.0)	($220.0)
Earnings before interest and taxes (EBIT)	$ 0.0	$ 40.0	$ 80.0

II. Situation if Debt/Assets (D/A) = 0%

EBIT (from Section I)	$ 0.0	$ 40.0	$ 80.0
Less interest	(0.0)	(0.0)	(0.0)
Earnings before taxes (EBT)	$ 0.0	$ 40.0	$ 80.0
Taxes (40%)	(0.0)	(16.0)	(32.0)
Net income	$ 0.0	$ 24.0	$ 48.0
Earnings per share (EPS) on 10,000 shares[a]	$ 0.0	$ 2.40	$ 4.80
Expected EPS		$ 2.40	
Standard deviation of EPS		$ 1.52	
Coefficient of variation		0.63	

III. Situation if Debt/Assets (D/A) = 50%

EBIT (from Section I)	$ 0.0	$ 40.0	$ 80.0
Less interest (0.12 × $100,000)	(12.0)	(12.0)	(12.0)
Earnings before taxes (EBT)	($ 12.0)	$ 28.0	$ 68.0
Taxes (40%; tax credit on losses)	4.8	(11.2)	(27.2)
Net income	($ 7.2)	$ 16.8	$40.8
Earnings per share (EPS) on 5,000 shares[a]	($ 1.44)	$ 3.36	$ 8.16
Expected EPS		$ 3.36	
Standard deviation of EPS		$ 3.04	
Coefficient of variation		0.90	

[a]The EPS figures can also be obtained using the following formula, in which the numerator amounts to an income statement at a given sales level laid out horizontally:

$$\text{EPS} = \frac{(\text{Sales} - \text{Fixed costs} - \text{Variable costs} - \text{Interest})(1 - \text{Tax rate})}{\text{Shares outstanding}} = \frac{(\text{EBIT} - I)(1 - T)}{\text{Shares outstanding}}$$

For example, with zero debt and Sales = $200,000, EPS is $2.40:

$$\text{EPS}_{D/A = 0} = \frac{(\$200,000 - \$40,000 - \$120,000 - 0)(0.6)}{10,000} = \$2.40$$

With 50 percent debt and Sales = $200,000, EPS is $3.36:

$$\text{EPS}_{D/A = 0.5} = \frac{(\$200,000 - \$40,000 - \$120,000 - \$12,000)(0.6)}{5,000} = \$3.36$$

The sales level at which EPS will be equal under the two financing policies, or the indifference level of sales, S_I, can be found by setting $\text{EPS}_{D/A = 0}$ equal to $\text{EPS}_{D/A = 0.5}$ and solving for S_I:

$$\text{EPS}_{D/A = 0} = \frac{(S_I - \$40,000 - 0.6S_I - 0)(0.6)}{10,000} = \frac{(S_I - \$40,000 - 0.6S_I - \$12,000)(0.6)}{5,000} = \text{EPS}_{D/A = 0.5}$$

$$S_I = \$160,000$$

By substituting this value of sales into either equation, we can find EPS_I, the earnings per share at this indifference point. In our example, $\text{EPS}_I = \$1.44$.

we assume both sales and operating costs are independent of financial leverage. Therefore, the three EBIT figures ($0, $40,000, and $80,000) will always remain the same, no matter how much debt OptiCap uses.[5]

Section II of Table 11-4, the zero-debt case, calculates OptiCap's earnings per share at each sales level under the assumption that the company continues to use no debt. Net income is divided by the 10,000 shares outstanding to obtain EPS. If sales are as low as $100,000, EPS will be zero, but it will rise to $4.80 at a sales level of $300,000. The EPS at each sales level is then multiplied by the probability of that sales level and summed to calculate the expected EPS, which is $2.40. We also calculate the standard deviation of EPS and the coefficient of variation as indicators of the firm's risk at a zero debt/assets ratio: σ_{EPS} = $1.52, and CV_{EPS} = 0.63.[6]

Section III of the table shows the financial results that could be expected if OptiCap were financed with a debt/assets ratio of 50 percent. In this situation, $100,000 of the $200,000 total capital would be debt. The interest rate on the debt, 12 percent, is taken from Table 11-3. With $100,000 of 12 percent debt outstanding, the company's interest expense in Table 11-4 would be $12,000 per year. This is a fixed cost — it is the same regardless of the level of sales — and it is deducted from the EBIT values as calculated in the top section. With debt = 0, there would be 10,000 shares outstanding. However, if half of the equity were replaced by debt so that debt = $100,000, there would be only 5,000 shares outstanding, and we must use this fact to determine the EPS figures that would result at each of the three possible sales levels.[7] With a debt/assets ratio of 50 percent, the EPS figure would be −$1.44 if sales were as low as $100,000; it would rise to $3.36 if sales were $200,000; and it would soar to $8.16 if sales were as high as $300,000.

---

[5]In the real world, capital structure *does* at times affect EBIT. First, if debt levels are excessive, the firm probably will not be able to finance at all if its earnings are low at a time when interest rates are high. This could lead to stop-start construction and research and development programs, as well as to the necessity of passing up good investment opportunities. Second, a weak financial condition (i.e., too much debt) could cause a firm to lose sales. For example, prior to the time that its huge debt forced Eastern Airlines into bankruptcy, many people refused to buy Eastern tickets because they were afraid the company would go bankrupt and leave them holding unusable tickets. Third, financially strong companies are able to bargain hard with unions as well as with their suppliers, whereas weaker ones may have to give in simply because they do not have the financial resources to carry on the fight. Finally, a company with so much debt that bankruptcy is a serious threat will have difficulty attracting and retaining managers and employees, or it will have to pay premium salaries. For all these reasons, it is not totally correct to say that a firm's financial policy has no effect on its operating income.

Note also that EBIT is dependent on operating leverage. If we were analyzing a firm with either more or less operating leverage, the top section of Table 11-4 would be quite different: Fixed and variable costs would be different, and the range of EBIT over the various sales levels would be narrower if the company had lower operating leverage but wider if it had more operating leverage.

[6]See Chapter 8 for a review of procedures for calculating standard deviations and coefficients of variation. Recall that the advantage of the coefficient of variation is that it permits better comparisons when the expected values of EPS vary, as they do here for the two capital structures.

[7]We assume in this example that the firm could change its capital structure by repurchasing common stock at its book value of $100,000/5,000 shares = $20 per share. However, the firm might actually have to pay a higher price to repurchase its stock on the open market. If Firm B had to pay $22 per share, then it could repurchase only $100,000/$22 = 4,545 shares, and in this case, expected EPS would be only $16,800/(10,000 − 4,545) = $16,800/5,455 = $3.08 rather than $3.36.

The EPS distributions under the two financial structures are graphed in Figure 11-2, where we use continuous distributions rather than the discrete distributions contained in Table 11-4. Although expected EPS would be much higher if financial leverage were employed, the graph makes it clear that the risk of low or even negative EPS would also be much higher.

Another view of the relationships among expected EPS, risk, and financial leverage is presented in Figure 11-3. The tabular data in the lower section were calculated in the manner set forth in Table 11-4, and the graphs plot these data. Here we see that expected EPS rises until the firm is financed with 50 percent debt. Interest charges rise, but this effect is more than offset by the declining number of shares outstanding as debt is substituted for equity. However, EPS peaks at a debt/assets ratio of 50 percent. Beyond this amount, interest rates rise so rapidly that EPS is depressed despite the falling number of shares outstanding.

The right panel of Figure 11-3 shows that risk, as measured by the coefficient of variation of EPS, rises continuously, and at an increasing rate, as debt is substituted for equity.

We see, then, that using leverage has both good and bad effects: Higher leverage increases expected earnings per share (in this example, until the D/A ratio equals 50 percent), but it also increases the firm's risk. Clearly, the debt/assets ratio should not exceed 50 percent, but where, in the range of 0 to 50 percent, should it be set? This issue is discussed in the following sections.

EPS Indifference Analysis

EPS INDIFFERENCE POINT
The level of sales at which EPS will be the same whether the firm uses debt or common stock financing.

Another way of considering the data on OptiCap's two financing methods is shown in Figure 11-4, which depicts the **EPS indifference point** — that is, the point at which EPS is the same regardless of whether the firm uses debt or common stock. At a low level of sales, EPS is much higher if stock rather than debt is

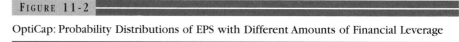

FIGURE 11-2

OptiCap: Probability Distributions of EPS with Different Amounts of Financial Leverage

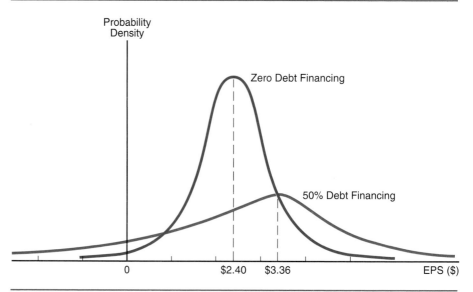

FIGURE 11-3

OptiCap: Relationships among Expected EPS, Risk, and Financial Leverage

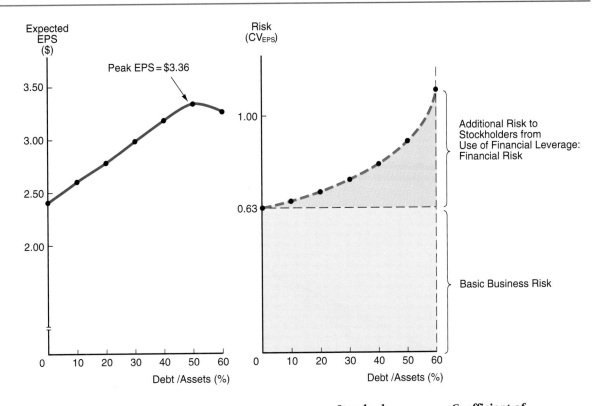

Debt/Assets Ratio	Expected EPS	Standard Deviation of EPS	Coefficient of Variation
0%[a]	$2.40[a]	$1.52[a]	0.63[a]
10	2.56	1.69	0.66
20	2.75	1.90	0.69
30	2.97	2.17	0.73
40	3.20	2.53	0.79
50[a]	3.36[a]	3.04[a]	0.90[a]
60	3.30	3.79	1.15

[a]Values for D/A = 0 and D/A = 50 percent are taken from Table 11-3. Values at other D/A ratios were calculated similarly.

used. However, the debt line has a steeper slope, showing that earnings per share will go up faster with increases in sales if debt is used. The two lines cross at sales of $160,000. Below that level, EPS would be higher if the firm uses more common stock; above it, debt financing would produce higher earnings per share.

If we were certain that sales would never again fall below $160,000, bonds would be the preferred method of financing any increases in assets. But we cannot know this for certain. In fact, investors know that in a number of previous years, sales have fallen below this critical level, and if any of several detrimental events should occur in the future, sales again would fall below $160,000. On the other hand, if sales continue to expand, higher earnings per share would result from the use of bonds, and this is an advantage that no investor would want to forgo.

FIGURE 11-4

Earnings per Share for Stock and Debt Financing for OptiCap

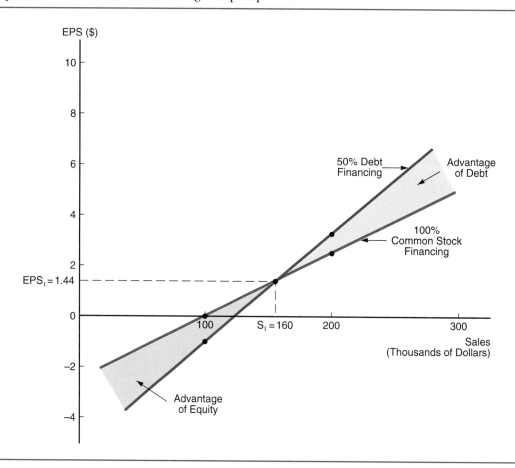

NOTES:

1. These values of the indifference level of sales, S_I and EPS_I, are the same as those obtained algebraically in Table 11-4. These relationships would be somewhat different if we did not assume that stock can be repurchased at book value.

2. We can also develop an equation to find the sales level at which EPS is the same under different degrees of financial leverage:

$$EPS_1 = \frac{S_I - F - VC - I_1}{Shares_1} = \frac{S_I - F - VC - I_2}{Shares_2} = EPS_2$$

Here, EPS_1 and EPS_2 are the EPSs at two debt levels; S_I is the sales indifference level at which $EPS_1 = EPS_2 = EPS_I$; I_1 and I_2 are interest charges at the two debt levels; $Shares_1$ and $Shares_2$ are shares outstanding at the two debt levels; F is the fixed costs; and VC = variable costs = Sales × V, where V is the variable cost percentage. Solving for S_I, we obtain this expression:

$$S_I = \left[\frac{(Shares_2)(I_1) - (Shares_1)(I_2)}{Shares_2 - Shares_1} + F \right]\left(\frac{1}{1 - v} \right)$$

In our example,

$$S_I = \left[\frac{(5,000)(0) - (10,000)(\$12,000)}{-5,000} + \$40,000 \right]\left(\frac{1}{0.4} \right)$$

$$= \$160,000$$

The Effect of Capital Structure on Stock Prices and the Cost of Capital

As we saw in Figure 11-3, OptiCap's expected EPS is maximized at a debt/assets ratio of 50 percent. Does this mean that OptiCap's optimal capital structure calls for 50 percent debt? The answer is a resounding no — *the optimal capital structure is the one that maximizes the price of the firm's stock, and this always calls for a debt/assets ratio that is lower than the one that maximizes expected EPS.* As we shall discover shortly, the primary reason this relationship exists is because P_0 reflects changes in risk that accompany changes in capital structures and affect cash flows long into the future, while EPS generally measures only the expectations for the near term. Current EPS does not generally capture future risk, while P_0 should be indicative of all future expectations.

This statement is demonstrated in Table 11-5, which develops OptiCap's estimated stock price and weighted average cost of capital at different debt/assets ratios. The debt cost and EPS data in Columns 2 and 3 were taken from Table 11-3 and Figure 11-3. The beta coefficients shown in Column 4 were estimated.

TABLE 11-5

Stock Price and Cost of Capital Estimates for OptiCap with Different Debt/Assets Ratios

Debt/ Assets (1)	k_d (2)	Expected EPS (and DPS[a]) (3)	Estimated Beta (4)	$k_s = [k_{RF} + (k_M - k_{RF})\beta_s]$[b] (5)	Estimated Price[c] (6)	Resulting P/E Ratio (7)	Weighted Average Cost of Capital, WACC[d] (8)
0%	—	$2.40	1.50	12.0%	$20.00	8.33	12.00%
10	8.0%	2.56	1.55	12.2	20.98	8.20	11.46
20	8.3	2.75	1.65	12.6	21.83	7.94	11.08
30	9.0	2.97	1.80	13.2	22.50	7.58	10.86
40	10.0	3.20	2.00	14.0	22.86	7.14	10.80
50	12.0	3.36	2.30	15.2	22.11	6.58	11.20
60	15.0	3.30	2.70	16.8	19.64	5.95	12.12

NOTES:

[a]OptiCap pays all of its earnings out as dividends, so EPS = DPS.

[b]We assume that $k_{RF} = 6\%$ and $k_M = 10\%$. Therefore, at debt/assets equal to zero, $k_s = 6\% + (10\% - 6\%)1.5 = 6\% + 6\% = 12\%$. Other values of k_s are calculated similarly.

[c]Because all earnings are paid out as dividends, no retained earnings will be plowed back into the business, and growth in EPS and DPS will be zero. Hence, the zero growth stock price model developed in Chapter 7 can be used to estimate the price of OptiCap's stock. For example, at debt/assets = 0,

$$\hat{P}_0 = \frac{\widehat{DPS}}{k_s} = \frac{\$2.40}{0.12} = \$20$$

Other prices were calculated similarly.

[d]Column 8 is found by use of the weighted average cost of capital (WACC) equation developed in Chapter 10:

$$WACC = w_d k_d (1 - T) + w_s k_s$$
$$= (D/A)(k_{dT}) + (1 - D/A)k_s$$

For example, at D/A = 40%,

$$WACC = 0.4[(10\%)(0.6)] + 0.6(14.0\%) = 10.80\%$$

Recall from Chapter 8 that a stock's beta measures its relative volatility compared with the volatility of an average stock. It has been demonstrated both theoretically and empirically that a firm's beta increases with its degree of financial leverage. The exact nature of this relationship for a given firm is difficult to estimate, but the values given in Column 4 do show the approximate nature of the relationship for OptiCap.

Assuming that the risk-free rate of return, k_{RF}, is 6 percent and that the required return on an average stock, k_M, is 10 percent, we can use the CAPM equation to develop estimates of the required rates of return, k_s, for OptiCap as shown in Column 5. Here we see that k_s is 12 percent if no financial leverage is used, but k_s rises to 16.8 percent if the company finances with 60 percent debt.

Figure 11-5 graphs OptiCap's required rate of return on equity at different debt levels. The figure also shows the composition of OptiCap's required return; the risk-free rate of 6 percent and the premiums for both business and financial risk, which were discussed earlier in this chapter. As you can see from the graph, the business

---

FIGURE 11-5

OptiCap's Required Rate of Return on Equity at Different Debt Levels

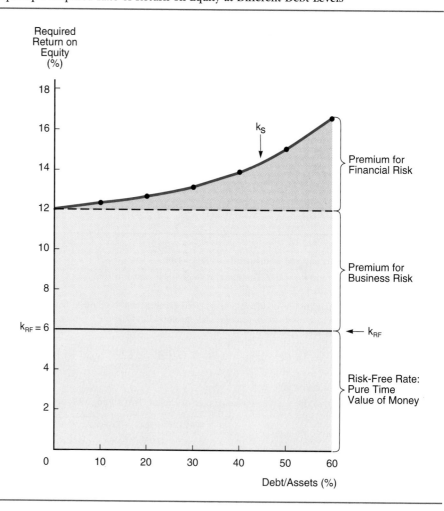

risk premium does not depend on the debt level—it remains constant at 6 percent at all debt levels. However, the financial risk premium varies depending on the debt level—the higher the debt level, the greater the premium for financial risk.

The zero growth stock valuation model developed in Chapter 7 is used in Table 11-5, along with the Column 3 values of DPS and the Column 5 values of k_s, to develop the estimated stock prices shown in Column 6. Here we see that the expected stock price first rises with financial leverage, hits a peak of $22.86 at a debt/assets ratio of 40 percent, and then begins to decline. *Thus, OptiCap's optimal capital structure calls for 40 percent debt.*

The price/earnings (P/E) ratios shown in Column 7 were calculated by dividing the price in Column 6 by the expected earnings given in Column 3. We use the pattern of P/E ratios as a check on the "reasonableness" of the other data. Other things held constant, P/E ratios should decline as the riskiness of a firm increases (market price declines), and that pattern does exist in our illustrative case. Thus, the data in Column 7 reinforce our confidence in the reasonableness of the estimated prices shown in Column 6.

Finally, Column 8 shows OptiCap's weighted average cost of capital, WACC, calculated as described in Chapter 10, at the different capital structures. If the company uses zero debt, its capital is all equity, so $WACC = k_s = 12\%$. As the firm begins to use lower-cost debt, its weighted average cost of capital declines. However, as the debt/assets ratio increases, the costs of both debt and equity rise, and the increasing costs of the two components begin to offset the fact that larger amounts of the lower-cost component are being used. At 40 percent debt, WACC hits a minimum, and it rises after that as the debt/assets ratio is increased.

The EPS, cost of capital, and stock price data shown in Table 11-5 are plotted in Figure 11-6. As the graph shows, the debt/assets ratio that maximizes OptiCap's expected EPS is 50 percent. However, the expected stock price is maximized, and the cost of capital is minimized, at a 40 percent debt/assets ratio. Thus, *the optimal capital structure calls for 40 percent debt and 60 percent equity. Management should set its target capital structure at these ratios, and if the existing ratios are off target, it should move toward the target when new security offerings are made.*

Self-Test Questions

Explain the following statement: "Using leverage has both good and bad effects."

What does the EPS indifference point show? What occurs at sales below this point? What occurs at sales above this point?

Is the optimal capital structure the one that maximizes expected EPS? Explain.

Explain the following statement: "At the optimal capital structure, a firm has minimized its cost of capital." Do stockholders want the firm to minimize its cost of capital?

Liquidity and Capital Structure

There are some practical difficulties with the type of analysis described in the previous section, including the following:

1. It is virtually impossible to determine exactly how either P/E ratios or equity capitalization rates (k_s values) are affected by different degrees of financial

FIGURE 11-6

Relationship between OptiCap's Capital Structure and Its EPS,
Cost of Capital, and Stock Price

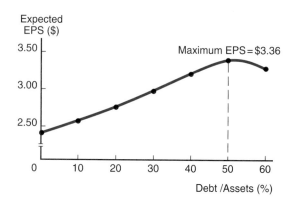

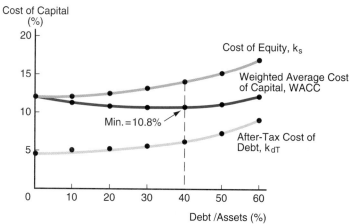

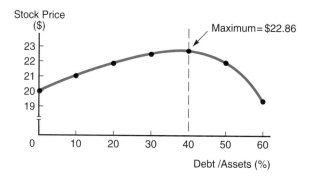

leverage. The best we can do is make educated guesses about these relationships. Therefore, management rarely, if ever, has sufficient confidence in the
type of analysis set forth in Table 11-5 and Figure 11-6 to use it as the sole
determinant of the target capital structure.

2. The managers might be more or less conservative than the average stockholder, so management might set a somewhat different target capital structure
than the one that would maximize the stock price. The managers of a publicly

owned firm never would admit this, because unless they owned voting control, they would be removed from office very quickly. However, in view of the uncertainties about what constitutes the value-maximizing capital structure, management could always say that the target capital structure employed is, in its judgment, the value-maximizing structure, and it would be difficult to prove otherwise. Still, if management is far off target, especially on the low side, then chances are very high that some other firm or management group will take over the company, increase its leverage, and thereby raise its value.

3. Managers of large firms, especially those that provide vital services such as electricity or telephones, have a responsibility to provide continuous service; therefore, they must refrain from using leverage to the point where the firms' long-run viability is endangered. Long-run viability might conflict with short-run stock price maximization and capital cost minimization.[8]

TIMES-INTEREST-EARNED (TIE) RATIO
A ratio that measures the firm's ability to meet its annual interest obligations; calculated by dividing earnings before interest and taxes by interest charges.

For all these reasons, managers are concerned about the effects of financial leverage on the risk of bankruptcy, and an analysis of this factor is therefore an important input in all capital structure decisions. Accordingly, managements give considerable weight to financial strength indicators such as the **times-interest-earned (TIE) ratio**, which is computed by dividing earnings before interest and taxes by interest expense. The TIE ratio provides an indication of how well the firm can cover its interest payments with operating income (EBIT) — the lower this ratio, the higher the probability that a firm will default on its debt and be forced into bankruptcy.

The tabular material in the lower section of Figure 11-7 shows OptiCap's expected TIE ratio at several different debt/assets ratios. If the debt/assets ratio was only 10 percent, the expected TIE would be very high at 25 times, but the interest coverage ratio would decline rapidly if the debt/assets ratio was increased. Note, however, that these coverages are expected values at different debt/assets ratios; the actual TIE for any debt/assets ratio will be higher if sales exceed the expected $200,000 level, but lower if sales fall below $200,000.

The variability of the TIE ratio is highlighted in the graph in Figure 11-7, which shows the probability distributions of the TIEs for OptiCap at debt/assets ratios of 40 percent and 60 percent. The expected TIE is much higher if only 40 percent debt is used. In general, we know that with less debt, there is a much lower probability of a TIE of less than 1.0, the level at which the firm is not earning enough to meet its required interest payment and thus is seriously exposed to the threat of bankruptcy.[9]

---

[8]Recognizing this fact, most public service commissions require utilities to obtain the commission's approval before issuing long-term securities, and Congress has empowered the SEC to supervise the capital structures of public utility holding companies. However, in addition to concern over the firms' safety, which suggests low debt ratios, both managers and regulators recognize a need to keep all costs as low as possible, including the cost of capital. Because a firm's capital structure affects its cost of capital, regulatory commissions and utility managers try to select capital structures that will minimize the cost of capital, subject to the constraint that the firm's financial flexibility not be endangered.

[9]Note that cash flows, which include depreciation, can be sufficient to cover required interest payments even though the TIE is less than 1.0. Thus, at least for a while, a firm might be able to avoid bankruptcy even though its operating income is less than its interest charges. However, most debt contracts stipulate that firms must maintain the TIE ratio above some minimum level, say, 2.0 or 2.5, or else they cannot borrow any additional funds, which can severely constrain operations. Such potential constraints, as much as the threat of actual bankruptcy, limit the use of debt.

FIGURE 11-7

OptiCap: Probability Distributions of Times-Interest-Earned Ratios
with Different Capital Structures

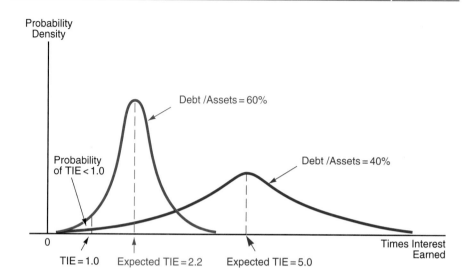

Debt/Assets	Expected TIE[a]
0%	Undefined
10	25.0
20	12.0
30	7.4
40	**5.0**
50	3.3
60	**2.2**

[a]TIE = EBIT/Interest. For example, when debt/assets = 50%, TIE = $40,000/$12,000 = 3.3. Data are from Tables 11-3 and 11-4.

Self-Test Question

Why do managers give considerable weight to the TIE ratio when they make capital structure decisions? Why not just use the capital structure that maximizes the stock price?

Capital Structure Theory

Over the years, researchers have proposed numerous theories to explain what firms' capital structures should be and why firms have different capital structures. The general theories of capital structure have been developed along two main lines: (1) tax benefit/bankruptcy cost trade-off theory and (2) signaling theory. These two theories are discussed in this section.

Trade-Off Theory

Modern capital structure theory began in 1958, when Professors Franco Modigliani and Merton Miller (hereafter referred to as MM) published what is considered by many to be the most influential finance article ever written.[10] MM proved, under a very restrictive set of assumptions — including there exist no personal income taxes, no brokerage costs, and no bankruptcy — that due to the tax deductibility of interest on corporate debt, a firm's value rises continuously as more debt is used, and hence its value will be maximized by financing almost entirely with debt.

Because several of the assumptions outlined by MM obviously were, and are, unrealistic, MM's position was only the beginning of capital structure research. Subsequent researchers, and MM themselves, extended the basic theory by relaxing the assumptions. Other researchers attempted to test the various theoretical models with actual data to see exactly how stock prices and capital costs are affected by capital structure. Both the theoretical and the empirical results have added to our understanding of capital structure, but none of these studies has produced results that can be used to precisely identify a firm's optimal capital structure. A summary of the theoretical and empirical research to date is expressed graphically in Figure 11-8. Here are the key points in the figure:

1. The fact that interest is a tax-deductible expense makes corporate debt less expensive than common or preferred stock. In effect, the government pays, or subsidizes, part of the cost of debt capital, thus using debt causes more of the firm's operating income (EBIT) to flow through to investors. So, the more debt a company uses, the higher its value. Under the assumptions of the original MM paper, their analysis led to the conclusion that the firm's stock price will be maximized if it uses virtually 100 percent debt, and the line labeled "Pure MM Result" in Figure 11-8 expresses their relationship between stock prices and debt.

2. The MM assumptions do not hold in the real world. First, interest rates rise as the debt/assets ratio increases. Second, expected tax rates fall at high debt levels, and this also reduces the expected value of the debt tax shelter. And, third, the probability of bankruptcy, which brings with it lawyers' fees and other costs, increases as the debt/assets ratio increases.

3. There is some threshold level of debt, labeled D/A_1 in Figure 11-8, below which the effects noted in Point 2 are immaterial. Beyond D/A_1, however, the bankruptcy-related costs, especially higher interest rates on new debt, become increasingly important, and they reduce the tax benefits of debt at an increasing rate. In the range from D/A_1 to D/A_2, bankruptcy-related costs reduce but do not completely offset the tax benefits of debt, so the firm's stock price rises (but at a decreasing rate) as the debt/assets ratio increases. However, beyond D/A_2 bankruptcy-related costs exceed the tax benefits, so from this point on increasing the debt/assets ratio lowers the value of the stock. Therefore, D/A_2 is the optimal capital structure.

---

[10]Franco Modigliani and Merton H. Miller, "The Cost of Capital, Corporation Finance, and the Theory of Investment," *American Economic Review,* June 1958, 261-297, and "Corporate Income Taxes and the Cost of Capital," *American Economic Review,* June 1963, 433-443. Modigliani and Miller both won Nobel Prizes for their work.

FIGURE 11-8

Effect of Leverage on the Value of OptiCap's Stock

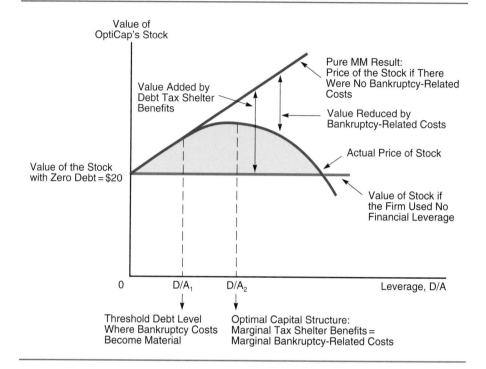

4. Both theory and empirical evidence support the preceding discussion. However, researchers have not been able to identify points D/A_1 and D/A_2 precisely, so the graphs shown in Figures 11-6 and 11-8 must be taken as approximations, not as precisely defined functions.

5. Another disturbing aspect of capital structure theory as expressed in Figure 11-8 is the fact that many large, successful firms, such as Microsoft, use far less debt than the theory suggests. This point led to the development of signaling theory, which is discussed next.

Signaling Theory

SYMMETRIC INFORMATION
The situation in which investors and managers have identical information about the firm's prospects.

ASYMMETRIC INFORMATION
The situation in which managers have different (better) information about their firm's prospects than do outside investors.

MM assumed that investors have the same information about a firm's prospects as its managers — this is called **symmetric information**, because both those who are inside the firm (managers and employees) and those who are outside the firm (investors) have identical information. However, we know that in fact managers often have better information about their firms than outside investors. This is called **asymmetric information**, and it has an important effect on decisions to use either debt or equity to finance capital projects. To see why, consider two situations, one in which the company's managers know that its prospects are extremely favorable (Firm F) and one in which the managers know that the future looks very unfavorable (Firm U).

Suppose, for example, that Firm F's research and development labs have just discovered a cure for the common cold, but the product is not patentable. Firm F's managers want to keep the new product a secret for as long as possible to delay competitors' entry into the market. New plants and distribution facilities must be built to exploit the new product, so capital must be raised. How should Firm F's management raise the needed capital? If the firm sells stock, then, when profits from the new product start flowing in, the price of the stock will rise sharply, and the purchasers of the new stock will have made a bonanza. The current stockholders (including the managers) also will do well, but not as well as they would have if the company had not sold stock before the price increased, because then they would not have had to share the benefits of the new product with the new stockholders. *Therefore, one would expect a firm with very favorable prospects to try to avoid selling stock and, rather, to raise any required new capital by other means, including using debt beyond the normal target capital structure.*[11]

Now let's consider Firm U. Suppose its managers have information that new orders are off sharply because a competitor has installed new technology that has improved its products' quality. Firm U must upgrade its own facilities, at a high cost, just to maintain its existing sales level. As a result, its return on investment will fall (but not by as much as if it took no action, which would lead to a 100 percent loss through bankruptcy). How should Firm U raise the needed capital? Here the situation is just the reverse of that facing Firm F, which did not want to sell stock so that it could avoid having to share the benefits of future developments. *A firm with unfavorable prospects would want to sell stock, which would mean bringing in new investors to share the losses!*[12]

The conclusions from all this are that firms with extremely bright prospects prefer not to finance through new stock offerings, whereas firms with poor prospects do like to finance with outside equity. How would you, as an investor, react to this conclusion? You ought to say, "If I see that a company plans to issue new stock, this should worry me, because I know that management would not want to issue stock if future prospects looked good, but it would want to issue stock if things looked bad. Therefore, I should lower my estimate of the firm's value, other things held constant, if I read an announcement of a new stock offering." Of course, the negative reaction would be stronger if the stock sale was by a large, established company such as GM or IBM, which surely has many financing options, than if it was by a small company such as USR Industries. For USR, a stock sale might mean truly extraordinary investment opportunities that were so large that they just could not be financed without a stock sale.

If you gave the above answer, your views are completely consistent with those of many sophisticated portfolio managers of institutions such as Morgan Guaranty Trust. *So, in a nutshell, the announcement of a stock offering by a mature firm that seems to have multiple financing alternatives is taken as a* **signal** *that the firm's prospects as seen by its management are not bright.* This, in turn, suggests that when a mature firm announces a new stock offering, the price of its stock should decline. Empirical studies have shown that this situation does indeed exist.

What are the implications of all this for capital structure decisions? The answer is that firms should, in normal times, maintain a **reserve borrowing capacity**

SIGNAL
An action taken by a firm's management that provides clues to investors about how management views the firm's prospects.

RESERVE BORROWING CAPACITY
The ability to borrow money at a reasonable cost when good investment opportunities arise; firms often use less debt than specified by the MM optimal capital structure to ensure that they can obtain debt capital later if they need to.

---

[11]It would be illegal for Firm F's managers to purchase more shares on the basis of their inside knowledge of the new product. They could be sent to jail if they did.

[12]Of course, Firm U would have to make certain disclosures when it offered new shares to the public, but it might be able to meet the legal requirements without fully disclosing management's worst fears.

that can be used in the event that some especially good investment opportunities come along. *This means that firms should generally use less debt than would be suggested by the tax benefit/bankruptcy cost trade-off expressed in Figure 11-8.*

If you find our discussion of capital structure theory somewhat imprecise, you are not alone. In truth, no one knows how to precisely identify the optimal capital structure for a firm or how to precisely measure the effect of the firm's capital structure on either its value or its cost of capital. In real life, capital structure decisions must be made more on the basis of judgment than numerical analysis. Still, an understanding of the theoretical issues as presented here is essential to making sound judgments on capital structure issues.

Self-Test Questions

What does it mean when one hears, "The MM capital structure theory involves a trade-off between the tax benefits of debt and costs associated with actual or potential bankruptcy"?

Explain how asymmetric information and signals affect capital structure decisions.

What is meant by reserve borrowing capacity, and why is it important for firms?

Variations in Capital Structures among Firms

As might be expected, wide variations in the use of financial leverage occur both across industries and among the individual firms in each industry. Table 11-6 illus-

---

TABLE 11-6

Capital Structure Percentages, 1997: Five Industries Ranked by Common Equity Ratios[a]

Industry	Common Equity (1)	Preferred Stock (2)	Total Debt (3)	Long-Term Debt (4)	Short-Term Debt (5)	Times-Interest-Earned Ratio (6)	Return on Equity (7)
Drugs	67.7%	0.6%	31.7%	13.7%	18.0×	−15.8×	−22.1×[b]
Industrial machinery	64.5	0.0	35.5	13.0	22.5	19.9	2.3
Electronics	54.1	0.5	45.4	17.6	27.8	22.4	9.0
Retailing	45.4	0.7	53.9	24.2	29.7	10.5	9.4
Utilities	34.2	1.4	64.4	46.7	17.7	1.7	8.5
Composite[c]	47.3	0.7	52.0	26.3	25.7	9.9	1.5

NOTES:

[a]These ratios are based on accounting, or book values. Stated on a market value basis, the equity percentages would be higher because most stocks sell at prices that are much higher than their book values.

[b]More than 60 percent of the ROEs in this industry were negative in 1997.

[c]These composite ratios include all industries, not just those listed above, except financial and professional service industries.

SOURCE: *Compustat PC Plus,* 1998.

trates differences for selected industries; the ranking is in descending order of common equity ratios, as shown in Column 1.

Drug and industrial machinery companies do not use much debt (their common equity ratios are high); the uncertainties inherent in industries that are cyclical, oriented toward research, or subject to huge product liability suits normally render the heavy use of debt unwise. On the other hand, utilities have traditionally used large amounts of debt, particularly long-term debt — their fixed assets make good security for mortgage bonds, and their relatively stable sales make it safe for them to carry more debt than would be true for firms with more business risk.

Particular attention should be given to the times-interest-earned (TIE) ratio because it gives a measure of how safe the debt is and how vulnerable the company is to financial distress. The TIE ratio depends on three factors: (1) the percentage of debt, (2) the interest rate on the debt, and (3) the company's profitability. Generally, the least leveraged industries, such as the drug and industrial machinery industries, have the highest coverage ratios, whereas the utility industry, which finances heavily with debt, has a low average coverage ratio. Table 11-6 shows that companies that manufacture industrial machinery have a high average TIE, while utilities have a very low TIE. Note, however, that drug companies had a negative TIE in 1997. This resulted because the industry had a particularly bad year — more than 60 percent of the companies in the industry experienced negative earnings during the year, which shows the degree of business risk inherent in the industry.

Wide variations in capital structures also exist among firms within given industries. For example, although the average common equity ratio in 1997 for the drug industry was 67.7 percent, Biopharmaceutics Inc.'s equity ratio was greater than 70 percent, but Matrix Pharmaceutical's equity ratio was about 15 percent. Thus, factors unique to individual firms, including managerial attitudes, play an important role in setting target capital structures.

Self-Test Question

Why do wide variations in the use of financial leverage occur both across industries and among the individual firms in each industry?

Dividend Policy

DIVIDENDS
Distributions made to stockholders from the firm's earnings, whether those earnings were generated in the current period or in previous periods.

We refer to the cash payments, or distributions, made to stockholders from the firm's earnings, whether those earnings were generated in the current period or in previous periods, as **dividends**. Consequently, a firm's *dividend policy* involves the decision to pay out earnings or to retain them for reinvestment in the firm. In this section, we examine how dividend policy affects the firm's capital structure and cost of capital, hence its value. We waited to discuss dividend policy until after we introduced the concepts of cost of capital and optimal capital structure because dividend policy decisions directly affect (1) capital structure — all else equal, retaining earnings rather than paying out dividends increases common equity relative to debt; and (2) cost of capital — financing with retained earnings is cheaper than issuing new common equity.

Dividend Policy and Stock Value

How do dividend policy decisions affect a firm's stock price? Academic researchers have studied this question extensively for many years, and they have yet to reach definitive conclusions. On the one hand, there are those who suggest that dividend policy is *irrelevant* because they argue a firm's value should be determined by the basic earning power and business risk of the firm, in which case value depends only on the income (cash) produced, not how the income is split between dividends and retained earnings (and hence growth). Proponents of this line of reasoning, called the **dividend irrelevance theory**, would contend that investors care *only* about the *total returns* they receive, not whether they receive those returns in the form of dividends or capital gains. Thus, *if dividend irrelevance theory is correct, there exists no* **optimal dividend policy,** *because dividend policy does not affect the value of the firm.*[13]

On the other hand, it is quite possible that investors prefer one dividend policy over another; if so, a firm's dividend policy is *relevant.* For example, it has been argued that investors prefer to receive dividends "today" because current dividend payments are more certain than the future capital gains that *might* result from investing retained earnings in growth opportunities, so k_s should decrease as the dividend payout is increased.[14]

Another factor that might cause investors to prefer a particular dividend policy is the tax effect of dividend receipts. Investors must pay taxes at the time dividends and capital gains are received. Thus, depending on his or her tax situation, an investor might prefer either a payout of current earnings as dividends, which would be taxed in the current period, or capital gains associated with growth in stock value, which would be taxed when the stock is sold, perhaps many years in the future. Investors who prefer to delay the impact of taxes would be willing to pay more for low payout companies than for otherwise similar high payout companies, and vice versa.

Those who believe the firm's dividend policy is relevant are proponents of the **dividend relevance theory**, which asserts that dividend policy can affect the value of a firm through investors' preferences.

DIVIDEND IRRELEVANCE THEORY
The theory that a firm's dividend policy has no effect on either its value or its cost of capital.

OPTIMAL DIVIDEND POLICY
The dividend policy that strikes a balance between current dividends and future growth and maximizes the firm's stock price.

DIVIDEND RELEVANCE THEORY
The value of a firm is affected by its dividend policy — the optimal dividend policy is the one that maximizes the firm's value.

Self-Test Questions

Differentiate between the dividend irrelevance and dividend relevance theories.

How might taxes affect investors' preferences concerning the receipt of dividends and capital gains?

---

[13]The principal proponents of the dividend irrelevance theory are Miller and Modigliani (MM), who outlined their theory in "Dividend Policy, Growth, and the Valuation of Shares," *Journal of Business,* October 1961, 411–433. The assumptions MM made to develop their dividend irrelevance theory are similar to those they introduced in their capital structure theory mentioned earlier in the chapter. Such assumptions are made to afford them the ability to develop a manageable theory.

[14]Myron J. Gordon, "Optimal Investment and Financing Policy," *Journal of Finance,* May 1963, 264–272; and John Lintner, "Dividends, Earnings, Leverage, Stock Prices, and the Supply of Capital to Corporations," *Review of Economics and Statistics,* August 1962, 243–269.

Investors and Dividend Policy

Although researchers cannot tell corporate decision makers precisely how dividend policy affects stock prices and capital costs, the research has generated some thoughts concerning investors' reactions to dividend policy changes and why firms have particular dividend policies. Three of these views are discussed in this section.

Information Content, or Signaling

If investors expect a company's dividend to increase by 5 percent per year, and if, in fact, the dividend is increased by 5 percent, then the stock price generally will not change significantly on the day the dividend increase is announced. In Wall Street parlance, such a dividend increase would be "discounted," or *anticipated,* by the market. However, if investors expect a 5 percent increase, but the company actually increases the dividend by 25 percent — say, from $2 to $2.50 — this generally would be accompanied by an increase in the price of the stock. Conversely, a less-than-expected dividend increase, or a reduction, generally would result in a price decline.

It is a well-known fact that corporations are extremely reluctant to cut dividends and, therefore, *managers do not raise dividends unless they anticipate higher, or at least stable, earnings in the future to sustain the higher dividends.* This means that a larger-than-expected dividend increase is taken by investors as a "signal" that the firm's management forecasts improved future earnings, whereas a dividend reduction signals a forecast of poor earnings. Thus, it can be argued that investors' reactions to changes in dividend payments do not show that investors prefer dividends to retained earnings; rather, the stock price changes simply indicate important information is contained in dividend announcements — in effect, dividend announcements provide investors with information previously known only to management. This theory is referred to as the **information content**, or **signaling, hypothesis**.

INFORMATION CONTENT (SIGNALING) HYPOTHESIS
The theory that investors regard dividend changes as signals of management's earnings forecasts.

Clientele Effect

It has also been shown that it is very possible that a firm sets a particular dividend payout policy, which then attracts a *clientele* consisting of those investors who like the firm's dividend policy. For example, some stockholders, such as retired individuals, prefer current income to future capital gains, so they want the firm to pay out a higher percentage of its earnings. Other stockholders have no need for current investment income, so they favor a low payout ratio. If investors could not invest in companies with different dividend policies, it might be very expensive for them to achieve their investment goals — investors who prefer capital gains could reinvest any dividends they receive, but they first would have to pay taxes on the income. In essence, then, a **clientele effect** might exist if firms' stockholders are attracted to companies because they have particular dividend policies — those investors who desire current investment income can purchase shares in high-dividend-payout firms, whereas those who do not need current cash income can invest in low-payout firms. Consequently, we would expect the

CLIENTELE EFFECT
The tendency of a firm to attract the type of investor who likes its dividend policy.

stock price of a firm to change if it changes its dividend policy, because investors will adjust their portfolios to include firms with the desired dividend policy.

Free Cash Flow Hypothesis

If it is the intent of the financial manager to maximize the value of the firm, then investors should prefer that a firm pay dividends only after all acceptable capital budgeting opportunities have been purchased. We know that acceptable capital budgeting projects increase the value of the firm. We also know that because flotation costs are incurred when issuing new stock, it costs a firm more to raise funds using new common equity than it does using retained earnings. So, to maximize value, where possible, a firm should use retained earnings rather than issue new common stock to finance capital budgeting projects. Thus, dividends should be paid only when *free cash flows* in excess of capital budgeting needs exist. If management does otherwise, the firm's value will not be maximized. Thus, according to the **free cash flow hypothesis**, the firm should distribute any earnings that cannot be reinvested at a rate at least as great as the investors' required rate of return, k_s.

The free cash flow hypothesis might help to explain why investors react differently to identical dividend changes made by similar firms. For example, a firm's stock price will not change dramatically if it reduces its dividend for the purposes of investing in capital budgeting projects with positive NPVs. On the other hand, a company that reduces its dividend simply to increase free cash flows will experience a significant decline in the market value of its stock, because the dividend reduction is not in the best interests of the stockholders — in this case, an agency problem exists. Thus, the free cash flow hypothesis suggests the dividend policy can provide information about the firm's behavior with respect to wealth maximization.

FREE CASH FLOW HYPOTHESIS
All else equal, firms that pay dividends from cash flows that cannot be reinvested in positive net present value projects, which are termed *free cash flows,* have higher values than firms that retain free cash flows.

Self-Test Question

Define (1) the information content hypothesis (2) the clientele effect, and (3) the free cash flow hypothesis, and explain how each affects dividend policy.

Dividend Policy in Practice[15]

We have provided some insights concerning the relevance of dividend policy and how investors might view dividend payments from firms. However, no one has been able to develop a formula that can be used to tell management specifically how a given dividend policy will affect a firm's stock price. Even so, managements still must establish a dividend policy. This section discusses several alternative policies as well as experiences we observe in practice.

---

[15]The payment of dividends has a direct effect on the equity section of a company's balance sheet. We do not show the specific balance sheet effects of paying cash dividends in this chapter. Neither do we show the effects of paying stock dividends or stock splits, both of which impact the equity section of the balance sheet as well. These effects will be illustrated when we discuss financial statement analysis in Chapter 14.

Types of Dividend Payments

The dollar amounts of dividends paid by firms follow a variety of patterns. In general, though, firms pay dividends using one of the four payout policies discussed in this section.

RESIDUAL DIVIDEND POLICY   In practice, dividend policy is very much influenced by investment opportunities and by the availability of funds with which to finance new investments. This fact has led to the development of a **residual dividend policy**, which states that a firm should pay dividends only if more earnings are available than are needed to support its optimal capital budget. The word *residual* means "left over," and the residual policy implies that dividends should be paid only out of "leftover" earnings.

The basis of the residual policy is the fact that *investors prefer to have the firm retain and reinvest earnings rather than pay them out in dividends if the rate of return the firm can earn on reinvested earnings exceeds the rate investors, on average, can themselves obtain on other investments of comparable risk.* For example, if the corporation can reinvest retained earnings at a 14 percent rate of return, whereas the average stockholder can earn at best a 12 percent return on similar-risk investments, then stockholders prefer to have the firm retain the profits.

According to the residual dividend policy, a firm that has to issue new common stock to finance capital budgeting needs does not have residual earnings, and dividends will be zero. And, because both the earnings level and the capital budgeting needs of a firm vary from year to year, strict adherence to the residual dividend policy would result in dividend variability — one year the firm might declare zero dividends because investment opportunities were good, but the next year it might pay a large dividend because investment opportunities were poor. Thus, following the residual dividend policy would be optimal only if investors were not bothered by fluctuating dividends.

STABLE, PREDICTABLE DIVIDENDS   In the past, many firms set a specific annual dollar dividend per share and then maintained it, increasing the annual dividend only if it seemed clear that future earnings would be sufficient to allow the new dividend to be maintained. A corollary of that policy was this rule: *Never reduce the annual dividend.*

A fairly typical dividend policy, that of Eastman Kodak, is illustrated in Figure 11-9. From 1978 through 1982, Kodak's earnings were relatively stable, and so was the payout of dividends. But, after 1982, more intense global competition, major litigation, and changing economic periods caused a great deal of volatility in Kodak's earnings. Management stopped increasing the dividend when earnings fell, but did not cut the dividend, even when earnings failed to cover the payment. Maintaining the dividend was Kodak's way of signaling to stockholders that management was confident that any declines in earnings were only temporary and that earnings would soon resume their upward trend. This was indeed the case — since 1992, earnings have fluctuated, but have exhibited a positive upward trend. However, Kodak maintained a nearly constant dollar dividend during this period because the company underwent a major restructuring and its market share in the U.S. declined somewhat. As Kodak improves its market position, especially in

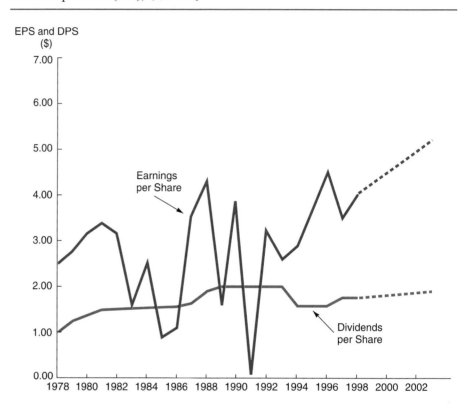

FIGURE 11-9

Eastman Kodak: Earnings per Share (EPS) and
Dividends per Share (DPS), 1978–2003

SOURCE: *Value Line,* June 1998. Projected values are shown as dashed lines.

digital photography, it is expected to again increase dividends, which is shown by
the dashed lines beyond 1998.

STABLE, PREDICTABLE DIVIDENDS
Payment of a specific dollar
dividend each year, or
periodically increasing the
dividend at a constant rate;
the annual dollar dividend
is relatively predictable by
investors.

There are two good reasons for paying **stable, predictable dividends** rather
than following the residual dividend policy. First, given the existence of the information content, or signaling, idea, a fluctuating payment policy would lead to
greater uncertainty, hence to a higher k_s and a lower stock price, than would exist
under a stable policy. Second, many stockholders use dividends for current consumption, and they would be put to trouble and expense if they had to sell part
of their shares to obtain cash if the company cut the dividend.

As a rule, stable predictable dividends imply more certainty than variable dividends, thus a lower k_s and a higher firm value. So, it is this dividend policy most
firms favor.

CONSTANT PAYOUT RATIO   It would be possible for a firm to pay out a constant percentage of earnings, but because earnings surely will fluctuate, this policy would
mean that the dollar amount of dividends would vary. For example, if Eastman
Kodak had followed the policy of paying a constant percentage of earnings per
share, say, 50 percent, the dividends per share paid since 1978 would have fluc-

tuated exactly the same as earnings per share as shown in Figure 11-9, and thus the company would have had to cut its dividend in several different years. Thus, with the constant payout ratio dividend policy, investors would have had much greater uncertainty concerning the expected dividends each year, and chances are k_s also would be greater, hence its stock price would be lower. Although Kodak's stock price has fluctuated somewhat, it has shown a general upward trend since the 1980s, in spite of substantial earnings fluctuations. Had it cut the dividend to keep the payout ratio constant, Kodak's stock price would have "fallen out of bed" several times if investors interpreted the dividend reduction as a signal that management thought the earnings declines were permanent.

LOW REGULAR DIVIDEND PLUS EXTRAS A policy of paying a low regular dividend plus a year-end extra in good years is a compromise between a stable dividend (or stable growth rate) and a constant payout rate. Such a policy gives the firm flexibility, yet investors can count on receiving at least a minimum dividend. Therefore, if a firm's earnings and cash flows are quite volatile, this policy might be its best choice. The directors can set a relatively low regular dividend — low enough so that it can be maintained even in low-profit years or in years when a considerable amount of retained earnings is needed — and then supplement it with an **extra dividend** in years when excess funds are available. Ford, General Motors, and other auto companies, whose earnings fluctuate widely from year to year, formerly followed such a policy, but in recent years they have joined the crowd and now follow our first choice of paying a stable, predictable dividend.

EXTRA DIVIDEND
A supplemental dividend paid in years when the firm does well and excess funds are available for distribution.

Payment Procedures

Dividends are normally paid quarterly, and, when conditions permit, the dividend is increased. For example, on June 12, 1998, the board of directors of Abbott Laboratories, an international pharmaceutical and health care products manufacturer, declared a 15¢ quarterly common stock dividend. Earlier in the year, Abbott's board indicated that it anticipated the annual dividend to be 60¢, which is 7.5¢ higher than the previous year.[16] So, Abbott's stockholders were not surprised when the 15¢ quarterly dividend was announced; they would have been shocked if the dividend had been eliminated, because Abbott has paid a dividend for 298 consecutive quarters, which is 74.5 years!

When Abbott declared the dividend, it issued the following statement:

> Abbott Park, Illinois, June 12, 1998 — The board of directors of Abbott Laboratories today declared a quarterly common dividend of 15 cents per share, . . . payable August 15, 1998, to shareholders of record at the close of business on July 15, 1998.[17]

The three dates mentioned in this announcement are important to current stockholders. These dates, as well as the ex-dividend date are defined as follows:

---

[16]Abbott Laboratories split its stock 2-for-1 in May 1998, so the amounts shown here are adjusted for the split. The total dividend paid in 1997 actually was $1.05 for each pre-split share, which equates to two shares following the stock split; thus, the after-split dividend per share is 52.5¢ = $1.05/2.

[17]This statement was the announcement Abbott posted on the company's Web site, which was located at http://www.abbott.com/news/.

DECLARATION DATE
The date on which a firm's board of directors issues a statement declaring a dividend.

1. Declaration date. On the **declaration date**, June 12, 1998, in Abbott's case, the board of directors meets and declares the regular dividend. For accounting purposes, the declared dividend becomes an actual liability on the declaration date, and if a balance sheet were constructed, the amount ($0.15) × (Number of shares outstanding) would appear as a current liability, and retained earnings would be reduced by a like amount.

**HOLDER-OF-RECORD DATE
(DATE OF RECORD)**
The date the company opens the ownership books to determine who will receive the dividend; the stockholders of record on this date receive the dividend.

2. Holder-of-record date. At the close of business on the **holder-of-record date**, or **date of record**, the company closes its stock transfer books and produces a list of shareholders as of that date. Thus, if Abbott Labs is notified of the sale and transfer of some stock before 5 P.M. on Wednesday, July 15, 1998, then the new owner receives the dividend. However, if notification is received after July 15, the previous owner of the stock gets the dividend check, because it is his or her name that appears on the company's ownership records.

3. Ex-dividend date. The securities industry has set up a convention of declaring that the right to the dividend remains with the stock until two business days prior to the holder-of-record date. This is to ensure the company is notified of the transfer in time to record the new owner and thus pay the dividend to him or her. The date when the right to receive the next dividend payment no longer goes with the stock — new purchasers will not receive the next dividend — is called the **ex-dividend date**. In the case of Abbott, the ex-dividend date is Monday, July 13, 1998, so any investor who purchases the stock on or after that date will not receive the next dividend payment associated with the stock. All else equal, then, we would expect the price of Abbott's stock to drop on the ex-dividend date approximately by the amount of the dividend — assuming no other price fluctuations, the price at which Abbott's stock opens on Monday, July 13 should be about 15¢ less than the close on Friday, July 10.

EX-DIVIDEND DATE
The date on which the right to the next dividend no longer accompanies a stock; it usually is two business days prior to the holder-of-record date.

PAYMENT DATE
The date on which a firm actually mails dividend checks.

4. Payment date. Abbott will pay dividends to the holders of record on August 15, 1998 — this is the **payment date**. Recently, many firms have started paying dividends electronically.

Dividend Reinvestment Plans

DIVIDEND REINVESTMENT PLAN (DRIP)
A plan that enables a stockholder to automatically reinvest dividends received back into the stock of the paying firm.

Today, most larger companies offer **dividend reinvestment plans (DRIPs)**, whereby stockholders can automatically reinvest dividends received to purchase more stock of the paying corporation.[18] As you will see, some DRIPs (referred to as "drips") directly affect the capital structures of the firms that offer them. Thus, in this section, we discuss the basics of DRIPs.

There are two types of DRIPs: (1) plans that involve only "old" stock that already is outstanding and (2) plans that involve newly issued stock. In either case, the stockholder must pay income taxes on the amount of the dividends even though stock rather than cash is received.

Under the "old-stock" type of plan, the stockholder chooses between receiving dividend checks or having the company use the dividends to buy more stock in the corporation. If the stockholder elects reinvestment, a bank, acting as trustee, takes the total funds available for reinvestment, purchases the corporation's stock

---

[18]See Richard H. Pettway and R. Phil Malone, "Automatic Dividend Reinvestment Plans," *Financial Management,* Winter 1973, 11–18, for an excellent discussion of this topic.

on the open market, and allocates the shares purchased to the participating stockholders' accounts on a pro rata basis. The transactions costs of buying shares (brokerage costs) are low because of volume purchases, so these plans benefit small stockholders who do not need cash dividends for current consumption.

The "new-stock" type of DRIP provides for dividends to be invested in newly issued stock; hence these plans raise new capital for the firm. AT&T, Florida Power & Light, Union Carbide, and many other companies have used such plans to raise substantial amounts of *new* equity capital. Such DRIP plans directly affect the capital structure of the firm — common equity is "issued," and the firm receives funds to invest in capital projects. No fees are charged to stockholders, and many companies offer stock at a discount below the actual market price. The companies absorb these costs as a trade-off against the flotation costs that would have been incurred had they sold stock through investment bankers rather than through the dividend reinvestment plans.[19]

Self-Test Questions

Explain the logic of the residual dividend policy and why it is more likely to be used to establish a long-run payout target than to set the actual year-by-year payout ratio.

Describe the stable, predictable dividend policy, and give two reasons a firm might follow such a policy.

Explain what a low-regular-dividend-plus-extras policy is and why a firm might follow such a policy.

Describe the constant payout ratio dividend policy. Why is this policy probably not as popular as a stable, predictable dividend policy?

Why is the ex-dividend date important to investors?

Differentiate between the two types of dividend reinvestment plans.

Factors Influencing Dividend Policy

In addition to managements' beliefs concerning which dividend theory is most correct, there are a number of other factors that are considered when a particular dividend policy is chosen. The factors firms take into account can be grouped into four broad categories:

1. **Constraints on dividend payments.** The amount of dividends a firm can pay might be limited due to (a) debt contract restrictions, which often stipulate that no dividends can be paid unless certain financial measures, such as the

---

[19]One interesting aspect of DRIPs is that they have forced corporations to reexamine their basic dividend policies. A high participation rate in a DRIP suggests that stockholders might be better off if the firm simply reduced cash dividends, as this would save stockholders some personal income taxes.

Also, it should be noted that companies either use or stop using new-stock DRIPs depending on their need for equity capital. For example, once it had completed a nuclear-powered generating plant, Florida Power & Light (now part of FPL Group) stopped offering a new-stock DRIP because its need for equity capital had declined.

times-interest-earned ratio, exceed stated minimums; (b) the fact that dividend payments cannot exceed the balance sheet item "retained earnings" (this is known as the *impairment of capital rule,* which is designed to protect creditors by prohibiting the company from distributing assets to stockholders before debtholders are paid); (c) cash availability, because cash dividends can be paid only with cash; and (d) restrictions imposed by the IRS on improperly accumulated retained earnings. If the IRS can demonstrate that a firm's dividend payout ratio is being held down deliberately to help its stockholders avoid personal taxes, the firm is subject to heavy tax penalties. But, this factor generally is relevant only to privately owned firms.

2. **Investment opportunities**. Firms that have large numbers of acceptable capital budgeting projects generally have low dividend-payout ratios, and vice versa. But, if a firm can accelerate or postpone projects (flexibility), then it can adhere more closely to a target dividend policy.

3. **Alternative sources of capital.** When a firm needs to finance a given level of investment, and flotation costs are high, k_e will be well above k_s, making it better to set a low payout ratio and to finance through retention rather than through sale of new common stock. Also, if the firm can adjust its debt/assets ratio without raising capital costs sharply, it can maintain a stable dollar dividend, even if earnings fluctuate, by using a variable debt/assets ratio. Another factor considered by management when making financing decisions is ownership dilution — if management is concerned about maintaining control, it might be reluctant to sell new stock, hence the company might retain more earnings than it otherwise would.

4. **Effects of dividend policy on k_s.** The effects of dividend policy on k_s might be considered in terms of four factors: (a) stockholders' desire for current versus future income, (b) perceived riskiness of dividends versus capital gains, (c) the tax advantage of capital gains over dividends, and (d) the information content of dividends (signaling). Because we discussed each of these factors earlier, we need only note here that the importance of each factor in terms of its effect on k_s varies from firm to firm depending on the makeup of its current and possible future stockholders.

It should be apparent from our discussions that dividend policy decisions truly are exercises in informed judgment, not decisions that can be quantified precisely. Even so, to make rational dividend decisions, financial managers must consider all of the points discussed in the preceding sections.

Self-Test Questions

Identify the four broad categories of factors that affect dividend policy.

What constraints affect dividend policy?

How do investment opportunities affect dividend policy?

How does the availability and cost of outside capital affect dividend policy?

Capital Structures and Dividend Policies Around the World

As you might expect, when we examine the capital structures of companies around the world we find wide variations. Table 11-7 illustrates capital structure

TABLE 11-7

Capital Structure Percentages for Selected Countries
Ranked by Common Equity Ratios, 1995

Country	Equity	Total Debt	Long-Term Debt	Short-Term Debt
United Kingdom	68.3%	31.7%	N/A	N/A
United States	48.4	51.6	26.8%	24.8%
Canada	47.5	52.5	30.2	22.7
Germany	39.7	60.3	15.6	44.7
Spain	39.7	60.3	22.1	38.2
France	38.8	61.2	23.5	37.7
Japan	33.7	66.3	23.3	43.0
Italy	23.5	76.5	24.2	52.3

NOTE: The percentages were computed from financial data that were stated in domestic currency. For example, the amount of total assets for French companies was stated in francs.

SOURCE: *OECD Financial Statistics, Part 3: Non-Financial Enterprises Financial Statements, 1996.*

differences for selected countries; the ranking is in descending order of common equity ratios, as shown in the column labeled "Equity." As you can see, companies in Italy and Japan use much greater proportions of debt than companies in the United States or Canada, and companies in the United Kingdom use the lowest proportion of debt of all the countries listed. Of course, different countries use somewhat different accounting conventions, which make comparisons difficult. Still, even after adjusting for accounting differences, researchers find that Italian and Japanese firms use considerably more financial leverage than U.S. and Canadian companies. The gap among the countries has narrowed somewhat during the past couple of decades. In the early 1970s, companies in Canada and the United States had debt/assets ratios of about 40 percent, and companies in Japan and Italy had debt/assets ratios of more than 75 percent (Japanese companies averaged nearly 85 percent leverage).

The dividend policies of companies around the world also vary considerably. A recent study found the dividend payout ratios of companies range from 10.5 percent in the Philippines to nearly 70 percent in Taiwan.[20] Even the countries listed in Table 11-7 exhibit some great differences — as a percentage of earnings, the dividends paid out in Canada, France, Italy, and the United States range from 20 percent to 25 percent, in Spain and the United Kingdom the range is from 30 percent to 40 percent, in Germany the rate is about 43 percent, and it is more than 50 percent for Japanese companies.

Why do international differences in financial leverage and dividend policies exist? It seems logical to attribute the differences to dissimilar tax structures. Although the interest on corporate debt is deductible in each country, and though individuals must pay taxes on interest received, both dividends and capital gains are taxed differently around the world. The tax codes in most developed countries

---

[20]Rafael La Porta, Florencio Lopez-de-Silanes, Andrei Shleifer, and Robert W. Vishny, "Agency Problems and Dividend Policies Around the World," unpublished manuscript, Harvard University, November 1997.

encourage personal investing and savings more than the U.S. Tax Code. For example, Germany, Italy, and many other European countries do not tax capital gains, and in most other developed countries, including Japan, France, and Canada, capital gains are not taxed unless they exceed some minimum amount. Further, in Germany and Italy, dividends are not taxed as income, and in most other countries some amount of dividends is tax exempt. The general conclusions we can make, then, are: (1) From a tax standpoint, corporations should be equally inclined to use debt in most developed countries. (2) In countries where capital gains are not taxed, investors should show a preference for stocks compared with countries that have capital gains taxes. (3) Investor preferences should lead to relatively low equity capital costs in those countries that do not tax capital gains, and this, in turn, should cause firms in those countries to use significantly more equity capital than their U.S. counterparts. But, for the most part, this is exactly the opposite of the actual capital structures we observe, so differential tax laws cannot explain the observed capital structure differences. Also, it has been found that differences in taxes do not explain the differences in dividend payout ratios among the countries.

If tax rates cannot explain the different capital structures or dividend policies, what else might be an appropriate explanation? Another possibility relates to risk, especially bankruptcy costs. Actual bankruptcy, and even the threat of potential bankruptcy, imposes a costly burden on firms with large amounts of debt. Note, though, that the threat of bankruptcy is dependent on the probability of bankruptcy. In the United States, equity monitoring costs are comparatively low because corporations produce quarterly reports, pay quarterly dividends, and must comply with relatively stringent audit requirements. These conditions are less prevalent in the other countries. On the other hand, debt monitoring costs are probably lower in such countries as Germany and Japan than in the United States because most of the corporate debt consists of bank loans as opposed to publicly issued bonds. More importantly, though, the banks in many European and developed Asian countries are closely linked to the corporations that borrow from them, often holding major equity positions in, and having substantial influence over the management of, the debtor firms. Given these close relationships, the banks are much more directly involved with the debtor firms' affairs, and, as a result, they also are more accommodating than U.S. bondholders in the event of financial distress. This, in turn, suggests that any given amount of debt gives rise to a lower threat of bankruptcy than for a U.S. firm with the same amount of business risk. Thus, an analysis of both bankruptcy costs and equity monitoring costs leads to the conclusion that U.S. firms should have more equity and less debt than firms in countries such as Japan and Germany, which is what we typically observe.

A study by Rafael La Porta, Florencio Lopez-de-Silanes, Andrei Shleifer, and Robert W. Vishny offers some insight into the dividend policy differences that exist around the world. They suggest that, all else equal, companies pay out greater amounts of earnings as dividends in countries with measures that help protect the rights of minority stockholders. In such countries, though, firms with many growth opportunities tend to pay lower dividends, which is to be expected, because the funds are needed to finance the growth and shareholders are willing to forgo current income in hopes of greater future benefits. On the other hand, in countries where shareholders' rights are not well protected, investors prefer dividends because there is great uncertainty about whether management will use earnings for self-gratification rather than for the benefit of the firm — investors in these countries accept any dividends they can get.

We cannot state that one financial system is better than another in the sense of making the firms in one country more efficient than those in another. However, as U.S. firms become increasingly involved in worldwide operations, they must become increasingly aware of worldwide conditions, and they must be prepared to adapt to conditions in the various countries in which they do business.

Self-Test Questions

Why do international differences in financial leverage exist?

Why do dividend payout ratios of companies differ among different countries?

SMALL BUSINESS

Dividend Policy for Small Businesses

The dividend policy decision involves determining the amount of earnings to distribute to stockholders. While most large, mature firms pay out a portion of earnings each year, many small, rapidly growing firms pay no dividends at all. As the small firm grows, so does its need for financing, and because small businesses have limited access to the capital markets, they rely on internal financing (retained earnings) to a greater extent than larger firms. Over time, though, as the firm and its products mature, its access to the capital markets improves, its growth slows, its financing requirements lessen, and at some point it begins to pay dividends.

Apple Computer can be used to illustrate this process. Apple was founded in 1977, and its first year sales were $660,000. In 1978, sales increased by 550 percent, to $3.6 million, and the company earned a profit of $660,000. Growth continued at a rapid pace in the following years. Initially, all of the stock was owned by the founders and a few venture capitalists. These investors wanted to ensure the company's success, and they also were more interested in capital gains than in taxable dividends, so the firm did not pay any dividends. Indeed, from 1978 through 1986, all earnings were plowed back and used to support growth, which averaged about 50 percent annually. We should also point out that, until 1994, Apple never issued debt; it chose instead to support its early growth by retaining earnings and by occasionally issuing additional shares of common stock. Apple had 128 million shares of stock outstanding in late 1997, up from 33 million in 1978.

By 1988, new competitors had entered the market, and Apple's growth was slowing down. *Value Line's*

analysts estimated that Apple's revenues would grow at an annual rate of 26 percent during the period 1988 to 1993. While a growth rate of 26 percent per year is well above average, it is far below Apple's earlier growth rate of 50 percent. On the basis of these growth forecasts, Apple's board of directors met early in 1987 and declared an annual dividend of $0.24 per share. The stock price reacted favorably, so the annual dividend was raised in 1988 to $0.32 and on up to $0.48 by 1994. Unfortunately, since that time, Apple has encountered financial difficulty, primarily because of lost market share, and in 1997 dividend payments were suspended. This shows how business risk can affect dividend policy.

This story illustrates three points. First, small, rapidly growing firms generally need to retain all their earnings, and also to obtain additional capital from outside sources, to support growth. Growth requires cash, and even highly profitable companies such as Apple have difficulty generating enough cash from earnings both to support rapid growth and to pay dividends. Second, as the firm matures, its growth will slow down, and its need for funds will diminish. Thus, when Apple's growth began to slow down, it no longer needed to retain all of its earnings, so it began to pay a small dividend. Third, the market recognizes that new, profitable firms often grow so fast that they must raise needed funds through new issues of common stock, and such issues can be considered indications that the firm's managers anticipate extraordinarily good investment opportunities.

Summary

In this chapter we discussed the concept of optimal capital structure, and examined the effects of financial leverage on stock prices, earnings per share, and the cost of capital. We also examined dividend policy decisions, and we discovered such decisions can have either favorable or unfavorable effects on the price of a firm's stock. The key concepts covered in the chapter are listed below.

- A firm's **optimal capital structure** is that mix of debt and equity that maximizes the price of the firm's stock. At any point in time, the firm's management has a specific **target capital structure** in mind, presumably the optimal one, although this target might change over time. Although it is theoretically possible to determine the optimal capital structure, as a practical matter we cannot estimate this structure with precision.
- Several factors influence a firm's capital structure decisions. These factors include the firm's (1) **business risk**, (2) **tax position**, (3) need for **financial flexibility**, and (4) **managerial conservatism or aggressiveness**.
- **Business risk** is the uncertainty associated with projections of a firm's future returns on equity. A firm will tend to have low business risk if the demand for its products is stable, if the prices of its inputs and products remain relatively constant, if it can adjust its prices freely when costs increase, and if a high percentage of its costs are variable and hence decrease as its output and sales decrease. Other things the same, the lower a firm's business risk, the higher its optimal debt/assets ratio.
- **Financial leverage** is the extent to which fixed-income securities (debt and preferred stock) are used in a firm's capital structure. **Financial risk** is the added risk to stockholders that results from financial leverage.
- The **EPS indifference point** is the level of sales at which EPS will be the same whether the firm uses debt or common stock financing. Equity financing will be better if the firm's sales end up below the EPS indifference point, whereas debt financing will be better at higher sales levels.
- Modigliani and Miller developed a **trade-off theory of capital structure**, where debt is useful because interest payments are **tax deductible**, but debt brings with it costs associated with actual or potential bankruptcy. Under MM's theory the optimal capital structure strikes a balance between the tax benefits of debt and the costs associated with bankruptcy.
- An alternative (or, really, complementary) theory of capital structure relates to the **signals** given to investors by a firm's decision to use debt or stock to raise new capital. The use of stock is a negative signal, while using debt is a positive, or at least a neutral, signal. Therefore, companies try to maintain a **reserve borrowing capacity**, and this means using less debt in "normal" times than the MM trade-off theory would suggest.
- The **optimal dividend policy** is the policy that strikes a balance between current dividends and future growth to maximize the price of the firm's stock.
- The **dividend irrelevance theory** holds that a firm's dividend policy has no effect either on the value of its stock or on its cost of capital.
- Those who believe in **dividend relevance** suggest that a particular dividend policy might be preferred because dividends are considered less risky than potential capital gains, personal tax implications associated with dividends, and so on.

- Because **empirical tests** of the theories have been **inconclusive**, *academicians simply cannot tell corporate managers how a change in dividend policy will affect stock prices and capital costs.* Thus, actually determining the optimal dividend policy is a matter of judgment.

- Dividend policy should reflect the existence of the **information content of dividends (signaling)**, **the clientele effect**, and/or **the free cash flow effect**. The information content, or signaling, hypothesis states that investors regard dividend changes as a signal of management's forecast of future earnings. According to the clientele effect, a firm attracts investors who like its dividend policy. And, the free cash flow effect suggests that firms with few capital budgeting opportunities and great amounts of cash should have higher dividend payout ratios if the value maximization goal is pursued.

- In practice, most firms try to follow a policy of paying a **stable, predictable dividend**. This policy provides investors with a stable, dependable income, and it also gives investors information about management's expectations for earnings growth through signaling effects.

- Other dividend policies used include: (1) the **residual dividend policy**, in which dividends are paid out of earnings left over after the capital budget has been financed; (2) the **constant payout ratio policy**, in which a constant percentage of earnings is targeted to be paid out; and (3) the **low-regular-dividend-plus-extras policy**, in which the firm pays a constant, low dividend that can be maintained even in bad years and then pays an extra dividend in good years.

- A **dividend reinvestment plan (DRIP)** allows stockholders to have the company automatically use their dividends to purchase additional shares of the firm's stock. DRIPs are popular with investors who do not need current income because the plans allow stockholders to acquire additional shares without incurring normal brokerage fees.

- Other factors, such as **legal constraints, investment opportunities, availability of other types of capital**, and the **effect on k_s**, are considered by managers when they establish dividend policies.

- Capital structures and dividend policies vary widely around the world. It seems the primary reason for such variation is the **risk** associated with firms' operations and financing arrangements.

- Small, rapidly growing firms generally need to **retain all their earnings** — and obtain additional capital from outside sources — to support growth. As the firm matures, its growth will slow down, and its need for funds will diminish. The market recognizes that new, profitable firms often grow so fast they simply must issue common stock and that such issues indicate the firms' managers anticipate extraordinarily good investment opportunities.

Questions

11-1 "One type of leverage affects both EBIT and EPS. The other type affects only EPS." Explain what this statement means.

11-2 Explain why the following statement is true: "Other things the same, firms with relatively stable sales are able to carry relatively high debt/assets ratios."

11-3 If a firm went from zero debt to successively higher levels of debt, why would you expect its stock price to first rise, then hit a peak, and then begin to decline?

11-4 Why is the debt level that maximizes a firm's expected EPS generally higher than the one that maximizes its stock price?

11-5 When the Bell System was broken up, the old AT&T was split into a new AT&T plus seven regional telephone companies. The specific reason for forcing the breakup was to increase the degree of competition in the telephone industry. AT&T had a monopoly on local service, long distance, and the manufacture of all the equipment used by telephone companies, and the breakup was expected to open most of these markets to competition. In the court order that set the terms of the breakup, the capital structures of the surviving companies were specified, and much attention was given to the increased competition telephone companies could expect in the future. Do you think the optimal capital structure after the breakup should be the same as the pre-breakup optimal capital structure? Explain your position.

11-6 Your firm's R&D department has been working on a new process that, if it works, can produce oil from coal at a cost of about $5 per barrel versus a current market price of $20 per barrel. The company needs $10 million of external funds at this time to complete the research. The results of the research will be known in about a year, and there is about a 50-50 chance of success. If the research is successful, your company will need to raise a substantial amount of new money to put the idea into production. Your economists forecast that although the economy will be depressed next year, interest rates will be high because of international monetary problems. You must recommend how the currently needed $10 million should be raised — as debt or as equity. How would the potential impact of your project influence your decision?

11-7 As an investor, would you rather invest in a firm that has a policy of maintaining (a) a constant payout ratio, (b) a stable, predictable dividend per share with a target dividend growth rate, or (c) a constant regular quarterly dividend plus a year-end extra when earnings are sufficiently high or corporate investment needs sufficiently low? Explain your answer, stating how these policies would affect your required rate of return, k_s. Also, discuss how your answer might change if you were a student, a 50-year-old professional with peak earnings, or a retiree.

11-8 How would each of the following changes tend to affect the average dividend payout ratios for corporations, other things held constant? Explain your answers.
a. An increase in the personal income tax rate.
b. A rise in interest rates.
c. A decline in corporate investment opportunities.
d. Permission for corporations to deduct dividend payments for tax purposes as they now can do with interest charges.
e. A change in the Tax Code so that both realized and unrealized capital gains in any year were taxed at the same rate as dividends.

11-9 "The cost of retained earnings is less than the cost of new outside equity capital. Consequently, it is totally irrational for a firm to sell a new issue of stock and to pay dividends during the same year." Discuss this statement.

11-10 Would it ever be rational for a firm to borrow money in order to pay dividends? Explain.

11-11 One position expressed in the financial literature is that firms set their dividends as a residual after using income to support new investment.
a. Explain what a residual dividend policy implies.
b. Could the residual dividend policy be consistent with (1) a stable, predictable dividend policy, (2) a constant payout ratio policy, and/or (3) a low-regular-dividend-plus-extras policy? Answer in terms of both short-run, year-to-year consistency and longer-run consistency.

Self-Test Problems   *Solutions Appear in Appendix B*

Key terms   **ST-1**   Define each of the following terms:

a. Target capital structure; optimal capital structure

b. Business risk; financial risk; total risk

c. Financial leverage

d. EPS indifference point

e. Times-interest-earned (TIE) ratio

f. Symmetric information; asymmetric information

g. Trade-off theory; signaling theory

h. Reserve borrowing capacity

i. Optimal dividend policy

j. Dividend irrelevance theory; dividend relevance theory

k. Information content, or signaling, hypothesis; clientele effect; free cash flow hypothesis

l. Residual dividend policy; stable, predictable dividend policy; constant payout ratio policy; low-regular-dividend-plus-extra policy

m. Declaration date; holder-of-record date; ex-dividend date; payment date

n. Dividend reinvestment plan (DRIP)

Financial leverage   **ST-2**   Gentry Motors Inc., a producer of turbine generators, is in this situation: EBIT = $4 million; tax rate = T = 35%; debt outstanding = $2 million; k_d = 10%; k_s = 15%; shares of stock outstanding = 600,000; and book value per share = $10. Because Gentry's product market is stable and the company expects no growth, all earnings are paid out as dividends. The debt consists of perpetual bonds.

a. What are Gentry's earnings per share (EPS) and its price per share (P_0)?

b. What is Gentry's weighted average cost of capital (WACC)?

c. Gentry can increase its debt by $8 million, to a total of $10 million, using the new debt to buy back and retire some of its stock at the current price. Its interest rate on debt will be 12 percent (it will have to call and refund the old debt), and its cost of equity will rise from 15 percent to 17 percent. EBIT will remain constant. Should Gentry change its capital structure?

d. What is Gentry's TIE coverage ratio under the original situation and under the conditions in part c of this question?

Alternative dividend policies   **ST-3**   Components Manufacturing Corporation (CMC) has an all-common-equity capital structure. It has 200,000 shares of $2 par value common stock outstanding. When CMC's founder, who was also its research director and most successful inventor, retired unexpectedly to the South Pacific in late 1999, CMC was left suddenly and permanently with materially lower growth expectations and relatively few attractive new investment opportunities. Unfortunately, there was no way to replace the founder's contributions to the firm. Previously, CMC found it necessary to plow back most of its earnings to finance growth, which averaged 12 percent per year. Future growth at a 5 percent rate is considered realistic, but that level would call for an increase in the dividend payout. Further, it now appears that new investment projects with at least the 14 percent rate of return required by CMC's stockholders (k_s = 14%) would amount to only $800,000 for 2000 in comparison to a projected $2,000,000 of net income. If the existing 20 percent dividend payout were continued, retained earnings would be $1.6 million in 2000, but, as noted, investments that yield the 14 percent cost of capital would amount to only $800,000.

The one encouraging thing is that the high earnings from existing assets are expected to continue, and net income of $2 million is still expected for 2000. Given the dramatically changed circumstances, CMC's management is reviewing the firm's dividend policy.

a. Assuming that the acceptable 2000 investment projects would be financed entirely by earnings retained during the year, calculate DPS in 2000, assuming that CMC uses the residual payment policy.

b. What payout ratio does your answer to part a imply for 2000?

c. If a 60 percent payout ratio is adopted and maintained for the foreseeable future, what is your estimate of the present market price of the common stock? How does this compare with the market price that should have prevailed under the assumptions existing just before the news about the founder's retirement? If the two values of P_0 are different, comment on why.

d. What would happen to the price of the stock if the old 20 percent payout were continued? Assume that if this payout is maintained, the average rate of return on the retained earnings will fall to 7.5 percent and the new growth rate will be

$$g = (1.0 - \text{Payout ratio}) \times (\text{ROE})$$

$$= (1.0 - 0.2)(7.5\%) = (0.8)(7.5\%) = 6.0\%$$

Problems

Risk analysis   **11-1**   **a.** Given the following information, calculate the expected value for Firm C's EPS: $E(\text{EPS}_A) = \$5.10$, $\sigma_A = \$3.61$; $E(\text{EPS}_B) = \$4.20$, $\sigma_B = \$2.96$; and $\sigma_C = \$4.11$.

	Probability				
	0.1	0.2	0.4	0.2	0.1
Firm A: EPS_A	($1.05)	$1.80	$5.10	$8.40	$11.70
Firm B: EPS_B	(1.20)	1.50	4.20	6.90	9.60
Firm C: EPS_C	(2.40)	1.35	5.10	8.85	12.60

b. Discuss the relative riskiness of the three firms' (A, B, and C) earnings.

Financing alternatives   **11-2**   Wired Communications Corporation (WCC) produces radio/television tuners for use with personal computers. The tuners sell for $288 per set, and this year's sales are expected to be 45,000 units. Variable production costs for the expected sales under present production methods are estimated at $10,200,000, and fixed production (operating) costs at present are $1,560,000. WCC has $4,800,000 of debt outstanding at an interest rate of 8 percent. There are 240,000 shares of common stock outstanding, and there is no preferred stock. The dividend payout ratio is 70 percent, and WCC is in the 40 percent marginal tax bracket.

The company is considering investing $7,200,000 in new equipment. Sales would not increase, but variable costs per unit would decline by 20 percent. Also, fixed operating costs would increase from $1,560,000 to $1,800,000. WCC could raise the required capital by borrowing $7,200,000 at 10 percent or by selling 240,000 additional shares at $30 per share.

a. What would be WCC's EPS (1) under the old production process, (2) under the new process if it uses debt, and (3) under the new process if it uses common stock?

b. At what unit sales level would WCC have the same EPS, assuming it undertakes the investment and finances it with debt or with stock? Hint: V = variable cost per unit = $8,160,000/45,000, and EPS = $[(P \times Q - V \times Q - F - I)(1 - T)]/\text{Shrs}$. Set $\text{EPS}_{\text{Stock}} = \text{EPS}_{\text{Debt}}$ and solve for Q.

c. At what unit sales level would EPS = 0 under the three production/financing setups — that is, under the old plan, the new plan with debt financing, and the new plan with stock financing? (Hint: Note that $V_{\text{Old}} = \$10,200,000/45,000$, and use the hints for part b, setting the EPS equation equal to zero.)

d. On the basis of the analysis in parts a, b, and c, which plan is the riskiest, which has the highest expected EPS, and which would you recommend? Assume here that there is a fairly high probability of sales falling as low as 25,000 units, and determine EPS_{Debt} and $\text{EPS}_{\text{Stock}}$ at that sales level to help assess the riskiness of the two financing plans.

Financing alternatives   **11-3**   The Strasburg Company plans to raise a net amount of $270 million to finance new equipment and working capital in early 2000. Two alternatives are being considered: Common stock may be sold to net $60 per share, or bonds yielding 12 percent may be issued. The balance sheet and income statement of the Strasburg Company prior to financing are as follows:

The Strasburg Company:
Balance Sheet as of December 31, 1999
(millions of dollars)

Current assets	$ 900.00	Accounts payable	$ 172.50
Net fixed assets	450.00	Notes payable to bank	255.00
		Other current liabilities	225.00
		Total current liabilities	$ 652.50
		Long-term debt (10%)	300.00
		Common stock, $3 par	60.00
		Retained earnings	337.50
Total assets	$1,350.00	Total liabilities and equity	$1,350.00

The Strasburg Company:
Income Statement for Year Ended
December 31, 1999
(millions of dollars)

Sales	$2,475.00
Operating costs	(2,227.50)
Earnings before interest and taxes (EBIT) (10%)	$ 247.50
Interest on short-term debt	(15.00)
Interest on long-term debt	(30.00)
Earnings before taxes (EBT)	$202.50
Taxes (40%)	(81.00)
Net income	$ 121.50

The probability distribution for annual sales is as follows:

Probability	Annual Sales (millions of dollars)
0.30	$2,250
0.40	2,700
0.30	3,150

Assuming that EBIT is equal to 10 percent of sales, calculate earnings per share under both the debt financing and the stock financing alternatives at each possible level of sales. Then calculate expected earnings per share and σ_{EPS} under both debt and stock financing. Also, calculate the debt/assets ratio and the times-interest-earned (TIE) ratio at the expected sales level under each alternative. The old debt will remain outstanding. Which financing method do you recommend?

Alternative dividend policies   **11-4**   In 1999 the Sirmans Company paid dividends totaling $3,600,000 on net income of $10.8 million. 1999 was a normal year, and for the past 10 years, earnings have grown at a constant rate of 10 percent. However, in 2000, earnings are expected to jump to $14.4 million, and the firm expects to have profitable investment opportunities of $8.4 million. It is predicted that Sirmans will not be able to maintain the 2000 level of earnings growth — the high 2000 earnings level is attributable to an exceptionally profitable new product line introduced that year — and the company will return to its previous 10 percent growth rate. Sirmans's target debt/assets ratio is 40 percent.

a. Calculate Sirmans's total dividends for 2000 if it follows each of the following policies:

   (1) Its 2000 dividend payment is set to force dividends to grow at the long-run growth rate in earnings.

   (2) It continues the 1999 dividend payout ratio.

   (3) It uses a pure residual dividend policy (40 percent of the $8.4 million investment is financed with debt).

   (4) It employs a regular-dividend-plus-extras policy, with the regular dividend being based on the long-run growth rate and the extra dividend being set according to the residual policy.

b. Which of the preceding policies would you recommend? Restrict your choices to the ones listed, but justify your answer.

c. Assume that investors expect Sirmans to pay total dividends of $9,000,000 in 2000 and to have the dividend grow at 10 percent after 2000. The total market value of the stock is $180 million. What is the company's cost of equity?

d. What is Sirmans's long-run average return on equity? [Hint: g = (Retention rate) × (ROE) = (1.0 − Payout rate) × (ROE).]

e. Does a 2000 dividend of $9,000,000 seem reasonable in view of your answers to parts c and d? If not, should the dividend be higher or lower?

Dividend policy and capital structure   **11-5**   Ybor City Tobacco Company has for many years enjoyed a moderate but stable growth in sales and earnings. However, cigarette consumption and consequently Ybor's sales have been falling recently, primarily because of an increasing awareness of the dangers of smoking to health. Anticipating further declines in tobacco sales for the future, Ybor's management hopes eventually to move almost entirely out of the tobacco business and into a newly developed, diversified product line in growth-oriented industries. The company is especially interested in the prospects for pollution-control devices because its research department has already done much work on the problems of filtering smoke. Right now the company estimates that an investment of $15 million is necessary to purchase new facilities and to begin operations on these products, but the investment could be earning a return of about 18 percent within a short time. The only other available investment opportunity totals $6 million and is expected to return about 10.4 percent.

The company is expected to pay a $3.00 dividend on its 3 million outstanding shares, the same as its dividend last year. The directors might, however, change the dividend if there are good reasons for doing so. Total earnings after taxes for the year are expected to be $14.25 million; the common stock is currently selling for $56.25; the firm's target debt/assets ratio is 45 percent; and its marginal tax rate is 40 percent. The costs of various forms of financing are as follows:

- New bonds, $k_d = 11\%$. This is a before-tax rate.
- New common stock sold at $56.25 per share will net $51.25.
- Required rate of return on retained earnings, $k_s = 14\%$.

a. Calculate Ybor's expected payout ratio, the break point at which the marginal cost of capital (MCC) rises, and its MCC above and below the point of exhaustion of retained earnings at the current payout. (Hint: k_s is given, and $\hat{D}_1/P_0$ can be found. Then, knowing k_s and $\hat{D}_1/P_0$, g can be determined.)

b. How large should Ybor's capital budget be for the year?

c. What is an appropriate dividend policy for Ybor? How should the capital budget be financed?

d. How might risk factors influence Ybor's cost of capital, capital structure, and dividend policy?

e. What assumptions, if any, do your answers to the preceding parts make about investors' preferences for dividends versus capital gains (in other words, what are investors' preferences regarding the $\hat{D}_1/P_0$ and g components of k_s)?

Exam-Type Problems

The problems included in this section are set up in such a way that they could be used as multiple-choice exam problems.

Financial leverage effects   **11-6**   Firms HL and LL are identical except for their leverage ratios and interest rates on debt. Each has $20 million in assets, earned $4 million before interest and taxes in 1999, and has a 40 percent marginal tax rate. Firm HL, however, has a leverage ratio (D/TA) of 50 percent and pays 12 percent interest on its debt, whereas LL has a 30 percent leverage ratio and pays only 10 percent interest on debt.

a. Calculate the rate of return on equity (net income/equity) for each firm.

b. Observing that HL has a higher return on equity, LL's treasurer decides to raise the leverage ratio from 30 to 60 percent, which will increase LL's interest rate on all debt to 15 percent. Calculate the new rate of return on equity for LL.

Financial leverage effects   **11-7**   The Damon Company wishes to calculate next year's return on equity under different leverage ratios. Damon's total assets are $14 million, and its marginal tax rate is 40 percent. The company is able to estimate next year's earnings before interest and taxes for three possible states of the world: $4.2 million with a 0.2 probability, $2.8 million with a 0.5 probability, and $700,000 with a 0.3 probability. Calculate Damon's expected return on equity, standard deviation, and coefficient of variation for each of the following leverage ratios, and evaluate the results:

Leverage (Debt/Assets)	Interest Rate
0%	—
10	9%
50	11
60	14

External equity financing   **11-8**   Northern California Heating and Cooling Inc. has a 6-month backlog of orders for its patented solar heating system. To meet this demand, management plans to expand production capacity by 40 percent with a $10 million investment in plant and machinery. The firm wants to maintain a 40 percent debt/assets ratio in its capital structure; it also wants to maintain its past dividend policy of distributing 45 percent of last year's net income. In 1999, net income was $5 million. How much external equity must Northern California seek at the beginning of 2000 to expand capacity as desired?

Dividend payout   **11-9**   The Garlington Corporation expects next year's net income to be $15 million. The firm's debt/assets ratio currently is 40 percent. Garlington has $12 million of profitable investment opportunities, and it wishes to maintain its existing debt/assets ratio. According to the residual dividend policy, how large should Garlington's dividend payout ratio be next year?

Dividend payout   **11-10**   The Scanlon Company's optimal capital structure calls for 50 percent debt and 50 percent common equity. The interest rate on its debt is a constant 10 percent; its cost of common equity from retained earnings is 14 percent; the cost of equity from new stock is 16 percent; and its marginal tax rate is 40 percent. Scanlon has the following investment opportunities:

Project A: Cost = $5 million; IRR = 20%
Project B: Cost = $5 million; IRR = 12%
Project C: Cost = $5 million; IRR = 9%

Scanlon expects to have net income of $7,287,500. If Scanlon bases its dividends on the residual policy, what will its payout ratio be?

Integrative Problems

Optimal capital structure **11-11** Assume that you have just been hired by Adams, Garitty, and Evans (AGE), a consulting firm that specializes in analyses of firms' capital structures and dividend policies. Your boss has asked you to examine the capital structure of Campus Deli and Sub Shop (CDSS), which is located adjacent to the campus. According to the owner, sales were $1,350,000 last year, variable costs were 60 percent of sales, and fixed costs were $40,000. Therefore, EBIT totaled $500,000. Because the University's enrollment is capped, EBIT is expected to be constant over time. Because no expansion capital is required, CDSS pays out all earnings as dividends. The management group owns about 50 percent of the stock, which is traded in the over-the-counter market.

CDSS currently has no debt — it is an all equity firm — and its 100,000 shares outstanding sell at a price of $20 per share. The firm's marginal tax rate is 40 percent. On the basis of statements made in your finance text, you believe that CDSS's shareholders would be better off if some debt financing were used. When you suggested this to your new boss, she encouraged you to pursue the idea, but to provide support for the suggestion.

You then obtained from a local investment banker the following estimates of the costs of debt and equity at different debt levels (in thousands of dollars):

Amount Borrowed	k_d	k_s
$ 0	—	15.0%
250	10.0%	15.5
500	11.0	16.5
750	13.0	18.0
1,000	16.0	20.0

If the firm were recapitalized, debt would be issued, and the borrowed funds would be used to repurchase stock. Stockholders, in turn, would use funds provided by the repurchase to buy equities in other fast-food companies similar to CDSS. You plan to complete your report by asking and then answering the following questions:

a. (1) What is business risk? What factors influence a firm's business risk?

(2) What is operating leverage, and how does it affect a firm's business risk?

b. (1) What is meant by the terms *financial leverage* and *financial risk?*

(2) How does financial risk differ from business risk?

c. Now, to develop an example that can be presented to CDSS's management as an illustration, consider two hypothetical firms, Firm U, with zero debt financing, and Firm L, with $10,000 of 12 percent debt. Both firms have $20,000 in total assets and a 40 percent marginal tax rate, and they face the following EBIT probability distribution for next year:

Probability	EBIT
0.25	$2,000
0.50	3,000
0.25	4,000

(1) Complete the following partial income statements and the set of ratios for Firm L.

	Firm U			Firm L		
Assets	$20,000	$20,000	$20,000	$20,000	$20,000	$20,000
Equity	$20,000	$20,000	$20,000	$10,000	$10,000	$10,000
Probability	0.25	0.50	0.25	0.25	0.50	0.25
Sales	$ 6,000	$9,000	$12,000	$6,000	$9,000	$12,000
Operating costs	(4,000)	(6,000)	(8,000)	(4,000)	(6,000)	(8,000)
Earnings before interest and taxes	$ 2,000	$ 3,000	$ 4,000	$ 2,000	$ 3,000	$ 4,000
Interest (12%)	(0)	(0)	(0)	(1,200)		(1,200)
Earnings before taxes	$ 2,000	$ 3,000	$ 4,000	$ 800	$	$ 2,800
Taxes (40%)	(800)	(1,200)	(1,600)	(320)		(1,120)
Net income	$ 1,200	$ 1,800	$ 2,400	$ 480	$	$ 1,680
ROE	6.0%	9.0%	12.0%	4.8%	%	16.8%
TIE	∞	∞	∞	1.7×	×	3.3×
Expected ROE		9.0%			10.8%	
Expected TIE		∞			2.5×	
σ_{ROE}		2.1%			4.2%	
σ_{TIE}		0×			0.6×	

    (2) What does this example illustrate concerning the impact of financial leverage on expected rate of return and risk?

d. With the preceding points in mind, now consider the optimal capital structure for CDSS.

    (1) To begin, define the term *optimal capital structure*.

    (2) Describe briefly, without using numbers, the sequence of events that would occur if CDSS decided to change its capital structure to include more debt.

    (3) Assume that shares could be repurchased at the current market price of $20 per share. Calculate CDSS's expected EPS and TIE at debt levels of $0, $250,000, $500,000, $750,000, and $1,000,000. How many shares would remain after recapitalization under each scenario?

    (4) What would be the new stock price if CDSS recapitalizes with $250,000 of debt? $500,000? $750,000? $1,000,000? Recall that the payout ratio is 100 percent, so g = 0.

    (5) Considering only the levels of debt discussed, what is CDSS's optimal capital structure?

    (6) Is EPS maximized at the debt level that maximizes share price? Why?

    (7) What is the WACC at the optimal capital structure?

e. Suppose you discovered that CDSS had more business risk than you originally estimated. Describe how this would affect the analysis. What if the firm had less business risk than originally estimated?

f. What are some factors that should be considered when establishing a firm's target capital structure?

g. How does the existence of asymmetric information and signaling affect capital structure?

Dividend policy   **11-12** Now your boss wants you to evaluate the dividend policy of Information Systems Inc. (ISI), which develops software for the health care industry. ISI was founded 5 years ago by Donald Brown and Margaret Clark, who are still its only stockholders. ISI has now reached the stage where outside equity capital is necessary if the firm is to achieve its growth targets yet still maintain its target capital structure of 60 percent equity and 40 percent debt. Therefore, Brown and Clark have decided to take the company public. Until now, Brown and Clark have paid themselves reasonable salaries but routinely reinvested all after-tax earnings in the firm, so dividend policy has not been an issue. However, before talking with potential outside investors, they must decide on a dividend policy.

Your boss has asked you to make a presentation to Brown and Clark in which you review the theory of dividend policy and discuss the following questions.

a. (1) What is meant by the term *dividend policy?*

   (2) The terms *irrelevance* and *relevance* have been used to describe theories regarding the way dividend policy affects a firm's value. Explain what these terms mean, and briefly discuss the relevance of dividend policy.

   (3) Explain the relationships between dividend policy and (a) stock price and (b) the cost of equity under each dividend policy theory.

   (4) What results have empirical studies of the dividend theories produced? How does all this affect what we can tell managers about dividend policy?

b. Discuss (1) the information content, or signaling, hypothesis, (2) the clientele effect, (3) the free cash flow hypothesis, and (4) their effects on dividend policy.

c. (1) Assume that ISI has an $800,000 capital budget planned for the coming year. You have determined that its present capital structure (60 percent equity and 40 percent debt) is optimal, and its net income is forecasted at $600,000. Use the residual dividend policy approach to determine ISI's total dollar dividend and payout ratio. In the process, explain what the residual dividend policy is, and use a graph to illustrate your answer. Then, explain what would happen if net income were forecasted at $400,000, or at $800,000.

   (2) In general terms, how would a change in investment opportunities affect the payout ratio under the residual payment policy?

   (3) What are the advantages and disadvantages of the residual policy? (Hint: Don't neglect signaling and clientele effects.)

d. What are some other commonly used dividend payment policies? What are their advantages and disadvantages? Which policy is most widely used in practice?

e. What is a dividend reinvestment plan (DRIP), and how do they work?

Computer-Related Problems

Work the problem in this section only if you are using the computer problem diskette.

Effects of financial leverage   **11-13**   Use the first model in File C11 to solve this problem.

a. Rework Problem 11-3, assuming that the old long-term debt will not remain outstanding but, rather, that it must be refinanced at the new long-term interest rate of 12 percent. What effect does this have on the decision to refinance?

b. What would be the effect on the refinancing decision if the rate on long-term debt fell to 5 percent or rose to 20 percent, assuming that all long-term debt must be refinanced?

c. Which financing method would be recommended if the stock price (1) rose to $105 or (2) fell to $30? (Assume that all debt will have an interest rate of 12 percent.)

d. With $P_0 = \$60$ and $k_d = 12\%$, change the sales probability distribution to the following:

Alternative 1		Alternative 2	
Sales	**Probability**	**Sales**	**Probability**
$2,250	0	$ 0	0.3
2,700	1.0	2,700	0.4
3,150	0	7,500	0.3

What are the implications of these changes?

Dividend policy
and capital structure

11-14 Use the second model in File C11 to solve this problem. Refer back to Problem 11-5. Assume that Ybor's management is considering a change in the firm's capital structure to include more debt; thus, management would like to analyze the effects of an increase in the debt/assets ratio to 60 percent. The treasurer believes that such a move would cause lenders to increase the required rate of return on new bonds to 12 percent and that k_s would rise to 14.5 percent.

    a. How would this change affect the optimal capital budget?

    b. If k_s rose to 16 percent, would the low-return project be acceptable?

    c. Would the project selection be affected if the dividend was reduced to $1.88 from $3.00, still assuming k_s = 16 percent?

CHAPTER 12

Working Capital Management

In December 1993, Trans World Airlines (TWA) was labeled the best domestic airline for long flights and the second best for short flights by American business travelers. TWA received this accolade just one month after emerging from bankruptcy court. The future seemed rosy — employees had agreed to salary concessions in exchange for an equity position in the company, the airline had restructured its liabilities and lowered its cost structure, and the employees, with their new ownership position, appeared to possess a new-found motivation and concern for company success. Unfortunately, the nation's seventh largest airline discovered that its "new lease on life" was not a long-term contract. By the summer of 1994, TWA was struggling to find ways to cover a $135 million shortfall expected for the year. Many analysts believed the company was headed toward a second, and perhaps final, bankruptcy, primarily because it was in an extremely precarious position with respect to liquidity. The company's cash reserves were not sufficient to carry TWA through the lean sales that were expected during the coming months, and analysts were very pessimistic that needed funds could be raised with a stock or bond issue or by selling off assets. Investors also recognized TWA's liquidity problems — the company's stock fell about 50 percent in less than four months. It was obvious that TWA needed to improve its liquidity position to ensure future survival. The answer for TWA has been to reduce costs by laying off employees, by eliminating some of its flights, and by replacing outdated airplanes with more fuel-efficient airplanes.

TWA has emerged from its second bankruptcy and has regained its designation as the best domestic airline for long flights, but its financial position is still very tenuous. Unforeseen circumstances, including a tragic crash and labor difficulties, have resulted in large losses in recent years. For instance, in 1996, TWA lost $285 million and, in 1997, the loss was $110 million. But, TWA has taken actions to improve its liquidity position — recently, revenues have begun to increase, while operating expenses have decreased (1998 revenues are up 3 percent, and operating expenses are down about 2 percent). In addition, TWA improved its short-term liquidity position in 1998 by increasing cash and other liquid assets by nearly 33 percent.

Continued

> Firms strive to maintain a balance between current assets and current liabilities and between sales and each category of current assets in an effort to provide sufficient liquidity to survive — to live to maximize value in the future. As long as a good balance is maintained, current liabilities can be paid on time, suppliers will continue to provide needed inventories, and companies will be able to meet sales demands. However, if the financial situation gets out of balance, liquidity problems surface and often multiply into more serious problems, perhaps even bankruptcy. As you read this chapter, consider how important liquidity, thus proper management of working capital, is to the survival of a firm. Also, consider the fact that many start-up firms never make it past the first few months of business primarily because such firms do not have formal working capital policies in place.

WORKING CAPITAL MANAGEMENT
The management of short-term assets (investments) and liabilities (financing sources).

In this chapter, we discuss *short-term financial management,* also termed **working capital management,** which involves decisions about the current (short-term) assets and current (short-term) liabilities of a firm. As you read this chapter, you will realize that a firm's value cannot be maximized in the long run unless it survives the short run. The principal reason firms fail is because they are unable to meet their working capital needs; consequently, *sound working capital management is a requisite for firm survival.*

Working Capital Terminology

It is useful to begin the discussion of working capital policy by reviewing some basic definitions and concepts:

WORKING CAPITAL
A firm's investment in short-term assets — cash, marketable securities, inventory, and accounts receivable.

1. The term **working capital,** sometimes called gross working capital, generally refers to current assets.

NET WORKING CAPITAL
Current assets minus current liabilities; the amount of current assets financed by long-term liabilities.

2. **Net working capital** is defined as current assets minus current liabilities, while the *current ratio* is calculated by dividing current assets by current liabilities. Both measures are intended to measure a firm's liquidity. However, neither a high current ratio nor a positive net working capital ensures that a firm will have the cash required to meet its needs. If inventories cannot be sold, or if receivables cannot be collected in a timely manner, then the apparent safety reflected by these measures could be illusory. The best and most comprehensive picture of a firm's liquidity position is obtained by examining its *cash budget,* which forecasts cash inflows and outflows, because it focuses on the firm's ability to generate sufficient cash inflows to meet its required cash outflows. Cash budgeting is discussed in Chapter 14.

WORKING CAPITAL POLICY
Decisions regarding (1) the target levels for each current asset account and (2) how current assets will be financed.

3. **Working capital policy** refers to the firm's basic policies regarding (a) target levels for each category of current assets and (b) how current assets will be financed.

4. Only those current liabilities that are specifically used to finance current assets are included in working capital decisions. Current liabilities that represent (a) current maturities of long-term debt, (b) financing associated with a construc-

tion program that will be funded with the proceeds of a long-term security issue after the project is completed, or (c) the use of short-term debt to finance fixed assets are not working capital decision variables in the current period because they resulted from past long-term debt financing decisions. Although such accounts are not part of a firm's working capital decision process, they cannot be ignored because they are *due* in the current period, and they must be taken into account when managers assess the firm's ability to meet its current obligations (its liquidity position).

Self-Test Question

Why is it important to properly manage short-term assets and liabilities?

The Requirement for External Working Capital Financing

In this section and throughout the chapter, we use the financial statements of Argile Textiles, a North Carolina textile manufacturer, to illustrate working capital analyses and decisions. First, let's examine balance sheets for Argile constructed at three different dates, which are given in Table 12-1. According to the definitions given earlier, Argile's December 31, 1999 working capital (current assets) was $470 million, and its net working capital was $340 million. Also, Argile's year-end 1999 current ratio was 3.62. Argile's production/sales operations are very seasonal, typically peaking in September and October. Thus, at the end of September Argile's inventories are significantly higher than they are at the end of the calendar year. Because of this sales surge, Argile's receivables are much higher at the end of September than at the end of December.

Consider what is expected to happen to Argile's current assets and current liabilities from December 31, 1999 to September 30, 2000. Current assets are expected to increase from $470 million to $690 million, or by $220 million, which must be supported with new financing. The higher volume of purchases, plus labor expenditures associated with increased production, will cause accounts payable and accruals to increase spontaneously from a total of $90 million ($30 million payables and $60 million accruals) to $190 million ($90 million payables and $100 million accruals), or by only $100 million during this period. This leaves a projected $120 million current asset financing requirement — the amount not covered by the increase in payables and accruals — which Argile expects to finance primarily by an $89 million increase in notes payable (from $40 million to $129 million). Note that from December 1999 to September 2000, Argile's net working capital is expected to increase from $340 million to $371 million, but its current ratio is expected to fall from 3.62 to 2.16. This occurs because most, but not all, of the funds invested in current assets are expected to come from current liabilities. Thus, *when current liabilities increase (decrease) by the same, or nearly the same, dollar amount as current assets, the current ratio decreases (increases).*

The fluctuations in Argile's working capital position shown in Table 12-1 result from seasonal variations. Similar fluctuations in working capital requirements, and hence in financing needs, also occur during business cycles — working capital needs typically decline during recessions but increase during booms. For some companies, such as those involved in agricultural products, seasonal fluctuations

TABLE 12-1

Argile Textiles: Historical and Projected Balance Sheets (millions of dollars)

	12/31/99 Historical	9/30/00 Projected	12/31/00 Projected
Cash and marketable securities	$ 20	$ 30	$ 22
Accounts receivable	180	250	198
Inventories	270	410	297
Total current assets (CA)	$470	$ 690	$517
Net plant and equipment	380	410	418
Total assets	$850	$1,100	$935
Accounts payable	$ 30	$ 90	$ 33
Accruals	60	100	66
Notes payable	40	129	46
Total current liabilities (CL)	$130	$ 319	$145
Long-term bonds	297	305	305
Total liabilities	$427	$ 624	$450
Common stock	130	156	156
Retained earnings	293	320	329
Total owners' equity	$423	$ 476	$485
Total liabilities and equity	$850	$1,100	$935
Net working capital = CA − CL	$340	$ 371	$372
Current ratio = CA/CL	3.62	2.16	3.57

are much greater than business cycle fluctuations, but for other companies, such as appliance or automobile manufacturers, cyclical fluctuations are larger. In the following sections we look in more detail at the requirement for working capital financing, and we examine some alternative working capital policies.

Self-Test Question

Under normal circumstances, when does the working capital position of a firm change? Explain.

The Cash Conversion Cycle

To summarize the working capital management process that Argile Textiles faces, consider the following activities:

1. Argile orders and then receives materials it needs to produce the products its sells. Argile purchases from its suppliers on credit, so an account payable is created for the credit purchase. The purchase has no immediate cash flow effect because payment is not made until some later date.
2. Labor is used to convert the materials (cotton and wool) into finished goods (cloth products, thread, etc.). However, wages are not fully paid at the time the work is done, so accrued wages build up (maybe for a period of one or two weeks).

3. The finished products are sold, but on credit, so sales create receivables, not immediate cash inflows.

4. At some point during the cycle, Argile pays its suppliers and employees. *If these payments are made before Argile has collected cash from its receivables, a net cash outflow will occur, and this outflow must be financed.*

5. The cycle is completed when Argile's receivables are collected (perhaps in 30 days). At that time, the company is in a position to pay off the credit that was used to finance production of the product, and it can then repeat the cycle.

The activities outlined here give you an indication of the relationships among the various working capital accounts. To illustrate these relationships, we can formalize the process Argile faces by examining its **cash conversion cycle,** which focuses on the length of time between when the company makes payments, or invests in the manufacture of inventory, and when it receives cash inflows, or realizes a cash return from its investment in production.[1] The following terms are used in the model:

CASH CONVERSION CYCLE
The length of time from the payment for the purchase of raw materials to manufacture a product until the collection of accounts receivable associated with the sale of the product.

1. The *inventory conversion period* is the average length of time required to convert materials into finished goods and then to sell those goods; it is the amount of time the product remains in inventory in various stages of completion. The inventory conversion period is calculated as follows:

$$\text{12-1} \quad \begin{matrix} \text{Inventory} \\ \text{conversion} \\ \text{period} \end{matrix} = \frac{\text{Inventory}}{\left(\begin{matrix}\text{Cost of goods} \\ \text{sold per day}\end{matrix}\right)} = \frac{\text{Inventory}}{\left(\dfrac{\text{Annual cost of goods sold}}{360}\right)}$$

If we assume Argile's cost of goods sold was $1,220 in 1999, its inventory conversion period would be[2]:

$$\begin{matrix}\text{Argile's inventory} \\ \text{conversion period}\end{matrix} = \frac{\$270 \text{ million}}{\left(\dfrac{1,220 \text{ million}}{360}\right)} = \frac{\$270}{\$3.389}$$

$$= 79.7 \text{ days}$$

Thus, according to its 1999 operations, it takes Argile nearly 80 days to manufacture and sell its products.

2. The *receivables collection period* is the average length of time required to convert the firm's receivables into cash — that is, to collect cash following a

---

[1]See Verlyn Richards and Eugene Laughlin, "A Cash Conversion Cycle Approach to Liquidity Analysis," *Financial Management,* Spring 1980, 32–38.

[2]In the computations that follow, as well as other ratio computations in this book, we assume there are 360 days in the year. This assumption is made to simplify computations only — 360 is divisible by more integer values than 365. This assumption changes neither the meaning nor the application of the computations.

sale. The receivables collection period is also called the days sales outstanding (DSO), and it is calculated as follows:

12-2
$$\text{Receivables collection period} = \frac{\text{Receivables}}{\text{Average daily credit sales}} = \frac{\text{Receivables}}{\left(\dfrac{\text{Annual credit sales}}{360}\right)}$$

If we assume sales were $1,500 million in 1999, Argile's receivables collection period (DSO) was

$$\text{Receivables collection period} = \frac{\$180 \text{ million}}{\left(\dfrac{\$1,500 \text{ million}}{360}\right)} = \frac{\$180}{\$4.167}$$

$$= 43.2 \text{ days}$$

Thus, on average, the cash payments associated with credit sales are not collected until 43.2 days after the sale.

3. The *payables deferral period* is the average length of time between the purchase of raw materials and labor and the payment of cash for them. It is computed as follows:

12-3
$$\text{Payables deferral period} = \frac{\text{Accounts payable}}{\text{Credit purchases per day}} = \frac{\text{Accounts payable}}{\left(\dfrac{\text{Cost of goods sold}}{360}\right)}$$

Thus, Argile's payables deferral period would be:

$$\text{Payable deferral period} = \frac{\$30 \text{ million}}{\left(\dfrac{\$1,220 \text{ million}}{360}\right)} = \frac{\$30}{\$3.389}$$

$$= 8.9 \text{ days}$$

So, Argile pays its suppliers an average of about nine days after materials are purchased.[3]

4. The *cash conversion cycle* computation nets out the three periods just defined, resulting in a value that equals the length of time between when the

---

[3]The computation for the payables deferral period shown here is the traditional method used to determine the value used in the calculation of the cash conversion cycle. However, if we recognize that the intent of the computation is to determine the length of time between the purchase of raw materials *and* the labor used to produce inventory and the payment for these inputs, the payables deferral period would more appropriately be written to include consideration of accrued wages.

firm pays for (invests in) productive resources (materials and labor) and when it receives cash (a return) from the sale of products. The cash conversion cycle thus equals the average length of time a dollar is tied up in current assets.

We can now use these definitions to analyze Argile's cash conversion cycle. First, the concept is diagrammed in Figure 12-1. Each component is given a number, and the cash conversion cycle can be expressed by this equation:

12-4						
	Cash		Inventory	Receivables		Payables
	conversion	=	conversion	+ collection	–	deferral
	cycle		period	period		period

$$= 79.7 \text{ days} + 43.2 \text{ days} - 8.9 \text{ days}$$

$$= 114.0 \text{ days}$$

In this case, the cash conversion cycle is 114 days. The *receipt* of cash from manufacturing and selling the products will be delayed by about 123 days because (1) the product will be "tied up" in inventory for almost 80 days, and (2) the cash from the sale will not be received until about 43 days after the selling date. But, the *disbursement* of cash for the raw materials purchased will be delayed by 9 days because Argile does not pay cash for the raw materials when they are purchased. Consequently, the net delay in cash receipts associated with an investment (cash disbursement) in inventory is 114 days. Therefore, Argile knows when it starts processing its textile products that it will have to finance the manufacturing and other operating costs for a 114-day period, which is nearly one-third of a year.

The firm's goal should be to shorten its cash conversion cycle as much as possible without hurting operations. This would improve profits because the longer the cash conversion cycle, the greater the need for external financing, such as bank loans, and such financing has a cost. The cash conversion cycle can be shortened by (1) reducing the inventory conversion period by processing and selling goods more quickly, (2) reducing the receivables collection period by speeding up collections, or (3) lengthening the payables deferral period by slowing down Argile's own payments. To the extent that these actions can be taken *without harming the return* associated with the management of these accounts, they should be carried out. We discuss some actions that can be taken to reduce the cash conversion cycle when we discuss the specific working capital accounts later in the chapter. As you read the chapter, you should keep the cash conversion cycle concept in mind.

Self-Test Questions

What steps are involved in estimating the cash conversion cycle?

What do the following terms mean?

(1) Inventory conversion period.

(2) Receivables collection period.

(3) Payables deferral period.

FIGURE 12-1

The Cash Conversion Cycle

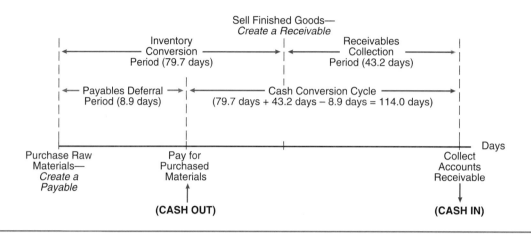

What is the cash conversion cycle model? How can it be used to improve current asset management?

Working Capital Investment and Financing Policies

Working capital policy involves two basic questions: (1) What is the appropriate level for current assets, both in total and by specific accounts, and (2) how should current assets be financed?

Alternative Current Asset Investment Policies

RELAXED CURRENT ASSET
INVESTMENT POLICY
A policy under which
relatively large amounts of
cash and marketable
securities and inventories
are carried and under
which sales are stimulated
by a liberal credit policy
that results in a high level
of receivables.

Figure 12-2 shows three alternative policies regarding the total amount of current assets carried. Essentially, these policies differ in that different amounts of current assets are carried to support any given level of sales. The line with the steepest slope represents a **relaxed current asset investment** (or "fat cat") **policy,** where relatively large amounts of cash, marketable securities, and inventories are carried and where sales are stimulated by the use of a credit policy that provides liberal financing to customers and a corresponding high level of receivables. Conversely, with the **restricted current asset investment** (or "lean-and-mean") **policy,** the holdings of cash, securities, inventories, and receivables are minimized. The **moderate current asset investment policy** lies between the two extremes.

The more certain a firm is about its sales, costs, order lead times, payment periods, and so forth, the lower the level of current assets it requires for operations. But, if there is a great deal of uncertainty about operations, then the firm requires some minimum amount of cash and inventory based on expected payments, expected sales, expected order lead times, and so on, plus additional amounts, or *safety stocks,* that enable it to deal with departures from the expected values. Similarly, accounts receivable levels are determined by credit terms, and the tougher

RESTRICTED CURRENT ASSET
INVESTMENT POLICY
A policy under which
holdings of cash and
marketable securities,
inventories, and receivables
are minimized.

MODERATE CURRENT ASSET
INVESTMENT POLICY
A policy that is between the
relaxed and restricted
policies.

the credit terms, the lower the receivables for any given level of sales. With a restricted current asset investment policy, the firm would hold minimal levels of safety stocks for cash and inventories, and it would have a tight credit policy even though this would mean running the risk of losing sales. A restricted, lean-and-mean current asset investment policy generally provides the highest expected return on investment, but it entails the greatest risk, while the reverse is true under a relaxed policy. The moderate policy falls in between the two extremes in terms of both expected risk and return.

In terms of the cash conversion cycle, a restricted investment policy would tend to reduce the inventory conversion and receivables collection periods, resulting in a relatively short cash conversion cycle. Conversely, a relaxed policy would create higher levels of inventories and receivables, longer inventory conversion and receivables collection periods, and a relatively long cash conversion cycle. A moderate policy would produce a cash conversion cycle somewhere between the two extremes.

FIGURE 12-2

Alternative Current Asset Investment Policies (millions of dollars)

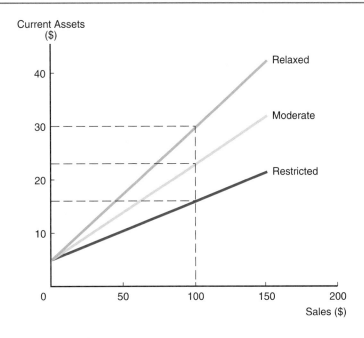

Policy	Current Assets to Support Sales of $100
Relaxed	$30
Moderate	23
Restricted	16

NOTE: The sales/current assets relationship is shown here as being linear, but the relationship is often curvilinear.

Alternative Current Asset Financing Policies

Most businesses experience seasonal and/or cyclical fluctuations. For example, construction firms have peaks in the spring and summer, retailers peak around Christmas, and the manufacturers who supply both construction companies and retailers follow similar patterns. Similarly, virtually all businesses must build up current assets when the economy is strong, but they then sell off inventories and have net reductions of receivables when the economy slacks off. Still, current assets rarely drop to zero, and this realization has led to the development of the idea that some current assets should be considered **permanent current assets** because their levels remain stable no matter the seasonal or economic conditions. **Temporary current assets,** on the other hand, are those amounts of current assets that vary with respect to the seasonal or economic conditions of a firm — during off-season periods, temporary assets will be zero, while during peak-season periods they will be very high. For example, Table 12-1 shows the level of current assets for Argile Textiles is expected to be $690 million in September 2000 and only $517 in December 2000. Because the height of Argile's selling season is in the fall, most of the difference between the levels of current assets at these two dates results from changes in temporary current assets.

The manner in which the permanent and temporary current assets are financed is called the firm's *current asset financing policy.* In general, the approach a firm uses to finance current assets is referred to as (1) *maturity matching,* (2) *aggressive,* or (3) *conservative.*

MATURITY MATCHING, OR "SELF-LIQUIDATING," APPROACH   The **maturity matching, or "self-liquidating," approach** calls for matching asset and liability maturities. This strategy minimizes the risk that the firm will be unable to pay off its maturing obligations *if* the liquidations of the assets can be controlled to occur on or before the maturities of the obligations. At the limit, a firm could attempt to match exactly the maturity structure of its assets and liabilities. Inventory expected to be sold in 30 days could be financed with a 30-day bank loan; a machine expected to last for 5 years could be financed by a 5-year loan; and so forth. Actually, of course, two factors prevent this exact maturity matching: (1) There is uncertainty about the lives of assets, thus when cash inflows will be received, and (2) some common equity must be used, and common equity has no maturity.

AGGRESSIVE APPROACH   A firm that follows the **aggressive approach** finances all of its fixed assets and some of its permanent current assets with long-term capital; the remainder of the permanent current assets and all of the temporary current assets are financed with such short-term financing as bank loans. There can be different *degrees* of aggressiveness — one firm might finance nearly all its permanent current assets with short-term credit, while another firm might finance relatively little of its current permanent assets with the same type of credit. The aggressive approach is riskier than either of the other two approaches because the short-term credit used to finance the permanent current assets must be renewed each time it comes due; thus, the firm is subject to dangers from rising interest rates as well as to loan renewal problems. However, short-term debt often is cheaper than long-term debt, and some firms are willing to sacrifice safety for the chance of higher profits.

PERMANENT CURRENT ASSETS
Current asset balances that do not change due to seasonal or economic conditions; these balances exist even at the trough of a firm's business cycle.

TEMPORARY CURRENT ASSETS
Current assets that fluctuate with seasonal or economic variations in a firm's business.

MATURITY MATCHING, OR "SELF-LIQUIDATING," APPROACH
A financing policy that matches asset and liability maturities. This would be considered a moderate current asset financing policy.

AGGRESSIVE APPROACH
A policy where all of the fixed assets of a firm are financed with long-term capital, but some of the firm's permanent current assets are financed with short-term nonspontaneous sources of funds.

CONSERVATIVE APPROACH
A policy where all of the fixed assets, all of the permanent current assets, and some of the temporary current assets of a firm are financed with long-term capital.

CONSERVATIVE APPROACH With the **conservative approach,** permanent, or long-term, capital is used to finance all permanent asset requirements and also to meet some or all of the seasonal demands, hence to finance temporary current assets. At the extreme, a firm could finance all of its seasonal needs with long-term financing alternatives and thus eliminate the need to use short-term financing. This would be a difficult, if not impossible, task to accomplish. Most firms that follow this approach use some amounts of short-term credit to meet financing needs during peak-season periods. Even so, firms that use this strategy will have "extra" permanent funds during off-peak periods, which allows them to "store liquidity" in the form of short-term investments, called marketable securities, during the off-season. As the name implies, this is a very safe, conservative current asset financing policy and generally is not as profitable as the other two approaches.

Self-Test Questions

What two key issues does working capital policy involve?

What are three alternative current asset investment policies? Is one best?

What are three alternative current asset financing policies? Is one best?

What distinguishes "permanent current assets" from "temporary current assets"?

Advantages and Disadvantages of Short-Term Financing

The three possible financing policies described in the preceding section are distinguished by the relative amounts of short-term debt used under each policy. The aggressive policy calls for the greatest use of short-term debt, while the conservative policy requires the least, and maturity matching falls in between. Some of the pros and cons of short-term financing are considered in this section.

Speed

A short-term loan can be obtained much faster than long-term credit. Lenders will insist on a more thorough financial examination before extending long-term credit, and the loan agreement will have to be spelled out in considerable detail because much can happen during the life of a 10- or 20-year loan.

Flexibility

If the needs for funds are seasonal or cyclical, a firm might not want to commit itself to long-term debt because (1) the cost of issuing long-term debt is considerably greater than for short-term credit, (2) some long-term loans have expensive penalties for paying off the debt prior to maturity, and (3) long-term loan agreements contain provisions, or covenants, that constrain the firm's future actions, whereas short-term credit agreements usually are much less onerous in this regard. In general, then, short-term financing alternatives are more flexible than long-term financing alternatives.

Cost of Long-Term versus Short-Term Debt

As we discussed in Chapter 2, the yield curve normally is upward sloping, indicating that interest rates generally are lower on short-term debt than on long-term debt. Thus, interest costs normally will be lower if the firm borrows on a short-term rather than on a long-term basis.

Risk of Long-Term versus Short-Term Debt

A disadvantage of short-term debt is that it subjects the firm to more risk than does long-term debt. This occurs for two reasons: (1) If a firm borrows on a long-term basis, its interest costs will be relatively stable, perhaps even fixed, over time; but if it uses short-term credit, its interest expense will fluctuate, at times reaching very high levels, such as the early 1980s when short-term rates were 20 percent and higher. (2) If a firm borrows heavily on a short-term basis, it could find itself unable to repay this debt, and it might be in such a weak financial position that the lender will not extend the loan; this could force the firm into bankruptcy.

Self-Test Questions

What are some advantages of short-term debt over long-term debt as a source of capital?

What are some disadvantages of short-term debt?

Sources of Short-Term Financing

SHORT-TERM CREDIT
Any liability originally scheduled for repayment within one year.

Statements about the flexibility, cost, and riskiness of short-term debt versus long-term debt depend, to a large extent, on the type of short-term credit that is used. **Short-term credit** is defined as any liability originally scheduled for payment within one year. There are numerous sources of short-term funds, and in the following section we briefly describe five major types: (1) accruals, (2) accounts payable (trade credit), (3) bank loans, (4) commercial paper, and (5) secured short-term loans. In addition, we discuss the cost of short-term financing.

Accruals

ACCRUALS
Continually recurring short-term liabilities; liabilities such as wages and taxes that increase spontaneously with operations.

A firm generally pays employees on a weekly, biweekly, or monthly basis, so its balance sheet typically shows some accrued wages. Similarly, the firm's own estimated income taxes, the Social Security and income taxes withheld from employee payrolls, and the sales taxes collected generally are paid on a weekly, monthly, or quarterly basis, so the balance sheet typically also shows some accrued taxes. These **accruals** increase automatically, or spontaneously, as a firm's operations expand. Further, this type of debt generally is considered "free" in the sense that no explicit interest is paid on funds raised through accruals. However, a firm ordinarily cannot control its accruals: The timing of wage payments is set by economic forces and industry custom, while tax payment dates are established by law.

Accounts Payable (Trade Credit)

TRADE CREDIT
The term given to the credit created when one firm buys on credit from another firm.

Most firms purchase from other firms (their suppliers) on credit, recording the debt as an *account payable*. This type of financing, which is called **trade credit,** is the largest single category of short-term debt, representing about 40 percent of the current liabilities for the average nonfinancial corporation.[4] Trade credit is a *spontaneous* source of financing in the sense that it arises from ordinary business transactions. The amount of trade credit used by a firm depends on the terms of the credit purchase and the size of the firm's operations. For example, lengthening the credit period, as well as expanding sales and purchases, generates additional trade credit.

Short-Term Bank Loans

Commercial banks, whose loans generally appear on a firm's balance sheet as notes payable, are second in importance to trade credit as a source of short-term financing.[5] The banks' influence actually is greater than it appears from the dollar amounts they lend because banks provide *nonspontaneous* funds. As a firm's financing needs increase, it specifically requests additional funds from its bank. If the request is denied, the firm might be forced to abandon attractive growth opportunities. Bank loans include the key features described next.

MATURITY   Bank loans to businesses frequently are written as 90-day notes, so the loan must be repaid or renewed at the end of 90 days. Of course, if a borrower's financial position has deteriorated, the bank might refuse to renew the loan.

PROMISSORY NOTE
A document specifying the terms and conditions of a loan, including the amount, interest rate, and repayment schedule.

PROMISSORY NOTE   When a bank loan is approved, the agreement is executed by signing a **promissory note** that specifies (1) the amount borrowed; (2) the interest rate; (3) the repayment schedule; (4) whether collateral, or security, is required; and (5) any other terms and conditions to which the bank and the borrower have agreed.

COMPENSATING BALANCE (CB)
A minimum checking account balance that a firm must maintain with a bank to borrow funds — generally 10 to 20 percent of the amount of loans outstanding.

COMPENSATING BALANCES   Banks often require firms to maintain an average checking account balance, called a **compensating balance (CB),** equal to from 10 to 20 percent of the amount of the loan. In effect, the compensating balance is a charge by the bank for *servicing* the loan (bookkeeping, maintaining a line of credit, and so on).

LINE OF CREDIT
An arrangement in which a bank agrees to lend up to a specified maximum amount of funds during a designated period.

LINE OF CREDIT   A **line of credit** is an agreement between a bank and a borrower indicating the maximum credit the bank allows a borrower to have outstanding at any point in time. For example, a bank loan officer might indicate to a financial

---

[4]In a credit sale, the seller records the transaction as a receivable; the buyer, as a payable. We examine accounts receivable as an asset investment later in the chapter. We might also note that if a firm's accounts payable exceed its receivables, it is said to be *receiving net trade credit,* whereas if its receivables exceed its payables, it is *extending net trade credit.* Smaller firms frequently receive net credit; larger firms generally extend it.

[5]Although commercial banks remain the primary source of short-term loans, other sources are available. For example, in 1998 GE Capital Corporation (GECC) had several billion dollars in commercial loans outstanding. Firms such as GECC, which was initially established to finance consumers' purchases of GE's durable goods, often find business loans to be more profitable than consumer loans.

REVOLVING CREDIT AGREEMENT
A line of credit in which the funds are guaranteed, or committed, by the bank or other lending institution.

COMMITMENT FEE
A fee charged on the *unused* balance of a revolving credit agreement to compensate the bank for guaranteeing that the funds will be available when needed by the borrower.

COMMERCIAL PAPER
Unsecured, short-term promissory notes issued by large, financially sound firms to raise funds.

SECURED LOAN
A loan backed by collateral; for short-term loans, the collateral is often either inventory or receivables, or both.

PLEDGING RECEIVABLES
Using accounts receivable as collateral for a loan.

FACTORING
The outright sale of receivables.

RECOURSE
The lender can seek payment from the borrowing firm when receivables' accounts used to secure a loan are uncollectible.

manager that the bank regards the firm as being "good" for up to $200,000 during the forthcoming year, which means the firm can have at most a $200,000 balance of loans outstanding from this source at any time during the year. When a line of credit arrangement is *guaranteed,* it is called a **revolving credit agreement.** A revolving credit agreement is similar to a regular line of credit, except the bank has a *legal obligation* to provide funds requested by the borrower. The bank generally charges a **commitment fee** for guaranteeing the availability of the funds. The commitment fee is usually charged on the unused balance of the credit line because, in order to guarantee the funds are available when requested, the bank must keep the funds where they can be accessed very quickly, which means safe investments that provide relatively low returns. Neither the legal obligation nor the fee exists under the typical line of credit; instead, a "regular" credit line provides the funds only if they are available at the bank.

Commercial Paper

Commercial paper is a type of unsecured promissory note *issued* by large, financially strong firms, and it is sold primarily to other firms, to insurance companies, to pension funds, to money market mutual funds, and to banks. The use of commercial paper is restricted to a comparatively small number of firms that are *exceptionally* good credit risks. Maturities of commercial paper vary from one to nine months, with an average of about five months.[6] Using commercial paper permits a corporation to tap a wider range of credit sources, including financial institutions across the country, and this can reduce interest costs. One potential problem with commercial paper is that a debtor who is in temporary financial difficulty might receive little help because commercial paper dealings generally are less personal than are bank relationships.

Secured Loans

Most loans can be secured if this is deemed necessary or desirable. Given a choice, it is usually better to borrow on an unsecured basis because the bookkeeping costs of **secured loans** are often high. However, weak firms might find that they can borrow only if they put up some type of security, or that by using security they can borrow at a lower rate.

Most secured short-term business loans involve the use of short-term assets, such as accounts receivable or inventories, as collateral. When receivables are used as collateral for a short-term loan, the firm is said to be **pledging** its receivables. When receivables are *sold* to a financial institution, the firm is said to be **factoring** its receivables, and the buyer is called a *factor.* A principal difference between the two arrangements is that when receivables are pledged, the lender has both a claim against the receivables and **recourse** to the borrower. Thus, if a customer that represents an account receivable does not pay, the selling firm that has pledged the receivables rather than the lender must take the loss. With most factoring arrangements, the factor that buys the receivables must take the loss.

---

[6]The maximum maturity without SEC registration is 270 days. Also, commercial paper can only be sold to "sophisticated" investors; otherwise, SEC registration would be required even for maturities of 270 days or less.

Therefore, it is not uncommon for the factor to provide a credit department for the borrower to carry out the credit investigation of its customers.

A substantial amount of credit is secured by business inventories. If a firm is a relatively good credit risk, the mere existence of the inventory might be a sufficient basis for receiving an unsecured loan. However, if the firm is a relatively poor risk, the lending institution might insist upon security in the form of a *lien* against the inventory. There are three major types of inventory liens: (1) A *blanket lien* gives the lending institution a lien against all of the borrower's inventories without limiting the ability of the borrower to sell the inventories. A blanket lien is generally used when the inventory put up as collateral is relatively low priced, fast moving, and difficult to identify individually. (2) A *trust receipt* is an arrangement in which the goods are held in trust for the lender, perhaps stored in a public warehouse or held on the premises of the borrower. A trust receipt arrangement generally is used for goods that are relatively high priced, slow moving, and easy to identify individually (e.g., serial numbers, models, and so on are different). When the goods that are covered by this lien are sold, proceeds from the sale must be transmitted to the lender. Automobile dealer financing is one of the best examples of trust receipt financing. (3) *Warehouse receipt financing* refers to arrangements in which inventory used as collateral is physically separated from the borrower's other inventory and then stored in a secured site located either on the premises of the borrower (*field warehousing*) or in a public warehouse (*terminal warehousing*). To provide inventory supervision, the lending institution employs a third party in the arrangement, a warehousing company, that acts as its agent in the oversight and the sale of the inventory.

Self-Test Questions

What types of short-term sources of funds are classified as accruals?

What is trade credit?

How does a revolving line of credit differ from a regular line of credit?

What is commercial paper? What types of companies can use commercial paper to meet their short-term financing needs?

What is a secured loan?

What two types of current assets are pledged as security for short-term loans?

Differentiate between pledging accounts receivable and factoring accounts receivable.

Describe three methods of inventory financing (types of liens).

Computing the Cost of Short-Term Credit

For any type of short-term credit, we can compute the interest rate, or cost, for the period the funds are used with the following equation:

12-5

$$\text{Interest rate per period (cost)} = \frac{\text{Dollar cost of borrowing}}{\text{Amount of usable funds}}$$

In this equation, the numerator represents the dollar amount that must be paid for using the borrowed funds, which includes the interest paid, application fees, charges for commitment fees, and so forth. The denominator represents the amount of the loan that actually can be used (spent) by the borrower, which is not necessarily the same as the amount borrowed because discounts or other costs might be deducted from the loan proceeds. As we will see shortly, when loan restrictions prevent the borrower from using the entire amount of the loan, the effective annual rate paid for the loan increases.

Using Equation 12-5, we can compute the effective annual rate and the annual percentage rate, which we showed in Chapter 6, as follows:

12-6

$$\frac{\text{Effective}}{\text{annual rate}} = \text{EAR} = \left[1 + \left(\frac{\text{Interest rate}}{\text{per period}}\right)\right]^m - 1.0$$

12-7

$$\frac{\text{Annual}}{\text{percentage rate}} = \text{APR} = \left(\frac{\text{Interest rate}}{\text{per period}}\right) \times m = i_{\text{SIMPLE}}$$

Here m is the number of borrowing periods in one year (i.e., if the loan is for one month, m = 12). Remember from our discussion in Chapter 6 that the EAR incorporates interest compounding in the computation while the APR does not. Both computations measure the cost of short-term borrowing on a percentage basis.

To illustrate the application of these equations, consider the credit terms of 2/10, net 30, which allows a firm to take a 2 percent discount from the purchase price if payment is made on or before Day 10 of the billing cycle; otherwise, the entire bill is due by Day 30. Therefore, if the firm does not take the discount, it effectively pays 2¢ to borrow 98¢ for a 20-day period, so the cost of using the funds for an additional 20 days is

$$\text{Interest rate per period} = \frac{\$0.02}{\$0.98} = 0.020408 \approx 2.041\%$$

Because there are m = 18 20-day periods in a 360-day year, the APR, or simple interest rate, associated with the trade credit is

$$\text{APR} = i_{\text{SIMPLE}} = 0.02041 \times 18 = 0.367 = 36.7\%$$

DISCOUNT INTEREST LOAN
A loan in which the interest, which is calculated on the amount borrowed (principal), is paid at the beginning of the loan period; interest is paid in advance.

And, the effective annual cost (rate) of using trade credit with these terms as a source of short-term financing is

$$\frac{\text{Effective}}{\text{annual rate}} = (1 + 0.02041)^{18} - 1.0 = 1.439 - 1.0 = 0.439 = 43.9\%$$

Now let's consider what happens when a firm finances with a **discount interest loan** from the bank. With this type of loan, the interest due is deducted "up front" so that the borrower receives less than the principal amount, or face value, of the loan. Assume Argile Textiles received a $10,000 discount interest loan with a 12 percent quoted (simple) interest rate and the funds will be used for a period of nine months. The interest payment on this loan is $10,000 × 0.12 × (9/12) = $900. Note that interest is paid only for the portion of the year the loan is outstanding, which is nine months in this case. Because the interest is paid in advance, Argile has only $9,100 = $10,000 − $900 available for use. Thus, the nine-month interest rate paid for the loan is

$$\frac{\text{Interest rate}}{\text{per period}} = \frac{\text{Nine-month}}{\text{interest rate}} = \frac{\$10,000 \times 0.12 \times \left(\frac{9}{12}\right)}{\$10,000 - \left[\$10,000 \times 0.12 \times \left(\frac{9}{12}\right)\right]}$$

$$= \frac{\$900}{\$9,100}$$

$$= 0.0989 = 9.89\%$$

The APR for the loan is

$$\text{APR} = 9.89\% \times \left(\frac{12}{9}\right) = 13.19\%$$

And, the EAR is

$$\text{EAR} = (1.0989)^{(12/9)} - 1 = 0.1340 = 13.40\%$$

What do you think the cost of the loan described here would be if Argile's bank charged a $50 fee to cover the costs of processing the loan? To answer this question, first take a look at Equation 12-5 and determine whether the payment affects the numerator (i.e., the dollar cost of borrowing), the denominator (i.e., the amount of usable funds), or both. The general rule is that the numerator is affected by any expense associated with the loan, and the denominator is affected if funds must be put aside (e.g., to satisfy a compensating balance requirement) or costs are paid out of the proceeds at the beginning of the loan period. Thus, if Argile uses the proceeds from the loan to pay the $50 fee, both the numerator and the denominator are affected, and the nine-month interest rate is

$$\frac{\text{Interest rate}}{\text{per period}} = \frac{\text{Nine-month}}{\text{interest rate}} = \frac{\$900 + \$50}{\$9,100 - \$50}$$

$$= \frac{\$950}{\$9,050}$$

$$= 0.1050 = 10.50\%$$

Check to see that the APR and the EAR are now 14.0 percent and 14.2 percent, respectively.

From the examples we presented here, you should recognize that the cost (percentage) of short-term financing is higher when the dollar expenses, such as those associated with interest, clerical efforts, loan processing, and so forth, are higher or when the amount of the original loan (i.e., the principal) that can actually be used by the borrower is lower.

Self-Test Questions

What is the difference between APR and EAR?

All else equal, what causes the APR and EAR to increase?

Managing Cash and Marketable Securities

In Chapter 7, we discovered that value, which we want to maximize, is based on cash flows. Thus, managing cash flows is an extremely important task for a financial manager. Part of this task is determining how much cash a firm should have on hand at any time to ensure that normal business operations continue uninterrupted. In this section, we discuss some of the factors that affect the amount of cash firms hold, and we describe some of the cash management techniques currently used by businesses.

Cash Management

For the purposes of our discussion, the term *cash* refers to the funds a firm holds that can be used for immediate disbursement — this includes the amount a firm holds in its checking account as well as the amount of actual currency it holds. Cash is a "nonearning, or idle, asset" that is required to pay bills. When possible, cash should be "put to work" by investing in assets that have positive expected returns. Thus, the goal of the cash manager is to minimize the amount of cash the firm must hold for use in conducting its normal business activities, yet, at the same time, to have sufficient cash to (1) pay suppliers, (2) maintain its credit rating, and (3) meet unexpected cash needs.

Firms hold cash for the following reasons:

TRANSACTIONS BALANCE
A cash balance necessary for day-to-day operations; the balance associated with routine payments and collections.

1. Cash balances are necessary in business operations because payments must be made in cash, and receipts are deposited in a cash account. Cash balances associated with routine payments and collections are known as **transactions balances.**

2. As discussed earlier, a bank often requires a firm to maintain a *compensating balance* on deposit to help offset the costs of providing services such as check clearing, cash management advice, and so forth.

PRECAUTIONARY BALANCE
A cash balance held in reserve for unforeseen fluctuations in cash flows.

3. Because cash inflows and outflows are somewhat unpredictable, firms generally hold some cash in reserve for random, unforeseen fluctuations in cash flows. These "safety stocks" are called **precautionary balances** — the less predictable the firm's cash flows, the larger such balances should be. However, if the firm has easy access to borrowed funds — that is, if it can borrow on short notice (e.g., via a line of credit at the bank) — its need for precautionary balances is reduced.

SPECULATIVE BALANCE
A cash balance that is held to enable the firm to take advantage of any bargain purchases that might arise.

4. Sometimes cash balances are held to enable the firm to take advantage of bargain purchases that might arise. These funds are called **speculative balances.** As with precautionary balances, though, firms that have easy access to borrowed funds are likely to rely on their ability to borrow quickly rather than on cash balances for speculative purposes.

Although the cash accounts of most firms can be thought of as consisting of transactions, compensating, precautionary, and speculative balances, we cannot calculate the amount needed for each purpose, sum them, and produce a total desired cash balance because the same money often serves more than one purpose. For instance, precautionary and speculative balances can also be used to satisfy compensating balance requirements. Firms do, however, consider all four factors when establishing their target cash positions.

In addition to these four motives, a firm maintains cash balances to preserve its credit rating by keeping its liquidity position in line with those of other firms in the industry. A strong credit rating enables the firm to both purchase goods from suppliers on favorable terms and maintain an ample line of credit with its bank.

Cash Management Techniques

Most cash management activities are performed jointly by the firm and its primary bank, but the financial manager is ultimately responsible for the effectiveness of the cash management program. Effective cash management encompasses proper management of both the cash inflows and the cash outflows of a firm, which entails consideration of the factors discussed next.

CASH FORECASTS   The most critical ingredient to proper cash management is the cash forecast, often referred to as the cash budget. A firm needs to predict the timing of the cash inflows and the cash outflows to plan for investment and borrowing activities. If a cash shortfall is projected during a particular period, arrangements can be made to borrow the needed funds before a crisis erupts. At the same time, if a cash surplus is projected, plans can be made to temporarily invest the funds rather than letting them sit idle. We discuss the cash budget in greater detail in Chapter 14.

SYNCHRONIZED CASH FLOWS
A situation in which cash inflows coincide with cash outflows, thereby permitting a firm to hold low transactions balances.

CASH FLOW SYNCHRONIZATION   It would be ideal if the receipt of a cash payment from a customer occurred at exactly the same time a bill needed to be paid; that portion paid out never would be idle and any excess could be invested quickly to reduce the time it is idle. Recognizing this point, companies try to arrange it so that cash inflows and outflows are matched as well as possible — customers are billed so their "billing cycles" coordinate with when the firm pays its own bills. Having **synchronized cash flows** enables a firm to reduce its cash balances, decrease its bank loans, lower interest expenses, and boost profits. The more predictable the timing of the cash flows, the greater the synchronization that can be attained — utilities and credit card companies generally have a high degree of cash flow synchronization.

FLOAT
The difference between the balance shown in a firm's (or individual's) checkbook and the balance on the bank's records.

DISBURSEMENT FLOAT
The value of checks that have been written and disbursed but that have not yet fully cleared through the banking system and thus have not been deducted from the account on which they were written.

FLOAT   **Float** is defined as the difference between the balance shown in a firm's (or individual's) checkbook and the balance on the bank's records. Suppose a firm writes, on the average, checks in the amount of $5,000 each day, and it normally takes six days from the time the check is mailed until it is cleared and deducted from the firm's bank account. This will cause the firm's own checkbook to show a balance $30,000 = $5,000 × 6 days smaller than the balance on the bank's records; this difference is called **disbursement float.** Now suppose the firm also receives checks in the amount of $5,000 daily, but it loses four days

COLLECTIONS FLOAT
The amount of checks that have been received and deposited but that have not yet been credited to the account in which they were deposited.

NET FLOAT
The difference between disbursement float and collections float; the difference between the balance shown in the checkbook and the balance shown on the bank's books.

LOCKBOX ARRANGEMENT
A technique used to reduce float by having payments sent to post office boxes located near customers.

PREAUTHORIZED DEBIT SYSTEM
A system that allows a customer's bank to periodically transfer funds from that customer's account to a selling firm's bank account for the payment of bills.

CONCENTRATION BANKING
A technique used to move funds from many bank accounts to a more central cash pool in order to more effectively manage cash.

while they are being deposited and cleared. This will result in $20,000 of **collections float**. In total, the firm's **net float** — the difference between $30,000 positive disbursement float and the $20,000 negative collections float — will be $10,000, which means the balance the bank shows in the firm's checking account is $10,000 greater than the balance the firm shows in its own checkbook.

Delays that cause float arise because it takes time for checks (1) to travel through the mail (mail delay), (2) to be processed by the receiving firm (processing delay), and (3) to clear through the banking system (clearing, or availability, delay). Basically, the size of a firm's net float is a function of its ability to speed up collections on checks received and to slow down collections on checks written. Efficient firms go to great lengths to speed up the processing of incoming checks, thus putting the funds to work faster, and they try to delay their own payments as long as possible.

ACCELERATION OF RECEIPTS   A firm cannot use customers' payments until they are received *and* converted into a spendable form, such as cash or an increase in a checking account balance. Thus, it would benefit the firm to accelerate the collection of customers' payments and the conversion of those payments into cash.

Although some of the delays that cause float cannot be controlled directly, the following techniques are used to manage collections:

1. A **lockbox arrangement** requires customers to send their payments to a post office box located in an area near where they live rather than directly to the firm. The firm arranges for a local bank to collect the checks from the post office box, perhaps several times a day, and to immediately deposit them into the company's checking account. By having lockboxes close to the customers, a firm can reduce float because, at the very least, (a) the mail delay is less than if the payment had to travel farther and (b) checks are cleared faster because the banks the checks are written on are in the same Federal Reserve district.

2. If a firm receives regular, repetitious payments from its customers, it might want to establish a **preauthorized debit system** (sometimes called preauthorized payments). With this arrangement, the collecting firm and its customer (paying firm) enter into an agreement whereby the paying firm's bank periodically transfers funds from the paying firm's account to the collecting firm's account, even if that account is located at another bank. Preauthorized debiting accelerates the transfer of funds because mail and check-clearing delays are completely eliminated, and much of the processing delay is eliminated.

3. **Concentration banking** is a cash management arrangement used to mobilize funds from decentralized receiving locations, whether they are lockboxes or decentralized company locations, into one or more central cash pools. The cash manager then uses these pools for short-term investing or reallocation among the firm's banks. By pooling its cash, the firm is able to take maximum advantage of economies of scale in cash management and investment — often commissions are less per dollar on large investments, and there are instances where investments of larger dollar amounts earn higher returns than smaller investments.

DISBURSEMENT CONTROL Accelerating collections represents one side of cash management, and controlling funds outflows, or disbursements, represents the other side. Three methods commonly used to control disbursements include the following:

1. Centralizing the processing of payables permits the financial manager to evaluate the payments coming due for the entire firm and to schedule the availability of funds to meet these needs on a companywide basis, and it also permits more efficient monitoring of payables and the effects of float. A disadvantage to a *centralized disbursement system* is that regional offices might not be able to make prompt payment for services rendered, which can create ill will and raise the company's operating costs. But, as firms become more electronically proficient, the centralization of disbursements can be coordinated more effectively and such situations should be reduced substantially.

ZERO-BALANCE ACCOUNT (ZBA)
A special checking account used for disbursements that has a balance equal to zero when there is no disbursement activity.

2. A **zero-balance account (ZBA)** is a special disbursement account that has a balance equal to zero when there is no disbursement activity. Typically, a firm establishes several ZBAs in its concentration bank and funds them from a master account. As checks are presented to a ZBA for payment, funds are automatically transferred from the master account.

CONTROLLED DISBURSEMENT ACCOUNTS (CDA)
Checking accounts in which funds are not deposited until checks are presented for payment, usually on a daily basis.

3. Whereas ZBAs typically are established at concentration banks, **controlled disbursement accounts (CDAs)** can be set up at any bank. Such accounts are not funded until the day's checks are presented against the account. The firm relies on the bank that maintains the CDA to provide information in the morning (before 11 A.M., New York time) concerning the total amount of the checks that will be presented for payment that day. This permits the financial manager (a) to transfer funds to the controlled disbursement account to cover the checks presented for payment or (b) to invest excess cash at midday, when money market trading is at a peak.

Marketable Securities

Realistically, the management of cash and marketable securities cannot be separated — management of one implies management of the other because the amount of marketable securities held by a firm depends on its short-term cash needs.

MARKETABLE SECURITIES
Securities that can be sold on short notice without loss of principal or original investment.

Marketable securities, or *near-cash* assets, are extremely liquid, short-term investments that permit the firm to earn positive returns on cash that is not needed to pay bills immediately but will be needed sometime in the near term, perhaps in a few days, weeks, or months. Although such investments typically provide much lower yields than operating assets, nearly every large firm has them. The two basic reasons for owning marketable securities are as follows:

1. Marketable securities serve as a *substitute for cash balances.* Firms often hold portfolios of marketable securities, liquidating part of the portfolio to increase the cash account when cash is needed because the *marketable securities offer a place to temporarily put cash balances to work earning a positive return.* In such situations, the marketable securities could be used as a substitute for some transactions balances, for precautionary balances, for speculative balances, or for all three.

2. Marketable securities are also used as a *temporary investment* (a) to finance seasonal or cyclical operations and (b) to amass funds to meet financial

TABLE 12-2

Securities Available for Investment of Surplus Cash

Security	Typical Maturity at Time of Issue	Approximate Yields		
		01/29/77	01/29/82	01/29/98
I. Suitable as Near-Cash Reserves				
U.S. Treasury bills	91 days to 1 year	4.8%	13.4%	5.0%
Commercial paper	Up to 270 days	4.9	14.5	5.4
Negotiable CDs	Up to 1 year	4.9	14.6	5.5
Money market mutual funds	Instant liquidity	5.0	14.3	5.5
Eurodollar time deposits	Up to 1 year	5.2	15.1	5.5
II. Not Suitable as Near-Cash Reserves				
U.S. Treasury notes	1 to 10 years	6.9%	14.5%	5.6%
U.S. Treasury bonds	10 to 30 years	7.6	14.4	6.0
Corporate bonds (AAA)[a]	Up to 40 years	8.2	16.1	6.7
Municipal bonds (AAA)[a, b]	Up to 30 years	5.2	12.2	4.9
Preferred stocks (AAA)[a, b]	Unlimited	7.5	13.1	7.2
Common stocks[c]	Unlimited	22.6	−4.8	25.1

NOTES:

[a]Rates shown for corporate and municipal bonds and for preferred stock are for longer maturities rated AAA. Lower rated, higher risk securities have higher yields.

[b]Rates are lower on municipal bonds because the interest they pay is exempt from federal income taxes, and the rate on preferred stocks is low because 70 percent of the dividends paid on them is exempt from federal taxes for corporate owners, who own most preferred stock.

[c]The returns given for common stocks represent the average yield that would have been earned in the stock market during the previous 52-week period. Individual common stock returns vary considerably, even at one point in time.

requirements in the near future. For example, if the firm has a conservative financing policy as we discussed earlier, then its long-term capital will exceed its permanent assets, and marketable securities will be held when inventories and receivables are low and not as much funding is needed.

Table 12-2 lists the major types of securities available for investment, with an indication of how widely the yields on these securities have fluctuated during the past couple of decades. Depending on how long they will be held, the financial manager decides on a suitable set of securities, and a suitable maturity pattern, to hold as *near-cash reserves* in the form of marketable securities. As noted in the table, long-term securities are not appropriate investments for marketable securities as we have described in this section — safety, especially maintenance of principal, should be paramount when putting together a marketable securities portfolio.[7]

Self-Test Questions

Why is cash management important?

What are the motives for holding cash?

[7]For descriptions of the characteristics of the financial assets given in Table 12-2, see Chapter 4.

What is float? How do firms use float to increase cash management efficiency?

What are some methods firms can use to accelerate receipts?

What are some techniques for controlling disbursements?

What are some securities commonly held as marketable securities? Why are such securities held by firms?

Credit Management

If you ask financial managers if they would prefer to sell their products for cash or for credit, you would expect them to respond by saying something like: "If sales levels are not affected, cash sales are preferred because payment is certain and immediate, and because the costs of granting credit and maintaining accounts receivable would be eliminated." Ideally, then, firms would prefer to sell for cash only. So, why do firms sell for credit? The primary reason most firms offer credit sales is because their competitors offer credit. Consider what you would do if you had the opportunity to purchase the same product for the same price from two different firms, but one firm required cash payment at the time of the purchase while the other firm allowed you to pay for the product one month after the purchase without any additional cost. From which firm would you purchase the product? Like you, firms would prefer to delay their payments, especially if there are no additional costs associated with the delay.

Effective credit management is extremely important because too much credit is very costly in terms of the investment in, and maintenance of, accounts receivables, while too little credit could result in the loss of profitable sales. Carrying receivables has both direct and indirect costs, but it also has an important benefit — granting credit should increase profits. Thus, to maximize shareholders' wealth, a financial manager needs to understand how to effectively manage the firm's credit activities.

In this section, we discuss (1) the factors considered important when determining the appropriate credit policy for a firm, (2) procedures for monitoring the credit policy to ensure it is being administered properly, and (3) how to evaluate whether credit policy changes will be beneficial to the firm.

Credit Policy

CREDIT POLICY
A set of decisions that includes a firm's credit standards, credit terms, methods used to collect credit accounts, and credit monitoring procedures.

CREDIT STANDARDS
Standards that indicate the minimum financial strength a customer must have to be granted credit.

The major controllable variables that affect demand for a company's products are sales prices, product quality, advertising, and the firm's **credit policy.** The firm's credit policy, in turn, includes the following factors:

1. **Credit standards** refer to the strength and creditworthiness a customer must exhibit in order to qualify for credit. The firm's credit standards are applied to determine which customers qualify for the regular credit terms and how much credit each customer should receive. The major factors considered when setting credit standards relate to the likelihood that a given customer will pay slowly or perhaps even end up as a bad debt loss. Determining the credit quality, or creditworthiness, of a customer probably is the most difficult part of credit management. But, credit evaluation is a well-established practice, and a good credit manager can make reasonably accurate judgments of the probability of default exhibited by different classes of customers by examining a firm's current financial position and evaluating factors that might affect the financial position in the future.

TERMS OF CREDIT
The payment conditions offered to credit customers; the terms include the length of the credit period and any cash discounts offered.

2. **Terms of credit** are the conditions of the credit sale, especially with regard to the payment arrangements. Firms need to determine when the **credit period** begins, how long the customer has to pay for credit purchases before the account is considered delinquent, and whether a cash discount for early payment should be offered. An examination of the credit terms offered by firms in the United States would show great variety across industries — credit terms range from cash before delivery (CBD) and cash on delivery (COD) to offering **cash discounts** for early payment. Because of the competitive nature of trade credit, most financial managers follow the norm of the industry in which they operate when setting credit terms.

CREDIT PERIOD
The length of time for which credit is granted; after that time, the credit account is considered delinquent.

3. **Collection policy** refers to the procedures the firm follows to collect its credit accounts. The firm needs to determine when, and how, notification of the credit sale will be conveyed to the buyer. The quicker a customer receives an invoice, the sooner the bill can be paid. In today's world, firms have turned more to the use of electronics to "send" invoices to customers. One of the most important collection policy decisions is how the past-due accounts should be handled. For example, a letter might be sent to customers when a bill is 10 days past due; a more severe letter, followed by a telephone call, might be used if payment is not received within 30 days; and the account might be turned over to a collection agency after 90 days.

CASH DISCOUNT
A reduction in the invoice price of goods offered by the seller to encourage early payment.

COLLECTION POLICY
The procedures followed by a firm to collect its accounts receivables.

Receivables Monitoring

Once a firm sets its credit policy, it wants to operate within the policy's limits. Thus, it is important that a firm examine its receivables periodically to determine whether customers' payment patterns have changed to the extent that credit operations are outside the credit policy limits. For instance, if the balance in receivables increases either because the amount of "bad," or uncollectible, sales increases or because the average time it takes to collect existing credit sales increases, the firm should consider making changes in its credit policy. **Receivables monitoring** refers to the process of evaluating the credit policy to determine if a shift in the customers' payment patterns occurs.

RECEIVABLES MONITORING
The process of evaluating the credit policy to determine if a shift in the customers' payment patterns occurs.

Traditionally, firms have monitored accounts receivables by using methods that measure the amount of time credit remains outstanding. Two such methods are the *days sales outstanding (DSO)* and the *aging schedule:*

DAYS SALES OUTSTANDING (DSO)
The average length of time required to collect accounts receivable; also called the *average collection period.*

1. **Days sales outstanding (DSO),** which is sometimes called the *average collection period,* represents the average time it takes to collect credit accounts. The computation for DSO was given in Equation 12-2 earlier in the chapter when we described the receivables collection period. At that point, we found that the receivables collection period, or DSO, for Argile was 43.2 days in 1999. The DSO of 43.2 days can be compared with the credit terms offered by Argile. If Argile's credit terms are 2/10, net 30, then we know there are customers that are delinquent when paying their accounts. In fact, if many customers are paying within 10 days to take advantage of the discount, the others would, on average, have to be taking much longer than 43.2 days.

2. One way to check the possibility of customers taking more or less time to pay is to use an aging schedule. An **aging schedule** is a breakdown of a firm's receivables by age of account. Table 12-3 contains the December 31, 1999 aging schedule for Argile Textiles. The standard format for aging schedules generally includes age categories broken down by month because banks and financial analysts usually want companies to report the ages of the receivables in this form. However, more precision, thus better monitoring information, can be attained by using narrower age categories (e.g., one or two weeks).

According to Argile's aging schedule, only 40 percent of the credit sales in 1999 were collected within the credit period of 30 days; thus, 60 percent of the credit sales collections were delinquent. Some of the payments were delinquent by only a few days, while others were delinquent by three to four times the 30-day credit period.

Management should constantly monitor the days sales outstanding and the aging schedule to detect trends to see how the firm's collection experience compares with its credit terms and to see how effectively the credit department is operating in comparison with other firms in the industry. If the DSO starts to lengthen or if the aging schedule begins to show an increasing percentage of past-due accounts, then the firm's credit policy might need to be tightened.

We must be careful when interpreting changes in DSO or the aging schedule, however, because if a firm experiences sharp seasonal variations, or if it is growing rapidly, then both measures could be distorted. For example, recall from earlier in the chapter that Argile's peak selling season is in the fall. Table 12-1 showed that forecasted receivables are expected to be high, at $250 million, in September 2000, which is during the peak season, and receivables are expected to be much lower, at $198 million, at the end of December 2000. If sales are expected to be $1,650 million in 2000, Argile's DSO will be $250/($1,650/360) = 54.5 days on September 30 but only $198/($1,650/360) = 43.2 days on December 31, 2000. This decline in DSO would not indicate that Argile had tightened its credit policy, only that its sales had fallen due to seasonal factors. Similar problems arise with the aging schedule when sales fluctuate widely. Therefore, *a change in either the DSO or the aging schedule should be taken as a signal to investigate further, but not necessarily as a sign that the firm's credit policy has weakened.* If a firm generally experiences widely fluctuating sales patterns, some type of modified

---

TABLE 12-3

Argile Textiles: Receivables Aging Schedule for 1999

Age of Account (in days)	Net Amount Outstanding	Fraction of Total Receivables	Average Days
0–30	$ 72,000	40%	18
31–60	90,000	50	55
61–90	10,800	6	77
Over 90	7,200	4	97
	$180,000	100%	

DSO = 0.40 (18 days) + 0.50 (55 days) + 0.06 (77 days) + 0.04 (97 days)
  = 43.2 days

aging schedule should be used to correctly account for these fluctuations.[8] Still, days sales outstanding and the aging schedule are useful tools for reviewing the credit department's performance.

Analyzing Proposed Changes in Credit Policy

The key question when deciding on a proposed credit policy change is this: Will the firm realize a net benefit? If the added benefits expected from a credit policy change do not exceed the added costs, then the policy change should not be made.

To illustrate how we can evaluate whether a proposed change in a firm's credit policy is appropriate, let's examine what would happen if Argile Textiles makes changes to reduce its average collection period. Argile's financial manager has proposed that this task be accomplished in 2000 by (1) billing customers sooner and exerting more pressure on delinquent customers to pay their bills and (2) tightening existing credit standards slightly — the credit department will more closely examine the financial positions of credit customers and suspend the credit of customers who are considered "habitually delinquent." It is apparent that both of these actions will result in a direct increase in the costs associated with Argile's credit policy; in fact, credit evaluation and collection costs are expected to increase from $16 million to $17 million. At the same time, even though Argile has an extremely loyal customer base, it is expected that $2 million in annual sales will be lost to competitors because some customers will have their credit decreased or even eliminated; therefore, forecasted sales will drop from $1,650 million to $1,648 million. But, because the credit policy changes will have little, if any, effect on the "good" credit customers, the financial manager does not expect there to be a change in the proportion of customers (20 percent) who currently take advantage of the cash discount. If the proposed credit policy changes are approved, the financial manager believes the average collection period, or DSO, for receivables can be reduced from 43.2 days to 35.6 days — this is more in line with the credit terms offered by Argile (2/10, net 30), and it is closer to the industry average of 34.1 days. Also, if the average collection period is reduced, the amount "carried" in accounts receivable is reduced, which means less funds are "tied up" in receivables. Table 12-4 summarizes the information about Argile's existing credit policy and the financial manager's proposed changes.

Should Argile adopt the financial manager's proposal? To answer this question, we need to compute the marginal costs and benefits associated with changing the existing credit policy to determine if the proposal is more advantageous than the current policy. The obvious costs to the firm include the $2 million decrease in sales and the $1 million increase in credit and collection costs, which, in combination, will decrease taxable earnings by $3 million. But, the decline in sales will also reduce variable operating costs by $2 million × 0.8133 = $1.63 million. In addition, decreases in both credit sales and the average collection period mean less funds will be "tied up" in receivables; thus, the opportunity, or carrying, cost of receivables will also be less.

---

[8] See Eugene F. Brigham, Louis C. Gapenski, and Phillip R. Daves, *Intermediate Financial Management,* 6th ed. (Fort Worth, Tex.: The Dryden Press, 1999), Chapter 18, for a more complete discussion of the problems with the DSO and aging schedule and how to correct for them.

TABLE 12-4

Argile Textiles: Existing and Proposed Credit Policies Expected for 2000
(millions of dollars)

	Existing Policy	Proposed Policy
Credit terms	2/10, net 30	2/10, net 30
Credit sales (S)	$1,650.0	$1,648.0
Cash discount[a]	$6.6	$6.6
Variable cost ratio (V)	81⅓%	81⅓%
Bad debts	$0	$0
Credit evaluation and collection costs	$16	$17
Days sales outstanding (DSO)	43.2 days	35.6 days

[a]Argile offers credit terms of 2/10, net 30; 20 percent of its customers take advantage of the cash discount, so the total cash discount is $6.6 million = (0.20) (0.02) ($1,650.0 million). Customers who take the discount will not be affected by the credit policy changes that are aimed at delinquent customers; thus, the amount of the discount will be the same under either credit policy.

To compute the carrying cost, we need to determine how much Argile has invested in receivables and the "cost" of this investment. The amount invested in receivables can be computed by determining the amount Argile paid for the products that were sold on credit but for which cash payment has not been received:

12-8

$$\frac{\text{Receivables}}{\text{investment}} = \frac{\text{Average accounts}}{\text{receivable balance}} \times \frac{\text{Variable}}{\text{cost ratio}}$$

$$= \left[\text{DSO} \times \left(\frac{\text{Sales}}{\text{per day}} \right) \right] \times \frac{\text{Variable}}{\text{cost ratio}}$$

$$= \left[\text{DSO} \times \left(\frac{S}{360} \right) \right] \times V$$

Only variable costs enter the calculation because it is this amount that represents the funds the firm has "tied up" in receivables, which is the amount that must be financed. For Argile, the receivables investments associated with the existing and the proposed credit policies in 2000 are as follows:

$$\text{Receivables investment}_{\text{Current}} = \left[43.2 \text{ days} \times \left(\frac{\$1,650 \text{ million}}{360} \right) \right] \times (0.8133)$$

$$= \$198.0 \text{ million} \times 0.8133$$

$$= \$161.0 \text{ million}$$

$$\text{Receivables investment}_{\text{Proposal}} = \left[35.6 \text{ days} \times \left(\frac{\$1,648 \text{ million}}{360} \right) \right] \times (0.8133)$$

$$= \$163.0 \text{ million} \times 0.8133$$

$$= \$132.6 \text{ million}$$

Once the investment in receivables is computed, the receivables carrying (opportunity) cost can be computed by determining how much return these funds would have earned if they were invested elsewhere:

12-9

$$\text{Receivables carrying cost} = \text{Receivables investment} \times \text{Opportunity cost of funds}$$

$$= \left[\text{DSO} \times \left(\frac{S}{360} \right) \times V \right] \times k_{AR}$$

Here k_{AR} represents the opportunity cost associated with the funds "tied up" in accounts receivable. Therefore, if Argile's opportunity cost for funds invested in receivables is 10 percent, the cost of carrying receivables with the existing policy and with the proposal would be

$$\text{Receivables carrying cost}_{\text{Current}} = \$161.0 \text{ million} \times 0.10 = \$16.1 \text{ million}$$

$$\text{Receivables carrying cost}_{\text{Proposal}} = \$132.6 \text{ million} \times 0.10 = \$13.3 \text{ million}$$

If the proposed credit policy changes are adopted, the required investment in receivables will decrease by $161.0 million − $132.6 million = $28.4 million, which will decrease the cost of carrying receivables by $2.8 million, from $16.1 million to $13.3 million.

Table 12-5 summarizes the results of the analysis we just described, and it illustrates the general idea behind credit policy analysis. The combined effect of all the changes in credit policy is a projected $800,000 annual increase in after-tax revenues, which suggests the credit policy changes would be beneficial for Argile. There might, of course, be corresponding changes on the projected balance sheet — the lower sales might necessitate somewhat less cash and inventories. These changes, as well as any other changes, also would have to be considered in the analysis. For simplicity, we assume the only changes relevant to the decision to change the credit policy are those discussed here and contained in Table 12-5.

The analysis in Table 12-5 provides Argile's managers with a vehicle for considering the impact of credit policy changes on the firm's income statement and balance sheet variables. However, a great deal of judgment must be applied to the decision because both customers' and competitors' responses to credit policy changes are very difficult to estimate. Nevertheless, this type of numerical analysis can provide a good starting point for credit policy decisions.

Self-Test Questions

What are the four credit policy variables? Describe how each variable affects sales and profitability.

Define days sales outstanding (DSO). What can be learned from it? How is it affected by sales fluctuations?

TABLE 12-5

Argile Textiles: Analysis of Changing Credit Policy (millions of dollars)

	Projected 2000 Revenues/Costs under Current Credit Policy	Projected 2000 Revenues/Costs under Proposed Credit Policy	Income Effect of Credit Policy Change
Sales	$1,650.0	$1,648.0	($2.0)
Less: Cash discounts	(6.6)	(6.6)	0.0
Net sales	1,643.4	1,641.4	(2.0)
Variable cost of goods sold	(1,342.0)	(1,340.4)	1.6
Bad debts	(0.0)	(0.0)	0.0
Credit evaluation and collection costs	(16.0)	(17.0)	(1.0)
Receivables carrying costs	(16.1)	(13.3)	2.8
Revenues net of variable production costs and credit costs	$ 269.3	$ 270.7	$1.4
Tax impact (40%)	(107.7)	(108.3)	(0.6)
After-tax revenues	$ 161.6	$ 162.4	$0.8

What is an aging schedule? What can be learned from it? How is it affected by sales fluctuations?

Describe the procedure used to evaluate a change in credit policy.

Inventory Management

If it could, a firm would prefer to have no inventory at all because, while products are in inventory, they do not generate returns and they must be financed. However, most firms find it necessary to maintain inventory in some form because (1) demand cannot be predicted with certainty and (2) it takes time to produce a product that is ready for sale. And, while excessive inventories are costly to the firm, so are insufficient inventories because customers might purchase from competitors if products are not available when demanded, and future business could be lost.

Although inventory models are covered in depth in production management courses, it is important to understand the basics of inventory management because proper management requires coordination among the sales, purchasing, production, and finance departments. Lack of coordination among these departments, poor sales forecasts, or both, can lead to financial ruin. Therefore, in this section, we describe the general concepts of inventory management.

Types of Inventory

RAW MATERIALS
The inventories purchased from suppliers that will ultimately be transformed into finished goods.

An inventory item can be classified according to one of the following stages of completion:

1. **Raw materials** include new inventory purchased from suppliers; it is the material a firm purchases to transform into finished products for sale. As long as the firm has an inventory of raw materials, delays in ordering and delivery from suppliers do not affect the production process.

WORK-IN-PROCESS
Inventory in various stages of completion; some work-in-process is at the very beginning of the production process while some is at the end of the process.

2. Work-in-process refers to inventory items that are at various stages of the production process. If a firm has work-in-process at every stage of the production process, then it will not have to completely shut down production if a problem arises at one of the earlier stages.

3. Finished goods inventory represents products that are ready for sale. Firms carry finished goods to ensure that orders can be filled when they are received. If there are no finished goods, the firm has to wait for the completion of the production process before inventory can be sold, thus demand might not be satisfied when it arrives. When a customer arrives and there is no inventory to satisfy that demand, a **stockout** exists, and the firm might lose the demand to competitors, perhaps permanently.

FINISHED GOODS
Inventories that have completed the production process and are ready for sale.

Optimal Inventory Level

STOCKOUT
Occurs when a firm runs out of inventory and customers arrive to purchase the product.

The goal of inventory management is to provide the inventories required to sustain operations at the lowest possible cost. Thus, the first step in determining the optimal inventory level is to identify the costs involved in purchasing and maintaining inventory, and then we need to determine at what point those costs are minimized.

INVENTORY COSTS We generally classify inventory costs into three categories: those associated with carrying inventory, those associated with ordering and receiving inventory, and those associated with running short of inventory (stockouts). First, let's look at the two costs that are most directly observable — carrying costs and ordering costs:

CARRYING COSTS
The costs associated with having inventory, which include storage costs, insurance, cost of tying up funds, depreciation costs, and so on; these costs generally increase in proportion to the average amount of inventory held.

1. Carrying costs include any expenses associated with having inventory, such as rent paid for the warehouse where inventory is stored, insurance on the inventory, and so forth, and they generally increase in direct proportion to the average amount of inventory carried.

2. Ordering costs are those expenses associated with placing and receiving an order for new inventory, which include the costs of generating memos, fax transmissions, and so forth. For the most part, the costs associated with each order are fixed regardless of the order size.[9]

ORDERING COSTS
The costs of placing an order; the cost of each order is generally fixed regardless of the average size of the inventory.

If we assume that the firm knows how much inventory it needs and sales are distributed evenly during each period, then we can combine the total carrying costs, TCC, and the total ordering costs, TOC, to find total inventory costs, TIC, as follows:

---

[9]In reality, both carrying and ordering costs can have variable- and fixed-cost elements, at least over certain ranges of average inventory. For example, utilities charges probably are fixed in the short run over a wide range of inventory levels. Similarly, labor costs in receiving inventory could be tied to the quantity received, hence could be variable. To simplify matters, we treat all carrying costs as variable and all ordering costs as fixed.

12-10

$$\text{Total inventory} \atop \text{costs (TIC)} = \text{Total carrying costs} + \text{Total ordering costs}$$

$$= \begin{pmatrix} \text{Carrying cost} \\ \text{per unit} \end{pmatrix} \times \begin{pmatrix} \text{Average units} \\ \text{in inventory} \end{pmatrix} + \begin{pmatrix} \text{Cost per} \\ \text{order} \end{pmatrix} \times \begin{pmatrix} \text{Number of} \\ \text{orders} \end{pmatrix}$$

$$= (C \times PP) \times \left(\frac{Q}{2}\right) + O \times \left(\frac{T}{Q}\right)$$

The variables in the equation are defined as follows:

C = carrying costs as a percent of the purchase price of each inventory item.
PP = purchase price, or cost, per unit.
Q = number of units purchased with each order.
T = total demand, or number of units sold, per period.
O = fixed costs per order.

According to Equation 12-10, the average investment in inventory depends on how frequently orders are placed and the size of each order. If we order every day, average inventory will be much smaller than if we order once a year and inventory carrying costs will be low, but the number of orders will be large and inventory ordering costs will be high. We can reduce ordering costs by ordering greater amounts less often, but then average inventory, thus the total carrying costs, will be high. This trade-off between carrying costs and ordering costs is shown in Figure 12-3. Note from the figure that there is a point where the total inventory cost, TIC, is *minimized;* this is called the **economic (optimum) ordering quantity (EOQ).**

ECONOMIC ORDERING QUANTITY
The optimal quantity that should be ordered; it is this quantity that will minimize the total inventory costs.

THE ECONOMIC ORDERING QUANTITY (EOQ) MODEL The EOQ is found by using calculus to find the point where the slope of the TIC curve in Figure 12-3 is perfectly horizontal; thus it equals zero. The result is the following equation:

12-11

$$\text{Economic ordering} \atop \text{quantity} = EOQ = \sqrt{\frac{2 \times O \times T}{C \times PP}}$$

EOQ MODEL
A formula for determining the order quantity that will minimize total inventory costs:

$$EOQ = \sqrt{\frac{2 \times O \times T}{C \times PP}}$$

The primary assumptions of the **EOQ model** given by Equation 12-11 are that (1) sales are evenly distributed throughout the period examined and can be forecasted perfectly, (2) orders are received when expected, and (3) the purchase price of each item in inventory is the same regardless of the quantity ordered.[10]

---

[10]The EOQ model can also be written as

$$EOQ = \sqrt{\frac{2(O)\,(T)}{C^*}}$$

where C^* is the annual carrying cost per unit expressed in dollars.

FIGURE 12-3

Determination of the Optimal Order Quantity

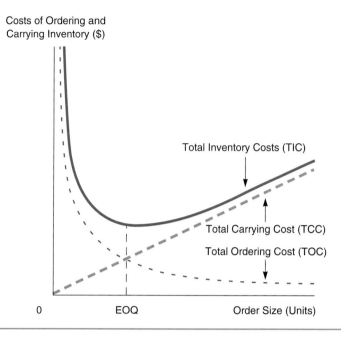

To illustrate the EOQ model, consider the following data supplied by Cotton Tops Inc., a distributor of custom-designed T-shirts that supplies concessionaires at Daisy World:

T = 78,000 shirts per year.
C = 25 percent of inventory value.
PP = $3.84 per shirt. (The shirts sell for $9, but this is irrelevant for our purposes here.)
O = $260 per order.

Substituting these data into Equation 12-11, we find an EOQ of 6,500 units:

$$\text{EOQ} = \sqrt{\frac{2(\$260)\,(78{,}000)}{(0.25)\,(\$3.84)}}$$

$$= \sqrt{42{,}250{,}000} = 6{,}500 \text{ units}$$

If Cotton Tops orders 6,500 shirts each time it needs inventory, it will place 78,000/6,500 = 12 orders per year and carry an average inventory of 6,500/2 = 3,250 shirts. Thus, at the EOQ amount, Cotton Tops' total inventory costs would equal $6,240:

$$TIC = (C \times PP)\left(\frac{Q}{2}\right) + O\left(\frac{T}{Q}\right)$$

$$= [0.25(\$3.84)]\left(\frac{6,500}{2}\right) + (\$260)\left(\frac{78,000}{6,500}\right)$$

$$= \$3,120 + \$3,120 = \$6,240$$

Note these two points: (1) Because we assume the purchase price of each inventory item does not depend on the amount ordered, TIC does *not* include the 78,000($3.84) = $299,520 annual cost of purchasing the inventory itself. (2) As we see both in Figure 12-3 and in the numbers here, at the EOQ, total carrying cost (TCC) equals total ordering cost (TOC). This property is not unique to our Cotton Tops illustration; it always holds.

Table 12-6 contains the total inventory costs that Cotton Tops would incur at various order quantities, including the EOQ level. Note that (1) as the amount ordered increases, the total carrying costs increase but the total ordering costs decrease, and vice versa; (2) if less than the EOQ amount is ordered, then the higher ordering costs more than offset the lower carrying costs; and (3) if greater than the EOQ amount is ordered, the higher carrying costs more than offset the lower ordering costs.

EOQ MODEL EXTENSIONS It should be obvious that some of the assumptions necessary for the basic EOQ to hold are unrealistic. To make the model more useful, we can apply some simple extensions. First, if there is a delay between the time inventory is ordered and when it is received, the firm must reorder before it runs out of inventory. For example, if it normally takes two weeks to receive orders, then Cotton Tops should reorder when two weeks of inventory is left. Cotton

TABLE 12-6

Cotton Tops Inc.: Total Inventory Costs for Various Order Quantities

	Quantity	Number of Orders	Total Ordering Costs	Total Carrying Costs	Total Inventory Costs
	3,000	26	$6,760	$ 1,440	$ 8,200
	5,200	15	3,900	2,496	6,396
	6,000	13	3,380	2,880	6,260
EOQ	**6,500**	**12**	**3,120**	**3,120**	**6,240**
	7,800	10	2,600	3,744	6,344
	9,750	8	2,080	4,680	6,760
	13,000	6	1,560	6,240	7,800
	78,000	1	260	37,440	37,700

NOTE: T = annual sales = 78,000 shirts
C = carrying cost = 25 percent
PP = purchase price = $3.84/shirt
O = ordering cost = $260/order

REORDER POINT
The level of inventory at which an order should be placed.

SAFETY STOCKS
Additional inventory carried to guard against changes in sales rates or production/shipping delays.

QUANTITY DISCOUNT
A discount from the purchase price offered for inventory ordered in large quantities.

Tops sells 78,000/52 = 1,500 shirts per week, so its **reorder point**, in this case, is when inventory drops to 3,000 shirts. Even if Cotton Tops orders additional inventory at the appropriate reorder point, unexpected demand might cause it to run out of inventory before the new inventory is delivered. To avoid this, the firm could carry **safety stocks,** which represent additional inventory that helps guard against stockouts. The amount of safety stock a firm holds generally *increases* with (1) the uncertainty of demand forecasts, (2) the costs (in terms of lost sales and lost goodwill) that result from stockouts, and (3) the chances that delays will occur in receiving shipments. The amount of safety stock *decreases* as the cost of carrying this additional inventory increases.

Another factor a firm might need to consider when determining appropriate inventory levels is whether its suppliers offer discounts to purchase large quantities. For example, if Cotton Tops' supplier offered a 1 percent discount for purchases equal to 13,000 units or more, the total reduction in the annual cost of purchasing large quantities of inventory would be [0.01($3.84)] × 78,000 = $2,995.20. Looking in Table 12-6, we see that the total inventory cost at 13,000 units is $7,800, which is $7,800 − $6,240 = $1,560 greater than the cost at the EOQ level of 6,500 units. But, the net benefit of taking advantage of the **quantity discount** is $2,995.20 − $1,560.00 = $1,435.20. Therefore, under these circumstances, each time Cotton Tops orders inventory, it will be more beneficial to order 13,000 units rather than the 6,500 units prescribed by the basic EOQ model.

In cases in which it is unrealistic to assume that the demand for the inventory is uniform throughout the year, the EOQ should not be applied on an annual basis. Rather, it would be more appropriate to divide the year into the seasons within which sales are relatively constant, say, the summer, the spring and fall, and the winter. Then, the EOQ model can be applied separately to each period.

Although we did not explicitly incorporate the extensions we mentioned here into the basic EOQ, our discussion should give you an idea of how the EOQ amount should be adjusted to determine the optimal inventory level if any of the conditions mentioned here exist.

Inventory Control Systems

RED-LINE METHOD
An inventory control procedure in which a red line is drawn around the inside of an inventory-stocked bin to indicate the reorder point level.

COMPUTERIZED INVENTORY CONTROL SYSTEM
A system of inventory control in which a computer is used to determine reorder points and to adjust inventory balances.

The EOQ model can be used to help establish the proper inventory level, but inventory management also involves the establishment of an *inventory control system.* Inventory control systems run the gamut from very simple to extremely complex, depending on the size of the firm and the nature of its inventories. For example, one simple control procedure is the **red-line method** — inventory items are stocked in a bin, a red line is drawn around the inside of the bin at the level of the reorder point, and the inventory clerk places an order when the red line shows. This procedure works well for parts such as bolts in a manufacturing process or for many items in retail businesses.

Most firms employ some type of **computerized inventory control system.** Large companies, such as Wal-Mart, often have fully integrated computerized inventory control systems in which the computer adjusts inventory levels as sales are made, orders inventory when the reorder point is reached, and records the receipt of an order. The computer records also can be used to determine if the usage rates of inventory items change, and thus adjustments to reorder amounts can be made.

JUST-IN-TIME SYSTEM
A system of inventory control in which a manufacturer coordinates production with suppliers so that raw materials or components arrive just as they are needed in the production process.

A relatively new approach to inventory control that requires a coordinated effort between the supplier and the buyer is called the **just-in-time system,** which was refined by Japanese firms many years ago. With this system, materials are delivered to the company at about the same time they are needed, perhaps a few hours before they are used. Another important development related to inventories is **out-sourcing,** which is the practice of purchasing components rather than making them in-house. For example, if GM arranged to buy radiators rather than making them itself, it would be out-sourcing. Out-sourcing is often combined with just-in-time systems to reduce inventory levels.

OUT-SOURCING
The practice of purchasing components rather than making them in-house.

Inventory control systems require coordination of inventory policy with manufacturing/procurement policies. Companies try to minimize total production and distribution costs, and inventory costs are just one part of total costs. Still, they are an important cost, and financial managers should be aware of the determinants of inventory costs and how they can be minimized.

Self-Test Questions

What are the types of inventory?

What are the three categories of inventory costs?

What is the purpose of the EOQ model?

What are safety stocks, and why are they required?

Describe some inventory control systems used in practice.

Multinational Working Capital Management

For the most part, the methods used to manage short-term assets and liabilities in multinational corporations are the same as those used in purely domestic corporations. But, multinational corporations face a far more complex task because they operate in many different business cultures, political environments, economic conditions, and so forth. In this section we discuss some of the differences between multinational and domestic working capital management.

Cash Management

Like a purely domestic company, a multinational corporation wants (1) to speed up collections and to slow down disbursements where possible, (2) to shift cash as rapidly as possible to those areas where it is needed, and (3) to try to put temporary cash balances to work earning positive returns. Multinational companies use the same general procedures for achieving these goals as domestic firms, but, because of longer distances and more serious mail delays, lockbox systems and electronic funds transfers are even more important.

One potential problem a multinational company faces that a purely domestic company does not is the chance that a foreign government will restrict transfers of funds out of the country. Foreign governments sometimes limit the amount of cash that can be taken out of the country because they want to encourage investment domestically. Even if funds can be transferred without limitation, deteriorating exchange rates might make it unattractive for a multinational firm to move funds to its operations in other countries.[11]

Once it has been determined what funds can be transferred out of the various nations in which a multinational corporation operates, it is important to get those funds to locations where they will earn the highest returns. Whereas domestic corporations tend to think in terms of domestic securities, multinationals are more likely to be aware of investment opportunities all around the world. Most multinational corporations use one or more global concentration banks, located in money centers such as London, New York, Tokyo, Zurich, or Singapore, and their staffs in those cities, working with international bankers, are able to take advantage of the best rates available anywhere in the world.

Credit Management

Credit policy is generally more important for a multinational corporation than for a purely domestic firm for two reasons. First, much U.S. trade is with poorer, less-developed nations, and in such situations granting credit is usually a necessary condition for doing business. Second, and in large part as a result of the first point, developed nations whose economic health depends on exports often help their manufacturing firms compete internationally by granting credit to foreign countries. In Japan, for example, government agencies help firms identify potential export markets and also help potential customers arrange credit for purchases from Japanese firms. The U.S. government has programs that help domestic firms export products, but it does not provide the degree of financial assistance available to many multinationals based in other countries from their local governments.

When granting credit, the multinational firm faces a riskier situation than purely domestic firms because, in addition to the normal risks of default, (1) political and legal environments often make it more difficult to collect defaulted accounts, and (2) the multinational corporations must worry about exchange rate changes between the time a sale is made and the time a receivable is collected.

By pointing out the risks in granting credit internationally, we are not suggesting that such credit is bad. Quite the contrary — the potential gains from international operations far outweigh the risks, at least for companies (and banks) that have the necessary expertise.

Inventory Management

Inventory management in a multinational setting is more complex than in a purely domestic firm because of logistical problems that arise with handling inventories. For example, should a firm concentrate its inventories in a few strategic centers located worldwide? Such a strategy might minimize the total amount of, thus the investment in, inventories needed to operate the global business; but, it also might cause delays in getting goods from central storage locations to user locations all around the world. It is clear, however, that both working stocks and safety stocks will have to be maintained at each user location, as well as at the strategic storage centers.

---

[11]The term "exchange rate" refers to the amount of one currency that another currency can be *exchanged* for (into). For example, to buy British pounds, you might need $2.50 in U.S. dollars.

Exchange rates can significantly influence inventory policy. For example, if a local currency was expected to rise in value against the dollar, a U.S. company operating in that country would want to increase stocks of local products before the rise in the currency, and vice versa. Another factor that must be considered is the possibility of import or export quotas or tariffs. Quotas restrict the quantities of products firms can bring into a country, while tariffs, like taxes, increase the prices of products that are allowed to be imported. Both quotas and tariffs are designed to restrict the ability of foreign corporations to compete with domestic companies; at the extreme, foreign products are excluded altogether.

Another danger in certain countries is the threat of expropriation, or government takeover of the firm's local operations. If the threat of expropriation is large, inventory holdings will be minimized, and goods will be brought in only as needed. Similarly, if the operation involves extraction of raw material, processing plants might be moved offshore rather than located close to the production site.

Taxes also must be considered, and they have two effects on multinational inventory management. First, countries often impose property taxes on assets, including inventories, and when this is done, the tax is based on holdings as of a specific date, say, January 1 or March 1. Such rules make it advantageous for a multinational firm (1) to schedule production so that inventories are low on the assessment date and (2) if assessment dates vary among countries in a region, to hold safety stocks in different countries at different times during the year.

In general, then, multinational firms use techniques similar to those described in this chapter to manage working capital, but their job is more complex because business, legal, and economic environments can differ significantly from one country to another.

Self-Test Questions

What are some factors that make cash management especially complicated in a multinational corporation?

Why is granting credit especially risky in an international context?

What are some factors that make inventory management in multinational firms more complex than in purely domestic firms?

ETHICAL DILEMMA

Money Back Guarantee, No Questions Asked

TradeSmart Inc. operates 1,200 discount electronics stores throughout the United States. TradeSmart has been quite successful in a highly competitive industry primarily because it has been able to offer brand name products at prices lower than can be found at other discount outlets. Because of its size, TradeSmart can purchase bulk inventory directly from manufacturers, and the economies of scale it derives from such purchases can be passed on to consumers in the form of lower prices.

In addition to low prices, TradeSmart offers an extremely liberal product return policy. Customers are permitted to return products for virtually any reason and with little regard to the time period covered by manufacturers' warranties. In fact, just a few days ago, a customer returned a digital pager that was more than two years old. TradeSmart gave the customer a full refund even though the pager appeared to have been run over by a car, which, if true, clearly would have voided the manufacturer's warranty. In another instance, a customer was given a refund when he returned the camcorder he had purchased three days earlier to record his daughter's wedding festivities. The customer could not describe the camcorder's malfunction—he said "it just didn't work right." The customer refused an offer to replace the camcorder; instead, he insisted on a full refund, which he was given. The manager of the customer relations department suspected that the customer had "purchased" the camcorder intending all along to return it after his daughter's wedding. But, TradeSmart's return policy does not dissuade customers from this practice. According to Ed Davidson, vice-president of customer relations, TradeSmart is willing to stand behind every product it sells, regardless of the problem, because the company believes such a policy is needed to attract and keep loyal customers in such a competitive industry. The company's motto—"Customer Satisfaction Is Our Business"—is displayed prominently throughout TradeSmart stores.

With such a liberal return policy, how does TradeSmart keep its prices so low? Actually, TradeSmart ships the returned products back to the manufacturers as defective products, so the return costs are passed on to the manufacturers. According to manufacturers, only one out of every six products returned by TradeSmart actually is defective. But, when the manufacturers complain about such returns as used products or products that have no mechanical problems, TradeSmart reminds them that the company does not have a service department, so its personnel are not knowledgeable concerning the technical circuitry of the products—the products are returned to the manufacturers with the customers' complaints attached. TradeSmart's inventory manager would contend that the company does not intentionally deceive or take advantage of the manufacturers' return policies and warranties. Do you agree with TradeSmart's return policy? Is it ethical? What action would you take if you were one of TradeSmart's suppliers?

SMALL BUSINESS

Growth and Working Capital Needs

Working capital is the requirement that entrepreneurs most often underestimate when seeking funds to finance a new business. The entrepreneur generally plans for research and development and for the plant and equipment required for production. Working capital, however, frequently comes as a surprise to the entrepreneur, who probably expects to develop a product the market will immediately accept and for which the market will pay a substantial premium. This premium will, he or she assumes, lead to high profit margins, which will then "finance" all of the firm's other needs. As naive as this point of view seems, it nevertheless is common among founders of new businesses.

Rick was one of the founders of a new microcomputer software company that began seeking venture capital to support its products in early 1999. When speaking with a venture capitalist, who was concerned about the low level of funding being sought, Rick explained that the company's products had such a high profit margin that the company essentially would be self-financing. Rick claimed there would be no need for financing once the marketing was under way because the profits would generate more than enough cash to pay for new product development.

Sally, a venture capitalist approached by Rick, was disconcerted by Rick's reasoning. She explained to Rick that the selling price of his product would not be received fully by his company because distributors and wholesalers were involved. She also pointed out that most of the sales would be on credit, so the revenues received by his company initially would be added to accounts receivable — not received as cash — and probably not collected, on average, for about 45 to 60 days. Meanwhile, Rick would have to write checks to pay for overhead, for high research and development expenses, for a marketing staff, for advertising, and so on. So instead of cash flowing in, the firm would be, on balance, paying cash out for the first few years of its life.

Rapid growth consumes cash; it does not generate cash. Rapid growth might generate profits, but profits do not pay the bills — cash does. Consider what a firm must do to sustain a high growth rate. If it is a manufacturer,

Continued

Continued

the components of its assets include raw materials inventory, work-in-process inventory, finished goods inventory, and accounts receivable, as well as fixed assets. With the exception of fixed assets, these items all are components of gross working capital. When the firm produces a product, it makes an investment in each of these working capital items before any cash is received from collection of receivables, assuming all sales are credit sales.

Consider a small firm that finances its activities solely through the funds it generates. If the firm has a cash conversion cycle of 180 days, cash is "turned over" only twice per year. If the company earns, say, 3 percent on its sales dollar, it has about 3 percent more money available after each cash cycle than before. With two cycles per year, about 6 percent more is available for investment at the end of the year than at the beginning. Thus, annual growth of approximately 6 percent can be supported internally; so if the company is growing at a rate of 20 percent per year, it must either obtain funds externally or face enormous pressures.

Generally, a firm can fund more rapid growth internally either by raising the profit margin or by shortening the cash conversion cycle (increasing the number of cycles per year). To raise the profit margin, the company must raise prices, cut costs, or both. Raising prices might reduce growth (because customers will be less eager to buy at higher prices), but it might also help bring growth and financial resources more into balance. Shortening the cash conversion cycle requires reducing inventory, collecting receivables more efficiently, or paying suppliers more slowly. For example, if the cash turnover changes to four times per year from two, internally fundable growth doubles (12 percent rather than 6 percent). Improving the cash conversion cycle and thus increasing the rate at which the firm can support growth internally reduces the firm's needs for outside funds to a more manageable level.

For the small business with serious constraints on obtaining outside funds, these discretionary policies can help bring the firm's rate of growth into balance with its ability to finance that growth. Furthermore, such control on the part of management might impress bankers and others who have funds, and this might help the firm get the outside financing it would have preferred to have had all along.

Summary

This chapter examined working capital management, the relationship between working capital accounts, alternative ways of financing current assets, and ways to manage and evaluate the various working capital accounts. In addition, we provided an indication of the complexities faced by multinational firms when managing working capital around the world. The key concepts covered in this chapter are listed below.

- **Working capital** refers to current assets, and **net working capital** is defined as current assets minus current liabilities. **Working capital policy** refers to decisions relating to the level of current assets and the way they are financed. Decisions affecting one working capital account have an impact on other working capital accounts.
- The **inventory conversion period** is the average length of time required to convert raw materials into finished goods and then to sell them.
- The **receivables collection period** is the average length of time required to convert the firm's receivables into cash, and it is equal to the days sales outstanding.
- The **payables deferral period** is the average length of time between the purchase of raw materials and labor and paying for them.

- The **cash conversion cycle** is the length of time between paying for purchases and receiving cash from the sale of finished goods. The cash conversion cycle can be calculated as follows:

$$\begin{array}{c} \text{Cash} \\ \text{conversion} \\ \text{cycle} \end{array} = \begin{array}{c} \text{Inventory} \\ \text{conversion} \\ \text{period} \end{array} + \begin{array}{c} \text{Receivables} \\ \text{collection} \\ \text{period} \end{array} - \begin{array}{c} \text{Payables} \\ \text{deferral} \\ \text{period} \end{array}$$

- Under a **relaxed current asset investment policy,** a firm holds relatively large amounts of each type of current asset. Under a **restricted current asset investment policy,** the firm holds minimal amounts of these items.
- **Permanent current assets** are those current assets that the firm holds even during slack times, whereas **temporary current assets** are the additional current assets that are needed during seasonal or cyclical peaks.
- The methods used to finance permanent and temporary current assets constitute the firm's current asset financing policy. A **moderate approach** to current asset financing involves matching, to the extent possible, the maturities of assets and liabilities so that temporary current assets are financed with short-term spontaneous debt and permanent current assets and fixed assets are financed with long-term debt or equity plus nonspontaneous debt. Under an **aggressive approach,** some permanent current assets and perhaps even some fixed assets are financed with short-term debt. A **conservative approach** would be to use long-term capital to finance all permanent assets and some of the temporary current assets.
- The advantages of short-term credit are (1) the **speed** with which short-term loans can be arranged, (2) increased **flexibility,** and (3) the fact that short-term **interest rates** are generally **lower** than long-term rates. The principal disadvantage of short-term credit is the **extra risk** that the borrower must bear because (1) the lender can demand payment on short notice and (2) the cost of the loan will increase if interest rates rise.
- **Short-term credit** is defined as any liability originally scheduled for payment within one year. Five major sources of short-term credit include (1) accruals, (2) accounts payable, (3) bank loans, (4) commercial paper, and (5) secured loans.
- **Accruals,** which are continually recurring short-term liabilities, represent free, spontaneous credit.
- **Accounts payable,** or **trade credit,** is the largest category of short-term debt. This credit arises spontaneously as a result of purchases on credit.
- **Bank loans** are an important source of short-term credit. When a bank loan is approved, a **promissory note** is signed. It specifies (1) the amount borrowed, (2) the percentage interest rate, (3) the repayment schedule, (4) the collateral, and (5) any other conditions to which the parties have agreed.
- **Commercial paper** is unsecured short-term debt issued by a large, financially strong corporation.
- Sometimes a borrower will find it necessary to borrow on a **secured basis,** in which case the borrower pledges assets such as inventories or accounts receivable as collateral for the loan.
- Accounts receivable financing involves either **pledging** or **factoring** receivables. Under a *pledging* arrangement the lender not only gets a claim against the receivables but also has recourse to the borrower. *Factoring* involves the purchase of accounts receivable by the lender, generally without recourse to the borrower.

- There are three primary methods of inventory financing: (1) A **blanket lien** gives the lender a lien against all of the borrower's inventories. (2) A **trust receipt** is an instrument that acknowledges that goods are held in trust for the lender. (3) **Warehouse receipt financing** is an arrangement under which the lender employs a third party to exercise control over the borrower's inventory and to act as the lender's agent.

- In general, the **effective cost** and the **annual percentage rate** of a short-term borrowing are computed as follows:

$$\text{Effective annual rate} = \text{EAR} = \left[1 + \left(\frac{\text{Interest rate}}{\text{per period}} \right) \right]^{m} - 1.0$$

$$\text{Annual percentage rate} = \text{APR} = \left(\frac{\text{Interest rate}}{\text{per period}} \right) \times m$$

where m is the number of borrowing (compounding) periods in one year. The interest rate per period is computed using the following equation:

$$\frac{\text{Interest rate}}{\text{per period (cost)}} = \frac{\text{Dollar cost of borrowing}}{\text{Amount of usable funds}}$$

- The **primary goal of cash management** is to reduce the amount of cash held to the minimum necessary to conduct business.

- The **transactions balance** is the cash necessary to conduct day-to-day business, whereas the **precautionary balance** is a cash reserve held to meet random, unforeseen needs. A **compensating balance** is a minimum checking account balance that a bank requires as compensation either for services provided or as part of a loan agreement. Firms also hold **speculative balances,** which allow them to take advantage of bargain purchases.

- **Effective cash management** encompasses the proper management of cash inflows and outflows, which entails (1) synchronizing cash flows, (2) using float, (3) accelerating collections, (4) determining where and when funds will be needed and ensuring that they are available at the right place at the right time, and (5) controlling disbursements.

- **Disbursement float** is the amount of funds associated with checks written by a firm that are still in process and hence have not yet been deducted by the bank from our account. **Collections float** is the amount of funds associated with checks written to the firm that have not been cleared and hence are not yet available for use. **Net float** is the difference between disbursement float and collections float, and it is also equal to the difference between the balance in a firm's checkbook and the balance on the bank's records. The larger the net float, the smaller the cash balances we must maintain, so net float is good.

- Two techniques that can be used to speed up collections are (1) **lockboxes** and (2) **pre-authorized debits.** Also, a **concentration banking system** consolidates cash into a centralized pool that can be managed more efficiently than a large number of individual accounts.

- Three techniques for controlling disbursements are (1) **payables centralization,** (2) **zero-balance accounts,** and (3) **controlled disbursement accounts.**

- Firms can reduce cash balances by holding **marketable securities,** which can be sold easily on short notice at close to their original purchase prices.

Marketable securities serve both as a substitute for cash and as a temporary investment for funds that will be needed in the near future. Safety is the primary consideration when selecting marketable securities.

- When a firm sells goods to a customer on credit, an **account receivable** is created.

- Firms can use an **aging schedule** and the **days sales outstanding (DSO)** to help keep track of their receivables position and to help avoid an increase in bad debts.

- A firm's **credit policy** consists of four elements: (1) credit standards, (2) credit terms, (3) collection policy, and (4) monitoring receivables.

- A firm should change its credit policy only if the costs of doing so will be more than offset by the benefits.

- **Inventory management** involves determining how much inventory to hold, when to place orders, and how many units to order.

- **Inventory** can be grouped into three categories: (1) raw materials, (2) work-in-process, and (3) finished goods.

- **Inventory costs** can be divided into three types: carrying costs, ordering costs, and stock-out costs. In general, carrying costs increase as the level of inventory rises, but ordering costs and stock-out costs decline with larger inventory holdings.

- The **economic ordering quantity (EOQ)** model is a formula for determining the order quantity that will minimize total inventory costs:

$$EOQ = \sqrt{\frac{2 \times O \times T}{C \times PP}}$$

Here O is the fixed cost per order, T is sales in units, C is the percentage cost of carrying inventory, and PP is the purchase price per unit.

- The **reorder point** is the inventory level at which new items must be ordered. **Safety stocks** are held to avoid shortages (1) if demand increases or (2) if shipping delays are encountered. If suppliers offer **quantity discounts** to purchase materials, it might be beneficial for the firm to order more than the EOQ amount.

- Firms use inventory control systems such as the **red-line method,** as well as **computerized inventory control systems,** to help them keep track of actual inventory levels and to ensure that inventory levels are adjusted as sales change. **Just-in-time (JIT) systems** and **out-sourcing** are also used to hold down inventory costs and, simultaneously, to improve the production process.

- **Multinational firms** use techniques similar to purely domestic firms to manage working capital, but they face more complex situations due to differences in the business, economic, and legal environments of various countries.

Questions

12-1   Describe the relationships among accounts payable, inventories, accounts receivable, and the cash account by tracing the impact on these accounts of a product manufactured and sold by a company. Start with the purchase of raw materials, and conclude with the collection for the sale of the product.

12-2   Describe the cash conversion cycle. How can a financial manager use knowledge of the cash conversion cycle to better manage the working capital of a firm?

12-3 What are the advantages of matching the maturities of assets and liabilities? What are the disadvantages?

12-4 From the standpoint of the borrower, is long-term or short-term credit riskier? Explain. Would it ever make sense to borrow on a short-term basis if short-term rates were above long-term rates?

12-5 Is it true that both trade credit and accruals represent a spontaneous source of capital for financing growth? Explain.

12-6 What kinds of firms use commercial paper? Could Mama and Papa Gus's Corner Grocery borrow using this form of credit?

12-7 Can you think of some firms that might allow you to purchase on credit but that probably would factor your receivables account?

12-8 What are the principal reasons for holding cash?

12-9 Discuss why it is important for a financial manager to understand the concept of float in order to effectively manage the firm's cash.

12-10 Why would a lockbox plan make more sense for a firm that makes sales all over the United States than for a firm with the same volume of business but concentrated where the corporate headquarters are located?

12-11 In general, does a firm wish to speed up or slow down collections of payments made by its customers? Why? How does the same firm wish to manage its disbursements? Why?

12-12 What does the term "liquidity" mean? Which would be more important to a firm that held a portfolio of marketable securities as precautionary balances against the possibility of losing a major lawsuit — liquidity or rate of return? Explain.

12-13 Firm A's management is very conservative whereas Firm B's is more aggressive. Is it true that, other things the same, Firm B would probably have larger holdings of marketable securities? Explain.

12-14 When selecting securities for portfolio investments, corporate treasurers must make a trade-off between risk and returns. Is it true that most treasurers are willing to assume a fairly high exposure to risk to gain higher expected returns?

12-15 What are the four elements of a firm's credit policy? To what extent can firms set their own credit policies as opposed to having to accept policies that are dictated by "the competition"?

12-16 What are aging schedules, and how can they be used to help the credit manager more effectively manage accounts receivable?

12-17 Indicate by a (+), (−), or (0) whether each of the following events would probably cause accounts receivable (A/R), sales, and profits to increase, decrease, or be affected in an indeterminant manner:

	A/R	Sales	Profits
The firm tightens its credit standards.	_____	_____	_____
The credit terms are changed from 2/10, net 30, to 3/10, net 30.	_____	_____	_____
The credit manager gets tough with past-due accounts.	_____	_____	_____

12-18 Describe the three classifications of inventory, and indicate the purpose for holding each type.

12-19 Indicate by a (+), (−), or (0) whether each of the following events would probably cause average annual inventories to rise, fall, or be affected in an indeterminant manner:

Suppliers switch from delivering by train to air freight. _____
A change from producing just-in-time to meet seasonal sales
  to steady, year-round production. (Sales peak at Christmas.) _____
Competition in the markets in which we sell increases. _____
The rate of general inflation increases. _____
Interest rates rise; other things are constant. _____

12-20 "Every firm should use the EOQ model to determine the optimal level of inventory to maintain." Discuss the accuracy of this statement with respect to the form of the EOQ model presented in this chapter.

Self-Test Problems   *Solutions Appear in Appendix B*

Key terms   **ST-1** Define each of the following terms:
  a. Working capital; net working capital; working capital policy
  b. Permanent current assets; temporary current assets
  c. Cash conversion cycle; inventory conversion period; receivables collection period; payables deferral period
  d. Relaxed current asset investment policy; restricted current asset investment policy; moderate current asset investment policy
  e. Moderate, or maturity matching, current asset financing policy; aggressive current asset financing policy; conservative current asset financing policy
  f. Accruals; trade credit
  g. Promissory note; line of credit; revolving credit agreement
  h. Compensating balance (CB); commitment fee
  i. Commercial paper; secured loan
  j. Pledging receivables; factoring
  k. Inventory blanket lien; trust receipt; warehouse receipt financing
  l. Transactions balance; precautionary balance; speculative balance
  m. Synchronized cash flows
  n. Net float; disbursement float; collections float
  o. Lockbox plan; pre-authorized debit
  p. Marketable securities; near-cash reserves
  q. Credit policy; credit terms; collection policy
  r. Aging schedule
  s. Carrying costs; ordering costs; total inventory costs
  t. Economic ordering quantity (EOQ); EOQ model
  u. Reorder point; stock-out cost
  v. Just-in-time system; out-sourcing

Working capital policy   **ST-2** The Calgary Company is attempting to establish a current assets policy. Fixed assets are $600,000, and the firm plans to maintain a 50 percent debt/assets ratio. The interest rate is 10 percent on all debt. The three alternative current asset policies under consideration are to carry current assets that total 40, 50, and 60 percent of projected sales. The company expects to earn 15 percent before interest and taxes on sales of $3 million. Calgary's marginal tax rate is 40 percent. What is the expected return on equity under each alternative? (Hint: Return on equity is computed by dividing net income by the dollar amount of equity.)

Trade credit versus bank credit   **ST-3** Gallinger Corporation projects an increase in sales from $1.5 million to $2 million, but it needs an additional $300,000 of current assets to support this expansion. The money can be obtained from the bank using a 13 percent discount interest loan; no compensating balance is required. Alternatively, Gallinger can finance the expansion by no longer taking discounts, thus increasing accounts payable. Gallinger purchases under terms of 2/10, net 30, but it can delay payment for an additional 35 days — paying in 65 days and thus becoming 35 days past due — without a penalty because of its supplier's current excess capacity problems.

a. Based strictly on effective annual interest rate comparisons, how should Gallinger finance its expansion?

b. What additional qualitative factors should Gallinger consider before reaching a decision?

Change in credit policy **ST-4** The Boca Grande Company expects to have sales of $10 million this year under its current operating policy. Its variable costs as a percentage of sales are 80 percent, and its cost of short-term funds is 16 percent. Currently, Boca Grande's credit policy is net 25 (no discount for early payment). However, its DSO is 30 days, and its bad debt loss percentage is 2 percent. Boca Grande spends $50,000 per year to collect bad debts, and its marginal tax rate is 40 percent.

The credit manager is considering two alternative proposals for changing Boca Grande's credit policy. Find the expected change in net income, taking into consideration anticipated changes in carrying costs for accounts receivable, the probable bad debt losses, and the discounts likely to be taken, for each proposal. Should a change in credit policy be made?

Proposal 1: Lengthen the credit period by going from net 25 to net 30. Collection expenditures will remain constant. Under this proposal, sales are expected to increase by $1 million annually, and the bad debt loss percentage on all sales is expected to rise to 3 percent. In addition, the DSO is expected to increase from 30 to 45 days on all sales.

Proposal 2: Shorten the credit period by going from net 25 to net 20. Again, collection expenses will remain constant. The anticipated effects of this change are a decrease in sales of $1 million per year, a decline in the DSO from 30 to 22 days, and a decline in the bad debt loss percentage to 1 percent on all sales.

EOQ and total inventory costs **ST-5** The Homemade Bread Company buys and then sells (as bread) 2.6 million bushels of wheat annually. The wheat must be purchased in multiples of 2,000 bushels. Ordering costs are $5,000 per order. Annual carrying costs are 2 percent of the purchase price of $5 per bushel. The delivery time is 3 weeks.

a. What is the EOQ?

b. At what inventory level should an order be placed?

c. What are the total inventory costs?

Problems

Disbursement float **12-1** The Garvin Company is setting up a new checking account with Barngrover National Bank. Garvin plans to issue checks in the amount of $1.6 million each day and to deduct them from its own records at the close of business on the day they are written. On average, the bank will receive and clear (i.e., deduct from the firm's bank balance) the checks at 5 P.M. the fourth day after they are written; for example, a check written on Monday will be cleared on Friday afternoon. The firm's agreement with the bank requires it to maintain a $1.2 million average compensating balance; this is $400,000 greater than the cash balance the firm would otherwise have on deposit. It makes a $1.2 million deposit, which clears immediately, at the time it opens the account.

a. Assuming that the firm makes deposits at 2 P.M. each day (and the bank includes them in that day's transactions), how much must it deposit daily to maintain a sufficient balance once it reaches a steady state? (To do this, set up a table that shows the daily balance recorded on the company's books and the daily balance at the bank until a steady state is reached.) Indicate the required deposit on Day 1, Day 2, Day 3, Day 4, if any, and each day thereafter, assuming that the company will write checks for $1.6 million on Day 1 and each day thereafter.

b. How many days of float does Garvin carry?

c. What ending daily balance should the firm try to maintain (1) on the bank's records and (2) on its own records?

d. Explain how net float can help increase the value of the firm's common stock.

Collection float   **12-2** Durst Corporation began operations 5 years ago as a small firm serving customers in the Denver area. However, its reputation and market area grew quickly so that today Durst has customers throughout the entire United States. Despite its broad customer base, Durst has maintained its headquarters in Denver and keeps its central billing system there. Durst's management is considering an alternative collection procedure to reduce its mail time and processing float. On average, it takes 5 days from the time customers mail payments until Durst is able to receive, process, and deposit them. Durst would like to set up a lockbox collection system, which it estimates would reduce the time lag from customer mailing to deposit by 3 days — bringing it down to 2 days. Durst receives an average of $1,400,000 in payments per day.

a. How many days of collection float now exist (Durst's customers' disbursement float), and what would it be under the lockbox system? What reduction in cash balances could Durst achieve by initiating the lockbox system?

b. If Durst has an opportunity cost of 10 percent, how much is the lockbox system worth on an annual basis?

c. What is the maximum monthly charge Durst should pay for the lockbox system?

Cost of bank loans   **12-3** The UFSU Corporation intends to borrow $450,000 to support its short-term financing requirements during the next year. The company is evaluating its financing options at the bank where it maintains its checking account. The financing alternatives offered by the bank include:

Alternative 1:   A discount interest loan with a simple interest of 9.5 percent.

Alternative 2:   A bank loan with 10.5 percent interest that is paid at the maturity of the loan (at the end of the year).

Alternative 3:   A $1 million revolving line of credit with interest of 9.25 percent paid on the amount borrowed at the end of the year and a 0.25 percent commitment fee paid on the unused balance.

Compute both the APR and the effective cost of each financing alternative assuming UFSU borrows $450,000. Which alternative should UFSU use?

Cost of bank loans   **12-4** Gifts Galore Inc. borrowed $1.5 million from National City Bank. The loan was made at an annual interest rate of 9 percent, but it was outstanding for only 3 months. Interest was due when the loan was repaid. A 20 percent compensating balance requirement raised the effective interest rate.

a. The approximate interest rate on the loan was 11.25 percent. What is the true effective rate?

b. What would be the effective cost of the loan if the note required discount interest?

Relaxing collection efforts   **12-5** The Pettit Corporation has annual credit sales of $2 million. Current expenses for the collection department are $30,000, bad debt losses are 2 percent, and the days sales outstanding is 30 days. Pettit is considering easing its collection efforts so that collection expenses will be reduced to $22,000 per year. The change is expected to increase bad debt losses to 3 percent and to increase the days sales outstanding to 45 days. In addition, sales are expected to increase to $2.2 million per year.

Should Pettit relax collection efforts if the opportunity cost of funds is 12 percent, the variable cost ratio is 75 percent, and its marginal tax rate is 40 percent?

Easing credit terms **12-6** Bey Technologies is considering changing its credit terms from 2/15, net 30, to 3/10, net 30, in order to speed collections. At present, 40 percent of Bey's customers take the 2 percent discount. Under the new terms, discount customers are expected to rise to 50 percent. Regardless of the credit terms, half of the customers who *do not take the discount* are expected to pay on time, whereas the remainder will pay 10 days late. The change does not involve a relaxation of credit standards; therefore, bad debt losses are not expected to rise above their present level of 2 percent of sales. However, the more generous cash discount terms are expected to increase sales from $2 million to $2.6 million per year. Bey's variable cost ratio is 75 percent, the interest rate on funds invested in accounts receivable is 9 percent, and the firm's marginal tax rate is 40 percent.

a. What is the days sales outstanding before and after the change?

b. Calculate the discount costs before and after the change.

c. Calculate the dollar cost of carrying receivables before and after the change.

d. Calculate the bad debt losses before and after the change.

e. What is the incremental profit from the change in credit terms? Should Bey change its credit terms?

Inventory cost **12-7** Computer Supplies Inc. must order computer diskettes from its supplier in lots of 1 dozen boxes. Given the following information, complete the table and determine the economic ordering quantity of diskettes for Computer Supplies Inc.:

Annual demand: 26,000 dozen
Cost per order placed: $30.00
Carrying cost: 20%
Price per dozen: $7.80

Order Size (dozens)	250	500	1,000	2,000	13,000	26,000
Number of orders	___	___	___	___	___	___
Average inventory	___	___	___	___	___	___
Carrying cost	___	___	___	___	___	___
Order cost	___	___	___	___	___	___
Total cost	___	___	___	___	___	___

EOQ and inventory costs **12-8** The following inventory data have been established for the Thompson Company:

(1) Orders must be placed in multiples of 100 units.

(2) Annual sales are 338,000 units.

(3) The purchase price per unit is $6.

(4) Carrying cost is 20 percent of the purchase price of goods.

(5) Fixed order cost is $48.

(6) One week is required for delivery.

a. What is the EOQ?

b. How many orders should Thompson place each year?

c. At what inventory level should an order be made?

d. Calculate the total cost of ordering and carrying inventories if the order quantity is (1) 4,000 units, (2) 4,800 units, or (3) 6,000 units. (4) What are the total costs if the order quantity is the EOQ?

Exam-Type Problems

The problems included in this section are set up in such a way that they could be used as multiple-choice exam problems.

Cash conversion cycle

12-9 The Saliford Corporation has an inventory conversion period of 60 days, a receivables collection period of 36 days, and a payables deferral period of 24 days.

    a. What is the length of the firm's cash conversion cycle?

    b. If Saliford's annual sales are $3,960,000 and all sales are on credit, what is the average balance in accounts receivable? (Hint: The accounts receivable balance should equal the average age of receivables, which is the collection period, times the daily sales.)

    c. What would happen to Saliford's cash conversion cycle if, on average, the length of time products are in inventory is shortened to 45 days?

Cost of bank credit

12-10 Susan Visscher, owner of Visscher's Hardware, is negotiating with First Merchant's Bank for a $50,000, 1-year loan. First Merchant's has offered Visscher the following alternatives. Calculate the effective interest rate for each alternative. Which alternative has the lowest effective interest rate? Assume any compensating balances are taken out of the loan proceeds.

    a. A 12 percent annual rate on a bank loan with no compensating balance required and interest due at the end of the year.

    b. A 9 percent annual rate on a bank loan with a 20 percent compensating balance required and interest due at the end of the year.

    c. An 8.75 percent annual rate on a discounted loan with a 15 percent compensating balance.

Cost of credit

12-11 Boles Corporation needs to raise $500,000 for one year to supply working capital to a new store. Boles buys from its suppliers on terms of 3/10, net 90, and it currently pays on Day 10 and takes discounts, but it could forgo discounts, pay on Day 90, and get the needed $500,000 in the form of costly trade credit. Alternatively, Boles could borrow from its bank on a 12 percent discount interest rate basis. What is the effective annual interest rate of the lower cost source?

Computation of float

12-12 Clearwater Glass Company has examined its cash management policy, and it has found that it takes an average of 5 days for checks the company writes to reach its bank and thus be deducted from its checking account balance (i.e., disbursement delay, or float, is 5 days). On the other hand, it is an average of 4 days from the time Clearwater Glass receives payments from its customers until the funds are available for use at the bank (i.e., collection delay, or float, is 4 days). On an average day, Clearwater Glass writes checks that total $70,000, and it receives checks from customers that total $80,000.

    a. Compute the disbursement float, collection float, and net float in dollars.

    b. If Clearwater Glass has an opportunity cost equal to 10 percent, how much would it be willing to spend each year to reduce collection delay (float) by 2 days? (Hint: Assume any funds that are freed up are invested at 10 percent annually.)

Receivables investment

12-13 Morrissey Industries sells on terms of 3/10, net 30. Total sales for the year are $900,000. Forty percent of the customers pay on Day 10 and take discounts; the other 60 percent pay, on average, 40 days after their purchases.

    a. What is the days sales outstanding?

    b. What is the average amount of receivables?

    c. What would happen to average receivables if Morrissey toughened up on its collection policy with the result that all nondiscount customers paid on the 30th day?

Tightening credit terms **12-14** Helen Bowers, the new credit manager of the Muscarella Corporation, was alarmed to find that Muscarella sells on credit terms of net 50 days while industry-wide credit terms have recently been lowered to net 30 days. On annual credit sales of $3 million, Muscarella currently averages 60 days' sales in accounts receivable. Bowers estimates that tightening the credit terms to 30 days would reduce annual sales to $2.6 million, but accounts receivable would drop to 35 days of sales, and the savings on investment in them should more than overcome any loss in profit.

Muscarella's variable cost ratio is 70 percent, and its marginal tax rate is 40 percent. If the interest rate on funds invested in receivables is 11 percent, should the change in credit terms be made?

Cost of carrying receivables **12-15** The McCollough Company has a variable operating cost ratio of 70 percent, its cost of capital is 10 percent, and current sales are $10,000. All of its sales are on credit, and it currently sells on terms of net 30. Its accounts receivable balance is $1,500. McCollough is considering a new credit policy with terms of net 45. Under the new policy, sales will increase to $12,000, and accounts receivable will rise to $2,500. If McCollough changes its credit policy to net 45, by how much will its cost of carrying receivables increase? Assume a 360-day year and that all customers pay on time.

EOQ model **12-16** Green Thumb Garden Centers sells 240,000 bags of lawn fertilizer annually. The optimal safety stock (which is on hand initially) is 1,200 bags. Each bag costs Green Thumb $4, inventory carrying costs are 20 percent, and the cost of placing an order with its supplier is $25.
a. What is the economic ordering quantity?
b. What is the maximum inventory of fertilizer? (Hint: Include the safety stock.)
c. What will Green Thumb's average inventory be? (Hint: Remember to include the safety stock.)
d. How often must the company order?

Integrative Problems

Cash management **12-17** Ray Smith, a retired librarian, recently opened a sportsman's shop called Smitty's Sports Paradise (SSP). Ray decided at age 62 that he wasn't quite ready to stay at home, living the life of leisure. It had always been his dream to open an outdoor sportsman's shop, so his friends convinced him to go ahead. Because Ray's educational background was in literature and not in business, he hired you, a finance expert, to help him with the store's cash management. Ray is very eager to learn, so he developed a set of questions to help him understand cash management. Now answer those questions:
a. What is the goal of cash management?
b. For what reasons do firms hold cash?
c. What is meant by the terms "precautionary" and "speculative" balances?
d. What are some specific advantages for a firm holding adequate cash balances?
e. How can a firm synchronize its cash flows, and what good would this do?
f. You have been going through the store's checkbook and bank balances. In the process, you discovered that SSP, on average, writes checks in the amount of $10,000 each day and that it takes about 5 days for these checks to clear. Also, the firm receives checks in the amount of $10,000 daily, but loses 4 days while they are being deposited and cleared. What is the firm's disbursement float, collections float, and net float?
g. How can a firm speed up collections and slow down disbursements?
h. Why would a firm hold marketable securities?

i. What factors should a firm consider in building its marketable securities portfolio? What are some securities that should and should not be held?

Credit policy   **12-18** Ray also wants you to examine his company's credit policy to determine if changes are needed because one of his employees, who graduated recently with a finance major, has recommended that the credit terms be changed from 2/10, net 30, to 3/20, net 45, and that both the credit standards and the collection policy be relaxed. According to the employee, such a change would cause sales to increase from $3.6 million to $4.0 million.

Currently, 62.5 percent of SSP's customers pay on Day 10 of the billing cycle and take the discount, 32 percent pay on Day 30, and 5.5 percent pay (on average) on Day 60. If the new credit policy is adopted, Ray thinks that 72.5 percent of customers would take the discount, 10 percent would pay on Day 45, and 17.5 percent would pay late, on Day 90. Bad debt losses for both policies are expected to be trivial.

Variable operating costs are currently 75 percent of sales, the cost of funds used to carry receivables is 10 percent, and its marginal tax rate is 40 percent. None of these factors would change as a result of a credit policy change.

To help decide whether or not to adopt the new policy, Ray has asked you to answer the following questions.

a. What four variables make up a firm's credit policy? In what direction would each be changed if the credit policy were to be relaxed? How would each variable tend to affect sales, the level of receivables, and bad debt losses?

b. How are the days sales outstanding (DSO) and the average collection period (ACP) related to one another? What would the DSO be if the current credit policy is maintained? If the proposed policy is adopted?

c. What is the dollar amount of discounts granted under the current and the proposed credit policies?

d. What is the dollar cost of carrying receivables under the current and the proposed credit policies?

e. What is the expected incremental profit associated with the proposed change in credit policy? Based on the analysis, should the change be made?

f. Suppose the company makes the proposed change, but its competitors react by making changes in their own credit terms, with the net result being that gross sales remain at the $3.6 million level. What would be the impact on the company's after-tax profits?

g. (1) What does the term "monitoring accounts receivable" mean?
(2) Why would a firm want to monitor its receivables?
(3) How might the DSO and the aging schedule be used in this process?

EOQ model   **12-19** Now Ray wants you to take a look at the company's inventory position. He thinks that inventories might be too high as a result of the manager's tendency to order in large quantities. Ray has decided to examine the situation for one key product — fly rods, which cost $320 each to purchase and prepare for sale. Annual sales of the product are 2,500 units (rods), and the annual carrying cost is 10 percent of inventory value. The company has been buying 500 rods per order and placing another order when the stock on hand falls to 100 fly rods. Each time SSP orders, it incurs a cost equal to $64. Sales are uniform throughout the year.

a. Ray believes that the EOQ model should be used to help determine the optimal inventory situation for this product. What is the EOQ formula, and what are the key assumptions underlying this model?

b. What is the formula for total inventory costs?

c. What is the EOQ for the fly rods? What will the total inventory costs be for this product if the EOQ is produced?

d. What is SSP's added cost if it orders 500 fly rods rather than the EOQ quantity? What if it orders 750 rods each time?

e. Of course, there is uncertainty in SSP's usage rate, as well as in order delays, so the company must carry a safety stock to avoid running out of the fly rods and having to lose sales. If a safety stock of 100 rods is carried, what effect would this have on total inventory costs?

f. For most of SSP's products, inventory usage is not uniform throughout the year but, rather, follows some seasonal pattern. Could the EOQ model be used in this situation? If so, how?

g. How would these factors affect the use of the EOQ model?
   (1) "Just-in-time" (JIT) procedures.
   (2) The use of air freight for deliveries.
   (3) Computerized inventory control systems.

Short-term financing **12-20** Finally, Ray has asked you to review the company's short-term financing policies and to prepare a report to help him with SSP's future working capital financing decisions. To help you get started, Ray has prepared some questions that, when answered, will give him a better idea of the company's short-term financing policies.

a. What is short-term credit, and what are the major sources of this credit?

b. Is there a cost to accruals, and do firms have much control over them? What is trade credit?

c. Like most small companies, SSP has two primary sources of short-term debt: trade credit and bank loans. One supplier, which supplies SSP with $500,000 of materials a year, offers SSP terms of 2/10, net 50.
   (1) What are SSP's net daily purchases from this supplier?
   (2) What is the average level of SSP's accounts payable to this supplier if the discount is taken? What is the average level if the discount is not taken?
   (3) What is the approximate cost if SSP does not take the discount? What is its effective annual cost?

d. In discussing a possible loan with the firm's banker, Ray has found that the bank is willing to lend SSP up to $800,000 for 1 year at a 9 percent simple, or quoted, rate. However, he forgot to ask what the specific terms would be.
   (1) Assume the firm will borrow $800,000. What would be the effective interest rate if the loan required interest to be paid at the end of the year (not a discount interest loan)? If the loan had been an 8 percent interest loan for 6 months rather than for 1 year, would that have affected the effective annual rate?
   (2) What would be the effective rate if the loan were a discount interest loan?
   (3) Now assume that the bank requires interest to be paid at the end of the year, but it requires the firm to maintain a 20 percent compensating balance. What is the effective annual rate on the loan? Assume SSP takes the compensating balance amounts from the loan proceeds.

e. SSP is considering using secured short-term financing. What is a secured loan? What two types of current assets can be used to secure loans?

f. What are the differences between pledging receivables and factoring receivables? Is one type generally considered better?

g. What are the differences among the three forms of inventory financing? Is one type generally considered best?

CHAPTER 13

Analysis of Financial Statements

U.S. firms are required to make "full and fair" disclosure of their operations by publishing various financial statements and other reports required by the Securities and Exchange Commission, the Financial Accounting Standards Board, and the American Institute of Certified Public Accountants. Unfortunately, these groups often do not consult with each other concerning the disclosure requirements. As a result, the average size of the annual reports sent to stockholders continues to increase each year. In fact, according to a study conducted by Ernst & Young (a large national accounting firm) a few years ago, from 1972 to 1992, the average size of an annual report of a large, national company increased from 35 to 65 pages, the number of pages of footnotes to the financial statements increased from 4 to 17, and the amount of space management uses for its discussions grew from 3 to 12 pages — if this growth continues, it won't be long before the length of the average annual report exceeds 100 pages!

In most cases, annual reports are used to convey more than financial results; some firms use the annual report as an opportunity to showcase top management and sell the future of the company, without regard to the financial information. Work on the report often begins as much as six months before its publication, and most firms hire professional designers and writers to ensure that the final product looks sharp and reads well. Some firms pride themselves on the unique packaging designs used. For example, since 1977, McCormick & Company has used one of the spices and seasonings it produces to scent the paper on which its annual report is printed — the scent for 1993 was Chinese Five Spice and, in 1997, it was peppermint. Also in 1993, Eskimo Pie Corporation fashioned its annual report to resemble an ice cream bar, complete with a stick.

In most instances, the puffery contained in annual reports detracts from the primary purpose of providing objective financial information about the firm. For that reason, Wall Street analysts and other sophisticated investors prefer more straightforward financial disclosure documents, such as 10-Ks, which contain more detailed and unadorned information and which must by law be filed with the Securities and Exchange Commission.

Continued

Of course, there are companies that use the annual report as originally intended — to communicate the financial position of the firm. One such firm is Berkshire Hathaway, whose legendary chairman Warren Buffett says, "I assume I have a very intelligent partner who has been away for a year and needs to be filled in on all that's happened." Consequently, in his letters he often admits mistakes and emphasizes the negative. Buffett also uses his letters to educate his shareholders and to help them interpret the data presented in the rest of the report. Berkshire Hathaway's annual reports contain no photographs, colored ink, bar charts, or graphs, freeing readers to focus on the company's financial statements and Buffett's interpretation of them. Some CEOs might contend that such a barebones approach is too dull for the average stockholder and, further, that some readers may actually be intimidated by the information overload. But, the manner in which Chairman Buffett presents financial information for Berkshire Hathaway seems to work because the stockholders are considered more sophisticated than average investors. If you would like to examine some of the statements made by Warren Buffett, visit their web site at http://berkshirehathaway.com.

More and more, firms are recognizing that the "slick" annual report has (1) lost its credibility with serious seekers of financial information and (2) become increasingly more expensive to produce. For example, Johnson & Johnson saved more than $400,000 by decreasing the size of its annual report by 18 pages and mailing it using third class postage; Pfizer's report was trimmed by 10 pages; and, U.S. Surgical decided to eliminate its annual report by including the required information with the annual proxy statements sent to shareholders.

As you read this chapter, think about the kinds of information corporations provide their stockholders. Do the basic financial statements provide adequate data for investment decisions? What other information might be helpful? Also, consider the pros and cons of Chairman Buffett's decision to include frank, and frequently self-critical letters in his company's annual reports. Would you suggest that other companies follow suit?

Financial statement analysis involves a comparison of a firm's performance with that of other firms in the same line of business, which is often identified by the firm's industry classification. Generally speaking, the analysis is used to determine the firm's financial position in order to identify its current strengths and weaknesses and to suggest actions the firm might enact to take advantage of its strength and correct its weaknesses.

Financial statement analysis is not only important for the firm's managers, it also is important for the firm's investors and creditors. Internally, financial managers use the information provided by financial analysis to help make financing and investment decisions to maximize the firm's value. Externally, stockholders and creditors use financial statement analysis to evaluate the attractiveness of the firm as an investment by examining its ability to meet its current and expected future financial obligations.

In this chapter, we discuss how to evaluate a firm's current position. For the most part, this chapter should be a review of what you learned in accounting. However, accounting focuses on how financial statements are made, whereas our focus is on how they are used by management to improve the firm's performance and by investors (either stockholders or creditors) to examine the firm's financial position when evaluating its attractiveness as an investment.

Financial Statements and Reports

ANNUAL REPORT
A report issued annually by a corporation to its stockholders. It contains basic financial statements as well as management's opinion of the past year's operations and the firm's future prospects.

Of the various reports corporations issue to their stockholders, the **annual report** is probably the most important. Two types of information are given in this report. First, there is a verbal section, often presented as a letter from the chairman, that describes the firm's operating results during the past year and then discusses new developments that will affect future operations. Second, the annual report presents four basic financial statements — the *income statement,* the *balance sheet,* the *statement of retained earnings,* and the *statement of cash flows.* Taken together, these statements give an accounting picture of the firm's operations and financial position. Detailed data are provided for the two most recent years, along with historical summaries of key operating statistics for the past five or ten years.[1]

The quantitative and verbal information contained in the annual report are equally important. The financial statements report what actually has happened to the firm's financial position and to its earnings and dividends over the past few years, whereas the verbal statements attempt to explain why things turned out the way they did. For example, Table 13-1 shows that Argile Textiles' earnings decreased by nearly $5 million in 1999, to $59.4 million versus $64.1 million in 1998. In the annual report, management reported that the 7.3 percent earnings drop resulted from losses associated with a poor cotton crop and from increased costs due to a three-month strike and a retooling of the factory. However, management then went on to paint a more optimistic picture for the future, stating that full operations had been resumed, that several unprofitable businesses had been eliminated, and that profits in the year 2000 were expected to rise sharply. Of course, an increase in profitability might not occur, and analysts should compare management's past statements with subsequent results to determine if management's optimism is justified. In any event, *the information contained in an annual report is used by investors to form expectations about future earnings and dividends.* Therefore, the annual report obviously is of great interest to investors.

For illustrative purposes, we will use data taken from Argile Textiles, the textile manufacturer we introduced in the last chapter. Formed in 1980 in North Carolina, Argile has grown steadily and has earned a reputation for selling quality products.

---

[1] Firms also provide quarterly reports, but these are much less comprehensive than the annual reports. In addition, larger firms file even more detailed statements, giving breakdowns for each major division or subsidiary, with the Securities and Exchange Commission (SEC). These reports, called *10-K reports,* are made available to stockholders upon request to a company's corporate secretary. Finally, many larger firms also publish *statistical supplements,* that give financial statement data and key ratios going back 10 to 20 years.

TABLE 13-1

Argile Textiles: Comparative Income Statements for Years Ending December 31
(millions of dollars, except per-share data)

	1999	1998
Sales	$ 1,500.0	$ 1,435.0
Cost of goods sold	(1,220.0)[a]	(1,167.1)
Gross profit	$ 280.0	$ 267.9
Fixed operating expenses except depreciation	(90.0)	(85.0)
Depreciation	(50.0)	(40.0)
Earnings before interest and taxes (EBIT)	$ 140.0	$ 142.9
Interest	(41.0)	(36.0)
Earnings before taxes (EBT)	$ 99.0	$ 106.9
Taxes (40%)	(39.6)	(42.8)
Net income	$ 59.4	$ 64.1
Preferred dividends	0.0	0.0
Earnings available to common shareholders	$ 59.4	$ 64.1
Common dividends	(29.0)	(27.0)
Addition to retained earnings	$ 30.4	$ 37.1
Per Share Data:		
Common stock price	$23.00	$24.00
Earnings per share (EPS)[b]	$ 2.38	$ 2.56
Dividends per share (DPS)[b]	$ 1.16	$ 1.08

[a]Parentheses are used to denote negative numbers.

[b]Argile has 25,000,000 shares of common stock outstanding.

The Income Statement

INCOME STATEMENT
A statement summarizing
the firm's revenues and
expenses over an
accounting period,
generally a quarter or a
year.

The **income statement**, often referred to as the profit and loss statement, presents the results of business operations during a specified period of time such as a quarter or a year. The statement summarizes the revenues generated and the expenses incurred by the firm during the accounting period. Table 13-1 gives the 1998 and 1999 income statements for Argile Textiles. Sales are shown at the top of each statement, after which various costs, including income taxes, are subtracted to obtain the net income available to common stockholders. A report on earnings and dividends per share is given at the bottom of the statement. In managerial finance, earnings per share (EPS) is called "the bottom line," denoting that of all the items on the income statement, EPS is the most important. Argile earned $2.38 per share in 1999, down from $2.56 in 1998, but it still raised the per share dividend from $1.08 to $1.16.

It is important to remember that not all of the amounts shown on the income statement represent cash flows. Recall from what you learned in accounting, that for most corporations, the income statement is generated using the accrual method of accounting. This means revenues are recognized when they are earned, not when the cash is received, and expenses are realized when they are incurred, not when the cash is paid. This point will be addressed further later in the chapter.

The Balance Sheet

BALANCE SHEET
A statement of the firm's financial position at a specific point in time.

The **balance sheet** shows the financial position of a firm at a specific point in time. This financial statement indicates the investments made by the firm in the form of assets and the means by which the assets were financed, whether the funds were raised by borrowing (liabilities) or by selling ownership shares (equity). Argile's year-end 1998 and 1999 balance sheets are given in Table 13-2. The top portion of the balance sheet shows that on December 31, 1999, Argile's assets totaled $850.4 million, while the bottom portion shows the liabilities and equity, or the claims against these assets. The assets are listed in order of their "liquidity," or the length of time it typically takes to convert them to cash. The claims are listed in the order in which they must be paid: Accounts payable generally must be paid within 30 to 45 days, accruals are payable within 60 to 90 days, and so on, down to the stockholders' equity accounts, which represent ownership and need never be "paid off."

Some additional points about the balance sheet are worth noting:

1. **Cash versus other assets.** Although the assets are all stated in terms of dollars, only cash represents actual money. Receivables are bills others owe Argile; inventories show the dollars the company has invested in raw materials, work-in-process, and finished goods available for sale; and net fixed assets reflect the amount of money Argile paid for its plant and equipment when it acquired

---

TABLE 13-2

Argile Textiles: December 31 Comparative Balance Sheets (millions of dollars)

		1999		1998
Assets				
Cash and marketable securities		$ 20.4		$ 40.0
Accounts receivable		180.0		160.0
Inventories		270.0		200.0
Total current assets		470.4		400.0
Gross plant and equipment	680.0		600.0	
Less: Accumulated depreciation	300.0		250.0	
Net plant and equipment		380.0		350.0
Total assets		$850.4		$750.0
Liabilities and Equity				
Accounts payable		$ 30.0		$15.0
Accruals		60.0		55.0
Notes payable		40.0		35.0
Total current liabilities		130.0		105.0
Long-term bonds		300.0		255.0
Total liabilities		430.0		360.0
Common stock (25,000,000)		130.0		130.0
Retained earnings		290.4		260.0
Owners' equity		420.4		390.0
Total liabilities and equity		$850.4		$750.0

NOTE: Argile has no preferred stock, so owners' equity includes common equity only.

those assets less the amount that has been written off (depreciated) since the acquisition of those assets. The noncash assets should produce cash over time, but they do not represent cash in hand, and the amount of cash they would bring if they were sold today could be higher or lower than the values at which they are carried on the books (their book values).

2. **Liabilities versus stockholders' equity.** The claims against assets are of two types — liabilities (or money the company owes) and the stockholders' ownership position.[2] The balance sheet must *balance,* so the **common stockholders' equity, or net worth**, is a residual that represents the amount stockholders would receive if all of the firm's assets could be sold at their book values and all of the liabilities could be paid at their book values. Argile's 1999 net worth is $420.4 million. But, suppose assets decline in value, perhaps because some of the accounts receivable are written off as bad debts. If liabilities remain constant, the value of the stockholders' equity must decline. Therefore, the risk of asset value fluctuations is borne by the stockholders. Note, however, that if asset values rise, these benefits will accrue exclusively to the stockholders. The change in the firm's net worth is reflected by changes in the retained earnings account; if bad debts are written off on the asset side of the balance sheet, the retained earnings balance is reduced on the liabilities and equity side.

3. **Breakdown of the common equity account.** The common equity section is divided into three accounts — common stock, paid-in capital, and retained earnings. The **retained earnings** account is built up over time as the firm "saves," or reinvests, a part of its earnings rather than paying everything out as dividends. The other two common equity accounts arise from the issuance of stock to raise capital.

The breakdown of the common equity accounts shows whether the company actually earned the funds reported in its equity accounts or whether the funds came mainly from selling stock. This information is important both to creditors and to stockholders. For instance, a potential creditor would be interested in the amount of money the owners put up, while stockholders would want to know the form in which the money was put up.

4. **Accounting alternatives.** Not every firm uses the same method to determine the account balances shown on the balance sheet. For instance, Argile uses the FIFO (first-in, first-out) method to determine the inventory value shown on its balance sheet. It could have used the LIFO (last-in, first-out) method. During a period of rising prices, compared with LIFO, FIFO will produce a higher balance sheet inventory value but a lower cost of goods sold, thus a higher net income.

In some cases, a company uses one accounting method to construct financial statements provided to stockholders and another accounting method for tax purposes, internal reports, and so on. For example, a company will use the most accelerated method permissible to calculate depreciation for tax purposes because accelerated methods lower the current taxable income. At the same time, the company might use straight line depreciation for constructing financial statements reported to stockholders because a higher net income

COMMON STOCKHOLDERS'
EQUITY (NET WORTH)
The capital supplied by
common stockholders —
capital stock, paid-in capital,
retained earnings, and,
occasionally, certain
reserves.

RETAINED EARNINGS
That portion of the firm's
earnings that has been
saved rather than paid out
as dividends.

---

[2]One could divide liabilities into (1) debts owed to someone and (2) other items, such as deferred taxes, reserves, and so on. Because we do not make this distinction, the terms *debt* and *liabilities* are used synonymously.

results. There is nothing illegal or unethical with this practice, but, when evaluating firms, users of financial statements must be aware that more than one accounting alternative is available for constructing financial statements.

5. **The time dimension.** The balance sheet can be thought of as a snapshot of the firm's financial position *at a point in time.* The income statement, on the other hand, reports on operations over *a period of time.* The balance sheet changes every day as inventories are increased or decreased, as fixed assets are added or retired, as liabilities are increased or decreased, and so on. Companies whose businesses are seasonal have especially large changes in their balance sheets during the year. For example, most retailers have large inventories just before Christmas but low inventories and high accounts receivable just after Christmas. Therefore, firms' balance sheets will change over the year, depending on the date on which the statement is constructed.

Statement of Retained Earnings

STATEMENT OF RETAINED EARNINGS
A statement reporting the change in the firm's retained earnings as a result of the income generated and retained during the year. The balance sheet figure for retained earnings is the sum of the earnings retained for each year the firm has been in business.

Changes in the common equity accounts between balance sheet dates are reported in the **statement of retained earnings.** Argile's statement is shown in Table 13-3. The company earned $59.4 million during 1999, it paid out $29 million in common dividends, and it retained $30.4 million for reinvestment in the business. Thus, the balance sheet item "Retained earnings" increased from $260.0 million at the end of 1998 to $290.4 million reported at the end of 1999. Note that the balance sheet account "Retained earnings" represents a claim *against assets,* not assets per se. Further, firms retain earnings primarily to expand the business, and this means investing in plant and equipment, in inventories, and so forth, *not* necessarily in a bank account. Changes in retained earnings represent the recognition that income generated by the firm during the accounting period has been reinvested in assets rather than paid out as dividends to stockholders. *Thus, retained earnings as reported on the balance sheet do not represent cash and are not "available" for the payment of dividends or anything else.*[3]

TABLE 13-3

Argile Textiles: Statement of Retained Earnings for the Year Ending December 31, 1999 (millions of dollars)

Balance of retained earnings, December 31, 1998	$260.0
Add: 1999 net income	59.4
Less: 1999 dividends to stockholders	(29.0)
Balance of retained earnings, December 31, 1999	$290.4

---

[3]A positive number in the retained earnings account indicates only that in the past, according to generally accepted accounting principles, the firm has earned an income, but its dividends have been less than its reported income. Even though a company reports record earnings and shows an increase in the retained earnings account, it still may be short of cash.

The same situation holds for individuals. You might own a new BMW (no loan), lots of clothes, and an expensive stereo, and, hence, have a high net worth, but if you had only 23 cents in your pocket plus $5 in your checking account, you would still be short of cash.

Accounting Income versus Cash Flow

When you studied the construction of income statements in accounting, the emphasis was probably on determining the net income of the firm. In finance, however, as we discussed in previous chapters, we focus on *cash flows* because the value of an asset (or a whole firm) is determined by the cash flows it generates. The firm's net income is important, but cash flows are even more important, because cash is needed to continue normal business operations such as the payment of financial obligations, the purchase of assets, and the payment of dividends.

As we discussed in Chapter 5, the goal of the firm should be to maximize the price of its stock. And, as we discovered in Chapter 7, the value of any asset, including a share of stock, depends on the cash flows produced by the asset. Thus, managers should strive to maximize cash flows available to investors over the long run. A business's **cash flows** include the cash receipts and the cash disbursements. The income statement contains revenues and expenses, some of which are cash items and some of which are noncash items. Generally the largest noncash item included on the income statement is depreciation, which is an operating cost. We need to understand the role of depreciation for the recognition of income, as well as the impact depreciation has on cash flows.

CASH FLOWS
The cash receipts and the cash disbursements, as opposed to the revenues and expenses reported for the computation of net income, generated by a firm during some specified period.

Depreciation results because we want to match revenues and expenses to compute the income earned by the firm during a specific accounting period — not because we want to match cash inflows and cash outflows. When a firm purchases a long-term asset, it is intended to be used to produce revenues for many years in the future. The cash payment for the asset occurs on the date of purchase. But, because the productive capacity of the asset is not used up in the year of purchase, its full cost is not recognized as an expense in that year. Rather, the value of the asset is expensed away over its lifetime as it is used to generate revenues and its value declines. Depreciation is the means by which the reduction in the asset's value, which is an operating cost, is matched with the revenues the asset helps to produce. The bottom line is that *depreciation is a noncash charge used to compute net income, so, if net income is used to obtain an estimate of the net cash flow from operations, the amount of depreciation must be added back to the income figure.*

ACCOUNTING PROFIT
A firm's net income as reported on its income statement.

Cash flows generally are related to **accounting profit**, which is simply net income reported on the income statement. Although companies with relatively high accounting profits generally have relatively high cash flows, the relationship is not precise. Therefore, investors are concerned with cash flow projections as well as profit projections.

Firms can be thought of as having two separate but related bases of value: *existing assets,* which provide profits and cash flows, and *growth opportunities,* which represent opportunities to make new investments that will increase future profits and cash flows. The ability to take advantage of growth opportunities often depends on the availability of the cash needed to buy new assets and the cash flows from existing assets are often the primary source of the funds used to make profitable new investments. This is another reason both investors and managers are concerned with cash flows as well as profits.

OPERATING CASH FLOWS
Those cash flows that arise from normal operations; the difference between cash collections and cash expenses.

For our purposes, it is useful to divide cash flows into two classes: (1) *operating cash flows* and (2) *other cash flows.* **Operating cash flows** are those that arise from normal operations, and they are, in essence, the difference between cash collections and cash expenses, including taxes paid. Other cash flows arise from borrowing, from the sale of fixed assets, or from the repurchase of common stock. Our focus here is on operating cash flows.

Operating cash flows can differ from accounting profits (or net income) for two primary reasons:

1. All the taxes reported on the income statement might not have to be paid during the current year, or, under certain circumstances, the actual cash payments for taxes might exceed the tax figure deducted from sales to calculate net income. The reasons for these tax cash flow differentials are discussed in detail in accounting courses.
2. Sales might be on credit, hence not represent cash, and some of the expenses (or costs) deducted from sales to determine profits might not be cash costs. Most important, depreciation is not a cash cost.

Thus, operating cash flows could be larger or smaller than accounting profits during any given year.

The Cash Flow Cycle

As we discussed in the last chapter, the production/sales functions of companies generally go through the cycle of (1) purchasing materials, which leads to (a) an increase in inventories and (b) a reduction in cash or an increase in payables, and (2) selling the finished product, which leads to (a) a reduction of inventories, (b) an increase in cash or accounts receivable, and (c) a profit, if the sales price exceeds the cost of the item sold. So, when Argile sells its products, both the income statement and the balance sheet are affected. It is critical that you understand (1) businesses deal with physical units such as autos, computers, or aluminum, (2) physical transactions are translated into dollar terms through the accounting system, and (3) the purpose of financial analysis is to examine the accounting numbers to determine how efficiently the firm produces and sells physical goods and services and to evaluate the financial position of the firm.

Several factors make financial analysis difficult. One of them is the variations that exist in accounting methods among firms, as was discussed previously. Another factor involves timing — an action is taken at one point in time, but its full effects cannot be accurately measured until some later period.

CASH FLOW CYCLE
The way in which actual net cash, as opposed to accounting net income, flows into or out of the firm during some specified period.

To understand how timing influences the financial statements, we must understand the **cash flow cycle** as set forth in Figure 13-1. In the figure, rectangles represent balance sheet accounts — assets and claims against assets — whereas circles represent income items and cash flow activities that affect balance sheet accounts. Each rectangle can be thought of as a reservoir, and there is a certain amount of the asset or liability in the reservoir (account) on each balance sheet date. Various transactions cause changes in the accounts, just as adding or subtracting water changes the level in a reservoir. The direction of the change in each reservoir is indicated by the direction of the arrow(s) connected to that reservoir. For example, because collecting an account receivable reduces the receivables reservoir but increases the cash reservoir, an arrow goes *from* the accounts receivable reservoir *to* the collections circle, then *from* the collections circle *to* the cash and marketable securities reservoir.

FIGURE 13-1

Cash and Materials Flows within Argile, 1999 (millions of dollars)

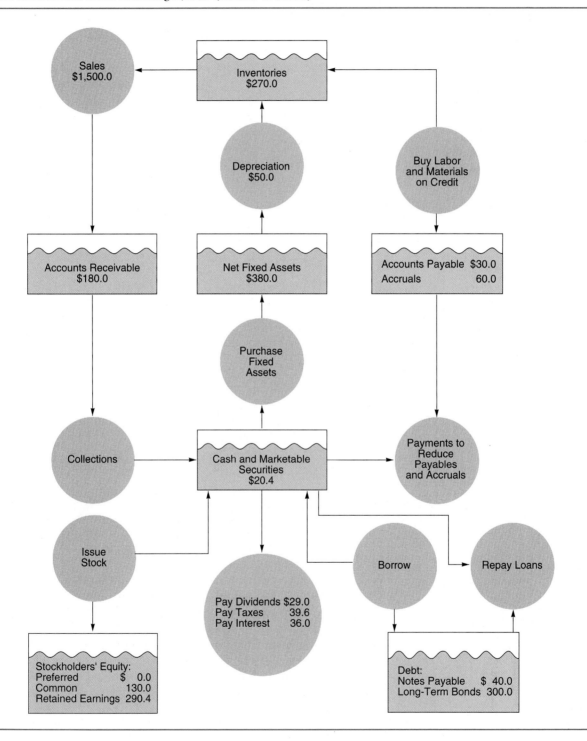

The cash account is the focal point of the figure. Certain events, such as collecting accounts receivable or borrowing money from the bank, cause the cash account to increase, while the payment of taxes, interest, dividends, and accounts payable cause it to decline. Similar comments could be made about all the balance sheet accounts — their balances rise, fall, or remain constant depending on events that occur during the period under study, which for Argile is January 1, 1999, through December 31, 1999.

Projected increases in sales might require the firm to raise cash by borrowing from its bank or by selling new stock. For example, if Argile anticipates an increase in sales, it will (1) expend cash to buy or build fixed assets; (2) step up purchases of raw materials, thereby increasing both raw materials inventories and accounts payable; (3) increase production, which will lead to an increase in both accrued wages and work-in-process; and (4) eventually build up its finished goods inventory. Some cash will have been expended and hence removed from the cash account, and the firm will have obligated itself to expend still more cash within a few weeks to pay off its accounts payable and its accrued wages. These cash-using events will have occurred *before* any new cash has been generated from sales. Even when the expected sales do occur, there will still be a lag in the generation of cash until receivables are collected. Depending on how much cash the firm had at the beginning of the buildup, the length of its production/sales cycle, and how long it can delay payment of its own payables and accrued wages, Argile might have to obtain substantial amounts of additional cash by selling stock or bonds or by borrowing from the bank. This is the concept called the cash conversion cycle that we described in Chapter 12.

If a firm runs out of cash and cannot obtain enough to meet its obligations, then it cannot operate, and it will have to declare bankruptcy. In fact, every year, thousands of companies are forced to do just that. Therefore, an accurate cash flow forecast is a critical element in managerial finance.[4] Financial analysts are well aware of all this, and they use the analytical techniques discussed in the remainder of this chapter to help discover cash flow problems before they become serious.

Statement of Cash Flows

STATEMENT OF CASH FLOWS
A statement reporting the impact of a firm's operating, investing, and financing activities on cash flows over an accounting period.

The graphic cash flow analysis set forth in Figure 13-1 is converted into numerical form and reported in annual reports as the **statement of cash flows**. This statement is designed to show how the firm's operations have affected its cash position by examining the investment (uses of cash) and financing decisions (sources of cash) of the firm. The information contained in the statement of cash flows can help answer questions such as these: Is the firm generating the cash needed to purchase additional fixed assets for growth? Does the firm have excess cash flows that can be used to repay debt or to invest in new products? This information is useful both for financial managers and investors, so the statement of cash flows is an important part of the annual report.

Constructing a statement of cash flows is relatively easy. First, to some extent, the cash flow effects of a firm's operations are shown in its income statement. For example, Argile reported its 1999 net income as $59.4 million, which we know

---

[4]The mechanics of a cash forecast are explained in Chapter 14.

includes a $50 million depreciation expense that is a noncash operating cost. So, if the $50 million depreciation expense is added back to the $59.4 million net income, we have an *estimate* of cash flows from normal operations equal to $109.4 million. But, for most firms, some of the reported revenues have not been collected and some of the reported expenses have not been paid at the time the income statement is constructed. To adjust the estimate of cash flows obtained from the income statement and to account for cash flows not reflected in the income statement, we need to examine the impact of changes in the balance sheet accounts during the year in question, which is fiscal year 1999 for Argile. Looking at the changes in the balance sheet accounts from the beginning to the end of the year, we want to identify which items provided cash (source) and which items used cash (use) during the year. To determine whether a change in a balance sheet account was a source or a use of cash, we can use the following simple rules:

Sources of Cash	**Uses of Cash**
Increase in a Liability or Equity Account	***Decrease in a Liability or Equity Account***
Borrowing funds or selling stock provides the firm with cash	Paying off a loan or buying back stock uses cash
Decrease in an Asset Account	***Increase in an Asset Account***
Selling inventory or collecting receivables provides cash	Buying fixed assets or buying more inventory uses cash

Using these rules, we can identify which changes in Argile's balance sheet accounts provided cash and which changes used cash during 1999. Table 13-4

TABLE 13-4

Argile Textiles: Cash Sources and Uses during 1999 (millions of dollars)

			Change	
	12/31/99	12/31/98	Sources	Uses
Balance Sheet Changes				
Cash and marketable securities	$ 20.4	$40.0	$ 19.6	
Accounts receivable	180.0	160.0		$20.0
Inventory	270.0	200.0		70.0
Gross plant and equipment	680.0	600.0		80.0
Accounts payable	30.0	15.0	15.0	
Accruals	60.0	55.0	5.0	
Notes payable	40.0	35.0	5.0	
Long-term bonds	300.0	255.0	45.0	
Common stock (25,000,000)	130.0	130.0		
Income Statement Information				
Net income	$ 59.4			
Add: Depreciation	50.0			
Gross cash flow from operations	$109.4		109.4	
Dividend payment	29.0			29.0
Totals			$199.0	$199.0

shows the results of this identification. In addition, the table includes the cash flow information contained in Argile's 1999 income statement.

The information contained in Table 13-4 can be used to construct the statement of cash flows shown in Table 13-5.[5] Each balance sheet change in Table 13-4 is classified as resulting from (1) operations, (2) long-term investments, or (3) financing activities. Operating cash flows are those associated with the production and sale of goods and services. The amount of net income plus depreciation is the primary operating cash flow, but changes in accounts payable, accounts receivable, inventories, and accruals are also classified as operating cash flows because these accounts are directly affected by the firm's day-to-day operations. Investment cash flows arise from the purchase or sale of plant, property, and equipment. Financing cash inflows result from issuing debt or common stock, while financing outflows occur when the firm pays dividends or repays debt. The cash inflows and outflows from these three activities are summed to determine their impact on the firm's liquidity position, which is measured by the change in the cash and marketable securities accounts.

The top part of Table 13-5 shows cash flows generated by and used in operations — for Argile, operations provided net cash flows of $39.4 million. The operating cash flows are generated principally from the day-to-day operations of the firm, and this amount can be determined by adjusting the net income figure to account for noncash items. The day-to-day operations of Argile in 1999 provided $109.4 million of funds; however, the increases in inventories and investment in receivables during the year accounted for a combined use of funds equal to more than 80 percent of this amount. The second section shows long-term investing activities. Argile purchased fixed assets totaling $80 million; this was its only investment activity during 1999. Argile's financing activities, shown in the lower section of Table 13-5, included borrowing from banks (notes payable), selling new bonds, and paying dividends to its common stockholders. Argile raised $50 million by borrowing, but it paid $29 million in dividends, so its net inflow of funds from financing activities during 1999 was $21 million.

When all of these sources and uses of cash are totaled, we see that Argile had a $19.6 million cash shortfall during 1999. It met that shortfall by drawing down its cash and marketable securities holdings by $19.6 million, as shown in Table 13-2, the firm's balance sheet, and Table 13-4.

Argile's statement of cash flows should be of some concern to the financial manager and to outside analysts. The company generated $39.4 million cash from operations, it spent $80 million on new fixed assets, and it paid out another $29 million in dividends. It covered these cash outlays by borrowing heavily, by selling off marketable securities, and by drawing down its bank account. Obviously, this situation cannot continue year after year, so something will have to be done. We will consider some of the actions the financial manager might recommend, but first we must examine the financial statements in more depth.

---

[5]There are two different formats for presenting the cash flow statement. The method we present here is called the *indirect method*. Cash flows from operations are calculated by starting with net income, adding back expenses not paid out of cash, and subtracting revenues that do not provide cash. Using the *direct method*, operating cash flows are found by summing all revenues that provide cash and then subtracting all expenses that are paid in cash. Both formats produce the same result, and both are accepted by the Financial Accounting Standards Board.

TABLE 13-5

Argile Textiles: Statement of Cash Flows for the Period ending December 31, 1999
(millions of dollars)

CASH FLOWS FROM OPERATING ACTIVITIES

Net income	$59.4	
Additions to Net Income		
Depreciation[a]	50.0	
Increase in accounts payable	15.0	
Increase in accruals	5.0	
Subtractions from Net Income		
Increase in accounts receivable	(20.0)	
Increase in inventory	(70.0)	
Net cash flow from operations		$39.4

CASH FLOWS FROM LONG-TERM INVESTING ACTIVITIES

Acquisition of fixed assets		($80.0)

CASH FLOWS FROM FINANCING ACTIVITIES

Increase in notes payable	$5.0	
Increase in bonds	45.0	
Dividend payment	(29.0)	
Net cash flow from financing		$21.0
Net change in cash		($19.6)
Cash at the beginning of the year		40.0
Cash at the end of the year		$20.4

---

[a]Depreciation is a noncash expense that was deducted when calculating net income. It must be added back to show the correct cash flow from operations.

Self-Test Questions

Identify the two types of information given in the annual report.

Describe these four basic financial statements: (1) the income statement, (2) the balance sheet, (3) the statement of retained earnings, and (4) the statement of cash flows.

Explain the following statement: "Retained earnings as reported on the balance sheet do not represent cash and are not 'available' for the payment of dividends or anything else."

Differentiate between operating cash flows and other cash flows.

List two reasons operating cash flows can differ from net income.

In accounting, the emphasis is on the determination of net income. What is emphasized in finance, and why is that emphasis important?

Assuming that depreciation is the only noncash cost, how can someone calculate the cash flow of a business?

Describe the general rules for identifying whether changes in balance sheet accounts represent sources or uses of cash.

Ratio Analysis

Financial statements provide information about a firm's position at a point in time as well as its operations over some past period. However, the real value of financial statements lies in the fact that they can be used to help predict the firm's financial position in the future and to determine expected earnings and dividends. From an investor's standpoint, *predicting the future is what financial statement analysis is all about,* while from management's standpoint, *financial statement analysis is useful both as a way to anticipate future conditions and, more important, as a starting point for planning actions that will influence the future course of events.*

An analysis of the firm's ratios is generally the first step in a financial analysis. The ratios are designed to show relationships between financial statement accounts *within* firms and *between* firms. Translating accounting numbers into relative values, or ratios, allows us to compare the financial position of one firm with another, even if their sizes are significantly different. For example, Firm A might have debt of $5,248,760 and interest charges of $419,900, while Firm B might have debt of $52,647,980 and interest charges of $3,948,600. Which company is stronger? The true burden of these debts, and the companies' ability to repay them, can be ascertained (1) by comparing each firm's debt with its assets and (2) by comparing the interest it must pay with the income it has available for payment of interest. Such comparisons are made by ratio analysis.

In the paragraphs that follow, we calculate the 1999 financial ratios for Argile Textiles and then evaluate those ratios in relation to the industry averages.[6] We should note that there exist many more ratios than we include here, but, because our intent is to give you an overview of financial statement analysis, we present a few of the more common ratios used by analysts. Also, note that all dollar amounts in the ratio calculations given here are in millions, except where per share values are used.

Liquidity Ratios

LIQUID ASSET
An asset that can be easily converted into cash without significant loss of its original value.

In the previous chapter, we discovered that a **liquid asset** is one that can be easily converted to cash without significant loss of its original value. Converting assets, especially current assets such as inventory and receivables, to cash is the primary means by which a firm obtains the funds needed to pay its current bills. Therefore, a firm's "liquid position" deals with the question of how well the firm is able to meet its current obligations. Short-term, or current, assets are more easily converted to cash (more liquid) than long-term assets. So, in general, one firm would be considered more liquid than another firm if it has a greater proportion of its total assets in the form of current assets.

Argile has debts totaling $130 million that must be paid off within the coming year. Will it have trouble satisfying those obligations? A full liquidity analysis

---

[6]In addition to the ratios discussed in this section, financial analysts employ a tool known as common size balance sheets and income statements. To form a *common size* balance sheet, one simply divides each asset and liability item by total assets and then expresses the result as a percentage. The resultant percentage statement can be compared with statements of larger or smaller firms or with those of the same firm over time. To form a common size income statement, one simply divides each income statement item by sales.

LIQUIDITY RATIOS
Ratios that show the relationship of a firm's cash and other current assets to its current liabilities.

requires the use of cash budgets (described in the next chapter), but by relating the amount of cash and other current assets to the firm's current obligations, ratio analysis provides a quick, easy-to-use measure of liquidity. Two commonly used **liquidity ratios** are discussed in this section.

CURRENT RATIO   The **current ratio** is calculated as follows:

$$\text{Current ratio} = \frac{\text{Current assets}}{\text{Current liabilities}}$$

$$= \frac{\$470.4}{\$130.0} = 3.6 \text{ times}$$

Industry average = 3.1 times

CURRENT RATIO
This ratio is calculated by dividing current assets by current liabilities. It indicates the extent to which current liabilities are covered by assets expected to be converted to cash in the near future.

If a company is getting into financial difficulty, it begins paying its bills (accounts payable) more slowly, borrowing more from its bank, and so forth. If current liabilities are rising faster than current assets, the current ratio will fall, and this could spell trouble. Because the current ratio provides the best single indicator of the extent to which the claims of short-term creditors are covered by assets that are expected to be converted to cash fairly quickly, it is the most commonly used measure of short-term solvency. Care must be taken when examining the current ratio, however, just as it should be when examining any ratio individually. For example, just because a firm has a low current ratio, even one below 1.0, this does not mean the current obligations cannot be met.

Argile's current ratio of 3.6 is above the average for its industry, 3.1, so, according to this measure, its liquidity position is somewhat stronger than the average textile firm. Because current assets are scheduled to be converted to cash in the near future, it is highly probable that they can be liquidated at close to their stated value. With a current ratio of 3.6, Argile could liquidate current assets at only 28 percent of book value and still pay off current creditors in full.[7]

Although industry average figures are discussed later in some detail, it should be noted at this point that an industry average is not a magic number that all firms should strive to maintain — in fact, some very well-managed firms are above the average while other good firms are below it. However, if a firm's ratios are far removed from the average for its industry, an analyst should be concerned about why this deviation occurs. Thus, a significant deviation from the industry average should signal the analyst (or management) to *check further*, even if the deviation is considered to be in the "good" direction. For example, we know that Argile's current ratio is a little above average. But, what would you conclude if Argile's current ratio actually was nearly twice that of the industry, perhaps 6.0×? Is this good? Maybe not. Because current assets, which are liquid, safe assets, generally generate lower rates of return than long-term assets, it might be argued that firms with too much liquidity are not investing wisely.

QUICK (ACID TEST) RATIO
This ratio is calculated by deducting inventories from current assets and dividing the remainder by current liabilities. The quick ratio is a variation of the current ratio.

QUICK, OR ACID TEST, RATIO   The **quick**, or **acid test, ratio** is calculated as follows:

---

[7]Argile's current ratio is 3.62 if the computation is carried to two decimal places (1/3.62 = 0.276, or nearly 28 percent). Note that 0.276($470.4) = $130, which is the amount of current liabilities.

$$\text{Quick, or acid test, ratio} = \frac{\text{Current assets} - \text{Inventories}}{\text{Current liabilities}}$$

$$= \frac{\$470.4 - \$270.0}{\$130.0} = \frac{\$200.4}{\$130.0} = 1.5 \text{ times}$$

Industry average = 1.9 times

Inventories typically are the least liquid of a firm's current assets, hence they are the assets on which losses are most likely to occur in the event of liquidation. Therefore, a measure of the firm's ability to pay off short-term obligations without relying on the sale of inventories is important.

The industry average quick ratio is 1.9, so Argile's ratio value of 1.5 is somewhat less than the industry's quick ratio, which suggests its level of inventories is high. Still, if the accounts receivable can be collected, the company can pay off its current liabilities even without having to liquidate its inventory.

Even though the current ratio is above the industry norm, the value of its quick ratio suggests that Argile's liquidity position is perhaps a little lower than the average firm in the industry. To get a better idea of why Argile is in this position, we must examine its asset management ratios.

Asset Management Ratios

ASSET MANAGEMENT RATIOS
A set of ratios that measures how effectively a firm is managing its assets.

The second group of ratios, the **asset management ratios**, measures how effectively the firm is managing its assets. These ratios are designed to answer this question: Does the total amount of each type of asset as reported on the balance sheet seem reasonable, too high, or too low in view of current and projected sales levels? Firms invest in assets to generate revenues both in the current period and in future periods. To purchase their assets, Argile and other companies must borrow or obtain funds from other sources. If they have too many assets, their interest expenses will be too high, hence their profits will be depressed. On the other hand, because production is affected by the capacity of assets, if assets are too low, profitable sales might be lost because the firm is unable to manufacture enough products.

INVENTORY TURNOVER RATIO
The ratio calculated by dividing cost of goods sold by inventories.

INVENTORY TURNOVER   The **inventory turnover ratio** is defined as follows[8]:

$$\text{Inventory turnover ratio} = \frac{\text{Cost of goods sold}}{\text{Inventories}}$$

$$= \frac{\$1,220.0}{\$270.0} = 4.5 \text{ times}$$

Industry average = 7.5 times

[8]Some compilers of financial ratio statistics, such as Dun & Bradstreet, use the ratio of sales to inventories carried at cost to represent inventory turnover. If this form of the inventory turnover ratio is used, we must recognize that the true turnover will be overstated because sales are stated at market prices while inventories are carried at cost.

As a rough approximation, each item of Argile's inventory is sold out and restocked, or "turned over," 4.5 times per year, which is considerably lower than the industry average of 7.5 times.[9] This suggests that Argile is holding excessive stocks of inventory; excess stocks are, of course, unproductive and represent an investment with a low or zero rate of return. Argile's low inventory turnover ratio makes us question the current ratio. With such a low turnover, we must wonder whether the firm is holding damaged or obsolete goods (e.g., textile types and patterns from previous years) not actually worth their stated value.

DAYS SALES OUTSTANDING (DSO)
The ratio calculated by dividing accounts receivable by average sales per day; indicates the average length of time it takes the firm to collect for credit sales.

Care must be used when calculating and using the inventory turnover ratio because purchases of inventory, thus the cost of goods sold figure, occur over the entire year, whereas the inventory figure is for one point in time. For this reason, it is better to use an average inventory measure.[10] If the firm's business is highly seasonal, or if there has been a strong upward or downward sales trend during the year, it is essential to make such an adjustment. To maintain comparability with industry averages, however, we did not use the average inventory figure in our computations.

DAYS SALES OUTSTANDING   **Days sales outstanding (DSO)**, also called the average collection period (ACP), is used to evaluate the firm's ability to collect its credit sales in a timely manner. DSO is calculated as follows[11]:

$$\text{DSO} = \frac{\text{Days sales}}{\text{outstanding}} = \frac{\text{Receivables}}{\text{Average sales per day}} = \frac{\text{Receivables}}{\left[\dfrac{\text{Annual sales}}{360}\right]}$$

$$= \frac{\$180.0}{\left[\dfrac{\$1,500.0}{360}\right]} = \frac{\$180.0}{\$4.167} = 43.2 \text{ days}$$

$$\text{Industry average} = 34.1 \text{ days}$$

The DSO represents the average length of time that the firm must wait after making a sale before receiving cash, which is the average collection period. Argile has about 43 days' sales outstanding, somewhat above the 34-day industry average.

---

[9]"Turnover" is a term that originated many years ago with the old Yankee peddler, who would load up his wagon with goods, then go off on his route to peddle his wares. The merchandise was his "working capital" because it was what he actually sold, or "turned over," to produce his profits, whereas his "turnover" was the number of trips he took each year. Annual sales divided by inventory equaled turnover, or trips per year. If he made 10 trips per year, stocked 100 pans, and made a gross profit of $5 per pan, his annual gross profit would be (100)($5)(10) = $5,000. If he went faster and made 20 trips per year, his gross profit would double, other things held constant.

[10]Preferably, the average inventory value should be calculated by summing the monthly figures during the year and dividing by 12. If monthly data are not available, one can add the beginning-of-year and end-of-year figures and divide by 2; this will adjust for growth but not for seasonal effects. Using the approach, Argile's average inventory for 1999 would be $235 = ($200 + $270)/2, and its inventory turnover would be 5.2 = $1,220/$235, which still is well below the given industry average.

[11]To compute DSO using this equation, we have to assume all of the firm's sales are credit. We usually compute DSO in this manner because information on credit sales is generally unavailable, so total sales must be used. Because all firms do not have the same percentage of credit sales, there is a chance that the days sales outstanding will be somewhat in error. Also, note that by convention the financial community generally uses 360 rather than 365 as the number of days in the year for purposes such as this.

The DSO also can be evaluated by comparison with the terms on which the firm sells its goods. For example, Argile's sales terms call for payment within 30 days, so the fact that sales are outstanding an average of 43 days indicates that customers, on the average, are not paying their bills on time. If the trend in DSO over the past few years has been rising, but the credit policy has not been changed, this would be even stronger evidence that steps should be taken to improve the time it takes to collect accounts receivable. This seems to be the case for Argile, because its 1998 DSO was about 40 days.

FIXED ASSETS TURNOVER RATIO
The ratio of sales to net fixed assets.

FIXED ASSETS TURNOVER The **fixed assets turnover ratio** measures how effectively the firm uses its plant and equipment to help generate sales. It is computed as follows:

$$\text{Fixed assets turnover ratio} = \frac{\text{Sales}}{\text{Net fixed assets}}$$

$$= \frac{\$1,500.0}{\$380.0} = 3.9 \text{ times}$$

Industry average = 4.0 times

Argile's ratio of 3.9 times is almost equal to the industry average, indicating that the firm is using its fixed assets about as intensively (efficiently) as are the other firms in the industry. Argile seems to have neither too much nor too few fixed assets in relation to other firms.

Care should be taken when using the fixed assets turnover ratio to compare different firms. Recall from accounting that most balance sheet accounts are stated in terms of historical costs. Inflation might cause the value of many assets that were purchased in the past to be seriously understated. Therefore, if we were comparing an old firm that acquired many of its fixed assets years ago at low prices with a new company that acquired its fixed assets only recently, we probably would find that the old firm had a higher fixed assets turnover. Because financial analysts typically do not have the data necessary to make inflation adjustments to specific assets, they must simply recognize that a problem exists and deal with it judgmentally. In Argile's case, the issue is not a serious one because all firms in the industry have been expanding at about the same rate; thus, the balance sheets of the comparison firms are indeed comparable.

TOTAL ASSETS TURNOVER RATIO
The ratio calculated by dividing sales by total assets.

TOTAL ASSETS TURNOVER The final asset management ratio, the **total assets turnover ratio,** measures the turnover of all of the firm's assets. It is calculated as follows:

$$\text{Total assets turnover ratio} = \frac{\text{Sales}}{\text{Total assets}}$$

$$= \frac{\$1,500.0}{\$850.4} = 1.8 \text{ times}$$

Industry average = 2.2 times

Argile's ratio is somewhat below the industry average, indicating that the company is not generating a sufficient volume of business given its investment in total assets. To become more efficient, sales should be increased, some assets should be disposed of, or a combination of these steps should be taken.

Our examination of Argile's asset management ratios shows that its fixed assets turnover ratio is very close to the industry average, but its total assets turnover is below average. The fixed assets turnover ratio excludes current assets, while the total assets turnover ratio does not. Therefore, comparison of these ratios suggests that Argile seems to have a liquidity problem. The fact that the inventory turnover ratio and the average collection period are worse than the industry averages suggests, at least in part, that there might be problems with inventory and receivables management. Slow sales and slow collections of credit sales suggest Argile might rely more heavily on external funds, such as loans, than the industry to pay current obligations. Examining the debt management ratios will help us to determine if this actually is the case.

Debt Management Ratios

The extent to which a firm uses debt financing has three important implications: (1) By raising funds through debt, stockholder ownership is not diluted. (2) Creditors look to the equity, or owner-supplied funds, to provide a margin of safety; if the stockholders have provided only a small proportion of the total financing, the risks of the enterprise are borne mainly by its creditors. (3) If the firm earns more on investments financed with borrowed funds than it pays in interest, the return on the owners' capital is magnified, or "leveraged."

FINANCIAL LEVERAGE
The use of debt financing.

Financial leverage, or borrowing, affects the expected rate of return realized by stockholders for two reasons: (1) The interest on debt is tax deductible while dividends are not, so paying interest lowers the firm's tax bill, all else equal; and, (2) usually the rate a firm earns from its investments in assets is different from the rate at which it borrows. If the firm has healthy operations, it generally invests the funds it raises at a rate of return that is greater than the interest rate on its debt. In combination with the tax advantage debt has compared with stock, the higher investment rate of return produces a magnified positive return to the stockholders. Under these conditions, leverage works to the advantage of the firm and its stockholders. Unfortunately, financial leverage is a two-edged sword. When the firm experiences poor business conditions, typically, sales are lower and costs are higher than expected, but the cost of borrowing still must be paid. The *costs* (interest payments) associated with borrowing are contractual and do not vary with sales, and they must be paid to keep the firm from potential bankruptcy. Therefore, the required interest payments might be a very significant burden for a firm that has liquidity problems. In fact, if the interest payments are high enough, a firm with a positive operating income actually could end up with a negative return to stockholders. Under these conditions, leverage works to the detriment of the firm and its stockholders.

A detailed discussion of financial leverage is given in the next chapter. For the purposes of ratio analysis, we need to understand that firms with relatively high debt ratios have higher expected returns when the business is normal or good, but they are exposed to risk of loss when the business is poor. Thus, firms with low debt ratios are less risky, but they also forgo the opportunity to leverage up their return on equity. The prospects of high returns are desirable, but investors are averse to risk. Therefore, as we discovered in Chapter 11, decisions about the use of debt require firms to balance higher expected returns against increased risk. For the purposes of our discussion here, we look at two procedures analysts use to examine the firm's debt in a financial statement analysis: (1) They check balance sheet ratios to determine the extent to which borrowed funds have been used to finance assets, and (2) they review income statement ratios to determine how well operating profits can cover fixed charges such as interest. These two sets of ratios are complementary, so analysts use both types.

DEBT RATIO
The ratio of total debt to total assets. It is a measure of the percentage of funds provided by creditors.

DEBT RATIO   The **debt ratio** measures the percentage of the firm's assets financed by creditors (borrowing), and it is computed as follows:

$$\text{Debt ratio} = \frac{\text{Total debt}}{\text{Total assets}}$$

$$= \frac{\$130.0 + \$300.0}{\$850.4} = \frac{\$430.0}{\$850.4} = 0.506 = 50.6\%$$

Industry average = 46.2%

Total debt includes both current liabilities and long-term debt. Creditors prefer low debt ratios because the lower the ratio, the greater the cushion against creditors' losses in the event of liquidation. The owners, on the other hand, can benefit from leverage because it magnifies earnings, thus the return to stockholders. But, too much debt often leads to financial difficulty, which eventually might cause bankruptcy.

Argile's debt ratio is 50.6 percent; this means that its creditors have supplied about half the firm's total financing. Because the average debt ratio for this industry is 46.2 percent, Argile might find it difficult to borrow additional funds without first raising more equity capital through a stock issue. Creditors might be reluctant to lend the firm more money, and management would be subjecting the firm to a greater chance of bankruptcy if it sought to increase the debt ratio much further by borrowing additional funds.[12]

TIMES-INTEREST-EARNED (TIE) RATIO
The TIE ratio is computed by dividing earnings before interest and taxes (EBIT) by interest charges; measures the ability of the firm to meet its annual interest payments.

TIMES INTEREST EARNED   The **times-interest-earned (TIE) ratio** is defined as follows:

$$\text{Times-interest-earned (TIE) ratio} = \frac{\text{EBIT}}{\text{Interest charges}}$$

---

[12]The ratio of debt to equity also is used in financial analysis. The debt-to-assets (D/A) and debt-to-equity (D/E) ratios are simply transformations of each other because total debt plus total equity must equal total assets:

$$D/E = \frac{D/A}{1 - D/A} \text{ and } D/A = \frac{D/E}{1 + D/E}$$

$$= \frac{\$140.0}{\$41.0} = 3.4 \text{ times}$$

$$\text{Industry average} = 5.4 \text{ times}$$

The TIE ratio measures the extent to which earnings before interest and taxes (EBIT), which represents the firm's operating income, can decline before the firm is unable to meet its annual interest costs. Failure to meet this obligation can bring legal action by the firm's creditors, possibly resulting in bankruptcy. Note that earnings before interest and taxes, rather than net income, is used in the numerator. Because interest is paid with pre-tax dollars, the firm's ability to pay current interest is not affected by taxes.

Argile's interest is covered 3.4 times. Because the industry average is 5.4 times, compared with firms in the same business, Argile is covering its interest charges by a low margin of safety. Thus, the TIE ratio reinforces our conclusion based on the debt ratio that Argile would face difficulties if it attempted to borrow additional funds.

FIXED CHARGE COVERAGE RATIO
This ratio expands the TIE ratio to include the firm's annual long-term lease payments and sinking fund payments.

FIXED CHARGE COVERAGE   The **fixed charge coverage ratio** is similar to the TIE ratio, but it is more inclusive because it recognizes that many firms lease assets and also must make sinking fund payments.[13] Leasing is widespread in certain industries, making this ratio preferable to the TIE ratio for many purposes. Argile's annual long-term lease payments are $10 million, and it must make an annual $8 million sinking fund payment to help retire its debt. Because sinking fund payments must be paid with after-tax dollars, whereas interest and lease payments are paid with pre-tax dollars, the sinking fund payment must be divided by (1 − Tax rate) to find the before-tax income required to pay taxes and still have enough left to make the sinking fund payment.[14]

Fixed charges include interest, annual long-term lease obligations, and sinking fund payments, and the fixed charge coverage ratio is defined as follows:

$$\text{Fixed charge coverage ratio} = \frac{\text{EBIT} + \text{Lease payments}}{\text{Interest charges} + \text{Lease payments} + \left[\dfrac{\text{Sinking fund payments}}{(1 - \text{Tax rate})} \right]}$$

$$= \frac{\$140.0 + \$10.0}{\$41.0 + \$10.0 + \left[\dfrac{\$8.0}{(1 - 0.4)} \right]} = 2.3 \text{ times}$$

$$\text{Industry average} = 4.8 \text{ times}$$

---

[13]Generally, a long-term lease is defined as one that extends for more than one year. Thus, rent incurred under a six-month lease would not be included in the fixed charge coverage ratio, but rental payments under a one-year or longer lease would be defined as a fixed charge and would be included. A sinking fund is a required annual payment designed to reduce the balance of a bond or preferred stock issue.

[14]Note that $8/(1 − 0.4) = $13.33. Therefore, if the company had pre-tax income of $13.33, it could pay taxes at a 40 percent rate and have exactly $8 left with which to make the sinking fund payment. Thus, to pay an $8 sinking fund requirement, Argile needs $13.33 of pre-tax income. Dividing by (1 − T) is called "grossing up" an after-tax value to find the corresponding pre-tax value.

In the numerator of the fixed charge coverage ratio, the lease payments are added to EBIT because we want to determine the firm's ability to cover its fixed charges from the income generated before any fixed charges are deducted. The EBIT figure represents the firm's operating income, net of lease payments, so the lease payments must be added back.

Argile's fixed charges are covered only 2.3 times, as opposed to an industry average of 4.8 times. Again, this indicates that the firm is weaker than average, and this points out the difficulties Argile probably would encounter if it attempted to increase its debt.

Our examination of Argile's debt management ratios indicates that the company has a debt ratio that is *above* the industry average, and it has coverage ratios that are *below* the industry averages. This suggests that Argile is in a somewhat dangerous position with respect to leverage (debt). In fact, Argile might have great difficulty borrowing additional funds until its debt position improves. If Argile cannot pay its current obligations as a result, it might be forced into bankruptcy. To see how Argile's debt position has affected its profits, we next examine the profitability ratios.

PROFITABILITY RATIOS
A group of ratios showing the effect of liquidity, asset management, and debt management on operating results.

Profitability Ratios

Profitability is the net result of a number of policies and decisions. The ratios examined thus far provide some information about the way the firm is operating, but the **profitability ratios** show the combined effects of liquidity, asset management, and debt management on operating results.

NET PROFIT MARGIN ON SALES
This ratio measures net income per dollar of sales; it is calculated by dividing net income by sales.

NET PROFIT MARGIN ON SALES The **net profit margin on sales**, which gives the profit per dollar of sales, is calculated as follows:

$$\text{Profit margin on sales} = \frac{\text{Net income}}{\text{Sales}}$$

$$= \frac{\$59.4}{\$1,500.0} = 0.040 = 4.0\%$$

Industry average = 4.9%

Argile's profit margin is below the industry average of 4.9 percent, indicating that costs are too high relative to sales revenues. Remember that, according to the debt ratio, Argile has a greater proportion of debt than the industry average, and the times interest earned ratio shows that Argile's interest payments on its debt are not covered as well as the rest of the industry. This is one of the reasons Argile's profit margin is low. To see this, we can compute the ratio of EBIT (operating income) to sales, which is called the *operating profit margin*. Argile's operating profit margin of 9.3 percent is exactly the same as the industry, so the cause of the low net profit margin is the relatively high interest attributable to the firm's above-average use of debt.

RETURN ON TOTAL ASSETS   The ratio of net income to total assets measures the **return on total assets (ROA)** after interest and taxes:

$$\text{Return on total} \atop \text{assets (ROA)} = \frac{\text{Net income}}{\text{Total assets}}$$

$$= \frac{\$59.4}{\$850.4} = 0.070 = 7.0\%$$

Industry average = 10.7%

RETURN ON TOTAL ASSETS (ROA)
The ratio of net income to total assets; provides an idea of the overall return on investment earned by the firm.

Argile's 7.0 percent return is well below the 10.7 percent average for the industry. This low return results from the company's above-average use of debt.

RETURN ON COMMON EQUITY   The ratio of net income to common equity measures the **return on common equity (ROE),** or the *rate of return on stockholders' investment*[15]:

$$\text{Return on common} \atop \text{equity (ROE)} = \frac{\text{Net income available to common stockholders}}{\text{Common equity}}$$

$$= \frac{\$59.4}{\$420.4} = 0.141 = 14.1\%$$

Industry average = 16.9%

RETURN ON COMMON EQUITY (ROE)
The ratio of net income to common equity; measures the rate of return on common stockholders' investment.

Argile's 14.1 percent return is below the 16.9 percent industry average. This result is due to the company's greater use of debt (leverage), a point that is analyzed further later in this chapter and the next chapter.

Our examination of Argile's profitability ratios shows that its operating results have suffered due to its tenuous liquidity position, its poor asset management, and its above-average debt. In the final group of ratios, we examine Argile's market value ratios to get an indication of how investors feel about the company's current position.

Market Value Ratios

MARKET VALUE RATIOS
A set of ratios that relate the firm's stock price to its earnings and book value per share.

The **market value ratios** represent a group of ratios that relate the firm's stock price to its earnings and book value per share. These ratios give management an indication of what investors think of the company's past performance and future

---

[15]Net income available to common stockholders is computed by subtracting preferred dividends from net income. Because Argile has no preferred stock, the net income available to common stockholders is the same as the net income.

prospects. If the firm's liquidity, asset management, debt management, and profitability ratios are all good, then its market value ratios will be high, and its stock price will probably be as high as can be expected. Of course, the opposite also is true.

PRICE/EARNINGS (P/E) RATIO
The ratio of the price per share to earnings per share; shows the dollar amount investors will pay for $1 of current earnings.

PRICE/EARNINGS RATIO The **price/earnings (P/E) ratio** shows how much investors are willing to pay per dollar of reported profits. To compute the P/E ratio, we need to know the firm's earnings per share (EPS):

$$\text{Earnings per share} = \frac{\text{Net income available to common stockholders}}{\text{Number of common shares outstanding}}$$

$$= \frac{\$59.4}{25} = \$2.38$$

Argile's stock sells for $23, so with an EPS of $2.38 its P/E ratio is 9.7:

$$\text{Price/earnings (P/E) ratio} = \frac{\text{Market price per share}}{\text{Earnings per share}}$$

$$= \frac{\$23.00}{\$2.38} = 9.7 \text{ times}$$

Industry average = 11.0 times

Other things held constant, P/E ratios are higher for firms with high growth prospects, but they are lower for riskier firms. Because Argile's P/E ratio is below those of other textile manufacturers, this suggests that the company is regarded as being somewhat riskier than most, as having poorer growth prospects, or both. From our analysis of its debt management ratios, we know Argile has above-average risk associated with leverage, but we do not know if its growth prospects are poor.

MARKET/BOOK RATIO The ratio of a stock's market price to its book value gives another indication of how investors regard the company. Companies with relatively high rates of return on equity generally sell at higher multiples of book value than those with low returns. First, we find Argile's book value per share:

$$\text{Book value per share} = \frac{\text{Common equity}}{\text{Number of common shares outstanding}}$$

$$= \frac{\$420.4}{25} = \$16.82$$

Now we divide the market value per share by the book value per share to get a **market/book (M/B) ratio** of 1.4 times for Argile:

$$\text{Market/book ratio} = \frac{\text{Market price per share}}{\text{Book value per share}}$$

MARKET/BOOK (M/B) RATIO
The ratio of a stock's market price to its book value.

$$= \frac{\$23.00}{\$16.82} = 1.4$$

Industry average = 2.0

Investors are willing to pay less for Argile's book value than for that of an average textile manufacturer. This should not be surprising; as we discovered previously, Argile has generated below-average returns with respect to both total assets and common equity. Generally, the stocks of firms that earn high rates of return on their assets sell for prices well in excess of their book values. For very successful firms, the market/book ratio can be as much as 10 to 15 times.

Our examination of Argile's market value ratios indicates that investors are not excited about the future prospects of its common stock as an investment. Perhaps the investors believe Argile is headed toward bankruptcy if actions are not taken to correct its liquidity and asset management problems and to improve its leverage position. A method used to get an indication of the direction a firm is headed is to evaluate the trends of the ratios over the past few years to answer the question: Is the firm's position improving or deteriorating?

Trend Analysis

TREND ANALYSIS
An analysis of a firm's financial ratios over time; used to determine the improvement or deterioration in its financial situation.

The analysis of its ratios indicates that Argile's current financial position is somewhat poor when compared with the industry norm. But, this analysis does not tell us whether Argile's financial position is better or worse than previous years. To determine in which direction the firm is headed, it is important to analyze trends in ratios. By examining the paths taken in the past, **trend analysis** provides information about whether the firm's financial position is more likely to improve or deteriorate in the future. A simple approach to trend analysis is to construct graphs containing both the firm's ratios and the industry averages for the past five years. Using this approach, we can examine both the direction of the movement in, and the relationships between the firm's ratios and the industry averages. Figure 13-2 shows that Argile's return on equity has declined since 1996, even though the industry average has steadily increased at a moderate rate. Other ratios could be analyzed similarly. If we were to compare Argile's ratios from 1999 with those from 1998, we would discover Argile's financial position has deteriorated, not strengthened — this is not a good trend.

Summary of Ratio Analysis: The Du Pont Chart

DU PONT CHART
A chart designed to show the relationships among return on investment, asset turnover, the profit margin, and leverage.

Table 13-6 summarizes Argile's ratios, and Figure 13-3, which is called a **Du Pont chart** because that company's managers developed the general approach, shows the relationships between return on investment, asset turnover, the profit margin, and leverage. The left side of the chart develops the profit margin on sales.

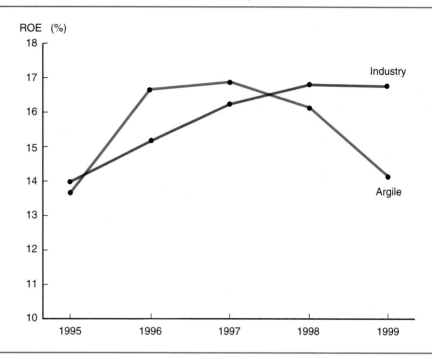

FIGURE 13-2

Return on Equity for Argile Textiles and the Industry

The various expense items are listed and then summed to obtain Argile's total costs, which are subtracted from sales to obtain the company's net income. When we divide net income by sales, we find that 4.0 percent of each sales dollar is left over for stockholders. If the profit margin is low or trending down, one can examine the individual expense items to identify and then correct problems.

DU PONT EQUATION
A formula that gives the rate of return on assets by multiplying the profit margin by the total assets turnover.

The right side of Figure 13-3 lists the various categories of assets, totals them, and then divides sales by total assets to find the number of times Argile "turns its assets over" each year. The company's total assets turnover ratio is 1.8 times.

The profit margin times the total assets turnover is called the **Du Pont equation**, and it gives the rate of return on assets (ROA)[16]:

13-1

$$ROA = \text{Net profit margin} \times \text{Total assets turnover}$$
$$= \frac{\text{Net income}}{\text{Sales}} \times \frac{\text{Sales}}{\text{Total assets}}$$

$$= \frac{\$59.4}{\$1,500.0} \times \frac{\$1,500.0}{\$850.4} = 4.0\% \times 1.8 \approx 7.0\%$$

[16]The numbers reported here are rounded to the nearest decimal place, so the ROA does not equal 7.0 percent if the rounded results for the net profit margin and the total assets turnover are used. If the ratios' values are carried out to three decimal places the Du Pont computation would be ROA = $0.0396 \times 1.764 = 0.0699 \approx 7.0\%$.

TABLE 13-6

Argile Textiles: Summary of Financial Ratios (millions of dollars, except per-share dollars)

Ratio	Formula for Calculation	Calculation	Ratio	Industry Average	Comment
Liquidity					
Current	$\dfrac{\text{Current assets}}{\text{Current liabilities}}$	$\dfrac{\$470.4}{\$130.0}$	= 3.6×	3.1×	Good
Quick, or acid test	$\dfrac{\text{Current assets} - \text{Inventories}}{\text{Current liabilities}}$	$\dfrac{\$200.4}{\$130.0}$	= 1.5×	1.9×	Low
Asset Management					
Inventory turnover	$\dfrac{\text{Cost of goods sold}}{\text{Inventories}}$	$\dfrac{\$1{,}220.0}{\$270.0}$	= 4.5×	7.5×	Low
Days sales outstanding (DSO)	$\dfrac{\text{Receivables}}{\left[\dfrac{\text{Annual sales}}{360}\right]}$	$\dfrac{\$180.0}{\$4.167}$	= 43.2 days	34.1 days	Poor
Fixed assets turnover	$\dfrac{\text{Sales}}{\text{Net fixed assets}}$	$\dfrac{\$1{,}500.0}{\$380.0}$	= 3.9×	4.0×	OK
Total assets turnover	$\dfrac{\text{Sales}}{\text{Total assets}}$	$\dfrac{\$1{,}500.0}{\$850.4}$	= 1.8×	2.2×	Low
Debt Management					
Debt ratio	$\dfrac{\text{Total debt}}{\text{Total assets}}$	$\dfrac{\$430.0}{\$850.4}$	= 50.6%	46.2%	Poor
Times interest earned (TIE)	$\dfrac{\text{EBIT}}{\text{Interest charges}}$	$\dfrac{\$140.0}{\$36.0}$	= 3.4×	5.4×	Low
Fixed charge coverage	$\dfrac{\text{EBIT} + \text{Lease payments}}{\dfrac{\text{Interest}}{\text{charges}} + \dfrac{\text{Lease}}{\text{payments}} + \left[\dfrac{\text{Sinking fund pmt}}{(1 - \text{Tax rate})}\right]}$	$\dfrac{\$150.0}{\$64.33}$	= 2.3×	4.8×	Low
Profitability					
Profit margin on sales	$\dfrac{\text{Net income}}{\text{Sales}}$	$\dfrac{\$59.4}{\$1{,}500.0}$	= 4.0%	4.9%	Poor
Return on total assets (ROA)	$\dfrac{\text{Net income}}{\text{Total assets}}$	$\dfrac{\$59.4}{\$850.4}$	= 7.0%	10.7%	Poor
Return on common equity (ROE)	$\dfrac{\text{Net income available to common stockholders}}{\text{Common equity}}$	$\dfrac{\$59.4}{\$420.4}$	= 14.1%	16.9%	Poor
Market Value					
Price/earnings (P/E)	$\dfrac{\text{Market price per share}}{\text{Earnings per share}}$	$\dfrac{\$23.00}{\$2.38}$	= 9.7×	11.0×	Low
Market/book	$\dfrac{\text{Market price per share}}{\text{Book value per share}}$	$\dfrac{\$23.00}{\$16.82}$	= 1.4×	2.0×	Low

FIGURE 13-3

FIGURE 13-3

Du Pont Chart Applied to Argile Textiles, 1999 (millions of dollars)

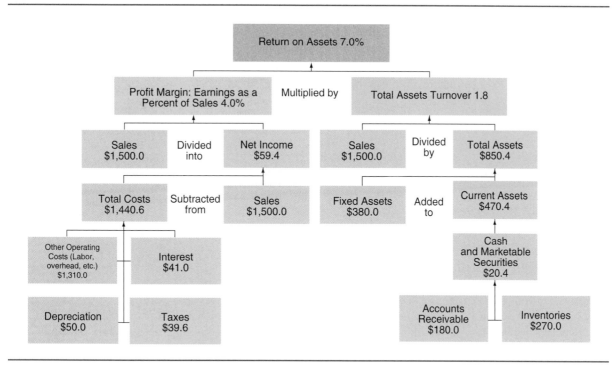

Argile made about 4.0 percent, or 4 cents, on each dollar of sales, and assets were "turned over" nearly 1.8 times during the year, so the company earned a return of 7 percent on its assets.

Argile's management can use the Du Pont system to analyze ways of improving the firm's performance. Focusing on the left, or "profit margin," side of its Du Pont chart, Argile's marketing people can study the effects of raising sales prices (or lowering them to increase volume), of moving into new products or markets with higher margins, and so on. The company's cost accountants can study various expense items and, working with engineers, purchasing agents, and other operating personnel, seek ways of holding down costs. On the "turnover" side, Argile's financial analysts, working with both production and marketing people, can investigate ways of minimizing the investment in various types of assets.

As a result of such an analysis, Sarah Allen, Argile's president, recently announced a series of moves designed to cut operating costs by more than 20 percent per year. Allen also announced that the company intends to concentrate its capital in markets where profit margins are reasonably high, and that if competition increases in certain of its product markets (such as the low-price end of the textiles market), Argile will withdraw from those markets. Argile is seeking a high return on equity, and Allen recognizes that if competition drives profit margins too low in a particular market, it then becomes impossible to earn high returns on the capital invested to serve that market. Therefore, if it is to achieve a high ROE, Argile might have to develop new products and shift capital into new areas. The company's future depends on this type of analysis, and if it succeeds in the future, then the Du Pont system will have helped it achieve that success.

Self-Test Questions

Identify two ratios that are used to analyze a firm's liquidity position, and write out their equations.

Identify four ratios that are used to measure how effectively a firm is managing its assets, and write out their equations.

Identify three ratios that are used to measure the extent to which a firm uses debt financing, and write out their equations.

Identify three ratios that show the combined effects of liquidity, asset management, and debt management on profitability, and write out their equations.

Identify two ratios that relate a firm's stock price to its earnings and book value per share, and write out their equations.

Explain how the Du Pont equation and chart combine different ratios to reveal the basic determinants of ROA.

Comparative Ratios

COMPARATIVE RATIO ANALYSIS
An analysis based on a comparison of a firm's ratios with those of other firms in the same industry.

The preceding analysis of Argile Textiles involved a **comparative ratio analysis** because the ratios calculated for Argile were compared with those of other firms in the same industry. Comparative ratios for a large number of industries are available from a number of sources, including Dun & Bradstreet (D&B), Robert Morris Associates, and the U.S. Commerce Department. Trade associations and individual firms' credit departments also compile industry average financial ratios. Finally, financial statement data for thousands of publicly owned corporations are available from various databases, and because brokerage houses, banks, and other financial institutions have access to these data, security analysts can and do generate comparative ratios tailored to their specific needs. Table 13-7 provides a sample of the ratios provided by the *Almanac of Business and Industrial Financial Ratios.*

Each of the data-supplying organizations uses a somewhat different set of ratios designed for its own purposes. For example, D&B deals mainly with small firms, many of which are proprietorships, and it sells its services primarily to banks and other lenders. Therefore, D&B is concerned largely with the creditor's viewpoint, and its ratios emphasize current assets and liabilities, not market value ratios. Therefore, when you select a comparative data source, you should be sure that your emphasis is similar to that of the agency whose ratios you plan to use. Additionally, there are often definitional differences in the ratios presented by different sources, so before using a source, be sure to verify the exact definitions of the ratios to insure consistency with your work.

Self-Test Questions

How is comparative ratio analysis carried out?

How does it compare with trend analysis?

TABLE 13-7

Ratios for Selected Industries

SIC Code, Line of Business, Number of Firms	Current Ratio	Quick Ratio	Debt Ratio	Days Sales Outstanding	Inventory Turnover	Total Asset Turnover	Profit Margin	Return on Assets	Return on Equity
	×	×	%	Days	×	×	%	%	%
2050 Bakery products (1,423)	1.1	0.7	52.3	35.4	11.9	1.6	2.6	7.8	8.5
2735 Book publishing (5,344)	1.6	1.0	61.0	40.9	6.0	1.0	6.7	11.9	16.9
2830 Drugs (784)	1.0	0.7	59.0	68.9	7.7	0.6	13.2	12.4	17.4
3140 Footwear (113)	3.0	1.6	45.0	36.4	6.1	1.5	4.9	12.0	13.2
5030 Lumber and construction (9,118)	1.7	0.9	60.1	35.9	10.1	3.4	2.5	12.4	21.4
5251 Hardware stores (6,803)	2.8	0.8	50.5	16.3	6.5	2.3	2.6	8.8	12.9

NOTE: SIC codes are Standard Industrial Classification codes used by the U.S. government to classify companies.

SOURCE: *Almanac of Business and Industrial Financial Ratios, 1998.*

Uses and Limitations of Ratio Analysis

As noted earlier, ratio analysis is used by three main groups: (1) *managers,* who employ ratios to help analyze, control, and thus improve the firm's operations; (2) *credit analysts,* such as bank loan officers or bond rating analysts, who analyze ratios to help ascertain a company's ability to pay its debts; and (3) *security analysts* (or *investors*), including both stock analysts, who are interested in a company's efficiency and growth prospects, and bond analysts, who are concerned with a company's ability to pay interest on its bonds as well as with the liquidating value of the assets in the event the company fails.

While ratio analysis can provide useful information concerning a company's operations and financial condition, it does have inherent problems and limitations that necessitate care and judgment. Some potential problems are listed here:

1. Many large firms operate a number of different divisions in quite different industries, and in such cases it is difficult to develop a meaningful set of industry averages for comparative purposes. This tends to make ratio analysis more useful for small, narrowly focused firms than for large, multidivisional ones.

2. Most firms want to be better than average, so merely attaining average performance is not necessarily good. As a target for high-level performance, it is best to focus on the industry leaders' ratios.

3. Inflation might distort firms' balance sheets — if recorded values are historical, they could be substantially different from "true" values. Further, because inflation affects both depreciation charges and inventory costs, profits are also affected. Thus, a ratio analysis for one firm over time, or a comparative analysis of firms of different ages, must be interpreted with judgment.

4. Seasonal factors can also distort a ratio analysis. For example, the inventory turnover ratio for a textile firm will be radically different if the balance sheet figure used for inventory is the one just before versus the one just after the close of the fall fashion season. This problem can be minimized by using monthly averages for inventory (and receivables) when calculating ratios such as turnover.

5. Firms can employ **"window dressing" techniques** to make their financial statements look stronger. To illustrate, a Chicago builder borrowed on a two-year basis on December 28, 1999, held the proceeds of the loan as *cash* for a few days, and then paid off the loan ahead of time on January 2, 2000. This improved the company's current and quick ratios, and made its year-end 2000 balance sheet look good. However, the improvement was strictly window dressing; a week later the balance sheet was back at the old level.

6. Different accounting practices can distort comparisons. As noted earlier, inventory valuation and depreciation methods can affect financial statements and thus make comparisons among firms difficult.

7. It is difficult to generalize about whether a particular ratio is "good" or "bad." For example, a high current ratio might indicate a strong liquidity position, which is good, or excessive cash, which is bad (because excess cash in the bank is a nonearning asset). Similarly, a high fixed assets turnover ratio might denote either a firm that uses its assets efficiently or one that is undercapitalized and cannot afford to buy enough assets.

8. A firm might have some ratios that look "good" and others that look "bad," making it difficult to tell whether the company is, on balance, strong or

"WINDOW DRESSING" TECHNIQUES
Techniques employed by firms to make their financial statements look better than they actually are.

weak. However, statistical procedures can be used to analyze the net effects of a set of ratios. Many banks and other lending organizations use statistical procedures to analyze firms' financial ratios, and, on the basis of their analyses, classify companies according to their probability of getting into financial trouble.[17]

Ratio analysis is useful, but analysts should be aware of these problems and make adjustments as necessary. Ratio analysis conducted in a mechanical, unthinking manner is dangerous, but, used intelligently and with good judgment, it can provide useful insights into a firm's operations. Probably *the most important and most difficult input to successful ratio analysis is the judgment used when interpreting the results to reach an overall conclusion about the firm's financial position.*

Self-Test Questions

Name three types of users of ratio analysis. What type of ratio does each group emphasize?

List several potential problems with ratio analysis.

Stock Dividends and Stock Splits

Before we conclude this chapter, we need to discuss the effect stock splits and stock dividends have on the financial statements of a firm. Because the number of shares of stock outstanding changes with either a stock split or a stock dividend, the EPS, P/E, and price of the stock are affected. Therefore, it is important to understand how a stock split or a stock dividend affects a firm and the value of its stock.

The rationale for stock dividends and splits can best be explained through an example. We will use Porter Electronic Controls Inc., a $700 million electronic components manufacturer, for this purpose. Since its inception, Porter's markets have been expanding, and the company has enjoyed growth in sales and earnings. Some of its earnings have been paid out in dividends, but some are also retained each year, causing earnings per share and market price per share to grow. The company began its life with only a few thousand shares outstanding, and, after some years of growth, each of Porter's shares had a very high EPS and DPS. When a "normal" P/E ratio was applied, the derived market price was so high that few people could afford to buy a "round lot" of 100 shares. This limited the demand for the stock and thus kept the total market value of the firm below what it would have been if more shares, at a lower price, had been outstanding. To correct this situation, Porter "split its stock."

[17]The technique used is discriminant analysis. For a discussion, see Edward I. Altman, "Financial Ratios, Discriminant Analysis, and the Prediction of Corporate Bankruptcy," *Journal of Finance,* September 1968, 589–609, or Eugene F. Brigham, Louis C. Gapenski, and Phillip R. Daves, *Intermediate Financial Management,* 6th ed. (Fort Worth, Tex.: The Dryden Press, 1999), Chapter 20.

Stock Splits

STOCK SPLIT
An action taken by a firm to increase the number of shares outstanding, such as doubling the number of shares outstanding by giving each stockholder two new shares for each one formerly held.

Although there is little empirical evidence to support the contention, there is nevertheless a widespread belief in financial circles that an *optimal, or psychological, price range* exists for stocks. "Optimal" means that if the price is within this range, the price/earnings ratio, hence the value of the firm, will be maximized. Many observers, including Porter's management, believe that the best range for most stocks is from $20 to $80 per share. Accordingly, if the price of Porter's stock rose to $80, management probably would declare a two-for-one **stock split**, thus doubling the number of shares outstanding, halving the earnings and dividends per share, and thereby lowering the price of the stock. Each stockholder would have more shares, but each share would be worth less. If the post-split price were $40, Porter's stockholders would be exactly as well off as they were before the split because they would have twice as many shares at half the price as before the split. However, if the price of the stock were to stabilize above $40, stockholders would be better off. Stock splits can be of any size — for example, the stock could be split two-for-one, three-for-one, one-and-a-half-for-one, or in any other way.[18]

TABLE 13-8

Porter Electronic Controls Inc.: Stockholders' Equity Accounts, Pro Forma, December 31, 2000 (millions of dollars, except per-share value)

I.   Before a Stock Split or Stock Dividend

Common stock (5 million shares outstanding, $1 par)	$ 5
Additional paid-in capital	10
Retained earnings	285
Total common stockholders' equity	$300
Book value per share	$60.00

II.   After a Two-for-One Stock Split

Common stock (10 million shares outstanding, $0.50 par)	$ 5
Additional paid-in capital	10
Retained earnings	285
Total common stockholders' equity	$300
Book value per share	$30.00

III.   After a 20 Percent Stock Dividend

Common stock (6 million shares outstanding, $1 par)[a]	$ 6
Additional paid-in capital[b]	89
Retained earnings[b]	205
Total common stockholders' equity	$300
Book value per share	$50.00

---

[a]Shares outstanding are increased by 20 percent, from 5 million to 6 million.

[b]A transfer equal to the market value of the new shares is made from the retained earnings account to the additional paid-in capital *and* common stock accounts; thus, the transfer = (5 million shares)(0.2)($80) = $80 million. Of this $80 million, ($1 par)(1 million shares) = $1 million goes to common stock and $79 million to paid-in capital.

---

[18]Reverse splits, which reduce the shares outstanding, can even be used. For example, a company whose stock sells for $5 might employ a one-for-five reverse split, exchanging one new share for five old ones and raising the value of the shares to about $25, which is within the optimal range. LTV Corporation did this after several years of losses had driven its stock price down below the optimal range.

Stock Dividends

Stock dividends are similar to stock splits in that they "divide the pie into smaller slices" without affecting the fundamental position of the current stock-holders. On a 5 percent stock dividend, the holder of 100 shares would receive an additional 5 shares (without cost); on a 20 percent stock dividend, the same holder would receive 20 new shares; and so on. Again, the total number of shares is increased, so EPS, DPS, and the market price per share all decline. If a firm wants to reduce the price of its stock, should it use a stock split or a stock dividend? Stock splits generally are used after a sharp price run-up to produce a large price reduction. Stock dividends typically are used on a regular annual basis to keep the stock price more or less constrained. For example, if a firm's earnings and dividends were growing at about 10 percent per year, its stock price would tend to go up at about that same rate, and it would soon be outside the desired trading range. A 10 percent annual stock dividend would maintain the stock price within the optimal trading range.

Balance Sheet Effects

Although the economic effects of stock splits and stock dividends are virtually identical, accountants treat them somewhat differently. On a two-for-one split, the shares outstanding are doubled, and the stock's par value is halved. This treatment is shown in Section II of Table 13-8 for Porter Electronic Controls, using a pro forma 2000 balance sheet.

Section III of Table 13-8 shows the effect of a 20 percent stock dividend. With a stock dividend, the par value is not reduced, but an accounting entry is made transferring capital from the retained earnings account to the common stock and paid-in capital accounts. The transfer from retained earnings is calculated as follows:

$$\begin{array}{c}\text{Dollars transferred}\\\text{from retained earnings}\end{array} = \binom{\text{Number of shares}}{\text{outstanding}} \times \binom{\text{Stock dividend}}{\text{as a percent}} \times \binom{\text{Market price}}{\text{of the stock}}$$

13-2

Porter has 5 million shares outstanding that sell for $80 each, so a 20 percent stock dividend would require the transfer of $80 million:

$$\text{Dollars transferred} = 5 \text{ million shares} \times 0.2 \times \$80 = \$80 \text{ million}$$

As shown in Table 13-8, $1 million of this $80 million is added to the common stock account and $79 million to the additional paid-in capital account. The retained earnings account is reduced from $155 million to $75 million.

Price Effects

Several empirical studies have examined the effects of stock splits and stock dividends on stock prices.[19] These studies suggest that investors see stock splits and

[19]See C. A. Barker, "Evaluation of Stock Dividends," *Harvard Business Review,* July–August 1958, 99–114. Barker's study has been replicated several times in recent years, and his results are still valid — they have withstood the test of time. Another excellent study, using an entirely different methodology, that reached similar conclusions, is Eugene F. Fama, Lawrence Fisher, Michael C. Jensen, and Richard Roll, "The Adjustment of Stock Prices to New Information," *International Economic Review,* February 1969, 1–21.

stock dividends for what they are — *simply additional pieces of paper.* If stock dividends and splits are accompanied by higher earnings and cash dividends, then investors will bid up the price of the stock. However, if stock dividends are not accompanied by increases in earnings and cash dividends, the dilution of EPS and DPS causes the price of the stock to drop by the same percentage as the stock dividend. Thus, the fundamental determinants of price are the underlying earnings and cash dividends per share, and stock splits and stock dividends merely cut the pie into thinner slices.

Self-Test Questions

What is the rationale for a stock split? What is the effect of stock splits and dividends on stock prices?

Differentiate between the accounting treatments for stock splits and stock dividends.

ETHICAL DILEMMA

Hocus-Pocus — Look, an Increase in Sales!

Dynamic Energy Wares (DEW) manufactures and distributes products that are used to save energy and to help reduce and reverse the harmful environmental effects of atmospheric pollutants. DEW relies on a relatively complex distribution system to get the products to its customers — large companies, which account for nearly 30 percent of total sales, purchase directly from DEW, while smaller companies and retailers that sell to individuals are required to purchase from one of the 50 independent distributors that are contractually obligated to *exclusively* sell DEW's products.

DEW's accountants have just finished the financial statements for the third quarter of the fiscal year, which ended three weeks ago. The results are terrible — profits are down 30 percent from this time last year when a downturn in sales began. Profits are depressed primarily because DEW continues to lose market share to a competitor that started business nearly two years ago.

Senior management has decided it needs to take action that will boost sales in the fourth quarter so that year-end profits are "more acceptable." So, starting immediately, DEW will (1) eliminate all direct sales, which means large companies now must purchase from DEW's distributors like the smaller companies and retailers, (2) require distributors to maintain certain minimum inventory levels, which are much higher than previous levels, and (3) form a task force to study and propose ways the firm can recapture lost market share.

The financial manager, who is your boss, has asked you to attend a hastily called meeting of DEW's distributors to announce the implementation of the changes in operations. At the meeting, the distributors will be informed that they must increase inventory to the required minimum level before the end of DEW's current fiscal year or face losing the distributorship. According to your boss, the reason for this requirement is to ensure distributors can meet the increased demand they will gain because the large companies no longer will be allowed to purchase directly from DEW. But, the sales forecast you have been working on for the past couple of months indicates distributors' sales are expected to decline by almost 10 percent during the next year, thus the added inventories might be extremely burdensome to the distributors. When you approached your boss about this, she said, "Tell the distributors not to worry! We won't require payment for six months, and any of the additional inventory that remains unsold after nine months can be returned. But, they *must* take delivery of the inventory within the next two months."

It appears the actions implemented by DEW will produce favorable year-end sales results for the current fiscal year. Do you agree with the decisions made by DEW's senior management? Will you be comfortable announcing the decisions to DEW's distributors? How would you respond to a distributor who says "DEW doesn't care about us, the company just wants to look good, no matter who gets hurt—that's unethical"? What are you going to say to your boss? Are you going to the distributors' meeting?

Financial Analysis in the Small Firm

Financial ratio analysis is especially useful for small businesses, and readily available sources provide comparative data by size of firm. For example, Robert Morris Associates provides comparative ratios for a number of small-firm classes, including the size range of zero to $250,000 in annual sales. Nevertheless, analyzing a small firm's statements presents some unique problems. We examine here some of those problems from the standpoint of a bank loan officer, one of the most frequent users of ratio analysis.

When examining a small-business credit prospect, a banker is essentially making a prediction about the ability of the company to repay its debt. In making this prediction, the banker will be concerned about indicators of liquidity and about continuing prospects for profitability, especially with respect to the firm's ability to generate cash flows. Bankers like to do business with a new customer if it appears that loans can be paid off on a timely basis and that the company will remain in business and therefore be a customer of the bank for some years to come. Thus, both short-run and long-run viability are of interest to the banker. At the same time, the banker's perceptions about the business are important to the owner-manager because the bank probably will be the firm's primary source of funds.

The first problem the banker is likely to encounter is that, unlike the bank's bigger customers, the small firm may not have audited financial statements. Further, the statements that are available may have been produced on an irregular basis (e.g., in some months or quarters but not in others). If the firm is young, it may have historical financial statements for only one year, or perhaps none at all. Also, the financial statements may not have been produced by a reputable accounting firm but by the owner's brother-in-law.

The quality of its financial data may therefore be a problem for a small business that is attempting to establish a banking relationship. This could keep the firm from getting credit even though it is really on solid financial ground. Therefore, it is in the owner's interest to make sure that the firm's financial data are credible, even if it is more expensive to do so. Furthermore, if the banker is uncomfortable with the data, the firm's management should also be uncomfortable. Because many managerial decisions depend on the numbers in the firm's accounting statements, those numbers should be as accurate as possible.

For a given set of financial ratios, a small firm might be riskier than a larger one. Small firms often produce a single product or rely heavily on a single customer, or both. For example, several years ago a company called Yard Man Inc. manufactured and sold lawn equipment. Most of Yard Man's sales were attributable to the business relationship it had with Sears. When Sears decided to drop Yard Man as a supplier, the company was left without its most important customer. The original Yard Man company is no longer in business. Because large firms typically have a broad customer base, they do not rely as much on a single customer.

A similar danger applies to a single-product company. Just as the loss of a key customer can be disastrous for a small business, so can a shift in the tides of consumer interest in a particular fad. For example, Coleco manufactured and sold the extremely popular Cabbage Patch dolls. The phenomenal popularity of the dolls was a great boon for Coleco, but the public is fickle. One can never predict when such a fad will die out, leaving the company with a great deal of capacity to make a product that no one will buy, and with a large amount of overvalued inventory. Exactly that situation hit Coleco, and it was forced into bankruptcy.

The extension of credit to a small company, and especially to a small owner-managed company, often involves yet another risk that is less of a problem for larger firms — namely, dependence on the leadership of a single key individual whose unexpected death could

Continued

Continued

cause the company to fail. For such a firm, it is important to have a plan of management succession clearly specified so creditors are assured the business will continue without interruption if some sort of disaster befalls the "key" manager. In addition, the firm could carry "key person insurance," payable to the bank or other creditor for the purposes of retiring the loan in the event of the key person's death.

In summary, to determine the financial strength of a small firm, the financial analyst must "look beyond the ratios" and analyze the viability of the firm's products, customers, management, and market. Ratio analysis is only the first step in a sound evaluation of the firm's ability to repay its debt and meet its other financial obligations.

Summary

The primary purposes of this chapter were (1) to describe the basic financial statements and (2) to discuss techniques used by investors and managers to analyze the statements. The key concepts covered in the chapter are listed below.

- The four basic statements contained in the annual report are the **balance sheet**, the **income statement**, the **statement of retained earnings**, and the **statement of cash flows**. Investors use the information provided in these statements to form expectations about the future levels of earnings and dividends, and about the firm's riskiness.
- **Operating cash flows** differ from reported **accounting income**. Investors should be more interested in a firm's projected cash flows than in reported earnings because it is cash, not paper profits, that is paid out as dividends and plowed back into the business to produce growth.
- **Financial statement analysis** generally begins with the calculation of a set of **financial ratios** designed to reveal the relative strengths and weaknesses of a company as compared to other companies in the same industry, and to show whether the firm's position has been improving or deteriorating over time.
- **Liquidity ratios** show the relationship of a firm's current assets to its current liabilities, and thus indicate the firm's ability to meet its current obligations.
- **Asset management ratios** measure how effectively a firm is managing its assets.
- **Debt management ratios** reveal (1) the extent to which the firm is financed with debt and (2) its likelihood of defaulting on its debt obligations.
- **Profitability ratios** show the combined effects of liquidity, asset management, and debt management policies on operating results.
- **Market value ratios** relate the firm's stock price to its earnings and book value per share, providing an indication of how investors regard the firm's future prospects.
- **Trend analysis** is important because it reveals whether the firm's ratios are improving or deteriorating over time.
- The **Du Pont chart** is designed to show how the profit margin on sales, the assets turnover ratio, and the use of debt interact to determine the rate of return on equity.

- A **stock split** is an action taken by a firm to increase the number of shares outstanding. Normally, splits reduce the price per share in proportion to the increase in shares because splits merely *divide the pie into smaller slices*. A **stock dividend** is a dividend paid in additional shares of stock rather than in cash. Both stock dividends and splits are used to keep stock prices within an "optimal," or psychological, range.
- In analyzing a small firm's financial position, ratio analysis is a useful starting point. However, the analyst must also (1) examine the **quality of the financial data**, (2) ensure that the firm is **sufficiently diversified** to withstand shifts in customers' buying habits, and (3) insure that the firm has a **plan for the succession of its management**.

Ratio analysis has limitations, but used with care and judgment, it can be very helpful. The interpretation of the computed ratio values is the most important ingredient for reaching a conclusion regarding both the existing and the prospective financial position of a firm.

Questions

13-1 What four finanical statements are contained in most annual reports?

13-2 If a "typical" firm reports $20 million of retained earnings on its balance sheet, could its directors declare a $20 million cash dividend without any qualms whatsoever? Explain why, or why not.

13-3 Describe the changes in balance sheet accounts that would constitute sources of funds. What changes would be considered uses of funds?

13-4 Financial ratio analysis is conducted by four groups of analysts: managers, equity investors, long-term creditors, and short-term creditors. What is the primary emphasis of each of these groups in evaluating ratios?

13-5 What are some cares that must be taken when using ratio analysis? What is the most important aspect of ratio analysis?

13-6 Profit margins and turnover ratios vary from one industry to another. What differences would you expect to find between a grocery chain such as Safeway and a steel company? Think particularly about the turnover ratios and the profit margin, and think about the Du Pont equation.

13-7 If a firm's ROE is low and management wants to improve it, explain how using more debt might help. Could using too much debt be a detriment?

13-8 How might (a) seasonal factors and (b) different growth rates distort a comparative ratio analysis? Give some examples. How might these problems be alleviated?

13-9 The balance sheets for Batelan Corporation for the fiscal years 1998 and 1999 follow. In the column to the right of the balance sheet amounts, indicate whether the change in the account balance represents a source or a use of cash for the firm. Place a (+) in the space provided to indicate a source of funds, a (−) to indicate a use of funds, and a (0) if it cannot be determined whether the change was a source or a use of cash.

	1999	1998	Source (+) or Use(–)?
Cash	$ 400	$ 500	_____
Accounts receivable	250	300	_____
Inventory	450	400	_____
Current assets	1,100	1,200	
Net property and equipment	1,000	950	_____
Total assets	$2,100	$2,150	
Accounts payable	$ 200	$ 400	_____
Accruals	300	250	_____
Notes payable	400	200	_____
Current liabilities	900	850	
Long-term debt	800	900	_____
Total liabilities	1,700	1,750	
Common stock	250	300	_____
Retained earnings	150	100	_____
Total equity	400	400	
Total liabilities and equity	$2,100	$2,150	

From these balance sheets, can you tell whether Batelan generated a positive or negative net income during 1999? Can you tell if dividends were paid? Explain.

13-10   Indicate the effects of the transactions listed in the following table on total current assets, current ratio, and net income. Use (+) to indicate an increase, (–) to indicate a decrease, and (0) to indicate either no effect or an indeterminate effect. Be prepared to state any necessary assumptions, and assume an initial current ratio of more than 1.0. (Note: A good accounting background is necessary to answer some of these questions; if yours is not strong, just answer the questions you can handle.)

	Total Current Assets	Current Ratio	Effect on Net Income
a. Cash is acquired through issuance of additional common stock.	_____	_____	_____
b. Merchandise is sold for cash.	_____	_____	_____
c. Federal income tax due for the previous year is paid.	_____	_____	_____
d. A fixed asset is sold for less than book value.	_____	_____	_____
e. A fixed asset is sold for more than book value.	_____	_____	_____
f. Merchandise is sold on credit.	_____	_____	_____
g. Payment is made to trade creditors for previous purchases.	_____	_____	_____
h. A cash dividend is declared and paid.	_____	_____	_____
i. Cash is obtained through short-term bank loans.	_____	_____	_____
j. Short-term notes receivable are sold at a discount.	_____	_____	_____
k. Marketable securities are sold below cost.	_____	_____	_____
l. Advances are made to employees.	_____	_____	_____
m. Current operating expenses are paid.	_____	_____	_____
n. Short-term promissory notes are issued to trade creditors in exchange for past due accounts payable.	_____	_____	_____
o. Ten-year notes are issued to pay accounts payable.	_____	_____	_____

	Total Current Assets	Current Ratio	Effect on Net Income
p. A fully depreciated asset is retired.	_____	_____	_____
q. Accounts receivable are collected.	_____	_____	_____
r. Equipment is purchased with short-term notes.	_____	_____	_____
s. Merchandise is purchased on credit.	_____	_____	_____
t. The estimated taxes payable are increased.	_____	_____	_____

13-11 Most firms would like to have their stock selling at high P/E ratio values, and they would also like to have a large number of different shareholders. Explain how stock dividends or stock splits might help achieve these goals.

13-12 What is the difference between a stock dividend and a stock split? As a stockholder, would you prefer to see your company declare a 100 percent stock dividend or a two-for-one split? Assume that either action is feasible.

Self-Test Problems   *Solutions Appear in Appendix B*

Key terms   **ST-1**   Define each of the following terms:
  a.   Annual report; income statement; balance sheet
  b.   Equity, or net worth; paid-in capital; retained earnings
  c.   Cash flow cycle
  d.   Statement of retained earnings; statement of cash flows
  e.   Depreciation; inventory valuation methods
  f.   Liquidity ratios; current ratio; quick, or acid test, ratio
  g.   Asset management ratios; inventory turnover ratio; days sales outstanding (DSO); fixed assets turnover ratio; total assets turnover ratio
  h.   Financial leverage; debt ratio; times-interest-earned (TIE) ratio; fixed charge coverage ratio
  i.   Profitability ratios; profit margin on sales; return on total assets (ROA); return on common equity (ROE)
  j.   Market value ratios; price/earnings (P/E) ratio; market/book (M/B) ratio; book value per share
  k.   Trend analysis; comparative ratio analysis
  l.   Du Pont chart; Du Pont equation
  m.   "Window dressing"; seasonal effects on ratios
  n.   Stock split; stock dividend

Debt ratio   **ST-2**   K. Billingsworth & Co. had earnings per share of $4 last year, and it paid a $2 dividend. Total retained earnings increased by $12 million during the year, while book value per share at year-end was $40. Billingsworth has no preferred stock, and no new common stock was issued during the year. If Billingsworth's year-end debt (which equals its total liabilities) was $120 million, what was the company's year-end debt/assets ratio?

Ratio analysis   **ST-3**   The following data apply to A. L. Kaiser & Company (millions of dollars):

Cash and marketable securities	$100.00
Fixed assets	$283.50
Sales	$1,000.00
Net income	$50.00
Quick ratio	2.0×
Current ratio	3.0×
DSO	40.0 days
ROE	12.0%

Kaiser has no preferred stock — only common equity, current liabilities, and long-term debt.

a. Find Kaiser's (1) accounts receivable (A/R), (2) current liabilities, (3) current assets, (4) total assets, (5) ROA, (6) common equity, and (7) long-term debt.

b. In part a, you should have found Kaiser's accounts receivable (A/R) = $111.1 million. If Kaiser could reduce its DSO from 40 days to 30 days while holding other things constant, how much cash would it generate? If this cash were used to buy back common stock (at book value) and thus reduced the amount of common equity, how would this affect (1) ROE, (2) ROA, and (3) total debt/total assets ratio?

Problems

Ratio analysis   **13-1**   Data for Argile Textiles' 1998 financial statements are given in Table 13-1 and Table 13-2 in the chapter.

a. Compute the 1998 values of the ratios indicated below:

Ratio	Argile	Industry
	1998 Values	
Current ratio	_____	3.9×
Days sales outstanding	_____	33.5 days
Inventory turnover	_____	7.2×
Fixed asset turnover	_____	4.1×
Debt ratio	_____	45.0%
Net profit margin on sales	_____	4.6%
Return on assets	_____	9.9%

b. Briefly comment on Argile's 1998 financial position. Can you see any obvious strengths or weaknesses?

c. Compare Argile's 1998 ratios with its 1999 ratios, which are presented in Table 13-6 in the chapter. Comment on whether you believe Argile's financial position improved or deteriorated during 1999.

d. What other information would be useful for projecting whether Argile's financial position is expected to get better or worse in the future?

Ratio analysis   **13-2**   Data for Campsey Computer Company and its industry averages follow.

a. Calculate the indicated ratios for Campsey.

b. Construct the Du Pont equation for both Campsey and the industry.

c. Outline Campsey's strengths and weaknesses as revealed by your analysis.

d. Suppose Campsey had doubled its sales as well as its inventories, accounts receivable, and common equity during 1999. How would that information affect the validity of your ratio analysis? (Hint: Think about averages and the effects of rapid growth on ratios if averages are not used. No calculations are needed.)

Campsey Computer Company: Balance Sheet as of December 31, 1999

Cash	$ 77,500	Accounts payable	$129,000
Receivables	336,000	Notes payable	84,000
Inventories	241,500	Other current liabilities	117,000
Total current assets	$655,000	Total current liabilities	$330,000
Net fixed assets	292,500	Long-term debt	256,500
		Common equity	361,000
Total assets	$947,500	Total liabilities and equity	$947,500

**Campsey Computer Company: Income Statement
for Year Ended December 31, 1999**

Sales	$1,607,500
Cost of goods sold	(1,353,000)
Gross profit	254,500
Fixed operating expenses except depreciation	(143,000)
Depreciation	(41,500)
Earnings before interest and taxes	70,000
Interest	(24,500)
Earnings before taxes	45,500
Taxes (40%)	(18,200)
Net income	$ 27,300

Ratio	Campsey	Industry Average
Current ratio	_____	2.0×
Days sales outstanding	_____	35 days
Inventory turnover	_____	5.6×
Total assets turnover	_____	3.0×
Profit margin on sales	_____	1.2%
Return on assets	_____	3.6%
Return on equity	_____	9.0%
Debt ratio	_____	60.0%

Balance sheet analysis   13-3   Complete the balance sheet and sales information in the table that follows for Isberg Industries using the following financial data:

Debt ratio: 50%

Quick ratio: 0.80×

Total assets turnover: 1.5×

Days sales outstanding: 36 days

Gross profit margin on sales: (Sales − Cost of goods sold)/Sales = 25%

Inventory turnover ratio: 5×

Balance Sheet

Cash	_____	Accounts payable		_____
Accounts receivable	_____	Long-term debt		60,000
Inventories	_____	Common stock		_____
Fixed assets	_____	Retained earnings		97,500
Total assets	$300,000	Total liabilities and equity		_____
Sales	_____	Cost of goods sold		_____

Du Pont analysis   13-4   The Finnerty Furniture Company, a manufacturer and wholesaler of high-quality home furnishings, has experienced low profitability in recent years. As a result, the board of directors has replaced the president of the firm with a new president, Elizabeth Brannigan, who has asked you to make an analysis of the firm's financial position using the Du Pont chart. The most recent industry average ratios, and Finnerty's financial statements, are as follows:

Industry Average Ratios

Current ratio	2×	Fixed assets turnover	6×
Debt ratio	30%	Total assets turnover	3×
Times-interest-earned	7×	Profit margin on sales	3%
Inventory turnover	8.5×	Return on total assets	9%
Days sales outstanding	24 days	Return on common equity	12.9%

Finnerty Furniture Company: Balance Sheet as of December 31, 1999 (millions of dollars)

Cash	$ 45	Accounts payable	$ 45
Marketable securities	33	Notes payable	45
Net receivables	66	Other current liabilities	21
Inventories	159	Total current liabilities	$111
Total current assets	$303	Long-term debt	24
		Total liabilities	$135
Gross fixed assets	225		
Less depreciation	78	Common stock	114
Net fixed assets	$147	Retained earnings	201
		Total stockholders' equity	$315
Total assets	$450	Total liabilities and equity	$450

Finnerty Furniture Company: Income Statement for Year Ended December 31, 1999 (millions of dollars)

Net sales	$795.0
Cost of goods sold	(660.0)
Gross profit	$135.0
Selling expenses	(73.5)
Depreciation expense	(12.0)
Earnings before interest and taxes	$ 49.5
Interest expense	(4.5)
Earnings before taxes (EBT)	45.0
Taxes (40%)	(18.0)
Net income	$ 27.0

a. Calculate those ratios that you think would be useful in this analysis.

b. Construct a Du Pont equation for Finnerty, and compare the company's ratios to the industry average ratios.

c. Do the balance sheet accounts or the income statement figures seem to be primarily responsible for the low profits?

d. Which specific accounts seem to be most out of line in relation to other firms in the industry?

e. If Finnerty had a pronounced seasonal sales pattern, or if it grew rapidly during the year, how might that affect the validity of your ratio analysis? How might you correct for such potential problems?

Ratio analysis **13-5** The Cary Corporation's forecasted 2000 financial statements follow, along with some industry average ratios.

a. Calculate Cary's 2000 forecasted ratios, compare them with the industry average data, and comment briefly on Cary's projected strengths and weaknesses.

b. What do you think would happen to Cary's ratios if the company initiated cost-cutting measures that allowed it to hold lower levels of inventory and substantially decreased the cost of goods sold? No calculations are necessary. Think about which ratios would be affected by changes in these two accounts.

Cary Corporation: Forecasted Balance Sheet as of December 31, 2000

Cash	$ 72,000
Accounts receivable	439,000
Inventories	894,000
Total current assets	$1,405,000
Land and building	238,000
Machinery	132,000
Other fixed assets	61,000
Total assets	$1,836,000
Accounts and notes payable	$ 432,000
Accruals	170,000
Total current liabilities	$ 602,000
Long-term debt	404,290
Common stock	575,000
Retained earnings	254,710
Total liabilities and equity	$1,836,000

Cary Corporation Forecasted Income Statement for 2000

Sales	$4,290,000
Cost of goods sold	(3,580,000)
Gross operating profit	$ 710,000
General administrative and selling expenses	(236,320)
Depreciation	(159,000)
Miscellaneous	(134,000)
Earnings before taxes (EBT)	$ 180,680
Taxes (40%)	(72,272)
Net income	$ 108,408
Number of shares outstanding	23,000

Per-Share Data

EPS	$4.71
Cash dividends	$0.95
P/E ratio	5×
Market price (average)	$23.57

Industry Financial Ratios (2000)[a]

Quick ratio	1.0×
Current ratio	2.7×
Inventory turnover[b]	5.8×
Days sales outstanding	32 days
Fixed assets turnover[b]	13.0×
Total assets turnover[b]	2.6×
Return on assets	9.1%
Return on equity	18.2%
Debt ratio	50.0%
Profit margin on sales	3.5%
P/E ratio	6.0×

[a]Industry average ratios have been constant for the past four years.

[b]Based on year-end balance sheet figures.

Stock dividend **13-6** The McLaughlin Corporation just declared a 6 percent stock dividend. Construct a pro forma balance sheet showing the effect of this action. The stock was selling for $37.50 per share, and a condensed version of McLaughlin's balance sheet as of December 31, 1999, before the dividend, follows (millions of dollars):

Cash	$ 112.5	Debt	$1,500
Other assets	2,887.5	Common stock (75 million	
		shares outstanding, $1 par)	75
		Paid-in capital	300
		Retained earnings	1,125
Total assets	$3,000.0	Total liabilities and equity	$3,000

Exam-Type Problems

The problems included in this section are set up in such a way that they could be used as multiple-choice exam problems.

Ratio calculation **13-7** Assume you are given the following relationships for the Zumwalt Corporation:

Sales/total assets	1.5×
Return on assets (ROA)	3%
Return on equity (ROE)	5%

Calculate Zumwalt's profit margin and debt ratio.

Liquidity ratios **13-8** The Hindelang Company has $1,312,500 in current assets and $525,000 in current liabilities. Its initial inventory level is $375,000, and it will raise funds as additional notes payable and use them to increase inventory. How much can Hindelang's short-term debt (notes payable) increase without pushing its current ratio below 2.0? What will be the firm's quick ratio after Hindelang has raised the maximum amount of short-term funds?

Ratio calculations **13-9** The W. F. Bailey Company had a quick ratio of 1.4, a current ratio of 3.0, and inventory turnover of 5 times, total current assets of $810,000, and cash and marketable securities of $120,000 in 1999. If the cost of goods sold equaled 86 percent of sales, what were Bailey's annual sales and its DSO for 1999?

Times-interest-earned ratio **13-10** Wolken Corporation has $500,000 of debt outstanding, and it pays an interest rate of 10 percent annually. Wolken's annual sales are $2 million; its average tax rate is 20 percent; and its net profit margin on sales is 5 percent. If the company does not maintain a TIE ratio of at least 5 times, its bank will refuse to renew the loan, and bankruptcy will result. What is Wolken's TIE ratio?

Return on equity **13-11** Coastal Packaging's ROE last year was only 3 percent, but its management has developed a new operating plan designed to improve things. The new plan calls for a total debt ratio of 60 percent, which will result in interest charges of $300 per year. Management projects an EBIT of $1,000 on sales of $10,000, and it expects to have a total assets turnover ratio of 2.0. Under these conditions, the average tax rate will be 30 percent. If the changes are made, what return on equity will Coastal earn? What is the ROA?

Return on equity **13-12** Earth's Best Company has sales of $200,000, a net income of $15,000, and the following balance sheet:

Cash	$ 10,000	Accounts payable	$ 30,000
Receivables	50,000	Other current liabilities	20,000
Inventories	150,000	Long-term debt	50,000
Net fixed assets	90,000	Common equity	200,000
Total assets	$300,000	Total liabilities and equity	$300,000

a. The company's new owner thinks that inventories are excessive and can be lowered to the point where the current ratio is equal to the industry average, 2.5×, without affecting either sales or net income. If inventories are sold off and not replaced so as to reduce the current ratio to 2.5×, if the funds generated are used to reduce common equity (stock can be repurchased at book value), and if no other changes occur, by how much will the ROE change?

b. Now suppose we wanted to take this problem and modify it for use on an exam, that is, to create a new problem which you have not seen to test your knowledge of this type of problem. How would your answer change if (1) We doubled all the dollar amounts? (2) We stated that the target current ratio was 3.0×? (3) We said that the company had 10,000 shares of stock outstanding, and we asked how much the change in part a would increase EPS? (4) What would your answer to (3) be if we changed the original problem to state that the stock was selling for twice book value, so common equity would not be reduced on a dollar-for-dollar basis?

c. Now explain how we could have set the problem up to have you focus on changing accounts receivable, or fixed assets, or using the funds generated to retire debt (we would give you the interest rate on outstanding debt), or how the original problem could have stated that the company needed *more* inventories and it would finance them with new common equity or with new debt.

Statement of cash flows   **13-13**   The consolidated balance sheets for the Lloyd Lumber Company at the beginning and end of 1999 follow. The company bought $50 million worth of fixed assets. The charge for depreciation in 1999 was $10 million. Net income was $33 million, and the company paid out $5 million in dividends.

a. Fill in the amount of the source or use in the appropriate column.

Lloyd Lumber Company: Balance Sheets at Beginning and End of 1999 (millions of dollars)

			Change	
	Jan. 1	Dec. 31	Source	Use
Cash	$ 7	$ 15	_____	_____
Marketable securities	0	11	_____	_____
Net receivables	30	22	_____	_____
Inventories	53	75	_____	_____
Total current assets	$ 90	$123		
Gross fixed assets	75	125	_____	_____
Less accumulated depreciation	25	35	_____	_____
Net fixed assets	$ 50	$ 90		
Total assets	$140	$213		
Accounts payable	$ 18	$ 15	_____	_____
Notes payable	3	15	_____	_____
Other current liabilities	15	7	_____	_____
Long-term debt	8	24	_____	_____
Common stock	29	57	_____	_____
Retained earnings	67	95	_____	_____
Total liabilities and equity	$140	$213		

NOTE: Total sources must equal total uses.

b. Prepare a statement of cash flows.

c. Briefly summarize your findings.

Income and cash flow analysis **13-14** The Montejo Corporation expects 2000 sales to be $12 million. Operating costs other than depreciation are expected to be 75 percent of sales, and depreciation is expected to be $1.5 million in 2000. All sales revenues will be collected in cash, and cost other than depreciation must be paid during the year. Montejo's interest expense is expected to be $1 million, and it is taxed at a 40 percent rate.

a. Set up an income statement and a cash flow statement (use two columns on one page) for Montejo. What is the expected cash flow from operations?

b. Suppose Congress changed the tax laws so that Montejo's depreciation expenses doubled in 2000, but no other changes occurred. What would happen to the new income and cash flow from operations expected in 2000?

c. Now suppose Congress, rather than increasing Montejo's 2000 depreciation, reduced it by 50 percent. How would the income and cash flows be affected?

d. If this company belonged to you, would you prefer Congress increase or decrease the depreciation expense allowed your company? Explain.

Stock split **13-15** After a five-for-one stock split, the Swensen Company paid a dividend of $0.75 per new share, which represents a 9 percent increase over last year's pre-split dividend. What was last year's dividend per share?

Integrative Problem

Financial statement analysis **13-16** Donna Jamison was recently hired as a financial analyst by Computron Industries, a manufacturer of electronic components. Her first task was to conduct a financial analysis of the firm covering the last two years. To begin, she gathered the following financial statements and other data.

Balance Sheets	1999	1998
Assets		
Cash	$ 52,000	$ 57,600
Accounts receivable	402,000	351,200
Inventories	836,000	715,200
Total current assets	$1,290,000	$1,124,000
Gross fixed assets	$ 527,000	$ 491,000
Less accumulated depreciation	166,200	146,200
Net fixed assets	$ 360,800	$ 344,800
Total assets	$1,650,800	$1,468,800
Liabilities and Equity		
Accounts payable	$ 175,200	$ 145,600
Notes payable	225,000	200,000
Accruals	140,000	136,000
Total current liabilities	$ 540,200	$ 481,600
Long-term debt	$ 424,612	$ 323,432
Common stock (100,000 shares)	$ 460,000	$ 460,000
Retained earnings	225,988	203,768
Total equity	$ 685,988	$ 663,768
Total liabilities and equity	$1,650,800	$1,468,800

Income Statements	1999	1998
Sales	$3,850,000	$3,432,000
Cost of goods sold	(3,250,000)	(2,864,000)
Other expenses	(430,300)	(340,000)
Depreciation	(20,000)	(18,900)
Total operating costs	($3,700,300)	($3,222,900)
EBIT	$ 149,700	$ 209,100
Interest expense	(76,000)	(62,500)
EBT	$ 73,700	$ 146,600
Taxes (40%)	(29,480)	(58,640)
Net income	$ 44,220	$ 87,960
EPS	$ 0.442	$ 0.880

Statement of Cash Flows (1999):

OPERATING ACTIVITIES

Net income	$ 44,220

Other Additions (Sources of Cash)

Depreciation	20,000
Increase in accounts payable	29,600
Increase in accruals	4,000

Subtractions (Uses of Cash)

Increases in accounts receivable	(50,800)
Increase in inventories	(120,800)
Net cash flow from operations	($ 73,780)

LONG-TERM INVESTING ACTIVITIES

Investment in fixed assets	($ 36,000)

FINANCING ACTIVITIES

Increase in notes payable	$ 25,000
Increase in long-term debt	101,180
Payment of cash dividends	(22,000)
Net cash flow from financing	104,180
Net reduction in cash account	($ 5,600)
Cash at beginning of year	57,600
Cash at year end	$ 52,000

Other Data

December 31 stock price	$ 6.00	$ 8.50
Number of shares	100,000	100,000
Dividends per share	$ 0.22	$ 0.22
Lease payments	$ 40,000	$ 40,000

Ratio	Industry Average
Current	2.7×
Quick	1.0×
Inventory turnover	6.0×
Days sales outstanding (DSO)	32.0 days
Fixed assets turnover	10.7×
Total assets turnover	2.6×
Debt ratio	50.0%
TIE	2.5×
Fixed charge coverage	2.1×
Profit margin on sales	3.5%
ROA	9.1%
ROE	18.2%
Price/earnings	14.2×
Market/book	1.4×

Assume that you are Donna Jamison's assistant, and that she has asked you to help her prepare a report that evaluates the company's financial condition. Then answer the following questions.

a. What can you conclude about the company's financial condition from its statement of cash flows?

b. What is the purpose of financial ratio analysis, and what are the five major categories of ratios?

c. What are Computron's current and quick ratios? What do they tell you about the company's liquidity position?

d. What are Computron's inventory turnover, days sales outstanding, fixed assets turnover, and total assets turnover ratios? How does the firm's utilization of assets stack up against that of the industry?

e. What are the firm's debt, times-interest-earned, and fixed charge coverage ratios? How does Computron compare to the industry with respect to financial leverage? What conclusions can you draw from these ratios?

f. Calculate and discuss the firm's profitability ratios — that is, its profit margin, return on assets (ROA), and return on equity (ROE).

g. Calculate Computron's market value ratios — that is, its price/earnings ratio and its market/book ratio. What do these ratios tell you about investors' opinions of the company?

h. Use the Du Pont equation to provide a summary and overview of Computron's financial condition. What are the firm's major strengths and weaknesses?

i. Use the following simplified 1999 balance sheet to show, in general terms, how an improvement in one of the ratios, say, the DSO, would affect the stock price. For example, if the company could improve its collection procedures and thereby lower the DSO from 37.6 days to 27.6 days, how would that change "ripple through" the financial statements (shown in thousands below) and influence the stock price?

Accounts receivable	$ 402	Debt	$ 965
Other current assets	888		
Net fixed assets	361	Equity	686
Total assets	$1,651	Total liabilities and equity	$1,651

j. Although financial statement analysis can provide useful information about a company's operations and its financial condition, this type of analysis does have some potential problems and limitations, and it must be used with care and judgment. What are some problems and limitations?

Computer-Related Problem

Work the problem in this section only if you are using the computer problem diskette.

Ratio analysis   **13-17**   Use the computerized model in File C13 to solve this problem.

a. Refer to Problem 13-5. Suppose Cary Corporation is considering installing a new computer system that would provide tighter control of inventories, accounts receivable, and accounts payable. If the new system is installed, the following data are projected (rather than the data given in Problem 13-5) for the indicated balance sheet and income statement accounts:

Accounts receivable	$ 395,000
Inventories	700,000
Other fixed assets	150,000
Accounts and notes payable	275,000
Accruals	120,000
Cost of goods sold	3,450,000
Administrative and selling expenses	248,775
P/E ratio	6×

How do these changes affect the projected ratios and the comparison with the industry averages? (Note that any changes to the income statement will change the amount of retained earnings; therefore, the model is set up to calculate 2000 retained earnings as 1999 retained earnings plus net income minus dividends paid. The model also adjusts the cash balance so that the balance sheet balances.)

b. If the new computer were even more efficient than Cary's management had estimated and thus caused the cost of goods sold to decrease by $125,000 from the projections in part a, what effect would that have on the company's financial position?

c. If the new computer were less efficient than Cary's management had estimated and caused the cost of goods sold to increase by $125,000 from the projections in part a, what effect would that have on the company's financial position?

d. Change, one by one, the other items in part a to see how each change affects the ratio analysis. Then think about, and write a paragraph describing, how computer models like this one can be used to help make better decisions about the purchase of such things as a new computer system.

Financial Planning and Control

CHAPTER 14

A MANAGERIAL PERSPECTIVE

In November 1994, Sony Corporation, the Japanese consumer electronics firm, wrote off more than $3.2 billion in assets, causing the book value of its assets to immediately decrease by about 30 percent and the market value of its stock to decrease by 13 percent within a one-week period. The write-off was directly attributed to Sony Pictures, the motion picture business that had been formed five years earlier with the $5 billion purchase of Columbia Pictures and TriStar Pictures from Coca-Cola Company. According to most analysts, the success of Sony's 1988 purchase of CBS Records, one of the world's largest record companies, teased the company into expanding its entertainment operations to the "Hollywood scene." Unfortunately, Sony did not follow the old adage: "Look before you leap." Company executives seemingly did not have a formal financial plan or control mechanism for the movie business. Michael Schulhof, chairman of Sony Corporation of America, was put in charge of Sony Pictures, even though he was unknown in the motion picture industry. He hired two movie producers, neither of whom had previous experience running a movie studio, to head the production facilities. From 1989 to 1994 more than $1 billion was spent on refurbishing studio lots and on executive perquisites such as fresh flowers, antiques, private chefs, and lavish parties. But, Sony Pictures' movie-production companies, Columbia and TriStar, were unable to consistently produce hit movies; in fact, most of the pictures were expensive flops, including *Last Action Hero, I'll Do Anything,* and *Mary Shelley's Frankenstein.* Was Sony Pictures just unlucky? Not according to Chuck Goto, an analyst with Smith Barney (now Salomon Smith Barney Holdings), who noted that "[i]f you look at it very objectively, it's clear the company mismanaged shareholders' money" by not planning adequately. It seems the only plan Sony had was to pour money into movies, and this strategy was destined to fail because there was not adequate forecasting and control to head off any problems that arose.

Even though it replaced the management and reorganized the operational structure of its motion picture business at the end of 1994, Sony had additional write-offs in 1995. Since that time, however, Sony Pictures Entertainment (SPE) has produced some hit motion pictures that have helped

Continued

SPE weather the rocky financial storm it inherited from the previous managers. In fact, in 1997, the Columbia TriStar Motion Picture Group (the monicker that was born with the reorganization) broke revenue records in the motion picture industry by grossing nearly $1.3 billion in U.S. theaters and more than $2.3 billion internationally. Some of the movies that helped SPE achieve this success included *Men in Black, My Best Friend's Wedding,* and *Air Force One.*

Many of the problems Sony Pictures originally experienced could have been avoided or reduced significantly if Sony Corporation had had a financial plan in place before it entered the movie industry. Most analysts agree that the value of Sony Pictures had decreased by about 50 percent from 1989 to 1994 when Sony began "biting the bullet" and initiated efforts to turn around its motion picture business. At that time, Sony had to evaluate the effects on forecasted earnings and stock prices of cutting certain costs, writing off assets, and controlling the finances associated with the motion picture businesses — a *plan* was devised to salvage Sony Pictures, which provided encouragement to Sony Corporation's investors and potential investors and proved successful, at least so far.

FINANCIAL PLANNING The projection of sales, income, and assets based on alternative production and marketing strategies, as well as the determination of the resources needed to achieve these projections.

In the last chapter, we focused on how to use financial statement analysis to evaluate the existing financial position of a firm. In this chapter, we see how a financial manager can use some of the information obtained through financial statement analysis for financial planning and control of the firm's future operations.

Well-run companies generally base their operating plans on a set of forecasted financial statements. The **planning process** begins with a sales forecast for the next few years. Then the assets required to meet the sales targets are determined, and a decision is made concerning how to finance the required assets. At that point, income statements and balance sheets can be projected, and earnings and dividends per share, as well as the key ratios, can be forecasted.

FINANCIAL CONTROL The phase in which financial plans are implemented; control deals with the feedback and adjustment process required to ensure adherence to plans and modification of plans because of unforeseen changes.

Once the "base-case" forecasted statements and ratios have been prepared, top managers want to know (1) how realistic the results are, (2) how to attain the results, and (3) what effect changes in operations would have on the forecasts. At this stage, which is the **control phase,** the firm is concerned with implementing the financial plans, or forecasts, and dealing with the feedback and adjustment process that is necessary to ensure the goals of the firm are pursued appropriately.

The first part of the chapter is devoted to financial planning using projected financial statements, or forecasts, and the second part of the chapter focuses on financial control using budgeting and the analysis of leverage and cash flows to determine how changes in operations affect financial forecasts.

Sales Forecasts

Forecasting is an essential part of the planning process, and a *sales forecast* is the most important ingredient of financial forecasting. The **sales forecast** generally starts with a review of sales during the past five to ten years, which can be expressed in a graph such as that in Figure 14-1. The first part of the graph shows five years of historical sales for Argile Textiles, the textile and clothing manufac-

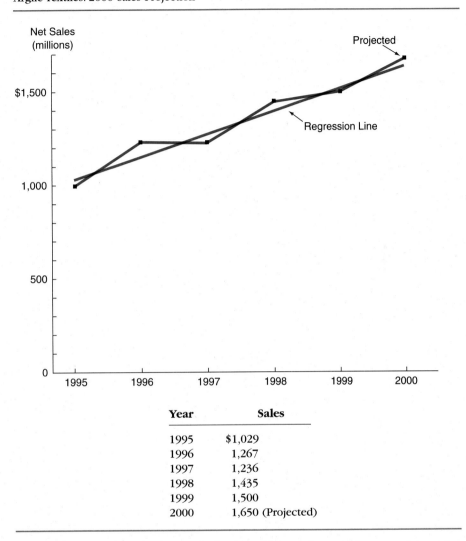

FIGURE 14-1

Argile Textiles: 2000 Sales Projection

Year	Sales
1995	$1,029
1996	1,267
1997	1,236
1998	1,435
1999	1,500
2000	1,650 (Projected)

SALES FORECAST
A forecast of a firm's unit and dollar sales for some future period; generally based on recent sales trends plus forecasts of the economic prospects for the nation, region, industry, and so forth.

turer we analyzed in the last two chapters. The graph could have contained ten years of sales data, but Argile typically focuses on sales figures for the latest five years because the firm's studies have shown that future growth is more closely related to the recent than to the distant past.

Argile had its ups and downs during the period from 1995 to 1999. In 1997, poor cotton production in the United States and diseased sheep in Australia resulted in low textile production, which caused sales to fall below the 1996 level. Then, a significant increase in both the supply of cotton and the supply of wool in 1998 pushed sales up by 16 percent. Based on a regression analysis, Argile's forecasters determined that the average annual growth rate in sales over the past five years was nearly 10 percent. To determine the forecasted sales growth for 2000, some of the factors that Argile considered included projections of expected economic activity, competitive conditions, and product development and distribution both in the markets in which Argile currently operates and in the markets it plans to enter in the future. Often, firms develop mathematical models such as regression equations to take into consideration such factors when forecasting future sales. Based on its historical sales trend, plans for new product and market introductions, and Argile's forecast for the economy, the firm's planning committee has projected a 10 percent growth rate for sales during 2000. So, 2000 sales are expected to be $1,650 million, which is 10 percent higher than 1999 sales of $1,500 million.

If the sales forecast is inaccurate, the consequences can be serious. First, if the market expands significantly *more* than Argile has geared up for, the company probably will not be able to meet demand. Customers will buy competitors' products, and Argile will lose market share, which will be hard to regain. On the other hand, if the projections are overly optimistic, Argile could end up with too much plant, equipment, and inventory. This would mean low turnover ratios, high costs for depreciation and storage, and, possibly, write-offs of obsolete or unusable inventory. All of this would result in a low rate of return on equity, which, in turn, would depress the company's stock price. If Argile had financed an unnecessary expansion with debt, its problems would, of course, be compounded. Remember from our analysis of its 1999 financial statements in the previous chapter, that Argile's current financial position is somewhat tenuous. Thus, an accurate sales forecast is critical to the well-being of the firm.[1]

Self-Test Questions

How do past trends affect a sales forecast?

Briefly explain why an accurate sales forecast is critical to profitability.

Projected (Pro Forma) Financial Statements

Any forecast of financial requirements involves (1) determining how much money the firm will need during a given period, (2) determining how much money the firm will generate internally during the same period, and (3) subtracting the funds generated from the funds required to determine the external financial requirements. One method used to estimate external requirements is the *projected, or pro forma, balance sheet method,* which is discussed in this section.

ADDITIONAL FUNDS NEEDED (AFN)
Funds that a firm must raise externally through borrowing or by selling stock to support forecasted sales.

The projected balance sheet method is straightforward — simply project the asset requirements for the coming period, then project the liabilities and equity that will be generated under normal operations, and subtract the projected liabilities and equity from the required assets to estimate the **additional funds needed (AFN)** to support the level of forecasted operations. The steps in the procedure are explained below.

---

[1] A sales forecast is actually the *expected value of a probability distribution* with many possible levels of sales. Because any sales forecast is subject to a greater or lesser degree of uncertainty, for financial planning we are often just as interested in the degree of uncertainty inherent in the sales forecast (σ sales) as we are in the expected value of sales. The concepts of probability distribution measures were discussed in Chapter 8.

Step 1. Forecast the 2000 Income Statement

PROJECTED BALANCE SHEET
METHOD
A method of forecasting
financial requirements
based on forecasted
financial statements.

The **projected balance sheet method** begins with a forecast of sales. Next, the income statement for the coming year is forecasted in order to obtain an initial estimate of the amount of retained earnings the company will generate during the year. This requires assumptions about the operating cost ratio, the tax rate, interest charges, and the dividends paid. In the simplest case, the assumption is made that costs will increase at the same rate as sales; in more complicated situations, cost changes are forecasted separately. Still, the objective of this part of the analysis is to determine how much income the company will earn and then retain for reinvestment in the business during the forecasted year.

Table 14-1 shows Argile's actual 1999 income statement and the initial forecast of the 2000 income statement if the conditions just mentioned exist. To create the 2000 income forecast, we assume that sales and variable operating costs will be 10 percent greater in 2000 than in 1999. In addition, it is assumed that Argile currently operates at full capacity, so it will need to expand its plant capacity in 2000 to handle the additional operations. Therefore, in Table 14-1, the 2000 forecasts of sales, *all* operating costs, and depreciation are 10 percent greater than their 1999 levels. The result is that earnings before interest and taxes (EBIT) is forecasted to be $154 million in 2000.

TABLE 14-1

Argile Textiles: Actual 1999 and Projected 2000 Income Statements (millions of dollars, except per-share data)

	1999 Results	2000 Forecast Basis[a]	Initial Forecast
Net sales	$ 1,500.0	×1.10	$ 1,650.0
Cost of goods sold	(1,220.0)	×1.10	(1,342.0)
Gross profit	$ 280.0		$ 308.0
Fixed operating costs except depreciation	(90.0)	×1.10	(99.0)
Depreciation	(50.0)	×1.10	(55.0)
Earnings before interest and taxes (EBIT)	$ 140.0		$ 154.0
Less interest	(41.0)		(41.0)[b]
Earnings before taxes (EBT)	$ 99.0		$ 113.0
Taxes (40%)	(39.6)		(45.2)
Net income	$ 59.4		$ 67.8
Common dividends	(29.0)		(33.0)[c]
Addition to retained earnings	$ 30.4		$ 34.8
Earnings per share	$ 2.38		$ 2.71
Dividends per share	$ 1.16		$ 1.32
Number of common shares (millions)	25		25

[a]×1.10 indicates "times $(1 + g)$"; used for items that grow proportionally with sales.

[b]Indicates a 1999 figure carried over for the preliminary forecast.

[c]Indicates a projected figure. See text for explanation.

To complete the initial forecast of 2000 income, we assume no change in the financing of the firm because, at this point, it is not known if additional financing is needed. But, it is apparent that the 2000 interest expense will change if debt (borrowing) is needed to support the forecasted increase in operations changes. To forecast the 2000 dividends, we simply assume the dividend payout will be similar to what it was in 1999, about 45 to 50 percent of earnings per share. So, the dividend per share for 2000 is forecasted to be $1.32. If the DPS_{2000} = $1.32, the total common dividends forecasted for 2000 would be (25 million shares) × $1.32 = $33.0 million if no additional common stock is issued. Like the interest expense amount, however, the amount of total dividends used to create this initial forecast will change if Argile decides to sell new stock to raise any additional financing necessary to support the new operations.

From the initial forecast of 2000 income contained in Table 14-1, we can see that $34.8 million is expected to be added to retained earnings in 2000. As it turns out, this addition to retained earnings represents the amount Argile is expected to invest in itself (internally generated funds) to support the increase in operations in 2000. So, the next step is to determine what impact this level of investment will have on Argile's forecasted 2000 balance sheet.

Step 2. Forecast the 2000 Balance Sheet

If we assume the 1999 end-of-year asset levels were just sufficient to support 1999 operations, then, in order for Argile's sales to increase in 2000, its assets also must grow. Because the company was operating at full capacity in 1999, *each* asset account must increase if the higher sales level is to be attained: More cash will be needed for transactions, higher sales will lead to higher receivables, additional inventory will have to be stocked, and new plant and equipment must be added for production.

Further, if Argile's assets are to increase, its liabilities and equity must also increase — the additional assets must be financed in some manner. Some liabilities will increase spontaneously due to normal business relationships. For example, as sales increase, so will Argile's purchases of raw materials, and these larger purchases will spontaneously lead to higher levels of accounts payable. Similarly, a higher level of operations will require more labor, while higher sales will result in higher taxable income. Therefore, both accrued wages and accrued taxes will

SPONTANEOUSLY GENERATED FUNDS
Funds that are obtained from routine business transactions.

increase. In general, these current liability accounts, which provide **spontaneously generated funds,** will increase at the same rate as sales.

Notes payable, long-term bonds, and common stock will not rise spontaneously with sales; rather, the projected levels of these accounts will depend on conscious financing decisions that will be made later. Therefore, for the initial forecast, it is assumed these account balances remain unchanged from their 1999 levels.

Table 14-2 contains Argile's 1999 actual balance sheet and an initial forecast of its 2000 balance sheet. The mechanics of the balance sheet forecast are similar to those used to develop the forecasted income statement. First, those balance sheet accounts that are expected to increase directly with sales are multiplied by 1.10 to obtain the initial 2000 forecasts. Thus, 2000 cash is projected to be $20.4(1.10) = $22.4 million, accounts receivable are projected to be $180.0(1.10) = $198.0 million, and so on. In our example, all assets increase with sales, so once the individual assets have been forecasted, they can be summed to complete the asset side of the forecasted balance sheet.

TABLE 14-2

Argile Textiles: Actual 1999 and Projected 2000 Balance Sheets (millions of dollars)

	1999 Balances	Forecast Basis[a]	2000 Initial Forecast
Cash	$ 20.4	×1.10	$ 22.4
Accounts receivable	180.0	×1.10	198.0
Inventories	270.0	×1.10	297.0
Total current assets	$470.4		$517.4
Net plant and equipment	380.0	×1.10	418.0
Total assets	$850.4		$935.4
Accounts payable	$ 30.0	×1.10	$ 33.0
Accruals	60.0	×1.10	66.0
Notes payable	40.0		40.0[b]
Total current liabilities	$130.0		$139.0
Long-term bonds	300.0		300.0[b]
Total liabilities	$430.0		$439.0
Common stock	130.0		130.0[b]
Retained earnings	290.4	+$34.8[c]	325.2
Total owners' equity	$420.4		$455.2
Total liabilities and equity	$850.4		$894.2
Additional funds needed (AFN)			$ 41.2[d]

[a]×1.10 indicates "times $(1 + g)$"; used for items that grow proportionally with sales.

[b]Indicates a 1999 figure carried over for the initial forecast.

[c]The $34.8 million represents the "addition to retained earnings" from the 2000 Projected Income Statement given in Table 14-1.

[d]The "additional funds needed (AFN)" is computed by subtracting the amount of total liabilities and equity from the amount of total assets.

Next, the spontaneously increasing liabilities (accounts payable and accruals) are forecasted. Then those liability and equity accounts whose values reflect conscious management decisions — notes payable, long-term bonds, and stock — *initially are forecasted* to remain at their 1999 levels. Thus, the amount of 2000 notes payable initially is set at $40 million, the long-term bond account is forecasted at $300 million, and so forth. The forecasted 2000 level of retained earnings will be the 1999 level plus the forecasted addition to retained earnings, which was computed as $34.8 million in the projected income statement we created in Step 1 (Table 14-1).

The forecast of total assets in Table 14-2 is $935.4 million, which indicates that Argile must add $85 million of new assets (compared with 1999 assets) to support the higher sales level expected in 2000. However, according to the initial forecast of the 2000 balance sheet, the total liabilities and equity total only $894.2 million, which is an increase of only $43.8 million. So, the amount of total assets exceeds the amount of total liabilities and equity by $41.2 million = $935.4 million − $894.2 million. This indicates that $41.2 million of the forecasted increase in total assets will not be financed by liabilities that spontaneously increase with sales (accounts payable and accruals) or by an increase in retained earnings. Argile can raise the additional $41.2 million, which we designate *additional funds needed (AFN),* by borrowing from the bank as notes payable, by issuing long-term bonds, by selling new common stock, or by some combination of these actions.

The initial forecast of Argile's financial statements has shown us that (1) higher sales must be supported by higher asset levels, (2) some of the asset increases can be financed by spontaneous increases in accounts payable and accruals and by retained earnings, and (3) any shortfall must be financed from external sources, either by borrowing or by selling new stock.

Step 3. Raising the Additional Funds Needed

Argile's financial manager will base the decision of exactly how to raise the $41.2 million additional funds needed on several factors, including its ability to handle additional debt, conditions in the financial markets, and restrictions imposed by existing debt agreements. The decisions concerning how to best finance the firm were discussed in Chapter 11. At this point, it is important to understand that, regardless of how Argile raises the $41.2 million AFN, the initial forecasts of both the income statement and the balance sheet will be affected. If Argile takes on new debt, its interest expenses will rise; if additional shares of common stock are sold, total dividend payments will increase if the same dividend per share is paid to all common stockholders. Each of these changes, which we term *financing feedbacks,* will affect the amount of additional retained earnings originally forecasted, which, in turn, will affect the amount of additional funds needed.

Remember from our ratio analysis in the previous chapter that we concluded Argile has a below-average debt position. Consequently, Argile has decided any additional funds needed to support future operations will be raised primarily by issuing new common stock. Following this financing policy should help improve Argile's debt position as well as its overall profitability.

Step 4. Financing Feedbacks

FINANCING FEEDBACKS
The effects on the income statement and balance sheet of actions taken to finance forecasted increases in assets.

As mentioned in Step 3, one complexity that arises in financial forecasting relates to **financing feedbacks.** The external funds raised to pay for new assets create additional expenses that must be reflected in the income statement; this lowers the initially forecasted addition to retained earnings, which means more external funds are needed to make up for the lower amount added to retained earnings. In other words, if Argile raised the $41.2 million AFN by issuing new debt and new common stock, it would find that both the interest expense and the total dividend payments would be higher than the amounts contained in the forecasted income statement shown in Table 14-1. Consequently, after adjusting for the higher interest and dividend payments, the forecasted addition to retained earnings would be lower than the initial forecast of $34.8 million. Because the retained earnings will be lower than projected, a financing shortfall will exist even after the original AFN of $41.2 million is considered. So, in reality, Argile must raise more than $41.2 million to account for the financing feedbacks that affect the amount of internal financing expected to be generated from the increase in operations. To determine the amount of external financing actually needed, we have to adjust the initial forecasts of both the income statement (Step 1) and the balance sheet (Step 2) to reflect the impact of raising the additional external financing. This process has to be repeated until AFN = 0 in

Table 14-2, which means Step 1 and Step 2 might have to be repeated several times to fully account for the financing feedbacks.

Table 14-3 contains the adjusted 2000 preliminary forecasts for the income statement and the balance sheet of Argile Textiles after all of the financing effects are considered. To generate the adjusted forecasts, it is assumed that of the total external funds needed, 65 percent will be raised by selling new common stock at $23 per share, 15 percent will be borrowed from the bank at an interest rate of 7 percent, and 20 percent will be raised by selling long-term bonds with a coupon interest of 10 percent. Under these conditions, it can be seen from Table 14-3 that Argile actually needs $43.6 million to support the forecasted increase in operations, not the $41.2 million contained in the initial forecast. The additional $2.4 million is needed because the added amounts of debt and common stock will cause interest and dividend payments to increase, which will decrease the contribution to retained earnings by $2.4 million.[2]

Analysis of the Forecast

The 2000 forecast as developed in this section represents a preliminary forecast because we have completed only the first stage of the total forecasting process. Next, the projected statements must be analyzed to determine whether the forecast meets the firm's financial targets. If the statements do not meet the targets, then elements of the forecast must be changed.

Table 14-4 shows Argile's 1999 ratios as they were reported back in Table 13-6 in the previous chapter, plus the projected 2000 ratios based on the preliminary forecast and the industry average ratios. As we noted in Chapter 13, the firm's financial condition at the close of 1999 was weak, with many ratios being well below the industry averages. The preliminary final forecast for 2000 (after financing feedbacks are considered), which assumes that Argile's past practices will continue into the future, shows an improved debt position. But, the overall financial position still is somewhat weak, and this condition will persist unless management takes some actions to improve things.

Argile's management actually plans to take steps to improve its financial condition. The plans are to (1) close down certain operations, (2) modify the credit policy to reduce the collection period for receivables, and (3) better manage inventory so that products are turned over more often. These proposed operational changes will affect both the income statement and the balance sheet, so the preliminary forecast will have to be revised again to reflect the impact of such changes. When this process is complete, management will have its final forecast. To keep things simple, we do not show the final forecast here; instead, for the remaining discussions, we assume the preliminary forecast is not substantially different and use it as the final forecast for Argile's 2000 operations.

As we have shown, forecasting is an iterative process, both in the way the financial statements are generated and in the way the financial plan is developed. For planning purposes, the financial staff develops a preliminary forecast based on a continuation of past policies and trends. This provides the executives with a starting point, or "straw man" forecast. Next, the model is modified to see what effects alternative operating plans would have on the firm's earnings and financial condition. This results in a revised forecast.

---

[2]Appendix 14A gives a more detailed description of the iterations required to generate the final forecasts.

TABLE 14-3

Argile Textiles: 2000 Adjusted Forecast of Financial Statements (millions of dollars)

	Initial Forecast	Adjusted Forecast	Financing Adjustment
INCOME STATEMENT			
Net sales	$1,650.0	$1,650.0	
Cost of goods sold	(1,342.0)	(1,342.0)	
Gross profit	$ 308.0	$ 308.0	
Fixed operating costs except depreciation	(99.0)	(99.0)	
Depreciation	(55.0)	(55.0)	
Earnings before interest and taxes (EBIT)	$ 154.0	$ 154.0	
Less interest	(41.0)	(42.3)	($1.3)
Earnings before taxes (EBT)	$ 113.0	$ 111.7	(1.3)
Taxes (40%)	(45.2)	(44.7)	0.5
Net income	$ 67.8	$ 67.0	(0.8)
Common dividends	(33.0)	(34.6)	(1.6)
Addition to retained earnings	$ 34.8	$ 32.4	($2.4)[a]
Earnings per share	$ 2.71	$ 2.55	
Dividends per share	$ 1.32	$ 1.32	
Number of common shares (millions)	25.0	26.2	
BALANCE SHEET			
Cash	$ 22.4	$ 22.4	
Accounts receivable	198.0	198.0	
Inventories	297.0	297.0	
Total current assets	$ 517.4	$ 517.4	
Net plant and equipment	418.0	418.0	
Total assets	$ 935.4	$ 935.4	
Accounts payable	$ 33.0	$ 33.0	
Accruals	66.0	66.0	
Notes payable	40.0	46.5	$ 6.5
Total current liabilities	$ 139.0	$ 145.5	
Long-term bonds	300.0	308.7	8.7
Total liabilities	$ 439.0	$ 454.2	
Common stock	130.0	158.4	28.4
Retained earnings	325.2	322.8	(2.4)[a]
Total owners' equity	$ 455.2	$ 481.2	
Total liabilities and equity	$ 894.2	$ 935.4	
Additional funds needed (AFN)	$ 41.2	$0.0	$41.2[b]

[a]The financing adjustment for the addition to retained earnings in the income statement is the same as the financing adjustment for retained earnings in the balance sheet.

[b]The total AFN, or external funding needs, equal $41.2 million plus the $2.4 million decrease in the change in retained earnings from the initial forecast.

TABLE 14-4

Argile Textiles: Key Ratios

	1999	Adjusted Preliminary 2000	Industry Average
Current ratio	3.6×	3.6×	3.1×
Inventory turnover	4.5×	4.5×	7.5×
Days sales outstanding	43.2 days	43.2 days	34.1 days
Total assets turnover	1.8×	1.8×	2.2×
Debt ratio	50.6%	48.6%	46.2%
Times interest earned	3.4×	3.6×	5.4×
Profit margin	4.0%	4.1%	4.9%
Return on assets	7.0%	7.2%	10.7%
Return on equity	14.1%	13.9%	16.9%

Self-Test Questions

What is the AFN, and how is the projected balance sheet method used to estimate it?

What is a financing feedback, and how do financing feedbacks affect the estimate of AFN?

Why is it necessary for the forecasting process to be iterative?

Other Considerations in Forecasting

We presented a very simple method for constructing pro forma financial statements under rather restrictive conditions. In this section, we describe some other conditions that should be considered when creating forecasts.

Excess Capacity

The construction of the 2000 forecasts for Argile was based on the assumption that the firm's 1999 operations were at full capacity, so any increase in sales would require additional assets, especially plant and equipment. If Argile did *not* operate at full capacity in 1999, then plant and equipment would only have to be increased if the additional sales (operations) forecasted in 2000 exceeded the unused capacity of the existing assets. For example, if Argile actually utilized only 80 percent of its fixed assets' capacity to produce 1999 sales of $1,500 million, then

$$\$1,500.0 \text{ million} = 0.80 \times (\text{Plant capacity})$$

$$\text{Plant capacity} = \frac{\$1,500.0 \text{ million}}{0.80} = \$1,875.0 \text{ million}$$

In this case, then, Argile could increase sales to $1,875 million, or by 25 percent of 1999 sales, before full capacity is reached and plant and equipment would have to be increased. In general, we can compute the sales capacity of the firm if it is known what percent of assets are utilized to produce a particular level of sales:

$$\text{Full capacity sales} \; = \; \frac{\text{Sales level}}{\left(\begin{array}{c}\text{Percent of capacity used}\\\text{to generate sales level}\end{array}\right)}$$

If Argile does not have to increase plant and equipment, fixed assets would remain at the 1999 level of $380 million, so the amount of AFN would be $3.2 million, which is $38 million (10 percent of $380 million fixed assets) less than the initial forecast reported in Table 14-2.

In addition to the excess capacity of fixed assets, the firm could have excesses in other assets that can be used for increases in operations. For instance, in the previous chapter, we concluded that perhaps Argile's inventory level at the end of 1999 was greater than it should have been. If true, some increase in 2000 forecasted sales can be absorbed by the above-normal inventory, and production would not have to be increased until inventory levels are reduced to normal — this requires no additional financing.

In general, excess capacity means less external financing is required to support increases in operations than would be needed if the firm previously operated at full capacity.

Economies of Scale

There are economies of scale in the use of many types of assets, and when economies occur, a firm's variable cost of goods sold ratio is likely to change as the size of the firm changes (either increases or decreases) substantially. Currently, Argile's variable cost ratio is $81\frac{1}{3}$ percent of sales, but the ratio might decrease to 80 percent of sales if operations increase significantly. If everything else is the same, changes in the variable cost ratio affect the addition to retained earnings, which, in turn, affects the amount of AFN.

Lumpy Assets

LUMPY ASSETS
Assets that cannot be acquired in small increments; instead, they must be obtained in large, discrete amounts.

In many industries, technological considerations dictate that if a firm is to be competitive, it must add fixed assets in large, discrete units; such assets often are referred to as **lumpy assets.** For example, in the paper industry, there are strong economies of scale in basic paper mill equipment, so when a paper company expands capacity, it must do so in large, lumpy increments. Lumpy assets primarily affect the turnover of fixed assets and, consequently, the financial requirements associated with expanding. For instance, if, instead of $38 million, Argile needed an additional $50 million in fixed assets to increase operations 10 percent, the AFN would be much greater. With lumpy assets, it is possible that a small projected increase in sales would require a significant increase in plant and equipment, which would require a very large financial requirement.

Self-Test Question

Discuss three factors that might cause "spontaneous" assets and liabilities to change at a different rate than sales.

Financial Control—Budgeting and Leverage

In the previous section, we focused on financial forecasting, emphasizing how growth in sales requires additional investment in assets, which, in turn, generally requires the firm to raise new funds externally. In the sections that follow, we consider the planning and control systems used by financial managers when implementing the forecasts. First, we look at the relationship between sales volume and profitability under different operating conditions. These relationships provide information that is used by managers to plan for changes in the firm's level of operations, financing needs, and profitability. Later, we examine the control phase of the planning and control process because a good control system is essential both to ensure that plans are executed properly and to facilitate a timely modification of plans if the assumptions upon which the initial plans were based turn out to be different than expected.

The planning process can be enhanced by examining the effects of changing operations on the firm's profitability, both from the standpoint of profits from operations and from the standpoint of profitability after financing effects are considered.

When Jack Smith became CEO at General Motors in 1992, he and his management team examined the operations that existed at GM at that time. They found the company's performance to be dismal, especially in North America, which produced almost a $5 billion loss in earnings before interest and taxes. Part of the solution to GM's problems was to reduce operating and financing costs in order to create more efficient operations — the hope was to break even, or to bring operating income up to zero, by 1993. That goal was accomplished, and in 1997 operating income from North American operations exceeded $3 billion. To achieve this turnaround, Smith and his staff at GM had to evaluate the impact on sales and net income of reducing costs through layoffs, savings in materials purchases, lowering debt, and so forth. In the next few sections, we look at some of the areas Smith might have evaluated to provide information about the effects of changing GM's operations.

Self-Test Question

How can the planning process be enhanced with a good financial control system?

Operating Breakeven Analysis

OPERATING BREAKEVEN ANALYSIS
An analytical technique for studying the relationship among sales revenues, operating costs, and profits.

The relationship between sales volume and operating profitability is explored in cost-volume-profit planning, or operating breakeven analysis. **Operating breakeven analysis** is a method of determining the point at which sales will just cover operating costs; that is, the point at which the firm's operations will break even. But, it also shows the magnitude of the firm's operating profits or losses if sales exceed or fall below that point. Breakeven analysis is important in the planning and control process because the cost-volume-profit relationship can be influenced greatly by the proportion of the firm's investment in assets that are fixed. A sufficient volume of sales must be anticipated and achieved if fixed and variable costs are to be covered, or else the firm will incur losses from operations. In other words, if a firm is to avoid accounting losses, its sales must cover all costs — those that vary directly with production and those that remain constant even when production levels change. Costs that vary directly with the level of production generally include the labor and materials needed to produce and sell the product, while the fixed operating costs generally include costs such as depreciation, rent, and insurance expenses that are incurred regardless of the firm's production level.

Operating breakeven analysis deals only with the upper portion of the income statement — the portion from sales to net operating income (NOI), or earnings before interest and taxes (EBIT). This portion generally is referred to as the *operating section* because it contains only the revenues and expenses associated with the normal production operations of the firm. Table 14-5 gives the operating section of Argile's forecasted 2000 income statement, which was shown in Table 14-3. For the discussion that follows, we assume that all of Argile's products sell for $15 each and the variable cost of goods sold per unit is $12.20, which is $81\frac{1}{3}$ percent of the selling price.

Breakeven Graph

Table 14-5 shows the net operating income (also referred to as the earnings before interest and taxes, or EBIT) for Argile if 110 million products are produced and sold during the year. But, what if Argile doesn't sell 110 million products? Certainly, the firm's net operating income will be something other than $154 million. Figure 14-2 shows the total revenues and total operating costs for Argile at various levels of sales, beginning with zero. According to the information given in Table 14-5, Argile has fixed costs, which include depreciation, rent, insurance, and so on, equal to $154 million. This amount must be paid even if the firm produces

---

TABLE 14-5

Argile Textiles: 2000 Forecasted Operating Income (millions of dollars)

Sales (S)	$1,650.0
Variable cost of goods sold (VC)	(1,342.0)
Gross profit (GP)	308.0
Fixed operating costs (F)	(154.0)
Net operating income (NOI)	$ 154.0

NOTES:

Sales in units = 110 million units.

Selling price per unit = $15.00.

Variable costs per unit = $1,342/110 = $12.20 = $15.00(0.8133).

Fixed operating costs = $154 million, which includes $55 million depreciation and $99 million in other fixed costs such as rent, insurance, and general office expenses.

FIGURE 14-2

Argile Textiles: Operating Breakeven Chart

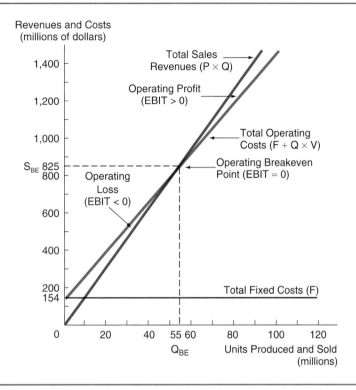

NOTES:

S_{BE} = operating breakeven in dollars.

Q = sales in units; Q_{BE} = operating breakeven in units.

F = fixed costs = $154 million.

V = variable costs per unit = $12.20.

P = price per unit = $15.00.

OPERATING BREAKEVEN POINT
Represents the level of production and sales where operating income is zero; it is the point where revenues from sales just equal total operating costs.

and sells nothing, so the $154 million fixed cost is represented by a horizontal line. If Argile produces and sells nothing, its sales revenues will be zero; but, *for each unit sold,* the firm's sales will increase by $15. Therefore, the total revenue line starts at the origin of the X and Y axes, and it has a slope equal to $15 to account for the dollar increase in sales for each additional unit sold. On the other hand, the line representing the total operating costs intersects the Y axis at $154 million, which represents the fixed costs incurred even when no products are sold, and it has a slope equal to $12.20, which is the cost directly associated with the production of each additional unit sold. The point at which the total revenue line intersects the total cost line is the **operating breakeven point**; this is where the revenues generated from sales just cover the *total operating costs* of the firm. Note that prior to the breakeven point, the total cost line is above the total revenue line, which shows Argile will suffer operating losses because the total costs cannot be covered by the sales revenues. And, after the breakeven point, the total revenue line is above the total cost line because revenues are more than sufficient to cover total operating costs, so Argile will realize operating profits.[3]

Breakeven Computation

Figure 14-2 shows that Argile must sell 55 million units to be at the operating breakeven point. If Argile sells 55 million products, it will generate $825 million in sales revenues, which will be just enough to cover the $825 million total operating costs — $154 million fixed costs and $671 million variable costs (55 million units at $12.20 per unit). If we do not have a graph like Figure 14-2, how can the operating breakeven point be computed? Actually, it is rather simple. Remember, the operating breakeven point is where the revenues generated from sales just cover the total operating costs, which include both the costs directly attributable to producing each unit and the fixed operating costs that remain constant no matter the production level. As long as the selling price of each unit (the slope of the total revenue line) is greater than the variable operating cost of each unit (the slope of the total operating cost line), each unit sold will generate revenues that contribute to covering the fixed operating costs. For Argile, this contribution (termed the *contribution margin*) is $2.80, which is the difference between the $15 selling price and the $12.20 variable cost of each unit. To compute the operating breakeven for Argile then, we have to determine how many units need to be sold to cover the fixed operating cost of $154 million if each unit has a contribution margin equal to $2.80. Just divide the $154 million fixed cost by the $2.80 contribution, and you will discover the breakeven point is 55 million units, which equates to $825 million in sales revenues.

More formally, the operating breakeven point can be found by setting the total revenues equal to the total operating costs so that net operating income (NOI) is zero. In equation form, NOI = 0 if

$$\begin{matrix} \text{Sales} \\ \text{revenues} \end{matrix} = \begin{matrix} \text{Total} \\ \text{operating} \\ \text{costs} \end{matrix} = \begin{matrix} \text{Total} \\ \text{variable} \\ \text{costs} \end{matrix} + \begin{matrix} \text{Total} \\ \text{fixed} \\ \text{costs} \end{matrix}$$

$$(P \times Q) = \text{TOC} = (V \times Q) + F$$

where P is the sales price per unit, Q is the number of units produced and sold, V is the variable operating cost per unit, and F is the total fixed operating costs.

---

[3]In Figure 14-2, we assume the operating costs can be divided into two distinct groups — fixed costs and variable costs. It should be noted that there are costs that are considered semivariable (or semifixed). These costs are fixed for a certain range of operations, but change if operations are either higher or lower. For the analysis that follows, we assume there are no semivariable costs, so that the operating costs can be separated into either a fixed component or a variable component.

Solving for the quantity that needs to be sold, Q, produces a formula that can be used to find the number of units that need to be sold to achieve operating breakeven:

14-1

$$Q_{OpBE} = \frac{F}{P - V} = \frac{F}{\text{Contribution margin}}$$

Thus, the operating breakeven point for Argile is

$$Q_{OpBE} = \frac{\$154.0 \text{ million}}{\$15.00 - \$12.20} = \frac{\$154.0 \text{ million}}{\$2.80} = 55.0 \text{ million units.}$$

In the remainder of the chapter, we omit the word "million" in the computations and include it only in the final answer.

From Equation 14-1, we can see that the operating breakeven point is lower (higher) if the numerator is lower (higher) or if the denominator is higher (lower). Therefore, all else equal, one firm will have a lower operating breakeven point than another firm if its fixed costs are lower, if selling price of its product is higher, if its variable operating cost per unit is lower, or if some combination of these exists. For instance, if Argile could increase the sales price per unit from $15.00 to $16.05 without affecting either its fixed operating costs ($154 million) or its variable operating cost per unit ($12.20), then its operating breakeven point would fall to 40 million units.

The operating breakeven point also can be stated in terms of the total sales revenues needed to cover total operating costs. At this point, we just need to multiply the sales price per unit by the breakeven quantity we found using Equation 14-1, which yields $825 million for Argile. Or, we can restate the contribution margin as a percent of the sales price per unit (this is called the *gross profit margin*), and then apply Equation 14-1. In other words,

14-2

$$S_{OpBE} = \frac{F}{1 - \left(\dfrac{V}{P}\right)} = \frac{F}{\text{Gross profit margin}}$$

Solving Equation 14-2 for Argile, the operating breakeven based on dollar sales is

$$S_{OpBE} = \frac{\$154.0}{1 - \left(\dfrac{\$12.20}{\$15.00}\right)} = \frac{\$154.0}{1 - 0.8133} = \frac{\$154.0}{0.1867} = \$825.0 \text{ million}$$

Equation 14-2 shows that 18.67¢ of every $1 of sales revenues goes to cover the fixed operating costs, so $825 million worth of the product must be sold to break even.

Breakeven analysis based on dollar sales rather than on units of output is useful in determining the breakeven volume for a firm that sells many products at varying prices. This analysis requires only that total sales, total fixed costs, and total variable costs at a given level are known.

Using Operating Breakeven Analysis

Operating breakeven analysis can shed light on three important types of business decisions: (1) When making new product decisions, breakeven analysis can help determine how large the sales of a new product must be for the firm to achieve profitability. (2) Breakeven analysis can be used to study the effects of a general expansion in the level of the firm's operations; an expansion would cause the levels of both fixed and variable costs to rise, but it also would increase expected sales. (3) When considering modernization and automation projects, where the fixed investment in equipment is increased in order to lower variable costs, particularly the cost of labor, breakeven analysis can help management analyze the consequences of purchasing these projects.

However, care must be taken when using operating breakeven analysis. To apply breakeven analysis as we have discussed it here requires that the sales price *per unit*, the variable cost *per unit*, and the *total* fixed operating costs do not change with the level of the firm's production and sales. Within a narrow range of production and sales, this assumption is probably not a major issue. But what if the firm expects either to produce a much greater (or fewer) number of products than normal or to expand its plant and equipment significantly? Will the numbers change? Most likely the answer is yes. Therefore, use of a single breakeven chart such as the one presented in Figure 14-2 is impractical — such a chart provides useful information, but the fact that it cannot deal with changes in the price of the product, with changing variable cost rates, and with changes in fixed cost levels suggests the need for a more flexible type of analysis. Today, such analysis is provided by computer simulation. Functions such as those expressed in Equations 14-1 and 14-2 (or more complicated versions of them) can be put into a spreadsheet or similarly modeled with other computer software, and then variables such as sales price, P, the variable cost rate, V, and the level of fixed costs, F, can be changed. The model can instantaneously produce new versions of Figure 14-2, or a whole set of such graphs, to show what the operating breakeven point would be under different production setups and price-cost situations.

Self-Test Questions

Is interest paid considered in operating breakeven analysis? Why or why not?

Give the equations used to calculate the operating breakeven point in units and in dollar sales.

Give some examples of business decisions for which operating breakeven analysis might be useful.

Identify some limitations to the use of a single operating breakeven chart.

Operating Leverage

OPERATING LEVERAGE
The existence of fixed operating costs, such that a change in sales will produce a larger change in operating income (EBIT).

If a high percentage of a firm's total operating costs are fixed, the firm is said to have a high degree of **operating leverage.** In physics, leverage implies the use of a lever to raise a heavy object with a small amount of force. In politics, people who have leverage can accomplish a great deal with their smallest word or action. *In business terminology, a high degree of operating leverage, other* *things held constant, means that a relatively small change in sales will result in a large change in operating income.*

Operating leverage arises because the firm has fixed operating costs that must be covered no matter the level of production. The impact of the leverage, however, depends on the actual operating level of the firm. For example, Argile has $154.0 million in fixed operating costs, which are covered rather easily because the firm currently sells 110 million products; thus, it is well above its operating breakeven point of 55 million units. But what would happen to the operating income if Argile sold more or less than forecasted? To answer this question we need to determine the *degree of operating leverage (DOL)* associated with Argile's 2000 forecasted operations.

DEGREE OF OPERATING LEVERAGE (DOL)
The percentage change in NOI (or EBIT) associated with a given percentage change in sales.

Operating leverage can be defined more precisely in terms of the way a given change in sales volume affects net operating income (NOI). To measure the effect of a change in sales volume on NOI, we calculate the **degree of operating leverage (DOL),** which is defined as the percentage change in NOI (or EBIT) associated with a given percentage change in sales[4]:

$$14\text{-}3 \qquad DOL = \frac{\text{Percentage change in NOI}}{\text{Percentage change in sales}} = \frac{\left(\dfrac{\Delta NOI}{NOI}\right)}{\left(\dfrac{\Delta\,Sales}{Sales}\right)} = \frac{\left(\dfrac{\Delta\,EBIT}{EBIT}\right)}{\left(\dfrac{\Delta\,Sales}{Sales}\right)} = \frac{\left(\dfrac{\Delta\,EBIT}{EBIT}\right)}{\left(\dfrac{\Delta\,Q}{Q}\right)}$$

Remember, the symbol Δ means "change." Thus, in effect, the DOL is an index number that measures the effect of a change in sales on operating income or EBIT.

Table 14-5 showed the NOI for Argile is $154.0 million at production and sales equal to 110 million units. If the number of units produced and sold increases to 121 million, the operating income (in millions of dollars) would be

$$NOI = 121(\$15.00 - \$12.20) - \$154.0 = \$184.8 \text{ million}$$

Therefore, the degree of operating leverage associated with this change is 2.0:

$$DOL = \frac{\left(\dfrac{\$184.8 - \$154.0}{\$154.0}\right)}{\left[\dfrac{\$15.00\,(121 - 110)}{\$15.00\,(110)}\right]} = \frac{\left(\dfrac{\$30.2}{\$154}\right)}{\left(\dfrac{11}{110}\right)} = \frac{0.20}{0.10} = \frac{20.0\%}{10.0\%} = 2.0\times$$

To interpret the meaning of the value of the degree of operating leverage, remember we computed the percent change in operating income and then divided the result by the percent change in sales. Taken literally, then, Argile's DOL of 2.0 indicates that the percent change in operating income will be 2.0 times the percent change in sales from the current 110 million units ($1,650.0 million). Thus, if the number of units sold increases from 110 million to 121 million, or by 10 percent, Argile's operating income should increase by 2.0 times 10 percent, or by 20.0 percent; at 121 million units, operating income should be 20.0 percent greater than the $154.0 million generated at 110 million units of sales; the new

[4]Remember the net operating income (NOI) is the same as the earnings before interest and taxes (EBIT).

TABLE 14-6

Argile Textiles: Operating Income at Sales Levels of 110 Million Units and 121 Million Units (millions of dollars)

	2000 Forecasted Operations	Sales Increase	Unit Change	Percent Change
Sales in units (millions)	110	121	11	+10.0%
Sales revenues	$1,650.0	$1,815.0	$165.0	+10.0%
Variable cost of goods sold	(1,342.0)	(1,476.2)	(134.2)	+10.0%
Gross profit	308.0	338.8	30.8	+10.0%
Fixed operating costs	(154.0)	(154.0)	(0.0)	0.0%
Net operating income (EBIT)	$ 154.0	$ 184.8	$ 30.8	+20.0%

operating income should be $184.8 million = 1.20 × $154 million. Table 14-6 shows a comparison of the operating incomes generated at the two different sales levels.

The results contained in Table 14-6 show that Argile's *gross profit* would increase by $30.8 million, or by 10 percent, if sales increase 10 percent. The fixed operating costs remain constant at $154.0 million, so EBIT also increases by $30.8 million, and the total impact of a 10 percent increase in sales is a 20 percent increase in operating income. If the fixed operating costs were to increase in proportion to the increase in sales — that is, 10 percent — then the net operating income also would increase by 10 percent because all revenues and costs would have changed by the same proportion. But, in reality, fixed operating costs will not change (a 0 percent increase), thus a 10 percent increase in Argile's forecasted 2000 sales will result in an *additional* 10 percent increase in operating income. The total increase is 20 percent, which results because operating leverage exists.

Equation 14-3 can be simplified so the degree of operating leverage at a particular level of operations can be calculated as follows[5]:

---

[5]Equation 14-4 can be derived by restating Equation 14-3 in terms of the variables we have defined previously, and then simplifying the result. Starting with Equation 14-3, we have

$$\text{DOL} = \frac{\text{Percentage change in NOI}}{\text{Percentage change in sales}} = \frac{\left(\dfrac{\Delta \text{NOI}}{\text{NOI}}\right)}{\left(\dfrac{\Delta \text{Sales}}{\text{Sales}}\right)} = \frac{\left(\dfrac{\Delta \text{EBIT}}{\text{EBIT}}\right)}{\left(\dfrac{\Delta Q}{Q}\right)} \tag{14-3}$$

EBIT can be stated as the gross profit, $Q(P - V)$, minus the fixed operating costs, F. So, if we use Q to indicate the level of operations forecasted for 2000 and Q^* to indicate the level of operations that would exist if operations were different, the percent change in EBIT is stated as

$$\% \, \Delta \, \text{EBIT} = \frac{[Q^* (P - V) - F] - [Q (P - V) - F]}{Q (P - V) - F} = \frac{(Q^* - Q)(P - V)}{Q (P - V) - F}$$

Substituting into Equation 14-3, restating the denominator, and solving, yields

$$\text{DOL} = \frac{\left[\dfrac{(Q^* - Q)(P - V)}{Q (P - V) - F}\right]}{\left[\dfrac{Q^* - Q}{Q}\right]} = \frac{(Q^* - Q)(P - V)}{Q (P - V) - F} \times \left(\frac{Q}{Q^* - Q}\right) = \frac{Q (P - V)}{Q (P - V) - F} \tag{14-4}$$

14-4
$$DOL_Q = \frac{Q(P - V)}{Q(P - V) - F}$$

or, rearranging the terms, DOL can be stated in terms of sales revenues as follows:

14-4a
$$DOL_S = \frac{(Q \times P) - (Q \times V)}{(Q \times P) - (Q \times V) - F} = \frac{S - VC}{S - VC - F} = \frac{\text{Gross profit}}{\text{EBIT}}$$

To solve Equation 14-4 or Equation 14-4a, we only need information from Argile's forecasted operations; we do not need information about the possible change in forecasted operations. Thus, Q represents the forecasted 2000 level of production and sales, and S and VC are the sales and variable operating costs, respectively, at that level of operations. For Argile, the equation solution for DOL would be

$$DOL_{Allied} = \frac{110(\$15.00 - \$12.20)}{110(\$15.00 - 12.20) - \$154} = \frac{\$1,650 - \$1,342}{\$1,650 - \$1,342 - \$154}$$

$$= \frac{\$308}{\$154} = 2.0\times$$

Equation 14-4 is normally used to analyze a single product, such as GM's Chevrolet Cavalier, whereas Equation 14-4a is used to evaluate an entire firm with many types of products and for which "quantity in units" and "sales price" are not meaningful.

The DOL of 2.0× indicates that *each* 1 percent *change* in sales will result in a 2 percent *change* in operating income. What would happen if Argile's sales decrease, say, by 10 percent? According to the interpretation of the DOL figure, Argile's operating income would be expected to decrease by 20 percent. Table 14-7 shows that this actually would be the case. Therefore, the DOL value indicates the *change* (increase or decrease) in operating income resulting from

TABLE 14-7

Argile Textiles: Operating Income at Sales Levels of 110 Million Units and 99 Million Units (millions of dollars)

	2000 Forecasted Operations	Sales Decrease	Unit Change	Percent Change
Sales in units (millions)	110	99	(11)	−10.0%
Sales revenues	$1,650.0	$1,485.0	($165.0)	−10.0%
Variable cost of goods sold	(1,342.0)	(1,207.8)	134.2	−10.0%
Gross profit	308.0	277.2	(30.8)	−10.0%
Fixed operating costs	(154.0)	(154.0)	(0.0)	0.0%
Net operating income (EBIT)	$ 154.0	$ 123.2	($ 30.8)	−20.0%

a *change* (increase or decrease) in the level of operations. It should be apparent that the greater the DOL, the greater the impact of a change in operations on operating income, whether the change is an increase or a decrease.

The DOL value found by using Equation 14-4 is the degree of operating leverage only for a specific initial sales level. For Argile, that sales level is 110 million units, or $1,650 million. The DOL value would differ if the initial (existing) level of operations differed. For example, if Argile's operating cost structure was the same, but only 60 million units were produced and sold, the DOL would have been

$$\text{DOL}_{60} = \frac{(60)(\$15.00 - \$12.20)}{[(60)(\$15.00 - \$12.20)] - \$154.0} = \frac{\$168.0}{\$14.0} = 12.0\times$$

The DOL at 60 million units produced and sold is six times greater than the DOL at 110 million units. Thus, from base sales of 60 million units, a 10 percent increase in sales, from 60 million to 66 million units, would result in a $12 \times 10\%$ = 120% increase in operating income, from $14.0 million to $30.8 million. This shows that when Argile's operations are closer to its operating breakeven point of 55 million units, its degree of operating leverage is higher.

In general, given the same operating cost structure, if a firm's level of operations is decreased, its DOL increases; stated differently, the closer a firm is to its operating breakeven point, the greater is its degree of operating leverage. This occurs because, as Figure 14-2 indicates, the closer a firm is to its operating breakeven point, the more likely it is to incur an operating loss due to a decrease in sales — there is not a very large buffer in operating income to absorb a decrease in sales and still be able to cover the fixed operating costs. Similarly, at the same level of production and sales, a firm's degree of operating leverage will be higher the lower the contribution margin for its products — the lower the contribution margin, the less each product sold is able to help cover the fixed operating costs, and the closer the firm is to its operating breakeven point. Therefore, the higher the DOL for a particular firm, it generally can be concluded the closer the firm is to its operating breakeven point, and the more sensitive its operating income is to a change in sales volume. *Greater sensitivity generally implies greater risk; thus, it can be stated that firms with higher DOLs generally are considered to have riskier operations than firms with lower DOLs.*

Operating Leverage and Operating Breakeven

The relationship between operating leverage and the operating breakeven point is illustrated in Figure 14-3, where various levels of operations are compared for Argile and two other textile manufacturers. One firm has a higher contribution margin than Argile and the other firm has lower fixed operating costs, so we know the other two firms have operating breakeven points that are less than Argile's. Allied Cloth has the lowest operating breakeven point because it has the highest contribution margin relative to its fixed costs. Argile has the highest operating breakeven point because it uses the greatest relative amount of operating leverage of the three firms. Consequently, all else equal, of the three textile manufacturers, Argile's operating income would be magnified the most if actual sales turned out to be greater than forecasted, but it also would experience the greatest decrease in operating income if actual sales turned out to be less than expected.

FIGURE 14-3

Operating Leverage

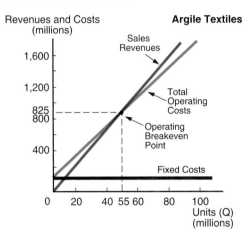

Argile Textiles

Selling price = $15.00
Variable cost per unit = $12.20
Fixed costs = $154 million
Operating breakeven = 55 million units
= $825 million

| Sales Level | | Total | Operating | |
Units (Q)	Revenues ($)	Operating Costs	Profit (EBIT)	DOL
30	$ 450	$ 520	($ 70)	
60	900	886	14	12.0
110	1,650	1,496	154	2.0
150	2,250	1,984	266	1.6

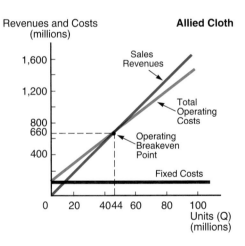

Allied Cloth

Selling price = $15.00
Variable cost per unit = $11.50
Fixed costs = $154 million
Operating breakeven = 44 million units
= $660 million

| Sales Level | | Total | Operating | |
Units (Q)	Revenues ($)	Operating Costs	Profit (EBIT)	DOL
30	$ 450	$ 499	($ 49)	
60	900	844	56	3.8
110	1,650	1,419	231	1.7
150	2,250	1,879	371	1.4

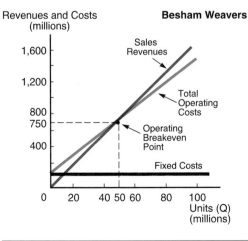

Besham Weavers

Selling price = $15.00
Variable cost per unit = $12.20
Fixed costs = $140 million
Operating breakeven = 50 million units
= $750 million

| Sales Level | | Total | Operating | |
Units (Q)	Revenues ($)	Operating Costs	Profit (EBIT)	DOL
30	$ 450	$ 506	($ 56)	
60	900	872	28	6.0
110	1,650	1,482	168	1.8
150	2,250	1,970	280	1.5

Self-Test Questions

What does the term "high degree of operating leverage" imply, and what are some implications of having a high degree of operating leverage?

Give the general equation used to calculate the degree of operating leverage.

What is the association between the concepts of operating breakeven and operating leverage?

Financial Breakeven Analysis

FINANCIAL BREAKEVEN ANALYSIS
Determining the operating income (EBIT) the firm needs to just cover all of its fixed financing costs and produce earnings per share equal to zero.

Operating breakeven analysis deals with evaluation of production and sales to determine at what level the firm's sales revenues will just cover its operating costs; the point where the operating income is zero. **Financial breakeven analysis** is a method of determining the operating income, or EBIT, the firm needs to just cover all of its *financing costs* and produce earnings per share equal to zero. Typically, the financing costs involved in financial breakeven analysis consist of the interest payments to bondholders and the dividend payments to preferred stockholders. Usually these financing costs are fixed, and, in every case, they must be paid before dividends can be paid to common stockholders.

Financial breakeven analysis deals with the lower portion of the income statement — the portion from operating income (EBIT) to earnings available to common stockholders. This portion of the income statement is generally referred to as the *financing section* because it contains the expenses associated with the financing arrangements of the firm. The financing section of Argile's 2000 forecasted income statement is contained in Table 14-8.

Breakeven Graph

FINANCIAL BREAKEVEN POINT
The point at which EPS equals zero.

Figure 14-4 shows the earnings per share (EPS) for Argile at various levels of EBIT. The point at which EPS equals zero is referred to as the **financial breakeven point.** As the graph indicates, the financial breakeven point for Argile is where EBIT equals $42.3 million. At this EBIT level, the income generated from operations is just sufficient to cover the financing costs, including income taxes; thus

---

TABLE 14-8

Argile Textiles: 2000 Forecasted Earnings per Share (millions of dollars)

Earnings before interest and taxes (EBIT)	$154.0
Interest	(42.3)
Earnings before taxes (EBT)	111.7
Taxes (40%)	(44.7)
Net income	67.0
Preferred dividends	(0.0)
Earnings available to common stockholders	$ 67.0

NOTES:
Number of common shares = 26.2 million.

Earnings per share = $67.0/26.2 = $2.55 (actual number of shares is 26.24 million).

EPS equals zero. To see this is true, we can compute the EPS when EBIT is $42.3 million:

Earnings before interest and taxes (EBIT)	$42.3
Interest	(42.3)
Earnings before taxes (EBT)	0.0
Taxes (40%)	(0.0)
Net income	0.0
Earnings available to common stockholders (EAC)	$ 0.0

EPS = $0/26.2 = $0

Breakeven Computation

The results obtained from Figure 14-4 can be translated algebraically to produce a relatively simple equation that can be used to compute the financial breakeven point of any firm. First, remember the financial breakeven point is defined as the level of EBIT that generates EPS equal to zero. Therefore, at the financial breakeven point,

14-5

$$EPS = \frac{\text{Earnings available to common stockholders}}{\text{Number of common shares outstanding}} = 0$$

$$= \frac{(\text{EBIT} - \text{I})(1 - \text{T}) - \text{D}_{ps}}{\text{Shrs}_C} = 0$$

FIGURE 14-4

Argile Textiles: Financial Breakeven Chart

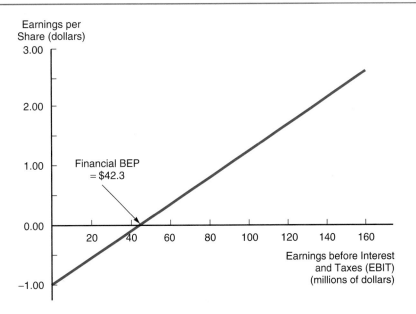

Here EBIT is the earnings before interest and taxes, I represents the interest payments on debt, T is the marginal tax rate, D_{ps} is the amount of dividends paid to preferred stockholders, and $Shrs_C$ is the number of common shares outstanding. Note that EPS equals zero if the numerator in Equation 14-5, which is the earnings available to common stockholders, equals zero; thus, the financial breakeven point also can be stated as follows:

$$(EBIT - I)(1 - T) - D_{ps} = 0$$

Rearranging this equation to solve for EBIT gives the solution for the level of EBIT needed to produce EPS equal to zero. Therefore, the computation for a firm's financial breakeven point is

14-6

$$EBIT_{FinBE} = I + \frac{D_{ps}}{(1 - T)}$$

Using Equation 14-6, the financial breakeven point for Argile Textiles in 2000 is

$$EBIT_{FinBE} = \$42.3 + \frac{\$0}{1 - 0.4} = \$42.3$$

which is the same result shown in Figure 14-4.

According to Equation 14-6, the amount of preferred stock dividends must be stated on a before-tax basis to determine the financial breakeven point. If a firm has no preferred stock, though, the firm only needs to cover its interest payments, so the financial breakeven point simply equals the interest expense. This is the case for Argile because it has no preferred stock. Because most corporations in the United States do not have preferred stock outstanding, we will not include preferred dividends in the discussions that follow.

Using Financial Breakeven Analysis

Financial breakeven analysis can be used to help determine the impact of the firm's financing mix on the earnings available to common stockholders.[6] When the firm uses financing alternatives that require fixed financing costs such as interest, financial leverage exists. Financial leverage affects the financing section of the income statement like operating leverage affects the operating section. This point is discussed in the next section.

Self-Test Questions

Define the financial breakeven point. How does the financial breakeven point differ from the operating breakeven point?

Why is it important to carry out financial breakeven analysis?

---

[6]The effect of financing the firm with various proportions of debt and equity was discussed in detail in Chapter 11.

Financial Leverage

FINANCIAL LEVERAGE
The existence of fixed financial costs such as interest; when a change in EBIT results in a larger change in EPS.

DEGREE OF FINANCIAL LEVERAGE (DFL)
The percent change in EPS that results from a given percent change in EBIT.

While operating leverage considers how changing sales volume affects operating income, **financial leverage** considers the impact changing operating income has on earnings per share, or earnings available to common stockholders. Thus, operating leverage affects the operating section of the income statement, whereas financial leverage affects the financing section of the income statement. *Financial leverage takes over where operating leverage leaves off, further magnifying the effects on earnings per share of changes in the level of sales.* For this reason, operating leverage sometimes is referred to as *first-stage leverage* and financial leverage as *second-stage leverage.*

Like operating leverage, financial leverage arises because fixed costs exist; in this case, the fixed costs are associated with how the firm is financed. The **degree of financial leverage (DFL)** is defined as the percent change in earnings per share (EPS) that results from a given percent change in earnings before interest and taxes (EBIT), and it is computed as follows:

14-7
$$DFL = \frac{\text{Percent change in EPS}}{\text{Percent change in EBIT}} = \frac{\left(\frac{\Delta\ EPS}{EPS}\right)}{\left(\frac{\Delta\ EBIT}{EBIT}\right)}$$

Table 14-9 shows the results of increasing Argile's EBIT 20 percent. The increase in EPS is 27.6 percent, which is 1.38 times the change in EBIT; therefore, the DFL for Argile equals 1.38.

TABLE 14-9

Argile Textiles: Earnings per Share at Sales Levels of 110 Million Units and 121 Million Units (millions of dollars, except per-share data)[a]

	2000 Forecasted Operations	Sales Increase	Dollar Change	Percent Change
Sales in units (millions)	110	121		
Earnings before interest and taxes (EBIT)	$154.0	$184.8	$30.8	+20.0%
Interest (I)	(42.3)	(42.3)	(0.0)	+ 0.0%
Earnings before taxes (EBT)	111.7	142.5	30.8	+27.6%
Taxes (40%)	(44.7)	(57.0)	(12.3)	+27.6%
Net income	$ 67.0	$ 85.5	$18.5	+27.6%
Earnings per share (26.2 million shares)	$2.55	$3.26	$0.71	+27.6%

NOTE:
[a]A spreadsheet was used to generate the results in this table. Only the final results are rounded; thus, there might be some rounding differences if you rely on some of the values in the table, which are rounded to one decimal place, to compute the other values.

The degree of financial leverage at a particular level of EBIT can be computed easily by using the following equation[7]:

14-8

$$DFL = \frac{EBIT}{EBIT - I} = \frac{EBIT}{EBIT - (Financial\ BEP)}$$

Using Equation 14-8, the DFL for Argile Textiles at EBIT equal to $154.0 million (sales of 110 million units) is

$$DFL_{110} = \frac{\$154.0}{\$154.0 - \$42.3} = \frac{\$154.0}{\$111.7} = 1.38\times$$

The interpretation of the DFL value is the same as for the degree of operating leverage, except the starting point for evaluating financial leverage is the earnings before interest and taxes (EBIT) and the ending point is earnings per share (EPS). Because the DFL for Argile is 1.38, the company can expect a 1.38 percent change in EPS for every 1 percent change in EBIT; a 20 percent increase in EBIT

---

[7]Equation 14-8 can be derived easily by expanding Equation 14-7, rearranging the terms, and then simplifying the results. If we use EPS and EBIT to indicate the 2000 forecasted EPS and EBIT, respectively, and EPS* and EBIT* to indicate the EPS and EBIT that would exist after a change in sales volume, then

$$DFL = \frac{\left(\dfrac{\Delta\ EPS}{EPS}\right)}{\left(\dfrac{\Delta\ EBIT}{EBIT}\right)} = \frac{\left(\dfrac{EPS^* - EPS}{EPS}\right)}{\left(\dfrac{EBIT^* - EBIT}{EBIT}\right)}$$

The computation for 2000 forecasted earnings per share is

$$EPS = \frac{(EBIT - I)(1 - T)}{Shrs_C}$$

where $Shrs_C$ is the number of common shares outstanding. The percent change in EPS can be written and simplified as follows:

$$\Delta EPS = \frac{\left[\dfrac{(EBIT^* - I)(1 - T)}{Shrs_C}\right] - \left[\dfrac{(EBIT - I)(1 - T)}{Shrs_C}\right]}{\left[\dfrac{(EBIT - I)(1 - T)}{Shrs_C}\right]} = \frac{(EBIT^* - I)(1 - T) - (EBIT - I)(1 - T)}{(EBIT - I)(1 - T)}$$

$$= \frac{EBIT^* - EBIT}{(EBIT - I)}$$

Substituting this relationship into the computation of DFL, we have

$$DFL = \frac{\left[\dfrac{(EBIT^* - EBIT)}{EBIT - I}\right]}{\left[\dfrac{(EBIT^* - EBIT)}{EBIT}\right]} = \frac{(EBIT^* - EBIT)}{(EBIT - I)} \times \frac{EBIT}{(EBIT^* - EBIT)} \qquad \textbf{(14-8)}$$

$$= \frac{EBIT}{EBIT - I} = \frac{EBIT}{EBIT - (Financial\ BEP)}$$

If a firm has preferred stock, the relationship given in Equation 14-6 can be substituted in this equation for the financial breakeven point.

results in a 27.6 percent (20 percent × 1.38) increase in earnings available to common stockholders, thus the same percent increase in EPS (the number of common shares outstanding do not change). Unfortunately, the opposite also is true — if Argile's 2000 EBIT is 20 percent below expectations, its EPS will be 27.6 percent below the forecast of $2.55, or $1.85. To prove this result is correct, construct the financing section of Argile's income statement when EBIT equals $123.2 million = 0.80 × $154 million.

The value of the degree of financial leverage found using Equation 14-8 pertains to one specific initial EBIT level. If the level of sales changes, and thus the EBIT changes, so does the value computed for DFL. For example, at sales equal to 80 million units, Argile's EBIT would be [80 ($15.00 − $12.20)] − $154.0 = $70.0 million, and the DFL value would be

$$DFL_{80} = \frac{\$70.0}{\$70.0 - \$42.3} = \frac{\$70.0}{\$27.7} = 2.52\times$$

Compared with sales equal to 110 million units, at sales equal to 80 million units Argile would have greater difficulty covering the fixed financing costs, so its DFL is much greater. At EBIT equal to $70.0 million, Argile is close to its financial breakeven point — EBIT equal to $42.3 million — and its degree of financial leverage is high. So, the more difficulty a firm has covering its fixed financing costs with operating income, the greater its degree of financial leverage. In general, then, the higher the DFL for a particular firm, the closer the firm is to its financial breakeven point and the more sensitive its earnings per share is to a change in operating income. *Greater sensitivity implies greater risk; thus, it can be stated that firms with higher DFLs generally are considered to have greater financial risk than firms with lower DFLs.*

Self-Test Questions

What does the term "high degree of financial leverage" imply, and what are some implications of having a high degree of financial leverage?

Give the general equation used to calculate the degree of financial leverage. Compare the equation for DFL with the equation for times-interest-earned given in Chapter 13.

Combining Operating and Financial Leverage

Our analysis of operating leverage and financial leverage has shown that *(1) the greater the degree of operating leverage, or fixed operating costs for a particular level of operations, the more sensitive EBIT will be to changes in sales volume, and (2) the greater the degree of financial leverage (or fixed financial costs for a particular level of operations), the more sensitive EPS will be to changes in EBIT.* Therefore, if a firm has a considerable amount of both operating and financial leverage, then even small changes in sales will lead to wide fluctuations in EPS. Look at the effect leverage has on Argile's 2000 forecasted operations. We found that if the sales volume increases by 10 percent, Argile's EBIT would increase by 20 percent; if EBIT increases by 20 percent, its EPS would increase by 27.6 percent. So, in combination, a 10 percent increase in sales

DEGREE OF TOTAL LEVERAGE (DTL)
The percent change in EPS resulting from a change in sales.

volume would result in a 27.6 percent increase in EPS. This shows the impact of total leverage, which is the combination of both operating leverage and financial leverage, with respect to Argile's current operations.

The **degree of total leverage (DTL)** is defined as the percent change in EPS resulting from a change in sales volume. This relationship can be written as follows:

$$14\text{-}9$$

$$\text{Degree of total leverage} = \text{DTL} = \frac{\left(\dfrac{\Delta \text{ EPS}}{\text{EPS}}\right)}{\left(\dfrac{\Delta \text{ Sales}}{\text{Sales}}\right)} = \frac{\left(\dfrac{\Delta \text{ EBIT}}{\text{EBIT}}\right)}{\left(\dfrac{\Delta \text{ Sales}}{\text{Sales}}\right)} \times \frac{\left(\dfrac{\Delta \text{ EPS}}{\text{EPS}}\right)}{\left(\dfrac{\Delta \text{ EBIT}}{\text{EBIT}}\right)} = \text{DOL} \times \text{DFL}$$

Combining the equations for DOL (Equations 14-4 and 14-4a) and for DFL (Equation 14-8), Equation 14-9 can be restated as follows:

$$14\text{-}10$$

$$\text{DTL} = \frac{\text{Gross profit}}{\text{EBIT}} \times \frac{\text{EBIT}}{\text{EBIT} - (\text{Financial BEP})} = \frac{\text{Gross profit}}{\text{EBIT} - (\text{Financial BEP})}$$

$$= \frac{S - VC}{\text{EBIT} - I} = \frac{Q(P - V)}{[Q(P - V) - F] - I}$$

Using Equation 14-10, the degree of total leverage for Argile would be

$$\text{DTL}_{110} = \frac{110(\$15.00 - \$12.20)}{[110(\$15.00 - \$12.20) - \$154.0] - \$42.3}$$

$$= \frac{\$308.0}{\$154.0 - \$42.3} = \frac{\$308.0}{\$111.7}$$

$$= 2.76\times$$

According to Equation 14-9, we could have arrived at the same result for DTL by multiplying the degree of operating leverage by the degree of financial leverage, so, the DTL for Argile would be 2.0 × 1.38 = 2.76. This value indicates that for every one percent change in sales volume, Argile's EPS will change by 2.76 percent; a 10 percent increase in sales will result in a 27.6 percent increase in EPS. This is exactly the impact expected.

The value of DTL can be used to compute the new earnings per share (EPS*) after a change in sales volume. We already know that Argile's EPS will change by 2.76 percent for every 1 percent change in sales. So, EPS* resulting from a 10 percent increase in sales can be computed as follows:

$$\text{EPS*} = \text{EPS}[1 + (0.10)(2.76)] = \$2.55 \times (1 + 0.276) = \$3.25 \text{ (rounding)}$$

which is the same result given in Table 14-9.

The degree of combined (total) leverage concept is useful primarily for the insights it provides regarding the joint effects of operating and financial leverage on earnings per share. The concept can be used to show management, for example, that a decision to automate a plant and to finance the new equipment with debt would result in a situation where a 10 percent decline in sales would result in a nearly 50 percent decline in earnings, whereas with a different operating and financial package, a 10 percent sales decline would cause earnings to decline only by 15 percent. Having the alternatives stated in this manner gives decision makers a better idea of the ramifications of alternative actions with respect to the firm's level of operations and how those operations are financed.

Self-Test Questions

What information is provided by the degree of total (combined) leverage?

What does the term "high degree of total leverage" imply?

Using Leverage and Forecasting for Control

From the discussion in the previous sections, it should be clear what the impact on income would be if the 2000 sales forecast for Argile Textiles is different than expected. If sales are greater than expected, both operating and financial leverage will magnify the "bottom line" impact on EPS (DTL = 2.76). But the opposite also holds. Consequently, if Argile does not meet its forecasted sales level, leverage will result in a magnified loss in income compared with what is expected. This will occur because production facilities might have been expanded too greatly, inventories might be built up too quickly, and so on; the end result might be that the firm suffers a significant income loss. This loss will result in a lower than expected addition to retained earnings, which means the plans for additional external funds needed to support the firm's operations will be inadequate. Likewise, if the sales forecast is too low, then, if the firm is at full capacity, it will not be able to meet the additional demand, and sales opportunities will be lost — perhaps forever. In the previous sections, we showed only how changes in operations (2000 forecasts) affect the income generated by the firm; we did not continue the process to show the impact on the balance sheet and the financing needs of the firm. To determine the impact on the financial statements, the financial manager needs to repeat the steps discussed in the first part of this chapter. It is at this stage that the financial manager needs to evaluate and act on the feedback received from the forecasting and budgeting processes. In effect, then, the forecasting (planning) and control of the firm is an ongoing activity, a vital function to the long-run survival of any firm.

The forecasting and control functions described in this chapter are important for several reasons. First, if the projected operating results are unsatisfactory, management can "go back to the drawing board," reformulate its plans, and develop more reasonable targets for the coming year. Second, it is possible that the funds required to meet the sales forecast simply cannot be obtained; if so, it is obviously better to know this in advance and to scale back the projected level of operations than to suddenly run out of cash and have operations grind to a halt. Third, even if the required funds can be raised, it is desirable to plan for their acquisition well in advance. Finally, any deviation from the projections needs to be dealt with to improve future forecasts and the predictability of the firm's operations to ensure the goals of the firm are being pursued appropriately.

Self-Test Question

Why is it important that the forecasting and control of the firm be an ongoing activity?

Cash Budgeting

One of the most important procedures in budgeting and control is construction of a cash budget. The cash budget helps management plan investment and borrowing strategies, and it also is used to provide feedback and control to improve the efficiency of financial management in the future.

The firm estimates its general needs for cash as a part of its overall budgeting, or forecasting, process. First, it forecasts its operating activities such as expenses and revenues for the period in question. Then, the financing and investment activities necessary to attain that level of operations must be forecasted. Such forecasts entail the construction of *pro forma* financial statements, which we discussed earlier in this chapter. The information provided from the *pro forma* balance sheet and income statement is combined with projections about the delay in collecting accounts receivable, the delay in paying suppliers and employees, tax payment dates, dividend and interest payment dates, and so on. All of this information is summarized in the **cash budget,** which shows the firm's projected cash inflows and outflows over some specified period. Generally, firms use a monthly cash budget forecasted over the next year plus a more detailed daily or weekly cash budget for the coming month. The monthly cash budgets are used for planning purposes and the daily or weekly budgets for actual cash control.

The cash budget provides much more detailed information concerning a firm's future cash flows than do the forecasted financial statements. Looking again at Argile Textiles' forecasted financial statements, we find net income in 2000 is predicted to be $67.0 million and, according to the forecasts given in Table 14-3, we find the net cash flow (in millions of dollars) generated from operations in 2000 is expected to be

> **CASH BUDGET**
> A schedule showing cash receipts, cash disbursements, and cash balances for a firm over a specified time period.

Net income	$ 67.0
Add: Noncash expenses (depreciation)	55.0
Gross cash flow from operations	$122.0
Adjustments to gross cash flow (change from 1999 balance sheet):	
Increase in accounts receivable	(18.0)
Increase in inventories	(27.0)
Increase in accounts payable	3.0
Increase in accruals	6.0
Total adjustments to gross cash flow	$ (36.0)
Net cash flow from operations	$ 86.0

Therefore, in 2000, it is expected Argile will generate $86 million cash inflow through normal production and sales operations. Much of this $86 million will be used to satisfy the financing and investment activities of the firm. Even after these activities are considered, Argile's cash account is projected to increase by $2.4 million in 2000. Does this mean that Argile will not have to worry about cash shortages during 2000? To answer this question, we must construct Argile's cash budget for 2000.

To simplify the construction of Argile's cash budget, we only consider the last half of 2000 (July through December). Further, we do not list every cash flow that is expected to occur, but instead focus on the operating flows. Remember that Argile's sales peak is in September and October. All sales are made on terms that allow a 2 percent cash discount for payments made within 10 days, and, if the discount is not taken, the full amount is due in 30 days. However, like most companies, Argile finds that some of its customers delay payment for more than 90 days. Experience has shown that payment on 20 percent of Argile's *dollar sales* is made within 10 days of the sale — these are the discount sales. On 70 percent of sales, payment is made during the month immediately following the month of sale, and payment is made on 10 percent of sales two months or more after the initial sales. To simplify the cash budget, though, we assume the last 10 percent of sales is collected in the second month following the sale.

The costs to Argile of cotton, wool, and other cloth-related materials average 60 percent of the sales prices of the finished products. These purchases are generally made one month before the firm expects to sell the finished products. In 2000, Argile's suppliers have agreed to allow payment for materials to be delayed for 30 days after the purchase. Accordingly, if July sales are forecasted at $150 million, then purchases during June will amount to $90 million, and this amount actually will be paid in July.

Other cash expenses such as wages and rent are also built into the cash budget, and Argile must make estimated tax payments of $16 million on September 15 and $10 million on December 15, while a $20 million payment for a new plant must be made in October. Assuming that Argile's **target, or minimum, cash balance** is $5 million and that it projects $8 million to be on hand on July 1, 2000, what will the firm's monthly cash surpluses or shortfalls be for the period from July to December?

TARGET (MINIMUM) CASH BALANCE
The minimum cash balance a firm desires to maintain in order to conduct business.

Argile's 2000 cash budget for July through December is presented in Table 14-10. The approach used to construct this cash budget generally is termed the **disbursements and receipts method** (also referred to as **scheduling**) because the cash disbursements and cash receipts are estimated to determine the net cash flow expected to be generated each month. The format used in Table 14-10 is quite simple — it is much like balancing a checkbook; the cash receipts are lumped into one category and the cash disbursements are lumped into another category to determine the net effect monthly cash flows have on the cash position of the firm. More detailed formats can be used, depending on how the firm prefers to present the cash budget information.

DISBURSEMENTS AND RECEIPTS METHOD (SCHEDULING)
The net cash flow is determined by estimating the cash disbursements and the cash receipts expected to be generated each period.

The first line of Table 14-10 gives the sales forecast for the period from May through December. These estimates are necessary to determine collections for July through December. Similarly, the second line of the table gives the credit purchases expected each month based on the sales forecasts so that the monthly payments for credit purchases can be determined.

The cash receipts category shows cash collections based on credit sales originating in three months — sales in the current month and in the previous two months. Take a look at the collections expected in July. Remember that Argile expects 20 percent of the dollar sales to be collected in the month of the sales, and thus, to be affected by the 2 percent cash discount offered; 70 percent of the dollar sales will be collected one month after the sales; and, the remaining 10 percent of the dollar sales will be collected two months after the sales (it is assumed there are no bad debts). In July, then, $0.20 \times (1 - 0.02) \times \$150$ million = \$29.4 million

TABLE 14-10

Argile Textiles: 2000 Cash Budget (millions of dollars)

	May	June	July	Aug	Sept	Oct	Nov	Dec
Credit sales	$100.0	$125.0	$150.0	$200.0	$250.0	$180.0	$130.0	$100.0
Credit purchases = 60% of next month's sales		90.0	120.0	150.0	108.0	78.0	60.0	
Cash Receipts								
Collections from this month's sales = 0.2 × 0.98 × (current sales)			29.4	39.2	49.0	35.3	25.5	19.6
Collections from previous month's sales = 0.7 × (previous month's sales)			87.5	105.0	140.0	175.0	126.0	91.0
Collections from sales two months previously = 0.1 × (sales 2 months ago)			10.0	12.5	15.0	20.0	25.0	18.0
Total cash receipts			$126.9	$156.7	$204.0	$230.3	$176.5	$128.6
Cash Disbursements								
Payments for credit purchases (1-month lag)			$ 90.0	$120.0	$150.0	$108.0	$ 78.0	$ 60.0
Wages and salaries (21⅓% of monthly sales)			32.0	42.7	53.3	38.4	27.7	21.3
Rent			9.0	9.0	9.0	9.0	9.0	9.0
Other expenses			7.0	8.0	11.0	10.0	5.0	4.0
Taxes					16.0			10.0
Payment for plant construction						20.0		
Total cash disbursements			$138.0	$179.7	$239.3	$185.4	$119.7	$104.3
Net cash flow (Receipts − Disbursements)			($ 11.1)	($ 23.0)	($ 35.3)	$ 44.9	$ 56.8	$ 24.3
Beginning cash balance			$ 8.0	($ 3.1)	($ 26.1)	($ 61.4)	($ 16.5)	$ 40.3
Ending cash balance			(3.1)	(26.1)	(61.4)	(16.5)	40.3	64.6
Target (minimum) cash balance			5.0	5.0	5.0	5.0	5.0	5.0
Surplus (shortfall) cash			($ 8.1)	($ 31.1)	($ 66.4)	($ 21.5)	$ 35.3	$ 59.6

collections will result from sales in July; $0.70 \times \$125$ million $= \$87.5$ million will be collected from sales that occurred in June, and $0.10 \times \$100$ million $= \$10.0$ million will be collected from sales that occurred in May. Thus, the total collections received in July represent 20 percent of July sales (minus the discount) plus 70 percent of June sales plus 10 percent of May sales, or $126.9 million in total.

The cash disbursements category shows payments for raw materials, wages, rent, and so on. Raw materials are purchased on credit one month before the finished goods are expected to be sold, but payments for the materials are not made until one month later (i.e., the month of the expected sales). The cost of the raw materials is expected to be 60 percent of sales. July sales are forecasted at $150 million; Argile will purchase $90 million of materials in June and pay for these purchases in July. Similarly, Argile will purchase $120 million of materials in July to meet August's forecasted sales of $200 million. Additional monthly cash disbursements include employees' salaries, which equal $21\frac{1}{3}$ percent of monthly sales; rent, which remains constant; and other operating expenses, which vary with respect to production levels. Cash disbursements that are not expected to occur monthly include taxes (September and December) and payment for the construction of additional facilities (October).

The line labeled net cash flow shows whether Argile's operations are expected to generate positive or negative net cash flows each month. But this is only the beginning of the story. We need to examine the firm's cash position based on the cash balance existing at the beginning of the month and based on the *target (minimum) cash balance* desired by Argile. The bottom line provides information as to whether Argile can expect a monthly cash surplus that can be invested temporarily in marketable securities or a monthly cash shortfall that must be financed with external sources of funds.

At the beginning of July, Argile will have cash equal to $8 million. During July, Argile is expected to generate a negative $11.1 million net cash flow; thus, July cash disbursements are expected to exceed cash receipts by $11.1 million. Because Argile only has $8 million cash to begin July, ignoring any financing requirements, the cash balance at the end of July is expected to be a negative $3.1; effectively, if the firm doesn't find additional funding, its checking account will be overdrawn by $3.1 million. To make matters worse, Argile has a target cash balance equal to $5 million, so, without any additional financing, its cash balance at the end of July is expected to be $8.1 million short of its target. Therefore, Argile must make arrangements to borrow $8.1 million in July to bring the cash account balance up to the target balance of $5 million. Assuming that this amount is indeed borrowed, loans outstanding will total $8.1 million at the end of July. (We assume that Argile did not have any loans outstanding on July 1 because its beginning cash balance exceeded the target balance.)

The cash surplus or required loan balance (shortfall) is given on the bottom line of the cash budget. A positive value indicates a cash surplus, whereas a negative value (in parentheses) indicates a loan requirement. Note that the bottom line surplus cash or loan requirement shown is a *cumulative amount.* Thus, Argile must borrow $8.1 million in July; it has a cash shortfall during August of $23.0 million as reported on the Net cash flow line, so its total loan requirement at the end of August is $8.1 million + $23.0 million = $31.1 million, as reported on the bottom line for August. Argile's arrangement with the bank permits it to increase its outstanding loans on a daily basis, up to a prearranged maximum (line of credit), just as you could increase the amount you owe on a credit card. Argile will use any surplus funds it generates to pay off its loans, and because the loan can be paid down at any time, on a daily basis, the firm will never have both a cash surplus and an outstanding loan balance. If Argile actually does have a cash surplus bottom line, these funds will be invested in marketable securities.

This same procedure is used in the following months. Sales will peak in September, accompanied by increased payments for purchases, wages, and other items. Receipts from sales will also go up, but the firm will still be left with a $35.3 million net cash outflow during the month. The total loan requirement at the end of September will hit a peak of $66.4 million, the cumulative cash plus the target cash balance.[8] This amount also is equal to the $31.1 million needed at the end of August plus the $35.3 million cash deficit for September.

Sales, purchases, and payments for past purchases will fall sharply in October, but collections will be the highest of any month because they will reflect the high September sales. As a result, Argile will enjoy a healthy $44.9 million net cash gain during October. This net gain can be used to pay off borrowings, so loans outstanding will decline by $44.9 million, to $21.5 million.

Argile will have an even larger cash surplus in November, which will permit it to pay off all of its loans. In fact, the company is expected to have $35.3 million in surplus cash by the month's end, and another cash surplus in December will swell the excess cash to $59.6 million. With such a large amount of unneeded funds, Argile's treasurer will certainly want to invest in interest-bearing securities or to put the funds to use in some other way. Various types of investments into which Argile might put its excess funds were discussed in Chapter 12.

Before concluding our discussion of the cash budget, we should make some additional points:

1. For simplicity, our illustrative budget for Argile omitted many important cash flows that are anticipated for 2000, such as dividends, proceeds from stock and bond sales, and additions to fixed assets. Some of these are projected to occur in the first half of the year, but those that are projected for the July through December period could easily be added to the example. The final cash budget should contain all projected cash inflows and outflows.

2. Our cash budget example does not reflect interest on loans or income from investing surplus cash. This refinement could easily be added.

3. If cash inflows and outflows are not uniform during the month, we could seriously understate the firm's peak financing requirements. The data in Table 14-10 show the situation expected on the last day of each month, but on any given day during the month it could be quite different. For example, if all payments had to be made on the fifth of each month, but collections came in uniformly throughout the month, the firm would need to borrow much larger amounts than those shown in Table 14-10. In this case, we would have to prepare a cash budget identifying requirements on a daily basis.

---

[8]This figure is calculated easily as follows:

$$\text{CASH}_{Sept} = \frac{\text{Beginning cash}}{\text{balance in July}} + \text{Net CF}_{July} + \text{Net CF}_{Aug} + \text{Net CF}_{Sept} - \frac{\text{Target cash}}{\text{balance}}$$

$$= \$8 - \$11.1 - \$23.0 - \$35.3 - \$5.0 = (\$66.4)$$

4. Because depreciation is a noncash charge, it does not appear on the cash budget other than through its effect on taxable income, hence on taxes paid.

5. Because the cash budget represents a forecast, all the values in the table are *expected* values. If actual sales, purchases, and so on are different from the forecasted levels, then the projected cash deficits and surpluses will also differ.

6. Computerized spreadsheet programs are particularly well suited for constructing and analyzing cash budgets, especially with respect to the sensitivity of cash flows to changes in sales levels, collection periods, and the like. We could change any assumption, say, the projected monthly sales or the time that customers pay, and the cash budget would automatically and instantly be recalculated. This would show us exactly how the firm's borrowing requirements would change if various other things changed. Also, with a computer model, it is easy to add features such as interest paid on loans, interest earned on marketable securities, and so on.

7. Finally, we should note that the target cash balance will probably be adjusted over time, rising and falling with seasonal patterns and with long-term changes in the scale of the firm's operations. Thus, Argile will probably plan to maintain larger cash balances during August and September than at other times, and, as the company grows, so will its required cash balance. Also, the firm might even set the target cash balance at zero — this could be done if it carried a portfolio of marketable securities that could be sold to replenish the cash account or if it had an arrangement with its bank that permitted it to borrow any funds needed on a daily basis. In that event, the target cash balance would simply be equal to zero. Note, though, that most firms would find it difficult to operate with a zero-balance bank account, just as you would, and the costs of such an operation would, in most instances, offset the costs associated with maintaining a positive cash balance. Therefore, most firms do set a positive target cash balance.

Self-Test Questions

What is the purpose of a cash budget?

Suppose a firm's cash flows do not occur uniformly throughout the month. What impact might this have on the accuracy of the forecasted borrowing requirements?

How is uncertainty handled in a cash budget?

Is depreciation reflected in a cash budget? Explain.

ETHICAL DILEMMA

Competition-Based Planning — Promotion or Payoff?

A few months ago, Kim Darby, financial manager of Republic Communications Corporation (RCC), contacted you about a job opening in the financial planning division of the company. RCC is a well-established firm that has offered long-distance phone service in the United States for more than three decades. But recent deregulation in the telecommunications industry has RCC concerned because competition has increased significantly — today there are many more firms offering long-distance services than five years ago. In fact, RCC has seen its profits decline along with market share since deregulation began. Kim Darby indicated that RCC wants to reverse this trend by improving the company's planning function so that long-distance rates can be set to better attract and keep customers in the future. According to her, that is the reason she contacted you.

When she first called, Kim told you RCC would like to hire you because you are one of the "up-and-comers" in the telecommunications industry. You have worked at National Telecommunications Inc. (NTI), one of RCC's fiercest competitors, since you graduated from college four years ago, helping to develop their rate-setting program, which many consider the best in the industry.

Taking the position at RCC would be comparable to a promotion with a $30,000 salary increase and provide greater chances for advancement than your current position at NTI. So, after interviewing with RCC and talking to friends and family, a couple of days ago you informally accepted the job at RCC—you have not yet notified NTI of your decision.

Earlier today, Kim called to see if you could start your new position in a couple of weeks. RCC would like you to start work as soon as possible because it wants to begin a redesign of its rate-setting plan in an effort to regain market share. During the conversation, Kim mentioned that it would be helpful if you could bring the rate-setting program and some rate-setting information with you to your new job — it will help RCC rewrite its rate-setting program. In an attempt to allay any reservations you might have, Kim told you that NTI sells its software to other companies and any rate-setting information is available to the public through states' public service commissions, so everything you bring really is well known in the industry and should be considered in the public domain. And, according to Kim, RCC is not going to copy the rate-setting program — her attitude is "what is wrong with taking a look at it as long as we don't copy the program?" If you provide RCC with NTI's rate-setting program, you know it will help the company to plan better, and better planning will lead to increased market share and higher stock prices. An improved rate-setting plan might net RCC as much as $200 million each year, and RCC has a very generous bonus system to reward employees that help the company improve its market position. If you do not provide the software, you might start your new job "off on the wrong foot." What should you do?

Summary

The first part of this chapter described in broad outline how firms project their financial statements and determine their capital requirements. The second part of the chapter included a discussion of how we can evaluate the effects of changes in forecasts on the income of the firm. The key concepts covered in the chapter are listed below.

- **Financial planning** involves making projections of sales, income, and assets based on alternative production and marketing strategies and then deciding how to meet the forecasted financial requirements.
- **Financial control** deals with the feedback and adjustment process that is required (1) to ensure that plans are followed or (2) to modify existing plans in response to changes in the operating environment.
- Management establishes a **target balance sheet** on the basis of ratio analysis.
- **The projected, or pro forma, balance sheet method** is used to forecast financial requirements.
- A firm can determine the amount of **additional funds needed (AFN)** by estimating the amount of new assets necessary to support the forecasted level of sales and then subtracting from that amount the spontaneous funds that will be generated from operations. The firm can then plan to raise the AFN through bank borrowing, by issuing securities, or both.
- **Operating breakeven analysis** is a method of determining the point at which sales will just cover operating costs, and it shows the magnitude of the firm's operating profits or losses if sales exceed or fall below that point.

- The **operating breakeven point** is the sales volume at which total operating costs equal total revenues and operating income (EBIT) equals zero. The equation used to compute the operating breakeven point is

$$Q_{OpBE} = \frac{F}{P - V} = \frac{F}{\text{Contribution margin}}$$

- **Operating leverage** is a measure of the extent to which fixed costs are used in a firm's operations. A firm with a high percentage of fixed costs is said to have a high degree of operating leverage.

- The **degree of operating leverage (DOL)** shows how a change in sales will affect operating income. Whereas *breakeven analysis* emphasizes the volume of sales the firm needs to be profitable, the *degree of operating leverage* measures how sensitive the firm's profits are to changes in the volume of sales. The equation used to calculate the DOL is

$$DOL_Q = \frac{Q(P - V)}{Q(P - V) - F}$$

- **Financial breakeven analysis** is a method of determining the point at which EBIT will just cover financing costs, and it shows the magnitude of the firm's earnings per share (EPS) if EBIT exceeds or falls below that point.

- The **financial breakeven point** is the level of EBIT that produces EPS = 0. The equation used to compute the financial breakeven point is

$$EBIT_{FinBE} = I + \frac{D_{ps}}{(1 - T)}$$

- **Financial leverage** is a measure of the extent to which fixed financial costs exist in a firm's operations. A firm with a high percentage of fixed financial costs is said to have a high degree of financial leverage.

- The **degree of financial leverage (DFL)** shows how a change in EBIT will affect EPS. The equation used to calculate the DFL is

$$DFL = \frac{EBIT}{EBIT - I} = \frac{EBIT}{EBIT - (\text{Financial BEP})}$$

- **Total (combined) leverage** is a measure of the extent to which total fixed costs (operating and financial) exist in a firm's operations. A firm with a high percentage of total fixed financial costs is said to have a high degree of total leverage.

- The **degree of total leverage (DTL)** shows how a change in sales will affect EPS. The equation used to calculate the DTL is

$$DTL = \frac{S - VC}{EBIT - I} = \frac{Q(P - V)}{Q(P - V) - F - I} = \frac{Q(P - V)}{EBIT - EBIT_{FinBE}}$$

- A critical ingredient in the budgeting and control process is the **cash budget**, which provides information about the timing of the firm's expected cash inflows and cash outflows.

The forecasting and control functions require continuous attention to ensure the goals of the firm are being met. Forecasting and control provide the foresight needed to implement adjustments to future operations so that the firm moves in the intended direction and wealth maximization is achieved.

Questions

14-1 Certain liability and net worth items generally increase spontaneously with increases in sales. Put a check (✓) by those items that typically increase spontaneously:

Accounts payable	_____
Notes payable to banks	_____
Accrued wages	_____
Accrued taxes	_____
Mortgage bonds	_____
Common stock	_____
Retained earnings	_____

14-2 Suppose a firm makes the following policy changes. If the change means that external, nonspontaneous financial requirements (AFN) will increase, indicate this by a (+); indicate a decrease by a (−); and indicate indeterminate or no effect by a (0). Think in terms of the immediate, short-run effect on funds requirements.

a. The dividend payout ratio is increased. _____

b. The firm contracts to buy, rather than make, certain components used in its products. _____

c. The firm decides to pay all suppliers on delivery, rather than after a 30-day delay, to take advantage of discounts for rapid payment. _____

d. The firm begins to sell on credit (previously all sales had been on a cash basis). _____

e. The firm's profit margin is eroded by increased competition; sales are steady. _____

f. Advertising expenditures are stepped up. _____

g. A decision is made to substitute long-term mortgage bonds for short-term bank loans. _____

h. The firm begins to pay employees on a weekly basis (previously it had paid at the end of each month). _____

14-3 What benefits can be derived from breakeven analysis, both operating and financial? What are some problems with breakeven analysis?

14-4 Explain how profits or losses will be magnified for a firm with high operating leverage as opposed to a firm with lower operating leverage.

14-5 Explain how profits or losses will be magnified for a firm with high financial leverage as opposed to a firm with lower financial leverage.

14-6 What data are necessary to construct an operating breakeven chart?

14-7 What data are necessary to construct a financial breakeven chart?

14-8 What would be the effect of each of the following on a firm's operating and financial breakeven point? Indicate the effect in the space provided by placing a (+) for an increase, a (−) for a decrease, and a (0) for no effect. When answering this question, assume everything except the change indicated is held constant.

	Operating Breakeven	**Financial Breakeven**
a. An increase in the sales price.	_____	_____
b. A reduction in variable labor costs.	_____	_____
c. A decrease in fixed operating costs.	_____	_____
d. Issuing new bonds.	_____	_____

	Operating Breakeven	Financial Breakeven
e. Issuing new preferred stock.	_____	_____
f. Issuing new common stock.	_____	_____

14-9 Assume that a firm is developing its long-run financial plan. What period should this plan cover — 1 month, 6 months, 1 year, 3 years, 5 years, or some other period? Justify your answer.

14-10 What is a cash budget? For what purposes should cash budgets be created?

14-11 Why is a cash budget important even when there is plenty of cash in the bank?

Self-Test Problems   *Solutions Appear in Appendix B*

Key terms   **ST-1** Define each of the following terms:
  a. Sales forecast
  b. Projected balance sheet method
  c. Spontaneously generated funds
  d. Dividend payout ratio
  e. Pro forma financial statement
  f. Additional funds needed (AFN)
  g. Financing feedback
  h. Financial planning; financial control
  i. Operating breakeven analysis; operating breakeven point, Q_{OpBE}
  j. Financial breakeven analysis; financial breakeven point; EPS level
  k. Operating leverage; degree of operating leverage (DOL)
  l. Financial leverage; degree of financial leverage (DFL)
  m. Combined (total) leverage; degree of total leverage (DTL)
  n. Cash budget

Operating leverage and breakeven analysis   **ST-2** Olinde Electronics Inc. produces stereo components that sell for P = $100. Olinde's fixed costs are $200,000; 5,000 components are produced and sold each year; EBIT is currently $50,000; and Olinde's assets (all equity financed) are $500,000. Olinde estimates that it can change its production process, adding $400,000 to investment and $50,000 to fixed operating costs. This change will (1) reduce variable costs per unit by $10 and (2) increase output by 2,000 units, but (3) the sales price on all units will have to be lowered to $95 to permit sales of the additional output. Olinde has tax loss carryforwards that cause its tax rate to be zero. Olinde uses no debt, and its average cost of capital is 10 percent.
  a. Should Olinde make the change?
  b. Would Olinde's degree of operating leverage increase or decrease if it made the change? What about its operating breakeven point?
  c. Suppose Olinde were unable to raise additional equity financing and had to borrow the $400,000 to make the investment at an interest rate of 8 percent. Use the Du Pont equation given in Chapter 13 to find the expected ROA of the investment. Should Olinde make the change if debt financing must be used?
  d. What would Olinde's degree of financial leverage be if the $400,000 was borrowed at the 8 percent interest rate?

Problems

Pro forma statements and ratios   **14-1** Magee Computers makes bulk purchases of small computers, stocks them in conveniently located warehouses, and ships them to its chain of retail stores. Magee's balance sheet as of December 31, 1999, is shown here (millions of dollars):

Cash	$ 3.5	Accounts payable	$ 9.0
Receivables	26.0	Notes payable	18.0
Inventories	58.0	Accruals	8.5
Current assets	$ 87.5	Current liabilities	$ 35.5
Net fixed assets	35.0	Long-term bonds	6.0
		Common stock	15.0
		Retained earnings	66.0
Total assets	$122.5	Total liabilities and equity	$122.5

Sales for 1999 were $350 million, while net income for the year was $10.5 million. Magee paid dividends of $4.2 million to common stockholders. Sales are projected to increase by $70 million, or 20 percent, during 2000. The firm is operating at full capacity. Assume that all ratios remain constant.

a. Construct Magee's pro forma balance sheet for December 31, 2000. Assume that all external capital requirements are met by bank loans and are reflected in notes payable. Do not consider any financing feedback effects.

b. Now calculate the following ratios, based on your projected December 31, 2000, balance sheet. Magee's 1999 ratios and industry average ratios are shown here for comparison:

	Magee Computers 12/31/00	Magee Computers 12/31/99	Industry Average 12/31/99
Current ratio	_____	2.5×	3.0×
Debt/total assets	_____	33.9%	30.0%
Return on equity	_____	13.0%	12.0%

c. Now assume that Magee grows by the same $70 million but that the growth is spread over 5 years — that is, that sales grow by $14 million each year. Do not consider any financing feedback effects.

(1) Construct a pro forma balance sheet as of December 31, 2000, using notes payable as the balancing item.

(2) Calculate the current ratio, total debt/total assets ratio, and rate of return on equity as of December 31, 2004. [Hint: Be sure to use total sales, which amount to $1,960 million, to calculate retained earnings but 2004 profits to calculate the rate of return on equity — that is, return on equity = (2004 profits)/(12/31/04 equity).]

d. Do the plans outlined in parts a and/or c seem feasible to you? That is, do you think Magee could borrow the required capital, and would the company be raising the odds on its bankruptcy to an excessive level in the event of some temporary misfortune?

Additional funds needed **14-2** Noso Textile's 1999 financial statements are shown below.

Noso Textile:
Balance Sheet as of December 31, 1999 (thousands of dollars)

Cash	$ 1,080	Accounts payable	$ 4,320
Receivables	6,480	Accruals	2,880
Inventories	9,000	Notes payable	2,100
Current assets	$16,560	Current liabilities	$ 9,300
Net fixed assets	12,600	Long-term bonds	3,500
		Common stock	3,500
		Retained earnings	12,860
Total assets	$29,160	Total liabilities and equity	$29,160

Noso Textile:
Income Statement for December 31, 1999 (thousands of dollars)

Sales	$36,000
Operating costs	(32,440)
Earnings before interest and taxes	$ 3,560
Interest	(560)
Earnings before taxes	$ 3,000
Taxes (40%)	(1,200)
Net income	$ 1,800
Dividends (45%)	$ 810
Addition to retained earnings	$ 990

a. Suppose 2000 sales are projected to increase by 15 percent over 1999 sales. Determine the additional funds needed. Assume that the company was operating at full capacity in 1999, that it cannot sell off any of its fixed assets, and that any required financing will be borrowed as notes payable. Also, assume that assets, spontaneous liabilities, and operating costs are expected to increase by the same percentage as sales. Use the projected balance sheet method to develop a pro forma balance sheet and income statement for December 31, 2000. (Do not incorporate any financing feedback effects. Use the pro forma income statement to determine the addition to retained earnings.)

b. Use the financial statements developed in part a to incorporate the financing feedback as a result of the addition to notes payable. (That is, do the next financial statement iteration.) For the purpose of this part, assume that the notes payable interest rate is 10 percent. What is the AFN for this iteration?

Degree of leverage   **14-3**   Van Auken Lumber's 1999 income statement is shown below.

Van Auken Lumber:
Income Statement for December 31, 1999 (thousands of dollars)

Sales	$36,000
Cost of goods sold	(25,200)
Gross profit	$10,800
Fixed operating costs	(6,480)
Earnings before interest and taxes	$ 4,320
Interest	(2,880)
Earnings before taxes	$ 1,440
Taxes (40%)	(576)
Net income	$ 864
Dividends (50%)	$ 432

a. Compute the degree of operating leverage (DOL), degree of financial leverage (DFL), and degree of total leverage (DTL) for Van Auken Lumber.

b. Interpret the meaning of each of the numerical values you computed in part a.

c. Briefly discuss some ways Van Auken can reduce its degree of total leverage.

External financing requirements   **14-4**   The 1999 balance sheet and income statement for the Woods Company are shown below.

Woods Company:
Balance Sheet as of December 31, 1999 (thousands of dollars)

Cash	$ 80	Accounts payable	$ 160
Accounts receivable	240	Accruals	40
Inventories	720	Notes payable	252
Current assets	$1,040	Current liabilities	$ 452
Fixed assets	3,200	Long-term debt	1,244
		Common stock	1,605
		Retained earnings	939
Total assets	$4,240	Total liabilities and equity	$4,240

Woods Company:
Income Statement for the Year Ending December 31, 1999 (thousands of dollars)

Sales	$8,000
Operating costs	(7,450)
Earnings before interest and taxes	$ 550
Interest	(150)
Earnings before taxes	$ 400
Taxes (40%)	(160)
Net income	$ 240

Per-share data	
Common stock price	$16.96
Earnings per share (EPS)	$1.60
Dividends per share (DPS)	$1.04
Number of shares	150

a. The firm operated at full capacity in 1999. It expects sales to increase by 20 percent during 2000 and expects 2000 dividends per share to increase to $1.10. Use the projected balance sheet method to determine how much outside financing is required, developing the firm's pro forma balance sheet and income statement, and use AFN as the balancing item.

b. If the firm must maintain a current ratio of 2.3 and a debt ratio of 40 percent, how much financing, after the first pass, will be obtained using notes payable, long-term debt, and common stock?

c. Make the second pass financial statements incorporating financing feedbacks, using the ratios in part b. Assume that the interest rate on debt averages 10 percent.

Operating breakeven analysis   **14-5**   The Weaver Watch Company manufactures a line of ladies' watches that is sold through discount houses. Each watch is sold for $25; the fixed costs are $140,000 for 30,000 watches or less; variable costs are $15 per watch.

a. What is the firm's gain or loss at sales of 8,000 watches? Of 18,000 watches?

b. What is the operating breakeven point? Illustrate by means of a chart.

c. What is Weaver's degree of operating leverage at sales of 8,000 units? Of 18,000 units? (Hint: Use Equation 14-4 to solve this problem.)

d. What happens to the operating breakeven point if the selling price rises to $31? What is the significance of the change to the financial manager?

e. What happens to the operating breakeven point if the selling price rises to $31 but variable costs rise to $23 a unit?

Operating breakeven analysis   **14-6**   The following relationships exist for Dellva Industries, a manufacturer of electronic components. Each unit of output is sold for $45; the fixed costs are $175,000, of which $110,000 are annual depreciation charges; variable costs are $20 per unit.

a. What is the firm's gain or loss at sales of 5,000 units? Of 12,000 units?

b. What is the operating income breakeven point?

c. Assume Dellva is operating at a level of 4,000 units. Are creditors likely to seek the liquidation of the company if it is slow in paying its bills? Explain.

Financial leverage **14-7** Gordon's Plants has the following partial income statement for 1999:

Earnings before interest and taxes	$4,500
Interest	(2,000)
Earnings before taxes	$2,500
Taxes (40%)	(1,000)
Net income	$1,500
Number of common shares	1,000

a. If Gordon's has no preferred stock, what is its financial breakeven point? Show that the amount you come up with actually is the financial breakeven point by recreating the portion of the income statement shown above for that amount.

b. What is the degree of financial leverage for Gordon's? What does this value mean?

c. If Gordon's actually has preferred stock that requires payment of dividends equal to $600, what would be the financial breakeven point? Show that the amount you compute is the financial breakeven point by recreating the portion of the income statement shown above for that amount. What is the degree of financial leverage in this case? (Hint: See footnote 7.)

Cash budgeting **14-8** Patricia Smith recently leased space in the Southside Mall and opened a new business, Smith's Coin Shop. Business has been good, but Smith has frequently run out of cash. This has necessitated late payment on certain orders, which, in turn, is beginning to cause a problem with suppliers. Smith plans to borrow from the bank to have cash ready as needed, but first she needs a forecast of just how much she must borrow. Accordingly, she has asked you to prepare a cash budget for the critical period around Christmas, when needs will be especially high.

Sales are made on a cash basis only. Smith's purchases must be paid for during the following month. Smith pays herself a salary of $4,800 per month, and the rent is $2,000 per month. In addition, she must make a tax payment of $12,000 in December. The current cash on hand (on December 1) is $400, but Smith has agreed to maintain an average bank balance of $6,000 — this is her target cash balance. (Disregard till cash, which is insignificant because Smith keeps only a small amount on hand in order to lessen the chances of robbery.)

The estimated sales and purchases for December, January, and February are shown below. Purchases during November amounted to $140,000.

	Sales	Purchases
December	$160,000	$40,000
January	40,000	40,000
February	60,000	40,000

a. Prepare a cash budget for December, January, and February.

b. Now suppose Smith were to start selling on a credit basis on December 1, giving customers 30 days to pay. All customers accept these terms, and all other facts in the problem are unchanged. What would be the company's loan requirements be at the end of December in this case? (Hint: The calculations required to answer this question are minimal.)

Cash budgeting   **14-9**   Carol Moerdyk, owner of Carol's Fashion Designs Inc., is planning to request a line of credit from her bank. She has estimated the following sales forecasts for the firm for parts of 2000 and 2001:

May 2000	$180,000
June	180,000
July	360,000
August	540,000
September	720,000
October	360,000
November	360,000
December	90,000
January 2001	180,000

Collection estimates obtained from the credit and collection department are as follows: collections within the month of sale, 10 percent; collections the month following the sale, 75 percent; collections the second month following the sale, 15 percent. Payments for labor and raw materials are typically made during the month following the one in which these costs have been incurred. Total labor and raw materials costs are estimated for each month as follows:

May 2000	$ 90,000
June	90,000
July	126,000
August	882,000
September	306,000
October	234,000
November	162,000
December	90,000

General and administrative salaries will amount to approximately $27,000 a month; lease payments under long-term lease contracts will be $9,000 a month; depreciation charges will be $36,000 a month; miscellaneous expenses will be $2,700 a month; income tax payments of $63,000 will be due in both September and December; and a progress payment of $180,000 on a new design studio must be paid in October. Cash on hand on July 1 will amount to $132,000, and a minimum cash balance of $90,000 will be maintained throughout the cash budget period.

a. Prepare a monthly cash budget for the last 6 months of 2000.

b. Prepare an estimate of the required financing (or excess funds) — that is, the amount of money Carol will need to borrow (or will have available to invest) — for each month during that period.

c. Assume that receipts from sales come in uniformly during the month (i.e., cash receipts come in at the rate of 1/30 each day), but all outflows are paid on the 5th of the month. Will this have an effect on the cash budget? In other words, would the cash budget you have prepared be valid under these assumptions? If not, what can be done to make a valid estimate of peak financing requirements? No calculations are required, although calculations can be used to illustrate the effects.

d. Carol produces on a seasonal basis, just ahead of sales. Without making any calculations, discuss how the company's current ratio and debt ratio would vary during the year assuming all financial requirements were met by short-term bank loans. Could changes in these ratios affect the firm's ability to obtain bank credit?

Exam-Type Problems

The problems in this section are set up in such a way that they could be used as multiple-choice exam problems.

Operating leverage   **14-10** The Niendorf Corporation produces tea kettles, which it sells for $15 each. Fixed costs are $700,000 for up to 400,000 units of output. Variable costs are $10 per kettle.

a. What is the firm's gain or loss at sales of 125,000 units? Of 175,000 units?

b. What is the breakeven point? Illustrate by means of a chart.

c. What is Niendorf's degree of operating leverage at sales of 125,000 units? Of 150,000 units? Of 175,000 units? (Hint: You may use either Equation 14-4 or 14-4a to solve this problem.)

Degree of operating leverage   **14-11** *a.* Given the following graphs, calculate the total fixed costs, variable costs per unit, and sales price for Firm A. Firm B's fixed costs are $120,000, its variable costs per unit are $4, and its sales price is $8 per unit.

b. Which firm has the higher degree of operating leverage? Explain.

c. At what sales level, in units, do both firms earn the same profit?

Breakeven Charts for Problem 14-11

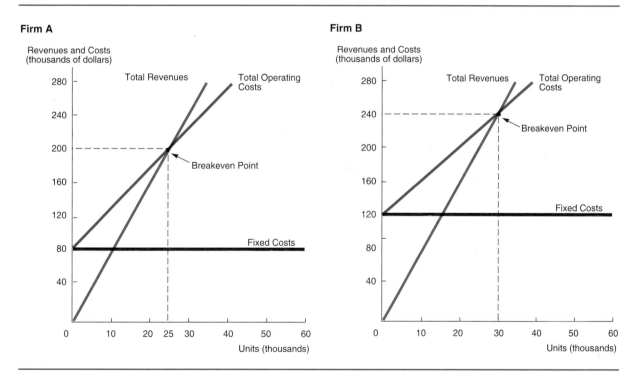

Long-term financing needed   **14-12** At year-end 1999, total assets for Shome Inc. were $1.2 million and accounts payable were $375,000. Sales, which in 1999 were $2.5 million, are expected to increase by 25 percent in 2000. Total assets and accounts payable are proportional to sales, and that relationship will be maintained. Shome typically uses no current liabilities other than accounts payable. Common stock amounted to $425,000 in 1999, and retained earnings were $295,000. Shome plans to sell new common stock in the amount of $75,000. The firm's profit margin on sales is 6 percent; 40 percent of earnings will be paid out as dividends.

a. What was Shome's total debt in 1999?

b. How much new, long-term debt financing will be needed in 2000? (Hint: AFN − New stock = New long-term debt.) Do not consider any financing feedback effects.

Additional funds needed   **14-13** The McGill Company's sales are forecasted to increase from $1,000 in 1999 to $2,000 in 2000. Here is the December 31, 1999, balance sheet (dollars in thousands):

Cash	$ 100	Accounts payable	$ 50
Accounts receivable	200	Notes payable	150
Inventories	200	Accruals	50
Current assets	$500	Current liabilities	$ 250
Net fixed assets	500	Long-term debt	400
		Common stock	100
		Retained earnings	250
Total assets	$1,000	Total liabilities and equity	$1,000

McGill's fixed assets were used to only 50 percent of capacity during 1999, but its current assets were at their proper levels. All assets except fixed assets increase at the same rate as sales, and fixed assets would also increase at the same rate if the current excess capacity did not exist. McGill's after-tax profit margin is forecasted to be 5 percent, and its payout ratio will be 60 percent. What is McGill's additional funds needed (AFN) for the coming year? Ignore financing feedback effects.

Breakeven analysis and leverage   **14-14** Straight Arrow Company manufactures golf balls. The following income statement information is relevant for Straight Arrow in 2000:

Selling price per sleeve of balls (P)	$5.00
Variable cost of goods sold (% of price)	75%
Fixed operating costs	$50,000
Interest expense	$10,000
Marginal tax rate	40%
Number of common shares	20,000

a. What level of sales does Straight Arrow need to achieve in 2000 to break even with respect to operating income?

b. At its operating breakeven, what will be the EPS for Straight Arrow?

c. How many sleeves of golf balls (units) does Straight Arrow need to sell in 2000 in order to attain the financial breakeven point? [Hint: An easy way to look at this problem is to consider how many sleeves of balls (units) beyond those needed for operating breakeven Straight Arrow needs to sell to cover its fixed financial charges. Note that Straight Arrow has no preferred stock.]

d. If Straight Arrow expects its sales to be $300,000 in 2000, what is its degree of operating leverage, its degree of financial leverage, and its degree of total (combined) leverage? Based on the degree of total leverage, compute the earnings per share you would expect in 2000 if sales actually turn out to be $270,000.

Integrative Problem

Forecasting, breakeven,   **14-15** Sue Wilson is the new financial manager of Northwest Chemicals (NWC), an Ore-
and leverage   gon producer of specialized chemicals sold to farmers for use in fruit orchards. She

is responsible for constructing financial forecasts and for evaluating the financial feasibility of new products.

Part I. Financial Forecasting

Sue must prepare a financial forecast for 2000 for Northwest. NWC's 1999 sales were $2 billion, and the marketing department is forecasting a 25 percent increase for 2000. Sue thinks the company was operating at full capacity in 1999, but she is not sure about this. The 1999 financial statements, plus some other data, are given in Table IP14-1.

Assume that you were recently hired as Sue's assistant, and your first major task is to help her develop the forecast. She asked you to begin by answering the following set of questions:

a. Assume that NWC was operating at full capacity in 1999 with respect to all assets. Estimate the 2000 financial requirements using the projected financial statement approach, making an initial forecast plus one additional "pass" to determine the effects of "financing feedbacks." Assume that (1) each type of asset, as well as payables, accruals, and fixed and variable costs, grows at the same rate as sales; (2) the payout ratio is held constant at 30 percent; (3) external funds needed are financed 50 percent by notes payable and 50 percent by long-term debt (no new common stock will be issued); and (4) all debt carries an interest rate of 8 percent.

b. Calculate NWC's forecasted ratios, and compare them with the company's 1999 ratios and with the industry averages. How does NWC compare with the average firm in its industry, and is the company expected to improve during the coming year?

c. Suppose you now learn that NWC's 1999 receivables and inventories were in line with required levels, given the firm's credit and inventory policies, but that excess capacity existed with regard to fixed assets. Specifically, fixed assets were operated at only 75 percent of capacity.

    (1) What level of sales could have existed in 1999 with the available fixed assets? What would the fixed assets/sales ratio have been if NWC had been operating at full capacity?

    (2) How would the existence of excess capacity in fixed assets affect the additional funds needed during 2000?

d. Without actually working out the numbers, how would you expect the ratios to change in the situation where excess capacity in fixed assets exists? Explain your reasoning.

e. Based on comparisons between NWC's days sales outstanding (DSO) and inventory turnover ratios with the industry average figures, does it appear that NWC is operating efficiently with respect to its inventories and accounts receivable? If the company were able to bring these ratios into line with the industry averages, what effect would this have on its AFN and its financial ratios?

f. How would changes in these items affect the AFN? (1) The dividend payout ratio, (2) the profit margin, (3) the plant capacity, and (4) NWC begins buying from its suppliers on terms which permit it to pay after 60 days rather than after 30 days. (Consider each item separately and hold all other things constant.)

Part II. Breakeven Analysis and Leverage

One of NWC's employees recently submitted a proposal that NWC should expand its operations and sell its chemicals in retail establishments such as Home Depot, Builder's Square, Scotty's, and so on. To determine the feasibility of the idea, Sue needs to perform a breakeven analysis. The fixed costs associated with producing and selling the chemicals to retail stores would be $60 million, the selling price per unit is expected to be $10, and the variable cost ratio would be the same as it is currently.

TABLE IP14-1

Financial Statements and Other Data on NWC (millions of dollars)

A. 1999 Balance Sheet

Cash and securities	$	20	Accounts payable and accruals	$	100
Accounts receivable		240	Notes payable		100
Inventories		240	Total current liabilities	$	200
Total current assets	$	500	Long-term debt		100
			Common stock		500
Net fixed assets		500	Retained earnings		200
Total assets	$	1,000	Total liabilities and equity	$	1,000

B. 1999 Income Statement

Sales	$2,000.00
Less: Variable costs	(1,200.00)
Fixed costs	(700.00)
Earnings before interest and taxes	$ 100.00
Interest	(16.00)
Earnings before taxes	$ 84.00
Taxes (40%)	(33.60)
Net income	$ 50.40
Dividends (30%)	(15.12)
Addition to retained earnings	$ 35.28

C. Key Ratios

	NWC	Industry	Comment
Profit margin	2.52	4.00	
Return on equity	7.20	15.60	
Days sales outstanding (360 days)	43.20 days	34.00 days	
Inventory turnover	5.00×	8.00×	
Fixed assets turnover	4.00×	5.00×	
Total assets turnover	2.00×	2.50×	
Total debt ratio	30.00%	36.00%	
Times interest earned	6.25×	9.40×	
Current ratio	2.50×	3.00×	
Payout ratio	30.00%	30.00%	

a. What is the operating breakeven point both in dollars and in number of units for the employee's proposal?

b. Draw the operating breakeven chart for the proposal. Should the employee's proposal be adopted if NWC can produce and sell 20 million units of the chemical?

c. If NWC can produce and sell 20 million units of its product to retail stores, what would be its degree of operating leverage? What would be NWC's percent increase in operating profits if sales actually were 10 percent higher than expected?

d. Assume NWC has excess capacity, so it does not need to raise any additional external funds to implement the proposal — that is, its 2000 interest payments remain the same as 1999. What would be its degree of financial leverage and its degree of total leverage? If the actual sales turned out to be 10 percent greater than expected, as a percent, how much greater would the earnings per share be?

e. Explain how breakeven analysis and leverage analysis can be used for planning the implementation of this proposal.

Computer-Related Problem

Work the problem in this section only if you are using the computer problem diskette.

Forecasting   **14-16** Use the model in File C14 to solve this problem. Stendardi Industries' 1999 financial statements are shown in the following table.

Stendardi Industries:
Balance Sheet as of December 31, 1999 (millions of dollars)

Cash	$ 4.0	Accounts payable	$ 8.0
Receivables	12.0	Notes payable	5.0
Inventories	16.0	Current liabilities	$13.0
Current assets	$32.0	Long-term debt	12.0
		Common stock	20.0
Net fixed assets	40.0	Retained earnings	27.0
Total assets	$72.0	Total liabilities and equity	$72.0

Stendardi Industries:
Income Statement for December 31, 1999 (millions of dollars)

Sales	$80.0
Operating costs	(71.3)
Earnings before interest and taxes	$ 8.7
Interest	(2.0)
Earnings before taxes	$ 6.7
Taxes (40%)	(2.7)
Net income	$ 4.0
Dividends (40%)	$1.60
Addition to retained earnings	$2.40

Assume that the firm has no excess capacity in fixed assets, that the average interest rate for debt is 12 percent, and that the projected annual sales growth rate for the next 5 years is 15 percent.

a. Stendardi plans to finance its additional funds needed with 50 percent short-term debt and 50 percent long-term debt. Using the projected balance sheet method, prepare the pro forma financial statements for 2000 through 2004, and then determine (1) additional funds needed, (2) the current ratio, (3) the debt ratio, and (4) the return on equity.

b. Sales growth could be 5 percentage points above or below the projected 15 percent. Determine the effect of such variances on AFN and the key ratios.

c. Perform an analysis to determine the sensitivity of AFN and the key ratios for 2004 to changes in the dividend payout ratio as specified in the following, assuming sales grow at a constant 15 percent. What happens to AFN if the dividend payout ratio (1) is raised from 40 to 70 percent or (2) is lowered from 40 to 20 percent?

APPENDIX 14A   Projected Financial Statements—Including Financing Feedbacks

In the chapter, we discussed the procedure used to construct pro forma financial statements. The first step is to estimate the level of operations and then project the impact such operations will have on the financial statements of the firm. We found that when a firm needs additional external financing, its existing interest and dividend payments will change; thus the values initially projected for the financial statements will be affected.

Therefore, to recognize these *financing feedbacks,* the construction of projected financial statements needs to be an iterative process. In this appendix, we give an indication of the iterative process for constructing the pro forma statements for Argile. Table 14A-1 contains the initial projected statements shown in Table 14-1 and Table 14-2 of the chapter, then some of the subsequent "passes" used to adjust the forecasted statements are given.

According to the discussion given in the chapter, the forecasted statements are first constructed assuming only retained earnings and spontaneous financing are available to support the forecasted operations. This "first pass" is necessary to provide an indication of the

TABLE 14A-1						
Argile Textiles: 2000 Forecast of Financial Statements (millions of dollars)						
	Initial Pass	**Feedback**	**Second Pass**		**Final Pass**	
INCOME STATEMENT						
Earnings before interest and taxes (EBIT)	$154.00		$154.00		$154.00	
Less interest	(41.00)	+ 1.26	(42.26)	+0.07	(42.33)	
Earnings before taxes (EBT)	$113.00		$111.74		$111.67	
Taxes (40%)	(45.20)	− 0.50	(44.70)	−0.03	(44.67)	
Net income	$ 67.80		$ 67.05		$ 67.00	
Common dividends	(33.00)	+ 1.54	(34.54)	+0.09	(34.63)	
Addition to retained earnings	$ 34.80	− 2.29	$ 32.51	−0.14	$ 32.37	
Earnings per share	$2.71		$2.56		$2.55	
Dividends per share	$1.32		$1.32		$1.32	
Number of common shares (millions)	25.00		26.17		26.24	
BALANCE SHEET						
Cash	$ 22.44		$ 22.44		$ 22.44	
Accounts receivable	198.00		198.00		198.00	
Inventories	297.00		297.00		297.00	
Total current assets	$517.44		$517.44		$517.44	
Net plant and equipment	418.00		418.00		418.00	
Total assets	$935.44		$935.44		$935.44	
Accounts payable	$ 33.00		$ 33.00		$ 33.00	
Accruals	66.00		66.00		66.00	
Notes payable	40.00	+ 6.19	46.19	+0.35	46.54	
Total current liabilities	$139.00		$145.19		$145.54	
Long-term bonds	300.00	+ 8.25	308.25	+0.49	308.74	
Total liabilities	$439.00		$453.43		$454.28	
Common stock	130.00	+26.81	156.81	+ 1.58	158.39	
Retained earnings	325.20	− 2.29	322.91	−0.14	322.77	
Total owners' equity	$455.20		$479.71		481.16	
Total liabilities and equity	$894.20	+38.95	$933.15	+2.29	$935.44	
Additional funds needed (AFN)	$ 41.24		$ 2.29		$ 0.00	

NOTE:

The results in this table are carried to two decimal places to show some of the more subtle changes that occur. Even so, you will find some rounding differences when summing the feedback amounts.

additional external funds that are needed — Argile needs $41.2 million. But, if Argile raises this additional amount by borrowing from the bank and by issuing new bonds and new common stock, then its interest and dividend payments will increase. This can be seen by examining the income statement that was constructed in the second pass to show the effects of raising the $41.2 million additional funds needed. Because Argile would have additional debt, it would have to pay $1.26 million more interest; because it has more shares of common stock outstanding, it would have to pay $1.54 million more dividends. Consequently, as the second pass balance sheet shows, if Argile only raises the $41.2 million AFN (additional funds needed) initially computed, it would find there still would be a need for funds — the AFN would be $2.3 million — because the addition to retained earnings would be lower than expected originally. As it turns out, Argile actually would need to raise $43.6 million to support the forecasted 2000 operations — $6.5 million from notes, $8.7 million from bonds, and $28.4 million from stock.

PART IV

Investor Decision Making

CHAPTER 15

Investment Concepts

"Maximize return and minimize risk." Should this be the battle cry of all investors? Perhaps. But not all individuals invest for the same reasons, and not all investors manage their portfolios the same. Many investors are relentless when it comes to achieving their investment goals. They brag that they can consistently outperform the market — and indeed, they can back up their claims. How do they do it? It might be hard to believe, but many investors do not make decisions about specific securities to include in their portfolios when pursuing their goals; instead they often employ professional investment advisors. And because there are a great number of investment professionals competing for investors' funds, investors have been known to create competitive environments among the various investment advisors who handle their money by continuously monitoring their positions and then, at least indirectly, letting each professional know how well he or she has performed relative to the others. The advisors/managers who lag behind the others are then asked to explain why their performances are not "up to par." If investment returns do not improve within a particular period, say, six months or a year, then funds are moved to other firms. If you were the person who was in jeopardy of losing an investment account, you would probably "bend over backwards" to find a way to keep it, especially if the investments were worth millions of dollars. In addition, you wouldn't want it to be known that you lost the account due to lackluster performances, because "reputation" is everything in this milieu.

Investors can still be savvy about their investments' positions, even if they don't make specific decisions about which securities are included in their portfolios, as long as they understand the fundamentals of investing. In most cases, experts would suggest that investment positions should be fairly consistent; that while investing is a dynamic process, significant changes in portfolio composition to chase exorbitant returns could prove disastrous. This doesn't mean you have to be overly conservative. It does mean you should not exceed your risk tolerance level — take risks that are in line with your risk attitudes. Follow the advice that has proven successful for others who use investment advisors/managers: (1) Ask friends for advice about

Continued

their experiences with investment advisors, (2) examine past performances, and (3) interview prospective candidates. Look for consistency in performance, a disciplined and focused work ethic, and a degree of enthusiasm for the profession.

In this chapter, we provide you with some basic investment concepts. As you read the chapter, think about why the approach we described here to manage investments might help you achieve your investment goals.

INVESTORS
Individuals who purchase investments with current savings in anticipation of relatively stable growth on average, or in the long term.

From an economic standpoint, we can define an investor as a person who forgoes current consumption to increase future wealth and thus to increase future consumption. If you ask investors why they invest, you will get many different responses — retirement, savings, house purchase, supplemental income, and so forth are some of the reasons people give. But, if you really think about it, there are only two general types of "investors," thus two major reasons people purchase financial assets: (1) Most people view investments as instruments that produce growth over a long period of time. Those who purchase investments with current savings in anticipation of relatively stable growth on average, or in the long term, are usually referred to as **investors**. (2) On the other hand, some people buy or sell "investments" in the short run because they believe such assets are not correctly valued in the financial markets, thus quick profits can be made as prices are corrected. Those who try to make a quick profit based on short-term market adjustments are called **speculators** because they gamble, or *speculate,* on whether financial assets are actually mispriced and market prices will adjust accordingly. Speculating is riskier than investing.

SPECULATORS
Individuals who try to make a quick profit based on short-term market adjustments; they gamble on whether the prices of financial assets believed to be mispriced will adjust accordingly in the market.

In this chapter and the next, we describe some investment concepts and evaluation techniques. Our discussions focus on investing, not speculating, and on individuals rather than institutions (e.g., pension funds, insurance companies, and so forth). In these chapters, we provide only a general overview of investing — you can learn more about investing by taking a course that is devoted solely to investment topics.

The Investment Process

Investing should be viewed as a continuous process that includes the steps outlined in this section and shown in Figure 15-1.

Investment Objectives

As we discovered in Chapter 4, there are many different financial instruments, each of which serves a somewhat different purpose, available to investors. Thus, before an investor can determine what investments to purchase, he or she must identify the reason(s) for investing. Some of the more common reasons given for investing include the following:

1. The major reason people invest is *retirement planning.* Even though most of us do not begin retirement planning early enough, when we do, we generally make choices about how to best invest to supplement Social Security or pen-

FIGURE 15-1

The Investment Process

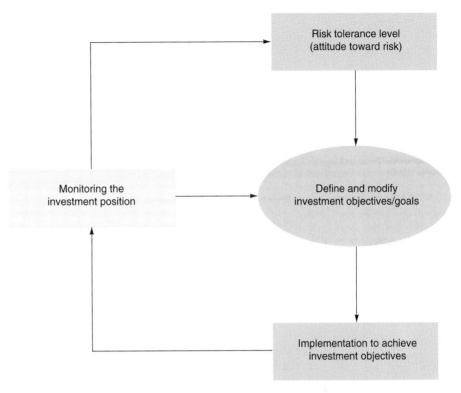

sion and retirement plans set up by employers or other organizations. Depending on what point in your career you start planning for your own retirement, the strategy you follow will differ. If you begin planning early in your career, you can invest in instruments that promise long-term growth; if you don't begin planning until later, you might have to invest in instruments that offer greater short-term stability.

2. People also use investments to *supplement current income,* especially if they are already retired. Appropriate investments include those that offer steady dividend or interest payments, which are called **income securities.** Preferred stock and interest-bearing bonds generally are considered good income-producing investments.

INCOME SECURITIES
Investments, such as preferred stock and corporate bonds, that offer steady dividend or interest payments.

3. Another reason people invest is to *shelter current income from taxes* using tax write-offs or other provisions of the Tax Code. Often, investors attempt to legally defer or avoid paying taxes on income if it is not needed in the current period. For example, the Tax Code provides that contributions to qualified employee pension plans and individual retirement accounts (IRAs) can be made from pre-tax income dollars such that taxes do not have to be paid until withdrawals are made at retirement. In addition, some investments, such as rental property, might allow you to take advantage of such tax write-offs as depreciation, which reduces the amount of taxes paid on income generated from the investments.

4. Finally, people often save current income to *achieve future goals* such as purchasing a house, sending their kids to college, traveling around the world, and so forth. If the need for, or the dedication toward, the future goal is great, an investor will probably select financial instruments that are safe enough to ensure the financial needs are met.

Investor's Attitude toward Risk

When we first discussed risk in Chapter 8, we indicated that, for the most part, investors are risk averse; thus, they demand greater returns for taking on greater levels of risk. We also stated that the degree of risk aversity exhibited by investors varies among individuals at any point in time and changes for individuals across time. For example, if you ask the students in your class what investments they would choose if they had $10,000 to invest, you would receive a wide range of answers — some would be willing to take on great risks in an effort to increase their investment quickly, while others would be more conservative because they want to preserve their investment and achieve steady, long-term growth. If you posed the same question at a reunion of your class in 40 years, you would receive very different answers — even those who are willing to take on great risks today would be more conservative in 40 years, most likely preferring to hold income producing instruments to help supplement their retirement income rather than riskier, high-growth-oriented investments.

To determine what instruments are appropriate to achieving your investment objectives, it is important that you examine your ability and willingness to take on risk when investing. Clearly, everyone strives to maximize the returns associated with their investments. But remember, higher returns are accompanied by higher risks. For most people, a good rule of thumb to follow when determining risk tolerance is this: *If you lose sleep over your investments or are more concerned about the performance of your portfolio than your job performance, then your investment position probably is too risky.* Generally speaking, your ability and willingness to tolerate risk, which is called your **risk tolerance level,** depends on existing economic conditions, your current socioeconomic position (wealth, income, etc.), and your expectations about your socioeconomic position in the future. For instance, when the economy is performing well and you have funds that are not needed for current expenses or for existing investment goals, you probably would be willing to invest in riskier securities than if the economy is performing poorly and the funds are needed for specific reasons.

RISK TOLERANCE LEVEL
An investor's ability and willingness to tolerate, or accept, risk.

Implementation to Achieve Investment Objectives

Once realistic goals have been formulated based on investment objectives and risk attitudes, it is necessary to implement the decisions that have been made. Implementation involves the selection and purchase of specific investment instruments to achieve the desired goals. This is a costly process because transaction costs, or commissions, must be paid to acquire investments. The transaction costs of some investment instruments, including savings accounts, certificates of deposit, and so forth, are small and indirect because only time, effort, and gas or telephone calls are involved; other transaction costs are more direct and larger because, in addition to time, effort, and phone calls, broker commissions are incurred. But, unless the investment strategy is implemented, which requires

TRANSACTION COSTS
The costs associated with trading securities, which include the costs of time, effort, and phone calls, as well as broker commissions that are incurred.

some amount of **transactions costs** to be paid, investment goals cannot be accomplished.

Depending on your risk tolerance level and your propensity to control your own investment decisions, you might prefer to either select your own investments or rely on the advice of an investment professional when implementing your investment strategy. If you choose to *actively manage* your investment portfolio, you must be able to commit the time and effort necessary to properly examine and select investment instruments appropriate to meeting investing goals. If you cannot make such a commitment or are not confident you have the ability to make cogent investment decisions, you probably should follow a more *passive management* style by purchasing investments that are managed by professionals, such as mutual funds, or by hiring a professional investment advisor.

INVESTMENT PORTFOLIO
A combination of investment instruments.

Whether you are active or passive in the management of your investments, you should always be aware of the composition of your **investment portfolio,** or the combination of investment assets you hold, because the allocation of your investment funds to various types of assets in your portfolio is an important decision. When determining the appropriate **asset allocation,** or proportion of funds invested in various types of assets, you should always keep in mind what your investment goal is. If your investment goal is to generate income, then your portfolio should include more income-producing investments than assets with returns that are primarily based on capital gains, or growth.

ASSET ALLOCATION
The proportion of funds invested in various categories of assets, such as money market instruments, long-term debt, stocks, and real estate.

In most cases, investors allocate funds according to three basic categories of financial assets: (1) short-term debt instruments, or money market securities (cash and near-cash items); (2) long-term debt, or bonds; and (3) stocks. You might think asset allocation is an easy task because there are only three categories among which your funds need to be allocated. But asset allocation is an important decision that affects the return you earn on your investment portfolio, and it is a continuous dynamic process. As conditions in the financial markets change, so do the asset allocations in investment portfolios. For instance, when the markets become more unstable and unpredictable than normal, many professional investment managers shift their allocations into the asset categories that are considered safer, such as money market instruments and debt. Similarly, as we noted earlier, as individuals move through life, there is a tendency to become more conservative, and thus, there is a shift into less risky asset categories. Table 15-1 provides an indication of asset allocations recommended by investment experts. Note that the allocation recommendations shift from riskier investments (i.e., stocks) to less risky investments (i.e., bonds and cash) as the individual investor gets closer to retirement.

TABLE 15-1

Recommended Asset Allocations Based on Risk Tolerance/Position in Life

Risk Tolerance	Description	Cash	Bonds	Stocks
High risk	Young investors	70–80%	15–25%	0–5%
Moderate risk	Investors near retirement	60	30–40	0–10
Low risk	Retired investors	40–50	40–50	5–20
	Investors older than 70	20–30	60	10–20

SOURCE: William Reichenstein, "Basic Truths about Asset Allocation: A Consensus View among Experts," *American Association of Individual Investors*, October 1996.

Monitoring the Investment Position

After the investment strategy has been implemented, the investment position must be monitored to ensure the goals are being met. Because economic and legal conditions change continuously and new investment instruments are created periodically, investors should systematically evaluate their investment position to determine whether they are in the best position to achieve their objectives. In addition, as individuals' attitudes toward risk or their socioeconomic positions change, their investment strategies also change. Thus, it is vitally important that investors regularly reexamine their goals and strategies and their investment positions to determine whether modifications are needed.

Self-Test Questions

What steps are involved in the investment process?

Explain why risk attitudes differ among investors at a particular point in time and why the risk attitude of an individual investor changes over time.

Why is it important to monitor, or periodically evaluate, your investment position?

Investment Alternatives

Remember from our description of financial assets in Chapter 4 that there are many different instruments available to help individuals meet their investment goals. For example, individuals who prefer low risk and want to invest for short periods can purchase money market instruments, such as Treasury bills, certificates of deposit, and so forth; those who have longer-term goals can purchase capital market instruments that are expected to exhibit stable, long-term growth, such as the stocks or bonds of large, well-established firms; and those who prefer greater risk can gamble with their money in the derivatives markets by purchasing options or futures. Although there are so many different types of investment instruments that it seems an investment exists to meet any investment goal imaginable, new investments continue to evolve as investors' needs (demands) change. For example, money market mutual funds were created in the mid-1970s when investors withdrew from the capital markets because interest rates were relatively high and there was great uncertainty about the stability of the long-term financial markets. Clearly, new financial instruments will continue to evolve in the future as investors' demographics change.

Self-Test Question

Do you believe new investment alternatives (instruments) will be created in the future? For what reason(s)?

Securities Transactions

Most of the investment transactions you enter that are not related to savings instruments from financial institutions require the help of a middleman, or agent,

BROKER
A middleman, or agent, who helps investors trade financial instruments such as stocks, bonds, and derivatives.

called a **broker.** The role of the broker is to help his or her clients trade financial instruments, especially stocks, bonds, and derivatives. For example, *stock brokers,* or account executives as they are called by many brokerage firms, help both individual and institutional investors buy and sell financial assets, and they earn commissions in the process. To trade securities for other investors, and thus be a broker, an individual must be licensed by the exchanges on which the traded securities are listed. In addition, a broker must abide by any licensing or registration requirements of the state in which he or she trades and by ethical standards established by the Securities and Exchange Commission.

Because brokerage firms play an important role in the financial markets and the implementations of the investment goals of individuals, in this section we describe some of the services such organizations traditionally provide. In addition, we give you an indication of how trading securities is accomplished.

Brokerage Firms versus Financial Intermediaries

First, we should note that, in the strictest sense, a brokerage firm is not considered a financial intermediary. Remember from the definition and descriptions we provided in Chapter 3 that financial intermediaries literally *manufacture* a variety of financial products, such as mortgages, automobile loans, NOW accounts, or pension funds, to allow savers to *indirectly* provide funds to borrowers (users of funds). Brokerage firms, on the other hand, do not create savings instruments, or financial securities; rather, they help investors trade such securities, which are created by corporations and governments. Thus, brokers allow savers to *directly* provide their funds to users of those funds — this process is not part of the intermediation process we discussed in Chapter 3. For instance, if you call a broker and purchase Microsoft common stock, you have invested in a security created by Microsoft, not by a bank, thrift institution, or other financial intermediary. In contrast, if you purchased a mutual fund that included Microsoft stock, then you have participated in the intermediary process because, in reality, you do not own Microsoft; instead, your investment is in the security created by the mutual fund company that actually owns Microsoft.

FULL-SERVICE BROKERAGE FIRM
A brokerage firm that offers a variety of services to its clients, including research information, monthly publications that contain investment recommendations, advisory services, and so forth.

Although their traditional role has been to help investors buy and sell stocks, bonds, and other securities, recently, many brokerage firms have ventured into areas we customarily associate with financial intermediaries. For example, some brokerage firms offer their own money market funds with limited checking privileges, credit cards, and other services that have traditionally been viewed as products of banks, mutual funds, or other financial intermediaries. In the future, we will probably see brokerage firms offer even more financial products that are considered "nontraditional" in an effort to better compete in the financial marketplace.

Types of Brokerage Firms

DISCOUNT BROKERAGE FIRM
A brokerage firm that offers clients only the basic services associated with trading securities; in some cases, the services provided include only trade execution and related reporting requirements.

In general, we classify brokerage firms into one of two categories: *full-service brokerage firms* or *discount brokerage firms.* As the name implies, a **full-service brokerage firm** offers a variety of services to its clients, including the results from various research projects, monthly publications that contain investment recommendations, and advisory services. In contrast, a **discount brokerage firm** offers clients only the basic services associated with trading securities, which means that, in some cases, the services provided include only trade executions and related reporting requirements. Because discount brokers offer fewer amenities than full-service brokers and the overall cost of their operations is less, they charge substantially lower commissions to execute trades. In fact, there are instances where the commissions charged by a "bare-bones" discount broker are only 20 percent of the commissions charged by a full-service broker. The commissions charged by full-service brokers average nearly $95 for 100 shares of stock with a purchase price of $50 per share. On the other hand, the commissions charged by discount brokers for the same trade range from $15 to $75, with an average of about $35. "Deep-discount" brokers often offer execution of similar trades for commissions less than $10.

Although most security trades are completed either by telephone or in person, many large brokerage firms now offer electronic trading. One advantage to trading electronically is that you can place an order any time, even when the markets are closed. Although orders placed when the markets are closed generally are not executed until the beginning of the next trading day, the ability to place orders at any time provides convenience to investors. Another advantage to electronic trading is that commissions are generally lower than dealing with a traditional stock broker, even when a discount broker is used, because, in effect, electronic orders can be placed directly with the representative of the brokerage firm that completes the trade. It is estimated that by the year 2000 perhaps 60 percent of the commissions generated by discount brokers and 10 percent of full-service brokerage commissions will be produced by online trading activities. Although most commissions will still be derived from traditional trading mechanisms, it is evident that a "virtual Wall Street" is evolving.

Table 15-2 lists the ten largest securities brokerage firms in the United States. Although these firms are classified as full-service brokers, most also have discount broker operations. In addition, they offer investment banking operations and other financial services.

TABLE 15-2

Ten Largest Brokerage Firms in the United States, 1998 (millions of dollars)

Company	Value of Capital	Value of Assets
1 Merrill Lynch	$40,004	$291,588
2 Morgan Stanley Dean Witter	32,646	302,355
3 Credit Suisse First Boston	28,693	238,625
4 Salomon Smith Barney Holdings	27,591	166,886
5 Goldman Sachs	21,774	127,343
6 Lehman Brothers Holdings	21,715	151,705
7 Bear Stearns	14,789	137,511
8 PaineWebber Group	5,615	57,065
9 Donaldson, Lufkin & Jenrette	4,481	69,988
10 BT Alexander Brown	2,250	16,349

SOURCE: *The Wall Street Journal, Interactive Edition,* September 28, 1998. Web site address: http://interactive.wsj.com

Trading Securities

Whether you use a full-service broker, a discount broker, or trade electronically, executing a trade involves the same general process — instructions must be given concerning the security to be traded. Generally speaking, besides identifying the security to be traded, trade instructions include an indication of the number of units, or shares, to be traded, when the trade should take place, and any limitations associated with the trade.

ROUND LOTS
Multiples of 100 shares of a security.

ODD LOTS
The term given to trades with shares that are not in multiples of 100.

TRADING QUANTITIES   When securities are traded on exchanges, they are traded in **round lots,** or multiples of 100 shares. This does not mean that an investor must buy or sell 100 shares, or in multiples of 100 shares, each time he or she trades. Investors can trade in **odd lots,** which is the term given to trades with shares that are not in multiples of 100. Because only round lots are traded on the exchanges, though, odd-lot trades are handled by special dealers, called *odd-lot dealers,* who effectively "bundle together" odd lots to create round lots that can be traded on the exchanges. Thus, odd-lot trading involves additional processing that increases the relative cost compared with round-lot trades.

MARKET ORDER
An order to execute a transaction at the best price available when the transaction reaches the market.

STOP ORDER
An order that specifies the price at which an order to buy or sell at the market price (a market order) is initiated.

LIMIT ORDER
An order to buy or sell a stock at no worse than a specified price.

TYPES OF ORDERS   Transactions to buy and sell stocks are executed according to orders submitted by investors. There are many different types of orders available to the investing public. The most common type of order is a **market order,** which is an order to execute a transaction at the best price available when the transaction reaches the market. Thus, if an investor submits a market order to buy IBM, he or she has instructed the broker to buy IBM at the lowest possible price as soon as the transaction reaches the trading floor.

Conditions and limitations concerning how and when a buy or sell transaction can be executed can also be included in an order. For example, stop orders and limit orders are used to specify the price at which a market order is executed or restrict the price of the transaction. More specifically, a **stop order** specifies the price at which an order to buy or sell at the market price (a market order) is initiated. If IBM is currently selling at \$115 and an investor submits an order to *BUY IBM 120 STOP,* the order to buy IBM will not be initiated until the price of IBM reaches \$120. A stop order instructs the broker when to begin executing a transaction; it does not guarantee, or limit, the price of the transaction. For example, the stop order to buy IBM simply instructs the broker to begin executing a market buy order when the price of IBM's stock reaches \$120. By the time the order actually is executed the price of IBM might be much higher or much lower than \$120. To restrict the price of a transaction, an investor can use a **limit order,** which is an order to buy or sell a stock at no worse than a specified price. For example, an investor who wants to buy IBM, but does not want to pay more than \$122 can submit an order to *BUY IBM 122 LIMIT,* which instructs the broker to buy the stock as long as the price is no higher than \$122. If the price of IBM is $122\frac{1}{4}$ when the order reaches the market, it will not be executed. Often, a stop order and a limit order are combined into a single order. If the previous orders for IBM are combined, the investor would submit an order to *BUY IBM 120 STOP 122 LIMIT.* In this case, a buy market order would be initiated when the price of IBM reaches \$120, but no stock would be purchased above \$122.

Orders that have price restrictions can also have time limitations. For example, a stop order can be placed so that it is canceled if the price conditions are not

DAY ORDER (DO)
Instruction to cancel an order if the price conditions are not met by the end of the trading day.

GOOD 'TIL CANCELED (GTC)
Indicates an order is active until the price limitations are met or until the investor cancels it.

FILL OR KILL ORDER
Instructs the broker to cancel the order if it cannot be executed immediately.

STREET NAME STOCK
Stock that is registered to the brokerage firm.

met by the end of the trading day — this is called a **day order (DO).** Or the order can remain **good 'til canceled (GTC),** which means the order is active until the price limitations are met or until the investor cancels it. In reality, however, the broker reconfirms a GTC order every six months to ensure the investor wants the order to remain outstanding. An investor can also place a **fill or kill order,** which instructs the broker to cancel the order if it cannot be executed immediately. Sometimes a time limit, such as 15 minutes, is placed on a fill or kill order.

EVIDENCE OF OWNERSHIP   When you buy stock from a broker, you will be asked whether you want the stock certificate, which is evidence of ownership, to be delivered to you or to be kept by the brokerage firm. If you choose to have the certificate delivered to you, then you will have physical possession of shares that are registered in your name and, when you sell the stock in the future, you will have to transfer ownership just like you would if you were selling a car (i.e., you need notarized signatures, and so on). On the other hand, if you allow the brokerage firm to hold your stock for you, generally it will be kept in **street name,** which means the stock is registered to the brokerage firm. The brokerage firm's records will indicate that you are the "real" owner of the stock and evidence of your ownership will be sent to you via periodic statements from the broker that indicate you own the shares. Dividends, annual reports, and other information that the company distributes to its shareholders are sent to the brokerage firm, which then distributes the payment or materials to its clients who own the stock. So, even though the stock is held in street name, you receive the same distributions as all other owners, regardless of how their shares are held. Actually, in most cases, it is better for you to allow the brokerage firm to hold your stock in street name for two reasons. First, it is easier to transfer the shares when they are sold than if they are registered in your name. And second, by retaining custody of the stock, in effect, the brokerage firm offers safekeeping for your investment.

SECURITY INSURANCE   Nearly every brokerage firm, including discount brokers, purchases insurance through the Securities Investor Protection Corporation (SIPC), which insures the cash and securities of investors held by the brokerage company from theft or loss (loss of the security, not loss in value). Each investor is covered to a maximum of $500,000. Some firms also purchase additional coverage from private organizations.

Self-Test Questions

How does a traditional brokerage firm differ from financial intermediaries such as those we described in Chapter 3?

What are the two major types of brokerage firms? What is the primary difference between them?

What is a round-lot trade? What is an odd-lot trade?

What types of instructions can investors specify when placing security orders?

Why would investors allow the stock they purchased to be kept in street name by the brokerage firm?

What is SIPC insurance?

Investment Information

Whether you choose to actively manage your investments or hire an investment advisor/manager, you should be informed about your choices. *Ignorance can be very costly when it comes to making investment decisions.* It is important that you understand what you are investing in before committing large sums of money. As a general rule, you should take time to investigate both the advantages and disadvantages of any investment you make. In Chapter 4, we described some of the more common investment instruments; in this section, we describe some of the sources and the uses of investment information related to those investments.

Sources of Investment Information

There are many sources and forms of investment information. Newspapers, magazines, company reports, investment research organizations, and the Internet provide volumes of data and information about various investments. For example, as we discussed in Chapter 13, a publicly traded company is required to prepare and publish annual reports that contain financial statements and other information about the firm and the nature of its operations during the year. Sources such as *Value Line Investment Survey, Moody's Investment Services,* and *Standard and Poor's,* among others, provide similar financial data as well as some of the results from analyses conducted by their research staffs. General business and economic news and quotations for stocks, bonds, and other securities can be found in local and national newspapers. The newspapers of larger cities, such as the *New York Times,* have large sections devoted entirely to financial reporting. *The Wall Street Journal, Barron's,* and *Investor's Business Daily* are "newspapers" that report only financial news and related business information for investors. More general business news and information are contained in various magazines, including *Business Week, Forbes, Fortune,* and *Money,* to name a few.

In addition to newspapers and business magazines, the Internet provides a mechanism for investors to find and contact numerous additional sources. Most large companies have web sites that provide information about operations, products, and personnel, as well as current and recent historical financial statements. And, many brokerage firms and investment services have web sites that provide specific information about companies and more general information about the economy and various financial markets. The U.S. government and various government agencies are very good sources if you want recent data relating to economic and general financial conditions. For example, the SEC and the Federal Reserve both have extensive amounts of data that can be downloaded and evaluated by anyone with a fairly standard personal computer.

As investors have become more proficient at moving information electronically, the personal computer (PC) has evolved as an important part of investment decision making. Numerous databases and programs to analyze them are now available on the Internet. Some of the services require a subscription, while others are free. In any event, it is evident that the PC has revolutionized the ability of individual investors to evaluate investment strategies and alternatives available to meet investment goals. A consequence of the proliferation of PCs and greater accessibility to a variety of software packages and financial databases is that individual investors are able to perform much more sophisticated investment analyses today than 20 or 30 years ago, and, as a result, make more informed investment decisions. And, as the electronic processing of information improves in the future, the analyses are certain to become even more sophisticated.

Price Information—Quotations

In the next section, we describe how to compute the return associated with an investment. First, however, we have to determine what the price of the investment is — that is, we have to be able to read the investment's price quotation. For the most part, it is easy to look in any newspaper and determine the current price of a stock or bond; but there are some items presented in the quotations that should be explained. In this section, we show you both stock quotes and bond quotes, and explain what the numbers actually mean.

Many investors consider *The Wall Street Journal* to be the premier source of daily quotations for stocks and bonds.[1] Therefore, we use information from *The Wall Street Journal* to describe how stock and bond quotations work.

STOCK QUOTES   Figure 15-2 shows a portion of the quotations published on Thursday, October 8, 1998, for stocks traded on the New York Stock Exchange (NYSE). Because these quotes appeared in *The Wall Street Journal* on October 8, they represent trading activity that occurred on Wednesday, October 7, 1998.

As you can see from the quotes in Figure 15-2, stock prices are denominated to the nearest $\frac{1}{16}$ of a dollar but stated as a simplified fraction (i.e., $\frac{8}{16}$ is simplified to $\frac{1}{2}$).[2] To explain the information contained in the stock quotations, let's look at the quote for Wal-Mart, which is highlighted. The labels above the columns indicate what the data represent, and they are fairly easy to read once you understand their meanings.

The "Hi" and "Lo" columns beneath the "52 Weeks" headline give the highest price and the lowest price at which the stock has traded during the 52-week period *preceding* the current trading day (i.e., the current quote is not included in the 52-week period). Therefore, excluding October 7, 1998, the highest price Wal-Mart sold for during the previous year was $69\frac{13}{16}$, which is approximately $69.81; during the same period, the lowest price was $30\frac{1}{4}$, which equals $30.25.

As you can see, the third column in Figure 15-2 shows the name of the stock, which is abbreviated where necessary. For instance, the stock immediately below Wal-Mart is listed as "WaldnResd," which is an abbreviation for Walden Residential Properties Inc., a real estate investment trust company. The column next to the company's name gives the **stock symbol,** which represents the trading initials of the company. Wal-Mart's stock symbol is WMT. The stock symbol is the reference used by brokers when trades are made and when price quotes are retrieved. The "running" market quotations you see at the top or the bottom of your television

STOCK SYMBOL
Designation that represents the trading initials of the company.

---

[1] *The Wall Street Journal* is published every day the stock markets are open during the year; thus, it is published Monday through Friday, except on holidays when the markets are closed.

[2] The minimum price movement, called the tick size, allowed by the NYSE was changed from $\frac{1}{8}$ to $\frac{1}{16}$ on June 24, 1997. From its inception more than 200 years ago, the minimum variation in price has been $\frac{1}{8}$; so, this was a monumental occasion for the NYSE.

FIGURE 15-2

Stock Price Quotations

52 Weeks Hi	Lo	Stock	Sym	Div	Yld %	PE	Vol 100s	Hi	Lo	Close	Net Chg
23	15½ ♣	Wackenhut B		.30	1.8	cc	331	17	16 11/16	16 11/16	−5/16
36	15 ♣	WacknhutCorr	WHC		...	32	1004	20 15/16	20 3/16	20 3/16	−11/16
n 28	16 7/16	Waddell&Reed A	WDR	.53	3.0	...	2019	18 3/8	17 13/16	17 7/8	−½
69 13/16	30¼	WalMart	WMT	.31	.5	34	41718	59½	58 3/8	58 3/4	−3/4
▼ 27 1/8	21 1/16 ♣	WaldnResd	WDN	1.93	9.4	39	478	21 1/8	20½	20 5/8	−1¼
30½	26 5/16	WaldnResd pfB		2.29	8.2	...	1	28	28	28	+½
49 15/16	24 1/8	Walgreen	WAG	.25	.6	39	7542	43 7/16	41	42 1/8	+3/16
40 3/8	15 7/16	WallaceCS	WCS	.64f	3.6	10	1779	17 11/16	17 3/8	17 9/16	...
22 5/8	11 3/8	WalterInd	WLT		...	12	1210	12½	11 5/8	11 7/8	−9/16
44 7/16	18½	Warnaco	WAC	.36	1.7	43	2676	22 1/8	21¼	21 7/16	−9/16
s 85 15/16	36 1/8	WarnerLamb	WLA	.64	1.0	53	45849	70½	63 9/16	66	−5 3/16
31 3/8	23 1/16	WA GasLt	WGL	1.20	4.3	17	1050	27 3/4	27 3/16	27 3/4	+1/8
6¼	3½	WA Homes	WHI	.15	3.3	9	69	4 3/4	4½	4½	−5/16
605½	426 3/8	WashPost B	WPO	5.00	1.0	12	1234	498 5/16	485½	498 5/16	+11 15/16
26 11/16	25 1/8	WA Wtr TOPrS A		1.97	7.5	...	13	26¼	26	26¼	+1/8
24 7/8	16 1/8	WA Wtr	WWP	1.24	6.3	14	2493	19 3/4	19 7/16	19 11/16	+¼
58 3/16	32 5/8	WasteMgt	WMI		...	26	171746	44 3/16	36 11/16	39	−8 3/16
11½	5 3/8	WstMgtInt ADR	WME		...	...	9257	11 3/8	11 3/16	11¼	−1/16
19 15/16	2 3/8	WtrInkInc	WI K		...	10	399	2 13/16	2 5/8	2 11/16	−1/16

NOTES:

♣ Indicates that the company's annual report and most current quarterly report are available at no cost. Investors Communications Business Inc. has an Internet site (www.icbinc.com) with links to other services that offer more than 3,500 free annual reports.

▼ The closing price for the day represents a new 52-week low. On Wednesday, October 7, 1998, the stock of Walden Residential Properties closed at 20⅝ ($20.625), which was below its previous 52-week low of 21 1/16 ($21.0625). If the symbol points up, ▲ , then the closing price represents a new 52-week high.

n The stock was initially issued within the last 52 weeks, thus its "Hi" and "Lo" prices only represent the highest and the lowest prices since the time the stock began trading publicly, not for the entire 52-week period.

s The stock was affected by a stock split or a stock dividend within the last year (52-week period).

pf Indicates that the stock listed is preferred stock. For example, Walden Residential Properties is listed twice, and the second listing has "pfB" next to the company's name. This listing is for a special class of preferred stock offered by the company.

f Represents the annualized dividend rate based on the most recent dividend declaration, which was higher than the previous dividend. Thus, the last dividend declared for WallaceCS (Wallace Computer Services Inc.) was $0.16 per quarter, which was increased from the previous quarterly dividend of $0.14.

cc The P/E ratio is 100× or more. Wackenhut Corrections Corporation class B stock, listed as Wackenhut B, had a price/earnings ratio greater than 100× in 1998.

x Indicates the stock is selling ex-dividend. Remember from Chapter 11 that investors who purchase a stock after it goes ex-dividend do not receive the next dividend payment because there is not enough time for their names to be registered in the company's ownership books before the date used to determine who is entitled to the dividend payment (the date of record).

vi The firm is in bankruptcy or being reorganized under bankruptcy laws.

z The amount listed for sales volume, "Vol," is the actual trading volume, not the round-lot volume.

SOURCE: *The Wall Street Journal,* October 8, 1998.

on financial channels or in brokers' offices are reported using company stock symbols because it is less cumbersome to include initials than the full names of the stocks.[3]

The column next to the stock symbol shows the dollar amount of the cash dividend per share, on an annual basis, that was last declared by the company. For example, the dividend reported for Wal-Mart was $0.31, which represented the dividend declared by the Board of Directors earlier in the year. Next to the amount of the dividend is the dividend yield, which is simply the dollar dividend divided by the current stock price. Thus, on October 7, 1998, Wal-Mart's dividend yield was $0.31/$58.75 = 0.00527 ≈ 5.0%. The price-to-earnings, or P/E, ratio, which is computed by dividing the current price by the earnings per share (EPS) most recently reported by the company, is given in the next column. Wal-Mart's P/E ratio was 34, which indicates that its stock price was 34 times higher than its EPS. Wal-Mart's stock price at the close of trading on October 7, 1998, was $58.75 (given in the "Close" column), which indicates its most recent EPS was $1.73 = $58.75/34. According to Wal-Mart's January 31, 1998, annual report, 1997 EPS was $1.56; thus, the growth in earnings was 11 percent on an annual basis for the first three quarters of Wal-Mart's 1998 fiscal year.

The last five columns in Figure 15-2 report information about the trading activity for the stock for the most recent trading day. The column labeled "Vol" gives the number of round-lot shares that were traded. On October 7, 1998, investors traded 41,718 round lots, or 4,171,800 shares of Wal-Mart stock. The columns labeled "Hi," "Lo," "Close," and "Net Chg" indicate the effect of the day's trading activity on the company's stock price. Thus, according to the numbers given in Figure 15-2, on Wednesday, October 7, 1998, the highest price Wal-Mart stock traded for was $59\frac{1}{2}$, or $59.50, and the lowest trading price for the stock was $58\frac{3}{8}$, or $58.375. At the end of the trading day, Wal-Mart's price was $58\frac{3}{4}$, or $58.75, which was $\frac{3}{4}$, or $0.75, less than the price at the end of the previous day — on Tuesday, October 6, 1998, Wal-Mart stock closed at $59\frac{1}{2}$, or $59.50. Note that the high price and the low price show the range within which the stock traded during the day, which gives investors some indication of the variability, or risk, of the stock during the trading period. On October 7, 1998, the trading range of Wal-Mart's stock was $59\frac{1}{2} - 58\frac{3}{8} = 1\frac{1}{8}$, which represented about 2 percent of its closing price. On the same day, however, the high and low prices for Waste Management's stock were $44\frac{3}{16}$ and $36\frac{11}{16}$, respectively, and the difference of $7\frac{1}{2}$ was more than 19 percent of the closing price, which implies much greater risk.

If you look in the first few columns of Figure 15-2, you notice there are symbols, such as ▲ and ♣, and letters, such as n and s, reported with some of the quotes. These symbols and letters are used to disclose special information about the stock, and their definitions are given in the explanatory notes published along with the stock quotes. There are nearly 40 symbols and letters, or footnotes as they are called, listed in *The Wall Street Journal*. A few of the more common footnotes are described in the notes to Figure 15-2.

In addition to the symbols and letters included in the quotes, note that some of the quotations are either bolded or underlined. Boldfaced quotes indicate that

---

[3]Stock symbols are also called *ticker symbols* because the first device used to continuously report stock prices to brokers' offices made a "ticking" sound when the quotes were printed.

the company's stock price changed by at least 5 percent compared with the previous closing price. For example, the price of Waste Management stock decreased from $47.19 (47³⁄₁₆) on October 6, 1998, to $39.00 on October 7, 1998, which represented a decline of more than 17 percent. Underlined quotes highlight stocks that show significant trading volume compared with their averages during the last 65 trading days. For example, the trading volume for Waste Management stock was 171,746 rounds lots, or more than 17 million shares, on October 7, 1998, which made it the third most actively traded stock on that day — Compaq and Coca Cola were the first and second most active stocks, respectively, with around 20 million shares traded.

Although our explanations of stock quotes apply to stocks listed on the NYSE, they are also valid for stocks listed on the American Stock Exchange and the NASDAQ, as well as most regional stock exchanges. The information provided for over-the-counter (OTC) stocks differs slightly; generally only the dividend, volume, latest trading price, and the change in price are provided.

BOND QUOTES   Figure 15-3 shows some quotes published on October 8, 1998, for corporate bonds traded on the NYSE. The interpretation of the bond quotations is somewhat different than the stock quotations.

There are three pieces of information in the first column of the bond quotation — issuer's name, coupon interest rate, and year of maturity. For example, if we examine the last bond quote for AT&T, we see the first column contains "ATT 8⅝31." The numbers indicate that the bond has a coupon rate equal to 8⅝, and it matures in the year 2031. Thus, an investor who buys this bond will be paid $1,000 × 0.08625 = $86.25 interest per year for each $1,000 face-value bond he or she owns.

The column labeled "Cur Yld." gives the current yield for the bond, which is computed by dividing the coupon interest payment by the current price of the bond. On October 7, 1998, the current yield was 7.8 percent for the AT&T bond. We show you the computation for the current yield after we discuss the rest of the quotation. The column labeled "Vol." gives the number of bonds traded; on October 7, 1998, 15 AT&T 8⅝ percent coupon bonds were traded. The closing "price" of the bond is given in the next column. This price does not represent a dollar amount because *bond values are stated as a percentage of the face value*. If AT&T's bond has a face value equal to $1,000, which is common, then, the price of the bond we are examining was $1,107.50 at the close of trading on October 7, 1998. To arrive at this value, we multiplied the "price" quote of 110¾ percent, or 1.1075, by $1,000. According to the last column in Figure 15-3, labeled "Net Chg.," the price of this bond decreased by ¼ from the previous day; thus, the October 6, 1998 closing quote was 111, which equates to a price of $1,110.

Now that we understand how to read the "price" quote, we can compute the current yield for the bond. The annual interest payment on a $1,000 face-value bond is $86.25, and the closing price on October 7, 1998 was $1,107.50; hence the current yield was $86.25/$1,107.50 = 0.0779 ≈ 7.8%, which is the figure reported in Figure 15-3.

Like the stock quotes we discussed earlier, there are explanatory notes for bond quotes, which are designated by letters included with the quotation information. Some of the more common explanatory notes are described in the notes to Figure 15-3.

FIGURE 15-3

Corporate Bond Quotations

CORPORATION BONDS
Volume, $17,124,000

Bonds	Cur Yld.	Vol.	Close	Net Chg.
ATT 4⅜99	4.4	30	99⁵/₁₆	+ ⁵/₃₂
ATT 6s00	6.0	210	100⅜	− ⅛
ATT 5⅛01	5.1	120	99¾	− ¼
ATT 6¾04	6.3	125	107⅜	+ ¾
ATT 7s05	6.5	82	108½	+ ⅜
ATT 7½06	6.6	25	113¼	− ⅜
ATT 7¾07	6.6	30	116⅝	− ¼
ATT 8⅛22	7.5	728	108⅞	...
ATT 8⅛24	7.5	88	108¼	...
ATT 8.35s25	7.5	10	112	...
ATT 8⅝31	7.8	15	110¾	− ¼
Aames 10½02	35.0	81	30	− 40
AlldC zr2000	...	4	90¼	...
AlldC zr05	...	5	66	...
AlldC zr09	...	210	50⅛	− ¼
Alza 5s06	cv	8	120	+ 2⅜
AMedia 11⅝04	11.5	2	101	− 4
Amresco 8¾99	15.9	496	55	− 5
Amresco 10s03	28.6	329	35	− 1⅛
Amresco 10s04	25.0	258	40	+ 8
Anhr 8⅝16	8.4	30	102⅞	...
AnnTaylr 8¾00	8.7	365	101⅛	+ ¼
Argosy 12s01	cv	35	93	− ½
Argosy 13¼04	12.6	22	105⅛	− ⅛

NOTES:

cv Designates a convertible bond. For example, the bond issued by Alza Corporation, which is a pharmaceutical preparation firm, is a convertible bond. (According to Alza's financial statements, each $1,000 bond can be converted into about 26 shares of common stock.)

cld Indicates that the bond has been called by the issuer.

t The bond is a floating rate bond with variable interest payments, depending on the conditions outlined in the bond contract (indenture).

zr Designates a zero coupon bond. For example, each of the bonds listed for Allied Chemical Corporation (AlldC) is a zero coupon, which means no interest is paid; thus, the returns on the bonds are derived solely from price appreciation.

SOURCE: *The Wall Street Journal,* October 8, 1998.

The prices of bonds issued by the Treasury and government agencies, such as the Federal National Mortgage Association, or FNMA (Fannie Mae), and the Tennessee Valley Authority (TVA) are quoted differently than the corporate bonds shown in Figure 15-3. Examples of the October 7, 1998, price quotes for Treasury notes and bonds are contained in Figure 15-4. The rate given in the first column is the coupon rate of interest. The column labeled "Maturity" gives the month and the year in which the bond or note matures. If the letter "n" follows the maturity date, the issue is a note; otherwise, it is a bond. Remember from our discussion in Chapter 4 that the only difference between Treasury notes and bonds is their maturities when they are originally issued — notes have original maturities from greater than one year to ten years, and bonds have original maturities greater than ten years.

Like a corporate bond, the price of a Treasury bond (or note) is stated as a percentage of the face value; unlike corporate bonds, price fractions are always stated as 32nds and located to the right of the colon in the quotation. For example, the note that matures in January 2003 had a bid quote of 104:21, which represents $104^{21}/_{32}$ percent of the face value. Two prices are given in the quote — the "Bid" and the "Asked." These values are called dealer bid/asked prices because they represent the amount government bond dealers bid (what they are willing to pay) to purchase the bonds from investors and the amount they ask (what they are willing to take) for selling their bonds to investors. Thus, investors who wanted to purchase the January 2003 notes had to pay the dealer's ask price, or 104:23 ($104^{23}/_{32}$), which means each $100,000 note cost $100,000 × 1.0471875 = $104,718.75 on October 7, 1998.

Next to the asked quote is the change in the asked quote from the previous trading day stated in 32nds. Thus, the asked price of the January 2003 note decreased by $^{9}/_{32}$ on October 7, 1998, compared with the closing price on October 6, 1998. The last column in Figure 15-4 gives the yield for the note or bond assuming it is purchased at the asked price and held to maturity. Therefore, an investor who purchased the January 2003 note on October 7, 1998, for $104,718.75 and held it until its maturity date would expect an average annual yield equal to 4.29 percent. In this case, the investor would receive $100,000 ×

FIGURE 15-4

Treasury Notes and Bonds Quotations

GOVT. BONDS & NOTES

Rate	Maturity Mo/Yr	Bid	Asked	Chg.	Ask Yld.
$5^{1}/_{2}$	Jan 03n	104:21	104:23	-9	4.29
$6^{1}/_{4}$	Feb 03n	107:23	107:25	-9	4.27
$10^{3}/_{4}$	Feb 03	125:01	125:07	-10	4.33
$5^{1}/_{2}$	Feb 03n	104:25	104:27	-10	4.28
$5^{1}/_{2}$	Mar 03n	105:00	105:02	-9	4.25
$5^{3}/_{4}$	Apr 03n	106:00	106:02	-10	4.27
$10^{3}/_{4}$	May 03	126:10	126:16	-10	4.34
$5^{1}/_{2}$	May 03n	105:03	105:05	-10	4.26
$5^{3}/_{8}$	Jun 03n	104:28	104:29	-11	4.22
$5^{1}/_{4}$	Aug 03n	104:29	104:30	-11	4.12
$5^{3}/_{4}$	Aug 03n	106:16	106:18	-10	4.24
$11^{1}/_{8}$	Aug 03	129:10	129:16	-15	4.32
$11^{7}/_{8}$	Nov 03	133:30	134:04	-14	4.34
$5^{7}/_{8}$	Feb 04n	107:22	107:24	-11	4.24
$7^{1}/_{4}$	May 04n	114:16	114:20	-14	4.29
$12^{3}/_{8}$	May 04	139:13	139:19	-15	4.34
$7^{1}/_{4}$	Aug 04n	115:00	115:04	-16	4.30
$13^{3}/_{4}$	Aug 04	148:00	148:06	-16	4.34
$7^{7}/_{8}$	Nov 04n	118:25	118:29	-18	4.32
$11^{5}/_{8}$	Nov 04	138:14	138:20	-17	4.35
$7^{1}/_{2}$	Feb 05n	117:14	117:18	-16	4.31
$6^{1}/_{2}$	May 05n	112:17	112:21	-16	4.28
$8^{1}/_{4}$	May 00-05	105:30	106:00	-4	4.33
12	May 05	143:02	143:08	-14	4.38

SOURCE: *The Wall Street Journal*, October 8, 1998.

0.055 = $5,500 interest each year ($2,750 every six months), but the value of the investment would decline from a current value of $104,718.75 to its $100,000 face value at maturity. Because the note is selling for more than its face value (at a premium), the yield to maturity is less than its coupon rate (YTM = 4.29% < Coupon rate = 5.50%).

Self-Test Questions

Name some sources of financial and investment information. Do you think that each source provides daily investment information?

In Figure 15-2, what is the difference between the "Hi" and "Lo" prices listed to the left of the company's name and the "Hi" and "Lo" prices listed to the right of the name?

How might an investor use information such as the daily high and low prices when evaluating the attractiveness of stocks?

How are bond prices reported?

What is the meaning of the current yield for a bond? What is the asked yield for a government bond?

Computing Investment Returns

An important part of monitoring investments includes determining the return that has been earned. In this section, we discuss techniques used to calculate the *historical* return earned by holding an individual investment and an investment portfolio over a period of time.

Computing the Return on an Individual Security

As we discovered in Chapter 7, the return on an investment is generated by (1) any *income* produced by the investment and (2) any *change in the value,* or the price, of the investment. Thus, the dollar return earned from an investment is simply the income received plus any change in value, which can be stated as follows:

$$\begin{array}{ccccc} \text{Dollar} & \text{Income} & \text{Ending value} & \text{Beginning value} \\ \text{return} = & \text{received} + & \text{of investment} - & \text{of investment} \\ \\ = & \text{INC} + & P_1 & - & P_0 \end{array}$$

In this equation, INC represents the income received from the investment, whether it is interest from a bond or dividends from a stock, P_1 is the investment's value at the end of the period for which the return is computed, and P_0 is the value of the investment at the beginning of the period for which the return is computed.

The *rate of return* on an investment for a particular period can then be computed as follows:

> **15-1**
>
> $$\text{Rate of return} = \bar{k} = \frac{\text{Income received} + \left(\begin{array}{c}\text{Ending value} - \text{Beginning value} \\ \text{of investment} \quad \text{or investment}\end{array}\right)}{\text{Beginning value of investment}}$$
>
> $$= \frac{\text{INC} + (P_1 - P_0)}{P_0} = \text{Holding period return (HPR)}$$

HOLDING PERIOD RETURN (HPR)
The return earned over the period of time an investment is held, which might be six months, five years, or some other period.

The computation given in this equation is often referred to as the **holding period return (HPR)** because we use it to calculate the return earned over the period of time the investment was held, which might be six months, five years, or some other period. The holding period return is the *actual,* or *realized, rate of return* we described in Chapter 7; thus, we use the same designation here, $\bar{k}$.

As you can see from the equation, the numerator includes the income received from the investment and the change in value, or the *capital gain (loss),* associated with the investment. To illustrate how to compute the HPR, let's examine the performance of Ingersoll-Rand, which is the world's leading manufacturer of air compressors and related equipment, from January 2, 1998, through October 1, 1998. During this period, Ingersoll-Rand paid its stockholders cumulative dividend payments equal to 45¢ — a 15¢ payment was made on March 1, June 1, and August 1 — and, on October 1, 1998, the stock price was $36.81. Any investors who purchased Ingersoll-Rand on January 2, 1998, when the price was $40.50, earned a nine-month HPR equal to

$$\text{Nine-month HPR}_{\text{Ingersoll}} = \frac{3\,(\$0.15) + (\$36.81 - \$40.50)}{\$40.50}$$

$$= \frac{\$0.45}{\$40.50} + \frac{(-\$3.69)}{\$40.50}$$

$$= 0.011 + (-0.091) = -0.08 = -8.0\%$$

This computation shows that investors who purchased Ingersoll-Rand at the beginning of 1998 and held it until October 1998 earned a nine-month return equal to −8.0 percent. In our calculation, we broke the return into two components: the part of the return associated with (1) the dividends paid by the firm, which is called the **dividend yield,** and (2) the change in the market value of the stock, which is called the **capital gain (loss).** Note that dividend payments contributed 1.1 percent to the return, but the value of Ingersoll-Rand's stock decreased by $3.69, which generated a −9.1 percent capital loss; thus, the total return associated with holding the stock for the first nine months of 1998 was −8.0 percent.

DIVIDEND YIELD
The part of the total return associated with the dividends paid by the firm; it is computed by dividing the amount of dividends paid by the stock price.

CAPITAL GAIN (LOSS)
A change in the market value of a security.

In most cases, we prefer to state returns on an annual basis so that alternative investments are more easily compared. Therefore, we need to adjust Equation 15-1 to account for the possibility that an investor's holding period might not equal exactly one year. To ensure the return is stated on an annual basis, then, Equation 15-1 can be rewritten as follows:

15-1a

$$\text{Annualized rate of return} = \bar{k} = \frac{INC + (P_1 - P_0)}{P_0} \times \left(\frac{360}{T}\right)$$

In Equation 15-1a, all the variables are as previously defined, and T represents the number of days the investment is held such that 360/T "annualizes" the HPR (i.e., adjusts the return so that it is stated on an annual basis). Note that we use 360 days in our computation for simplicity only because the number 360 is divisible by more values than 365.

Returning to the Ingersoll-Rand example, we found that the return for the first nine months of 1998 was −8.0 percent. Thus, the equivalent annual return is −8.0% × 360/270 = −10.7%. The same result is found by applying Equation 15-1a:

$$\text{Annualized return} = \bar{k} = \frac{3(\$0.15) + (\$36.81 - \$40.50)}{\$40.50} \times \left(\frac{360}{270}\right)$$

$$= -0.08 \times 1.33 = -0.1067 = -10.7\%$$

Generally, when we examine the returns associated with an investment that has been held for many years, we want to know the *average annual return.* For instance, you may have heard someone state that an investment he or she has had for a long time, say, five or ten years, has earned an average return (or grown by an average) of 15 percent per year. How do we calculate the average annual return? First, we must compute the annual HPR for each year the investment was held. Thus, if an investment was held for five years, we would compute five annual returns. Then, after the annual returns have been calculated, we find the average. There are two techniques for computing the average return on an investment that has been held for more than one year (period) — the *simple arithmetic average* and the *geometric average.*[4]

The **simple arithmetic average return** is computed by summing each return and then dividing by the number of returns. Thus, the calculation for the simple arithmetic average return is

SIMPLE ARITHMETIC AVERAGE RETURN
Computed by summing each return and then dividing by the number of returns; it does not consider compounding.

15-2

$$\text{Simple arithmetic average return} = \bar{K}_A = \frac{\bar{k}_1 + \bar{k}_2 + \cdots + \bar{k}_N}{N}$$

$$= \frac{\sum_{t=1}^{N} \bar{k}_t}{N}$$

In this equation, $\bar{K}_A$ is the simple arithmetic average return, $\bar{k}_t$ is the holding period return for year t, and n is the number of years the investment has been held.

[4]Both the simple arithmetic average and the geometric average can be applied to holding periods other than one year — e.g., one month, six months, and so forth. Because it is more common to compare average returns on an annual basis, our calculations are based on annual returns only.

To illustrate the application of Equation 15-2, let's consider the data given in Table 15-3, which shows the end-of-year market prices (including dividends) and the annual holding period returns for the common stock of TreeTop Landscape Services from 1994 to 1999. Thus, the simple arithmetic average return is

$$\overline{K}_{A_{TreeTop}} = \frac{50.0\% + 10.0\% + 4.0\% + 2.0\% + (-42.9\%)}{5}$$

$$= \frac{23.1\%}{5} = 4.6\%$$

which suggests that the average return per year was 4.6 percent during the five-year period from January 1995 to December 1999. But, the computation for the simple arithmetic average return does not include consideration of compounded rates.

GEOMETRIC AVERAGE RETURN
Computed by taking the n'th root of the growth multiple $(1 + \overline{k}_1) \times (1 + \overline{k}_2) \times \cdots \times (1 + \overline{k}_N)$ and subtracting 1.0; it does consider compounding.

The **geometric average return** does consider compounded rates because it assumes that a dollar invested today will grow to $1(1 + \overline{k}_1)$ at the end of one year; this amount will be reinvested to grow to $[\$1(1 + \overline{k}_1)](1 + \overline{k}_2)$ at the end of the second period; and so on. Thus, the multiple by which an investment of $1 (or any other amount) grows over many years is $[(1 + \overline{k}_1) \times (1 + \overline{k}_2) \times \cdots \times (1 + \overline{k}_N)]$. For example, as we discovered in Chapter 6, if $1 is invested today at a 15 percent rate for five years, it will grow by $2.0114 \approx (1.15)^5$ times. To find the annual average, then, we have to reverse the compounding process by taking the Nth root of the growth multiple and subtracting 1.0. Therefore, we can state the geometric average return as follows:

15-3

$$\text{Geometric average return} = \overline{K}_G = [(1 + \overline{k}_1) \times (1 + \overline{k}_2) \times \cdots \times (1 + \overline{k}_N)]^{\frac{1}{N}} - 1.0$$

$$= \left[\prod_{t=1}^{n} (1 + \overline{k}_t) \right]^{\frac{1}{N}} - 1.0$$

In this equation $\overline{K}_G$ is the geometric average return, and all of the other variables are the same as defined in Equation 15-2. The Greek symbol π, which is pronounced

TABLE 15-3

Market Prices and Returns for TreeTop Landscape Services, 1994–1999

Year	End-of-Year Price	One-Year Holding Period Return[a]
1994	$200.00	—
1995	300.00	50.0%
1996	330.00	10.0
1997	343.20	4.0
1998	350.18	2.0
1999	200.00	-42.9

[a]TreeTop Landscape paid no dividends during this period; therefore, the annual holding period returns are based on price changes only.

"pie," means to multiply, or take the product of, a series of numbers. And, when an equation is raised to the 1/N power, it means take the Nth root of the result, which can be accomplished by using the y^x key on your calculator.[5]

If we apply Equation 15-3, the geometric average return for TreeTop Landscape Services is computed as follows:

$$\overline{K}_{G_{TreeTop}} = [(1 + 0.500)(1 + 0.100)(1 + 0.040)(1 + 0.020)(1 - 0.429)]^{\frac{1}{5}} - 1.0$$

$$= [(1.500)(1.100)(1.040)(1.020)(0.571)]^{\frac{1}{5}} - 1.0$$

$$= (1.00)^{0.2} - 1.0 = 0.00 = 0.0\%$$

which indicates TreeTop Landscape showed no growth from January 1995 to December 1999.

As you can tell from our results, the computations for the simple arithmetic average return and the geometric average return give different answers — 4.6 percent versus 0.0 percent. Which one is correct? In this case, we can find the answer very simply by computing the five-year holding period return. Remember that the $200 price that existed when the stock market closed at the end of 1994 (Friday, December 30) was also the price of the stock when the market reopened at the beginning of 1995. Therefore, if an investor bought Treetop Landscape on Monday, January 2, 1995, he or she would have paid $200 per share. Because an investor could have bought the stock for the same price on Friday, December 31, 1999, the actual growth over the five-year holding period was zero. The stock price fluctuated each of the five years, but any investor who purchased TreeTop Landscape at the beginning of 1995 and then sold it five years later was returned the amount originally invested; thus, neither a gain nor a loss was realized. Consequently, we can conclude the geometric average return shows the correct change in value during the five-year period being examined.

Because the simple arithmetic average return does not consider compounding, its value will always be equal to or greater than the geometric average return. From your knowledge of time value of money concepts, which were presented in Chapter 6, you should understand that this relationship exists because, all else equal, it takes a greater rate of return to reach a particular future value if funds are not compounded. The simple arithmetic average return and the geometric average return will be equal only if the annual returns are constant.

Although the simple arithmetic average return should not be used to compute the average annual return for an investment over a multiple-year period, such as five years, it can be used to compute the average return for a group of investments at one point in time. For example, if you wanted to determine the average return on stocks from a particular industry, you would use the simple arithmetic average because you are not concerned with growth over time; instead, you are examining returns at a specific point in time.

Computing the Return on a Portfolio

In Chapter 8, we stated that the *expected return* on a portfolio is the weighted average of the expected returns on the individual stocks included in the portfolio. The same principal applies when computing the historical return of a portfo-

[5]See Chapter 6 for further discussion about using the y^x key on your calculator.

lio — we simply need to determine the weighted average of the actual returns on each individual stock, with the weights being the fraction of the total portfolio invested in each stock at the *beginning of the investment (holding) period*. Therefore, we compute the historical return of a portfolio using the following equation:

$$15\text{-}4 \qquad \bar{k}_p = \left(\frac{\text{Value of Security 1}}{\text{Portfolio value}}\right)\bar{k}_1 + \left(\frac{\text{Value of Security 2}}{\text{Portfolio value}}\right)\bar{k}_2 + \cdots + \left(\frac{\text{Value of Security N}}{\text{Portfolio value}}\right)\bar{k}_n$$

$$= w_1\bar{k}_1 + w_2\bar{k}_2 + \cdots + w_n\bar{k}_n$$

$$= \sum_{j=1}^{n} w_j\bar{k}_j$$

Here the w_j's are the weights based on market values at the beginning of the investment period, and there are n stocks in the portfolio.

To illustrate the use of Equation 15-4, let's examine Sue Hogan's portfolio of stocks for the last two years. The brokerage firm has provided Sue with the following information:

Stock	Market Value		
	1/1/98	12/31/98	12/31/99
Microtech	$1,500	$1,800	$1,980
Unicity	2,500	2,750	3,300
Hywall	1,000	950	1,425
Portfolio value	$5,000	$5,500	$6,705

To help Sue evaluate her investments, we can first compute the annual holding period returns for each stock using Equation 15-1. These computations yield the following results:

Stock	Return	
	1998	1999
Microtech	20.0%	10.0%
Unicity	10.0	20.0
Hywall	−5.0	50.0

If we apply Equation 15-4, the portfolio return for 1998 is calculated as follows:

$$\bar{k}_{p,1998} = \left(\frac{\$1,500}{\$5,000}\right)(20.0\%) + \left(\frac{\$2,500}{\$5,000}\right)(10.0\%) + \left(\frac{\$1,000}{\$5,000}\right)(-5.0\%)$$

$$= 0.3(20.0\%) + 0.5(10.0\%) + 0.2(-5.0\%)$$

$$= 6.0\% + 5.0\% + (-1.0\%)$$

$$= 10.0\%$$

Note that Hywall lost 5 percent in 1998; because the amount invested in Hywall represented only 20 percent of the entire portfolio, the total return was reduced by only 1 percent.

To compute the 1999 portfolio return, we again apply Equation 15-4, but, the weights for each stock are based on their values at the beginning of 1999 (end of 1998) rather than the original values. Therefore, because Hywall's value decreased during 1998, its weight, or influence on the portfolio's return, also decreased. The computation of the 1999 portfolio return is

$$\bar{k}_{p,1999} = \left(\frac{\$1,800}{\$5,500}\right)(10.0\%) + \left(\frac{\$2,750}{\$5,500}\right)(20.0\%) + \left(\frac{\$950}{\$5,500}\right)(50.0\%)$$

$$= 0.3273(10.0\%) + 0.50(20.0\%) + 0.1727(50.0\%)$$

$$= 3.3\% + 10.0\% + 8.6\%$$

$$= 21.9\%$$

Note that the weight of Hywall dropped from 20 percent at the beginning of 1998 to 17.3 percent at the beginning of 1999. Consequently, even though the price of Hywall's stock increased by 50 percent during 1999, its contribution to the portfolio return was less than Unicity, which earned 20 percent for one-half (50 percent) of the portfolio's funds.

We could have computed the annual returns for the portfolio by determining the change in the total value of the portfolio each year. In other words, we could have computed the portfolio returns by applying Equation 15-1 as follows:

$$\bar{k}_{p,1998} = \frac{\$5,500 - \$5,000}{\$5,000} = 0.100 = 10.0\%$$

$$\bar{k}_{p,1999} = \frac{\$6,705 - \$5,500}{\$5,500} = 0.219 = 21.9\%$$

The returns are the same as those we computed using Equation 15-4. When we aggregate the returns, however, it is not necessary to compute the weights associated with each stock because this information is included in the aggregated value. Therefore, if we simply want to compute an overall return for a portfolio, we can use Equation 15-1. If we want to determine the returns associated with the individual stocks and their contribution to the portfolio's return, then Equation 15-4 should be used.

Self-Test Questions

What does it mean when an investor states that his or her holding period return was 15 percent?

What is a capital gain (loss)?

Differentiate between the simple arithmetic average return and the geometric average return. Under what circumstances should each be used?

What is the difference between computing the return on a portfolio using Equation 15-1 versus Equation 15-4?

Indexes — Measuring Market Returns

In the previous section, we examined methods used to measure returns on individual assets such as stocks and bonds. In this section, we discuss market indexes, which are used to measure the returns for combinations of securities, or "baskets" of investments, such as stock markets and bond markets.

Market indexes measure performance in the financial markets much like economic indexes measure performance in the economy. One of the most often quoted market indexes is the Dow Jones Industrial Average, or DJIA, which measures the aggregate return, or performance, for the 30 largest industrial firms in the United States. Started by Charles Dow in 1896, the DJIA is the oldest known stock market index. The index, which originally included only 12 large firms, was created to gauge the overall performance of the stock market. Table 15-4 shows the composition of the Dow when it was started and the companies included in the DJIA today. Only one company that was in the original Dow is still in it today — General Electric. Even though the DJIA includes only 30 stocks, which is about 1 percent of the total number of stocks listed on the NYSE, many people believe it provides a very good picture of the stock market's performance because the companies in the Dow are extremely large industrial firms that account for nearly one-fourth of the total market value of NYSE firms.

There are many other market indexes in addition to the Dow that either have been created to measure different "baskets" of investments or use different methods of computation. For example, another very well-known family of indexes includes those published by Standard & Poor's — the S&P 500, S&P 400, S&P Industrials, and so forth. Certainly, the S&P indexes are more general, with broader coverage, than the DJIA because they include more companies. Indexes with even broader coverage exist. For example, all the major stock markets have composite indexes that include all the stocks listed on the exchanges; e.g., there is the NYSE index, the AMEX index, and the NASDAQ index. In addition, the Russell 3000 (3,000 securities) and the Wilshire 5000 (5,000 securities) are indexes that were created in an attempt to measure the performance of more general groups of stocks, not just those listed on particular exchanges. Still, you probably hear the DJIA quoted more often than any other index — it is published in nearly every newspaper, and local and national newscasts quote the Dow every night to provide listeners with an indication of the daily performance of the stock markets. The Dow is considered the stock market's bellwether barometer.

Table 15-5 lists a few of the market indexes that are published in *The Wall Street Journal* every day; it includes the return on stocks in 1998 according to each index measure. Notice that the returns differ fairly significantly. There are two major reasons for the differences. First, as we indicated earlier, not every index measures the same group of stocks. In such cases, it makes sense there would be some variation among the different index results. For example, compared with the firms that are included in the DJIA, the firms included in the NASDAQ index are very small. But, even if the indexes included the same "basket" of securities, there would still be some differences in the results because the indexes are not

TABLE 15-4

Composition of the Dow Jones Industrial Average, 1896 and 1998

I. ORIGINAL DJIA, 1896

Company	What Happened to the Company?
American Cotton Oil	Became CPC International; now named Bestfoods
American Sugar	Became Amstar Holdings; now named Long Wharf Maritime Center
American Tobacco	1911 antitrust action resulted in a breakup — American brands and RJR Tobacco evolved
Chicago Gas	Acquired in 1897 by Peoples Gas, which is now a subsidiary of TECO Energy Inc.
Distilling & Cattle Feeding	Became Quantum Chemical, which is now a subsidiary of Millennium Chemicals Inc.
General Electric	Still part of the DJIA
Laclede Gas	Operates under the same name, removed from the DJIA in 1899
National Lead	Named NL Industries today
North American	A utility monopoly that was broken up in the 1940s
Tennessee Coal & Iron	Acquired by U.S. Steel in 1907; U.S. Steel is now USX
U.S. Leather (preferred)	Liquidated in 1952
U.S. Rubber	Became Uniroyal, which is now a subsidiary of Michelin

II. CURRENT DJIA, 1998

Company	Date First Included	Comments
AlliedSignal Inc.	1925	Formed as Allied Chemical in 1920; current name was adopted in 1985
Aluminum Co. of America	1959	
American Express Co.	1982	
AT&T Corp.	1916	Replaced in 1928; included again in 1939; deregulated in 1980s
Boeing Co.	1987	
Caterpillar Inc.	1991	
Chevron Corp.	1930	Changed name from Standard Oil of California in 1984
Citigroup	1997	Renamed in 1998 when Travelers Group and Citicorp merged
Coca-Cola Co.	1932	Replaced in 1935; included again in 1987
DuPont Co.	1924	Replaced in 1925; included again in 1935
Eastman Kodak Co.	1930	
Exxon Corp.	1928	Changed name from Standard Oil of New Jersey in 1972
General Electric	1896	Replaced in 1898; included again in 1899; replaced in 1901; included again in 1907
General Motors Corp.	1915	Replaced in 1916; included again in 1925
Goodyear Tire & Rubber Co.	1930	
Hewlett-Packard Co.	1997	
IBM	1932	Replaced in 1939; included again in 1979
International Paper Co.	1956	
J.P. Morgan & Co.	1991	
Johnson & Johnson	1997	
McDonald's Corp	1985	
Merck & Co.	1979	
Minnesota Mining & Manuf.	1976	
Philip Morris Cos.	1985	
Procter & Gamble Co.	1932	
Sears, Roebuck & Co.	1924	
Union Carbide Corp.	1928	
United Technologies Corp.	1933	Replaced in 1934; included again in 1939; changed name from United Aircraft in 1975
Wal-Mart Stores Inc.	1997	
Walt Disney Co.	1991	

NOTES:

(1) In the comments, the term "replaced" indicates the stock was taken out of the DJIA.

(2) The number of stocks included in the DJIA was increased from 12 to 20 in 1916.

(3) The number of stocks included in the DJIA was increased from 20 to 30 in 1928.

SOURCES: *The Dow Jones Averages, 1885-1995,* Phyllis S. Pierce, editor (Burr Ridge, IL: Irwin Professional Publishing, 1996). Dow Jones Company web site: http://averages.dowjones.com

TABLE 15-5

Various Market Indexes, 1998

Index Name	Composition	Method of Computation	1998 Return
Dow Jones Industrial Average	30 largest industrial firms in the United States	Price-weighted	16.1%
NYSE Composite	More than 2,700 common stocks traded on the NYSE (excludes other types of securities)	Value-weighted	16.6
S&P 500	500 large companies traded on the NYSE and NASDAQ from different industrial sectors	Value-weighted	26.7
NASDAQ Composite	All common stocks of domestic companies traded on NASDAQ	Value-weighted	39.6
Russell 3000	3,000 largest companies in the United States based on market capitalization — represents about 98 percent of all investable stocks	Value-weighted	21.5
Wilshire 5000	More than 7,000 common stocks (originally 5,000) traded on the NYSE, AMEX, and OTC — the broadest market measure	Value-weighted	23.4

all constructed the same. While a detailed discussion of the computational differences among the various indexes is beyond the scope of this section, we can give you an indication of how the indexes differ with a simple example.

Table 15-6 contains information for the prices associated with three fictional companies for a one-year period. We can use this information to construct two different types of indexes: a price-weighted index and a value-weighted index. To construct a simple *price-weighted index*, we simply add the price of one share of each stock and then divide by three. According to the values given in Table 15-6, the value of the index was 80 at the end of 1998 and 77 at the end of 1999. Therefore, according to this measure, the three stocks generated a 3.75 percent loss during 1999. If you look at the column in the table labeled "One-Year Return," you can see that only one stock actually had a loss; the other two stocks earned rather substantial returns. But, because Wotterup is a very high priced stock, its change in price influenced the index more than the other two stocks, which have much smaller prices (Wotterup's price is more than 80 percent of the combined prices in 1998). This is a major criticism of price-weighted indexes.

One way to mitigate the influence high-priced securities have on the value of a price-weighted index is to compute a value-weighted index. A *value-weighted index* is based on the total market value of the stock of each firm rather than the price of a single share. For example, according to the information in Table 15-6, the total market value, referred to as **market capitalization,** of Amber Inc. was $50,000 in 1998, and the value of Wotterup was $40,000. Thus, even though Amber's per share stock price was $190 less than, or 5 percent of, the stock price of Wotterup, its total market capitalization was $10,000, or 25 percent, greater. The

MARKET CAPITALIZATION
The total market value of a firm's stock, which can be computed by multiplying the number of shares outstanding by the market price per share.

TABLE 15-6

Constructing Market Indexes (values are at the end of the year)

Stock	Shares Outstanding	1998		1999		One-Year Return
		Price	Market Capital	Price	Market Capital	
Amber Inc	5,000	$ 10	$ 50,000	$ 15	$ 75,000	50.0%
B&B Design	500	30	15,000	36	18,000	20.0
Wotterup Inc	200	200	40,000	180	36,000	−10.0
Totals		$240	$105,000	$231	$129,000	

I. Calculating a simple price-weighted index, I_W:

$I_{W,1998} = \$240/3 = 80$

$I_{W,1999} = \$231/3 = 77$

1999 return based on $I_W = (77 - 80)/80$

$$= -0.0375 = -3.75\%$$

II. Calculating a simple value-weighted index, I_V:

$I_{V,1998} = \$105,000/3 = 35,000$

$I_{V,1999} = \$129,000/3 = 43,000$

1999 return based on $I_V = (43,000 - 35,000)/35,000$

$$= 0.2286 = 22.86\%$$

NOTE: The value-weighted index is often computed by dividing the combined market value of the stocks from one year by the market value of the previous year, and then the result is multiplied by 100. In our illustration, the computation would be:

$$I_V = (\$129,000/\$105,000) \times 100 = 122.86$$

As you can see, this result is 22.86 percent greater than a base year value of 100.

value-weighted index shown in Table 15-6 is in a very simple form. It shows you, though, that the method used to construct an index can make a considerable difference in the results that are indicated for market performance. Note that the value-weighted index suggests the combined performance of the three companies was very good in 1999 — the return for the year was almost 23 percent. This result is significantly different from the result given by the price-weighted index primarily because the loss experienced by Wotterup did not influence the index as much as the positive returns associated with the other two stocks — in 1998, the market value of Wotterup was less than 40 percent of the combined market capitalization of the three stocks.

We mention these two methods to construct market indexes so that you are aware that the indexes reported in the papers or on the nightly news do not always measure the same event. If you hold equal numbers of shares in every stock you own, then you might want to compare the returns on your portfolio with a price-weighted index such as the DJIA; otherwise, it might be better to use a value-weighted index such as the S&P 500 for the comparison. In reality, however, market indexes are very highly correlated, regardless of how they are constructed or the specific group of securities used. Figure 15-5 shows the movements of five indexes since 1971. As you can see, for the most part, the indexes move in tandem. If we showed a single graph of the annual market returns measured by each of the indexes (i.e., changes in the values given in Figure 15-5), it would be very difficult to identify the returns of the individual indexes because their lines would overlap for most of the years.

Indexes have several important uses. First, because market indexes are used as gauges for determining how well the stock market is performing, they also provide investors with an indication of how well the general economy is doing. When the market is rising we call it a **bull market,** which suggests the economy is performing well; when the market is falling we call it a **bear market,** which suggests the economy is performing poorly. In addition to gauging the economy, market indexes are used as benchmarks by individual investors and mutual fund managers when determining how well their portfolios have performed. Have you ever heard someone say they outperformed the market? To make such a statement, they must have compared their portfolio's return with the return on the market using one of the market indexes. Indexes are also used to estimate the betas for securities. Remember from our discussion in Chapter 8 that beta represents the relationship between a stock's returns and the market's returns; thus, it is a measure of the systematic risk associated with the stock. And, finally, indexes are used as investments and as the basis for other investments, such as options.

BULL MARKET
A rising stock market.

BEAR MARKET
A falling stock market.

FIGURE 15-5

Market Indexes, 1971–1998

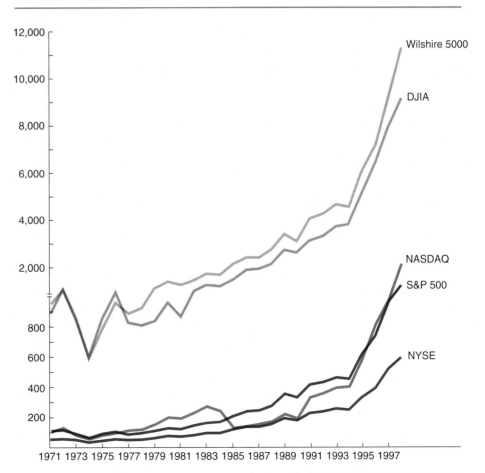

Self-Test Questions

What does a market index measure?

What are some examples of market indexes that are published in *The Wall Street Journal?*

Are the market returns computed using different indexes always the same? Why, or why not?

What are some uses for market indexes? How might you as an individual investor use indexes?

Alternative Investment Strategies

BUY-AND-HOLD STRATEGY
Strategy allowing investors to purchase securities with the intent to hold them for a long period, perhaps a number of years.

Investors construct investment portfolios by holding different positions in different financial assets. To achieve their investment goals, most individual investors follow a **buy-and-hold strategy,** which means they purchase securities with the intent to hold them until either their goals are met or modifications are needed in their portfolios to ensure future goals are met. A buy-and-hold strategy is usually considered a long-term rather than a short-term investment position. When investors buy securities, regardless of the intended holding period, they are said to be *going long* and, clearly, they hope that prices increase. On the other hand, when investors sell securities they own, they are said to be *going short,* which generally occurs when they believe prices will drop in the future.

When investors expect prices to increase, they can go long and magnify their return by borrowing funds from brokerage firms, or *margin trading,* so that they can invest amounts greater than they have saved. On the other side of the coin, when investors expect prices to decline, they can make money by *short selling,* which involves selling securities they do not own and replacing them at some future date. If prices fall, the securities can be repurchased at lower prices and investors can keep the difference between short selling prices and the repurchase prices.

In this section, we describe both margin trading and short selling to give you an idea of alternative investment arrangements that can be made with a broker. We must caution you, though, that such arrangements should not be used unless they are fully understood; in other words, *caveat investor* — let the investor beware.

MARGIN TRADING
Type of trade that allows an investor to borrow from his or her broker some portion of the funds needed to purchase an investment.

Margin Trading

Margin trading permits an investor to borrow from his or her broker some portion of the funds needed to purchase securities. The amount that can be borrowed is based on the **margin requirement,** which represents the minimum amount of personal funds (initial equity) an investor must have to purchase securities. For example, if the margin requirement is 60 percent, the investor must provide at least 60 percent of a security's purchase price; hence the maximum amount the broker will lend the investor is 40 percent. The margin requirement, which is set by the Federal Reserve, is currently 50 percent.[7]

MARGIN REQUIREMENT
The minimum percent of the total purchase price an investor must have to buy stock (or other investments) on margin.

---

[7]In 1946, the margin requirement was 100 percent, meaning an investor could not borrow to make stock purchases. The lowest margin requirement was 40 percent in the late 1930s. With a 40 percent

HYPOTHECATION AGREEMENT
Assigns securities as collateral for a margin loan.

When an investor borrows funds from a brokerage firm to purchase securities, he or she signs a **hypothecation agreement,** which assigns the securities as collateral for the margin loan. In essence, the hypothecation agreement allows the broker to liquidate the stocks to repay the loan if the investor defaults. Like other borrowers, investors who borrow funds to purchase securities are charged interest on their margin loans. The interest rate, which is called the **broker loan rate,**

BROKER LOAN RATE
The rate charged by brokers to borrow funds for margin trading.

is based on the rate a brokerage firm is charged by its lenders. Because an investor pays a specified rate to borrow funds from his or her broker, margin trading magnifies the gains when the value of the investment increases at a rate *greater than* the broker loan rate; but, margin trading also magnifies losses associated with a decline in value.

To illustrate margin trading, consider Karen Lambert who has $6,000 of her own funds to invest in MVP Corporation, which is currently selling for $50 a share. With her funds, Karen can purchase 120 shares ($6,000/$50) of MVP stock. MVP does not pay dividends. Thus, if the value of MVP's stock increases to $60 in one year, Karen will gain $10 per share and the total gain on her investment will be $1,200, or 20 percent ($1,200/$6,000 = 0.20) If the value of MVP's stock drops to $40, Karen will lose $10, and the value of her investment will decrease by 20 percent to $4,800.

The brokerage firm that handles Karen's trades allows margin trading with a margin requirement equal to 60 percent plus a 10 percent broker loan rate.[8] So, if Karen *margins* her position, she can purchase greater than the 120 shares of MVP stock she could purchase using only her own funds. To determine the amount of MVP stock Karen can purchase on margin, let's first consider how the actual margin, or percent investor's equity, is computed:

15-5	$$\frac{\text{Actual}}{\text{margin}} = \frac{\text{Percentage of}}{\text{investor's equity}} = \frac{\text{Investor's equity}}{\text{Market value of investment}}$$

The *actual margin* must equal the margin requirement when the stock is purchased; hence the maximum amount Karen can purchase is

$$\frac{\text{Actual}}{\text{margin}} = 0.60 = \frac{\$6,000}{\text{Market value of investment}}$$

$$\frac{\text{Market value}}{\text{of investment}} = \frac{\$6,000}{0.60} = \$10,000$$

Therefore, Karen can purchase $10,000, or 200 shares, of MVP if she margins her position. To do so, she must borrow $4,000 from the broker to add to her $6,000. If the value of MVP's stock increases to $60, the total value of the 200 shares will

margin, an investor could borrow 60 percent of the amount of stock purchased. The margin requirement has been 50 percent since 1974.

[8]A brokerage firm can establish its margin requirement greater than the amount set by the Federal Reserve, but it cannot offer a lower margin requirement.

equal $12,000. Karen cannot keep the entire $12,000 if she liquidates her position because she has to give the broker $4,400 to repay the $4,000 she borrowed and to pay $0.10 \times \$4,000 = \$400$ interest charged on the loan. Thus, Karen can keep $12,000 − $4,400 = $7,600, which is $1,600 greater than the $6,000 she had to invest. The return on *her* funds is 26.7 percent, which is greater than the 20 percent she would earn without margin trading:

$$\text{One-year HPR} = \frac{\$1,600}{\$6,000} = 0.267 = 26.7\%$$

On the other hand, if the value of MVP's stock drops to $40, the value of the 200 shares will be $8,000. Karen still has to pay the broker $4,400 to repay the loan with interest, so she is left with $8,000 − $4,400 = $3,600, a 26.7% loss on her investment (−$1,600/$8,000). As this example shows, both gains and losses are magnified by margin trading.

Note that the amount Karen owes the broker does not change when the market value of the stock changes. Thus, when the stock price increases, Karen has greater equity, or ownership, in the investment position; when the stock price decreases, she has less equity. At any point, an investor's equity position is represented by the actual margin associated with the existing market price of the stock. To compute an investor's equity position, Equation 15-5 can be expanded such that

15-5a

$$\frac{\text{Actual}}{\text{margin}} = \frac{\text{Investor's equity}}{\text{Market value of investment}}$$

$$= \frac{\left[\left(\begin{array}{c}\text{Number}\\\text{of shares}\end{array}\right) \times \left(\begin{array}{c}\text{Price per}\\\text{share}\end{array}\right)\right] - \begin{array}{c}\text{Amount}\\\text{borrowed}\end{array}}{\left(\begin{array}{c}\text{Number}\\\text{of shares}\end{array}\right) \times \left(\begin{array}{c}\text{Price per}\\\text{share}\end{array}\right)}$$

Thus, when the value of MVP's stock is $60, Karen has an equity position equal to 66.7 percent because the actual margin is

$$\begin{array}{c}\text{Actual margin:}\\(\text{Price} = \$60)\end{array} = \frac{(200 \times \$60) - \$4,000}{(200 \times \$60)} = \frac{\$8,000}{\$12,000} = 0.667 = 66.7\%$$

On the other hand, when the value of MVP's stock is $40, the actual margin is 50 percent because Karen owes the broker half the $40 \times 200 = \$8,000$ value of the MVP stock.

MARGIN CALL
A call from the broker to add more funds to a margined account.

If the price of a stock drops too much, a margined investor might be tempted to abandon his or her position in the stock and not repay the broker's loan. To ensure this does not happen, the broker will require the investor to provide additional funds when the *actual margin* decreases to a certain percentage or lower. At this point, the broker *calls* for more funds by issuing a **margin call.** The price at which a margin call is issued depends on the **maintenance margin,** which represents the lowest actual margin, or percentage equity, the brokerage firm permits its margined investors to possess at any time. To determine the price at which a margin call will be issued, we can set the *actual margin*

MAINTENANCE MARGIN
The lowest actual margin the broker will permit margined investors to have at any time.

in Equation 15-5a equal to the *maintenance margin* and rearrange the equation as follows[9]:

15-6

$$\text{Margin call price (per share)} = \frac{\text{Amount borrowed}}{(\text{Number of shares}) (1- \text{Maintenance margin})}$$

Therefore, if the maintenance margin is 45 percent, Karen Lambert will receive a margin call when the price of MVP falls to $36.36 per share:

$$\text{Margin call price (per share)} = \frac{\$4,000}{200 \times (1- 0.45)} = \$36.36$$

If the price of MVP drops below $36.36, the total value of the 200 shares Karen purchased will be less than $200 \times \$36.36 = \$7,272$, and her actual margin position will be less than the 45 percent maintenance margin. If Karen does get a margin call, she will have to provide additional funds to increase the actual margin; if she doesn't provide the funds, some or all of her stock will be liquidated to satisfy the margin call. Remember, in margin trading, the stock is put up as collateral for the investment position, so it can be sold by the broker if necessary.

Of course, Karen would prefer that the price of MVP stock increases so that her return is magnified by margin trading. If she thought MVP's stock was going to decrease in value, she might *short sell,* which is the investment arrangement we discuss next.

SHORT SELLING
Type of trade that allows an investor to borrow the stock of another investor and then sell it, but with a promise to replace the stock at a later date.

Short Selling

If an investor believes the price of a stock (or other security) is going to decrease in the future, he or she could make a profit by **short selling** the stock.[10] To *short sell,* an investor borrows the stock of another investor and then

---

[9]Equation 15-6 is derived as follows:

$$\text{Maintenance margin} = \frac{\left[\left(\substack{\text{Number of}\\\text{shares}}\right) \times \left(\substack{\text{Price per}\\\text{share}}\right)\right] - \substack{\text{Amount}\\\text{borrowed}}}{\left(\substack{\text{Number of}\\\text{shares}}\right) \times \left(\substack{\text{Price per}\\\text{share}}\right)} = 1 - \frac{\text{Amount borrowed}}{\left(\substack{\text{Number of}\\\text{shares}}\right) \times \left(\substack{\text{Price per}\\\text{share}}\right)}$$

$$\left(1- \substack{\text{Maintenance}\\\text{margin}}\right) = \frac{\text{Amount borrowed}}{\left(\substack{\text{Number of}\\\text{shares}}\right) \times \left(\substack{\text{Price per}\\\text{share}}\right)}$$

$$\left(1- \substack{\text{Maintenance}\\\text{margin}}\right) \times \left(\substack{\text{Number of}\\\text{shares}}\right) \times \left(\substack{\text{Price per}\\\text{share}}\right) = \text{Amount borrowed}$$

$$\substack{\text{Margin call}\\\text{price (per share)}} = \frac{\text{Amount borrowed}}{\left(\substack{\text{Number of}\\\text{shares}}\right) \left(1- \substack{\text{Maintenance}\\\text{margin}}\right)}$$

[10]Securities other than stock can be *shorted.* However, because it generally is easier to discuss short selling with respect to stock trading, we discuss only stocks here.

sells it, promising to replace, or repay, the borrowed stock at a later date. If the price of the borrowed stock falls, the investor can buy it back and replace it at a lower price, hence make a profit. In essence, then, the objective of short selling is to "sell high and buy low." For example, if Karen expects MVP's stock to decrease in value, she could borrow 100 shares from her broker and sell them for the current price of $50 each. If the price per share decreases to $40, Karen would buy back the shares at $40 each and return them to her broker; her profit, not considering commissions and other costs, would be $10 per share, or $1,000 total. But, if the price of MVP increases to $60, Karen would lose $10 per share, or $1,000 total, because she would have to repurchase the stock for $10 more than it was shorted.

There are restrictions to short selling that make it unattractive to many investors. An important restriction is that an investor cannot short sell a stock if its latest trade results in a price decrease, which is called a **downtick.** Therefore, short sales can be placed only after *uptick* or *zero-plus tick* trades. An **uptick** trade is where the price of the most recent trade is higher than the previous trade, and a **zero-plus tick** trade occurs when the price of the most recent trade equals the price of the previous trade but exceeds the price from one trade earlier. A second restriction is that the initial proceeds generated from the short sale cannot be used freely by the investor; instead, the proceeds are kept by the broker as collateral for the stock that was borrowed. In addition, the investor must "deposit" funds with the brokerage firm to ensure the stock can be repurchased if its price increases. The amount of the deposit is generally a function of the margin requirement, subject to some minimum amount, say, $2,000. For example, if Karen wants to short sell 100 shares of MVP stock when its price is $50, the proceeds from the sale would be $5,000. Not only would the broker keep this money in a deposit account, but Karen probably would have to deposit $5,000 × 0.60 = $3,000 of her own funds with the broker to ensure the short position can be covered if the stock's price increases. If the price of the stock increases by too much, the investor will receive a "margin call" from the brokerage firm that will require him or her to provide additional funds to cover possible future price increases.[11] Any amount left in the brokerage account will be given to the investor when the short position is covered, which occurs when the stock is returned to its original owner.

Actually, when an investor short sells a stock, the owner of the stock generally does not know his or her stock has been sold because street name stock is used. In any event, because the owner of the stock technically does not have the shares any longer, the short seller must pay any dividends distributed by the company during the period the stock is shorted; in reality, investors whose stocks are short sold should not be concerned that they technically do not own the shares during the shorting period.

At times, investors short sell stock they also own. When this investment position is taken, the investor is said to be **shorting against the box.** The name originated in earlier times when an investor held securities in a safety deposit

---

DOWNTICK
A decrease in price from one trade to another.

UPTICK
Occurs when the price of the most recent trade is higher than the previous trade.

ZERO-PLUS TICK
Occurs when the price of the latest trade equals the price of the previous trade but exceeds the price from one trade earlier.

SHORTING AGAINST THE BOX
Occurs when an investor short sells a stock he or she also owns.

---

[11]The accounts in which funds or securities are held as collateral for, or to insure the safety of, various investment positions are usually referred to as margin accounts because, even if the investor is not specifically margin trading, the position involves some type of borrowing or leverage activity. For instance, short selling involves borrowing securities.

box at the bank or strong box at home or work; thus, this investment strategy involved short selling the same stock that was held in "the box." In the past, investors "shorted against the box" to delay tax payments associated with liquidating an investment until some future period. Suppose, for example, that Ed Rampart purchased 100 shares of stock five years ago for $25 per share, and the price of the stock is $75 today, which is December 10. Ed would like to capture the $50 per share gain he realized from holding the stock, but he would prefer to delay payment of taxes until next year. If Ed short sells 100 shares of the stock today, he would "lock in" the profit for as long as he maintains the short sale position in combination with ownership of the stock. If the price of the stock increases by $1, Ed will realize a $100 gain from the stock he owns, but he will lose exactly $100 on his short sale position. The opposite will occur if the price of the stock drops by $1 — he will lose on the stock he owns and gain on the short sale position. Suppose in January, Ed sells the stock and closes his short sale position at the same time the price of the stock is $60 per share.[12] At that time, Ed would receive $60 × 100 shares = $6,000 from the sale of his stock and ($75 − $60) × 100 = $1,500 from the short sale position; thus, Ed would receive a total of $7,500, which is the same amount he would have received if he sold the stock in December. The big difference is that Ed delayed recognition of his gain until the next tax year.

According to the example given here, shorting against the box sounds like a good method to delay tax payments. Unfortunately, revisions made to the Tax Code in 1997 essentially eliminated the tax benefits associated with such an investment strategy. Therefore, fewer investors are able to use this strategy to delay taxes.

The restrictions along with the unpredictability of stock price movements make short selling a very risky investment strategy. Short selling is an investment strategy used by sophisticated investors. If you ever consider short selling a security, be sure you understand what you are doing and the possibility that you can lose large amounts of money. How much can you lose on a short sale? To answer this question, we pose another question: How high can the value of a stock rise?

Self-Test Questions

What is a buy-and-hold investment strategy?

What do we mean when we say an investor is "going long"? What does "going short" mean?

What is margin trading? How can margin trading help magnify returns?

How do investors short sell? What are some of the restrictions to short selling?

What does it mean to "short against the box"?

---

[12]An investor who shorts against the box can liquidate his or her position by selling the stock he or she owns and then purchasing the stock needed to cover the short position. The investor will incur two commissions. On the other hand, the investor can generally save commissions by using the stock he or she owns to cover the short position. In most cases, as long as the short sale and the stocks that are owned are handled by the same brokerage firm, the final transaction will not be charged commissions.

Summary

In this chapter, we discussed some fundamental investment concepts. A basic understanding of these concepts is necessary for individuals to be knowledgeable about their investments. The key topics covered in the chapter are listed below.

- Investing is a continuous process that includes decisions about the (1) **investment objective,** (2) **attitude toward risk,** (3) **implementation of investment goals,** and (4) **monitoring the investment position.**
- There are many different **investment instruments** available to meet investment goals. Many of these securities were discussed in Chapter 4.
- Most securities transactions that involve individuals require the use of a **broker,** who helps clients trade financial assets.
- **Brokerage firms differ from financial intermediaries** because they permit savers to provide their funds directly, rather than indirectly, to users of those funds.
- Brokerage firms can be classified either as a **full-service broker** or as a **discount broker.** The cost of trading securities is lower with a discount broker, but a full-service broker provides such services as investment analysis and advice.
- Securities are traded in **round lots,** or multiples of 100 shares.
- Investors can place different types of orders with their brokers. The most common order is the **market order,** which instructs the broker to trade at the best price available when the order reaches the market. Restrictions can be included with orders — price restrictions can be given in the form of a **stop order** or a **limit order,** while time restrictions can be given in the form of a **day order, good 'til canceled order,** or a **fill or kill order.**
- Stock certificates, which represent ownership in a firm, often are kept in **street name** so that ownership transfer is easier when the stock is sold.
- **Investment information** comes in a variety of forms — via newspapers, magazines, and television. Stock and bond quotes published in financial newspapers provide much more information than just the current market values of the securities.
- It is important that investors know how to compute rates of returns earned from their investments. The **holding period return,** which represents the return earned for the time period the investment was held, is calculated as follows:

$$\frac{\text{Holding period}}{\text{rate of return}} = \bar{k} = \frac{\text{Income received} + \left(\frac{\text{Ending value}}{\text{of investment}} - \frac{\text{Beginning value}}{\text{of investment}}\right)}{\text{Beginning value of investment}}$$

$$= \frac{\text{INC} + (P_1 - P_0)}{P_0}$$

A portion of the total return earned from an investment comes from the **income** generated by the investment and a portion comes from the **capital gain (loss)** associated with changes in the investment's market value.

- There are two approaches that are used to compute the average return per year (period): **simple arithmetic average return** and **geometric average return.** The simple arithmetic average return does not consider compounding; the geometric average return does consider compounding.

- The **return on a portfolio** is computed by determining the weighted average of the returns of the securities in the portfolio.
- **Market indexes** are used (1) to gauge how well the market and the economy are doing, (2) as benchmarks when determining how well investments have performed, (3) to estimate betas for stocks, and (4) as investments.
- A rising market is called a **bull market,** and a falling market is called a **bear market.**
- Not all indexes are computed the same. Some indexes, such as the Dow Jones Industrial Average, are **price-weighted indexes,** while other indexes, such as the S&P 500, are **value-weighted indexes.**
- If an investor follows a **buy-and-hold strategy,** he or she generally purchases securities with the intent to hold them for more than one year.
- **Margin trading** permits an investor to borrow a portion of the investment funds from the brokerage firm. When an investor borrows funds from a broker, a **hypothecation agreement** is signed so that the securities can be used as collateral for the loan. The interest rate charged on the margined funds is called the **broker loan rate.**
- Margin trading permits an investor to leverage, thus to **magnify (either up or down) the returns** associated with an investment position. If the margin position deteriorates, the investor receives a **margin call** that requires him or her to provide more funds to the broker.
- Investors can earn positive returns when the price of a security is declining by **short selling.** When an investor short sells, he or she borrows securities from another investor and sells the shares in the market. The securities have to be repurchased at some later date so that they can be replaced. During the short sale period, the short seller is responsible for paying the investor who owned the stock any dividends made by the firm. A short sale can occur only after the price of the security has increased from a previous trade; such a price reaction is called an **uptick.**
- An investor is said to be **shorting against the box** when he or she short sells securities that he or she also owns.

Questions

15-1   Outline the "investment process," and indicate the types of decisions that are necessary at each step of the process.

15-2   Why is it important for every investor to monitor his or her investment position on a continuous basis? What would happen if the monitoring function is ignored?

15-3   According to its traditional role, why is a stock brokerage firm not considered a financial intermediary? Differentiate between the role of a brokerage firm and an intermediary.

15-4   Identify some of the instructions that investors can give brokers when trading securities. Under what circumstances would a limit order be appropriate? Why would an investor ever use a good 'til canceled (GTC) order?

15-5   What types of information can investors get from stock and bond quotations?

15-6   Explain the difference between a dividend yield and a capital gain (loss). Which is preferable from an investor's standpoint?

15-7 What is the difference between the simple arithmetic average return and the geometric average return? Under what circumstances is it appropriate to use each method?

15-8 What are the major uses of market indexes?

15-9 When they are used to measure returns, do all market indexes yield the same results? What are some reasons different indexes might give different results? Give some examples.

15-10 What is the difference between a price-weighted index and a value-weighted index? Which is a better computational method?

15-11 Explain how margin trading magnifies an investor's returns.

15-12 How, and why, does an investor short sell a security?

15-13 What are the possible gains and losses that can occur when an investor short sells a security?

15-14 Can you think of instances where an investor would benefit from short selling even if he or she expects the price of the security to increase during the short sale period?

15-15 How do you think transactions costs affect decisions about implementing investment goals?

Self-Test Problems *Solutions Appear in Appendix B*

Key terms   **ST-1**   Define each of the following terms:
  a. Investors; speculators
  b. Risk tolerance level
  c. Transactions costs
  d. Asset allocation
  e. Full-service brokerage firm; discount brokerage firm
  f. Market order; stop order; limit order; day order; fill or kill order
  g. Street name stock
  h. Stock symbol
  i. Holding period return (HPR); dividend yield; capital gain
  j. Market index; bull market; bear market
  k. Margin requirement; maintenance margin; margin call
  l. Hypothecation agreement; broker loan rate
  m. Uptick; downtick; zero-plus tick

Margin trading   **ST-2**   Lance Underwood is considering his options for investing the $19,800 inheritance he just received, so he contacted a broker who was recommended by a friend. The broker told Lance that he could either invest the $19,800 or borrow from the brokerage firm and invest more. The margin requirement at the brokerage firm is 55 percent, the maintenance margin is 40 percent, and the broker loan rate is 12 percent. Lance has decided he wants to invest in Microsoft because his close friends have told him how well the stock has performed over the past 15 years. Currently, Microsoft has a market price equal to $120, and the company does not pay dividends.
  a. Assuming Lance does not margin, how many shares of Microsoft stock could he purchase? What holding period return would he earn if the price of Microsoft increases to $150 in one year? What would be the return if the price drops to $105?

b. Assuming Lance margins by borrowing the maximum amount allowed by the broker, how many shares of the Microsoft stock could he buy? What would be the holding period return that he would earn if the price of Microsoft increases to $150 in one year? What would be the return if the price drops to $105?

c. If Lance margins, how far can the price of Microsoft stock drop before he could expect a margin call? Assume Lance margins the maximum amount.

Portfolio return **ST-3** Lucy Ramissaw invested $10,000 in 4 stocks 3 years ago. She just received a statement from Bestvest Brokerage Inc., which is the firm with which she trades, that summarized her investment portfolio as follows:

	Date				
Investment Name	**1/2/96**	**12/31/96**	**12/31/97**	**12/31/98**	**12/31/99**
Mateo Computers	$ 2,000	$ 2,400	$ 2,760	$ 2,484	$ 3,726
Northern Water	4,000	4,100	4,900	5,635	6,762
AMN Motors	1,000	900	1,080	1,350	1,404
Farley Argicorp	3,000	2,850	3,420	3,762	3,762
Portfolio value	$10,000	$10,250	$12,160	$13,231	$15,654

a. Compute the 4-year holding period return and the annual returns for each stock. That is, compute the overall return for the entire 4-year period, and then compute the return for each year.

b. Based on the market values given in the table, compute the weights (proportion) of each stock in the portfolio for each year.

c. Compute the 4-year holding period return and the annual returns for the portfolio based on (1) the market values given for the total portfolio and (2) the annual returns for each individual stock computed in part a and the weights computed in part b.

Problems

The problems in this section do not take into consideration the impact of taxes or commissions on investment returns. For simplicity, we assume there are no taxes and no commissions.

Rates of return **15-1** Nancy Cotton bought 400 shares of NeTalk for $15 per share. One year later, Nancy sold the stock for $21, just after she received a 90¢ cash dividend from the company.

a. What is the total dollar return earned by Nancy for the year?

b. What is the rate of return Nancy earned?

c. Separate the rate of return computed in part b into the dividend yield and the capital gain. In other words, compute the dividend yield and the capital gain that Nancy earned by holding NeTalk for one year.

Rates of return **15-2** Janis Rafferty purchased 100 shares of Gold Depot common stock at the beginning of January for $25. Janis received a $1.25 dividend payment from the Gold Depot at the end of December, and, at that time, the stock was selling for $27.50.

a. Compute the dollar return that Janis earned during the year.

b. Compute the rate of return Janis earned.

c. What was the dividend yield and the capital gain generated by Gold Depot during the year?

d. Compute the rate of return Janis would have earned if she had purchased 500 shares instead of 100 shares of Gold Depot at the beginning of the year.

Arithmetic and geometric returns **15-3**   According to the NYSE Composite Index, the stock market returns from 1995 through 1999 were as follows:

Year	NYSE Return
1995	31.3%
1996	19.1
1997	30.1
1998	−1.5
1999	3.9

a. Compute the simple arithmetic average return for the NYSE for the 5-year period.

b. Compute the geometric average return for the NYSE for the 5-year period.

c. Based on your answer in part b, compute the dollar value an investor would have at the end of 1999 if he or she invested $2,000 in the NYSE index at the beginning of 1995.

d. Using the annual returns given in the table, compute the value of a $2,000 initial investment at the end of each year.

Rates of return   **15-4**   George K. Rice is reviewing the performance of the portfolio he has held for the past five years. He has decided to compare his portfolio returns with the market returns measured by the S&P 500 Index. The market values of his portfolio and the S&P 500 Index from 1994 through 1999 are given in the following table:

End of Year	Portfolio Value	S&P 500 Index
1994	$17,000.00	459.27
1995	20,400.00	615.93
1996	22,440.00	740.74
1997	23,562.00	970.43
1998	27,096.30	1017.01
1999	37,934.82	1078.03

a. Compute the annual returns for both the portfolio and the market.

b. Compute the simple arithmetic average return for both the portfolio and the market.

c. Compute the geometric average return for both the portfolio and the market.

d. Explain why the simple arithmetic average return is greater than the geometric average return for both the portfolio and the market.

e. Evaluate the performance of George's portfolio compared with the market.

Short selling   **15-5**   Abby Deere took the advice of a close friend and short sold 100 shares of Techware common stock when its market price was $105.

a. What will Abby gain or lose (in dollars) if the price of Techware is $120 when she repurchases the stock to close her short sale position?

b. What will Abby gain or lose (in dollars) if the price of Techware is $95 when she repurchases the stock to close her short sale position?

c. What is the most Abby can gain from her short sale position? Explain why.

d. What is the most Abby can lose from her short sale position? Explain why.

Portfolio return   **15-6**   Harold Rawlings computed the returns he earned last year from each of the stocks he holds in his portfolio. The individual returns as well as the amounts he invested in each stock at the beginning of the year are as follows:

Stock	Return	Amount Invested
AT&T	22.5%	$5,200
GM	12.3	5,520
Danka	-44.7	1,200
Suiza Foods	100.0	3,080

a. Compute the return Harold earned on his portfolio during the year.

b. Harold decided to keep Danka in his portfolio, even though it had financial difficulty and performed very poorly last year, because he expects a significant turnaround that will generate a 25 percent return next year. Suppose that Harold is correct. Assuming the returns from the other stocks remain the same as last year, compute the return on the portfolio for next year. (Hint: The portfolio weights for the stocks change based on the returns earned last year; i.e., the values of the stocks at the end of the year should be used to compute the new weights.)

Margin trading   **15-7**   Assume Warner-Lambert Company, a pharmaceutical manufacturer, is currently selling for $75 per share. You have $7,500 of your own funds to invest. The brokerage firm that you use for your stock trades will allow you to borrow funds to buy the stock with an initial margin equal to 62.5 percent, a maintenance margin of 40 percent, and a broker loan rate equal to 12 percent. In 1 year, you expect the per share price of Warner-Lambert's stock to be 20 percent higher than it is today, and, at that time, the company will pay shareholders a cash dividend equal to $2.00 per share.

a. If your expectations for the coming year are correct, what return would you earn if you invested your $7,500 and did not borrow any funds from the brokerage firm?

b. If you borrowed the maximum amount allowable from the brokerage firm, how much can you invest in Warner-Lambert?

c. If your expectations for the coming year are correct, what return would you earn if you invested your $7,500 and borrowed the maximum funds allowable from the brokerage firm?

d. Compute the return you would earn if the stock's price drops to $70 per share at the end of the year and you borrowed to invest the maximum amount possible.

Holding period return   **15-8**   Three years ago Sparky Lewis purchased 200 shares of Andrinap Inc. for $80 per share. The company does not pay dividends. Now the market value of the stock is $128.08.

a. Compute the total dollar return Sparky has earned since he bought Andrinap.

b. Compute Sparky's 3-year holding period return.

c. Compute the average annual return Sparky earned. (Hint: You know the beginning value and ending value of the stock, so you can use the time value of money concepts we discussed in Chapter 6 to solve this problem.)

Margin trading, short selling,   **15-9**   Abby Cowler bought 300 shares of INV stock 4 years ago when it was selling for
and returns $10 per share. At that time, she really believed the stock was "a diamond in the rough," so she borrowed to purchase the maximum amount she could. The initial margin requirement was 55 percent, and the broker loan rate was 10 percent. Today, the stock is selling for $30 per share, and the margin requirements are the same as when Abby first purchased INV. INV reinvests all of its earnings in capital budgeting projects, so it has not paid dividends since its stock began trading publicly.

Even though INV's stock currently is selling for $30, its price has dropped from a historically high price of $38 just a few months ago. Abby doesn't want to sell the stock because she believes it will regain its upward trend within the next few months. For that reason, Abby is considering taking the advice of one of her friends, who suggested that she short sell 100 shares of INV to protect a portion of her gains if the stock price drops further in future months. Her friend explained that if she decides to sell her stock after further declines, the short sale position will help offset some of the losses she will earn on her long position in the stock.

    a. Assume the price of INV is $20 per share in 1 year and that Abby does not short sell the stock. What return would Abby earn on the stock for the year? Remember that Abby is in a margined position.

    b. Assume the price of INV is $20 per share in 1 year and that Abby short sells 100 shares of the stock at the beginning of the year. What return would Abby earn on the stock for the year?

    c. Compute Abby's 5-year holding period return given the situation presented in part a.

    d. Compute Abby's 5-year holding period return given the situation presented in part b.

    e. Rework parts a through d assuming the price of INV is $40 in 1 year.

Constructing market indexes　**15-10**　The following table gives information about the five stocks that have traded on the Small Investors Stock Exchange (SISE) since it started 2 years ago:

Stock	Number of Shares	Price per Share		
		Beginning of Year 1	End of Year 1	End of Year 2
Startab	500	$ 75.00	$ 82.50	$100.00
Oakorn	100	450.00	454.50	460.00
Teeduff	1000	30.00	40.00	38.50
Amxy	5000	7.50	6.75	13.50
Zaxive	300	150.00	165.00	148.50

None of the stocks pays a dividend.

    a. Using all the stocks, construct a simple price-weighted market index and compute the market returns for each year. (Hint: See Table 15-6.)

    b. Using all the stocks, construct a value-weighted market index and compute the market returns for each year. (Hint: See Table 15-6.)

    c. Explain why the returns computed in parts a and b are not identical.

Exam-Type Problems

The problems included in this section are set up in such a way that they could be used as multiple-choice exam problems.

Short selling　**15-11**　Assume that IBM is selling for $110 per share and that you short sell 200 shares of the stock.

    a. What would be your dollar return if the price of IBM stock drops to $95 per share?

    b. What would be your dollar return if the price of IBM stock increases to $120 per share?

    c. Is there a limit to your gains? Is there a limit to your losses? Explain.

Margin trading　**15-12**　Robin wants to purchase 1000 shares of Anatop Inc., which is selling at $5 per share. Anatop does not pay dividends because all earnings are reinvested in the firm to maintain its successful R&D department. The brokerage firm will allow Robin to borrow funds with an initial margin requirement equal to 70 percent and a maintenance margin of 35 percent. The broker loan rate is 14 percent. Assume that Robin borrows the maximum allowed by the brokerage firm to purchase the Anatop stock.

a. How much of her own money must Robin provide to purchase 1,000 shares of Anatop?

b. To what price can Anatop drop before Robin receives a margin call from her broker?

c. If the price of Anatop's stock is $7.50 in 1 year, what rate of return would Robin earn from her investment position?

d. If the price of Anatop's stock is $4.00 in 1 year, what rate of return would Robin earn from her investment position?

Holding period return **15-13** Mary Anderson bought 250 shares of Dishport stock when it was selling at $50 per share, and she sold the stock for $55 per share 6 months later. During the time she held the stock, Mary received two $1 dividend payments from the firm.

a. What was Mary's 6-month holding period return?

b. On an annual basis, what return did Mary earn?

Portfolio return **15-14** Ralph Saunderson's portfolio includes both stocks and a corporate bond. The total amount of funds Ralph has invested is $50,000, with $40,000 invested in stocks. The names of the stocks and their most recent 1-year returns are given in the following table:

Stock	Return
Abbott Inc.	20.1%
Randicorp	12.5
Salvidore Co.	−2.4

Of the $40,000 invested in the stocks, 50 percent is invested in Randicorp, and the rest is divided equally between Abbott Inc. and Salvidore Company. The most recent 1-year return on the bond was 6 percent.

a. How much does Ralph have invested in each of the stocks?

b. If Ralph's portfolio included only the stocks, what would be his most recent 1-year return?

c. What is the most recent 1-year return Ralph earned on the entire portfolio?

Integrative Problem

Rates of return, margin trading, and short selling **15-15** Suppose you have just been hired by Jamestown Financial Services (JFS) as an investment advisor. Your boss, Susan Canton, has to write a report for an important client, so she has decided to give you "on-the-job training" by asking you to answer the following questions and complete the appropriate computations:

a. What questions would you ask our client to determine her investment objectives and how to best achieve them?

b. How would you determine the appropriate asset allocation for the client? Under what conditions should the asset allocation be changed?

c. What is a stockbroker, and what role does a broker play in securities transactions?

d. Should JFS recommend that the client use a full-service broker or a discount broker when she trades securities in her portfolio?

e. What types of orders can be placed with a broker? When should restrictions, either time limits or price limits, be used when placing trading orders?

f. Where can our client get investment and other financial information so that she can stay current with her investment position?

g. One year ago our client inherited a portfolio of stocks. The following table gives information about the inherited stocks:

Stock	Number of Shares Inherited	Value of Shares When Inherited	Current Value of Shares[a]
Borman	3,000	$ 45,500	$ 43,225
Capnow	185	18,500	24,050
Exytor	500	30,000	33,000
Orteck	120	6,000	9,000
		$100,000	$109,275

[a]Includes any dividends paid during the year.

What return did our client earn on each stock and on the portfolio?

b. Our client wants to compare the returns on her stocks with the market return. Jamestown generally uses the S&P 500 Index for such comparisons. When our client received her inheritance, the value of the S&P 500 was 1017.01, and today its value is 1080.53. What was the market's return for the year?

i. Our client's stockbroker told her that his firm allows margin trading and short selling. Our client does not understand these investment positions. Explain the concepts of margin trading and short selling so that our client can better understand the risks she would be taking if she decided to pursue either position.

j. Our client is quite interested in purchasing MacroTech because she has observed the extraordinary growth the stock has experienced during the past decade. In particular, our client wants to know what returns she could earn if she borrowed from her brokerage firm to buy MacroTech. The brokerage firm has an initial margin requirement equal to 60 percent, a maintenance margin of 35 percent, and a broker loan rate of 10 percent. Assume our client borrows the maximum she can from the broker. Also assume that MacroTech does not pay a dividend.

(1) How much can our client invest in MacroTech if she has $18,600 of her own money to invest? How many shares of MacroTech can she buy if the stock price is $100?

(2) If the price of MacroTech stock increases from $100 to $125 over a 1-year period, what rate of return would our client earn?

(3) If the price of MacroTech stock decreases from $100 to $90 over a 1-year period, what rate of return would our client earn?

(4) What is a margin call? At what price would our client receive a margin call for the MacroTech stock?

(5) If the price of MacroTech drops to $61 and a margin call is issued such that our client has to provide enough funds to increase her actual margin to 50 percent, how much money must she give to the broker?

k. Our client is also thinking about short selling 200 shares of TNT Fireworks, which is currently selling at $35. TNT does not pay dividends.

(1) If the brokerage firm requires our client to provide a deposit, or "good faith funds," based on the initial margin requirement, how much money will she have to give to the broker to short sell TNT?

(2) What will be the dollar return on the short sale position if the price of TNT drops to $28 per share?

(3) What will be the dollar return on the short sale position if the price of TNT increases to $40 per share?

l. If you had to give our client one piece of advice about investing, what would it be?

CHAPTER 16

Security Valuation and Selection

Throughout history, the investment adage "buy low, sell high" has been repeated again and again. Following this advice is not as difficult as it might seem because, historically, the stock market has trended upward over the long term. Thus, if you invest in a basket of securities today and you hold your position for a long period, say, 10 to 20 years, chances are that you will be able to sell the securities for much higher prices. In fact, if you earn the historical market average return, your original investment will double every five to six years.

In today's world, the many technological advances that have been made in processing and delivering information have increased the interests of individuals in managing their own investment portfolios. Of course every person who manages his or her own investments wants to find stocks that will become "winners" after they are purchased, and thus result in investment bonanzas. Some investors use extreme measures in their attempts to identify such stocks. Therefore, perhaps the old adage should be revised to state: "Beat the market — buy lower, sell higher."

Investors who try to "beat the market" on a risk-adjusted basis use various approaches in their attempts to identify stocks that are either mispriced or promise very high growth rates. These two groups of stock are referred to as *value stocks* and *growth stocks*. Some professional investors believe value stocks produce greater return potentials than growth stocks, while other professionals believe the opposite. Which side is correct?

According to a recent article in *Forbes,* value stocks perform better than growth stocks, and their risks are substantially less. The article provides evidence that growth stocks, which are also called glamour stocks, have performed slightly better than the S&P 500 index since the late 1970s. During the same period, firms with small market capitalizations and low price-earnings (P/E) ratios, or value stocks, did much better. The return on value stocks averaged more than 20 percent annually from 1978 to 1998, while the average return on growth stocks was nearly 4 percent lower. In addition, the results show that mutual funds that contained value stocks outperformed

Continued

mutual funds that contained growth stocks in almost all of the cases that were examined.

So, why haven't the growth stocks performed as well as the value stocks? The answer is not clear-cut. Although the strategy of investing in growth stocks is founded on a well-grounded principle — invest in stocks of companies with growth rates that exceed the norm — most growth stocks sell for prices that exceed 20 to 30 times earnings, which is quite a premium for future growth that is not guaranteed. Of course, future growth could turn out to be greater than originally forecasted, in which case substantial gains would be realized. But, the opposite can also occur, in which case the returns would be substantially less than expected because lower-than-expected growth *in any future period* lowers the forecasts of all subsequent cash flows, even if the growth predictions of later years come true. In addition, according to the *Forbes* article, "when the growth funds do well, it is usually only for a brief spurt, and brief spurts aren't the key to long-term success."

Value stocks, on the other hand, tend to be stocks of small firms that have not received the glamour of the growth stocks because few, if any, analysts or professional investors follow them. It is felt that these types of companies produce above-average returns because most of the information that comes out of the firms is considered "good news" and is a surprise to the market; thus, stock prices often increase significantly. In addition, it appears there are more value stocks to choose from than growth stocks, which suggests there is less chance that the prices of value stocks will be inflated relative to growth stocks.

Forbes is quick to point out that proponents of growth stocks and proponents of value stocks will remain divided for years to come. There are substantial returns to be made in either camp, and most professional advisors tell investors to look for both good growth prospects and bargains. So, it seems the question every investor wants answered is, "How can I pick the winners?" Unfortunately, there is no concrete answer to this question. In fact, you might discover that this question really cannot be answered. But, in this chapter, we attempt to give you an idea of some of the approaches used by investors to value and select securities — that is, to pick the winners.

SOURCE: James M. Clash and Mary Beth Grover, "The Wallflower Strategy," *Forbes*, February 9, 1998, 114-117.

How do we value investments? In Chapter 7, we described the concept of valuation and its general application to both financial assets, such as stocks and bonds, and real assets, such as buildings and equipment. And, as we learned at that point, the value of any asset can be described simply as the present value of the cash flows expected to be generated by the asset during its life. Unfortunately, as we discovered in Chapters 8 and 9, predicting future cash flows is not always an easy task. Estimating cash flows is much easier in situations in which a legal contract obligates an individual or a firm to make specific payments at specific times than where there is an implied contract that cash distributions eventually will be made at some time in the future. For instance, we know that a traditional corporate bond obligates the firm to make interest payments that are defined in a legal document called an *indenture;* thus, the future cash flows associated with a bond are generally easy to estimate. On the other hand, common stock does not legally obligate the firm to make any future cash distributions; rather, investors view common stock as an *implied contract* with the firm that value will be maximized and cash distributions will be made when the firm exhausts its positive growth opportunities. Thus, even though the concept of valuation is fairly intuitive, in reality, trying to determine the value of investments such as common stock is not so straightforward; in fact, it can be a formidable task.

In this chapter, we describe some of the approaches that are used to value and select securities such as common stock. We can only provide you with an overview of available valuation and selection methods; it is beyond the scope of this chapter to provide detailed discussions of such techniques. More detailed descriptions can be attained by taking a course that is specifically dedicated to the subject of investments.

Fundamental Analysis versus Technical Analysis

FUNDAMENTAL ANALYSIS
The practice of evaluating the information contained in financial statements, industry reports, and economic factors to determine the intrinsic value of a firm.

INTRINSIC VALUE
The "true," or economic, value of the firm.

FUNDAMENTALISTS
Analysts who utilize fundamental analysis in an attempt to forecast future stock price movements.

Traditionally, the techniques used to value common stock have been divided into one of two categories — *fundamental analysis* or *technical analysis.* Therefore, we begin our discussion with a description of both these approaches, and then we provide you with an overview of some of the popular valuation techniques used by both types of analysts.

Fundamental analysis is the practice of evaluating the information contained in financial statements, industry reports, and economic factors to determine the *intrinsic value* of a firm. The term **intrinsic value** refers to the "true," or economic, value of the firm. If the market value and the intrinsic value are not the same, then the stock is said to be *mispriced.* **Fundamentalists,** which refers to analysts who utilize fundamental analysis, attempt to forecast future stock price movements by examining factors that are believed related to the market values of stocks. The factors that are examined can be grouped into one of three categories: (1) company conditions, such as earnings, financial strength, products, management, labor relations, and so forth; (2) industry conditions, such as maturity, stability, competitive conditions, and so on; and (3) economic and market conditions. Thus, fundamental analysis entails integrating evaluations of the company, its industry, and the economy.

TECHNICAL ANALYSIS
Examination of supply and demand for securities to determine trends in price movements of stocks or financial markets.

TECHNICIANS
The term given to analysts who examine stocks and financial markets using technical analysis.

In a general sense, technical analysis includes any method that does not incorporate the fundamental investment concepts and evaluation of those factors believed to be the basis for establishing the market values of securities. More specifically, **technical analysis** is based on analyses of supply/demand relationships for securities to determine trends in price movements of stocks or financial markets. Technical analysts, who are called **technicians,** search for trends by examining charts or by using computer programs that evaluate information about historical movements in trading volume and prices for stocks and for financial markets as a whole. In the past, technicians have been referred to as *chartists* because they have been known to pore over charts, or plots, that contain historical trading volume and prices in an attempt to find patterns that can be expected to repeat in the future. In fact, if technical analysts have a rallying cry, it would be "history repeats itself." The approach technicians take is based on their belief that movements in the financial markets are caused by investors' attitudes toward various economic and financial factors and other psychological circumstances, which, in many instances, result in actions that, although not always rational, are fairly predictable. According to technicians, investors' actions are predictable because humans are creatures of habit — when faced with situations such as ones that occurred in the past, current investors will take actions similar to those of past investors. For example, reactions to emotions such as greed and fear generally can be anticipated — in bull markets, investors pour more and more money into the stock market as a result of their greed; in bear markets, fear causes these same investors to pull their money out of the markets. In essence, then, investors have a tendency to "jump on the bandwagon" when the markets are performing well, but they quickly "abandon ship" when the markets turn around.

In the sections that follow, we describe some of the techniques both fundamentalists and technicians use to make decisions about the values of stocks and financial markets. Most of the chapter is devoted to methods (analyses) that are generally considered part of fundamental analysis principally because such approaches are consistent with the general concepts of valuation. Later in the chapter we provide a brief overview of methods used in technical analysis. Although our focus throughout the chapter is on stocks, most of the techniques we describe can also be used for evaluation of debt instruments and other financial assets.

Self-Test Questions

Differentiate between the general approach a fundamental analyst and a technical analyst would take to value a particular security or financial market.

Is the market value of a stock always equal to its intrinsic value? What do you think will happen if the two values are not equal?

Economic Analysis

BUSINESS CYCLE
The movement in aggregate economic activity as measured by the gross domestic product (GDP).

Clearly, the condition of the economy affects the performances of businesses and thus their securities in the financial markets. When the economy is growing, financial markets generally increase because individuals are willing to invest their savings in stocks and bonds, which provides firms with funds needed for expansionary projects. Of course, the opposite occurs when the economy is stagnant or in a decline. Therefore, it is important to assess the future of the economy when forecasting movements of the financial markets and the performances of firms. In this section, we provide a brief overview of areas that should be examined when analyzing economic conditions.

EXPANSION
Increasing economic activity.

Forecasting Business Cycles

CONTRACTION
Decreasing economic activity.

GROSS DOMESTIC PRODUCT (GDP)
A measure of all the goods and services produced in the economy during a specific time period.

When we forecast economic conditions, what we really want to determine is when to expect changes in the *business cycle*. The **business cycle** is defined as the direction in which aggregate economic activity is moving. Increasing economic activity is called an **expansion,** while decreasing economic activity is called a **contraction.** We generally gauge economic activity using the **gross domestic product (GDP),** which is a measure of all the goods and services produced in the economy during a specific time period. The GDP is stated both in nominal terms, which means the value is not adjusted for inflation, and in real terms, which means the value is inflation adjusted. The real GDP allows economists to determine the actual growth in the economy.

We know that movements in the financial markets are closely related to business cycles. Thus, if we can get good estimates of changes in the business cycle, we should be able to forecast movements in financial markets such as the stock market and the bond market. Unfortunately, past business cycles have been irregular, which makes it difficult to use historical economic information to predict future cycles. To make matters worse, the financial markets are not perfectly related to business cycles. For example, Figure 16-1 shows the movements in the stock market since 1970, with those periods in which the economy was in a *recession* highlighted. Economists define a **recession** as two consecutive quarters of economic contraction, or decline, in the GDP. According to the National Bureau of Economic Research, there have been five recessions since 1970. Note from Figure 16-1 that the stock market decreased during each of the recessions, but that the two most notable declines in the market within the last 20 years actually occurred during economic expansions — stocks declined 30 percent from September 1987 through November 1987 and 16 percent from July 1998 through August 1998. But, as you can also see from the graph, the stock market performed very well during the 1990s; the market increased about 220 percent

RECESSION
Two consecutive quarters of economic contraction, or decline, in the GDP.

FIGURE 16-1

Recessions and Stock Price Movements, 1970–1998

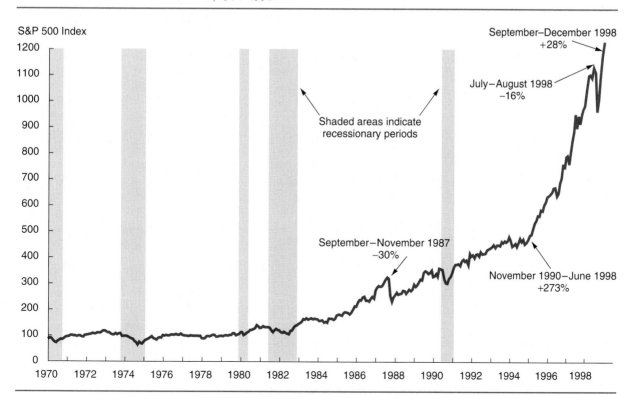

SOURCES: U.S. Department of Commerce, Bureau of Economic Analysis, and Standard & Poor's Compustat.

TABLE 16-1

Recessionary Periods since 1970

Recession Period		Recession Duration (months)	Time since Previous Recession (months)	Average Annual Change in Real GDP
Beginning Date	**Ending Date**			
December 1969	November 1970	11	105	−0.09%
November 1973	March 1975	16	36	−2.97
December 1979	June 1980	6	57	−1.92
June 1981	December 1982	18	12	−1.12
June 1990	March 1991	9	90	−2.67

SOURCE: Bureau of Economic Analysis

from the beginning of 1990 until the end of 1998 and, since the middle of the 1990–1991 recession when the market began a general rebound, the increase has been more than 300 percent.

Table 16-1 gives information about the recessions that have occurred since 1970. Clearly there is no pattern associated with these recessions — their lengths and effects as well as the times between recessions (expansionary periods) have varied considerably. As we write this text at the end of 1998, the economy has been in a 93-month expansionary period that is not forecasted to end in the near term. But, if there is no pattern to when and how long recessions occur, how can such predictions be made? The answer can be found by examining economic indicators published by the government and by determining the general tenor of professional analysts.

ECONOMIC INDICATORS   The Bureau of Economic Analysis (BEA), which is part of the U.S. Department of Commerce, collects a compendium of economic measures, such as the GDP, price indexes, personal and business income figures, and so on. These measures, as well as various analyses performed by the BEA, are published in the *Survey of Current Business,* which is available at nearly every university library and in most public libraries.[1] Perhaps the most often cited barometers of business activity compiled by the BEA are the *composite indexes,* which are aggregate measures that include various economic variables grouped into one of three categories — leading, lagging, or coincident — depending on the timing of their movements relative to business cycles. Rather than rely on a single indicator in each category, the BEA forms composite measures of multiple indicators, which provide better gauges of general economic patterns because then spurious movements are averaged out.

As the name implies, movements in **leading economic indicators** tend to precede, or lead to, movements in the economy. Similarly, **lagging economic indicators** generally follow, or lag, economic movements. And, the **coincident indicators** tend to mirror, or move at the same time as, business cycles. The economic indicators that comprise each of the three composite indexes are shown in Table 16-2.

LEADING ECONOMIC INDICATORS
Economic measures that tend to move prior to, or precede, movements in the business cycle.

LAGGING ECONOMIC INDICATORS
Economic measures that tend to move after, or follow, movements in the general economy (business cycles).

COINCIDENT INDICATORS
Economic measures that tend to mirror, or move at the same time as, business cycles.

[1] The Bureau of Economic Analysis also has a web site located at www.bea.doc.gov.

TABLE 16-2

Business Cycles Indicators—Leading, Coincident, and Lagging Composite Indexes

Index and Measures Included[a]	Rationale/Explanation
I. Index of Leading Indicators	
Average workweek, production	Workweek hours increase (decrease) as firms try to produce more (less) to meet forecasted higher (lower) future demand.
Average first-time claims for unemployment insurance	Claims for unemployment decrease (increase) when recoveries (contractions) are expected.
New orders of manufacturers — consumer goods and materials	As the economy expands (contracts), new orders increase (decrease).
Manufacturers' new orders of nondefense capital goods	As the economy expands (contracts), companies expand (contract) plant and equipment.
Vendor delivery performance	Deliveries slow (speed up) during expansion (contraction) periods because products are not as (more) readily available.
New private building permits	Expectations of good (bad) times entice individuals to build new (stay in their existing) homes.
Money supply, M2	An increase (decrease) in the money supply causes interest rates to decrease (increase), thus the economy is affected.
Interest-rate spread: 10-year Treasury bonds yield less federal funds rate	Interest rates are based on expectations — when longer-term and shorter-term rates converge (diverge), investors have greater (less) confidence in the financial markets and are willing to take greater (less) risks.
Stock prices — S&P 500 index	The prices of stocks depend on cash flows expected in the future.
Index of consumer expectations	Constructed by the Survey Research Center at the University of Michigan — if consumers expect an improved (worse) economy, they will spend more (less).
II. Index of Coincident Indicators	
Number of employees on nonagricultural payrolls	Employees are hired (let go) as business improves (deteriorates).
Personal income — salaries	Salaries generally increase (decrease) as the economy expands (contracts).
Industrial production	Most significant movements in the manufacture of products occur at the same time as economic movements; orders precede actual production.
Manufacturing and trade sales	Increased (decreased) sales to distributors, retailers, and so on, occur during economic expansions (contractions).
III. Index of Lagging Indicators	
Average length of unemployment	As the economy rebounds from an economic contraction, laid-off employees rehired, and vice versa; those unemployed for longer periods are called first.
Ratio of inventories divided by sales — manufacturers and trade	Sales begin to increase (decrease) and inventories decrease (increase) as the economy recovers from a contraction (expansion).
Change in labor costs per unit of output for manufacturers	Lower (higher) unemployment causes labor costs to increase (decrease) as the economy rebounds from a contraction (expansion).
Prime rate at banks	Banks usually don't change the prime rate until the general demand for funds (loans) changes.
Loans to commerce and industry	Borrowing increases (decreases) to support financing required for *sustained* increases (decreases) in operations.
Percent of personal income consumers have outstanding in installment loans/credit	Individuals borrow more (less) based on their personal incomes during expansions (contractions); but, only after they recognize the economic situation/conditions.
Change in the consumer price index for services	Prices change only after business conditions change.

Source: *The Conference Board News*, located at http://domino.stat-usa.gov/bea.

[a]

As you can see, the composite index of leading indicators includes ten measures, such as manufacturers' new orders, new building permits for residential housing, money supply, and so forth. Perhaps the most familiar leading indicator included in this composite index is stock prices. Stock prices have long been considered a leading economic indicator because, as we pointed out in Chapter 7, the prices of stocks are based on *forecasted* future cash flows. As you can imagine, the composite index of leading indicators gets a great deal of attention, especially from the news media, because it is viewed as a prophecy of the future of the economy. Unfortunately, it is difficult to predict the timing of economic movements relative to changes in the composite index of leading indicators because the lead time has not been consistent over time. Figure 16-2 shows a graph of the three composite indexes published by the BEA. As you can see, for the most part, the indexes have performed as expected — the index of leading indicators began declining prior to the start of recessionary periods, the index of coincident indicators started declining when the recessions began, and the index of lagging indicators started declining after recessionary periods began and sometimes not until after the recessions ended. Thus, for the most part, the composite indexes seem to provide indications of general business cycles, but, the timings and magnitudes

FIGURE 16-2

Business Cycle Indicators — Composite

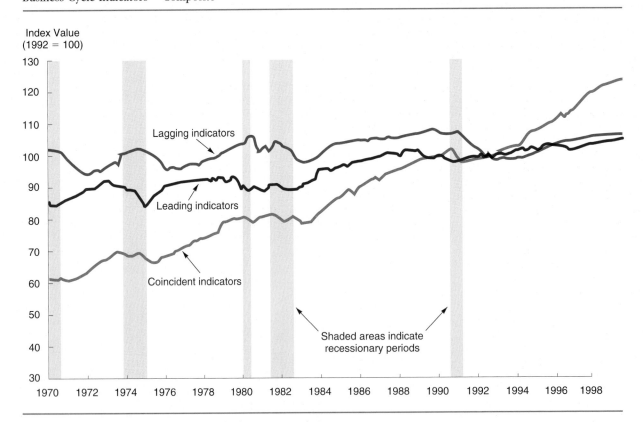

SOURCE: U.S. Department of Commerce, Bureau of Economic Analysis.

of the cycles are very difficult to forecast — the lead and lag times vary from one recession to another.

PROFESSIONAL FORECASTERS' OPINIONS   In addition to the economic information published by the government, most large brokerage firms and financial service organizations have divisions that analyze economic data to provide their clients with estimates of future business activity. While the specific results of the analyses are usually available only to clients, these companies often release their general economic forecasts to the public. In addition, analysis' forecasts are regularly contained in business publications such as *The Wall Street Journal, BusinessWeek,* and so on. By examining a number of experts' forecasts, you can form your own opinion about expected economic movements based on the consensus of professionals' analyses.

Business Cycles — Monetary Policy and Fiscal Policy

The monetary policy carried out by the Federal Reserve and the fiscal policy of the government can significantly affect business cycles. Remember from our discussion in Chapter 3 that **monetary policy** refers to the means by which the Federal Reserve influences economic conditions by managing the nation's money supply. The Fed changes the money supply through reserves at financial institutions in its effort to promote stable economic conditions with moderate growth. For example, when the economy is in a recession, the Fed generally attempts to increase business activity by easing credit via lower interest rates, which is accomplished by increasing reserves (money supply). While the actions taken by the Fed have not always been the same in like economic situations, investors should evaluate existing economic conditions and form opinions about future actions the Fed might take because, clearly, the financial markets will be affected.

Fiscal policy refers to government spending, which is primarily supported by the government's ability to tax individuals and businesses. Conceptually, government fiscal policy should have the same goal as monetary policy — promote economic stability with moderate growth. Since the 1960s, the fiscal policy in the United States has been dominated by **deficit spending,** which occurs when the government spends more than it collects in taxes (i.e., expenses exceed revenues). Many economists believe that deficit spending results in higher than normal prices or interest rates because either more money has to be printed or greater amounts have to be borrowed by the government to finance the additional spending. Clearly, then, evaluating the government's spending behavior is important when determining economic expectations. Such an assessment is especially critical when examining a multinational corporation. For instance, recently, exposure of the corrupt practices of governments in southeast Asia resulted in substantial declines in stock markets throughout the world. Even in the United States, the market declined considerably because investors feared that Asian companies would dump products at "cut-rate" prices and thus make international markets less accessible to U.S. firms.

From our discussion here, it should be apparent that economic conditions affect financial markets, and thus it is important to perform an economic analysis, even if it is very cursory, when making investment decisions. The next step in our analysis is to determine how industries are influenced by economic conditions and their general financial and competitive positions.

MONETARY POLICY
The means by which the Federal Reserve influences economic conditions by managing the nation's money supply.

FISCAL POLICY
Government spending, which is primarily supported by the government's ability to tax individuals and businesses.

DEFICIT SPENDING
Situation that occurs when the government spends more than it collects in taxes.

Self-Test Questions

What is a business cycle? Identify two types of business cycles.

Describe the three types (categories) of economic indicators.

How do monetary and fiscal policies affect the economy?

Why is it important to perform an economic analysis before making investment decisions?

Industry Analysis

The stock market consists of many different segments called industries, which include companies with like characteristics. Although industries are usually defined by product classifications, we also differentiate firms according to their general sectors — industrial, service, technology, financial, and so forth. As you can imagine, all industries do not perform the same in different business cycles; some industries perform better than others during expansionary periods, and vice versa. Therefore, we need to examine industry conditions to determine the attractiveness of the firms classified in the industry relative to firms in other industries. A basic industry analysis should include evaluations to determine (1) the relationship between the general performance of the industry and economic conditions and (2) the potential for future growth with respect to where the industry is in its life cycle.

Industry Performance and Economic Conditions

In Chapter 8, we indicated that every firm is affected by economic, or market, conditions. Also, we noted that changes in business cycles do not affect every firm the same. Clearly then, we would expect that different industries react differently to shifts in the economy. For example, industries that include durable goods manufacturers, such as construction and automobile manufacturers, generally are more sensitive to interest rate changes than industries that include staple goods firms, such as food retailers and consumer services. Some industries are referred to as **cyclical industries** because they tend to be directly related to business cycles such that they perform best during expansions and worst during contractions. In contrast, some industries are **defensive, or countercyclical, industries** because they tend to be the best-performing industries when the economy is in a contraction or recession, but they are generally the poorest-performing industries in expanding economies. Can you think of examples of both cyclical and countercyclical industries? Automobile manufacturing and construction usually are considered cyclical industries, while automobile parts manufacturers and home improvement suppliers are considered countercyclical industries.

To determine the sensitivity of an industry to the economy, we can use computer models that are based on sophisticated statistical methods, or we can simply observe the direction an industry's stock prices move when major economic factors, such as interest rates and consumer prices, change. It is fairly easy to use a spreadsheet to plot the relationship between industry sales and a particular economic variable or to run a relatively simple regression analysis. For example, Figure 16-3 gives the results of fitting a trend line showing the relationship

CYCLICAL INDUSTRIES Industries that tend to be directly related to business cycles such that they perform best during expansions and worst during contractions.

DEFENSIVE, OR COUNTERCYCLICAL, INDUSTRIES Industries that tend to perform best when the economy is in a contraction or recession, but are generally the poorest performers in expanding economies.

FIGURE 16-3

Trend Line — Relationship of Housing Starts with Interest Rates, 1965–1998

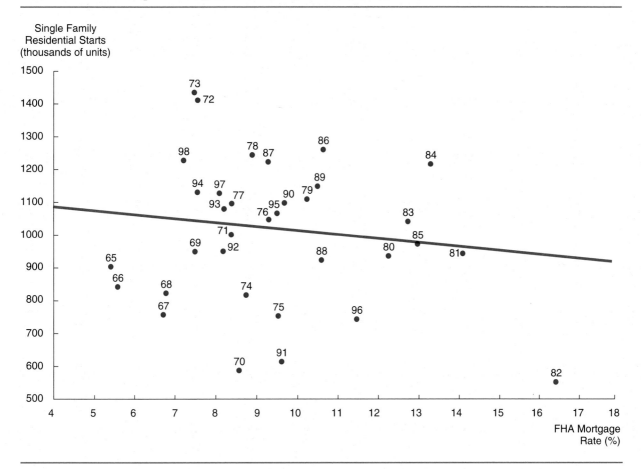

SOURCE: U.S. Department of Commerce, Bureau of Economic Analysis, and the Federal Reserve Board.

between housing starts and mortgage rates. Note that the line has a negative slope, which indicates that housing starts increase as interest rates fall, and vice versa. This suggests that individuals are more (less) inclined to purchase houses when interest rates are low (high) than when rates are high (low). Other factors, such as salary levels and prices, also affect housing starts, but Figure 16-3 gives you an idea of one method we can use to determine the relationship between economic conditions and industry activity.

Industry Life Cycle

INDUSTRY LIFE CYCLE
The various phases of an industry with respect to its growth in sales and its competitive conditions.

When we examine the history of business and industry, we discover that industries go through life cycles that are comparable to the human life cycle. The cycle begins when the industry is born and firms are weak and susceptible to competition, it progresses through periods of strengthening and growth, and it ends with the death of the industry. More specifically, the **industry life cycle** follows various stages of growth with respect to the product and the competitive condi-

FIGURE 16-4

The Industry Life Cycle

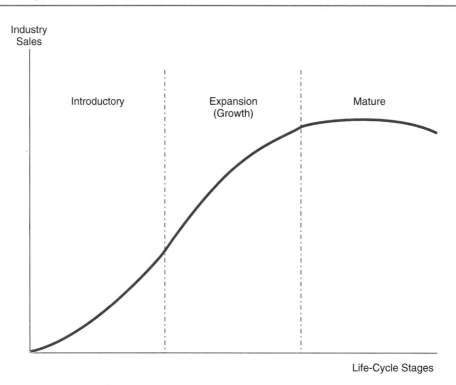

tions within the industry. Generally, we can identify three distinct stages in the life of an industry. The three stages, which are depicted in Figure 16-4, are described as follows:

1. The *introductory stage* begins with the birth of the industry. In this stage, growth is very rapid, there are few barriers to keep new competition from entering the industry, and survivorship is relatively low. Most firms have "bare bones" operations because they are trying to carve out a competitive niche. For this reason, generally all earnings are reinvested in the firm to support growth. Note from Figure 16-4 that industry sales are growing at an increasing rate in this stage of the life cycle, which suggests there exist numerous growth opportunities (i.e., investments with positive net present values).

2. The *expansion stage* includes firms that survived the introductory stage. Operations become more sophisticated as firms move into larger facilities to meet their expanded needs. In this stage, however, growth begins to slow because the product is no longer a novelty. Sales are still increasing, but at a decreasing rate (see Figure 16-4). Competitive barriers increase because firms have begun to carve their competitive niches and customers become more brand loyal. Because there are fewer investment growth opportunities, it is in this stage (probably near the end) that firms generally begin to pay dividends.

3. The *mature stage* is characterized by firms that are well entrenched because, in essence, they have "paid their dues." It is difficult for newcomers to enter the industry because competitive niches that are hard to penetrate have been established — competitive barriers are high. Growth in the industry begins to flatten, thus much of the earnings is paid out as dividends.

Industries do not progress through the life-cycle stages at the same pace. Some industries, such as biotechnology, move through the stages relatively quickly compared with industries such as automobile manufacturing or utilities. Also, industries that continuously produce large amounts of innovative technology might never reach the mature stage of the industry life cycle.

It is important for an investor to understand where in the life cycle an industry is currently operating. The survivorship of the industry, its chances for growth, and expectations about its future depend on where in the life cycle the industry is positioned. Further, investors should evaluate the characteristics of the investment opportunities in each of the three stages. The introductory stage is characterized by small, growth-oriented firms, many of which will be lucky to survive and move to the expansion stage. Therefore, investing in this stage is considered very risky, but potentially very rewarding, because those that do survive generally grow very rapidly. Consider, for example, the gain you would have earned if you had purchased Microsoft stock when it was first sold to the public in March 1986 for $21 a share. The value of one share of the *original* stock was worth almost $10,000 at the end of 1998.[2] The total holding period return for the stock was more than 47,000 percent. On the other hand, if you had purchased the stock of one of the other startup software companies that existed in 1986, your holding period gain would likely have been −100 percent, because many of those companies no longer exist today. As you can imagine, investing in industries in the expansion and mature stages is less risky than the introductory stage. In fact, industries in the mature stage are often characterized by large, stable firms with income-producing stocks (i.e., stable dividends).

Self-Test Questions

Describe the characteristics of a cyclical industry and a defensive industry.

What stages does an industry go through during its life cycle?

Explain why the introductory stage of the industry life cycle is considered the riskiest stage for investors.

Evaluating the Firm's Financial Position

Remember that the ultimate goal of investment analysis is to value the firm's security. And, as we already know, valuation requires an estimation of the future cash flows expected to be generated by the investment. Therefore, the next step

---

[2]From the time it was first sold to the public in 1986 and the end of 1998, Microsoft's stock was split seven times. There were five 2-for-1 splits and two 3-for-2 splits. Therefore, one share of the original stock is the equivalent of 72 shares of the 1998 stock. On December 31, 1998, Microsoft sold for $138\frac{11}{16}$ per share.

in investment analysis is to examine the current financial condition of the firm issuing the security and forecast its future prospects.

To evaluate the financial condition of a firm, we generally use financial statement analysis such as we described in Chapter 13. It is important for investors to examine the financial reports prepared by the firm to judge the firm's performance in the current period and in past periods in an effort to determine its future direction. From an investor's standpoint, the purpose of financial statement analysis is to determine the attractiveness of an investment by identifying the strengths and weaknesses of the firm and projecting how its operations will change in the future.

Because we discussed financial statement analysis in detail in Chapter 13, in this section we simply summarize the general concepts of such analyses. Remember from our earlier discussion that, in general, financial statement analysis involves a comparison of a firm's operating performance and financial position with that of other firms in the same line of business. Investors can use financial statement analysis to form expectations about the future of the firm, especially with regard to its cash flow distributions. Even though financial statement analysis is based on examinations of accounting statements, which often do not represent economic earnings, such assessments are useful in investment analysis for the following reasons:

1. A firm's business conditions can be compared with other similar firms to determine whether its current operations are average, below average, or above average.
2. Based on business conditions both in the current period and in recent past periods, we can forecast the direction the firm is likely to take in the future. In some instances, firms that are performing below average in the current period are considered attractive investments because their futures are forecasted to be much brighter, and vice versa.
3. By formulating forecasts about the future financial condition of the firm, we can predict earnings and dividends that can be used in security valuation models.
4. Examinations of current and forecasted business conditions can be used to form expectations regarding the risk of the firm's future operations. Recall that risk is an important ingredient in the determination of the rate of return investors require to invest in the firm's securities. It is this required rate of return that is used as the discount rate when calculating the present value of the future cash flows associated with the investment — that is, finding its value.

From our discussion here, it should be apparent that the primary use of financial statement analysis as an analytical tool is to help investors form expectations about the future cash flows and the risks associated with an investment. Before we leave our current discussion, however, we would be remiss if we did not repeat the comment we made in Chapter 13 concerning financial statement analysis: *The most important and most difficult input to successful ratio analysis is the judgment used when interpreting the results to reach an overall conclusion about the firm's financial position.*

In addition to financial statements, fundamental analysts examine qualitative factors, such as labor conditions, management tenure, brand loyalty, and so forth, when forming opinions about a firm's financial position. It is felt that examining the nature of existing qualitative factors such as these is important in predicting the future strength of the firm's financial position. Unfortunately, incorporating qualitative factors in the analysis of companies requires the analyst to apply a great deal of judgment.

Self-Test Question

What are some of the reasons financial statement analysis should be included in investment analysis?

Stock Valuation Techniques

As we indicated earlier, there are a number of valuation methods used by individual investors and professional analysts to evaluate common stocks. In this section, we describe three basic techniques used to value stock. The approaches we describe here are used by investors in their efforts to find mispriced stocks and fast-growing stocks as well as to make strategic decisions about the general compositions of their portfolios.

Dividend Discount Models

DIVIDEND DISCOUNT MODEL (DDM)
A model that utilizes the discounted cash flow principle to value common stock; value is represented by the present value of the dividends expected to be received from investing in the stock.

In Chapter 7, we discovered that the cash flows derived from investing in a common stock are called dividends. In addition, we determined that the market value of a stock can be found by computing the present value of all the dividends expected to be paid by the firm in the future. Clearly, according to our discussion throughout the book, finding the present value of, or discounting, future cash flows is the most appropriate approach to valuation.

Most existing stock valuation models were born from the **dividend discount model (DDM),** which applies the discounted cash flow principle to the dividends expected to be received from investing in a stock. In Chapter 7, we presented the general dividend discount model in Equation 7-4, which is stated as follows:

$$\text{7-4} \quad \text{Value of stock} = V_s = \hat{P}_0 = \text{PV of expected future dividends}$$

$$= \frac{\hat{D}_1}{(1 + k_s)^1} + \frac{\hat{D}_2}{(1 + k_s)^2} + \cdots + \frac{\hat{D}_\infty}{(1 + k_s)^\infty}$$

$$= \sum_{t=1}^{\infty} \frac{\hat{D}_t}{(1 + k_s)^t}$$

In this equation, $\hat{D}_t$ represents the dividend payment expected in period t, and k_s is the rate of return investors require for similar risk investments. Recall that if we assume the firm grows at a constant rate, the DDM given in Equation 7-4 is rewritten in the following simplified form:

$$\hat{P}_0 = \frac{\hat{D}_1}{k_s - g}$$

Here, g represents the constant growth rate in dividends. Although this is a very simple equation, applying it to get a good estimate of a stock's value is anything but simple for two reasons. First, correct application of the equation requires that the firm's growth is constant today and forever into the future. In reality, there probably is not one company in the world that strictly meets this criterion. Second, we must be able to estimate three variables: (a) next period's dividend payment, (b) the constant growth rate, and (c) the appropriate required rate of return. Thus, although this valuation process seems quite simple, it actually is a very formidable task.

Even with its problems and the inherent difficulties associated with forecasting the inputs necessary for its application, the DDM model can be used to get a ballpark value for common stock. For instance, if we can predict with some confidence the dividends expected to be paid by a firm for, say, the next ten years and we can use the Capital Asset Pricing Model (CAPM) to determine the appropriate rate of return, we can apply the nonconstant growth version of the DDM to estimate what the current stock price should be.

In Chapter 7 we discovered that we could value a stock that currently has nonconstant growth but is expected to achieve constant growth at some point in the future by proceeding as follows:

1. Compute the present value of the dividends that experience nonconstant growth, and then sum the results.
2. Find the price of the stock at the end of the nonconstant growth period, at which point it has become a constant growth stock, and discount this price back to the present.
3. Add the results of these two computations to find the intrinsic value of the stock, $\hat{P}_0$.

Summarizing these three steps, the nonconstant growth DDM is written as follows:

16-1

$$\hat{P}_0 = \frac{\hat{D}_1}{(1 + k_s)^1} + \frac{\hat{D}_2}{(1 + k_s)^2} + \cdots + \frac{\hat{D}_N + \hat{P}_N}{(1 + k_s)^N}$$

$$= \sum_{t=1}^{N} \frac{\hat{D}_t}{(1 + k_s)^t} + \frac{\hat{P}_N}{(1 + k_s)^N}$$

Here

$\hat{D}_1 \ldots \hat{D}_N$ = the expected dividends that are affected by nonconstant growth
$\hat{P}_N$ = the future stock price computed when constant growth begins (or when nonconstant growth ends)
k_s = the cost of equity, or the required rate of return of the stockholders.

To illustrate the use of the DDM technique for stock valuation, let's consider Philip Morris. In 1998, the dividend paid by the company was $1.76 per share, and its beta coefficient was 1.1. To evaluate Philip Morris, let's assume today's date is January 1, 1999, and that all dividend payments are made at the end of the year. Examining the past ten years of growth in earnings and dividends, we find (1) that *earnings* growth has averaged about 20 percent each year, and it has been 20 percent for the last couple of years, and (2) that *dividend* growth has averaged nearly 18 percent per year, and it has been about 19 percent for the last few years. Clearly, these growth rates cannot continue forever; otherwise the firm's earnings and dividends would double every three to four years. So, let's make a simple assumption: Let's suppose the firm's growth rate continues to be 20 percent for the next five years, and then it decreases by 1 percent each year until it settles at 5 percent, the rate at which it will continue to grow from that time on. In addition, let's assume future market conditions will not differ significantly from average conditions, which suggests the market return will be around 14 percent, and the average rate on long-term Treasury bonds is approximately 5.5 percent. We now have sufficient information to apply the DDM method to value Philip Morris stock. Table 16-3 shows the steps we took to value the stock and the results of the valuation.

Using the DDM, we estimate the value of Philip Morris to be \$57.81 at the beginning of 1999. The actual market price of Philip Morris stock at the end of 1998 hovered between \$54 and \$57 per share. Does this mean that the stock is correctly valued? Perhaps. But, surely not everyone will predict the same growth rates as we did; thus, because different analysts might reach completely different conclusions, different forecasts are likely. If we find that analysts arrive at substantially different predictions, which one is most reliable? It is very difficult, if not impossible, to answer this question. However, we do know that valuation methods such as the DDM are most effective when forecasts of future dividends are accurate and when the assumptions associated with the CAPM and the DDM are not violated. For example, to apply the constant growth model to find the price of Philip Morris in the year 2017, we had to assume dividends would grow at a constant rate of 5 percent from the year 2018 until infinity. Clearly, this assumption is not reasonable. Even so, the DDM approach provides analysts with estimates of the values of common stocks. Professional analysts, however, incorporate much more complex computations than we did in our example — more detailed information is used to better predict the future performance of a firm.

Valuation Using P/E Ratios

P/E RATIO
Ratio computed by dividing the current market price per share, P_0, by the earnings per share, EPS_0.

Many analysts consider the P/E ratio, also referred to as the *earnings multiplier,* to be a good indicator of the value of a stock in relative terms. The **P/E ratio** we refer to here is the same as what we described in Chapter 13, which is computed by dividing the current market price per share, P_0, by the earnings per share, EPS_0. The higher (lower) the P/E ratio, the more (less) investors are willing to pay for each dollar the firm earns.

In a sense, the P/E ratio is similar to the payback method we used in capital budgeting. For example, if a firm's P/E ratio is 12, then, *assuming the firm pays all earnings as dividends,* it would take 12 years for an investor to recover his or her initial investment. If we view P/E ratios as measures of payback, then, all else equal, lower earnings multipliers are better. In fact, it has been suggested that firms with low P/E ratios relative to other firms in their industries can earn above-average risk-adjusted returns, and vice versa. The rationale is that if the P/E ratio

TABLE 16-3

Using the DDM Technique to Value Philip Morris

Step 1. Compute the required rate of return associated with Philip Morris (PM) using the CAPM:

$$k_{PM} = k_{RF} + (k_M - k_{RF})\beta_{PM}$$

$$= 5.5\% + (14.0\% - 5.5\%)1.1 = 14.85\%$$

Step 2. Forecast the dividends based on the assumed future growth rates for the periods when nonconstant growth is expected. At the same time, we can find the present values of the dividends using the required return:

Year	Assumed Growth	Forecasted Dividend $\hat{D}_t = \hat{D}_{t-1}(1 + g_t)$	PV of the Dividend at 14.85%
1998	—	$ 1.760	—
1999	20.0%	2.112 = 1.760(1.20)	$1.839
2000	20.0	2.534 = 2.112(1.20)	1.921
2001	20.0	3.041 = 2.534(1.20)	2.007
2002	20.0	3.649 = 3.041(1.20)	2.097
2003	20.0	4.379 = 3.649(1.20)	2.191
2004	19.0	5.211 = 4.379(1.19)	2.271
2005	18.0	6.149 = 5.211(1.18)	2.333
2006	17.0	7.194 = 6.149(1.17)	2.376
2007	16.0	8.345 = 7.194(1.16)	2.400
2008	15.0	9.597 = 8.345(1.15)	2.403
2009	14.0	10.941 = 9.597(1.14)	2.386
2010	13.0	12.363 = 10.941(1.13)	2.347
2011	12.0	13.847 = 12.363(1.12)	2.289
2012	11.0	15.370 = 13.847(1.11)	2.212
2013	10.0	16.907 = 15.370(1.10)	2.119
2014	9.0	18.429 = 16.907(1.09)	2.011
2015	8.0	19.903 = 18.429(1.08)	1.891
2016	7.0	21.296 = 19.903(1.07)	1.762
2017	6.0	22.574 = 21.296(1.06)	1.626

PV of dividends = $40.481

Step 3. Compute the price of the stock after nonconstant growth ends in the year 2017:

$$P_{2017} = \frac{\hat{D}_{2017}(1 + g_n)}{k_s - g_n} = \frac{\hat{D}_{2018}}{k_s - g_n} = \frac{\$22.547(1.05)}{0.1485 - 0.05} = \frac{\$23.703}{0.0985} = \$240.640$$

Step 4. Compute the current price of the stock, which is the present value of the dividends computed in Step 2 plus the present value of the future price computed in Step 3:

$$P_0 = P_{1/99} = \$40.481 + \frac{\$240.640}{(1.1485)^{19}}$$

$$= \$40.481 + \$17.333 = \underline{\underline{\$57.814}}$$

is low relative to similar firms, earnings have not been fully captured in the existing stock value; thus, the price will be bid up. Similarly, if the P/E ratio is high relative to similar firms, the market has overvalued current earnings; thus, the price must decrease.

So, how can P/E ratios be used to value common stocks? Generally speaking, we examine whether the stock's P/E ratio is considered to be higher or lower than "normal" to decide if the price is too high or too low. If we can determine what value is appropriate for the P/E, we can then multiply that value by the firm's EPS to estimate the stock price. Determining the appropriate P/E requires judgment, so analysts do not always agree about what the value for a firm's P/E should be.

Depending on the company analysis, such as evaluation of financial statements, the P/E ratio might need to be adjusted to reflect expectations about the firm's performance in the future. The P/E ratio might be adjusted downward if the firm's future is considered less promising than the recent past because it would be expected that investors will not be willing to pay the same multiple for the earnings expected to be generated in the future. Although the adjustment process is somewhat arbitrary, we know that P/E ratios are higher (lower) for firms with higher (lower) expected earnings growth and lower (higher) expected required rates of return. For example, investors will place a higher value on the current earnings if the firm is expected to grow at rates greater than normal.

To illustrate the use of P/E ratios to determine the price of a stock, let's again examine Philip Morris. According to *The Wall Street Journal*, Philip Morris had a P/E ratio equal to approximately 21 at the end of 1998, which was much greater than the industry average of about 10 that existed at the same time. If we examine the P/E ratios during the past three years, we find that the average value for both the company and the industry was approximately 14. Thus, if we assume that a "normal" P/E ratio for Philip Morris is 14, we can multiply this number by the EPS expected for 1999 to estimate the price of Philip Morris stock. According to Zacks Investment Research, analysts estimate that the EPS for 1999 should be about $3.50. Therefore, using the P/E ratio method to value Philip Morris stock, we estimate the price to be around $3.50 × 14 = $49, which is much lower than the actual price at the end of 1998. One reason for the difference in our estimate and the actual price is that we used what might be considered a normal P/E ratio rather than adjusting the value to reflect expected future growth.

At the time we write this book, there are two important events that might require us to adjust the P/E ratio we used. First, Philip Morris announced it reached an agreement with 46 states to settle health claims and other lawsuits associated with their tobacco products. The proposed settlement reduces uncertainty about the future cash flows expected to be generated by the company. Second, Philip Morris agreed to buy three cigarette lines from another tobacco company. Both of these events might be considered advantageous to future growth. Thus, we should probably adjust the value of the P/E ratio we use, say, to 18. Using a P/E ratio equal to 18, we estimate the value of Philip Morris to be $3.50 × 18 = $63, which is not substantially greater than the existing price. For this reason, we might be inclined to conclude that Philip Morris stock is correctly valued. Keep in mind, however, that our estimate is based on an arbitrary adjustment to the P/E ratio. If we assumed the value of the current P/E ratio is appropriate, our estimate would be $3.50 × 21 = $73.50, which suggests that Philip Morris stock is undervalued. Interestingly, at the time we write this book, Martin Feldman, a well-known tobacco analyst who works for Salomon Smith Barney (part of Citigroup), projected the price of Philip Morris stock to reach $75 within a year. In addition, of the 14 brokers surveyed by Zacks Investment Research, 9 recommended that Philip Morris should be bought. Thus, it appears the experts consider Philip Morris to be a good investment prospect, at least at this point in time.

Evaluating Stocks Using the Economic Value Added (EVA) Approach

ECONOMIC VALUE ADDED (EVA)
Method used to evaluate if the earnings generated by a firm are sufficient to compensate the suppliers of funds — both the bondholders and the stockholders.

Economic value added (EVA) is one of the newest approaches used to measure financial performance and thus evaluate the attractiveness of a firm's stock. The basic approach, which was developed by Stern Stewart Management Services, is to utilize basic financial principles to analyze a company's performance to value the firm. Some of the companies that have used EVA include Coca-Cola, Eli Lily, AT&T, Sprint, and Quaker Oats, to name a few. Some companies, such as Coca-Cola, have used EVA since the early 1980s. So, what is EVA and how is it applied to make investment decisions?

EVA is based on the concept that the earnings from actions taken by a company must be sufficient to compensate the suppliers of funds — both the bondholders and the stockholders. This should sound like a familiar concept — it is closely related to the concept that projects must earn at least the weighted average cost of capital (WACC) of the firm to be acceptable, which we discussed in Chapters 9 and 10. What is different with the EVA approach, however, is that we make an adjustment to the earnings figure reported on the income statement to account for the costs associated with both the debt and the equity issued by the firm. Remember that the income statement includes interest expense, which is a reflection of the cost of debt, but compensation to common stockholders relative to the cost of equity is not included.

The general concept behind EVA is to determine how much a firm's economic value is increased by the decisions it makes. Thus, we can write the basic EVA equation as follows:

16-2

$$EVA = (IRR - WACC) \times \left(\frac{Invested}{capital}\right)$$

$$= EBIT(1 - T) - \left(WACC \times \frac{Invested}{capital}\right)$$

In this equation, IRR represents the firm's internal rate of return, WACC is the firm's weighted average cost of capital, T is the marginal tax rate, and "Invested capital" refers to the amount of funds provided by investors. Equation 16-2 can be used to evaluate the value of the firm as a whole or in terms of individual projects. If the EVA is positive, the actions of the firm increase its value, but if the EVA is negative, the actions of the firm decrease its value.

To illustrate the use of the EVA approach, let's again examine Philip Morris. First, we gathered the following information from the financial statements published by the company at the end of 1998:

Operating income, EBIT	$11.66 billion
Total capital = Long-term debt + Equity	$41.03 billion
Shares outstanding	2.42 billion
Marginal Tax rate	40%
Debt/assets ratio	73%

In addition, using information about the interest paid during the year and the amount of debt outstanding, we estimate that Philip Morris had a before-tax cost of debt, k_d, equal to approximately 6.5 percent. Assuming the cost of equity we computed earlier using the CAPM is correct, then the WACC is computed as follows:

$$WACC = [6.5\%(1 - 0.40)](0.73) + 14.85\%(0.27) = 6.86\%$$

If we apply Equation 16-2, we find the EVA for Philip Morris is equal to

$$EVA = \$11.66 \text{ billion}(1 - 0.40) - (0.0686 \times \$41.03 \text{ billion})$$

$$= \$7.00 \text{ billion} - \$2.81 \text{ billion}$$

$$= \$4.19 \text{ billion}$$

According to this computation, EVA suggests that investors demanded $2.81 billion in compensation for providing funds to the firm. But, because the firm generated approximately $7 billion in net operating profits after taxes to cover the compensation associated with financing, we can conclude that Philip Morris was able to use its funds to earn higher returns than those demanded by investors. Thus, the firm should be attractive to investors. Philip Morris stock should be especially attractive to common stockholders because they have the right to any amounts earned in excess of the required rate of return.

We can use the EVA concept to determine the maximum dividend that can be paid to stockholders before we would expect the firm's value to be threatened. The computation is simple — just divide the computed EVA by the number of outstanding shares. In the case of Philip Morris, the maximum dividend suggested by EVA is $4.19 billion ÷ 2.42 billion shares = $1.73. Remember that Philip Morris paid a dividend equal to $1.76 in 1998. Thus, the actual dividend and the EVA dividend are nearly identical. This might suggest that the value of the company will not change in the future. But, as with the other techniques we have discussed in this section, the EVA approach requires additional computations and predictions to achieve greater precision in the final result. For instance, Stern Stewart indicates that it has identified more than 160 possible adjustments to accounting values contained in financial statements to better estimate the true economic value of the firm's performance. We made none of these adjustments here.

The EVA approach has gained attention as a valuation technique because it is based on the fundamental principle of wealth maximization, which should be the goal of every firm. EVA is also attractive because it allows us to outline the value creation process in simple terms: (1) Changing the capital structure can change value because the WACC is affected, and (2) increasing the efficiency of the firm through reductions in operating expenses or increases in revenues will increase operating income and thus increase value. Prospective EVA users should be aware, though, that to get a precise estimate of the economic performance of a firm, it might be necessary to make many adjustments to the accounting numbers contained in the firm's financial statements. Knowing how to apply such adjustments often takes considerable expertise.

Self-Test Questions

Describe the general procedure involved with using the dividend discount model (DDM) to value stock.

How are P/E ratios used to estimate the value of common stock?

What is EVA? How can the EVA approach be used to determine the attractiveness of a firm?

In general, what are some of the difficulties that are involved with the application of the valuation techniques described in this section?

Technical Analysis

The valuation techniques described in the previous section rely on basic valuation principles by focusing on *what* factors determine values and *why* values change; thus, these techniques would be considered to be part of fundamental analysis. Technical analysis, on the other hand, focuses on predicting *when* values will change. Technical analysts believe it is possible to identify shifts in the supply/demand relationships associated with investments that result in persistent trends for either individual stocks or the market as a whole. More importantly, however, technical analysts believe that investors behave in a predictable manner when faced with current situations similar to ones that occurred in the past; in other words, "history repeats itself."

Technical analysts probably would not disagree with fundamental analysts who believe they can find the intrinsic values of firms. They would argue, however, that by the time technicians complete their evaluations of the economy, the respective industries, and the companies, it is probably too late to take advantage of any mispricings that are discovered. Therefore, technical analysts believe methods other than those used by fundamental analysts are needed to determine which investments should be bought and sold. In this section, we describe some of the approaches used by technical analysts to evaluate stocks and the stock market. The purpose of this section is to give you a general understanding of technical analysis. Thus, only a few of the numerous methods used by technical analysts are included here.

Charting — Using Charts and Graphs

BAR CHART
A graph that indicates the high, low, and closing price movements for a stock during a specified period.

As we have stated, technical analysis is based primarily on the belief that trends exist in the stock market. One of the ways technical analysts attempt to identify trends is by examining charts and graphs of historical prices, trading volume, and so on. To illustrate the use of charts, let's examine a **bar chart,** which is simply a graph that indicates the daily, weekly, or monthly high, low, and closing price movements for a firm's stock during a specified period. Figure 16-5 shows a bar

FIGURE 16-5

Bar Chart for Jacrad Corporation

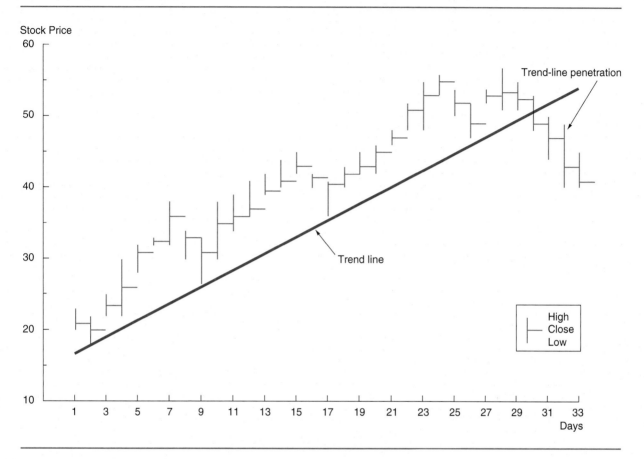

In Figure 16-5, we have drawn a **trend line**, which indicates the direction of
the stock price movement. The line in Figure 16-5 was drawn so that it touches
the low prices for some of the trading days. According to the trend line shown,

TREND LINE
A line that indicates the
direction of the stock price
movement; it is drawn so
that it touches either the
high prices or the low
prices for some of the
trading days.

chart for a hypothetical company named Jacrad Corporation. In the graph, the
trading line that is plotted for each day includes three pieces of information:
(1) the high price, which corresponds to the top of the line; (2) the low price,
which corresponds to the bottom of the line; and (3) the closing price, which is
represented by the portion that protrudes horizontally from the line. As you can
see from the graph, the height of the line indicates the range within which the
stock's price traded during the day. For example, on the sixth day of trading,
Jacrad's highest trading price was $33, its lowest trading price was $32, and the
closing price was $32.50; thus, the price range was very narrow. On the other
hand, on Day 32, the high price was $49, the low price was $40, and the closing
price was $43. This wider trading range suggests greater volatility occurred on
Day 32 than on Day 6.

there was a pattern of increased prices for the first 29 trading days included on the chart. But, note that on Day 30 the trading line crosses the trend line, and on Days 31 through 33 the trading lines are below the trend line. The point at which the trading line crosses the trend line is called the **trend line penetration.** If the penetration is either significant or persistent, the suggestion is that there is pressure for the previous trend to reverse. Therefore, according to the bar chart given in Figure 16-5, an investor should think about selling Jacrad Corporation on Day 31 or 32, even though the price is above $40 per share, which is more than twice its price one month earlier.

We showed only one example of the numerous types of charts technical analysts might use. But our illustration should give you an idea of the basic approach that is involved in charting. We should mention, however, that most of the graphs examined by technical analysts are much more complex and much more difficult to interpret than the example in Figure 16-5. The most critical, as well as the most difficult, part of charting is interpreting the graphs in an attempt to find trading patterns and to determine the timing reversals in any patterns that are found.

Measures and Indicators Used by Technical Analysts

Technical analysts use more than just charts and graphs to formulate their investment predications; they also use measures and indicators that they believe gauge both the trading activity and the tenor of the market. In this section, we describe some of the more common measures used by technical analysts.

THE DOW THEORY   As far as we can tell, structured technical analysis was introduced in the late 1890s by Charles Dow, who developed the **Dow theory.** According to the theory, there are three types of market movements: (1) a primary, or broad, trend that lasts from several months to many years; (2) a secondary, or intermediate, trend that lasts from a few weeks to three or four months; and (3) a short-term movement, which is represented by daily price movements. The basic objective of the Dow theory is to identify the reversal of primary trends by examining the movements of the Dow Jones Industrial Average, which includes stocks of the largest 30 industrial firms, and the Dow Jones Transportation Average, which includes stocks of 20 transportation firms. Those who follow the Dow theory believe that these two indexes reflect the most important factors that drive market movements, including market psychology, or the general attitude of investors. In essence, the theory states that as long as the industrial index and the transportation index move in the same direction, indications are that the market will continue its current trend. For example, in a bull market, if the two indexes consistently increase, then it is suggested that the market is strong, and it should continue its increase. On the other hand, when the indexes move in opposite directions, the suggestion is that the market is weakening, and a reversal of the current trend might be imminent.

MOVING AVERAGES   Technical analysts often examine the patterns of average stock prices for a fixed time frame, or window, over a particular period of time. Such measures are called **moving averages.** For example, suppose we want to compute a three-day moving average using the following series of prices:

TREND LINE PENETRATION
The point at which the trading line crosses the trend line.

DOW THEORY
A technique used to predict reversals in market patterns by examining the movements of the Dow Jones Industrial Average and the Dow Jones Transportation Average.

MOVING AVERAGES
Stock price averages for a fixed time frame, say, 100 days, computed for a particular period of time.

Day	Price	Three-Day Moving Average
1	$44.00	—
2	44.24	—
3	44.90	$44.38
4	45.02	44.72
5	45.14	45.02

The first three-day average that can be computed includes the prices for Days 1, 2, and 3. The result of the computation is ($44.00 + $44.24 + 44.90)/3 = $44.38. The second three-day average that can be computed includes the prices for Days 2, 3, and through 4; the computation is the same as the first three-day average, except the price for Day 1 is omitted and the price for Day 4 is included. As you can see, the window of prices used to compute the averages is always three days, but as the window "moves" through time, only the prices from the most recent three days are used.

The windows for the moving averages used by technical analysts generally range from 30 days to one year. For example, analysts might compute a 100-day moving average. The results of the moving average computations over a given period, say, six months, are then graphed. The graphs are interpreted much like bar charts — when the moving average crosses over, or penetrates, a previously established series, a reversal in the trend might be expected.

TECHNICAL INDICATORS
Measures used by technical analysts to forecast future movements in stock prices.

TECHNICAL INDICATORS **Technical indicators** are measures technical analysts use to help forecast future movements in stock prices. Technicians believe these indicators behave much like the leading economic indicators we discussed earlier in the chapter. Although there are many variations of technical indicators, there are two basic types — those that measure the *breadth* of the market and those that measure the *sentiment* of the market.

MARKET BREADTH INDICATORS
Technical indicators that are used to measure the trading volume and the range of trading that takes place in the market.

Market breadth indicators are used to measure the trading volume and the range of trading that takes place in the market. For example, one of the most often quoted measures is the **advance/decline line,** which is constructed by graphing the results of computing the difference between the number of advancing stocks and the number of declining stocks over a given time period. The advance/decline line is used to track whether there is upward or downward pressure in the market. As long as the advance/decline line moves in the same direction as the market, technicians would generally conclude that the market will continue in the same direction. But, if the advance/decline line moves opposite the market trend, the indication is that the market is weakening and a reversal might soon occur. Other breadth indicators, such as the overbought/oversold index, the traders' index, and various other volume indexes, are also used by technical analysts. In essence, technical analysts believe that changes in trading volume, thus measures based on trading volume, provide indications of future price changes in the market.

ADVANCE/DECLINE LINE
A graph that depicts the results of computing the difference between the number of advancing stocks and the number of declining stocks over some time period.

SENTIMENT INDICATORS
Technical indicators that are used to monitor the "mood," or psychology, of the market.

Sentiment indicators are used to monitor the "mood," or psychology, of the market. One group of sentiment measures is based on observations of the recommendations made to, and the behavior of, the *average individual investor*. Many technical analysts believe the average investor makes decisions to buy or sell in the stock market at the wrong time. Therefore, when odd-lot buying increases or recommendations made by investment newsletters subscribed to by investors are bullish, technical analysts would suggest that the market is expected to decline in the near term.[3] Another group of sentiment measures is based on observations of the trading behavior of investment *experts* and sophisticated investors. For example, technical analysts believe that the amount of short selling done by professional investors is a good indicator of which direction they expect the market to move — when the professionals increase their short positions, it is a sign that the market might decline in the future, and vice versa.

Even though we were able to briefly describe only a few of the many approaches used by technical analysts in this section, you should have a general idea of the basic factors technicians believe provide important signals about movements in stock prices. For the most part, however, fundamental analysts would argue that technical analysis can only reveal what we already know (the movements of historical prices), not what we want to know (the movement of future prices).

Self-Test Questions

Why are technical analysts often referred to as chartists?

What is a trend line?

How are moving averages computed?

What types of indicators are used by technical analysts?

Stock Selection Criteria

Through the years, many different criteria, or screening techniques, for selecting stocks have been developed by numerous investment professionals. Some of the approaches emphasize growth potential, while others focus on value and stability. Most of the factors that are evaluated are considered part of fundamental analyses, but some of the measures clearly would be classified as technical indicators. Even with their differences, the stock selection approaches used by well-known investment professionals do have some commonalities, which we describe in this section.

The discussion in this section focuses on an article presented in the November 1998 issue of the *AAII Journal,* which is published by the American Association of Individual Investors.[4] The article summarized and compared the stock selection criteria applied by ten well-known investment professionals. Some of the techniques, such those developed by Benjamin Graham and T. Rowe Price, were proposed decades ago but still evoke interest today. In this section we briefly

---

[3]In Chapter 15, we defined an odd-lot trade as a trade where the number of shares involved are not in multiples of 100. For instance, if an investor buys 60 shares of a particular stock, he or she is involved in an odd-lot trade. Only individuals trade odd-lot shares. Thus, when odd-lot trading increases, we know that trading by individuals has increased.

[4]Maria Crawford Scott, "The Common Traits of Successful Investment Strategies," *AAII Journal,* November 1998, vol. XX, no. 10, 11–15.

describe the general approaches and indicate the commonalities of the approaches included in the *AAII Journal.* Before we begin, however, we should make it clear that, to date, no one has discovered the "perfect" stock selection technique.

We should mention that many investors use the screening, or selection, techniques we refer to in this section in hopes that they can find stocks that will "beat the market" on a risk-adjusted basis. Such stocks can be classified in two categories — *growth stocks* and *value stocks,* both of which were referenced in the Managerial Perspective at the beginning of the chapter. Technically, **growth stocks** are defined as stocks of firms that have many positive net present value opportunities; that is, the firms' values should increase, or grow, as these projects are undertaken. More generally, though, we define growth stocks as the stocks of firms that exhibit sales and earnings growths that significantly exceed the industry averages. **Value stocks,** on the other hand, are defined as stocks of firms that are mispriced, especially those that are undervalued.

Table 16-4 lists the ten investment professionals discussed in the *AAII Journal* article and summarizes their general investment philosophies and the stock selection criteria they believe should be applied to achieve particular investment goals. In the table, we can only provide a very general indication of the investment philosophy of each professional. Consequently, we should note that each of the individuals listed in Table 16-4 outlines very clear-cut investment goals, and each also recommends that every investor should be disciplined in the pursuit of his or her investment goals.

If we examine the quantitative and qualitative criteria presented in the table, we find some interesting similarities among the different approaches. First, note that each of the stock selection criteria requires some type of an evaluation of the firm's earnings and that the P/E ratio appears to be the most commonly used valuation measure. It should not be a surprise that professional investors prefer firms that exhibit stable growth in earnings. Neither should it be a surprise that the criteria favor firms with financial strength — the best firms seem to be those that have low amounts of debt relative to the industry norm and the ability to meet current obligations. One element that is not consistent among the criteria is the amount of institutional ownership — ownership by pension funds, insurance companies, and so forth — that should be present. Those who favor institutional ownership believe it adds liquidity to a firm's stock, while those who prefer a lower institutional presence believe it is easier to find stocks that are selling at bargain prices if institutional ownership is relatively low.

If we examine the qualitative factors included in Table 16-4, we find there is a general consensus that an investor should have some knowledge and understanding of a company's product line and its general operations before investing in it. In fact, most of the professionals listed in the table would argue that you should not invest in companies you cannot understand because there is a good chance you will not be able to understand the reasons for stock price movements, even after they have occurred. The professionals also seem to favor firms that have carved competitive niches resulting from patents, brand loyalty, or other competitive barriers. If a company is faced with little competition, its future growth is generally more certain than for a company in a very competitive industry.

Perhaps the most interesting piece of information contained in Table 16-4 is located in the last column, Investment Horizon. In this column, we summarized

GROWTH STOCKS
Stocks of firms that have many positive net present value opportunities; in general, these firms exhibit sales and earnings growths that significantly exceed the industry averages.

VALUE STOCKS
Stocks of firms that are mispriced, especially those that are undervalued.

TABLE 16-4

Stock Selection Criteria of Investment Professionals (listed alphabetically)

Name	Investment Philosophy	Types of Stocks Included
Warren Buffett	Use the intrinsic value to select companies expected to generate long-run earnings	Any stock, but the selection criteria require the stocks to be from older companies
David Dreman	Examine investors' attitudes; trade on overreactions	Large and medium firms
Phillip Fisher	Look for firms that show growth higher than the market	Any stock
Benjamin Graham	Find firms with prices below their intrinsic values	Quality dividend-paying firms or unpopular large firms with good subsidiaries
Peter Lynch	Select firms that have good growth prospects at reasonable prices	Any stock
William O'Neil (CANSLIM)	Seek firms that exhibit favorable conditions for future price increases	Any stock, but smaller firms are preferred
James O' Shaughnessy	Whichever strategy is used, be disciplined; use approach that has exhibited success	Depends on the strategy used
T. Rowe Price	Select firms positioned early in their life cycle with good long-term growth prospects	Any stock, but smaller firms offer greater growth opportunities
Ralph Wanger	Find firms that have good value based on financial strength and growth prospects	Established firms that are relatively small
Geraldine Weiss	Select quality firms that pay dividends and are undervalued	Dividend-paying firms; high quality; great number of outstanding shares

SOURCE: Maria Crawford Scott, "The Common Traits of Successful Investment Strategies," *AAII Journal,* November 1998, vol. XX, no. 10, 11–15.

Selection Criteria		
Quantitative Characteristics	**Qualitative Characteristics**	**Investment Horizon**
Strong earnings with consistent upward trend; high retained earnings; high returns for 5 of the last 10 years	Firms should be easy to understand; have a competitive edge due to patents, brands, etc.	Hold until the firm's features are no longer attractive
Low P/E ratios with high dividend yields; high earnings growth compared with market; high ROE and current ratio; low debt	Understand the firm's business and which factors most affect earnings	Hold for a long term; sell if P/E ratios are near the market's P/E
Low P/E ratios relative to growth; good capital position; above-average profits and strong, stable growth in sales	Look for good R&D firms; depth in personnel; good relations with investors; strong market prospects	Hold until growth falls or firm's general features change
Low P/E and price-to-book ratios; stable growth in earnings; current ratio greater than 2.0; long-term debt less than 110 percent of current assets	Prefers to rely on quantitative measures, but seeks firms that are well managed historically	Hold for a long term; sell if price is well above intrinsic value
Low P/E ratios relative to industry and firm's historical growth, low debt/equity ratios, and low institutional ownership; stable earnings	Firms should be established and known by investor; boring; demand for product exists in all economies	Hold for a long term; sell when investment doesn't fit into goals
High, increasing earnings and growth in earnings; low debt; prices achieving new highs; low institutional ownership	Seek leading firms in innovative, growth-oriented industries	Monitor continuously; sell worst performers each quarter
For value-based strategies, choose market leaders with above average sales, dividend yields, etc.; for growth-based strategies, firms should have capitalization greater than $150 million, stable earnings, and high price strength	—	Hold stocks until they no longer meet investment goals
P/E low compared with historical norm; stable EPS growth; retains earnings to increase capital base; above-average profit margins	High degree of management ownership; in growth industry; good labor relations	Hold for a long term; sell when firm is no longer a growth firm
P/E ratio low relative to growth potential; cheap price relative to assets; good working capital; low debt; low institutional ownership	Good management; competitive edge; provide needs for future social and economic trends	Hold for a long term; sell when investment no longer fits goals
Stable earnings and dividends; low P/Es; dividend yields within 10 percent of all-time high; high current ratio; low debt/equity ratio; high institutional ownership	Have a knowledge of the firm's product, R&D, and marketing efforts	Hold until the dividend yield is within 10 percent of historical low

the general feelings of the professionals with respect to the length of time an investment should be held. It is clear that none of the professionals recommends that investors should speculate or try to time market movements; instead, the common theme is to hold an investment until it no longer satisfies the investor's goals. Thus, the consensus of the professionals is to "buy and hold" until either personal goals or market conditions change.

We can summarize the common factors contained in the advice of the investment professionals as follows:

1. Be disciplined with your investment approach. Give a particular strategy a chance to work; don't flip flop between approaches because you don't see immediate results.
2. Know the company in which you invest; make sure you have a basic understanding of the company and its operations before you invest.
3. Choose firms that are in strong financial positions and have good potential for future growth.
4. Stay in the investment until it no longer satisfies your investment goals. But don't use short-term performance evaluations to determine if your investment goals are being met.

Self-Test Questions

According to the investment selection criteria presented in Table 16-4, which measure is used most often to value stocks?

What is the most common qualitative factor included in the stock selection criteria?

How long do the professionals listed in Table 16-4 recommend investors hold stocks chosen using their selection criteria?

Investment Selection in Efficient Markets

Abnormal Returns
Returns that exceed the returns earned by investments with similar risks.

In Chapter 2, we described the concept of information efficiency in the financial markets. Remember that if the markets are efficient with respect to information, then investors cannot use investment selection criteria to *consistently* earn **abnormal returns,** which are defined as returns that exceed the returns earned by investments with similar risks. Thus, those who believe the markets are efficient might also believe that it is a waste of time to use the valuation and stock selection approaches we discussed in the previous sections to try to find mispriced securities. For that reason, in this section, we discuss the concept of information efficiency in the financial markets and the use of stock valuation and selection techniques suggested by both technical analysts and fundamental analysts.

Market Efficiency and Stock Analysis

Remember that the three general forms of market efficiency include weak form efficiency, semistrong form efficiency, and strong form efficiency.

WEAK FORM EFFICIENCY
Current market prices reflect all historical information, including any information that might be provided by examining past price movements and trading volume data.

WEAK FORM EFFICIENCY If **weak form efficiency** exists, then existing market prices reflect all historical information, including any information that might be provided by examining past price movements and trading volume data. Most of the results of various empirical tests of this form of market efficiency indicate that the markets are weak form efficient. This suggests that the charting techniques and other approaches used by technical analysts cannot be used to earn abnormal returns. In fact, some of the tests show that investors actually could do just as well if they select stocks randomly and follow a simple buy-and-hold strategy. Most fundamental analysts would agree that the markets are weak form efficient because they believe that the approaches used by technical analysts are analogous to sorcery or witchcraft.

SEMISTRONG FORM EFFICIENCY
Existing market prices reflect all publicly available information, including information contained in historical data and information contained in current financial statements.

SEMISTRONG FORM EFFICIENCY **Semistrong form efficiency** asserts that existing market prices reflect all publicly available information, including information contained in historical data and information contained in current financial statements. If the markets are semistrong form efficient, then using fundamental analysis techniques, such as examining financial statements, industry life cycles, and so on, to earn abnormal returns will prove futile. To date, tests of this form of market efficiency have been inconclusive — some of the results seem to prove semistrong form efficiency exists, while some of the results indicate such efficiency does not exist. On the one hand, many fundamental analysts would argue that it is their evaluations and the information they provide that helps make the markets efficient. But, some of the empirical evidence suggests that this argument might be flawed because pockets of information inefficiency are present in the markets. For instance, some researchers believe that stocks with low P/E ratios produce abnormal returns. Others believe that small firms perform better than large firms on a relative basis. Still others suggest that those who find such anomalies in the market are examining the wrong events or are using the wrong types of statistical tests.

STRONG FORM EFFICIENCY
Existing market prices reflect all information, whether it is public or private.

STRONG FORM EFFICIENCY **Strong form efficiency** asserts that existing market prices reflect all information, whether public or private. Thus, if the markets achieve this form of efficiency, then even corporate insiders would be unable to earn abnormal returns on a consistent basis. In a strong form efficient market, investors could not earn abnormal returns even if they had inside information. For the most part, empirical tests of the strong form of market efficiency have produced results that suggest insiders can consistently earn abnormal returns; thus, the evidence fails to prove strong form efficiency exists.

Investment Analysis and Strategy in Efficient Markets

What does the evidence about the efficiency of the financial markets suggest about selecting investments? If you believe the markets are efficient, should you simply randomly select securities and follow a buy-and-hold strategy? In an efficient market, are the approaches we discussed in this chapter useless? In general, the answer to the latter two questions is a resounding NO. The approaches we included in this chapter are useful for more reasons than to try to earn abnormal returns. There is no doubt that individual investors would love to earn abnormal returns if they could. But the evidence suggests it is difficult if not impossible to accomplish this objective on a consistent basis. Even if we accept that abnormal returns can be earned only with diligent evaluation of both fundamental and technical information, most of us would be inclined to follow buy-and-hold investment strategies because we are unable or unwilling to put the time and effort into seeking out mispriced securities knowing that we could be wrong.

If we accept that abnormal returns cannot be earned on a consistent basis, we still need to evaluate the investments we select to ensure our investment goals are being met. If you invest without conducting appropriate investment analysis, you might find you have constructed an investment portfolio that is either too risky or not risky enough. The valuation and selection approaches described in this chapter can be used to evaluate particular investments to determine whether they should be included in your portfolio. Thus, unless your goal is to earn about the same return as the market by investing in a portfolio with a large number of different securities, then it generally would not be wise to randomly select stocks. In summary, *you should always do your "investment" homework so you know what risks you are taking and whether your investment goals are being met.*

Self-Test Questions

What are the three forms of market efficiency?

If the markets are considered to be informationally efficient, is there a need to evaluate investments using the approaches we described in this chapter?

Summary

In this chapter we described some of the approaches used to evaluate and select securities. The key concepts covered in the chapter are listed below.

- Investment evaluation generally can be classified into one of two categories: (1) **Fundamental analysis** includes evaluation of economic information, industry reports, and company financial statements to find a stock's intrinsic value, and (2) **technical analysis** is based on the belief that history repeats itself in the financial markets such that identifiable trends exist.
- **Economic analysis** involves evaluation of business cycles and the role of government policies on economic conditions to determine which types of firms should be purchased; some firms perform best in good economic times (**cyclical firms**), while others perform best in poor economic times (**defensive firms**).
- **Economic indicators** are used to measure past, current, and future economic conditions. **Leading economic indicators** tend to precede movements in the economy, **lagging economic indicators** tend to follow, or lag, economic movements, and **coincident economic indicators** tend to mirror, or move at the same time as, business cycles.
- Economic movements are affected by the **monetary policy** established by the Federal Reserve when managing the money supply and by the **fiscal policy**, or spending habits, of the government.
- **Industry analysis** includes evaluation of how firms in a particular industry react to movements in the economy and where in its life cycle the industry is operating.
- The **industry life cycle** consists of three stages: (1) The **introductory stage** is characterized by the infancy of the industry when operations are lean,

competitive barriers are low, and sales are increasing at increasing rates; (2) in the **expansion stage,** firms begin to establish niches due to brand loyalty, the growth in sales begins to slow, competitive barriers increase, and firms begin to pay dividends; and (3) the **mature stage** includes firms that are entrenched, have hard-to-break competitive niches, and generally are paying fairly stable dividends.

- A firm's **financial position** can be evaluated using the approaches we discussed in Chapter 13, where we described financial statement analysis.

- Stock valuation techniques include: (1) **dividend discount models,** which are based on the general concept of determining the present value of the future cash flows associated with the investment; (2) the **P/E ratio** approach, which is used to determine whether the relationship between market price and earnings is above or below normal; and (3) **Economic Value Added (EVA) models,** which utilize fundamental financial principles to evaluate the impact of management decisions on the firm's value.

- Technical analysts are often called chartists because they examine charts and graphs such as **bar charts** and **trend lines.** In addition, technicians use approaches such as the **Dow theory, moving averages,** and **technical indicators** to assess when to expect reversals in existing price trends.

- Even though **professional investors** suggest different criteria for selecting investments, there are some common elements that each espouses. In general, the professionals agree that investors should be disciplined with their investments, know the companies they invest in, choose firms that are financially strong, and buy and hold until conditions change to the point that the investments no longer meet the investment goals.

- The three forms of informational efficiency that could exist in the financial markets are **weak form efficiency, semistrong form efficiency,** and **strong form efficiency.** The results of empirical testing are mixed, but they seem to suggest that the markets are somewhat semistrong form efficient.

- Even if the markets are informationally efficient, **an investor still needs to analyze investments to ensure the risk position of his or her portfolio is appropriate and the investment goals are being met.**

Questions

16-1   Differentiate between fundamental analysis and technical analysis approaches used for stock valuation and selection.

16-2   For each of the following cases, identify whether the economic variable leads, lags, or is coincidental with economic movements. Discuss your reasoning.

Economic Variable	Leading	Lagging	Coincident
a. New building permits	——	——	——
b. Stock market	——	——	——
c. Money supply	——	——	——
d. Prime interest rate	——	——	——
e. Consumer prices	——	——	——
f. Industrial production	——	——	——
g. Personal wages/salaries	——	——	——

16-3   Explain how the Federal Reserve manages the monetary policy of the United States. If the economy was in a recession with high interest rates, what actions might be taken by the Fed to exert downward pressure on interest rates?

16-4   Some economists contend that the deficit spending practices followed by the U.S. government artificially inflate prices and interest rates. Explain their rationale. Can you think of any arguments that can be used to defend deficit spending as a means to support economic activity?

16-5   Indicate whether the industries listed below should be classified as cyclical, defensive, or neither. As you make your classifications, consider the reason(s) you make such designations.

	Cyclical	Defensive	Neither
a. Automobile manufacturing	_____	_____	_____
b. Debt collection services	_____	_____	_____
c. Jewelry	_____	_____	_____
d. Food processing/groceries	_____	_____	_____
e. Personal computer software	_____	_____	_____
f. Appliance manufacturing	_____	_____	_____

16-6   Given the circumstances listed below, determine which stage of the industry life cycle individual investors would prefer. Include your rationale.

	Life-Cycle Stage		
	Introductory	Expansion	Mature
a. The purpose of the investments is to supplement retirement income.	_____	_____	_____
b. Susan recently graduated from college and is just beginning her career.	_____	_____	_____
c. Steve wants to use some of his lottery winnings to speculate in stocks.	_____	_____	_____
d. An investor wants a stock that pays dividends and also promises high future growth.	_____	_____	_____
e. Randy, who now is 12 years old, just received a small inheritance from his aunt.	_____	_____	_____

16-7   Describe the dividend discount model (DDM), P/E ratio, and the Economic Value Added (EVA) approaches used to value common stock. Under what conditions does each approach provide a good estimate of a stock's value?

16-8   Discuss the basic concepts upon which technical analysis is founded. What information does a technician hope to glean from his or her charts and graphs and the technical indicators?

16-9   Examine Table 16-4 in the chapter. Discuss the common themes that are found in the investment philosophies and selection criteria of the professional investors named in the table. Do these commonalties suggest anything about investment strategies and behaviors that should be followed by average investors?

16-10   Assume the financial markets are strong form efficient. Would there be any reason for investors to conduct investment analyses? Why?

Self-Test Problems   *Solutions Appear in Appendix B*

Key terms   **ST-1** Define each of the following terms:
  a. Fundamental analysis; fundamentalists
  b. Technical analysis; technicians
  c. Economic analysis; industry analysis; company analysis
  d. Business cycle; recession
  e. Economic indicators; leading economic indicators; lagging economic indicators; coincident economic indicators
  f. Monetary policy; fiscal policy; deficit spending
  g. Cyclical industry; defensive industry
  h. Industry life cycle
  i. Growth stocks; value stocks
  j. Dividend discount model (DDM); P/E ratio; Economic Value Added (EVA)
  k. Bar chart; trend line
  l. Dow theory; market breadth indicators; sentiment indicators
  m. Efficient markets; abnormal returns
  n. Weak form efficiency; semistrong form efficiency; strong form efficiency

Valuation using   **ST-2** American Transmitter (AT) is a telecommunications firm that currently does not pay
EVA and P/E ratio   a dividend. The following information about AT has been gathered from various sources:

Before-tax cost of debt	8.0%
Cost of equity	15.0%
EBIT	$600,000
Total capital	$2,000,000
Debt/assets ratio	65.0%
EPS	$2.64
Shares outstanding	100,000
Marginal tax rate	40.0%

  a. Compute AT's weighted average cost of capital.
  b. Compute the Economic Value Added (EVA) for AT in the current operating period. Is AT a good investment?
  c. Given the answer from part a, compute the EVA dividend that AT could pay without harming the value of the firm.
  d. Estimate the market price per share assuming AT normally has a P/E ratio equal to 15×.

Moving averages   **ST-3** The following table contains the closing prices for the common stock of Banquet
         Caterers for the last 10 days of trading:

Day	Price
1	$76.00
2	76.50
3	76.75
4	77.10
5	77.20
6	77.85
7	78.20
8	77.95
9	77.90
10	78.10

  a. Compute a 5-day moving average for the entire period. (Hint: You should have 6 moving average values when you are finished.)

b. Based on your series of moving averages, comment on whether you believe the stock price is trending upward or downward.

Problems

Constant dividend growth **16-1** Zycard Inc. has determined that stockholders require a 15 percent rate of return to invest in its common stock. The last dividend paid by the company was $2.50 per share.

a. What will be the value of Zycard's stock if investors expect future dividends to grow at a constant annual rate of (1) 0 percent, (2) 5 percent, and (3) 10 percent?

b. Describe what steps you might take to estimate the appropriate future growth rate for Zycard.

Stock valuation using DDM **16-2** Anchor Shipping has paid a dividend for more than 50 years, and this practice is expected to continue for a long time to come. Analysts have evaluated the financial position of Anchor and discovered that past dividends have grown by a constant rate of 6 percent each year. The most recent dividend payment, which was made yesterday, was $3.40 per share. The company has not been able to compute the rate of return required by its shareholders. But, the following information about market conditions has been gathered:

Risk-free rate	8.0%
Market return	18.0%
β for Anchor Shipping	1.6

a. According to the Capital Asset Pricing Model, what is the rate of return required by Anchor's stockholders?

b. Using the constant growth version of the dividend discount model (DDM), what should be the current value of Anchor's common stock?

Nonconstant growth stock valuation **16-3** Consumer-Friendly Collections (CFT) has grown at a rate of 30 percent in each of the last 5 years. This same growth rate is expected to continue for the next 3 years. After 3 years, growth will decline to 15 percent, where it will remain for 5 years, and then growth will decline to 5 percent, the rate at which the firm will grow for the remainder of its life. CFT's beta coefficient is 1.5, the expected market return is 14 percent, and the risk-free rate of return is 6 percent. Currently, the economy is experiencing normal growth, and economists' projections indicate that this type of economy will continue at least for the next 5 years.

a. Using the Capital Asset Pricing Model, compute the required rate of return for CFT stock.

b. What should be the market value of CFT's stock today if its most recently paid dividend was $2.40 per share?

c. If you suspected the economy was going to enter into a long-term recessionary period 1 year from now, would you make any adjustments to the expected growth rates given here? Explain why or why not.

Computing moving averages **16-4** The S&P 500 end-of-month closing prices from January 1997 through December 1998 are listed below.

Date	S&P 500	Date	S&P 500
January 1997	786.16	January 1998	980.28
February 1997	790.82	February 1998	1049.34
March 1997	757.12	March 1998	1101.75
April 1997	801.34	April 1998	1111.77
May 1997	848.28	May 1998	1090.82
June 1997	885.15	June 1998	1133.84
July 1997	954.31	July 1998	1120.67
August 1997	899.47	August 1998	957.53
September 1997	947.28	September 1998	1017.05
October 1997	914.62	October 1998	1098.67
November 1997	955.40	November 1998	1163.63
December 1997	970.43	December 1998	1229.23

a. Compute all the 6-month moving averages associated with this series of data.

b. Plot the results of your computations in part a. Describe any patterns, or trends, that seem to be apparent.

c. According to your interpretations of the graph, which direction do you think the market should move during 1999? (Note: At the time you work this problem, you should be able to compare your prediction with what actually happened in the market.)

P/E ratios and valuation   **16-5**   General Motors common stock currently is selling for $71.44, which is 19 times its earnings per share, EPS. The most recent dividend paid by GM was $2.00 per share.

a. What is GM's current EPS?

b. What is GM's current dividend payout ratio? (Hint: Remember that the payout ratio refers to the percent of earnings that is paid as dividends.)

c. Assume that GM has achieved constant growth and investors require a 12 percent return to invest in GM's stock. Compute both the dividend yield and the growth provided by GM's stock. (Hint: The dividend yield is the dividend divided by the current market price of the stock.)

d. The industry P/E ratio normally varies from around 11× to 14×. Using these industry averages, estimate the price at which GM should sell.

e. Discuss some factors that might justify GM's P/E being greater than the industry average.

EVA analysis   **16-6**   Consider the following operating information gathered from 3 firms that are identical except for their capital structures:

	Firm A	Firm B	Firm C
Total invested capital	$100,000	$100,000	$100,000
Debt/assets ratio	0.80	0.50	0.20
Shares outstanding	6,100	8,300	10,000
Before-tax cost of debt	0.14	0.12	0.10
Cost of equity	0.26	0.22	0.20
Operating income, EBIT	$25,000	$25,000	$25,000
Net income	$ 8,970	$12,350	$14,950
Marginal tax rate	0.35	0.35	0.35

a. Compute the weighted average cost of capital, WACC, for each firm.

b. Compute the Economic Value Added, EVA, for each firm.

c. Based on the results of your computations in part b, which firm would be considered the best investment? Why?

d. Assume the industry P/E ratio generally is 15×. Using the industry norm, estimate the price for each stock.

e. What factors would cause you to adjust the P/E ratio value used in part d so that it is more appropriate?

EVA analysis **16-7** Backhaus Beer Brewers (BBB) just announced that the current fiscal year's income statement reports its net income to be $1.2 million. BBB's marginal tax rate is 40 percent, and its interest expense for the year was $1.5 million. The company has $8.0 million of invested capital, of which 60 percent is debt. In addition, BBB tries to maintain a weighted average cost of capital, WACC, near 12 percent.

a. Compute the operating income, or EBIT, BBB earned in the current year.

b. What is BBB's Economic Value Added (EVA) for the current year?

c. BBB has 500,000 shares of common stock outstanding. According to the EVA value you computed in part b, how much can BBB pay in dividends per share before the value of the firm would start to decrease? If BBB does not pay any dividends, what would you expect to happen to the value of the firm?

Valuation using DDM and P/E ratios **16-8** The investment public has shown great interest in the stock of Rollover Beds Corporation because the company has been growing at an average annual rate equal to 25 percent. Jason Jackson decided to evaluate the company to determine whether he should include the stock in his investment portfolio. Jason's analysis has led him to conclude that the current rate of growth will not end within the next 30 years. He also has determined that the appropriate required rate of return for Rollover's stock is 20 percent. Some other information Jason examined is given below.

EBIT	$300,000
Net income	$120,000
Total dividends paid	$72,000
Shares outstanding	100,000
Industry P/E ratio	25×

a. Compute the most recent dividend per share, D_0. What is the dividend expected to be next year, D_1?

b. Using the information provided in the problem and the result of your computation in part a, apply the constant growth DDM to determine the current price of Rollover Beds.

c. Does your answer in part b make sense? Explain why you arrived at the answer you did. Given the information available, is there a more appropriate approach to estimating the price of the stock?

d. Apply the P/E ratio approach to value Rollover's stock. Compare the result of this computation to the result from part b. Which would you consider a better estimate for the price?

Exam-Type Problems

The problems included in this section are set up in such a way that they could be used as multiple-choice exam problems.

Stock valuation using DDM **16-9** The current price of ADM's stock, P_0, is $20, and the company is expected to pay a $2.20 dividend next year. If the appropriate required rate of return for ADM's stock is 15 percent, what should be the price of the stock in one year, P_1? Assume the company has achieved constant growth.

Nonconstant growth stock valuation **16-10** Steel Safety Corporation is still in the introductory stage of the industry life cycle; thus, its sales and earnings have grown rapidly in recent years. However, the company has chosen to retain all of its earnings rather than pay dividends. Analysts have projected that Steel Safety will continue to retain all earnings for another 10 years. It is expected that the company will pay its first dividend 11 years from today, which is predicted to be $25 per share. Analysts have also determined that the appropriate required rate of return on Steel Safety's stock is 16 percent.

a. Compute the value of the stock today assuming that once the dividend payments start the dollar amount remains constant at $25 per share per year. (Hint: Keep in mind that the first dividend is not paid until 11 years from today.)

b. Assuming the dividend will grow at a constant rate of 5 percent per year once the payments begin, what is the value of the stock today?

EVA analysis   **16-11**   J.D. Agribusiness has $500,000 invested capital, 60 percent of which is in the form of debt. With this capital structure, the company has a weighted average cost of capital equal to 12 percent. According to J.D.'s latest income statement, operating income is about $100,000, and its marginal tax rate is 40 percent. According to the EVA approach, is J.D. Agribusiness a good company in which to invest?

Valuation using P/E ratios   **16-12**   The stock of East/West Maps is currently selling for $122.40, which equates to a P/E ratio of 30×.

a. Using the P/E ratio, compute the current EPS of East/West.

b. Assume earnings next year increase by 20 percent, but the P/E ratio drops to 25×, which is more in line with the industry average. What will be the price of East/West stock next year?

c. If an investor purchases the stock today for $122.40 and sells it in one year at the price computed in part b, what rate of return would be earned?

EVA analysis   **16-13**   RJS Foods reported that its net income was $65,000 last year. Interest expense was reported to be $40,000, and its marginal tax rate was 35 percent. According to the company's balance sheet, invested capital equals $800,000.

a. Compute the operating income (EBIT) RJS Foods generated last year.

b. If the WACC for RJS Foods is 12 percent, what was its EVA last year?

Integrative Problem

Stock valuation and selection   **16-14**   Michelle Delatorre, the professional tennis player we first introduced in the Integrative Problem in Chapter 2, has returned to your office at Balik and Kiefer to ask some questions about stock valuation and selection. Ms. Delatorre intends to continue to retain your services as her investment advisor and manager, but she wants to "dabble" in the stock market with a small amount of the winnings she earned in tournaments last year. Therefore, Ms. Delatorre has posed some questions relating to stock valuation and selection that she would like help answering.

a. What is the difference between evaluating stocks using fundamental analysis and technical analysis?

b. What is a business cycle? What does it mean when we say the economy is in an expansion? What does it mean when we say the economy is in a contraction?

c. What approaches can we use to forecast business cycles? Is it difficult to predict business cycles? Why?

d. How are business cycles affected by the monetary policy carried out by the Federal Reserve and by the fiscal policy followed by the government?

e. Why is it necessary to evaluate the industry within which a company operates before making an investment decision? What factors should be examined when conducting an industry analysis?

f. How can knowledge of the industry life-cycle concept aid an individual with his or her investment decisions?

g. What is the primary reason an investor needs to examine the financial position of a firm?

h. Describe the three stock valuation techniques discussed in the chapter and indicate when it is appropriate to use each one.

i. Ms. Delatorre has been following a company that was recommended by one of her fellow tennis players. The more she investigates the company, which is named Omega Optical, the greater her interest becomes. But she does not know how to estimate the value of the company's stock. Ms. Delatorre has collected quite a bit of information about Omega through her own analysis. The results of her investigations have yielded the following information:

EBIT	$110,000
Net income	$60,060
Marginal tax rate	35%
Invested capital	$550,000
Before-tax cost of debt, k_d	8.0%
Cost of equity, k_s	18%
Debt/assets ratio	40%
Shares outstanding	40,000
Current dividend per share, D_0	$0

In addition to this information, Ms. Delatorre has given you some analysts' forecasts she has gathered from various investment information subscriptions she receives. The consensus of the experts is that Omega will initiate its first dividend payment 5 years from today when it pays each investor $4.00 per share. In the following year, the dividend payment will increase by 25 percent, but then the growth in dividends will decrease by 2 percent per year until it stabilizes at the constant, or normal, growth of 5 percent. In other words, dividend growth in Year 6 will be 25 percent, it will decrease to 23 percent in Year 7, it will decrease to 21 percent in Year 8, and so on, until Year 16, when dividend growth settles at 5 percent for the remaining life of the firm.

    (1) Using the dividend discount model, compute the value of Omega's common stock.

    (2) Ms. Delatorre's cache of information indicates that the average P/E ratio for firms with operations similar to Omega's is 25. Using the P/E valuation approach, what would be the estimate for the price of the stock?

    (3) Compute Omega's EVA. According to this computation, is Omega a good investment? Why?

j. Explain why the results you found in part i are not the same for each computation. What do you believe the value for the stock should be?

k. Describe some measures used by technical analysts that might be helpful to Ms. Delatorre's effort to value Omega's stock.

l. If you had to summarize the advice of the experts contained in Table 16-4 and give Ms. Delatorre three pieces of general advice about investing, what would you tell her?

m. Describe the concept of informational efficiency in the financial markets. If the markets are efficient, of what use is investment analysis? What investment advice would you give Ms. Delatorre about investing in an efficient market?

Computer-Related Problem

Work the problem in this section only if you are using the computer problem diskette.

EVA analysis   **16-15** Use the model in File C16 to solve this problem. Refer back to Problem 16-6. Rework parts a through d using the computerized model, but make the changes given below. Consider each change independent of the others; thus, in each case, assume all the values except those to be changed are the same as originally stated in Problem 16-6.

a. All else equal, except the debt/assets ratio is 70 percent for Firm A, 40 percent for Firm B, and 30 percent for Firm C.

b. All else equal, except the EBIT for each firm is $15,000.

c. All else equal, except the marginal tax rate for each firm is 40 percent.

APPENDIX A

Mathematical Tables

TABLE A-1

Present Value of $1 Due at the End of n Periods:

EQUATION:

FINANCIAL CALCULATOR KEYS:

$$PVIF_{i,n} = \frac{1}{(1 + i)^n}$$

n	i		0	1.0
N	I	PV	PMT	FV
		Table Value		

Period	1%	2%	3%	4%	5%	6%	7%	8%	9%	10%
1	.9901	.9804	.9709	.9615	.9524	.9434	.9346	.9259	.9174	.9091
2	.9803	.9612	.9426	.9246	.9070	.8900	.8734	.8573	.8417	.8264
3	.9706	.9423	.9151	.8890	.8638	.8396	.8163	.7938	.7722	.7513
4	.9610	.9238	.8885	.8548	.8227	.7921	.7629	.7350	.7084	.6830
5	.9515	.9057	.8626	.8219	.7835	.7473	.7130	.6806	.6499	.6209
6	.9420	.8880	.8375	.7903	.7462	.7050	.6663	.6302	.5963	.5645
7	.9327	.8706	.8131	.7599	.7107	.6651	.6227	.5835	.5470	.5132
8	.9235	.8535	.7894	.7307	.6768	.6274	.5820	.5403	.5019	.4665
9	.9143	.8368	.7664	.7026	.6446	.5919	.5439	.5002	.4604	.4241
10	.9053	.8203	.7441	.6756	.6139	.5584	.5083	.4632	.4224	.3855
11	.8963	.8043	.7224	.6496	.5847	.5268	.4751	.4289	.3875	.3505
12	.8874	.7885	.7014	.6246	.5568	.4970	.4440	.3971	.3555	.3186
13	.8787	.7730	.6810	.6006	.5303	.4688	.4150	.3677	.3262	.2897
14	.8700	.7579	.6611	.5775	.5051	.4423	.3878	.3405	.2992	.2633
15	.8613	.7430	.6419	.5553	.4810	.4173	.3624	.3152	.2745	.2394
16	.8528	.7284	.6232	.5339	.4581	.3936	.3387	.2919	.2519	.2176
17	.8444	.7142	.6050	.5134	.4363	.3714	.3166	.2703	.2311	.1978
18	.8360	.7002	.5874	.4936	.4155	.3503	.2959	.2502	.2120	.1799
19	.8277	.6864	.5703	.4746	.3957	.3305	.2765	.2317	.1945	.1635
20	.8195	.6730	.5537	.4564	.3769	.3118	.2584	.2145	.1784	.1486
21	.8114	.6598	.5375	.4388	.3589	.2942	.2415	.1987	.1637	.1351
22	.8034	.6468	.5219	.4220	.3418	.2775	.2257	.1839	.1502	.1228
23	.7954	.6342	.5067	.4057	.3256	.2618	.2109	.1703	.1378	.1117
24	.7876	.6217	.4919	.3901	.3101	.2470	.1971	.1577	.1264	.1015
25	.7798	.6095	.4776	.3751	.2953	.2330	.1842	.1460	.1160	.0923
26	.7720	.5976	.4637	.3607	.2812	.2198	.1722	.1352	.1064	.0839
27	.7644	.5859	.4502	.3468	.2678	.2074	.1609	.1252	.0976	.0763
28	.7568	.5744	.4371	.3335	.2551	.1956	.1504	.1159	.0895	.0693
29	.7493	.5631	.4243	.3207	.2429	.1846	.1406	.1073	.0822	.0630
30	.7419	.5521	.4120	.3083	.2314	.1741	.1314	.0994	.0754	.0573
35	.7059	.5000	.3554	.2534	.1813	.1301	.0937	.0676	.0490	.0356
40	.6717	.4529	.3066	.2083	.1420	.0972	.0668	.0460	.0318	.0221
45	.6391	.4102	.2644	.1712	.1113	.0727	.0476	.0313	.0207	.0137
50	.6080	.3715	.2281	.1407	.0872	.0543	.0339	.0213	.0134	.0085
55	.5785	.3365	.1968	.1157	.0683	.0406	.0242	.0145	.0087	.0053

TABLE A-1

continued

Period	12%	14%	15%	16%	18%	20%	24%	28%	32%	36%
1	.8929	.8772	.8696	.8621	.8475	.8333	.8065	.7813	.7576	.7353
2	.7972	.7695	.7561	.7432	.7182	.6944	.6504	.6104	.5739	.5407
3	.7118	.6750	.6575	.6407	.6086	.5787	.5245	.4768	.4348	.3975
4	.6355	.5921	.5718	.5523	.5158	.4823	.4230	.3725	.3294	.2923
5	.5674	.5194	.4972	.4761	.4371	.4019	.3411	.2910	.2495	.2149
6	.5066	.4556	.4323	.4104	.3704	.3349	.2751	.2274	.1890	.1580
7	.4523	.3996	.3759	.3538	.3139	.2791	.2218	.1776	.1432	.1162
8	.4039	.3506	.3269	.3050	.2660	.2326	.1789	.1388	.1085	.0854
9	.3606	.3075	.2843	.2630	.2255	.1938	.1443	.1084	.0822	.0628
10	.3220	.2697	.2472	.2267	.1911	.1615	.1164	.0847	.0623	.0462
11	.2875	.2366	.2149	.1954	.1619	.1346	.0938	.0662	.0472	.0340
12	.2567	.2076	.1869	.1685	.1372	.1122	.0757	.0517	.0357	.0250
13	.2292	.1821	.1625	.1452	.1163	.0935	.0610	.0404	.0271	.0184
14	.2046	.1597	.1413	.1252	.0985	.0779	.0492	.0316	.0205	.0135
15	.1827	.1401	.1229	.1079	.0835	.0649	.0397	.0247	.0155	.0099
16	.1631	.1229	.1069	.0930	.0708	.0541	.0320	.0193	.0118	.0073
17	.1456	.1078	.0929	.0802	.0600	.0451	.0258	.0150	.0089	.0054
18	.1300	.0946	.0808	.0691	.0508	.0376	.0208	.0118	.0068	.0039
19	.1161	.0829	.0703	.0596	.0431	.0313	.0168	.0092	.0051	.0029
20	.1037	.0728	.0611	.0514	.0365	.0261	.0135	.0072	.0039	.0021
21	.0926	.0638	.0531	.0443	.0309	.0217	.0109	.0056	.0029	.0016
22	.0826	.0560	.0462	.0382	.0262	.0181	.0088	.0044	.0022	.0012
23	.0738	.0491	.0402	.0329	.0222	.0151	.0071	.0034	.0017	.0008
24	.0659	.0431	.0349	.0284	.0188	.0126	.0057	.0027	.0013	.0006
25	.0588	.0378	.0304	.0245	.0160	.0105	.0046	.0021	.0010	.0005
26	.0525	.0331	.0264	.0211	.0135	.0087	.0037	.0016	.0007	.0003
27	.0469	.0291	.0230	.0182	.0115	.0073	.0030	.0013	.0006	.0002
28	.0419	.0255	.0200	.0157	.0097	.0061	.0024	.0010	.0004	.0002
29	.0374	.0224	.0174	.0135	.0082	.0051	.0020	.0008	.0003	.0001
30	.0334	.0196	.0151	.0116	.0070	.0042	.0016	.0006	.0002	.0001
35	.0189	.0102	.0075	.0055	.0030	.0017	.0005	.0002	.0001	*
40	.0107	.0053	.0037	.0026	.0013	.0007	.0002	.0001	*	*
45	.0061	.0027	.0019	.0013	.0006	.0003	.0001	*	*	*
50	.0035	.0014	.0009	.0006	.0003	.0001	*	*	*	*
55	.0020	.0007	.0005	.0003	.0001	*	*	*	*	*

*The factor is zero to four decimal places.

TABLE A-2

Present Value of an Annuity of $1 per Period for n Periods:

EQUATION:

$$PVIFA_{i,n} = \sum_{t=1}^{n} \frac{1}{(1+i)^t} = \frac{1 - \dfrac{1}{(1+i)^n}}{i} = \frac{1}{i} - \frac{1}{i(1+i)^n}$$

FINANCIAL CALCULATOR KEYS:

n	i		1.0	0
N	**I**	**PV**	**PMT**	**FV**

Table Value

Number of Periods	1%	2%	3%	4%	5%	6%	7%	8%	9%
1	0.9901	0.9804	0.9709	0.9615	0.9524	0.9434	0.9346	0.9259	0.9174
2	1.9704	1.9416	1.9135	1.8861	1.8594	1.8334	1.8080	1.7833	1.7591
3	2.9410	2.8839	2.8286	2.7751	2.7232	2.6730	2.6243	2.5771	2.5313
4	3.9020	3.8077	3.7171	3.6299	3.5460	3.4651	3.3872	3.3121	3.2397
5	4.8534	4.7135	4.5797	4.4518	4.3295	4.2124	4.1002	3.9927	3.8897
6	5.7955	5.6014	5.4172	5.2421	5.0757	4.9173	4.7665	4.6229	4.4859
7	6.7282	6.4720	6.2303	6.0021	5.7864	5.5824	5.3893	5.2064	5.0330
8	7.6517	7.3255	7.0197	6.7327	6.4632	6.2098	5.9713	5.7466	5.5348
9	8.5660	8.1622	7.7861	7.4353	7.1078	6.8017	6.5152	6.2469	5.9952
10	9.4713	8.9826	8.5302	8.1109	7.7217	7.3601	7.0236	6.7101	6.4177
11	10.3676	9.7868	9.2526	8.7605	8.3064	7.8869	7.4987	7.1390	6.8052
12	11.2551	10.5753	9.9540	9.3851	8.8633	8.3838	7.9427	7.5361	7.1607
13	12.1337	11.3484	10.6350	9.9856	9.3936	8.8527	8.3577	7.9038	7.4869
14	13.0037	12.1062	11.2961	10.5631	9.8986	9.2950	8.7455	8.2442	7.7862
15	13.8651	12.8493	11.9379	11.1184	10.3797	9.7122	9.1079	8.5595	8.0607
16	14.7179	13.5777	12.5611	11.6523	10.8378	10.1059	9.4466	8.8514	8.3126
17	15.5623	14.2919	13.1661	12.1657	11.2741	10.4773	9.7632	9.1216	8.5436
18	16.3983	14.9920	13.7535	12.6593	11.6896	10.8276	10.0591	9.3719	8.7556
19	17.2260	15.6785	14.3238	13.1339	12.0853	11.1581	10.3356	9.6036	8.9501
20	18.0456	16.3514	14.8775	13.5903	12.4622	11.4699	10.5940	9.8181	9.1285
21	18.8570	17.0112	15.4150	14.0292	12.8212	11.7641	10.8355	10.0168	9.2922
22	19.6604	17.6580	15.9369	14.4511	13.1630	12.0416	11.0612	10.2007	9.4424
23	20.4558	18.2922	16.4436	14.8568	13.4886	12.3034	11.2722	10.3711	9.5802
24	21.2434	18.9139	16.9355	15.2470	13.7986	12.5504	11.4693	10.5288	9.7066
25	22.0232	19.5235	17.4131	15.6221	14.0939	12.7834	11.6536	10.6748	9.8226
26	22.7952	20.1210	17.8768	15.9828	14.3752	13.0032	11.8258	10.8100	9.9290
27	23.5596	20.7069	18.3270	16.3296	14.6430	13.2105	11.9867	10.9352	10.0266
28	24.3164	21.2813	18.7641	16.6631	14.8981	13.4062	12.1371	11.0511	10.1161
29	25.0658	21.8444	19.1885	16.9837	15.1411	13.5907	12.2777	11.1584	10.1983
30	25.8077	22.3965	19.6004	17.2920	15.3725	13.7648	12.4090	11.2578	10.2737
35	29.4086	24.9986	21.4872	18.6646	16.3742	14.4982	12.9477	11.6546	10.5668
40	32.8347	27.3555	23.1148	19.7928	17.1591	15.0463	13.3317	11.9246	10.7574
45	36.0945	29.4902	24.5187	20.7200	17.7741	15.4558	13.6055	12.1084	10.8812
50	39.1961	31.4236	25.7298	21.4822	18.2559	15.7619	13.8007	12.2335	10.9617
55	42.1472	33.1748	26.7744	22.1086	18.6335	15.9905	13.9399	12.3186	11.0140

TABLE A-2

continued

Number of Periods	10%	12%	14%	15%	16%	18%	20%	24%	28%	32%
1	0.9091	0.8929	0.8772	0.8696	0.8621	0.8475	0.8333	0.8065	0.7813	0.7576
2	1.7355	1.6901	1.6467	1.6257	1.6052	1.5656	1.5278	1.4568	1.3916	1.3315
3	2.4869	2.4018	2.3216	2.2832	2.2459	2.1743	2.1065	1.9813	1.8684	1.7663
4	3.1699	3.0373	2.9137	2.8550	2.7982	2.6901	2.5887	2.4043	2.2410	2.0957
5	3.7908	3.6048	3.4331	3.3522	3.2743	3.1272	2.9906	2.7454	2.5320	2.3452
6	4.3553	4.1114	3.8887	3.7845	3.6847	3.4976	3.3255	3.0205	2.7594	2.5342
7	4.8684	4.5638	4.2883	4.1604	4.0386	3.8115	3.6046	3.2423	2.9370	2.6775
8	5.3349	4.9676	4.6389	4.4873	4.3436	4.0776	3.8372	3.4212	3.0758	2.7860
9	5.7590	5.3282	4.9464	4.7716	4.6065	4.3030	4.0310	3.5655	3.1842	2.8681
10	6.1446	5.6502	5.2161	5.0188	4.8332	4.4941	4.1925	3.6819	3.2689	2.9304
11	6.4951	5.9377	5.4527	5.2337	5.0286	4.6560	4.3271	3.7757	3.3351	2.9776
12	6.8137	6.1944	5.6603	5.4206	5.1971	4.7932	4.4392	3.8514	3.3868	3.0133
13	7.1034	6.4235	5.8424	5.5831	5.3423	4.9095	4.5327	3.9124	3.4272	3.0404
14	7.3667	6.6282	6.0021	5.7245	5.4675	5.0081	4.6106	3.9616	3.4587	3.0609
15	7.6061	6.8109	6.1422	5.8474	5.5755	5.0916	4.6755	4.0013	3.4834	3.0764
16	7.8237	6.9740	6.2651	5.9542	5.6685	5.1624	4.7296	4.0333	3.5026	3.0882
17	8.0216	7.1196	6.3729	6.0472	5.7487	5.2223	4.7746	4.0591	3.5177	3.0971
18	8.2014	7.2497	6.4674	6.1280	5.8178	5.2732	4.8122	4.0799	3.5294	3.1039
19	8.3649	7.3658	6.5504	6.1982	5.8775	5.3162	4.8435	4.0967	3.5386	3.1090
20	8.5136	7.4694	6.6231	6.2593	5.9288	5.3527	4.8696	4.1103	3.5458	3.1129
21	8.6487	7.5620	6.6870	6.3125	5.9731	5.3837	4.8913	4.1212	3.5514	3.1158
22	8.7715	7.6446	6.7429	6.3587	6.0113	5.4099	4.9094	4.1300	3.5558	3.1180
23	8.8832	7.7184	6.7921	6.3988	6.0442	5.4321	4.9245	4.1371	3.5592	3.1197
24	8.9847	7.7843	6.8351	6.4338	6.0726	5.4509	4.9371	4.1428	3.5619	3.1210
25	9.0770	7.8431	6.8729	6.4641	6.0971	5.4669	4.9476	4.1474	3.5640	3.1220
26	9.1609	7.8957	6.9061	6.4906	6.1182	5.4804	4.9563	4.1511	3.5656	3.1227
27	9.2372	7.9426	6.9352	6.5135	6.1364	5.4919	4.9636	4.1542	3.5669	3.1233
28	9.3066	7.9844	6.9607	6.5335	6.1520	5.5016	4.9697	4.1566	3.5679	3.1237
29	9.3696	8.0218	6.9830	6.5509	6.1656	5.5098	4.9747	4.1585	3.5687	3.1240
30	9.4269	8.0552	7.0027	6.5660	6.1772	5.5168	4.9789	4.1601	3.5693	3.1242
35	9.6442	8.1755	7.0700	6.6166	6.2153	5.5386	4.9915	4.1644	3.5708	3.1248
40	9.7791	8.2438	7.1050	6.6418	6.2335	5.5482	4.9966	4.1659	3.5712	3.1250
45	9.8628	8.2825	7.1232	6.6543	6.2421	5.5523	4.9986	4.1664	3.5714	3.1250
50	9.9148	8.3045	7.1327	6.6605	6.2463	5.5541	4.9995	4.1666	3.5714	3.1250
55	9.9471	8.3170	7.1376	6.6636	6.2482	5.5549	4.9998	4.1666	3.5714	3.1250

TABLE A-3

Future Value of $1 at the End of n Periods:

EQUATION:

$$FVIF_{i,n} = (1 + i)^n$$

FINANCIAL CALCULATOR KEYS:

n   i   1.0   0

N   **I**   **PV**   **PMT**   **FV**

Table Value

Period	1%	2%	3%	4%	5%	6%	7%	8%	9%	10%
1	1.0100	1.0200	1.0300	1.0400	1.0500	1.0600	1.0700	1.0800	1.0900	1.1000
2	1.0201	1.0404	1.0609	1.0816	1.1025	1.1236	1.1449	1.1664	1.1881	1.2100
3	1.0303	1.0612	1.0927	1.1249	1.1576	1.1910	1.2250	1.2597	1.2950	1.3310
4	1.0406	1.0824	1.1255	1.1699	1.2155	1.2625	1.3108	1.3605	1.4116	1.4641
5	1.0510	1.1041	1.1593	1.2167	1.2763	1.3382	1.4026	1.4693	1.5386	1.6105
6	1.0615	1.1262	1.1941	1.2653	1.3401	1.4185	1.5007	1.5869	1.6771	1.7716
7	1.0721	1.1487	1.2299	1.3159	1.4071	1.5036	1.6058	1.7138	1.8280	1.9487
8	1.0829	1.1717	1.2668	1.3686	1.4775	1.5938	1.7182	1.8509	1.9926	2.1436
9	1.0937	1.1951	1.3048	1.4233	1.5513	1.6895	1.8385	1.9990	2.1719	2.3579
10	1.1046	1.2190	1.3439	1.4802	1.6289	1.7908	1.9672	2.1589	2.3674	2.5937
11	1.1157	1.2434	1.3842	1.5395	1.7103	1.8983	2.1049	2.3316	2.5804	2.8531
12	1.1268	1.2682	1.4258	1.6010	1.7959	2.0122	2.2522	2.5182	2.8127	3.1384
13	1.1381	1.2936	1.4685	1.6651	1.8856	2.1329	2.4098	2.7196	3.0658	3.4523
14	1.1495	1.3195	1.5126	1.7317	1.9799	2.2609	2.5785	2.9372	3.3417	3.7975
15	1.1610	1.3459	1.5580	1.8009	2.0789	2.3966	2.7590	3.1722	3.6425	4.1772
16	1.1726	1.3728	1.6047	1.8730	2.1829	2.5404	2.9522	3.4259	3.9703	4.5950
17	1.1843	1.4002	1.6528	1.9479	2.2920	2.6928	3.1588	3.7000	4.3276	5.0545
18	1.1961	1.4282	1.7024	2.0258	2.4066	2.8543	3.3799	3.9960	4.7171	5.5599
19	1.2081	1.4568	1.7535	2.1068	2.5270	3.0256	3.6165	4.3157	5.1417	6.1159
20	1.2202	1.4859	1.8061	2.1911	2.6533	3.2071	3.8697	4.6610	5.6044	6.7275
21	1.2324	1.5157	1.8603	2.2788	2.7860	3.3996	4.1406	5.0338	6.1088	7.4002
22	1.2447	1.5460	1.9161	2.3699	2.9253	3.6035	4.4304	5.4365	6.6586	8.1403
23	1.2572	1.5769	1.9736	2.4647	3.0715	3.8197	4.7405	5.8715	7.2579	8.9543
24	1.2697	1.6084	2.0328	2.5633	3.2251	4.0489	5.0724	6.3412	7.9111	9.8497
25	1.2824	1.6406	2.0938	2.6658	3.3864	4.2919	5.4274	6.8485	8.6231	10.835
26	1.2953	1.6734	2.1566	2.7725	3.5557	4.5494	5.8074	7.3964	9.3992	11.918
27	1.3082	1.7069	2.2213	2.8834	3.7335	4.8223	6.2139	7.9881	10.245	13.110
28	1.3213	1.7410	2.2879	2.9987	3.9201	5.1117	6.6488	8.6271	11.167	14.421
29	1.3345	1.7758	2.3566	3.1187	4.1161	5.4184	7.1143	9.3173	12.172	15.863
30	1.3478	1.8114	2.4273	3.2434	4.3219	5.7435	7.6123	10.063	13.268	17.449
40	1.4889	2.2080	3.2620	4.8010	7.0400	10.286	14.974	21.725	31.409	45.259
50	1.6446	2.6916	4.3839	7.1067	11.467	18.420	29.457	46.902	74.358	117.39
60	1.8167	3.2810	5.8916	10.520	18.679	32.988	57.946	101.26	176.03	304.48

TABLE A-3

continued

Period	12%	14%	15%	16%	18%	20%	24%	28%	32%	36%
1	1.1200	1.1400	1.1500	1.1600	1.1800	1.2000	1.2400	1.2800	1.3200	1.3600
2	1.2544	1.2996	1.3225	1.3456	1.3924	1.4400	1.5376	1.6384	1.7424	1.8496
3	1.4049	1.4815	1.5209	1.5609	1.6430	1.7280	1.9066	2.0972	2.3000	2.5155
4	1.5735	1.6890	1.7490	1.8106	1.9388	2.0736	2.3642	2.6844	3.0360	3.4210
5	1.7623	1.9254	2.0114	2.1003	2.2878	2.4883	2.9316	3.4360	4.0075	4.6526
6	1.9738	2.1950	2.3131	2.4364	2.6996	2.9860	3.6352	4.3980	5.2899	6.3275
7	2.2107	2.5023	2.6600	2.8262	3.1855	3.5832	4.5077	5.6295	6.9826	8.6054
8	2.4760	2.8526	3.0590	3.2784	3.7589	4.2998	5.5895	7.2058	9.2170	11.703
9	2.7731	3.2519	3.5179	3.8030	4.4355	5.1598	6.9310	9.2234	12.166	15.917
10	3.1058	3.7072	4.0456	4.4114	5.2338	6.1917	8.5944	11.806	16.060	21.647
11	3.4785	4.2262	4.6524	5.1173	6.1759	7.4301	10.657	15.112	21.199	29.439
12	3.8960	4.8179	5.3503	5.9360	7.2876	8.9161	13.215	19.343	27.983	40.037
13	4.3635	5.4924	6.1528	6.8858	8.5994	10.699	16.386	24.759	36.937	54.451
14	4.8871	6.2613	7.0757	7.9875	10.147	12.839	20.319	31.691	48.757	74.053
15	5.4736	7.1379	8.1371	9.2655	11.974	15.407	25.196	40.565	64.359	100.71
16	6.1304	8.1372	9.3576	10.748	14.129	18.488	31.243	51.923	84.954	136.97
17	6.8660	9.2765	10.761	12.468	16.672	22.186	38.741	66.461	112.14	186.28
18	7.6900	10.575	12.375	14.463	19.673	26.623	48.039	85.071	148.02	253.34
19	8.6128	12.056	14.232	16.777	23.214	31.948	59.568	108.89	195.39	344.54
20	9.6463	13.743	16.367	19.461	27.393	38.338	73.864	139.38	257.92	468.57
21	10.804	15.668	18.822	22.574	32.324	46.005	91.592	178.41	340.45	637.26
22	12.100	17.861	21.645	26.186	38.142	55.206	113.57	228.36	449.39	866.67
23	13.552	20.362	24.891	30.376	45.008	66.247	140.83	292.30	593.20	1178.7
24	15.179	23.212	28.625	35.236	53.109	79.497	174.63	374.14	783.02	1603.0
25	17.000	26.462	32.919	40.874	62.669	95.396	216.54	478.90	1033.6	2180.1
26	19.040	30.167	37.857	47.414	73.949	114.48	268.51	613.00	1364.3	2964.9
27	21.325	34.390	43.535	55.000	87.260	137.37	332.95	784.64	1800.9	4032.3
28	23.884	39.204	50.066	63.800	102.97	164.84	412.86	1004.3	2377.2	5483.9
29	26.750	44.693	57.575	74.009	121.50	197.81	511.95	1285.6	3137.9	7458.1
30	29.960	50.950	66.212	85.850	143.37	237.38	634.82	1645.5	4142.1	10143.
40	93.051	188.88	267.86	378.72	750.38	1469.8	5455.9	19427.	66521.	*
50	289.00	700.23	1083.7	1670.7	3927.4	9100.4	46890.	*	*	*
60	897.60	2595.9	4384.0	7370.2	20555.	56348.	*	*	*	*

*FVIF > 99,999.

TABLE A-4

Future Value of an Annuity of $1 per Period for n Periods:

EQUATION:

$$FVIFA_{i,n} = \sum_{t=1}^{n} (1 + i)^{n-t} = \frac{(1 + i)^n - 1}{i}$$

FINANCIAL CALCULATOR KEYS:

n	i	0	1.0	
N	**I**	**PV**	**PMT**	**FV**
				Table Value

Number of Periods	1%	2%	3%	4%	5%	6%	7%	8%	9%	10%
1	1.0000	1.0000	1.0000	1.0000	1.0000	1.0000	1.0000	1.0000	1.0000	1.0000
2	2.0100	2.0200	2.0300	2.0400	2.0500	2.0600	2.0700	2.0800	2.0900	2.1000
3	3.0301	3.0604	3.0909	3.1216	3.1525	3.1836	3.2149	3.2464	3.2781	3.3100
4	4.0604	4.1216	4.1836	4.2465	4.3101	4.3746	4.4399	4.5061	4.5731	4.6410
5	5.1010	5.2040	5.3091	5.4163	5.5256	5.6371	5.7507	5.8666	5.9847	6.1051
6	6.1520	6.3081	6.4684	6.6330	6.8019	6.9753	7.1533	7.3359	7.5233	7.7156
7	7.2135	7.4343	7.6625	7.8983	8.1420	8.3938	8.6540	8.9228	9.2004	9.4872
8	8.2857	8.5830	8.8923	9.2142	9.5491	9.8975	10.260	10.637	11.028	11.436
9	9.3685	9.7546	10.159	10.583	11.027	11.491	11.978	12.488	13.021	13.579
10	10.462	10.950	11.464	12.006	12.578	13.181	13.816	14.487	15.193	15.937
11	11.567	12.169	12.808	13.486	14.207	14.972	15.784	16.645	17.560	18.531
12	12.683	13.412	14.192	15.026	15.917	16.870	17.888	18.977	20.141	21.384
13	13.809	14.680	15.618	16.627	17.713	18.882	20.141	21.495	22.953	24.523
14	14.947	15.974	17.086	18.292	19.599	21.015	22.550	24.215	26.019	27.975
15	16.097	17.293	18.599	20.024	21.579	23.276	25.129	27.152	29.361	31.772
16	17.258	18.639	20.157	21.825	23.657	25.673	27.888	30.324	33.003	35.950
17	18.430	20.012	21.762	23.698	25.840	28.213	30.840	33.750	36.974	40.545
18	19.615	21.412	23.414	25.645	28.132	30.906	33.999	37.450	41.301	45.599
19	20.811	22.841	25.117	27.671	30.539	33.760	37.379	41.446	46.018	51.159
20	22.019	24.297	26.870	29.778	33.066	36.786	40.995	45.762	51.160	57.275
21	23.239	25.783	28.676	31.969	35.719	39.993	44.865	50.423	56.765	64.002
22	24.472	27.299	30.537	34.248	38.505	43.392	49.006	55.457	62.873	71.403
23	25.716	28.845	32.453	36.618	41.430	46.996	53.436	60.893	69.532	79.543
24	26.973	30.422	34.426	39.083	44.502	50.816	58.177	66.765	76.790	88.497
25	28.243	32.030	36.459	41.646	47.727	54.865	63.249	73.106	84.701	98.347
26	29.526	33.671	38.553	44.312	51.113	59.156	68.676	79.954	93.324	109.18
27	30.821	35.344	40.710	47.084	54.669	63.706	74.484	87.351	102.72	121.10
28	32.129	37.051	42.931	49.968	58.403	68.528	80.698	95.339	112.97	134.21
29	33.450	38.792	45.219	52.966	62.323	73.640	87.347	103.97	124.14	148.63
30	34.785	40.568	47.575	56.085	66.439	79.058	94.461	113.28	136.31	164.49
40	48.886	60.402	75.401	95.026	120.80	154.76	199.64	259.06	337.88	442.59
50	64.463	84.579	112.80	152.67	209.35	290.34	406.53	573.77	815.08	1163.9
60	81.670	114.05	163.05	237.99	353.58	533.13	813.52	1253.2	1944.8	3034.8

TABLE A-4

continued

Number of Periods	12%	14%	15%	16%	18%	20%	24%	28%	32%	36%
1	1.0000	1.0000	1.0000	1.0000	1.0000	1.0000	1.0000	1.0000	1.0000	1.0000
2	2.1200	2.1400	2.1500	2.1600	2.1800	2.2000	2.2400	2.2800	2.3200	2.3600
3	3.3744	3.4396	3.4725	3.5056	3.5724	3.6400	3.7776	3.9184	4.0624	4.2096
4	4.7793	4.9211	4.9934	5.0665	5.2154	5.3680	5.6842	6.0156	6.3624	6.7251
5	6.3528	6.6101	6.7424	6.8771	7.1542	7.4416	8.0484	8.6999	9.3983	10.146
6	8.1152	8.5355	8.7537	8.9775	9.4420	9.9299	10.980	12.136	13.406	14.799
7	10.089	10.730	11.067	11.414	12.142	12.916	14.615	16.534	18.696	21.126
8	12.300	13.233	13.727	14.240	15.327	16.499	19.123	22.163	25.678	29.732
9	14.776	16.085	16.786	17.519	19.086	20.799	24.712	29.369	34.895	41.435
10	17.549	19.337	20.304	21.321	23.521	25.959	31.643	38.593	47.062	57.352
11	20.655	23.045	24.349	25.733	28.755	32.150	40.238	50.398	63.122	78.998
12	24.133	27.271	29.002	30.850	34.931	39.581	50.895	65.510	84.320	108.44
13	28.029	32.089	34.352	36.786	42.219	48.497	64.110	84.853	112.30	148.47
14	32.393	37.581	40.505	43.672	50.818	59.196	80.496	109.61	149.24	202.93
15	37.280	43.842	47.580	51.660	60.965	72.035	100.82	141.30	198.00	276.98
16	42.753	50.980	55.717	60.925	72.939	87.442	126.01	181.87	262.36	377.69
17	48.884	59.118	65.075	71.673	87.068	105.93	157.25	233.79	347.31	514.66
18	55.750	68.394	75.836	84.141	103.74	128.12	195.99	300.25	459.45	700.94
19	63.440	78.969	88.212	98.603	123.41	154.74	244.03	385.32	607.47	954.28
20	72.052	91.025	102.44	115.38	146.63	186.69	303.60	494.21	802.86	1298.8
21	81.699	104.77	118.81	134.84	174.02	225.03	377.46	633.59	1060.8	1767.4
22	92.503	120.44	137.63	157.41	206.34	271.03	469.06	812.00	1401.2	2404.7
23	104.60	138.30	159.28	183.60	244.49	326.24	582.63	1040.4	1850.6	3271.3
24	118.16	158.66	184.17	213.98	289.49	392.48	723.46	1332.7	2443.8	4450.0
25	133.33	181.87	212.79	249.21	342.60	471.98	898.09	1706.8	3226.8	6053.0
26	150.33	208.33	245.71	290.09	405.27	567.38	1114.6	2185.7	4260.4	8233.1
27	169.37	238.50	283.57	337.50	479.22	681.85	1383.1	2798.7	5624.8	11198.0
28	190.70	272.89	327.10	392.50	566.48	819.22	1716.1	3583.3	7425.7	15230.3
29	214.58	312.09	377.17	456.30	669.45	984.07	2129.0	4587.7	9802.9	20714.2
30	241.33	356.79	434.75	530.31	790.95	1181.9	2640.9	5873.2	12941.	28172.3
40	767.09	1342.0	1779.1	2360.8	4163.2	7343.9	22729.	69377.	*	*
50	2400.0	4994.5	7217.7	10436.	21813.	45497.	*	*	*	*
60	7471.6	18535.	29220.	46058.	*	*	*	*	*	*

*FVIFA > 99,999.

APPENDIX B

Solutions to Self-Test Problems

Note: We do not show an answer for ST-1 problems because they are verbal rather than quantitative in nature. For the ST-1 problems, you can refer to the marginal glossary definitions or relevant chapter sections to check your responses.

Chapter 2

ST-2   ***a.***   Average = $(6\% + 7\% + 8\% + 9\%)/4 = 30\%/4 = 7.5\%$.

      b. $k_{T\text{-bond}} = k^* + IP = 3.0\% + 7.5\% = 10.5\%$.

      c.   If the 5-year T-bond rate is 11 percent, the inflation rate is expected to average approximately $11\% - 3\% = 8\%$ during the next 5 years. Thus, the implied Year 5 inflation rate is 10 percent:

$$IP_5 = 8\% = (6\% + 7\% + 8\% + 9\% + Infl_5)/5$$

$$40\% = 30\% + Infl_5$$

$$Infl_5 = 10\%.$$

Chapter 3

ST-2   ***a.***   If the Fed wants to increase the money supply, it should *buy* Treasury securities, because it pays for the securities by increasing reserves at financial institutions. The amount of securities the Fed should buy is solved as follows:

$$\frac{\text{Maximum change in}}{\text{the money supply}} = \frac{\Delta \text{ Excess reserves}}{\text{Reserve requirement}} = \$135 \text{ million} = \frac{\Delta \text{ Excess reserves}}{0.10}$$

$$\Delta \text{ Excess reserves} = \$135 \text{ million} \times 0.10 = \$13.5 \text{ million}$$

$$\Delta \text{ Excess reserves} = \Delta \text{ Reserves} \left(1 - \frac{\text{Reserve}}{\text{requirement}}\right)$$

$$\Delta \text{ Reserves} = \frac{\Delta \text{ Excess reserves}}{\left(1 - \dfrac{\text{Reserve}}{\text{requirement}}\right)} = \frac{\$13.5 \text{ million}}{(1 - 0.10)} = \$15 \text{ million}$$

Thus, the Fed must purchase $15 million in Treasury securities. This action would create immediate excess reserves equal to $13.5 million, which would then create ($13.5 million)/(0.10) = $135 million in additional money.

b. Solve this problem the same as above, except substitute $54 million for the $135 million. The answer should be $6 million, which represents the amount of securities the Fed needs to *buy* in order to reduce the money supply by $54 million.

Chapter 4

ST-2   **a.** $100,000,000/10 = $10,000,000 per year. Because the $10 million will be used to retire (repay) the bonds immediately, no interest will be earned on it.

     b. The debt service requirements will decline. As the amount of bonds outstanding declines, so will the interest payments each year (amounts are in millions of dollars):

Payment Period (1)	Amount of Outstanding Bonds (2)	Sinking Fund Payment (3)	Interest Payment $0.12 \times (2) = (4)$	Total Debt Service $(3) + (4) = (5)$
1	$100	$10	$12.0	$22.0
2	90	10	10.8	20.8
3	80	10	9.6	19.6
.	.	.		
.	.	.		
.	.	.		
10	10	10	1.2	11.2

Note from the table that the total cash debt service requirement decreases by $1.2 million each year because there is $10 million less debt at the beginning of each year, which means $1.2 million less interest has to be paid each year.

     c. Annual debt service costs will be $100,000,000(0.12) + $6,582,009 = 18,582,009.

     d. If interest rates rose, causing the bond's price to fall, the company would use open market purchases. This would reduce its debt service requirements.

ST-3   **a.** Most firms have a continuing need for long-term debt to finance operations. Therefore, it would make sense for a business firm to issue bonds such as the Canadian bonds. From the standpoint of a viable firm, the only significant difference between a 30-year bond and a perpetual bond that is callable is a refinancing requirement for the regular bond at the end of 30 years. During a period of inflation, refinancing of inexpensive old debt at new high rates can significantly alter the embedded cost (coupon rate) of debt.

     b. The default risk of all four bonds can be considered nil. However, the bonds would be exposed to risk of fluctuating interest rates, and this risk for the non-Canadian types will increase with their expected time to maturity:

       (1) 5-year bond.
       (2) 50-year bond.
       (3) Regular perpetuity.

The Canadian-type perpetuity would be a perpetuity if interest rates rise, a 30-year bond if they fall. Thus, for investors, it's "heads I win, tails you lose," so we would assign the highest interest rate to the Canadian-type bond.

c. No. If bonds with a coupon of less than 3 percent could have been sold to replace the existing 3 percent bonds, it would have been in the best interest of the Canadian taxpayers to retire the more expensive bonds.

d. We need to answer why investors believed that the bonds would be called. If the information was based on unfounded rumor, then there was no reason to expect the Canadian public to foot the bill for investors' mistakes. On the other hand, the Canadian government also has a moral obligation to the holders of its bonds to prevent false information about its bonds from being deliberately passed on to investors. From a purely economic standpoint, unless the Canadian government wanted to reduce its overall debt, it would not make much sense to call the relatively inexpensive debt; to do so would require issuing new, more expensive debt.

If the government had originally sold the bonds to naive investors, and had somehow led them to think that the bonds would be retired, then fairness might indicate retirement. But, the original holders probably sold or otherwise disposed of their bonds years ago, and it would probably take more stupidity than naivete to buy the bonds expecting a call.

Chapter 5

ST-2 *Thompson's Taxes as a Corporation:*

Income before salary and taxes	$60,000.0	$90,000.0	$110,000.0
Less: salary	(40,000.0)	(40,000.0)	(40,000.0)
Taxable income, corporate	20,000.0	50,000.0	70,000.0
Total corporate tax	($ 3,000.0)[a]	($ 7,500.0)	($ 12,500.0)
Salary	$40,000.0	$40,000.0	$ 40,000.0
Less: exemptions and deductions	(17,100.0)	(17,100.0)	(17,100.0)
Taxable personal income	22,900.0	22,900.0	22,900.0
Total personal tax	($ 3,435.0)[b]	($ 3,435.0)	($ 3,435.0)
Combines corporate and personal tax	$ 6,435.0	$10,935.0	$ 15,935.0

Thompson's Taxes as a Proprietorship:

Total income	$60,000.0	$90,000.0	$110,000.0
Less: exemptions and deductions	(17,100.0)	(17,100.0)	(17,100.0)
Taxable personal income	42,900.0	72,900.0	92,900.0
Tax liability of proprietorship	$ 6,506.5[c]	$14,906.5	$ 20,506.5
Advantage to being a corporation	$ 71.5	$ 3,971.5	$ 4,571.5

[a]Corporate tax in 2000 = (0.15)($20,000) = $3,000.

[b]Personal tax (if Thompson incorporates) in 2000 = (0.15)($22,900) = $3,435.

[c]Proprietorship tax in 2000 = $6,352.5 + (0.28)($42,900 - $42,350) = $6,506.5

The corporate form of organization allows Thompson to pay the lowest taxes in each year; therefore, on the basis of taxes over the 3-year period, Thompson should incorporate his business. However, note that to get money out of the corporation so he can spend it, Thompson will have to have the corporation pay dividends, which will be taxed as personal income. Therefore, sometime in the future Thompson will have to pay additional taxes when corporate distributions are made.

Chapter 6

ST-2   **a.**   (1)

```
0   i = ?  1      2      3      4      5
|----------|------|------|------|------|
-5,500                              7,020
```

$$FV_n = PV(1 + i)^n$$

$$\$7,020 = \$5,500(1 + i)^5$$

$$FVIF_{i,5} = \frac{\$7,020}{\$5,500} = 1.2764$$

Use the Future Value of $1 table (Table A-3 in Appendix A) for 5 periods to find the interest rate corresponding to an FVIF of 1.2764. The closest value is 1.2763, which is in the 5% column; so the return is 5 percent.

To solve for the exact rate, use your calculator or solve algebraically. Using your calculator, enter N = 5, FV = 7,020, PV = −5,500, and then press the I key — you should find the result is 5.001. To solve algebraically, recognize that, according to the above computations, $(1 + i)^5 = 1.276364$ (carried to 6 places). Therefore,

$$(1 + i)^5 = 1.276364$$

$$i = (1.276364)^{\frac{1}{5}} = 0.05001 = 5.001\%$$

(2)

```
0   i = ?  1     2     3     4     5     6     7     8
|----------|-----|-----|-----|-----|-----|-----|-----|
-5,500                                            8,126
```

$$FV_n = PV(1 + i)^n$$

$$\$8,126 = \$5,500(1 + i)^8$$

$$FVIF_{i,8} = \frac{\$8,126}{\$5,500} = 1.4775$$

Looking in the Future Value of $1 table (Table A-3 in Appendix A) across 8 periods, we find that an FVIF of 1.4775 corresponds to 5 percent. Using your calculator or solving algebraically will yield the same result.

Because both investments yield the same return, you should be indifferent between them.

b.   If you believe there is greater uncertainty about whether the 8-year investment will pay the amount expected ($8,126) than about whether the 5-year investment will pay the amount expected ($7,020), then you should prefer the shorter-term investment. We will discuss the effects of risk on value in Chapter 8.

ST-3   **a.**

```
1/1/00  8%  1/1/01      1/1/02      1/1/03      1/1/04
|-----------|-----------|-----------|-----------|
         -1,000                            FV = ?
```

$1,000 is being compounded for 3 years, so your balance on January 1, 2004, is $1,259.71:

$$FV_n = PV(1 + i)^n = \$1,000(1 + 0.08)^3 = \$1,259.71.$$

b.

1/1/00	2%	1/1/01	1/1/02	1/1/03	1/1/04
		−1,000			FV = ?

The effective annual rate for 8 percent, compounded quarterly, is

$$\text{Effective annual rate} = \left(1 + \frac{0.08}{4}\right)^4 - 1.0$$
$$= (1.02)^4 - 1.0 = 0.0824 = 8.24\%.$$

Therefore, FV = $1,000(1.0824)^3 = $1,000(1.2681) = $1,268.10. Alternatively, use FVIF for 2%, $3 \times 4 = 12$ periods:

$$FV_{12} = \$1,000(FVIF_{2\%,12}) = \$1,000(1.2682) = \$1,268.20.$$

Alternatively, using a financial calculator, input N = 12, I = 2, PV = −1000, PMT = 0, and FV = ? FV = $1,268.24.

Note that since the interest factors are carried to only four decimal places, rounding differences occur.

c.

1/1/00	8%	1/1/01	1/1/02	1/1/03	1/1/04
		250	250	250	250
					FV = ?

As you work this problem, keep in mind that the tables assume that payments are made at the end of each period. Therefore, you may solve this problem by finding the future value of an annuity of $250 for 4 years at 8 percent:

$$FVA_4 = PMT(FVIFA_{8\%,4}) = \$250(4.5061) = \$1,126.53.$$

Alternatively, using a financial calculator, input N = 4, I = 8, PV = 0, PMT = −250, and FV = ?; FV = $1,126.53.

d.

1/1/00	8%	1/1/01	1/1/02	1/1/03	1/1/04
		?	?	?	?
					FV = 1,259.71

$$N = 4; I = 8\%; PV = 0; FV = \$1,259.71; PMT = ?; PMT = \$279.56.$$

$$PMT(FVIFA_{8\%,4}) = FVA_4$$

$$PMT(4.5061) = \$1,259.71$$

$$PMT = \$1,259.71/4.5061 = \$279.56.$$

Therefore, you would have to make 4 payments of $279.56 each to have a balance of $1,259.71 on January 1, 2000.

ST-4   a. Set up a time line like the one in the preceding problem:

Note that your deposit will grow for 3 years at 8 percent. The fact that it is now January 1, 2000, is irrelevant. The deposit on January 1, 2001, is the PV, and the FV is $1,000. Here is the solution:

$$N = 3; I = 8\%; PMT = 0; FV = \$1,000; PV = ?; PV = \$793.83.$$

$$FV_3(PVIF_{8\%,3}) = PV$$

$$PV = \$1,000(0.7938) = \$793.80 = \text{Initial deposit to accumulate } \$1,000.$$

(Difference due to rounding.)

b.

Here we are dealing with a 4-year annuity whose first payment occurs one year from today, on 1/1/01, and whose future value must equal $1,000. You should modify the time line to help visualize the situation. Here is the solution:

$$N = 4; I = 8\%; PV = 0; FV = \$1,000; PMT = ?; PMT = \$221.92.$$

$$PMT(FVIFA_{8\%,4}) = FVA_4$$

$$PMT = \frac{FVA_4}{(FVIFA_{8\%,4})}$$

$$= \frac{\$1,000}{4.5061} = \$221.92 = \text{Payment necessary to accumulate } \$1,000.$$

c. This problem can be approached in several ways. Perhaps the simplest is to ask this question: "If I received $750 on 1/1/01 and deposited it to earn 8 percent, would I have acquired $1,000 on 1/1/2000?" The answer is no:

$$FV_3 = \$750(1.08)^3 = \$944.78.$$

This indicates that you should let your father make the payments rather than accept the lump sum of $750.

You could also compare the $750 with the PV of the payments:

$$N = 4; I = 8\%; PMT = -\$221.92; FV = 0; PV = ?; PV = \$735.03.$$

$$PMT(PVIFA_{8\%,4}) = PVA_4$$

$$\$221.92(3.3121) = \$735.02 = \text{Present value at } 1/1/00$$
$$\text{of the required payments.}$$

(Difference due to rounding.)

This is less than the $750 lump sum offer, so your initial reaction might be to accept the lump sum of $750. However, this would be a mistake. The problem is that when you found the $735.02 PV of the annuity, you were finding the value of the annuity *today,* on January 1, 2000. You were comparing $735.02 today with the lump sum of $750 one year from now. This is, of course, invalid. What you should have done was take the $735.02, recognize that this is the PV of an annuity as of January 1, 2000, multiply $735.02 by 1.08 to get $793.82, and compare $793.82 with the lump sum of $750. You would then take your father's offer to make the payments rather than take the lump sum on January 1, 2001. If you solved the PV for an annuity due, you would find the same answer.

d.

1/1/00	i = ?	1/1/01	1/1/02	1/1/03	1/1/04

−750   1,000

$$N = 3; PV = -\$750; PMT = 0; FV = \$1,000; I = ?, I = 10.0642\%.$$

$$PV(FVIF_{i,3}) = FV$$

$$FVIF_{i,3} = \frac{FV}{PV}$$

$$= \frac{\$1,000}{\$750} = 1.3333.$$

Use the Future Value of $1 table (Table A-3 in Appendix A) for 3 periods to find the interest rate corresponding to an FVIF of 1.3333. Look across the Period 3 row of the table until you come to 1.3333. The closest value is 1.3310, in the 10 percent column. Therefore, you would require an interest rate of approximately 10 percent to achieve your $1,000 goal. The exact rate required, found with a financial calculator, is 10.0642 percent. Solving directly, $i = (1.3333)^{\frac{1}{3}} - 1 = 10.0642\%.$

e.

1/1/00	i = ?	1/1/01	1/1/02	1/1/03	1/1/04

                    186.29   186.29   186.29   186.29
                                                        FV = 1,000

$$N = 4; PV = 0; PMT = -\$186.29; FV = \$1,000; I = ?; I = 20.0\%.$$

$$PMT(FVIFA_{i,4}) = FVA_4$$

$$\$186.29(FVIFA_{i,4}) = \$1,000$$

$$FVIFA_{i,4} = \frac{\$1,000}{\$186.29} = 5.3680.$$

Using Table A-4 at the end of the book, we find that 5.3680 corresponds to a 20 percent interest rate.

f.

1/1/00	4%	1/1/01		1/1/02		1/1/03		1/1/04

$$400 \quad PMT \quad PMT \quad PMT \quad PMT \quad PMT \quad PMT$$
$$FV = 1,000$$

Find the future value of the original $400 deposit:

$$FV_6 = PV(FVIF_{4\%,6}) = \$400(1.2653) = \$506.12.$$

This means that on January 1, 2004, you need an additional sum of $493.88 = $1,000 − $506.12. This will be accumulated by making 6 equal payments which earn 8 percent compounded semiannually, or 4 percent each 6 months:

$$N = 6; I = 4\%; PV = 0; FV = \$493.88; PMT = ?; PMT = 74.46.$$

$$PMT(FVIFA_{4\%,6}) = FVA_6$$

$$PMT = \frac{FVA_6}{(FVIFA_{4\%,6})}$$

$$= \frac{\$493.88}{6.6330} = \$74.46.$$

Alternatively, using a financial calculator, input N = 6, I = 4, PV = −400, FV = 1000, and PMT = ? PMT = $74.46.

g.

$$\text{Effective annual rate} = \left(1 + \frac{i_{SIMPLE}}{m}\right)^m - 1.0$$

$$= \left(1 + \frac{0.08}{2}\right)^2 - 1 = (1.04)^2 - 1$$

$$= 1.0816 - 1 = 0.0816 = 8.16\%.$$

h.   There is a reinvestment rate risk here because we assumed that funds will earn an 8 percent return in the bank. In fact, if interest rates in the economy fall, the bank will lower its deposit rate because it will be earning less when it lends out the funds you deposited with it. If you buy certificates of deposit (CDs) that mature on the date you need the money (1/1/2004), you will avoid the reinvestment risk, but that would work only if you were making the deposit today.

ST-5   Bank A's effective annual rate is 8.24 percent:

$$\text{Effective annual rate} = \left(1 + \frac{0.08}{4}\right)^4 - 1.0$$

$$= (1.02)^4 - 1 = 1.0824 - 1$$

$$= 0.0824 = 8.24\%.$$

Now Bank B must have the same effective annual rate:

$$\left(1 + \frac{i}{12}\right)^{12} - 1.0 = 0.0824$$

$$\left(1 + \frac{i}{12}\right)^{12} = 1.0824$$

$$1 + \frac{i}{12} = (1.0824)^{1/12}$$

$$1 + \frac{i}{12} = 1.00662$$

$$\frac{i}{12} = 0.00662$$

$$i = 0.07944 = 7.94\%.$$

Thus, the two banks have different quoted rates — Bank A's quoted rate is 8 percent, while Bank B's quoted rate is 7.94 percent; however, both banks have the same effective annual rate of 8.24 percent. The difference in their quoted rates is due to the difference in compounding frequency.

Chapter 7

ST-2 **a.** This is not necessarily true. Because G plows back two-thirds of its earnings, its growth rate should exceed that of D, but D pays higher dividends ($6 versus $2). We cannot say which stock should have the higher price.

b. Again, we just do not know which price would be higher.

c. This is false. The changes in k_d and k_s would have a greater effect on G — its price would decline more.

d. The total expected return for D is $\hat{k}_D = \hat{D}_1/P_0 + g = 15\% + 0\% = 15\%$. The total expected return for G will have $\hat{D}_1/P_0$ less than 15 percent and g greater than 0 percent, but $\hat{k}_G$ should be neither greater nor smaller than D's total expected return, 15 percent, because the two stocks are stated to be equally risky.

e. We have eliminated a, b, c, and d, so e should be correct. On the basis of the available information, D and G should sell at about the same price, $40; thus, $\hat{k}_s$ = 15% for both D and G. G's current dividend yield is $2/$40 = 5%. Therefore, g = 15% − 5% = 10%.

ST-3 **a.** Pennington's bonds were sold at par; therefore, the original YTM equaled the coupon rate of 12%.

b. Five years have passed; with 25 years remaining until maturity, 25 × 2 = 50 interest payments remain:

$$V_d = \sum_{t=1}^{50} \frac{\$120/2}{\left(1 + \frac{0.10}{2}\right)^t} + \frac{\$1,000}{\left(1 + \frac{0.10}{2}\right)^{50}}$$

$$= \$60(PVIFA_{5\%,50}) + \$1,000(PVIF_{5\%,50})$$

$$= \$60(18.2559) + \$1,000(0.0872)$$

$$= \$1,095.35 + \$87.20 = \$1,182.55.$$

Alternatively, with a financial calculator, input the following: N = 50, I = 5, PMT = 60, FV = 1000, and PV = ? PV = $1,182.56.

c.
$$\text{Current yield} = \text{Annual coupon payment/Price}$$

$$= \$120/\$1,182.55$$

$$= 0.1015 = 10.15\%.$$

$$\text{Capital gains yield} = \text{Total yield} - \text{Current yield}$$

$$= 10\% - 10.15\% = -0.15\%.$$

d.
$$\$916.42 = \sum_{t=1}^{13} \frac{\$60}{(1 + k_d/2)^t} + \frac{\$1,000}{(1 + k_d/2)^{13}}.$$

Using Equation 7-3, the approximate YTM is:

$$YTM \approx \frac{\$60 + \left(\dfrac{\$1,000 - \$916.42}{13} \right)}{\left[\dfrac{2(\$916.42) + \$1,000}{3} \right]}$$

$$\approx 7\%$$

At $k_{d/2} = 7\%$:

$$V_d = INT(PVIFA_{7\%,13}) + M(PVIF_{7\%,13})$$

$$\$916.42 = \$60(8.3577) + \$1,000(0.4150)$$

$$= \$501.46 + \$415.00 = \$916.46.$$

Therefore, the YTM on July 1, 1999, was $7\% \times 2 = 14\%$. Alternatively, with a financial calculator, input the following: N = 13, PV = −916.42, PMT = 60, FV = 1000, and $k_{d/2}$ = I = ? Calculator solution = $k_{d/2}$ = 7.00%; therefore, k_d = 14.00%.

e.
$$\text{Current yield} = \$120/\$916.42 = 13.09\%$$

$$\text{Capital gains yield} = 14\% - 13.09\% = 0.91\%.$$

ST-4   The first step is to solve for g, the unknown variable, in the constant growth equation. Because $\hat{D}_1$ is unknown but D_0 is known, substitute $D_0(1 + g)$ as follows:

$$\hat{P}_0 = P_0 = \frac{\hat{D}_1}{k_s - g} = \frac{D_0(1 + g)}{k_s - g}$$

$$\$36 = \frac{\$2.40(1 + g)}{0.12 - g}.$$

Solving for g, we find the growth rate to be 5 percent:

$$\$4.32 - \$36g = \$2.40 + \$2.40g$$

$$\$38.4g = \$1.92$$

$$g = 0.05 = 5\%.$$

The next step is to use the growth rate to project the stock price 5 years hence:

$$\hat{P}_5 = \frac{D_0(1 + g)^6}{k_s - g}$$

$$= \frac{\$2.40(1.05)^6}{0.12 - 0.05}$$

$$= \$45.95.$$

[Alternatively, $\hat{P}_5 = \$36(1.05)^5 = \$45.95$.]

Therefore, Ewald Company's expected stock price 5 years from now, $\hat{P}_5$, is $45.95.

ST-5 ***a.*** (1) Calculate the PV of the dividends paid during the supernormal growth period:

$$\hat{D}_1 = \$1.1500(1.15) = \$1.3225.$$

$$\hat{D}_2 = \$1.3225(1.15) = \$1.5209.$$

$$\hat{D}_3 = \$1.5209(1.13) = \$1.7186.$$

PV of dividends = $1.3225(0.8929) + $1.5209(0.7972) + $1.7186(0.7118)

$$= \$1.1809 + \$1.2125 + \$1.2233$$

$$= \$3.6167 \approx \$3.62.$$

(2) Find the PV of Snyder's stock price at the end of Year 3:

$$\hat{P}_3 = \frac{\hat{D}_4}{k_s - g} = \frac{\hat{D}_3(1 + g)}{k_s - g}$$

$$= \frac{\$1.7186(1.06)}{0.12 - 0.06}$$

$$= \$30.36.$$

PV of $\hat{P}_3$ = $30.36(0.7118) = $21.61.

(3) Sum the two components to find the value of the stock today:

$$\hat{P}_0 = \$3.62 + \$21.61 = \$25.23.$$

Alternatively, the cash flows can be placed on a time line as follows:

Enter the cash flows into the cash flow register, I = 12, and press the NPV key to obtain P_0 = $25.23.

b. $\hat{P}_1$ = $1.5209(0.8929) + $1.7186(0.7972) + $30.36(0.7972)

$$= \$1.3580 + \$1.3701 + \$24.2030$$

$$= \$26.9311 \approx \$26.93.$$

(Calculator solution: $26.93.)

$\hat{P}_2$ = $1.7186(0.8929) + $30.36(0.8929)

$$= \$1.5345 + \$27.1084$$

$$= \$28.6429 \approx \$28.64.$$

(Calculator solution: $28.64.)

c.

Year	Dividend Yield	+	Capital Gains Yield	=	Total Return
1	$\dfrac{\$1.3225}{\$25.23} \approx 5.24\%$		$\dfrac{\$26.93 - \$25.23}{\$25.23} \approx 6.74\%$		$\approx 12\%$
2	$\dfrac{\$1.5209}{\$26.93} \approx 5.65\%$		$\dfrac{\$28.64 - \$26.93}{\$26.93} \approx 6.35\%$		$\approx 12\%$
3	$\dfrac{\$1.7186}{\$28.64} \approx 6.00\%$		$\dfrac{\$30.36 - \$28.64}{\$28.64} \approx 6.00\%$		$\approx 12\%$

Chapter 8

ST-2 a. The average rate of return for each stock is calculated by simply averaging the returns over the five-year period. The average return for each stock is 18.90 percent, calculated for Stock A as follows:

$$k_{Avg} = (-10.00\% + 18.50\% + 38.67\% + 14.33\% + 33.00\%)/5$$

$$= 18.90\%$$

The realized rate of return on a portfolio made up of Stock A and Stock B would be calculated by finding the average return in each year as k_A(% of Stock A) + k_B(% of Stock B) and then averaging these yearly returns:

Year	Portfolio AB's Return, k_{AB}
1995	(6.50%)
1996	19.90
1997	41.46
1998	9.00
1999	30.65
	$k_{Avg} = \underline{\underline{18.90\%}}$

b. The standard deviation of returns is estimated, using Equation 7-3a, as follows (see Footnote 3):

$$\text{Estimated } \sigma = S = \sqrt{\dfrac{\sum\limits_{t=1}^{n} (\bar{k}_t - \bar{k}_{Avg})^2}{n-1}} \tag{7-3a}$$

For Stock A, the estimated σ is 19.0 percent:

$$\sigma_A = \sqrt{\dfrac{(-10.00 - 18.9)^2 + (18.50 - 18.9)^2 + \cdots + (33.00 - 18.9)^2}{5-1}}$$

$$= \sqrt{\dfrac{1,445.92}{4}} = 19.0\%.$$

The standard deviation of returns for Stock B and for the portfolio are similarly determined, and they are as follows:

	Stock A	Stock B	Portfolio AB
Standard deviation	19.0	19.0	18.6

c. Because the risk reduction from diversification is small (σ_{AB} falls only from 19.0 to 18.6 percent), the most likely value of the correlation coefficient is 0.9. If the correlation coefficient were −0.9, the risk reduction would be much larger. In fact, the correlation coefficient between Stocks A and B is 0.92.

d. If more randomly selected stocks were added to the portfolio, σ_p would decline to somewhere in the vicinity of 15 percent; see Figure 8-7, σ_p would remain constant only if the correlation coefficient were +1.0, which is most unlikely. σ_p would decline to zero if the correlation coefficient, r, were equal to −1.0 and the proper proportions were held in a two-stock portfolio.

Chapter 9

ST-2   a. *Payback:*
To determine the payback, construct the cumulative cash flows for each project:

	Cumulative Cash Flows	
Year	Project X	Project Y
0	($10,000)	($10,000)
1	(3,500)	(6,500)
2	(500)	(3,000)
3	2,500	500
4	3,500	4,000

$$\text{Payback}_X = 2 + \frac{\$500}{\$3,000} = 2.17 \text{ years.}$$

$$\text{Payback}_Y = 2 + \frac{\$3,000}{\$3,500} = 2.86 \text{ years.}$$

Net present value (NPV):

$$\text{NPV}_X = -\$10,000 + \frac{\$6,500}{(1.12)^1} + \frac{\$3,000}{(1.12)^2} + \frac{\$3,000}{(1.12)^3} + \frac{\$1,000}{(1.12)^4}$$

$$= \$966.01.$$

$$\text{NPV}_Y = -\$10,000 + \frac{\$3,500}{(1.12)^1} + \frac{\$3,500}{(1.12)^2} + \frac{\$3,500}{(1.12)^3} + \frac{\$3,500}{(1.12)^4}$$

$$= \$630.72.$$

Alternatively, using a financial calculator, input the cash flows into the cash flow register, enter I = 12, and then press the NPV key to obtain $\text{NPV}_X = \$966.01$ and $\text{NPV}_Y = \$630.72$.

Internal rate of return (IRR):
To solve for each project's IRR, find the discount rates which equate each NPV to zero:

$$\text{IRR}_X = 18.0\%.$$

$$\text{IRR}_Y = 15.0\%.$$

b. The following table summarizes the project rankings by each method:

	Project Which Ranks Higher
Payback	X
NPV	X
IRR	X

Note that all methods rank Project X over Project Y. In addition, both projects are acceptable under the NPV and IRR criteria. Thus, both projects should be accepted if they are independent.

c. In this case, we would choose the project with the higher NPV at k = 12%, or Project X.

d. To determine the effects of changing the cost of capital, plot the NPV profiles of each project. The crossover rate occurs at about 6 to 7 percent (6.2%).

NPV Profiles for Projects X and Y

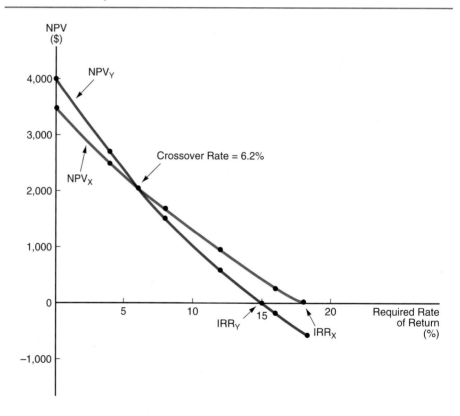

Required Rate of Return	NPV$_X$	NPV$_Y$
0%	$3,500	$4,000
4	2,545	2,705
8	1,707	1,592
12	966	631
16	307	(206)
18	5	(585)

If the firm's required rate of return is less than 6 percent, a conflict exists because $NPV_Y > NPV_X$, but $IRR_X > IRR_Y$. Therefore, if k were 5 percent, a conflict would exist.

e. The basic cause of the conflict is differing reinvestment rate assumptions between NPV and IRR. NPV assumes that cash flows can be reinvested at the cost of capital, while IRR assumes reinvestment at the (generally) higher IRR. The high reinvestment rate assumption under IRR makes early cash flows especially valuable, and hence short-term projects look better under IRR.

ST-3 **a.** *Estimated investment outlay:*

Price	($50,000)
Modification	(10,000)
Change in net working capital	(2,000)
Total investment outlay	($62,000)

b. *Incremental operating cash flows:*

	Year 1	Year 2	Year 3
1. After-tax cost savings[a]	$12,000	$12,000	$12,000
2. Depreciation[b]	19,800	27,000	9,000
3. Depreciation tax savings[c]	7,920	10,800	3,600
Net cash flow (1 + 3)	$19,920	$22,800	$15,600

[a]$20,000(1 − T) = $20,000 (1 − 0.40) = $12,000

[b]Depreciable basis = $60,000, the MACRS percentage allowances are 0.33, 0.45, and 0.15 in Years 1, 2, and 3, respectively; hence, depreciation in Year 1 = 0.33($60,000) = $19,800, and so on. There will remain $4,200, or 7 percent, undepreciated after Year 3; it would normally be taken in Year 4.

[c]Depreciation tax savings = T(Depreciation) = 0.4($19,800) = $7,920 in Year 1, and so on.

c. *Terminal cash flow:*

Salvage value	$20,000
Tax on salvage value[a]	(6,320)
Net working capital recovery	2,000
	$15,680

[a]Sales price	$20,000
Less book value	(4,200)
Taxable income	$15,800
Tax at 40%	$ 6,320

Book value = Depreciable basis − Accumulated depreciation
= $60,000 − $55,800 = 44,200.

d. *Project NPV:*

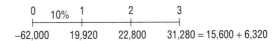

$$NPV = -\$62,000 + \frac{\$19,920}{(1.10)^1} + \frac{\$22,800}{(1.10)^2} + \frac{\$31,280}{(1.10)^3}$$

$$= -\$1,547.$$

Alternatively, using a financial calculator, input the cash flows into the cash flow register, enter I = 10, and then press the NPV key to obtain NPV = −$1,547. Because the earthmover has a negative NPV, it should not be purchased.

ST-4 *First determine the initial investment outlay:*

Purchase price	($8,000)
Sale of old machine	3,000
Tax on sale of old machine	(160)[a]
Change in net working capital	(1,500)[b]
Total investment	($6,660)

[a]The market value is $3,000 − $2,600 = $400 above the book value. Thus, there is a $400 recapture of depreciation, and Dauten would have to pay 0.40($400) = $160 in taxes.

[b]The change in net working capital is a $2,000 increase in current assets minus a $500 increase in current liabilities, which nets to $1,500.

Now, examine the operating cash inflows:

Sales increase	$1,000
Cost decrease	1,500
Increase in pretax operating revenues	$2,500

After-tax operating revenue increase:

$$\$2,500(1 - T) = \$2,500(0.60) = \$1,500.$$

Depreciation:

Year	1	2	3	4	5	6
New[a]	$1,600	$2,560	$1,520	$ 960	$ 880	$ 480
Old	350	350	350	350	350	350
Change	$1,250	$2,210	$1,170	$ 610	$ 530	$ 130
Depreciation						
Tax savings[b]	$ 500	$ 884	$ 468	$ 244	$ 212	$ 52

[a]Depreciable basis = $8,000. Depreciation expense in each year equals depreciable basis times the MACRS percentage allowances of 0.20, 0.32, 0.19, 0.12, 0.11, and 0.06 in Years 1–6, respectively.

[b]Depreciation tax savings = T(Δ Depreciation) = 0.4(Δ Depreciation).

Now recognize that at the end of Year 6 Dauten would recover its net working capital investment of $1,500, and it would also receive $800 from the sale of the replacement machine. However, because the machine would be fully depreciated, the firm must pay 0.40($800) = $320 in taxes on the sale. Also, by undertaking the replacement now, the firm forgoes the right to sell the old machine for $500 in Year 6; thus, this $500 in Year 6 must be considered an opportunity cost in that year. No tax would be due because the $500 salvage value would equal the old machine's Year 6 book value.

Finally, place all the cash flows on a time line:

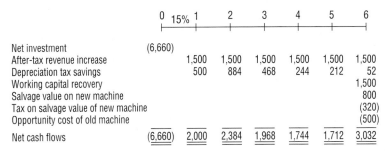

	0 15% 1	2	3	4	5	6
Net investment	(6,660)					
After-tax revenue increase	1,500	1,500	1,500	1,500	1,500	1,500
Depreciation tax savings	500	884	468	244	212	52
Working capital recovery						1,500
Salvage value on new machine						800
Tax on salvage value of new machine						(320)
Opportunity cost of old machine						(500)
Net cash flows	(6,660)	2,000	2,384	1,968	1,744	1,712	3,032

The net present value of this incremental cash flow stream, when discounted at 15 percent, is $1,335. Thus, the replacement should be made.

ST-5 a. First, find the expected cash flows:

Year	Expected Cash Flows
0	$0.2(-\$100,000) + 0.6(-\$100,000) + 0.2(-\$100,000) = (\$100,000)$
1	$0.2(\$20,000) \quad + 0.6(\$30,000) \quad + 0.2(\$40,000) \quad = \quad \$30,000$
2	$\$30,000$
3	$\$30,000$
4	$\$30,000$
5	$\$30,000$
5*	$0.2(\$0) \quad + 0.6(\$20,000) \quad + 0.2(\$30,000) \quad = \quad \$18,000$

```
0    10%   1        2        3        4        5
|---------|--------|--------|--------|--------|
-100,000  30,000   30,000   30,000   30,000   48,000
```

Next, determine the NPV based on the expected cash flows:

$$NPV = -\$100,000 + \frac{\$30,000}{(1.10)^1} + \frac{\$30,000}{(1.10)^2} + \frac{\$30,000}{(1.10)^3}$$

$$+ \frac{\$30,000}{(1.10)^4} + \frac{\$30,000}{(1.10)^5} = \$24,900.$$

Alternatively, using a financial claculator, input the cash flows in the cash flow register, enter I = 10, and the press the NPV key to obtain NPV = $24,900.

b. For the worst case, the cash flow values from the cash flow column farthest on the left are used to calculate NPV:

```
0    10%   1        2        3        4        5
|---------|--------|--------|--------|--------|
-100,000  20,000   20,000   20,000   20,000   20,000
```

$$NPV = -\$100,000 + \frac{\$20,000}{(1.10)^1} + \frac{\$20,000}{(1.10)^2} + \frac{\$20,000}{(1.10)^3}$$

$$+ \frac{\$20,000}{(1.10)^4} + \frac{\$20,000}{(1.10)^5} = \$24,184.$$

Similarly, for the best case, use the values from the column farthest on the right. Here the NPV is $70,259.

If the cash flows are perfectly dependent, then the low cash flow in the first year will mean a low cash flow in every year. Thus, the probability of the worst case occurring is the probability of getting the $20,000 net cash flow in Year 1, or 20 percent. If the cash flows are independent, the cash flow in each year can be low, high, or average, and the probability of getting all low cash flows will be

$$0.2(0.2)(0.2)(0.2)(0.2) = 0.2^5 = 0.00032 = 0.032\%.$$

c. The base case NPV is found using the most likely cash flows and is equal to $26,142. This value differs from the expected NPV of $24,900 because the Year 5 cash flows are not symmetric. Under these conditions, the NPV distribution is as follows:

P_r	NPV
0.2	($24,184)
0.6	26,142
0.2	70,259

Thus, the expected NPV is 0.2(−$24,184) + 0.6($26,142) + 0.2($70,259) = $24,900. As is generally the case, the expected NPV is the same as the NPV of the expected cash flows found in Part a. The standard deviation is $29,904:

$$\sigma^2_{NPV} = 0.2(-\$24,184 - \$24,900)^2 + 0.6(\$26,142 - \$24,900)^2$$
$$+ 0.2(\$70,259 - \$24,900)^2$$
$$= \$894,261,126.$$
$$\sigma_{NPV} = \sqrt{\$894,261,126} = \$29,904.$$

The coefficient of variation, CV, is $29,904/$24,900 = 1.20.

d. Because the project's coefficient of variation is 1.20, the project is riskier than average, and hence the project's risk-adjusted cost of capital is 10% + 2% = 12%. The project now should be evaluated by finding the NPV of the expected cash flows, as in Part a, but using a 12 percent discount rate. The risk-adjusted NPV is $18,357, and therefore the project should be accepted.

Chapter 10

ST-2 a. A break point will occur each time a low-cost type of capital is used up. We establish the break points as follows, after first noting that LEI has $24,000 of retained earnings:

$$\text{Retained earnings} = (\text{Total earnings})(1.0 - \text{Payout})$$
$$= \$34,285.72(0.7)$$
$$= \$24,000.$$

$$\text{Break point} = \frac{\text{Total amount of low-cost capital of a given type}}{\text{Proportion of this type of capital in the capital structure}}.$$

Capital Used Up	Break Point Calculation		Break Number
Retained earnings	$BP_{RE} = \dfrac{\$24,000}{0.60}$	$= \$40,000$	2
10% flotation common	$BP_{10\%E} = \dfrac{\$24,000 + \$12,000}{0.60}$	$= \$60,000$	4
5% flotation preferred	$BP_{5\%P} = \dfrac{\$7,500}{0.15}$	$= \$50,000$	3
12% debt	$BP_{12\%D} = \dfrac{\$5,000}{0.25}$	$= \$20,000$	1
14% debt	$BP_{14\%D} = \dfrac{\$10,000}{0.25}$	$= \$40,000$	2

Summary of break points

(1) There are three common equity costs and hence two changes and, therefore, two equity-induced breaks in the MCC. There are two preferred costs and hence one preferred break. There are three debt costs and hence two debt breaks.

(2) The numbers in the third column of the table designate the sequential order of the breaks, determined after all the break points were calculated. Note that the second debt break and the break for retained earnings both occur at $40,000.

(3) The first break point occurs at $20,000, when the 12 percent debt is used up. The second break point, $40,000, results from using up both retained earnings and the 14 percent debt. The MCC curve also rises at $50,000 and $60,000, as preferred stock with a 5 percent flotation cost and common stock with a 10 percent flotation cost, respectively, are used up.

b. Component costs within indicated total capital intervals are as follows: Retained earnings (used in interval $0 to $40,000):

$$k_S = \frac{\hat{D}_1}{P_0} + g = \frac{D_0(1 + g)}{P_0} + g$$

$$= \frac{\$3.60(1.09)}{\$60} + 0.09$$

$$= 0.0654 + 0.09 \qquad\qquad = 15.54\%.$$

Common with F = 10% ($40,001 to $60,000):

$$k_e = \frac{\hat{D}_1}{P_0(1.0 - F)} + g = \frac{\$3.924}{\$60(0.9)} + 9\% \qquad = 16.27\%.$$

Common with F = 20% (over $60,000):

$$k_e = \frac{\$3.924}{\$60(0.8)} + 9\% \qquad = 17.18\%.$$

Preferred with F = 5% ($0 to $50,000):

$$k_{ps} = \frac{D_{ps}}{P_0 - \text{Flotation costs}} = \frac{\$11}{\$100(0.95)} \qquad = 11.58\%.$$

Preferred with F = 10% (over $50,000):

$$k_{ps} = \frac{\$11}{\$100(0.9)} \qquad = 12.22\%.$$

Debt at k_d = 12% ($0 to $20,000):

$$k_{dT} = k_d(1 - T) = 12\%(0.6) \qquad = 7.20\%.$$

Debt at k_d = 14% ($20,001 to $40,000):

$$k_{dT} = 14\%(0.6) \qquad = 8.40\%.$$

Debt at k_d = 16% (over $40,000):

$$k_{dT} = 16\%(0.6) \qquad = 9.60\%.$$

c. WACC calculations within indicated total capital intervals:
   (1) $0 to $20,000 (debt = 7.2%, preferred = 11.58%, and retained earnings [RE] = 15.54%):

$$WACC_1 = w_d k_{dT} + w_{ps} k_{ps} + w_s k_s$$
$$= 0.25(7.2\%) + 0.15(11.58\%) + 0.60(15.54\%) = 12.86\%.$$

   (2) $20,001 to $40,000 (debt = 8.4%, preferred = 11.58%, and RE = 15.54%):

$$WACC_2 = 0.25(8.4\%) + 0.15(11.58\%) + 0.60(15.54\%) = 13.16\%.$$

   (3) $40,001 to $50,000 (debt = 9.6%, preferred = 11.58%, and equity = 16.27%):

$$WACC_3 = 0.25(9.6\%) + 0.15(11.58\%) + 0.60(16.27\%) = 13.90\%.$$

   (4) $50,001 to $60,000 (debt = 9.6%, preferred = 12.22%, and equity = 16.27%):

$$WACC_4 = 0.25(9.6\%) + 0.15(12.22\%) + 0.60(16.27\%) = 14.00\%.$$

   (5) Over $60,000 (debt = 9.6%, preferred = 12.22%, and equity = 17.18%):

$$WACC_5 = 0.25(9.6\%) + 0.15(12.22\%) + 0.60(17.18\%) = 14.54\%.$$

d. IRR calculation for Project E:

$$PVIFA_{k,6} = \frac{\$20,000}{\$5,427.84} = 3.6847.$$

This is the factor for 16 percent, so $IRR_E = 16\%$.
Alternatively, N = 6, PV = $-$ 20000, PMT = 5427.84, and I = ? I = 16.00%.

e. See the following graph of the MCC and IOS schedules for LEI.

LEI: MCC and IOS Schedules

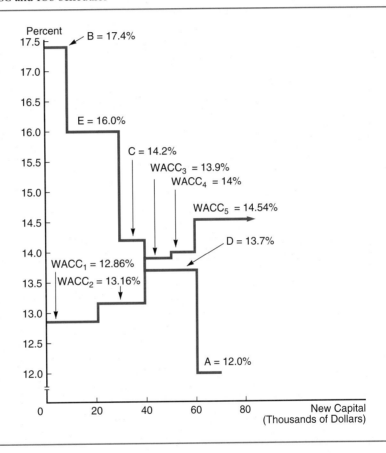

f. LEI should accept Projects B, E, and C. It should reject Projects A and D because their IRRs do not exceed the marginal costs of funds needed to finance them. The firm's capital budget would total $40,000.

Chapter 11

ST-2 **a.**

EBIT	$4,000,000
Interest ($2,000,000 × 0.10)	(200,000)
Earnings before taxes (EBT)	$3,800,000
Taxes (35%)	(1,330,000)
Net income	$2,470,000

$$EPS = \$2,470,000/600,000 = \$4.12.$$

$$P_0 = \$4.12/0.15 = \$27.47.$$

b.

$$Equity = 600,000 \times (\$10) = \$6,000,000.$$

$$Debt = \$2,000,000$$

$$Total\ capital = \$8,000,000.$$

$$WACC = w_d[k_d(1 - T)] + w_s k_s$$

$$= (2/8)[(10\%)(1 - 0.35)] + (6/8)(15\%)$$

$$= 1.63\% + 11.25\%.$$

$$= 12.88\%.$$

c.

EBIT	$4,000,000
Interest ($10,000,000 × 0.12)	(1,200,000)
Earnings before taxes (EBT)	$2,800,000
Taxes (35%)	(980,000)
Net income	$1,820,000

Shares (shrs) bought and retired:

$$\Delta Shrs = \Delta Debt/P_0 = \$8,000,000/\$27.47 = 291,227.$$

New outstanding shares:

$$Shrs_1 = Shrs_0 - \Delta Shrs = 600,000 - 291,227 = 308,773.$$

New EPS:

$$EPS = \$1,820,000/308,773 = \$5.89.$$

New price per share:

$$P_0 = \$5.89/0.17 = \$34.65\ versus\ \$27.47.$$

Therefore, Gentry should change its capital structure.

d.

$$TIE = \frac{EBIT}{I}.$$

$$Original\ TIE = \frac{\$4,000,000}{\$200,000} = 20\ times.$$

$$New\ TIE = \frac{\$4,000,000}{\$1,200,000} = 3.33\ times.$$

ST-3 a.

Projected net income	$2,000,000
Less projected capital investments	(800,000)
Available residual	$1,200,000
Shares outstanding	200,000

$$\text{DPS} = \$1,200,000/200,000 \text{ shares} = \$6 = \hat{D}_1.$$

b. EPS = $2,000,000/200,000 shares = $10.

Payout ratio = DPS/EPS = $6/$10 = 60%, or

Total dividends/NI = $1,200,000/$2,000,000 = 60%.

c. Currently, $P_0 = \dfrac{\hat{D}_1}{k_s - g} = \dfrac{\$6}{0.14 - 0.05} = \dfrac{\$6}{0.09} = \$66.67.$

Under the former circumstances, $\hat{D}_1$ would be based on a 20 percent payout on $10 EPS, or $2. With $k_s = 14\%$ and $g = 12\%$, we solve for P_0:

$$P_0 = \frac{\hat{D}_1}{k_s - g} = \frac{\$2}{0.14 - 0.12} = \frac{\$2}{0.02} = \$100.$$

Although CMC has suffered a severe setback, its existing assets will continue to provide a good income stream. More of these earnings should now be passed on to the shareholders, as the slowed internal growth has reduced the need for funds. However, the net result is a 33 percent decrease in the value of the shares.

d. If the payout ratio were continued at 20 percent, even after internal investment opportunities had declined, the price of the stock would drop to $2/(0.14 − 0.06) = $25 rather than to $66.67. Thus, an increase in the dividend payout is consistent with maximizing shareholder wealth.

Because of the downward-sloping IOS curve, the greater the firm's level of investment, the lower the average ROE. Thus, the more money CMC retains and invests, the lower its average ROE will be. We can determine the average ROE under different conditions as follows:

Old situation (with founder active and 20 percent payout):

$$g = (1.0 - \text{Payout ratio})(\text{Average ROE})$$

$$12\% = (1.0 - 0.2)(\text{Average ROE})$$

$$\text{Average ROE} = 12\%/0.8 = 15\% > k_s = 14\%.$$

Note that the *average* ROE is 15 percent, whereas the *marginal* ROE is presumably equal to 14 percent.

New situation (with founder retired and a 60 percent payout):

$$g = 6\% = (1.0 - 0.6)(\text{ROE})$$

$$\text{ROE} = 6\%/0.4 = 15\% > k_s = 14\%.$$

This suggests that the new payout is appropriate and that the firm is taking on investments down to the point at which marginal returns are equal to the cost of capital.

Chapter 12

ST-2 **The Calgary Company: Alternative Balance Sheets**

	Restricted (40%)	Moderate (50%)	Relaxed (60%)
Current assets[a]	$1,200,000	$1,500,000	$1,800,000
Fixed assets	600,000	600,000	600,000
Total assets	$1,800,000	$2,100,000	$2,400,000
Debt (50% of assets)	$ 900,000	$1,050,000	$1,200,000
Equity	900,000	1,050,000	1,200,000
Total liabilities and equity	$1,800,000	$2,100,000	$2,400,000

The Calgary Company: Alternative Income Statements

	Restricted	Moderate	Relaxed
Sales	$3,000,000	$3,000,000	$3,000,000
EBIT	450,000	450,000	450,000
Interest (10%)	(90,000)	(105,000)	(120,000)
Earnings before taxes (EBT)	$ 360,000	$ 345,000	$ 330,000
Taxes (40%)	(144,000)	(138,000)	(132,000)
Net income	$ 216,000	$ 207,000	$ 198,000
ROE	24.0%	19.7%	16.5%

[a]Current assets = Sales × 40% = $3,000,000 × 0.40 = $1,200,000.

ST-3 *a.*

$$EAR = \left[1 + \left(\frac{\text{Interest rate}}{\text{per period}}\right)\right]^m - 1.0$$

$$\frac{\text{Interest rate}}{\text{per period}} = \frac{\text{Dollar cost of borrowing}}{\text{Amount of usable funds}}$$

Effective cost of the bank loan:

$$\frac{\text{Interest rate}}{\text{per period}} = \frac{\$300,000(0.13)}{\$300,000 - \$300,00(0.13)} = \frac{0.13}{1 - 0.13}$$

$$= 0.1494 = 14.94\%$$

Because the maturity of the bank loan is 1 year, the effective annual rate (EAR) is also 14.94 percent.

Effective cost of the trade credit:

Terms: 2/10, net 30. But the firm plans delaying payments 35 additional days, which is the equivalent of 2/10, net 65. Therefore, Gallinger plans to use its funds for an additional 55 days beyond the discount period, and the EAR of delaying payment is:

$$\frac{\text{Interest rate}}{\text{per period}} = \frac{0.02}{0.98} = 0.02041 = 2.041\%$$

$$\text{EAR} = (1 + 0.02041)^{\frac{360}{55}} - 1.0 = 0.1414 = 14.14\%$$

Comparing interest costs, Gallinger Corporation might be tempted to expand its payables rather than obtain financing from a bank.

b. The interest rate comparison favors trade credit. But Gallinger Corporation should take into account how its trade creditors would look upon being 35 days delinquent in making payments. Gallinger would become a "slow pay" account, and in times when suppliers were operating at full capacity, Gallinger would be given poor service and would also be forced to pay on time.

ST-4   Under the current credit policy, the Boca Grande Company has no discounts, has collection expenses of $50,000, has bad debt losses of (0.02)($10,000,000) = $200,000, and has average accounts receivable of (DSO)(Average sales per day) = (30)($10,000,000/360) = $833,333. The firm's cost of carrying these receivables is (Variable cost ratio)(A/R)(Cost of capital) = (0.80)($833,333)(0.16) = $106,667. It is necessary to multiply by the variable cost ratio because the actual *investment* in receivables is less than the dollar amount of the receivables.

Proposal 1: Lengthen the credit period to net 30 so that

1. Sales increase by $1 million.
2. Discounts = $0.
3. Bad debt losses = (0.03)($10,000,000) = $300,000
4. DSO = 45 days on all sales.
5. New average receivables = (45)($11,000,000/360) = $1,375,000.
6. Cost of carrying receivables = (V)(k)(Average accounts receivable)
$$= (0.80)(0.16)($1,375,000)$$
$$= $176,000.$$
7. Collection expenses = $50,000.

Analysis of proposed change:

	Income Statement under Current Policy	Income Statement under New Policy	Effect of Change
Gross sales	$10,000,000	$11,000,000	$1,000,000
Less discounts	(0)	(0)	(0)
Net sales	10,000,000	11,000,000	1,000,000
Production costs (80%)	(8,000,000)	(8,800,000)	(800,000)
Profit before credit costs and taxes	2,000,000	2,200,000	200,000
Credit-related costs			
Cost of carrying receivables	(106,667)	(176,000)	(69,333)
Collection expenses	(50,000)	(50,000)	(0)
Bad debt losses	(200,000)	(300,000)	(100,000)
Profit before taxes	1,643,333	1,674,000	30,667
Taxes (40%)	(657,333)	(669,600)	(12,267)
Net income	$ 986,000	$ 1,004,400	$ 18,400

The proposed change appears to be a good one, assuming the assumptions are correct.

Proposal 2: Shorten the credit period to net 20 so that

1. Sales decrease by $1 million.
2. Discount = $0.
3. Bad debt losses = (0.01)($9,000,000) = $90,000.
4. DSO = 22 days.
5. New average receivables = (22)($9,000,000/360) = $550,000.
6. Cost of carrying receivables = (V)(k)(Average accounts receivable)
$$= (0.80)(0.16)(\$550,000)$$
$$= \$70,400.$$
7. Collection expenses = $50,000.

Analysis of proposed change:

	Income Statement under Current Policy	Income Statement under New Policy	Effect of Change
Gross sales	$10,000,000	$9,000,000	($1,000,000)
Less discounts	(0)	(0)	(0)
Net sales	$10,000,000	$9,000,000	($1,000,000)
Production costs (80%)	(8,000,000)	(7,200,000)	800,000
Profit before credit costs and taxes	$2,000,000	$1,800,000	($200,000)
Credit-related costs			
Cost of carrying receivables	(106,667)	(70,400)	36,267
Collection expenses	(50,000)	(50,000)	(0)
Bad debt losses	(200,000)	(90,000)	110,000
Profit before taxes	$ 1,643,333	$1,589,600	($ 53,733)
Taxes (40%)	(657,333)	(635,840)	21,493
Net income	$ 986,000	$ 953,760	($ 32,240)

This change reduces net income, so it should be rejected. Boca Grande will increase profits by accepting Proposal 1 to lengthen the credit period from 25 days to 30 days, assuming all assumptions are correct. This may or may not be the *optimal,* or profit-maximizing, credit policy, but it does appear to be a movement in the right direction.

ST-5 *a.*

$$EOQ = \sqrt{\frac{2(O)(T)}{(C)(PP)}}$$

$$= \sqrt{\frac{(2)(\$5,000)(2,600,000)}{(0.02)(\$5.00)}}$$

$$= 509,902 \text{ bushels.}$$

Because the firm must order in multiples of 2,000 bushels, it should order in quantities of 510,000 bushels.

b.

$$\text{Average weekly sales} = 2,600,000/52$$

$$= 50,000 \text{ bushels.}$$

$$\text{Reorder point} = 3 \text{ weeks' sales}$$

$$= 3(50,000)$$

$$= 150,000 \text{ bushels.}$$

c. Total inventory costs:

$$\text{TIC} = [(\text{C})\text{PP}]\left(\frac{Q}{2}\right) + O\left(\frac{T}{Q}\right)$$

$$= [(0.02)(\$5)]\left(\frac{510,000}{2}\right) + (\$5,000)\left(\frac{2,600,000}{510,000}\right)$$

$$= \$25,500 + \$25,490.20$$

$$= \$50,990.20.$$

Chapter 13

ST-2 Billingsworth paid $2 in dividends and retained $2 per share. Since total retained earnings rose by $12 million, there must be 6 million shares outstanding. With a book value of $40 per share, total common equity must be $40(6 million) = $240 million. Because Billingsworth has $120 million of debt, its debt ratio must be 33.3 percent:

$$\frac{\text{Debt}}{\text{Assets}} = \frac{\text{Debt}}{\text{Debt} + \text{Equity}} = \frac{\$120 \text{ million}}{\$120 \text{ million} + \$240 \text{ million}}$$

$$= 0.333 = 33.3\%.$$

ST-3 **a.** In answering questions such as this, always begin by writing down the relevant definitional equations, then start filling in numbers. Note that the extra zeros indicating millions have been deleted in the calculations below.

(1)
$$\text{DSO} = \frac{\text{Accounts receivable}}{\text{Sales}/360}$$

$$40 = \frac{\text{A/R}}{\$1,000/360}$$

$$\text{A/R} = 40(\$2.778) = \$111.1 \text{ million.}$$

(2)
$$\text{Quick ratio} = \frac{\text{Current assets} - \text{Inventories}}{\text{Current liabilities}} = 2.0$$

$$= \frac{\text{Cash and marketable securities} + \text{A/R}}{\text{Current liabilities}} = 2.0$$

$$2.0 = \frac{\$100 + \$111.1}{\text{Current liabilities}}$$

$$\text{Current liabilities} = (\$100 + \$111.1)/2 = \$105.6 \text{ million.}$$

(3)
$$\text{Current ratio} = \frac{\text{Current assets}}{\text{Current liabilities}} = 3.0$$

$$= \frac{\text{Current assets}}{\$105.6} = 3.0$$

$$\text{Current assets} = 3.0(\$105.6) = \$316.7 \text{ million.}$$

(4)   Total assets = Current assets + Fixed assets

$$= \$316.7 + \$283.5 = \$600.1 \text{ million.}$$

(5) $$\text{ROA} = \frac{\text{Net income}}{\text{Total assets}}$$

$$= \frac{\$50}{\$600.1} = 0.0833 = 8.33\%.$$

(6) $$\text{ROE} = \frac{\text{NI}}{\text{Equity}}$$

$$12.0\% = \frac{\$50}{\text{Equity}}$$

$$\text{Equity} = \frac{\$50}{0.12}$$

$$= \$416.7 \text{ million.}$$

(7)   Total assets = Total liabilities = $600.1 million

Current liabilities + Long-term debt + Equity = $600.1 million

$105.6 + Long-term debt + $416.7 = $600.1 million

Long-term debt = $600.1 − $105.6 − $416.7 = $77.8 million.

b. Kaiser's average sales per day were $1,000/360 = $2.8 million. Its DSO was 40, so A/R = 40($2.8) = $111.1 million. Its new DSO of 30 would cause A/R = 30($2.8) = $83.3 million. The reduction in receivables would be $111.1 − $83.3 = $27.8 million, which would equal the amount of cash generated.

(1)   New equity = Old equity − Stock bought back

$$= \$416.7 - \$27.8$$

$$= \$388.9 \text{ million.}$$

Thus,

$$\text{New ROE} = \frac{\text{Net income}}{\text{New equity}}$$

$$= \frac{\$50}{\$388.9}$$

$$= 12.86\% \text{ (versus old ROE of 12.0\%).}$$

(2) $$\text{New ROA} = \frac{\text{Net income}}{\text{Total assets} - \text{Reduction in A/R}}$$

$$= \frac{\$50}{\$600.1 - \$27.8}$$

$$= 8.74\% \text{ (versus old ROA of 8.33\%).}$$

(3) The old debt is the same as the new debt:

$$\text{Debt} = \text{Total liabilities} - \text{Equity} = \text{Current liabilities} + \text{Long-term debt}$$

$$= \$600.1 - \$416.7 = \$183.4 \text{ million} = \$105.6 + \$77.8$$

Old total assets = \$600.1 million.

New total assets = Old total assets − Reduction in A/R

$$= \$600.1 - \$27.8$$

$$= \$572.3 \text{ million.}$$

Therefore,

$$\frac{\text{Debt}}{\text{Old total assets}} = \frac{\$183.4}{\$600.1} = 30.6\%,$$

while

$$\frac{\text{New debt}}{\text{New total assets}} = \frac{\$183.4}{\$572.3} = 32.0\%.$$

Chapter 14

ST-2 *a.* (1) Determine the variable cost per unit at present, using the following definitions and equations:

$$Q = \text{units of output (sales)} = 5{,}000.$$

$$P = \text{average sales price per unit of output} = \$100.$$

$$F = \text{fixed operating costs} = \$200{,}000.$$

$$V = \text{variable costs per unit.}$$

$$\text{EBIT} = P(Q) - F - V(Q)$$

$$\$50{,}000 = \$100(5{,}000) - \$200{,}000 - V(5{,}000)$$

$$5{,}000V = \$250{,}000$$

$$V = \$50.$$

(2) Determine the new EBIT level if the change is made:

$$\text{New EBIT} = P_2(Q_2) - F_2 - V_2(Q_2)$$

$$= \$95(7{,}000) - \$250{,}000 - \$40(7{,}000)$$

$$= \$135{,}000.$$

(3) Determine the incremental EBIT:

$$\Delta \text{EBIT} = \$135{,}000 - \$50{,}000 = \$85{,}000.$$

(4) Estimate the approximate rate of return on the new investment:

$$\Delta ROA = \frac{\Delta EBIT}{Investment} = \frac{\$85,000}{\$400,000} = 21.25\%.$$

Because the ROA exceeds Olinde's average cost of capital, which is 10 percent, this analysis suggests that Olinde should go ahead and make the investment.

b.
$$DOL = \frac{Q(P - V)}{Q(P - V) - F}$$

$$DOL_{Old} = \frac{5,000(\$100 - \$50)}{5,000(\$100 - \$50) - \$200,000} = 5.00.$$

$$DOL_{New} = \frac{7,000(\$95 - \$40)}{7,000(\$95 - \$40) - \$250,000} = 2.85.$$

This indicates that operating income will be less sensitive to changes in sales if the production process is changed; thus the change would reduce risks. However, the change would increase the breakeven point. Still, with a lower sales price, it might be easier to achieve the higher new breakeven volume.

$$Old: Q_{BE} = \frac{F}{P - V} = \frac{\$200,000}{\$100 - \$50} = 4,000 \text{ units.}$$

$$New: Q_{BE} = \frac{F}{P_2 - V_2} = \frac{\$250,000}{\$95 - \$40} = 4,545 \text{ units.}$$

c. The incremental ROA is:

$$\Delta ROA = \frac{\Delta Profit}{\Delta Sales} \times \frac{\Delta Sales}{\Delta Assets}.$$

Using debt financing, the incremental profit associated with the investment is equal to the incremental profit found in Part a minus the interest expense incurred as a result of the investment:

$$\Delta Profit = \text{New profit} - \text{Old profit} - \text{Interest}$$

$$= \$135,000 - \$50,000 - 0.08(\$400,000)$$

$$= \$53,000.$$

The incremental sales is calculated as:

$$\Delta Sales = P_2Q_2 - P_1Q_1$$

$$= \$95(7,000) - \$100(5,000)$$

$$= \$665,000 - \$500,000$$

$$= \$165,000.$$

$$ROA = \frac{\$53,000}{\$165,000} \times \frac{\$165,000}{\$400,000} = 13.25\%.$$

The return on the new equity investment still exceeds the average cost of funds (10%), so Olinde should make the investment.

d.
$$DFL = \frac{EBIT}{EBIT - I}$$

$$DFL_{New} = \frac{\$135,000}{\$135,000 - \$32,000}$$

Chapter 15

ST-2 **a.** Number of shares $= \dfrac{\$19,800}{\$120} = 165$ shares

If $P_1 = \$150$,

$$HPR = \frac{(\$150 - \$120)165}{\$19,800} = \frac{\$4,950}{\$19,800} = 0.250 = 25.0\%.$$

If $P_1 = \$105$,

$$HPR = \frac{(\$105 - \$120)165}{\$19,800} = \frac{-\$2,475}{\$19,800} = -0.125 = -12.5\%.$$

b. If Lance borrowed the maximum amount allowed, he could purchase $36,000 worth of Microsoft stock.

$$\frac{\text{Maximum that}}{\text{can be invested}} = \frac{\$19,800}{\text{Margin requirement}}$$

$$= \frac{\$19,800}{0.55} = \$36,000.$$

Thus, Lance can purchase $36,000/$120 = 300 shares of Microsoft.

Because Lance borrows $36,000(1 − 0.55) = $16,200, he will have to pay interest equal to $16,200 × 0.12 = $1,944 at the end of the year. Therefore, the return he will earn if Microsoft's price is $150 or $105 at the end of the year is

If $P_1 = \$150$,

$$HPR = \frac{(\$150 - \$120)300 - \$1,944}{\$19,800}$$

$$= \frac{\$7,056}{\$19,800} = 0.356 = 35.6\%.$$

If $P_1 = \$105$,

$$HPR = \frac{(\$105 - \$120)300 - \$1,944}{\$19,800}$$

$$= \frac{-\$6,444}{\$19,800} = -0.325 = -32.5\%.$$

c.

$$\frac{\text{Margin}}{\text{call price}} = \frac{\text{Amount borrowed}}{(\text{Number of shares})\left(1 - \dfrac{\text{Maintenance}}{\text{margin}}\right)}$$

$$= \frac{\$16,200}{300(1 - 0.40)} = \$90.00.$$

ST-3 a. The annual return is computed as follows:

$$\frac{\text{Annual}}{\text{return}} = \frac{P_1 - P_0}{P_0}.$$

Thus, the 1996 return for Mateo Computers is:

$$\frac{\text{Mateo Computers'}}{1996 \text{ return}} = \frac{\$2,400 - \$2,000}{\$2,000} = \frac{\$400}{\$2,000} = 0.20 = 20\%.$$

Using the same approach, the annual returns for the stocks are:

	1996	1997	1998	1999
Mateo Computers	20.0%	15.0%	−10.0%	50.0%
Northern Water	2.5	19.5	15.0	20.0
AMN Motors	−10.0	20.0	25.0	4.0
Farley Argicorp	−5.0	20.0	10.0	0.0
Portfolio	2.5	18.6	8.8	18.3

The 4-year HPR for Mateo Computers is

$$\frac{\text{Mateo Computers'}}{4\text{-year HPR}} = \frac{P_{1/31/99} - P_{1/1/96}}{P_{1/1/96}}$$

$$= \frac{\$3,726 - \$2,000}{\$2,000} = \frac{\$1,726}{\$2,000} = 0.863 = 86.3\%.$$

The 4-year HPRs for the other companies and the portfolio are:

Northern Water = \$ 6,762/\$ 4,000 − 1 = 69.1%
AMN Motors   = \$ 1,404/\$ 1,000 − 1 = 40.4%
Farley Argicorp = \$ 3,762/\$ 3,000 − 1 = 25.4%
Portfolio   = \$15,654/\$10,000 − 1 = 56.5%

b. The weights for the stocks each year are computed by dividing the market value of the stock by the market value of the portfolio.

1996 Weights
Mateo Computers = \$ 2,000/\$10,000 =   20.0%
Northern Water = \$ 4,000/\$10,000 =   40.0%
AMN Motors   = \$ 1,000/\$10,000 =   10.0%
Farley Argicorp = \$ 3,000/\$10,000 =   30.0%
Portfolio   = \$10,000/\$10,000 = 100.0%

1997 Weights

Mateo Computers = $ 2,400/$10,250 = 23.4%
Northern Water = $ 4,100/$10,250 = 40.0%
AMN Motors   = $ 900/$10,250 = 8.8%
Farley Argicorp = $ 2,850/$10,250 = 27.8%
Portfolio   = $10,250/$10,250 = 100.0%

1998 Weights

Mateo Computers = $ 2,760/$12,160 = 22.7%
Northern Water = $ 4,900/$12,160 = 40.3%
AMN Motors   = $ 1,080/$12,160 = 8.9%
Farley Argicorp = $ 3,420/$12,160 = 28.1%
Portfolio   = $12,160/$12,160 = 100.0%

1999 Weights

Mateo Computers = $ 2,484/$13,231 = 18.8%
Northern Water = $ 5,635/$13,231 = 42.6%
AMN Motors   = $ 1,350/$13,231 = 10.2%
Farley Argicorp = $ 3,762/$13,231 = 28.4%
Portfolio   = $13,231/$13,231 = 100.0%

c. The 4-year HPR and the annual returns for the portfolio based on the market values given in the table are shown with the above computations. Using the weights for each stock each year to compute the annual returns, we have:

$$1996 \text{ portfolio return} = 20.0\%(0.20) + 2.5\%(0.40) + (-10.0\%)(0.10) \\ + (-5.0\%)(0.30) = 2.5\%.$$

$$1997 \text{ portfolio return} = 15.0\%(0.234) + 19.5\%(0.400) + 20.0\%(0.088) \\ + 20.0\%(0.278) = 18.6\%.$$

$$1998 \text{ portfolio return} = (-10.0\%)(0.227) + 15.0\%(0.403) + 25.0\%(0.089) \\ + 10.0\%(0.281) = 8.8\%.$$

$$1999 \text{ portfolio return} = 50.0\%(0.188) + 20.0\%(0.426) + 4.0\%(0.102) \\ + 0.0\%(0.284) = 18.3\%.$$

These results are the same as reported earlier. Using this same method, the 4-year HPR is

$$4\text{-year HPR} = 86.3\%(0.20) + 69.1\%(0.40) + 40.4\%(0.10) + 25.4\%(0.30) \\ = 56.6\% \text{ (rounding difference)}.$$

Chapter 16

ST-2 *a.* If $k_d = 10.0\%$, $k_s = 15.0\%$, $T = 40.0\%$, and Debt/assets = 65.0%,

$$WACC = [10.0\%(1 - 0.40)](0.65) + 15.0\%(0.35) = 9.15\%.$$

b.
$$EVA = EBIT(1 - T) - (WACC \times \text{Invested capital}) \\ = \$600,000(1 - 0.40) - (0.0915 \times \$2,000,000) \\ = \$360,000 - \$183,000 \\ = \$177,000.$$

c.
$$\text{EVA dividend} = \text{EVA}/(\text{Shares outstanding})$$
$$= \$177,000/100,000$$
$$= \$1.77.$$

d. First, we must compute the net income for American Transmitter.

EBIT	$600,000
Interest[a]	(130,000)
Earnings before taxes	470,000
Taxes (40%)	(188,000)
Net income	$282,000

[a]Remember $k_d = 10.0\%$. But, to compute interest, we need to know the amount of debt, which equals $\$2,000,000 \times 0.65 = \$1,300,000$. Therefore, the annual interest expense is $\$1,300,000 \times 0.10 = \$130,000$.

$$\text{EPS} = (\text{Net income})/(\text{Shares outstanding})$$
$$= \$282,000/100,000$$
$$= \$2.82.$$

$$\hat{P}_0 = \text{EPS} \times \text{P/E}$$
$$= \$2.82 \times 15$$
$$= \$42.30.$$

ST-3   a. The average price for the first series, Day 1 through Day 5, is computed as follows:

$$\frac{\text{Average price for}}{\text{Day 1 through Day 5}} = \frac{\$76.00 + \$76.50 + \$76.75 + \$77.10 + \$77.20}{5}$$

$$= \$76.71.$$

The average price for each 5-day period is computed as a simple average such as above. The results are given in the following table:

Series	5-day Period	Average
1	Day 1 - Day 5	$76.71
2	Day 2 - Day 6	77.08
3	Day 3 - Day 7	77.42
4	Day 4 - Day 8	77.66
5	Day 5 - Day 9	77.82
6	Day 6 - Day 10	78.00

b. If you plot the series of 5-day moving averages, you will find that the line is upward sloping, which suggests the stock price is trending upward.

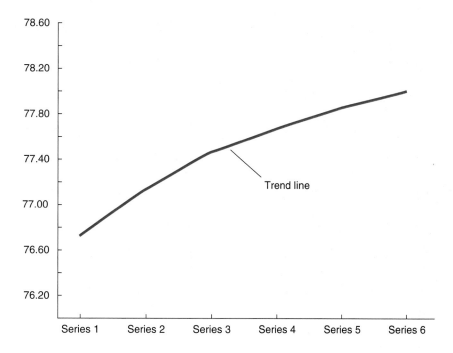

APPENDIX C

Answers to End-of-Chapter Problems

We present here some intermediate steps and final answers to selected end-of-chapter problems. Please note that your answer may differ slightly from ours due to rounding errors. Also, although we hope not, some of the problems may have more than one correct solution, depending upon what assumptions are made in working the problem. Finally, many of the problems involve some verbal discussion as well as numerical calculations; this verbal material is not presented here.

2-1 *a.* $1,050,000.
    b. ($3,450,000).

2-2 *a.* $k_1 = 9.20\%$; $k_5 = 7.20\%$.

2-4 *a.* 4.8%.
    b. 6.8%.
    c. 5-yr bond = 7.3%.

2-5 600,000 shares.

2-6 *a.* k_1 in Year 2 = 13%.

2-7 k_1 in Year 2 = 15%; Year 2 inflation = 11%.

2-8 6.0%.

3-1 *a.* 4.5%.
    b. 5.5%.
    c. $444.4 billion.

3-2 *a.* $20 billion.
    b. $12 billion.

3-3 *a.* $451 billion.
    b. $2.951 trillion.
    c. $3.0 billion.
    d. $95.1 billion.

3-4 *a.* $225 billion.
    b. 25.0%.
    c. −$150 billion.

3-5 $1,035 billion.

3-6 *a.* $2,280 billion.
    c. $120 billion.
    d. $0.

3-7 *a.* −$2,280 billion.
    b. −$1,080 billion.

3-8 $12 billion.

3-9 $55.8 million.

4-1 *a.* ≈7,930 bonds.
    b. Annual debt service = $0.

4-2 *b.* 20,000 shares.
    d. $EPS_{Meyer} = \$2.52$; $EPS_{Haugen} = \$2.50$.

4-3 *a.* $20.

4-4 *c.* Alternative 1 EPS = $0.60;
        Alternative 2 EPS = $0.64.
    d. Alternative 2.

4-5 *a.* +$300.
    b. −$200.
    c. At $P_0 = \$18$, −$300; at $P_0 = \$13$, +$200.

4-6 *b.* $4,252,500.
    c. At $0.60/mark, cost = $4,500,000;
        at $0.54/mark, cost = $4,050,000.

5-2 $Tax_{1999} = \$0$; Initial $tax_{2001} = \$4,500$;
    Initial $tax_{2002} = \$15,450$; Final $tax_{2001} = \$0$.

5-3 *a.* 2000 advantage as a corporation = $500.50.
2001 advantage = $3,100.50.
2002 advantage = $4,400.50

5-4 *a.* Personal tax = $18,608.50.
c. IBM after-tax yield = 7.59%;
choose the Florida bonds.
d. 18.18%.

5-5 *a.* Personal tax = $5,913.50.
b. Loan interest is not tax deductible.

5-6 *a.* Taxes = $14,052.50.
b. Taxes = $6,262.50.

5-7 *a.* Tax = $61,250.
b. Tax = $15,600.
c. Tax = $4,680.

5-8 Tax = $107,855; Net income = $222,145;
Average tax rate = 33.76%.

5-9 *a.* Tax = $155.
b. Tax = $300.
c. Tax = $2,430.

5-10 *a.* Tax = $40.
b. Tax = $40.
c. Tax = $70.

6-1 *a.* $530.
d. $445.

6-2 *a.* $895.40.
b. $1,552.90.
c. $279.20.
d. $500.03; $867.14.

6-3 *a.* ≈ 10 years.
c. ≈ 4 years.

6-4 *a.* $6,374.96.
d. (1) $7,012.46.

6-5 *a.* $2,457.84.
c. $2,000.
d. (1) $2,703.62.

6-6 *a.* Stream A: $1,251.21.

6-7 *b.* 7%.
c. 9%.
d. 15%.

6-8 *a.* $881.15.
b. $895.40.
c. $903.05.
d. $908.35.

6-9 *b.* $279.20.
c. $276.85.
d. $443.70.

6-10 *a.* $5,272.40.
b. $5,374.00.

6-11 *a.* 1st City = 7%; 2nd City = 6.66%.

6-12 *a.* PMT = $6,594.94.
b. $13,189.87.

6-13 *a.* Z = 9%; B = 8%.
b. Z = $558.39; $135.98; 32.2%; B = $548.33;
$48.33; 9.7%.

6-14 *a.* $61,203.
b. $11,020.
c. $6,841.

6-15 *a.* $176,792.
b. $150,257.

6-16 PV of $2,000 = $911.20.

6-17 *a.* 15% (or 14.87%).

6-18 APR = 8.0%; EAR = 8.24%.

6-19 12%.

6-20 9%.

6-21 *a.* $50,808.
b. $39,364.74 and $0.

6-22 $1,808.32.

6-23 ≈ 15 years.

6-24 5 years; $1,885.09.

6-25 $PV_{7\%}$ = $1,428.57;
$PV_{14\%}$ = $714.29.

6-26 $984.88 ≈ $985.

6-27 $1,901.

6-28 *a.* $260.73.
b. $263.34.

6-29 k_{SIMPLE} = 15.19%.

6-30 $4,971.

7-1 *a.* $1,251.26.
b. $898.90.

7-2 *a.* $1,250.
b. $833.33
d. At 8%, V_d = $1,196.31.

7-3 *b.* PV = $5.29.
d. $30.01.

7-4 *a.* 7%.
b. 5%.
c. 12%.

7-5 *a.* (1) $9.50.
(2) $13.33.
b. (1) Undefined.

7-6 *a.* $7.20.
b. $41.60.
c. $35.28.

7-7 **a.** $1,000.
    b. IBM = $812.59; GM = $711.89.
    d. 5.0%.

7-8 **a.** Dividend 2002 = $2.66.
    b. P_0 = $39.42.
    c. Dividend yield 2000 = 5.10%; 2004 = 7.00%.

7-9 **a.** P_0 = $54.11.

7-10 **a.** P_0 = $21.43.
    b. P_0 = $26.47.
    d. P_0 = $40.54.

7-11 **a.** V_L at 5 percent = $1,518.97; V_L at 8 percent = $1,171.15; V_L at 12 percent = $863.79.

7-12 **a.** 8.02%.

7-13 **a.** YTM at $829 ≈ 15%.

7-14 **a.** 13.3%.
    b. 10%.
    c. 8%.
    d. 5.7%.

7-15 $23.75.

7-16 $25.03.

7-17 IBM bond = 9.33%.

7-18 10.2%.

7-19 P_0 = $19.89.

7-20 **a.** $53,410.60.
    b. $49,601.50.

8-1 **a.** $0.5 million.

8-2 **a.** 13.5%.
    b. 1.8.
    c. k_F = 8% + 5.5%β_F.
    d. 17.9%.

8-3 **a.** $\bar{k}_A$ = 11.30%.
    c. σ_A = 20.8%; σ_P = 20.1%.

8-4 **a.** $\hat{k}_M$ = 13.5%; $\hat{k}_J$ = 11.6%.
    b. σ_M = 3.85%; σ_J = 6.22%.
    c. CV_M = 0.29; CV_J = 0.54.

8-5 **a.** $\hat{k}_Y$ = 14%.
    b. σ_X = 12.20%.

8-6 **a.** β_B = 2.
    b. k_B = 12.5%.

8-7 **a.** k_X = 15.5%.
    b. (1) k_X = 16.5%.
    c. (1) k_X = 18.1%.

8-8 β_{New} = 1.16.

8-9 β_p = 0.7625; k_p = 12.1%.

8-10 4.5%.

9-1 **b.** NPV = $7,486.20.
    d. DPP = 6.51 yrs.

9-2 **b.** IRR_A = 17.8%; IRR_B = 24.0%.

9-3 **a.** IRR_A = 20%; IRR_B = 16.7%; Crossover rate ≈ 16%.

9-4 **a.** NPV_A = $14,486,808; NPV_B = $11,156,893; IRR_A = 15.03%; IRR_B = 22.26%.

9-5 **a.** ($178,000).
    b. $52,440; $60,600; $40,200.
    c. $48,760.
    d. ($19,544).

9-6 **a.** ($126,000).
    b. $42,560; $47,477; $35,186.
    c. $51,268.
    d. $11,389.

9-7 **a.** ($52,000).
    b. $18,560; $22,400; $12,800; $10,240.
    c. $1,500.
    d. $1,021.

9-8 **a.** ($776,000).
    b. $199,000; $255,400; $194,300; $161,400; $156,700.
    c. $115,200.
    d. $436.77.

9-9 **a.** Expected CF_A = $6,750; σ_A = $474.34; CV_A = 0.0703.
    b. NPV_A = $10,037.

9-10 **a.** 14%.

9-11 NPV_T = $409; IRR_T = 15%; Accept; NPV_P = $3,318; IRR_P = 20%; Accept.

9-12 NPV_E = $3,861; IRR_E = 18%; NPV_G = $3,057; IRR_G = 18%; Purchase electric-powered forklift; it has a higher NPV.

9-13 NPV_S = $448.86; NPV_L = $263.89; IRR_S = 15.24%; IRR_L = 14.29%.

9-14 **a.** PV_C = −$556,717; PV_F = −$493,407; Forklift should be chosen.

9-15 IRR_Q = 15.6%; NPV_Q = $92.89.

9-16 Accept Project Y; NPV_Y = $886.21.

9-17 NPV = $15,301.

9-18 NPV = $22,329.

9-19 **a.** 16%.
    b. NPV = $411; accept.

9-20 **a.** 15%.
    b. New β_{Firm} = 1.48; new k_{Firm} = 15.4%; new $k_{Division}$ = 17%.

10-1 **a.** 16.3%.
    b. 15.4%.
    c. 16%.

10-2 **a.** 8%.
    b. $2.81.
    c. 15.8%.

10-3 **a.** $18 million.
    b. BP = $45 million.
    c. BP_1 = $20 million; BP_2 = $40 million.

10-4 **a.** g = 3%.
    b. EPS = $5.562.

10-5 **a.** $67,500,000.
    c. k_s = 12%; k_e = 12.4%.
    d. $27,000,000.
    e. $WACC_1$ = 9%; $WACC_2$ = 9.2%.

10-6 **a.** k_{dT} = 5.4%; k_s = 14.6%.
    b. WACC = 10.92%.
    d. WACC = 11.36%.

10-7 **a.** 3 breaks; BP_{D_1} = $1,111,111;
    BP_{RE} = $1,818,182; BP_{D_2} = $2,000,000.
    b. $WACC_1$ = 10.96%;
    $WACC_2$ = 11.50%;
    $WACC_3$ = 12.14%;
    $WACC_4$ = 12.68%.
    c. IRR_1 = 16%; IRR_3 = 14%.

10-8 **a.** 13%.
    b. 10.4%.
    c. 8.58%.

10-9 7.92%.

10-10 11.94%.

10-11 **a.** F = 10%.
    b. k_e = 15.8%.

10-12 WACC = 12.72%.

10-13 $10 million.

10-14 $42,000.

10-15 $62,000.

10-16 **a.** 14.40%.
    b. 10.62%.

10-17 7.2%.

10-18 k_e = 16.5%.

11-1 **a.** $5.10.

11-2 **a.** EPS_{Old} = $2.04; New: EPS_D = $4.74;
    EPS_S = $3.27.
    b. 33,975 units.
    c. $Q_{New,Debt}$ = 27,225 units.

11-3 Debt used: E(EPS) = $5.78; σ_{EPS} = $1.05;
    E(TIE) = 3.49×.

Stock used: E(EPS) = $5.51; σ_{EPS} = $0.85;
E(TIE) = 6.00×.

11-4 **a.** (1) $3,960,000.
    (2) $4,800,000.
    (3) $9,360,000.
    (4) Regular = $3,960,000;
        Extra = $5,400,000.
    c. 15%.
    d. 15%.

11-5 **a.** PO = 63.16%; BP = $9.55 million;
    $WACC_1$ = 10.67%; $WACC_2$ = 10.96%.
    b. $15 million.

11-6 **a.** ROE_{LL} = 14.6%; ROE_{HL} = 16.8%.
    b. ROE_{LL} = 16.5%.

11-7 No leverage: $\widehat{ROE}$ = 10.5%; σ = 5.4%;
    CV = 0.51; 60% leverage: $\widehat{ROE}$ = 13.7%;
    σ = 13.5%; CV = 0.99.

11-8 $3,250,000.

11-9 Payout = 52%.

11-10 Payout = 31.39%.

12-1 **a.** $1,600,000.
    c. Bank = $1,200,000; books = −$5,200,000.

12-2 **b.** $420,000.
    c. $35,000.

12-3 Alternative 1 EAR = 10.50%;
    Alternative 3 EAR = 9.56%.

12-4 **a.** 11.73%.
    b. 12.09%.

12-5 ΔNI = +$13,350.

12-6 **a.** DSO_O = 27.0 days; DSO_N = 22.5 days.
    b. D_O = $15,680; D_N = $38,220.
    c. C_O = $10,125; C_N = $10,969.
    e. ΔNI = +$68,770.

12-7 EOQ = 1,000.

12-8 **a.** EOQ = 5,200.
    b. 65.
    c. 6,500.
    d. (3) TIC = $6,304.

12-9 **a.** 72 days.
    b. $396,000.
    c. Decrease to 57 days.

12-10 **a.** 12%.
    b. 11.25%.
    c. 11.48%.

12-11 N/P EAR = 13.64%.

12-12 **a.** Net float = $30,000.
    b. $16,000.

12-13 *a.* DSO = 28 days.
     b. $70,000.

12-14 ΔNI = ($60,578).

12-15 $70.

12-16 *a.* EOQ = 3,873.
     b. 5,073 bags.
     c. 3,137 bags.
     d. Every 6 days.

13-1 *a.* Current ratio = 3.81×; DSO = 40.14 days;
     TA turnover = 4.10×; Debt ratio = 48%.

13-2 *a.* Current ratio = 1.98×; DSO = 75 days; Total
     assets turnover = 1.7×; Debt ratio = 61.9%.

13-3 A/P = $90,000; Inv = $67,500; FA = $160,500.

13-4 *b.* Net profit margin = 3.4%;
     TA turnover = 1.77×; ROA = 6.0%.

13-5 *a.* Quick ratio = 0.85×; DSO = 37 days; ROE =
     13.1%; Debt ratio = 54.8%.

13-6 ΔShares = +4.5 million; CS = $79.50;
     Paid-in capital = $464.25; RE = $956.25.

13-7 $\dfrac{\text{NI}}{\text{S}} = 2\%; \dfrac{\text{D}}{\text{A}} = 40\%.$

13-8 $262,500; 1.19×.

13-9 Sales = $2,511,628; DSO = 37 days.

13-10 TIE = 3.5×.

13-11 ROE = 24.5%; ROA = 9.8%.

13-12 *a.* +5.54%.
     b. (2) +3.21%.

13-13 Total sources = $102; Net increase in cash and
marketable securities = $19.

13-14 *a.* NI = $900,000; CF = $2,400,000.
     b. CF = $3,000,000.

13-15 $3.44.

14-1 *a.* Notes payable = $31.44 million.
     b. Current ratio = 2.00×; ROE = 14.2%.
     c. (1) −$14.28 million.
        (2) Total assets = $147 million; Notes
            payable = $3.72 million.
        (3) Current ratio = 4.25×; ROE = 10.84%.

14-2 *a.* Total assets = $33,534; AFN = $2,128.
     b. Notes payable = $4,228; AFN = $70;
     ΔInterest = $213.

14-3 *a.* DOL = 2.5; DFL = 3.0.

14-4 *a.* First pass AFN = $667.
     b. Increase in notes payable = $51; Increase in
     CS = $368.

14-5 *a.* (1) −$60,000.
     b. Q_{OpBE} = 14,000.
     c. (1) −1.33.

14-6 *a.* (2) $125,000.
     b. Q_{OpBE} = 7,000.

14-7 *a.* $2,000.
     b. DFL = 1.8.
     c. $3,000.

14-8 *a.* December = ($4,400); February = $2,000.
     b. $164,400.

14-9 *b.* October loan = $22,800;
     November investment = $118,500.

14-10 *a.* (1) −$75,000.
        (2) $175,000.
     b. Q_{OpBE} = 140,000.
     c. (1) −8.3.
        (2) 15.0.
        (3) 5.0.

14-11 *a.* FC_A = $80,000; VC_A = $4.80/unit; P_A =
     $8.00/unit.

14-12 *a.* $480,000.
     b. $18,750.

14-13 AFN = $360.

14-14 *a.* 40,000.
     b. ($0.30).
     c. 48,000.
     d. DOL = 3.0; DFL = 1.7; $EPS_{\$270,000}$ = $0.225.

15-1 *a.* $2,760.
     b. 46%.
     c. Capital gains = 40%; Dividend yield = 6%.

15-2 *a.* $375.
     b. 15%.
     d. 15%.

15-3 *a.* $\overline{K}_A$ = 16.58%.
     b. K_G = 15.80%.
     c. FV_{1999} = $4,164.60.

15-4 *a.* $k_{\text{p, 1997}}$ = 5%; $k_{\text{S\&P 1997}}$ = 31.01%.
     b. $\overline{K}_{A, P}$ = 18.00%; $\overline{K}_{A, \text{S\&P500}}$ = 19.24%.
     c. $\overline{K}_{G, P}$ = 17.41%; $\overline{K}_{G, \text{S\&P500}}$ = 18.61%.

15-5 *a.* −$1,500.
     b. +$1,000.

15-6 *a.* 29.283%.
     b. 43.938%.

15-7 *a.* 22.7%.
     b. $12,000.
     c. 29.1%.
     d. −34.9%.

15-8 *a.* $9,616.00.
     b. 60.1%.
     c. 17%.

15-9   **a.** −34.8%.
     b. −23.7%.
     c. 77.5%.
     d. 244.2%.

15-10   **a.** $k_{W,2}$ = 1.57%.
     b. $k_{V,1}$ = 7.67%.

15-11   **b.** −$2,000.

15-12   **a.** $3,500.
     b. $2.31.
     d. −34.6%.

15-13   **a.** 14.0%.

15-14   **a.** Amount invested in Randicorp = $20,000.
     b. 10.675%.
     c. 9.74%.

16-1   **a.** (2) P_0 = $26.25.

16-2   **a.** 24.0%.
     b. $20.02.

16-3   **b.** $46.41.

16-5   **a.** $3.76.
     c. Divided yield = 2.8%.
     d. At P/E = 14×, P_0 = $52.64.

16-6   **a.** $WACC_A$ = 12.48%; $WACC_B$ =14.90%;
        $WACC_C$ = 17.30%.
     b. EVA_A = $3,770; EVA_B = $1,350;
        EVA_C = −$1,050.
     d. P_B = $22.32.

16-7   **a.** $3.5 million.
     b. EVA = $1.14 million.

16-8   **a.** D_0 = $0.72; $\hat{D}_1$ = $0.90.
     b. P_0 = −$18, which does not make sense.

16-9 P_1 = $20.80.

16-10   **a.** P_0 = $35.42.
     b. P_0 = $54.10.

16-11   EVA = $0.

16-12   **a.** EPS_0 = $4.08.
     b. P_0 = $122.40.
     c. k = 0%.

16-13   **a.** EBIT = $140,000.
     b. EVA = −$5,000.

A P P E N D I X   D
Selected Equations

Chapter 2

$k = k^* + IP + DRP + LP + MRP = k_{RF} + DRP + LP + MRP.$

$k_{RF} = k^* + IP.$

$IP_n = \dfrac{I_1 + I_2 + \ldots I_n}{n}.$

Chapter 3

$\dfrac{\text{Maximum change}}{\text{in money supply}} = \dfrac{\text{Excess reserves}}{\text{Reserve requirement}}.$

Chapter 4

$\text{Conversion price} = \left(\dfrac{\text{Face}}{\text{value}}\right)\left(\dfrac{\text{Conversion}}{\text{ratio}}\right).$

Chapter 5

$\dfrac{\text{Equivalent \textbf{pretax} yield}}{\text{on taxable investment}} = \dfrac{\substack{\text{Yield on tax-free} \\ \text{investment}}}{1 - T}.$

Chapter 6

$FV_n = PV(1 + i)^n = PV(FVIF_{i,n}).$

$PV = FV_n\left[\dfrac{1}{(1 + i)^n}\right] = FV_n(1 + i)^{-n} = FV_n(PVIF_{i,n}).$

$PVIF_{i,n} = \dfrac{1}{FVIF_{i,n}}.$

$$FVIFA_{i,n} = \frac{(1+i)^n - 1}{i}.$$

$$PVIFA_{i,n} = \frac{1 - \dfrac{1}{(1+i)^n}}{i} = \frac{1 - (1+i)^{-n}}{i}.$$

$$FVA_n = PMT(FVIFA_{i,n}).$$

$$FVA(DUE)_n = PMT[FVIFA(DUE)_{i,n}] = PMT[(FVIFA_{i,n})(1+i)].$$

$$PVA_n = PMT(PVIFA_{i,n}).$$

$$PVA(DUE)_n = PMT[PVIFA(DUE)_{i,n}] = PMT[(PVIFA_{i,n})(1+i)].$$

$$PVP = \frac{Payment}{Interest\ rate} = \frac{PMT}{i}.$$

$$PV_{Uneven\ stream} = \sum_{t=1}^{n} CF_t \left(\frac{1}{1+i}\right)^t = \sum_{t=1}^{n} CF_t(PVIF_{i,t}).$$

$$FV_{Uneven\ stream} = \sum_{t=1}^{n} CF_t(1+i)^{n-t} = \sum_{t=1}^{n} CF_t(FVIF_{i,n-t}).$$

$$FV_n = PV\left(1 + \frac{i_{SIMPLE}}{m}\right)^{m \times n}.$$

$$Effective\ annual\ rate = EAR = \left(1 + \frac{i_{SIMPLE}}{m}\right)^m - 1.0.$$

$$Periodic\ rate = \frac{i_{SIMPLE}}{m}.$$

$$i_{SIMPLE} = APR = (Periodic\ rate)(m).$$

Chapter 7

$$Asset\ value = V = \sum_{t=1}^{N} \frac{\hat{CF}_t}{(1+k)^t}.$$

$$V_d = \sum_{t=1}^{N} \frac{INT}{(1+k_d)^t} + \frac{M}{(1+k_d)^N}.$$

$$= INT(PVIFA_{k_d,N}) + M(PVIF_{k_d,N}).$$

$$V_d = \sum_{t=1}^{2N} \frac{INT/2}{(1+k_d/2)^t} + \frac{M}{(1+k_d/2)^{2N}} = \left(\frac{INT}{2}\right)(PVIFA_{k_d/2,2N}) + M(PVIF_{k_d/2,2N}).$$

$$\begin{array}{c} Approx.\ yield \\ to\ maturity \end{array} = \frac{INT + \left(\dfrac{M - V_d}{N}\right)}{\left[\dfrac{2(V_d) + M}{3}\right]}.$$

$$Current\ yield = \frac{INT}{V_d}.$$

$$\begin{array}{c} Capital\ gains \\ yield \end{array} = \frac{\left(\begin{array}{c} Beginning \\ bond\ value \end{array}\right) - \left(\begin{array}{c} Ending \\ bond\ value \end{array}\right)}{\left(\begin{array}{c} Beginning \\ bond\ value \end{array}\right)}.$$

$$\text{Price of callable bond} = \sum_{t=1}^{N_C} \frac{\text{INT}}{(1 + k_d)^t} + \frac{\text{Call price}}{(1 + k_d)^{N_c}}.$$

$$\frac{\text{Stock}}{\text{value}} = \sum_{t=1}^{\infty} \frac{\hat{D}_t}{(1 + k_s)^t}$$

$$V_{ps} = \frac{D_{ps}}{k_{ps}}.$$

$$k_{ps} = \frac{D_{ps}}{V_{ps}}.$$

$$\hat{P}_0 = \frac{D_0(1 + g)}{k_s - g} = \frac{\hat{D}_1}{k_s - g} \text{ if growth, g, is constant.}$$

$$\hat{k}_s = \frac{\hat{D}_1}{P_0} + g.$$

Chapter 8

$$\text{Expected rate of return} = \hat{k} = \sum_{i=1}^{n} Pr_i k_i.$$

$$\text{Variance} = \sigma^2 = \sum_{i=1}^{n} (k_i - \hat{k})^2 Pr_i.$$

$$\text{Standard deviation} = \sigma = \sqrt{\sum_{i=1}^{n}(k_i - \hat{k})^2 Pr_i}.$$

$$\text{CV} = \frac{\sigma}{\hat{k}}.$$

$$\hat{k}_p = \sum_{j=1}^{n} w_j \hat{k}_j.$$

$$\beta_p = \sum_{j=1}^{n} w_j \beta_j.$$

$$\text{SML} = k_j = k_{RF} + (k_M - k_{RF})\beta_j = k_{RF} + (RP_M)\beta_j.$$

Chapter 9

$$\text{Payback} = \left(\begin{array}{c} \text{Year before full} \\ \text{recovery of} \\ \text{original investment} \end{array} \right) + \left(\frac{\text{Unrecovered cost at start of full-recovery year}}{\text{Total cash flow during full-recovery year}} \right).$$

$$\text{NPV} = \widehat{CF}_0 + \frac{\widehat{CF}_1}{(1 + k)^1} + \frac{\widehat{CF}_2}{(1 + k)^2} + \cdots + \frac{\widehat{CF}_n}{(1 + k)^n}$$

$$= \sum_{t=0}^{n} \frac{\widehat{CF}_t}{(1 + k)^t}.$$

$$\text{IRR:} \widehat{CF}_0 + \frac{\widehat{CF}_1}{(1 + IRR)^1} + \frac{\widehat{CF}_2}{(1 + IRR)^2} + \cdots + \frac{\widehat{CF}_n}{(1 + IRR)^n} = 0$$

$$\sum_{t=0}^{n} \frac{\widehat{CF}_t}{(1 + IRR)^t} = 0.$$

$$\text{MIRR: PV costs} = \sum_{t=0}^{n} \frac{COF_t}{(1 + k)^t} = \frac{\sum_{t=0}^{n} CIF_t(1 + k)^{n-t}}{(1 + MIRR)^n} = \frac{TV}{(1 + MIRR)^n}.$$

Net cash flow = NI + Depr.

$$\text{Incremental operating cash flow} = \Delta NI_t + \Delta Depr_t$$

$$= (\Delta S_t - \Delta OC_t) \times (1 - T) + T(\Delta Depr_t).$$

$$E(NPV) = \sum_{i=1}^{n} Pr_i (NPV_i).$$

$$\sigma_{NPV} = \sqrt{\sum_{i=1}^{n} Pr_i [NPV_i - E(NPV)]^2}.$$

$$CV_{NPV} = \frac{\sigma_{NPV}}{E(NPV)}.$$

$$k_{Project} = k_{RF} + (k_M - k_{RF})\beta_{Project}.$$

Chapter 10

After-tax component cost of debt = $k_{dT} = k_d(1 - T)$.

$$\text{Component cost of preferred stock} = k_{ps} = \frac{D_{ps}}{NP} = \frac{D_{ps}}{P_0 - \text{Flotation costs}}.$$

$$k_s = k_{RF} + RP = \frac{\hat{D}_1}{P_0} + g = \hat{k}_s.$$

$$k_s = k_{RF} + (k_M - k_{RF})\beta_s.$$

k_s = Bond yield + Risk premium.

$$k_e = \frac{\hat{D}_1}{P_0(1 - F)} + g = \frac{\hat{D}_1}{NP} + g.$$

$$WACC = w_d k_{dT} + w_p k_p + w_s(k_s \text{ or } k_e).$$

$$BP = \frac{\text{Total amount of lower-cost capital of a given type}}{\text{Proportion of this type of capital in the capital structure}}.$$

Chapter 11

$$EPS = \frac{(S - F - VC - I)(1 - T)}{\text{Shares outstanding}} = \frac{(EBIT - I)(1 - T)}{\text{Shares outstanding}}.$$

$$EPS_{Indifference}: S_I = \left[\frac{(\text{Shares}_2)(I_1) - (\text{Shares}_1)(I_2)}{\text{Shares}_2 - \text{Shares}_1} + F \right]\left(\frac{1}{1 - V} \right).$$

$$TIE = \frac{EBIT}{INT}.$$

$$EPS_1 = EPS_0[1 + (DTL)(\%\Delta Sales)].$$

Chapter 12

$$\begin{pmatrix} \text{Account} \\ \text{balance} \end{pmatrix} = \begin{pmatrix} \text{Amount of} \\ \text{daily activity} \end{pmatrix} \times \begin{pmatrix} \text{Average life} \\ \text{of the account} \end{pmatrix}.$$

$$\begin{matrix} \text{Inventory conversion} \\ \text{period} \end{matrix} = \frac{\text{Inventory}}{\text{CGS}/360}.$$

$$\begin{matrix} \text{Receivables collection} \\ \text{period} \end{matrix} = \text{DSO} = \frac{\text{Receivables}}{\text{Sales}/360}.$$

$$\begin{matrix} \text{Payables} \\ \text{deferral period} \end{matrix} = \text{DPO} = \frac{\text{Accounts payable}}{\text{CGS}/360}.$$

$$\begin{matrix} \text{Cash} \\ \text{conversion} \\ \text{cycle} \end{matrix} = \begin{matrix} \text{Inventory} \\ \text{conversion} \\ \text{period} \end{matrix} + \begin{matrix} \text{Receivables} \\ \text{collection} \\ \text{period} \end{matrix} - \begin{matrix} \text{Payables} \\ \text{deferral} \\ \text{period} \end{matrix}.$$

$$\begin{matrix} \text{Interest rate} \\ \text{per period (cost)} \end{matrix} = \frac{\text{Dollar cost of borrowing}}{\text{Amount of usable funds}}.$$

$$\text{EAR} = \left[1 + \left(\frac{\text{Interest rate}}{\text{per period}} \right) \right]^m - 1.0.$$

$$\text{APR} = \left(\frac{\text{Interest rate}}{\text{per period}} \right) \times m.$$

$$\begin{matrix} \text{Receivables} \\ \text{investment} \end{matrix} = \left[\text{DSO} \times \left(\frac{S}{360} \right) \right] \times V.$$

$$\text{Receivables cost of carrying} = [(\text{DSO})(\text{Sales}/360)(V)](k_{AR}) = \left(\begin{matrix} \text{Receivables} \\ \text{investment} \end{matrix} \right) \times k_{AR}.$$

$$\begin{matrix} \text{Total} \\ \text{carrying cost} \end{matrix} = \text{TCC} = (C)(PP)\left(\frac{Q}{2} \right).$$

$$\begin{matrix} \text{Total} \\ \text{ordering cost} \end{matrix} = \text{TOC} = O\left(\frac{T}{Q} \right).$$

$$\begin{matrix} \text{Total} \\ \text{inventory cost} \end{matrix} = \text{TIC} = \text{TCC} + \text{TOC}$$

$$= (C)(PP)\left(\frac{Q}{2} \right) + O\left(\frac{T}{Q} \right).$$

$$\begin{matrix} \text{Economic ordering} \\ \text{quantity} \end{matrix} = \text{EOQ} = \sqrt{\frac{2(O)(T)}{(C)(PP)}}.$$

Chapter 13

$$\text{Current ratio} = \frac{\text{Current assets}}{\text{Current liabilities}}.$$

$$\text{Quick, or acid test, ratio} = \frac{\text{Current assets} - \text{Inventories}}{\text{Current liabilities}}.$$

$$\text{Inventory turnover ratio} = \frac{\text{Cost of goods sold}}{\text{Inventories}}.$$

$$\text{DSO} = \frac{\text{Days sales}}{\text{outstanding}} = \frac{\text{Receivables}}{\text{Average sales per day}} = \frac{\text{Receivables}}{\text{Annual sales}/360}.$$

$$\text{Fixed assets turnover ratio} = \frac{\text{Sales}}{\text{Net fixed assets}}.$$

$$\text{Total assets turnover ratio} = \frac{\text{Sales}}{\text{Total assets}}.$$

$$\text{Debt ratio} = \frac{\text{Total debt}}{\text{Total assets}}.$$

$$\text{Times-interest-earned (TIE) ratio} = \frac{\text{EBIT}}{\text{Interest charges}}.$$

$$\frac{\text{Fixed charge}}{\text{coverage ratio}} = \frac{\text{EBIT} + \text{Lease payments}}{\text{Interest charges} + \text{Lease payments} + \left[\dfrac{\text{Sinking fund payments}}{(1 - \text{Tax rate})}\right]}.$$

$$\text{Profit margin on sales} = \frac{\text{Net income}}{\text{Sales}}.$$

$$\text{Return on total assets (ROA)} = \frac{\text{Net income}}{\text{Total assets}}.$$

$$\text{DuPont equation: ROA} = \left(\frac{\text{Profit}}{\text{margin}}\right)\left(\frac{\text{Total assets}}{\text{turnover}}\right) = \left(\frac{\text{Net income}}{\text{Sales}}\right)\left(\frac{\text{Sales}}{\text{Total assets}}\right).$$

$$\text{Return on common equity (ROE)} = \frac{\text{Net income available to common stockholders}}{\text{Common equity}}.$$

$$\text{Price/earnings (P/E) ratio} = \frac{\text{Market price per share}}{\text{Earnings per share}}.$$

$$\frac{\text{Earnings}}{\text{per share}} = \frac{\text{Net income available to common stockholders}}{\text{Number of common shares outstanding}}.$$

$$\text{Book value per share} = \frac{\text{Common equity}}{\text{Shares outstanding}}.$$

$$\text{Market/book (M/B) ratio} = \frac{\text{Market price per share}}{\text{Book value per share}}.$$

$$\frac{\text{Dollars transferred}}{\text{from retained earnings}} = \left(\begin{array}{c}\text{Number of}\\ \text{shares}\\ \text{outstanding}\end{array}\right) \times \left(\begin{array}{c}\text{Stock dividend}\\ \text{as a percent}\end{array}\right) \times \left(\begin{array}{c}\text{Market price}\\ \text{of the stock}\end{array}\right).$$

Chapter 14

$$\text{Full capacity sales} = \frac{\text{Sales level}}{\begin{array}{c}\text{Percentage of capacity used}\\\text{to generate sales level}\end{array}}.$$

$$TC = F + VQ.$$

$$Q_{\text{OpBE}} = \frac{F}{P - V} = \frac{F}{\text{Contribution margin}}.$$

$$S_{\text{OpBE}} = PQ_{\text{BE}} = \frac{FC}{1 - \dfrac{V}{P}} = \frac{F}{\text{Gross profit margin}}.$$

$$DOL = \frac{\left(\dfrac{\Delta EBIT}{EBIT}\right)}{\left(\dfrac{\Delta Q}{Q}\right)}.$$

$$DOL_Q = \frac{Q(P - V)}{Q(P - V) - F}.$$

$$DOL_S = \frac{S - VC}{S - VC - F} = \frac{\text{Gross profit}}{EBIT}.$$

$$EBIT = PQ - VQ - F.$$

$$EBIT_{\text{FinBE}} = I + \frac{D_{ps}}{(1 - T)}.$$

$$DFL = \frac{\left(\dfrac{\Delta EPS}{EPS}\right)}{\left(\dfrac{\Delta EBIT}{EBIT}\right)}.$$

$$DFL = \frac{EBIT}{EBIT - I}; \text{ if preferred stock} = 0.$$

$$DFL = \frac{EBIT}{EBIT - [\text{Financial BEP}]}.$$

$$DTL = DOL \times DFL = \frac{S - VC}{EBIT - I}; \text{ if preferred stock} = 0.$$

$$DTL = \frac{\text{Gross profit}}{EBIT - [\text{Financial BEP}]}.$$

Chapter 15

$$\begin{array}{c}\text{Dollar}\\\text{return}\end{array} = \begin{array}{c}\text{Income}\\\text{received}\end{array} + \begin{array}{c}\text{Ending value}\\\text{of investment}\end{array} - \begin{array}{c}\text{Beginning value}\\\text{of investment}\end{array}.$$

$$\begin{array}{c}\text{Per period}\\\text{rate of return}\end{array} = \bar{k} = \frac{\text{Dollar return}}{\text{Beginning value of investment}} = \frac{INC + (P_1 - P_0)}{P_0}.$$

$$\begin{array}{c}\text{Annualized}\\\text{rate of return}\end{array} = \frac{INC + (P_1 - P_0)}{P_0}\left(\frac{360}{T}\right) = APR.$$

$$\text{Simple arithmetic average return} = \frac{\sum_{t=1}^{n} \bar{k}_t}{n}.$$

$$\text{Geometric average return} = \left[\prod_{t=1}^{n} (1 + \bar{k}_t) \right]^{\frac{1}{n}} - 1.0.$$

$$\bar{k}_p = \sum_{j=1}^{n} w_j \bar{k}_j.$$

$$\text{Price-weighted index} = I_W = \frac{\sum_{j=1}^{n} P_{jt}}{n}.$$

$$\text{Value-weighted Index} = I_V = \frac{\sum_{j=1}^{n} (P_{jt} \times \text{Shares})}{n}.$$

$$\frac{\text{Actual}}{\text{margin}} = \frac{\text{Investor's equity}}{\text{Market value of investment}} = \frac{\left[\binom{\text{Number}}{\text{of shares}} \times \binom{\text{Price}}{\text{per share}} \right] - \frac{\text{Amount}}{\text{borrowed}}}{\binom{\text{Numbers}}{\text{of shares}} \times \binom{\text{Price}}{\text{per share}}}.$$

$$\frac{\text{Margin}}{\text{call price}} = \frac{\text{Amount borrowed}}{\binom{\text{Number}}{\text{of shares}} \times \left(1 - \frac{\text{Maintenance}}{\text{margin}} \right)}.$$

Chapter 16

$$V_s = P_0 = \sum_{t=1}^{\infty} \frac{\hat{D}_t}{(1 + k_s)^t} = \sum_{t=1}^{N} \frac{\hat{D}_t}{(1 + k_s)^t} + \frac{\hat{P}_n}{(1 + k_s)^N}.$$

$$P_0 = EPS_0 \times P/E \text{ ratio.}$$

$$EVA = EBIT(1 - T) - \left(WACC \times \frac{\text{Invested}}{\text{capital}} \right).$$

Index